日本外交文書

占領期 第一巻
（占領政策への対応）

外務省

序

外務省では、明治維新以降のわが国外交の経緯を明らかにし、あわせて外交交渉上の先例ともなりうる基本的史料を提供する目的で、昭和十一年に『日本外交文書』第一巻を公刊した。以来、既に明治・大正期の刊行を終え、昭和については、満州事変、海軍軍縮問題、日中戦争、および太平洋戦争等の特集とともに、昭和期Ⅰ（昭和二―六年）、昭和期Ⅱ（昭和六―十二年）、および昭和期Ⅲ（昭和十二―二十年）の刊行を終え、戦前期の刊行は完結した。

他方、戦後期についても、サンフランシスコ平和条約シリーズ全三巻を既に刊行したが、今般、これに続いて、占領期第一巻から第三巻を刊行する。占領期シリーズ全三巻は、外交史料館の所蔵史料などから、平和条約関連を除く、昭和二十年から二十七年における主要な関係文書を選定し、編纂・刊行するもので、これら三巻をもって『日本外交文書』の通算刊行冊数は二一九冊となる。

激動の時代といわれる昭和期を顧みるにあたって、本巻が正確な史実を提供し、外交問題の歴史的研究に資するとともに、現在の国際関係を考察する上でも貢献できれば幸いである。

平成二十九年一月

外務省外交史料館長

例　言

占領期(昭和二十一—二十七年)については、既に「サンフランシスコ平和条約」全三巻を刊行済みである。占領期第一巻から第三巻では、平和条約関連を除く、当該期の諸問題に関する主要な文書を、三巻に分けて事項ごとに収録する。

1　収録文書は、基本的に外交史料館の所蔵史料によった。

2　収録文書は、原則として原文のままとしたが、明らかな誤字と認められる箇所については、正しい文字に置き換えた。

3　収録文書には、一連文書番号および件名を付し、事項ごとに日付順に配列した。

4　収録文書中発電月日不明の電報は、着電の日付を記し、1月(15)日のように丸括弧を付して区別した。

5　収録文書中右肩に付した(1)(2)(3)等の記号は、同一番号の電報が分割されて発電されたことを示す。なお、収録にあたっては、文章の区切りではなくとも分割された箇所をもって改行した。

6　収録文書に付した書誌情報中にある発受信者などの人名については、初出の場合のみ姓名を表示し、以後は姓のみにとどめた。また発受信者名に付す国名・地名は、原則として辞令に基づく在勤地とした。

7　採録にあたって加えた注記は、(編注)として当該箇所に明記し、その文面は各文書の末尾に記載した。

8　原文書に欄外記入や付箋がある場合は、(欄外記入)(付箋)として当該箇所に明記し、その文面は

各文書の末尾に記載した。
9 収録文書中(省略)(ママ)等の括弧を付したルビは、収録にあたって記したものである。
10 原文書で印字不鮮明等の理由により判読不明な文字は□とし、(一字不明)のようにルビを付した。
11 押印については、公印と私印をそれぞれ㊞と(印)に区別して記した。
12 占領期第二巻末尾に占領期第一巻から第二巻の全収録文書の日付順索引を、占領期第三巻末尾に占領期第一巻から第三巻の全収録文書の日付順索引を付した。

目 次

一 占領政策への対応 1

　1 降伏文書調印と初期占領政策への対応（昭和20年9月〜10月） ... 3

　2 民主化・非軍事化政策への対応（昭和20年10月〜21年5月） ... 206

　3 経済諸施策への対応（昭和21年5月〜24年4月） ... 458

　4 制限緩和に向けた対応（昭和24年5月〜27年4月） ... 701

（以上、第一巻）

二 外交権の停止

三 日本国憲法の制定

四 中間賠償

　1 対象施設の決定と撤去に向けた対応

　2 賠償の緩和から中止までの対応

五　「マッカーサー・ライン」をめぐる漁業問題

　六　極東国際軍事裁判開廷までの対応

　日本外交文書　占領期　第一巻～第二巻　日付索引

　七　邦人の引揚げ問題

　　1　一般問題

　　2　ソ連軍占領地域

　　3　中国

　　4　南方地域

　日本外交文書　占領期　第一巻～第三巻　日付索引

（以上、第二巻）

（以上、第三巻）

一　占領政策への対応

Ⅱ．古墳文化への志向

1 降伏文書調印と初期占領政策への対応（昭和20年9月〜10月）

1 降伏文書

昭和20年9月2日 調印

付記一 右和訳文
二 昭和二十年七月二十六日発表「ポツダム宣言」
三 右和訳文

INSTRUMENT OF SURRENDER

We, acting by command of and in behalf of the Emperor of Japan, the Japanese Government and the Japanese Imperial General Headquarters, hereby accept the provisions set forth in the declaration issued by the heads of the Governments of the United States, China and Great Britain on 26 July 1945, at Potsdam, and subsequently adhered to by the Union of Soviet Socialist Republics, which four powers are hereafter referred to as the Allied Powers.

We hereby proclaim the unconditional surrender to the Allied Powers of the Japanese Imperial General Headquarters and of all Japanese armed forces and all armed forces under Japanese control wherever situated.

We hereby command all Japanese forces wherever situated and the Japanese people to cease hostilities forthwith, to preserve and save from damage all ships, aircraft, and military and civil property and to comply with all requirements which may be imposed by the Supreme Commander for the Allied Powers or by agencies of the Japanese Government at his direction.

We hereby command the Japanese Imperial General Headquarters to issue at once orders to the Commanders of all Japanese forces and all forces under Japanese control wherever situated to surrender unconditionally themselves and all forces under their control.

We hereby command all civil, military and naval officials

3

to obey and enforce all proclamations, orders and directives deemed by the Supreme Commander for the Allied Powers to be proper to effectuate this surrender and issued by him or under his authority and we direct all such officials to remain at their posts and to continue to perform their non-combatant duties unless specifically relieved by him or under his authority.

We hereby undertake for the Emperor, the Japanese Government and their successors to carry out the provisions of the Potsdam Declaration in good faith, and to issue whatever orders and take whatever action may be required by the Supreme Commander for the Allied Powers or by any other designated representative of the Allied Powers for the purpose of giving effect to that Declaration.

We hereby command the Japanese Imperial Government and the Japanese Imperial General Headquarters at once to liberate all allied prisoners of war and civilian internees now under Japanese control and to provide for their protection, care, maintenance and immediate transportation to places as directed.

The authority of the Emperor and the Japanese Government to rule the state shall be subject to the Supreme Commander for the Allied Powers who will take such steps as he deems proper to effectuate these terms of surrender.

Signed at TOKYO BAY, JAPAN at 0904 on the SECOND day of SEPTEMBER, 1945.

重光 葵

By Command and in behalf of the Emperor of Japan and the Japanese Government.

梅津美治郎

By Command and in behalf of the Japanese Imperial General Headquarters.

Accepted at TOKYO BAY, JAPAN at 0908 on the SECOND day of SEPTEMBER, 1945, for the United States, Republic of China, United Kingdom and the Union of Soviet Socialist Republics, and in the interests of the other United Nations at war with Japan.

Douglas MacArthur

Supreme Commander for the Allied Powers.

C. W. Nimitz

1　降伏文書調印と初期占領政策への対応（昭和20年9月～10月）

(付記１)

降伏文書

下名ハ茲ニ合衆國、中華民國及「グレート、ブリテン」國ノ首班ガ千九百四十五年七月二十六日「ポツダム」ニ於テ發シ後ニ「ソヴィエト」社會主義共和國聯邦ガ參加シタル宣言ノ條項ヲ日本國天皇、日本國政府及日本帝國大本營ノ命ニ依リ且之ニ代リ受諾ス右四國ハ以下之ヲ聯合國ト稱ス

下名ハ茲ニ日本帝國大本營並ニ何レノ位置ニ在ルヲ問ハズ一切ノ日本國軍隊及日本國ノ支配下ニ在ル一切ノ軍隊ノ聯合國ニ對スル無條件降伏ヲ布告ス

下名ハ茲ニ何レノ位置ニ在ルヲ問ハズ一切ノ日本國軍隊及日本國臣民ニ對シ敵對行爲ヲ直ニ終止スルコト、一切ノ船舶、航空機竝ニ軍用及非軍用財產ヲ保存シ之ガ毀損ヲ防止スルコト及聯合國最高司令官又ハ其ノ指示ニ基キ日本國政府ノ諸機關ノ課スベキ一切ノ要求ニ應ズルコトヲ命ズ

下名ハ茲ニ日本帝國大本營ガ何レノ位置ニ在ルヲ問ハズ一切ノ日本國軍隊及日本國ノ支配下ニ在ル一切ノ軍隊ノ指揮官ニ對シ自身及其ノ支配下ニ在ル一切ノ軍隊ガ無條件ニ降伏スベキ旨ノ命令ヲ直ニ發スルコトヲ命ズ

United States Representative
徐　永　昌
Republic of China Representative
Bruce Fraser
United Kingdom Representative
Lieutenant-General K. Derevyanko
Union of Soviet Socialist Republics Representative
T. A. Blamey
Commonwealth of Australia Representative
L. Moore Cosgrave
Dominion of Canada Representative
Leclerc
Provisional Government of the French Republic Representative
C. E. L. Helfrich
Kingdom of the Netherlands Representative
L. M. Isitt
Dominion of New Zealand Representative

下名ハ茲ニ一切ノ官廳、陸軍及海軍ノ職員ニ對シ聯合國最高司令官ガ本降伏實施ノ爲適當ナリト認メテ自ラ發シ又ハ其ノ委任ニ基キ發セシムル一切ノ布告、命令及指示ヲ遵守シ且之ガ施行スルコトヲ命ジ並ニ右職員ガ聯合國最高司令官ニ依リ又ハ其ノ委任ニ基キ特ニ任務ヲ解カレザル限リ各自ノ地位ニ留リ且引續キ各自ノ非戰鬪的任務ヲ行フコトヲ命ズ

下名ハ茲ニ「ポツダム」宣言ノ條項ヲ誠實ニ履行スルコト竝ニ右宣言ヲ實施スル爲聯合國最高司令官又ハ其ノ他特定ノ聯合國代表者ガ要求スルコトアルベキ一切ノ命令ヲ發シ且斯ル一切ノ措置ヲ執ルコトヲ天皇、日本國政府及其ノ後繼者ノ爲ニ約ス

下名ハ茲ニ日本國政府及日本帝國大本營ニ對シ現ニ日本國ノ支配下ニ在ル一切ノ聯合國俘虜及被抑留者ヲ直ニ解放スルコト竝ニ其ノ保護、手當、給養及指示セラレタル場所ヘノ即時輸送ノ爲ノ措置ヲ執ルコトヲ命ズ

天皇及日本國政府ノ國家統治ノ權限ハ本降伏條項ヲ實施スル爲適當ト認ムル措置ヲ執ル聯合國最高司令官ノ制限ノ下ニ置カルルモノトス

千九百四十五年九月二日午前九時四分日本國東京灣上ニ於テ署名ス

大日本帝國天皇陛下及日本國政府ノ命ニ依リ且其ノ名ニ於テ

重光　葵

日本帝國大本營ノ命ニ依リ且其ノ名ニ於テ

梅津美治郎

千九百四十五年九月二日午前九時八分東京灣上ニ於テ合衆國、中華民國、聯合王國及「ソヴィエト」社會主義共和國ノ聯邦ノ爲ニ竝ニ日本國ト戰爭狀態ニ在ル他ノ聯合諸國家ノ利益ノ爲ニ受諾ス

聯合國最高司令官　ダグラス、マックアーサー

合衆國代表者　シー、ダブリュー、ニミッツ

中華民國代表者　徐永昌

聯合王國代表者　ブルース、フレーザー

「ソヴィエト」社會主義共和國聯邦代表者　クズマ、エヌ、ヂェレヴィヤンコ

「オーストラリア」聯邦代表者　ティー、エー、ブレーミー

6

1　降伏文書調印と初期占領政策への対応(昭和20年9月～10月)

「カナダ」代表者　エル、コスグレーヴ

「フランス」代表者　ジャック、ルクレルク

「オランダ」國代表者　シェルフ、ヘルフリッヒ

「ニュー、ジーランド」代表者　エル、エム、イシット

編注　本訳文は、昭和二十年九月二日付「官報號外」の布告欄に依拠したが、署名部分の明らかな誤字は改めた。

(付記1)

Proclamation of the Three Powers,
the United States, Great Britain and China.

(Potsdam, July 26, 1945)

1. We the President of the United States, the President of the National Government of the Republic of China, and the Prime Minister of Great Britain, representing the hundreds of millions of our countrymen, have conferred and agreed that Japan shall be given an opportunity to end this war.

2. The prodigious land, sea and air forces of the United States, the British Empire and of China, many times reinforced by their armies and air fleets from the West, are poised to strike the final blows upon Japan. This military power is sustained and inspired by the determination of all the Allied Nations to prosecute the war against Japan until she ceases to resist.

3. The result of the futile and senseless German resistance to the might of the aroused free peoples of the world stands forth in awful clarity as an example to the people of Japan. The might that now converges on Japan is immeasurably greater than that which, when applied to the resisting Nazis, necessarily laid waste to the lands, the industry and the method of life of the whole German people. The full application of our military power, backed by our resolve, will mean the inevitable and complete destruction of the Japanese armed forces and just as inevitably the utter devastation of the Japanese homeland.

4. The time has come for Japan to decide whether she will continue to be controlled by those self-willed militaristic advisers whose unintelligent calculations have brought the Empire of Japan to the threshold of annihilation, or whether she will follow the path

of reason.

5. The following are our terms:

We will not deviate from them. There are no alternatives. We shall brook no delay.

6. There must be eliminated for all time the authority and influence of those who have deceived and misled the people of Japan into embarking on world conquest, for we insist that a new order of peace, security and justice will be impossible until irresponsible militarism is driven from the world.

7. Until such a new order is established and until there is convincing proof that Japan's war making power is destroyed, points in Japanese territory to be designated by the Allies shall be occupied to secure the achievement of the basic objectives we are here setting forth.

8. The terms of the Cairo Declaration shall be carried out and Japanese sovereignty shall be limited to the islands of Honshu, Hokkaido, Kyushu, Shikoku and such minor islands as we determine.

9. The Japanese military forces, after being completely disarmed, shall be permitted to return to their homes with the opportunity to lead peaceful and productive lives.

10. We do not intend that the Japanese shall be enslaved as a race or destroyed as a nation; but stern justice shall be meted out to all war criminals, including those who have visited cruelties upon our prisoners. The Japanese Government shall remove all obstacles to the revival and strengthening of democratic tendencies among the Japanese people. The freedom of speech, of religion, and of thought as well as respect for the fundamental human rights shall be established.

11. Japan shall be permitted to maintain such industries as will sustain her economy and permit the exaction of just reparations in kind, but not those which would enable her to rearm for war. To this end, access to, as distinguished from control of, raw materials shall be permitted. The eventual Japanese participation in world trade relations shall be permitted.

12. The occupying forces of the Allies shall be withdrawn from Japan as soon as these objectives have been accomplished and there has been established, in accordance with the freely ex-

8

1 降伏文書調印と初期占領政策への対応（昭和20年9月〜10月）

pressed will of the Japanese people, a peacefully inclined and responsible government.

13. We call upon the Government of Japan to proclaim now the unconditional surrender of all the Japanese armed forces, and to provide proper and adequate assurances of their good faith in such action. The alternative for Japan is prompt and utter destruction.

〔付記三〕

米、英、支三國宣言

（千九百四十五年七月二十六日「ポツダム」ニ於テ）

一　吾等合衆國大統領、中華民國政府主席及「グレート、ブリテン」國總理大臣ハ吾等ノ數億ノ國民ヲ代表シ協議ノ上日本國ニ対シ今次ノ戰爭ヲ終結スルノ機會ヲ與フルコトニ意見一致セリ

二　合衆國、英帝國及中華民國ノ巨大ナル陸、海、空軍ハ西方ヨリ自國ノ陸軍及空軍ニ依ル數倍ノ増強ヲ受ケ日本國ニ対シ最後的打撃ヲ加フルノ態勢ヲ整ヘタリ右軍事力ハ日本國ガ抵抗ヲ終止スルニ至ル迄同國ニ対シ戰爭ヲ遂行スルノ一切ノ聯合國ノ決意ニ依リ支持セラレ且鼓舞セラレ居ルモノナリ

三　蹶起セル世界ノ自由ナル人民ノ力ニ対スル「ドイツ」國ノ無益且無意義ナル抵抗ノ結果ハ日本國國民ニ対シ先例ヲ極メテ明白ニ示スモノナリ現在日本國ニ対シ集結シツツアル力ハ抵抗スル「ナチス」ニ対シ適用セラレタル場合ニ於テ全「ドイツ」國人民ノ土地、産業及生活様式ヲ必然的ニ荒廢セシメタル力ニ比シ測リ知レザル程更ニ強大ナルモノナリ吾等ノ決意ニ支持セラルル吾等ノ軍事力ノ最高度ノ使用ハ日本國軍隊ノ不可避且完全ナル壊滅ヲ意味スベク又同様必然的ニ日本國本土ノ完全ナル破壊ヲ意味スベシ

四　無分別ナル打算ニ依リ日本帝國ヲ滅亡ノ淵ニ陷レタル我儘ナル軍國主義的助言者ニ依リ日本國ガ引續キ統御セラルベキカ又ハ理性ノ經路ヲ日本國ガ履ムベキカヲ日本國ガ決定スベキ時期ハ到來セリ

五　吾等ノ條件ハ左ノ如シ吾等ハ右條件ヨリ離脱スルコトナカルベシ右ニ代ル條件存在セズ吾等ハ遅延ヲ認ムルヲ得ズ

六　吾等ハ無責任ナル軍國主義ガ世界ヨリ驅逐セラルルニ至ル迄ハ平和、安全及正義ノ新秩序ガ生ジ得ザルコトヲ主張スルモノナルヲ以テ日本國國民ヲ欺瞞シ之ヲシテ世界征服ノ擧ニ出ヅルノ過誤ヲ犯サシメタル者ノ權力及勢力ハ永久ニ除去セラレザルベカラズ

七　右ノ如キ新秩序ガ建設セラレ且日本國ノ戰爭遂行能力ガ破碎セラレタルコトノ確證アルニ至ル迄ハ聯合國ノ指定スベキ日本國領域内ノ諸地點ハ吾等ノ茲ニ指示スル基本的目的ノ達成ヲ確保スル爲占領セラルベシ

八　「カイロ」宣言ノ條項ハ履行セラルベク又日本國ノ主權ハ本州、北海道、九州及四國並ニ吾等ノ決定スル諸小島ニ局限セラルベシ

九　日本國軍隊ハ完全ニ武裝ヲ解除セラレタル後各自ノ家庭ニ復歸シ平和的且生產的ノ生活ヲ營ムノ機會ヲ得シメラルベシ

十　吾等ハ日本人ヲ民族トシテ奴隸化セントシ又ハ國民トシテ滅亡セシメントスルノ意圖ヲ有スルモノニ非ザルモ吾等ノ俘虜ヲ虐待セル者ヲ含ム一切ノ戰爭犯罪人ニ對シテハ嚴重ナル處罰加ヘラルベシ日本國政府ハ日本國國民ノ間ニ於ケル民主主義的傾向ノ復活强化ニ對スル一切ノ障礙ヲ除去スベシ言論、宗教及思想ノ自由並ニ基本的人權ノ尊重ハ確立セラルベシ

十一　日本國ハ其ノ經濟ヲ支持シ且公正ナル實物賠償ノ取立ヲ可能ナラシムルガ如キ產業ヲ維持スルコトヲ許サルベシ但シ日本國ヲシテ戰爭ノ爲再軍備ヲ爲スコトヲ得シムルガ如キ產業ハ此ノ限ニ在ラズ右目的ノ爲原料ノ入手（其ノ支配トハ之ヲ區別ス）ヲ許可サルベシ日本國ハ將來世界貿易關係ヘノ參加ヲ許サルベシ

十二　前記諸目的ガ達成セラレ且日本國國民ノ自由ニ表明セル意思ニ從ヒ平和的傾向ヲ有シ且責任アル政府ガ樹立セラルルニ於テハ聯合國ノ占領軍ハ直ニ日本國ヨリ撤收セラルベシ

十三　吾等ハ日本國政府ガ直ニ全日本國軍隊ノ無條件降伏ヲ宣言シ且右行動ニ於ケル同政府ノ誠意ニ付適當且充ナル保障ヲ提供センコトヲ同政府ニ對シ要求ス右以外ノ日本國ノ選擇ハ迅速且完全ナル壞滅アルノミトス

1 降伏文書調印と初期占領政策への対応（昭和20年9月～10月）

2 昭和20年9月2日 連合国最高司令官総司令部より 日本政府宛

指令第1号（1般命令第1号）

付記 一般命令第1号和訳文

OFFICE OF THE SUPREME COMMANDER
FOR THE ALLIED POWERS

2 September 1945

DIRECTIVE
NUMBER 1

Pursuant to the provisions of the Instrument of Surrender signed by representatives of the Emperor of Japan and of the Japanese Imperial Government and of the Japanese Imperial General Headquarters, 2 September 1945, the attached "General Order Number 1, Military and Naval" and any necessary amplifying instructions, will be issued without delay to Japanese and Japanese-controlled Armed Forces and to affected civilian agencies, for their full and complete compliance.

By direction of the Supreme Commander for the Allied Powers:

R. K. SUTHERLAND,
Lieutenant General, U. S. Army,
Chief of Staff.

1 incl: General Order No. I,
Military and Naval.

GENERAL ORDER No. I

Military and Naval

I. The Imperial General Headquarters by direction of the Emperor, and pursuant to the surrender to the Supreme Commander for the Allied Powers of all Japanese Armed Forces by the Emperor, hereby orders all of its Commanders in Japan and abroad to cause the Japanese Armed Forces and Japanese-controlled Forces under their command to cease hostilities at once, to lay down their arms, to remain in their present locations and to surrender unconditionally to Commanders acting on behalf of the United States, The Republic of China, The United Kingdom and the British Empire, and the Union of Soviet Socialist Republics, as indicated hereafter or as may be further directed by the Supreme Commander for the Allied Powers. Immediate contact will be made with the indicated Commanders, or their designated representatives, subject to any changes in detail prescribed by the Supreme Commander for the Allied Powers, and their instructions will be completely and immediately carried out.

(a) The senior Japanese Commanders and all ground, sea, air and auxiliary forces within China, (excluding Manchuria), Formosa and French Indo-China North of 16 degrees North latitude, shall surrender to Generalissimo Chiang Kai-Shek.

(b) The senior Japanese Commanders and all ground, sea, air and auxiliary forces within Manchuria, Korea North of 38 degrees North latitude, Karafuto, and the Kurile Islands, shall surrender to the Commander-in-Chief of Soviet Forces in the Far East.

(c) (1) The senior Japanese Commanders and all ground, sea, air and auxiliary forces within the Andamans, Nicobars, Burma, Thailand, French Indo-China South of 16 degrees North latitude, Malaya, Sumatra, Java, Lesser Sundas (including Bali, Lombok, and Timor), Boeroe, Ceram, Ambon, Kai, Aroe, Tanimbar and islands in the Arafura Sea, Celebes, Halmahera and Dutch New Guinea shall surrender to the Supreme Allied Commander, South East Asia Command.

(2) The senior Japanese Commanders and all ground, sea, air and auxiliary forces within Borneo, British New Guinea, the Bismarcks and the Solomons shall surrender to the Commander-in-Chief, Australian Military Forces.

(d) The senior Japanese Commanders and all ground, sea, air and auxiliary forces in the Japanese mandated Islands, Bonins, and other Pacific Islands shall surrender to the Commander-in-Chief, U. S. Pacific Fleet.

(e) The Imperial General Headquarters, its Senior Commanders, and all ground, sea, air and auxiliary forces in the main islands of Japan, minor Islands adjacent thereto, Korea South

1　降伏文書調印と初期占領政策への対応（昭和20年9月〜10月）

of 38 degrees North latitude, Ryukyus, and the Philippines shall surrender to the Commander-in-Chief, U.S. Army Forces, Pacific.

(f) The above indicated Commanders are the only representatives of the Allied Powers empowered to accept surrender, and all surrenders of Japanese Forces shall be made only to them or to their representatives.

The Japanese Imperial General Headquarters further orders its Commanders in Japan and abroad to disarm completely all forces of Japan or under Japanese control wherever they may be situated, and to deliver intact and in safe and good condition all weapons and equipment at such times and at such places as may be prescribed by the Allied Commanders indicated above.

Pending further instructions, the Japanese Police Force in the main Islands of Japan will be exempt from this disarmament provision. The Police Force will remain at their posts and shall be held responsible for the preservation of Law and Order. The strength and arms of such Police Force will be prescribed.

II. The Japanese Imperial General Headquarters shall furnish to the Supreme Commander for the Allied Powers, without delay after receipt of this order, complete information with respect to Japan and all areas under Japanese control, as follows:

(a) Lists of all land, naval, air and anti-aircraft units showing locations and strengths in Officers and Men.

(b) Lists of all aircraft, Military, Naval and Civil, giving complete information as to the number, type, location and condition of such aircraft.

(c) Lists of all Japanese and Japanese-controlled Naval Vessels, surface and submarine and Auxiliary Naval Craft, in or out of commission and under construction, giving their positions, condition and movement.

(d) Lists of all Japanese and Japanese-controlled Merchant Ships of over 100 gross tons, in or out of commission and under construction, including Merchant Ships formerly belonging to any of the United Nations which are now in Japanese hands, giving their positions, condition and movement.

(e) Complete and detailed information, accompanied by maps, showing locations and layouts of all mines, minefields, and other obstacles to movement by land, sea or air, and the safety lanes in connection therewith.

(f) Locations and descriptions of all military installations and establishments, including airfields, seaplane bases, antiaircraft defenses, ports and naval bases, storage depots, permanent and temporary land and coast fortifications, fortresses and other fortified areas.

(g) Locations of all camps and other places of detention of United Nations Prisoners of War and Civilian Internees.

III. Japanese Armed Forces and Civil Aviation Authorities will insure that all Japanese Military, Naval and Civil Aircraft remain on the ground, on the water, or aboard ship, until further notification of the disposition to be made of them.

IV. Japanese or Japanese-controlled Naval or Merchant vessels of all types will be maintained without damage and will undertake no movement pending instructions from the Supreme Commander for the Allied Powers. Vessels at sea will immediately render harmless and throw overboard explosives of all types. Vessels not at sea will immediately remove explosives of all types to safe storage ashore.

V. Responsible Japanese or Japanese-controlled Military and Civil Authorities will insure that:

(a) All Japanese mines, minefields and other obstacles to movement by land, sea and air, wherever located, be removed according to instructions of the Supreme Commander for the Allied Powers.

(b) All aids to navigation be reestablished at once.

(c) All safety lanes be kept open and clearly marked pending accomplishment of (a) above.

VI. Responsible Japanese and Japanese-controlled Military and Civil Authorities will hold intact and in good condition pending further instructions from the Supreme Commander for the Allied Powers the following:

(a) All arms, ammunition, explosives, military equipment, stores and supplies, and other implements of war of all kinds and all other war material (except as specifically prescribed in section IV of this order).

(b) All land, water and air transportation and communication facilities and equipment.

14

1 降伏文書調印と初期占領政策への対応(昭和20年9月～10月)

(c) All Military installations and establishments, including airfields, seaplane bases, anti-aircraft defenses, ports and naval bases, storage depots, permanent and temporary land and coast fortifications, fortresses and other fortified areas, together with plans and drawings of all such fortifications, installations and establishments.

(d) All factories, plants, shops, research institutions, laboratories, testing stations, technical data, patents, plans, drawings and inventions designed or intended to produce or to facilitate the production or use of all implements of war and other material and property used by or intended for use by any military or paramilitary organization in connection with its operations.

VII. The Japanese Imperial General Headquarters shall furnish to the Supreme Commander for the Allied Powers, without delay after receipt of this order, complete lists of all the items specified in paragraphs (a), (b), and (d) of section VI above, indicating the numbers, types and locations of each.

VIII. The manufacture and distribution of all arms, ammunition and implements of war will cease forthwith.

IX. With respect to United Nations Prisoners of War and Civilian Internees in the hands of Japanese or Japanese-controlled authorities:

(a) The safety and well-being of all United Nations Prisoners of War and Civilian Internees will be scrupulously preserved, to include the administrative and supply services essential to provide adequate food, shelter, clothing, and medical care until such responsibility is undertaken by the Supreme Commander for the Allied Powers.

(b) Each camp or other place of detention of United Nations Prisoners of War and Civilian Internees together with its equipment, stores, records, arms, and ammunition, will be delivered immediately to the command of the senior officer or designated representative of the Prisoners of War and Civilian Internees.

(c) As directed by the Supreme Commander for the Allied Powers, Prisoners of War and Civilian Internees will be transported to places of safety where they can be accepted by Allied authorities.

(d) The Japanese Imperial General Headquarters will furnish to the Supreme Commander for the Allied Powers, without delay after receipt of this order, complete lists of all United Nations Prisoners of War and Civilian Internees, indicating their locations.

X. All Japanese and Japanese-controlled Military and Civil Authorities shall aid and assist the occupation of Japan and Japanese-controlled areas by forces of the Allied Powers.

XI. The Japanese Imperial General Headquarters and appropriate Japanese Officials shall be prepared, on instructions from Allied Occupation Commanders, to collect and deliver all arms in the possession of the Japanese Civilian population.

XII. This and all subsequent instructions issued by the Supreme Commander for the Allied Powers or other Allied Military Authorities will be scrupulously and promptly obeyed by Japanese and Japanese-controlled Military and Civil Officials and private persons. Any delay or failure to comply with the provisions of this or subsequent orders, and any action which the Supreme Commander for the Allied Powers determines to be detrimental to the Allied Powers, will incur drastic and summary punishment at the hands of Allied Military Authorities and the Japanese Government.

XIII. The Japanese Imperial General Headquarters will immediately advise the Supreme Commander for the Allied Powers the earliest date and time at which information called for in Parts II, VII and IX (d) can be submitted.

（付記）

一般命令第一號（陸、海軍）

一 帝國大本營ハ茲ニ勅命ニ依リ且勅命ニ基ク一切ノ日本國軍隊ノ聯合國最高司令官ニ對スル降伏ノ結果トシテ日本國國内及國外ニ在ル一切ノ指揮官ニ對シ其ノ指揮下ニ在ル日本國軍隊及日本國ノ支配下ニ在ル軍隊ヲシテ敵對行爲ヲ直ニ終止シ其ノ武器ヲ措キ現位置ニ留リ且左ニ指示セラレ又ハ聯合國最高司令官ニ依リ追テ指示セラルルコトアルベキ合衆國、中華民國、聯合王國及「ソヴィエト」社會主義共和國聯邦ノ名ニ於テ行動スル各指揮官ニ對シ無條件降伏ヲ爲サシムベキコトヲ命ズ指示セラレタル指揮官又ハ其ノ指名シタル代表者ニ對シテハ即刻連絡

1 降伏文書調印と初期占領政策への対応（昭和20年9月～10月）

スベキモノトス但シ細目ニ關シテハ聯合國最高司令官ニ依リ變更ノ行ハルルコトアルベク右指揮官又ハ代表者ノ命令ハ完全ニ且即時實行セラルベキモノトス

(イ)支那（滿洲ヲ除ク）、臺灣及北緯十六度以北ノ佛領印度支那ニ在ル日本國ノ先任指揮官竝ニ一切ノ陸上、海上、航空及補助部隊ハ蔣介石總帥ニ降伏スベシ

(ロ)滿洲、北緯三十八度以北ノ朝鮮、樺太及千島諸島ニ在ル日本國ノ先任指揮官竝ニ一切ノ陸上、海上、航空及補助部隊ハ「ソヴィエト」極東軍最高司令官ニ降伏スベシ

(ハ)(一)「アンダマン」諸島、「ニコバル」諸島、「ビルマ」、「タイ」國、北緯十六度以南ノ佛領印度支那、「マライ」、「スマトラ」、「ジャヴァ」、小「スンダ」諸島(「バリ」、「ロンボク」及「チモール」ヲ含ム)、「ブル」、「セラム」、「アンボン」、「カイ」、「アル」、「タニンバル」及「アラフラ」海ノ諸島、「セレベス」諸島、「ハルマヘラ」諸島竝ニ蘭領「ニュー、ギニア」ニ在ル日本國ノ先任指揮官竝ニ一切ノ陸上、海上、航空及補助部隊ハ東南亞細亞軍司令部最高司令官ニ降伏スベ

(二)「ボルネオ」、英領「ニュー、ギニア」、「ビスマルク」諸島及「ソロモン」諸島ニ在ル日本國ノ先任指揮官竝ニ一切ノ陸上、海上、航空及補助部隊ハ濠洲陸軍最高司令官ニ降伏スベシ

(ホ)日本國委任統治諸島、小笠原諸島及他ノ太平洋諸島ニ在ル日本國ノ先任指揮官竝ニ一切ノ陸上、海上、航空及補助部隊ハ合衆國太平洋艦隊最高司令官ニ降伏スベシ

(ニ)日本國大本營竝ニ日本國本土、之ニ隣接スル諸小島、北緯三十八度以南ノ朝鮮、琉球諸島及「フィリピン」諸島ニ在ル先任指揮官竝ニ一切ノ陸上、海上、航空及補助部隊ハ合衆國太平洋陸軍部隊最高司令官ニ降伏スベシ

(ヘ)前記各指揮官ノミガ降伏ヲ受諾スルノ權限ヲ付與セラレタル聯合國代表者ニシテ日本國軍隊ノ降伏ハ總テ右指揮官又ハ其ノ代表者ノミニ對シテ爲サルベシ

日本國大本營ハ更ニ日本國國内及國外ニ在ル其ノ指揮官ニ對シ何レノ位置ニ在ルヲ問ハズ一切ノ日本國軍隊又ハ

日本國ノ支配下ニ在ル軍隊ヲ完全ニ武裝解除シ且前記聯合國指揮官ニ依リ指定セラルル時期及場所ニ於テ一切ノ兵器及裝備ヲ現狀ノ儘且安全ニシテ良好ナル狀態ニ於テ引渡スベキコトヲ命ズ

追テ指示アル迄日本國本土內ニ在ル日本國警察機關ハ武裝解除規定ノ適用ヲ免ルルモノトス警察機關ハ其ノ部署ニ留ルモノトシ法及秩序ノ維持ニ付其ノ責ニ任ズベシ右警察機關ノ人員及武器ハ規定セラルルモノトス

二、日本國大本營ハ聯合國最高司令官ニ對シ本命令受領ノ後遲滯ナク日本國及日本國ノ支配下ニ在ル一切ノ地域ニ於ケル左ノ諸點ニ關スル完全ナル情報ヲ提供スベシ

（イ）一切ノ陸上、海上、航空及防空部隊ノ位置及將兵ノ數ヲ示ス表

（ロ）一切ノ陸軍、海軍及非軍用航空機ノ數、型式、位置及其ノ狀態ニ關シ完全ナル情報ヲ與フル表

（ハ）日本國及日本國ノ支配スル一切ノ水上及潛水海軍艦艇並ニ補助海軍艦艇ニシテ就役中ノモノ又ハ就役中ニ非ザルモノ及建造中ノモノノ位置、狀態及運行ヲ示ス表

（ニ）日本國及日本國ノ支配スル一切ノ總噸數百噸ヲ超ユル商船（營テ聯合國ノ何レカニ屬シ現ニ日本國ノ權內ニ在ルモノヲ含ム）ニシテ就役中ノモノ又ハ就役中ニ非ザルモノ及建造中ノモノノ位置、狀態及運行ヲ示ス表

（ホ）一切ノ機雷、機雷原其ノ他ノ陸上、海上又ハ空中ノ行動ニ對スル障害物ノ位置及施設狀況並ニ右ニ關聯スル安全通路ニ關スル完全且詳細ナル地圖附情報

（ヘ）飛行場、水上機基地、對空防備施設、港、海軍基地、物資貯藏所、常設及假設ノ陸上及沿岸防備施設、要塞其ノ他ノ防備地域ヲ含ム一切ノ軍事施設及建造物ノ位置及說明

（ト）聯合諸國ノ俘虜及被抑留者ノ一切ノ收容所其ノ他ノ抑留所ノ位置

三、日本軍及民間航空所管當局ハ一切ノ日本國ノ陸軍、海軍及非軍用航空機ガ追テ其ノ處理ニ關シ通告アル迄陸上、海上又ハ艦上ニ留ルコトヲ保障スルモノトス

四、日本國ノ又ハ日本國ノ支配スル一切ノ型式ノ海軍艦艇及商船ハ聯合國最高司令官ノ指示アル迄之ヲ毀損スルコ

18

1 降伏文書調印と初期占領政策への対応（昭和20年9月～10月）

トナク保全シ且移動ヲ企圖セザルモノトス航海中ノ船舶ニ於テハ直ニ一切ノ種類ノ爆發物ヲ無害ト爲シ海中ニ抛棄スルモノトス航海中ニ非ザル船舶ニ於テハ直ニ一切ノ種類ノ爆發物ヲ沿岸ノ安全ナル貯藏所ニ移轉スルモノトス

五　責任アル日本國ノ及日本國ノ支配下ニ在ル軍及行政當局ハ左記ヲ保障スルモノトス
　(イ)一切ノ日本國ノ機雷、機雷原其ノ他ノ陸上、海上及空中ノ行動ニ對スル障害物ハ何レノ位置ニ在ルヲ問ハズ聯合國最高司令官ノ指示ニ從ヒ之ヲ除去
　(ロ)航海ヲ便ナラシムル一切ノ施設ハ直ニ之ヲ復活ス
　(ハ)前記(イ)ノ實施迄一切ノ安全通路ハ之ヲ開放シ且明瞭ニ標示ス

六　責任アル日本國ノ及日本國ノ支配下ニ在ル軍及行政當局ハ聯合國最高司令官ヨリ追テ指示アル迄左記ヲ現狀ノ儘且良好ナル狀態ニ於テ保持スルモノトス
　(イ)一切ノ兵器、彈藥、爆發物、軍用ノ裝備、貯品及需品其ノ他一切ノ種類ノ戰爭用具及他ノ一切ノ戰爭用資材（本命令第四項ニ特ニ規定スルモノヲ除ク）

　(ロ)一切ノ陸上、水上及空中運輸及通信ノ施設及裝置
　(ハ)飛行場、水上機基地、對空防備施設、港及海軍基地、物資貯藏所、常設及假設ノ陸上及沿岸防備施設、要塞其ノ他ノ防備地域ヲ含ム一切ノ軍事施設及建造物並ニ一切ノ此等ノ防備施設、軍事施設及建造物ノ設計及圖面
　(ニ)一切ノ戰爭用具竝ニ軍事機關又ハ準軍事機關ガ其ノ運營ニ關シ現ニ使用シ又ハ使用セントスル他ノ資材及資産ヲ製造スル爲又ハ此等ノ製造ヲ容易ナラシムル爲計畫セラレ又ハ之ニ充當セラレタル一切ノ工場、製造場、工作場、研究所、實驗所、試驗所、技術上ノ要目（「データ」）特許、設計、圖面及發明

七　日本國大本營ハ聯合國最高司令官ニ對シ本命令受領ノ後遲滯ナク前記第六項(イ)、(ロ)及(ニ)ニ揭グル一切ノ項目ニ關シ其ノ數量、型式及位置ヲ示ス完全ナル表ヲ提供スベシ

八　一切ノ兵器、彈藥及戰爭用具ノ製造及分配ハ直ニ之ヲ終止スルモノトス

九　日本國ノ又ハ日本國ノ支配下ニ在ル官憲ノ權內ニ在ル

(イ)聯合諸國ノ俘虜及被抑留者ニ關シテハ

一切ノ聯合諸國ノ俘虜及被抑留者ノ安全及福祉ハ細心ノ注意ヲ以テ之ヲ保持スルモノトシ右ハ聯合國最高司令官ガ其ノ責任ヲ引繼グニ至ル迄適當ナル聯合國最高司令官ガ其ノ責任ヲ引繼グニ至ル迄適當ナル食糧、住居、被服及醫療ヲ確保スルニ必要ナル管理及補給ノ業務ヲ含ムモノトス

(ロ)聯合諸國ノ俘虜及被抑留者ノ收容所其ノ他ノ抑留所夫々其ノ設備、貯藏品、記錄、武器及彈藥ト共ニ直ニ之ヲ右俘虜及被抑留者中ノ先任將校又ハ指定セラレタル代表者ニ引渡シ其ノ後聯合國官憲ガ之ヲ引取リ得ベキ安全ナル場所ニ輸送セラルルモノトス

(ハ)聯合國最高司令官ノ指示スル所ニ從ヒ俘虜及被抑留者ハ聯合國官憲ガ之ヲ引取リ得ベキ安全ナル場所ニ輸送セラルルモノトス

(ニ)日本國大本營ハ聯合國ノ最高司令官ニ對シ本命令受領ノ後遲滯ナク一切ノ聯合國ノ俘虜及被抑留者ノ所在ヲ示ス完全ナル表ヲ提供スルモノトス

十 一切ノ日本國ノ及日本國ノ支配下ニ在ル軍及行政當局ハ聯合國軍隊ノ日本國及日本國ノ支配スル地域ノ占領ヲ援助スベシ

十一 日本國大本營及日本國當該官憲ハ聯合國占領軍指揮官ノ指示アル際一般日本國民ノ所有スル一切ノ武器ヲ蒐集シ且引渡ス爲ノ準備ヲ爲シ置クベシ

十二 日本國ノ及日本國ノ支配下ニ在ル軍及行政官憲並ニ私人ハ本命令及爾後聯合國最高司令官又ハ他ノ聯合國軍官憲ノ發スル一切ノ指示ニ誠實且迅速ニ服スルモノトス本命令若ハ爾後ノ命令ノ規定ヲ遵守スルニ遲滯アリ又ハ之ヲ遵守セザルトキ及聯合國最高司令官ガ聯合國ニ對シ有害ナリト認ムル行爲アルトキハ聯合國軍官憲及日本國政府ハ嚴重且迅速ナル制裁ヲ加フルモノトス

十三 日本國大本營ハ聯合國最高司令官ニ對シ前記第二項、第七項及第九項(ニ)ニ要求セラルル情報ヲ提供シ得ベキ最モ速ナル日時ヲ直ニ通報スルモノトス

昭和20年9月2日 閣議了解

3 「聯合國最高司令官ノ要求ニ係ル一般命令ノ實施ニ關スル件」

付記 昭和二十二年十二月二十六日、外務省作成

20

1　降伏文書調印と初期占領政策への対応（昭和20年9月～10月）

終戦処理会議・終戦連絡中央事務局その他の設置に関する調書

聯合國最高司令官ノ要求ニ係ル一般命令ノ實施ニ關スル件

（昭和二〇、九、二、閣議了解）

聯合國最高司令官ノ要求ニ係ル一般命令所定ノ事項中ニハ統帥關係以外ノ事項存スルモ、之ガ實施ニ付テハ、此ノ際特別ノ法律制定ノ手續ヲ執ルコトナク、行政上ノ措置ニ依リ充分之ガ目的ノ達成ニ努ムルモノトシ、今後ノ事態ニ依リ特ニ必要ヲ生ジタル場合ニ於テ其ノ際ニ緊急勅令ノ制定等所要ノ立法措置ヲ講ズルモノトス

付　記

終戦処理会議その他に関する件

（一九四七、一二、二六）

A、終戦処理會議及び終戦事務連絡委員會

(イ)終戦處理會議

(一)設立年月日

　一九四五年八月二十二日

(二)構成員

　内閣總理大臣
　外務大臣
　陸軍大臣
　海軍大臣
　近衞國務大臣
　參謀總長
　軍令部總長
　幹事　内閣書記官長
　ただし審議事項の性質に応じ、必ずしも全構成員による審議を要せず、また上記以外の各大臣をも出席せしめる。

(三)目的

　終戦に関する重要事項の審議

(四)解散年月日

　自然消滅

(ロ)終戦事務連絡委員會

(一)設立年月日

　一九四五年八月二十二日

(二) 構成員

委員長　外務大臣

副委員長　內閣書記官長

委員　外務省政務局長

委員　內務省警保局長

幹事　各省高等官若干名

厚生省勤勞局長

運輸省企畫局長

軍需省總動員局長

農林省總務局長

大藏省總務局長

陸軍省軍務局長

海軍省軍務局長

(三) 目的

終戰事務を正確且つ迅速に實施勵行するため大本營及び政府の連絡機關として終戰處理會議の下に設置せられ、その具體的事務としては停戰協定事項を正確に實施するため同事項に關する大本營及び政府各機關の分擔事務の確定及びその實施促進に關する事項を掌理する。

(四) 解散年月日

終戰連絡事務局の運營に伴い自然消滅す。

B、終戰連絡中央事務局及び地方事務局

(一) 終戰連絡中央事務局

(イ) 設置年月日　一九四五年八月二十六日

(ロ) 終戰連絡地方事務局　第(二)項參照

(二) 當初における終戰連絡地方事務局の數及び所在地

(イ) 事務局

事務局名	所在地	設置年月日	備考
橫濱事務局	橫濱市	一九四五、九、三	
仙臺事務局	仙臺市	一九四五、一〇、一〇	一九四六、一〇、一四東北事務局と改稱
札幌事務局	札幌市	一九四五、一〇、一四	一九四六、一〇、一四北海道事務局と改稱
名古屋事務局	名古屋市	一九四五、一一、九	一九四六、一〇、一四東海北陸事務局と改稱
京都事務局	京都市	一九四五、九、三	
大阪事務局	大阪市	一九四五、一二、一〇	
吳事務局	吳市	一九四五、一〇、九	一九四六、一〇、一四中國事務局と改稱
館山事務局	館山市	一九四五、一二、六	

22

1　降伏文書調印と初期占領政策への対応（昭和20年9月〜10月）

（ロ）出張所

出張所	所在地	設置年月日	備考
鹿屋事務局	鹿屋町	一九四五、一一、九	
佐世保事務局	佐世保市	一九四五、一〇、一〇	
福岡事務局	福岡市	一九四五、一二、九	
松山事務局	松山市	一九四五、一二、九	
和歌山事務局	和歌山市	一九四五、一一、九	
計　一四事務局			

出張所名	所在地	設置年月日	備考
長崎出張所	長崎市	一九四五、一二、一	
立川出張所	立川市	一九四五、九、一〇	
厚木出張所	厚木町	一九四五、九、四	
計　三出張所			

（三）その後一九四六年十二月三十一日までにおける終戦連絡地方事務局の増減

（イ）事務局の新設または廃止

事務局名	所在地	設置年月日	廃止年月日	備考
高松事務局	高松市	一九四六、一二、三		一九四六、一〇、一四　四國事務局と改稱
九州事務局	福岡市	一九四六、一二、一		
岡山事務局	岡山市	一九四六、一二、一		

事務局名	所在地	設置年月日	廃止年月日	備考
千葉事務局	千葉市	一九四六、一二、二三		
熊本事務局	熊本市	一九四六、三、二〇		
神戸事務局	神戸市	一九四六、四、一		
久留米事務局	久留米市	一九四六、六、一〇		
館山事務局	（前掲）			
松山事務局	（前掲）			
鹿屋事務局	（前掲）	一九四六、三、二三		
福岡事務局	（前掲）	一九四六、三、二〇	一九四六、九、一五	
計　新設　七　廃止　五				
一九四六年十二月三十一日現在数　一六				

（ロ）出張所の新設または廃止

出張所名	所在地	設置年月日	廃止年月日	備考
松山出張所	松山市	一九四六、二、二三		松山事務局廃止とともに出張所を新設す
金澤出張所	金澤市	一九四六、四、一		
福井出張所	福井市	一九四六、四、一		
奈良出張所	奈良市	一九四六、四、一		
大津出張所	大津市	一九四六、四、一	一九四六、一一、五	
舞鶴出張所	舞鶴市	一九四六、四、一	一九四六、一〇、三一	
浦和出張所	浦和市	一九四六、五、一三	一九四六、六、一五	
山口出張所	山口市	一九四六、五、一三		
鹿児島出張所	鹿児島市	一九四六、五、一〇		

備考	一九四六年十二月三十一日現在數	計　新設　廃止	大分出張所	青森出張所	小倉出張所
その後一九四七年一月一日以降現在(一九四七、一、二〇)までに事務局四(佐世保、千葉、和歌山及び岡山)、出張所八(厚木、金澤、奈良、舞鶴、松山、長崎、福井及び青森)を廃止した結果右兩者の現在數は前者一二一、後者四である。		一二一　一二　三	大分市　一五六、二二九	青森市　一五六、六二二	小倉市　一五六、六一七

C、一九四五年八月連合軍受入のため設けられた受入委員會

(一)横濱地區連合軍受入設營委員會

(イ)構成員

　委員長　秋山特命全權公使

　副委員長　藤原神奈川縣知事

　事務總長　鈴木特命全權公使

　委員　内閣綜合計畫局、内務、陸軍、海軍、遞信、運輸、軍需、大藏の各省及び關係地方廳より各一名あて

(ロ)連合軍受入場所　神奈川縣横濱地區

(二)厚木地區連合軍受入設營委員會

(イ)構成員

　委員長　有末陸軍中將

　委員　外務、内務、陸軍、海軍、遞信、運輸、軍需、大藏の各省及び關係地方廳より各一名あて

(ロ)連合軍受入場所　神奈川縣厚木地區

(三)館山地區連合軍受入設營委員會

(イ)構成員

　委員長　林總領事

　委員　内務、陸軍、海軍、遞信、運輸、軍需、大藏の各省及び關係地方廳より各一名あて

(ロ)連合軍受入場所　千葉縣館山地區

(四)鹿屋地區連合軍受入設營委員會

1　降伏文書調印と初期占領政策への対応（昭和20年9月～10月）

4　内地における外国人捕虜および被抑留者の解放に関する指令

昭和20年9月2日　連合国最高司令官総司令部より日本政府宛

(イ) 構成員
　委員長　伊東大使館参事官
　委員　内務、陸軍、海軍、遞信、運輸、軍需、大藏の各省及び關係地方廳より各一名あて

(ロ) 連合軍受入場所
　鹿兒島縣鹿屋地區

付記　右和訳文

OFFICE OF THE SUPREME COMMANDER
FOR THE ALLIED FORCES

2 September 1945

MEMORANDUM FOR THE JAPANESE GOVERNMENT
THROUGH: Central Liaison Office Number 1.
FROM: The Supreme Commander for the Allied Powers.

1. The Japanese Government is ordered to alert the Japanese authorities in each of the Allied Prisoner of War and Civilian Internee Camps indicated on the attached sheet, for evacuation of all personnel therein on or about 3 September 1945.

2. On such date or soon thereafter the Japanese camp commander at each of the camps listed will be contacted by a representative of the United States Army. The local representative of the Japanese Government will act under the orders of the United States Army representative and will furnish transportation for all personnel from the camps to the evacuation point or points designated by the United States Army representative.

3. Camp commanders will make an estimate of the transportation required at each camp and will hold such transportation available until contacted by the representative of the United States Army.

FOR THE SUPREME COMMANDER

Harold Fair
Lt. Col., A.G.D.
Asst Adj. General

Incl 1 - List of POW and Civ Internee Camps

編　注　別紙は省略。別紙の内容については本文書付記参照。

（付記）

日本政府ニ對スル覺書　九月二日附
中央連絡事務局經由第一號
聯合國最高司令官發

一、日本政府ハ別紙所揭ノ聯合國俘虜及抑留者ノ各收容所ノ日本官憲ニ對シ九月三日頃全收容者ヲ引揚ゲシムル為待機スル様命令スベシ。

二、同日又ハ其ノ後間モナク別紙所揭各收容所ノ日本人所長ハ米國陸軍ノ代表者ヨリ連絡ヲ受クベシ。日本政府ノ地方官憲ハ米國陸軍代表者ノ命令ノ下ニ行動シ全收容者ノ為收容所ヨリ米國陸軍代表者ニ依リ指示セラルル引揚地點迄ノ輸送ヲ提供スベシ。

三、收容所長ハ各收容所ニ於テ必要トスル輸送量ノ見積リヲ為シ米國陸軍ノ代表者ヨリ連絡ヲ受クル迄常ニ右輸送量ヲ確保シ置クベシ。

（別紙）

聯合國俘虜及抑留者收容所ノ表

俘虜

仙臺第一乃至第十一
東京第三、第三B、第四、第五、第七、第十三、第十五、第十六
名古屋第一、第三、第六、第七、第八、第九、第十○、第十一
北海道本所、第一乃至第四

抑留者

福島、北海道、神奈川第一、埼玉、宮城

5

昭和20年9月2日

連合国最高司令官総司令部布告第一号

付記　右和訳文

GENERAL HEADQUARTERS
SUPREME COMMANDER FOR THE ALLIED POWERS

1　降伏文書調印と初期占領政策への対応（昭和20年9月～10月）

PROCLAMATION NO. 1

TO THE PEOPLE OF JAPAN:

As Supreme Commander for the Allied Powers, I do hereby proclaim as follows:

The unconditional surrender of the Imperial Japanese Government to the Allied Powers has brought to an end the armed conflict which has long existed between these forces. By the terms of the Instrument of Surrender, signed by command of and in behalf of the Emperor of Japan, the Japanese Government and the Japanese Imperial General Headquarters, the victorious military forces under my command will today occupy the territory of Japan.

By virtue of the authority vested in me as Supreme Commander for the Allied Powers, I hereby establish military control over all of Japan and the inhabitants thereof, and announce the following conditions of the occupation:

ARTICLE I

All powers of the Imperial Japanese Government, including the executive, legislative and judicial, will henceforth be exercised under my authority.

ARTICLE II

All governmental, public and honorary functionaries and employees, as well as all officials and employees, paid or voluntary, of all public utilities and services, including public welfare and public health, and all other persons engaged in essential services, shall continue to perform their usual functions and duties subject to my order, and shall preserve and safeguard all records and property.

ARTICLE III

All persons will obey promptly all my orders and orders issued under my authority. Acts of resistance to the occupying forces or any acts which may disturb public peace and safety will be punished severely.

ARTICLE IV

Your personal and property rights and religious beliefs will be respected. You will pursue your normal occupations, except as I shall otherwise order.

ARTICLE V

For all purposes during the military control, English will be

27

the official language. In event of any ambiguity or diversity of interpretation or definition between any English and Japanese text, the English text shall prevail.

ARTICLE VI

Definition of "military control" as used herein and in all other official communications and publications includes "Military Administration".

ARTICLE VII

Further proclamations, ordinances, regulations, notices, directives and enactments will be issued by me or under my authority, and will specify what is required of you and what you are forbidden to do.

Given under my hand at YOKOHAMA.
THIS SECOND DAY OF SEPTEMBER 1945.

/s/ DOUGLAS MacARTHUR
General of the Army of the United States
Supreme Commander for the Allied Powers

聯合國最高司令官總司令部

日本國民ニ告ク

布告第一號

第一條

本官ハ茲ニ聯合國最高司令官トシテ左ノ通布告ス

日本帝國政府ノ聯合國最高司令官ニ對スル無條件降伏ニ依リ日本國軍ト聯合國軍トノ間ニ長期ニ亙リ行ハレタル武力紛爭ハ茲ニ終局ヲ告ゲタリ日本國天皇、日本國政府及大本營ノ命ニ依リ且其名ニ於テ署名セラレタル降伏文書ノ諸條項ニ基キ本官ノ指揮下ニアル戰勝軍ハ本日ヲ以テ日本國ノ領土ヲ占領セントス

本官ハ聯合國最高司令官トシテ賦與セラレタル權限ニ基キ茲ニ日本國全領域竝其ノ住民ニ對シ軍事管理ヲ設定シ左ノ占領條件ヲ布告ス

第二條

行政、司法及立法ノ三權ヲ含ム日本帝國政府ノ一切ノ權能ハ爾今本官ノ權力下ニ行使セラルルモノトス

一切ノ官公吏、名譽職及雇傭員竝ニ公共福祉及公衆衞生ヲ含ム各種公共施設及業務ニ從事スル一切ノ有給及無給ノ役

（付記）

1 降伏文書調印と初期占領政策への対応（昭和20年9月～10月）

第三條

職員其ノ他必須業務ニ従事スル一切ノ者ハ本官ノ命令ニ基キ其ノ平素ノ職務及義務ヲ引續キ遂行シ一切ノ記録及財產ノ保存及保全ニ任スヘシ

第四條

一切ノ私人ハ本官ノ命令及本官ノ委任ニ基キ發セラルル一切ノ命令ヲ速ニ遵守スヘシ占領軍ニ對スル抵抗行為又ハ公共ノ安寧ヲ紊スカ如キ一切ノ行為ニ出ツル者ハ嚴重ニ處罰セラルヘシ

第五條

日本國國民ノ人權、財產權及宗教上ノ信仰ハ之ヲ尊重スヘシ日本國國民ハ本官ノ別段ノ命令ナキ限リ其ノ日常ノ業務ヲ繼續スヘシ

第六條

軍事管理期間中ハ英語ヲ以テ一切ノ目的ニ使用セラルル公用語トス英文及日本文ノ間ニ解釋若ハ意義ノ分明ナラサルモノアルトキハ英文ニ從フモノトス

本布告及其他ノ一切ノ公文並公表ニ使用セラルル「軍事管理」ナル語ノ意義ハ「軍政」ヲモ含ムモノトス

第七條

爾後ノ諸布告、軍命令、規則、告示、訓令、條令ハ本官ニ依リ又ハ本官ノ委任ニ基キ布告セラルヘク日本國民ニ對ス
ル要求事項若ハ禁止事項ヲ明示スルモノトス

一九四五年九月二日

横濱ニ於テ

聯合國最高司令官

「アメリカ」合衆國陸軍元帥　ダグラス、マックアーサー

6　連合国最高司令官総司令部布告第二号

昭和20年9月2日

付記　右和訳文

GENERAL HEADQUARTERS

SUPREME COMMANDER FOR THE ALLIED POWERS

PROCLAMATION NO. 2

CRIMES AND OFFENSES

TO THE PEOPLE OF JAPAN:

In order to make provision for the security of the armed forces under my command and for the maintenance of public peace, order and safety in the occupied area, as Supreme Commander for the Allied Powers, I do hereby proclaim as follows:

ANY PERSON WHO:

Violates the provisions of the Instrument of Surrender, or any proclamation, order, or directive given under the authority of the Supreme Commander for the Allied Powers, or does any act to the prejudice of good order or the life, safety, or security of the persons or property of the United States or its Allies or does any act calculated to disturb public peace and order or prevent the administration of justice, or wilfully does any act hostile to the Allied Forces, shall, upon conviction by a Military Occupation Court, suffer death or such other punishment as the Court may determine.

Given under my hand at YOKOHAMA

THIS SECOND DAY OF SEPTEMBER 1945

/s/ DOUGLAS MacARTHUR

General of the Army of the United States

（付記）

聯合國最高司令官總司令部

布告第二號

犯罪及罪科

日本國民ニ告ク

本官ハ茲ニ聯合國最高司令官トシテ本官麾下ノ軍隊ノ安全ノ確保並ニ占領地域ニ於ケル公共ノ平和、秩序及安寧保持ノ爲ノ規定ヲ設クル目的ヲ以テ左ノ通布告ス

降伏文書若ハ聯合國最高司令官ノ權限ニ基キ發セラルル一切ノ布告、命令若ハ指示ノ諸項ニ違犯シ又ハ善良ナル秩序ヲ害シ若ハ「アメリカ」合衆國若ハ其ノ聯合國ニ屬スル人若ハ財產ニ對シ生命、安全若ハ安寧ヲ害スル行爲ヲ爲シ又ハ公共ノ平和及秩序ヲ攪亂シ若ハ裁判ヲ妨害スル行爲ヲ以テ行動シ又ハ故意ニ聯合國ニ對シ敵意アル行動ヲ爲シ一切ノ私人ハ占領軍裁判所ノ判決ニ基キ死刑若ハ當該裁判所ノ判決スル其ノ他ノ刑ニ處セラルヘシ

一九四五年九月二日　横濱ニ於テ

1 降伏文書調印と初期占領政策への対応(昭和20年9月～10月)

7

昭和20年9月2日

連合国最高司令官総司令部布告第三号

付記　右和訳文

〰〰〰〰〰〰〰〰〰〰

聯合國最高司令官

「アメリカ」合衆國陸軍元帥　ダグラス、マックアーサー

GENERAL HEADQUARTERS
SUPREME COMMANDER FOR THE ALLIED POWERS

PROCLAMATION NO. 3

CURRENCY

TO THE PEOPLE OF JAPAN:

As Supreme Commander for the Allied Powers, I hereby proclaim as follows:

Article I

1. Supplemental military yen currency, marked "B", issued by the Military Occupation Forces is legal tender in Japan for the payment of all yen debts public or private.

2. Supplemental military yen currency, marked "B", issued by the Military Occupation Forces, regular yen currency issued by the Bank of Japan and Japanese state notes and coin shall be equivalent in all respects and interchangeable at their face value.

Article II

JAPANESE MILITARY CURRENCY

3. All military and all occupational currency which has been issued by the Japanese Government, Army or Navy, is void and valueless and the giving or accepting of such currency in any transaction is prohibited.

Article III

EXPORT AND IMPORT OF CURRENCY PROHIBITED

4. All foreign financial transactions, including the export and import of currency, coin and securities, are prohibited except as authorized by me.

5. All financial transactions shall be deemed to be foreign except those between Honshu, Hokkaido, Shikoku, Kyushu, and the adjacent waters.

Article IV

REGULATION OF OTHER CURRENCY

6. Currency of the United States of America and the Allied Powers and all other currency, except that mentioned in Article I, is not legal tender in Japan and the delivery or acceptance of such currency is prohibited, except as authorized by me.

Article V.

PENALTIES

7. Any person violating the provisions of this proclamation shall, upon conviction by a Military Occupation Court, suffer such punishment as the Court shall determine.

Given under my hand at YOKOHAMA this SECOND day of SEPTEMBER 1945.

/s/ DOUGLAS MacARTHUR
General of the Army of the United States
Supreme Commander for the Allied Powers.

布告第三號

通　貨

本官ハ茲ニ聯合國最高司令官トシテ左ノ通布告ス

日本國民ニ告ク

第一條

一、占領軍ノ發行スル「B」ノ記號ヲ附シタル軍用補助通貨ヲ以テ一切ノ公私ノ圓貨債務ノ支拂ヲ爲シ得ル日本法貨トス

二、占領軍ノ發行スル「B」ノ記號ヲ附シタル軍用補助通貨、日本銀行ノ發行スル法定通貨並ニ日本政府發行紙幣及硬貨ハ凡ユル點ニ於テ同價値トシ額面價格ニ依リ相互ニ兩替シ得ルモノトス

第二條　日本軍用通貨

三、日本國政府及陸海軍ノ發行シタル一切ノ軍用及占領地通貨ハ無效且無價値トシ如何ナル取引ニ於テモ右通貨ノ受授ヲ禁止ス

第三條　通貨ノ輸出入禁止

四、通貨、硬貨、證券ノ輸出入ヲ含ム一切ノ對外金錢取引ハ之ヲ禁止ス但シ本官ノ許可アルトキハ此ノ限ニ非ス

（付記）

聯合國最高司令官總司令部

1 降伏文書調印と初期占領政策への対応（昭和20年9月～10月）

五、本州、北海道、四國、九州及近海相互間ノモノヲ除キ金銭取引ハ總テ之ヲ對外取引ト看做ス

　第四條　其他ノ通貨ニ關スル規則

六、「アメリカ」合衆國及聯合國ノ通貨竝ニ他ノ一切ノ通貨ニ非サルモノトシ右通貨ノ受授ハ之ヲ禁止ス但シ本官ノ許可アルトキハ此ノ限ニ非ス

　第五條　罰則

七、本布告ノ規定ニ違犯シタル者ハ占領軍裁判所ノ有罪判決ヲ俟チ當該裁判所ノ決定スル刑ニ處セラルヘシ

右布告ス

　　一九四五年九月二日
　　　橫濱ニ於テ
　　　　聯合國最高司令官
　　　「アメリカ」合衆國陸軍元帥
　　　　　ダグラス、マックアーサー

8　〔重光（葵）外務大臣マッカーサー連合国最高司令官〕会談

昭和20年9月3日

重光・マッカーサー会談

重光外務大臣マッカーサー會見
昭和二十年九月三日
自一〇時三〇分至一二時
於橫濱連合軍最高司令部

大臣より昨日ポツダム宣言を敷衍せる降伏文書等の解釋に付貴方に充分明確に説明し置く必要ありと存し來訪せりと述へたる上要旨左の如く陳述す

一、日本政府の地位

政府はポツダム宣言受諾及降伏文書署名により生する義務及責任を完全に履行する堅き決心と實力を有す而して今日迄事態の急變に伴ひ生せる甚大なる困難を克服し來り今や皇族を主班とする內閣迄組織せられ敗戰に伴ふ多くの命令規則を發布する義務を勇敢に實行する決意を以て既に多くの命令規則を發布し且つ國民に對し之を充分徹底せしむる為議會をも召集せり右は九月一日の筈なりしも進駐延期に伴ひ再會も延期せられ四日五日の兩日となりしか之を通し國民に政府の明確なる態度を表示し充分の理解を求むる心算なり

國民も今の所政府を信賴し其の力を信じ居れり。

三、然るに此の義務履行を主張する政府の努力は今や非常に大なる難關に逢着す此れ即ち貴方の布告案なり右は之迄の例に反し日本政府を飛び越えて直接に日本國民に號令するものなり實は今日迄日本政府はポツダム宣言又は昨日の降伏文書にて米側は日本政府に要求をなし政府は之を實現する義務あるものと了解し又實際之等文書の内容も斯くの如く成り居るものと思へり之れ我方の解釋なるか最高司令官も其意味にて詔書及降伏文書と共に命令第一號を發せるものと考ふる處右は昨日旣に詔書及降伏文書と共に命令第一號を發せられ國民に之を實行を命したり斯く日本政府と共に公布せられ國民に之を實行を命したり斯く日本政府を通して總ての命令及要求を實現する事か之迄の方法にて右は良くウワークし得るものと思ふ然るに今囘の布告案は全然之に反し政府を抜きにして直接國民に命令し居り然も其の内容は受諾出來さるもの多し若し之か公布を見は國民の政府に對する信賴は全然無くなり行政上の混亂生し其の結果國内の混亂自然生す又日本政府の義務を履行せんとする力も無くなる次第にて其の結果か如何に成り行くや豫測をも許さす

三、布告案の内容を見るに今日にては旣に不必要の事も多く又昨日の文書にて國民も知らしめられ居るものも多し、通貨の問題も相互に理解を持たは解決し得へし尙し必要ありとせは從來と同樣のフォーミュラを以て政府に對する最高司令官の命令として發せられるれは可ならん然らは政府は誠實に此れを履行すへく萬一政府か履行せさるか又は占領軍か滿足せさる場合は國民に對する義務を出すも良からんか之れを爲さすして今直に斯かる布告を出す事は司令官の希望も政府の考へも實現出來さる事となるへし今日は以上の點を明確に述へて司令官の考を變す貰はんか爲に來訪せるなり云々

右に對しマックアーサーは左の如く囘答せり

昨日の演說にて述へし如く旣に勝敗に依り事態は決した譯にして日本側に課したる義務は完全に履行せられさる可からす之れを囘避し又は反對する事は到底許し難し日本側に於て凡ての義務を飽く迄忠實に履行する事を期待す而して自分等は日本國を破壞し國民を奴隷とする考は全然なし寧ろ何とか日本の困難を救助し度しと考へ居るものにて日本政府かグッドフエイスを充分示しくるれは

1 降伏文書調印と初期占領政策への対応(昭和20年9月～10月)

問題は簡単になり要するに政府及國民の出方一つにて之の問題は如何ともなるものなり布告の内容は日本側の手に依り充分履行し貰ひ差支なし。

之の時同席のサザランド参謀長口を挿み右は今朝會議にて議論したる布告案の事なるか外相の意見は之れを日本政府に對する命令とし貰ひ度しと謂ふに在りと説明せり。

右に對しマックアーサーは外相の言ふ如くして差支なきものなりやと述へたるに付大臣より布告案を示し日本側の同意し難き諸點を指摘せり。

右に依り結局マックアーサーは然らは之れを日本政府に對する司令官の命令に變更したる案と變へて提出ありたく本日中に作り得へきやと尋ねたるに付大臣より明日の畫迄に作る旨を答へ且之れを参謀長に手交する事に話合ひたり。

右の後更に各般の問題に付要旨左の如く會談せり

(イ)大臣より元帥は何日頃東京に來らるるやと尋ねたるに付要旨左の如く會談せり。

(ロ)大臣より目下の大問題の一は大陸方面より軍隊引揚の件

(ハ)大臣より本日は司令官の要求を完全に履行せんか爲其の援助及協力を求むる爲來訪せる次第なるか御話により目的を大体達成せりと思ふ今や日本に課せられたる義務の履行は日本國民の名譽に係る問題となり居る次第なりと述へたるに元帥は了解せり今後も何時にても來訪せられ度米軍は日本を苦しめに来れるに非す敗北せる國民の困難は何處に於ても同様なれは寧ろ之を助けんとし来れるものなり尚日本側の忠實なる義務履行は其の精神的方面を滿足せしむるのみならす物質的にも樂になることを意味すと答へたるに付大臣より右の點は了解する旨述へたり。

(二)元帥より陛下は宮城に居らるるやガードは如何になり居るやと尋ねたるに付大臣は宮城燒失せる為極く狹き所に御座所を設け居り近衛師團は軍隊の一部として解散せ

右に依り船も無く又武装解除後は多数の人間の食糧も安全も危惧されテスパレートの状態なりと述へたるに、司令官は船は日本のものなく聯合國には其の餘裕なしと答へたり。依りて大臣より然らは日本の破損船舶を修理し使ふ外なき旨述へたるに元帥之を肯定せり

らるるに付宮内省直屬のポリスガード組織せらるる筈なりと答へたり。

(ホ) 元帥より食糧狀態如何との問あり大臣は之か現在のナイトメーヤーにて今は配給を繼續し居るも本年の作柄は平年以下なる上外國よりの輸入は杜絕し且農具肥料の生產も一般命令第一號第七條により停止し居る次第なり、と述へ且元帥の質問に答へ元來國內需要の約五分の一程度は主として滿洲、朝鮮、泰、佛印より輸入し居たるか之か全面的に停止せられたる次第を說明せり。右に對し元帥は其の點は考慮すへきか農具の生產は始めて差支なしと述へ大臣より船舶も約八〇萬噸弱殘存するも航行に堪ゆるものは三十數萬噸なるも日本の如き島國にては船かなくてはいかんともならす食糧問題は緊迫せりと述へたるに參謀長は船は直く解除する旨述へたり。

(ヘ) 大臣より右に付ては造船所も復活し船の修理を爲ささるへからす戰前は造船能力月十萬噸を遙か上廻り居たるも問題は鋼鐵にして此の方も手當をせさるへからす又右は鐵道の修理にも必要なるか製鋼能力は月五〇萬噸位ある筈なりと述へたるに元帥は然らはどしどし始めたら宜し

(ト) 依りて大臣より米側の意向は了解せるに付平和產業はどしどし開始すへく若し平和產業なりや否やに疑問ある場合は米側の解釋を問ひ合はすこととすへしと述へたるに元帥は既に方針は極りて付疑ひ等なかるへしと言ひたるか大臣は兎に角必要あらは米側にて監察官を出すことも差支なきに付日本國民の息の止まらぬ樣にして貰ひ度しと述へ置けり。

〰〰〰〰〰

かるへく米側には日本國民の息か止まるか如き措置をなす意向なく寧ろ之を助けんとするものなりと答へたり。

9

昭和20年9月3日　大本營より連合国最高司令官宛

外国人捕虜および被抑留者に関する情報提供について

付記　右和文原案

From the Japanese Imperial General Headquarters to the Supreme Commander for the Allied Powers.

With reference to the information concerning the Allied Prisoners of War and Civilian Internees requested in accordance

1　降伏文書調印と初期占領政策への対応（昭和20年9月〜10月）

with General Order No.1 Paragraph XIII and with reference to sub-paragraph g of Paragraph II and subparagraph d of Paragraph IX of General Order No.1, the Japanese Imperial General Headquarters and Japanese Government wish to inform that

1) The list of the Allied Prisoners of War and Civilian Internees in the main islands of Japan will be submitted by 15.00 hours, September 5.

2) With regard to the list of the Allied Prisoners of War and Civilian Internees located in other places than the main islands of Japan, the Japanese Military Authorities in each locality were instructed to deliver it on the spot to the Allied authorities, since it is now impossible in Japan to gather correct information owing to difficulties of transportation and communication. However, lists compiled as of November 1, 1944 (except the lists for the Philippines and Borneo, which were not received at that time owing to the severance of transportation, and that for the War Prisoners' Camp at Shanghai, from where all inmates but 25 were later transferred to Japan) will be submitted for your reference by 15.00 hours September 5.

The lists of the Civilian Internees in China (except the list of the Weihsien（マヽ）Camp which was burned during a recent airraid) will be submitted by 15.00 hours September 5 only with such data as are available in Japan at present, because the latest information is impossible to obtain on account of the severance of transportation and communication.
September 3rd, 1945

（付　記）

大本營發聯合國最高司令官宛

第　　號（九月三日）

俘虜及被抑留者ニ關スル情報提供ニ關スル件

一般命令第一號第十三項ニヨリ聯合國ノ俘虜及被抑留者ニ關シテ要求セラレ居ル情報（一般命令第一號第二項ノ（ト）及第九項ノ（ニ）參照）ニ關シテハ

一、日本内地ニ於ケル俘虜及被抑留者ノ名簿ハ九月五日十五時ニ提出シ得ヘシ

二、日本内地以外ノ地域ニ於ケル俘虜及被抑留者ノ名簿ニ付テハ最近ノ交通通信狀況窮迫セルニヨリ正確ナル資料ヲ

3 September 1945

DIRECTIVE
NUMBER 2

PART I
GENERAL

1. a. The Japanese Imperial Government and the Japanese Imperial General Headquarters are hereby directed to comply, or to insure the compliance as the case may be, with the requirements of the Supreme Commander for the Allied Powers stated in this Directive.

b. This Directive and such amplifying instructions by the Japanese Imperial Government and the Japanese Imperial General Headquarters as may prove necessary thereunder, shall apply to Japanese and Japanese-controlled Armed Forces and appropriate civil agencies in the main islands of JAPAN and adjacent off-shore islands to include TSUSHIMA ISLAND, KOREA south of 38 degrees north latitude, and the RYUKYUS.

c. The requirements imposed by this Directive are designed to facilitate and insure the prompt and orderly establish-

---

指令第二号

昭和20年9月3日　連合国最高司令官総司令部より
　　　　　　　　日本政府、大本営宛

付　記　右和訳文

OFFICE OF THE SUPREME COMMANDER
FOR THE ALLIED POWERS
APO 500

10

提出スルコト不可能ナル為各現地日本軍當局ニ於テ夫々聯合國側ニ手交スヘキ様指示シアリ、但シ昭和十九年十一月一日現在ニテ調製セラレタル俘虜名簿（當時輸送杜絶ノタメ比島俘虜收容所、「ボルネオ」俘虜收容所ノ分ハ送付ナク及其ノ後收容俘虜二五名ヲ殘シ他ノ全員ヲ内地ヘ移管シタル上海俘虜收容所ノ分ヲ除ク）アルヲ以テ参考ノ為九月五日十五時提供スヘシ
尚支那ニ於ケル被抑留者ノ名簿（先般戰禍ヲ蒙リ燒失シタル濰縣 Weishen ノ分ヲ除ク）ハ先般來ノ交通通信ノ途絶ヘ最近ノモノヲ入手シ得サルニ付差當リ手元ニテ間ニ合フ範圍ノモノヲ九月五日十五時提供スヘシ

38

1 降伏文書調印と初期占領政策への対応（昭和 20 年 9 月～10 月）

ment of the Occupation Forces of the Supreme Commander for the Allied Powers in designated objectives within its area of application, and to establish certain controls over disarmament and demobilization of Japanese Armed Forces deemed necessary to insure orderly compliance with terms of surrender.

d. Additional requirements will be imposed from time to time as deemed necessary to carry out the above objectives.

2. a. The term "Japanese Armed Forces" as used herein shall be defined as all Japanese and Japanese-controlled Army and Naval Forces including their Air Forces, Auxiliaries and quasi-military organizations, as well as all personnel employed by or attached to any of the foregoing, but shall not include civil police.

b. The term "Allied Representative" as used herein shall be defined as any Commander of Occupation Forces, or any Subordinate Commander, Staff Officer, or Agent acting under authority of the Supreme Commander for the Allied Powers, or a Commander of Occupation Forces.

3. The Supreme Commander for the Allied Powers, who is also Commander-in-Chief, United States Army Forces, Pacific, has designated Commanders of Occupation Forces in areas of JAPAN Proper and KOREA south of 38 degrees north latitude, as shown in detail on Map, Annex "A", which will be regarded as a part of this Directive. All orders or instructions issued by or under authority of these Commanders shall be regarded as being by authority of the Supreme Commander for the Allied Powers within the area indicated.

4. The official text of all Proclamations, Orders and Instructions issued by authority of the Supreme Commander for the Allied Powers shall be in English. When a Japanese translation is also issued and any discrepancies occur, the English text will govern. When any question arises as to the meaning of any instructions issued, the interpretation of the issuing authority shall be final.

5. Commanding Officers of all organizations, units, or subdivisions of the Japanese Armed Forces will be held personally responsible by the Supreme Commander for the Allied Powers or the Commanders of Occupation Forces concerned, for the prompt and complete execution of instructions issued by Allied Representatives and applicable within the sphere of responsibility of

such Japanese Commanding Officers.

6. Unless otherwise specified, time limits contained in this Directive are reckoned from receipt of this Directive by Japanese Imperial General Headquarters. Required reports will be submitted in English.

PART II

JAPANESE ARMED FORCES

1. The Japanese Imperial General Headquarters will, without delay, adjust boundaries of control of the First Japanese General Army to coincide with the Eighth United States Army and of the Second Japanese General Army to coincide with the Sixth United States Army, as outlined on Map, Annex "A", hereto.

2. a. The Commanding General, First Japanese General Army will report in person to the Commanding General, Eighth United States Army, in the TOKYO area at hour and place designated by the latter, for instructions covering the entry of Occupation Forces into the area of responsibility of the Eighth United States Army.

b. The Commanding General, Second Japanese General Army will report by radio, without delay, to the Commanding General, Sixth United States Army, for instructions covering the entry of Occupation Forces into the area of responsibility of the Sixth United States Army. Initial radio contact through the facilities of the Supreme Commander for the Allied Powers, subsequent direct contact as directed by the Commanding General, Sixth United States Army.

c. The Commanding General, Seventeenth Japanese Area Army, KEIJO, will report to the Commanding General, United States Army Forces, Korea (Commanding General, XXIV United States Army Corps), for detailed instructions covering entry of United States Army Occupation Forces into KOREA south of 38 degrees north latitude, in accordance with instructions previously transmitted to the Japanese Imperial General Headquarters.

d. A senior representative of the Chief, Japanese Imperial Naval General Staff, will report in person to a designated naval representative of the Supreme Commander for the Allied Powers, in the TOKYO area at hour and place designated by the latter, for

40

1　降伏文書調印と初期占領政策への対応（昭和20年9月〜10月）

instructions covering the entry of United States Naval Forces into water areas and naval establishments of JAPAN Proper and KOREA.

　　e.　Japanese Commanders in the RYUKYUS will receive, at appropriate times, direct instructions from the Commanding General, Tenth United States Army, covering occupation of those Islands by United States Forces.

3.　The Japanese Imperial General Headquarters will submit to the Supreme Commander for the Allied Powers on demand:

　　a.　Detailed information regarding the current location of the Japanese Imperial General Headquarters and all its departments, branches, and agencies. Locations will be accurately marked on maps to scale not smaller than 1:100,000. The complete official name and address of each department, branch, and agency of the Imperial General Headquarters will be given, together with the name and appointment or office of the Senior Officer or official of each such department, branch, or agency.

　　b.　Detailed organization charts of the Japanese Armed Forces showing the chain of command to the level of divisions and independent brigades and comparable Naval units.

4.　The Japanese Imperial General Headquarters will provide the Supreme Commander for the Allied Powers, without delay, the following information pertaining to each General Army, Area Army, Army, Division, Independent Brigade (all types), and Independent Regiment (all types), and comparable Naval units:

　　a.　Designation and code name and number.
　　b.　Specific location of Headquarters.
　　c.　Commander's name.
　　d.　Home depot.
　　e.　Table of organization strength.
　　f.　Actual strength, as of latest date for which strength reports have been received.

5.　a.　In the execution of the provisions of Part I, "General Order No.1, Military and Naval," relating to disarmament of the Japanese Armed Forces, the Japanese Imperial General Headquarters shall remain responsible for the full and unqualified performance of such disarmament by Japanese Armed Forces.

b. Detailed instructions as to delivery of armaments to the occupation forces will be given directly to Japanese Commanders concerned by:

(1) Commanding General, Eighth United States Army, Commanding General, Sixth United States Army and Commanding General, United States Army Forces, KOREA, within their respective areas of responsibility in the case of munitions stocks, armaments of the Japanese Army, and Naval and Merchant ships and armaments taken over by Army Forces.

(2) Designated Naval Representatives of the Supreme Commander for the Allied Powers in the case of Naval vessels, shore establishments, supplies and equipment taken over by the United States Navy.

6. a. The Japanese Imperial General Headquarters shall conduct the speedy and orderly demobilization of all Japanese Armed Forces.

b. Processes of demobilization, to include surveillance, rate of discharge of personnel and designation of units for demobilization, are subject to supervision by the Commander of the Occupation Forces in the area in which units are to be demobilized.

7. The Japanese Imperial General Headquarters is responsible for continuing the maintenance and administration of Japanese Armed Forces until demobilized, and for the maintenance and preservation of all records and archives until relieved of this responsibility by Allied Representatives.

8. The Japanese Imperial General Headquarters shall issue instructions:

a. That the following tasks be accomplished without delay:

(1) All boom defenses at all ports and harbors will be opened and kept open; they will be removed within fourteen (14) days.

(2) All controlled minefields at all ports and harbors will be disconnected and rendered harmless.

(3) All demolition charges in all ports and harbor

42

1 降伏文書調印と初期占領政策への対応(昭和20年9月～10月)

works will be removed, or rendered harmless and their presence clearly marked.

b. That all aids to sea and air navigation be re-established. Pending the accomplishment of this task, the existing war system of navigational lighting will be maintained except that all dimmed lights will be shown at full brilliancy.

c. That all pilotage services continue to operate and all pilots, equipped with charts, remain at their normal stations ready for service.

d. That Japanese personnel concerned in the operation of sea and air ports remain at their stations and continue to carry out their normal duties pending further instructions.

e. That all warships and merchant ships whether in port or at sea immediately train all weapons fore and aft and render them inoperative.

9. The Japanese Imperial General Headquarters shall direct that, except as may be required otherwise in the execution of tasks assigned by Allied representatives, all personnel in Japanese warships, auxiliaries, merchant ships, and other craft remain on board their ships pending further instructions.

10. The Japanese Imperial General Headquarters will deliver to the Supreme Commander for the Allied Powers without delay the following information:

a. Details of coastal convoy routes and searched channels and of buoys, lights, and other navigational aids in Japanese and Korean waters.

b. Detailed lists of naval ammunition and naval fuel stocks, including furnace diesel, gasoline, and coal, as last reported to the Japanese Navy Ministry.

c. A list of all hospital ships giving location, condition, and bed capacity.

d. Ten copies each of the latest published editions of all nautical and aviation charts and other hydrographic publications of whatever classification, covering the main islands of JAPAN and adjacent Islands, the RYUKYUS, CHINA, KOREA, and other territory occupied by the Japanese.

e. Triangulation and tidal data for the MARIANAS and CAROLINE ISLANDS.

43

11. The Japanese Imperial Government and the Japanese Imperial General Headquarters will deliver to the Supreme Commander for the Allied Powers within 21 days the following maps and documents:

a. Two copies each of the latest editions of topographic maps of all scales and of whatever classification published under the authorities of the Japanese Imperial General Headquarters; the Japanese General Staff and the Imperial Land Survey, pertaining to JAPAN, CHINA, KOREA, MANCHURIA and all other areas which have been occupied by the Japanese military and naval forces. Maps shall be arranged in separate folios to scale and area, and shall be accompanied by graphical indices showing the contents of each folio. All additional copies of such maps in possession of the Japanese Imperial General Headquarters and its subordinate agencies shall be held in safe custody pending further instructions by the Supreme Commander for the Allied Powers, as to their ultimate disposition.

b. Two copies each of all records of geodetic positions and descriptions of triangulation stations and bench marks established in connection with topographic surveys of JAPAN, KOREA, CHINA and MANCHURIA and all other areas occupied by Japanese military and naval forces.

c. All survey data of the PHILIPPINE ISLANDS captured by the Japanese Forces during their occupation of MANILA.

12. Immediate steps will be taken to mark clearly all mines, minefields, and other obstacles to movement by land, sea, and air, wherever located in the area covered by this Directive.

13. The Japanese Imperial General Headquarters will insure that all minesweeping vessels immediately carry out prescribed measures of disarmament, fuel as necessary, and remain available for minesweeping service. Submarine mines in Japanese and Korean waters will be swept as directed by designated Naval Representatives of the Supreme Commander for the Allied Powers.

14. All Japanese land mines, land minefields, and other obstacles to include demolition charges, concealed explosives, and booby-traps, shall be made safe, and shall be removed at the earliest practicable date. Pending completion of the foregoing, all

44

1 降伏文書調印と初期占領政策への対応（昭和20年9月〜10月）

safety lanes shall be clearly marked and kept open.

15. The Japanese Imperial Government and the Japanese Imperial General Headquarters will insure that:

　a. Arrangements are made to provide on call by the Supreme Commander for the Allied Powers complete information with respect to:

　　(1) All overseas international electrical communication facilities including cables, radio telegraph, radio telephone and radio broadcasting facilities.

　　(2) All long distance and main line electrical communication facilities interconnecting the principal points on HOKKAIDO, HONSHU, SHIKOKU, KYUSHU, KOREA and FORMOSA and the RYUKYUS and KURILE ISLAND groups.

　b. All overseas international and internal electrical communication facilities (including cables, radio telegraph, radio telephone and radio broadcasting facilities) in the area covered by this Directive are maintained intact and continued in operation with the existing personnel (whether military, naval and/or civilian).

　c. Access is provided upon demand by the representatives of the Supreme Commander for the Allied Powers to the above-mentioned facilities for such censorship and supervision as circumstances may dictate to be necessary.

　d. The senior representatives of the government, civil, air, naval and military signal communication agencies are made available on call to the Chief Signal Officer on the staff of the Supreme Commander for the Allied Powers for instructions.

16. The Japanese Imperial General Headquarters will submit a report to the Supreme Commander for the Allied Powers without delay, furnishing the following information:

　a. Detailed statement regarding health of the Japanese Armed Forces.

　b. A station list of field and fixed hospitals controlled by the Japanese Armed Forces, showing location of each hospital and capacity in beds.

17. The Japanese Imperial Government will insure that

the names of all towns, municipalities, and cities are posted in English on both sides of each inter-city highway entrance and on railroad station platforms, using letters at least six (6) inches high. Transcription of names into English shall be in accord with the Modified Hepburn (Romaji) system.

18. The Japanese Imperial General Headquarters will make available on demand detailed information concerning recruiting and discharge methods employed in the Japanese Armed Forces.

PART III

ALLIED PRISONERS OF WAR AND CIVILIAN INTERNEES

1. a. The term "Prisoners of War" as used herein shall be construed as including all personnel held in Japanese custody:

(1) Who are or have been members of, or persons accompanying or serving with, the armed forces of any of the United Nations, or

(2) Who, as members of the armed forces of countries occupied by Japan, have been captured by the Japanese while engaged in serving the cause of the United Nations, and who, under terms of the Geneva (Prisoner of War) Convention of 27 July 1929, are entitled to be treated as prisoners of war even though such convention was not ratified by Japan, or

(3) Who are or have been members of or serving with the merchant marine of any of the United Nations.

(4) The term "Prisoners of War" does not include such personnel who, although formerly held in Japanese custody as Prisoners of War, have accepted release from the status in exchange for employment in or by Japan.

b. The term "Civilian Internees" as used herein shall be construed as including all persons without military status, detained by the Japanese Government, who are not nationals of the Japanese Empire as constituted on 10 July 1937.

c. The term "Prisoner of War and Civilian Internee Camp" as used herein shall be construed as including any camp,

46

1　降伏文書調印と初期占領政策への対応（昭和20年9月～10月）

prison, ship, billet, hospital or other place of confinement or detention of Prisoners of War or Civilian Internees.

　　d. The term "Camp Commander" as used herein shall be construed to include the commanding officer of any unit, detachment, or other element of the Japanese Armed Forces or their Auxiliaries or any civil warden or other official charged with the custody of Prisoners of War or Civilian Internees.

　2. The Japanese Imperial Government and the Japanese Imperial General Headquarters shall furnish to the Supreme Commander for the Allied Powers within forty-eight (48) hours the following information, if not heretofore submitted:

　　a. A list of Prisoner of War and Civilian Internee Camps as defined in paragraph 1 above, showing for each:

　　　(1) Official name or designation.
　　　(2) Location with respect to the nearest prominent geographical point.
　　　(3) Latitude and longitude in degrees and minutes.
　　　(4) Total number of Prisoners of War and Civilian Internees, including, where appropriate, the number of females included in the totals.
　　　(5) Geographical location of nearest railway station.
　　　(6) Name and geographical location, dimensions, and condition of runways of nearest airfield.
　　　(7) Approximate number of Prisoners of War or Civilian Internees requiring hospitalization.

　　b. A marked map or maps of 1:1,000,000 scale on which the location of each camp is accurately plotted.

　　c. Marked maps of 1:100,000 or larger scale of each area in which Prisoner of War and Civilian Internee Camps are located, showing accurately the location of each camp.

　3. The Japanese Imperial Government and the Japanese Imperial General Headquarters upon receipt of this Directive shall dispatch to each Camp Commander by the most rapid means available the following instructions:

　　a. Assemble all Prisoners of War and Civilian Internees at the earliest opportunity and read the following statement in English and such other languages as may be required:

　　"The formal surrender of Japan to the Allied Powers was

signed on 2 September 1945. General of the Army Douglas MacArthur has been named Supreme Commander for the Allied Powers. United Nations Forces are proceeding as rapidly as possible with the occupation of the Japanese Home Islands and Korea. The relief and recovery of Allied Prisoners of War and Civilian Internees will be accomplished with all possible speed.

"Pending the arrival of Allied Representatives the command of this camp and its equipment, stores, records, arms, and ammunition are to be turned over to the Senior Prisoner of War or a designated Civilian Internee, who will thenceforth give instructions to the Camp Commander for maintenance of supply and administrative services and for the amelioration of local conditions. The Camp Commander will be responsible to the Senior Prisoner of War or designated Civilian Internee for maintaining his command intact.

"Allied Representatives will be sent to this Camp as soon as possible to arrange for your removal and eventual return to your homes."

b. Turn over complete control of the camp to the Senior Prisoner of War or Civilian Internee, together with all equipment, stores, administrative and other records, arms, and ammunition, unless such items as may be designated by the Senior Prisoner of War or Civilian Internee for the use of the Japanese Camp Officials in the discharge of their functions as specified below.

c. Under the supervision of the Senior Prisoner of War or designated Civilian Internee, discharge the necessary administrative and supply functions, to include requisition of government or military stocks available locally, to insure:

    (1) Rations equivalent to the highest scale available locally to Japanese Armed Forces or civilian personnel.

    (2) The best medical care available, together with all necessary medical supplies.

    (3) Adequate shelter, clothing and bathing facilities.

d. This Directive will constitute authority to requisition such government or military supplies available in the vicinity of the camp as are required for the discharge of the responsibilities specified herein.

1　降伏文書調印と初期占領政策への対応（昭和 20 年 9 月～10 月）

e. Maintain camp organization intact and account to the Senior Prisoner of War or Civilian Internee for all camp personnel, camp administrative records, rosters, and records of transfer, hospitalization, and decease of individual Prisoners of War and Civilian Internees who are or have been confined in the camp.

f. Be prepared to supply, or to requisition from local government or military sources, transportation and supplies and to accomplish administrative arrangements for such movement of Prisoners of War and Civilian Internees as may be directed locally by Allied Representatives.

g. Under the supervision of the Senior Prisoner of War or Civilian Internee, prepare and dispatch the following information to the Supreme Commander for the Allied Powers through the Japanese Imperial General Headquarters:

(1) Complete lists of all Prisoners of War and Civilian Internees present, showing names, rank or position, nationality, next of kin, home address, age, sex, and physical condition.

(2) Extracts from available records on deceased or transferred Prisoners of War and Civilian Internees, showing name, rank or position, nationality, next of kin, home address, date of death or transfer, and destination or in the case of deceased persons, place of burial.

4. The Japanese Imperial General Headquarters shall transmit to the Supreme Commander for the Allied Powers without delay all information forwarded by Camp Commanders in response to the instructions specified in paragraph 3 g., above.

PART IV

RESOURCES

1. General

The Japanese Imperial Government will place at the disposal of the Occupation Forces of the Allied Powers all local resources required for their use as directed by authorized representatives of the Supreme Commander for the Allied Powers, or the Commanders of Occupation Forces within their respective areas.

2. Control

The Japanese Imperial Government will establish one central agency and required sub-agencies in each of the major occupied areas, whose primary function will be to provide information concerning, and to receive requisitions for, areas and facilities required for occupation forces.

3. Petroleum

Provisions will be made to furnish Allied Occupation Forces with petroleum products, storage and distribution facilities as required to the limit of availability. Specific requirements will be submitted at a later date.

4. Labor

   a. Labor Supply

   The Japanese Imperial Government will provide, through central government agencies established in each of the major occupied areas, labor in quantities and with the training and skills and at the time and places designated by the Supreme Commander for the Allied Powers, or the Commanders of the Occupation Forces within their respective areas. The agencies supplying labor will insofar as possible maintain the integrity of working groups such as construction gangs and longshoremen teams in order to secure maximum efficiency in control and production.

   b. Labor Requirements

   Labor requirements supplied by the Japanese Imperial Government for the Occupation Forces will include the following:

   (1) General labor.

   (2) Technical and semi-skilled labor.

   (3) Stevedoring and cargo handling.

   (4) Repair of roads, railroads, docks and other facilities.

   (5) Construction of housing and related facilities for Allied Occupation Forces.

5. Housing

The Japanese Imperial Government will be prepared to furnish to the Occupation Forces all buildings suitable for and required by these forces. Requirements will include the following

50

1 降伏文書調印と初期占領政策への対応（昭和20年9月〜10月）

general categories: Office buildings, hospitals, living quarters, warehousing and storage, shops, transportation and communication installations. Specific requirements will be submitted at a later date. Buildings will, insofar as possible, be of fireproof construction, equipped with running water, sewage disposal facilities, electricity, heating plants and situated on all-weather access roads.

6. Airfields

Selected airfields will be made available to Occupation Forces as required. The runways, dispersal areas and service aprons will be cleared of Japanese planes and the runways improved, if required, to provide a hard surfaced landing area of maximum proportions with a minimum length of 5,000 feet. Passenger and freight terminals, maintenance, servicing and communications facilities will be made available at each field. All Japanese aircraft and equipment will be safeguarded pending further instructions. Complete lists of all types of serviceable operating and maintenance equipment, and facilities, will be prepared by type and areas and presented to Allied Representatives upon demand.

PART V MISCELLANEOUS

1. The Japanese Imperial General Headquarters will make immediately available in the TOKYO area, to the Chief Signal Officer on the staff of the Supreme Commander for the Allied Powers, a radio-photo and still-photo laboratory complete with equipment and operating personnel.

2. Appropriate representatives of the Japanese Imperial General Headquarters will report to the Chief Signal Officer on the staff of the Supreme Commander for the Allied Powers within 48 hours with full information concerning available photographic personnel, equipment, processed and unprocessed film, and film and print libraries for both aerial and ground photography, which will thereafter be made available as demanded.

3. All agencies, civil and military, engaged in the collection, dissemination, and recording of weather information will continue normal operation pending further instructions. All meteorological data files and all equipment will be preserved intact. A station list of all weather installations will be submitted to the Supreme Commander for the Allied Powers without delay,

showing international index numbers, geographical location, and classification (forecast, research, central, or observing).

4. The Japanese Imperial Government shall, without delay, furnish to the Chief Surgeon on the staff of the Supreme Commander for the Allied Powers the following information:

   a. A comprehensive description of public health measures in force, with lists of principal officials, organizations and facilities.

   b. Nature, location, and seriousness of current epidemics, including control measures in effect.

   c. Last reported status of supply of drugs, medicines, and other sanitary supplies.

   d. A list of all civilian hospitals, sanitariums, and other medical institutions, giving locations and bed capacities.

5. All voice broadcasts for public information, in languages other than the Japanese, will be discontinued forthwith.

By direction of The Supreme Commander for the Allied Powers:

R.K. SUTHERLAND,

Lieutenant General, U.S. Army,
Chief of Staff.

DISTRIBUTION:

Action:	Japanese Imperial General H.Q.	(5)
"	Japanese Imperial Government	(5)
Information:	Staff, CINCAFPAC	(15)
"	CINCPAC	(5)
"	CG, Eighth Army	(3)
"	CG, Sixth Army	(3)
"	CG, XXIV Corps	(3)
"	CG, FEAF	(1)
"	CG, USASTAF	(1)
"	CG, AFWESPAC	(1)
"	CG, Tenth Army	(1)
"	WARCOS	(8)
"	Com Third Fleet	(3)
"	Com Fifth Fleet	(3)
"	Com Seventh Fleet	(3)

1　降伏文書調印と初期占領政策への対応（昭和20年9月～10月）

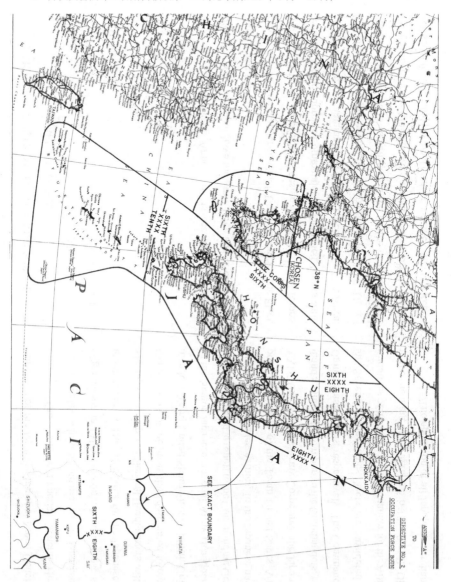

OFFICE OF THE SUPREME COMMANDER FOR THE
ALLIED POWERS

APO 500

3 September 1945

ANNEX "B"

TO

DIRECTIVE

NUMBER 2

1. The following Annex "B" is herewith appended to Directive No.2 and shall have the same force and effect and become a part thereof.

2. The Commander-in-Chief, United States Pacific Fleet, with Headquarters at GUAM, is designated as the Naval Representative for the Supreme Commander for the Allied Powers within the meaning of Paragraph 2 d, Part II, Directive No.2. A Naval Liaison Group representing the Commander-in-Chief, United States Pacific Fleet, is established in the Office of the Supreme Commander for the Allied Powers, and the Senior Officer thereof will serve for local and personal contact with the Chief and Representatives of the Japanese Imperial Naval General Staff.

3. The Japanese Imperial General Headquarters will, without delay, adjust boundaries of the Japanese Imperial Naval Organization in JAPAN to correspond to those set forth in Paragraph 1, Part II, Directive No.2 for the Japanese Imperial Army. The Japanese Imperial General Headquarters will direct the Naval Commanders of the areas thus designated to report to the Commanders, Third United States Fleet and Fifth United States Fleet, as the Senior Japanese Imperial Army Headquarters in the same areas are directed to report to the Commanding Generals, Sixth and Eighth United States Armies. In the Japanese naval areas corresponding to those of the Tenth United States Army area and the XXIV United States Army Corps area, the Japanese Naval Commanders thereof will report to the Commanders, Fifth and Seventh United States Fleets, respectively. The Commanders, Third, Fifth and Seventh United States Fleets, are considered as Naval Representatives of the Supreme Commander for the Allied Powers within the meaning of Paragraph 5 b (2), Part II, Directive No.2.

4. The operation of all Japanese merchant vessels of over

54

1　降伏文書調印と初期占領政策への対応（昭和20年9月～10月）

100 gross tons will be subject to the supervision of the Supreme Commander for the Allied Powers. The Japanese Imperial Government and the Japanese Imperial General Staff will report such vessels fully manned to the Commander-in-Chief, United States Pacific Fleet (or representatives designated by him), who is charged with the direction and supervision of their operation.

5. The terms "Commanders of Occupation Forces", as used in Paragraph 2 b, Paragraph 3 and paragraph 5, part I, and Paragraph 6, Part II, of Directive No.2, will include the Commanders, Third, Fifth and Seventh United States Fleets, within their respective areas of responsibility, relating to Naval Occupation Forces and to disarmament and demobilization of naval units.

（付　記）

聯合國最高司令官司令部
指令第二號　千九百四十五年九月三日

第一章　總　則

一、（イ）日本帝國政府及日本帝國大本營ハ茲ニ本指令ニ掲グル聯合國最高司令官ノ要求ニ付場合ニ應ジ自ラ之ニ從ヒ又ハ之ニ應ゼシムル様保證スルコトヲ指令セラル

（ロ）本指令並ニ之ニ伴ヒ必要ナルコト判明スルコトアルベキ日本帝國政府及日本帝國大本營ノ擴充ノ訓令ハ日本國本土並ニ對馬島、北緯三十八度以南ノ朝鮮及琉球ヲ含ム隣接海岸諸島ニ在ル日本國及日本國ノ支配下ニ在ル軍隊並ニ當該行政機關ニ適用セラルベシ

（ハ）本指令ニ依ツテ課セラレタル要請事項ハ指示セラレタル事項ニ付其ノ適用範圍内ニ於テ聯合國最高司令官ニ依リ占領軍ノ迅速且秩序アル設置ヲ容易ニシ且確保スルコトヲ目的トスルト共ニ降服條件ノ秩序アル遵守ヲ確保スルニ必要ナリト認メラルル日本武裝軍ノ武裝解除及復員ニ一定ノ監視ヲ行ハントスルニ在リ

（ニ）前記目的ヲ達成スル爲必要ト認ムルトキハ隨時追加要求事項ヲ課スルモノトス

二、（イ）茲ニ用ヒラレタル本指令ニ使用セラルル「日本國軍隊」ナル語ハ總テ日本國及日本國ノ支配下ニ在ル陸軍及海軍ヲ謂ヒ其ノ空軍補助機關及準軍事組織並ニ前記ノ何レカニ依リ雇傭セラレ又ハ之ニ附屬スル一切ノ者ヲ含ムモノトス但シ民普通警察ヲ含マズ

（ロ）本指令ニ使用セラルル「聯合軍代表」ナル語ハ占領軍指揮官若ハ下級指揮官、参謀將校又ハ聯合軍最高司令官若ハ占領軍指揮官ノ權限ノ下ニ行動スル機關ヲ謂フ

三、聯合軍最高司令官兼米國太平洋陸軍總司令官ハ本指令ノ一部ト看做サルベキ附屬「甲」ノ地圖ニ詳細ニ示サル日本國本土竝ニ北緯三十八度以南ノ朝鮮ノ地域ニ於ケル占領軍最高指揮官ヲ指名セリ右指揮官ニ依リ若ハ其ノ權限ノ下ニ發セラルル一切ノ命令及訓令ハ右ニ示メサレタル地域内ニ於テ聯合國最高司令官ノ權限ニ依リ爲サレタルモノト看做サルベシ

四、聯合國最高指揮官ノ權限ニ依リ發セラルル一切ノ布告、命令及訓令ノ正文ハ英語ニ依ルベシ。日本語ノ翻譯文ヲ同時ニ發布シ文意相違セル場合ニハ英文ニ從フモノトス。發セラレタル一切ノ訓令ノ意義ニ關シ疑義發生スルトキハ發令者ノ解釋ヲ最終ノモノトスベシ

五、日本國軍隊ノ一切ノ機關、部隊又ハ分隊ノ指揮官ハ聯合國代表ニ依リ發セラレ且右日本國ノ指揮官ノ責任ノ範圍内ニ於テ適用セラルル訓令ノ迅速且完全ナル實行ニ付聯合國最高司令官若ハ當該占領軍指揮官ニ對シ個人的ニ責任ヲ負フモノトス

六、別段ノ指示ナキ限リ本指令ニ定ムル時間制限ハ日本帝國大本營ニ依ル本指令受領ノ時ヨリ起算セラルルモノトス。要求セラルル報告ハ英語ニ依リ提出セラルルモノトス。

第二章　日本國軍隊

一、日本國大本營ハ日本國第一總軍ノ管轄ノ限界ヲ合衆國第八軍ニ符合セシムル樣又日本國第二總軍ノ管轄ノ限界ヲ合衆國第六軍ニ符合セシムル樣附屬セシムル樣附屬イ地圖ニ示サルル如ク遲滯ナク調整スルモノトス

二、イ、日本國第一總軍指揮官ハ合衆國第八軍ノ責任地區ノ占領軍ノ進入ニ關聯スル指示ヲ俟ツ爲東京地區ニ在ル合衆國第八軍指揮官ニ指示セラルル時及場所ニ於テ右指揮官ト自ラ遲滯ナク連絡スルモノトス。

ロ、日本國第二總軍指揮官ハ合衆國第六軍ノ占領軍ノ進入ニ關聯スル指示ヲ俟ツ爲合衆國第六軍ノ責任地區ヘノ指揮官「ラヂオ」ニ依リ遲滯ナク連絡スルモノトス指揮官「ラヂオ」ニ依リ連絡ハ聯合國最高司令官ノ施最初ノ「ラヂオ」ニ依リ連絡ハ合衆國第六軍ノ指揮官ガ指設ニ依リ爾後ノ直接連絡ハ合衆國第六軍ノ指揮官ガ指示スル所ニ從ヒ行ハルルモノトス

1 降伏文書調印と初期占領政策への対応（昭和20年9月〜10月）

八、在京城日本國第十七地區軍指揮官ハ前以テ日本帝國大本營ニ傳達セラルル指示ニ從ヒ北緯三十八度以南ノ朝鮮ヘノ合衆國占領軍ノ進入ニ關聯スル詳細ナル指示ヲ俟ツ爲朝鮮合衆國軍隊指揮官ト連絡スヘシ

二、日本帝國海軍軍令部總長ノ先任代表者ハ合衆國海軍ノ日本本土及朝鮮ノ水域及海運施設ヘノ進入ニ關聯スル指示ヲ俟ツ爲東京地區ニ在ル聯合國最高司令官ノ指名セラレタル海軍代表者ニ依リ指示セラルル時及場所ニ於テ右代表者ト連絡スルモノトス

ホ、琉球諸島ニ在ル日本國指揮官ハ合衆國軍隊ニ依ル右諸島ノ占領ニ關聯スル合衆國第十軍指揮官ヨリノ直接ノ指示ヲ適當ナル時ニ於テ受クルモノトス

三、日本帝國大本營ハ聯合國最高司令官ニ對シ要求アル際ハ左記ヲ提供スルモノトス

イ、日本帝國大本營並ニ其ノ一切ノ部、局及機關ノ現位置ニ關スル詳細ナル情報（位置ハ縮尺十萬分ノ一ヨリ小ナラザル圖上ニ之ヲ明示スルモノトス帝國大本營ノ各部、局及機關ノ完全ナル公ノ名稱及宛先ハ右ノ各部、局又ハ機關ノ先任將校又ハ官員ノ姓名及任務又ハ職務

ト共ニ之ヲ示スモノトス）

ロ、師團及獨立旅團並ニ右ニ相當スル海軍部隊ニ至ルマデノ指揮系統ヲ示ス日本國軍隊ノ詳細ナル組織圖

四、日本帝國大本營ハ聯合國最高司令官ニ對シ各總軍、地區軍、軍、師團、獨立旅團並ニ右ニ相當スル海軍部隊及獨立聯隊（一切ノ形式ノモノ）並ニ右ニ相當スル海軍部隊ニ關聯スル左ノ情報ヲ遲滯ナク提供スルモノトス

イ、名稱並ニ暗號呼出名及番號

ロ、本營ノ特定ノ位置

ハ、指揮官ノ姓名

ニ、原隊ノ所在地

ホ、組織上ノ兵力表

ヘ、現兵力（兵力量ノ報告ガ受領セラレタル最近ノ日時ニ依ルモノ）

五、イ、日本國軍隊ノ武裝解除ニ關スル「一般命令第一號（陸、海軍）」第一項ノ規定ノ實施ニ當リ日本帝國大本營ハ日本國軍隊ノ斯ル武裝解除ノ十分ニシテ且無條件ナル履行ニ對シ責ニ任ズベシ

ロ、占領軍ニ對スル武裝ノ引渡ニ關スル詳細ナル指示ハ

左ノ指揮官ヨリ當該日本國指揮官ニ對シ直接之ヲ與フルモノトス

(一)合衆國陸軍ノ手中ニ入ル日本軍ノ彈藥、兵器、軍用品及装備ニ付テハ合衆國第八軍司令官、合衆國第六軍司令官ノ各責任地區ニ於テ當該司令官

(二)合衆國海軍ノ手中ニ入ル海軍艦艇、沿岸施設、軍需品及装備ニ付テハ聯合國最高司令官ノ指定海軍代表

(複數)

六、イ、日本帝國大本營ハ一切ノ日本國軍隊ノ急速且秩序アル動員解除ヲ行フベシ

ロ、動員解除諸手續(右ノ監督、人員ノ解除率及動員解除セラルル部隊ノ指定ヲ含ム)ハ右部隊ガ動員解除セラルベキ地域ニ在ル占領軍指揮官ノ監督ヲ受クルモノトス

七、日本帝國大本營ハ動員解除ノ終了迄日本國軍隊ノ維持及經理ヲ繼續スル責任ヲ有シ且聯合國代表ニ依リ責任ヲ解除セラルル迄一切ノ記録及文書ノ維持及保存ノ責任ヲ有ス

八、日本帝國大本營ハ左ノ訓令ヲ發スベシ

イ、左ノ事業ハ遲滯ナク成就セラルベシ

(一)一切ノ港及泊地ニ於ケル防材ニ依リ防禦ハ開放セラレ且開放シ置カルルモノトス右防材ハ十四日以内ニ撤去セラルルモノトス

(二)一切ノ港及泊地ニ於ケル一切ノ監理機雷原ハ連絡ヲ斷チ且無害タラシムルモノトス

(三)一切ノ港及泊地ノ施設内ニアル爆破装薬ハ撤去セラレ若ハ無害タラシメラレ且之カ存在ハ明識セラルルモノトス

ロ、一切ノ航行、航空、補助施設ハ復活セラルルモノトス右復活ノ完了迄現行ノ戰時航路標示照明ハ維持セラルベキ尤モ現在ノ微光燈ハ之ヲ全光度ヲ以テ照明スルモノトス

ハ、一切ノ水先案内業ハ繼行セラルベク水先案内人ハ何レモ海圖ヲ携帶シ其ノ職場ニ待機スルモノトス

ニ、海港、空港ニ於テ業務ニ服スル日本人職員ハ追テ指示アル迄其ノ職場ニ留リ現業ヲ繼行スベシ

ホ、一切ノ軍艦及商船ハ其ノ停泊中ナルト航行中ナルト

58

1 降伏文書調印と初期占領政策への対応(昭和20年9月～10月)

九、日本帝國大本營ハ日本軍艦、補助艦、商船及其ノ他ノ船舶ノ乗組員ガ聯合國代表(複数)ニ依リ指定セラレタル事業ノ遂行ニ付別段ノ要請ヲ受ケタル者ヲ除キ全員追テ指示アル迄艦船上ニ留ル事ヲ命ズベシ

一〇、日本帝國大本營ノ聯合國最高司令官ニ對シ遲滯ナク左ノ事項ニ關スル情報ヲ提供スルモノトス

イ、日本ノ沿岸海域及朝鮮海域ニ於ケル沿岸航路及探知セラレタル水路並ニ浮標、照明及其ノ他ノ航行補助施設ニ關スル細目

ロ、日本國海軍省ヘノ最近ノ報告ニ依ル海軍彈藥貯藏品及燃料貯藏品(汽罐用「ディーゼル」油、「ガソリン」及石炭ヲ含ム)ニ關スル細目表

ハ、一切ノ病院船ニ付其ノ位置、狀態及寢臺收容力ヲ示セル表

二、日本國本土及隣接諸島、琉球、支那、朝鮮及日本軍ニ依リ占領セラレタル他ノ領域ニ關スル一切ノ航海圖、航空圖及他ノ一切ノ種類ノ河海測量出版物中最近出版セラレタル三角標及據點標ノ測量ノ位置及記述ノ全記録各二部

ロ、日本朝鮮支那及滿洲並ニ日本陸海軍部隊ニ依リ占領セラレタル一切ノ他ノ地域ノ地形調査ニ關連シテ建設セラレタル凡ユル縮尺及種類ノ地形學的地圖各二部、右地圖ハ縮尺及地區別ニ從ヒ區別セラレタル各葉ニ調整セラル可ク且各葉ノ内容ヲ指示スル圖ヲ附スベシ日本帝國大本營及右ニ從屬スル機關ニ歸屬スル斯ル地圖ノ一切ノ追加部本ハ聯合國最高司令官ガ其ノ最終的措置ニ關シ追テ指示アル迄安全ニ保管ス可シ

イ、日本帝國大本營、参謀本部及帝國陸地測量部ニ依リ又ハ其ノ監輯ノ下ニ發行セラレタル日本、支那、浦潮及日本陸海軍ニヨリ占領セラレタル他ノ一切ノ地域ニ對シ二一日以内ニ左ノ地圖及資料ヲ提出スルモノトス

十二、日本帝國政府及日本帝國大本營ハ聯合國最高司令官ニ及海流資料

ホ、「マリアナ」及「カロリン」諸島ニ關スル三角測量ノモノ各十部

八、日本軍ノ「マニラ」占領中獲得シタル「フィリピ

59

ン）諸島ニ關スル一切ノ測量資料

十三、一切ノ機雷、機雷原及本指令ニ關スル地域ノ何處ニアルヲ問ハズ陸上、海上及空中ニ於ケル行動ノ障害物ヲ明瞭ニ表示スルノ措置ヲ直ニ執ルベシ

十三、日本帝國大本營ハ一切ノ掃海艇ガ所定ノ武裝解除ノ方法ヲ實行シ所要ノ燃料ヲ補給シ掃海事業ニ役立チ得ル如ク保存スベシ

日本國及朝鮮水域ニ於ケル水中機雷ハ聯合國最高司令官ノ所定ノ海軍代表ニ依リ指示セラルル所ニ從ヒ掃海セラルベシ

十四、日本國ノ一切ノ地雷、地雷源及破壞用爆藥、隱匿セラレタル爆發物、穿ヲ含ム其ノ他ノ障害物ノ安全状態ト爲シ出來得ル限リ速カニ之ヲ除去スベシ右作業ノ完了迄ハ一切ノ安全通路ハ明瞭ニ表示セラレ且開カレ在ルベシ

十五、日本帝國政府及日本帝國大本營ハ左ノ事項ヲ保證スルモノトス

イ、聯合國最高司令官ノ要求アル場合次ノ事項ニ關スル完全ナル情報ヲ提供スルコト

（一）海底電線、無線電信、無線電話、無線放送施設ヲ含

ム一切ノ對外國際電氣通信施設

（二）北海道、本州、四國、九州、朝鮮、臺灣、琉球諸島、千島諸島ノ主要地點ヲ結ブ一切ノ長距離幹線電氣通信施設

ロ、本指示ノ關スル地域内ニ在ル一切ノ對外及對内電氣通信施設（海底電線、無線電信、無線電話及無線放送施設ヲ含ム）ハ其ノ盡維持セラレ現在人員（陸軍、海軍、民間タルトヲ問ハズ）ニ依テ操作ヲ繼續セラルベシ

ハ、聯合國最高司令官ノ代表者ノ要求アル場合上記ノ施設ニ對シ情況ノ必要トスル檢閱及監督ヲ可能ナラシムベシ

ニ、政府、民、空、海、陸ノ通信機關ノ上級代表者ハ訓令ヲ受クル爲聯合國最高司令官司令部通信部長ノ呼出ニ應ズベシ

十六、日本帝國大本營ハ聯合國最高司令官ニ對シ遲滯ナク左記情報ヲ提供スル詳細ナル記述

イ、日本國軍隊ノ健康ニ關スル報告ヲ提出スベシ

ロ、日本國軍隊ニ依リ管理セラルル野戰及固定病院ノ所在地表、右ハ各病院ノ位置及收容能力（寢臺數）ヲ示ス

60

1　降伏文書調印と初期占領政策への対応（昭和20年9月～10月）

モノトス

七、日本帝國政府ハ一切ノ市町村ノ名稱ヲ之等都市ヲ結ブ幹線道路ノ入口ノ兩側並ニ停車場歩廊ニ英字ヲ以テ掲グル事、右ニ使用スル英字ハ少クトモ六「インチ」以上ナル事ヲ要シ名稱ヲ英字ニテ記ス場合ハ修正「ヘボン」式「ローマ」字ニ依ルモノトス

六、日本帝國大本營ハ要求アルトキハ日本國軍隊ニ於テ使用セラルル徴集及除隊ノ方法ニ關スル詳細ナル情報ヲ入手シ得シムルモノトス

第三章　聯合國俘虜及被抑留者

一、イ、茲ニ使用セラルル「俘虜」ナル語ハ日本ノ收容下ニ在リ左ノ各項ニ掲グル總テノ人員ヲ含ムモノト解セラルベシ

（一）聯合諸國ノ何レカノ軍隊ノ隊員又ハ隨件者若ハ從業員タル者若クハタリシ者

（二）日本國ニ依リ占領セラレタル諸國ノ軍隊ノ一員トシテ聯合諸國ノ爲ニ勤務中日本人ニ依リ逮捕セラレ一九二九年七月二十七日ノ「ジェネバ」條約（俘虜ニ關スルモノ）ノ規定ニ從ヒ俘虜トシテ扱ハルル權利

ヲ有スルモノ（コノ條約ガ日本ニ依リ批准シ居ラザリシコトハ關係ナシ）

（三）聯合諸國ノ何レカノ商船隊ノ乗員タルカ若ハ乗員タリシ者又ハ之ニ從業スルモノ若ハ從事シタル者

（四）「俘虜」ナル語ハ嘗テ俘虜トシテ日本ノ收容下ニ置カレタルモ日本ニ於テ又ハ日本ニ依ル雇傭ヲ條件トシテ俘虜ノ身分ヨリノ釋放ヲ承諾シタル者ヲ含マズ

ロ、茲ニ使用セラルル「被抑留者」ナル語ハ日本政府ニ依リ留置セラレ一九三七年七月十日當時ノ日本帝國ノ臣民タラザルモノニシテ軍人タルノ身分ヲ有セザルモノ總テヲ含ムモノト解セラルベシ

八、茲ニ使用セラルル「俘虜及被抑留者收容所」ナル語ハ總テノ收容所、監獄、船舶、宿舎、病院其他俘虜或ハ被抑留者ノ監禁又ハ抑留ノ他ノ場所ヲ含ムモノト解セラルベシ

二、茲ニ使用セラルル "收容所長" ナル語ハ日本國軍隊若ハ其ノ補助隊ノ各部隊、分遣隊若ハ他ノ單位ノ指揮官又ハ各看守長若ハ其ノ他ノ官憲ニシテ俘虜若ハ被抑留者ノ收容ノ責ヲ負フ者ヲ含ムモノト解セラルベシ

三、日本帝國政府及日本帝國大本營ハ聯合國最高司令官ニ對シ未ダ提出セラレザル場合ニハ四十八時間內ニ左ノ諸情報ヲ提供スベシ

イ、各別ニ左ノ諸項ヲ表示スル前記第一項ニ於テ定義セラレタル俘虜及被抑留者收容所ノ表

(1) 公式ノ名稱又ハ呼稱

(2) 眞近ノ著名ナル地理的地點トノ關係ニ於ケル所在地

(3) 度、分ニ於ケル緯度及經度

(4) 俘虜及被抑留者ノ總數(該當ノ場合ニハ總數中ニ於ケル女子ノ數ヲ含ム)

(5) 眞近ノ鐵道停車場ノ地理的位置

(6) 眞近ノ飛行場ノ名稱及地理的位置、廣サ、竝ニ滑走路ノ狀態

(7) 入院ヲ要スル俘虜又ハ被抑留者ノ概數

ロ、各收容所ノ位置ガ正確ニ劃セラレタル百萬分ノ一ノ素圖(單數及複數)

ハ、各收容所ノ位置ヲ正確ニ示ス俘虜及被抑留者收容所ノ所在スル各地區ノ百萬分ノ一縮尺又ハ更ニ大ナル縮尺ノ素圖(複數)

三、日本帝國政府及日本帝國大本營ハ本指示受領後利用可能ノ最モ迅速ナル方法ニ依リ各收容所長ニ對シ次ノ諸訓令ヲ傳達スベシ

イ、俘虜及被抑留者全員ヲ最モ早キ機會ニ集合シ且次ノ聲明ヲ英語及要求セラルベキ他ノ言語ニテ讀ムコト

「日本ノ聯合國ニ對スル正式降伏ハ一九四五年九月二日ニ署名セラレタリ『ダグラス、マクアーサー』將軍ハ聯合國最高司令官ニ任命セラレタリ、聯合諸國軍ハ可能ナル限リ速ニ日本本土及朝鮮ノ占領ヲ進メツツアリ、聯合國俘虜及被抑留者ノ救濟及開放ハ可能ナル限リ速ニ達成セラルベシ

聯合國代表者(複數)ノ到着ニ到ル迄本收容所竝ニ設備、貯品記錄、武器及彈藥ハ先任俘虜又ハ指定セラレタル被抑留者ニ對シ引渡サルベク此等ノ者ハ爾今補給及管理ノ業務ノ維持竝ニ地方的狀態ノ緩和ノ爲收容所長ニ對シ指令ヲ與フベシ

收容所長ハ先任俘虜又ハ指定セラレタル被抑留者ニ對シ其ノ指揮ヲ其ノ儘維持スルコトニ關シ責任ヲ有スベシ其ノ代々ノ指揮

1 降伏文書調印と初期占領政策への対応（昭和20年9月～10月）

聯合國代表者ハ諸君ノ移轉及諸君ノ家ヘノ究極的歸還ヲ準備スルヲ爲本收容所ニ派遣セラルベシ

ロ、收容所ノ完全ナル支配ヲ、設備、貯品、管理及他ノ記録、武器及彈藥ト共ニ先任俘虜又ハ被抑留者ニ引渡スコト、但シ先任俘虜又ハ被抑留者ニ依リ後ニ掲グル職務ノ遂行上收容所日本人官憲ガ使用スルモノトシテ指定セラルベキ物件ヲ除ク

ハ、先任俘虜及指定セラレタル被抑留者ノ監督ノ下ニ左ノ諸項ヲ確保スル爲必要ナル管理及補給ノ業務（地方的ニ入手シ得ベキ政府及軍ノ貯藏品ノ徵發ヲ含ム）ヲ行フコト

(1)日本國軍隊又ハ民間人ニ於トリ地方的ニ可能ナル最高限ニ相應スル食量

(2)凡テノ必要ナル醫藥的補給ト共ニ可能ナル最善ノ醫療

(3)適當ナル住居、被服、及浴場設備

二、本指示ハ茲ニ掲ゲラレタル諸責任ヲ履行スル爲ニ必要ニシテ收容所ノ近隣ニ於テ入手可能ナル政府及軍ノ補給品ヲ徵發スルノ權限ヲ設定スルモノトス

ホ、收容所機構ヲ其ノ儘ニ保持シ且先任俘虜又ハ被抑留者ニ對シ收容所ノ全員、收容所ノ管理記錄、作業名簿(Rasters)及、收容所ニ在リ又ハ在リタル各俘虜及被抑留者ノ移送、入院、及病氣ノ記錄ニ關シ説明スルコト

ヘ、地方的ニ聯合國代表者（複數）ニ依リ指令セラルベキ俘虜及被抑留者ノ移動ノ爲輸送手段及需品ノ補給ヲ又ハ地方政府又ハ軍機關ヨリ之ヲ徵發シ且行政的諸準備ヲ完成スル準備ヲ爲スベキコト

ト、先任俘虜又ハ被抑留者ノ監督ノ下ニ日本帝國大本營ヲ通ジ聯合國最高司令官ニ對シ次ノ情報ヲ準備シ且送付スルコト

(1)姓名、階級又ハ地位、國籍、最近親、家ノ宛名、年齡、性及健康狀況ヲ示ス俘虜及被抑留者現在員全部ノ完全ナル表（複數）

(2)姓名、階級又ハ地位、國籍、最近親、家ノ宛名、死亡又ハ移送ノ日附、及行先又ハ死亡セル者ノ場合ハ埋葬場所ヲ示セル死亡若ハ移送俘虜又ハ被抑留者ニ關スル利用シ得ベキ記錄ヨリノ拔萃

四、日本帝國大本營ハ前記第三項ト、ニ掲ゲラレタル指令ニ

應ジ收容所長ヨリ提出セラレタル凡テノ情報ヲ遲滯ナク聯合國最高司令官ニ移送スベシ

　第四章　資　源

一、總　則

日本帝國政府ハ聯合國最高司令官ノ委任ヲ受ケタル代表者又ハ各地域ニ於ケル占領軍指揮官ノ指示ニ從ヒ聯合國占領軍ノ要求スル為要求セラルベキ一切ノ地方的資源ヲ聯合國占領軍ノ處分ニ委ヌベシ

二、統　制

日本帝國政府ハ、各主要占領地域ニ一ノ中央事務所及要求セラルル下級事務所ヲ設置スベク、該事務所ノ主要職務ハ占領軍ノ要求スル地域及施設ニ關スル情報ヲ提供シ且要求ヲ受領スルニ在リ

三、石　油

聯合國占領軍ニ對シ其ノ要求スル石油製品、貯藏品及配給施設ヲ出來得ル限リ供給スルノ準備ヲ爲スベシ。具体的ノ要求ハ追テ提示セラルベシ

四、勞　務

(イ) 勞務ノ供給

日本帝國政府ハ、各主要占領地域毎ニ設置セラルル中央政府機關ヲ通ジ聯合國最高司令官又ハ各地域ニ於ケル占領軍指揮官ノ指示スル量、熟練度、技倆並ニ期日及場所ニ適合スル勞務ヲ供給スベシ勞務供給事務所ノ如キ勞務者群ノ統一ヲ出來得ル限リ保持スベシ組ノ如キ勞務者群ノ統一ヲ出來得ル限リ保持スベシ

(ロ) 必要ナル勞務

日本帝國政府ニ依リ占領軍ニ提供セラルル必要ナル勞務ハ下記ヲ含ムモノトス

(1) 一般勞務

(2) 技術的勞働及半熟練勞働

(3) 荷揚及仲仕

(4) 道路、鐵道、埠頭其他ノ施設ノ修理

(5) 聯合國占領軍用ノ住居及其ノ關聯施設ノ建造

五、住　居

日本帝國政府ハ占領軍ノ為適當ニシテ且占領軍ノ要求スル一切ノ建築物ヲ提供スル準備ヲ為スベシ、右要求ハ次ノ一般ノ項目ヲ含ムモノトス、事務所、病院、宿舍、倉庫及貯藏所、店舖、運輸通信施設、具体的ノ要求ハ追テ提

1 降伏文書調印と初期占領政策への対応（昭和20年9月〜10月）

六、飛行場

特定ノ飛行場ハ占領軍ノ要求ニ應ジ其ノ利用ニ供セラルベシ。滑走路、航空機分散地帶及前庭ヨリ日本機ヲ除去シ且滑走路ハ要求ニ應ジ最小限五、〇〇〇呎ヲ下ラザル最大ノ補裝着陸地ヲ有スルガ如ク改良セラルベシ。貨物ニ關スル設備、經理、運用及通信ノ施設ハ各飛行場ニ於テ利用シ得ルガ如クスベシ。一切ノ日本航空機及裝置ハ追テ指示アル迄保全セラルベシ。使用可能ナル一切ノ種類ノ運轉及維持ノ裝置及設備ノ完全ナル目錄ヲ種別及地域別ニ準備シ要求ニ應ジ聯合國代表ニ提示スベシ

第五章　雜　則

一、日本國大本營ハ直ニ東京地域ニ於テ無線電送寫眞及普通寫眞實驗室ヲ其附屬設備及作業員全部ト共ニ聯合國最高司令官司令部ノ通信部長ノ使用ノ爲提供スルモノトス

二、日本國大本營ノ權限アル代表者ハ聯合國最高司令官司令部通信部長ニ對シ其ノ使用ニ提供シ得ヘキ寫眞作業員、

示セラルベシ。建築物ハ出來得ル限リ耐火建築ニシテ水道、下水、電力、煖房ノ設備ヲ有シ且如何ナル天候ニ於テモ使用シ得ル道路ニ接スルモノタルベシ

設備、使用濟及未使用「フイルム」及印畫紙ノ蒐集物ニ關シ一切ノ情報ヲ四十八時間以内ニ報告スルモノトス此等ハ爾後要求ニ應シ現實ニ提供セラルルモノトス

三、氣象情報ノ蒐集、配布及記錄ニ從事スル軍用及非軍用ノ一切ノ機關ハ追テ指示アル迄通常通リノ作業ヲ繼續スヘシ一切ノ測候ニ關スル「データ」「ファイル」及一切ノ設備ハ現狀ノ儘保存セラルルモノトス、聯合國最高司令官ニ關シ一切ノ測候施設ヲ列記セル表ヲ遲滯ナク提出スルモノトス右表ニ於テハ國際索引數字、地理的位置種類（豫報、調査、中央又ハ觀測）ヲ記述スルモノトス

四、日本國政府ハ聯合國最高司令官司令部醫務部長ニ對シ遲滯ナク左記情報ヲ提供スベシ

（イ）現在實施中ノ公共衞生措置ノ網羅的ノ記述並ニ主要職員、機關及施設ノ表

（ロ）現在發生中ノ流行病ノ性質、發生場所及危險性並ニ右ニ對シ實施中ノ對策

（ハ）最近ノ報告ニ基ク醫藥品及他ノ衞生用品ノ狀況

（ニ）位置及寢臺能力ヲ記述セル一切ノ軍用以外ノ病院療養

所及其ノ他ノ醫療施設ノ表

五、日本語以外ノ言語ニヨル一切ノ公開音聲放送ハ即時中止セラルルモノトス

聯合國最高司令官ノ命ニ依リ

參謀長米國陸軍中將

アール、ケー、スザーランド

本命令配布先

指令先　日本國大本營（五部）

日本國政府（五部）

指令第二號附屬「ロ」

一、下記附屬「ロ」ハ指令第二號ニ附屬シ右指令ト同一效力ヲ有スヘク且其ノ一部ヲ成スモノトス

三、「グアム」ニ司令部ヲ置ク合衆國太平洋艦隊最高司令官ハ指令第二號第二章第二項㈡ノ意味ニ於ケル聯合國最高司令官ノ海軍代表者ニ指名セラレタリ聯合國最高司令官內二合衆國太平洋艦隊最高司令官ヲ代表スル海軍連絡團ヲ設置シ同團ノ先任將校ハ日本帝國海軍軍令部ノ總長及代表者ト地方ノ且個人的ノ連絡ニ當ルモノトス

三、日本帝國大本營ハ日本帝國陸軍ニ對スル指令第二號第二章第一項ノ規定スル所ト照應スルガ如ク日本國ニ於ケル日本帝國海軍組織ノ境界ヲ遲滯ナク調整スヘシ日本帝國大本營ハ斯クシテ定メラレタル區域ノ海軍指揮官ニ對シ合衆國第三艦隊及第五艦隊指揮官ニ連絡スルコトヲ命スルコトニ恰モ同一區域內ニアル先任日本帝國陸軍司令部ニ對シ合衆國第六軍及第八軍ノ指揮官ニ連絡スルコトヲ命シ如クナルヘシ合衆國第十軍區域及合衆國第二十四軍區域ニ對應スル日本海軍區域ニ於テハ同區域ノ日本海軍指揮官ハ夫々合衆國第五及第七艦隊ニ連絡スヘシ第三、第五及第七合衆國艦隊指揮官ハ指令第二號第二章第五項（ロ）ノ意味ニ於ケル聯合國最高司令官ノ海軍代表者ト看做サル

四、一切ノ日本商船ニシテ百噸ヲ超ユルモノノ行動ハ聯合國最高司令官ノ監督ニ服スヘシ、日本帝國政府及日本帝國大本營ハ全員搭乘ノ此ノ種船舶ニ付此等船舶ノ行動ノ指揮及監督ノ任ヲ有スル合衆國太平洋艦隊最高司令官（又ハ同最高司令官ノ任命スル代表者）ニ連絡スヘシ

五、指令第二號第一章第二項二（ロ）、第三項及第五項並ニ第二

1 降伏文書調印と初期占領政策への対応（昭和20年9月～10月）

11

重光・サザーランド会談

昭和20年9月4日　重光外務大臣　サザーランド連合国最高司令官総司令部参謀長　会談

付記一　右会談録別紙第一号和文原案
二　右会談録別紙第二号和文原案
三　右会談録別紙第三号和文原案
四　作成日不明

布告第三号に対する日本政府対案

外務大臣「サザーランド」参謀長會談要旨

三〇、六、四、於横濱聯合軍總司令部
岡崎及「マンソン」大佐同席

編注　「附屬甲」の地図は和訳文には添付されていない。

モノトス

章第六項ニ用ヒラルル「占領軍指揮官」ナル語ハ海軍占領軍竝ニ海軍部隊ノ武装解除及復員ニ關シテハ各自ノ責任區域ニ在ル合衆國第三、第五及第七艦隊指揮官ヲ含ム

一、大臣ヨリ別紙第一號ヲ示シ貴方ノ布告案ハ昨日モオ話ノ通リ面白カラサルニ付日本側ノ作成セル案ヲ持参セルニ付研究アリ度シ要スルニ日本政府ハ誠実ニ義務履行ノ決心アリ且實力ヲ有ス政府ヲ通シ凡テノ要求ヲ出サルルコト最モ實際的ナリト述ヘ詳細其點ヲ説明セリ之ニ對シ参謀長ハ昨日以來ノ話ハヨク了解セリ自分モ米國ノ手テ行フヨリモ日本政府ヲ通スル方カ能率的ニシテ且政府ノ機構ハ完全ニ働キ居ルコトヲ認メ居レリ武装解除ニシテモ日本側ハ十月十日迄ニ完了ノ旨述ヘラレ居ル處米國側ノ手ニテ之ヲ行ハハ到底斯カル短時日ニテ實行出來ス自分等ノ希望ハ米軍ハ静カニ駐屯シ凡テノ必要事項ハ日本側ニオ願スルコトニアリ從ッテ貴方ノ「フォームユラ」ハ結構ナリト思フ又今後モ凡テノ同様ノ形式ヲ採リヘク只其ノ内容ニ付テハ米側ノ要求ヲ全部含マレ居ルヤ否ヤ研究ヲ要スト述ヘタルニ付岡崎ヨリ先方原案ヲ示シ之ト對照セシメタルカ直チニ諾否ヲ云ハス依リテ大臣ヨリ米國側ハ凡テノ要求及命令ヲ日本政府ニ出サレ政府大臣ニ於テ十分之ヲ實行シ得サルカ如キ場合ニ於テノミ米國自身ニテ命令ヲ出スモ已ムヲ得サルカ政府ハ必ス眞面目ニ義務ヲ

履行スヘキニ付御心配御無用ナリト述ヘタルニ參謀長ハ其通リナリトテ之ヲ肯定セリ結局案文ノ形式ハ日本側ノ主張通リトナル公算大ナルモ内容ニ付テハ問題アルヘシト思料セラル

三、大臣ヨリ通貨ノ問題ニ付テハ目下專門家ノ間ニ話合進行中ナレハ米側ノ布告案モ其ノ結果ヲ見テ何分ノ決定ヲ致シタク或ハ話合ノ結果ニテハ布告モ命令モ必要ナキニ至ルヤトモ考ヘ居レリト述ヘタルニ參謀長ハ之ヲ肯定シ話合ハ圓滿ニ進行居ルノ模樣ナレハ御說ノ通リ暫ク模樣ヲ見テ何分ノ決定ヲシ度シト答ヘタリ。之ニテ米國側布告案ノ乃至三ハ何レモ差當リ直チニ實施セス其ノ內容ヲ實現スル場合モ先ツ日本政府ヲ通シテナサントスル意向明確トナレリ。依テ大臣ヨリ斯ノ如ク先ツ日本側ト話合ハレタル後命令等ヲ出サルルニ於テハ凡テ圓滿且實際ニ運フコトトナリ甚夕滿足ナリト述ヘタルニ參謀長モ其通リニテ實ハ昨日交付セル命令第二號モズット以前ニ印刷セルモノニテ中ニハ實狀ニ合ハヌ點モアリ又ハ既ニ日本側ニテ實行濟ノモノモアリ且實行ノ方法ニ付テモ日本側ニヨリ良キ案モアルヘシト思ヒ之等ノ點ニ付テハ遠慮ナク申出アラハ考慮シ出來ル丈ケ日本ノ意嚮ニ沿フ樣致スヘシト附言シテ之ヲ渡セル次第ニテ本日中ニモ日本側ヨリ打合セノ申出アルコトヲ期待シ居レリト答ヘタリ。外務大臣ヨリ日本政府ニ對スル指令其ノ物ハ今後ハ發表ヲ要セスヤ其ノ內容ヲ日本政府若ハ大本營ニ於テ實行ニ當リ必要ナル國民ニ對スル命令措置ヲ發表シ然ルヘキヤト述ヘタルニ先方ハ其ノ通リ取計ハレ然ルヘシト述ヘタリ

三、大臣ヨリ別紙第二號ヲ示シ之ハ日本ノ經濟狀況ノ概況ニテ細カキ數字ハ更ニ提出スヘキモ一應硏究アリ度シト述ヘタルニ參謀長ハ之ヲ一讀シ平和產業卽チ消費物資(コンシューマー、グッヅ)ノ生產ハ日本ニモ緊急缺クヘカラサルモノト思フニ付大臣ヨリ特ニ差支ナク且ノ生產ニ必要ナル農具及肥料ノ生產ヲ開始セラレタルニ付キテハ南方諸地域モ綿糸布ノ需要大ナルモ供給者ナク困リ居ルニ付近ク命令第三號等ヲ以テ日本紡績ノ再開ヲ要求スルヤモ知レスト述ヘ或ハ之カ製品ヲ賠償ノ一部ト付キテハ參謀長ハ勿論之カ生產ハ宜シカラン特ニ紡績ニ績ニシロ、ドシドシ始メラルルカ宜シカラン特ニ紡績ニル處參謀長ハ勿論之カ生產ハ宜シカラン特ニ紡績ニ

1 降伏文書調印と初期占領政策への対応(昭和20年9月～10月)

シテ取上ケントスル考ヘナルヤノ感觸ヲ得タリ尚絹ニ付テハ却ツテ澁リ居ル樣子ニテ一定限度ノ生産ニ留メ度口振リヲ示シタルカ之ハ米國内「ナイロン」生産等トノ競爭問題ヲ考慮シ居ルニ非ルヤト考ヘラレタリ

四、大臣ヨリ別紙第三號ヲ示シ日本ノ船舶運航停止ノ爲食料、石炭其ノ他ノ問題何レモ窮迫シ居ル事情ヲ詳細説明セル處參謀長ハ日本國民ノ困ルコトハ即チ米國側モ困ルコトナリ依リテ船舶ノ運航ハ直ニ許容スル心算ナレハ總司令部海軍代表「バランタイン」少將ニ連絡シ如何ナル船カ何時何處ニ行キ何ヲ積ミテ來ルヤ等ノ事項ヲ記シタル「アプリケーション」ヲ提出スレハ一定ノ地域ヲ航行セサル條件ヲ附シテ直ニ許可スヘシト述ヘ一定地域トハ例ヘハ米艦隊ノ泊地等ヲ意味スルモノナリト説明セリ尚參謀長ヨリ漁船モ速カニ出漁スルコトヲ希望ス又損傷セル船舶ノ修理モ直ニ取掛リテ差支ナク要スルニ日本側ノ有スル凡ユル船力運航ヲ開始スルコトカ米國側ノ希望ナリト答ヘタリ大臣ヨリ支那其他ノ外地ニアル軍隊及居留民ノ引揚ニモ多數ノ船舶ヲ要シ誠ニ困難ナル問題ナリト述ヘタルニ參謀長ハ困難ハヨク了承スルモ米

國側モ復員交替等ノ爲ニ船腹不足ラサル狀況ニテ差當リ聯合國ノ船舶ヲ日本側ニ提供スルカ如キハ不可能ナリト明瞭ニ斷リタリ

五、(イ)大臣ヨリ飛行機ニ依リ旅客「サーヴィス」ヲ行ヒ度キ旨申出テラレ參謀長トノ間ニ使用可能ノ飛行機數等ニ付問答アリ先方ハ民間航空モ船舶鐵道等ト共ニ日本側ニ取リ必要缺クヘカラサルモノナルヘシトテ同情的態度ヲ示セルカ結局本件ハ日本側ヨリノ具體案提出ヲ待チテ研究スルコトトナレリ

(ロ)岡崎ヨリ命令第二號ニ基キ日本語ヲ除ク海外放送ハ四日零時ヨリ停止セル旨ヲ述ヘタルニ參謀長ハ右ハ專ラ對外宣傳ヲ防止セントスル爲ナリ從テ國內放送ヲ禁スル考ヘニアラスト述ヘタルニ付然ラハ今ハ一時停止シ居ルモ後ニ至リ米側ヨリ檢閲官ヲ派遣シ宣傳ノ放送ヲ防止スレハ再開セシムルモ宜シカラスヤト述ヘタルニ右ハ將來研究スヘシト答ヘタリ

(ハ)米兵ノ警察官ニ對スル暴行阻止ノ爲一定ノ腕章ヲ作ルコト如何トノ我方申出ニ對シ參謀長賛成シ主任官ト具體的ニ話合フコトトセリ其ノ際參謀長ハ机上ノ書類ヲ

（別紙第一號）

General Order No. 2

Administration

The Imperial Japanese Government shall proclaim in conformance with the order of the Supreme Commander for the Allied Powers as follows:

1. All governmental, public and honorary functionaries and employees, as well as all officials and employees, paid or voluntary, of all public utilities and services, including public welfare and public health, and all other persons engaged in essential services, shall continue to perform their usual functions and duties, preserving and safeguarding all records and property.

2. The Japanese people shall obey promptly all the orders of the Supreme Commander for the Allied Powers and orders issued under his authority. Acts of resistance to the occupying forces or any acts which may disturb public peace and safety shall be punished severely.

3. The Japanese people shall pursue their normal occupations. Their personal and property rights and religious beliefs are to be respected.

4. The Imperial Japanese Government shall punish severely any person who violates the provisions of the Instrument of Surrender, order, or directive given under the authority of the Supreme Commander for the Allied Powers, or does any act to the prejudice of good order or the life, safety, or security of the persons or property of the United States or its Allies or does any act calculated to disturb public peace and order or prevent the administration of justice, or willfully does any act hostile to the Allied Forces.

示シ日本側ヨリ非常ニ多クノ事件ノ報告アルモ何等證據トナルモノヲ示ササルニ付殆ト取締ノ方法ナシ司令部ハ極力事故發生防止ノ措置ヲ取リ居ルモ部隊ハ本土上陸作戰ヲ豫期シ死ヲ決シタル戰鬭部隊ナルヲ以テ一應落着ク迄事件ノ發生絶無ヲ期シ難キモ他國ノ軍隊ヨリハ成績良好ナリト考ヘラレサルニ非ス卜述ヘ居タリ

70

1　降伏文書調印と初期占領政策への対応(昭和20年9月～10月)

(別紙第二號)

Memorandum

The following is a frank statement of the present economic conditions in Japan.

1) Food Problem

Japan proper, densely populated and yet with comparatively limited area for cultivation, depended even before the war on imports from abroad for feeding its population. Since the war broke out, great effort was exerted on expanding the domestic production of staple food, and at the same time considerable quantity of rice from Formosa, Korea and Southern regions and various kinds of cereal foods from Manchuria were to be imported yearly to meet demand. But as the transportation across the sea became increasingly difficult and even the import from Manchuria began to encounter serious obstacles, Japan was forced to take steps this July of decreasing the daily basic ration for adult from 330 grams to 300 grams, of which at least fifty percent consists of substitute cereals. The supply conditions of miso (bean paste) and shoyu (soy sauce), which depend for raw materials upon staple food products, are no less serious. As for the auxiliary food, the condition has been even worse, with the marked decline in the production of fresh vegetables and marine products. As for meat, even the rationing has long been stopped for the general populace.

While we depend for protein (which is indispensable for the maintenance of health) upon such products as fish, shell-fish, miso, and other soy bean products, the continued supply of these products depends entirely upon the maintenance of fishing industry and the importation of Manchurian soy-beans.

Domestic supply of salt meets only one-third of the need, while that of sugar will be nil when Formosa and Mandated Islands lost to Japan.

The prospects of food supply in the early winter present a serious problem to us, inasmuch as we had a poor crop of wheat this spring and since we must expect also the same in the case of rice.

2) Fuel Problem

(a) Japan's Main Island depends for its supply of coal

71

upon Kyushu and Hokkaido. And the transportation of coal to big city areas (such as the Tokyo-Yokohama area, the Osaka-Kobe area, and the Nagoya area) has been supplied by means of ships and railroad, especially the former. Now that the water transportation has practically been suspended, the coal supply is severely curtailed, causing the almost complete cessation of gas-supply.

(b) Liquid fuel has always been the weakest point. The present stock has been reduced to a negligible quantity, and the prospect of new supply is equally dark, inasmuch as the production of alcohol in Japan has to compete in its raw materials with the pressing demand for staple food.

(c) Domestic fuel supply, namely charcoal and firewoods, is also expected to be far short of the minimum demand, mainly owing to the transportation difficulties. In particular, it is feared that those who are living in temporary huts (later to be described) would have to face a severest winter.

3) <u>Clothings</u>

As for cotton and wool, our stocks have dwindled to a negligible quantity and we must depend entirely upon importation for future supplies. The production of staple fibre and rayon will have to be kept at the minimum on account of the shortage of supply of industrial salt, while the production of silk, too, is expected to decline because of the curtailment of mulberry acreage in favor of food crops.

Furthermore, not only have people had, during the war time, no opportunity to replace their worn-out clothings, but in addition many of them have lost a greater part of what they had through the bombing which became intensified since the end of the last year. Thus the supplying of raw materials for the production of clothings is a most urgent task before us.

4) <u>Housing</u>

Already before the war, housing shortage, especially in big cities, was acute enough. On top of this, the bombing since the end of last year has completely burned or destroyed upwards of two million houses, making ten million persons homeless, forcing them either to crowd into other houses or to devise temporary huts barely good enough to provide shelter.

Winter being not far away, the housing problem for

72

1 降伏文書調印と初期占領政策への対応(昭和20年9月〜10月)

the victims of air-raid calls for an immediate solution, and yet the shortage of raw materials and the lack of various processing equipments render the solution of the problem extremely difficult. Although we are determined to make the best of the domestic supply of lumber resources, we still wish to appeal for the careful consideration of the Allied Powers as regards the transportation bottleneck to which the next section is devoted.

5) Transportation

Because of her geographical configuration and of the lack of raw materials at home, Japan has depended greatly upon the marine transportation. Before the war, the monthly transportation of goods on sea including importation from abroad and Korea and Formosa used to exceed six million tons. During the war, however, the loss of shipping far exceeded the new construction, and the sea lanes were exposed to constant danger of Allied attacks, and towards the end of the war even the coastal shipping was in the state of paralysis.

In order to meet this situation, we attempted to shift a part of the transportation burden from the water to the land. But the freight facilities of the railroad have also suffered greatly from air-raids; and also because of the negligence of replacement since the beginning of the China Incident (1937), the transportation capacity of the railroad has declined rapidly in the recent past.

In addition to this, the order of the Supreme Commander for the Allied Forces has made it impossible for ships of more than 100 tons to navigate after 6 o'clock p.m., August 24th. This action has caused, inter alia, such hardships as:- The stoppage of coal supply to the Tokyo-Yokohama, the Osaka-Kobe, and the Nagoya areas (normally supplied from Hokkaido and Kyushu), the stoppage of supply of newsprint from Hokkaido, the cessation of the transportation of salt from the southern Korea, the further tightening of food situation in the Osaka-Kobe area which normally depends heavily on Shikoku islands, the stoppage of supply of lumber needed for emergency housing, the complete stoppage of the transportation of essential civilian goods for those (about one million) who live on small islands along the coast of Japan, a serious hindrance to the demobilization of soldiers and labor-recruits due to the suspension of inland sea lines, etc. Unless the suspension of water transportation be quickly relinquished, the civilian life of Japan in many aspects will be dangerously threatened and it is even feared that the maintenance of internal peace and order may become extremely difficult.

（別紙第三號）

Memorandum

1. Major portion of the nations necessaries of life and industrial materials are transported by sea. Before the war 6,000,000 tons per month were actually carried by cargo boats (June 1936), and 1,300,000 tons per month by motor sailing vessels.

However, July last, owing to the drastic reduction of bottom there was transported only 870,000 tons by steamships and 400,000 tons by motor vessels. Over taxing of the railways to the extreme has proved of little avail to relieve the situation. Now with the order of prohibiting the operation of vessels more than 100 gross tons, the country is confronted by a grave situation, having virtually no means of transportation and communication by sea. Reopening of transportation services is desired to meet the specially urgent requirements, for which there should be a general lifting of the ban on the operation of all available cargo and passenger boats and of vessels of more than 100 tons.

2. Coal is scarce. The railways have in hand only enough to last for a few days, cities have to get along without gas factories manufacturing civil goods are at standstill; and these few ships that are in service are also in want of fuel. While we must meet the urgent requirements along all these lines, we must also transport coal for the manufacture of fertilizers, articles of food, medical supplies, and textile goods, from Hokkaido to Tokyo-Yokohama area and from Kyushu to Osaka-Kobe area; to the amount, it is estimated, of 400,000 tons by steamboats and 350,000 tons by motor sailing vessels every month. (The figures for pre-war time are respectively 2,800,000 tons and 1,230,000 tons, while those for July this year are 300,000 tons and 360,000 respectively.)

The estimated volume to be transported by steam boats for coming months is made larger than the actual figure for July this year, it being intended to restore sea transportations to its old time supremacy over land transportation and to devote railway

1　降伏文書調印と初期占領政策への対応（昭和20年9月～10月）

facilities chiefly to the purposes of demobilization of armed forces and conscript labor.

It should be added that the above-mentioned amounts of coal supply do not cover what is needed for the supply of electricity as fuel for general consumption, cement manufacture, mines and foundries, and especially for the supply of electricity which will be totally impossible.

Transportation of newspaper is another important item in view of the importance of guiding postwar public opinion in the right direction.

The minimum amount required is 20,000 tons per month to be transported from Hokkaido to Tokyo and Yokohama area, which is barely sufficient to maintain the present level of single sheet papers. (450,000 tons in the pre-war time; 6,000 tons for July last, under special control.)

3.　Scarcity of food institutes a serious menace to the nation. Among the immediate requirements, mention may be made of the transportation of 30,000 tons of rice and wheat from Shikoku to Osaka and Kobe and of 10,000 tons of salt from the Seto Inland Sea to the Osaka, Kobe and other areas and especially the importation of 28,000 tons of cereals and 37,000 tons of salt from Southern Korea (pre-war figures: 310,000 tons for cereals and 170,000 tons for salt. July last: 290,000 tons for cereals, and 120,000 tons for salt.)

4.　In order to relieve stringency in the supply of supplementary food stuffs it is necessary to transport immediately at least 40,000 tons of canned foods and dried fish now awaiting shipment in Hokkaido.

5.　Great number of houses have been burned down during the war, which is a cause of greatest apprehension and unrest. The transportation of lumber is a matter of urgent necessity, the shipping of at least 40,000 tons from Hokkaido to Tokyo-Yokohama area, being required immediately, although it will suffice only for the building of 10,000 standardised emergency houses: (Pre-war figure for lumber: 400,000 tons June last: none.)

6.　200,000 Japanese women and children who are congregated now in South Korea must be quickly brought back home. But in view of the above stated requirements for goods transportation, it is considered desirable to transport for the present 30,000 people a month by applying 45,000 dead weight tons to that purpose.

7. There is no prospect of possibility for the transportation of such necessaries of life and materials for reconstructions as iron (Pre War figure: 970,000 tons. July last: 23,000 tons), non ferrous metals (Pre war figure: 370,000 tons. July last: 44,000 tons), cement (Pre war figure: 650,000 tons), sugar (Pre war figure 30,000 tons), fodder (Pre war figure: 20,000 tons. July last: 17,000 tons), fertilizers (Pre war figure: 40,000 tons), fat and oil (Pre war figure: 50,000 tons and general merchandise (Pre war figure: 58,000 tons).

8. In view of the indispensable character of the Seto Inland routes for the demobilization of armed forces and conscript labor and as the principal avenues of communication between Hondo, Shikoku and Kyushu and other islands, and the ban on navigation has produced considerable confusion. The cancellation of the order prohibiting all shipping service under 31 is urgently desired.

Likewise the cancellation is desired of the order under 30 regarding shipping services to and from isolated islands, since these services constitute the only means between isolated islands, and their suspension is a direct menace to the lives of 1,000,000 people residing on these islands.

9. The order prohibiting the operation of oil tankers is causing great difficulties through the stoppage of the transportation of fuel for ships and automobiles, and food and insecticide oils. The lifting of the ban will make it possible to ship from Akita, Funakawa and the Seto Inland area the urgently need oils to the amount of 32,000 tons (pre war figure: 500,000 tons. July last: 50,000 tons).

（付記１）

一般命令第二號　行政

日本國政府ハ聯合國最高司令官ノ命令ニ遵ヒ下記ノ如ク聲明スヘシ

一、一切ノ官公吏、名譽職及雇傭員並ニ公共福祉及公衆衛生ヲ含ム各種公共施設及業務ニ從事スル一切ノ有給及無給ノ役職員其ノ他必須業務ニ從事スル一切ノ者ハ其ノ平素ノ職務及義務ヲ引續キ遂行シ一切ノ記錄及財產ノ保存及

1 降伏文書調印と初期占領政策への対応(昭和20年9月～10月)

保全ニ任スヘシ

二、帝國臣民ハ聯合國最高司令官ノ命令及同司令官ノ委任ニ基キ發セラルル一切ノ命令ヲ速ニ遵守スヘシ、占領軍ニ對スル抵抗行爲又ハ公共ノ安寧ヲ紊スカ如キ一切ノ行爲ニ出ツル者ハ嚴重ニ處罰セラルヘシ

三、帝國臣民ハ日常ノ業務ヲ繼續スヘシ、帝國臣民ノ人權及財產權及宗教上ノ信仰ハ尊重セラルヘシ

四、帝國政府ハ降伏文書若ハ聯合國最高司令官ノ權限ノ下ニ發セラルル命令及指令ニ違反シ又ハ善良ナル秩序ヲ害シ若ハ合衆國若ハ其ノ聯合國ノ人若ハ財產ニ對シ其ノ生命、安全若ハ安寧ヲ害スル行爲ヲ爲シ又ハ公共ノ平和及秩序ヲ攪亂シ若ハ裁判ヲ妨害スルノ目的ヲ以テ行動シ又ハ故意ニ聯合國軍ニ對シ敵意アル行動ヲ爲ス者ハ嚴罰ニ處セラルヘシ

（付記二）

覺　書

以下ハ現下ニ於ケル日本ノ經濟狀態ヲ卒直ニ述ヘタルモノナリ

一、食糧問題

日本本土ハ人口極メテ稠密ナルモ耕地狹小ニシテ、食糧生產量ハ人口ヲ養フニ足ラス戰前ニ於テモ多量ノ食糧ヲ海外ニ仰キタリ、戰爭開始後ニ於テハ國內ノ主要食糧增產ニ極力努メタルモ尙ホ多量ノ米ヲ臺灣、朝鮮及南方諸地域ヨリ又ハ中ノ少クトモ五〇％ハ米以外ノ代用品ヲ混入シ居ル實情ナリ、主要食糧ヲ原料トスル味噌醬油ノ狀況モ亦樂觀ヲ許サス、副食物ノ狀況ハ主食物以上ニ惡化シ居リ蔬菜ノ生產ハ減少シ魚介類モ亦燃料油、漁具等ノ資材ノ不足、漁船ノ減少ノ結果生產ハ著シク低位ニ在リ、肉類ニ至リテハ一般ニ對スル配給ハ皆無ナリ

國民保健上缺クヘカラサル蛋白質ノ供給源ハ魚介類及味噌等豆類ニ俟タサルヘカラサル處之カ供給ノ繼續ハ漁業ノ維持及滿洲大豆ノ輸入ヲ必須條件トス

鹽ノ生產ハ食料鹽需要ノ三分ノ一弱ニ過キス、砂糖モ亦臺

77

灣及南洋委任統治領ヲ喪失スル曉ニ於テハ需要量ノ殆ト全部ヲ輸入ニ俟タサル可カラス

本端境期ニ於ケル食糧狀況ハ今年麥ノ減產、稻作ノ不況ニ依リ極メテ憂慮スヘキ狀態ニシテ、相當量ノ米及雜穀ヲ輸入シ得サルニ於テハ國民生活ニ大ナル支障ヲ生スルニ至ルヘシ

三、燃料問題

イ、日本本土ニ於ケル石炭生產ハ九州及北海道ヲ主トスル爲京濱、阪神、名古屋等ノ石炭需給ハ殆ト之ヲ右兩地方ヨリ船舶及鐵道就中前者ニ依ル輸送ニ依存シ居ル處、船舶運航停止ノ爲前記需要地ニ於ケル配炭ハ極度ニ壓迫サレ瓦斯ノ供給ノ如キハ全ク杜絕シ居ル狀況ナリ

ロ、液體燃料ハ日本ノ最大弱點ナルカ、旣ニ現有「ストック」ハ少量ニシテ且今後ノ供給ノ望極メテ薄ク又「アルコール」ニ付テハ食糧狀況極メテ悲觀スヘキモノアルハ他項ニ於テ說明ノ通ニ從ッテ「アルコール」原料ノ供給ニ困難ニ豫想セラル

ハ、家庭用燃料卽チ木炭及薪ニ付テハ主トシテ輸送力ノ關係上相當ノ不足ヲ豫想セラレ、殊ニ今冬ニ於テハ他項ニ述フル如キ假小屋生活ノ爲一層困難ナル問題ヲ提供スヘシ

三、衣類問題

棉花及羊毛ハ僅少ナル「ストック」ヲ保有スルノ外今後輸入ニ俟タサレハ供給皆無ニシテ「ステープルファイバー」及「レーヨン」ノ生產ハ工業鹽ノ缺乏ニ依リ極度ニ壓縮セラルヘク絹ニ付テモ食糧增產ノ爲桑畑減少シ繭ノ生產ハ減退ヲ豫想セラル

而モ多年ニ亘ル戰爭期間中民家ノ衣類ノ補充ハ殆ト不可能ナリシニ加へ、昨年末以來ノ空襲ニ依リ手持ノ全部又ハ大部分ヲ喪失セルモノ多數ニシテ纖維製品ノ急速ナル生產ハ國民生活上ノ緊要事ナルカ原料ノ供給ニ付急速ニ措置スル要アリ

四、住宅問題

戰爭前ニ於テ旣ニ住宅ハ不足ニシテ、特ニ都市ニ於テ右傾向顯著ナリシ處、昨年末以來ノ空襲ニヨリ全燒及全壞家屋ハ二百萬戶ヲ越スニ至リ、約一千萬人ニ達スル民衆ハ家ヲ失ヒテ或ハ他家ニ寄寓シ或ハ燒跡ニ辛ウシテ雨露ヲ凌ク程度ノ假小屋ヲ構築シテ住居シ居ル狀況ナリ

1 降伏文書調印と初期占領政策への対応（昭和20年9月～10月）

冬ノ到來ヲ控ヘテ、罹災者ノ住宅問題ハ最モ急速ニ解決ヲ要スル問題ナルカ、木材ノ窮乏製材能力ノ減退及建築用諸材料ノ缺乏トニ鑑ミ其ノ解決ハ極メテ困難ナルヘシ、國内木材資源ノ徹底的利用ニ依リ極力善處スルトスルモ尚他項記述ノ如ク輸送上ノ便宜ニ付聯合國軍側ノ考慮ヲ要請セサルヲ得ス

　五、輸送問題

日本ハ其ノ地理的情況ト國内ノ資源不足ニ鑑ミ海上輸送ニ依存スルコト極メテ大ニシテ戰前ニ於テハ船舶ニ依ル物資輸送ハ海外ヨリノ輸移入ヲ含ミ六百萬噸ヲ越ヘタリ、然ルニ第二次世界大戰中ニ於ケル船舶ノ損耗ハ遙ニ建造ヲ凌駕シ、海上交通ハ聯合國側ノ攻撃ニ依リ常ニ多大ノ危險ニサラサレ、殊ニ戰爭末期ニ於テハ日本近海ノ海上交通モ殆ト不可能ノ狀態ニ陷リタリ

右事情ニ對應スル爲海上輸送ノ一部ヲ陸上輸送ニ轉嫁スル等ノ措置ヲ執リタルモ鐵道モ亦昨年以來ノ空襲ニ依リ車輛及陸上施設ニ大ナル被害ヲ受ケ、支那事變發生以來補修資材及勞務ノ不足ニ依リ既ニ衰損著シカリシ鐵道ノ輸送能力ハ急速ニ低下スルニ至レリ

然ルニ八月二十八日十八時以降聯合軍最高司令官ノ指令ニ依リ百總屯以上ノ各種船舶ハ全テ其ノ運行ヲ停止セラレタル結果北海道及九州ヨリ需要地タル京濱、阪神及名古屋方面ヘノ石炭輸送ハ杜絶シ、北海道ヨリノ新聞用紙ノ供給ハ不可能トナリ、南朝鮮ヨリノ鹽ノ輸送亦不可能ニ陷リ主トシテ四國方面ヨリノ輸送ニ依存シ居リタル阪神ノ食糧事情ハ頗ル急迫シ空襲ニ依リ家ヲ喪ヒタル民家ノ應急住宅ノ建築モ亦木材ノ供給杜絶ニ依リ困難ヲ極ムルニ至レリ、加フルニ本土周邊ノ島嶼ノ居住者ハ唯一ノ交通路ヲ失ヒタル結果生活必需物資ノ流入ニ完全ニ停止シ約百萬ノ之等島嶼居住者ハ其ノ生活ハ根本的ニ脅カサレ、又瀬戸内航路ノ停止ニ依リ軍人及徵用工ノ復員ハ大ナル支障ヲ來タシツツアル情況ニシテ若シ船舶ノ航行停止ニシテ速ニ解除セラレサルニ於テハ日本ノ國民生活ハ根本的ニ脅威セラレ治安ノ維持スラ不可能ニ至ルノ懼ナシトセサル次第ナリ

　　（付記三）

　　　　覺　　書

一、我國ニ於ケル國民生活物資及產業資材ハ其ノ大部ヲ海上

輸送ニ依存シ戰前ニ於テハ貨物船ニ依ルモノ月六百萬噸（昭和十六年六月）ノ實績ヲ示セル狀況ナリ然ルニ其後船腹ノ激減ニ逢ヒ本年七月ニ於テハ汽船ハ僅カニ八十七萬噸、機帆船八四十萬噸ヲ輸送セルニ止リ鐵道ニ過度ノ輸送轉嫁ヲ行ヒ苦況打開ニ努メタルモ國民生活破綻ヲ招キツツアル狀況ナリ而モ今般百總噸以上ノ船舶ノ航行禁止ヲ命セラレ海上運輸及交通杜絕シ國內狀況眞ニ憂慮スヘキモノアリ

而シテ特ニ事態急迫シ卽刻輸送ヲ開始スル要アルモノ左ノ如シ、之カ爲就航可能ノ貨物船及貨客船及百總噸以上ノ機帆船ノ航行禁止ヲ全面的ニ解除スルコトヲ要望ス

三、鐵道用燃料石炭窮迫シ漸ク數日分ヲ支フルニ過ギズ又都市ノ瓦斯供給停止ノ狀況亦逼迫セルヲ以テ取敢ヘズ之等ヲ充ト共ニ船舶用燃料炭ニアル外民需工場用炭杜絕セスト共ニ一部肥料、食料、藥品、繊維等ノ製造用トシテ北海道ヨリ京濱へ又九州ヨリ阪神へ汽船ニ依リ四十萬噸機帆船ニ依リ三十五萬噸（戰前ハ汽船二百八十萬噸、機帆船百二十三萬噸、本年七月ハ汽船三十萬噸、機帆船三

十六萬噸、汽船ガ七月ノ實績ヨリ增加セシメントスルハ鐵道轉嫁ハ卽急ニ之ヲ海運ニ還元シ鐵道ハ復員輸送ニ重點ヲ置カシムルヲ要スルニ因ル）ヲ輸送スルヲ要ス右ノ程度ノ輸送ニ在リテハ電力、一般燃料「セメント」鑛山鑄物等ニ供給スル餘力ナク冬期ニ向フ準備（特ニ電力）ハ全ク不可能ナリ

新聞紙供給困難トナリ戰後ニ於ケル國民指導ニ由々シキ事態惹起スル慮アルヲ以テ北海道ヨリ京濱へ月二百噸ヲ輸送スルヲ要ス、コノ程度ニテハ現在ノニ頁新聞ヲ辛ジテ維持シ得ル程度ナリ。（戰前八四十五萬噸、七月八六千噸但シ特ニ抑制セルモノナリ）

三、食料ノ不足ハ國民ニ重大ナル脅威ヲ與ヘ居ルヲ以テ取敢ズ四國ノ米麥三萬噸ヲ阪神ヘ、瀨戶內海ノ鹽一萬噸ヲ阪神其ノ他ヘノ滯貨穀類二萬八千噸、鹽三萬七千噸ヲ積取ルコト緊要ナリ（戰前ニ於テハ穀類三十一萬噸、鹽十七萬噸、七月八穀類二十九萬噸、鹽十二萬噸）

四、內地ノ副食物ハ極度ノ逼迫ヲ緩和スル爲北海道滯貨罐詰及干魚四萬噸中少クトモニ萬噸ヲ至急積取ル必要アリ

1 降伏文書調印と初期占領政策への対応（昭和20年9月～10月）

五、家屋ノ戰災燒失ハ特ニ冬期ニ向ヒ國民生活不安ノ最大原因タルニ鑑ミ木材輸送ヲ促進スルノ要アリ、取敢ヘズ北海道ヨリ京濱阪神等ヘ少クモ四萬噸ヲ輸送スルヲ要ス但シコノ程度ニテハ標準家屋一萬戸ヲ建造シ得ルニ過ギズ（木材ハ戰前四十萬噸、七月ハ殆ンドナシ）

六、南鮮ニ滯留セル老幼婦女子二十萬名ヲ至急還送スルニ非ザレバ食料不足ニ依リ餓死スル者モ生ズル狀況ナルモ前記ノ如ク物資輸送ニ使用セバ四萬五千重量噸ヲ使用シ得ルニ過ギズ斯クテハ月三萬人ヲ輸送シ得ルニ過ギズ

七、以上ノ程度ナルヲ以テ戰（戰前九十七萬噸、七月八十二萬三千噸）非鐵（戰前三十七萬噸、七月四萬四千噸）「セメント」（戰前六萬五千噸）砂糖（戰前三萬噸）肥料（戰前十二萬噸、七月一萬七千噸）飼料（戰前四萬噸）油飼（戰前五萬噸）雜貨（戰前五十八萬噸）等生活必需用又ハ復興用トシテ不可缺ナルモノノ目途立タザル狀況ナリ

八、瀨戶内海航路ハ華人徴用工ノ復員輸送ノミナラズ島嶼、本土、四國、九州間ノ主要ナル交通路トシテ不可缺ナルニ不拘航行禁止ニ依リ混亂ヲ招キツツアルヲ以テ三十一ノ航路全部ノ禁止ヲ解除スルヲ希望ス

九、油槽船ノ航行禁止ニ依リ船舶用燃料、自動車燃料、食油、殺虫油等ノ輸送停止シ著シキ支障ヲ來シツツアルヲ以テ直ニ之ヲ解除スルコト、之ニ依リ秋田、船川、瀨戶内海方面ヨリ緊急必要ナルモノ三萬二千粁ヲ輸送シ得ベシ（戰前ハ五十萬以上、七月ハ五萬）

離島航路ハ離島相互及本土トノ間ノ唯一ノ交通線トシテ人員及生活必需物資輸送ノ生命線ナルニ不拘之ガ停止ノ為百萬島民ノ生命ヲ脅カシツツアルヲ以テ三十ノ航路ノ全部解除スルヲ希望ス

（付記四）

布告第三號ニ對スル對案

日本政府ハ聯合國最高司令官ノ指示ニ基キ通貨ニ關シ左ノ通リ布告ス

第一條

一、占領軍ハ其ノ駐屯ニ必要トスル經費支辨ノ為日本銀行ノ發行スル法定通貨竝ニ日本政府發行紙幣及硬貨ヲ使用ス

二、占領軍將兵ノ既ニ所持シ又ハ占領軍ニ於テ既ニ將兵ニ支給セルB式補助軍用通貨ニ付テハ占領軍ニ代リ日本政府

本布告ノ規定ニ違反シタルモノハ處罰セラルベシ

了解事項（不發表）

昭和二十年九月　日附日本政府布告第　號ニ關シ聯合國最高司令官ト日本政府間ニ於テ左ノ通リ了解ス

一、上記布告第二條第三條及第四條ニ規定セル大藏大臣ノ許可ハ其ノ一般的方針ニ關シ聯合國最高司令官ノ指示ニ從フコト

二、第三條ニ關シテハ海外ヨリノ引揚者ニ對シ通貨、鑄貨及有價證券ノ輸出入ニ付例外的且有利ナル考慮ヲ認ムル要アルコト

第一総軍に対する米国陸軍第八軍の指令案

昭和20年9月4日　米国陸軍第八軍総司令部作成

付　記　右に対する日本側回答

HEADQUARTERS EIGHTH ARMY

United States Army

Office of the Commanding General

ニ於テ出來得ル限リ速ニ日本銀行ヲシテ回收セシム

三、占領軍ハ日本通貨使用ニ同意シ且前記補助軍用通貨ノ收促進ニ協力スベキコトヲ約ス

第二條　日本軍用通貨

四、日本國政府及陸海軍ノ發行シタル一切ノ軍用及占領地通貨ハ如何ナル取引ニ於テモ右通貨ノ授受ヲ禁止ス　但シ大藏大臣ノ許可アルトキハ此ノ限リニ非ズ

第三條　通貨ノ輸出入禁止

五、通貨、硬貨、證券ノ輸出入ヲ含ム一切ノ對外金錢取引ハ之ヲ禁止ス、但シ大藏大臣ノ許可アルトキハ此ノ限リニ非ズ

六、本州、北海道、四國、九州及近海相互間ノモノヲ除キ金錢取引ハ總テ之ヲ對外取引ト看做ス

第四條　其ノ他ノ通貨ニ關スル規則

七、「アメリカ」合衆國及聯合國ノ通貨竝ニ他ノ一切ノ通貨ハ日本國ニ於ケル法貨ニ非ザルモノトシ右通貨ノ授受ハ之ヲ禁止ス、但シ大藏大臣ノ許可アルトキハ此ノ限リニ非ス

第五條　罰則

1　降伏文書調印と初期占領政策への対応（昭和20年9月～10月）

APO 343

4 September 1945

INSTRUCTIONS TO BE PRESENTED TO THE COMMANDING GENERAL, FIRST JAPANESE GENERAL ARMY ON 5 SEPTEMBER 1945

I. GENERAL:

1. The Commanding General, First Japanese General Army, is furnished the following list of instructions as a guide for the procedure by which the provisions of Directive No. 2 from the Supreme Commander for the Allied Powers may be initiated.

2. A second conference of principal staff officers of the United States and Japanese Armies will be held at 0800/I, 6 September 1945, at which the Japanese will furnish the information required in the remaining portions of this document.

3. Such of these functions as are not within the prerogatives of the Commanding General, First Japanese General Army, to supervise will be so indicated by him on a written list. This list will show the names of the persons responsible for the supervision of the excepted functions and the Commanding General, First Japanese General Army, will insure that instructed representatives of the appropriate agencies are present at the conference scheduled for 0800/I, 6 September 1945.

II. JAPANESE ARMED FORCES:

1. The Commanding General, First Japanese General Army, will furnish to the Commanding General, Eighth United States Army, the following detailed information:

a. Location of the following units within the area of the First Japanese General Army, accurately plotted on a map, scale not smaller than 1/50,000.

(1) Headquarters of departments, branches and agencies of the Japanese Imperial General Headquarters;

(2) Headquarters, First Japanese General Army;

(3) All major units down to and including independent regiments (all types).

b. Home depot for each of the units listed in "a" above.

c. Table of organization strength for all units.

d. Actual strength as of latest date for which strength

83

reports have been received.

    e. Status of demobilization within each unit as of 2 September 1945.

    f. Location of demobilization depots, together with names of commanders.

    g. Location of all minefields, land mines and other obstacles to movement overland with the present status of them. Immediately take steps to deactivate all such fields, booby traps and other demolitions, marking with conspicuous signs any which have not been rendered harmless.

    h. Four copies of the latest edition of all topographic maps of all scales of the area of the First Japanese General Army.

    i. A line route map of all long distance and main line electric communication facilities within the First Japanese General Army area.

    2. The Commanding General, First Japanese General Army, will direct the senior commander of Japanese armed forces within each of the designated regimental boundaries to report immediately to the senior commander of the United States Army Forces in his area for such instructions as may be necessary.

    a. At that time local Japanese commanders will present to the local United States Army commanders detailed station lists of all armed force units remaining within the area together with the status of demobilization.

    3. Steps will be taken immediately to disarm all members of the Japanese armed forces including those acting as special or military police. All arms and ammunition collected as a result of this action will be assembled at such places as may be directed by the local commander of the United States Army Forces.

    4. The Commanding General, First Japanese General Army, will notify all Japanese military commanders and civilian officials within the area of the First Japanese General Army that effective 0800/I, 6 September 1945, reconnaissance parties may be expected to proceed to selected points within the area of that command. The Commanding General, First Japanese General Army will be notified of these points seventy-two (72) hours in advance of the movement of the reconnaissance parties.

    a. Actual movement of troops into the selected areas

1　降伏文書調印と初期占領政策への対応(昭和20年9月～10月)

mentioned above may be expected after the reconnaissance parties have finished their mission. The Commanding General, First Japanese General Army, will receive forty-eight (48) hours advance notice prior to such troop movements.

5. A liaison officer of colonel's rank will remain on duty with the Headquarters, Eighth United States Army.

III. TRANSPORTATION:

 1. GENERAL:

  a. The Commanding General, First Japanese General Army will designate one representative in each of the following categories who will be empowered to speak and make decisions for the Commanding General, First Japanese General Army in his respective field within the Eighth Army area of occupation as set forth in Annex A to Directive No. 2, Office of the Supreme Commander for the Allied Powers:

   (1) Railway transportation;
   (2) Motor transportation;
   (3) Water transportation (including ports and harbors and waterfront facilities).

  b. These representatives will report to the Commanding General, Eighth United States Army without delay and will remain on duty with Headquarters, Eighth United States Army at Yokohama until further notice.

  c. The Transportation Officer, Eighth United States Army (Colonel R. P. Shea) is designated as the representative of the Commanding General, Eighth United States Army, in all matters pertaining to transportation.

 2. RAILWAY TRANSPORTATION:

  a. It is intended that the operation and maintenance of all railways, local, interurban and national, will be conducted by the appropriate Japanese agency, under the general supervision of the Commanding General, Eighth United States Army. All rail transportation as listed above will continue in operation as presently scheduled and managed until further notice.

  b. The movement of United States Army or Navy personnel, supplies and equipment by rail will be effected by the presentation of a demand to the Japanese Railway representative for the movement of such personnel, supplies and equipment. This demand will state:

(1) Number of personnel;

(2) Amount and description of supplies;

(3) Description, dimensions and weight of any unusual packages;

(4) List of equipment, giving size and weight;

(5) Origin and destination of such personnel, supplies and equipment;

(6) Time and date at which movement is to begin;

(7) Time and date at which movement must be completed.

c. The detailed plan for the movement by rail of personnel, supplies and equipment will be furnished the Transportation Officer, Eighth United States Army, at least twenty-four (24) hours prior to the time the movement is to commence. This plan will include:

(1) Type and number of cars or trains to be employed;

(2) Route to be followed;

(3) Schedule of the movement in detail;

(4) Any exceptional or unusual circumstances or conditions which may affect the move.

3. WATER:

a. It is expected that the debarkation of occupation forces, their supplies and equipment will utilize all of the harbor facilities in all major ports within the Eighth United States Army area of occupation. Therefore, all wharves, piers, jetties, overwater warehouses, sheds and adjacent storage facilities must be reserved for United States Army use except those specifically allocated to the United States Navy by the Supreme Commander for the Allied Powers.

b. It is expected that the resupply program and later schedules of troop movements will not require all facilities, and accordingly various facilities will be released to the proper Japanese agency.

c. The Japanese authorities will designate competent representatives at each port who will perform the following functions:

86

1 降伏文書調印と初期占領政策への対応(昭和20年9月～10月)

    (1) Harbor Master;

    (2) Chief Pilot;

    (3) Stevedore and Waterfront Labor Superintendent.

  d. A list of one hundred (100) tons or more located in or employed in coastwise or inter-island trade within the Eighth United States Army area of occupation will be furnished together with a schedule, if any, under which these craft are now operated. It is anticipated that if such service is in operation carrying commercial cargo, that its continued operation will be approved. With the exception of craft that may be employed as outlined above, no craft over one hundred (100) tons may depart or enter any port within the Eighth United States Army area of occupation without prior approval from this headquarters in each instance.

  4. MOTOR TRANSPORTATION:

    a. The Commanding General, First Japanese General Army, will furnish within seventy-two (72) hours of receipt of this document a complete and accurate list of all Japanese Army vehicles located within the Eighth United States Army area of occupation. They will furnish also a list of all truck companies, highway transportation groups, if any, or any similar military units. The same information is required with relation to motor vehicle maintenance units of any description.

    b. An inventory will be made and furnished to the Commanding General, Eighth United States Army, of all private, municipal, prefectural or national bus or truck operating organizations. This list will include:

    (1) Number and type vehicles;

    (2) Number operating in each case;

    (3) Type of fuel;

    (4) Routes and schedules or areas served.

    c. It is anticipated that various transportation units of the First Japanese General Army may be utilized for the overland transportation of United States Army personnel, equipment and supplies. It is therefore directed that no such organization be demobilized within the Eighth United States Army area of occupation without prior approval of this headquarters in each instance.

d. Demands for the use of private and municipal, prefectural or national motor transportation organizations, if any, will be handled in the same manner as outlined above for rail transportation.

5. The authority of the Commanding General, Eighth United States Army, to requisition, supervise or operate any of the facilities, equipment or agencies involved or engaged in transportation activities may be delegated at any time to subordinate commands. Notice of delegation of such authority will be given the appropriate Japanese representative on duty with this headquarters in writing, and all matters not specifically delegated are reserved to this headquarters.

IV. ALLIED PRISONERS OF WAR AND CIVILIAN INTERNEES: This subject has been covered in detail in papers already submitted.

R. L. EICHELBERGER,
Lieutenant General, USA,
Commanding.

(付記)

Note Verbale

RE APO 343, INSTRUCTIONS PRESENTED TO THE COMMANDING GENERAL, FIRST JAPANESE GENERAL ARMY ON 5 SEPTEMBER 1945.

(欄外記入)

1. a) The Instructions involve several functions which are not within the prerogatives of the Commanding General, First Japanese General Army, but are in charge of the Japanese Government. The officials of the Japanese Government concerned will be present at the conference of September 6, as directed, but direct consultation with the Government is desired hereafter regarding matters pertaining to the affairs in charge of the Government.

b) Consultations have already been under way on railway transportation between General Besson of the Eighth Army and officials of the Ministry of Communications.

On the question of water transportation conversation is also in progress between the Allied General Headquarters and the representatives of the Japanese Government. It is desired, therefore, that in arranging transportation questions within the 8th

1　降伏文書調印と初期占領政策への対応（昭和20年9月～10月）

Army area the result of these conversations will be taken into consideration.

2. With reference to Article II Paragraph 2, it will be more practical that a Commander of the Army concerned or, if necessary, by Division Commanders on the spot will report to the Senior Commander of the United States Army Forces in his area for instructions, in the place of a regimental Commander.

This point has been explained directly by the Japanese General Headquarters to the Supreme Commander for the Allied Powers.

3. With reference to Article II, Paragraph 3, it is requested to alter that part of the Instructions ordering disarmament of military police, because it will cause many difficulties in the maintenance of peace and order.

4. With reference to Article II, Paragraph 4, it is desired that the reconnaissance party will be sent after the disarming of troops in the area concerned has been completed.

5. With reference to Article III, Paragraph 3, subparagraph a, it is requested that the Commander of the Eighth Army will allow some exceptions for the civilian requirements even at the initial stage of the debarkation of the occupation troops. On this point concrete explanations will be made in due course.

（欄外記入）
九月六日午前八時會議ニ於テ鈴木公使ヨリ先方ニ説明

林（安）館山地区連合軍受入設営委員会委員長より
岡崎（勝男）終戦連絡中央事務局長官宛

13　昭和20年9月4日

館山地区占領に関する米国軍送付文書の和訳転送について

付記　昭和二十年九月四日付日本政府より連合国最高司令官総司令部宛公信和文原案
館山地区での米国軍の措置に対する抗議

館山公第二號
昭和二十年九月四日

在館山
林委員長〔印〕

岡崎終戰連絡中央事務局長官殿

米側所持ノ文書譯文送付ノ件

九月三日舘山公第一號ヲ以テ送付セル米側ノ所持セル文書
譯文別添送付スルニ付右御査收相成度

（別 添）

司令部第一一二RCT APO五〇三、一九四五年九月三日

表題、米國軍ニヨル舘山灣地區ノ占領

相手方、日本武裝軍隊ノ責任アル軍指揮官及責任アル行政
當局官憲

一、米國政府及日本國政府間ノ協定ニ從ヒ本軍ハ舘山灣地區
ヲ左ノ目的ヲ以テ占領スルモノトス
　a．或種ノ軍用資材ヲ確保シ且處分スルコト
　b．對象トナレル地區ニ於ケル行政ヲ監督スルコト
　c．俘虜及軍以外ノ被抑留者ヲ釋放スルコト
二、上記目的ノ達成ノ爲、前記協定ニ從ヒ、當地區ノ責任アル
軍指揮官及行政官憲ハ能フ限リ當司令部ト協力スベキコ
トヲ期待ス

三、依テ左ノ通リ指示ス
　a．本通知ヲ受領シタル後廿四時間以內ニ左ノ情報供給
ノ爲指示セラルルコトアルベキ説明資料ヲ附シタル地
圖又ハ素圖ヲ提出スベシ
　(1) 西ヶ崎鴨川ノ線ヨリ南ノ總テノ軍（陸海軍）施設ノ所
在地
　(2) 斯カル施設ニ於ケル武器、守備隊、軍需品及一切ノ
種類ノ補給品
　(3) 通信施設、道路、鐵道、電話、電信、無電及Radar
裝置
　(4) 物資集積所（戰鬪用ニ臨時堆積セル軍需品ヲ含ム）
　(5) 銀行、郵便局、公共營造物、發電所、水道、警察署、
官廳建物ノ所在地
　(6) 化學的戰爭資材
　(7) 精油及人造燃料工場
　(8) 刑務所、留置所等
　(9) 俘虜收容所
　(10) 祕密結社ノ本部、隣組、其他
　(11) 食糧、衣類、燃料集積所（民用）

1 降伏文書調印と初期占領政策への対応（昭和20年9月～10月）

⑿軍事施設ノ破壊ニ對スル豫備計畫（若シアラバ）

四、貴下ニ對シ更ニ左ノ通リ通告ス

a. 本司令部ハ左ノ諸項ヲ含ム民行政監督ノ任ニ當ルベキ軍政參謀課ヲ設置ス

　(1) 裁判所、金融、財産ノ保管管理、教育、情報
　(2) 公衆福利施設、民間ニ對スル給與
　(3) 公衆ノ安寧、商品統制、物價、配給
　(4) 公共營造物、運輸、商工業
　(5) 公衆ノ保健及衛生
　(6) 勞働

五、貴下ニ對シ當司令部ノ麾下ニアル職員ハ左ノ指示ヲ受ケ居ル旨ヲ通知ス

a. 軍人タルト一般人民タルトヲ問ハズ、地方住民ト交歡ヲ爲サザルコト

b. 如何ナル場合ト雖モ米兵ハ神社内ニ立入ラザルコト

c. 文化及藝術品及宗教的意義アル場所ハ保護セラルベキコト

d. 米兵ハ娼家ニ立入ルコトヲ禁止サレ居ルコト

e. 一般人ハ米軍ノ職務執行ヲ妨害セザル限リ危害ヲ加ヘラルルコトナシ

六、左ノ事項ハ直ニ實施セラルベシ

a. 一切ノ學校ヲ閉鎖スルコト

b. 醜業婦ハ警察ニ依リ隔離セシメラルルコト

c. 一切ノ酒場ヲ閉鎖スルコト

d. 麻薬ノ販賣制限ニ關スル日本國ノ諸規則ハ依然有效タルコト

e. 總テノ市町村民ハ一切ノ武器及彈藥ヲ最寄ノ警察ニ差出スコト

f. 一切ノ劇場ハ閉鎖セラルベキコト

g. 各個人ハ毎日十九時ヨリ六時迄當司令部ヨリ特ニ書面ヲ以テ許可セラレタル者ノ外各自ノ自宅ニ留マルコト

h. 一時二十人以上公共ノ場所ニ集合セザルコト

原則トシテ米國政府ヲ代表スル本司令部ノ命令ヲ遵守スルノ協力的態度及積極的意思ヲ公然表示スル文官ヲ在職セシムルコトヲ提議ス

米國陸軍指揮官准將　ジュリアン・W・カニンガム

日本政府發聯合國總司令部宛覺書

昭二〇、九、四

千葉縣館山ニ派遣セラレ居ル地方連絡事務局長林安男爵ノ終戰連絡中央事務局長官ニ對スル報告ニ依レハ九月三日館山ニ上陸セル米國陸軍指揮官「カニンガム」代將（Brigadier General Cunningham）ハ林氏ニ對シ別添ノ如キ命令ヲ手交シ其ノ卽時執行方指令セル趣ナリ右報告ハ深刻ナル危懼ト不安トヲ釀シツツアリ

日本政府ハ右カ聯合國總司令部ノ警察ヲ含ム日本政府ノ機能ヲ存續シ尊重スルト云フ一般方針ニ矛盾スルノミナラス一切ノ學校ヲ閉鎖スルカ如キハ國民ノ教育ヲ進步トノ見地ヨリ忍ヒ難キコトナル點ヲ得ス聯合國總司令部カ此ノ點ニ深甚ナル注意ヲ拂ヒ適當ナル指示ヲ在館山米國陸軍指揮官ニ對シ發セラレンコトヲ要望ス（了）

（付 記）

編 注 本文書ノ別添ハ見當ラナイガ、第13文書ノ別添ガソノ和訳文ニ当ルト思ワレル。

---

14 昭和20年9月5日
岡崎終戦連絡中央事務局長官
サザーランド連合国最高司令官
（総司令部参謀長）会談

指令第二号などに関する岡崎・サザーランド会談

付 記 昭和二十年九月五日付、作成者不明

岡崎長官「ス」参謀長會談要點

「命令第二號ニ關スル質疑」

（二〇、九、五）

一、Directive No.2 は No.1 の間違ひなり（No.1 を中止せる口實なるやに推量せらる）

一、四八時間延長期間の問題

「可及的早ければ早い程よし」の意味なり

一、商船の問題

(a)「アドミラル、バランタイン」に申入れよ、特定の場所（艦隊の泊地等）を除き航行を許可す

(b) 修繕は直ちに許可す—之に關し「報告」提出要求す

(c) 建造中のものは報告を提出せよ考慮すべし

尚以上の問題に付「バランタイン」に話したる處

1　降伏文書調印と初期占領政策への対応（昭和20年9月～10月）

「其の通りなり、但し之に關する折衝は一元的に海軍の連絡委員中村中將又は其の部下のものが必ず附添ひ政府の意向なることを明確にして筋一本にて行はれたし」と〔（リスト）〕の報告は司令部へ出頭の要なし、送付にて可

（第二總司令部は大阪にて可なる由）

一、"Subordinate Agency"は橫濱以外に差當り京都に置く、之以外將來要求するやも知れず

陸海軍側の質問

一、字句質問―省略

一、長野縣を第一總軍管區に入れられ度しとの件に付きては復員問題に關しては認む

一、設營等の要求は前廣に行はれたしとの日本側の申入れは了承す、學校、官廳、縣廳等の建物使用囘避の件も承認す

一、伊豆列島は小笠原の南迄第八軍管區とす

設營其の他の問題に關しては元通り第六軍管區とす

一、海軍保安隊保持の件に付ては

岡崎長官より「將來普通警察官を三倍に増し之に代らしめんとし居る處、復員軍人を直ちに之に當らしめたらば貴方に於ても不都合ならんとも察せらるるにより、目下民間人を之が爲訓練中にして之が期間中保安隊の保持を許され度し」と助言せる處漸次減少の建前ならは考慮するものの如し

一、「空港の整備」の目的如何の質問に對し

不時着の爲の準備なる故、其れに必要なる限度の人のみ止め置けばよく、この空港は軍用民用を問はずと囘答せり

一、軍艦に乘せる人間の問題に關し

最少限度の人間の意味なりと

「マ」〔マッカーサー〕重光會談其の後の成行に關しては囘答なし

日本政府に對する「ディレクティヴ」となすことに同意せるか我方提出の案文に付て未た先方の意思表示なし

一、大本營解散問題に關し

復員完了時の十月一日乃至十日が豫定さるるも在外地軍隊の處理の主體を如何にするやの問題に對し

岡崎長官より

陸海軍省のみを殘す形式にて之が處理に當らしめては如

何と提案せるに対し先方は

「在外地日本軍處理は時間的に何時終了するや予想不可能なるに付、かかる不確定の條件では陸海軍省の存續を許す譯には行かぬ尠くとも處理に移されざるを得ぬならん――之が殘務整理の計畫に關し立案し報告せられよ」と囘答せり

一、在外地日本軍使用軍票處理問題に關し岡崎長官より、久保外資局長に

第二條に關しては

「中央部に於て軍票の失效を宣言するも現地に中央の實力の及ばぬ現狀にあつては何等措置を講じ得ず、極めて不合理なるに付各地現地司令官に於て適宜裁量の上處理せらるる如く取計ひたし」との意見を先方に開陳すること可然旨說示し

久保局長は鈴木公使立會の上此の「ライン」に沿ひ話を進めたる模樣なり

一、館山、立川の問題に關し岡崎長官としては

Remindはするが競々なる進駐軍の心理に發したる過渡的豫防的措置ならん館山地區に於ても陸軍側にて報告以上の憲兵を殘置しありたるを發見せられたる事實あるに徵するも右の如く思考し從つて未だ先方に話し居らす

館山に關する書面申入は九月六日に提出の筈

（丁）

（付記）

命令第二號に關する質疑（二〇、九、五午後四時）

日本側 有末中將、横山少將、岡崎長官

米側 「サザランド」參謀長、「チェーンパース」少將

一、命令第二號は第一號の誤り

二、制限時間四十八時間トアルモ可能ナル範圍ニテ急速ニ實行スレバ宜シ（我方ノ俘虜抑留者ノ情報ハ既ニ接到、先方ハ迅速ナルニ滿足ノ意ヲ表ス）

三、商船ニ關シテハ(イ)就航可能ノモノハ「バランタイン」ヲ出サハ許可ノ筈(ロ)海軍少將ニ「アツプリケーション」ヲ出サハ許可ノ筈

1 降伏文書調印と初期占領政策への対応(昭和20年9月～10月)

破損セルモノハ直ニ修理シ差支ナキモ其ノ具體的ノ事項ヲ報告スベク(ハ)建造中ノモノハ其ノ工事進捗程度等具體的事項ヲ示シ参謀長ノ許可ニ書類ヲ提供セハ考慮スヘシ(ニ)各地ノ船舶ハ命令記載ノ如ク一々最寄ノ海軍司令官ノ許ニ運航シ報告スルノ要ナク一括シテ日本政府ヨリ米總司令部ニ通報アラハ足ル

四、中央事務局ノ分局ハ差當リ横濱及京都トス尚第二總軍司令部ヲ廣島ヨリ大阪ニ移ス件ハ承知ス第六軍司令部ハ京都ノ筈其ノ他勞働力集結ノ困難、官廳建物乃至學校ヲ徵用セサルコト等ニ付適宜申入レタリ

五、長野縣ハ復員ニ關スル限リ第一總軍ノ管轄トシ差支ナシ他ノ問題ニ付テハ命令書記載ノ通リトスルモ一應日本側ノ申出ハ研究スヘシ伊豆七島ハ八丈島南方迄ヲ第八軍管轄内ニ入レ差支ナシ

六、空港(Ⅱ8a)、空港ハ民間ノモノ及陸海軍空軍基地ヲ含ム目的ハ不時着機ノ保護ニ在ルニ付之ニ必要ノ人員ヲ殘セハ足ル尚飛行機ニ付テハ極東空軍司令部(本部ハ東京ノ筈)ト航空總軍トノ直接折衝ニ委ス

七、掃海作業ノ爲海防艦ヲ使用ノ件ハ米海軍ニテ承認セ

ハ總司令部ハ異議ナシ

八、海軍保安隊ハ海軍側ニテ各地ノ保有數及復員計畫ヲ示シタル報告書提出セハ考慮スヘシ(岡崎ヨリ警察官ノ増員ハ訓練等ノ關係アリ急速ニ運ハサルニ付保安隊留置ノ必要アルコトヲ強調シ置ケリ)

九、其ノ他「テクニカルターム」ノ意味ハ專門家ノ間ニ質疑ノコトトシ又地圖其ノ他情報ノ提供ハ可能ノ範圍ニテ差支ナシ

附記 直接質疑事項ニ非ラサルモ諸問題討議ノ間ニ於テ米側ハ(イ)復員完了迄ハ大本營ヲ殘置スルモ其ノ後ハ之ヲ解體セシメ(ロ)結局ハ海外軍隊歸還等ノ事務ハ文官ニ之ヲ委セ度キモ(ハ)其ノ間ノ過渡的機關トシテ陸海軍省ヲ殘置スルコトニハ大體異存ナキ模様ナリ尤モ海外兵員ノ歸還ハ三年位ヲ要スルヤモ知レサルモ夫レ迄陸海軍省ヲ殘スコトハ認メ得ス又其ノ必要モナシトノ意向ナルヤニ觀取セラレタリ然シテ本件ハ速ニ日本側ヨリ案ヲ具シテ協議アリ度シト要求セリ

昭和20年9月5日

重光外務大臣より
在スイス加瀬（後一）公使、在スウェーデン岡本（季正）公使他宛（電報）

降伏条項の実施状況について

本　省　9月5日後7時発

合第七一二號（至急）

一、八月二十日聯合國側ハ馬尼剌ニ於テ帝國全權委員ニ對シ差當リ帝國ノ執ルヘキ措置ニ付各般ノ指令ヲ文書ニテ手交セルガ其ノ後右文書ニ示サレタル米軍ノ進駐ハ天候ノ為ニ日遅延セルモ二十八日以降東京灣地區鹿屋地區（鹿兒島縣）ニ於テ豫定ノ如ク行ハレ「マクアーサー」司令部ハ近ク横濱ヨリ東京ニ移駐スルコトトナレリ、現在迄ノ處聯合國軍本土進駐ハ順調ニ進ミ居リ國内ニ於テハ米兵ノ個々ノ行動ニ多少遺憾ノ點アルモ大ナル不祥事ノ發生ヲ見ス（九月四日現在）

一、大東亞地域ニ於ケル降伏條項ノ履行、就中武裝解除、傷病兵老幼婦女子ノ引揚ヲ繞ル問題等ハ當面ノ困難ナル懸案ナルモ我方ニ於テ十分ナル誠意ヲ以テ之ガ處理ニ當リ、各地ニ於テ概ネ圓滑ニ實施セラレ居ル模樣ニシテ尚今後

モ我方ニ於テ銳意之ガ解決ニ努ムベク萬全ノ措置ヲ講ジツツアリ、特ニ滿洲、蒙疆、北鮮、北支ノ一部竝ニ南樺太ニ於テハ日本軍及邦人ノ安否ニ付憂フヘキ事態認メラレタルニ付至急事態改善方申入レ中ナリ米軍ハ九月八日京城地區ニ進駐ノ予定ナリ

（二）俘虜及抑留者ノ情報蒐集ニ關シテハ目下ノ不自由ナル通信狀況ニ鑑ミ中央ニ於テ一括正確ナル情報ヲ蒐集先方ニ提供スルコト至難ナルニ付内地以外ノ各地ニ於ケル俘虜及抑留者關係情報供與ハ各地毎ニ彼我當該官憲間ニ於テ情報提供方協定ヲ見タリ

一、帝國政府ノ正式降伏ノ調印式ハ九月二日午前九時四分東京灣上ノ米戰艦「ミズーリ」號上ニ於イテ開始セラレ、日本側ヨリ政府代表本大臣陸海軍代表梅津参謀總長ノ兩全權出席シ署名セル降伏文書ニ對シ聯合國最高司令官「マックアーサー」元帥初メ、米・支・英・蘇・濠・加・佛・和・新西蘭各聯合國代表之ニ署名シ九時十五分無事終了セリ

一、右帝國政府ノ正式降伏ノ調印終了ニ關シ畏クモ天皇陛下ニ於セラレテハ國民ニ對シ降伏文書ノ一切ノ條項竝ニ帝

1　降伏文書調印と初期占領政策への対応（昭和20年9月～10月）

16　昭和20年9月6日　米国政府より
マッカーサー連合国最高司令官宛

連合国最高司令官への米国政府通達（和訳文）

連合國最高司令官の權限に關するマッカーサー元帥への通達

一九四五年九月六日

1　天皇及び日本政府の國家統治の權限は、連合國最高司令官としての貴官に從屬する。貴官は、貴官の使命を實行するため貴官が適當と認めるところに從つて貴官の權限を行使する。われわれと日本との關係は、契約的基礎の上に立つているのではなく、無條件降伏を基礎とするものである。貴官の權限は最高であるから、貴官は、そ

の範圍に關しては日本側からのいかなる異論をも受け付けない。

2　日本の管理は、日本政府を通じて行われるが、これは、このような措置が滿足な成果を擧げる限度内においてである。このことは、必要があれば直接に行動する貴官の權利を妨げるものではない。貴官は、實力の行使を含む貴官の發した命令を認めるような措置を執ることによって、貴官が必要と認めるような措置を強制することができる。

3　ポツダム宣言に含まれている意向の聲明は、完全に實行される。しかし、それは、われわれがその文書の結果として日本との契約的關係に拘束されていると考えるからではない。それは、ポツダム宣言が、日本に關して、又極東における平和及び安全に關して、誠意をもって示されているわれわれの政策の一部をなすものであるから、尊重され且つ實行されるのである。

編注一　本文書は米国大統領の承認を経て、九月六日にマッカーサー司令官に伝達された。

二　本文書は、昭和二十四年一月、外務省特別資料部作成

97

「日本占領及び管理重要文書集」第一巻より抜粋。

17 昭和20年9月6日　連合国最高司令官総司令部より　日本政府宛

B号円表示軍票を法貨とする旨の指令

付　記　右和訳文

OFFICE OF THE SUPREME COMMANDER

FOR THE ALLIED POWERS

6 September 1945.

AG 123 (6 Sep 45)

SCAPIN 8

MEMORANDUM FOR THE JAPANESE GOVERNMENT.

THROUGH: Central Liaison Office Number 1.

SUBJECT: Legal Tender.

1. It is desired that the Japanese Imperial Government place in effect immediately as a law, decree or other appropriate measure the following, which will have application within Honshu, Hokkaido, Shikoku, Kyushu and adjacent waters:

a. "Supplemental military yen currency, marked "B", issued by the Military Occupation Forces is legal tender in Japan for the payment of all yen debts public or private.

b. "Supplemental military yen currency, marked "B", issued by the Military Occupation Forces, regular yen currency issued by the Bank of Japan and Japanese state notes and coin shall be equivalent in all respects and interchangeable at their face value.

c. "All military and all occupational currency which has been issued by the Japanese Government, Army or Navy, is void and valueless and the giving or accepting of such currency in any transaction is prohibited."

2. You are advised to bring to the attention of the proper authorities that such penalties as may be necessary to secure enforcement of the above will be prescribed by the Japanese Government and it is requested that the list of maximum and minimum penalties to be imposed for approval.

FOR THE SUPREME COMMANDER:

(signed)

HAROLD FAIR,

1　降伏文書調印と初期占領政策への対応（昭和20年9月～10月）

（付　記）

Lt Colonel, A.G.D.
Asst. Adjutant General.

聯合國最高司令官發帝國政府宛覺書
（九月六日發中央聯絡事務局經由）（AG 一二三）

法貨ニ關シ

1、帝國政府ニ於テ直チニ本州、北海道、四國、九州及右ニ接近スル海域ニ於テ適用セラルヘキ下記ノ如キ法律命令若シクハ其他適當ノ手段ヲ執ラルル樣希望ス

A、占領軍ニヨリ發行セラルル「B」ノ標記シアル補助軍票圓ヲ公私凡テノ圓債務支拂ノ爲日本ノ法貨タリ

B、「B」ノ標記シアル補助軍票圓ノ標記シアル其他ノ硬貨ハ凡ユル點ニ於テ額面價ニ於テ正常ノ圓通貨其他凡テノ圓通貨ト等價且交換シ得ルモノトス

C、日本政府陸軍又ハ海軍ノ發行シタル凡テノ軍票ハ無效且無價値ニシテ如何ナル取引ニ於テモ右通貨ノ授受ハ禁止セラルヘキモノトス

2、帝國政府ニ於テ上記ノ執行ヲ確保スルニ必要ナル刑罰ヲ規定スル樣適當ナル當局ノ注意ヲ喚起セラレ度ク及上記ニ違反セル場合ニ適用スヘキ最大及最少ノ刑罰表ヲ本司令部ニ提出シ承認ヲ求メラレ度

副官代理「エフヤー」中佐

～～～～～～

18　**南西諸島における降伏文書**

昭和20年9月7日　調印

Headquarters Tenth Army

7 September 1945

Surrender

The undersigned Japanese Commanders, in conformity with the general surrender executed by the Imperial Japanese Government, at Yokohama, on 2 September 1945, hereby formally render unconditional surrender of the islands in the Ryukyus within the following boundaries:

30° North 126° East, thence 24° North 122° East, thence 24° North 133° East, thence 29° North 131° East, thence 30° North 131° 30' East, thence to point of origin.

箭見敏郎　Toshiro Nomi　Lieutenant General　Commander Japanese Forces
崎島具登　Sakishima Gunto
高田利貞　Toshisada Takada　Major General　Commander Japanese Army Forces
奄美具登　Amami Gunto
加藤唯雄　Tadao Kato　Rear Admiral　Commander Japanese Navy Forces
奄美具登　Amami Gunto

Accepted: Joseph W. Stilwell
J.W. Stilwell
General, United States Army
Commanding

河辺（虎四郎）参謀次長　　　　　　　　　　　　　　　　　会談
サザーランド連合国最高司令官
総司令部参謀長

19
昭和20年9月8日

河辺・サザーランド会談

付記　昭和二十年九月九日、終戦連絡中央事務局第
　　　一部作成

［連絡會議議事録］

昭二十、九、八　政一

河邊参謀次長「スザーランド」参謀長會談録

河邊参謀次長ハ九月八日「スザーランド」参謀長ヲ往訪個
人的會見ヲ逐ケタルカ會談要旨左ノ通（永井少將ヨリ連絡）

一、河邊「マックアーサー」總司令部ノ他ノ連合國軍ニ對
スル權限如何
「ス」　何等指揮ノ權限ナシ、調印ト降伏ノ遣リ方ヲ定メ
ル權限ヲ有スルノミ、右以外ノ權限トシテハ米軍ノ日
本本土進駐ニ關スル事項アルノミ

二、河邊　日本ハ四國ヲ對手トスルコトトナルモ、支「ソ」
ニ對シ米側ハ斡旋出來サルヤ
「ス」（當惑セル面持ニテ）米側トシテモ困リ居ルモ斡旋

1　降伏文書調印と初期占領政策への対応（昭和20年9月～10月）

ハ出來ス、自分ハ天津ニ居タコトアリ、支那ニモ困リ居レリ、「ソ」連ニ對シテモ困リ居レリ、獨ニ對スル場合ト同様、「ソ」連ノ遣リ方ハ相當酷イ樣ナリ

三、河邊　今後ノ進駐豫定地域及兵力如何

四、河邊　大本營ハ既ニ不要ノモノトナレルカ、参謀本部ハ殘ルモノト思考ス

［ス］　第一總軍、第二總軍等モ不要ニ非スヤ

河邊　實ハ指令第二號ニ基キ第一、第二總軍ヲ米第八、第六軍ノ管轄範圍ト合致セシムル爲急遽編成替ヲ實施セル許リナリ

五、河邊　滿洲、北鮮方面八十萬ノ居留民ノ保護ニ付テハ政府モ大本營モ心痛シ居レリ、名案ナキヤ

［ス］　併シソウ長ク存續セシムル要ナカルヘシ

［ス］　近ク指示スヘシ

［ス］　右ハ大問題ニテ日本側モ困リ居ラルルコトト思フモ名案ナシ

河邊　右ニ付キ赤十字、宗教團体又ハ南鮮派遣米軍ノ援助ハ期待シ得サルヤ

［ス］　赤十字、宗教團体ハ活用セラレ可ナルヘシ、米側

六、河邊　日本ニハ自動車僅少ニ付キ多クヲ提供シ得ス、米側ニテ持チ來ル譯ニ行カサルヤ

［ス］　承知セリ

河邊　宿舎提供ノ問題モ惱ミノ種ナリ、勞務ハ提供シ得ルニ付キ木材ハ米側ニテ輸入シ得サルヤ

［ス］　米側トシテモ困リ居レリ、㯰テ組立家屋ノ材料ヲ取リ寄セヘキモ右ハ輸送力及時間ノ問題ナリ

七、河邊　米側ハ何故斯クモ多數ノ兵力ヲ日本ニ進駐セシムルヤ、日本ハ忠實ニ降伏文書ヲ實施シ居ルニ非スヤ

［ス］　ソノ疑問ハ良ク判ル、併シ米トシテハ太平洋ノ主兵力ヲ全部日本ニ入ルル考ヘナリ、十二月ニ最高潮ニ達スヘシ、爾後ハ狀況ノ如何ニ依ル

八、河邊　米兵ノ進駐ニ依リ國民ニ對米憎惡心ヲ生シ將來ノ日米關係ニ惡影響ヲ及ス虞ナキヤ

［ス］　當初ハ致シ方ナシ、併シ後一ケ月經テ見ラレタシ

九、河邊　日本軍人ハ武裝解除サルルコトトナルモ軍刀ハ軍人ノ家ニ取リテハ家寶ナリ、軍刀ハ外スモ猶之ヲ家ニ所藏スルヲ認ムル寛大サヲ有セラレサルヤ

「ス」其ノ氣持ハ判ル、近ク何分ノ指令ヲ出スヘシ

10、「ス」（河邊次長辭去ニ際シ）貴下ハ近ク軍籍ヲ離ルルコトトナリ淋シサヲ感セラルヘシ、貴下ノ幸福ト繁榮ヲ祈ル、猶今後用事アラハ遠慮ナク申シ出テラレタシ

終連第一部

連絡會議議事錄（九、九）

（付記）

一、河邊スザーランド會談（政一長）
要點
(1) 聯合國最高司令部の各聯合軍に對する指揮權は殆んどなく司令部自體も困り居れり
(2) 在滿八十萬の救出については司令部にも名案なし
(3) 太平洋方面米兵力は全部十二月中に日本に入れるか其後の情況を見て引揚げるか否やを定める

二、谷川憲兵司令官（？）米軍會談（政一長）
(1) 神奈川縣憲兵二、三〇〇の倍增の要求に對し差當りは三、五〇〇位は認む
(2) 憲兵たりしものが警察に入ることは一時的には認むるも永續的には認めず

三、外務省窓口を統一する件

四、南方等に於ける軍一本建と外務出先機關との關係（政一長）
(1) 聯合國側が軍一本建を要求する場合
(2) 現地軍、外務間に話合のつきたる場合
(3) 一般命令に依り外務機關から課せられ居る外務等では外務機關の活動分野大なるべく
(4) 停戰協定後の先方の出方如何によりては居留民關係事項等は外務機關にやらす向便利且有利なることあるべく今日より軍も極力外務機關の活用、存置を考慮の度

右趣旨軍より出先に電報の筈

五、緒方、ブリガデイア、ジェネラル、ソープ會談（稻垣よりの連絡一部長）
(1) 宣傳、啓發に關しては別に「指令」を出す
(2) 資料を供給するに付き適宜新聞等にのせろ
(3) 檢閱規則揭載禁止事項等詳細提出せよ
(4) 橫濱に二名、第八軍司令部に一名の連絡者を差出せ
(5) 中央郵便局に人を入れ海外通信を檢閱する、國內通信

1　降伏文書調印と初期占領政策への対応（昭和20年9月～10月）

は隨時檢閲すべし

(6) フイルムを供給する故映画をやれ

(7) 宣傳啓發關係は情報局を使ってやる

六、在外軍隊及居留民の引揚（四部二課長）

船腹五六萬噸中一四は要修理、現在航行可能四二中不取敢二八を引揚に使用することとせば民需は極度に窮屈になる鐵道は一割運行停止、造船所も止まるやも不知、二八で行くか否か火曜閣議で決定の筈但し主食は來年四月頃には非道いことになる故資料を取揃へ聯合軍に陳情の予定（本點は經濟局、終連三部にて擔當急速實施のこと）

七、在外軍隊武裝解除後は定着せしめ度陸軍の意嚮なり

(1) 本件に關し且將來のこともあり至急連絡者を大陸及南方へ派遣し度右に關する飛行機を出され度

(2) 先づ誰を何しにやるか政務局で定められ度（終連二部長）

八、連絡飛行に關する件

(1) 國内は簡單に許可すべきに付き計畫書を出せ

(2) 京城へは米側でやる

(3) 其他の國外は連合軍で計畫中それは一寸待たれ度

(4) 註、太田三部長の話によれば中華航空機は現に福岡迄は飛行實施中にして之に關する連絡は横田監督課長とやればよい 由本件三部より別途現狀問報のことに打合済

九、船舶運行狀況

終連三部に於て海軍と連絡の上現實に動いて居るや否か確かめ報告すること

10、在外同胞保護委員會の件（管理局）

20　昭和20年9月8日

米英ソの外交基調に關する觀測報告

在スウェーデン岡本公使より　重光外務大臣宛（電報）

ストックホルム　9月8日後4時45分發

本　省　9月11日前9時40分着

第五七一號

諜報者報告（四日及七日）

一、對日戰ノ終了ト共ニ英米カ對蘇外交攻勢ヲ開始シ居ルコトハ屢次所報ノ通リニシテ獨逸處理ニ付テモ英米一部ニ

於テハ獨逸ノ高度ニ發達セル工業ヲ破壞シ之ヲ農業國化スルハ無謀ナリトノ聲昂マリ居ルノミナラス自由選擧ノ實施ニ依リ對蘇防壁トシテノ獨逸ノ再建ヲ促進セントスルノ氣運スラ察セラレ政府トシテモ蘇聯ニ對シ既ニ確約セル以上ノ讓步ハ行ハサル態度ヲ示シ居ルモノト觀測セラル

二、英米外交ノ攻勢ニ對抗スル蘇聯邦政策ノ基調ハ第一ニ歐洲並ニ東亞ニ於テ武力占領ニヨリ最大限度ニ於ケルコト第二ニ英米殊ニ米トノ正面衝突ヲ極力避ケ必要ナルコト第三ニ國內ノ社會的對立相剋ヲ利用シ親蘇分子共產黨及急進派勢力ヲ強化シ之ヲ利用スルコト第四ニ主トシテ亞細亞ニ於テハ英米ノ帝國主義ニ對抗シテ民族解放運動ヲ利用スルコトニアリト觀測スル

三、九月二日「スターリン」ノ饒舌ハ當地ニ於テモ劃期的意義ヲ有スルモノトシテ論議サレ居リ一部ニハ蘇聯ノ政策力既ニ國際的ノ共產主義ヲ棄テ國家主義的帝國主義ニ立戾リタルモノニシテ既ニ資本主義國家ノ「イデオロギー」

的障碍除去サレタリト觀ル者アル處蘇聯邦カ最近國家主義的宣傳及階級制度ノ強化ヲ行ヒ居ルハ事實ナルモ之ヲ以テ直ニ蘇聯邦ノ根本的「イデオロギー」ニ變化ヲ來シタルモノト見ルハ早計ナルヘシ尤モ蘇聯ノ野心ハ帝政露西亞ノ野望ト全然其ノ方向ヲ同フシ居ルヲ以テ蘇聯ハ右ノ野心達成ノ爲ニハ共產主義ノ「イデオロギー」ヲ利用シテ大衆ヲ引摺リ國際的ニハ共產ラントシ居ルモノト觀測セリ

四、英米ノ資本主義的政治組織ハ蘇聯ニ取リ政治的浸透ノ可能性アルノミナラス之等兩國ノ武力攻擊ヲ懼ルル必要ナク一方日獨ノ敗戰ニ依リ蘇聯ノ政治的浸透ヲ許ササリシ政治組織並ニ其ノ脅威タリシ尨大ナル軍備除去セラレ蘇聯ハ今ヤ平和產業ノ充實國民生活ノ改善ニ勢力ヲ注キ得ルニ至レルカ日獨兩國ノ再起不能ナラシムルコトハ蘇聯ノ安全上取リ絕對必要條件ナルヲ以テ蘇聯ハ蘇聯ヲ目標トシテ英米獨或ハ日英米力接近スルコトヲ懼レ最近蘇聯ハ新聞「ラジオ」ヲ通シ日本特ニ其ノ支配階級ニ對シ猛烈ナル攻擊ヲ行ヒ居ル處今後共日英米ノ接近ヲ防止スル爲對日條件ノ苛酷化ヲ要求シ其ノ結果トシテ生スヘキ日

1　降伏文書調印と初期占領政策への対応（昭和20年9月～10月）

21

昭和20年9月10日　連合国最高司令官総司令部より日本政府宛

新聞・放送の検閲方針に関する指令

OFFICE OF THE SUPREME COMMANDER
FOR THE ALLIED POWERS

10 September 1945

SCAPIN 16

MEMORANDUM FOR THE IMPERIAL JAPANESE GOVERNMENT

THROUGH: YOKOHAMA LIAISON OFFICE

FROM: The Supreme Commander for the Allied Powers.

1. The Japanese Imperial Government will issue the necessary orders to prevent dissemination of news, through newspapers, radio broadcasting or other means of publication, which fails to adhere to the truth or which disturbs public tranquility.

2. The Supreme Commander for the Allied Powers has decreed that there shall be an absolute minimum of restrictions upon freedom of speech. Freedom of discussion of matters affecting the future of Japan is encouraged by the Allied Powers, unless such discussion is harmful to the efforts of Japan to emerge from defeat as a new nation entitled to a place among the peace-loving nations of the world.

3. Subjects which cannot be discussed include Allied troop movements which have not been officially released, false or destructive criticism of the Allied Powers, and rumors.

4. For the time being, radio broadcasts will be primarily of a news, musical and entertainment nature. News, commentation and informational broadcasts will be limited to those originating at Radio Tokyo studios.

5. The Supreme Commander will suspend any publication or radio station which publishes information that fails to adhere to the truth or disturbs public tranquility.

For the SUPREME COMMANDER:

HAROLD FAIR,
Lt Col, A.G.D.,
Asst Adjutant General

本ノ窮迫ニ乗シ其ノ勢力伸張ヲ圖ラントスルモノト觀測セラル

22 昭和20年9月10日　連合国最高司令官総司令部より　大本営、陸軍省、海軍省宛

大本営廃止に関する指令

AG 091 (10 Sep 45) CS
SCAPIN 17
MEMORANDUM:
TO: Imperial Japanese General Headquarters
Imperial Japanese Ministry of War
Imperial Japanese Ministry of the Navy

10 September 1945

1. It is directed that the Imperial Japanese General Headquarters be abolished on or before 2400, 13 September 1945.

2. Acknowledgment of receipt of this directive is desired.

For the Supreme Commander:

R. K. SUTHERLAND,
Lieutenant General, U. S. Army,
Chief of Staff.

23 昭和20年9月12日　連合国最高司令官総司令部より　日本政府宛

B号円表示軍票、米ドルおよび外貨の使用に関する指令

AG 123 (September 12, 1945) MG
Memorandum
To: The Japanese Imperial Government
Through: Central Liaison Committee, Yokohama.
Subject: Use of Supplemental Yen (Type B) U. S. Dollars and Other Foreign Currency.

1. The Japanese Imperial Government has not yet complied with directions given them in the memorandum, AG 123 (6 September 1945) that Supplemental (Type B) be decreed legal tender in Japan.

2. Further, directly at variance with the desire of the Supreme Commander expressed to the representatives of the Japanese Imperial Government from the Central Liaison Office, the Ministry of Finance and the Bank of Japan, that currency of the United

1　降伏文書調印と初期占領政策への対応（昭和20年9月～10月）

24　昭和20年9月13日　連合国最高司令官総司令部より　大本営、陸軍省、海軍省宛

大本営解消後の連絡に関する指令

OFFICE OF THE SUPREME COMMANDER
FOR THE ALLIED POWERS

AG 091 (13 Sep 45) CS
SCAPIN 25
MEMORANDUM FOR:

13 September 1945

編　注　本文書の別添は省略。

Incl: Proposed Statement of Declaration.

For the Supreme Commander:

Harold FAIR
Lt. Col. ADG
Asst. Adjt. General

States, currencies of the Allied Powers and other foreign currencies be not permitted to circulate in Japan, a statement was issued to the press "From the authorities of the Ministry of Finance" that dollars would be exchanged for Yen at the bank, (Mainichi Shinbun Morning Edition 9 September 1945). In addition a radio broadcast on 8 September stated that exchange of dollar notes can be made at the rate of 4 yen 25 sen to the dollar.

3. It is directed that the Japanese Imperial Government, through the Japanese Ministry of Finance, issue the attached statement formally to the press and radio, publish it prominently in Post Offices, Railway Stations, Banks and other financial institutions and public places, such as within and without Imperial Government, Prefectural and Municipal Buildings.

4. It is further directed that the Japanese Government prohibits the giving or taking of United States currency or the currency of any Allied Power or any other foreign currency in any transaction.

5. In the event that any further delay occurs in the declaration of Supplemental Yen as legal tender immediately by decree, the Supreme Commander for the Allied Powers will take such action as he deems appropriate.

IMPERIAL JAPANESE GENERAL HEADQUARTERS
JAPANESE MINISTRY OF WAR
JAPANESE MINISTRY OF THE NAVY.

THROUGH: Central Liaison Office, Yokohama.

1. It is directed that upon the abolition of the Imperial Japanese General Headquarters, pursuant to the Memorandum from the Supreme Commander for the Allied Powers, dated 10 September 1945, the functions charged to the Imperial Japanese General Headquarters will be executed by the respective Ministries concerned.

2. It is further directed that the existing Liaison Commission continue to function, but with respect to the Ministries of War and Navy instead of Imperial Japanese General Headquarters.

3. Acknowledgement of receipt of this directive is desired.

FOR THE SUPREME COMMANDER:

signed.

HAROLD FAIR,
Lt. Colonel, A.G.D.,
Asst. Adjutant General.

25　昭和20年9月13日　連合国最高司令官総司令部より　日本政府宛

連合国および枢軸国財産の保全に関する指令

OFFICE OF THE SUPREME COMMANDER
FOR THE ALLIED POWERS

13 September 1945

AG 091.112 (13 Sep 45) MG

SCAPIN 26

MEMORANDUM FOR: IMPERIAL JAPANESE GOVERNMENT

THROUGH: Central Liaison Office, Yokohama

SUBJECT: Protection of Allied and Axis Property

1. The Imperial Japanese Government will impound immediately and report within fifteen days all property and other assets, books of account and other records owned or controlled, in whole or in part, directly or indirectly, by the Governments or any nationals, within or without Japan, of Germany, Italy, Bulgaria, Finland, Thailand, Rumania and Hungary.

2. The Imperial Japanese Government will cause to be preserved in good order and condition all property and other assets,

1　降伏文書調印と初期占領政策への対応（昭和20年9月〜10月）

books of account and other records, owned or controlled in whole or in part by the Governments or any national of any of the United Nations on December 7, 1941 and make a complete report to the Supreme Commander within one week.

3. Acknowledgement of this directive is requested.

FOR THE SUPREME COMMANDER:

HAROLD FAIR
Lt Colonel, AGD.,
Asst. Adjutant General.

26　日本占領政策に関するマッカーサー司令官の声明

昭和20年9月14日　連合国最高司令官総司令部発表

General of the Army Douglas MacArthur's Statement concerning the Occupation Policy for Japan

September 14, 1945

I have noticed some impatience in the press based upon the assumption of a so-called soft policy in Japan. This can only arise from an erroneous concept of what is occurring.

The first phase of the occupation must of necessity be based upon military considerations which involve the deployment forward of our troops and the disarming and demobilization of the enemy. This is coupled with the paramount consideration of withdrawing our former prisoners of war and war internees from the internment camps and evacuating them to their homes. Safety and security require that these steps shall proceed with precision and completeness lest calamity may be precipitated. The military phase is proceeding in an entirely satisfactory way. Over half of the enemy's force in Japan proper is now demobilized and the entire program will be practically complete by the middle of October. During this interval of time safety and complete security must be assured.

When the first phase is completed the other phases as provided in the surrender terms will infallibly follow. No one need have any doubt about the prompt, complete and entire fulfillment of the terms of surrender. The process, however, takes time. It is well understandable in the face of atrocities committed by the enemy that there should be impatience. This natural impulse, however, should be tempered by the fact that security and military expediency still require an exercise of some restraint. The surrender terms are not soft and they will not be applied in kid gloved fashion.

Economically and industrially, as well as militarily, Japan is completely exhausted and depleted. She is in a condition of utter collapse. Her governmental structure is controlled completely by the occupation forces and is operating only to the extent necessary to insure such an orderly and controlled procedure as will prevent social chaos, disease and starvation.

The overall objectives for Japan have been clearly outlined in the surrender terms and will be accomplished in an orderly, concise and comprehensive way without delays beyond those imposed by the magnitude of the physical problems involved.

It is extraordinarily difficult for me at times to exercise that degree of patience which is unquestionably demanded if the long time policies which have been decreed are to be successfully accomplished without repercussions which would be detrimental to the well-being of the world but I am restraining myself to the best of my ability and am generally satisfied with the progress being made.

編注　本文書は、昭和二十四年三月、外務省特別資料部作成「日本占領及び管理重要文書集」第二巻より抜粋。

27

昭和20年9月15日　連合国最高司令官総司令部より　日本政府宛

非軍需工場における生産につき情報報告方指令

OFFICE OF THE SUPREME COMMANDER
FOR THE ALLIED POWERS

15 September 1945

AG 091 (15 Sep 45) MG
(SCAPIN-29)

MEMORANDUM FOR: IMPERIAL JAPANESE GOVERNMENT
THROUGH: Central Liaison Office, Yokohama
SUBJECT: Production in Non-War Plants

1. The Japanese Government will, within thirty days, after

1　降伏文書調印と初期占領政策への対応（昭和20年9月～10月）

receipt of this directive, report to the Supreme Commander, machinery and measures which have been maintained or established for the development, administration and enforcement of programs for:

　a. Production of essential commodities for domestic consumption

　b. Control of prices, salaries and wages

　c. The equitable distribution and rationing of essential commodities

　d. The elimination of black markets and discriminatory practices

　e. The useful employment of the Japanese people along lines adapted to and devoted to peace and in conformity with the objectives of occupation.

　2. The Japanese Government will be prepared to submit to the Supreme Commander upon request, the following data:

　　a. A list including statistical details of economic control plans and measures taken

　　b. A list of industrial plants, other than war materials plants as defined in General Directive No.1, showing location, ownership, products being or to be produced, condition of plant, present and planned capacity, capital equipment and stocks of raw materials, finished goods and goods in process

　　c. Quantities of industrial and agricultural products available in each prefecture for civilian consumption with a compilation by month for twelve months of future estimated needs, matched against the planned productivity of the commodities

　　d. Estimates of raw materials available per month over a twelve month period

　3. The Japanese Government will initiate, maintain and enforce production and other economic programs that serve the following purposes:

　　a. The avoidance of acute economic distress;

　　b. The assurance of a just and impartial distribution of available supplies;

　　c. Compliance with the requirements of reparations and deliveries agreed upon by the Allied Governments;

　　d. The restoration of Japanese Economy in order that

the reasonable peacetime requirements of the population can be satisfied.

4. The Japanese Government will use all means at its disposal within limitations made by directives from the Supreme Commander, to encourage:

a. The production and processing of all foodstuffs, including fisheries products;

b. The manufacture of soap, insecticides, fungicides, medical, dental and sanitation supplies;

c. The production of coal, charcoal and other solid fuels and crude petroleum;

d. The production of fertilizer;

e. The production of clothing, footwear and other textiles for domestic consumption;

f. The production of cement, timber, asphalt and ceramics required for emergency constructions and repair;

g. The production of items required for the operation, maintenance and repair of rail and road transportation and of coastal water transportation within the limitation of directives from the Supreme Commander;

h. The production of items required for the operation, maintenance and repair of public utilities and communications facilities within Japan; and,

i. The production of such other items as the Supreme Commander approves as consistent with the aims of occupation.

5. All food processing, fertilizer and medical and sanitation supply plants and facilities will immediately be placed in maximum operation. Delays in operation of such facilities due to lack of fuel, raw materials or labor will be reported immediately to the Supreme Commander.

6. The responsibility for administration and execution of economic controls and the responsibility for any breakdown of such controls will rest entirely with the Japanese Government.

FOR THE SUPREME COMMANDER:

/s/ Harold Fair
/t/ HAROLD FAIR
Lt Colonel, A.G.D.
Asst Adjutant General.

112

1　降伏文書調印と初期占領政策への対応（昭和20年9月～10月）

28　昭和20年9月17日　在ポルトガル森島（守人）公使より吉田（茂）外務大臣宛（電報）

日本占領の進捗状況に関する報道振り報告

リスボン　9月17日後11時54分発
本　省　9月19日前8時30分着

第三六二號

一、十四日東京發「ニュースクロニクル」「パーシバル」特電ハ「エイケル、バーガー」中將ハ日本ノ占領ニハ米軍四十萬ニテ充分ニシテ英軍ノ駐屯ヲ必要トセス又自分個人的意見ニテハ既ニ日本ニハ陸海空軍ナク重要産業破壞サレ原料ナキ第五流國ニ墮シタルモノニシテ隨ツテ一個年以上占領ヲ繼續スルコトヲ必要トセス爾後ハ米國專門家ノ滯留ニテ充分ナル旨聲明セル旨報シ居レリ

二、尚「マックアーサー」ハ日本軍ノ武裝解除順調ニ進捗中ニシテ十月中旬完了スヘク降服條件カ急速且完全ニ履行サルヘキコト疑フヘキ餘地ナシ残虐行爲ニ對シ輿論ノ激昂ハ當然ナルモ治安及軍事上ノ必要ヨリ自制ヲ要スル點アルハ免レストル旨報セラル

29　昭和20年9月18日　原（馨）経済局第一課長作成

船舶問題に関する総司令部との協議要旨

九月十八日（經濟一、原）

九月十八日十二時半第一相互事務本部ニ「クレーマー」大佐ヲ訪問シ建造中及修理中ノ船舶「リスト」ヲ持參シ至急許可發出方求メタル處先方ハ内容及數字ヲ一覽シニ、三ノ質問ヲナシタル後着手方命令セヨト要求セリ、因ニ右「リスト」ニ記載セル修理船ハ合計二一四〇隻五三七、七七五總噸ニシテ建造中ノモノハ一二二隻三七一、五三〇總噸兩者合計約九一萬噸ナルヲ以テ右完成ノ曉（大體二、三ケ月以内）ニハ逼迫セル現在ノ海上輸送ハ余程緩和スルモノト豫測セラル。

其際「ク」ハ經濟情報提供方ニ關スル日本側ノ行動ヲ今少シク敏速ニセラレタシト要求スルト共ニ米國側ハ日本國民ノ少クトモ最低必要ヲ充サシムルカ爲ニ努力シ居ル次第ナルヲ説明シ「ク」ノ指揮シ居ル「經濟及科學部」ノ任務ヲ規定セル總司令部示達ヲ見セ米國ノ政策ニ對スル日本側ノ心

新聞報道の規範に関する指令

OFFICE OF THE SUPREME COMMANDER
FOR THE ALLIED POWERS

19 September 1945

Ag 000.73 (18 Sep 45) CI
SCAPIN 33

MEMORANDUM FOR: IMPERIAL JAPANESE GOVERNMENT.
THROUGH: Central Liaison Office, Tokyo.
SUBJECT: Press Code For Japan.

1. News must adhere strictly to the truth.

2. Nothing shall be printed which might, directly or by inference, disturb the public tranquility.

3. There shall be no false or destructive criticism of the Allied Powers.

4. There shall be no destructive criticism of the Allied Forces of Occupation and nothing which might invite mistrust or resentment of those troops.

5. There shall be no mention or discussion of Allied troops movements unless such movements have been officially released.

配ヤ取越苦勞ハ無用ナリトノ印象ヲ與ヘムトスル樣子見受ケラレタリ。

尚右示達ハ占領軍總司令部「サザランド」參謀長ノ名ヲ以テ關係部局ヘ配布セルモノニシテ其内容ハ拾ヒ讀ノ程度ニテ其全貌ヲ捉フルノ暇ナカリシモ大體左ノ如キモノナリ。

一、經濟及科學部(以下經濟部ト稱ス)ハ日本及朝鮮ノ經濟政策ニ付總司令部ニ意見ヲ具申シ若クハ必要ナル措置ヲ採ル

二、之カ爲產業、鑛業、金融、公共事業、「カルテル」等ノ現狀ヲ調査ス

三、日本產業ノ解體及移轉ニ付テハ總司令部ノ許可ヲ要ス

四、金及銀、地金、通貨、證券等ハ之カ輸出入ヲ禁止ス

五、經濟統計ニ關スル情報ハ外國ニ公表セサルコト

六、日本國民ノ生活必要ヲ充足シ且占領軍ノ不便ヲ尠クスル爲メ日本ノ生產力ヲ高メ且「インフレ」ヲ防止スルニ努ムヘシ

30　昭和20年9月19日
　　連合国最高司令官総司令部より
　　日本政府宛

1 降伏文書調印と初期占領政策への対応(昭和20年9月〜10月)

6. News stories must be factually written and completely devoid of editorial opinion.

7. News stories shall not be colored to conform with any propaganda line.

8. Minor details of a news story must not be over-emphasized to stress or develop any propaganda line.

9. No news story shall be distorted by the omission of pertinent facts or details.

10. In the make-up of the newspaper no news story shall be given undue prominence for the purpose of establishing or developing any propaganda line.

For the SUPREME COMMANDER:

HAROLD FAIR,
Lt. Col., A.G.D.,
Asst. Adjutant General.

31 昭和20年9月20日 公布

勅令「ポツダム」宣言ノ受諾ニ伴ヒ發スル命令

二關スル件」(いわゆるポツダム緊急勅令)

付記 昭和二十年九月二十日公布

勅令「昭和二十年勅令第五百四十二號施行ニ關スル件」

朕茲ニ緊急ノ必要アリト認メ樞密顧問ノ諮詢ヲ經テ帝國憲法第八條第一項ニ依リ「ポツダム」宣言ノ受諾ニ伴ヒ發スル命令ニ關スル件ヲ裁可シ之ヲ公布セシム

御名 御璽

昭和二十年九月二十日

内閣總理大臣 男爵 鈴木貫太郎
※
内閣總理大臣 公爵近衞 文麿
國務大臣 米内 光政
海軍大臣 米内 光政
運輸大臣 小日山直登
大藏大臣 津島 壽一
司法大臣 岩田 宙造
農林大臣 千石興太郎
國務大臣 緒方 竹虎
内務大臣 山崎 巖
商工大臣 中島知久平

115

勅令第五百四十二號

政府ハ「ポツダム」宣言ノ受諾ニ伴ヒ聯合國最高司令官ノ爲ス要求ニ係ル事項ヲ實施スル爲特ニ必要アル場合ニ於テハ命令ヲ以テ所要ノ定ヲ爲シ及必要ナル罰則ヲ設クルコトヲ得

　　附　則

本令ハ公布ノ日ヨリ之ヲ施行ス

　外務大臣　吉田　茂
　陸軍大臣　下村　定
　國務大臣　小畑敏四郎
　文部大臣　前田　多門
　厚生大臣　松村　謙三

（付　記）

勅令第五百四十三號

昭和二十年勅令第五百四十二號ニ於テ命令トハ勅令、閣令又ハ省令トス

前項ノ閣令及省令ニ規定スルコトヲ得ル罰ハ三年以下ノ懲役又ハ禁錮、五千圓以下ノ罰金、科料及拘留トス

　　附　則

本令ハ公布ノ日ヨリ之ヲ施行ス

〜〜〜〜〜〜〜〜〜〜〜〜〜〜〜〜

32　吉田・マッカーサー会談

付記一　昭和二十年九月二十二日付吉田外務大臣より
マッカーサー連合国最高司令官宛書簡
再度面談方要請

二　昭和二十年九月二十四日
吉田・マッカーサー会談要旨

吉田外務大臣「マッカーサー」元帥會談録

九月二十日十一時「マ」元帥往訪（面談ニ先チ武内書記官ヨリ朝米司令部ニテハ侍從長來訪ノ砌　陛下自ラ御來訪ノコトヲ申出サレタル場合ニ付長ク協議セルカ如シト耳話セ

編　注　本文書および本文書付記は、「官報號外　昭和二十年九月二十日」から抜粋。

付記一　昭和20年9月20日　吉田外務大臣　マッカーサー連合国最高司令官　会談

1　降伏文書調印と初期占領政策への対応（昭和20年9月～10月）

リ）先ツ本日侍從長ハ　陛下ノ御使トシテ御思召ヲ體シ　陛下ノ御來訪ヲ豫期シ居リタルカ如シ）

「マ」元帥ノ入京ニ對スル挨拶ヲ傳達スル爲貴元帥ヲ來訪スル次第ナルカ本大臣モ親シク貴元帥ニ面會シ　陛下ノ懇篤ナル思召ヲ傳達スル爲來訪セル次第ナリト云ヘルニ　陛下ノ元帥ニ懇篤ノ謝意言上ヲ願フト答フ尙ホモジモジシ何カ云ヒ度様子ニ付本大臣ノ參考トシテ承知シタキハ貴元帥ニ於テ　陸下ノ御訪問ヲ期待セラルル次第ナリヤト述ヘタルニ同元帥ハ期待セストハ云ハスニ　陛下ニ御目ニカカルコトハ自分ノ最モ喜ハシキコトナルカ自分ハ　陛下ヲ「インバラス」又ハ「ヒューミリエート」スルコトヲ願ハストモヘタルニ付大臣ヨリ　陛下ニ於カレテモ來訪スルコトハ貴元帥ヲ「インバラス」スルコトナキヤトノ思召モアリト述ヘタルニ同元帥ハ更ニ　陛下ヲ「インバラス」スルコトハ最モ希望セサル所ト繰返タリ大臣ヨリ若シ　陛下ノ御來訪アルトシテ其ノ他ニ付希望アリヤト尋ネタルニ一二　陛下ノ御都合ニヨルヘシ場所ハ司令部ヨリ米國大使館ノ方可ナラスヤト云ヘルカ本件交渉ニ付受命シ居ラサリシニ付話ハ之ニテ打切リタリ（終戰連絡事務局武内第二部長内話耳打ニヨレハ司令部側ニ於テハ朝來長ク協議シ居リ

　　　　陛下ノ御來訪ヲ豫期シ居リタルカ如シ）

次ニ大臣ヨリ近來米國新聞論調日本及貴元帥ニ對シ面白カラヌ其ノ理由如何「マ」ハ比律賓等ニ於ケル日本軍ノ俘虜虐待ノ報道傳ハリ各方面ニ衝動ヲ與ヘ又日本ノ各新聞カ米國ニ對シ種々宜敷カラサル爲メト答ヘタルニ「マ」ハ之ヲ肯定セリ

次ニ「マ」ハ日本ノ愚カナル軍閥指導者ハ愚カナル作戰ヲ爲シ今日ノ敗戰トナレリト我軍部ヲ攻擊シタル後先ツ選擧權ヲ擴大シ新聞言論ノ自由ヲ認ムルノ要アリ陸海軍人等ノ復員行ハルレハ七百萬人ノ軍人等カ放出セラレ之ヲ如何ニ吸收スルヤ卽チ失業問題カ大問題ナリ此等ノ大問題ヲ處理スルコトハ少數ノ指導者ニハ到底不可能ナリト述ヘ「デモクラッシー」ノ效能ヲ強調シタルニ大臣ハ敢テ日本ノ歷史ヲ研究セストモ十數年以前ノ日本ノ狀勢又ハ第一次世界大戰後ノ世界ノ狀況ヲ見レハ直チニワカルコトナルカ當時ハ「デモクラッシー」カ世界ヲ風靡シ日本ニ於テモ「デモクラッシー」ハ極端ト思ハルル迄ニ進

ミタリ政政黨政治モ極端ニ迄進ミ當時軍人ハ勳章ヤ劍ヲ付ケテ汽車ヤ電車ニ乘ルコトヲモ躊躇セリ云ハハ軍ト云フモノハナカリシナリ然ルニ一九二九年ノ世界ノ不況ノ爲事態ハ全然逆トナリ獨逸、伊太利、蘇聯等ニ於テハ或ハ「ナチ」或ハ「ファッショ」或ハ共產主義トナリ日本ニ於テハ軍國主義擡頭スルニ至レルナリ「ナチ」ト云ヒ「ファッショ」ト云フモ孰レモ國貧シキカ故ニ起ルモノニシテ「デモクラッシー」ハ富メル國ノ產物ナリ「デモクラッシー」實現ノ爲ニハ先ツ以テ國民ニ食ヘサセ國民ニ職ヲ與ヘ其ノ生活ノ安定向上ヲ圖ルコト肝要ナリ日本ニ於テハ軍國主義ヲ成ルモノニアラストラ述フシテ成ルモノニアラスト述フ尙「マ」ヨリ日本ノ敎育ニ付論シ特ニ敎科書惡シト述ヘタルモ時間ノ餘裕ナカリシヲ以テ大臣ハ之ニ應酬スルコトナク辭去セリ

（付記一）

Dear General MacArthur,

In connection with the conversation we had on 20 Septem-

ber, I should like to see you again at your earliest convenience. I shall be pleased if you could let me know the date.

Yours Sincerely,

(S. Yoshida)

General Douglas MacArthur
General of the Army

（付記二）

九月二十四日「マックアーサー」往訪、陛下御訪問、阿部大將引渡、池田顧問官終戰連絡事務局總裁任命等ノ件ヲ述ヘ阿部大將ハ病氣中ハ措置ヲ執ラサルコトトナリ池田顧問官ノ件ニ付テハ「マ」ハ諒解セルニ付履歷書送付アリタシト述フ

33

昭和20年9月20日 連合国最高司令官総司令部より
日本政府宛

歳入歳出および財政機構等につき報告方指令
OFFICE OF THE SUPREME COMMANDER
FOR THE ALLIED POWERS

1 降伏文書調印と初期占領政策への対応(昭和 20 年 9 月～10 月)

AG 091 (20 Sep 45) ESS
SCAPIN 38

A.P.O. 500
20 September 1945

MEMORANDUM FOR: IMPERIAL JAPANESE GOVERNMENT.

THROUGH: Central Liaison Office, Tokyo.

SUBJECT: Information Concerning Government Finances, Financial Institutions, and Financial Restriction.

1. The Imperial Japanese Government will make a report within two weeks containing all pertinent information of the following:

 a. All receipts and expenditures of the Japanese Imperial Government for each month, January to August 1945.

 b. The budget of the Japanese Imperial Government for the fiscal year ending 31 March 1946 as approved by the Diet and including any alterations which may have been made subsequently by decree or otherwise.

 c. An approved or proposed revised budget for the remainder of the fiscal year ending 31 March 1946.

 d. A financial statement of the Japanese Imperial Government as of the close of business 1 September 1945.

 e. All receipts and expenditures of the Imperial Household for each month, January to August 1945.

 f. The budget of the Imperial Household for the fiscal year ending 31 March 1946.

 g. A revised budget of the Imperial Household for the remainder of the fiscal year ending 31 March 1946.

 h. A financial statement of the Imperial Household as of the close of business 1 September 1945.

2. The Imperial Japanese Government will forward to the Supreme Commander within one week:

 a. Sworn Statements of Condition as of 1 September 1945 of all banks, trust companies, national policy companies, insurance companies, and similar financial institutions, incorporated or unincorporated, operating in Japan. Such Statements of Condition will show, separately, assets and liabilities outside Japan.

 b. The Imperial Japanese Government will, at the same time, forward to the Supreme Commander lists of all directors and responsible officials of all such financial institutions and lists of all owners of one thousand shares or more of stock in such institutions whether in the name of the owner or that of another, and the owners of five (5) percent or more of the stock in such institutions.

3. The Imperial Japanese Government will forward, within two weeks, to the Supreme Commander, a report of all financial agreements in force on 7 December 1941, or subsequently ratified between the Imperial Japanese Government, the Bank of Japan or any other bank, national policy company or similar financial institution, controlled or directed by the Imperial Japanese Government, and any other government or any bank, or other financial institution controlled or directed by any other government.

4. The Imperial Japanese Government will promptly forward to the Supreme Commander copies of all laws, decrees, ordinances, or other enactments concerning:

a. Compulsory savings.

b. Limitations on the amounts of salaries, bonuses, dividends, or other income.

c. Limitations on withdrawals from or the use of bank deposits, trust funds, insurance payments or any other savings.

d. Limitations on the use of the proceeds of the sale of movable or immovable property, liquidations, inheritances or realization of any other capital assets.

e. Restrictions on the investment of capital in and the extensions of credit for industrial, commercial, and agricultural activities.

f. Transactions in gold, silver, foreign securities, foreign currencies, foreign exchange and external assets.

g. Any other restrictions on the use of income or capital.

FOR THE SUPREME COMMANDER:

Harold Fair
For B. M. FITCH,
Brigadier General, U.S. Army,
Adjutant General.

34 昭和20年9月20日 連合国最高司令官総司令部より日本政府宛

物価および労務賃金につき報告方指令

1　降伏文書調印と初期占領政策への対応（昭和20年9月～10月）

OFFICE OF THE SUPREME COMMANDER
FOR THE ALLIED POWERS
A.P.O. 500

20 September 1945

MEMORANDUM FOR: IMPERIAL JAPANESE GOVERNMENT.
THROUGH: Central Liaison Office, Tokyo.
SUBJECT: Prices of Commodities and Rates for Services.

It is desired that the Imperial Japanese Government furnish the information outlined in the attached.

1 Incl: Info Desired

R. C. KRAMER
Colonel, GSC
Chief, Economic and
Scientific Section

DESIRED INFORMATION

1. Prices of principal commodities in the following form:

Commodity	Average Price Oct/Dec 1930	Price 15 Sep 45 (or near date)
Rice		
Fresh Fish		
Timned Fish		
Vegetables		
Fertilizers		
Grey Cloth		
Staple Fibre		
Paper		
Lumber		
Charcoal		
Coal		

2. Rates charged for services in customary units:

Service	Average Rate Oct/Dec 1930	Rates 15 Sep 45
Electricity for Lighting		
Electricity for Power		
Passenger Fares - State Railways		
Passenger Fares - Suburban Railways		

Passenger Fares - Street
Railways
Telegrams
Telephones - Local
Telephones - Long Distance
Postage
Common Labor

35　昭和20年9月20日　連合国最高司令官総司令部より　日本政府宛

検閲連絡代表者の任命に関する指令

OFFICE OF THE SUPREME COMMANDER
FOR THE ALLIED POWERS

20 September 1945

AG 311.7 (20 Sep 45) CI

MEMORANDUM FOR: IMPERIAL JAPANESE GOVERNMENT.
THROUGH: Central Liaison Office, Tokyo.
SUBJECT: Censorship Liaison Representatives.

1. It is desired that English-speaking liaison representatives be accredited to the Civil Censorship Officer, AFPAC, from the Board of Communications and the Board of Information, to be available as desired in the various installations of Civil Censorship Detachment. Names of these representatives are to be forwarded to the Supreme Commander for Allied Powers.

2. Both representatives are to be familiar with peace-time and war-time censorship restrictions imposed by the Japanese government.

3. They are to report to the Civil Censorship Officer, AFPAC, on the sixth floor of the Radio Tokyo building.

4. Directions are to be issued by the Japanese government to existing censorship organizations and communications services to cooperate with AFPAC censorship personnel.

5. The liaison representatives will be informed of types of communications to be censored, and will make arrangements that these are available for censorship.

FOR THE SUPREME COMMANDER:

HAROLD FAIR,
Lt. Col., A.G.D.,

1 降伏文書調印と初期占領政策への対応（昭和20年9月～10月）

Asst. Adjutant General.

36

昭和20年9月20日

在スウェーデン岡本公使より
吉田外務大臣宛（電報）

米英の対日世論につき報告

ストックホルム　9月20日後6時20分発
本　　省　9月22日前7時0分着

第五九二號

一、最近日本處理手緩シトノ論米英ニ擡頭シ居ルハ注意ヲ要ス
ル處其ノ要點左ノ通リ參考迄

一、日本降伏ヲ獨逸ノ場合ト同樣ナリトカ又ハ同樣ナルヘキナリト考フルモノ多ク獨逸カ嚴重ニ占領サレ居ルニ不拘日本カ政府ノ存續ヲ許サレ行政權ヲ略完全ニ施行シ居ルハ不可解ナリトノ思想ヨリ發足シ日本官邊又ハ知名ノ士ノ言說ニ神經ヲ尖カラシテ一々之ヲ詮索シ現狀ニ於テハ日本カ敗北ヲ自認シタルモノトハ認メ得サルヲ以テ更ニ峻嚴ナル取扱ヲナスヘシト要求シ居レリ「マックアーサー」及占領軍當事者ノ發表ニ對シテモ極メテ辯解的ニシテ手緩シ「ダルラン」的對日處理ナリトシ非難ノ聲ヲ擧

ケ居レリ

二、皇室ニ關スル論說亦少カラス結局皇室ニ對スル國民ノ尊崇現在ノ如クナレハ日本ノ民主主義ハ行ハレス却テ日本カ戰爭ニ敗レタルニアラスシテ　陛下ノ大御心ニ依リテ終戰シタルモノナリトノ思想ヲ助長シ軍國トシテノ日本ノ再建ヲ容易ナラシムルモノナリトシテ　陛下ヲ神ナリトスル考ヲ減殺スル樣占領軍ニ於テ硬ノ態度ヲ執ルヘシト論シ居リ現ニ「ヘラルドトリビューン」ノ如キ右ノ趣旨ヲ繰返ヘシ革命コソ日本ニ必要ナルノミナラス占領軍ハ皇室擁護ナル逆方向ニ向ヒ居レリトサヘ極論シ又上院議員「ラッセル」ノ如キハ　陛下ヲ戰爭犯罪人ト述ヘ居レリ

三、日本ハ經濟的ニ獨逸程完全ナル破壞ヲ喫セス國力ニ相當ノ潛在ノ餘裕ヲ殘シ居ルヲ以テ之ヲ徹底的ニ押ヘツヘクシトノ論モ亦既ニ散見セラレ今後政治問題ト竝ヒテ活潑トナルヘシ

四、日本朝野ノ態度カ敗戰ト同時ニ極メテ鄭重懇勲ニシテ百八十度ノ轉回ヲ示シ民主主義ニ走ラントノ動向ヲ示シ居ルヲ見テ一部ニハ是ハ「トリック」ニハアラスヤトノ疑

123

第三六七號

念ヲ以テ見居ルカ如シ
五、要スルニ現在表面化シツツアル米英ノ對日態度ハ日本ノ捕虜等ニ對シテ行ヘル慘虐行爲ニ刺戟セラレ之ニ人種的偏見モ手傳ヒ且將來日本ノ復讐ヲ懼ルルノ餘リ戰勝ノ醉ヲ驅テ出來ル限リ日本ヲ苛メツケ再ヒ起ツテ仇ヲ爲ス餘地無カラシメントスルヲ主眼トシ此ノ際日本ヲ獨逸並ニ取扱度キ感情論ト思考サレ具體的且打算ノニ日本ノ政治形態經濟形態ヲ如何ニセハ可ナルヤノ實際問題ニ付テハ米國政府カ未タ無策ニシテ徒ラニ「ソフトピース」的の遣方ヲ爲シ居ルコトニ對スル不滿トカ合流シ居ルモノト見ラレ從テ此種輿論ハ少ク共當分ノ間ハ減セサルモノト觀測ス

37

昭和20年9月21日

在ポルトガル森島公使より
吉田外務大臣宛（電報）

占領軍の必要人数に関するマッカーサー司令官発言の反響振り報告

リスボン　9月21日後11時59分発
本　省　9月23日前8時38分着

日本占領軍ハ二十萬ニテ足ルトノ「マッカーサー」ノ言明ハ米國朝野ノ論議ヲ惹起シ居リ國務長官代理ハ事前ニ協議ナカリシ旨ヲ言明占領軍ノ數ハ政策ノ如何ニ依リ決定セラルヘキモノナリトノ趣旨ヲ以テ國務省側ノ不滿ヲ露骨ニ表明シ又大統領ハ一度簡單ニ豫定以下ノ兵數ヲ喜フ旨ヲ述ヘタルモ其ノ後輿論ノ動キニ鑑ミ態度ヲ曖昧ニシ居ルカ如ク英紙所報ヲ綜合スルニ對日政策ヲ「マッカーサー」限リテ決定シ居ルカ如キ點ニ關シ一般ニ不滿アリ反動ノ來ル恐アルヤニ受取ラル

38

昭和20年9月22日

連合国最高司令官総司令部より
日本政府宛

指令第三号

付記一　右和訳文

二　昭和二十年九月二十六日、終戰連絡中央事務局第三部作成

「聯合軍總司令部指令第三號ノ解釋ニ關スル件」

1　降伏文書調印と初期占領政策への対応（昭和20年9月〜10月）

三　昭和二十年九月二十六日付
右解釈に関するクレーマー連合国最高司令官
総司令部経済科学局長覚書和訳文

OFFICE OF THE SUPREME COMMANDER
FOR THE ALLIED POWERS

APO 500
22 September, 1945

DIRECTIVE
NO. 3

1. *General.* The Japanese Imperial Government is hereby directed to comply, or to insure the compliance as the case may be, with the requirements of the Supreme Commander for the Allied Powers stated in this directive.

2. *Economic Controls.*

　a. You are responsible for initiating and maintaining a firm control over wages and prices of essential commodities.

　b. You are responsible for initiating and maintaining a strict rationing program for essential commodities in short supply, to insure that such commodities are equitably distributed.

　c. You will report to the Supreme Commander all details of existing economic control machinery and procedures covering the objectives outlined in paragraphs "a" and "b" above within ten days after the receipt of this directive. You will include data on wage schedules and ration allowances of essential commodities in short supply. You will include a statement as to the manner in which such economic control measures are operating and the reasons for inadequacies, if any.

3. *Production.*

　a. You will stimulate and encourage the immediate maximum production of all essential consumers' commodities, including industrial, agricultural, and fisheries products, and commodities necessary to the production of such essential consumers' goods. Priority in allocation of materials, fuel, equipment, and labor will be given to the production of commodities necessary to the feeding, clothing, and housing of the population.

　b. Where conversion is considered necessary, of plants heretofore engaged in the production of items prohibited by Par. 4, below, to the production of essential consumers' commodities, you will submit individual application for such conversion of each plant concerned.

4. *Prohibited items.* No production will be permitted of the following types of items:

a. Arms, ammunition, or implements of war. Applications will be presented for the use or manufacture of such industrial explosives as may be deemed necessary, accompanied by complete supporting data as to its essentiality and methods by which their distribution and use will be controlled.

b. Parts, components or ingredients especially designed or produced for incorporation into arms, ammunition, or implements of war.

c. Combat naval vessels.

d. All types of aircraft, including those designed for civilian use.

e. Parts, components, and materials especially designed or produced for incorporation into aircraft of any type.

5. You will preserve and maintain in good condition for inspection and such disposition as may be directed by this Headquarters all plants, equipment, patents, and other property, and all books, records, and documents of Japanese Imperial Government or private industrial companies and trade and research associations which have manufactured any of the items listed in paragraph 4 of this directive or any of the following items:

a. Iron and steel.

b. Chemicals.

c. Non-ferrous materials.

d. Aluminium.

e. Magnesium.

f. Synthetic rubber.

g. Synthetic oil.

h. Machine tools.

i. Radio and electrical equipment.

j. Automotive vehicles.

k. Merchant ships.

l. Heavy machinery and important parts thereof.

and of any companies, associations or cartels which contributed to or were essential to the Japanese war effort or were essential to the Japanese economy.

126

1　降伏文書調印と初期占領政策への対応（昭和 20 年 9 月～10 月）

6. *Inventory and Records Required.* You will as rapidly as possible submit to this Headquarters an inventory of significant plants producing or intending to produce products in the industries listed in paragraphs 4 and 5 of this directive. This inventory will include detailed reports specifying condition and equipment and capacity of plants, and the extent of the stocks of fuel, raw materials, finished goods, and goods in process available.

7. *Imports and Exports.* No imports to, or exports from, Japan of any goods, wares or merchandise will be permitted, except with the prior approval of this Headquarters.

8. a. You will submit a report of all laboratories, research institutes, and similar scientific and technological organizations which will include the following information:

(1) Name.
(2) Location.
(3) Ownership.
(4) Description of facilities.
(5) Number of employees.
(6) Detailed list of all projects by agency that are currently being studied by these agencies and projects studied since 1940.

b. You will direct such agencies to be open for inspection by duly authorized Allied representatives at all times.

c. You will direct such agencies to render a report as of the first day of each month to this Headquarters through your office stating in detail the projects on which their facilities and personnel have been engaged during the preceding month and the results of such work.

d. You will prohibit all research or development work which has as its object effecting mass separation of Uranium 235 from Uranium or effecting mass separation of any other radioactively unstable elements.

9. All reports required in this directive will be submitted typewritten in English, on white paper—size 8½ by 11 inches, in five copies.

R.K. SUTHERLAND
Lieutenant General, United States Army,
Chief of Staff.

OFFICIAL:

(Sgd.) Harold Fair

For B.M. FITCH,

Brigadier General, U.S. Army,

Adjutant General.

編　注　本文書は、昭和二十四年一月、外務省特別資料部作成「日本占領及び管理重要文書集」第一巻より抜粋。

（付記一）

聯合國最高司令官司令部

指令第三號　千九百四十五年九月二十二日

一、總則　日本帝國政府ハ茲ニ本指令ニ掲クル聯合國最高司令官ノ要求ニ付場合ニ應シ自ラ之ニ從ヒ又ハ之ニ應セシムル樣保證スルコトヲ指令セラル

二、經濟統制

（イ）日本帝國政府ハ賃銀及必需品ノ價格ニ付確固タル統制ヲ設定シ及維持スベキ責任ヲ負フ

（ロ）日本帝國政府ハ供給不足セル必需品ノ公正ナル分配ヲ保證スル爲此等ノ商品ノ嚴重ナル割當ヲ設定シ及維持スベキ責任ヲ負フ

（ハ）日本帝國政府ハ最高司令官ニ對シ本指令接受後十日以内ニ（イ）及（ロ）ニ掲ケラレタル目的ヲ有スル現存經濟統制機構及手續ニ關スル一切ノ詳細ヲ報告スベシ右報告ニハ賃銀表及供給不足セル必需品ノ割當量ニ關スル資料ヲ含マシムベシ右ノ如キ經濟統制措置カ現ニ如何ニ適用セラレツツアリヤ其ノ理由如何ニ關スル陳述ヲ含マシムベシ若シ何等不十分ノ點アリトセハ其ノ理由如何ニ關スル陳述ヲ含マシムベシ

二十三日午後四時接受

三、生　產

（イ）日本帝國政府ハ工業、農業及漁業生産品ヲ含ム一切ノ消費者用必需品竝ニ右ノ如キ有費者用必需貨物ノ生産ニ必要ナル商品ヲ直ニ最大限度迄生産スル樣刺戟シ及獎勵スベシ原料、燃料、施設及勞働ノ割當ニ當リテハ住民ノ食、衣及住ニ必要ナル商品ノ生産ニ優先順位與ヘラルベシ

（ロ）下記四ニヨリ禁止セラルル品目ノ生産ニ現在迄從事シ居リタル工場ヲ消費者用必需品ノ生産ニ轉換セシムル

128

1　降伏文書調印と初期占領政策への対応（昭和20年9月～10月）

ノ要ヲ認ムル場合ニ於テハ日本帝國政府ハ各當該工場ニ付個別的ニ轉換ノ願書ヲ提出スベシ

四、禁止品目

次ノ種類ノ品目ノ生產ハ許可セラレズ

(イ)武器、彈藥又ハ戰爭用具

必要ト認メラルル工業用爆藥ノ使用又ハ製造ニ付キテハ其ノ必要缺クベカラザルコト及其ノ分配及使用ノ統制方法ニ關スル完全ナル說明資料ヲ附シテ願書ヲ提出スベシ

(ロ)武器、彈藥又ハ戰爭用具ノ生產ニ使用スル爲ニ特ニ設計シ又ハ生產セラルル部品、組成品又ハ成分

(ハ)戰鬪用海軍艦艇

(ニ)民間用トシテ設計セラレタルモノヲ含ミ一切ノ型式ノ航空機

(ホ)一切ノ型式ノ航空機ノ生產ニ使用スル爲特ニ設計シ又ハ生產セラルル部品、組成品及材料

五、日本帝國政府ハ點檢竝ニ本司令部ニ依リ指示セラルベキ處分ヲ受クル爲本指令ノ四ニ揭ゲラレタル品目ノ何レカ又ハ左ニ揭グル品目ノ何レカヲ製造シ居リタル日本帝國

政府又ハ私有工業會社竝ニ商會及硏究團體ノ工場、設備、特許及其ノ他ノ財產竝ニ一切ノ帳簿、記錄及文書ヲ良好ナル狀態ニ於テ保存シ及維持スベシ

(イ)鐵及鋼
(ロ)化學製品
(ハ)非鐵材料
(ニ)「アルミニユーム」
(ホ)「マグネシウム」
(ヘ)合成護謨
(ト)人造石油
(チ)工作機械
(リ)「ラジオ」及電氣器具
(ヌ)自動車類
(ル)商船
(ヲ)重量機械及其ノ重要部品

日本戰爭努力ニ貢獻シ又ハ日本經濟ニ必須ナリシ會社、團体又ハ「カルテル」ニ付テモ右ニ同ジ

六、財產目錄及記錄要求

日本帝國政府ハ出來得ル限リ速ニ本司令部ニ對シ本指令

四及五ニ掲ゲラレ居ル生產物ヲ現ニ生產シ居リ又ハ生產セントシ居ル主ナル工場ノ財產目錄ヲ提出スベシ右財產目錄ハ工場ノ狀況設備及能力竝ビニ燃料手持高原料、完成品及製造過程ニアル商品ヲ具體的ニ示ス詳細ナル報告ヲ含ムベシ

七、輸入及輸出　本司令部ノ事前ノ承認ナキ限リ日本ヨリ又ハ日本ヘノ如何ナル製品、商品ノ輸出入ヲモ許可セズ

八、(イ)日本帝國政府ハ一切ノ實驗所、研究所竝ニ同種ノ科學及技術機關ニ付左記情報ヲ含ム報告書ヲ提出スベシ

(1)名稱
(2)位置
(3)所有者
(4)施設ノ說明
(5)使用人數
(6)現在此等ノ機關ニ依リ研究セラレ居ル一切ノ企畫及一九四○年以降研究セラレタル企畫ニ關スル詳細ナル表

(ロ)日本帝國政府ハ此等機關ニ對シ正當ナル權限ヲ有スル聯合軍代表ノ視察ニ常ニ應ズル樣指令スベシ

(ハ)日本帝國政府ハ此等機關ニ對シ每月一日現在ヲ以テ前月中ニ當該機關ノ施設及所屬員ガ其ノ爲ニ使用セラル諸企畫及其ノ業績ヲ詳細ニ陳述セル報告書ヲ中央連絡事務局ヲ通ジテ本司令部ニ提出スル樣指令スベシ

(ニ)日本帝國政府ハ「ウラニウム」ヨリ「ウラニウム」二三五ノ大量分離ヲ來サシムルカ又ハ如何ナル他ノ電波活動上ノ不安定要素ノ大量分離ヲモ來サシムルコトヲ目的トスル一切ノ研究又ハ實驗作業ヲ禁止スベシ

九、本指令ニ於テ要請セラルル一切ノ報告書ハ英語ヲ以テ縱十一吋、橫八吋半ノ白紙ニ「タイプ」シタルモノ五部提出セラルベシ

參謀總長
米國陸軍中將「アル・ケイ・サザランド」

關係係官「ハロルド、フエヤ」署名
米國陸軍副官「ビー、エム、フイッチ」代將ニ代リ

(付記二)
聯合軍總司令部指令第三號ノ解釋ニ關スル件
二〇、九、二六

1 降伏文書調印と初期占領政策への対応(昭和20年9月〜10月)

終戦事務局第三部

指令第三號ノ眞意釋明ニ關スル件

昭和二十年九月二十六日

首題ノ件九月二十五日終戰連絡中央事務局第三部長及聯合軍總司令部「クレーマー」大佐會談ノ結果明確トナリタル點左ノ如シ

一、左ノ三點ニ關シ覺書ヲ以テ說明アリタリ

(一) 第五號(ル)ノ商船トハ百總噸ヲ超ユル一切ノ形式ノ非戰鬪用船舶ノミヲ包含スルモノトス

(二) 第六號ニ於テ要求スル財產目錄ハ一九四五年九月一日現在ニ於テ生產シアリ又ハ生產ノ意圖ヲ有シ或ハ生產能力アリタル一切ノ事業場(プラント)ヲ包含スルモノトス

(三) 第六號ノ主ナル作業場ニハ當該產業量事業場ヲ生產量大ナルモノヨリ順次ニトリソノ合計ガ當該產業ノ總生產量ノ八五％以上ニ達スル範圍マデヲ包含スルモノトス
但シ當該產業ノ總生產量ノ二％未滿ノ生產額ヲ有スル作業場ハ除外ス

(付記三)

一、指令第三號ニ就テ幾分誤解ト誤譯トガ生ジテ來テ居リ同指令ハ賃銀及必需物資ノ價格ニ對シ嚴重ナル統制ニ著手シ且維持スルコト從ツテ必需物資ノ供給ガ窮屈ナル場合確固タル配給制ヲ實施スルコトヲ日本政府ニ要求スルモノデアル

二、コノ指令ノ持ツ目標ハ二ツアル卽チ

(イ) 一般必需品ヲ取得スルニ際シ一般市民ハ裕福ナル人ト同等ノ機會ヲ與ヘラルル事ヲ確保スルコト

(ロ) 一般市民ニ對シテソノ生活ニ破綻的結果ヲ生ゼシムル「インフレーション」ノ發生ヲ防止スルコト

三、統制センガ爲ニ統制ヲ強ヒル意志ハ盲頭(モウ)ナイ一般市民ニ對シテ統制ガ實施セラレザルヨリモ行フ方ガ有益ナル結果ヲモタラスト確信セラレタル時ニ於テコソ統制ガ實施サレル統制ガ存在スルヨリモ然ラザル場合ノ方ガヨリヨキ結果ヲ生ズル見透ガ認メラレタル時ハ臨機應變ニ統制ヲ緩和又ハ廢止スル

四、平常時ノ生活ニ於テ市民ガ自己ノ收入ヲ個々ノ判斷デ最

適ノ用途ニ消費スル權利ヲ制限スルガ如キコトハ米國ノ諸主義ニ悖ル勤勞者ガ取得スルコトヲ認メラレル賃金ヲ政府ガ統制スルコトハ團体契約ヲ認メル亞米利加ノ諸主義ニ相反スルノデアル

五、從ツテ市民生活ニ對スル統制ハ非常處置デアツテ根本原則ヲ示スモノデナイ非常時局ガ解消スレバ諸種ノ統制ハ除去サレル或ハ又統制ヲ實施スルヨリモソノ非常時ヲ突破スル爲ニ統制ヨリモ優越セル手段ガ考究サルレバソノ方法ガ適用サレル

六、日本ニ於テハ政府當局ニ依ル統制ノ問題ハ非常ナル重要性ヲ帶ビルコトデアリ同時ニ日本政府ニヨル一般ノ市民ノ諸活動ニ對スル統制ハ我ガ米國ノ固執スル諸主義ニ相反スルコトデアルガ故ニ次ノ點ヲ貴方ニ要求スルモノデアル、卽チ

貴方ノ掌握シテ居ル情報機關ヲ通シテコノ問題ト之レニ對スル處理方法ノ諸理由及ビ日本市民ノ各階級ニ對スル當司令部ノ將來採ラントスル方針ヲ一般ニ理解セシムルコト

七、コノ點ニ關聯シテ去ル九月二十六日朝行ハレタル次ノ放

送ニ貴方ノ關心ヲ喚起シタイ、日本政府ハ十月一日ヨリ生鮮食糧品ニ對シ價格ノ最高標準ノ統制ヲ撤去スル予定ナリシモ前述ノ第一項ニ明示セル指令第三號ニ基キ同統制ハ尙存續セントノ放送シテオル事實デアル、コノ放送ガ與ヘタ印象ヲ除去スル手段ヲ採ラルベキコト及コレラノ方針ハ充分說明セラル可キニ付該放送ノ全文ヲ小生ノ手許ニナキ爲メ、ソノ入手方ヲ御手配相成ル樣希望スルモノデアル。

小生ハ貴方ガコノ種事務ニ管掌セシメオラルル諸官トコノ問題ニ付キ尙進ンデ討議スルコトヲ希望シ期待スルモノデアル。

〰〰〰〰〰〰〰〰〰〰

39

「降伏後ニ於ケル米國ノ初期ノ對日方針」（和訳文）

昭和20年9月22日　米国政府発表

付　記　昭和二十年九月三十日、外務省作成「降伏後ニ於ケル米國ノ初期ノ對日方針」說明

降伏後ニ於ケル米國ノ初期ノ對日方針

1 降伏文書調印と初期占領政策への対応（昭和20年9月～10月）

本文書ノ目的

千九百四十五年九月二十二日

本文書ハ降伏後ノ日本國ニ對スル初期ノ全般的政策ニ關スル聲明ナリ本文書ハ大統領ノ承認ヲ經タルモノニシテ聯合國最高司令官及米國關係各省及機關ニ對シ指針トシテ配布セラレタリ本文書ハ日本國占領ニ關スル諸問題中政策決定ヲ必要トスル一切ノ事項ヲ取扱ヒ居ルモノニ非ズ本文書ニ含マレズ又ハ充分盡サレ居ラザル事項ハ既ニ別個ニ取扱ハレ又ハ將來別個ニ取扱ハルベシ

第一部 究極ノ目的

日本國ニ關スル米國ノ究極ノ目的ニシテ初期ニ於ケル政策ガ從フベキモノ左ノ如シ

(イ)日本國ガ再ビ米國ノ脅威トナリ又ハ世界ノ平和及安全ノ脅威トナラザルコトヲ確實ニスルコト

(ロ)他國ノ權利ヲ尊重シ國際聯合憲章ノ理想ト原則ニ示サレタル米國ノ目的ヲ支持スベキ平和的且責任アル政府ヲ究極ニ於テ樹立スルコト、米國ハ斯ル政府ガ出來得ル限リ民主主義的自治ノ原則ニ合致スルコトヲ希望スルモ自由ニ表示セラレタル國民ノ意思ニ支持セラレザル如何ナ

ル政治形態ヲモ日本國ニ強要スルコトハ聯合國ノ責任ニ非ズ

此等ノ目的ハ左ノ主要ナル手段ニ依リ達成セラルベシ

(イ)日本國ノ主權ハ本州、北海道、九州、四國並ニ「カイロ」宣言及米國ガ既ニ参加シ又ハ將來参加スルコトアルベキ他ノ協定ニ依リ決定セラルベキ周邊ノ諸小島ニ限ラルベシ

(ロ)日本國ハ完全ニ武裝解除セラレ且非軍事化セラルベシ軍國主義者ノ權力ト軍國主義ノ影響力ハ日本國ノ政治生活、經濟生活及社會生活ヨリ一掃セラルベシ軍國主義及侵略ノ精神ヲ表示スル制度ハ強力ニ抑壓セラルベシ

(ハ)日本國國民ハ個人ノ自由ニ對スル欲求並ニ基本的人權特ニ信教、集會、言論及出版ノ自由ノ尊重ヲ増大スル樣獎勵セラルベク且民主主義的及代議ノ組織ノ形成ヲ獎勵セラルベシ

(ニ)日本國國民ハ其ノ平時ノ需要ヲ充シ得ルガ如キ經濟ヲ自力ニ依リ發達セシムベキ機會ヲ與ヘラルベシ

第二部 聯合國ノ權限

一 軍事占領

降伏條項ヲ實施シ上述ノ究極目的ノ達成ヲ促進スル為日本國本土ハ軍事占領セラルベシ右占領ハ日本國トノ戰爭狀態ニ在ル聯合國ノ利益ノ爲行動スル主要聯合國ノ爲ノ軍事行動タルノ性質ヲ有スベシ右ノ理由ニ因リ對日戰爭ニ於テ指導的役割ヲ演ジタル他ノ諸國ノ軍隊ノ占領ヘノ參加ハ歡迎セラレ且期待セラルルモ占領軍ハ米國ノ任命スル最高司令官ノ指揮下ニ在ルモノトス協議及適當ナル諸問機關ノ設置ニ依リ主要聯合國ヲ滿足セシムベキ日本國ノ占領及管理ノ實施ノ爲ノ政策ヲ樹立スル爲有ラユル努力ヲ盡スベキモ主要聯合國ノ意見ノ不一致ヲ生ジタル場合ニ於テハ米國ノ政策ニ從フモノトス

二　日本國政府トノ關係

天皇及日本國政府ノ權限ハ降伏條項ヲ實施シ且日本國ノ占領及管理ノ施行ノ爲樹立セラレタル政策ヲ實行スル爲必要ナル一切ノ權力ヲ有スル最高司令官ニ從屬スルモノトス日本社會ノ現在ノ性格竝ニ最小ノ兵力及資源ニ依リ目的ヲ達成セントスル米國ノ希望ニ鑑ミ最高司令官ハ米國ノ目的達成ヲ滿足ニ促進スル限リニ於テハ　天皇ヲ含ム日本政府機構及諸機關ヲ通ジテ其權限ヲ行使スベシ日本國政府ハ最高司令官ノ指示ノ下ニ國內行政事項ニ關シ通常ノ政治機能ヲ行使スルコトヲ許容セラルベシ但シ右方針ハ　天皇又ハ他ノ日本國ノ權力者ガ降伏條項實施上最高司令官ノ要求ヲ滿足ニ果サザル場合最高司令官ガ政府機構又ハ人事ノ變更ヲ要求シ又ハ直接行動スル權利及義務ニ依リ制限セラルルモノトス更ニ又右方針ハ最高司令官ヲシテ米國ノ目的達成ニ指向スル革新的變化ニ抗シテ　天皇又ハ他ノ日本國ノ政府機關ヲ支持スル樣拘束スルモノニ非ズ卽チ右方針ハ日本國ニ於ケル現存ノ政治形態ヲ利用セントスルモノニシテ之ヲ支持セントスルモノニ非ズ封建的及權威主義的ノ傾向ヲ修正セントスル政治形態ノ變更ハ日本國政府ニ依ルト日本國國民ニ依ルトヲ問ハズ許容セラレ且支持セラルベシ變更ノ實現ノ爲日本國國民又ハ日本國政府ガ其ノ反對者抑壓ノ爲實力ヲ行使スル場合ニ於テハ最高司令官ハ麾下部隊ノ安全竝ニ占領ノ他ノ一切ノ目的ノ達成ヲ確實ニスルニ必要ナル場合ニ於テノミ之ニ干涉スルモノトス

三　政策ノ周知

日本國國民及世界一般ハ占領ノ目的及政策竝ニ其ノ達成上ノ進展ニ關シ完全ナル情報ヲ與ヘラルベシ

1 降伏文書調印と初期占領政策への対応(昭和20年9月～10月)

第三部　政治

一　武裝解除及非軍事化

武裝解除及實行セラルベシ日本國國民ニ對シテハ其ノ現在及將來ノ苦境招來ニ關シ陸海軍指導者及其ノ協力者ガ爲シタル役割ヲ徹底的ニ知ラシムル爲一切ノ努力ガ爲サルベシ

本國ハ陸海空軍、祕密警察組織又ハ何等ノ民間航空ヲ保有スルコトナシ日本國ノ地上、航空及海軍兵力ハ武裝ヲ解除セラレ且解體セラルベク日本國大本營、參謀本部(軍令部)及一切ノ祕密警察組織ハ解消セシメラルベシ陸海軍資材、陸海軍艦船、陸海軍施設並ニ陸海軍及民間航空機ハ引渡サレ且最高司令官ノ要求スル所ニ從ヒ處分セラルベシ日本國大本營及參謀本部(軍令部)ノ高級職員、日本國政府ノ他ノ陸海軍高級職員、超國家主義的及軍國主義的組織ノ指導者並ニ他ノ軍國主義及侵略ノ重要ナル推進者ハ拘禁セラレ將來ノ處分ヲ爲留置セラルベシ軍國主義及好戰的國家主義ノ積極的ノ推進者タリシ者ハ公職及公ノ又ハ重要ナル私的責任アル如何ナル地位ヨリモ排除セラルベシ超國家主義的又ハ軍國主義的ノ社會上、政治上、職業上及商業上ノ團體及機關ハ解散セラレ且禁止セラルベシ理論上及實踐上ノ軍國主義及超國家主義(準軍事的訓練ヲ含ム)ハ教育制度ヨリ除去セラルベシ職業的舊陸海軍將校及下士官竝ニ他ノ一切ノ軍國主義及超國家主義ノ推進者ハ監督的及教育的地位ヨリ排除セラルベシ

二　戰爭犯罪人

最高司令官又ハ適當ナル聯合國機關ニ依リ戰爭犯罪人トシテ告發セラレタル者(聯合國ノ俘虜其ノ他ノ國民ヲ虐待セル廉ニヨリ告發セラレタル者ヲ含ム)ハ逮捕セラルベシ裁判ニ付サレ有罪ノ判決アリタルトキハ處罰セラルベシ聯合國中ノ他ノ國ヨリ其ノ國民ニ對スル犯罪ノ爲又ハ證人トシテ又ハレタル者ノ最高司令官ニ依リ裁判ノ理由トシテ要求セラレタル者ノ最高司令官ニ依リ必要トセラレザル限リ當該國ニ引渡サレ拘禁セラルベシ

三　個人ノ自由及民主主義過程ヘノ翼求ノ獎勵

宗教的ノ信仰ノ自由ハ占領ト共ニ直ニ宣言セラルベシ同時ニ日本人ニ對シ超國家主義的及軍國主義的ノ組織及運動ハ宗敎ノ外被ニ隱ルルヲ得ザル旨明示セラルベシ日本國國民ハ米國及他ノ民主主義國家ノ歴史、制度、文化又ハ軍國主義的ノ

及其ノ成果ヲ知ル機會ヲ與ヘラレ且此等ノ獎勵セラルベシ占領軍人員ノ日本人トノ交際ハ所要ノ限度ニ於テノミ占領政策及占領目的ヲ促進スル爲統制セラルベシ集會及公開討論ノ權利ヲ有スル民主的政黨ハ獎勵セラルベシ但シ占領軍ノ安全ヲ保持スル必要ニ依リ制限セラルベシ人種、國籍、信仰又ハ政治ノ見解ヲ理由ニ差別待遇ヲ規定スル法律、命令及規則ハ廢止セラルベシ又本文書ニ述ベラレタル諸目的及諸政策ニ矛盾スルモノハ廢止、停止又ハ必要ニ應ジ修正セラルベシ此等諸法規ノ實施ヲ特ニ其ノ任務トスル諸機關ハ廢止又ハ適宜改組セラルベシ政治的理由ニ因リ日本國當局ニ依リ不法ニ監禁セラレ居ル者ハ釋放セラルベシ個人ノ自由及人權ヲ保護スル爲司法制度、法律制度及警察制度ハ第三部ノ一及三ニ揭ゲラレタル諸政策ニ適合セシムル樣能フ限リ速ニ改革セラルルベク且爾後漸進的ニ指導セラルベシ

第四部　經濟

一　經濟上ノ非軍事化

日本軍事力ノ現存經濟基礎ハ破壞セラレ且再興ヲ許與セラレザルヲ要ス從テ特ニ下記諸項ヲ含ム計畫ガ實施セラルベシ

軍隊又ハ軍事施設ノ裝備、維持又ハ使用ヲ目的トスル一切ノ物資又ハ軍事施設ノ生產ノ卽時停止及將來ニ於ケル禁止
海軍艦船及一切ノ型式ノ航空機ヲ含ム軍用器材ノ生產又ハ修理ノ爲ノ一切ノ專門的施設ノ禁止
隱蔽又ハ擬裝セラレタル軍備ヲ防止スル爲日本國ノ經濟活動ニ於ケル特定部門ニ對スル監察管理制度ノ設置
日本國ニトリ其ノ價値ガ主トシテ戰爭準備ニ在ルガ如キ特定產業又ハ生產部門ノ除去
戰爭遂行力ノ增進ニ指向セラレタル專門的ノ硏究及敎育ノ禁止
將來ノ平和的需要ノ限度ニ日本重工業ノ規模及性格ヲ制限スルコト
非軍事化目的ノ達成ニ必要ナル範圍ニ日本國商船ヲ制限スルコト

本計畫ニ從ツテ除去セラルベキ日本國ノ現存生產施設ノ終局的ノ處分ニ關シ用途轉換、外國ヘノ搬出、又ハ屑鐵化ノ何レトスベキヤハ明細表ニ基キテ決定セラルベシ右決定ニ至ル迄ノ間ニ於テハ容易ニ民需生產ニ轉換シ得ル施設ハ非常

1 降伏文書調印と初期占領政策への対応（昭和20年9月〜10月）

ノ場合ヲ除キ破壞セラルベカラズ

二　民主主義勢力ノ助長

民主主義ノ基礎ノ上ニ組織セラレタル勞働、産業及農業ニ於ケル組織ノ發展ハ之ヲ奬勵支持スベシ所得竝ニ生產及商業手段ノ所有權ヲ廣範圍ニ分配スルコトヲ得シムル政策ハ之ヲ支持スベシ

日本國國民ノ平和的傾向ヲ强化シ且經濟活動ヲ軍事的目的ノ爲ニ支配シ又ハ指導スルコトヲ困難ナラシムルト認メラルル經濟活動、經濟組織及指導ノ各形態ハ之ヲ支持スベシ

右目的ノ爲最高司令官ハ左ノ政策ヲ執ルベシ

(イ)將來ノ日本國ノ經濟活動ヲ專ラ平和ノ目的ニ向ヶテ指導セザル者ハ之ヲ經濟界ノ重要ナル地位ニ留メ又ハ斯ル地位ニ選任スルコトヲ禁止スルコト

(ロ)日本國ノ商工業ノ大部分ヲ支配シ來リタル產業上及金融上ノ大「コンビネーション」ノ解體計畫ヲ支持スベキコト

三　平和的ノ經濟活動ノ再開

日本國ノ政策ハ日本國國民ニ經濟上ノ大破滅ヲ齎シ且日本國國民ヲ經濟上ノ困難ト苦惱ノ見透シニ直面セシムルニ至

レリ日本ノ苦境ハ日本國自ラノ行爲ノ直接ノ結果ニシテ聯合國ハ其ノ蒙リタル損害復舊ノ負擔ヲ引受ケザルベシ右損害ハ日本國國民ガ一切ノ軍事的目的ヲ抛棄シ孜々且專心平和的生活樣式ニ向ヒ努力スル曉ニ於テノミ復舊セラルベシ日本國ハ物質的再建ニ着手スルト其ノ經濟活動及經濟制度ヲ徹底的ニ改革シ且日本國國民ヲ平和ヘノ線ニ沿ヒ有益ナル職業ニ就カシムルコト必要ナリ聯合國ハ適當ナル期間內右諸措置ガ實現セラルルコトヲ妨ゲルコトアルベキ條件ヲ課セントスル意圖ナシ

占領軍ノ必要トスル物資及役務ノ調達ニ關シテハ之ガ爲飢餓、廣範圍ノ疾病及甚シキ肉體的苦痛ヲ生ゼザル程度ニ於テ日本國ガ調達センコトヲ期待ス

日本國當局ニ對シテハ左ノ目的ニ役立ツ計畫ヲ續行シ、進展シ、實施スルコトヲ期待スルモノニシテ必要アル場合ニ於テハ之ヲ命令スベシ

(イ)甚シキ經濟上ノ苦痛ヲ避クルコト

(ロ)入手シ得ル物資ノ公正ナル配給ヲ確實ナラシムルコト

(ハ)聯合諸國政府間ニ協定セラルル賠償引渡要求ニ應ズルコト

(二)日本國國民ノ合理的ナル平和的需要ヲ充シ得ルガ如ク日本經濟ノ再建ヲ促進スルコト

右ニ關シ日本國當局ハ自己ノ責任ニ於テ必須國家公共事業、財政、金融並ニ必需物資ノ生產及分配ヲ含ム經濟活動ノ統制ヲ設ケ且實施スルコトヲ許サルベシ但シ占領目的ニ合致スルコトヲ確實ナラシムル爲右統制ハ最高司令官ノ承認及審査ヲ受クルモノトス

四　賠償及返還

賠償

(イ)日本國ノ侵略ニ對スル賠償方法ハ左ノ如シ

日本國ノ保有スベキ領域外ニ在ル日本國財產ノ關係聯合國當局ノ決定ニ從ヒ引渡スコト

(ロ)平和ノ爲ノ日本經濟又ハ占領軍ニ對スル補給ノ爲必要ナラザル物資又ハ現存資本設備及施設ヲ引渡スコト

賠償勘定ニ於テ又ハ返還トシテ輸出方指令セラレタルモノノ外荷受國ガ其ノ見返リトシテ必要ナル輸入品ノ提供ニ同意シ又ハ外國爲替ニ依リ支拂ニ同意スル場合ニノミ輸出ヲ許容ス日本國ノ非軍事化計畫ト矛盾シ又ハ之ニ支障ヲ來スガ如キ種類ノ賠償ヲ強要

スルコトナカルベシ

返還

一切ノ識別シ得ル掠奪財產ハ之ヲ完全且速ニ返還スルヲ要ス

五　財政、貨幣及銀行政策

日本國當局ハ依然國內ノ財政、貨幣及信用政策ノ管理及指導ノ責任ヲ保持スベシ但シ最高司令官ノ承認及審査ニ服スルモノトス

六　國際通商及金融關係

日本國ハ終局的ニハ諸外國トノ正常ナル通商關係ノ再開ヲ許容セラルベキモ占領期間中適當ナル統制ノ下ニ外國ヨリト竝ニ許容セラレタル一切ノ商品輸入ヲナス爲ノ商品ヲ購入スル平和的目的ノ爲ニ必要トスル原料及他ノ商品輸入及對外支拂ヲナス爲ノ商品輸出ヲ許可セラルベシ一切ノ商品輸出入、外國爲替及金融取引ニ對シ統制ヲ維持スベキ處右統制實施ノ爲ニ執ルベキ政策及其ノ實際ノ運營ハ何レモ占領軍當局ノ政策ニ違反セズ且特ニ日本國ノ獲得スル一切ノ對外購買力ガ日本國ノ缺クベカラザル必要ノ爲ニノミ利用セラルルコトヲ確實ナラシムル爲最高司令官ノ承認及監督ヲ受クベシ

1　降伏文書調印と初期占領政策への対応（昭和20年9月～10月）

(付記)

編　注　本文書は、昭和二十四年一月、外務省特別資料部作成「日本占領及び管理重要文書集」第一巻より抜粋。

七　在外日本國資產

日本國ノ現存在外資產及降伏條項ニ依リ日本國ヨリ分離セシメラレタル地域ニ在ル日本國ノ現存資產ハ全部又ハ一部皇室及政府ノ所有ニ屬スル資產ヲ含ミ占領軍當局ニ明示セラレ且聯合國當局ノ決定ニ依ル處分ヲ待ツベシ

八　日本國內ニ於ケル外國企業ニ對スル機會均等

日本國當局ハ如何ナル外國ノ企業ニ對シテモ排他的若ハ優先的ノ機會若ハ條件ヲ與ヘラレ又ハ日本國ノ產業組織ガ右機會若ハ條件ヲ與フルコトヲ許可セザルベク又外國企業ニ對シ經濟活動ノ如何ナル重要部門ノ統制權ヲモ讓渡セザルベシ

九　皇室ノ財產

皇室ノ財產ハ占領目的ノ達成ニ必要ナル如何ナル措置ヨリモ免除セラルルコトナカルベシ

昭二〇、九、三〇

「降伏後ニ於ケル米國初期ノ對日方針」說明

目　次

甲、本文書ニ關スル一般的說明

乙、逐條的說明

第一部　究極ノ目的
第二部　聯合國ノ權力
第三部　政　治
第四部　經　濟

丙、國体及政体ニ關スル米國ノ態度

(省略)

[參考]

第一、本文書ト「ヴェルサイユ」條約ニ於ケル對獨措置トノ比較

第二、本文書ト獨「ポツダム、コンミユニケ」トノ比較

甲、本文書ニ關スル一般的說明

(1) 米國乃至聯合軍ノ對日方針乃至政策ハ「ポツダム」宣言發出後ノ和平交涉ノ際シ國體問題ニ關シテハ相當ノ解明ヲ見タル外占領軍ノ到着迄其細部ハ明カニセラレズ占領

軍及最高司令官到着後ニ於テハ重光大臣ヲ初メ各方面ニ於テ之ト接觸セル他聯合軍ニ依リ發セラレタル諸種ノ命令、指令等ニ依リ斷片的、部分的ニ明瞭ノ度ヲ加ヘ來リタルモ尚根本ノ對日軍事的處理ノ段階ハ彼等ノ豫想以上ニ圓滑ニ進展シ其ノ成功ノ目途確立シ所謂政治及經濟處理ノ段階ニ入リツツアリ然ルニ米側ヨリ觀ルニ日本側ノ態度ハ其ノ首腦部乃至支配階級ガ對內關係ニ控制セラルル點アリト雖モ尚甚シク米側ノ意圖ノ諒解ニ缺クル點アリ米側ノ期待スル日本民衆モ依然積極ノ企圖ニ出ツル能力微弱ナルヲ以テ米側トシテハ日本政府等ノ所謂支配階級ニ對シ米國側ノ意圖乃至方針ヲ一層明確ニシ其ノ反省、自覺ヲ促ストスルト共ニ日本民衆ニ對スル刺戟乃至眠氣覺シヲ與ヘントセルコト本文書發表ノ重要ナル動機ト推測セラル

(2) 又米文書公表ニ關スル米國ノ國內ノ原因トシテハ九月十七日「マクアーサー」ノ日本本土占領軍ハ六月內ニ二十萬以下ニ減少シ得ヘシトノ聲明ニ關聯シ國務次官「アチソン」ヲ初メ國內諸方面ニ各種ノ論議ヲ誘發セル結果之ニ關シ明確ナル米國政府ノ對日方針ヲ發表スルヲ可トセルコトヲ考慮シ得ヘシ

註一、右「マ」元帥聲明ニ關シ米國內及聯合諸國間ニ所謂軟弱政策ニ過クトノ非難アリタル他米國內ニ於テハ國務省、軍部間ニ本件ヲ以テ所謂「政策決定ヲ要スル問題」ナリトシ政策決定ハ出先軍司令官ノ權限外ナリト爲シ權限問題ニ關スル紛爭アリタリ

更ニ本文書ノ公表カ米國ノ對外關係ノ考慮ヨリスルモ適當且必要トセラレタルモノナルヘシ

(1) 卽チ一面ニ於テ諸外國就中蘇及濠洲等ニ於ケル所謂軟弱政策ノ批難ニ對スル回答トシテ之カ公表ヲ有利トセルコト

(2) 他面降服後ノ日本卽チ日本本土ノ處理方針ニ關シテハ米國ノ政策カ支配スヘキコト(第二部1)ヲ明確ニスルヲ有利トセルコト(註二、及註三)

註二、元來米國カ現實政策上日本ヲ其ノ支配下ニ置カントスルハ當然ナル處(歐洲就中波蘭及「バルカン」

1　降伏文書調印と初期占領政策への対応(昭和20年9月～10月)

諸國處理ニ關スル蘇聯トノ對立ニヨル苦キ經驗ニ鑑ミ特ニ然リ)他面對日戰爭カ大部分米國ニヨリ負擔セラレタル事ニ基キ米國ハ英蘇等トノ間ニ「ポツダム」會談當時乃至日本ノ降服前後ニ於テ

(イ)占領地域ノ分擔(即チ日本ノ主要部分タル本土カ米ニ依リ占領セラルヘキコト從ツテ降服ニヨリ屬領ヲ事實上腕キ取ラレタル日本ノ處理カ米國ノ支配的發言下ニ實施セラルヘキコト

(ロ)日本處理方針ノ內容

(ハ)所謂聯合國最高司令官ノ權限特ニ其ノ他聯合國軍ニ對スル權限及

等ニツキテハ話合ヲッケタルモノナルヘキモ

(二)占領後ノ日本本土ニ於ケル處理方針ノ實施ニ關スル他聯合國ノ發言ノ許容ノ限度

ニ關シテハ明確ナル話合成立シ居ラサリシモノト推測セラル右ニ關聯シ倫敦外相會議ニ於ケル「モロトフ」ノ發言及右ニ對スル「トルーマン」大統領ノ記者會談及「マックアーサー」ノ最高司令官

任命當時ニ於ケル蘇米間意見不一致ニ關スル歐洲新聞報道等ハ注意セラルルヘシ

註三、米國カ日本ノ國際共產主義ニ依リ蘇聯ノ支配下ニ陷ルコトヲ好マサルヘキハ當然ニシテ本文書中ニ於テモ「革命」(revolution)ナル語ハ避ケラレ居ル他蘇聯「エイヂエンシー」(共產黨ニ非ス)ノ暗躍ハ各種口實ヲ設ケ彈壓シ行クヘキハ勿論ナルヘシ

本文書公表ハ米國內ニ於テ極メテ好評ヲ以テ迎ヘラレ各紙共本文書ニ示サレタル方針ヲ以テ妥當且適切ナルモノト爲シ居レリ

(3)右事實ニ鑑ミ我方トシテハ本文書ノ諸方針ヲ明確ニ理解把握シ上之ヲ積極的自發的ニ實踐シ行ク必要アリ若シ從來ノ我方ノ諒解ト一致セサル諸點アルニ於テハ必要ニ應シ先方ニ質問ノ上之ニ關スル我方態度ヲ決定スヘク他面本件公表ニ依リ財界其ノ他ニ於テ相當動搖ヲ來シ居ルヲ以テ細部ニ關シテモ可及的疑議ヲ解明スル必要アルヘシ

(4)尙本文書ハ「ポツダム」宣言ノ方針ヲ詳密化セルモ

141

乙、逐條解釋

本文書ノ目的

先ツ本文書ハ米國政府カ其ノ内部諸機關ニ對シ與ヘタル指針ニシテ國務、海軍、陸軍三省ノ協議ニ依リ作成セラレ大統領ノ承認ヲ得タルコトヲ明カニシ居ルモ他ノ聯合國トノ間ニ如何ナル程度ノ了解アリタルヤニ付テハ何等觸ルル所ナシ（前記甲參照）

本文書ハ降伏後ノ日本ニ對スル「初期」(initial)政策ニ關スルモノニシテ且「日本占領ニ關スル諸問題中政策決定ヲ必要トスルモノヲ網羅シ居ラ」サルモノトセラレ居リ從テ今後モ更ニ本文書同樣ノ政策指針ノ發表ヲ豫期セラルルル次第ナルカ本文書カ一應日本占領方針ノ大綱ヲ揭ケ居リ且ノニシテ「ポツダム」宣言ノ各條項ハ全部本文書中ニ網羅セラレアリ此ノ點獨逸ニ關スル「クリミヤ」宣言ト七月「ポツダム」會談ニ於テ發表セラレタル「獨逸管理政策」聯合國聲明トノ關係ニ類似スルモノナリ（尚「カイロ」宣言「ポツダム」宣言ト本書トノ比較研究本文書ト「獨逸管理政策」ニ關スル聯合國聲明トノ比較ニ付テハ別稿ニ讓ル）

「ポツダム」宣言ノ規定スル諸問題即チ㈠軍國主義的權力及勢力ノ驅逐㈡占領㈢軍隊ノ武裝解除㈣戰爭犯罪人ノ處罰及民主主義的傾向ノ復活、強化㈥產業ニ對スル制限（世界貿易ヘノ參加）ヲ悉ク「カバー」シ居リ（日本占領軍撤退後ノ問題ハ暫ク置キ）從テ日本占領ニ關シ今後更ニ政策決定ヲ要スルモノトハ或ハ日本ノ最後的政治形態ニ關シ日本國民ノ自由ニ意思ヲ表現スルノ方式、帝國カ其ノ主權ヲ喪失スヘキ地域ニ關スル最後的歸屬ノ決定、海軍、商船隊、對獨「ポツダム」宣言參照）其ノ他内外ニ存スル日本ノ資產ノ處分方法、賠償方法ノ細目、占領軍費ノ問題等既ニ本文書其ノ他ニ於テ大綱ヲ決セラレ居ル問題ノ細目ノ點ナラヤト思考セラル。他面又「マクアーサー」カ日本占領軍ノ數ヲ今後六ケ月間ニ二十萬ニテ充分ナリトノ聲明ヲナシタルニ對シ國務次官「デイーン・アチソン」ハ斯ル決定ハ米國政府ノ行フヘキ所ナリト反駁シタル事件等ヨリ本文書ニ揭記セラレサル細目ノ點ニ付テモ所謂「政策決定ヲ要スルモノ」ニ付テハ必スシモ最高司令官ノ權限ニ全部委任セラレタルモノニ非スシテ米國政府ノ決定スヘキモノナルコトヲ保留スルノ意向ニ於テ「網羅的ナラス」トスルノ字句ヲ

1 降伏文書調印と初期占領政策への対応（昭和20年9月〜10月）

挿入シ最高司令官ノ獨斷專行ヲ抑制セントスル暗示シ居ルモノトモ解セラル

第一部 究極ノ目的

「日本ニ關スル米國ノ究極ノ目的ニシテ當初ノ時期ニ於ケル政策カ遵フヘキモノ」トシテA、B二點ヲ舉ケ居ル處Bノ「聯合國憲章ノ理想ト原則ニ示サレタル米國ノ目的ヲ支持スヘキ平和的且責任アル政府」ノ樹立ナル字句ハ注意ヲ要スヘシ

蓋シ「聯合國憲章ノ理想ト原則」トハ去ル六月二十六日「サンフランシスコ」ニ於テ成レル聯合國憲章 (United Nations Charter) ノ前文ニ揭ケラレ居ル左ノ字句ヲ云フモノニシテ日本ハ未タ右 United Nations 参加スルコトヲ許サレサルモ（獨伊ト同樣完全ニ平和的民主的國家トナリタル後ニ於テハ結局之ニ加ハルヲ得ルモノト思考セラル）茲ニ初メテ間接ノ乍ラ聯合國憲章ニ對スル尊重支持ヲ要求セラルルコトトナレル次第ナリ

"The peoples of the United Nations, determined to save the succeeding generations from the scourge of war, which twice in our lifetime has brought untold sorrow to mankind, to reaffirm faith in fundamental human rights, in the dignity and worth of the human person, in the equal rights of men and women of nations large and small; to establish conditions under which justice and respect for the obligations arising from treaties and other sources of international law can be maintained; and to promote social progress and better standard of life in larger freedom; and for these ends, to practice tolerance and live together in peace with one another as good neighbors, to unite our strength to maintain international peace and security; to insure, by the acceptance of principles and the institution of methods, that armed force shall not be used, save in the common interest; to employ international machinery for the promotion of the economic and social advancement of all peoples, have resolved to combine our efforts to accomplish those aims."

更ニ米國ハ斯ル平和的且責任アル政府カ「出來得ル限リ民主主義ノ自治ノ原則ニ合致スルコトヲ希望スルモ自由ニ表示セラレタル國民ノ意思ニ支持セラレサルカ如キ政體ヲ日本ニ強要スルコトハ聯合國ノ責任ニ非ス」ト述ヘ居ル處右ハ「ポツダム」宣言受諾ノ際帝國政府申入ニ對スル米國政

143

府ノ回答中ノ"The ultimate form of government of Japan shall be established by the freely expressed will of the Japanese people"ニナル表現ト對比シ深キ含蓄ヲ有スルモノト認メラルル即チ「ポツダム」宣言、將又本文書ニ於テ米國並ニ聯合國ノ他ノ本ニ民主主義的ノ自治ニ基ク平和的且責任アル政府ノ出現ヲ希望スルモノナルカ右ハ民主主義的ノ名ニ附サレタル如何ナル政府ヲモ支持スルト云フニ非スシテ民主主義的ノ政府ノ中ニテモ「自由ニ表現セラレタル」日本國民ノ意志カ之ヲ希望スルモノノミヲ認ムルコトヲ以テ聯合國（單ニ米國ノミナラス蘇聯等ヲモ含ム）ノ責務ナリトスル建前ヲトルモノニシテ右ハ「バルカン」諸國等ニ於テ蘇聯カ勝手ニ所謂民主主義的政府ヲ樹立シテ自己ノ勢力ノ伸張ヲ計リタル經驗ニ照シ斯ノ如キコトヲ日本ニ於テハ防止セントスルノ企圖ヲ含ムモノナルヘシ
而シテ第一部後段ニ於テハ右究極ノ目的ヲ達成スルニ爲メ四ツノ手段カ列擧セラレ居ル處右ハ概ネ「ポツダム」宣言中ニ含マレ居ル所其ノ内Aニ於テ日本附近島嶼ノ主權ニ關スル決定ノ問題ハ「カイロ」宣言及米國カ既ニ參加シ又ハ「將來參加スルコトアルヘキ他ノ協定ニ依リ」決定セラルヘキ

旨規定シ居ルハ新聞ニモ傳ヘラルルカ如キ米國ノ海軍基地要求其ノ他ノ諸問題アリテ本件ニ關シ未タ聯合國側ノ合意ノ存セサルヲ證明スルモノナリ
尚Bノ「軍國主義及侵略ノ精神ヲ表示スル制度」トハ如何ナルモノヲ意味スヘキヤハ結局本文書中ノ「日本政府トノ關係」（二部二）「武裝解除及非軍國主義化（三部ノ一）「個人ノ自由及民主主義過程ヘノ希求ノ獎勵」（二部三）等ノ諸項ヨリ推測スルノ外ナカルベシ而シテ茲ニ最モ重大ナル問題ハ天皇制度ノ問題ナリ（前記甲及内參照）然レドモ此ノ點ニ付テハ米國側ノ意圖明確ナラズ。天皇制度ソノモノカ絶對的ノ「軍國主義及侵略ノ精神ヲ表示スル制度」ナリトハ言ヒ難カルベク結局ハ運用ノ問題ニ歸スベキナリ蓋シ維新以來所謂「軍國主義及侵略ノ精神ヲ表示スル制度」ノ最重要機關タリシ統帥部ノ解體ハ日本ノ國家制度ヲ新ナル觀點ヨリ再檢討シ眞ノ民主主義トノ關聯ニ於テ日本自身決定改正シ行ク機會ヲ與フルモノナリ。

第二部　聯合國ノ權力

1　軍事占領

今次占領ノ法律的性質ニ付テハ種々ノ解釋ヲ生スルモノナ

1　降伏文書調印と初期占領政策への対応（昭和20年9月〜10月）

ルカ右占領カ一九〇七年海牙條約ニ規定スルカ如キ戰時占領ト異リ占領國ト被占領國トノ間ノ合意ニ基キ行ハルル特殊ノ占領ナルハ疑問ノ余地ナキ所ナリ。而シテ斯ル占領モ軍事力ヲ以テ行ハルル意味ニ於テハ軍事占領ナルモ占領ノ内容（占領者ノ權利、義務等）カ占領者ト被占領者ノ合意ニ依リ決定セラルル點ニ於テ特殊性ヲ有スルモノト謂フヘキ處本章ニ於テ日本本土ノ軍事占領ハ「主要聯合國ノ為ノ軍事行動タルノ性質ヲ有ス」ヘキモノト定義セラル右占領内容カ戰爭中ニ行ハルル戰時占領ニ近キモノナリトノ米側見地ヲ明ニセルモノト云フヘシ

右ノ他本節ハ日本本土ノ占領及管理ノ施行ニ關スル米國トノ他ノ聯合國トノ關係、換言セハ日本本土卽チ日本ノ占領及處理ノ施行乃至實施（就中實際上ノ具体的細目）ニ關シテハ米國ノ政策カ支配スヘキコトヲ明確ニ主張セントスルモノト解セラル（甲(1)註二註三參照）

尚茲ニ軍事占領ノ範圍ニ付日本本土ト明示シ居ルハ最高司令官ノ從來ノ實際ノ措置振ニ照應シ興味アル所ニシテ惟フニ本文書ノ規定スル所ハ一般命令第一號ニ於テ聯合各國ノ日本諸領土占領ノ分擔ト對應シ米國軍ノ一應占領セル地域ヲ指スモノト思ハレス

（但シ朝鮮南半ヲ含マス）ヲ目途トシ居ルモノト解セラルルシテ此ノ地域ニ於テ「對日戰爭ニ指導的役割ヲ演シタル他ノ諸國ノ軍隊ノ占領ヘノ參加」ヲ歡迎シ居ルハ多分ニ對英、蘇、支政治的「ヂエスヂユアー」ヲ感セラル。

又「日本ノ占領及管理ノ施行ニ關シ」「適當ナル諮問機關ヲ設ク」ル旨言及シ居ルハ新ナル日本占領方式トシテ注目ノ要アリ、最近聯合國外相會議ニ於ケル蘇聯外相「モロトフ」ノ日本管理委員會設置ノ提案ト關聯シ對蘇「アピーズメント、ポリシー」トモ考ヘラルル處米國ノ意圖スル本機關ハ飽迄諮問機關ニシテ「萬一聯合諸國ノ意見ノ不一致ヲ生シタル場合ニ於テハ米國政策ニ從フ」モノタルコトヲ明ニシ尠クトモ日本其ノモノノ占領ニ對シテハ他國ニ對スル米國ノ優越性ヲ維持セントシ居ル點歐洲ニ於ケル蘇聯ノ活躍ト對照スル場合興味多シ。

「米國ノ政策ニ從フ」コトヲ明言シ居ルモ本點ニ付テ關係各國トノ了解成立シ居ルヤニ付テハ何等言及シ居ラサルコト前述ノ如クニシテ「モロトフ」外相ノ提案ヨリ察スルモ本點ハ米國獨自ノ見解ニシテ他ノ聯合國ト完全ナル話合ヲ遂ケタルモノトハ思ハレス

2　日本政府トノ關係

降伏文書ハ「天皇及日本國政府ノ國家統治ノ權限ハ本降伏條項ヲ實施スル爲適當ト認ムル措置ヲ執ルヘキ聯合國最高司令官ノ制限ノ下ニ置カルルモノトス」ト定ムルノミニシテ　天皇竝ニ帝國政府ノ統治權ノ認メラルル具體的範圍ノ如何ナルモノナリヤ、又最高司令官ハ「ポツダム」宣言ノ目的ヲ達成スル爲如何ナル範圍ニ於テ直接帝國國民ヲ命令、強制スルモノナリヤニ付テ明瞭ヲ缺キ居リタル次第ナルカ玆ニ「日本政府ハ最高司令官ノ指示ノ下ニ國内行政事項ニ關シ通常ノ統治權ヲ行使スルコトヲ許容セラルヘシ」トシ他方若シ日本側ニ於テ「最高司令官ノ要求ヲ滿足ニ果ササル」場合ニ於テノミ同司令官カ日本ノ政府機構ニ干涉シ又直接其ノ權力ヲ行使スヘキ旨ヲ定メ居リ斯クテ帝國政府ニ認メラルル統治權ノ範圍並ニ最高司令官カ直接其ノ權力ヲ行フ場合カ一應明カニセラレタリ。

然レトモ國内事項ニ關スル通常ノ統治權ナル語ノ具體的内容ニ付テハ事ニ當リテ認定ノ困難ナルコトアリ得ヘク殊ニ右ノ規定ニ於テ帝國ノ外交權ハ認メラレ居ラサルヤ否ヤノ疑ヲ存ス。

蓋シ　ノ語ニハ外交權ノ行使ヲ含マサルモノト解スルヲ妥當トスヘク（第四部經濟五、六參照）從テ帝國ニ對シ外交權ノ認メラルルヤ否ヤノ問題ハ此ノ字句ヨリハ明ニスルヲ得ス、「ポツダム」宣言其ノ他ノ文書ヨリ別ニ判斷セラルヘキモノナルヘシ

本節ニ於テ最モ注目スヘキハ最高司令官ノ　天皇竝ニ日本政府機關ノ現在ニ於ケル利用ハ決シテ將來ニ對シ之ヲ支持スルモノニ非サル事ヲ明ニセル點ナリ。

曩ニ帝國政府ノ「ポツダム」宣言受諾ニ當リ　天皇ノ大權ニ付聯合國側ノ保障ヲ求メタルニ對シ聯合國側ヲ代表シ米國政府ハ "The ultimate form of government of Japan shall, in accordance with the Potsdam Declaration, be established by the freely expressed will of the Japanese people" ト答ヘタリ。

右ヲ以テ　天皇ノ大權ニ對スル將來ノ保障カ與ヘラレタルモノト解スヘキヤ否ヤニ付テハ議論ノ分レタル所ナルカ玆ニ米國政府ハ最モ直截明瞭ナル形ニ於テ之ニ對スル回答ヲ與ヘタルモノト云フヘシ。

右ノ規定ヲ第一部前段Bノ「自由ニ表示セラレタル國民ノ意思ニ支持セラレサルカ如キ政體ヲ日本ニ強要スルコトハ

1 降伏文書調印と初期占領政策への対応（昭和20年9月〜10月）

聯合國ノ責任ニ非ス」トノ規定ト綜合判斷スレハ米國政府ハ我皇室制度ノ存續ニ關シ將來ノ如何ナル保障ヲモ與フルコトヲ拒ムモノナルト共ニ、天皇制度ノ廢止ニ付テモ右カ自由ナル民意ニ依ラサル限リ敢テ之ヲ行フ意思ナキ建前ナルコトヲ明ニシ居レリ。

然レ共續イテ「封建的又ハ權力主義ノ傾向ヲ修正セントスル統治形式」ノ強力ニ依ル變更ヲ認メ暗ニ慫慂シ居ルハ米國ノ眞意ヲ暗示スモノナルヘシ。

蓋シ米國政府ハ日本ニ於ケル國際共產主義勢力ノ滲透、支配ハ喜ハサル處ナルモサリトテ日本ノ「封建的又ハ權力主義的傾向」ノ象徵トシテ　天皇制度ノ存續ヲモ希望セサルモノト解セラルル節アリ。（然レトモ同時ニ對內的ノ「アピーズメント・ポリシー」ノ「ゼスチユアー」モアリ眞意ノ捕捉困難ナルハ勿論ナリ）然シテ我國体ノ變革ハ自ラ手ヲ下シテ之ヲ行フコトヲ避ケ出來得レハ日本國民自身カ內部ヨリコレヲ崩壞セシムルヲ希望スルモノナルヘシテシテ兹ニ「封建的又ハ權力主義的傾向」トハ如何ナル傾向ヲ謂フヘキヤ。米國ノ意圖スル所明確ナラサルモ華族制度、貴族院制度又ハ樞密院及重臣等ニ付イテハ封建的又ハ權力主義的傾向ト認メ居ルコトハ殆ント疑ナカルヘシ。此ノ字句中ニ、天皇ヲ含ム皇室制度ヲ包含シ居ルヤハ明白ナラズ、然レトモ包含セラレストモ解スルハ困難ナリ。此ノ點ハ英國ノ場合ヲ想起スルトキ米國ノ意圖カ制度乃至組織ソノモノヲ問題トスルニ非スシテ其ノ代表スル思想及ビ運用ノ如何ヲ重視シ居ルモノニ非サルカヲ思ハシム結局我方トシテハ本字句ハ「民主主義傾向」ノ反對字句トシテ取上ケタルモノト解シ　天皇制度ノ存置ヲ堅持シ所要ノ改正ニ邁進スルヲ要スベシ

第三部　政治

一、武裝解除及非軍國主義

本節ハ日本國民ノ泣ニ精神的武裝解除ヲ行ハントスルモノナリ。然シテ其ノ前提トシテ日本國民ニ對シ「其ノ現在及將來ニ關シ陸海軍指導者及其ノ協力者カ為シタル役割ヲ徹底的ニ知ラシムル」コトナシ得ル處右ニ對獨シ」トナシ得ル處右ニ對獨「ポツダム」宣言カ「トナシ得ル處右ニ對獨「ポツダム」宣言カ國人民ヲシテ軍事的ニ喫シタルコト並ニ自己ノ無慈悲ナル戰爭遂行ト狂信的ナル「ナチ」ノ抵抗トカ「ドイツ」國ノ經濟ヲ破壞シ且混亂及受難ヲ不可避ノモノトセルモ

ナルニ依リ自ラ招キタル結果ニ付テハ責任ヲ免ルルコト能ハサルコトヲ首肯セシムルコトトシテ「ナチ」ノミナラス獨逸國民ノ責任ヲモ問ヒ居ル點ト對比シテ注目ニ價スルモノナルヘシ。

次イテ「日本ノ陸海軍、祕密警察組織」ノ解體、「陸海軍資材、陸海軍艦船、陸海軍施設及陸海軍竝ニ民間航空機」ノ引渡、高級軍人竝ニ「國家主義的竝ニ軍國主義的組織ノ指導者」等ノ拘禁ヲ定メ斯クテ組織主義、資材、人間ノ三方面ヨリ日本ノ軍國主義ノ潰滅ヲ期スルモノナリ。

「拘禁セラレ將來ノ處分ノ爲ニ抑留セラル」ヘキ者ノ中戰爭犯罪人トシテ裁判ヲ受クルモノアルハ勿論ナルカ其ノ範圍ハ必スシモ戰爭犯罪人ニ限ルモノニ非ストモ思考セラル。

(對獨「ポツダム」宣言政治的原則(五)參照)

更ニ「軍國主義竝ニ好戰的國家ノ積極的代表人物」カ公的竝ニ重要ナル私的地位ヨリ排除セラレ又ハ陸海軍ノ職業的將校竝ニ下士官其ノ他ノ者カ「凡テ監督的及教育的地位」ヨリ排除セラルヘキモノトセリ。最近ノ海外通信ニヨレハ聯合國管理委員會ハ獨逸軍需會社ノ再開ニ關シ「ナチ」黨員カ單ナル勞働者以上ノ地位ヨリ一掃セラルヘシト

ノ指令ヲ發セル趣ナルカ右ト關聯シ監督的及教育的地位(supervisory and teaching position)トアル逸國民ノ地位上斯ル監督的ノ指令ヘラレタルモノニ非スシテ社會的ノ指述ヘラレタルモノニ非スシテ社會的ノ及教育ノ地位ニ立ツコトヲモ排除セントスルノ趣旨ニ解セラル。然リトセハ官廳、會社等ノ上級地位ハ勿論、社會ニ於ケル如何ナル指導的ノ地位ニ立ツコトモ困難ト云ハサルヘカラス

三、戰爭犯罪人

戰爭犯罪ニ關スル「モスコー」宣言ハ殘虐ノ行爲ヲ行ヒタル者カ右殘虐行爲ノ行ハレタル國ニ送ラレ其ノ國ノ裁判ヲ受クルヲ原則トシ地理的制限ナキ重大犯罪人ニ付テノミ國際裁判ニ附スヘキ旨定メ居ル處本節ノ規定ハ寧ロ聯合國裁判所ノ裁判ヲ主トシ聯合各國ノ國內裁判ハ從トスルモノノ如ク最高司令官ニヨリ「裁判ヲ爲又ハ證人トシテ或ハ其ノ他ノ理由ニ依リ必要トセラレザル」モノノミカ關係國ノ國內裁判ヲ受クルモノトセリ。

三、個人ノ自由及民主主義過程ヘノ希求ノ獎勵

「日本國民ハ米國及其ノ他ノ民主主義國家ノ歷史、制度、文化及成果ヲ知ル機會ヲ與ヘラレ且其ノ事ヲ獎勵セラルベ

1 降伏文書調印と初期占領政策への対応（昭和20年9月～10月）

シ〕トシテ米國ハ日本ノ徹底的「アメリカナイズ」ヲ企圖シ居ルカ如ク又（中略）統制セラルベシ」トナスハ獨逸ニ於テ傳ヘラルルカ（如キカ）ク獨逸住民トノ交驩禁止令トハ寧ロ反對ニ所要ノ限度ニ於テノミ」統制セラルルニ過ギズシテ一般ニソノ交渉ヲ認メタルモノト解スルヲ安當トス（占領軍ニヨリ啓蒙ヲ暗示ス）

「民主的政黨ハ獎勵セラルヘシ但シ占領軍ノ安全ヲ保持スル必要ニ依リ制限セラルヘシ」トアル處民主的政黨ノ中ニ共產主義的政黨モ包含セラルルヤ否ヤノ問題ニ付テハ勿論之ヲ肯定スルニ解スルヲ妥當トスベシ、而シテ占領軍ノ行フベキ後段ノ制限ハ占領軍ノ安全ヲ理由トスベキモノナルニ現實ニ於テハ之ガ政治的ニ利用セラルルコトモ有リ得ベシ。

「人種、國籍、信教又ハ政治的見解ヲ理由ニ差別待遇ヲ規定スル法律、命令及規則」及「本文書ニ逃ベラレアル諸目的ノ竝ニ諸政策ト矛盾スル法令」ハ「此等諸法規ノ實施ヲ特ニ其ノ任務トスル諸機關」ト共ニ廢止セラルベキモノナリトセラレ居ル處右ハ對獨「ポツダム」宣言中ニ「ヒトラー」政體ノ基礎ヲ提供シ又ハ人種、宗敎的信條若ハ政治的

意見ニ基ク差別ヲ設ケタル「ナチ」ノ一切ノ法令ハ廢止セラルベシ」トアルニ對應スルモノナリ。而シテ獨逸ニ於テハ「ユダヤ」人其ノ他ニ對スルカ此ノ種法令カ多數ニ存在シ居リタルコトハ容易ニ考ヘ得ル所ナルモ我國ニ於テハ積極的ニ斯ノ如キ差別待遇ヲ規定スル法令ハ甚ダ少ク殊ニ朝鮮、臺灣等カ帝國ノ主權ノ下ニ立タザルニ至レバ愈々少キモノトナルベシ。唯治安維持法、思想犯保護觀察法、出版法（第二十六條）等ノ國體變革ノ罪ヲ對象トスルモノハ廢止セザルベカラザルベシ

「政治的理由ニヨリ日本當局ニヨリ不法ニ監禁セラレ居ル者ハ釋放セラルベシ」トセラレ居ル處治安維持法ニ依リ拘禁乃至處刑中ノ者ハ右ニ該當スルモノナルベシ。更ニ「司法、法律及警察組織ハ第三部ノ一（武裝解除及非軍國主義化）及三（個人ノ自由及民主主義的過程ヘノ希求ノ獎勵）ニ於テ揭ケラレタル諸政策ニ適合セシムル爲出來得ル限リ速ニ改革」セラルベキモノトセラレ居ル處右ハ軍法會議、軍律會議、憲兵、特務機關等、軍ト直接關係アル機關ノ解體ノ他、更ニ廣ク樞密院行政裁判所、貴族院、選擧制度、特高制度等々ノ改革ヲモ含ムモノナルヤニモ思考セラル。但

149

本章ノ規定ハ對獨「ポツダム」宣言ノ規定ト酷似スルモノアリ、獨逸ニ對スル考ヘ方ガ直ニ我方ニ適用セラレ居ルガ如キ節モアリ日本ト獨逸ノ國情ノ相違ヨリ具體的ナル遙庭アルヲ餘儀ナクセラルルモノト思惟ス。

　第四部　經　　濟

本第四部ハ之ヲ「ポツダム」宣言ノ諸條項及第一部(就中后段A乃至D)及最高司令官ノ發シタル諸命令類ト比較對照シ考究スルトキソノ意義ヲ一層明確ニシ得ヘシ全般ヲ通シ(1)經濟面ニ於ケル日本ノ戰爭遂行能力及可能性ノ徹底的除去及管理最モ支配的ニシテ一、三、六、八、等ハ何レモ右趣旨ニ出ツルモノナルヘク(2)他面最低限度(獨逸ノ場合ニ於テハ英蘇ヲ除ク全歐洲諸國ノ平均水準ナル指標アルハ注意ヲ要ス)ノ生活水準ヲ有スル所謂平和的經濟活動ヲ保證(三、四、―B六)賠償等ニツキ方針ヲ示スモノナリ特ニ注意ヲ要スルハ所謂米國ノ二大目的ノ一ナル民主主義ノ實現ノ爲ニ必要ナル我國特ニ農村ノ封建的(高度資本主義ノ組織タル財閥ニ非ス)經濟組織ニ改革ニ關シ殆ント何等ノ方針ノ明示セラレ居ラサル點ニシテ我國ノ軍國主義乃至侵略主義化ノ大源動力タル本點ニ關スル正策ノ缺除ハ米國ノ民主主義化ノ理想主義的性格ニ不安ヲ抱カシムルモノアリ

一、經濟上ノ非軍事化

本項ニ關シテハ具體的ノ限界明瞭ナラサル諸表現使用セラレアルモ右限界ニ關シテハ本方針ニ基キ最高司令部ノ發シタル諸命令就中指令第三號ト對照考究ヲ可トスヘシ

二、民主主義勢力ノ助長

本項ノ内容ハ必シモ經濟上ノ民主主義勢力ノ助長ト言フヨリハ寧ロ經濟上ノ乃至非軍國主義化ノ爲メ諸方途ヲ示セルモノト言フヘシ后段Aハ第三部一ノ軍閥指導者ノ排除ト對照シ經濟上ノ軍國主義ノ指導者ノ排除ニ關スル者ナル處軍閥ノ場合ニ比シ過去ヲ問題トセサル點緩和セラレ

后段Bハ其意義明ナラサルモ有力且有能ナル財閥乃至獨占組織ヲ解體シ經濟力ノ弱化ヲ圖ルモノト看做シ得ヘシ解體ヲ「支持スヘシ」ト爲シ解體スヘシト爲シ居ラサル點注意ヲ要ス

三、平和的經濟活動ノ再開

「ポツダム」宣言第十一項ニ相應スルモノナルヘキ處

1　降伏文書調印と初期占領政策への対応（昭和20年9月〜10月）

(1) 聯合軍ノ原則トシテ日本經濟復興ニ助力ヲ與ヘサルヘキコト

(2) 聯合軍ハ但シソノ物資調達等ニ關シテモ日本國民最低生活水準ヲ侵カサザルヘキコト

(3) 日本當局ノ經濟行政ノ目標及權（一字分アキ）ヲ明ニシ居ルモノナリ

四、賠償竝ニ返還

冒頭「侵略」トアルハ日本國的ニ於ケル權利ノ侵犯ヲモ含ムコト當然ナルヘシ

前段Bニ關シテハ前記三、ノ場合ト同樣先ツ日本ノ平和的經濟ノ水準卽日本人ノ生活水準ニ關スル科學的標準ノ決定ヲ先決問題トスヘシ

末尾ノ一項ノ解釋ニ關シテハ第一次世界大戰後ノ獨逸處理ニ於ケル失敗ニ鑑ミ例バ軍事的用途ニ轉換シ得ル如キ巨大ナル製鋼業等ノ存續バ賠償物資生產ノ爲ニ容認スル意圖ナキヤ明確ニセルモノナルヘシ

本項全般ヲ通シ賠償ノ規模乃至限度ニ關スル明確ナル說明ハ見出シ得サルモ（右ハ勿論今後ニ於ケル聯合各國ノ要求ニ基キ聯合國間ニ協定セラルヘキモノナルヘシ）前段Bニ於テ平和的日本經濟ノ爲ニ必要ナル物資及設備ノ國內留保ヲ明示セル點及賠償勘定ニ於ケル輸出卽現物賠償ヲ暗示セル點及輸入ノ承認等ヲ揭ケアルハ聯合國少クトモ米國ノ賠償ニ關スル現實的方針ヲ暗示スルモノト解シ得ヘシ

五、財政、貨幣竝ニ銀行政策

六、七、ニ照應考慮スルニ、對外關係ヲ有スル經濟活動ハ少クトモ差當リノ間ハ聯合軍ノ直接管理下ニ於カルルモノナルニ反シ國內ニ關スル限リ日本當局ニ統制及指導ヲ委ヌル點ニ注意ヲ要ス

註　尙指令第三號ニ於テ米側ノ極度ニ「インフレーション」ヲ囘避セントシ居ルハ注意ヲ要スヘシ

六、國際通商及金融關係

(1) 「ポツダム」宣言第十一項ニ該當スルモノニシテ「必シモ「バーター」制ニ依ラサル點

(2) 又聯合軍ノ監督下ニ實施サルル點ニ注意スヘシ

七、在外日本財產

(1) 皇室財產ニツキ免除セサルハ特ニ九、皇室財產ニ強調セラレル點ト合セ米軍及經濟當局ノ日本皇室ニ對ス

ラレタル日本國民ノ狂信的特質ノ根源ヲ為スヲ以テ日本處理方針トシテハ宜シク之ヲ廢止スヘシトノ為セルニ對シ一部ニ於テハ聯合國軍ノ犠牲ヲ最少限ニ止メツツ戰爭ノ終結ヲ促進シ且戰後ノ處理ヲ秩序（序カ）ヲ以テ容易ナラシムル為ニハ天皇制ヲ維持乃至利用スルニ如カストノ論スルモノアリタル斯ル輿論ヲ背景トシツツ日本ニ對スル最後ノ條件トシテ起草セラレタル「ポツダム」宣言ハ國体及政体ノ問題ニ關シテハ單ニ其ノ第十二項ニ於テ聯合國ノ占領兵力ハ同宣言ニ掲ケラレタル目的ノ達成セラレ且「日本國民ノ自由ニ表明スル意思ニ基キ平和的傾向ヲ有スル責任アル政府ノ樹立ヲ見タル場合」直ニ撤退セラルヘシト述フルニ止メ居レリ（但日本ノ平和主義合理主義民主主義化ノ要請宣言全般ニ亘リ支配シ居ルコト勿論ナリ）

三、「ポツダム」宣言ノ條項受諾ニ當リ我方ヨリ國体問題ニ關シテ照會ヲ行ヒタルニ對シ聯合國ノ名ニ於テ米國ヨリ發シタル回答ハ其ノ第一項ニ於テ天皇及日本政府ノ國家統治ノ權限ハ降伏條項實施ノ為必要ト認ムル措置ヲ執ル最高司令官ノ制限ノ下ニ置カルルコトヲ明ニスルト共ニ第四項ハ「ポツダム」宣言ノ趣旨ヲ繰返シ「最終的ノ日本

観方ヲ暗示スル有力ナル指針ト言フヘシ

（2）在外財産中私有財産ノ處分ニ關シテハ問題アルヘキ處本點ニ關シテハ「聯合國當局ノ決定ニ從ヒ處分」セラルヘシト為シ明確ナラサルモ四賠償1At照應スルニ少クトモ其主要ナルモノハ私有財産ト雖モ賠償物資トシテ引渡サルヘキコト略確實ナルヘシ

八、日本國内ニ於ケル外國企業ニ對スル機會均等

（1）例ヘハ日本銀行等半國家的性質ヲ有スル日本企業ト外國企業トノ差別待遇ヲモ否定スルモノニハ非ルヘク專ラ諸外國間ノ機會均等ヲ目的トシ居ルモノト解セラル右ハ米ノ滿々タル自信ヲ示ト共ニ他面日本支配ノ意圖ヲ露呈スルモノナリ

九、皇室財産

特ニ本項ヲ明示セルハ意味深重ナリト言フヘク所謂日本皇室ノ財閥的性格ノ除去ノ意圖ヲ示スモノナルヘシ

内、國体及政体問題ニ對スル米國ノ態度

一、日本ノ國体及政体ノ問題ハ戰爭終結以前ヨリ聯合國間ニ必スシモ意見ノ一致ヲ見ス聯合國輿論ハ大勢トシテ天皇制ハ畢ニ非民主主義的ナルノミナラス戰場ニ於テ顯示セ

1　降伏文書調印と初期占領政策への対応（昭和20年9月〜10月）

國ノ統治形態ハ「ポツダム」宣言ニ遵ヒ日本國國民ノ自由ニ表明スル意思ニ依リ決定セラルヘキモノトス」ト述ヘ居レリ。「國民ノ自由ニ表明スル意思」ニ依リ統治形態ヲ決定スルハ大西洋憲章第三條カ「各國民カ其ノ統治形式ヲ撰擇スル權利ヲ尊重ス」ト述フルト軌ヲ一ニシ日本ノ國體ハ日本人自體ノ決定スヘキ問題ナリト爲スモノト認メラレタリ

三、九月二十二日米國政府ノ公表セル「初期ノ對日方針」ニ依リ聯合國ノ日本ノ國體及政體ニ對スル方針及現在ノ日本政府ニ對スル方針ハ一層明確ノ度ヲ加フルニ到リタリ

右公表文中ニ強調セラレ居ル點左ノ如シ

(1) 米國ハ現在（九月二十九日當時）ノ日本政府乃至日本統治形式ヲ以テ「他國家ノ權利ヲ尊重シ聯合國憲章ノ理想ト原則ニ示サレタル米國ノ目的ヲ支持スヘキモノニシテ且責任アル政府」（第一部前段）ト認メ居ラス且「封建的又ハ權力主義的ノ傾向」（第二部2）ヲ有スルモノト爲シ居リ之ヲ支持スルノ意圖ヲ有セス「日本社會ノ現在ノ性格及最少限ノ兵力及資材ニ依リ目的ヲ達成セントスル米國ノ希望」（第一部2）ニ依リ卽單ニ便宜

上「米國ノ目的達成ヲ滿足ニ促進スル限リニ於テ　天皇ヲ含ム日本政府機關及諸機關（第二部2）」卽「現在ノ日本政治形式ヲ利用（第二部2）」セントスル丈ノ話ナリ從ッテ

(イ)「天皇及日本政府ノ權力」ヲ對等ノ地位ニ置キ承認スルモノニ非ス之ヲ以テ「最高司令官ニ」屬（第二部2）」スルモノト爲スノミナラス「政治機構又ハ人事ノ變更ヲ要求シ乃至ハ直接行動スル權利要求ヲ滿足ニ果ササル場合」最高司令官ハ「最高司令官ノ(一字分アキ)

(ロ) 現在ノ日本統治機構ハ改革ヲ要スルヲ以テ「米國ノ目的ノ達成」ノ線ニ沿フ「前進的改革」ヲ抑ヘカラスト爲シ又日本政府自身又ハ國民ニ依リ「封建的又ハ權力主義的ノ傾向修正」ノ爲ノ統治形式ノ變更ヲ支持スヘク斯カル變更ヲ爲ノ強力行使ニ對シ最高司令官ハ「麾下部隊ノ安全竝ニ占領ノ目的ノ達成ノ保障ノ爲必要」ナラサル限リ干渉スヘカラストスル米國ノ希望ニ付本文書中ニ明ニセラレ居ル點左ノ如シ

(2) 現存統治形式變革ノ方向ニ關スル米國ノ希望ニ付本文

(イ)米國ノ二大究極目的ノ一トシテ「他國家ノ權利ヲ尊重シ聯合國憲章ノ理想ト原則ニ示サレタル米國ノ目的(乙、逐條説明中當該部分參照)ヲ支持スヘキ平和的且責任アル政府(第一部前段B)」ノ樹立ヲ擧ケ

(ロ)米國トシテハ右政府カ「出來得ル限リ民主主義的自治ノ原則ニ合致スルコト」ヲ希望スルコト(第一部前段B)

(ハ)軍國主義及侵略ノ精神ヲ表示スル制度ハ強力ニ抑壓セラルヘキコト(第一部後段B)

(ニ)「封建主義的又ハ權力主義的傾向」(乙、逐條説明當該部分參照)ヲ修正セントスル統治形式ノ變革ヲ支持スヘキコト(第一部2)

(ホ)右諸點ノ外米國ノ二究極目的ノ一カ日本ノ再ヒ米國又ハ世界ノ平和及安全ノ脅威トナラサルコトニアル以上(第一部前段A)右ノ線ニ添フヘキコト當然ナリ

右各項目ノ詳細ノ説明ハ乙、逐條説明ニ讓ルモ以上ヲ綜合スルニ米國ノ希求スル方向ハ

(1)平和主義化(非軍國主義化、非侵略主義化)

(2)民主主義化(非封建主義化、非權力主義化、個人權利及自由尊重化)

(3)右ノ爲ノ合理主義化(神話的、神格的性格ノ排除)

三點ニアリト言ヒ得ヘク右ヲ稍具體的ニ我國現在ノ統治形式就中所謂國體ニ關聯シ考察スヘシ

(1)平和主義化

所謂國體ノ護持ハ「萬世一系ノ天皇ニ依ル統治」ヲ確保シ且右統治ニ對シ國民ノ歸一服從ヲ確保スルコトナルヘキ處本文書ニ於テ所謂統治形式ナル表現ハ勿論右ノ意味ニ於ケル國體及政體(兩者ニ關スル觀念ノ區別ナカルヘシ)ヲ含ムヨリ廣汎ナル觀念卽議會制度、政府制度、統治制度、皇室制度等ヲ含ム統治形式乃至統治組織ト解スヘシ

右解釋ニ依ルトキハ所謂國體ナルモノハ一種ノ容器乃至枠ニシテ之ニ盛ラルヘキ内容ハ實質的ニハ國内諸政治勢力ノ均衡關係及形式ノ乃至制度上ヨリハ天皇ノ統治ニ對スル輔弼制度、政府制度、議會制度、統治制度如何ニ依リ定マルモノト言フヘシ而シテ我現存統治形式ヲ以テ平和主義化ニ非ストハ爲ス者ノ中右ノ如キ觀念ノ整理ヲ有セス近年ニ於テ我國ノ輔弼制度、政府

1　降伏文書調印と初期占領政策への対応（昭和20年9月～10月）

制會、統帥制度ノ缺陷及右ニ乘スル國内政治勢力ノ不均衡ニ依リ我國ノ軍國主義ノ非平和的ナリシ事實ヲ目シ廣キ意味ニ於ケル我統治形式カ平和主義的ニ非ストシテ右統治形式カ平ラ爲シ而シテ右統治形式カ平和的ニ非ストスル爲スアルモ右ハ誤解ト言ハサルヘカラス近年ニ於ケル我國ノ軍國主義化ハ寧ロ統帥制度等ノ缺陷及之ニ乘スル軍國主義的政治勢力ノ支配（更ニソノ根底的原因ヲ爲スモノハ我國ノ封建的社會經濟組織ニアリ）ニ依ルモノニシテ　天皇統治制度ソノモノニ非ス（但シ(3)ニ於テ評述スル如キ意味ニ於テ我統治形式中特ニ　天皇統治制度ヲ平和主義的ノナラスト爲ス者アリ(3)(イ)參照）右ノ點明ラカナル限リ米國ノ我統治形式ノ平和主義化ノ希求ハ必シモ　天皇統治制度ソノモノノ變革ヲ固執セスモ廣義ノ意味ニ於ケル統治形式ノ平和主義化ヲ以テ滿足スルモノナルヘシト信セラル（例ハ統帥制度ノ撤廢等ノ制度上ノ變革及實質上軍國主義的分子ノ排除等）

(2)民主主義化

完全ナル民主主義ノ諸原則カ　天皇統治制度ヲ好マサルコトハ容易ニ理解シ得ヘキ也

我國ノ　天皇統治制度及廣義ノ統治形式例ハ憲法ノ欽定、大權事項ノ範圍ノ擴大、元老制度、貴族院制度、選舉制度等ニ於キ法制上（慣習法ヲ含ム）非民主主義的色彩濃厚ナルハ否ミ難シ（但シ右ハ勿論我國ノ農村等ニ於ケル封建的經濟組織之ヲ基底トスル封建主義的思想、之ニ基ク封建主義的政治勢力右ノ如キ統治形式ノ非民主主義性格ヲ克服シ得ス逆ニ之カ濫用ヲ許シ來リタルコトニ寧ロ從來ノ我國ノ非民主主義的性格ノ眞ノ根因ナルコトヲ否定スルモノニ非ス）而シテ米國ノ前記ノ如キ民主主義化ノ強キ希求ヲ我　天皇統治制度ソノモノヲ好マサルコトハ明ナルヘク歐洲ニ於ケル君主ノ諸國ニ於テ君主ノ統治權行使ヲ事實上（政治慣習上及法制上）民主主義的輔弼機構ニ依リ殆ト完全ニ調整シ居ル實例ニモ鑑ミ少クトモ大權行使ニ關スル輔弼機構ノ民主主義化（內閣更迭等ノ最高政治ノ所謂閣取引廢止）ハ要求セラルヘク右ト同時ニ廣義ノ統治形式ノ前記ノ如キ諸種ノ封建的非民主主義的諸制度ノ變革モ要請セラルルモノト信ス又所謂「封建主義ノ權力

主義的」存在トシテノ貴族ノ政治上ノ特權及財閥(家族的)ノ排斥カ皇室制度及皇室財産制度ニ觸レ來ルハ不得已所ナリト謂フヘシ

註 本文書第四部七及九ニ於ケル皇室財産ヲ賠償等占領目的ノ爲ノ必要上例外ノ取扱乃至免除セサルコトヲ特ニ明記シ居ル點ハ注意ヲ要スヘシ

(3) 合理主義化

本點ニ關スル米國ノ希求ハ (1) 及 (2) ニ關聯乃至從屬スルモノト看ルヲ妥當トスヘシ卽

(イ) 誤レル神國思想八紘一宇思想ニ基ク軍國主義及侵略主義ノ根源カ我 天皇制度ニアリトシ非軍國主義化ノ爲ニ 天皇制度ヲ除去乃至合理主義化スヘシトナスモノニシテ神國思想八紘一宇思想選民思想カ軍國主義ニ誤用サレタル過去ノ事實ハ否定シ得ス又斯種思想ガ我 天皇制度ノ本質卽萬世一系ノ 天皇ニ依ル統治ト紙一重ノ關係ニ在ルコトモ否ミ得スシテ我國ニ於テ萬世一系ノ 天皇ニ依ル統治ノ行ハル所以ハ我國ノ歷史ノ事實及之ニ對スル國民ノ愛着乃至信仰(國民感情)及之カ基礎ヲ爲ス現在我國ニ於

テ行ハレツツアル如キ我民族ノ歷史ノ解釋ハ之ヲ必シモ合理主義的ナルモノト言ヒ得サルヘキモ民族ノ存スル以上必シモ不合理ト言フヘキニ非ルノミナラス而モ之等ノ愛着及信仰ハ夫レ自體何等軍國主義的乃至侵略ノモノニ非ス「正常ナル民族ノ誇」ニ止マリ得ヘキモノト信ス而シテ此限度ニ於テハ米國トシテモ許容スルモノナルヘシ

但シ我 天皇制度ニ隨伴スル神格的神話ノ性格カ容易ニ侵略主義乃至軍國主義ノ手段ニ轉化シ得ヘキ危險ヲ包藏スルハ否ミ得サルヘク米國トシテハ少クトモ 天皇制度ニ隨伴スル斯種性格ノ除去ヲ强ク希望スル所ナルヘシ

註 右ニ關シ本文書第三部三ニ於テ宗敎ノ自由ノ宣言及 Ultranationalistic 卽極端ナル(?) 國家主義並ニ軍國主義組織及運動ハ宗敎ノ外被ノ陰ニ隱ルルヲ得サル旨日本人ニ對シ明示セラルヘシトシナシ居ルハ神道ニ關スルモノトモ解シ得ヘク注目ニ價スヘシ

(ロ) 天皇制度カ本質的ニ民主主義的ナル存在ニ非ルコト

156

1 降伏文書調印と初期占領政策への対応(昭和20年9月～10月)

モ論議ノ餘地ナシト雖モ特ニ我國ニ於テハ獨特ノ神話的ノ神格的性格ヲ帶ヒ居リ而モ右諸性格カ從來我國ノ政治ヲ支配シ來リタル封建的ノ政治勢力ニ依リ實現然ナル程度ニ迄強調利用セラレ來リタル結果民主主義ノ根本原則タル個人ノ權利及自由ノ自覺乃至認識及之カ健全ナル發展展開ニ對スル障害トナリ居リタル事實ハ否ムヘカラス少クトモ斯種不自然ナル神話的ノ性格、神格的性格ヲ除去若合理主義的ニ修正スルニ非レハ所謂理性（「リーズン」）ニ基ク思想ノ展開、就中個人人格乃至個人ノ權利及個人ノ自由ノ發展ハ望ミ難カルベシ（權力ニ對スル盲從）

　註　右ニ關聯シ本文書第三部政治三「個人ノ自由及民主主義過程ヘノ希求ノ獎勵」ノ諸項目就中「政治的見解ヲ理由ニ差別待遇ヲ規定スル」法令及「本文書ニ述ヘラレタル諸目的竝ニ諸政策ト矛盾スル」法令ノ改廢及政治犯人ノ釋放等ヲ掲ケアルハ注意ヲ要スベシ

(3) 現存統治形式變革ノ過程乃至方式

即米國ハ右ノ如キ方向ニ向ヒ日本ノ現存統治形式ノ變

革セラルルコトヲ希望シ居ルモノナルモ米國トシテハ右變革ヲ外部ヨリ強要スルノ方式ヲ避ケ極力日本政府乃至日本國民ノ自由ナル意思ニ基ク方式ニ依リ、實現セントスル建前ヲトリ居ルコトハ米國ノ對蘇、對英考慮等力表面上斯カル建前ヲ執ルハ米國ノ對蘇、對英考慮等（米國自身ノ利害打算ハ米國政府カ大西洋憲章「ポツダム」宣言等ニ於テ與ヘタル「コミットメント」ノ關係ヲモ含ム）ニ基クモノニ過キス、右方式乃至建前ノ許ス範圍ニ於テ米國カ將來實際ニ如何ナル程度迄其本心ニ於テ抱ク前諸變革希望ノ實現ヲ試ムルヤハ今後ニ於ケル米側ノ出方及我方ノ態度ニ依ルヘキモ、本文書中ニ於テモ

(イ)「自由ニ表示セラレタル國民ノ意志ニ支持セラレルカ如キ政體ヲ日本ニ強要スルコトハ聯合國ノ責任ニアラス」（第一部前段B末尾）ト爲ス點及

(ロ)「封建的又ハ權力主義的ノ傾向ヲ修正セントスル統治形式ノ變更ハ政府ニ依ルト國民ニ依ルトヲ問ハス許容シ支援スヘク之カ實現ノ爲ノ強力行使ハ占領軍ノ安全及占領目的ノ達成ノ保障上必要ナル限度ニ於テ

ノミ干渉セラルヘシ」(第二部ニ末尾)トナシ居ル點ハ特ニ注目ヲ要スル點ナリ

右(イ)ハ「強要セス」ナル字句ニ力點ヲ置クヨリハ寧ロ「自由ニ表示セラレタル國民ノ意志」ナル字句ニ重點アリ即チ米國トシテハ先ツ政體ニ關シ眞ニ自由ナル國民ノ意志ヲ表示セシメ(註一)タル上斯カル國民意志ニ支持セラレサル政體ヲ強要セストナスモノニシテ本文書第一部各段Cノ(信教、集會、言論、出版ノ自由ノ促進及民主主義的及代議的組織ノ獎勵)及第三部三「政治3個人ノ自由及民主主義過程ヘノ希求ノ獎勵」中ニ評述セラレアル諸點(法令撤廢取締機關ノ撤廢等)ハ右ノ意味ニ解セラルヘク「自由ナル國民ノ意志」トハ國體及私有財產論議ノ取締ヲ許容スルモノニ非サルヘシ(事實上本點ニ關スル最高司令部ノ態度ハ極メテ積極的ナリ)

右(ロ)ハ一面ニ於テ政府ニ依ル明治維新的自發變更ヲ慫憑スルト共ニ他面ニ於テ國民ニ依ル變更カ強力行使ヲ伴フ場合ニ於テモ米軍ノ好マサル限リ干渉スヘカラストナシ寧ロ之ヲ暗示シ居ルモノト解シ得ヘシ

他面ニ於テ米國及日本カ國際共產主義化シ蘇聯支配下ニ當ルコトヲ好マサルハ當然ニシテ本文書中ニ於テモ「革命」(Revolution)ナル語ハ避ケ居ル點「政府又ハ日本國民ニ依ル統治形式ノ變更」ヲ許容且支持シ居ル點(第二部2後段)等ハ注意スヘキモノナルヘシ

結論

(1)米國ノ我現存統治形式ニ對スル認識之カ變革方向及右變革ノ方式乃至過程ニ關スル意嚮ハ概ネ右ノ如クニシテ米國ハ今日ノ天皇制度ヲ含ム日本統治形式ヲ支持セス現在ハ便宜上之ヲ利用シ得ルニ過キス之ヲ前記ニ末段ニ述ヘタル方向ニ向ヒ變革セントスル底意乃至キ希望ヲ抱キ居ルモノニシテ過去ノ經緯並ニ自己ノ利害打算上右變革ヲ外部ヨリ強要スルノ形式ヲ極力避ケ日本政府乃至日本國民ノ自發的「自由」意思ノ方式ニ依リ右變革ノ底意乃至希望ヲ達セントシ居ルモノナリ

(2)我方特ニ我政府トシテハ(前記二、3、參照)現下ノ冷嚴ナル實情ヲ明確ニ認識ノ上(特ニ本文書公表ノ動機ニ關スル甲、一般ノ說明一、參照)從來ノ如キ後手ニ廻ルコトヲ避ケ速カニ前記ニ、就中(2)末段ノ諸點ニ向ヒ積極果敢

1　降伏文書調印と初期占領政策への対応（昭和20年9月～10月）

編　注　本文書末尾にあるポツダム宣言第十二項と「降伏後ニ於ケル米國ノ初期ノ對日方針」との字句比較は省略した。

40　連合国と友好関係にある諸国の財産保護に関する指令

昭和20年9月22日　連合国最高司令官総司令部より　日本政府宛

AG 091.112（21 Sep 45）MG
SCAPIN-39

MEMORANDUM FOR: IMPERIAL JAPANESE GOVERNMENT
THROUGH: Central Liaison Office, Tokyo.
SUBJECT: Protection of Property of Friendly Nations and Their Nationals.

1. The Imperial Japanese Government shall be responsible for the protection of all property in which nations friendly to the Allied Powers, or the nationals thereof, have any right, title or interest and shall take all measures necessary to guard such property against wanton destruction and depredation.

2. The provisions of Paragraph 1 above shall apply to all such property situated in the four (4) main islands of Japan and adjacent offshore islands including Tsushima Island.

FOR THE SUPREME COMMANDER:

/s/ Harold Fair,
/t/ HAROLD FAIR,
Lt. Colonel, A.G.D.,
Asst Adjutant General.

22 September 1945

二　所要措置ヲ講スルコト内外ノ情勢ニ鑑ミ大局上是非共必要ナリト信セラル

（欄外記入）

（欄外記入）
本件スキャピンはCLCOのファイル中に見当らず、日本政府側に於て受領したか否か不明である、日本連絡部土屋参事官を通じAGにて調べて貰つた結果、AG側のレコードには日本政府に渡したことになっている趣である（本コピーは最近特財一課にて先方から入手したもの）1949年2月26日（吉岡印）

159

41 ラジオ放送の規範に関する指令

昭和20年9月22日 連合国最高司令官総司令部より 日本政府宛

OFFICE OF THE SUPREME COMMANDER
FOR THE ALLIED POWERS

AG 000.77 (22 Sep 45) CI
SCAPIN 43

22 September 1945

MEMORANDUM FOR: THE IMPERIAL JAPANESE GOVERNMENT.

THROUGH: Central Liaison Office, Tokyo.

SUBJECT: Radio Code for Japan.

1. News Broadcasts

a. Newscasts must adhere strictly to the truth.

b. Nothing shall be broadcast which might, directly or indirectly, disturb public tranquillity.

c. There shall be no false or destructive criticism of the Allied Powers.

d. There shall be no destructive criticism of the Allied Forces of Occupation and nothing which might invite mistrust or resentment of those troops.

e. No announcement shall be made concerning movement of Allied troops unless such movements have been officially released.

f. Newscasts must be factual and completely devoid of editorial opinion.

g. Newscasts shall not be colored to conform to any propaganda line.

h. Minor details of a newscast must not be over-emphasized to stress or develop any propaganda line.

i. No newscast shall be distorted by the omission of pertinent facts or details.

j. Presentation of news items in newscasts shall not be so arranged as to give undue prominence to an item for the purpose of establishing or developing any propaganda line.

k. News commentary, analysis and interpreting of the news shall strictly conform to the above require-

1　降伏文書調印と初期占領政策への対応（昭和20年9月～10月）

ments.

2. <u>Entertainment Programs</u>

 Programs of entertainment which include plays, skits, dramatizations, poetry, variety shows, comedy, etc. shall conform to the requirements set forth in paragraph 1-A on News broadcasts with particular emphasis on the following:

a. Themes shall not be used which may be construed as fostering any propaganda line.

b. Themes shall not be used which, directly or indirectly disparage the Armed Forces or peoples of the Allied Powers; nor will themes be permitted which would tend, directly or indirectly to ridicule those Allied Forces and peoples.

3. <u>Programs of Information and Education</u>

 Programs of Information and Education, which include lectures and talks on subjects such as agriculture, forestry, mining, banking, etc.; lectures and talks on subjects such as history and geography; announcements of an informative nature from governmental agencies; and other allied types of programs, shall conform to the following:

a. Material shall be strictly factual and all interpreting and editorializing shall be founded in fact.

b. Material shall be free from any propagandizing.

c. Remarks or statements that would tend to disturb public tranquillity are prohibited.

d. Material shall not be used which can be construed as detrimental to relationships between Allied Powers, or which places any one of the Allied Powers in disrepute.

4. <u>Commercial Programs</u>

 In the event that commercial firms use the radio for advertising purposes, the script prepared by these firms shall conform strictly to the policies set forth above.

FOR THE SUPREME COMMANDER:

HAROLD FAIR,

Lt. Col., A.G.D.,

42

昭和20年9月22日　連合国最高司令官総司令部より
日本政府宛

金銀等の輸出入統制に関する指令

OFFICE OF THE SUPREME COMMANDER
FOR THE ALLIED POWERS
APO 500
22 September 1945

AG 091.3 (22 Sep 45) ESS
SCAPIN 44

MEMORANDUM FOR: The Imperial Japanese Government.

THROUGH: Central Liaison Office, Tokyo.

SUBJECT: Controls over exports and imports of Securities and financial instruments.

1. The Imperial Japanese Government will immediately make such amendments to its laws, and will take such other action as may be required, to prevent and prohibit, except pursuant to the permission of the Ministry of Finance, the exportation or withdrawal from Japan to any foreign country, or the importation into Japan from any foreign country, of any of the following:

(a) Gold or silver coin;

(b) Gold, silver or platinum bullion or alloy thereof in bullion form;

(c) Currency and securities;

(d) Checks, drafts, bills of exchange, promissory notes, payment instructions, transfer orders, or other financial instruments;

(e) Powers of attorney, proxies, or other authorizations or instructions to effect financial or property transactions within or outside of Japan;

(f) Any other evidence of indebtedness or evidence of ownership of property not specifically enumerated above.

2. No exportation or importation specified in the foregoing paragraph will be permitted by the Ministry of Finance without the prior approval of this Headquarters.

3. Six copies of the applicable laws, amended to comply with the provisions of the foregoing, shall be furnished to this

Asst. Adjutant General.

162

1　降伏文書調印と初期占領政策への対応(昭和20年9月～10月)

43　昭和20年9月22日　金融取引の統制に関する指令
連合国最高司令官総司令部より　日本政府宛

OFFICE OF THE SUPREME COMMANDER
FOR THE ALLIED POWERS
APO 500
22 September 1945

AG 130. (22 Sep 45) ESS
SCAPIN 45

MEMORANDUM FOR: The Imperial Japanese Government.
THROUGH: Central Liaison Office, Tokyo.

SUBJECT: Control of Financial Transactions.

1. The Imperial Japanese Government will immediately make such amendments to its laws and will take such other action as may be required to prevent and prohibit, without the prior permission of the Ministry of Finance, all transactions involving any of the following:

(a) Gold or silver coins;

(b) Gold, silver, or platinum bullion, or alloy thereof in bullion form;

(c) External assets owned, or controlled, directly or indirectly, in whole or in part, by any person in Japan;

(d) Property in Japan which is, or on or since 7 December 1941, has been, owned or controlled directly or indirectly, in whole or in part, by any person outside of Japan;

(e) Transactions in foreign exchange.

2. Definitions of the terms used in this memorandum are set forth in Appendix A attached hereto.

3. No transaction specified in the foregoing will be per-

4. An acknowledgment of this directive is requested.

FOR THE SUPREME COMMANDER:

HAROLD FAIR,
Lt Colonel, A.G.D.,
Asst. Adjutant General.

Headquarters. Such copies shall contain the English and Japanese texts.

mitted by the Ministry of Finance without the prior approval of the Supreme Commander.

4. Six copies of all applicable laws, as amended to comply with the foregoing provisions, shall be furnished to the Supreme Commander. Such copies shall contain both the English and Japanese texts.

5. An acknowledgment of this memorandum is requested.

FOR THE SUPREME COMMANDER:

HAROLD FAIR,
Lt Colonel, A.G.D.,
Asst. Adjutant General.

1 Incl: Appendix "A" -
Definitions of terms.

GENERAL HEADQUARTERS
UNITED STATES ARMY FORCES, PACIFIC

22 September 1945

APPENDIX A
DEFINITIONS

1. The term "laws" shall include, but not by way of limitation laws, decrees, ordinances, regulations and other enactments.

2. The term "person" shall include any individual, partnership, association, corporation, or other organization, and any government, including political subdivisions, agencies, or instrumentalities thereof;

3. The term "transaction" shall include any purchase, sale, acquisition, transfer, payment, withdrawal, disposition, importation, or exportation of, dealing in, or exercising any right, power, or privilege with respect to, any property.

4. The term "property" shall include money, checks, drafts, bullion, bank deposits, savings accounts, any debts, indebtedness or obligations, financial securities commonly dealt in by bankers, brokers and investment houses, notes, debentures, stocks, bonds, coupons, bankers' acceptances, mortgages, pledges, liens or other right in the nature of security, warehouse receipts, bills of lading, trust receipts, bills of sale, any other evidences of title, ownership, or indebtedness, goods, wares merchandise, chattels, stocks on hand, ships, goods on ships, real estate mortgages, ven-

164

1 降伏文書調印と初期占領政策への対応（昭和20年9月～10月）

dors sales agreements, land contracts, real estate and any interest therein, leaseholds, ground rents, options, negotiable instruments, trade acceptances, royalties, book accounts, accounts receivable, judgments, patents, trademarks, copyrights, contracts or licenses affecting or involving patents, trademarks or copyrights, insurance policies, safe deposit boxes and their contents, annuities, pooling agreements, contracts of any nature whatsoever, etcetera.

5. The term "transactions in foreign exchange" shall include, but not by way of limitation, any transaction involving any foreign currency, any payment or transfer to or from any foreign country, any transfer of credit, or payment of an obligation expressed in terms of a foreign currency, any purchase, sale, transfer or other dealing in any foreign currency, any financial or property transaction between a person in Japan and a person outside of Japan, whether or not expressed in terms of any foreign currency, and any transaction involving any obligation owed by any person in Japan to any person outside of Japan or owed by any person outside of Japan to any person in Japan.

6. The term "external assets" shall include, but not by way of limitation:

(1) Any property physically situated outside of Japan;

(2) Any claims, demands, bank deposits, savings accounts, and credits which are the obligations of persons outside of Japan;

(3) Any securities, checks, drafts, notes, receipts, insurance policies, or other evidences of ownership or indebtedness issued by, or which are the obligation of, any person outside of Japan;

(4) Any copyright, patents or trademarks, issued by any country other than Japan, and any contracts or licenses relating thereto;

(5) Any currency except supplemental yen currency, type "B", Bank of Japan notes and Japanese state notes and coins.

---

44 昭和20年9月22日　在ポルトガル森島公使より吉田外務大臣宛（電報）

連合国の対日処理方針に関する報道振り報告

45 昭和20年9月24日　連合国最高司令官総司令部より日本政府宛

新聞への政府統制排除に関する指令

SCAPIN 51

AG 000.76 (24 Sep 45) CI

MEMORANDUM FOR: IMPERIAL JAPANESE GOVERNMENT.

THROUGH: Central Liaison Office, Tokyo.

SUBJECT: Disassociation of Press from Government.

1. In order further to encourage liberal tendencies in Japan and establish free access to the news sources of the world, steps will be taken by the Japanese government forthwith to eliminate government-created barriers to dissemination of news and to remove itself from direct or indirect control of newspapers and news agencies.

2. No preferential treatment will be accorded to any news service now existing or which may be created. Foreign news ser-

---

リスボン　9月22日後11時59分発
本　省　9月24日前1時10分着

第三六九號

一、十九日華府發新聞電ハ陸海外三省ノ決定ニ基キ「マッカーサー」ニ對シ重工業ノ廢止ニ依ル平和産業ヘノ轉換、本件履行ニ對スル監督ノ強化、言論集會ノ自由及勞働組合組織ヲ害スル法規ノ廢止、政官界ニ於ケル實業界要人ノ引退ヲ命シタル旨ヲ傳ヘ右政策ノ決定ハ米政府ノ手ニ在ルコトヲ警告セルモノニシテ米政府ノ對日處理方針ハ強硬ニナルモノト報シ居レリ

二、九月十七日「クロニクル」所載輿論觀測所ノ調ヘニ依レハ　陛下ノ御退位ヲ可トスルモノ六割七分、否トスルモノ二割二分意見ナキモノ一割一分ナル最近着ノ米紙ハ日本降服ノ際提示セル　陛下ノ大權ニ關スル條件ニ付テハ米政界ノ意見ハ贊否半ハシ居ル旨報シ居レリ尚二十日東京發特電ハ　陛下ノ御退位ニ關スル噂乃至觀測ヲ傳ヘ甚タシキハ現ニ日米間ニ具體的話合アル旨ヲ傳フ

三、「マッカーサー」ハ記者ニ對シ　陛下ハ日本軍ノ解體迄御在位ノ筈ナリト聲明セル旨報セラル

1　降伏文書調印と初期占領政策への対応（昭和20年9月～10月）

vices of all nations will be permitted to serve the press of Japan to the extent that press desires.

　3. All communications facilities under government control shall be equally available to all national and international news agencies so that distribution of news within the Japanese home islands will not be the special privilege of one controlled organization.

　4. The government will rescind its prohibition on reception of incoming wireless telegrams (foreign news) by any agency except the Ministry of Communications. Interception by any agency of radio news broadcast by the United Nations as a public service will be permitted. The property rights of news transmitted by recognized press services will be observed.

　5. The present system of distribution of news within the home islands will be permitted under strict censorship until such time as private enterprise creates acceptable substitutes for the present monopoly.

　　　FOR THE SUPREME COMMANDER:

　　　　　R. U. Bolling

　　　　　　for HAROLD FAIR,
　　　　　　　Lt Colonel, A.G.D.,
　　　　　　　Asst. Adjutant General.

46　一般市民が所有する銃器刀剣類の回収に関する電信指令

昭和20年9月24日　連合国最高司令官総司令部より　日本政府宛

OFFICE OF THE SUPREME COMMANDER

FOR THE ALLIED POWERS

OPNL PRIORITY

SIGNAL CORPS MESSAGE　GC-P ADV　BWB/hrw

24 September 1945

FROM: THE SUPREME COMMANDER FOR THE ALLIED POWERS
TO: IMPERIAL JAPANESE GOVERNMENT

　1. Reference your CLO No. 73, dated 15 September 1945, it is noted that you report that your police authorities can collect revolvers and rifles in possession of civilian whenever necessary, and that these same authorities have already commenced the col-

lection of privately owned swords, except those having particular value as objects of art. In this connection you are now further directed, as follows: (ZAX-5981) –

a. All revolvers and rifles in possession of the civilian population shall be collected without delay.

b. Collection of swords in possession of the civilian population shall be continued and promptly completed. As regards swords considered to be objects of art, such distinction in this matter is approved but this designation shall only be applied in case the swords are actually objects of art and are in the hands of bona-fide civilians, as contrasted with demobilized members of the military services.

2. Regarding your request that private hunting guns be retained in the hands of the civilian population this is approved under the following conditions.

a. Licenses for retention of hunting guns shall be granted by the proper authorities only to persons who actually require such guns in order to acquire meat, hides, and skins, or to destroy harmful birds and beasts.

b. It shall be clearly explained to all persons granted such license under the regulations, that he will be held personally responsible in case of any deception in connection with the issuance of the license.

3. Further instructions covering in detail the subject of collection, delivery and disposition of civilian arms will be issued at a later date.

B. M. FITCH,
Brigadier General US Army,
Adjutant General.

APPROVED BY:
W. E. Chambers,
Brig. General, U.S. Army
Acting Asst. Chief of Staff, G-3

47 **日本軍から引き渡される軍需品の再交付に関する指令**
昭和20年9月24日 連合国最高司令官総司令部より 日本政府宛

1　降伏文書調印と初期占領政策への対応（昭和20年9月〜10月）

付記1　昭和二十年九月二十二日、終戦連絡中央事務局作成
［陸海軍軍需品引渡シニ關スル件］
二　作成日不明、外務省作成
［軍需品ノ引渡、引受ニ關スル日本及聯合側代表會談ノ概要］

OFFICE OF THE SUPREME COMMANDER
FOR THE ALLIED POWERS

24 September 1945

AG 402.5 (24 Sep 45) GD
SCAPIN 53
MEMORANDUM FOR: IMPERIAL JAPANESE GOVERNMENT
THROUGH: Central Liaison Office, Tokyo
SUBJECT: Materials, Supplies, and Equipment Received and to be Received from the Japanese Armed Forces.

　1. In furtherance of paragraph VI, General Order No. 1, dated 2 September 1945, it is desired that the Imperial Japanese Government take immediate steps to prepare to turn over on demand to the Commanding Generals, Sixth and Eighth United States Armies, XXIV Corps, and Commanders, Fifth and Seventh Fleets, all arms, ammunition, explosives, military equipment, stores, and supplies and other implements of war of all kinds and any equipment or other property belonging to, used by, or intended for use by the Japanese armed forces or any members thereof in connection with their operations. Japanese armed forces include all Japanese and Japanese controlled land, sea, and air forces and military and para-military organizations, formations, or units and their auxiliaries including Civilian Volunteer Corps wherever they may be located.

　2. United States Occupation Force Commanders have been directed to destroy all equipment which is essentially or exclusively for use in war or warlike exercises and which is not suitable for peacetime civilian uses. After operational requirements of Occupation Forces have been met, equipment and supplies of the Japanese armed forces which are not essentially for war or warlike exercises, including scrap from implements of war destroyed, are to be returned to the Japanese Government except that in Korea.

　3. The Home Ministry of the Imperial Japanese Govern-

ment is hereby designated as the official agency to receive and account for such supplies, materials and equipment of the Japanese armed forces as are being returned to your control.

4. In order to administer these transactions, it is desired that the Imperial Japanese Government take the following action:

a. Responsible Japanese Army and Navy Commanders will prepare inventories by location (generally corresponding to points at which the material is being assembled for turn over to the United States Occupation Forces) of all supplies, materials, and equipment in their possession. These inventories will be made available upon call to United States Occupational Force Commanders.

b. The Home Ministry of the Imperial Japanese Government will send representatives to the Commanding Generals, Sixth and Eighth United States Armies and Commander, Fifth Fleet, for the purpose of receiving supplies, materials, and equipment being returned to the Japanese Government. Sufficient personnel will be provided to accept these items at the locations where turned over by the Japanese armed forces.

c. The Home Ministry of the Imperial Japanese Government will maintain records of all property so received and account for this property in such form that the disposition of all supplies, materials, and equipment may be traced to the ultimate consumer. These records will be made available on call to the Supreme Commander for the Allied Powers, the United States Occupational Force Commanders, or authorized representatives.

5. You are informed that the supplies, materials, and equipment returned to your Government are for the purpose of civilian relief, and for use towards restoration of Japanese civil economy to the extent that it can provide the essentials of food, clothing, and shelter for the Japanese civilian population. The use of these supplies, materials, and equipment for any purposes other than the above is expressly forbidden.

FOR THE SUPREME COMMANDER:

HAROLD FAIR,
Lt. Col., A.G.D.,
Asst. Adjutant General

(Copy furnished Lt Gen Arisuye, Chairman, Liaison Committee,

1　降伏文書調印と初期占領政策への対応（昭和20年9月～10月）

Tokyo for Imperial Japanese Army and Navy）

（付記一）

陸海軍軍需品引渡シニ關スル件（二〇・九・二二）

一、二十二日午前十時求メニ依リ岡崎長官「イーストウッド」少將ヲ往訪セリ。折カラ有末中將會談中ナリシガ同中將ヲモ同席セシメタル上左ノ通リ述ベタリ。

（イ）米側ハ大體十月末迄ニ日本陸海軍ノ武器、彈藥、軍需品等ノ引渡ヲ受クル筈ナルガ、今般其ノ大部分ヲ日本政府ニ引渡スコトトセリ。

（ロ）右ノ中食糧、醫藥品、寢具等ハ之ヲ救濟事業ニ使用セラレ度、其ノ他ノ物資（「スクラップ」等ヲモ含ム）ハ之ヲ有效ニ使用セラレ差支ナシ。

（ハ）右引渡ヲ受クル官廳ハ混亂ヲ避クル爲一省又ハ一局トシ度、至急之ヲ決定シ通知アリ度シ。

（ニ）本件物資ガ闇ニ流レ、又ハ私腹ヲ肥ス事ナキヤウ充分注意アリ度、米國ニ於テモ其ノ行先ハ嚴重ニ「チェック」スル考ナリ。

（ホ）本件ニ關シ新聞發表等ハ當分之ヲ爲サザルヲ可トス。又發表スル場合ハ事前ニ米側ト協議シ、其ノ承諾ヲ得テ日米同時ニ之ヲ行フコトトシ度シ。

二、尚岡崎長官ノ質問ニ答ヘ

（イ）引渡ハ現在物資集積セラレ居ル場所ニ於テ之ヲ行フ（日本軍側提出ノ地圖ヲ示シ其ノ場所ノ非常ニ多キコトヲ説明セリ。）

（ロ）引渡ハ一齊ニ一行フニ非ズシテ順次ニ之ヲ爲ス。

（ハ）引渡ハ第八軍、第六軍ニ於テ實施スルニ付日本側ハ此等司令部ト實施ニ付打合ヲ遂グル必要アリ。

（ニ）陸海軍省ニ引渡ス事ハ希望セズ。

（ホ）米側ハ大砲其他若干ノ物ハ取除キ米國ニ記念品トシテ送附スル考ナルガ、殘リノ物ハ殆ド全部日本側ニ引渡ス意向ナリ。

三、二十二日午後終戰處理會議幹事會ニ於テ岡崎ヨリ右ノ次第ヲ報告シ、其ノ結果引渡ハ内務省ニテ引受クルコト最適ナリトノ結論ニ達シ、直ニ内務次官ヲ招致シ右ノ次第ヲ傳ヘタリ。（尚以上二、及三ノ外務大臣ニ報告シタルガ大臣ハ本件ヲ池田正彬氏ニ報告シ、其ノ指示ヲモ求ムベキ旨命ゼラレタルモ、池田氏ハ大磯ニ病臥中ノ爲、連

絡ノ時間ナク、書記官長ト協議シタル結果以上ノ如キ決定ヲ見タル次第ナリ。）

（付記二）

軍需品ノ引渡、引受ニ關スル日本及聯合側代表會談ノ概要

九月二十四日附聯合軍最高司令部覺書「日本軍隊ヨリ受領シ且受領スヘキ軍需資材、補給品及設備ニ關スル件」ニ基ク軍需品ノ引渡、引受ニ關シ同二十七日日本政府及陸海軍代表ト聯合軍最高司令部參謀部補給部（GIV）長「イーストウッド」准將トノ間ニ質疑應答行ハレタル處其ノ要旨左ノ通リ

尚日本政府側ヨリ大島内務省調査部長、武内中央連絡事務局第二部長、加藤内務書記官、陸軍側ヨリ有末中將、海軍側ヨリ横山少將出席シ聯合軍側ハ「イーストウッド」ノ他「ハッチンソン」大佐出席セリ

(一) 米第六軍、第八軍及米第五艦隊各指揮官ニ對スル内務省代表ノ派遣ハ京都ニ十月一日午前十時、横濱及横須賀ニハ夫々九月二十九日午前十時各指揮官ト會見シ得ルガ如

ク之ヲ行フ右代表者ノ氏名ハ京都ニ對シ大森氏ヲ派遣スル以外ハ未定ナルヲ以テ決定次第之ノ通知シ聯合軍最高司令部ヨリ各地指揮官ニ電報ス（二十八日朝全代表氏名連絡濟）

(二) 現地指揮官トノ連絡ノ爲内務省ガ特ニ支部ヲ設置スル要アリヤ否ヤニ關シテハ現地ニ於ケル軍需品ノ引渡狀況等ヲ考量シ且現地指揮官トノ協議ニ依リ之ヲ決スルモノトスルモ横須賀ノ如ク海軍關係軍需品引渡ハ破壊セラルヘキモ多ク其ノ要ナキヤモ知レス

(三) 陸海軍解體後ノ治安維持ノ爲警察力強化ノ要アル處之ニ要スル武器ハ軍需品ノ破壊ニ際シ特別ノ考慮ヲ拂フモ機關銃ノ如キ其ノ所有ハ許可困難ナルヤモ知レス尚内務省ハ右ノ目的ノ爲要スル武器彈藥ノ數量ヲ直チニ提出スル要アリ（二、三日中ニ提出スヘキ旨答フ）

(四) 水上警察ノ強化ニ要スル船艇モ亦軍需品ノ引渡ノ際シ十分ニ考慮セラルヘシ

(五) 軍需品ノ引渡、引受前後ノ保管ノ爲ニハ多數ノ人員ヲ要シ我警察力ノミヲ以テシテハ微弱ニ過クルヲ以テ現ニ陸海軍力之力警備ニ充テ居ル人員ヲ内務省ニ職員トシテ利

1 降伏文書調印と初期占領政策への対応（昭和20年9月～10月）

(六) 引受軍需品ノ記録ハ必シモ内務省ニ於テ之ヲ行フ要ナク地方縣廳ヲシテ行ハシムルコトヲ得ルモ内務省ハ要求アリ次第常ニ其ノ記録ヲ統一シ聯合軍側ニ供シ得ルコトヲ要ス

(七) 軍需品ノ引渡、引受ノ行動ハ九月二十六日附聯合軍最高司令部覺書ニテ其ノ公表禁止ヲ解カレタルモ右事實ノ發表方法ハ米國内ニ於ケル反響等モアリ政策問題ナルヲ以テ追テ何分ノ指示アルヘク更ニ軍需品ノ引渡、引受ノ細目ノ事實ノ發表ニ關シテハ現地指揮官ノ裁量ニ依リ之ヲ禁止スルコトモアリ得ヘシ

（註）本件ニ關シテハ會談終了後ノ陸、海、内ノ打合セノ席上陸軍側ヨリ當分發表ヲ差控フヘキ旨ノ提案アリ内務省側ハ之ニ對シ右ノ事實ノ發表ヲ全面的ニ見合スコトハ不可能ナルヘキモ其ノ發表方法ニ關シテハ米國内輿論ニ對スル反響ヲ考慮シ聯合軍側ノ特別ノ恩惠ナルコトヲ強調スルノ餘リ却ツテ逆効果ヲ來ササル樣嚴ニ注意スヘキ旨述フル所アリタリ

用スルコトトシ差支ナシ、聯合軍側モ之カ保全ニ付協力スルコトアルヘシ

(八) 米第八、第六軍等ニ對シテハ日本ニ對スル覺書内容ヨリ更ニ詳細ナル豫定表カ示サレアルモ右ハ軍機ナルヲ以テ之ヲ日本側ニ與ヘ得ス

(九) 引渡品目中ニハ施設（土地、建造物、製造、修理工場、工作機械等）ヲ含ミ equipment ナル語ハ之等ノ一切ノモノヲ意味スルモ先ツ第一、二ハ之等ノ中ニアル資材、補給品等ノ引渡ヲ完了セシメ次テ建造物、工場等ノ引渡ヲ實施スル手順ナリ

(十) 聯合軍ニテ破壊スルコトナク米本國ニ持チ歸ルモノト然ラサルモノトニ關シテハ大體ノ計畫ハ既ニ樹テラレアリ大砲（artillery）ハ概ネ記念品トシテ米本國ニ持チ歸ル方針ナルモ要塞砲ノ如キハ破壊スヘシ

(十一) 引渡、引受方法ハ現地軍指揮官ノ指示ニ依リ各軍需品集積所ニ於テ先ツ民需ニ振向ケ得ルモノト然ラサルモノノ區別シ後者ニ關シテハ之ヲ破壊乃至本國ニ持チ歸ルモノトニ分チ破壊セラレタル後民需ニ振向ケ得ルモノハ再ヒ嚮ニ區別セラレタル民需用物資ノ中ニ加ヘ之ヲ内務省ニ引受保管セシムルガ如クス右ノ細目ノ計畫ハ現地ニ於テ内務省（軍）代表ニ對シ時間ノ餘裕ヲ以テ指示スベキモ現

(十二)破壞ノ方法ハ日本軍ヨリ既ニ連絡濟ノモノヲ考慮シテ行フベキモ必ズシモ之ニ從ハズ小銃ノ如キハ石油ヲ用ヒテ之ヲ燒却シ彈藥ハ海中ニ投ズル等完全ナル破壞ヲ期スベシ

(十三)破壞ヲ實施スルハ日本側ナルモ(聯合軍之ニ協力ス)之ヲ命ズルハ現地各指揮官ナリ破壞ニ要スル勞力ハ陸、海、内及地方廳ノ協議ニ基キ之ヲ都合スベク、武器、彈藥ノ取扱ニ關シ熟練者ヲ要スルニ於テハ復員人トシテ之ニ從事スルモ差支ナシ軍人ト雖モ復員後民間人トシテ之ニ從事スルコトヲ妨ゲズ

(註)本會談後ノ打合セニ於テ軍人ヲ民間人ノ資格ニ於テ内務省ニ參加セシメ軍需品ノ引渡、引受ニ協力セシムルモ本件ハ成ル可ク聯合側ニ目立タサル樣行フベシトノ意見ノ開陳アリタリ

(十四)引渡、引受ノ際シ日本軍ヨリ提出ノ系統圖ニ依レバ衣服、食糧、醫療、獸醫、工作等各廠每ニ軍需品集積所アル處軍ノ帳簿ニ依リ實施スルヲ妨ゲズ

(註)陸、海、内ノ打合ニ於テ軍需品ノ集積所ハ多數ニ上リ之等ヲ圖示セルモノヲ陸、海ヨリ夫々内務側ニ

提供スルコトニ決セリ

(十五)引渡ハ十月中ニ終了スベシ

(十六)米第八軍、第六軍ハ引渡ノ完了迄ノ責任ヲ有ス

(十七)米第五艦隊ノ管轄ハ明確ナラザルモ奥地ニ於テ海軍需品ノ引渡引受ヲ行フ際米第八、第六軍指揮官代表ガ之ニ參加シ米陸海共當ルト雖モ米第五艦隊指揮官ニ於テ海軍共管ノ形式ヲトルベシ

(十八)掃海及外地ヨリ復員輸送ニ從事スル海軍艦艇乘リ組員ニ對スル衣糧等及之等艦艇ノ燃料ニ關シテハ米第五艦隊ヨリ直接支給セラルルカ又ハ内務省ノ引受分ヨリ之ヲ受クルカ何レニセヨ考慮セラルベシ但シ内務省ノ引受分ハ飽ク迄一般民間人ニシテ困窮シ居レル者及南方等ヨリ裸ノ近キ狀態ニテ歸還スル者ニ對シ優先的ニ頒ケ與ヘラルベキ性質ノモノニシテ軍人ハ靴、衣服等ニセヨ一般民間人ニ比シ遙カニ優レタルモノヲ所持シアル事實ニ鑑ミ優先スベキニアラズ

(註)陸、海、内ノ打合席上陸軍側ヨリ内務省引受品分配ニ當リ特ニ外地ヨリノ歸還者ニ對スル分ヲ別ニシ置クカ其ノ他適當ナル方法ヲ講ジ所謂早イ者勝チニ

地到着後迄ニ計畫表ヲ與ヘ得ルヤハ疑問ナリ

1　降伏文書調印と初期占領政策への対応（昭和20年9月～10月）

48

ロンドン外相会議における極東問題に関するソ連の提案について

昭和20年9月26日　在スウェーデン岡本公使より吉田外務大臣宛（電報）

ストックホルム　9月26日後4時40分発
本　省　9月27日後1時20分着

第五九八號

蘇聯ノ態度強硬且非妥協的ナル為各種問題ニ付事毎ニ行悩ミツツアル目下ノ倫敦外相會議ニ於テ「モロトフ」ノ軍政機關ノ一部トシテ聯合國委員會ヲ設置シ聯合國最高司令官ノ日本及太平洋地域ニ對スル政策決定ヲ援助セシムルコトヲ提案シテ英米ヲ愕カセタルカ「バーンズ」ハ歐洲問題ノミヲ論議スヘシトノ下ニ本會議ニ参加セルモノニシテ極東問題ノ専門家ヲ帯同シ居ラストノ理由ニテ本問題ノ論議ヲ拒絶セル趣ニシテ本二十六日ノ各紙ハ蘇聯ノ右提案ハ「マックアーサー」ノ對日政策ニ對スル不満ヲ表明スルト

共ニ日本問題ニ關シ蘇聯ノ干渉ヲ排除セントスル米國ノ態度ニ反對シ蘇聯トシテ極東ニ於テモ種々要求ヲ提出スル意圖アルコトヲ示スモノト觀ラルト報シ居レリ曩ニモ電報セル通リ蘇聯ノ態度ハ最モ危險ニシテ益々警戒ヲ要スルモノアリト思考ス

49

連合国の対日態度に関する観測報告

昭和20年9月26日　在ダブリン別府（節彌）総領事より吉田外務大臣宛（電報）

ダブリン　9月26日後　発
本　省　10月2日前11時45分着

第一三二號

新聞報道ヲ綜合セル本官ノ印象御参考迄
一、本邦ニ對スル聯合國ノ現在ノ措置ハ素ヨリ「ポツダム」條項ニ準據スヘキ處聯合國一般民衆ハ勿論政治家連モ右「ポツダム」條項ヲ通讀タニセス單ニ戦勝者トシテ日本ヲ其ノ意ノ儘ニ處分シ得ルモノト誤解シ勝手ナ議論ヲ吐キ居レリ殊ニ無條件降伏ニ基ク獨逸ニ對スル措置ヲ同様日本ニモ適用セントスル簡単ナル見方ヲスル傾向アリ

ナラザル様要望スル所アリタリ

二、米進駐軍當局ハ現地ノ事情ニ即シ秩序ヲ維持シ事端ノ發生ヲ避ケント努メ居ルト思ハルルモ聯合國ノ本國ニ於テハ右一ノ如キ傾向及戰爭直後ノ對日復讐心（當國外務次官補ヨリノ特派員電報ハ概ネ事實報道ヲ主トスルニ例ヘハ英本國ノ新聞雜誌論調ハ反日熱頗ル強キノミナラス邦ヨリノ最近本官ト會談ノ際右復讐心ヲ指摘セリ）強ク本（「タイムズ」「ディリーテレグラフ」等然リ）日本ヲ意ノ儘ニセントスル氣持強シ

三、尚英米蘇佛等ハ歐洲及地中海ニ於ケル國際問題解決ノ為各自ノ極東ニ於ケル利害關係乃至對日政策ニ關スル主張ヲ讓歩スルヲ厭ハサルコトアルハ豫想セラレ右ハ蘇聯カ伊太利領「トリポリタニア」ノ委任統治ヲ要求スルニ際シ米國ノ太平洋ニ於ケル我委任統治島嶼ノ獲得ヲ指摘セリト傳ヘラルルニモ窺ハル

四、我方トシテハ敵味方相互ノ「ポツダム」條項ノ遵守ヲ堅持シ右一及二ノ如キ情勢ヲ念頭ニ置クト共ニ無責任ナル俗論ニ迷ハサルルコト無ク忍耐ヲ以テ結束ヲ圖リ苟クモ他國ヲシテ乘セシメス且出來得ル限リノ範圍ニテ本邦ノ實情ニ即シタル自主的政治體制ヲ樹立セラルルコト切望セ

昭和天皇・マッカーサー会談

昭和20年9月27日 昭和天皇 マッカーサー連合国最高司令官 会談

付 記 昭和二十年九月二十五日、萩原（徹）儀典課長作成「天皇陛下「マクアーサー」將軍御訪問ニ關シ米軍側ト打合次第」

「マッカーサー」元帥トノ御會見錄

昭和二十年九月二十七日午前十時

於在京米國大使館

石渡宮内大臣、藤田侍從長、德大寺侍從

ラル

且左記二項ハ目下ノ急務ニアラサルヤト愚考ス
（イ）内政ノ一ト先ツ安定シタル上ハ臣下ノ内閣ヲシテ國體明徵及戰爭快癒ノ政務ヲ執ラシム
（ロ）對外的ニ主權國タルコトヲ徹底スル爲（岩波法律學小辭典五百二十八頁「主權國」參照）外務省ノ權限（終戰事務局ヲ含ム）ヲ内政上ナルヘク廣汎ニ擴大ス

1　降伏文書調印と初期占領政策への対応（昭和20年9月〜10月）

村山侍醫、筧行幸主務官、扈從

定刻米國大使館ニ御到着、玄關ヨリ「フェラーズ」准將ノ御先導ニテ館内ニ入ラセラレ、居室入口ニ於テ「マッカーサー」元帥御出迎申上グ。陛下ヨリ御握手ヲ賜ハレハ

「マ」本日ハ行幸ヲ賜リ光榮ニ存ジマス

陛下　御目ニカカリ大變嬉シク思ヒマス

元帥ノ御案内ニテ居室中央ニ立御、元帥其ノ向ツテ左側ニ立テ八米國軍寫眞師ハ寫眞三葉ヲ謹寫ス

更ニ元帥ノ御案内ニテ「ファイア、プレイス」ニ向ツテ左ノ椅子ニ陛下御着席アリ、元帥ハ右側ノ同様ナル椅子ニ着席ス。元帥ハ極メテ自由ナル態度ニテ

「マ」實際寫眞屋トイフノハ妙ナモノデパチヤヤ撮リマスガ、一枚カ二枚シカ出テ來マセン

陛下　永イ間熱帶ノ戰線ニ居ラレ御健康ハ如何デスカ

「マ」御蔭ヲ以テ極メテ壯健デ居リマス。私ノ熱帶生活ハモウ連續十年ニ及ヒマス

之ヨリ元帥ハ口調ヲ變ヘ、相當力強キ語調ヲ以テ約二十分ニ亘リ滔々ト陳述シタルガ其ノ要旨左ノ如シ（英語ノ性質ニ鑑ミ、此ノ部分ハ此處ニハ特ニ敬語ヲ省略シテ譯述ス）

「マ」戰爭手段ノ進歩、殊ニ強大ナル空軍力及原子爆彈ノ破壞力ハ筆紙ニ盡シ難イモノガアル、今後若シ戰爭カ起ルトスレバ其ノ際ハ勝者、敗者ノ論ナク齊シク破壞サレ盡シテ人類ノ絕滅ニ至ルテアラウ、現在ノ世界ニハ今猶憎惡ト復讐ノ混亂ヲ渦ヲ捲イテ居ルガ、世界ノ達見ノ士ハ宜シク此ノ混亂ヲ通ジテ遠キ將來ヲ達觀シ平和ノ政策ヲ以テ世界ヲ指導スルニ必要ガアル。

日本再建ノ途ハ困難ニ苦痛ニ充チテ居ルトト思フガ、夫レハ若シ日本ガ戰爭ヲ繼續スルコトニ依ツテ蒙ルベキ惨害ニ較ブレバ何テモ無イテアラウ、若シ日本ガ更ニ抗戰ヲ續ケテ居タナラバ日本全土ハ文字通リ殲滅シ何百萬トモ知レヌ人民ガ犠牲ニナツタデアラウ、自分ハラ日本ト相手ニ戰ツテ居ツタノデアルカラ日本ノ陸海軍ガ何ニ絕望的状態ニ在ツタカヲ充分知悉シテ居ル、終戰ニ當ツテノ陛下ノ御決意ハ國土ト人民ヲシテ測リ知レザル痛苦ヲ免レシメラレタ點ニ於テ誠ニ御英斷デアツタ。

世界ノ輿論ノ問題デアルガ、將兵ハ一旦終戰トナレバ普通ノ善イ人間ニナリ終ルノデアル。然シ其ノ背後ニハ戰爭ニ行ツタコトモ無イ幾百萬ノ人民ガ居テ憎惡ヤ復讐ノ

感情デ動イテ居ル、斯クシテ所謂輿論ガ簇出スルノデアルガ其ノ尖端ヲ行クモノガ新聞デアル、米國ノ輿論、英國ノ輿論、支那ノ輿論等々色々出テ來ルガ、「プレスノ自由」ハ今ヤ世界ノ趨勢トナッテ居ルノデ、其ノ取扱ハ仲々困難デアル。

陛下 此ノ戰爭ニ付テハ、自分トシテハ極力之ヲ避ケ度イ考デアリマシタガ戰爭トナルノ結果ヲ見マシタコトハ自分ノ最モ遺憾トスル所デアリマス。

「マ」陛下ガ平和ノ方向ニ持ッテ行ク爲御盡念アラセラレタ御胸中ハ自分ノ充分諒察申上グル所デアリマス。只一般ノ空氣ガ滔々トシテ或方向ニ向ヒツツアルトキ、別ノ方向ニ向ッテ之ヲ導クコトハ一人ノ力ヲ以テハ爲シ難イコトデアリマス。恐ラク最後ノ判斷ハ 陛下モ自分モ世ヲ去ッタ後、後世ノ歷史家及輿論ニ依テ下サルルヲ俟ツ他ナイデアリマシャウ。

陛下 私モ日本國民モ敗戰ノ事實ヲ充分認識シテ居ルコトハ申ス迄モアリマセン、今後ハ平和ノ基礎ノ上ニ新日本ヲ建設スル爲私トシテモ出來ル限リノカヲ盡シ度イト思ヒマス。

「マ」夫レハ崇高ナ御心持デアリマス、私モ同ジ氣持デアリマス。

陛下「ポツダム」宣言ヲ正確ニ履行シタイト考ヘテ居リマスコトハ先日侍從長ヲ通ジ閣下ニ御話シタ通リデアリマス。

「マ」終戰後 陛下ノ政府ハ誠ニ多忙ノ中ニ不拘凡ユル命令ヲ一々忠實ニ實行シテ居ス所ガ無イコト、又幾多ノ有能ナ官吏ガ着々任務ヲ遂行シテ居ルコトハ賞讚ニ値スル所デアリマス。

又聖斷一度下ッテ日本ノ軍隊モ日本ノ國民モ總テ整然之ニ從ッタ見事ナ有樣ハ是卽チ御稜威ノ然ラシムル所デアリマシテ、世界何レノ國ノ元首ト雖及バザル所デアリマス。之ハ今後ノ事態ニ處スルニ當リ 陛下ノ御氣持ヲ強ク力付ケテ然ルベキコトト存ジマス。

陛下程日本ヲ知リ日本ノ國民ヲ知ル者ハ他ニ御座イマセヌ、從テ今後 陛下ニ於カレ何等御意見乃至御氣附ノ點 opinions and advice モ御座イマセバ、侍從長其ノ他然ルベキ人ヲ通ジ御申聞ケ下サル樣御願ヒ致シマス、夫レハ私ノ參考トシテ特ニ有難ク存ズル

1　降伏文書調印と初期占領政策への対応（昭和20年9月～10月）

所デ御座イマス。勿論總テ私限リノ心得トシテ他ニ洩ラスガ如キコトハ御座イマセンカラ、何時タリトモ又如何ナル事デアラウト隨時御申聞ケ願ヒ度イト存ジマス。

陛下　閣下ノ使命ハ東亞ノ復興即チ其ノ安定及繁榮ヲ齎シ以テ世界平和ニ寄與スルニ在ルコトト思ヒマスガ、此ノ重大ナル使命達成ノ御成功ヲ祈リマス。

「マ」　夫レ（東亞ノ復興云々）ハ正ニ私ノ念願トスル所デアリマス。只私ヨリ上ノ權威（オーソリティ）ガ有ッテ私ハソレニ使ハレル出先（エイジェンシー）ニ過ギナイノデアリマス。私自身ガ其ノ權威デアレバト言フ氣持ガ致シマス。

陛下　閣下ノ指揮下ノ部隊ニ依ル日本ノ占領ガ何等ノ不祥事無ク行ハレタコトヲ滿足ニ存ジテ居リマス。此ノ點ニ於テモ今後共閣下ノ御盡力ニ俟ツ所大ナルモノガアルト存ジマス。

「マ」　私ノ部下ニハ苛烈ナ戰鬪ヲ經テ來タ兵士ガ多勢居リマシテ、戰爭直後ノ例トシテ上官ノ指示ニ背キ事件ヲ惹起スル者ガ間々居リマスガ、此ノ種事件ヲ最小限ニスル爲ニハ充分努力スルツモリデアリマス。

陛下　以前ニモ日本ニ御出ニナツタ樣ニ聞イテ居リマスガ、

何時頃デシタカ。

「マ」　私ハ東洋トノ關係ハモウ四十五年ニナリマス。最初ハ一九〇五年日露戰爭當時デ、父ガ大山元帥ノ下ニ從軍シ私ハ父ノ副官トシテ參リマシタ。其ノ關係デ大山元帥、兒玉元帥、乃木大將、黑木大將等數々ノ日本ノ偉大ナル人物ヲ知ッテ居リマス。黑木大將ガ米國ニ派遣セラレタトキハ私ハ父ト共ニ政府ノ命ヲ受ケテ案內ヲ致シマシタ、又「タウンセンド、ハリス」祭ニ出羽海軍大將ガ派遣セラレマシタ際ニモ接伴致シマシタ。此ノ前東京ニ參リマシタトキハ比島ノ「ケソン」大統領ト一緒ニ御座イマシテ此ノ米國大使館ニ居リマシタ。「ケソン」ガ謁見ヲ賜ハリマシタコトハ　陛下モ御記憶ノコトト存ジマス。ソレハ好ク覺エテ居リマス。

陛下　「ケソン」ハ肺ヲ病ンデ居リマシタ。戰爭勃發後比島ヲ去リ暫時豪洲ニ滯在ノ後米國ニ渡リマシタガ、病ジテ約一年前死去致シマシタ。「ケソン」ノ死ハ東洋ノ爲ニ大ナル損失ト存ジマス。彼ハ平和ノ士デアリ困難ナ事態ヲ穩ニ取纏メ得ル人物デアリマシタ。

陛下　夫人モ最近御到着ニナツタソウデアリマスガ、御元

氣ノコトト存ジマス。

「マ」御言葉有難ク存ジマス。又御花マデモ賜ハリ感激致シテ居リマス。實ハ七歳ニナル愚息モ參リマシテ「マニラ」ニ比ベテ此ノ氣候ヲ共ニ樂シンデ居リマス。愚息ハ近頃小サナ日本犬ヲ飼ヒ始メマシテ大悦ビデ御座イマス。

陛下 日本ノ秋ハヨイ氣候デアリマスカラ、夫人ノ爲ニモ亦永イ間酷熱ノ地ニ居ラレタ閣下ノ爲ニモ御氣持ノヨイコトト存ジマス。

「マ」有難ク存ジマス。日本ノ秋ニハ度々參リマシテ、其ノ好サハ充分存ジテ居リマス。只ココニ居リマスト周リノ荒廢ガ餘リヒドクテ昔ノ東京ノ氣分ハアリマセン。スコシ田舎ヘデモ車デ行ケバ破壞モ少ナク昔ノ懷シイ有様ニ接スルコトガ出來ルカモ知レマヌ(ヌカ)

陛下 日本ニ御滯在中モツト御會ヒスル機會モアルコトト存ジマスガ、御忙シイコトト思ヒマスカラ今日ハ之デ御別レシマス。

「マ」先刻モ申上ゲマシタ通リ今後何カ御意見ナリ御氣附ノ點モ御座イマシタナラバ、何時デモ御遠慮無ク御申聞ケ願ヒ度ク存ジマス。本日ハ行幸ヲ賜ハリ破格ノ光榮ト

存ジマス。

陛下ヨリ再ビ御握手ヲ賜ハリ、元帥ノ御案内ニテ控ヘノ間ニ玉歩ヲ進メ給ヒ、此處ニテ 陛下ヨリ元帥ニ對シ宮内大臣、侍従長、侍醫行幸主務官ヲ御紹介アリ、元帥夫々握手ヲ行ヒタル後玄關迄 陛下ヲ奉送ス。(此ノ間約三十七分。奥村謹記)

(付 記)

天皇陛下「マクアーサー」將軍御訪問ニ關シ米軍側ト打合次第

萩原儀典課長

九月二十五日午後四時岡崎終戰連絡事務局長官ト共ニ米軍司令部ニ「フエラース」準將ヲ往訪シ打合ノ結果ニ關シ書キ物一通リ打合ヲ遂ケ「フエラース」準將ノ意嚮ヲモ確メタル上再ヒ會見シタキ旨申出タルニ依リ午後六時再度往訪シタル處別紙ノ書キ物ヲ示シ更ニ打合ヲ遂ケタリ

以下ハ別紙ノ譯文ヲ記シ且「註」トシテ口頭ニテ打合セタル諸點乃至打合セノ經過ヲ記載セリ

1　降伏文書調印と初期占領政策への対応（昭和20年9月～10月）

記

一、時　日

陛下ハ九月二十七日木曜日午前十時米國大使館ニ御到着遊ハサル

二、鹵簿

鹵簿ハ「オートバイ」一臺及自動車五臺ヨリ成リ「オートバイ」及御警衞ノ乘車シ居ル第一車（前驅）及最後ノ車（後驅）大使館門前ニ於テ離脱シ第二、第三及第四ノミ大使館敷地內ニ入ル

陛下ハ侍從長ト共ニ第二車（御料車）ニ御乘リ遊ハサレコノ車カ大使館玄關ニ第一ニ到着ス

三、御到着

大使館玄關ニ於テ「フエラース」準將及「バウアー」大尉御出迎申上ケ　陛下及御通譯ヲ「マクアーサー」ノ所迄御案內申上ク

（註）「フエラース」準將及「バウアー」大尉ハ玄關前ノ階段ノ所ニ立チ居リ　陛下自動車ヨリ御下車ニナルヲ待チ敬禮シ「自分ハ『フエラー』準將テアリマス御案內申上ケマス」トノ意味ヲ述フ（右ハ通譯ヲ要セサルヘシ）

陛下御握手ヲ給ハレハ光榮ナリ大体「フエラース」カ　陛下ヲ御案內申上ケ（御通譯ハコレニ從フヲ要ス）「バウアー」カ宮內大臣以下ノ隨員ヲ案內スル形トナル

侍從、侍醫及行幸主任官ハ玄關ヲ入リタル所ノ廣間（ホール）又ハ其ノ隣ノ小書齋ニテ御待チスルコトニ打合セアリ

四、御會見

「マクアーサー」ハ客間（リビングルーム）ニ於テ　陛下ト御會見ス　一行ノ右以外ノ者ハ次ノ間（アンテルーム）ニ殘ル

（註）「マクアーサー」將軍ハ客間ノ入口（次ノ間トノ境）ノ邊ニテ　陛下ヲ御迎ヘシテ握手シ　陛下ト共ニ客間內ニ入ル（御通譯ノミ同行）

陛下ト「マクアーサー」ノ席ハ客間ノ「ファイヤープース」ヲ背ニシテ設ケアリ

次ノ間ニ殘留スルモノハ宮內大臣侍從長「フエラース」準將「バウアー」大尉ナリ

「フエラース」準將ノ話ニ依レハ客間ト次ノ間トノ間ニハ戸ヲ設ケアラス宮内大臣及侍從長ノオ待チシ居ル位置ハ　陛下ノ御座所ト餘リ離レ居ラス　陛下ノ御姿モ見エル筈ナリトノコトナリ（當初打合セニ際シテハ宮内大臣及侍從長カ侍立スルコトヲ希望スル旨ノ當方申出ヲ諒承シ居タルカ第二囘打合セニテ「マクアーサー」ノ希望ナリトテ右ノ通先方ヨリ申出タルモノナリ）

通譯ハ日本語英譯、英語和譯共ニ日本側通譯者（後藤式部官又ハ奥村參事官）ニ依リ行ハルルモノトス（第一囘打合セニ於テ米國側通譯「バウアー」大尉ヲモ用フル樣話合ヒタルモ「マクアーサー」ノ希望ナリトテ第二囘打合セノ際先方ヨリ訂正シ來レリ成ルヘク「インティメート」ナル形ニテ會見シ度キ「マクアーサー」ノ考ヘナルヤニ察セラル）

五、新聞發表

「マクアーサー」將軍及日本政府側双方ニ於テ御訪問終了後夫々新聞發表ヲ爲スモノトス

（註）米軍側ニテハ機密保持ニ十分注意スヘク目下ノ所

「マクアーサー」自身及「フエラース」準將以外ニ承知シ居ルモノナシ「バウアー」大尉及憲兵隊等ニモ當日ノ朝知ラスコトトスヘシト申シ居レリ

六、寫眞

米軍報導隊ノ一寫眞師カ　陛下及「マクアーサー」將軍ノ寫眞ヲ寫スコトトス

（註）寫眞師ハ一人、寫眞ハ一枚　陛下及「マクアーサー」將軍ノミノ寫眞ナリ寫眞ヲ發表スルヤ否ヤニ付テハ更ニ打合セヲ要ス

第一囘打合セニ於テ「フエラース」準將ヨリ　陛下ハ平素餘リ寫眞ヲ寫サシメラレサル樣承知シ居ルモ頗ル歴史的ナル會見ナルヲ以テ「マクアーサー」將軍カ希望スルカト考フル旨述ヘタルニ依リ式部長官打合ノ上第二囘打合ニ於テ同意ノ旨答ヘ置キタリ

七、御會見時間

御訪問ハ恐ラク十五分乃至三十分ヲ要スヘシ

（註）此ノ點ハ當方ヨリ先方ノ豫定ヲ尋ネタル處「フエラース」準將ハ全ク　陛下ノ御考ヘ次第ニシテ「マクアーサー」將軍ハ「頗ル打解ケテ且極メテ話シ易

1　降伏文書調印と初期占領政策への対応（昭和20年9月～10月）

八、御歸還

キ）態度ヲ採リ度キ考ナリト言ヒ居リ　陛下ノ御考
次ニテ何ヲ御話シニナリ何程ノ時間會談遊ハサ
ルモ御自由ナリト言ヒ居タルカ先ツ一應十五分乃至
三十分ト豫定シ置クコトトスヘシトテ斯ク記載セリ
其ノ際　陛下ヨリ軍装ヲ用ヒラレサルヘキ旨ヲ述ヘ置キタ
ル處第二囘會談ノ節「フェラース」準將ハ「其ノ旨「マクア
ーサー」將軍ニ報告セル處「マクアーサー」將軍ハ然ラハ
紳士對紳士ノ會見ナリト言ヒ居タリ」ト述ヘタリ
尚又御通路ノ交通整理乃至交通遮斷ニ付米軍ノ自動車等モ
盛ニ通ル所ナレハ米國憲兵モ協力アリタキ旨申入レタル處
「フェラース」準將ハ機密保持ノ爲當日朝ニ至リ警視廳内
ニ在ル米國憲兵隊「ホフマン」將軍ニ指令スヘキニ付警察
側ヨリ當日朝連絡アリ度キ旨述ヘタリ
右ニ關連シ第二囘打合ニ於テ「フェラース」準將ハ「マク
アーサー」將軍ニ話シタル處交通遮斷ハ米國ニ於テハ行フ
コトナク「マクアーサー」將軍自身モ日本ニ於テハルコト
ヲナシ居ラス米本國輿論ニ面白カラサル反響ヲ生スル虞ア
ルヲ以テ米國憲兵トシテハ交通整理ニ協力スルモ交通遮
斷ニハ協力シ難シトノ意嚮ナリト申出タリ
其ノ際「フェラース」ハ「マクアーサー」カ本國ノ對日輿
論ニ面白カラサルニ不拘日本國ノ爲ニ種々苦慮シ居ル次第ナ
ル旨ヲ洩シ居タリ

御料車ノ所迄御供スル筈ナリ
（註）「マクアーサー」將軍ハ會見ヲ終リ　陛下ト共ニ客
間ヨリ出テ來リ次ノ間ニ待チ居タル宮内大臣及侍從
長ニ握手スヘシ尤モ　陛下カ會談中適當ノ時期ニ又
ハ會談ノ終リニ隨員ヲ紹介スヘキ旨ヲ述ヘラレテ客
間ニ隨員ヲ呼ヒ入レラルルモ又ハ歸路ニ次ノ間ニテ
紹介セラルルモ御自由ナリト申シ居レリ

（以上）

尚右以外ニ何等儀式メキタルコト例ヘハ米國旗ニ對スル敬
禮トカ言フカ如キコトヲ期待シ居ラルルヤト確メタル處
「フェラース」準將ハ米國側トシテハ全然斯ル考ヘナク極
メテ打解ケタル會見トシ度ク「マクアーサー」將軍ハ二國

御別レ申上ケ「フェラース」準將及「バウアー」大尉カ
間ヨリ出テ來リ次ノ間ニ待チ居タル宮内大臣及侍從

ノ最高指揮官同士ノ打解ケタル會見ト考ヘ居ル旨述ヘ居タリ

51 昭和20年9月27日 連合国最高司令官総司令部より 日本政府宛

新聞および言論の制限撤廃に関する指令

OFFICE OF THE SUPREME COMMANDER
FOR THE ALLIED POWERS

AG 000.76 (27 Sep 45) CI

27 September 1945

SCAPIN 66

MEMORANDUM FOR: IMPERIAL JAPANESE GOVERNMENT

THROUGH: Central Liaison Office, Tokyo

SUBJECT: Further Steps toward Freedom of Press and Speech

1. The Japanese government forthwith will render inoperative the procedures for enforcement of peace-time and war-time restrictions on freedom of the press and freedom of communications.

2. Only such restrictions as are specifically approved by the Supreme Commander will be permitted in censorship of newspapers and other publications, wireless and trans-oceanic telephone, cable, internal telephone and telegraph, mail, motion pictures or any other form of the written or spoken word.

3. Pending repeal of laws imposing restrictions which have given the government complete control of all channels of expression of public opinion, their enforcement shall be suspended.

4. No punitive action shall be taken by the Japanese government against any newspaper or its publisher or employees for whatever policy or opinion it may express, unless ordered by the Supreme Commander. The power of the government to revoke permission to publish, to arrest without prior approval of the Supreme Commander, to impose fines on publications and to curtail paper supplies as a punishment for editorial comment shall not be exercised.

5. Compulsory organizations of publishers and writers will be discontinued.

6. No press bans will be issued by any government agency and no pressure, direct or indirect, will be exerted on any medium to compel it to conform to any editorial policy not its own.

7. Steps shall be taken to repeal such parts of existing peace-time and war-time laws as are inconsistent with the Sup-

1 　降伏文書調印と初期占領政策への対応（昭和20年9月〜10月）

reme Commander's directives of 10 September 1945 relating to dissemination of news, and of 24 September 1945 relating to association of press from government; subject laws including:

a. Shimbunshi-Ho
b. Kokka Sodoin-Ho
c. Shimbunshi-To-Keizai-Seigenrei
d. Shimbun-Jigyo-Rei
e. Genron, Shuppan, Shukai, Kessha To Rinji Torishimari-Ho
f. Genron, Shuppan, Shukai, Kessha To Rinji Torishimari-Ho Shiko Kisoku
g. Senji Keiji Tokubetsu-Ho
h. Kokubo Hoan-Ho
i. Gunki Hogo Ho
j. Fuon Bunsho Torishimari-Ho
k. Gunyo Shigen Himitsu Hogo Ho
l. Juyo Sangyo Dantai Rei Oyobi Juyo Sangyo Dantai Rei Shiko Kisoku

8. A report will be submitted to the Supreme Commander on the first and the sixteenth day of each month describing in detail the progressive steps taken by the Japanese government to comply with this order and the orders of 10 September and 24 September.

FOR THE SUPREME COMMANDER:

HAROLD FAIR,
Lt. Col., A.G.D.,
Asst. Adjutant General.

52

昭和20年9月28日　連合国最高司令官総司令部宛

地方総監府の廃止につき通報

付記　昭和二十年十一月一日付連合国最高司令官総司令部より日本政府宛覚書

　　　右承認の旨回答

To: Office of the Supreme Commander for the Allied Powers
From: Central Liaison Office
Subject: Abolishment of the Regional Government General

28 September 1945

C.L.O. No.97

付記

GENERAL HEADQUARTERS
SUPREME COMMANDER FOR THE ALLIED POWERS

1 November 1945

AG 091 (1 Nov 45) GS
SCAPIN 222

SUBJECT: Abolition of the Regional Governments General and Establishment of Regional Administrative Affairs Bureaus.

THROUGH: Central Liaison Office, Tokyo.

MEMORANDUM FOR: IMPERIAL JAPANESE GOVERNMENT.

The proposal of the Imperial Japanese Government to abolish the Regional Governments General and establish Regional Administrative Affairs Bureaus, as set forth in its memorandum of 28 September 1945, C.L.O. No. 97, on the above subject, is approved.

FOR THE SUPREME COMMANDER:

Tokyo.

This is to notify that the Imperial Japanese Government plans to abolish the Regional Government General in the early part of October.

The above Regional Government General was established in June of this year with the primary object of co-ordinating and controlling the various local administrations to cope with new developments arising in the war situation and its structure is purely wartime in nature. (The Regional Gov't General is a strictly bureaucratic structure and gives no provisions for autonomous local assemblies as existing in the prefectures, cities, towns and villages.) Consequently, the Imperial Japanese Government takes this opportunity to abolish this system.

To co-ordinate and adjust regional administration to meet peacetime needs the Imperial Japanese Government plans to establish a Regional Administration Office in a simplified form.

For the Director General
(T. Katsube)
Liaison Officer,
Central Liaison Office,

53 在外金融機関および戦時金融機関の閉鎖に関する指令

昭和20年9月30日　連合国最高司令官総司令部より　日本政府宛

OFFICE OF THE SUPREME COMMANDER
FOR THE ALLIED POWERS

30 September 1945

AG 091.3 (30 Sep 45) ESS
SCAPIN 74

MEMORANDUM FOR: IMPERIAL JAPANESE GOVERNMENT.
THROUGH: Central Liaison Office, Tokyo.
SUBJECT: Closing of Colonial and Foreign Banks and Special Wartime Institutions.

1. You will immediately close and not allow to reopen, except at the direction of this headquarters, the head offices, branches and agencies in Japan of the banks and other financial institutions enumerated in Inclosure 1, attached hereto.

2. You will immediately post signs on the premises declaring that the institutions are closed.

3. Guards will be posted at all the premises occupied by such institutions, and access to the premises will not be permitted except as directed by this headquarters.

4. Any books, records and papers of the institution which are not on the premises occupied by them will be taken into custody and delivered into the special custody of this headquarters.

5. You will impound all gold, silver, currency, securities, notes, mortgages, pledges and other assets of the institutions which are not located on the premises occupied by them.

6. You will take such action as is required to prevent and prohibit without the prior permission of the Ministry of Finance, any purchase, sale, transfer, withdrawal, or disposition of, or other transaction involving any assets of such institutions. No such transaction will be permitted by the Ministry of Finance without authorization of this headquarters.

H. W. ALLEN,
Colonel, A.G.D.,
Asst Adjutant General.

7. You will discharge and summarily remove from office the chairman of the board of directors, the president, the managing directors and the advisors of all institutions listed in Inclosure 1, and all other persons holding comparable posts in such institutions; and you will forbid them to enter into or to act for institutions with which they were associated. You will cancel the authority of all persons holding powers of attorney or signing authority and will not permit any authority or power to act on behalf of such institutions to be given to any other persons without the authorization of this headquarters. All the officers, directors and other officials of such institutions will remain available and will not change their address without the authorization of this headquarters.

8. a. You will safeguard and preserve, not remove or permit to be moved from their present location, any of the following:

(1) Any plates used for printing currency and stamps other than notes of the Bank of Japan, Japanese State notes, and stamps used solely within Japan.

(2) All stocks of manufactured currency and stamps other than notes of the Bank of Japan, Japanese State notes, and stamps used solely within Japan.

(3) All watermarked paper intended for the manufacture of currency and stamps, other than notes of the Bank of Japan, Japanese State notes, and stamps solely for use within Japan.

b. You will report to this headquarters by 0900 hours, 2 October 1945, the location of all of the items listed in "a" above.

9. You will report immediately to this headquarters the action taken to comply with these requirements.

10. An acknowledgment of the receipt of this memorandum is desired.

FOR THE SUPREME COMMANDER:

HAROLD FAIR,
Lt Colonel, A.G.D.,
Asst. Adjutant General.

1 Incl: As indicated in Paragraph 1.

INCLOSURE 1

LIST OF FINANCIAL INSTITUTIONS TO BE CLOSED BY

188

1　降伏文書調印と初期占領政策への対応（昭和20年9月～10月）

JAPANESE GOVERNMENT

1. Wartime Finance Bank.
2. United Funds Bank.
3. All branches and agencies in Japan of Bank of Chosen.
4. All branches and agencies in Japan of Bank of Taiwan.
5. Southern Development Bank.
6. Overseas Funds Bank.
7. Deutsche Bank fuer Ostasien.
8. Offices in Japan of Central Bank of Manchu.
9. Offices in Japan of Bank of China.
10. Banque Franco-Japonaise.
11. Oriental Development Company.
12. Nanyo Development Company.
13. North China Development Company.
14. Central China Development Company.
15. South Manchuria Railway Company.
16. Southern Development Company.
17. Taiwan Development Company.
18. Manchuria Development Company, Ltd.
19. Manchuria Heavy Industry Development Company, Ltd.
20. Chosen Colonization Bank.
21. National Financial Control Association.
22. All other banks, development companies, and institutions whose foremost purpose has been the financing of colonization and development activities in areas outside Japan or the financing of war production by the mobilization or control of financial resources in colonial or Japanese occupied territory.

~~~~~~~~~~

54　昭和20年10月1日　連合国最高司令官総司令部より　日本政府宛

出版言論の自由に関する政府措置につき通報

TO: OFFICE OF THE SUPREME COMMANDER FOR THE ALLIED POWERS
FROM: Central Liaison Office, Tokyo
C.L.O. 133   1 October 1945
SUBJECT: Semi-Monthly Report on Governmental Measures for

the Realization of Freedom of Speech and Publication

1) Referring to your order dated the 10th of September we beg to report to you that all the Regional Governors General and Prefectural Governors were duly notified of the order on the 11th and they were instructed to fully inform all the newspaper publishers under their jurisdiction of the same order.

2) With regard to the Shimbun Jigyo Rei, the Shuppan Jigyo Rei and the Shimbunshi-To-Keizai-Seigen Rei, their repeal was discussed and decided upon by the Council of the General Mobilization on the 29th of September and is expected to come into effect shortly.

Various restrictions based on the Shimbunshi-To-Keizai-Seigen Rei have ceased to be operative since the 25th of August. Applications for the publication of newspapers and other printed matters are now being accepted they are made even though the repeal of the above-mentioned ordinance has not taken effect.

3) The Nippon Shinbun Kosha, which has been the subsidiary governmental organ, was dissolved on the 27th of September and the Nippon Shinbun Renmei was newly established on the same date as a purely non-official organization by all the fifty-two Japanese daily news publishers in Japan.

4) After the termination of the war the Japanese Government has not granted any preferential treatment to any newspaper publisher or news agency by way of subsidies or other means.

5) After the termination of the war, every newspaper publisher or news agency has been allowed to receive foreign telegrams as freely as it desires. Although newspapers such as the Asahi and the Mainichi have already made contracts with foreign news services, the Government has not imposed any restrictions in regard to the above action.

The newspapers in general, however, being unable to bear the financial burden involved in contracts with the foreign news services, seem to be considering the joint establishment of an organ for receiving foreign telegrams.

The Government is preparing to revive the Doho Musen Dempo Kisoku (Regulation on Simultaneous Radiogram) in order to enable all news agencies to utilize equally the facilities

190

of the Doho Dempo (Simultaneous radiogram) in regard to the dissemination of news within the country.

6) With regard to the question of making equally available to all national and international news agencies the existing governmental communication facilities which have been loaned to the Domei News Agency, these facilities are so inadequate that it cannot be solved by simply placing them at the disposal of various news agencies. The question is now under study.

7) In regard to the reception of foreign broadcasts the Government has lately permitted all people to possess all-wave radio sets to enable any person to listen freely to these broadcasts.

8) The prohibition of the sale and distribution of various newspapers ordered on the 28th of September was lifted on the following day.

FOR THE DIRECTOR GENERAL,

(T. Katsube),

Liaison Officer,

Central Liaison Office.

---

55 昭和20年10月1日 連合国最高司令官総司令部より 日本政府宛

郵便の検閲に関する指令

OFFICE OF THE SUPREME COMMANDER

FOR THE ALLIED POWERS

1 October 1945

AG 311.7 (1 Oct 45) CI

SCAPIN 80

MEMORANDUM FOR: IMPERIAL JAPANESE GOVERNMENT

THROUGH: Central Liaison Office, Tokyo.

SUBJECT: Censorship of the Mails.

1. All postal communications are subject to censorship, to the extent deemed advisable by the Supreme Allied Commander.

2. Mails will be made available to Civil Censorship Detachment, AFPAC, and will be submitted for censorship as directed from time to time thru the liaison officer of the Board of Communications assigned to censorship.

FOR THE SUPREME COMMANDER:

HAROLD FAIR,

56

昭和20年10月2日　連合国最高司令官総司令部より
　　　　　　　　　日本政府宛

北緯二十九度以北の南方諸島の降伏に関する指令

GENERAL HEADQUARTERS
SUPREME COMMANDER FOR THE ALLIED POWERS

2 October 1945

AG 091 (2 Oct 45) GC-F ADV
SCAPIN 85

MEMORANDUM FOR: THE IMPERIAL JAPANESE GOVERNMENT.

THROUGH: Central Liaison Office, Tokyo.

SUBJECT: Status of NANPO SHOTO.

1. Reference is made to paragraph 1 d of inclosure to Directive No.1, Office of the Supreme Commander for the Allied Powers, dated 2 September 1945, to the Imperial Japanese Government concerning surrender of certain islands.

2. Islands in the Nanpo Shoto lying north of 29 degrees north latitude, to include O-Shima, are considered to have been included in the surrender of the Japanese Empire and no special surrender ceremonies for those individual islands are required.

3. The Nanpo Shoto as a whole are under the control of the Commander-in-Chief, U. S. Pacific Fleet.

FOR THE SUPREME COMMANDER:

H. W. ALLEN,
Colonel, A.G.D.,
Asst Adjutant General.

Lt. Col., A.G.D.,
Asst. Adjutant General.

57

昭和20年10月3日　在スウェーデン岡本公使より
　　　　　　　　　吉田外務大臣宛（電報）

ロンドン外相会議から見た国際情勢の観測報告

ストックホルム　10月3日後6時50分発
本　　　　省　10月4日前11時20分着

第六〇四號

一、倫敦外相會議ハ事毎ニ英米對蘇聯邦特ニ英蘇間ノ意見ノ

1　降伏文書調印と初期占領政策への対応（昭和20年9月～10月）

對立ニ依リ暗礁ニ乗リ上ケ「デイリーヘラルド」ノ如キモ吾人ハ兩眼ヲ見開ケル儘第三次大戰ノ方向ニ進ミツツアリト悲觀的論說ヲ揭ケ居ル程ニシテ一般ノ豫想通リ物別レトナレル處會談ノ經緯ヨリ見テ歐洲カ東歐ト西歐ニ英蘇ノ勢力範圍トシテ明瞭ニ二分セラレタルコト及英米對蘇聯邦相互間ノ猜疑心頗ル強ク此ノ調子ニテハ大國間ノ協力ヲ最重要基調トスル世界平和ノ如キハ前途遼遠ナルコトノ二點ハ今ヤ赤裸々ニ表面化セラレタルモノト觀察ス

三、會議中蘇聯邦ノ行キ方ハ押シノ一手ニテ次々ト英國ノ傳統的生命線ニ抵觸スルカ如キ要求ヲ提出シ英國ノ強硬ナル反對ヲ押シ切リ得サリシモ（ベビン）ト「モロトフ」トノ間ニハ卓ヲ叩イテ激論セル場面モアリ相當注意ヲ惹キタリト傳ヘラル）其ノ企圖セル所ハ英米國民カ此ノ際蘇聯邦ヲ相手ニ一戰ノ意氣無キヲ見越シ過大ノ要求ヲ押付ケ英米ヲ シテ應接ニ違無カラシメ其ノ間出來得ル限リノ情報ヲ獲得シ以テ此ノ際將來ニ對シ政略戰略兩面ニ於テ有利ナル地步ヲ固メントスルニアリシモノノ如シ將來東亞問題カ議セラルル際ニモ蘇聯邦ハ同一ノ手口ヲ用ヒ

日本ヲ徹底的ニ痛メ付ケルノ名目ノ下ニ意外ノ無理難題的ノ要求ヲ持出ス公算無シトセス我方トシテハ充分警戒ノ要アリト存ス

三、英國ニ於テハ獨蘇開戰以來ノ國民ノ親蘇熱ハ漸次下降シツツアリシ處最近ハ獨逸ニ於ケル赤軍ノ無規律「バルカン」ニ於ケル蘇聯邦ノ遣口等カ現金トナリ一層冷却セル模樣ニシテ新聞雜誌等ニ反蘇的記事モ散見スルニ至レルカ今次會談ニ於ケル蘇聯邦ノ態度ハ其ノ極メテ厄介ナル難物ナルコトヲ露骨ニ感セシメ英國民一般ニ對スル不安ヲ感シ蘇聯邦ニ對スル恐怖反感ヲ深ムルニ至ルヘク英政府ハ西歐聯合ノ結束ヲ急クト共ニ米國ト共同シテ蘇聯邦ノ強硬ナル要求ニ對抗シ之ニ引摺ラレ乍ラモ可及的ニ之ヲ緩和セントスル試ムル趨勢ト觀測セラル

〰〰〰〰〰〰〰〰〰〰〰

58

昭和20年10月4日

在ポルトガル森島公使より吉田外務大臣宛（電報）

日本管理理事会の設置に関するソ連の動向につき報告

付　記　昭和二十一年一月、條約局法規課作成東亞問題カ議セラルル際ニモ蘇聯邦ハ同一ノ手口ヲ用ヒ

「極東委員會及聯合國日本理事會ニ付テ」

リスボン　10月4日前1時40分発
本　省　10月6日前6時40分着

第三八九號

一、三日倫敦放送ニ依レハ二十九日米外相カ英米佛蘇及支ハ日本管理理事會設置ノ可否ヲ極東委員會ニ於テ決定スヘキ旨聲明セルニ對シ「モロトフ」ハ米外相宛書面ヲ以テ右聲明ハ正確ナラス蘇聯ハ日本管理會設置ニ贊成ニシテ且極東委員會成立前ニ之ヲ設置スルヲ要ストノ意見ナル旨明カニセリ

二、三日倫敦發UPニ依レハ英米間ニ軍事協力ニ關スル商議進捗中ニテ右ハ萬一ノ場合ニ備ヘ且國際會議ニ於ケル英米ノ主張ヲ支持スル目的ニ出ツト

「マックアーサー」ノ名ニ於テ行ハルル軍事占領ナリト觀念シ同司令官ノ執ルヘキ措置ハ悉ク作戰行動ノ性質ヲ帶ブルモノナルヲ以テ他ノ容喙ヲ許サズトナシ以テ日本管理ニ關スル總テユル權限ヲ一手ニ收メ且之ヲ專行セントシタルコトハ「八月十一日附四大國ノ名ニ於ケル合衆國政府ノ帝國政府ニ對スル回答」及降伏文書並ニ「降伏後ニ於ケル米國ノ初期ノ對日方針」ニ明ナル所カ同時ニ合衆國ハ日本降伏直後ヨリ「マックアーサー」ノ下ニ其ノ諮問機關ヲ設ケ日本ノ管理ニ關スル米國ノ「エクスクルーシブ」ナル權力ヲ保持シツツモ關係各國ニ發言ノ機會ヲ與ヘ之ヲ「アピーズ」セントノ意嚮ヲ有シタルハ「降伏後ニ於ケル米國ノ初期ノ對日方針」ニ於テ「日本ノ占領及管理ノ施行ニ關シ充分協議ヲ行フト共ニ適當ナル諮問機關ヲ設ケテ主要聯合諸國ヲ滿足セシムヘキ政策ヲ樹立スル樣有ラユル努力ヲ盡スヘキ」旨述ヘラレ居リ且客年十二月三十一日「バーンズ」國務長官カ「當初ヨリ我々ハ日本ノ管理ヲ聯合國ノ責任ト為スヘク計畫シ居リタリ八月二十日既ニ我々ハ蘇、英、支三國ニ對シ「ポツダム」宣言ノ目的ヲ降伏條項ノ遂行ノ為ニ我々ニ參加スル樣要請セリ」ト聲明シ居ルニ依リテモ明

（付　記）
極東委員會及聯合國日本理事會ニ付テ
（昭和二十一年一月　條約局法規課）

第一、極東委員會及聯合國日本理事會成立ノ經緯
降伏後ノ日本ノ管理ニ關シ合衆國カ之ヲ聯合國最高司令官

1 降伏文書調印と初期占領政策への対応(昭和20年9月～10月)

ナリ

右米國ノ態度ニ對スル關係諸國殊ニ蘇聯ノ反撥ハ直ニ表面化スルコトナカリシモ九月二十五日「ロンドン」ニ於ケル外相理事會ニ對シテ蘇聯代表「モロトフ」ハ突如

「聯合國對日管理委員會ヲ設置シ米、英、蘇、支四國委員ノ手ニ依リ聯合國ノ對日政策ヲ決定スヘシ」

トノ提議ヲナセリ又「モロトフ」外相ハ十月一日附ヲ以テ「バーンズ」國務長官ニ左ノ如キ書簡ヲ送付セリ

「蘇聯政府ハ戰爭力繼續シ日本軍隊力武裝解除セラレ居ラザル間ハ日本管理ニ關スル權能ハ當然聯合國最高司令官ノ手ニ委ネラルヘキナリト思考スルモ此ノ段階ヲ經過セル場合聯合國力意見ノ一致ヲ見タル政策ヲ遂行スルト共ニ共同ノ責任ヲ負ヒ得ヘキ聯合國機關ヲ創設スルコト不可避タルニ至ルヘシ蘇聯政府ハ聯合國諮問委員會トハ別ニ日本管理々事會ヲ創設スルコト賢明且有益ナリト思考ス極東諮問委員會委員長ハ米國代表カ就任シテ會合ヲ開キ四大國以外ニ對日戰ニ活動的役割ヲ演シタル諸國代表ヲ參加セシムヘキナリ、蘇聯政府ハ日本管理々事會力諮問委員會ニ先立チテ設立セラルヘキナリト思考ス云々」

右書簡ニ於ケル蘇聯ノ主張ハ

(一)「日本管理ノ段階ヲ「戰爭力繼續シ日本軍隊力武裝解除セラレ居ラザル」期間ト其ノ後ノ期間トニ分チ後期ニ於ケル管理方法ハ自ラ相異ル必要アルヲ説キ後期ニ於テ米國ノ提案ニ係ル對日戰ニ活動的役割ヲ演シタル全聯合國ヨリ成ル極東諮問委員會ノ設立及同委員會ニ於ケル合衆國ノ優位ニハ別ニ反對セサルモ

(二)米國ノ提案ニ係ル對日戰ニ活動的役割ヲ演シタル全聯合國ヨリ成ル極東諮問委員會ノ設立及同委員會ニ於ケル合衆國ノ優位ニハ別ニ反對セサルモ

(三)其ノ他ニ極東諮問委員會ノ上ニ立チ聯合國最高司令官ニ代リ之ト同樣ノ權限ヲ有スル日本管理々最高機關タル四大國ニ依ル日本管理々事會ヲ設立スヘシ

ト云フニアリ

蘇聯ノ斯カル提議ニ對シ合衆國ハ一方ニ於テ右提議力外相理事會ノ議題ニ非ストノ立場ヨリ之カ討議ヲ拒否シ又「マツクアーサー」ノ地位ヲ何等變更スル意思ナキコトヲ再三聲明スルト共ニ他方極東諮問委員會ノ設立ヲ進メ十月十日ヨリ極東諮問委員會ヲ十月二十三日華府ニテ開催シ英、蘇、支、佛、加、濠、新西蘭、和蘭、比島(其ノ後英國ノ要求ニ依リ印度追加セラル)ヲ招請スヘキ旨發表シ同時ニ左揭極東諮問委員會要綱ヲ公表セリ

195

一、設置

――國政府ハ參加國代表ヨリ成ル極東諮問委員會ヲ茲ニ設置ス

二、機能

(A)極東諮問委員會ハ參加國政府ニ對シ左ノ事項ニ付勸告ヲ行フヘシ

(1)降伏文書ニ依リ課セラレタル諸義務ノ日本ニ依ル嚴格ナル遂行ヲ確保スル爲ニ必要ナル措置竝ニ機關

(2)降伏文書ノ諸條項ノ日本ニ依リ履行ヲ決定スヘキ政策、原則竝ニ基準ノ確定

(3)參加國政府ノ合意ニ依リ附託セラルヘキ其ノ他ノ諸問題

(B)本委員會ハ軍事行動竝ニ領土的調整ニ關シ勸告ヲ行ハサルヘシ

三、他ノ協議方法

本委員會ノ設置ハ極東問題ニ關シ參加國政府カ他ノ協議方法ヲ使用スルヲ妨ケス

四、構成

極東諮問委員會ハ本協定ニ參加スヘキ各國代表一名ヨリ成ル本委員會ハ情況ニ應シ極東ニ所在シ又ハ極東ニ領土ヲ有スル他ノ聯合國代表ヲ追加增員セラルヘシ本委員會ノ構成員タラサル聯合國ハ委員會ニ於テ審議事項カ當該國ノ利益ニ主要ナル影響ヲ及ボスベシト認ムル場合當該國ノ合會ヘ出席ヲ招請セラルベシ加之委員會ハ其ノ審議事項カ當該國ニ特別關聯アル場合ニ於テハ構成員タラザル聯合國ト雖モ其ノ代表者ト充分ナル協議ヲ行フベキナリ

五、所在地及組織

極東諮問委員會ハ其ノ本部ヲ華府ニ置ク所要ニ應ジ他ノ場所ニテモ會合スルコトアルベシ

委員會ノ各代表ハ文武代表ヨリ成ル適當ナル隨員ヲ伴フコトヲ得ベシ

委員會ハ事務局ヲ組織シ必要ニ應ジ委員ヲ指名スベク其ノ他其ノ組織及手續ヲ整フベシ

六、廢止

極東諮問委員會ハ米英蘇支四國ノ中一國ニ依リ廢止通告ニ依リ其ノ機能ヲ中止スベク右廢止前ニ於テ委員會ト其ノ機能ノ中然ルベキモノヲ參加國政府ノ構成員タル暫定的又ハ恆久ノ安全保障機構ヘ移管スベシ

196

1　降伏文書調印と初期占領政策への対応（昭和20年9月～10月）

斯クテ極東諮問委員會ハ蘇聯ノ同委員會參加拒絶ニモ拘ラズ十月三十日華府ニ於テ蘇聯不參加ノ儘開催セラレタリ參加國及代表氏名左ノ如シ

米國代表　「マッコイ」少將（議長）
支那代表　魏道明駐米大使
濠洲代表　「エヴアット」外相
加奈陀代表　「ピアソン」駐米公使
佛蘭西代表　「ナジャール」前駐米公使
英國代表　「ハリファックス」駐米大使、蘇大使
印度代表　「ギルヤシャンカール、バイバイ」駐華府代表
和蘭代表　「ローソン」博士
新西蘭代表　「ベレンゼン」駐米公使
比島代表　「カルロス、ロムロ」代將

而シテ極東諮問委員會ト事務局、分科委員會ヲ設ケ活動ヲ開始シタルガ委員一行ハ日本視察ノ爲本年一月九日來京セリ

他方蘇聯ノ極東諮問委員會不參加及日本管理理事會設立ノ提議ニ關スル米蘇兩國間ノ意見ノ不一致ハ其ノ後頻繁ナル兩國間ノ交涉ノ對象トナリタルカ米蘇對立ノ要點ハ蘇聯ガ極東諮問委員會ノ如キ間接的ノ手段ヲ以テシテハ日本降伏ニ全的ノ努力ヲ拂ヒタル大國ノ希望發言ニ適當ナラズ米英蘇支四大國ノ同等發言權ヲ基礎トセル日本管理理事會ヲ設置シ直接日本ヲ管理スベシトナスニ對シ合衆國ハ政策遂行ニ當リ「マックアーサー」ヲ輔佐スル四大國委員會ノ設置ニ反對セザルモ四國ノ意見不一致ノ場合「マックアーサー」ガ決定權ヲ保有スベキナリトナシ蘇聯ニ拒否權ヲ與フルヲ欲セザルニアリ、其ノ後屢々兩國ノ歩ミ寄リ傳ヘラレ遂ニ今次「モスコー」會談ニ於テ妥協成立シ双方ノ主張ヲ折衷採用ノ結果日本管理ノ機關トシテ極東委員會及聯合國日本理事會ノ二機關設立セラルルニ至レルモノナリ
第二、極東委員會及聯合國日本理事會ノ性格
今次「モスコー」三國外相會議「コミユニケ」ニ依リ明カニセラレタル所左ノ通

A　極東委員會

（一）構成及議決方法

極東委員會ハ極東諮問委員會ニ代ルモノニシテ其ノ參加國ハ諮問委員會ニ同シ但シ蘇聯モ參加ス卽チ參加國

ハ米、英、蘇、支、佛、濠、加、新西蘭、印度、和蘭、比島ノ十一ケ國ナリ議決ノ方法ハ米、英、蘇、支四國ヲ含ム過半數ニ依リ表決セラルルヲ以テ全會一致ヲ要セザルモ四大國ニ拒否權ノ認メラレ居ル點ハ後述ノ如ク甚夕重要ナル意義ヲ有ス

(二) 權能及其ノ行使方式

(a) 極東委員會ノ最モ重要ナル權能ハ「日本カ降伏條件所定ノ義務ヲ履行スルニ當リ準則タルヘキ政策原則及基準ノ作成」（第二章第一條イ項）ナリ即チコノ點ニ於テ委員會ハ聯合國ノ日本管理ニ關スル立法機關ナリト云フヲ得ヘシ而シテ委員會ニ依リ日本管理政策ノ決定セラレタル時ハ合衆國政府ニ於テ之ニ適應スル指令ヲ作成スルコトトナリ居リ右指令ハ更ニ傳達セラレヘク最高司令官ヲ通シテ聯合國最高司令官ニ執行スル責任ニ負フモノナリ尚極東委員會ニ於ケル米國政府ノ役割ニ付テハ日本管理ニ關スル米國側從來ノ主導的地位ニモ鑑ミ深甚

ナル考慮拂ハレタルモノノ如ク「コミユニケ」中ニモ特ニ「合衆國政府ノ權能」ナル一章ヲ存スル次第ナリ而シテ之ニ依レハ米國政府ハ前記ノ如ク先ツ委員會ト最高司令官トノ連絡機關タルヘキモノナルカ更ニ

「合衆國政府ハ委員會カ既ニ決定セル政策ニ依リ規定セラレサル緊急問題發生シタル時ハ委員會ノ決定アル迄最高司令官ニ對シ暫定的指令ヲ發スルコトヲ得但シ日本ノ基本的ノ統治組織又ハ管理制度ノ根本的變革或ハ日本政府全體ノ變更ニ關スル總ユル指令ハ極東委員會ニ諮問シ且其ノ合意アリタル後ニ非レハ之ヲ發スルコトヲ得ス」（第三章第三條）

ト規定セラレ居レリ蓋シ合衆國政府カ聯合國最高司令官ニ發スヘキ指令ハ極東委員會ノ政策決定ニ從テ作成セラルルモ右規定後段ノ三問題ヲ除キテハ米國政府ニ於テ(一)緊急ノ問題ニ付(二)既ニ決定セラレタル政策ニ含マレサル(三)委員會ノ決定アル迄ノ暫定的ノ指令ヲ發シ得ルコトトナリ居リ殊ニ(二)ノ緊急

198

1　降伏文書調印と初期占領政策への対応（昭和20年9月～10月）

問題ナリヤ否ヤノ認定ハ合衆國政府ノ行フ所ナルヲ以テ合衆國政府ハコノ暫定的指令ヲ可成ハ自由ニ且廣キ範圍ニ亘リ發出スルコトヲ得ヘシ「バーンズ」國務長官カ客年十二月三十一日ノ演說ニ於テ「合衆國政府ハ必要アル場合總ユル緊急問題ニ關シ暫定的指令ヲ發スルノ自由ヲ有ス合衆國政府カ右指令ヲ發シ得サルハ僅ニ次ノ三問題ニ限ル」（前掲第三章第三條後段）ト述ヘ極東委員會ノ政策決定ニ基ク指令ヨリモ寧ロ暫定的指令ヲ原則ノ如ク取扱ヒタルハ甚タ示唆的ナリト云ヒ得ヘシ。

斯クテ極東委員會ノ日本管理政策決定機關トシテノ地位ハ合衆國政府ノ暫定的指令ニ發出權ニヨリ大ナル制限ヲ受ケ合衆國政府ノ委員會トノ連絡機關ナルト共ニ同時ニ暫定的指令發出權ヲ有ルヲ以テ其ノ限リニ於テ委員會ト竝ヒテ政策決定機關ナル特殊的地位承認セラレタリトスルモ他面右第三章第三條後段日本ノ基本的統治組織又ハ管理制度ノ根本的變革或ハ日本政府全體ノ變更ノ三問題ハ合衆國政府ノ暫定的指令ヲ以テ之ヲ處理スルコトヲ得

ス如何ナル場合ニ於テモ委員會ノ決定ヲ必要トス次第ナリ而モ前述ノ如ク四大國ハ委員會ノ表決ニ於テ拒否權ヲ有シ居リ一方ニ於テ合衆國政府ハ右三問題ニ關スル政策決定ニ當ツテ四大國ノ一トシテ其ノ同意ヲ與ヘサル限リ極東委員會ハ合衆國ノ意ニ反スル決定ヲナシ得サルノ保障ヲ有スルモ合衆國政府カ委員會ニ對シテ右三問題ニ關スル何ラカノ提案ヲ附議シ得ハ蘇聯ノ拒否權ノ行使ニヨリ否決セラルル方法ヲモ有セサルヘキ次第ニシテ右三問題ニ關シ合衆國政府ハ其ノ意思ヲ實施スヘキ如何ナル限リ合衆國政府ハ日本管理ニ關スル政策決定ニ於テ「フリーハンド」ヲ失ヒタルモノト言ヒ得ヘシ

(b)極東委員會ノ第二ノ機能ハ
「委員ノ要求アル場合合聯合國最高司令官宛ノ總ユル指令又ハ委員會ノ管轄內ニアル政策決定ニ關聯スル最高司令官ノ總ユル行為ノ審查」（第二章第一條ロ項）

ナリ前段ニ關シテハ更ニ
「總テノ發セラレタル指令ハ委員會ニ提出スルコト

ヲ要ス」（第三章第四條）ナル規定ヲ存シ合衆國政府ハ暫定的指令ヲ含ム總テノ最高司令官宛ノ指令ヲ委員會ニ提出スル義務ヲ負フモノニシテ其ノ委員會ニ適合シ居ルヤ否ヤヲ吟味スルコトヲ得又果シテ其ノ決定ニ適合シ居ルヤ否ヤヲ吟味スルコトヲ得又他ノ暫定的指令ノ濫發ヲ「コントロール」スルヲ得ヘシ而シテ「委員會力第二章第一條ロ項ノ規定ニ從ヒ指令又ハ行爲ヲ審査シ之力修正ヲ決定スル場合其ノ決定ハ政策決定ト看做ス」（第三章第二條）ナル規定ニ基ク事後修正權ハ本權能ヲ強化スルモノニシテ特ニ斯カル修正力暫定的指令ニヨリ再修正セラルルヲ封スル上ニ於テ意義大ナルヘシ

（c）尚委員會ハ「第五章第二條所定ノ表決手續ニ從テ參加國政府間ニ到達セラレタル合意ニ依リ委員會ニ附託セラルルコトアルヘキ他ノ諸問題ノ審議」（第二章第一條ハ項）ヲナス但シ

（三）其ノ他

（a）極東委員會ハ其ノ本部ヲ華府ニ置クモ東京其ノ他ノ地ニ於テモ會合スルコトヲ得尚最高司令官トモ協議シ得（第六章第一條參照）

（b）「委員會ノ設置ハ極東問題ニ關シ參加國政府力他ノ協議方法ヲ採用スルコトヲ妨ケス」（第四章）

（c）尚參加國以外ノ聯合國ノ極東委員會ヘノ招請並ニ之トノ協議、隨員、事務局、小委員會ニ關スル規定アリ（第五章第一條、第六章第二、三條參照）

（d）最後ニ委員會ノ終了ニ先立チ委員會ハ移管ニ適當ナル權能喪失ニ先立チ委員會ハ移管ニ適當ナル權

「委員會ハ軍事行動又ハ領土調整ニ關シ勸告ヲ行ハス」（第二章第二條）

又

「委員會ハ其ノ活動ニ際シ聯合國日本理事會力設置セラレ居ル事實ヲ前提トシ且合衆國政府ニ始マリ最高司令官ニ至ル一聯ノ命令系統ヲ含ム現存日本管理機構及占領軍ニ對スル最高司令官ノ指揮權ヲ尊重ス」（第二章第三條）

1　降伏文書調印と初期占領政策への対応（昭和20年9月～10月）

（四）極東諮問委員會ト極東委員會トノ比較

(a) 兩委員會ハ其ノ主タル權能カ能ヲ參加國カ構成員タル暫定的又ハ恆久的安全保障機構ニ移管スヘシ」（第七章）ナル規定ハ委員會終了ノ時ヲ同シクスルト考ヘ得ヘク其ノ際「移管ニ適當ナル機能」カ果シテ如何ナルモノナリヤ豫想困難ナルモ假ニ日本ノ再軍備其ノ他ニ對スル監視ノ如キモノトセハ之ヲ恐ラク國際聯合或ハ極東ニ於ケル聯合國組織ニ移管シ實行セラルルコトトナルヘシ

「日本カ降伏條件所定ノ義務ヲ履行スルニ當リ準則タルヘキ政策、原則及基準ノ作成」ナル點ニ於テ同一ナルモ決定セラレタル政策ノ法的效果ニ大ナル相異アリ卽チ諮問委員會ハ之ヲ單ニ勸告スルモノナルニ反シ極東委員會ノ決定ハ拘束力ヲ有スルモノナリ（極東委員會ノ決定ニハ表決ノ規定ヲ存シ諮問委員會ニ之ヲ有セサルハ右ノ相異ヨリ生スルモノナリ）

(b) 更ニ重要ナルハ前述ノ如ク極東委員會ニ於ケル政策

決定ニ當リ四大國カ拒否權ヲ有スル事ニシテ此ノ點合衆國ノ蘇聯ニ對スル重大ナル讓歩ナリトナシ得ヘシ

(c) 諮問委員會ノ勸告ハ參加國政府ニ對シテ爲サルルモノニシテ斯ル勸告カ如何ニシテ實行ニ移サルルヤノ手續規定セラレ居ラサルモ極東委員會ニ於テハ委員會決定カ合衆國政府ノ手ヲ經テ最高司令官ニ依リ執行セラルル迄ノ諸手續規定セラレ居リ諮問委員會ニ比シ遙カニ完備セルモノトナシ得ヘシ

(d) 諮問委員會ハ「降伏文書ノ諸條項ノ日本ニ依ル嚴格ナル遂行ヲ確保スルニ必要ナル措置並ニ機關」ニ關シ勸告ヲ行フ權能ヲ有シ卽チ日本管理ニ關スル政策ノ決定ノミナラス執行ニ關シテモ勸告ヲ行フニ反シ極東委員會ハ原則トシテ斯ル權能ヲ有セス政策執行ニ關シ最高司令官ニ協議勸告スルハ聯合國日本理事會之ヲ擔當ス　一註、但シ極東委員會ハ其ノ管轄内ニアル政策決定ニ關聯スル最高司令官ノ行爲ヲ審査修正シ得ヘク（第二章第一條ロ項、第三章第二條）又前記三問題ニ關スル委員會ノ政策決定ノ施行ニ關シ理

201

事會ト最高司令官トノ意見一致セサル場合委員會カ之ヲ最終的ニ決定ス（聯合國日本理事會規定第六條）

B、聯合國日本理事會

(一) 構成

理事會ハ聯合國最高司令官（又ハ其ノ代理）並ニ合衆國、蘇聯、中華民國ノ各代表及英、濠、新西蘭、印度ヲ通シテノ一代表ノ五員ニ依リ構成セラレ最高司令官議長ニ就任ス卽チ「マックアーサー」議長ノ外ニ合衆國ハ理事會ニ一代表ヲ有ス

「各代表ハ軍民顧問ヨリ成ル適當ナル隨員ヲ伴フコトヲ得」（第三條）

(二) 理事會ノ權能及聯合國最高司令官ノ地位

理事會ハ

「降伏條件、日本ノ占領及管理ノ實施並ニ之ニ附隨スル指令ノ實施ニ關シ最高司令官ト協議勸告シ日本協定所定ノ管理權ヲ行使スル」（第一條）

ヲ其ノ權能トス

斯ル權能ヲ有スル理事會ト聯合國最高司令官トノ關係ハ次ノ如ク規定セラル

「最高司令官ハ降伏條件、日本ノ占領及管理ノ實施並ニ之ニ附隨スル指令ノ實施ノ爲總ユル命令ヲ發スヘシ總ユル場合ニ於テ一切ノ行爲ハ日本ニ於ケル聯合國唯一ノ執行機關タル最高司令官ノ下ニ且之ヲ通シテ實施セラル最高司令官ハ事情ノ許ス限リ實體的事項ニ關スル命令發出ニ先立チ理事會ニ協議諮問スヘシ右事項ニ關スル最高司令官ノ決定ハ支配的タルモノトス」（第五條）

卽チ最高司令官ハ日本ニ於ケル聯合國ノ唯一ノ執行機關ニシテ理事會ハ斯カル地位ニ於ケル最高司令官ノ諮問機關ナリ極東委員會カ立法ノ權限ヲ有スルニ對シ理事會ノ職務ハ其ノ執行ニ直接關係スルヲ以テ聯合國最高司令部所在地タル東京ニ會合シ且最少限二週間ニ一度會議ヲ開ク（第一條第四條）

而シテ最高司令官ハ實體的ノ事項ニ關スル命令ノ發出ニ先立チ理事會ト協議シ且之ニ諮問スヘキ義務ヲ有スルモ「事態ノ許ス限リ」ナル限度ニ於テノミニシテ事態ノ許スヤ否ヤノ認定權ハモトヨリ最高司令官ニアリ諸

1　降伏文書調印と初期占領政策への対応（昭和20年9月～10月）

問セラレタル事項ニ關スル理事會ノ權能ハ後述三問題ニ關スル場合ヲ除キ最高司令官トノ協議及勸告ニ止マルモノニシテ支配的ナル決定ハ最高司令官之ヲナス此ノ點ニ於テ米官邊ガ今囘ノ協定ハ日本管理最高當事者タル「マックアーサー」ノ地位ヲ何等變スルモノニ非ズトナセルハ正當ナリト云フベシ更ニ注意スベキハ本協定ニ依リ設立セラレタル理事會ガ蘇聯ノ提唱セル米英蘇支四國ノ同等發言權ヲ基礎トシ「マックアーサー」ニ代リ直接日本ヲ管理スル管理理事會ト根本的ニ其ノ性格ヲ異ニスル點ニシテ聯合國日本理事會ハ「マックアーサー」議長ノ下ニ合衆國代表ヲ含ム四代表ヲ以テ構成セラルル諮問機關ニ過キズ直接日本ヲ管理スルモノニ非サルヲ以テ理事會ニ關スル限リ蘇聯ノ合衆國ニ對スル讓歩ナリトナシ得ベシ
理事會ガ唯一ノ實效ノ權限ヲ有スルハ
「日本ノ基本的統治組織又ハ管理態度ノ根本的變革或ハ日本政府全體ノ變更ニ關スル問題ニ付テノ極東委員會ノ政策決定ノ實施ニ關シ聯合國理事會ノ一員カ最高司令官（又ハ其ノ代理）ト意見ヲ異ニスル場合最高司令

官ハ極東委員會ニ於テ合意成立スル迄命令ノ發出ヲ留保ス」（第六條）
ヘキ義務ヲ有スル點ナリ卽チ合衆國政府ハ右三問題ニ關スル限リ其ノ政策決定ニ於テ極東委員會ノ合意ナクシテハ指令ヲ發シ得サルト共ニ最高司令官ハ右政策執行ニ關シ理事會ノ同意ヲ要求セラレ居ル次第ニシテ何レノ場合ニ於テモ四大國ノ一員ノ反對ヵ拘束力ヲ有ス
ルモノナルヲ以テ合衆國ハ右三問題ニ關スル立法上執行上ノ兩權能ヲ制限セラレ居ルモノナリ尚最高司令官ハ必要アレハ日本政府ノ個々ノ閣僚ノ變更其ノ缺員ノ補充ヲナシ得ルモ他ノ聯合國理事會代表ト事前ノ協議ヲ要ス（第七條）卽チ本條ハ第五條所定ノ「事情ノ許ス限リ」ナル條件ヲ特ニ排除シタル點ニ意味ヲ有ス然レトモ右ハ政府全體ノ變更ニ非サルヵ故ニ協議不調ノ場合最高司令官ハ尙決定權ヲ有スルヲ以テ結局本規定ノ價値ハ手續ヲ若干愼重化セルニ止マルモノト云ヒ得ヘシ

第三、新方式ノ下ニ於ケル日本管理
「モスコー」協定ニ依ル極東委員會及聯合國日本理事會ノ

成立ハ合衆國政府ガ日本管理政策ノ決定ヲナシ「マックアーサー」ガ其ノ執行ヲナシタル現在迄ノ日本管理方式ニ大ナル變化ヲ齎ラセルモノトシテ云フベシ而シテ兩機關成立ノ經緯、其ノ法的性格ハ既述ノ如クナルガ本協定ハ三國特ニ米蘇間ノ妥協ノ產物ナルヲ以テ本協定ニ於テ兩國ノ主張ガ如何ナル程度實現セラレタルヲ以テ本協定ノ理事會ハ理事會ノ成立ハ蘇聯ノ勝利ナルガ如ク見ユルモ實際以テ本理事會ノ成立ハ蘇聯ガ其ノ設立ヲ主張セシモノナルヲ聯合國日本理事會ハ蘇聯ガ其ノ設立ヲ主張セシカヲ考察スルヲ要スベシ蘇聯ノ妥協ノ產物ナルヲ以テ本協定ニ於テ兩國ノ主張ガ如ニ於テ蘇聯主張ノ理事會ハ本協定ニ於テ兩國ノ主張ガ如名稱ニ於テノミ同一ニシテ實体ニ於テ本協定ノ理事會ハ理事會ナル實現セラレザリシヲ以テ蘇聯ノ大讓步トナシ得ベシ次ニ極東委員會ニ關シテハ極東委員會力單ニ勸告機關ナルニ不滿ニシテ其ノ強化ヲ主張セシハ蘇聯ニ非ズシテ英國ナルガ右英國ノ主張ハ必ズシモ強固ニ唱ヘラレタル次第ニ非ザリシ事情ニ鑑ミ今回委員會ガ強化セラレシハ英國ノ代償ノ實現ト云フヨリハ寧ロ理事會ニ關スル蘇聯ノ讓步ノ代償ト看做スヲ適當トスベシ而シテ極東委員會ニ關シテ最モ問題トナルハ合衆國政府ガ暫定的指令權及四大國ノ拒否權ナルガ合衆國政府ガ極東委員會ノ政策決定ノ原則ニモ拘ラズ

暫定的指令ヲ利用シ得ベキコト既述ノ如シ又四大國ノ拒否權ニ關シテハ日本ノ基本的統治組織又ハ管理制度ノ根本的變革或ハ日本政府ノ全体トシテノ變更ノ三問題ニ關シテ特ニ問題トナルベク「バーンズ」國務長官ガ右ハ合衆國政府ノ未ダ企圖セシニ非ズト述ベタル如ク將來特ニ第一第二ノ點ニ關スル變革ハ寧ロ蘇聯ヨリ之ヲ提案ツ合衆國ガ拒否權ヲ行使スルノ公算大ナリト考ヘラル、從テ極東委員會ニ於テモ蘇聯ノ日本管理方式變更ノ企圖ハ其ノ實現ノ可能性甚ダ少ク結局蘇聯ハ極東委員會及聯合國日本理事會ノ雙方ニ於テ名ヲ採リテ實ヲ棄テタルモノトナスコトヲ得ベシ一方本協定ガ合衆國ノ現在迄ノ日本管理ノ權能ニ制限ヲ設ケタル事云フ迄モナク本協定ニ對スル「マックアーサー」ノ反對意見表明、並ニ米各新聞ノ合衆國政府ニ對スル非難此ノ意味ニ於テ當然ナリト謂フベシ然レドモ又合衆國ノ讓步ハ尚日本管理ニ於ケル合衆國ノ優越性ヲ消滅セシメタルモノニ非ザルコト論無シ然ラバ斯ク米蘇ノ互讓ニ依リ成立セル新方式ノ日本管理ガ現實ニ如何ニ運用セラルベキヤヲ按ズルニ其ノ豫想甚ダ困難ナリト雖モ少クトモ右ノ妥協ガ單ニ日本管理ノミナラス

1　降伏文書調印と初期占領政策への対応（昭和20年9月～10月）

歐洲、近東問題等ニ關スルニ兩國ノ全世界ノ對立ヲ背景トスルモノナル以上極東委員會或ハ聯合國理事ニ於テ蘇聯ガ合衆國ノ政策ニ反對ヲナス場合モ右ハ他ノ地域ニ於ケル問題ヲ有利ニ解決センガ爲ノ政治的懸引トシテ行ハルルコト多カルベク從テ又之ガ爲ノ考察ニ當リテモ常ニ全世界的見地ヨリ之ヲ爲サザルベカラザルコト明ナリ尚特ニ極東委員會參加小國中濠洲、新西蘭、比島等ノ對日態度特ニ強硬ニシテ且委員會ノ權限ヲ其ノ實際ノ運營ニ當リ增大セシメ日本管理ノ總ユル問題ヲ委員會ノ手ニ收メントスルノ意圖ヲ有スト思ハルルヲ以テコノ點ニ於テ合衆國トノ關係ハ注意ヲ要スベシ

2 民主化・非軍事化政策への対応（昭和20年10月～21年5月）

59 政治的民事的および宗教的自由に対する制限の撤廃に関する指令

昭和20年10月4日 連合国最高司令官総司令部より日本政府宛

付記　右和訳文

OFFICE OF THE SUPREME COMMANDER
FOR THE ALLIED POWERS

4 October 1945

SCAPIN 93

MEMORANDUM FOR: IMPERIAL JAPANESE GOVERNMENT.
THROUGH: Central Liaison Office, Tokyo.
SUBJECT: Removal of Restrictions on Political, Civil, and Religious Liberties.

1. In order to remove restrictions on political, civil and religious liberties and discrimination on grounds of race, nationality, creed or political opinion, the Imperial Japanese Government will:

　　a. Abrogate and immediately suspend the operation of all provisions of all laws, decrees, orders, ordinances and regulations which:

　　　(1) Establish or maintain restrictions on freedom of thought, of religion, of assembly and of speech, including the unrestricted discussion of the Emperor, the Imperial Institution and the Imperial Japanese Government.

　　　(2) Establish or maintain restrictions on the collection and dissemination of information.

　　　(3) By their terms or their application, operate unequally in favor of or against any person by reason of race, nationality, creed or political opinion.

　　b. The enactments covered in paragraph a, above, shall include, but shall not be limited to, the following:

　　　(1) The Peace Preservation Law (Chian Iji Hō, Law No. 54 of 1941, promulgated on or about 10 March 1941).

2 民主化・非軍事化政策への対応(昭和20年10月～21年5月)

(2) The Protection and Surveillance Law for Thought Offense (Shisō Han Hogo Kansatsu Hō, Law No. 29 of 1936, promulgated on or about 29 May 1936).

(3) Regulations Relative to Application of Protection and Surveillance Law for Thought Offense (Shisō Han Hogo Kansatsu Hō Shikō Rei, Imperial Ordinance No. 401 of 1936, issued on or about 14 November 1936).

(4) Ordinance Establishing Protection and Surveillance Stations, (Hogo Kansatsu-Jo Kansei, Imperial Ordinance No. 403 of 1936, issued on or about 14 November 1936).

(5) The Precautionary Detention Procedure Order (Yobo Kokin Tetsuzuki Rei, Ministry of Justice Order, Shiho Rei, No. 49, issued on or about 14 May 1941).

(6) Regulations for Treatment of Persons Under Precautionary Detention (Yobo Kokin Shogu Rei, Ministry of Justice Order, Shihosho Rei, No. 50, issued on or about 14 May 1941).

(7) The National Defense and Peace Preservation Law (Kokubo Hoan Hō, Law No. 49 of 1941, promulgated on or about 7 March 1941).

(8) National Defense and Peace Preservation Law Enforcement Order (Kokubo Hoan Hō Shiko Rei, Imperial Ordinance No. 542 of 1941, issued on or about 7 May 1941).

(9) Regulations for Appointment of Lawyers Under Peace Preservation Laws (Bengoshi Shitei Kitei, Ministry of Justice Order, Shihosho Rei, No. 47 of 1941, issued on or about 9 May 1941).

(10) Law for Safeguarding Secrets of Military Material Resources (Gunyō Shigen Himitsu Hogo Hō, Law No. 25 of 1939, promulgated on or about 25 March 1939).

(11) Ordinance for the Enforcement of the Law for Safeguarding Secrets of Military Material Resources (Gunyō Shigen Himitsu Hogo Hō Shiko Rei, Imperial Ordinance No. 413 of 1939, issued on or about 24 June 1939).

(12) Regulations for the Enforcement of the Law of Safeguarding Secrets of Military Material Resources (Gunyō Shigen Himitsu Hogo Hō Shiko Kisoku, Ministries of War and Navy Ordinance No. 3 of 1939, promulgated on or about 26 June

1939).

(13) Law for the Protection of Military Secrets (Gunki Hogo Hō, Law No. 72 of 1937, promulgated on or about 17 August 1937, revised by Law No. 58 of 1941).

(14) Regulations for the Enforcement of the Law for the Protection of Military Secrets (Gunki Hogo Hō Shiko Kisoku, Ministry of War Ordinance No. 59, issued on or about 12 December 1939 and revised by Ministry of War Ordinance Numbers 6, 20 and 58 of 1941).

(15) The Religious Body Law (Shukyō Dantai Hō, Law No. 77 of 1939, promulgated on or about 8 April 1939).

(16) All laws, decrees, orders, ordinances and regulations amending, supplementing or implementing the foregoing enactments.

c. Release immediately all persons now detained, imprisoned, under "protection or surveillance", or whose freedom is restricted in any other manner who have been placed in that state of detention, imprisonment, "protection and surveillance", or restriction of freedom:

(1) Under the enactments referred to in paragraph 1 a and b above.

(2) Without charge.

(3) By charging them technically with a minor offense, when, in reality, the reason for detention, imprisonment, "protection and surveillance", or restriction of freedom, was because of their thought, speech, religion, political beliefs, or assembly.

The release of all such persons will be accomplished by 10 October 1945:

d. Abolish all organizations or agencies created to carry out the provisions of the enactments referred to in paragraph 1 a and b above and that part of, or functions of, other offices or subdivisions of other civil departments and organs which supplement or assist them in the execution of such provisions. These include, but are not limited to:

(1) All secret police organs.

(2) Those departments in the Ministry of Home Affairs, such as the Bureau of Police, charged with supervision of

2 民主化・非軍事化政策への対応(昭和20年10月～21年5月)

publiciations, supervision of public meetings and organizations, censorship of motion pictures, and such other departments concerned with the control of thought, speech, religion or assembly.

(3) Those departments, such as the Special Higher Police (Tokubetsu Koto Keisatsu Bu), in the Tokyo Metropolitan Police, the Osaka Metropolitan Police, any other Metropolitan Police, the Police of the territorial administration of Hokkaido and the various Prefectural police charged with supervision of publications, supervision of public meetings and organizations, censorship of motion pictures, and such other departments concerned with the control of thought, speech, religion or assembly.

(4) Those departments, such as the Protection and Surveillance Commission, and all protection and surveillance stations responsible thereto, under the Ministry of Justice charged with Protection and Surveillance and control of thought, speech, religion, or assembly.

e. Remove from office and employment the Minister of Home Affairs, the Chief of the Bureau of Police of the Ministry of Home Affairs, the Chief of the Tokyo Metropolitan Police Board, the Chief of Osaka Metropolitan Police Board, the Chief of any other Metropolitan police, the Chief of the Police of the Territorial Administration of Hokkaido, the Chiefs of each Prefectural Police Department, the entire personnel of the Special Higher Police of all Metropolitan, Territorial, and Prefectural police departments, the Guiding and Protecting officials and all other personnel of the Protection and Surveillance Commission and of the Protection and Surveillance Stations. None of the above persons will be reappointed to any position under the Ministry of Home Affairs, the Ministry of Justice or any police organ in Japan. Any of the above persons whose assistance is required to accomplish the provisions of this directive will be retained until the directive is accomplished and then dismissed.

f. Prohibit any further activity by police officials, members of police forces, and other government, national or local, officials or employees which is related to the enactments referred to in paragraph 1 a and b above and to the organs and functions abolished by paragraph 1 d above.

g. Prohibit the physical punishment and mistreatment

of all persons detained, imprisoned, or under protection and surveillance, under any and all Japanese enactments, laws, decrees, orders, ordinances and regulations. All such persons will receive at all times ample sustenance.

h. Ensure the security and preservation of all records and any and all other materials of the organs abolished in paragraph 1 d. These records may be used to accomplish the provisions of this directive, but will not be destroyed, removed, or tampered with in any way.

i. Submit a comprehensive report to this Headquarters not later than 15 October 1945 describing in detail all action taken to comply with all provisions of this directive. This report will contain the following specific information prepared in the form of separate supplementary reports:

(1) Information concerning persons released in accordance with paragraph 1 c above. (to be grouped by Prison or institution in which held or from which released or by office controlling their protection and surveillance)

(a) Name of person released from detention or imprisonment or person released from protection and surveillance, his age, nationality, race and occupation.

(b) Specification of criminal charges against each person released from detention or imprisonment or reason for which each person was placed under protection and surveillance.

(c) Date of release and contemplated address of each person released from detention or imprisonment or from protection and surveillance.

(2) Information concerning organizations abolished under the provisions of this directive:

(a) Name of organization.

(b) Name, address, and title of position of persons dismissed in accordance with paragraph 1 e.

(c) Description by type and location of all files, records, reports, and any and all other materials.

(3) Information concerning the Prison System and Prison Personnel.

(a) Organization chart of the Prison System.

(b) Names and Location of all prisons, detention

210

centers and jails.

 (c) Names, rank and title of all prison officials (Governors and Assistant Governors, Chief and Assistant Chief Warders, Warders and Prison doctors).

 (4) Copies of all orders issued by the Japanese Government including those issued by the Governors of Prisons and Prefectural Officials in effectuating the provisions of this directive.

 2. All officials and subordinates of the Japanese Government affected by the terms of this directive will be held personally responsible and strictly accountable for compliance with and adherence to the spirit and letter of this directive.

FOR THE SUPREME COMMANDER:

    H. W. ALLEN,
    Colonel, A.G.D.,
    Asst Adjutant General.

（付　記）

政治的民事的及宗教的自由ニ對スル制限ノ撤廢ニ關スル覺書

（一九四五年十月四日）

一、日本帝國政府ハ政治的、民事的及宗教的自由ニ對スル制限竝ニ人種、國籍、信仰又ハ政見ヲ理由トスル差別待遇ヲ撤廢スルタメ

（イ）左記ノ事項ニ關スル一切ノ法律、勅令、省令、命令及規則ヲ廢止シ其ノ效力ヲ直ニ停止セシムルモノトス

（1）天皇、皇室及帝國政府ニ關スル自由ナル討議ヲ含ム思想、宗教、集會及言論ノ自由ニ對スル制限ヲ設定又ハ之ヲ維持スルモノ

（2）情報ノ蒐集及頒布ニ對スル制限ヲ設定シ又ハ之ヲ維持スルモノ

（3）法令ノ條文又ハ其ノ適用ニヨリ人種、國籍、信仰又ハ政見ヲ理由トシテ特定ノ者ニ對シ不當ナル恩惠又ハ不利ヲ與フルモノ

（ロ）上記ノ（イ）項ニ該當スル法規ハ左ノモノヲ含ム。但シ左ノモノニ限ラルルコトナシ

（1）治安維持法（昭和十六年法律第五十四號、同年三月十日頃公布）

(2) 思想犯保護觀察法(昭和十一年法律第二十九號、同年五月二十九日頃公布)

(3) 思想犯保護觀察法施行令(昭和十一年勅令第四百一號、同年十一月十四日頃公布)

(4) 保護觀察所官制(昭和十一年勅令第四百三號、同年十一月十四日頃公布)

(5) 予防拘禁手續令(司法省令第四十九號、昭和十六年五月十四日頃公布)

(6) 予防拘禁處遇令(司法省令第五十號、昭和十六年五月十四日頃公布)

(7) 國防保安法(昭和十六年法律第四十九號、同年三月七日頃公布)

(8) 國防保安法施行令(昭和十六年勅令第五百四十二號、同年五月七日頃公布)

(9) 弁護士指定規定(昭和十六年司法省令第四十七號、同年五月九日頃公布)

(10) 軍用資源祕密保護法(昭和十四年法律第二十五號、同年三月二十五日頃公布)

(11) 軍用資源祕密保護法施行令(昭和十四年勅令第四百

十三號、同年六月二十四日頃公布)

(12) 軍用資源祕密保護法施行規則(昭和十四年陸海軍省令第三號、同年六月二十六日頃公布)

(13) 軍機保護法(昭和十二年法律第七十二號、同年八月十七日頃公布、昭和十六年、法律第五八號ニ依リ改正)

(14) 軍機保護法施行規則(陸軍省令第五十九號、昭和十四年十二月十二日頃公布、昭和十六年陸軍省令第六二〇及五八號ニヨリ改正)

(15) 宗教團體法(昭和十四年法律第七十七號、同年四月八日頃公布)

(16) 上記ノ法規ヲ修正、補足若ハ實施ニ關スル一切ノ法律、勅令、省令、命令及規則

(八) 左記ノ理由ニヨリ拘留、投獄、保護觀察或ハ他ノ方法ニ依リ自由ヲ束縛サルル一切ノ者ヲ卽時釋放スルモノトス

(1) 上記第一項(イ)及(ロ)ニ示サレタル法規ニ基クモノ

(2) 何等ノ指定ナキモノ

(3) 拘留、投獄、保護觀察或ハ自由ノ束縛ノ眞ノ理由ガ

2 民主化・非軍事化政策への対応（昭和20年10月～21年5月）

其ノ者ノ思想、言論、宗教、政見又ハ集會ニ存スルニ拘ラズ技術的ニハ輕微ノ犯罪ヲ理由トシテ其ノ罪ヲ問フ場合

此等ノ者ノ釋放ハ昭和廿年十月十日迄ニ完了スベキモノトス

(ニ) 上記第一項(イ)及ビ(ロ)ニ示サレタル一切ノ組織又ハ機關、並ニ斯ル條項ヲ遂行スル上ニ於テ之ヲ補足若クハ援助スル他ノ官廳又ハ關係部局ハ機能ヲ廢止スベキモノトス、本項ノ適用ヲ受クルモノハ左ニ列擧スルモノヲ含ム、但シ之ニ限ラルルコトナシ

(1) 一切ノ祕密警察機關

(2) 内務省内ノ警保局ノ如キ出版物ノ取締、集會及結社ノ取締、映畫檢閲等ノ任務ヲ有スルモノ及思想、言論、宗教及集會ノ統制ニ任ズル其他ノ部局

(3) 出版物取締、集會及結社ノ取締、映畫檢閲等ニ當ル警視廳ノ特別高等警察部、大阪府其他ノ都市警察部、北海道廳警察部、及各府縣ノ警察部並ニ思想、言論、宗教又ハ集會ノ統制ニ任ズル他ノ各部局

(4) 保護觀察、思想、言論、宗教又ハ集會ノ統制ニ當ル司法省内ノ保護觀察審査會及之ニ隷屬スル一切ノ保護觀察所

(ホ) 内務大臣、内務省警保局長、警視總監、大阪府警察局長、(其ノ他ノ各都市警察署長)、北海道廳警察部長、(各都市)北海道及各府縣ノ特別高等警察課ノ全員、司法省保護觀察審査會並ニ保護觀察所ノ一切ノ官吏ヲ罷免スルモノトス。更ニ上記ノ者ハ總テ今後内務省、司法省其ノ他日本ニ於ケル如何ナル警察機關ニ於テモ再ビ登用サルルコトナキモノトス。上記ノ者ノ内其ノ援助ガ本指令ノ遂行ニ必要トサル場合ニハ本指令ノ履行ガ完了スル時ニ至ルマデ其ノ職ニ止マリ、爾後罷免サルルモノトス

(ヘ) 警察官吏、警官若ハ他ノ中央乃至地方官吏又ハ雇員ハ上記第一項(イ)及(ロ)並ニ第一項(ニ)ニ依リ廢止サルベキ機關及機能ニ關シ今後如何ナル行動ヲ採ルコトモ禁止スベキモノトス

(ト) 如何ナル日本政府ノ法規、法律、勅令、省令、命令規則ニ依リテモ拘留、投獄、保護觀察ヲ受ケタル一切ノ

私人ニ体刑又ハ不当ナル待遇ヲ与フルコトヲ禁止スベキモノトス。斯ル者ニ対シテハ総テ常ニ身体保持ニ充分ナル営養ヲ与フベシ

(チ) 第一項(ニ)ニ依リ廃止サルル機関ノ一切ノ記録其ノ他一切ノ資料ノ保存ニ必要ナル措置ヲ採ルベキモノトス。此等ノ記録ハ本指令ノ遂行ノ為ニ使用セラルベク其ノ破棄、移動、若ハ改竄ヲ行フコトヲ得ズ

(リ) 本指令ノ條項ニ遵ヒ採ラレタル凡ユル措置ノ細目ヲ示ス詳細ナル報告書ヲ当司令部ニ対シ昭和二十年十月十五日迄ニ提出スベキモノトス。此ノ報告書ハ別個ノ補足ノ報告ノ形式ニ依リ次ノ如キ特定ノ事項ヲ報告スルモノトス

(1) 上記第一項(ハ)ニ基キ釋放サルル者ニ関スル報告(拘留サレ又ハ釋放サレタル時ニ於ケル刑務所其ノ他ノ施設或ハ其ノ保護若ハ観察ヲ統轄スル官廳ニ依リ類別スルコト)

(い) 拘留若ハ入獄ヨリ釋放サレタル者若ハ保護観察ヨリ釋放サレタル者ノ氏名、年齡、國籍、人種及職業

(ろ) 拘留若クハ入獄ヨリ釋放サレタル者ニ対シ挙ゲラレタル罪状ノ種類又ハ保護観察ヲ行フル理由トシテ挙ゲラレタル罪状ノ種類

(は) 拘留入獄若クハ保護観察ヨリ釋放セラレタル者ニツキ其ノ釋放ノ行ハレタル日及釋放ヲ受クル者ノ予定スル住所

(2) 本指令ノ規定ニヨリ廃止サレタル機関ニ関スル報告

(い) 機関ノ名稱

(ろ) 第一項(ニ)ニ基キ罷免サレタル者ノ氏名、住所及職名

(は) 凡ユル書類、記録其ノ他一切ノ資料ノ種類及所在地

(3) 刑務所機構及刑務所人事ニ関スル報告

(い) 刑務所機構ノ概要

(ろ) 凡ユル監獄、刑務所、拘置所ノ名稱及所在地

(は) 凡ユル刑務所所員ノ氏名、官等及職名(刑務所所長、副所長、看守長、副長、看守及刑務所醫)

(4) 本指令ヲ遂行スルニ当リ日本政府ノ發セル凡ユル命令書、(刑務所長及縣廳官吏ノ發セルモノヲ含ム)

2 民主化・非軍事化政策への対応（昭和20年10月～21年5月）

60 政治等の自由制限撤廃指令に関する吉田・サザーランド会談

昭和20年10月5日

吉田外務大臣│
　　　　　　│会談
サザーランド連合国最高司令官総司令部参謀長│

付　記　昭和二十年十月五日、終戦連絡中央事務局第一部作成

右指令に関するマンソン大佐の内話要旨

〰〰〰〰〰〰〰〰〰〰〰

二、本指令ノ條項ニヨリ影響ヲ受ケル一切ノ日本政府官吏及其ノ從屬者ハ本指令ノ忠實ナル遵守遂行ニ對シ各自責任ヲ有シ嚴重ニ其ノ責任ヲ履行スルコトヲ要ス

〰〰〰〰〰〰〰〰〰〰〰

吉田外務大臣「サザーランド」参謀長會談録

十月五日「サザーランド」参謀長往訪、自分ヨリ前記「ベーリー」ニ對スルト同樣ノコトヲ述ヘタルニ「サ」ハ實ハ三人ノ共産黨員死刑ニ處セラレ米國新聞ニ相當ノ衝動ヲ與ヘタル結果昨日ノ覺書トナリタル次第ニテ如何トモスル能ハス此ノ遣リ方ハ遺憾ニ存ス今後ハ成ルヘク注意スヘシ當分カカル仕打ハナキコトト思フト述ヘタルニ付自分ヨリ

参考
「ベーリー」トノ會談録
「ユー、ピー」社長「ベーリー」ヨリ今囘ノ内閣總辭職ハ國民ニ對シ非常ナル「ショック」ナラントノ述ヘタルニ付自分ヨリ總辭職ヨリモ寧ロ昨日ノ「マ」司令部ノ覺書カ國民ニトリ非常ナル「ショック」ナリ恰モ日本ハ米軍々政下ニ在ルカ如キ感ヲ與ヘ其ノ結果トシテ現内閣ノ威信地ニ墜チ持續出來サルコトカ今次總辭職ノ原因ナリ自分ハ近來ノ「マ」司令部ノ態度ニ付諒解ス可ラサルモノアリ内務大臣其他警察機關ヲ撤去シ更ニ入獄中ノ政治犯人ヲ釋放セヨト云フニ赤色革命ヲ獎勵スルカ如キモノニシテ日本政府トシテハ平和秩序ヲ維持スルコトヲ得ス混亂状態ニ陷ルノ外ナシ斯クシテ如何ニシテ米軍ノ日本ニ對スル平和進駐ノ目的

新聞、「ラヂオ」等ニ發表スル以前ニ相互ニ「インサイド、インフオメーション」ノ交換ニ依リ急激ナル「ショック」ヲ避クルコトトシテハ如何ト述ヘタルニ「サ」ハ最モ然ルヘシ但シ「エマーゼンシー」ノ場合ハ此ノ限リニアラストシテ述フ

ヲ達シ得ルヤ反省ヲ促ササルヲ得スト述ヘ共産主義ニ關スル從來ノ政策將來ノ見透シヲ語リ更ニ天皇ノ戰爭責任及裁可權ニ付說明シタルニ「ベ」ハ若シ終戰ノ場合閣僚及統帥部カ戰爭繼續ニ一致セハ　天皇ハ御裁可相成ルヤト問ヒタルニ付自分ヨリ斯カル場合ハ　陛下ノ御意思ニ反スルモ御裁可アルヘシト答ヘタルニ先方ハ諒解セル如クニ見受ケラレタリ尙「ベ」ハ昨四日米側覺書ニ於テ內務大臣ノ罷免ヲ要求シタルハ米政府ノ眞意ヨリ少シ逸脱（デビエート）シ居ルカ如シト述ヘ自分ヨリ在英大使當時日英間ニ或種ノ諒解ヲ成立セシメ之ヲ通シテ日米關係ノ改善ニ資スル爲英政府ト話合ヲ行ヒタルモ日支事變ノ勃發ニ依リ不成功ニ終リタル經緯ヲ說明シ置キタリ

（付　記）
政治的、公民的及宗敎的自由ニ對スル制限除去ノ件

一、本件措置ヲ決定シ且詳細承知シ居ルハ「マックアーサー」、「スザランド」、軍政部長クリスト准將及情報敎育局長「ダイク」（但シ本人ハ小問題ノミ承知）ノ四名ノミナリ

二、GHQトシテハ本件措置ニ依リ現內閣ヲ崩壞セシムル意圖ナシ

三、然ラバ本件措置ヲ執リタル所以如何ト云ハバGHQノ態度ハ命令第一號及指令第二號ニ依リ夙ニ明カナル所ニシテ今ヤ之ヲ實現スル時期ニ達セリト認メタルガ故ナリ

四、GHQ內部又ハ華府乃至米紙其他ノ外部ヨリノ事情等政治ノ必要ニ基キ本件措置ガ執ラレタルヤトノ質問ニ對シテハ之ヲ否定セリ

五、而シテ本件措置ノ直接ノ動機ハ三木獄死其他事件ノ新聞公表ニ在リ

六、本件措置ノ及ボスベキ影響乃至共産主義ノ問題ニ付テハ充分之ヲ承知シ居ルモ今ヤ本件措置決行ノ時期ナリト認メラレタルナリ

「マンソン」大佐ノ山形公使ニ對スル內話左ノ通
（昭二〇、一〇、五）

昭和20年10月5日　外務省作成

「國体及共產主義ニ關スル米國ノ方針」

2　民主化・非軍事化政策への対応（昭和20年10月〜21年5月）

國体及共産主義ニ關スル米國ノ方針

（昭和二〇、一〇、五）

現在ノ帝國政府首腦者及政府當局（就中內務省司法省文部省等）ノ重大關心ハ所謂國体護持及共産主義ニ關スル米國ノ方針如何ノ問題ニ寄セラレアリ本稿ハ主トシテ右ニ關スル米側方針ノ說明ヲ目的トスルモノナリ（但右ハ飽迄モ米側方針ノ說明ニシテ我方ニ□ル說明乃至啓蒙ノ余地ナシ
（一字不明）
爲スモノニ非ス）

一、日本處理ニ關スル英・米・支ノ基本方針ヲ闡明セル「ポツダム」宣言ヲ貫ク原則カ日本ノ平和主義（乃至日本ノ非軍國主義化）民主主義、合理主義化ニアルコト明瞭ナル處最近米國ノ公表セル初期ノ對日方針ニ於テモコノ點ハ同様ナリ就中民主主義化ニ關シテハ本公表文書中

(1) 第一部前段Bニ於テ米國ノ二大究極目的ノ一ツトシテ
「他國家ノ權利ヲ尊重シ聯合國憲章ノ理想ト原則ニ示サレタル米國ノ目的ヲ支持スヘキ平和的且責任アル政府ヲ追而樹立スルコト」及「米國ハ斯ル政府カ出來得ル限リ民主主義的自治ノ原則ニ合致スルコトヲ希望スル」旨ヲ明ニシ

(2) 且右究極目的ノ達成ノ主要手段ガ日本國民ニ對スル個人ノ自由並ニ基本的人權ノ尊重就中信敎集會言論出版ノ自由ニ對スル欲求增大ノ獎勵及「民主主義的及代議的組織ノ形成ノ獎勵」（第一部前段C）ニアルコト

(3) 更ニ主要手段ガ政治面及經濟面ニ於テ主トシテ第三部政治三、個人ノ自由及民主主義過程ヘノ希求ノ獎勵及第四部經濟二、民主主義的勢力ノ助長ニ具体的ニ列擧セラレアルガ如キモノナルコト

(4) 又日本政府乃至日本國民ニヨル現在ノ日本統治形式
（天皇ヲ含ム）ノ封建的又ハ權力主義的傾向ノ修正ハ之ヲ許容支持シ斯ル修正乃至變革ノ爲ノ強力行使ニ對シテハ最高司令官ハ麾下部隊ノ安全及占領目的ノ達成上ニ必要ナキ限リ干涉スヘカラス（第二部二后段）トナシ居レリ

(5) 但シ米國ハ前記(1)ノ如キ究極目的ニ拘ラス建前トシテハ少クトモ自由ニ表現セラレタル日本國民ノ意志ニ支持セラレサル統治形式卽政体ヲ日本ニ强要セサルコトヲ明ニシ居レリ

二、先ツ右一(1)及(4)(5)ニ付考察スルニ

217

(1) 米國ノ對日處理方針カ日本支配ニアルコトハ勿論ニシテ換言セハ右一(1)ノ目的ハ米國ノ二大究極目的ノ他ノ一タル本文書第一部前段Ａ「日本カ再ヒ米國ノ脅威トナリ又ハ世界ノ平和ト安全ノ脅威トナルコトナキ様保證スルコト」ナル目的ニ從屬スルモノト言フヘシ

即右一(1)ノ目的ハ換言セハ民主主義的自治原則ニ合致スル政府ノ樹立ナル目的ノ為一面ニ於テ純理想主義的考慮ヲ含ミ居ルモノト他面ニ於テ統治形式ノ自治ニ依ル政府乃至統治形式カ獨裁的政府乃至統治形式ニ比シ本質的ニ平和的ナル事實及分割統治ノ意圖ニ基ク實利的考慮ヲモ含ミ居ルモノト推測シ得ヘシ(右ノ如キ平和化卽民主主義化ナル考ヘ方ハ例ハ第四部經濟ニ「民主主義的勢力ノ助長」ナル節ニ於テ右兩觀念カ混交サレ居ル事實ニモ之ヲ見出シ得ヘシ)

(2) 問題トナルハ

(イ) 前記一(2)ノ民主主義的自治ノ原則ニ合致スルコトニ關スル米國ノ希望モ果シテ國體卽チ天皇統治制度ノ變更ヲ含ムモノナリヤ否ヤノ點

(ロ) 然リトセハ右希望ノ強サ如何ノ點

ノニ點ナルヘシ

右ニ關シテハ別稿卽「國體及政體ニ關スル米國ノ態度」中ニ詳說シアルモ簡單ニ述フレハ

(3) 米國ノ右希望ハ

(イ) 過去ニ於ケル軍國主義的封建的勢力ニ依ル天皇統治制度ノ誤用ノ結果トシテ 天皇統治制度ノ誤解ヲ有シ居ルコト卽非平和的ノ皇國主義的存在ナリトノ誤解ヲ有シ居ルコト

(ロ) 我 天皇統治制度カ獨特ナル沿革ヲ有シ就中其神話的ノ性格ニ基キ所謂封建主義ノ權力盲從的性格ヲ帶ビ居リ右カ民主主義ノ根底タル個人人格乃至人權自由ノ覺醒認識ノ障害トナリ居ルコト

(ハ) 我 天皇制度就中其神話的性格カ誤レル神國ノ八紘一宇的侵略想想(思カ)ニ深キ關係ヲ有スルコト(右(ロ)(ハ)カ狂信的愛國心ノ發露ヲ齎ラセルコト)

等ニ鑑ミ且亦 天皇統治制度モノカ本質的ニ完全ナル民主主義ト相容レサル事實ニモ鑑ミ 天皇統治制度卽國體ノ變革ヲ希望モ含ミ居ルハ疑點ナカルヘシ

(4) 而シテ現在ノ 天皇制度乃至皇室制度ニ對スル米國ノ

2　民主化・非軍事化政策への対応（昭和20年10月〜21年5月）

變革希望ハ其ノ新聞論調及今日迄ノ米軍當局ノ表明セル態度ヨリ察スルニ極メテ根強キモノナルヘシ（例ハ「マ」元帥御訪問皇室財產制度）

然レトモ右ハ現在ノ儘ノ　天皇統治制度乃至皇室制度全般ニ對スル反感乃至變革希望ニシテ「　天皇ニ依ル統治」ソノモノノ繼續ハ所要ノ變革ヲ加フル限リ且眞ニ、自由ニ表現セラレタル日本國民ノ意志カ之ヲ希望スル限リ絕對的ニ之ヲ排除セントスルモノニハ非ルヘシ

（イ）所要ノ變革トシテ考慮セラルルコトハ先ツ神話的性格ノ排除乃至皇室財產制度ノ修正ノ他　天皇ニ依ル「統治」ノ內容乃至實質カ最モ機微且重要ナルヘキモ右ニ關シ強度ノ民主主義的調整ヲ加フルコトノ必要ナルヘク（而シテ右ハ事實上政治慣習ノ變革ヲ含ムヘシ）

（ロ）又眞ニ「自由ニ表現セラレタル國民意志」トハ治安維持法等ニ依ル共產黨取締ハ之ヲ容認セサルモノナリ

註右ニ關シテハ
（イ）民主主義ノ本質ヨリ見ルモ又米國內ニ於ケル共產黨取締ノ實情及共產黨ノ最近ノ綱領乃至方針、米蘇關係就中最近ニ於ケル倫敦外相會議ノ結果設立略確實視セラルル極東諮問委員會及日本管理委員會等ニ鑑ミ米軍當局ノ立場ヲ考察スル必要アルヘシ

（ロ）前記一（5）卽米國ハ日本國民ノ自由意志ニ反スル政体乃至統治形式ヲ強要セストナス點ニ關シ「強要セス」ノ點ヨリ寧ロ「自由ニ表現セラレタル意志」ノ點ニ重點ヲ置クヘキナリ

（5）就中前記一（4）ノ如キハ米國ハ我統治形式ノ「封建的、權力主義的傾向」ノ政府乃至國民ニ依ル變革、修正ニ關シテハ積極的慫慂ヲ暗示シ居ルモノト解セラルル次第ニシテ特ニ政府トシテハ最モ注意ヲ要スル點ナリ

（本點ヨリ見ルモ國体ニ關スル論議ヲ一切取締ラントスルカ如キハ明瞭ニ米國ノ方針ニ背反スル次第ナリ）

第三部三「個人ノ自由及民主主義過程ヘノ希求ノ獎勵」ノ考察

（1）第一項ニ於テハ（イ）宗敎的信仰ノ自由（ロ）民主主義諸國ノ智識ノ普及（ハ）占領軍人員ト日本人トノ交涉ノ不制限ヲ

述ヘ居ル處右ハ何レモ日本ニ於ケル現在ノ神話的、封建的非合理的迷夢ノ打破及啓蒙ニ依リ民主主義及合理主義ノ根底タル個人ノ人格ノ意識ヲ日本國民ニ植付ケルコトヲ以テ日本民主主義化ノ第一歩トナスノ米側見解ヲ表明スルモノト言フヘシ

即米側ニ於テハ日本ニ於ケル神話主義右ニ基ク日本國民ノ盲從ノ打破ニ依リ個人ノ人格ノ發見及意識ヘノ本ノ民主主義化平和主義化ノ第一歩トナスモノニシテ此ノ故ヲ以テ特ニ右(イ)(ロ)(ハ)ニナル一連ノ記述ヲ掲ケタルモノナルヘシ(然ラサル限リ特ニ宗教信仰ノ自由云々ノ(イ)ノ如キ記述ヲ理解シ得サルヘシ)

(イ)ハ即神道乃至神社禮拜ノ強制ノ廢止乃至停止ノ問題及場合ニ依リテハ神道ニ關スルニ以上ノ干渉ヲ招來スルモノト見サルヘカラス

(ロ)ハ一面ニ於テ人種差違等ニ依リ獨逸ニ於ケル如キ交歡禁止ノ必要ナキノミナラズ逆ニ米兵等ノ日本國民トノ接觸ヲ制限スルコトナク寧ロ之ニヨリ日本國民ノ神話的迷夢ノ啓蒙ヲ企圖スルモノナルヘシ

尚本項方針ハ日本ノ教育制度改善ニ關シテモ強ク要請セラルヘシ

(2)第二項即民主主義的政黨ノ獎勵ノ項ニ關シテハ(イ)共產黨カ右民主的政黨ノ中ニ含マルルヤ否ヤノ點先ツ問題トナルヘキ處米蘇關係米國國內ニ於ケル共產黨ノ容認及共產黨自身ノ當面採ルヘキ政策等ニ鑑ミ米國トシテハ少クトモ共產黨ノ正式ニ否認乃至禁壓スルコトニハ同意セサルヘシ(獨伊等ノ米軍占領地ニ於テモ共產黨ハ公認セラレアルモ事實上之ニ對スル支持ヘ適宜處理シアル趣ナリ)

(ロ)但シ但書ノ如ク占領軍ノ安全保持等ノ名目ニ依リ共產黨等ニ依ル過度ノ治安攪亂ノ虞アルニ到レハ之ヲ彈壓スルモノト信ス

(3)第三項中

(イ)「人種、國籍、信教又ハ政治的見解ヲ理由ニ差別待遇ヲ規定スル」法令ノ改廢ハ主トシテ獨逸管理方針ノ名殘リナルヘキモ政治的見解ナル語ハ結局國体ニ關スル見解ヲモ包含スヘク治安維持法等ハ問題トナリ來ル

2　民主化・非軍事化政策への対応（昭和20年10月～21年5月）

(ロ)「本文書ニ述ヘラレタル諸目的竝ニ諸政策ト矛盾スル法令」ノ改廢止及修正ニ付キテハ詳細ナル具体的檢討ヲ必要トスヘシ(國内主管官廳方針トシテハ明瞭ニシテ特ニ說明ノ要ナカルヘキモ治安維持法等國體ニ關スル取締法令ハ本文書ノ究極目的ノ一カ所謂「自由ニ表現セラレタル國民ノ意志ニ依ル政体ノ決定」ニアル以上當然問題トナリ來ルモノト思考ス(註一)

(ニ) 政治犯人ノ釋放
(イ)(ロ)ノ諸法令ノ實施ヲ特ニ其目的トスル機關ノ改廢止ニ付キテハ尚具体的研究未了ナリ

「不法ニ」ナル語ノ解釋ハ困難ナルモ事實上右不法ナリヤ否ヤノ解釋ハ米側ノ見解ニ依リ判斷セラルルコトナルヘク極右犯人ノ釋放、左翼犯人ノ拘禁繼續ノ如キハ採ラサル所ナルヘシ

(ホ) 司法法律及警察組織ノ改革及指導
具体的ニハ尚研究中ナルモ強權的性質(就中行刑、檢察、警察制度ニ於ケル)ハ所謂人權自由ノ尊重ノ建前ヨリ早急改革ヲ要スヘシ

註一　集會、言論、出版ノ自由カ米國ノ目的ノ一ナル處右自由ノ限度ニ關スル米側見解カ果シテ國体ノ護持乃至ニ私有財産制度ノ尊重ヲ含ムモノナリヤ否ヤノ點ニツキテハ米側見解ヲ確カムルニ非レハ確言シ得サルヘキモ從來ノ米側當局ノ態度ハ本文書ニ現ハレタル前記諸方針ヨリ推測スルニ之等ニ關スル取締ヲ許容セサル建前ヲ採ルコト略々確實ナリ

〰〰〰〰〰〰〰〰

62

昭和20年10月6日　連合国最高司令官総司令部より　日本政府宛

外国為替資産および関係事項の報告に関する指令

GENERAL HEADQUARTERS
SUPREME COMMANDER FOR THE ALLIED POWERS

6 October 1945

AG 123 (6 Oct 45) ESS
SCAPIN 96
MEMORANDUM TO: IMPERIAL JAPANESE GOVERNMENT.
THROUGH: Central Liaison Committee, Tokyo.
SUBJECT: Reports of Foreign Exchange Assets and related mat-

ters.

1. The definitions contained in Memorandum AG 130 (22 Sep 45) ESS dated 22 September 1945, Subject "Control of Financial Transactions" will apply to this memorandum. In addition, the following definitions will apply:

   a. The term "foreign exchange assets" will include gold and silver coins; gold, silver and platinum bullion and alloys thereof in bullion form; and external assets.

   b. The term "evidences of ownership" will include, but not by way of limitation, securities, title deeds, mortgages, bank books, receipts, checks, drafts, promissory notes, bills of exchange, certificates of indebtedness, copyrights, trademarks and patents.

2. You will immediately take appropriate action to require all banks, trust companies, insurance companies, securities brokers and other financial institutions within Japan to physically segregate all foreign exchange assets held by them whether for their own account or for the account of others, and all evidences of ownership thereof and books, documents and records relating thereto. You will take appropriate action to insure that such items are segregated, preserved and kept readily accessible to this Headquarters.

3. You will immediately take appropriate action to prevent the removal without the permission of this Headquarters of any foreign exchange assets or evidences of ownership thereof or books, documents and records relating thereto from safe deposit vaults and boxes or other places of safekeeping in financial institutions. You may permit the removal of such items for the purpose of preparing the reports provided in this memorandum, but any item so removed shall be delivered to the financial institution in which the item is held and segregated in accordance with the provisions of paragraph 2 above.

4. You will furnish to this Headquarters reports of all foreign exchange assets and evidences of ownership thereof owned and controlled by, or in the custody of, all persons within Japan in accordance with the following schedule:

   a. Within thirty days, you will furnish a complete report of all foreign exchange assets and evidences of ownership thereof

222

2　民主化・非軍事化政策への対応（昭和20年10月〜21年5月）

owned or controlled, directly or indirectly, in whole or in part, by the Japanese national, prefectural and local governments, and their agencies and instrumentalities, including all utilities, undertakings, public corporations and monopolies owned by any of them or in which they have a controlling interest.

b. Within thirty days, you will furnish a complete report of all foreign exchange assets and evidences of ownership thereof owned or controlled, directly or indirectly, in whole or in part, by the Imperial Household;

c. Within forty-five days, you will furnish a complete report of all foreign exchange assets and evidences of ownership thereof owned or controlled, directly or indirectly, in whole or in part, by all banks, trust companies, securities brokers, and other financial institutions;

d. Within sixty days you will furnish a complete report of all foreign exchange assets and evidences of ownership thereof owned or controlled, directly or indirectly, in whole or in part, by all other partnerships, corporations, associations, and business organizations;

e. Within seventy-five days you will furnish a complete report of all foreign exchange assets and evidences of ownership thereof owned or controlled, directly or indirectly, in whole or in part, by all other persons within Japan.

f. Within ninety days, you will furnish a complete report of all foreign exchange assets and evidences of ownership thereof which are held by or in the custody of any person in Japan and which have not been previously reported.

5. The holdings of each person will be reported separately in such form and manner as will be prescribed by this Headquarters. Within five days you will furnish this Headquarters with copies of the forms desired to be used by you for this purpose.

6. Six copies of all reports will be furnished.

7. Until further notice, the provisions of paragraph 2 of this memorandum will not apply to institutions closed by direction of this Headquarters. Request for permission to inspect the books and records of such institutions for the purpose of preparing the reports required will be addressed to the Ministry of Finance which in turn will refer the matter to this Headquarters.

8. You will report immediately to this Headquarters the action taken to comply with these requirements.

9. An acknowledgment of the receipt of this memorandum is desired.

FOR THE SUPREME COMMANDER:

H. W. ALLEN,
Colonel, A.G.D,
Asst Adjutant General.

63 昭和20年10月9日 政務局第一課作成

［自主的即決的施策ノ緊急樹立ニ關スル件］

自主的即決的施策ノ緊急樹立ニ關スル件（試案）

二〇、一〇、九 政一

国際情勢ハ帝國ノ國際管理實現ノ方向ニ向ヒツツアリ帝國ノ前途愈々多難ニシテ對米相互信賴感ヲ鞏化シツツ我方ノ自主的發意ニ依リ日本ノ變革更生ヲ具體的ニ實現スルコト焦眉ノ急務ナリ然ルニ降伏後ニ於ケル事態ノ進展ヲ観ルニ事實ハ右喫緊ノ要請ヨリ距ルコト遠ク進駐軍ハ「ポツダム」宣言及「降伏後ニ於ケル米國ノ初期ノ對日方針」等ニ體現セラレ居ル日本統治ニ關スル方針大綱ヲ綱領トスル革命勢力タルノ感アリ帝國ニシテ速ニ聯合國側ノ日本統治方針大綱ノ意圖スル所カ平和主義ト合理主義ヲ基調トスル民主主義日本ノ建設ニ在ルコトヲ明確且徹底的ニ把握シ日本ノ變革更生ノ主體性ヲ恢復シ自發的ニ統治制度ヲ初メ政治、経済、文化等各般ノ分野ニ亘リ急速ニ施策要綱ヲ樹立シ之ヲ強力ニ遂行スルニ非ラサレハ事毎ニ進駐軍側ヨリ命令ヲ與ヘラレ、受動的ニ之カ實施ヲ餘儀ナクセラレ政治経済ノ革新案ハ極端ニ走ルノ結果トナルヘク斯クテハ唯ニ施策ニ中正ヲ失フノミナラス國家ノ自主權ノ全面的喪失ヲ招來シ勢ヒノ趨ク所終戦決定當時「ポツダム」宣言ノ降伏條項ヲ受諾スルニ決シタル際ノ帝國ノ意圖ハ沒却セラレ降伏後ノ別逸ニ擇フ所ナキ狀態ニ立到ルノ惧レ極メテ大ナリ仍テ別紙要綱ニ據リ緊急ヲ要スル施策ヲ即決的ニ確立シ之ヲ聯合軍側ヘ連絡シテ其ノ協力ヲ求メ全力ヲ盡シテ之カ實施ニ邁進スルモノトス

（別紙）

2 民主化・非軍事化政策への対応（昭和20年10月〜21年5月）

自主的即決的施策確立要綱

一、最高指針

(1) 彼我双方ニ依ル「ポツダム」宣言ノ降伏條項ノ恪遵ト國際正義ノ厳守ヲ期スヘキコト

(2) 對米協調ニ徹シ相互ノ理解ト信頼感ヲ増大シ帝國更生ノ基礎ヲ鞏化スヘキコト

(3) 變革更生ニ至ル萬般ノ施策ハ進歩主義ヲ基調トシ民主主義、平和主義、合理主義ニ基ク政治經濟ノ社會化ニ重點ヲ指向シ國民大衆ノ生活確保ヲ第一義トスヘキコト

(4) 變革更生ノ斷行ニ當リ飽ク迄自主性ト主體性ヲ失ハス且ツ日本民族國有ノ美點ト好マシキ傳統ヲ常ニ其ノ基底ニ嚴存セシムヘキコト

二、細目

(1) 降伏條項ノ嚴守及國家生存權ノ確保

(イ)「ポツダム」宣言等ニ掲ケラレアル降伏條項ヲ忠實ニ履行スルト共ニ聯合國側ニ依リ右條項ノ範圍逸脱ヲ防止スルコト

(ロ) 徹底的日米協調ニ依リ米國ノ協力ノ下ニ圓滑ニ國内革新ノ實行ヲ圖ルコト

(ハ) 聯合國側ノ支援ヲ得テ差當リハ國民經濟維持上少クトモ最低限度ノ必要ヲ確保スルコト

(ニ) 帝國領土ノ割讓ノ合理的解決ヲ圖ルコト

(2) 統治制度及統治組織ノ改革

(イ) 皇室制度ノ合理化ヲ圖ルト共ニ大赦、皇室財産ノ御下付等ヲ行ヒ國民ノ皇室ニ對スル信仰ヲ新タニシ以テ國體ノ護持ヲ完カラシムルコト

(ロ) 憲法ヲ改正シ之カ運用上民主主義精神ニ依ル補弼制度ヲ確立スルモ大權ハ時ニ應シ能動的ノモノタラシムルコト

(ハ) 内大臣府、樞密院等ノ民主化ニ依リ［一字不明］高政治ノ公開ヲ圖ルコト

(ニ) 選擧法及貴族院令ノ民主主義的、進歩主義的改正ヲ行ヒ急速ニ總選擧ヲ行フコト

（選擧法ノ改正案ハ審議會ニ一ケ月ノ期限ヲ附シ主要點ノ改正案ヲ完了セシムヘク要スレバ暫定的改正ニテモ可ナリ）

(ホ) 内閣各省ノ統合簡素化ヲ行フト共ニ官制及官吏任用

制度ヲ根本的ニ改革スルコト
(ヘ)檢察制度ニ附着スル封建的殘渣ヲ一掃スルコト
(ト)國民經濟的諸條件ノ變移ニ應ジタル地方行政區劃ノ改正ヲ行ヒ且ツ地方自治制ヲ強化スルコト

(3)文化政策ノ刷新
(イ)神社神道ニ於ケル政治性ヲ拂拭シ神道カ極端ナル國家主義ト神話的日本選民思想ノ源泉タルヤノ疑ヒヲ一掃スルコト
(ロ)廣ク東西ノ古典ノ翻譯乃至註釋普及ヲ圖ルコト
(ハ)大學教育ニ眞理探究ノ自由ヲ認メ又個ノ完成ヲ目トスル全學校ノ再編成ニ關シ基本ノ方向ヲ闡明シ教材ノ根本的改正ヲ速カニ完了スルコト
(ニ)思想、宗教、文化等ニ關スル政府ノ統制ヲ廢スルト共ニ右ノ分野ニ於ケル民間諸團體ニ殘存スル軍國主義的、封建的性格ヲ一掃スルコト
(ホ)文化ノ中心ヲ首府ノミニ限定セズ地方的ニ分散スルコト

(4)國民大衆ノ生活確保
(イ)權威アル食糧需給計劃ヲ樹立シ配分制度ヲ合理化スルノ具體案及住宅政策ヲ確定シ即時實施ニ移スコト之カ爲ニ統制ヲ活用スルコト
(ロ)生產ノ增加ヲ圖ルト共ニ劃期的ナル財政施策ヲ實施シ購買力ノ吸收ノ爲ノ方法ヲ盡シ以テ「インフレーション」ノ進行ヲ阻止スルコト
(精密ナル數字ニ基ク明確ナル具體案ヲ速カニ聯合軍側ニ提示シテ支援ヲ得ル樣措置スヘシ)
(ハ)封建的ノ農村經濟組織ヲ打破スルト共ニ農業經營ニ近代的ノ技術ヲ導入シ之カ多角化ヲ圖ルコト
(ニ)傳統的ノ手工業ヲ存續助長スルコト
(ホ)修理經濟ノ急速復活ヲ促進スルコト
(ヘ)產業立國ノ重點ヲ農業ニ置クヘキヤ工業ニ置クヘキヤニ依ル人口ノ再配置ヲ圖ルコト

(5)國民經濟ノ社會化
(イ)勞働組合、農民組合、消費組合等ノ結成ヲ促進シ一般ニ組合運動ノ活發化ノ爲ノ措置ヲ講スルコト
(ロ)社會保險制度ノ擴充强化ヲ即時實施スルコト

2　民主化・非軍事化政策への対応(昭和20年10月～21年5月)

其ノ結果帝國ノ運命ハ危機ニ陥ルニ至ルコト豫見ニ難カラス

(イ)企業經營權ニ對スル干渉ヲ止ムルコト
(ロ)財產稅及高度ノ累進課稅ヲ課スルコト
(ハ)富ノ再分配、企業獨占ノ打破、産業支配權ノ社會化ヲ計リ且右ハ大財閥ノ解体ト並行セシムルコト
(ニ)輸入資金ノ造成及失業者ノ吸収
(6)
(イ)聯合國側ヨリ原料ノ提供ヲ得テ完成ノ品トシテ之ヲ給付シ輸入資金ノ獲得及賠償ノ一部ニ充當ヲ圖ルコト
(ロ)輸出ノ可能性ニ關スル調査ヲ速カニ完成シ輸出可能物資ノ外貨ヘノ換價及輸出産業ノ操業ヲ再開スルコト
(ハ)聯合軍側ト連絡シ所要ノ援助ヲ得ル樣努ムヘシト
(ニ)失業對策トシテ土木事業、「ダム」建設等ヲ即急實施スルコト
(註)前記諸項目ハ自發的、即決的ニ着手スルヲ要シ然ラスシテ徒ラニ時機ヲ失スルニ於テハ聯合軍側ヨリ先手ヲ打タレ實施命令ノ頻發ヲ見ルヘク□□□□舉カラスト看取セラルル場合ハ部分的軍管理ノ實施ニ至ル公算モアリ惹イテハ占領政策上 天皇及帝國政府ヲ活用セントノ當初ヨリノ米側ノ意嚮ハ放棄ヲ餘儀ナクセラレ〔四字不明〕

64　昭和20年10月9日　連合国最高司令官総司令部より日本政府宛

必需物資の輸入に関する指令

SCAPIN 110

AG (091.31) ESS　　　　　　　9 October 1945

GENERAL HEADQUARTERS
SUPREME COMMANDER FOR THE ALLIED POWERS

MEMORANDUM FOR: THE IMPERIAL JAPANESE GOVERNMENT.

THROUGH: Central Liaison Office, Tokyo.

SUBJECT: Import of Essential Commodities.

1. Several requests have been received from the central Liaison Committee of the Japanese Imperial Government for authorization to import commodities deemed by it to be essential for the maintenance of the civil population.

2. Requests to import commodities will not be submitted

to this headquarters unless:

   a. Such imports are vital to the maintenance of a minimum standard of living for the civil population.

   b. Credits have been established for payment of imports desired by means of exports, approved by this headquarters for this purpose.

3. The Japanese Imperial Government will promptly:

   a. Submit its plans for payment for approved essential imports including schedules of resources presently available to it for payment of imports and a forecast of such resources as will become available for this purpose by 31 December 1946.

   b. Submit a plan whereby resources may be made available to provide necessary foreign exchange. Present to this headquarters for approval its plan to conserve or prevent the use of resources in Japan, that are not essential to the maintenance of a minimum standard of living and which are suitable for export.

   c. Insure that all practicable measures are taken to achieve the maximum utilization of essential Japanese resources so that imports into Japan are limited to absolute minimum essentials. Such measures will specifically include, but are not limited to:

   (1) Provision for the maximum production of crude petroleum, foodstuffs, fuel, fertilizer, salt.

   (2) Establishment of such fiscal measures as are necessary for full implementation of this directive.

   (3) Establishment of such labor policies as are essential for full implementation of this directive.

   (4) Provision for priority of transport to such essential resources.

   d. Create an agency to be responsible for receiving and for the distribution of, imports so as to insure equitable distribution at a cost consistent with current wages to the public. No person will be appointed to a responsible position in this agency who has been an active exponent of militant nationalism and aggression.

FOR THE SUPREME COMMANDER:

H. W. ALLEN,

2　民主化・非軍事化政策への対応（昭和20年10月～21年5月）

65　政治等の自由制限撤廃指令に関する日本側照会への回答

昭和20年10月10日　連合国最高司令官総司令部より日本政府宛

OFFICE OF THE SUPREME COMMANDER
FOR THE ALLIED POWERS

10 October 1945

AG 091 (4 Oct 45) CIS
SCAPIN 115
MEMORANDUM FOR: IMPERIAL JAPANESE GOVERNMENT.
THROUGH: Central Liaison Office, Tokyo.
SUBJECT: Answer to Pro Memoria concerning The Memorandum of the Supreme Commander for the Allied Powers on Removal of Restrictions on Liberties dated 4 October 1945.

1. Officials who have been removed from positions of responsibility in one Department will not be transferred to positions of responsibility in another. Within the term "officials" as used herein are included Prefectural Police Chiefs and Section Chiefs and ranking assistants in the Special Higher Police. No dismissed personnel including minor officials of Special Higher Police referred to in paragraph 4 below will be placed in the Ministry of Education. If personnel is reemployed by other departments such information will be furnished this Headquarters.

2. Officials connected now with police affairs will not be permitted to hold positions in either the Ministry of Home Affairs or in the Ministry of Justice.

3. "Positions under the Ministry of Home Affairs, the Ministry of Justice···" includes all positions under those Ministries except for such minor positions in the Prefectural Government which are responsible in policy matters for other Ministries.

4. The entire personnel of the Special Higher Police will be dismissed and in no case be reemployed in any position of power or responsibility over the people.

5. All personnel connected with "Protection and Surveill-

Colonel, A.G.D.,
Asst Adjutant General.

ance" will be dismissed.

6. If the Chief of a Protection and Surveillance Station holds concurrently the office of Public Prosecutor, he will be removed from both positions.

7. An initial report will be furnished October 15th, containing such information as you have ready. Another report containing the balance of the required information will be submitted on October 22nd.

8. Police officials will not be retained longer than the time necessary to accomplish the provisions of the October 4th Memorandum.

9. You will inform this Headquarters by October 20th of the full details of the case of any individual who is held for both a criminal and political offense. Pending decision by this Headquarters, individuals may be retained in custody.

FOR THE SUPREME COMMANDER:

H. W. ALLEN,
Colonel, A.G.D.,
Asst Adjutant General.

昭和20年10月11日　幣原（喜重郎）内閣総理大臣　マッカーサー連合国最高司令官　会談

幣原・マッカーサー会談

付　記　右会談でマッカーサーが表明した改革意見

総理「マッカーサー」會談要旨　　昭二〇、一〇、一三

十月十一日午後五時総理大臣「マクアーサー」元帥ヲ聯合軍司令部ニ往訪セラル先方ハ「サザランド」参謀長同席ナリシカ総理ノ座ニ着セラルルヤ否ヤ先ツ「マ」元帥ニ於テ發言シ

今日御面會ノ機會ニ先ツ以テ日本政府ニ希望スルコトニ付申上ケ度シ決シテ無理ナルコトヲ期待シ居ルニハ非サルモ積リナルモ聞カレル貴下ニ於ハ或ハ「ハーシユ」ニ響クヤモ知レス然シ若シ無理又ハ實行不可能ト考ヘラルルコトアラバ忌憚ナク御指摘アリタシト述ヘ豫テ用意ノ書キ物（別紙ノ通リ）ヲ讀ミ上ケタリ之ニ對シ総理ヨリ

只今元帥ノ御意見トシテ承リタル五項目中アルモノハ組閣早々ノ閣議ニ於テ既ニ考慮シテ決定セルモノアリ擔當

2　民主化・非軍事化政策への対応（昭和20年10月～21年5月）

閣僚ト相談ノ要ハアルモ五項目ヲ通シテ差當リ實行全然不可能ト認メラルルモノ無ク安心セル次第ナリ

第一ノ婦人參政權ノ件ハ既ニ政府ニ於テハ之カ實施ヲ決心シ閣議ニ於テ内定ヲ見居レリ選擧權ノ問題ニ付テハ次ノ順序ニテ事ヲ運ブ予定ナリ卽チ現議會ハ選擧後數年ヲ經過シ居リ民意ヲ反映シ居ルモノナリヤ否ヤ疑ヲ有スル向鮮カラサルニ付現在ノ民意ヲ反映セシムル爲解散ニ進ミタシ解散ニ當リテハ現行ノ選擧法ヲ以テシテハ實際ニ選擧ヲ行ヒ得サル節アリ例ヘハ戰災ニ依リ疎開若ハ轉居セル家庭多數ニ上リ居ルコト記錄ヲ喪失セル役場ノ鮮カラサルコト等ノ事實アルノミナラス眞ノ民意ヲ議會ニ反映セシムル爲ニハ現行制度ニハ不適當ナル條意モ鮮カラズ婦人參政權ノ定メ無キモ其ノ一ナリ之等ノ改正ヲ行フニ當リ當面ノ改正ノミヲ取上ケ根本的ノ改正ハ之ヲ他日ニ讓ルヤ否ヤノ問題アリ苦心ヲ要スル所ナリ政府トシテハナルヘク根本的改正ト考ヘ見タルカ時日之ヲ許サス當面ノ必要問題ノミニ付改正ヲ加ヘ近々臨時議會ニ提出シ同意ヲ得レバナルヘク早ク議會ヲ解散シ之ニ依リ選擧ヲ行フ考ヘナリコノ際貴下ニ對シ一言致シ置キタキハ從來

行フ考ヘナリコノ際貴下ニ對シ一言致シ置キタキハ從來ノ日本ノ選擧ニ於テハ直接間接ニ何等カノ政府ノ干涉無カリシコトナキカノ如キ印象ヲ抱ケルモノ多ク其ノ爲當選セル議員ニシテ官選議員トノ惡評ヲ得タルモノアリ然ルニ今回ノ選擧ニ於テハ政府ハ絕對不干涉ノ方針ヲ實行スル堅キ決意ヲ有シ最モ自由且公正ナル民意ヲ反映セシメント念願シ居レリ

ト述ヘテ來レル時「マクアーサー」ハ語ヲ挾ミ全ク「エクセレント」ノ御考ナリ是非共左樣實行セラレタシ之ハ日本ノ爲最モ健全ナル方向ト思フ

次ニ賛意ヲ表シタリ次テ總理ヨリ次ニ勞働組合組織化ノ問題ハ余カ十數年前閣議ニ列シ居リタル頃議ニ上リタルコトアルモ或ル事情ニ依リ行ハレサリシ問題ナリ今日ニ於テ之カ實現ハ非常ナル困難アリトハ考ヘサル次第ナルモ具体的ニハ擔當閣僚ト相談ヲ要ストス考フ

學校ニ於テ自由主義ノ敎育ヲ施ス樣ニシタシトノ御希望ノ點ニ付テハ之亦閣議ニ於テ決定ヲ見政府ハ其ノ方針ヲ昨日發表シタル次第ナリ主義トシテ政府ニ於テ何等異議ナキ問題ナリ

次ニ祕密審問及其ノ濫用ニ依リ人民ニ恐怖ノ念ヲ與ヘタル制度ヲ廢止シ之ニ代フルニ公正ナル制度正義ヲ行フ制度ヲ以テセヨトノ御趣旨ハ當然ノコトナリ具體的ノ方法ハ當面ノ同僚ニ考ヘ貫フ積リナルカ方針其ノモノニ付テハ政府ハ之ヲ力實行ヲ決意シ居ルモノナリ

日本ノ産業ニ付現行ノ獨占的支配ノ行ハルル事態ヲ改ムルヲ要ストノ御趣旨ニ付テハ如何ナルコトヲ實際問題トシテ考ヘ居ラルルヤ不明ノ節アリ即チ現在ノ獨占ナルモノカ我カ國現行ノ法律制度ノ定ムルトコロトシテ存在シ居ルモノトハ考ヘラレヌ或ハ大工業家カ自己ノ努力又ハ設備ニ依リ事實問題トシテ他ノ競爭ヲ許ササルモノアルニ依ルモノナルヤモ知レサルモ之カ如何ニ改正セルヤ直接法律ノ規定スル結果ニ非サルモノトスレハ直チニ考ヘ及ハサル次第ナリ

ト述ヘタル處「マクアーサー」ハ本件ハ自分モ充分諒解シ居ラス多分「アンチ、トラスト」法ノ如キヲ制定セハ可ナル問題ニ非スヤ尤モ英國ニハ之トハ別ノ法律アル由ナリト答ヘタルニ付總理ヨリ

實ハ「アンチ、トラスト」法トカ之ニ類似ノ英國法律等ノ原文カ現在日本ニ於テ直チニ入手可能ナリヤ否ヤ思ヒ當ラス自分ハ嘗テ之ヲ所有シ居リタルモ戰災ニ依リ燒失セリ官廳若ハ圖書館ニ保存セラレタル文書モ燒失ノト思フ

ト述ヘタル處「マクアーサー」ハ早速米國ヨリ取リ寄スヘシト答ヘタリ次テ總理ヨリ日本ノ衣食住ノ問題ヲ早急ニ解決シ病氣餓死其ノ他社會的慘禍ヲ速ニ予防セヨトノ點竝ニ其ノ爲ニハ衣食住ニ關係アル勞働力ヲ充分ニ働カシムル要アリ今日此ノ方面ニ必スシモ勤勉且懸命ニ勞働力動員セラレ居ラサル模樣ナリトノ御意見ニ付テハ先ツ次ノニ點ノ考慮ヲ要ストテ考フ

其ノ一ハ今次戰爭ニ於テ日本ノ軍隊ノ完全ナル敗北下文官官僚ノヘマ續失ニ依リ日本カ今日ノ慘禍ヲ招キシモノナルコトニ付テハ國民全部カ充分ニ之ヲ認ムル所ナルモ其ノ結果トシテ多數ノ國民ハ國運ノ將來ヲ悲觀シ自暴自棄ニ陷レルカ或ハ呆然自失ノ狀況ニ在リ精神的ニ沈淪ノ

2 民主化・非軍事化政策への対応(昭和20年10月～21年5月)

極ニ在ル譯ニテ此ノ點米國國民ノ如キ戰勝國民ト異ル所アリ之等ノ人々ニ對シテハ希望ヲ興ヘテ奮發セシムル手段ヲ講スベキ所ナルカ彼等ニ奮發心ヲ起サシムルト言フモ必スシモ容易ナラサル次第ナリ

其ノ二ハ物質的ニ見テ生産原料窮乏ノ狀況甚シク原料ヲ如何ニ調達スルカ支拂方法ヲ如何ニスルカノ難問アリ之カ決定ヲ見スシテハ早急ニ事業ヲ復活スルモ中途挫折スルコトアルヘシトシ事業家モ勞働者モ躊躇シ居ル事情モ考慮セサル可ラス

然シ何レニセヨ本問題ハ政府トシテハ默視シ得ル所ニ非ス何等カノ方途ヲ講シテ國民ニ獎勵ヲ與ヘ「ユースフル、ワーク」ニ「フル、エンプロイメント」ヲ用フル樣極力努力スル決心ナリ

尙以上貴下ノ希望セラルル五項目ニ付日本側トシテ困難ハアルモ之カ排除ハ不可能ニ非スト見當ヲ就ケ得モノト考ヘラレ喜ハシキ次第ナリ

然シ玆ニ一言シタキハ政府ハ一旦引受ケタルコトハ他ノ之ヲ胡魔化シテ責任ヲ逃レントスルカ如キ意志毛頭無ク速ニ之ヲ實行シ行カントスル堅キ決意ヲ有ス今日迄貴下

ニ述フルヤ「マクアーサー」ハニ於テ日本人トノ間ニ或ハ如何ナル經驗ヲ經ラレシヤ承知セサルモ此ノ點ハ御安心ヲ願フト答フ次テ總理ヨリ

其ノ御言葉ヲ聞キ甚タ喜ハシキ次第ナリ

以上大體ノ御趣旨ハ日本ノ各般ノ制度ヲ民主主義化並ニ自由主義化スヘシトノ御意見ト考フ然ラハ實際ニハ余カ內閣ニ列シ居リタル十二三年前ニハ事實此ノ潮流カ日本ニ流レ居リタルモノナリ其ノ後滿洲事件ノ起リアリテ此ノ潮流ヲ逆轉セシメ有害ナル勢力カ時ノ勢ヲ占ムルヲ許サルルニ至リ(Malign influence was allowed to prevail)民主主義的潮流ノ發達ハ阻止セラレタリ然レ共最近ノ時局急轉ニ依リ此ノ阻害スル原因力全ク除去セラルルニ至リシ以上日本ハ既ニ二十數年以前萌シヲ見セタル方向ニ向ヒ再ヒ前進ヲ開始スルコト困難ニ非スト期待シ居レリ

但シ其ノ民主主義化ト稱シ自由主義化ト稱スル意味ハ如何ナルモノナリヤ民主主義自由主義ノ適用ハ各國夫々異ル所アリト考フ例ヘハ米國ノ「デモクラシー」ハ英國ノ「デモクラシー」ト異レリ「ソビエット」カ主張スル

233

「デモクラシー」ハ更ニ異ナリ從ツテ若シ貴下カ日本ニ對シ米國ト同様ノ体様ノ「デモクラシー」ヲ期待セラルルナラハ其ノ實現ノ時期ヲ期スルコト容易ニ非スト認メラル然ルニ一般大衆ノ意思ヲ尊重シ之ヲ反映スル政治上ノ主義ヲ意味セラルルナラハ既ニ二十數年前ニ萌芽ヲ見セタルコトアルモノニシテ之カ實現ヲ見ルハ敢テ遠キ將來ニモ非スト考フ日本ニ於テ「デモクラシー」カ成功スル以上ハ日本國民ノ長キ期間置カレ來リタル環境ニ適合スルモノナラサル可ラス主義ノ目的トスル所ハ民意ノ反映ニ在リ目的ハ此處ニ在ルモ形式ハ日本的「デモクラシー」トナルモノト考フ

ト述ヘ終リヤ「マクアーサー」ハ之ニ對シ右ハ至極尤モノコトナリ貴下等カ嘗テ局ニ當リ居ラレタル時代ノ状況ニ付テハ自分モ同様ノ情報ヲ與ヘラレ居リ之カ「インターラプト」セラレサリシナラハ今日ノ事態ニハ立チ至ラサリシナルヘシ此ノ點ヨリスルモ新政府ノ成功ヲ望ムモノナリト述ヘ會談ヲ終ヘタリ

（以上）

（付 記）

編 注 本文書に別紙は見当たらないが、本文書付記が別紙に当たると思われる。

十月十一日幣原首相ニ對シ表明セル「ポツダム」宣言ノ實現ニ當リテハ日本國民カ數世紀ニ亙リ隷屬セシメラレタル傳統的社會秩序ハ是正セラルルヲ要ス右ハ疑ヒモナク憲法ノ自由主義化ヲ包含スヘシ

日本國民ハ其ノ心理ヲ事實上奴隷化スル日常生活ニ關シテノ有ラユル形式ニ於ケル政府ノ祕密審問ヨリ解放セラレ思想、言論及信敎ノ自由ヲ抑壓スル有ラユル形式ノ統制ヨリ解放セラレサルヘカラス能率化ノ名ヲ藉リ又ハ其ノ必要ヲ理由トシテ爲サルル國民ノ組織化ハ政府ノ如何ナル名ニ於テ爲サルルモノモ一切廢止セラルルヲ要ス

斯ル諸要求ノ履行及諸目的ノ實現ノ爲日本ノ社會制度ニ對スル下記ノ諸改革ヲ日本社會ニ同化シ得ル限リ出來得ル限リ速ニ實行スルコトヲ期待ス

2　民主化・非軍事化政策への対応(昭和20年10月～21年5月)

一、參政權ノ賦與ニ依リ日本ノ婦人ヲ解放スルコト―婦人モ國家ノ一員トシテ各家庭ノ福祉ニ役立ツヘキ新シキ政治ノ概念ヲ齎スヘシ

二、勞働組合ノ組織奬勵―以テ勞働ニ威嚴ヲ賦與シ勞働者階級カ搾取ト濫用ヨリ己レヲ擁護シ生活程度ヲ向上セシムル爲大ナル發言權ヲ與ヘラルヘシ、之ト共ニ現存スル幼年勞働ノ惡弊ヲ是正スル爲必要ナル措置ヲ採ルコト

三、學校ヲヨリ自由主義的ナル教育ノ爲開校スルコト―國民カ事實ニ基礎付ケラレタル知識ニ依リ自身ノ將來ノ發展ヲ形成スルコトヲ得政府カ國民ノ主人ニアラスシテ使用人タルノ制度ヲ理解スルコトニ依リ解答スルヲ得ヘシ

四、國民ヲ祕密ノ審問ノ濫用ニ依リ絕エス恐怖ヲ與フル組織ヲ撤廢スルコト―故ニ專制的ノ恣意的且不正ナル手段ヨリ國民ヲ守ルヘキ正義ノ制度ヲ以テ之ニ代フ

五、日本ノ經濟制度ヲ民主主義化シ以テ所得並ニ生產及商業手段ノ所有權ヲ廣ク分配スルコトヲ保障スル方法ヲ發達セシムルコトニ依リ獨占的產業支配ヲ是正スルコト刻下ノ行政部面ニ就テハ國民ノ住宅、食糧、衣料ノ問題ニ關シ政府ノ力强ク且迅速ナル行動ニ出テ疫病、疾病、饑餓其他重大ナル社會ノ破局ヲ防止スルコトヲ希望ス、今冬ハ危機タルヘク來ルヘキ困難克服ノ道ハ總テノ人々ヲ有效ナル仕事ニ就業セシムルノ他ナシ

〜〜〜〜〜〜〜〜〜〜〜〜〜〜〜〜〜〜〜〜〜〜〜

67

警察力増強に関する日本側提議は不許可の旨

回答

昭和20年10月11日　連合国最高司令官総司令部より　日本政府宛

OFFICE OF THE SUPREME COMMANDER
FOR THE ALLIED POWERS

11 October 1945

AG 091.1 (11 Oct 45) DCSO
SCAPIN 119

MEMORANDUM FOR: IMPERIAL JAPANESE GOVERNMENT.
THROUGH: Central Liaison Committee, Tokyo.
SUBJECT: Japanese Government Proposal to Increase Domestic Police Force.

1. The proposal of the Japanese Government to increase

the strength and armament of the Japanese Police Force, including the provision of a mobile force and augmentation of the water police, as presented to the Deputy Chief of Staff for Operations on 5 October 1945, is not favorably considered.

2. There shall be no increase in the strength, organization or armament of the civil police force at this time.

FOR THE SUPREME COMMANDER:

H. W. ALLEN,
Colonel, A.G.D.,
Asst. Adjutant General.

68 東久邇宮内閣総辞職をめぐる国内情勢につき通報

昭和20年10月12日 吉田外務大臣より在スイス加瀬公使、在スウェーデン岡本公使他宛（電報）

本　省　10月12日後4時発

合第八一六號

一、東久邇宮内閣ハ成立以來終戰直後ノ急迫セル事態ニ處シ努力シ來タルカ特ニ陸海軍ノ復員及聯合軍進駐ハ極メテ順調ニ進展シ來リタルカ急轉セル事態ノ展開ニ對シ政府ノ施策ノ速度ハ兎角遲レ勝チニシテ漸ク内外ノ批判ヲ誘致シ終ニ思想言論ノ制限撤廢ニ關シ治安維持法以下諸法令ノ廢止並ニ内務大臣以下多数責任者ノ罷免要求ヲ直接ノ契機トシテ十月五日總辭職ヲ見ルニ至レリ

二、帝國ノ占領及管理ノ施行ニ關シテハ聯合國中米國カ主導的ノ役割ヲ果スヘキ處其ノ意圖ハ九月二十二日米政府カ「日本ニ對スル初期ノ全般的政策」ヲ公表スルニ至リ一段ト明確ノ度ヲ加フルニ至リタルカ右ニ依レハ米國ノ目的ハ日本ヲ非軍國主義化シ民主主義化シ合理主義化スルニ在リ　天皇及日本政府ハ此ノ見地ヨリ之ヲ利用スルニ止リテ之ヲ支持スルモノニアラス封建的權力主義的傾向ノ除去換言セハ民主主義化ノ爲ニハ有ラユル手段ヲ辭セサルト共ニ他面日本經濟ノ平和的活動ハ之ヲ促進シ國民生活ノ最低限ハ之ヲ侵害スル意圖ナキコトヲ述ヘ居レリ

三、此ノ間未會有ノ悲境ニ立チタル國民ハ戰時中ノ精神的困憊ト肉體的ノ疲勞ヨリ未タ脱却スル能ハス久シク國策ヲ指

2　民主化・非軍事化政策への対応（昭和20年10月～21年5月）

導シ來レル勢力ハ衰ヘ帝都以下本土ハ聯合軍ノ占領下ニ在ル事態ニ於テ一般ニ未タ新ナル建設的施策ノ着手ニ逢著スヘシト雖モ政治面ニ於テハ鳩山氏ヲ中心トスル自由黨ノ外日本社會黨、日本無產黨等結成ノ動キアル他アラス米側ノ指令ニ依リ思想言論集會結社ノ制限ハ急遽撤廢サレタリト雖モ政治面ニ於テハ鳩山氏ヲ中心トスル顯著ナル具体的ノ動キヲ見ズ、尚總選擧ハ選擧法改正選擧人名簿ノ作成等技術ノ必要モアリ前内閣ニ於テ明春ニ持越方決定セリ

四、他方國民生活ハ冬期ヲ迎ヘテ逼迫ヲ告ケ(イ)主要食糧ハ既ニ最低限ヲ下廻リ居ル上本年度米作豫想ハ五千五百萬石ニ達セス來年度ノ食生活維持ノ爲ニ二百五十萬乃至三百萬屯ノ穀類輸入ノ必要認メラルル他食鹽ノ不足著シク、(ロ)必要トセラルル船腹四百萬噸ニ對シ九月末稼動船腹五十一萬噸ニシテ鐵道輸送力モ既ニ過重ノ負擔ヲ負ハサレ戰災燒失家屋ハ二百二十萬戸現在掘立小屋居住者四十萬戸アルニ對シ本年內應急「バラック」(七坪余)三十萬戸建築計畫モ多大ノ困難ヲ豫想セラレ、(ハ)平時經濟維持ニ必要トセラルル船腹四百萬噸ニ對シ九月末稼動船腹五十萬噸ニシテ鐵道輸送力モ既ニ過重ノ負擔ヲ負ハサレ居ルモ現在稼動七千臺ニ過キス、(ニ)失業者モ軍需工場整理ニ依ルモノ四百五十萬軍隊復員內地四百萬外

地三百六十五萬ノ大東亞地域ヨリノ歸還邦人三百萬ノ內前職復歸等ニ依リ就職シ得ルモノヲ除キ將來五、六百萬ニ達スヘシト推定セラル、米軍當局ハ漸ク斯ル事態ヲ認識シ(イ)不足必需物資及賃銀ノ統制維持、(ロ)民需生產促進、(ハ)軍所有物資ノ民需轉用ノ爲ノ引渡、(ニ)船舶運航制限緩和並ニ船舶ノ修理及建造中ノモノノ工事繼續、(ホ)「トラック」ノ修理製造促進等ヲ指令シ日本經濟ノ自力更生ヲ刺戟スルヤウ努メツツアリ尚緊急必需物資ノ輸入ニ付目下種々話合ヲ行ヒ居レリ

五、尚海外派遣軍及居留民ノ引揚ハ極度ニ逼迫セル船腹事情ヨリ著シク困難ナル處（軍隊三百二十萬、居留民三百八十萬）我方ニ於テハ二百六萬噸ヲ之ニ振當ツヘク立案セルニ對シ聯合軍司令部ニ於テハ日本ノ經濟狀態ヨリシテ貨物船ヲ引揚ニ使用スルコトヲ禁シ(其結果充當船腹ハ十萬噸程度)他方殘存海軍艦船十余萬噸ヲ使用方指令セリ、現在內地釜山間十數隻內地支那大陸間數隻ヲ以テ極力引揚ニ努メ海軍艦船ハ南方諸地域ヨリノ引揚ニ使用シ居ルモ引揚ハ相當長期ニ亘ラサルヲ得ス、特ニ憂慮セラルルハ冬期ヲ控ヘテノ食糧衣料ノ問題ニシテ我方ニ於テ

69 日本軍の内地における復員完了に関するマッカーサー司令官の声明

昭和20年10月16日　連合国最高司令官総司令部発表

六、斯クノ如キ新内閣ハ疲弊セル國力ヲ以テ如何ニシテ逼迫セル國民生活ヲ再建スルヤノ焦眉ノ問題アルノミナラス今後政治経濟宗教教育各方面ニ亘リ聯合國ヨリノ要求ヲ如何ニ處置シ以テ帝國ノ再興ノ基ヲ開クヘキヤノ重大ナル責務ヲ課セラレ居ルモノト謂フヘシ

モ東京及現地ニ於テ極力對策樹立方聯合軍側ト折衝中ナルモ現在迄ノ所猶手持ヲ以テ賄ヒ居ル狀況ナリ、蘇聯軍占領地域ハ我方ノ苦心ニ拘ラス依然通信連絡ノ方法全クナク事態不明ニシテ憂慮セラレ居ルモ支那大陸ニ於テハ二三ノ地域ヲ除キ一般ニ治安ハサシテ悪化シ居ラス大ナル不祥事ヲ見居ラス

General of the Army Douglas MacArthur's Statement on the Completion of the Demobilization of Japanese Armed Forces.

October 16, 1945

Today the Japanese Armed Forces throughout Japan completed their demobilization and ceased to exist as such. These forces are now completely abolished. I know of no demobilization in history, either in war or in peace, by our own or by any other country, that has been accomplished so rapidly or so frictionlessly. Everything military, naval or air is forbidden to Japan. This ends its military might and its military influence in International affairs. It no longer reckons as a world power either large or small. Its path in the future, if it is to survive, must be confined to the ways of peace.

Approximately seven million armed men, including those in the outlying theaters, have laid down their weapons. In the accomplishment of the extraordinarily difficult and dangerous surrender in Japan, unique in the annals of history, not a shot was necessary, not a drop of Allied blood was shed. The vindication of the great decision of Potsdam is complete.

Nothing could exceed the abjectness, the humiliation and the finality of this surrender. It is not only physically thorough, but has been equally destructive on Japanese spirit. From swagger and

2 民主化・非軍事化政策への対応(昭和20年10月～21年5月)

arrogance, the former Japanese military have passed to servility and fear. They are thoroughly beaten and cowed and tremble before the terrible retribution the surrender terms impose upon their country in punishment for its great sins.

Again I wish to pay tribute to the magnificent conduct of our troops. With few exceptions, they could well be taken as a model for all time as a conquering army. No historian in later years when passions cool, can arraign their conduct. They could so easily —and understandably—have emulated the ruthlessness which their enemy freely practiced when conditions were reversed—but their perfect balance between their implacable firmness of duty on the one hand and resolute restraint from cruelness and brutalities on the other, has taught a lesson to the Japanese civil population that is startling in its impact. Nothing has so tended to impress Japanese thought—not even catastrophic fact of military defeat itself. They have for the first time seen the free man's way of life in actual action and it has stunned them into new thoughts and new ideas. The revolution, or more properly speaking the evolution, which will restore the dignity and freedom of the common man, has begun. It will take much time and require great patience, but if world public opinion will permit of these two essential factors— mankind will be repaid. Herein lies the way to true and final peace.

The Japanese army, contrary to some concepts that have been advanced, was thoroughly defeated before the surrender. The strategic manoeuvring of the Allies had so scattered and divided it, their thrusts had so immobilized, disintegrated and split its units, its supply and transportation lines were so utterly destroyed, its equipment was so exhausted, its morale so shattered, that its early surrender became inevitable. Bastion after bastion, considered by it as impregnable and barring our way, had been by-passed and rendered impotent and useless, while our tactical penetrations and envelopments resulted in piece-meal destruction of many isolated fragments. It was weak everywhere, forced to fight where it stood, unable to render mutual support between its parts and presented a picture of collapse that was complete and absolute. The basic cause of the surrender is not to be attributed to an arbitrary decision of authority. It was inevitable because of the strategic and tactical circumstances forced upon it. The situation had become hopeless. It was merely a question of when with our troops poised for final invasion. This invasion would have been annihilating but might well have cost hundreds of thousands of American lives.

The victory was a triumph for the concept of the complete integration of the three dimensions of war, ground, sea, and air. By a thorough use of each arm in conjunction with the corresponding utilization of the other two, the enemy was reduced to a condition of helplessness. By largely avoiding methods involving a separate use of the services and by avoiding methods of frontal assault as far as possible, our combined power forced collapse with relative light loss probably unparalleled in any campaigns in history. This latter fact indeed was the most inspiring and significant feature, the unprecedented saving in American life. It is for this we have to say truly—thank God. Never was there a more intensive application of the principle of the strategic-tactical employment of limited forces as compared with the accumulation of overwhelming forces.

Illustrating this concept, General Yamashita recently stated in an interview in Manila, explaining reasons for his defeat, that "diversity of Japanese command resulted in complete lack of cooperation and coordination between the services". He complained: "that he was not in supreme command, that the air forces were run by Field Marshal Terauchi at Saigon and the fleet run directly from Tokyo", that he "only knew of the intended Naval strike at Leyte Gulf five days before it got under way" and professed "ignorance of its details".

The great lesson for the future is that success in the Art of War depends upon a complete integration of the services. In unity will lie military strength. We cannot win with only backs and ends, and no line, however strong, can go alone. Victory will rest with the team.

編注　本文書は、昭和二十四年三月、外務省特別資料部作成「日本占領及び管理重要文書集」第二巻より抜粋。

70　昭和20年10月16日　連合国最高司令官総司令部より　日本政府宛

映画に対する日本政府の統制排除につき指令

GENERAL HEADQUARTERS

2 民主化・非軍事化政策への対応(昭和20年10月～21年5月)

SUPREME COMMANDER FOR THE ALLIED POWERS

16 October 1945

AG 000.76 (8 Oct 45) CI
SCAPIN 146

MEMORANDUM FOR: IMPERIAL JAPANESE GOVERNMENT

THROUGH: Central Liaison Office, Tokyo

SUBJECT: Elimination of Japanese Government Control of the Motion Picture Industry

1. Further to the directive of 27 September 45 from the Supreme Allied Commander, titled "Further Steps toward Freedom of Press and Speech," the Japanese Government forthwith will render inoperative the procedures for enforcement of peacetime and war-time restrictions on freedom of speech in motion pictures, including newsreels.

2. The directive of 4 October 45, titled "Removal of Restrictions on Political, Civil, and Religious Liberties," also shall apply.

3. Pending repeal of laws imposing restrictions on the motion picture industry, making it a channel for dissemination of propaganda, their enforcement shall be suspended.

4. No punitive action will be taken by the Japanese Government or any of its agencies against motion picture companies, producers, actors, directors or other persons or associations of persons engaged in the motion picture or legitimate theater industry for exercising their lawful freedom of speech.

5. Steps shall be taken to repeal the following laws and/or regulations which are inconsistent with the Supreme Commander's directives enumerated in paragraphs 1 and 2 of this order, subject laws including but not restricted to:

Eigaho, Horitsu Dai 66, 5 April, Showa 14 (1939)
Eigaho, Kaisei, Horitsu Dai 35, Showa 16 (1941)
Eigaho, Fusoku, Horitsu Dai 35, Showa 16 (1941)
Eigaho Shikkorei, Chokurei Dai 668, 26 Sept, Showa 14 (1939)
Eigaho, Kaisei, Chokurei 916, Showa 15 (1940)
Eigaho, Fusoku, Chokurei 916, Showa 15 (1940)
Eigaho, Shikko Kisoku; Naimu, Mombu, & Kosei Shorei Dai 1, 27 Sept, Showa 14 (1939)

241

Eigaho, Kaisei; Naimu, Mombu, & Kosei Shorei Dai 37, Sept, Showa 14 (1940)

Eigaho, Kakurei, Naimu, Mombu, Kosei Shorei Dai 1, December, Showa 15 (1940)

Eigaho, Kakurei, Naimu, Mombu, Kosei Shorei Dai 1, June, Showa 16 (1941)

Eigaho, Fusoku: Shorei Dai 37, September, Showa 15 (1940)

Eigaho, Kakurei, Naimu, Mombu, Kosei Shorei Dai 1, April, Showa 18 (1943)

Eigaho, Kakurei, Naimu, Mombu, Kosei Shorei Dai 1, December, Showa 18 (1943)

Eigaho, Kakurei, Naimu, Mombu, Kosei Shorei Dai 1, January, Showa 19 (1944)

Eigaho, Fusoku: Kakurei, Shorei, Dai 1, December, Showa 15 (1940)

Eigaho, Fusoku: Shorei, Dai 1, June, Showa 16 (1941)

Eigaho, Fusoku: April 13, Showa 18 (1943)

6. In addition to rendering the foregoing laws inoperative, necessary instructions will be issued to prefecture and metropolitan authorities, including police agencies, directing their repeal of any and all local censorship rules, regulations or laws, to insure that the spirit of the directives is observed by them.

7. Steps shall be taken to repeal the following Tokyo Metropolitan Police Regulations:

a. "Metropolitan Police Station Official Publication - (Supplement)

April 1, 1944 Showa 19

Saturday -- Metropolitan Police Rules # 9.

Rules and regulations governing all forms of public performances -- April 1, 1944 (Showa 19)"

(Sections 1 to 95)

b. "Metropolitan Police Rule # 10

Rules and Regulations governing all motion pictures - - April 1, 1944 (Showa 19)"

(Sections 1 to 40)

c. "Public Morality # 682 --

April 15, 1944 (Showa 19)

242

Notification of Rules and Regulations governing all public performances and motion pictures."

(Sections 1 to 25)

(Appendix)

"Rules and Regulations of executing the Motion Picture Law."

(Sections 1 to 28)

These laws, rules or regulations give broad supervisory powers to the police, in addition to their censorship provisions. Such powers include deciding who shall work in the industry, passing on the financial condition of an owner, checking on the behavior or attitude of an employee, controlling the proportion of foreign films exhibited, preventing actors from walking on the street in stage costume, determining the issuance of passes, and examining the minutes of a stockholder's meeting. These powers, no free people can entrust to a police.

8. The few sections of these rules which deal with matters of Safety Regulations and Building and Zoning restrictions shall remain in effect until the Japanese Government shall re-enact such regulations for the protection and safety of the public against fire and structural hazards in the motion picture industry.

9. Necessary instructions will be issued to Prefectural Authorities including all police agencies, directing the repeal of any and all similar local rules, regulations or laws which conflict with the spirit or intent of this directive.

10. It is the purpose and intent of this directive to free the Japanese motion picture industry from government domination and to permit the industry to reflect the democratic aspirations of the Japanese people. In due time (when the Japanese motion picture companies have demonstrated good faith), it is envisaged that they will establish an industry-wide committee which will act as a policing agency.

11. The report required of the Japanese Government in paragraph 8 of the directive of 27 September will include a statement of action taken to comply with this directive.

FOR THE SUPREME COMMANDER:

H. W. ALLEN,
Colonel, A.G.D.,

71 昭和20年10月20日 連合国最高司令官総司令部より 日本政府宛

主要な金融機関および企業の解体・整理に関する指令

GENERAL HEADQUARTERS
SUPREME COMMANDER FOR THE ALLIED POWERS

A.P.O. 500

20 October 1945

AG 091.3 (20 Oct 45) ESS
SCAPIN 162
MEMORANDUM FOR: IMPERIAL JAPANESE GOVERNMENT.
THROUGH: Central Liaison Office, Tokyo.
SUBJECT: Dissolution or Liquidation of Major Financial or Industrial Enterprises.

1. No approval will be given to plans or proposals submitted to you for the dissolution or liquidation of any holding company, "Zaibatsu," "Conzern," or major industrial or financial enterprise without prior submission to this headquarters.

2. When such plan or proposal is forwarded to this headquarters you will attach thereto the opinion of the Imperial Japanese Government on the plan or proposal.

FOR THE SUPREME COMMANDER:

H. W. ALLEN,
Colonel, A.G.D.,
Asst. Adjutant General.

72 昭和20年10月22日 連合国最高司令官総司令部より 日本政府宛

教育制度の方針に関する指令

OFFICE OF THE SUPREME COMMANDER
FOR THE ALLIED POWERS

22 October 1945

AG 350 (22 Oct) CI & E
SCAPIN 178
MEMORANDUM FOR: IMPERIAL JAPANESE GOVERNMENT.
THROUGH: Central Liaison Office, Tokyo.

2　民主化・非軍事化政策への対応（昭和20年10月～21年5月）

SUBJECT: Administration of the Educational System of Japan.

1. In order that the newly formed Cabinet of the Imperial Japanese Government shall be fully informed of the objectives and policies of the occupation with regard to Education, it is hereby directed that:

a. The content of all instruction will be critically examined, revised, and controlled in accordance with the following policies:

(1) Dissemination of militaristic and ultra-nationalistic ideology will be prohibited and all military education and drill will be discontinued.

(2) Inculcation of concepts and establishment of practices in harmony with representative government, international peace, the dignity of the individual, and such fundamental human rights as the freedom of assembly, speech, and religion, will be encouraged.

b. The personnel of all educational institutions will be investigated, approved or removed, reinstated, appointed, reorientated, and supervised in accordance with the following policies:

(1) Teachers and educational officials will be examined as rapidly as possible and all career military personnel, persons who have been active exponents of militarism and ultra-nationalism, and those actively antagonistic to the policies of the occupation, will be removed.

(2) Teachers and educational officials who have been dismissed, suspended, or forced to resign for liberal or antimilitaristic opinions or activities, will be declared immediately eligible for and if properly qualified will be given preference in reappointment.

(3) Discrimination against any student, teacher, or educational official on grounds of race, nationality, creed, political opinion, or social position, will be prohibited, and immediate steps will be taken to correct inequities which have resulted

245

from such discrimination.

(4) Students, teachers, and educational officials will be encouraged to evaluate critically and intelligently the content of instruction and will be permitted to engage in free and unrestricted discussion of issues involving political, civil, and religious liberties.

(5) Students, teachers, educational officials, and public will be informed of the objectives and policies of the occupation, of the theory and practices of representative government, and of the part played by militaristic leaders, their active collaborators, and those who by passive acquiescence committed the nation to war with the inevitable result of defeat, distress, and the present deplorable state of the Japanese people.

c. The instrumentalities of educational processes will be critically examined, revised, and controlled in accordance with the following policies:

(1) Existing curricula, textbooks, teaching manuals, and instructional materials, the use of which is temporarily permitted on an emergency basis, will be examined as rapidly as possible and those portions designed to promote a militaristic or ultra-nationalistic ideology will be eliminated.

(2) New curricula, textbooks, teaching manuals, and instructional materials designed to produce an educated, peaceful, and responsible citizenry will be prepared and will be substituted for existing materials as rapidly as possible.

(3) A normally operating educational system will be re-established as rapidly as possible, but where limited facilities exist preference will be given to elementary education and teacher training.

2. The Japanese Ministry of Education will establish and maintain adequate liaison with the appropriate staff section of the Office of the Supreme Commander for the Allied Powers, and upon request will submit reports describing in detail all action

2 民主化・非軍事化政策への対応(昭和20年10月～21年5月)

taken to comply with the provisions of this directive.

3. All officials and subordinates of the Japanese Government affected by the terms of this directive, and all teachers and school officials, both public and private, will be held personally accountable for compliance with the spirit as well as the letter of the policies enunciated in this directive.

FOR THE SUPREME COMMANDER:

H. W. ALLEN,
Colonel, A.G.D.,
Asst. Adjutant General.

73 昭和20年10月23日 連合国最高司令官総司令部より 日本政府宛

一般市民の武器引渡しに関する指令

GENERAL HEADQUARTERS
SUPREME COMMANDER FOR THE ALLIED POWERS

23 October 1945

AG 388.3 (23 Oct 45) CIS
SCAPIN 181

MEMORANDUM FOR: THE IMPERIAL JAPANESE GOVERNMENT

THROUGH: Central Liaison Office, Tokyo

SUBJECT: Instructions Concerning the Surrender of Arms by the Civilian Population of Japan.

1. The following instructions supplement those issued by this headquarters in a Radiogram to the Imperial Japanese Government, above subject, dated 24 September 1945:

a. The Imperial Japanese Government shall surrender all firearms, ammunition, swords, bayonets, daggers and other weapons, ammunition, explosives and components thereof collected from the civilian population to U.S. Army representatives in accordance with instructions issued by the Commanding Generals of the Sixth and Eighth Armies and the Commander of the Fifth Fleet, USN.

(1) The following exceptions will be allowed:

(a) Firearms and knives required for hunting purposes, and swords considered objects of art.

247

(b) Explosives required by legitimate business or industrial organizations.

(2) Individual licenses and permits covering the above exceptions will be issued by the Imperial Japanese Government and reported monthly, by list, to this headquarters, the Commanding Generals of the Sixth and Eighth Armies, the Commander of the Fifth Fleet, USN, or other appropriate Occupation Force Commanders.

(3) Individuals and organizations duly licensed to retain and use firearms and explosives, or components thereof, shall comply with such instructions as may be issued by the appropriate Occupation Force Commander in the area.

b. The Imperial Japanese Government shall take whatever action is necessary to comply with these instructions and prevent violations or deception in the issuance of licenses or permits. Initial collection of arms, ammunition and explosives and issuance of licenses for authorized retentions shall be completed by 1 December 1945. Such subsequent checks and inspections shall be conducted as are necessary to detect violations and evasions of these instructions.

2. The Imperial Japanese Government shall submit a complete report to this headquarters not later than 1 December 1945 and monthly thereafter, indicating the number of firearms and weapons and the amount of explosives or components thereof confiscated or licensed, by type and location, together with copies of instructions to prefectural Governors and Police Chiefs and proclamations issued to effectuate the instructions issued by this headquarters.

FOR THE SUPREME COMMANDER:

H. W. ALLEN,
Colonel, A.G.D.,
Asst. Adjutant General.

2 民主化・非軍事化政策への対応（昭和20年10月～21年5月）

昭和20年10月25日　条約局作成

「聯合國ノ對日要求ノ内容ト其ノ限界」

聯合國ノ對日要求ノ内容ト其ノ限界（研究素材）

（昭、二〇、一〇、二五條約局）

第一、聯合國ノ對日要求ノ内容

一、政治的要求

1、天皇及日本政府ノ權力ニ對スル制限

イ、右權力ノ聯合國最高司令官ヘノ從屬（八月十四日聯合國對日囘答（以下「對日囘答」ト稱ス）、「降伏後ノ日本ニ對スル米國ノ初期ノ政策」（以下「政策」ト稱ス）第二部

ロ、最高司令官ノ要求スル命令發出及措置實施ノ義務（同右）

2、現存日本統治形式ニ對スル不支持、右統治形式變更ノ企圖ノ許容及支持（政策第二部）

3、領土的要求

イ、太平洋諸島嶼ノ剝奪（「ポツダム」宣言（以下「宣言」ト稱ス）八、「カイロ」宣言）

ロ、滿洲、臺灣、澎湖島等ノ中國ヘノ返還（同右）

ハ、占領地ノ返還（同右）

ニ、朝鮮ノ獨立（同右）朝鮮ノ信託統治領代（十、二十「ヴインセント」極東部長聲明）

ホ、千島及樺太南半ノ「ソ」聯ヘノ割讓（「ソ」政府聲明）

4、軍國主義ノ抹殺及民主主義ノ助長ニ關スル要求（宣言六、一〇、政策第一部）

イ、軍國主義的勢力及權力ノ除去（宣言六、政策第一部）

軍國主義的又ハ極端ナル國家主義ノ團体、機關ノ解消、指導者ノ被免（政策第三部）宗教的外被ニ隠レタル軍國主義、極端ナル國家主義ノ禁絕（同右）

教育者中ノ右分子ノ除去（十、二三、最高司令官司令部覺書（以下「覺書」ト稱ス）

ロ、言論、宗教及思想ノ自由並ニ基本的人權ノ尊重（宣言十、政策第一部）

司法、法律、警察組織ノ民主主義的改革（政策第

三部、十、十一「マ」元帥要求）

思想、言論取締法令ノ撤廃、祕密警察組織ノ廢止、警察當局者ノ被免（十一、四覺書）

政治犯罪人ノ釋放（十、四覺書）

民主主義的政黨ノ獎勵（政策第三部）

人種、國籍、信敎又ハ政治的見解ニ依ル差別法令ノ撤廢及右法令實施機關ノ廢止（政策第三部）

敎育制度ノ改革（政策第三部、十、十一「マ」元帥要求、十、十二覺書）

二、婦人ノ政治參與（十、十一「マ」元帥要求）

戰爭責任者及戰爭犯罪人ノ處罰（宣言六、十、政策第三部）

外交權ニ對スル制限

在中立國日本外交使臣及領事官ノ召還、在外日本公館財産及文書ノ引渡要求（十、一二五覺書）

三、軍事的要求

1、全日本國軍隊ノ無條件降伏（宣言十三）

2、軍隊ノ武裝解除及武器引渡（宣言九、指令第二號）

陸海軍、大本營ノ施設ノ撤去（一般命令四、五、指令第二號）

艦船、航空機、施設、財產ノ處分、處分迄破壞ノ禁絕（一般命令一、四、六）

3、俘虜及被抑留者ノ釋放（一般命令九、指令第二號）

4、日本國領土ノ占領（宣言七、政策第二部）

占領ニ對スル日本當局ノ援助（一般命令十）

占領軍命令ノ遵守及違反者ノ處罰（一般命令十三）

物資ノ供出、勞務ノ提供、建築物施設ノ提供（指令第二號）

占領軍トノ聯絡機關ノ設置（指令第二號）

民間武器ノ蒐集及引渡（一般命令十一、九、二四指示）

5、軍事的情報ノ提供（一般命令二、七、指令第二號）

新聞、放送ノ取締（九、十覺書）

郵便、通信ノ檢閱（十一、一覺書）

三、經濟的要求

1、賠償ノ賦課及略奪財產ノ返還（宣言十一、政策第

四部）

250

2　民主化・非軍事化政策への対応（昭和20年10月～21年5月）

在外日本財產ノ引渡及處分（政策第四部）

國民經濟及占領軍ノ補給ニ必要ナラサル物資、資本、設備、施設ノ引渡（同右）

略奪財產ノ返還（同右）

2、軍需產業ノ禁絕（宣言十一、政策第四部）

兵器、彈藥、軍用艦船、軍用器具及其ノ部分品ノ生產禁止（指令第三號）

重工業ノ規模、性格ヲ平和的需要ニ制限（政策第四部）

偽裝平和產業ノ禁褐（遏カ）為ノ監視（同右）

戰爭遂行能力增進ヲ目的トスル專門的研究等ノ禁止（同右）

3、原料支配ノ禁絕（宣言十一）

4、占領軍ノ許可ナキ輸出入ノ禁止（指令第三號）

5、日本經濟ノ民主主義化（政策第四部、十、十一「マ」元帥要求）

產業、金融上ノ大財閥ノ解體（政策第四部）

非平和的經濟指導者ノ地位剝奪（同右）

生產及商業手段及之ヨリノ收益分配ノ廣範化（同右）

勞働、產業、農業ノ分野ニ於ケル民主主義的組織ノ獎勵（同右）

勞働組合ノ助長ノ要求（十、十一「マ」元帥要望）

6、財政、金融的要求

占領軍軍票ノ強制通用（指令第三號）

金、銀、證券ノ取引及輸出入ノ制限（九、一二二覺書）

外地特殊銀行等ノ閉鎖（九、一三〇覺書）

7、國民經濟維持ニ關スル要求（宣言十一）

配給ノ公正化（政策第四部）

國民經濟活動ノ管理、統制（政策第四部、指令第三號）

公共事業、財政、金融、必需物資ノ生產及分配ノ管理（政策第四部）

賃金、價格及配給統制（指令第三號）

生產ノ增進（政策第四部、指令第三號）

軍需品ノ民需ヘノ轉換（九、一二四覺書）

8、麻藥ノ栽培、製造ノ禁止（十、十二覺書）

9、經濟情報ノ提供（指令第三號）

10、日本國內ニ於ケル外國企業ノ機會均等（政策第四部）

11、皇室財產ニ對スル除外例ノ不承認(同右)

第二、聯合國ノ對日要求ニ對スル限界

一、聯合國自身「ポツダム」宣言等ニ於テ認メタル限界

(1) 政治的事項

(イ)日本ノ政體決定ヘノ不干涉(宣言十二、對日回答、政策第一部)

(ロ)現存日本政府ノ承認、直接軍政ノ不施行(聯合國最高司令官ノ權力ハ右司令官ノ要求ガ滿足ニ果サルル限リ、天皇及日本政府ヲ通ジテ行使セラルルノ原則)(宣言十、十三、政策第二部)

(ハ)日本ノ統治權ニ對スル制限ノ限界(天皇及日本政府ノ國家統治權ニ對スル制限ハ聯合國最高司令官ガ降伏條項實施ノ爲必要ト認ムル措置ノ範圍ニ限定)(對日回答)

(ニ)日本ヨリ剝奪スベキ領土ノ限界(宣言八、「カイロ」宣言)

(ホ)日本國民ヲ奴隸化乃至滅亡セシメザルノ誓約(宣言十)

(2) 軍事的事項

(イ)日本領土ノ占領目的、占領期間ノ限界、撤兵ノ豫約(宣言七、十二)

(ロ)日本國軍隊ノ家庭及平和的生業ヘノ復歸ノ承認(賠償二代ル勞役賦課ノ抑制)(宣言九)

(ハ)占領軍ニ依リ物資、勞務徵用ノ制限(飢餓、疫病ヲ招來スルガ如キ物資、勞務ノ調達ヲ爲サズ)(政策第四部)

(3) 經濟的事項

(イ)國民生活維持ノ爲ノ產業ノ承認(宣言十一、政策第一部、第四部)

(ロ)原料入手ノ承認(宣言十一)

(ハ)世界貿易ヘノ參加承認(宣言十一、政策第四部)

(ニ)賠償ニ對スル制限(國民經濟ノ保持、日本非軍事化ニ支障ヲ來スガ如キ賠償ヲ強要セズ)(政策第四部)

三、過去ニ於ケル聯合國側宣言、聲明等ニ依ル限界(乃至之トノ矛盾)

(1) 政治的事項

(イ)領土ノ問題

2 民主化・非軍事化政策への対応（昭和20年10月～21年5月）

（イ）世界通商及原料ノ機會均等（大西洋憲章第四項「戰勝國タルト敗戰國タルトヲ間ハズ一切ノ國ガ其ノ經濟的繁榮ニ必要ナル世界ノ通商及原料ノ均等條件ニ於ケル利用ヲ享有スルコトヲ促進スルニ努ムベシ」）

（ロ）國民經濟ノ維持向上（大西洋憲章第五項「改善セラレタル勞働基準、經濟的向上及社會的安全ヲ一切ノ國ノ爲ニ確保スル爲右一切ノ國ノ間ニ經濟的分野ニ於テ完全ナル協力ヲ生ゼシメンコトヲ欲ス」）

今次戰爭ニ關係ナク帝國ガ正當ニ取得シ且帝國ノ主權行使ニ付從來爭ナカリシ領土ノ割讓ノ問題
（聯合國ハ「領土的其ノ他ノ擴大ヲ求メズ」（大西洋憲章第一項）「自國ノ爲ニ何等ノ利得ヲ欲求スルモノニ非ズ又領土擴張ノ何等ノ念ヲ有スルモノニ非ズ」（「カイロ」宣言）
住民ノ意思ニ反シ領土ノ歸屬ヲ決シ得ルヤノ問題（大西洋憲章第二項「關係國民ノ自由ニ表明セル希望ト一致セザル領土的變更ノ行ハルルコトヲ欲セス」）

（ロ）統治形式ノ問題
日本國民ノ自由ニ表明セル意思ニ依リ現統治形式ノ存續ガ決セラレタル場合聯合國ハ之ニ干涉シ得ルヤノ問題（暗ニ統治形式ノ變更ヲ希望シ居ルヤニ窺ハルル「米國ノ初期ノ對日政策」第二部ノ條項ト「ポツダム」宣言第十二項及大西洋憲章第三項「一切ノ國民ガ其ノ下ニ生活セントスル政體ヲ選擇スルノ權利ヲ尊重ス」トノ矛盾）

（2）經濟的事項

三、既存條約ニ依ル限界（乃至之トノ矛盾）

（イ）委任統治地域ニ付
「カイロ」宣言―日本ガ「奪取シ又ハ占領シタル」モノトシテ「剝奪」ス
「ヴェルサイユ」條約、「ヤップ」島及他ノ赤道以北ノ太平洋委任統治諸島ニ關スル日米條約（我國ノ構成部分トシテ施政ヲ行フ）地域トシテ承認ス）トノ矛盾

（ロ）臺灣及澎湖列島ニ付

「カイロ」宣言―日本ガ清國ヨリ「盗取シタル地域」ナルヲ以テ中國ニ返還

日清講和條約、太平洋方面ニ於ケル島嶼タル屬地及領地ニ關スル四國條約及追加協定トノ矛盾

(ハ)朝鮮ニ付(日韓合併條約、韓國併合宣言ニ對シ今日迄米、英、蘇ノ何レヨリモ異議アリタルコトナシ)

(ニ)樺太、千島ニ付(樺太、千島交換協定、「ポーツマス」條約、太平洋方面ニ於ケル島嶼タル屬地及領地ニ關スル條約及追加協定、華府條約(千島ニ對スル我領土權ヲ保障スル明文アリ)高平「ルート」協定(日米兩國政府ハ相互ニ前記方面ニ於テ「他ノ一方ノ有スル所領ヲ尊重スルノ強固ナル決意ヲ有ス」等トノ矛盾)

四、一般國際法ニ依ル限界

1、聯合國側對日要求ノ法的根據ヨリ生スル限界

(右法的根據ハ「ポツダム」宣言、降伏文書、其ノ他ノ往復文書ヲ内容トスル彼我ノ合意ニ存ス(獨ノ場合トノ相違)右合意ハ彼我ノ合意ニ平等ニ拘束シ從テ聯合國側ノ要求ハ右合意ノ範圍ヲ逸脱スルヲ得ス)

2、占領ノ法的性質ヨリ生スル限界

イ、合意ニ基ク占領(海牙陸戰法規ノ定ムル如キ戰時占領トノ差異)ナルニ依リ占領軍ノ權力ハ右合意ニ依リ制約セラル

ロ、一九〇七年海牙條約ノ準用(合意ニ基ク占領ナリト雖モ右合意中ニ明定セラレサル限リ本條約ヲ準用スヘク同條約ノ人道的精神ハ之ヲ尊重シ出來得ル限リ之ニ準用ニ努メサルヘカラス(例ヘハ現行法令ノ尊重、私有財產ノ尊重、掠奪ノ嚴禁等)

3、主權制限規定ノ「制限的」解釋

一國ノ主權ヲ制約スル條項ニシテ疑義アル場合ハ之ヲ制約スヘキコト國際法上ノ確立セル原則ナリトス(從テ將來聯合國ノ要求ニシテ彼我ノ合意ヲ逸脱スル疑アル場合ハ右原則ヲ援用スルヲ得)

昭和20年10月26日 連合国最高司令官総司令部より 日本政府宛

紙類配給による新聞・出版統制の排除に関する指令

2 民主化・非軍事化政策への対応(昭和20年10月〜21年5月)

GENERAL HEADQUARTERS
SUPREME COMMANDER FOR THE ALLIED POWERS

26 October 1945

AG 461 (26 Oct 45) ESS RP
SCAPIN 195

MEMORANDUM FOR: IMPERIAL JAPANESE GOVERNMENT
THROUGH: Central Liaison Office, Tokyo.
SUBJECT: Elimination of Newspaper and Publishers' Associations Control over Distribution of Paper.

1. The Japanese Government will assume the responsibility of distributing newsprint and foreign-type papers to publishers as of 1 November 1945 or as soon thereafter as practicable.

2. The Japan Newspaper League (Nippon Shimbun Renmei) and Japan Publishers' Association (Nippon Shuppan Kyokai) now controlling the distribution of newsprint and foreign-type papers will no longer perform this function.

3. The Japanese Government will create a paper rationing organization consisting of two sections, one section to be responsible for distributing foreign paper for books and magazines, the other section to be responsible for distributing newsprint. Each section will be composed of (a) government officials (b) representatives of large and small publishers (c) at least three well-known disinterested individuals.

4. The Japanese Government will submit to the Supreme Commander for the Allied Forces within ten days after receipt of this directive the following information:

a. A statement of the principles and policies which will govern paper distribution.

b. The names of the individuals making up the rationing organization and whom they represent.

5. The Japanese Government will submit to the Supreme Commander for the Allied Powers at the end of each month a complete and detailed report of the paper distribution activities during that month. The report will include the following information relevant to (a) newsprint (b) foreign type paper:

a. Total quantity of newsprint and foreign-type paper available for distribution during the given month.

b. A description of the basis on which the publishers

255

were allocated papers

  c. The following facts about each publisher receiving allocation:

    (1) Name and location of company.
    (2) Amount of paper allocated.
    (3) Name of each publication and its circulation.
    (4) Present allocation expressed as percentage of average monthly amount received during period January 1944 through August 1945.

  d. A complete statement concerning rejected applicants for paper, including name, location, name and nature of proposed publication, amount requested and reason for rejection.

6. An acknowledgement of this memorandum is directed.

FOR THE SUPREME COMMANDER:

H. W. ALLEN,
Colonel, A.G.D.,
Asst. Adjutant General

---

76 昭和20年10月29日　終戦連絡中央事務局第一部作成

「英蘇支等軍隊ノ日本占領参加報道ニ關スル件」

吉田大臣ヨリ「マッカーサー」元帥ニ口頭申入ラレ度事項

廿、十、二十九　終連第一部

英、蘇、支等軍隊ノ日本占領参加報道ニ關スル件

一、近ク英、蘇、支等聯合國ヨリ日本占領参加ノ爲夫々部隊ヲ派遣スヘキ旨報セラレタル處日本國内ニ於テハ今ヤ復員力完了シ、戰時法令、戰時機關等ノ廢止、軍國主義者及過激國家主義者ヲ公共的地位ヨリ排除スルコト等ノ措置力進捗シツツアルノミナラス國民輿論カ民主主義的政治ノ確立ニ向ヒツツアル事御承知ノ通ナルカ今日新ニ多數ノ部隊カ日本占領ノ爲渡來シ混亂ニ導クコトナキヤ危惧ヲ生セサルヲ得ス

殊ニ滿鮮ニ於テ「ソ」聯軍ノ爲邦人カ暴虐ナル待遇ヲ受ケツツアル事實ニ鑑ミ同軍來日ノ報道ハ國民ニ多大ノ不安ヲ生セシメツツアリ國内ニ於ケル宿舎設備、食糧、燃料等ノ不足ノ結果困難ナル事情生シ居リ新ニ多數ノ軍隊ノ來駐ハ斯ル困難ナル事情ヲ更ニ惡化スル虞アリ

2　民主化・非軍事化政策への対応(昭和20年10月～21年5月)

77
教員・教育関係者の調査、適格審査および証明に関する指令

昭和20年10月30日　連合国最高司令官総司令部より
　　　　　　　　　　日本政府宛

三、上述ノ事情ニ鑑ミ萬一之等諸國ヨリノ進駐力實現スル場合ニ對スル當方ノ希望ノ開陳ヲ許サルルナラハ
（1）之等諸國ヨリハ象徴的部隊ノ進駐ニ止マル如ク御斡旋ヲ得度
（2）又之等部隊進駐ノ上ハ當然ニ聯合國最高司令官ノ指揮下ニ入ルモノト思考スル處之等部隊ノ日本側トノ接衝ニ關シテモ聯合國總司令部ヲ通シテ行フコトトシテ出來得ル限リ混亂ヲ避クルコトニ致度
（3）之等諸國ノ部隊ノ駐屯地域ニ付テハ米國軍部隊ト隔絶セル地域ヲ占據セシコトトナリテ歐洲ニ於ケル實例ニ鑑ミルモ各占領地域間ノ經濟的、社會的及政治的ノ割據分斷ヲ招來スル惧大ナルヲ以テ斯カル事態ノ發生ヲ避クル為何レモ米國軍駐屯地域内ニ混入收容スル如ク配慮相成度

GENERAL HEADQUARTERS
SUPREME COMMANDER FOR THE ALLIED POWERS

30 October 1945

AG 350 (30 Oct 45) CIE
SCAPIN 212

MEMORANDUM FOR: THE IMPERIAL JAPANESE GOVERNMENT.
THROUGH: Central Liaison Office, Tokyo.
SUBJECT: Investigation, Screening, and Certification of Teachers and Educational Officials.

1. In order to eliminate from the educational system of Japan those militaristic and ultra-nationalistic influences which in the past have contributed to the defeat, war guilt, suffering, privation, and present deplorable state of the Japanese people; and in order to prevent the teachers and educational officials having military experience or affiliation; it is hereby directed that:

　a. All persons who are known to be militaristic, ultra-nationalistic, or antagonistic to the objectives and policies of the occupation and who are at this time actively employed in the educational system of Japan, will be removed immediately and will be barred from occupying any position in the educational system of Japan.

b. All other persons now actively employed in the educational system of Japan will be permitted to retain their positions at the discretion of the Ministry of Education until further notice.

c. All persons who are members of or who have been demobilized from the Japanese Military forces since the termination of hostilities, and who are not at this time actively employed in the educational system of Japan, will be barred from occupying any position in the educational system of Japan until further notice.

2. In order to determine which of those persons who are now actively employed in or who may in the future become candidates for employment in the educational system of Japan are unacceptable and must be removed, barred, and prohibited from occupying any position in the educational system of Japan, it is hereby directed that:

a. The Japanese Ministry of Education will establish suitable administrative machinery and procedures for the effective investigation, screening, and certification of all present and prospective teachers and educational officials.

b. The Japanese Ministry of Education will submit to this Headquarters as soon as possible a comprehensive report describing all actions taken to comply with the provisions of this directive. This report will contain in addition the following specific information:

(1) A precise statement of how acceptability of the individual is to be determined, together with lists of specific standards which will govern the retention, removal, appointment or re-appointment of the individual.

(2) A precise statement of what administrative procedures and machinery are to be established in order to accomplish the investigation, screening, and certification of personnel, together with a statement of what provisions are to be made for review of appealed decisions and reconsideration of individuals previously refused certification.

3. All officials and subordinates of the Japanese Government affected by the terms of this directive, and all school officials, both public and private, will be held personally accountable for

2　民主化・非軍事化政策への対応(昭和20年10月～21年5月)

compliance with the spirit as well as the letter of the policies enunciated in this directive.

FOR THE SUPREME COMMANDER:

H. W. ALLEN,
Colonel, A.G.D.,
Asst. Adjutant General.

78　昭和20年10月31日　外務省作成

［新日本建設初期外交政策要綱案］

新日本建設初期外交政策要綱案

昭和二〇、一〇、三一

新日本建設外交ノ初期目標ヲ概ネ左ノ點ニ置ク

第一　目標

一、「ポツダム」宣言及降伏文書條項ノ履行ヲ可及的速ニ完了スルコト

右條項ノ實施内容ノ確定ニ當リ特ニ國體護持及民族生存ノ經濟的基盤確保ニ遺憾ナカラシムルコト

二、貿易ノ再開ヲ成ルヘク速ニ可能ナラシムルコト

三、成ルベク早期ニ妥當ナル平和條約ノ締結ヲ圖リ正常ナル國際關係ノ修復ヲ實現スルコト

第二　措置

1、「ポツダム」宣言及降伏文書條項ノ履行

(イ)軍國主義ノ排除ニ關スル事項

(ロ)帝國領土ノ占領ニ關スル事項

(ハ)領土ノ處理ニ關スル事項

(ニ)軍隊ノ武裝解除及復員ニ關スル事項

(ホ)戰爭犯罪人ニ關スル事項

(ヘ)民主主義的傾向ノ復活及強化ニ對スル障害ノ除去ニ關スル事項

(ト)言論、宗教及思想ノ自由竝ニ基本的人權ノ尊重ノ確立ニ關スル事項

(チ)産業經濟ニ關スル事項

(リ)賠償ニ關スル事項

(ヌ)平和的責任政府ノ樹立ニ關スル事項

(ル)占領軍ノ撤退ニ關スル事項

(ヲ)軍隊ノ無條件降伏ニ關スル事項

(ト)俘虜及被抑圧者ノ取扱ニ關スル事項
(カ)「ポツダム」宣言及降伏條項實施ノ為ノ聯合國側要求ニ關スル事項

2、自主的改革ノ斷行

(イ)戦争ノ勝敗如何ニ拘ラズ又聯合國側ノ要請如何ニ拘ルニ鑑ミ政治經濟文化等各般ニ亙リ自主的ニ所要ノ改革ヲ斷行スルコト

(ロ)改革ハ「ポツダム」宣言及降伏條項ノ實施トモ睨合セ非軍國主義化及民主主義化ノ線ニ沿フモノタルヲ要スルニ飽ク迄現實ノ缺陷是正ヲ主旨トシ日本民族ノ理想ヲ没却セサルモノタルヲ要スルコト

3、國體護持及民族生存ノ經濟的基盤確保

(イ)國體護持ニ遺憾ナカラシムル爲特ニ一君萬民立憲政體ヲ徹底的ニ純化スルノ措置ヲ講ジ日本的ナル民本政治ノ確立ヲ期スルコト

(ロ)民族生存ノ經濟的基盤確保ニ遺憾ナカラシムル爲特ニ許容産業ノ範圍内容ヲ成ルベク廣汎且多角的ナラシメ合理的ナル産業構成ヲ可能ナラシムル如ク努ムルト共ニ賠償問題ノ處理ニ當リテモ右趣旨ニ合致スルガ如ク調整スルニ努ムルコト
尚領土問題ノ處理ニ關シテモ民族生存ノ經濟的基盤確保上出來得ル限リ有利ナル條件ノ護得ヲ圖ルコト

4、實施促進

前記諸條項ノ履行ヲ可及的速ニ完了スル爲對外誓約實施ノ直接ノ責任官廳タル外務省ニ於テ主動的ニ實施ノ促進ヲ圖ルコト

二、貿易ノ再開

1、當面ノ緊要物資ノ輸入ノ急速實用ヲ圖ルコト

2、一般的輸出入貿易ノ早期再開ヲ期シ蠶糸、茶、繊維製品、工藝品其ノ他輸出産業ノ培養ニ努ムルト共ニ造船海運業ノ再建ニ付所要ノ措置ヲ講ズルコト

3、貿易ハ我國經濟維持ノ絕對要件ナルコトニ付聯合國側ノ理解ヲ深メシムル爲適當ノ措置ヲ執ルコト

三、平和條約ノ早期締結

1、對外誓約ノ遅滯ナキ履行及自主的國内革新ノ積極果敢ナル斷行ニ依リ國際ノ信用ノ恢復ヲ速カナラシメ以テ成ルベク早期ニ平和條約ノ締結ヲ見ルニ至ラシムル

2 民主化・非軍事化政策への対応（昭和20年10月～21年5月）

コト

2、平和條約ノ内容ヲ出來得ル限リ委當ナラシムル爲之ガ締結ニ至ル迄ノ期間ニ於ケル對外措置ニ付極力後腐リヲ殘サザル如ク留意スルト共ニ特ニ日米ノ間ニ基本的相互信賴感ヲ釀成スルニ努ムルコト

3、平和條約締結問題ニ付テハ豫メ之ガ準備ニ遺憾ナキヲ期スルコト

四、基本的態度

新日本建設外交ハ萬邦協和ヲ基調トスベク特ニ或國ニ偏倚シ他ノ國ニ反爭ノ態度ニ出ヅルガ如キコトハ極力之ヲ避クルヲ要スルモ現實ノ事態ニ鑑ミ當面凡ソ左ノ心組ヲ以テ對處スルコト

(イ) 聯合國ニ對日處理ニ付米ガ主導的地位ヲ占メ居ルニモ鑑ミ對米關係ガ主軸ヲ爲スハ當然ナルコト對米關係處理ニ當リテハ信義ニ則リ大局的建設的協調ヲ旨トスルモ苟クモ理不盡ナル要求ニ對シテハ屈セザルノ毅然タル態度ヲ失ハザルコト

(ロ) 日華提携ハ基本的ニハ對米（英）協調ト共ニ新日本建設外交ノ主軸タルベキモ當面ノ現實問題トシテハ中國ガ

聯合國ノ一員タル立場ニアル事實ニモ鑑ミ對支關係ハ性急ニ特殊ニ偏スルコトナク全般トノ關聯ニ於テ考慮處理セラルベキコト

(ハ) 對蘇關係ノ取扱ハ帝國ノ國際關係全局トノ關聯ニテ破壞的作用ヲ結果スルガ如キコトナキ樣愼重ナル戒心ヲ以テスルヲ要スルコト

(ニ) 大國ハ素ヨリ小國乃至被壓迫民族ノ動向等世界情勢ノ現實ノ動キニ付絶ヘズ周密ナル洞察ヲ怠ラズ之ガ將來ノ展望ノ判斷ニ誤算ナキヲ期スルコト

〰〰〰〰〰〰〰〰〰〰〰〰〰〰〰

79 「日本占領及び管理のための連合國最高司令官に對する降伏後における初期の基本的指令」（和訳文）

昭和20年11月1日　米国国務・陸軍・海軍三省承認

日本占領及び管理のための連合國最高司令官に對する降伏後における初期の基本的指令

一九四五年十一月一日

1　この指令の目的及び範圍

（い）この指令は、降伏後の初期の期間における日本の占領及び管理に當つて、貴官の有する權限及び貴官の指針となる政策を規定する。

（ろ）この指令にいう日本は、次のものを含むものと定められる。日本の主要な四島、すなわち北海道（エゾ）、本州、九州、四國及び對馬諸島を含む約一千の隣接小諸島。

（は）この指令は、第1部一般及び政治、第2部經濟及び民生物資、第3部財政金融にわかれる。

第1部　一般及び政治

2　軍事的權限の基礎及び範圍

日本に對する貴官の權限及び權限の基礎は、貴官を連合國最高司令官に任命する米國大統領の署名ある指令及び日本國天皇の命令によつて實施された降伏文書である。これらの文書は、更に一九四五年七月二六日のポツダム宣言、一九四五年八月一〇日の日本側通告に對する一九四五年八月一一日の國務長官の回答及び一九四五年八月一四日の最終の日本側通告に基礎を置いている。これらの文書に從つて、連合國最高司令官としての貴官の日本に對する權限は、

降伏實施という目的のために最高のものである。敵國領土の軍事占領者としての通例の權力の實施以外に、貴官は、降伏及びポツダム宣言の規定の實施に得策且つ適當と考えるいかなる措置をも執る權力を有する。しかしながら、貴官は、貴官が必要と認めるか又は反對の訓令を受けない限り、直接軍政を樹立することなく、貴官の使命達成と兩立する限り、日本國天皇又は日本政府を通じて貴官の權力を行使する。貴官の權力の行使に當つては、次の一般原則が貴官の指針となるであろう。

3　日本の軍事占領の基本的目的

（い）日本に關する連合國の終局の目的は、日本が再び世界の平和及び安全に對する脅威とならないためのできるだけ大きい保證を與え、又、日本が終局的には國際社會に責任あり且つ平和的な一員として參加することを日本に許すような諸條件を育成するにある。この目的の達成にとつて不可缺と考えられるある措置は、ポツダム宣言に述べられている。これらの措置は、特に、次の諸點を含んでいる。

カイロ宣言を履行すること及び日本の主權を主要

2 民主化・非軍事化政策への対応(昭和20年10月〜21年5月)

四島及び連合國の決定する諸小島に制限すること。あらゆる形態の軍國主義及び超國家主義を排除すること。

日本を非武装化し且つ非軍事化し、日本の戰爭遂行能力を引き續き抑制すること。

政治上、經濟上、社會上の諸制度における民主主義的傾向及び過程を強化すること。

日本における自由主義的政治傾向を獎勵し且つ支持すること。

米國は、日本政府が民主主義的自治の諸原則にできるだけ從ふことを希望するが、日本國民の自由に表明された意思によつて支持されないいかなる政治形態をも日本に強いることは占領軍の責任ではない。

(ろ) 連合國最高司令官としての貴官の使命は、降伏が強力に實施されることを確實にし且つ連合國の目的の達成に適當な行動を執るにある。

(は) この指令は、戰後の世界における日本の待遇に關する長期政策を最終的に形成しようとするものではなく、又、貴官の日本占領期間中降伏及びポツダム宣言の實

施に努力するに當つて貴官の執るべき措置を詳細に規定しようとするものでもない。これらの政策及びその實現のため適當な措置は、大部分日本における事態の發展によつて決定されるであらう。それ故、貴官は、常に日本の經濟、産業、財政金融、社會及び政治の狀態に關する調査を繼續し、これを本國政府の利用に供することが必要である。これらの調査を進めるに當つては、この指令に逃べられている初期の管理措置に變更を加え、又連合國の終局目的を促進する政策を逐次形成してゆくための基礎を築くようになされなければならない。必要に應じ、貴官に對して、補足指令が合同參謀本部を通じて發せられる。

4 日本に對する軍事的權限の確立

(い) 日本の降伏後直ちに貴官は、天皇、日本政府及び日本大本營に對して、日本の全軍隊及び日本の支配下にある全軍隊に戰闘行爲を停止して武器を引き渡すように命令を發し、且つ降伏文書及びポツダム宣言に逃べられている政策の實施に必要な他の命令を發するよう要求する。貴官は、天皇及び日本政府に對して、貴

官の使命の目的實現のために發せられるすべての命令が日本におけるすべての者によつて迅速且つ完全に遵守されることを確實にするのに必要なすべての措置を執るように要求する。

（ろ）貴官は、帝都東京及び貴官が日本政府に對する貴官の管理を容易ならしめるために必要と認める府縣の首都を占領する。貴官は、更に貴官の必要と認める戰略的な場所をも占領する。それ以外には、貴官は、日本のいかなる部分をも占領してはならない。しかしながら、貴官の使命實現の必要に應じて、日本のいかなる地域においても臨時に貴官の軍隊を使用することができる。下記第4節（は）の規定には從わなければならないが、貴官は、日本當局又は必要があれば貴官の軍隊による法律及び秩序の囘復及び維持を確實にするために迅速な行動をとる。

（は）降伏實施に行動が必要な場合には、貴官は、當初から直接に行動する權利を有する。それ以外には、天皇又は他の日本當局が有効に行動することを欲しないか又は有効に行動しないときに直接行動を執る最高司令官としての貴官の權利を常に留保して、貴官は、貴官の最高權限を天皇と中央及び地方における日本政府機構とを通じて行使する。この政策は、日本における現在の政治形態を利用するにあつて、これを支持するものではない。政府の封建的及び權威主義的傾向を修正しようとする變更は、許容され且つ支持される。この樣な變更の實現のために日本國民又はその反對者に對して實力を行使する場合には、貴官は、最高司令官として貴官の軍隊の安全及び他の一切の占領目的達成を確實にするに必要な場合にのみ干渉すべきである。貴官は、情勢の必要に應じて、直接軍政の施行を含めて、貴官の最高の權力及び權限を全面的に行使することができる。日本のいずれかの部分において直接軍政の實施が必要となつた場合には、貴官は、その後直ちに合同參謀本部に通報する。貴官は、合同參謀本部との事前の協議及び合同參謀本部を經て貴官になされる通達なしには天皇を排除したり又は天皇を排除しようとするいかなる措置をも執らない。

2　民主化・非軍事化政策への対応（昭和20年10月〜21年5月）

(に)　貴官は、(1)一九一四年世界大戰開始以後日本が委任統治その他の方法によつて奪取又は占領した太平洋諸島の全部、(2)滿洲、臺灣、澎湖諸島、(3)朝鮮、又樺太及び(5)今後の指令に完全に指定されることのあるような他の地域の日本からの完全な政治上及び行政上の分離を實施するために適當な措置を日本において執る。

(ほ)　貴官は、適當な方法によつて日本國民の全階層に對し、彼らの敗戰の事實を明らかにする。彼らの苦痛と敗北は日本の不法且つ無責任な侵略によつてもたらされたものであること、又、日本人の生活及び制度から軍國主義が排除されてはじめて日本は國際社會への參加を許されることを、彼らに認識させなければならない。彼らが他國民の權利と日本の國際義務とを尊重する非軍國主義的、民主主義的日本を發達させるように期待されていることを彼らに知らせなければならない。貴官は、日本の軍事占領は連合國の利益のために實施されているものであり、日本の侵略力及び潛在的戰爭能力の破壞のためと日本人に災禍をもたらした軍國主義及び軍國主義的制度の排除のために必要であることを明らかにする。この目的をもつて、且つ軍隊の安全を確實にするために、貴官が望ましいと認めるときに、又貴官が望ましいと認める限度において、日本に交際禁止政策を適用することができる。しかしながら、貴官の將兵は、米國及び連合國並びにそれらの代表者に對する信賴を深めるように日本人を扱わなければならない。

(へ)　貴官は、天皇に對し、ポツダム宣言に述べられている目的の達成を阻害するか、又は降伏文書若しくは合同參謀本部を通じて貴官に發せられることのある指令に抵觸するすべての法律、命令、規則を廢止するよう要求する。貴官は、特に政治的及び市民的自由の制限と、人種、國籍、信仰又は政見による差別とを設け且つ維持したすべての法律、命令、規則の廢止を確實にする。既に廢止され、又は廢止されるべき法規の執行を特に擔當している機關又は機關の一部は、即時廢止されなければならない。

(と)　貴官は、必要に應じ、占領軍に對する犯罪及び降伏

265

實施と兩立するような他の事項について管轄權を有する軍事裁判所を設置する。しかしながら、そうしないことを貴官が必要と認める場合を除き、日本の裁判所が貴官の軍隊の安全に直接且つ重大な關係を有しない事件については有效な裁判權を行使することを確實にする。

(ち) 米國政府又は他の連合國政府の非軍事機關代表者は、貴官の承認を得、且つその目的、期間及び範圍に關し合同參謀本部によつて貴官に通告される決定に從うのでなければ、占領に參加し又は日本國内で獨立して任務を遂行してはならない。

5 政治的及び行政的改組

(い) 地方、地域及び中央の行政機關は、その機能及び責任が占領目的と一致しないものを除き、下記第5節(ろ)に述べられている受け容れがたい官吏又は信頼を置きがたいことが確められた官吏を排除した上で機能繼續を許される。このような機關及びその人員は、行政について責任を負わされ、貴官の政策及び指令の實施の任務を課せられる。しかしながら、あらゆる場合に、又あらゆる事情の下において、貴官が貴官の指令を滿足しない場合、貴官自身で直接行動を執る權限を與えられる程度に應じて、貴官自身で直接行動を執る權限を與えられている。

(ろ) 下記第7節(は)に示されている場合を除き、好戰的國家主義及び侵略の積極的な推進者、日本の超國家主義的結社、暴力的結社又は愛國的祕密結社、その出先機關又は參加團體の有力な會員であつた者、下記第5節(と)に列擧されている他の團體の活動に勢力をもつていた者又は軍事占領目的に敵意を示した者は、いかなる私的企業における責任ある公職又は公的企業若しくは重要な私的企業における責任ある又は有力ないかなる他の地位をも保持することを許されない。

(は) 貴官は、現在の政治形態が維持される限り、あらゆる場合において、内大臣、樞密顧問、内閣總理大臣及び閣僚の地位が貴官の使命の目的を促進するものと信頼することができる人物によつてのみ占められることを確實にする。貴官は、大東亞省の即時廢止を要求するが、同省の機構及び人員のうち、上記第4節(に)に

2 民主化・非軍事化政策への対応(昭和20年10月～21年5月)

規定されている植民地分離の實施に必要なものは殘置することができる。貴官は、非武裝化及び復員の過程において陸軍省、海軍省、軍需省を逐次解體廢止する。

(に) 國の政策の地方的實施に對し地方に責任をもたせることは、獎勵される。

(ほ) 日本における通常の刑事及び民事裁判所は、貴官の決定する規則、監督及び統制に從つて機能繼續を許される。上記第5節(ろ)の規定によつて受け容れがたい裁判官その他の裁判所所員は、できるだけ速やかに排除される。このような官吏は、受け容れうる有資格者と取り換える。機能繼續を許されるすべての裁判所に對し、貴官は、全面的審査權を保有する。貴官は、貴官の使命の目的と一致しないすべての判決を拒否する。貴官は、上記第4節(へ)によつて廢止されるべき種類の法律又は規則のみによつて拘留されている者を釋放させるため、できる限りの措置を執る。

(へ) 司法及び普通警察機關並びに貴官が適當な監督の下に殘置することを適當と考えるような他の警察機關から信賴しがたい分子、好ましくない分子、特に超國家

主義的結社、暴力的結社及び愛國的祕密結社の會員を追放しなければならない。

(と) 日本全國を通じて、貴官は、大日本政治會、大政翼贊會、大政翼贊政治會、これらの參加團體及び出先機關又は後繼團體並びに日本のすべての超國家主義的結社、暴力的結社及び愛國的祕密結社、これらの出先機關及び參加團體の解散を確實にする。

(ち) 貴官は、國務省が合同參謀本部を通じて要求する日本の外交官、領事官、その他海外出先機關員の召還を日本政府に指令する。貴官は、又降伏實施の文書及び財產を連合國政府の正當に任命した代表者による管理に移す手配をするように日本政府に指令する。

(り) 上記第5節(と)に述べられている團體のいずれかの所有又は支配しているすべての動產及び不動產は、公有財產とみなされるべきである。なんらかの財產(例えば、半官會社又は日本政府若しくは日本皇室が重大利害を有する民間會社の資產)の公的地位について疑問がある場合には、それは、公有財產とみなされるべ

きである。皇室財産は、この指令に逃べられている目的の遂行に必要ないかなる措置からも免除されてはならない。

6 非軍事化

（い）貴官は、憲兵隊（但し、警察を含まない）、民間義勇隊及びすべての準軍事組織を含むすべての日本の武装部隊及びすべての準軍事組織の速やかな武装解除を確實にする。部隊の隊員は、捕虜としてではなく、彼ら自身の將校の下に武装解除された部隊として取り扱われ、貴官の發したか又は發することのある指令に従つて復員させられる。貴官は、日本へ送還されるいづれの者に對しても不公平であつて捕虜となつたい待遇又は權能はく奪を防止する規定が設けられるよう要求する。

（ろ）貴官は、軍事參議院、元帥府、大本營、參謀本部、軍令部、陸軍、海軍及び民間義勇隊、憲兵隊を含むすべての軍事組織及び準軍事組織並びに日本における軍事的傳統の保存に役立つことのあるすべての在郷軍人會その他の軍國主義的團體の恆久的解體を規定する。

但し、貴官は、降伏特に復員を實施するという限られた目的をもつて、上に列擧されたものを含む陸海軍機關を短期間利用することができる。陸海空における、すべての軍事的及び準軍事的訓練は禁止される。

（は）貴官は、すべての武器、彈薬、艦艇及び非軍事的用途に當てられる航空機を含む軍用器材を押收又は破壞し且つその生産を停止する。

（に）貴官は、この指令の第2部及び第3部に逃べられているように、日本の潜在的戰争能力を破壞するために適當な措置を執る。

7 日本人公職者の逮捕及び抑留

（い）次の者は、その處置について追つて訓令があるまで、戰争犯罪容疑者としてできる限り速やかに逮捕し且つ抑留する。

（1）軍事參議院、元帥府、大本營立びに參謀本部及び軍令部の構成員全部。

（2）憲兵隊の將校全部及び陸海軍將校のうち好戰的國家主義及び侵略の重要な推進者であつた者全部。

268

2　民主化・非軍事化政策への対応（昭和20年10月～21年5月）

（3）超國家主義的結社、暴力的結社及び愛國的祕密結社の樞要な會員全部。

（4）貴官が戰爭犯罪人と信ずる理由を有する者又はこれまで貴官に送達されたか又は送達されることのある戰爭犯罪容疑者の表の中にその姓名又は人相書が含まれている者全部。

（ろ）日本の侵略計畫の策定又は實行に當り積極的且つ支配的に政治上、經濟上、金融上その他重要な役割を演じた者全部並びに大日本政治會、大政翼贊會、大政翼贊政治會、これらの出先機關及び參加團體又は後繼團體の幹部全部は、追つて處置されるまで抑留される。

貴官は、貴官の使命達成の必要に應じ他の非軍人をも抑留することができる。

（は）しかしながら、貴官は、上記第7節の（い）の（1）及び（2）に列擧されている種類の人物中、日本武裝部隊の復員を確實にするために貴官が絕對に必要とする人物を、嚴重な監督の下に短期間利用することができる。

（に）貴官は、平和に對する罪及び人道に對する罪を犯した者を含む戰爭犯罪人に關する貴官の責任について、

さらに訓令を受ける。

（ほ）戰爭犯罪人として逮捕された非軍人又は軍人に對して、財產又は政治上、產業上その他の階級若しくは地位によつて、逮捕の方法又は拘留の狀態に關して差別を設け又は特別の考慮を與へてはならない。

（へ）第二次世界大戰において連合國のいずれかの敵國であるか又はあつたことのある日本以外の國（ブルガリア、フィンランド、ドイツ、ハンガリー、イタリー、ルーマニア、及びタイ）の國民はすべて調査登錄し、狀況の必要に應じ、抑留し又はその活動を制限することができる。このような國の外交官及び領事官は、保護抑留し、追つて處置するため留めておく。

（と）第7節の規定によつて抑留又は逮捕された人物の所有又は支配している動產及び不動產は、その終局の處置について指令があるまで貴官の管理下におく。

8　捕虜、連合國人、中立國人、その他の者

（い）貴官は、連合國の捕虜及び流民が保護され且つ送還されることを確實にする。

（ろ）中立國の國民は、適當な軍事當局に登錄するように

要求される。彼らは、貴官の設定することのある規則に從つて送還されることができる。しかしながら、連合國の一國に對する戰爭にいかなる方法によつてでも積極的に參加したすべての中立國人は、逮捕され、後に發せられる訓令に從つて處置される。中立國人は、その本國又は日本以外に居住する者との通信又は事業關係についていかなる特權をも與えられない。中立國の場合には、貴官によつて送還されることができる。しかしながら、連合國人の送還に優先權が與えられる。

（は）連合國人であつて日本に居住しているか又は抑留されているすべての非軍人は、調査し、綿密にじん問し、貴官が適當と認める場合には抑留し又は居住を制限する。右の中上記第7節（ろ）の規定に該當するすべての者は、戰爭犯罪容疑者として逮捕し且つ抑留しなければならない。一又は二以上の連合國に對する戰爭にいかなる方法によつてでも積極的に參加した他のすべての連合國人は、逮捕し、追つて處置するため留めておく。その後、彼らは、貴官に與えられるべき指令に從つて處置される。一般に、連合國人の健康及び福祉をに確實にするために實際的措置が執られる。

（に）貴官は、中國人たる臺灣人及び朝鮮人を、軍事上の安全の許す限り解放國民として取り扱う。彼らは、この指令に使用されている「日本人」という語には含まれないが、彼らは、日本臣民であつたのであり、必要の場合には、貴官によつて敵國人として取り扱われることができる。彼らは、もし希望するならば、貴官の定める規則によつて送還されることができる。しかしながら、連合國人の送還に優先權が與えられる。

（ほ）軍事情勢によつて必要とされる限度内において、貴官は、連合國及び連合國人の財産の保存及び保護に必要なすべての妥當な措置を執らなければならない。

9 政治活動

（い）日本の軍國主義的及び超國家主義的イデオロギーと宣傳とのいかなる形式における弘布も、禁止され且つ完全に抑壓される。貴官は、日本政府に對し國家神道施設への財政的その他の援助を停止するように要求する。

（ろ）貴官は、軍事的安全とこの指令に述べられている目

2 民主化・非軍事化政策への対応(昭和20年10月～21年5月)

的の達成のために必要な最低限度の統制及び檢閲を、郵便、無電、ラジオ、電話、電信、海底電信、映畫及び出版物を含む非軍事的通信に對し設ける。思想の自由は、利用しうるあらゆる弘報手段による民主主義の理想及び原理の弘布によって育成される。

(は)貴官は、現存するすべての政黨、政治團體、政治結社を即時統制の下に置く。そのうち軍事占領の要求及びその目的に一致した活動をしているものは、獎勵されるべきである。このような要求及び目的に一致しない活動をしているものは、廢止すべきである。占領軍の安全維持の必要には從わなければならないが、集會及び公開討論の權利を有する民主主義的政黨の結成及び活動は、獎勵される。代議的地方政府の自由な選擧は、できる限り早い時期に行われるべきであり、地域的及び全國的の自由な選擧は、貴官の勸告を考慮した後合同參謀本部を通じて指令されるところに從って行われるべきである。この項に述べられている計畫に關する貴官の行動は、占領の終局目的の一つ、すなわち日本國民の自由に表明された意思による平和的傾向を

有し且つ責任ある政府の樹立に照して執られなければならない。

(に)勞働、産業、農業における民主主義的團體の發達は、獎勵される。

(ほ)信教の自由は、日本政府によって速やかに宣言されるべきである。貴官の軍事占領の安全及びその目的の達成が害われない限度において、又上記第9節(い)及び(は)に從うことを條件として、貴官は、意見、言論、出版及び集會の自由を確實にする。

10 教育、美術及び文書

(い)教育機關は、できる限り速やかに再開される。好戰的國家主義及び侵略の積極的推進者であつたすべての教師及び軍事占領の目的に積極的に反對し續けているすべての教師は、受け容れうる有資格後繼者と取り換える。すべての學校における日本の軍事的及び準軍事的教育及び教練は、禁止される。貴官は、貴官に受け容れられる教科がすべての學校で採用され、そのうちには上記第3節(い)に示されている觀念を含むことを確保する。

11 占領期間中の日本の經濟問題に關する米國政府の政策は、次の諸目的の同時達成を企圖している。

(い) あらゆる種類の武器、軍需品又は軍用器材の生産を專門とする現存の施設を除去すること。

(ろ) 國際的平和に對して危險ないかなる軍備をもたらすにつくり又は維持する日本の經濟能力を破壞すること。

(は) 適當な連合國當局によつて決定されることのある賠償及び返還計畫を實行すること。

(に) 日本の平和的、民主的勢力の成長に貢獻するような

種類の經濟的慣行及び制度の日本國內における發達を獎勵すること。

(ほ) 日本の經濟的組織の運用と經濟的操作とが、占領の一般的目的に合致することを確實にし、且つ平和的貿易國家の列への日本の終局的復歸を可能とするように監督指導すること。

この指令の經濟的部分をなす訓令は、前途に控えている占領の最初且つ當面の期間においてこれらの目的を促進することを企圖している。これらの訓令は、貴官の遭遇する事態及び日本國民の行動に照して、追加改訂されることもある。

12 日本における連合國最高司令官としての貴官の最高權限は、經濟的分野におけるすべての事項に及ぶ。この權限の行使に當つては、貴官の目的の達成の許す限度で、貴官は、天皇及び日本政府の機構を貴官の目的達成に利用する。貴官は、彼らに對し、貴官の命令を遂行し、且つ、貴官の目的遂行上貴官の必要と思うような變更を經濟事項擔當の政府部門の行政組織に加えるように要求する。

第2部

甲 經濟

目的及び一般的基本原則

(ろ) 貴官は、すべての政府事業、準政府事業、重要な民間の金融、產業、製造及び商業會社竝びに上記第5節(へ)に述べられている日本の團體の記錄を、貴官の參考及び使用の目的のために保存させるべきである。

(は) 貴官は、できる限りすべての歷史的、文化的及び宗敎的物件を占領軍その他によつて略奪されないように保護させ且つ保存させる。

2 民主化・非軍事化政策への対応(昭和20年10月～21年5月)

貴官は、次の場合には、直接に行動しなければならない。

(い) 任務の性質そのものから貴官の経済的目的が有効に達成されない場合。

(ろ) 貴官の操作のいずれか特定の部面において日本政府を通ずる操作が満足すべき方法でないことが明らかとなる場合。

13 直接に行動するに当つては、貴官は、貴官がその任務を日本政府当局に委せても満足しうると考える時期まで、この指令に含まれている経済的措置を実施するか又は、その実施を確実にするために、日本の官吏及び機関から独立し且つこれに優越する行政機構を設置する。

貴官は、日本の経済の復興又は日本経済の強化についてなんらの責任をも負わない。貴官は、次のことを日本國民に明らかにする。

(い) 貴官が日本にいずれの特定の生活水準を維持し又は維持させるなんらの義務をも負わないこと。

(ろ) 生活水準は、日本がどれだけ徹底的にすべての軍國主義的野望をみずからすて、その人的及び天然資源の利用を全く且つ専ら平和的生活の目的に転換し、適当な経済的及び財政的統制を実施し、且つ占領軍及びその代表する諸政府と協力するかにかかつていること。日本がその努力及び資源によつて第11節に特記されている目的に合致する日本における生活状態を終局的に実現するのを妨げるのは、米國の政策ではない。

経済的非武装化

14 日本の経済的非武装化を実施するために、

(い) 貴官は、すべての武器、弾薬その他の軍用器材、海軍艦艇、非軍事的用途に向けられるものを含むあらゆる種類の航空機並びに前記のもののいずれかに合体させることを特に目的とする部分品、構成物及び資材の將來の生産、取得、発達、維持又は使用を即時停止し、且つ防止する。

(ろ) 貴官は、上記の品目中いずれかの生産又は使用されるか又は使用される目的を有する施設を保全するために貴官が必要と認める措置を執る。これらの施設は、終局的処理について追つて訓令あるまでは、緊急事態でなければ破壊されるべきでない。

（は）貴官は、合同參謀本部を通ずる特別の承認を得なければ、（い）項に特記されている禁止計畫の實施又は（ろ）項に從つて受ける訓令の執行を延期しない。しかしながら、萬一貴官が（い）項に列擧されている品目のいずれかの生產が貴官の軍事作戰、占領軍又は臨時の軍事的調查の要求をみたすために必要であると認める場合には、貴官は、合同參謀本部に適當な勸告をなし、合同參謀本部の決定があるまで、必要な最低限度まで生產の手配をなす權限を與えられる。

15 經濟的非武裝化、賠償、返還の計畫實施のために後に貴官に送付される訓令は、鐵、鋼、化學製品、非鐵金屬、アルミニウム、マグネシウム、人造ゴム、人造石油、工作機械、ラジオ、電氣器具、自動車りよう、商船、重機械及びこれらの重要部分のような、日本のある生產部門の縮減又は除去を含む。

しかしながら、これらの事項について最終的且つ特定の決定あるまで、貴官は、占領軍の需要及び人民の最少限度の平和的需要をみたすのに必要な最低限度まで、これらの產業における生產の繼續及び生產施設の修理を許

貴官は、生產の繼續又は生產施設の修理に關して與えられるいかなる許可も、日本經濟のいかなる部門に加えられることのある制限又は賠償若しくは返還として要求されることのある引渡についての最終的決定を害するものでないことを日本人に對し明らかにする。

16 貴官は、又第14節及び第15節に逃べられている種類を含む工場及び設備を必需消費財の生產に轉換することを許可することができる。貴官は、このような轉換の行われた場合そのいずれもが平和經濟への眞正な動きであり且つ軍事的目的のために生產能力を溫存しようとする擬裝された試みでないことを確める。

貴官は、又いずれのこのような轉換許可も、賠償若しくは返還による工場若しくは設備の撤去、又は第11節による安全上の理由のためのくず鐵化に關する後の決定を害するものでないことを日本人に對し明らかにする。

17 貴官は、
（い）第14節及び第15節に禁止されている種類の生產が隱蔽され又は擬裝された形で行われないことを確實にす

274

2　民主化・非軍事化政策への対応（昭和20年10月～21年5月）

るために、直ちに檢査制度及び統制を確立する。

(ろ) 第14節に網らされている生產物をこれまで生產してきたか又は今後生產する目的を有するすべての重要な施設及び第15節に特記されているすべての產業における重要な施設に關する明細目錄の報告をできるだけ速やかに作成させる。これらの報告は、工場及び施設の狀態、能力並びに手持原料、製品及び仕掛品の數量を明記しなければならない。貴官は、又日本商船隊の明細目錄を作成する。

貴官に、これらの報告を今後の經濟政策に關する今後の決定に必要な情報を供するために、貴官は、これらの報告を合同參謀本部に送る。

(は) 貴官の占領終了後日本の再軍備を防止する統制を立案し、合同參謀本部に勸告する。

18　貴官は、すべての實驗所、調查機關及び類似の技術機關が、貴官が占領目的のために必要と考えるものを除き、即時閉鎖されることを確實にする。貴官は、必要と認める場合にはこれらのものの物的施設の維持及び安全並びに貴官の技術的又は防諜的調查に利益ある人員の保持をはかる。貴官は、直ちにこのような閉鎖團體において行

われた研究及び調查の性質を調べ、明白に平和的目的を有する種類の研究及び調查の再開を、(1)許可される研究の特定の種類を定義し、(2)ひん繁な檢査を規定し、研究の結果を貴官に卒直に知らせることを要求し、(4)規則に違反した場合には違反機關の恒久的閉鎖を含む嚴罰を課する適當な規則の下にできるだけ速やかに許可する。

日本經濟制度の運用

19　日本當局は、自己の資源及び勞力によって次のことの達成を可能とする實行計畫を作成し且つ有效に實施するように期待される。

(い) 甚しい經濟的困窮を避けること。

(ろ) 利用しうる物資の適正公平な分配を確保すること。

(は) 占領軍の必要のための貴官の要求をみたすこと。

(に) 連合國政府の合意するような賠償引渡のための要求をみたすこと。

これらの目的達成のために、日本當局は、農業及び漁業生產物、石炭、木炭、家屋修理材料、衣料その他の必需品の生產を最大とするように最善をつくさなければな

らない。日本當局がそうするのを怠つた場合には、貴官は、日本當局に貴官が必要と判斷する措置を執るように指令する。

20 貴官は、飢餓、廣範圍の疾病及び甚しい肉體的苦痛をひきおこすことなしに行われうる限度内で、占領軍の必要をみたすために物資及びサーヴィスを供給することを日本當局に要求する。

21 日本當局は、第19節に明記されている經濟的目的の達成のために適當又は必要な經濟活動に對する統制を自己の責任において確立實施することを許されるべきである。これらの統制の政策と實施は双方とも、特にこれらの統制が第15節に矛盾する限りにおいて、貴官の承認及び監督を受けなければならない。この節は、貴官が第12節に規定されているところに從つて直接行動に出ることを妨げるものではない。

22 深刻なインフレーションは、占領の終局の目的の達成を大いに遲延させるであろう。それ故、貴官は、日本當局に對し、このようなインフレーションを囘避するためにあらゆる實行可能な努力を拂うように指令する。しかしながら、インフレーションの防止又は抑制は、賠償、返還、非軍事化又は經濟的非武裝化の計畫の實施に當り生產施設の撤去、破壞又は縮少を制限する理由としてはならない。

23 貴官は、好戰的國家主義及び侵略の積極的推進者であつたすべての者、この指令の第5節（と）（第1部、一般及び政治）に列擧されている團體に積極的に參加した者及び將來の日本の經濟的努力を專ら平和的目的の方向に向けないいかなる者をも、產業、金融、商業又は農業における重要な責任又は勢力ある地位に留め又は選任することを禁止する。（貴官にとつて滿足すべき反證のない限り、貴官は、一九三七年以來產業、金融、商業又は農業において高度の責任を有するか樞要な地位を占めたことのあるいかなる者も好戰的國家主義及び侵略の積極的推進者であつたものと推定する。）

24 貴官は、日本の戰爭努力又は經濟において重要な役割を演じたことのある日本の大產業及び金融會社並びに商業及び研究團體のすべての工場、設備、特許權、帳簿、

2　民主化・非軍事化政策への対応（昭和20年10月〜21年5月）

25　次のものを獎勵し且つこれに好意を示すのが米國政府の意向である。

（い）所得と生産及び商業手段の所有權とを廣く分配することを許す政策。

（ろ）勞働、産業、農業における民主主義的基礎の上に組織された團體の發達。

從つて、貴官は、

（1）日本側に對し、本國政府の軍事的及び經濟的目的に從つて日本財界を改組することに責任を持つ公的機關を設立するように要求する。貴官は、この機關に對し、日本の大規模な産業及び金融企業合同體又は他の私的事業支配の大集中を解體する計畫を貴官の承認をうるため提出するように要求する。

（2）滿足すべき改組案が承認されるまでの間、本國政府の軍事的經濟的目的との合致を確實にするため前記

記錄その他すべての重要財産を、この指令及び他の指令によつて決定されるような處置のために破壊から保全し且つ保全するように要求する。

日本經濟制度の民主化

（1）項に述べられている日本財界に對し監視を確立し且つ維持する。

（3）統制團體を解散する。從來これらの團體によつて行われていた公的機能であつて必要なものがあれば、貴官の承認し且つ監督する公的機關に移管されるべきである。

（4）改組されるべき産業へ商社が自由に加入することを制限する立法的又は行政的措置は、その目的又は效果が私的獨占を育成し且つ強化するものである場合には、すべて廢止する。

（5）私的國際カルテル又は他の制限的な私的國際契約若しくは取極への日本の参加をすべて終止し、禁止する。

（6）日本側に對し勞働に對する戰時の統制をできるだけ速やかに撤廢し、勞働保護立法を復活させるように要求する。

（7）民主的な線に沿う被使用者の組織の結成に對するすべての法的障害の撤廢を要求する。但し、これは、いかなる擬装の下における軍國主義的勢力の恆久化又は占領軍の目的及び作戰行動に敵意を抱くいかなる集團

の存續をも防止するのに必要な保障措置を執ることを妨げるものではない。

（8）罷業又は他の作業停止は、これらが占領軍の軍事行動を妨害するか又はその安全を直接危くすると貴官が認めた場合にのみ防止又は禁止する。

對外經濟取引

26　貴官は、商品及びサーヴィスについての日本の對外貿易全般に統制を確立する。このような統制は、初期の期間において次の諸政策を實施するように運營されなければならない。

（い）　輸出商品が國内の最低需要をみたすのに必要なことが明らかな場合には、輸出を承認してはならない。

（ろ）　工場及び設備の輸出は、それが賠償又は返還に必要とされるかどうかについて決定がなされるまでは、許可されてはならない。

（は）　賠償のため又は返還として積出を指令されたもの以外の輸出は、これらの輸出品の見返として必要な輸入品を供給することに同意するか又は輸出品の代價を外國爲替で支拂うことに同意する仕向國に對してのみ行

うことができる。

（に）　すべての輸出代金は、貴官が管理し、まず第一に、承認された輸入の支拂にあてなければならない。日本におけるいかなる者、會社又は團體も、貴官の特別の承認がなければ、いかなる種類の外國資産の取得をも許されてはならない。

（ほ）　この指令中の他の個所に述べられている經濟政策に明らかに一致する輸入にのみ承認を與えるべきである。

（へ）　輸入又は輸出（賠償のために行われることのある輸出を含む）の必要は、いかなる日本の産業部門をも日本の潜在的戰爭能力に著しく寄與し又は戰略物資に對する他國の對日從屬度を高めるような程度まで復興又は發展させることを要求し又は許可する理由と考えられてはならない。

27　日本當局は、事前に貴官と協議の上貴官の明示的承認を得なければ、外國政府又は業者との間にいかなる種類の經濟協定をも結ぶべきではない。いかなるこのような協定の提案も、その審議のために合同參謀本部に提出されなければならない。

2 民主化・非軍事化政策への対応(昭和20年10月〜21年5月)

賠償及び返還

28　貴官は、合同參謀本部によって貴官に通達される連合國の當該官憲の決定に從って、現物賠償計畫及び識別しうる略奪財産の返還計畫を實施することを確實にする。賠償は、次の方法によって實行される。

(い)　日本が保有すべき領域外にある日本資産を移轉すること。

(ろ)　平和的な日本經濟の運營又は占領軍に對する供給に必要でない商品、現存の工場、設備、施設を日本から移動すること。

日本の侵略の犠牲となった連合國から貴官の受理する賠償又は返還のすべての要求は、貴官の勸告を添えて合同參謀本部に報告する。

乙　民生物資供給及び救濟

民生物資供給方針及び供給基準

29(い)　貴官は、日本への輸入を嚴重に制限する目的をもって、日本の重要資源の最大限の利用を達成するために實行しうるすべての經濟及び警察措置が執られることを確實にする。このような措置は、生産と物價の統制、配給、やみ市場の取締、財政金融統制その他日本において利用しうる資源、施設及び資力の完全な使用を目的とする措置を含む。

(ろ)　貴官は、現地資源の補充のためにのみ、且つ占領軍を危うくするか軍事行動を妨げるような廣範圍の疾病又は民生不安の防止に必要な限度においてのみ、輸入物資の供給に責任を持つ。このような輸入は、食料、燃料、醫療及び衛生物資その他の必需品目の最低量に限定され、そのうちには、貴官がそれがなければ輸入しなければならないような物資の現地生産を可能ならしめる品目を含む。

(は)　上記第29節(ろ)によって輸入が必要な物資は、他のアジア及び太平洋地域から得られる餘剰物資からできるだけ入手する。このような餘剰物資が他の米軍司令官の管轄地域から供給しうる限度においては、貴官は、このような他の司令官と直接に取極を行うことができる。このような餘剰物資が米國以外の政府又はこのような政府の軍司令官の管轄下の地域において入手しうる限度においては、このような餘剰物資の入手に必要

分配の方法及び條件

30 貴官は、割一的配給基準による物資の公正な分配を確實にするためにすべての實行可能な措置を執るように要求する。

31 軍事的便宜に合致する最大限度まで、一般住民のための輸入物資は、實行可能であり且つ望ましい限りにおいて、貴官にとつて受け容れうるような日本の公的供給機關又は他の受託者に對し、且つ貴官の直接の監督又は統制の下に、引き渡されるべきである。このような引渡は、可能な場合には常に輸入港において行われるが、必要な場合には國内の適當な分配中心地で引渡を行うことができる。

（に）合同參謀本部に貴官の勸告を提出する

貴官が貴官の占領目的を達成するため、追加輸入をする責任を負うべきであると考えるときは、貴官は、情勢を合同參謀本部に報告する。このような外交代表が利用し得ない場合には、貴官は、貴官の勸告を添えて又はその承認を得て行われる。な交渉は、當該地域における現地米國外交代表により

32 滿足すべき公的供給機關が存在しないか又は作戰上若しくは他の理由によつて實行不可能である場合には、貴官は、直接卸賣業者又は他の商人に對し販賣することができる。貴官による分配が實行不可能である場合には民生物資のこのような直接的供給と分配をなるべく少くするために、貴官は、日本人が不必要に占領軍による責任に卷き込まないことを確實にすべきである。貴官による直接販賣が必要となる場合には、その代金は、貴官が國内經濟に適合すると決定する價格をもつて、購入者によつて現地通貨で支拂われる。

33 供給機關又は他の受託者に引き渡される物資は、それら機關によつて分配經路を通じ、且つ貴官にとつて滿足すべき分配方針に從い、又貴官が國内經濟に適合するように決定する價格によつて販賣される。軍事上の必要が要求する場合には、民生物資は、貴官の監督若しくは統制下にある供給機關による直接的救濟放出の對象とすることができる。

第3部 財政金融

2 民主化・非軍事化政策への対応（昭和20年10月〜21年5月）

34 財政金融の部門においては、貴官は、後に列擧されている政策及び計畫の有效な實施が許す限度まで日本政府を通じて行動するが、このような政策及び計畫を實施し又はそれらの有效な實施を確實にするに必要な限度において日本當局及びその機關に從屬しない行政機構を設置して、この指令の他の部分において述べられている原則を完全に適用する。貴官は、この指令の第40節、第41節、第45節、第46節及び第47節の規定を實施し又はそれらの有效な實施を確實にするために、このような獨立の行政機構を設置することを特に指令されている。

35 日本の金融機關及び財政制度は、日本の資源を基礎として機能するように期待される。貴官は、この指令に明記されている目的のために必要でない限り、日本の財政金融機構の維持、強化、又は運用を目的としたいかなる措置をも執らない。

36 貴官は、日本銀行又は他のいかなる銀行若しくは機關に對しても法貨である銀行券及び通貨を發行することを認可し又は要求することができる。このような認可がなければ、いかなる日本政府の又は民間の銀行又は機關も

銀行券又は通貨の發行を許されない。

37 貴官は、日本當局に對し無償で且つ貴官の軍事占領の費用を含む貴官の軍隊のすべての經費をまかなうに十分な數量の法貨である圓紙幣又は圓クレディットを貴官に提供するように要求する。

38（い）なんらかの理由によって正規の法貨である圓紙幣の適當な量が入手できない場合には、貴官は、軍布告に從って發行される補助圓軍票（B型）を使用する。補助圓は、法貨と宣言され、他の法貨である圓通貨と差別なしに等價で交換される。

（ろ）正規の圓通貨は、この地域において現在法貨である通貨を含む。

（は）日本によって占領された地域において流通させるために發行された日本の軍票は、法貨としないし、又通用力もなく、補助圓又は正規の圓通貨と交換することもできない。

39 貴官は、今後訓令を受理するまでは、一方において日本圓と、他方において米ドル及び他の通貨とのいかなる一般的交換率の使用又は發表をも布告し、實施し又は許

可しない。しかしながら、陸海軍人員に對する支拂及び陸海軍の會計の目的にのみ使用されるべき交換率、すなわち正規又は補助圓15は1ドルという比率は、すでに貴官に通達されている。

40　貴官は、好戰的國家主義及び侵略の積極的推進者であったか、又はこの指令の第7節に列擧されている團體に積極的に参加したすべての公的及び私的の財政金融機關又は團體における重要な責任又は勢力ある地位から罷免し且つ排除する。反證のない限りこのような機關又は團體のいずれかにおける框要な地位を占めたことがあるいかなる者も、好戰的國家主義及び侵略の積極的推進者であると一般に推定することができる。貴官は、又將來の財政金融活動を專ら平和的目的に向けない者を財政金融分野における重要な地位に留め又は選任することを阻止する。

41　貴官は、戰時生產の金融又は植民地若しくは日本の占領地域における財源の動員若しくは統制を最高の目的としていた銀行その他の金融機關を閉鎖し且つその再開を許さない。これらは、次のものを含む。

（い）　戰時金融金庫

（ろ）　全國金融統制會及びその會員である統制會

（は）　朝鮮銀行及び臺灣銀行の日本本土における營業所

（に）　日本本土外を活動舞臺としていた各種の銀行及び開發會社、例えば南洋興發會社、南方開發金庫並びに滿洲中央銀行、蒙疆銀行、中國聯合準備銀行及び中國中央儲備銀行の東京營業所等。貴官は、これらの銀行その他の機關のすべての帳簿及び記錄を保管する。

42　貴官は、貴官の軍事占領の目的達成に必要と考える財政金融措置を執る權限を與えられる。これは、特に次の措置を含むが、これに限るわけではない。

（い）　上記第41節に指示されているもの以外の銀行は、滿足すべき管理を行い、好ましくない人員を除き又はある種の勘定及び振替の封鎖、若しくは封鎖されるべき勘定の決定の計畫を實施するための措置を執るという目的のためか、又は他の軍事上の理由のために明らかに必要な場合にのみ閉鎖する。貴官は、上記第41節に述べられている以外のいずれの閉鎖された銀行をも前記目的の遂行と合致する限り速やかに再開しなければな

2 民主化・非軍事化政策への対応（昭和20年10月～21年5月）

（ろ）私的又は公的の證券又は不動産その他の財産の移轉その他の取引を禁止し又は制限する。

（は）貴官の軍事占領の目的遂行に明らかに必要な限度においてのみ、一般的又は部分的支拂猶豫令を施行する。

（に）株式取引所、保險會社及び類似の金融機關を貴官の適當と考える期間閉鎖する。

43 貴官は、次のものの支拂を禁止する。

（い）すべての軍人年金、その他の手當を禁止する。但し、受給者の勞働能力を制限する肉體的不具に對する補償は除くが、その率は、非軍事的な原因から生ずる同様の肉體的不具に對するものの最低より高くてはならない。

（ろ）次の者に授與されるすべての公的又は私的の年金その他の手當又は特典。

（1）大日本政治會、大政翼贊會、大政翼贊政治會、それらの参加團體及び出先機關、又は後繼若しくは類似團體並びにすべての日本の超國家主義的結社、暴力的結社及び愛國的祕密結社、これらの出先機關及び参加團體の會員であるか又はこれらのために盡力した者から罷免されたもの。

（2）この指令の第5節又は第40節に従つて官職又は地位から罷免されたもの。

（3）この指令の第7節に従つて拘禁された者は、拘禁期間中又はその後有罪と決定した場合には永久に。

44（い）課税又は他の財政金融の分野に關する法律、命令、規則又は慣行であつて國籍、人種、信條又は政見を理由にいずれかの者に對して有利又は不利な差別待遇を與えるものは、このような差別待遇を除去するのに必要な限度まで改正され、停止され又は廃止される。あらゆる種類の國家主義的、帝國主義的、軍國主義的又は反民主主義的結社のためのあらゆる種類の寄附金募集は、禁止される。

45 貴官は、日本の公的支出がこの指令の他の個所に述べられている目的と一致することを確實にする。

（ろ）貴官は、下に列記されている種類に入るすべての金銀、白金、通貨、證券、金融機關における勘定、クレデイツト、財産的價値ある書類その他すべての資産を押收し又は封鎖する。

（い）次のもののいずれかによって直接又は間接に、全部又は一部所有されている又は支配されている財産。

(1) 日本の中央、都道府縣及び市町村政府又はこれらのもののいずれかの出先機關若しくは手先。このうちには、これらのもののいずれかの支配下にあるすべての公共事業、企業、公園又は獨占事業を含む。

(2) ドイツ、イタリー、ブルガリア、ルーマニア、ハンガリーの政府、國民又は住民。このうちには、かつてこれら諸國及び日本の國民又は住民によって占領されていた地域の政府、國民又は住民を含む。

(3) 日本皇室。

(4) 大日本政治會、大政翼贊會、大政翼贊政治會、これらの參加團體及び出先機關又は後繼若くは類似の團體並びに日本のすべての國家主義的結社、暴力的結社及び愛國的祕密結社、これらの出先機關、參加團體並びにこれらの役員、幹部、支持者。

(5) 國家神道。

(6) 貴官の禁止し又は解散したすべての團體、クラブ又は他の協會。

(7) 連合國及び中立國の政府を含む日本以外の國籍を有する不在所有者及び日本以外にある日本人。

(8) 本州、北海道、九州、四國及び日本の支配下にあるすべての小諸島を除き、一八九四年以後いずれかの時期に日本の支配下にあった地域にあるいずれかの者又は會社。

(9) 第7節の規定により拘禁されるべき者及び表にのせるか又は他の方法によって軍政府が明示する他のすべての者。

（ろ）日本のすべての外國爲替（公有及び私有）及び日本の内外にあるあらゆる種類の對外資産。

（は）法律に從うと法律の形式に從うと稱する手續による沒收、はく奪又は略奪の不法行爲の對象となった財産とその他の方法によるとを問わず、強迫による讓渡、

（に）所有者のいかんを問わず、重要な文化的又は物質的價値を有する美術品。

貴官は、押收又は封鎖されたいずれの資産も、貴官に與えられることのある許可又は他の訓令によって許される通りに處理されることを確實にするような措置を執る。

2 民主化・非軍事化政策への対応(昭和20年10月〜21年5月)

特に上記(い)(1)によつて封鎖される財産の場合には、貴官は、このような財産を監視の下に置きながら、この指令に從つて貴官又は認可を得た者によるその使用を許すような許可制度を採用することに着手する。上記(は)によつて封鎖される財産の場合には、貴官は、この指令の目的に從い、且つ軍國主義的その他の好ましくない勢力の隠ぺいを防止するのに適當な保障の下において迅速な返還のための措置を執る。

貴官は、貴官が上記(ろ)に述べられているすべての資産の完全な披露を得るのに必要と考えるような報告を日本政府に要求する。

46 貴官は、日本の内外にある、すべての日本の外國爲替(公有及び私有)及びすべての種類の對外資産を探し出し、貴官によつて貴官の管理下に設けられる特別の機關の所有又は管理に歸せしめる。

47 輸出入から生ずるものを含むすべての外國爲替取引は、日本が潜在的戰爭能力を發展させるのを防止し、且つこの指令に述べられている他の目的を達成する目的をもつて管理される。これらの目的を遂行するために、貴官は、

(い) 規則又は許可によつて認められるものを除き金、銀、白金、外國爲替のすべての賣買及びあらゆる種類の外國爲替取引を禁止する。

(ろ) 輸出代金であるいかなる外國爲替も、この指令の目的の達成に直接必要な輸入の支拂にあてるし、又合同參謀本部を通ずる本國政府の特別の承認なくしては外國爲替資産を他のいかなる用途に當てることをも認可しない。

(は) 次のものを含むすべての外國爲替取引に關し有效な管理を實施する。

(1) 日本國内の者と日本國外の者との間の財産に關する取引。

(2) 日本國内の者が日本國外の者に對し有する負債、又は將來支拂うべき負債に關連する取引。

(3) いかなる外國爲替資産又は他の形式の財産の日本國への輸入又は日本からの輸出に關連する取引。

(に) 貴官は、日本のすべての在外及び對外資産に關し本國政府に完全な報告を提出する。

48 いかなる外國の者、機關又は政府による日本又は日本

人に對するいかなるクレディットの供與も、貴官の勸告に基き合同參謀本部を通じて本國政府により認可されない限り許されない。

49 貴官が日本銀行若しくはいかなる公的機關にも又はいかなる公的機關若しくは私的機關にもクレディットを供與することは豫期されていない。貴官の見解において、このような行動が不可缺となる場合には、貴官の適當と考える緊急行動を執ることができるが、そのような場合には、貴官はその事實を合同參謀本部を通じて本國政府に報告する。

50 貴官は、貴官の軍事占領の財政的運營を示すのに必要であるような經理と記錄を行い、合同參謀本部に對しそしての要求のある情報を提供する。このうちには、貴官の軍隊による通貨の使用、政府勘定によるすべての決濟、占領費及び貴官の軍隊の參加を伴う作戰又は活動から生ずる他の經費に關する情報を含む。

編注一　本文書は十一月八日に合同參謀本部からマッカーサー司令官に通達された。

二　本文書は、昭和二十四年一月、外務省特別資料部作成「日本占領及び管理重要文書集」第一卷より拔粹。

80

昭和20年11月4日　　大藏省より
　　　　　　　　　　連合国最高司令官総司令部宛

四大財閥の解体計画につき通報

4 November 1945

LOF 2

MEMORANDUM FOR: SUPREME COMMANDER FOR THE ALLIED POWERS.

THROUGH: Central Liaison Office, Tokyo.

SUBJECT: Dissolution of Holding Companies.

The firms of Mitsui Honsha, Yasuda Hozensha, Sumitomo Honsha, and Kabushiki Kaisha Mitsubishi Honsha, hereinafter referred to as the "Holding Companies", have been holding conversations with the Minister of Finance with a view to voluntary dissolution in accordance with the desires of the Supreme Commander for the Allied Powers.

The following plan is proposed for your approval to govern

2 民主化・非軍事化政策への対応（昭和20年10月〜21年5月）

the dissolution of these firms and such other firms of similar character as may volunteer for dissolution:

1. a. The Holding Companies will transfer to a Holding Company Liquidation Commission all securities owned by them and all other evidences of ownership or control of any interest in any firm, corporation or other enterprise.

b. The Holding Companies will cease to exercise direction or control, either directly or indirectly, of all financial, industrial, commercial or non-commercial enterprises whose securities they own or of which they hold any other evidences of ownership or control.

c. The directors and auditors of the Holding Companies will resign all offices held by them in such Holding Companies immediately after the transfer of the securities and other evidences of ownership referred to in paragraph "a" of this Memorandum and cease forthwith to exercise any influence, either directly or indirectly, in the management or policies of the Holding Companies affected by this dissolution.

d. All members of the Mitsui, Yasuda, Sumitomo and Iwasaki families will immediately resign all offices held by them in any financial, commercial, non-commercial or industrial enterprises and cease forthwith to exercise any influence, either directly or indirectly, in the management of policies of the enterprise affected by this dissolution.

2. The Imperial Japanese Government will establish a Holding Company Liquidation Commission whose functions among others shall be:

a. To proceed with the liquidation of all property transferred to it by the Holding Companies as rapidly as feasible.

b. To issue receipts to the Holding Companies in exchange for such transferred property. Such receipts will be non-negotiable, non-transferable and ineligible for use as collateral.

c. Pending the final disposition of the transferred property, to exercise the voting rights incident thereto but only to the extent necessary to insure proper methods of accounting and reporting and to accomplish changes in management, corporate practices and such other changes as are specifically desired by the Supreme Commander for the Allied Powers.

d. To redeem such receipts, upon the final liquidation of the transferred property, by delivery to the holders thereof, bonds of the Imperial Japanese Government, which bonds shall mature not less than ten years from the date of delivery and shall be non-negotiable, non-transferable except by inheritance, and in-eligible for use as collateral, except as the Holding Company Liquidation Commission may determine. Such exceptions will be limited to such matters as payment of taxes, death duties and comparable purposes. The Holding Company Liquidation Commission will be empowered to deliver negotiable bonds to small shareholders in the Holding Companies in redemption of their proportionate interest in such receipts in the event that such action is considered desirable by the Commission. The face value of the bonds given in redemption of the receipts shall not be in excess of the net proceeds derived in liquidation of the property transferred to it by the Holding Companies.

e. To protect the interests of small shareholders.

f. Determination of operating questions arising in the normal course of business of the holding companies such as disposition of funds received and payment of taxes and other debts.

3. When the securities, or other property transferred to the Holding Company Liquidation Commission are offered for sale, preference to purchase will be given to employees of the companies involved, and in the case of corporate shares the number of such shares that may be purchased by any single purchaser will be limited in order to insure maximum democratization of ownership.

4. Neither the Holding Companies nor any members of the Mitsui, Yasuda, Sumitomo or Iwasaki families will purchase or otherwise acquire title or ownership of, or any interest in, any of the transferred property when it is offered for sale by the Holding Company Liquidation Commission.

5. The books, records, accounts and meeting of the Holding Company Liquidation Commission will be open to the Supreme Commander for the Allied Powers at all times and all acts of such Commission will be subject to his approval or review.

6. Nominees for membership on the Holding Company Liquidation Commission will be submitted to the Supreme Commander for his approval before appointment. At any time the Sup-

2　民主化・非軍事化政策への対応(昭和20年10月〜21年5月)

reme Commander may appoint his own nominees to membership on such Commission.

7. Immediately subsequent to the time of the transfer to the Holding Company Liquidation Commission of the securities and other evidence of ownership and control, proceedings will be commenced for the dissolution of the Holding Companies.

8. The dissolution of the Holding Companies will be under the supervision of the Holding Company Liquidation Commission and the Commission, with the consent of the Supreme Commander, will be authorized to draw upon the assets of such companies in its possession to meet the debts of the companies, in event such companies do not have sufficient other assets to pay their creditors.

9. With the permission of the Supreme Commander for the Allied Powers, the bonds mentioned in paragraph 2. d. hereof, or any part thereof, may be delivered directly to the shareholders of the Holding Companies by the Holding Company Liquidation Commission in amounts proportionate to their various interest therein, in the event the dissolution of such Holding Companies is completed before such bonds or any part thereof, are issued and distributed.

The foregoing plan will be declared in immediate effect upon approval of the Supreme Commander for the Allied Powers.

IMPERIAL JAPANESE GOVERNMENT:

(Sgd.) K. Shibusawa
Viscount Keizo Shibusawa
Minister of Finance

編注　本文書は、昭和二十四年八月、外務省特別資料課作成「日本占領及び管理重要文書集」第三巻より抜粋。

81　財閥解体計画の承認および即時実施に関する指令

昭和20年11月6日　連合国最高司令官総司令部より　日本政府宛

GENERAL HEADQUARTERS
SUPREME COMMANDER FOR THE ALLIED POWERS

6 November 1945

AG 004 (6 Nov 45) ESS/ADM
SCAPIN 244
MEMORANDUM FOR: IMPERIAL JAPANESE GOVERNMENT.
THROUGH: Central Liaison Office, Tokyo.
SUBJECT: Dissolution of Holding Companies.

1. Receipt of the proposed plan for the dissolution of Mitsui Honsha, Yasuda Hozensha, Sumitomo Honsha and Kabushiki Kaisha Mitsubishi Honsha is acknowledged.

2. The plan proposed therein is approved in general and the Imperial Japanese Government will immediately proceed to effectuate it. No disposition of any property transferred to the Holding Company Liquidation Commission will be made without the prior approval of the Supreme Commander. You will submit the legislation through which the Holding Company Liquidation Commission will be created to the Supreme Commander for approval. It should be clearly understood that full freedom of action is retained by the Supreme Commander for the Allied Powers to elaborate or modify the proposed plan at any time and to supervise and review its execution.

3. The Imperial Japanese Government will immediately take such steps as are neccessary effectually to prohibit the sale, gift, assignment or transfer of any moveable or immoveable property, including securities and other evidences of ownership, indebtedness or control by Mitsui Honsha, Yasuda Hozensha, Sumitomo Honsha and Kabushiki Kaisha Mitsubishi Honsha and the members of the Mitsui, Iwasaki, Yasuda and Sumitomo families or by any person acting on their behalf.

4. The Imperial Japanese Government will deliver to the Supreme Commander for the Allied Powers, within fifteen days of the receipt of this memorandum, a report listing:

   a. All moveable or immoveable property, securities and other evidences of ownership, indebtedness and control in which the members of the Mitsui, Iwasaki, Yasuda and Sumitomo families had any right, title or interest as of November 1st, 1945.

   b. All transactions involving moveable or immoveable property, including securities and other evidences of ownership, indebtedness and control by any member of the Mitsui, Iwasaki, Yasuda and Sumitomo families since January 1st, 1945.

5. It is the intention of the Supreme Commander to dissolve the private industrial, commercial, financial and agricultural combines in Japan, and to eliminate undesirable interlocking directorates and undesirable intercorporate security ownership so as to:

a. Permit a wider distribution of income and of ownership of the means of production and trade.

b. Encourage the development within Japan of economic ways and institutions of a type that will contribute to the growth of peaceful and democratic forces. The plan proposed by the Imperial Japanese Government in the memorandum referred to in Paragraph 1 above will be considered only as a preliminary step toward these objectives.

6. Accordingly, the Imperial Japanese Government will promptly present for approval by the Supreme Commander for the Allied Powers:

a. Plans for the dissolution of industrial, commercial, financial and agricultural combines in addition to those mentioned in the communication acknowledged in Paragraph 1 hereof.

b. Its program to abrogate all legislative or administrative measures which create, foster or tend to strengthen private monopoly.

c. Its program for the enactment of such laws as will eliminate and prevent private monopoly and restraint of trade, undesirable interlocking directorates, undesirable intercorporate security ownership and the segregation of Banking from commerce, industry and agriculture and as will provide equal opportunity to firms and individuals to compete in industry, commerce, finance and agriculture on a democratic basis.

7. The Imperial Japanese Government will immediately take such steps as are necessary effectually to terminate and prohibit Japanese participation in private international cartels or other restrictive private international contracts or arrangements.

8. Acknowledgement of the receipt of this memorandum is directed.

FOR THE SUPREME COMMANDER:

H.W. ALLEN,
Colonel, A.G.D.,

82　昭和20年11月6日　終戦連絡中央事務局より連合国最高司令官総司令部宛

政治犯の釈放につき通報

Asst. Adjutant General.

Ministry of Justice
Ministry of the Navy
Ministry of War

To: Office of the Supreme Commander for the Allied Powers
From: Central Liaison Office.
Subject: Release of Political Offenders.

6 November 1945

C.L.O. No. 479 (1)

As already reported in the Memorandum C.L.O. Nos. 271 and 332 of 15 October and 22 October, 1945, respectively, in compliance with the Memorandum 1C of 4 October 1945, from the Supreme Allied Commander, the Japanese Government released all the political offenders under detention in Japan Proper by 10 October, 2400 hours, as follows:

Ministry Concerned.	Number of Released Political Offenders.
	439
	28
	1
Total	468

The only exceptions are those who have concurrently been charged with criminal offences.

It may be added that, as already reported, 39 persons of the Allied or neutral nationalities (including White Russians) charged with offences relating to espionage or speech and publication were released immediately after the termination of the war, and, in pursuance of the Supreme Allied Commander's Memorandum of 4 October, 1945, 2,026 persons were released from protection and surveillance, and 17 persons from precautionary detention. Thus, there remains now no person in this category, who is being subjected to any judicial measure.

The above-mentioned release of political offenders took place not as a consequence of the amnesty granted under date of 17 October. It was effectuated in the form of "suspension of sentences" or "suspension of detention" as an initial step pursuant to the Allied Memorandum of 4 October.

2 民主化・非軍事化政策への対応（昭和20年10月～21年5月）

Hereunder is given a description for information of the Allied Supreme Headquarters, of the legal effects which the amnesty has produced upon persons who had been released prior thereto.

1. All political offenders were released in compliance with the Allied Memorandum of 4 October - namely those who were involved with

   a) Offences against the Peace preservation Law.
   b) Offences against the National Defence and Peace Preservation Law.
   c) Offences against the Law for Safeguarding Military Secrets.
   d) Offences against the Law for Safeguarding Secrets of Military Material Resources.
   e) Offences against the Territorial Boundary Regulation Law.
   f) Offences against the Fortified Zones Law.
   g) Offences relating to external troubles under the Criminal Code.
   h) Offences relating to speech, publication, assembly and association.

With the sole exception of the offences (g) above, all these offences are pardoned under the General Amnesty Decree. Consequently, in cases where a sentence was declared in regard to any pardoned offence prior to the grant of the amnesty, such sentence has ceased to be operative thereafter and the offender will not be punished in the future. In other cases of pardoned offences, which were pending at the time the amnesty was granted, the right of public prosecution has ceased to exist, and no punitive action will be taken in connection with such offences.

2. Even in the case of an offence relating to external troubles under the Criminal Code in (g) above, the benefit of a special amnesty may be granted by taking into consideration the circumstances attending the offence, the personality and conduct of the offender, the circumstances following the crime, etc., if it has been established that the offence was committed, not from a private, but from a political motive. When, the benefit of a special amnesty is granted, any sentence that has been passed will cease to be opera-

83 必需物資の輸入に関する指令に基づく資料提出について

昭和20年11月8日　終戦連絡中央事務局より
　　　　　　　　　連合国最高司令官総司令部宛

付　記　昭和二十年十一月七日、終戦連絡中央事務局
　　　　第二部作成
　　　　「必需物資輸入ニ關スル件」

C.L.O. No. 507 (2)　　　　　　　　　8 November 1945
Subject: Import of Essential Commodities
From: Central Liaison Office
To: The Office of the Supreme Commander for the Allied Powers

In conformity with the directive of the Office of the Supreme Commander for the Allied Powers dated 9 October 1945 concerning the import of essential commodities, the Central Liaison Office submits herewith data on foodstuffs and fertilizers. Data on other commodities are now in preparation and will be submitted as soon as they are completed.

For the President,

(T. Katsube)
Chief of the Liaison Section,
Central Liaison Office.

Enclosure: Data on foodstuffs and Fertilizers

編　注　本文書の別添は省略。なお、食糧・肥料以外の資料は
　　　　同年十一月十五日付終戦連絡中央事務局より連合国最
　　　　高司令官総司令部宛CLO第五七七号をもって提出さ
　　　　れた。

(付　記)
　　必需物資輸入ニ關スル件

---

tive thereafter; and, as the case will be treated as if no sentence had been passed, the said sentence will not be carried into execution.

For the President,

(S. Iguchi)
Director of General Affairs,
Central Liaison Office.

(110、11、7)

2 民主化・非軍事化政策への対応（昭和20年10月～21年5月）

第一　方　針

昭和二十一米穀年度ニ於ケル食糧危機突破ノ爲國民生活維持繼續ニ最低限必要ニシテ且ツ可能ナル限度ニ於テ食糧輸入ヲ確保センガ爲聯合軍最高司令部ノ要求ニ基キ左記各項ヲ檢討シ向後一ケ年ノ我國經極的（濟カ）國力ノ推移ニ付一應ノ見透ヲ樹テタル上必要物資輸入ノ申入レヲ爲スモノトス

　　　　記

一、食糧輸入ト關聯シ海上輸送力ノ見地ヨリ觀タル國力ノ推移
二、食糧其他重要物資要輸入額
三、輸入資金捻出ノ爲ノ我輸出可能額
四、食糧、肥料、鹽、石炭、石油等ノ重要物資ニ付國内増産ノ爲必須ノ諸施策

第二　結論
一、我國民生活維持ノ鍵タル食糧ニ付テハ總ユル供給確保對策ヲ講ズルモ一九四六年ニ於テ六、五〇〇千「トン」ニ上ル不足ヲ豫想セラレ之ガ充足ヲ國外ヨリノ輸入ニ依存セザルヲ得ズ又鹽ニ付テモ國民生活繼續ヲ可能ナラシムル爲ニ早期ノ國外ヨリノ支援ヲ必要トス而シテ之等食生活確保ノ基礎ノ上ニ民生維持ヲ可能ナラシムベキ爾今産業ノ復興維持ヲ圖ラザルベカラザルノミナラズ國外期待物資ニ對スル支拂手段確保ノ爲輸出産業ノ振興ニ特段ノ方策ヲ講ズルノ要アリ斯クシテ食糧ヲ頂點トシテ右ノ如キ構造ヲ有スル我國民經濟ノ維持ノ爲尚諸他ノ物資ニシテ之ヲ輸入ニ俟タザルヲ得ザルモノ相當アリ食糧不足ノ絶對量ヲ充足スルハ固ヨリ緊切ナルモ其ノ取得先ノ状況外考慮スル外均衡アル經濟維持ノ爲必要トスル輸入物資ノ充足、竝ニ我國輸送力ノ現状ヲ要請スルモノトス、本要請ハ現下ノ我國力ノ輸入ヲ要請スルモノトス、本要請ハ現下ノ我國力ノ全体的痺麻状態ニ於テ其ノ破局ヲ辛ウジテ防止スベキヲ期待シ居ル程度ノモノニシテ固ヨリ必要最低限ヲ下廻ルモノナレドモ現國力ノ現状ニ於テ已ムナキモノナリ

品目　　數量（單位トン）　希望取得先

1、穀類　　三、三九〇、〇〇〇
　内譯　　八五〇、〇〇〇　朝鮮

2、鹽

内譯

一、二四六、〇〇〇　米、加
一、〇五〇、〇〇〇　泰
三五〇、〇〇〇　佛印
六〇〇、〇〇〇　滿洲
二五〇、〇〇〇　臺灣

内譯

一四〇、〇〇〇　臺灣
二二〇、〇〇〇　滿洲
六九〇、〇〇〇　北支

3、石油類

六五三、六〇〇キロリットル　米國
但シ昭和二十年度第三、四半期分トシテ右以外ニ二
七〇、〇〇〇「トン」ノ輸入ヲ要ス

4、燐礦石

三四〇、〇〇〇トン
但シ昭和二十年度第三、四半期分トシテ右以外ニ二
一五、六〇〇瓩ノ輸入ヲ要ス

内譯

八〇、〇〇〇　沖繩
一二〇、〇〇〇　北支
一二〇、〇〇〇　佛印
二〇、〇〇〇　米國

5、棉花

内譯

一八〇、〇〇〇　朝鮮
一〇、〇〇〇　北支
一五〇、〇〇〇　米國

6、油料種實（コプラ）四三、四〇〇　フィリツピン

7、石炭

内譯

一、一三〇、〇〇〇　北支
二一〇、〇〇〇　朝鮮
四二〇、〇〇〇　樺太

8、鐵礦石

内譯

八五〇、〇〇〇　北支
二〇〇、〇〇〇　中支
六五〇、〇〇〇　朝鮮

9、非鐵金屬

内譯

一二八、〇〇〇　朝鮮
四二、〇〇〇　滿洲

10、砂糖

八六、〇〇〇　臺灣

11、油脂

二〇〇、〇〇〇　馬來スマトラ

12、飼料

内譯

四〇、〇〇〇　中支
二〇、〇〇〇　中支

2　民主化・非軍事化政策への対応（昭和20年10月～21年5月）

（備考）希望取得先ハ状況ニ依リ振替可ナルモ満洲二〇、〇〇〇　北支

二、食糧需給ヨリ見テ穀類最少限三、〇〇〇千トンノ輸入ガ必要ナルモ満鮮、臺等ニハ輸出余力充分ナラザル見込ニシテ相當量ヲ米加拉ニ南方地域ニ仰ガザルベカラズ然ルトキハ我ガ保有スル海上輸送力ハ相當不足シ之ヲ強行セバ石炭、鐵鋼ヲ始メ爾余ノ産業ハ全面的休止ノ状態トナリ輸出余力ノ如キ殆ド皆無トナルベク更ニ船質船型ヨリ檢討スルモ我保有船ニテハ米大陸向航行可能船極メテ僅少ニシテ米洲物資輸入ハ外國船利用ハ不可避ノ状況ナリ

仍左ノ通リノ備船ニ付許可ヲ要請スルモノトス

一九四六年一月乃至三月　三三〇、〇〇〇重量トン
一九四六年四月乃至六月　六七〇、〇〇〇
一九四六年七月乃至九月　六七〇、〇〇〇

尚右時期以降ニ於テモ同様ノ状況ナルモ其ノ必要量ハ別途算出ノ上提出ス

三、重要輸入物資ノ國内増産ノ爲ニハ速急ニ凡ユル對策ヲ講ズベキモ特ニ産業ノ原動力タル石炭ノ生産確保ハ最モ喫緊ノ要務ニシテ之ガ爲ニハ華人、鮮人勞務者ノ取扱如何ガ現在ニ於テ其ノ生産ヲ左右シ居ル状態ナリ次ニ急激ニ狭隘化シタル國土ニ於テ尨大ナル復員歸還人口ヲ吸収スルコトガ我國現在ノ深刻ナル課題ナルノミナラズ、支拂能力貧弱ナル我國トシテ輸入代金ヲ極力低額ニ止メザルヲ得ズ仍テ可能ナル限リ原料ヨリ製品マデノ一貫工程ヲ國内ニ確保セザルヲ得ズ之等ノ點ニ基キ特ニ聯合國側ニ支援ヲ要望スベキ事項次ノ如シ

1. 石炭鉱業ニ關シ炭坑ノ治安確保ノ爲、華人、鮮人勞務者ノ速カナル送還ニ付支援ヲ要望スルト共ニ華人、鮮人勞務者在籍炭礦ニ米軍MPノ派遣ヲ要請スルコト

2. 石油事業ニ關シ極力原油ヲ輸入シ之ヲ國内ニ於テ精製スルコトノ承認ヲ受クルモノトシ之ガ爲裏ニ指令ヲ受ケタル國内原油處理ニ必要ナル限度以外ノ精製ノ停止ニ付再檢討ヲ要望スルコト

3. 前項事情ハ鐵鑛、輕金屬、非鐵金屬、機械工業等ニ付テモ同様ナルヲ以テ同様ノ方針ノ承認方要請スル

コト

四、必需物資輸入ノ支拂ニ對シテ我國輸出產業ノ振興ニ經タザルベカラザルモ右ハ先ヅ海外需要ノ最近ノ狀況ヲ的確ニ把握セザルベカラズ之ニ關シ聯合國側ノ支援ヲ必要トス

而シテ輸出ニ依リ支拂ニ付テハ輸出先ノ購買力ノ復興等自主的ニ決定シ難キ要素尠カラザルノミナラズ我國ニ於テ可能ナル限リノ輸出ヲ實現スルトシテモ尚相當ノ借越ヲ豫想セラルル狀況ニシテ輸入希望物資ノ緊要性ニ鑑ミ特ニ左ノ事項ニ對スル支援ヲ必要トス

1. 海外需要ノ動向、輸出品ノ種類、意匠等ニ關シ適切ナル指導ヲ與フル為聯合國側ヨリ專門家ヲ派遣スルコト

2. 現在我ガ保有スル金、銀、「ダイヤモンド」ヲ支拂手段ニ充當スルコトノ許可ヲ受クルコト

3. 輸入品、輸出品ノ時期的喰違ヒ不可避ナル前述ノ事情ニ基キ一定ノ時期ヲ限リテノ借越ヲ認ムルコト

第三、個別的檢討
（中略）

第四、聯合軍ニ對スル提出資料目次

一、必需輸入物資
次ノ必需輸入物資ニ付需給狀況、國內ニ於ケル最高度生產確保對策（必要財政手段ヲ含ム）輸入要請數量ヲ明ニス
(1) 食糧 (2) 肥料 (3) 鹽 (4) 石油 (5) 石炭 (6) 其他必需物資

二、輸送力ノ檢討
現下ノ民生維持ニ關シ最大ノ隘路ハ食糧トカビ輸送力ナルヲ以テ輸送力ノ檢討ヲ為シ其ノ不足量及傭船要積量ヲ明ニス

三、輸入資金ノ算定
必需物資輸入ニ要スル資金額ノ說明並ニ輸出ヲ以テ充當シ得ザル不足額ノ處理ニ關スル要望ヲ明ニス

四、必需物資輸入ニ對スル支拂計畫トシテノ輸出計畫
右計畫ハ輸入資金トシテ現在利用シ得ル物資表及一九四六年十二月三十一日迄ニ右目的ニ利用シ得ル物資ノ豫測ヲ含ム

五、前各項ノ總括
前各項ヲ總括シタル說明及聯合國ニ要請スベキ事項ヲ

2　民主化・非軍事化政策への対応(昭和20年10月～21年5月)

84

「終戦事務ノ連絡強化ニ關スル次官會議決定」

昭和20年11月15日　次官会議決定

終戦事務ノ連絡強化ニ關スル次官會議決定

（昭和二〇、一一、一五　外務省）

終戦ニ關聯スル聯合國側トノ折衝事務ハ今後愈々多岐ニ亙ルヘキ處右ニ關スル我方歩調ヲ統一スルコト必要ナルヲ以テ今後左記要領ニ依リ各省間ノ連絡ヲ強化スルコトト致度

記

一、重要事項及他省ニ關係アル事項ニ關シテハ各省ノ聯合國側トノ單獨折衝ハ之ヲ避ケ終戦連絡事務局ヲ經由スルモノトス

含ム

(1)輸出適格在日本資源ノ保存及使用ノ防止對策(2)現行賃銀ニ適應スル費用ヲ以テ一般民家ヘノ公平ナル分配ヲ確保スル爲ノ輸入物資ノ受入、配給機關ニ付テハ目下立案シツツアルヲ以テ計畫作成次第提出スルモノトス

〜〜〜〜〜〜〜〜〜〜

二、其他ノ事項ニ關シテハ關係省ニ於テ聯合國側ト折衝ヲ爲ス場合ハ事前事後ヲ問ハス終戦連絡事務局ニ連絡スルモノトス

三、終戦連絡事務局ト各省トノ連絡ヲ強化スル爲左記措置ヲ講スルモノトス

(1)終戦連絡事務局ニ於テ各省ニ對スル擔當連絡官數名ヲ決定シ置キ常時連絡ニ當リ得ル態勢ヲ執ルモノトス當連絡官在席シ非サル等ノ場合ハ總務部第一課長若ハ同課事務官連絡ニ當ル

（註）各省ト右擔當連絡官トノ間ニ直通電話ヲ架設ノ要アリ

(2)各省ニ於ケル連絡擔當官（終戦連絡部長等）ハ週一回終戦連絡事務局ニ會合シ各省ニ於ケル終戦事務ニ關スル打合セヲ行フ

（註）現在毎日終戦連絡事務局ニ於テ會合シ居ル各省終戦事務連絡會議ハ其儘存續ス

四、各省ヨリ聯合國側ニ提出セル資料ハ其ノ寫ヲ作成シ速ニ終戦連絡事務局總務部長宛送付スルモノトス

終戦連絡事務局ヨリ聯合國側ニ提出セル資料ニ付テモ其

85 昭和20年11月16日 大蔵省より連合国最高司令官総司令部宛

戦時利得の排除および国家財政の再編成について

ノ寫ヲ同局ヨリ關係省宛送付スルモノトス

LOF 4.

MEMORANDUM FOR: Supreme Commander for the Allied Powers.

THROUGH: Central Liaison Office, Tokyo.

SUBJECT: Elimination of War Profits and Reorganization of National Finances.

THE FINANCE MINISTRY
THE IMPERIAL JAPANESE GOVERNMENT

16 November 1945.

1. In conformance with our understanding of your objectives and with your directives and in order to contribute to the growth of peaceful and democratic forces in Japan; to lay the groundwork for the reconstruction of the national budget, the support of agriculture, the reorganization and democratization of the banking structure and continue the fight against inflation, the Imperial Japanese Government desires to proceed without delay with the following program:

   a. To create a new tax designed to eliminate and recapture all profits, corporate and individual, made during, in connection with, and as a result of, the war.

   b. To assess a universal capital levy, on a graduated scale.

2. Such tax and capital levy will operate in such a manner as to obtain the maximum yield through strict enforcement and prevention of evasions and abuses, protect the legitimate savings of the wage earner and the farmer, and otherwise prevent injustice to that portion of the population which most requires encouragement and support in the reorganization of our economy toward peaceful ends.

3. Pending enactment and collection of the new tax and capital levy, measures will be taken effectually to prevent the use of funds paid, and to be paid in satisfaction of claims arising from the production or supply of war materials or from war damage, ex-

cept for such purposes as may be approved by the Supreme Commander for the Allied Powers.

4. To establish equitable valuations and otherwise to insure the success of this program it is contemplated that a special board, composed of independent citizens will be created.

5. Your approval of this program is requested.

FOR THE MINISTRY OF FINANCE

Viscount Keizo Shibusawa
Minister of Finance

---

86 非民主主義的映画の排除に関する指令

昭和20年11月16日 連合国最高司令官総司令部より日本政府宛

GENERAL HEADQUARTERS
SUPREME COMMANDER FOR THE ALLIED POWERS

16 November 1945

AG 062.2 (16 Nov 45) CIE
SCAPIN 287
MEMORANDUM FOR: IMPERIAL JAPANESE GOVERNMENT.

THROUGH: Central Liaison Office, Tokyo.
SUBJECT: Elimination of Undemocratic Motion Pictures.

1. In the past, Japanese motion pictures have been utilized to propagate nationalistic, militaristic and feudalistic concepts; i.e., conformity to a feudal code, contempt for life, creation of the "Warrior Spirit", the uniqueness and superiority of the "Yamato" (Japanese race), the "special role of Japan in Asia", etc. Many such motion pictures are still being distributed and exhibited.

2. The Japanese Government is directed to:

   a. Take immediate action to insure against the present or future sale, exchange or exhibition of any of the motion pictures on the attached inclosure.

   b. Secure from the owners, producers or exhibitors of these pictures all prints of the same, whether positive or negative, sound or silent, in 16mm or 35mm width.

   c. Direct the placing of these motion pictures, prints and negatives in a safe, fire-proof place in Tokyo, subject to the disposition of this headquarters.

   d. Direct the producers to mark each film container with

the title of each container's contents in English and Japanese.

　　e. Provide this headquarters within ten (10) days with a list in duplicate showing the total number of prints and negatives of each of the motion pictures listed on the attached inclosure which have been placed in storage as directed by Paragraph 2c, above.

FOR THE SUPREME COMMANDER:

　　　　　　　　　　H. W. ALLEN,
　　　　　　　　　　Colonel, A.G.D.,
　　　　　　　　　　Asst Adjutant General.

1 Incl:
　Annex A, described above.

編注　本文書の別添は省略。

87　昭和20年11月17日　鈴木(九萬)終戦連絡横浜事務局長より児玉(謙次)終戦連絡中央事務局総裁宛

アイケルバーガー米国陸軍第八軍司令官との会談内容につき報告

濱連機密第五三號

昭和二十年十一月十七日

終戰連絡横濱事務局長　鈴木　九萬〔印〕

終戰連絡中央事務局
　總裁　兒玉　謙次殿

米國第八軍司令官「アイケルバーガー」中將ト會談ノ件

十一月十七日午后本官「アイケルバーガー」司令官往訪ノ際ノ會談中主要ナル點左ノ通報告申進ス

(一) 同司令官ハ今般發表サレタル第六軍ノ所謂「デアクティヴェーション」ニ關シ自分ハ十二月三十一日ヲ以テ第六軍ヲモ指揮スルコトトナルヘシ第六軍ノ「デアクティヴェーション」カ明年一月二十六日ニ行ハルヘシトハ新聞ニ發表サレシ通ナリ自分ハ歸國シ度キ希望ナリシカ之ニテ歸國出來ヌコトトナリタリ目下一時歸國中ノ參謀長「バイヤース」少將カ十二月一日ニ歸任ノ筈ナルニ付自分ハ十二月五日ヨリ十日迄ノ間ニ當地出發シ、二、三週間ノ予定ニテ一時歸國ノ予定ナリト内話ス(第六軍司令官

2 民主化・非軍事化政策への対応（昭和20年10月〜21年5月）

「クルーガー」ト「アイケルバーガー」中將カ相互關係必ラスシモ圓滑ナラス前者カ「トルーマン」大統領ト良ク同大統領カ前者ヲ「マックアーサー」最高司令官ノ御目附的ノ二日本ニ殘サムトセシカ後者（「アイケルバーガー」中將）ハ「マックアーサー」最高司令官ト良ク同司令官トシテハ「ア」中將ノ殘ルヲ希望シ終ニ「ア」中將カ殘ルコトニ決シタリトノ説アルコト御承知ノ通ナリ尚第六軍接收ノ結果第八軍司令部カ他ニ移動スルカ如キコト無カルヘキヤトノ問ニ對シテハ明答ヲ避ケタリ

（二）十一月十五日西山次長二面會シテ最高司令部側ヨリ陸海軍々人ノ恩給支拂停止ニ關スル指令發令サレムトシ居リ中央連絡事務局ニ於テ折角之カ阻止ノ爲御努力中ノ由承知シタルニ付事情ハ詳カニセサルモ兎モ角本官ノ私見トシテ既ニ終戦ノ結果數百萬人ノ軍人カ復員セムトシ居リ之カ就職乃至今後ノ生活ノ問題ハ既ニ大ナル社會問題ニテ之ヲウマク解決セサレハ共産主義等ニ走ラスル危険多分ニアル際右ノ如キ指令ヲ發セラルルニ於テハ更ニ問題ヲ複雑困難ナラシメ又文官ノ恩給ニモ影響ヲ及ホスヘク多大ノ衝動ヲ國民ニ多數ニ及ホスヘシ由來歐米等ノ軍人

ト異ナリ日本ニ於ケル職業軍人ハ比較的下級社會層ヨリ出テ居リ恩給額モ少ナク恩給カ退役後ノ殆ント唯一ノ収入ナリ又戰沒將士ノ遺家族等ニトリテハ扶助料カ唯一ノ生計ノ源泉トモ云フヘク之カ支拂ヲ停止スルハ重大問題ナリ旁々本件指令ノ發令ハ暫ラク延期シ最高司令部ト日本政府トノ間ニ忌憚無ク意見交換ヲ行ヒ恩給法ヲ適當ニ改正スルコト然ルヘキ旨ヲ力説セルニ「ア」中將ハ其ノ話ハ自分ハ全然知ラサリシカ了解シヘシ（誰レノ問題ナリヤトノ問ナリシニ付「クレーマー」大佐ノ方ヨリ出テ居ル話ノ由ナリト答フ）第八軍軍政局主任「ヴァンス」大佐ニハ既ニ話シタリヤ（未タナリト答ヘシニ）同大佐ノ頭ヘモ入レ置カレ度シト述ヘ居リタリ尚本會見ニハ右（二）ノ問題モアリシニ付「ア」中將ノ諒解ヲ得テ鎌田中將モ同道セリ

〜〜〜〜〜〜〜〜〜

88　昭和20年11月18日　連合国最高司令官総司令部より　日本政府宛

皇室財産の凍結に関する指令

GENERAL HEADQUARTERS
SUPREME COMMANDER FOR THE ALLIED POWERS
APO 500
18 November 1945

AG 091.3 (18 Nov 45) ESS/FI
SCAPIN 300
MEMORANDUM FOR: IMPERIAL JAPANESE GOVERNMENT.
THROUGH: Central Liaison Office, Tokyo.
SUBJECT: Imperial Household Property.

1. You will immediately take such action as may be required to insure that no transactions involving the Imperial Household property will be effected without the prior approval of this Headquarters.

2. You will nullify any transfers of Imperial Household property which were effected on or since the 15th day of August, 1945 and which were not incidental to the normal operations of the Imperial Household.

3. Except as may be further directed, all bureaus and offices, etc. of the Department of the Imperial Household may continue to exercise their normal functions, and may receive any payments and make any expenditures normally incidental to their operations; provided however that the following transactions may not be effected without the prior approval of this Headquarters;

 a. The disposition or acquisition of any capital assets, including but not limited to lands, estates, securities, buildings, and art objects;

 b. The voting, or the exercise of any voting rights, with respect to any securities owned by the Imperial Household;

 c. The exercising of any managerial or other control or authority in respect to any enterprise the securities of which are owned or controlled in whole or in part by the Imperial Household;

 d. The bestowal of any Imperial gifts or special money grants;

 e. The supplementing of any item of expenditure from Reserve Funds;

 f. Any loans between accounts;

 g. Any item of expenditure in excess of the sums allotted for such items in the budget;

h. Any item of expenditure not provided for in the budget;

i. Any expenditure from the First and Second Reserve Funds.

4. The main budget for the fiscal year 1946 shall be submitted to this Headquarters for approval not later than 15 December 1945. Additional Budgets shall be submitted to this Headquarters for approval each time as they may arise. No expenditure may be effected subsequent to the fiscal year, 1945, unless the budget covering such expenditure has been approved by this Headquarters.

5. Prior to the issuance of this memorandum, the Department of the Imperial Household informally furnished to this Headquarters statements of the property holdings of the Imperial Household. You will promptly examine the statements furnished and within fifteen days you will certify to the accuracy of such statements. If such statements are certified to be incomplete or inaccurate in any respect, you will furnish within such period such corrections or additions as are required.

6. You will report promptly to this Headquarters the action taken to comply with these requirements.

7. An acknowledgement of the receipt of this memorandum is directed.

FOR THE SUPREME COMMANDER:

H. W. ALLEN,
Colonel, A.G.D.,
Asst. Adjutant General.

GENERAL HEADQUARTERS
SUPREME COMMANDER FOR THE ALLIED POWERS
18 November 1945

89

昭和20年11月18日　連合国最高司令官総司令部より
　　　　　　　　　日本政府宛

商用および民間航空の廃止に関する指令

付記　昭和二十一年六月十二日付連合国最高司令官総司令部より日本政府宛公信SCAPIN第一〇一七号
右指令の変更について

AG 360 (18 Nov 45) ESS-E
SCAPIN 301

MEMORANDUM FOR: IMPERIAL JAPANESE GOVERNMENT.

THROUGH: Central Liaison Office, Tokyo.

SUBJECT: Commercial and Civil Aviation.

1. You will abolish by 31 December 1945 all governmental and semi-governmental bodies concerned with commercial or other civil aviation in any of its aspects except those activities specifically authorized for operation under the direction of the Supreme Commander.

2. You will take necessary measures by 31 December 1945 to effect the dissolution of all companies, partnerships, or associations of any kind which have been engaged in any way with relation to commercial air transport or other civilian air operations, or in pilot or other training related to aircraft design, construction, maintenance or operation.

3. You will submit to this headquarters not later than 15 December 1945 a register of officers, principal operating officials, professional engineering and research personnel, pilots and instructors of the organizations affected by the above dissolution.

4. On and after 31 December 1945 you will not permit any governmental agency or individual, or any business concern, association, individual Japanese citizen or group of citizens, to purchase, own, possess, or operate any aircraft, aircraft assembly, engine, or research, experimental, maintenance or production facility related to aircraft or aeronautical science including working models.

5. You will not permit the teaching of, or research or experiments in aeronautical science, aerodynamics, or other subjects related to aircraft or balloons.

6. Acknowledgment of receipt of this memorandum is directed.

FOR THE SUPREME COMMANDER:

H. W. ALLEN,
Colonel, A.G.D.,
Asst. Adjutant General

(付記)

2　民主化・非軍事化政策への対応(昭和20年10月～21年5月)

GENERAL HEADQUARTERS
SUPREME COMMANDER FOR THE ALLIED POWERS

APO 500
12 June 1946

AG 452 (12 Jun 46) ESS/ST
SCAPIN 1017
MEMORANDUM FOR: THE IMPERIAL JAPANESE GOVERNMENT.
THROUGH: Central Liaison Office, Tokyo.
SUBJECT: Amendment to Memorandum on "Commercial and Civil Aviation."

1. Reference is made to Memorandum, General Headquarters, Supreme Commander for the Allied Powers, AG 360 (18 Nov 45) ESS/E (SCAPIN 301) to the Imperial Japanese Government, subject: "Commercial and Civil Aviation."

2. Paragraphs 4, 5 and 6 of the above referenced memorandum are hereby deleted and the following paragraphs are added thereto:

"4. You will prohibit the manufacture, ownership, storage or operation by any public or private agency under your jurisdiction of any aircraft, or components or devices specifically designed therefor.

"5. You will permit no individual or group under your jurisdiction to develop or execute plans for the design, manufacture, procurement or operation of any aircraft, components or devices designed therefor; or for procurement outside Japan of such services, except as specifically authorized by the Supreme Commander for the Allied Powers.

"6. You will prohibit research and organized instruction having purposes directed towards activities forbidden by paragraphs 4 and 5 hereof.

"7. The provisions of Directive No.3 (SCAPIN 47) dated 22 September 1945 as amended by SCAPIN 984, 25 May 1946, continue to apply to the subjects covered by this memorandum, aircraft in all phases being classified for this purpose as implements of war."

FOR THE SUPREME COMMANDER:

JOHN B. COOLEY,
Colonel, AGD,

90 昭和20年11月19日 連合国最高司令官総司令部より 日本政府宛

連合国人の遺骸の所在地調査に関する指令

SUPREME COMMANDER FOR THE ALLIED POWERS
GENERAL HEADQUARTERS
APO 500

19 November 1945

AG 293 (19 Nov 45) QM
MEMORANDUM TO: IMPERIAL JAPANESE GOVERNMENT
THROUGH: Central Liaison Office, Tokyo
SUBJECT: Location of Remains of Allied Personnel

1. Remains of many Allied personnel have been cremated or buried within Japan during the war; Allied or U.S. Army personnel recovery parties have been unable to recover a large number of such remains. It is understood that in many cases information concerning the location of remains is not available in records of the Imperial Japanese Government, but is known to police officials or local individuals.

2. The Imperial Japanese Government is directed to take such steps as is necessary to furnish this Headquarters complete information regarding the location of the remains of such deceased Allied Personnel throughout Japan. Reports will be submitted prior to 15 December 1945 and will include the following information:

a. Name, rank, serial number of deceased
b. Date, place and cause of death
c. Exact present location of remains
d. Names and addresses of persons cognizant of the location of such remains
e. Any other pertinent data.

3. Receipt of this directive will be acknowledged.

FOR THE SUPREME COMMANDER:

H.W. ALLEN,
Colonel, A.G.D.
Asst Adjutant General.

Adjutant General.

91 ラジオ通信の統制に関する指令

昭和20年11月20日　連合国最高司令官総司令部より　日本政府宛

GENERAL HEADQUARTERS
SUPREME COMMANDER FOR THE ALLIED POWERS

20 November 1945

AG 676.3 (20 Nov 45) CCS
SCAPIN 321

MEMORANDUM FOR: IMPERIAL JAPANESE GOVERNMENT.
THROUGH: Central Liaison Office, Tokyo.
SUBJECT: Control of Radio Communications.

　1. Certain radio circuits and broadcasting stations now are being operated by the Japanese Government or by Japanese private agencies.

　2. No additions to any radio circuits or to the number of broadcasting stations will be made, and no changes in points of communication, in location of transmitting stations or associated central offices, or in call signs, frequencies, power output methods of communication, or in ownership of transmitting or receiving facilities will be made without registering such changes with the Civil Communications Section of this Headquarters, through the Japanese Imperial Government, at least ten (10) days in advance of the proposed date of institution of the additional operation or change. The document of registration shall be in English on 8 "by $10\frac{1}{2}$" paper typed or printed on one side only and authenticated by a competent official of the Japanese Imperial Government. It shall contain full details of the projected operation, and explanation of the need or reason for the change or additional service, and a bill of major materials if new construction is contemplated. The ten (10) day period of notice shall not commence to run until the document of registration has been delivered to this Headquarters and receipted for by an Officer signing for the Chief, Civil Communications Section. In the absence of disapproval by this Headquarters, the proposed addition or change may be instituted at the end of the ten (10) day period. However, the filing of the document of registration and the expiration of the ten (10) day period of notice without disapproval this Headquarters, will not be construed as approval by the Supreme Commander of the change or addition,

GENERAL HEADQUARTERS
SUPREME COMMANDER FOR THE ALLIED POWERS

21 November 1945

AG 311.7 (10 Nov 45) CIS
SCAPIN 326

MEMORANDUM FOR: IMPERIAL JAPANESE GOVERNMENT
THROUGH: Central Liaison Office, Tokyo
SUBJECT: Regulations Governing Communications over International, Foreign and External Telegraph, Telephone and Wireless Facilities.

1. It is the primary responsibility of the Japanese Government Communications Agency to see that all censorable messages are submitted to censorship for action either before being sent out of the country on any circuit, or before being delivered or further transmitted for delivery to the addressee after receipt in Japan. Censorable messages are (a) all communications transmitted by electrical means, entering or leaving the four main islands of Japan or the approximately 1,000 islands immediately contiguous thereto, and (b) domestic communications transmitted by electrical means which may disturb the public tranquillity, or are inimical to the interests of the Allied Powers and (c) any other messages which censorship may later require.

2. The following regulations will apply:

a. WIRELESS-TELEGRAPH AND CABLE MESSAGES

and will not prejudice his right to require modification or rescission of the change or addition at a later date.

3. Direct correspondence between the Civil Communications Section and the Board of Communications on matters within the scope of this memorandum is authorized.

FOR THE SUPREME COMMANDER:

H. W. ALLEN,
Colonel, A.G.D.,
Asst. Adjutant General.

---

92 国際電信、電話および無線施設による通信の統制に関する指令

昭和20年11月21日 連合国最高司令官総司令部より 日本政府宛

2　民主化・非軍事化政策への対応(昭和20年10月〜21年5月)

(1) No message will be accepted for transmission or delivery which is in any other language than English, Russian or Japanese.

(2) The full name and address of the addressee must appear on all incoming messages.

(3) The full name and address of both the sender and addressee must appear on all outgoing messages.

(4) Private, government or commercial codes may be used only upon approval of the Civil Censorship Officer, SCAP.

This shall include use of abbreviated or code names and/or addresses.

(5) The Communications Agency or its employees will not reveal to any person (except those connected with Censorship) the action taken by Civil Censorship Detachment, SCAP, on any message unless directed to do so by the censor. When a censor "cancels" a message, the Communication Agency's office of origin or receipt will return the message to the sender, advising that the message has been cancelled, and will refund any amount collected to the sender.

b. WIRELESS-TELEPHONE AND CABLE-TELEPHONE COMMUNICATIONS

(1) All international, external or foreign telephone calls must be approved by Civil Censorship Officer, SCAP before the parties to the call may be connected.

(2) Required Information.

Before establishing connection, the telephone agency shall furnish the following information to the censor, and obtain approval of the proposed call:

(a) The name and address of the person placing the call.

(b) The name and address of the person receiving the call.

(c) The subjects to be discussed during the call.

(d) The names of any other persons expected to join in the conversation.

c. GENERAL REGULATIONS

(1) The Civil Censorship Detachment, SCAP, may maintain censors in the operating rooms of the Communications Agency's offices and may inspect these operating rooms, files and records at any time. The Communication Agency's offices will submit any or all files and records for inspection at any time Censorship so requests. No records, files, no copies of messages will be destroyed without prior written approval.

(2) The Board of Communication, through its liaison representative, will furnish to the Civil Censorship Officer, at such time and place requested, any files, records, reports, or information as may be requested.

(3) No communication will be censored or reviewed by any person of any office or agency other than Civil Censorship Detachment, SCAP, except upon approval of the Supreme Commander for the Allied Powers.

(4) Operational interpretations of these regulations may be made from time to time by the Civil Censorship Officer, SCAP, and transmitted to the Board of Communications through the Japanese Liaison representative attached to the Civil Censorship Detachment, SCAP.

FOR THE SUPREME COMMANDER:

   H. W. ALLEN,
   Colonel, A.G.D.,
   Asst. Adjutant General.

昭和20年11月21日　連合国最高司令官総司令部発表

2 民主化・非軍事化政策への対応(昭和20年10月〜21年5月)

日本の警察政策改善に関するソープ民間諜報局長の見解

Brigadier General Elliot R. Thorpe's Observation on a Change in Japanese Police Policies

November 21, 1945

Adding emphasis to recent articles in the Japanese press dealing with a change in Japanese police policies, Brig. Gen. Elliot R. Thorpe, chief of the Counter-Intelligence section, SCAP, declared that the police must become the servant of the people rather than their master and must be trained "to keep order by wisdom and example, rather than by force, intimidation and inhumane prison conditions."

General Thorpe's remarks were addressed to a group of Japanese officials including Goro Koizumi, director of the police bureau of the Ministry of Home Affairs, and Kenji Hirooka, chief of the Police Bureau's affairs section, who were visiting his office to present him with a copy of the Home Minister's speech before a police chiefs' conference and a plan for reorganization of the Japanese police.

On the basis of reports received recently at headquarters, General Thorpe strongly censured the confiscation of foodstuffs from the populace on the pretext that the food is required by the occupation forces. As the forces live entirely on imported supplies, the general stated, "such pretexts are grossly false and serve only to line the pockets of the officials guilty of such confiscations."

The chief counter-intelligence officer declared that salaries paid the police must be commensurate with the dignity and position of service in the community. He stressed the point that the Supreme Commander expects prompt and efficient action in enforcing the law.

In conclusion, General Thorpe stated that proof of the good intentions of the Home Minister and the police official will be in the manner in which they are carried out.

編注 本文書は、昭和二十四年三月、外務省特別資料部作成「日本占領及び管理重要文書集」第二巻より抜粋。

313

94 昭和20年11月21日 終戦連絡中央事務局より
連合国最高司令官総司令部宛

治安警察法等の廃止につき通報

TO: GENERAL HEADQUARTERS OF THE SUPREME COMMANDER FOR THE ALLIED POWERS
FROM: Central Liaison Office, Tokyo
SUBJECT: Abrogation of Public Peace Police Law and Regulation.

C.L.O. No. 672 (1.3)

21 November 1945

In compliance with your Memorandum under date of October 4, 1945, Subject: "Removal of Restrictions on Political, Civil, and Religious Liberties, the Central Liaison Office begs to inform that the abrogation of the under-mentioned law, Imperial Ordinance and the Government General Ordinance of Korea was decided upon at the Cabinet meeting which was held on November 16th. The abrogation will be promulgated and put into force on about November 21st.

1. The Public Peace Police Law (Chian Keisatsu Ho)

2. Imperial Ordinance No.317 of 1925 (regarding the public peace police in Kwantung Province)

3. The Government General Ordinance regarding Peace Preservation (Ordinance No.2 of 1907, Korea)

FOR THE PRESIDENT,

(S. Iguchi),
Director of General Affairs
Central Liaison Office

---

95 昭和20年11月24日 連合国最高司令官総司令部より
日本政府宛

戦時利得の排除および国家財政の再編成に関する指令

GENERAL HEADQUARTERS
SUPREME COMMANDER FOR THE ALLIED POWERS
APO 500

24 November 1945

AG 121.7 (24 Nov 45) ESS-FI
SCAPIN 337
MEMORANDUM FOR: IMPERIAL JAPANESE GOVERNMENT.

2　民主化・非軍事化政策への対応(昭和20年10月〜21年5月)

THROUGH: Central Liaison Office, Tokyo.

SUBJECT: Elimination of War Profits and Reorganization of National Finances.

1. Reference is made to the memorandum of the Minister of Finance, dated 16 November 1945, (LOF 4), outlining a program for the elimination of war profits and the reorganization of national finances.

2. This program is approved in principle as only one of the steps leading to the development within Japan of ways and institutions which will contribute to the growth of peaceful and democratic forces. Certain Japanese interests have used unjustified and aggressive war to illegally enrich themselves for many years. You will demonstrate to all Japanese that war is financially unprofitable by insuring that the tax described in para 1 of your proposal includes the period not only dating from the perfidious attack on Pearl Harbor but includes the period prior to that date to the maximum extent possible.

3. The complete legislative proposal covering the program will be presented in the Diet for enactment during the first session to be held in 1946. A draft of the proposal will be submitted to this Headquarters for approval not later than 31 December 1945. The Imperial Household will not be exempt from such program.

4. Pending the enactment of the necessary legislation, no payments will be made by the Imperial Japanese Government, its sub-divisions, agencies or instrumentalities or any other person upon any claim arising from the production or supply of war materials, from WAR damage or from the construction or conversion of war plants, except upon the following conditions:

a. The amount of such payments shall be deposited in blocked accounts with the Bank of Japan in the name of the beneficiary.

b. No payment, transfer or withdrawal from such accounts may be effected without the approval of this Headquarters.

5. No credit will be extended by the Imperial Japanese Government, its sub-divisions, agencies or instrumentalities, or by any other person against:

a. Claims arising from the production or supply of war

materials, from war damage, or from the construction or conversion of war plants.

   b. Blocked accounts resulting from the payment of such claims.

6. Any accounts heretofore blocked in connection with the payment of claims arising from the production or supply of war materials, from war damage, or from the construction or conversion of war plants will remain blocked, except as authorized by this Headquarters. The provisions of Pars. 4 and 5 hereof shall apply to such accounts.

7. Any payments in excess of ¥5,000.00 to any one claimant, made by the Imperial Japanese Government, its sub-divisions, agencies or instrumentalities or any other person, on or since 15 August 1945 for any of the purposes stated in Par. 4 hereof, which have not been blocked or which have been released from a blocked account, in whole or in part, will be redeposited by the beneficiary in a blocked account with the Bank of Japan within 30 days from this date. If any of such funds have been invested in fixed assets or are otherwise not recoverable without undue hardship to the beneficiary, a report giving full details of the circumstances will be submitted to the Ministry of Finance for consideration by this Headquarters.

8. Except as authorized by this Headquarters, the Imperial Japanese Government, its sub-divisions, agencies or instrumentalities will not hereafter:

   a. Issue bonds or any other instruments of indebtedness.

   b. Obtain or extend credit in any form.

   c. Assume further guarantees of, or make any further commitment to pay, any obligation of any bank, insurance company, trust company, securities company, investment company, industrial or commercial concern, or other enterprise, whether publicly or privately owned.

   d. Grant any subsidies, tax exemptions, tax allotments, rebates, or any similar benefits, except that national revenues may be reallocated to political sub-divisions for purposes otherwise not prohibited by this directive.

   e. Sell or otherwise dispose of any interest in real estate or other fixed assets, utilities, and other public undertakings or en-

2　民主化・非軍事化政策への対応（昭和20年10月～21年5月）

96

恩給等の支払い終止に関する指令

昭和20年11月24日　連合国最高司令官総司令部より　日本政府宛

terprises.

9. Requests for approval required by this directive will be accompanied by the written recommendation of the Ministry of Finance.

10. Acknowledgment of the receipt of this memorandum is directed.

FOR THE SUPREME COMMANDER:

H. W. ALLEN,
Colonel, A.G.D.,
Asst. Adjutant General.

GENERAL HEADQUARTERS
SUPREME COMMANDER FOR THE ALLIED POWERS
APO 500
24 November 1945

AG 260 (24 Nov 45) ESS/FI

SCAPIN 338

MEMORANDUM FOR: IMPERIAL JAPANESE GOVERNMENT.
THROUGH: Central Liaison Office, Tokyo.
SUBJECT: Pensions and Benefits.

1. The Imperial Japanese Government is directed to take the necessary steps as rapidly as practicable and in no event later than 1 February 1946 to terminate all payments except as authorized by this Headquarters, of any public or private pensions or other emoluments or benefits of any kind granted or conferred to any person:

a. By reason of military service, including severance or retirement pay or similar bonus or allowance, except compensation for physical disability, limiting the recipients ability to work, at rates which are no higher than the lowest of those for comparable physical disability arising from non-military causes;

b. By reason of membership in or services to any association, society, or other organization dissolved or suspended as a result of any order of the Supreme

Commander for the Allied Powers;

c. Who has been removed from any office or position as a result of any order of the Supreme Commander for the Allied Powers;

d. Who has been interned or arrested as a result of any order of the Supreme Commander for the Allied Powers, during the term of internment or arrest, or permanently, in case of subsequent conviction.

2. The restriction in 1-a above shall not apply to current pay, subsistence, travel or other normal allowances accruing prior to discharge from the military service.

3. As rapidly as practicable and in any event by 1 February 1946, all certificates or other documents evidencing any right to, or deferred payment of, any pension or other emolument or benefit prohibited by this memorandum shall be declared void and any sums set aside or deposited for such payment shall be recovered forthwith by the government.

4. Within 10 days after receipt of this memorandum there shall be submitted to this Headquarters a full report with reference to:

a. Military pensions or other emoluments:

(1) Pensions

(a) Total amount due and payable during the period from August 15, 1945 to November 15, 1945;

(b) Total amount paid in cash during the period from August 15, 1945 to November 15, 1945;

(c) Total amounts represented by certificates or other documents evidencing rights to such payments and the total amounts of any sums set aside or deposited for such payments;

(2) Severance pay and retirement allowances, divided into the same categories as subdivision (1) above;

(3) Allowances, bonuses or benefits of any other nature, divided into the same categories as division a–(1) above;

b. Non-military public or private pensions and other

2　民主化・非軍事化政策への対応（昭和20年10月～21年5月）

97　昭和20年11月28日　連合国最高司令官総司令部より　日本政府宛

新通貨の発行統制および流通貨量の報告に関する指令

GENERAL HEADQUARTERS
SUPREME COMMANDER FOR THE ALLIED POWERS
APO 500

28 November 1945

AG 123 (26 Nov 45) ESS/FI

MEMORANDUM FOR: IMPERIAL JAPANESE GOVERNMENT.

THROUGH: Central Liaison Office, Tokyo.

SUBJECT: Control Over Issue of New Currency.

1. The Imperial Japanese Government will not print or issue, nor permit the printing or issuance of new types or series of Bank of Japan notes, state notes, subsidiary currency or any other currency without the previous consent of this Headquarters. No planning for or designing of new types or series of bank notes, state notes or other currency shall be initiated without first submitting a complete report to this Headquarters, stating the reasons for, and the types and quantities of new notes and currencies desired.

emolument or benefits prohibited by this memorandum, divided into the same categories as division a- (1) above;

c. Action taken to comply with this memorandum.

5. Six copies of the above report will be furnished to this Headquarters.

6. Any requests for authorizations required by this memorandum will be transmitted in writing through the Ministry of Finance and directed to the Supreme Commander for the Allied Powers.

7. Acknowledgement of receipt of this memorandum is directed.

FOR THE SUPREME COMMANDER:

H. W. ALLEN,
Colonel, A.G.D.,
Asst. Adjutant General.

2. On or before the tenth day of each month, the Ministry of Finance will submit a report to this Headquarters on the present note issue of the Bank of Japan as of the end of the previous month, showing for each denomination: Amount in Circulation, Amount Unissued, Amount Withdrawn and Cancelled, Total Amount Printed. The first report will be submitted on or before 10 December 1945. A sample of the report form will be submitted to this Headquarters for approval within five days from receipt of this memorandum.

3. The Ministry of Finance will submit one report on state notes and currency in circulation as of 30 September 1945 and containing the same type of information as required in paragraph 2 above. Subsequent reports will be delivered quarterly.

FOR THE SUPREME COMMANDER:

H. W. ALLEN,
Colonel, A.G.D.,
Asst. Adjutant General.

---

98 昭和20年11月28日 連合国最高司令官総司令部より 日本政府宛

雇用の平等に関する指令

GENERAL HEADQUARTERS
SUPREME COMMANDER FOR THE ALLIED POWERS

28 November 1945

AG 230.14 (28 Nov 45) ESS/LA
SCAPIN 360

MEMORANDUM FOR: IMPERIAL JAPANESE GOVERNMENT.
THROUGH: Central Liaison Office, Tokyo.
SUBJECT: Employment Policies.

1. The Imperial Japanese Government will insure that no discrimination will be exercised or permitted for or against any worker either in private or government work, in wages, hours or working conditions by reason of nationality, creed or social status.

2. Koreans, Formosans and Chinese nationals who elect to remain in Japan rather than to accept repatriation will be guaranteed the same rights, privileges and opportunities in employment as are extended to Japanese nationals in comparable circumst-

ances.

3. Koreans, Formosans and Chinese nationals awaiting repatriation will be furnished opportunities to work for the occupation forces without discrimination. All such workers will be paid by the Imperial Japanese Government at the same rates as Japanese workers and will be extended all benefits granted Japanese nationals working for the occupation forces.

4. The Imperial Japanese Government is directed to revoke, rescind and abrogate all laws, ordinances, rules, regulations and enactments of any kind or character which provide preferential employment and educational opportunities for demobilized military personnel solely on the basis of military service.

5. Acknowledgment of receipt of this memorandum and reports of action taken hereunder are directed.

FOR THE SUPREME COMMANDER:

H. W. ALLEN,
Colonel, A.G.D.,
Asst. Adjutant General.

99　昭和20年11月30日　吉田外務大臣よりマーシャル連合国最高司令官総司令部副参謀長宛

第一および第二復員省大臣の幣原首相兼任につき通報

Major General Richard J. Marshall,
Deputy Chief of Staff,
General Headquarters of the Supreme Commander for the Allied Powers

30 November 1945

My dear General,

With reference to the proposed First and Second Ministries of Demobilization I desire to tell you for your information that a decision has been made according to which the Prime Minister Baron Shidehara will serve concurrently as head of both Ministries.

It is confidently hoped that the above arrangement will prove on the whole satisfactory to the Allied Headquarters.

Sincerely yours,

100

昭和20年12月8日 連合国最高司令官総司令部より 日本政府宛

救済・厚生事業計画の立案に関する指令

Shigeru Yoshida,
Foreign Minister

GENERAL HEADQUARTERS
SUPREME COMMANDER FOR THE ALLIED POWERS

8 December 1945

AG 044 (8 Dec 45) GD
SCAPIN 404

MEMORANDUM FOR: IMPERIAL JAPANESE GOVERNMENT
THROUGH: Central Liaison Office, Tokyo.
SUBJECT: Relief and Welfare Plans.

1. Imperial Japanese Government will submit to this headquarters, by 31 December 1945, a detailed and comprehensive plan for providing food, clothing, housing, medical care, financial assistance, and welfare services to unemployed and other needy persons in Japan during the period January–June 1946.

2. The plan will include:

a. A statement of the basis used in calculating requirements;

b. A list, by prefecture, of the estimated number of persons who will monthly require direct assistance because of unemployment, physical incapacity, or other cause of dependency;

c. A description of the local administrative machinery to be used for investigating and meeting relief needs, including a statement of personnel policy;

d. The method of securing supplies, materials, and shelter from the overall sources available to the economy of Japan;

e. Estimated monthly cost of relief by prefecture.

3. It is the intention of this directive to require the development of adequate measures for the care of persons whose financial and/or other resources are inadequate to maintain minimum living standards during the period indicated. The Imperial Japanese Government will inaugurate immediately necessary measures to prevent any person or group of persons in japan from being discriminated against in the distribution of available supplies because of in-

ability to work, inability to obtain remunerative employment, or for political, religious or economic beliefs.

4. In the event that current relief legislation, appropriations and/or administrative facilities are believed to be inadequate to prevent discrimination against unemployed and other needy persons in the distribution of available supplies, the reply to this memorandum will set forth proposed new legislation, appropriations and/or improved relief administrative facilities which will be developed, with the anticipated date of their inauguration. If the Imperial Japanese Government considers current legislation, appropriation and relief administration adequate to meet probable relief needs during the period stated, the reply will make positive affirmation of this judgment and will cite appropriate references to current legislation, relief regulations and related material.

5. Acknowledgement of the receipt of this memorandum is directed.

FOR THE SUPREME COMMANDER:

H. W. ALLEN,
Colonel, A.G.D.,
Asst. Adjutant General.

101

昭和20年12月8日　連合国最高司令官総司令部より　日本政府宛

制限会社に対する規則につき指令

GENERAL HEADQUARTERS
SUPREME COMMANDER FOR THE ALLIED POWERS
APO 500

8 December 1945

AG 300.8 (8 Dec 45) ESS-AC
SCAPIN 408

MEMORANDUM FOR: THE IMPERIAL JAPANESE GOVERNMENT.
THROUGH: Central Liaison Office, Tokyo.
SUBJECT: Regulations Affecting Restricted Concerns.

1. Reference is made to Memorandum this Headquarters AG 004 (8 Dec 45) ESS, subject: Establishment of a Schedule of Restricted Concerns.

2. The Imperial Japanese Government will take immediate action to assure that except as otherwise authorized or directed

by this Headquarters each concern listed on the "Schedule of Restricted Concerns" will comply with the following directions:

a. All cash on hand other than that customarily required for payroll and petty cash expenditures will be promptly deposited in the accounts of such concerns with banks in Japan.

b. The proceeds of all sales and loans and all other receipts and income from every source will be promptly deposited upon receipt in the bank accounts of such concerns.

c. No payment, transfer, or withdrawal from any account will be made which is not incidental to the normal course of business of the concern.

d. No sale, transfer, or other disposition of any capital assets including lands, buildings, major items of equipment and securities will be made.

e. No other property will be sold, conveyed, distributed or otherwise disposed of except in the normal course of business and for adequate consideration, and no act will be performed for the purpose of or which has the effect of dissipating assets.

f. No new stock or other participating share interest, however described, will be authorized or issued, and the rights and privileges of any existing stock or other participating share interests will not be reduced or added to or otherwise modified.

g. No bonded indebtedness will be authorized or created and no loans of any other character will be obtained, except in the normal course of business.

h. No dividends will be paid or declared.

i. No salary payments in excess of those paid in June, 1945 will be made to the executive officers, including but not limited to, the president, vice-president, secretary, treasurer, directors, managers, advisors and auditors. No bonuses, retirement pay, severance allowances or other emoluments and benefits, except periodic salary payments, will be paid to such executive officers.

3. The Imperial Japanese Government will promptly obtain and furnish to this Headquarters statements from each firm listed on the "Schedule of Restricted Concerns" specifying all payments other than periodic salary payments made on or since 1 July 1945, to any person who on or since such date was an executive officer of such firm and the basis for such payments.

324

2 民主化・非軍事化政策への対応（昭和20年10月〜21年5月）

102

昭和20年12月9日　終戦連絡中央事務局第二部作成
［十二月九日總司令部ニ於テ石炭問題ニ關シ打合セノ件］

（欄外記入一）
十二月九日總司令部ニ於テ石炭問題ニ關シ打合セノ件
（昭和二〇、一二、九）

4. Request for approval of any transaction covered by paragraph 2 of this memorandum will be accompanied by the written recommendations of the Minister of Finance, and by such additional data as may be necessary for a thorough understanding of the transaction concerned.

5. The Imperial Japanese Government will acknowledge receipt of this memorandum and promptly report the action taken by it in compliance therewith.

FOR THE SUPREME COMMANDER

H. W. ALLEN,
Colonel, A.G.D.,
Asst. Adjutant General.

一、『石炭ノ「ストック」ハ平年消費ノ七〇％デ行ケバ來年二月末マデニハ無クナルガ日本政府ノ措置ハ總テ遅キ様ナリ何等カ急速ニ措置ヲ講ズベシ』トノ強キ要請アリ

二、當方ヨリスベテノ問題ノ解決ハ食糧ノ増配ニ在リ之ガ為ニハ南鮮ヨリノ食糧輸入ヲ考慮アリ度キ旨印象付ケ置キタルニ對シ「イーストウッド」准將了承シ居リタリ

三、北海道大夕張、昭和、奈井江炭礦ノ争議事情ニ付米側ヨリ情報ヲ求メタルニ付米側ガ日本側ハ何故強キ語調ニテ詰メ寄ラレタリ（會議後當方ヨリ調停委員會ニ依リ争議ヲ解決スル方法ヲ日本人ハ知ラザルコト既ニ二年アリ、善悪ハ別トシサウ簡單ニ委員會ヲ任命出來ルモノニ非ル旨説明シ置ケル處此ノ議論ニハ「イーストウッド」モ納得セル如シ）

四、『（イ）本日提出ノ資料及各種ノ資料ニ付之ヲ「フォーマライズ」スル様「ダイレクティブ」ヲ出スベシ又（ロ）争議調停ニ付「ダイレクティブ」ヲ出スベシ』

五、「鑛山局長ノ報告ノミニ全面ノ信ヲ措クベカラズ各方面ヨリノ情報ニ依リ十分ニ事情ヲ確メヨ」

六、『賃銀ノ「スケール」及物資配給ニ付炭礦夫ハ承知シ非ズ之ヲ十分ニ周知セシメハ爭議ノ幾分カハ防止シ得ズ』之ヲ十分ニ周知セシメハ爭議ノ幾分カハ防止シ得ズ進ムベシト當方述ベタリ

七、本日ノ會議ハ關係大臣ニモ十分報告シ急速ニ各種ノ施策ヲ進ムベシト當方述ベタリ

八、『各種産業ニ消費スル石炭ヲ切り下ゲテ辻褄ヲ合スガ如キ消極策ハ廢メテ積極的ニ増産ニ突キ當り行クベシ』

九、『爆藥ガ「ボトルネック」ニナリ居ラズヤ今後増産ニ伴ヒ火藥量モ増大スベキ處右ニ對スル用意アリヤ』

10、「徴用ノ準備如何何時頃カラ始ムルヤ」ノ問ニ對シ我方ヨリ準備ハ進ミ居リ十二月中ニハ發動セシムル豫定ト答フ（徴用ノ如キハ怪シカラヌトハ言ハズ黙認セルガ如キ印象ヲ得タリ

（欄外記入二）
〔一字不明〕
ル□ニ非ズヤ』

三、『賃銀ノ値上ニ付十一月十四日ニ總司令部ヨリ「オーソライズ」セルニモ拘ラズ何ヲ愚圖愚圖シ居レリヤ』ノ質問アリ爭議中ノ炭礦ハ「オーソライズ」サレタル額以上ヲ要求シ居ルモノニテ此ノ點ニ米側ノ誤解アリ又賃銀ノ計算ハ複雑ナルモノニテ簡單ニ手取リガ十二圓ニナルカドウカ判ラヌト云フ事情アル旨説明シ置ケリ

三、先方出席者 「イーストウッド」准將ト「カルビンスキー」「メイ」「コリンス」ソノ他

當方 岡崎燃料局長、山本、田口（商工省）
朝海、鈴木（連絡局）
片柳食管次長（農林省）

（欄外記入一）
十二月十日終戰委員會席上第二部ヨリ配布セルモノ

（欄外記入二）
之ハ反對ナリ
GHQハ戰後モ混亂期ニ於テハ戰時中ニ劣ラズ徴用ヲ必要トス
トノ意見ナリ 黃田

（欄外記入三）
厚生省ー連絡トレズ

103 昭和20年12月9日 連合国最高司令官総司令部より日本政府宛

農地改革プログラムの立案方指令

326

三、石炭廳ニ付質問アリ用意整ヒタル旨返事セリ

2 民主化・非軍事化政策への対応（昭和20年10月〜21年5月）

付記 昭和二十一年三月十五日付終戦連絡中央事務局より連合国最高司令官総司令部宛公信CL〇第一二二〇号

農地改革プログラムの提出について

GENERAL HEADQUARTERS
SUPREME COMMANDER FOR THE ALLIED POWERS

9 December 1945

AG 602.6 (9 Dec 45) CIE
SCAPIN 411
MEMORANDUM FOR: IMPERIAL JAPANESE GOVERNMENT.
THROUGH: Central Liaison Office, Tokyo.
SUBJECT: Rural Land Reform.

1. In order that the Imperial Japanese Government shall remove economic obstacles to the revival and strengthening of democratic tendencies, establish respect for the dignity of man, and destroy the economic bondage which has enslaved the Japanese farmer for centuries of feudal oppression, the Japanese Imperial Government is directed to take measures to insure that those who till the soil of Japan shall have a more equal opportunity to enjoy the fruits of their labor.

2. The purpose of this order is to exterminate those pernicious ills which have long blighted the agrarian structure of a land where almost half the total population is engaged in husbandry. The more malevolent of these ills include:

a. Intense overcrowding of land.

Almost half the farm households in Japan till less than one and one half acres each.

b. Widespread tenancy under conditions highly unfavorable to tenants.

More than three-fourths of the farmers in Japan are either partially or totally tenants, paying rentals amounting to half or more of their annual crops.

c. A heavy burden of farm indebtedness combined with high rates of interest on farm loans.

Farm indebtedness persists so that less than half the total farm households are able to support themselves on their agriculture income.

d. Government fiscal policies which discriminate

against agriculture in favor of industry and trade. Interest rates and direct taxes on agriculture are more oppressive than those in commerce and industry.

e. Authoritative government control over farmers and farm organizations without regard for farmer interests.

Arbitrary crop quotas established by disinterested control associations often restrict the farmer in the cultivation of crops for his own needs or economic advancement.

Emancipation of the Japanese farmer cannot begin until such basic farm evils are uprooted and destroyed.

3. The Japanese Imperial Government is therefore ordered to submit to this Headquarters on or before 15 March 1946 a program of rural land reform. This program shall contain plans for:

a. Transfer of land ownership from absentee land owners to land operators.

b. Provisions for purchase of farm lands from non-operating owners at equitable rates.

c. Provisions for tenant purchase of land at annual installments commensurate with tenant income.

d. Provisions for reasonable protection of former tenants against reversion to tenancy status. Such necessary safeguards should include:

(1) Access to long and short term farm credit at reasonable interest rates.

(2) Measures to protect the farmer against exploitation by processors and distributors.

(3) Measures to stabilize prices of agricultural produce.

(4) Plans for the diffusion of technical and information of assistance to the agrarian population.

(5) A program to foster and encourage an agricultural cooperative movement free of domination by non-agrarian interests and dedicated to the economic and cultural advancement of the Japanese

328

2　民主化・非軍事化政策への対応（昭和 20 年 10 月〜21 年 5 月）

e. The Japanese Imperial Government is requested to submit in addition to the above, such other proposals it deems necessary to guarantee to agriculture a share of the national income commensurate with its contribution.

FOR THE SUPREME COMMANDER:

H. W. ALLEN,
Colonel, A.G.D.,
Asst. Adjutant General.

（付 記）

TO: GENERAL HEADQUARTERS OF THE SUPREME COMMANDER FOR THE ALLIED POWERS.
FROM: Central Liaison Office, Tokyo.
SUBJECT: Rural Land Reform.

C.L.O. No. 1220 (EA)

15 March 1946

1. Reference: Your Memorandum AG 602.6 (9 Dec 45) CIE, subject as above.

2. The Imperial Japanese Government submits herewith enclosed the "Program of Rural Land Reform" for the rooting and destroying the feudalistic regime in the rural land and democratization of the agricultural system, prepared by the Ministry of Agriculture and Forestry in accordance with Paragraph 3 of the reference Memorandum.

FOR THE PRESIDENT:

(S. Iguchi)
Director of General Affairs,
Central Liaison Office.

Enclosure: 5 copies of the "Program of Rural Land Reform".

編 注　本文書の別添は見当たらない。

昭和 20 年 12 月 12 日　連合国最高司令官総司令部より日本政府宛

昭和二十年度追加予算承認および以後の予算案には総司令部の事前承認を要する旨指令

GENERAL HEADQUARTERS
SUPREME COMMANDER FOR THE ALLIED POWERS
APO 500

12 December 1945

AG 110.01 (12 Dec 45) ESS/FI
SCAPIN 427

MEMORANDUM FOR: IMPERIAL JAPANESE GOVERNMENT.

THROUGH: Central Liaison Office, Tokyo.

SUBJECT: Supplementary Budgets 1 and 2 for Fiscal Year 1945-46.

1. Reference is made to the memorandum of the Minister of Finance, dated 8 December 1945 (LOF 55), requesting approval of Supplementary Budgets Numbers 1 and 2 for the fiscal year 1945-46, to be introduced to the present session of the Diet.

2. There is no objection to the revenue and expenditure program contained in these budgets. The necessary borrowing is permitted.

3. Hereafter, all budgets of the Imperial Japanese Government, including amendments or revisions, will be submitted to this Headquarters before being submitted to the Diet.

4. An acknowledgment of the receipt of this memorandum is directed.

FOR THE SUPREME COMMANDER:

H. W. ALLEN,
Colonel, A.G.D.,
Asst. Adjutant General.

〜〜〜〜〜〜〜〜〜〜

昭和20年12月12日　連合国最高司令官総司令部より
　　　　　　　　　日本政府宛

国際郵便再開に関する日本側提議は不許可の
旨回答

105

AG 311.1 (12 Dec 45) AG
SCAPIN 429

MEMORANDUM FOR: THE IMPERIAL JAPANESE GOVERNMENT.

THROUGH: Central Liaison Office, Tokyo.

GENERAL HEADQUARTERS
SUPREME COMMANDER FOR THE ALLIED POWERS

12 December 1945

2 民主化・非軍事化政策への対応(昭和20年10月〜21年5月)

SUBJECT: Re-establishment of Civilian Mail Service.

Reference C.L.O. No. 566 (5), 14 November 1945, subject: "Opening of Communications For Japanese Nationals Overseas", the request that mail service he resumed between Japanese nationals and their families, residing in other countries, is not favorably considered at the present time.

FOR THE SUPREME COMMANDER:

H. W. ALLEN,
Colonel, A.G.D.,
Asst Adjutant General.

106

昭和20年12月15日　連合国最高司令官総司令部より　日本政府宛

神道の国家管理廃止に関する指令

GENERAL HEADQUARTERS
SUPREME COMMANDER FOR THE ALLIED POWERS

15 December 1945

AG 000.3 (15 Dec 45) CIE
SCAPIN 448

MEMORANDUM FOR: IMPERIAL JAPANESE GOVERNMENT.
THROUGH: Central Liaison Office, Tokyo.
SUBJECT: Abolition of Governmental Sponsorship, Support, Perpetuation, Control, and Dissemination of State Shinto (Kokka Shintō, Jinja Shintō)

1. In order to free the Japanese people from direct or indirect compulsion to believe or profess to believe in a religion or cult officially designated by the state, and

In order to lift from the Japanese people the burden of compulsory financial support of an ideology which has contributed to their war guilt, defeat, suffering, privation, and present deplorable condition, and

In order to prevent a recurrence of the perversion of Shinto theory and beliefs into militaristic and ultra-nationalistic propaganda designed to delude the Japanese people and lead them into wars of aggression, and

In order to assist the Japanese people in a rededication of their national life to building a new Japan based upon ideals of perpetual peace and democracy,

It is hereby directed that:

a. The sponsorship, support, perpetuation, control, and dissemination of Shinto by the Japanese national, prefectural, and local governments, or by public officials, subordinates, and employees acting in their official capacity are prohibited and will cease immediately.

b. All financial support from public funds and all official affiliation with Shinto and Shinto shrines are prohibited and will cease immediately.

(1) While no financial support from public funds will be extended to shrines located on public reservations or parks, this prohibition will not be construed to preclude the Japanese government from continuing to support the areas on which such shrines are located.

(2) Private financial support of all Shinto shrines which have been previously supported in whole or in part by public funds will be permitted, provided such private support is entirely voluntary and is in no way derived from forced or involuntary contributions.

c. All propagation and dissemination of militaristic and ultra-nationalistic ideology in Shinto doctrines, practices, rites, ceremonies, or observances, as well as in the doctrines, practices, rites, ceremonies, and observances of any other religion, faith, sect, creed, or philosophy, are prohibited and will cease immediately.

d. The Religious Functions Order relating to the Grand Shrine of Ise and the Religious Functions Order relating to State and other Shrines will be annulled.

e. The Shrine Board (Jinji-in) of the Ministry of Home Affairs will be abolished, and its present functions, duties, and administrative obligations will not be assumed by any other governmental or tax-supported agency.

f. All public educational institutions whose primary function is either the investigation and dissemination of Shinto or the training of a Shinto priesthood will be abolished and their physical properties diverted to other uses. Their present functions, duties, and administrative obligations will not be assumed by any other governmental or tax-supported agency.

g. Private educational institutions for the investigation and dissemination of Shinto and for the training of a priesthood for Shinto will be permitted and will operate with the same privileges and be subject to the same controls and restrictions as any other private educational institution having no affiliation with the government; in no case, however, will they receive support from public funds, and in no case will they propagate and disseminate militaristic and ultra-nationalistic ideology.

h. The dissemination of Shinto doctrines in any form by any means in any educational institution supported wholly or in part by public funds is prohibited and will cease immediately.

(1) All teachers' manuals and textbooks now in use in any educational institution supported wholly or in part by public funds will be censored, and all Shinto doctrine will be deleted. No teachers' manual or textbook which is published in the future for use in such institutions will contain any Shinto doctrine.

(2) No visits to Shinto shrines and no rites, practices, or ceremonies associated with Shinto will be conducted or sponsored by any educational institution supported wholly or in part by public funds.

i. Circulation by the government of "The Fundamental Principles of the National Structure" (Kokutai no Hongi), "The Way of the Subject" (Shinmin no Michi), and all similar official volumes, commentaries, interpretations, or instructions on Shinto is prohibited.

j. The use in official writings of the terms "Greater East Asia War" (Dai Tōa Sensō), "The Whole World under One Roof" (Hakkō Ichi-u), and all other terms whose connotation in Japanese is inextricably connected with State Shinto, militarism, and ultra-nationalism is prohibited and will cease immediately.

k. God-shelves (kamidana) and all other physical symbols of State Shinto in any office, school, institution, organization, or structure supported wholly or in part by public funds are prohibited and will be removed immediately.

1. No official, subordinate, employee, student, citizen, or resident of Japan will be discriminated against because of his failure to profess and believe in or participate in any practice, rite, ceremony, or observance of State Shintō or of any other religion.

m. No official of the national, prefectural, or local government, acting in his public capacity, will visit any shrine to report his assumption of office, to report on conditions of government or to participate as a representative of government in any ceremony or observance.

2. a. The purpose of this directive is to separate religion from the state, to prevent misuse of religion for political ends, and to put all religions, faiths, and creeds upon exactly the same legal basis, entitled to precisely the same opportunities and protection. It forbids affiliation with the government and the propagation and dissemination of militaristic and ultra-nationalistic ideology not only to Shintō but to the followers of all religions, faiths, sects, creeds, or philosophies.

b. The provisions of this directive will apply with equal force to all rites, practices, ceremonies, observances, beliefs, teachings, mythology, legends, philosophy, shrines, and physical symbols associated with Shintō.

c. The term State Shintō within the meaning of this directive will refer to that branch of Shintō (Kokka Shintō or Jinja Shintō) which by official acts of the Japanese Government has been differentiated from the religion of Sect Shintō (Shūha Shintō or Kyōha Shintō) and has been classified a non-religious national cult commonly known as State Shintō, National Shintō, or Shrine Shintō.

d. The term Sect Shintō (Shūha Shintō or Kyōha Shintō) will refer to that branch of Shintō (composed of 13 recognized sects) which by popular belief, legal commentary, and the official acts of the Japanese Government has been recognized to be a religion.

e. Pursuant to the terms of Article I of the Basic Directive on "Removal of Restrictions on Political, Civil, and Religious Liberties" issued on 4 October 1945 by the Supreme Commander for the Allied Powers in which the Japanese people were assured

2　民主化・非軍事化政策への対応（昭和20年10月〜21年5月）

complete religious freedom,

(1) Sect Shinto will enjoy the same protection as any other religion.

(2) Shrine Shinto, after having been divorced from the state and divested of its militaristic and ultra-nationalistic elements, will be recognized as a religion if its adherents so desire and will be granted the same protection as any other religion in so far as it may in fact be the philosophy or religion of Japanese individuals.

f. Militaristic and ultra-nationalistic ideology, as used in this directive, embraces those teachings, beliefs, and theories which advocate or justify a mission on the part of Japan to extend its rule over other nations and peoples by reason of:

(1) The doctrine that the Emperor of Japan is superior to the heads of other states because of ancestry, descent, or special origin.

(2) The doctrine that the people of Japan are superior to the people of other lands because of ancestry, descent or special origin.

(3) The doctrine that the islands of Japan are superior to other lands because of divine or special origin.

(4) Any other doctrine which tends to delude the Japanese people into embarking upon wars of aggression or to glorify the use of force as an instrument for the settlement of disputes with other peoples.

3. The Imperial Japanese Government will submit a comprehensive report to this Headquarters not later than 15 March 1946 describing in detail all action taken to comply with all provisions of this directive.

4. All officials, subordinates, and employees of the Japanese national, prefectural, and local governments, all teachers and education officials, and all citizens and residents of Japan will be held personally accountable for compliance with the spirit as well as the letter of all provisions of this directive.

FOR THE SUPREME COMMANDER:

H. W. ALLEN,
Colonel, A.G.D.,
Asst. Adjutant General.

昭和20年12月19日　連合国最高司令官総司令部発表

「連合國の日本占領の基本的目的と連合軍によるその達成の方法に關するマックアーサー元帥の管下部隊に對する訓令」（和訳文）

連合國の日本占領の基本的目的と連合軍によるその達成の方法に關するマックアーサー元帥の管下部隊に對する訓令

一九四五年十二月十九日

完全に敗亡した敵に對しそのやり方の誤りをただし且つ世界において尊敬を受ける地位を回復するために與えられつつある機會が極めてはつきりとここに述べられる。

連合國最高司令官の日本に對する權限は、降伏條項及びポツダム宣言の條項を實施するために完全なものとして引證される。日本及びその國民に對する管理は、實行可能な最大限度まで降伏條項に規定されている目的に適すると認められる天皇その他の日本政府機構を通じて行われるであろう。

連合國の政策が従うべき日本に關する究極の目的は、次の通りである。

日本が再び世界の平和及び安全に対する脅威とならないことを確實にすること。

他國の權利を尊重すべき平和的且つ責任ある政府を最終的に決定される最高司令官の目的を支持するであろう。この政府は、できるだけ嚴密に民主主義的自治の原則に合致するものでなければならない。政府のとる形態は、固定のものでも不變のものでもない。自由に表明された國民の意思に支持されないいかなる政治形態をも日本に強いることは、ポツダム條項に反する。最高司令官によって示された目的は、次の主要な方法によって達成されるであろう。

日本の主権は、本州、北海道、九州、四國の諸島及び對馬諸島を含む約一千の近接諸小島に制限されるであろ

336

2 民主化・非軍事化政策への対応（昭和20年10月～21年5月）

う。

日本は、完全に非武裝化され、且つ、非軍事化されるであろう。軍國主義者の權威と軍國主義の勢力は、日本の政治的、經濟的、社會的生活から全面的に除去されるであろう。軍國主義と侵略との精神を表現する諸制度は、強力に抑壓されるであろう。

日本國民は、個人的自由への希望及び基本的人權、特に宗教、集會、言論及び出版の自由の尊重を發展させるように獎勵されるべきである。民主主義的且つ代議的組織の形成が獎勵されなければならない。

人民の平時の需要をみたすことを許す經濟は、彼ら自身による上に述べたようなものの發達の機會から生れるべきである。

日本政府及び國民は、最高司令官の指令を強制されることなく實行するあらゆる機會を與えられるべきであるが、自發的な行動が執られない場合には、遵守を要求するために適當な管下部隊に命令が與えられるであろう。

占領軍は、主として最高司令官の指令の遵守を監視する機關として又必要があれば最高司令官が遵守を確實にするために用いる機關として行動する。

連合國及びその代表者に對する尊敬及び信賴は、實例と實際行動とによって高められるであろう。一般人民は、個人の自由及び財產權に對するあらゆる不當な干涉を受けることはないであろう。歷史的、文化的、宗敎的物件及び施設（數箇所の宮殿を含む）は、注意深く保護され且つ保存されるであろう。

占領軍は、國際法及び陸戰法規によって課せられた義務を遵守するであろう。

軍事的安全の要求には從わなければならないが、占領軍は、言論、出版、宗敎及び集會の自由を許し且つ獎勵するであろう。

編 注 本文書は、昭和二十四年一月、外務省特別資料部作成「日本占領及び管理重要文書集」第一卷より抜粹。

108

昭和20年12月26日
連合国最高司令官総司令部より日本政府宛

生活必需物資への価格・配給統制撤廃に関する

日本側提案は不承認の旨回答

GENERAL HEADQUARTERS
SUPREME COMMANDER FOR THE ALLIED POWERS
APO 500
26 December 1945

AG 130 (26 Dec 45) ESS/PC
SCAPIN 502

MEMORANDUM FOR: THE IMPERIAL JAPANESE GOVERNMENT.

THROUGH: Central Liaison Office, Tokyo.

SUBJECT: Abandonment of Price and Distribution Controls over Necessary Articles of Life.

1. Reference is made to CLO No. 616 (2) requesting permission to remove sundry essential items from price and distribution controls.

2. Reference is made to paragraphs 2 (a) and (b) of Directive No.3 (dated 22 September 1945) to the Imperial Japanese Government in which the Imperial Japanese Government is directed to maintain a firm control over prices and a strict rationing program for essential commodities. The request referred to in paragraph 1 above is denied for the following reasons:

   a. Abandonment of price controls would stimulate inflationary trends.

   b. Abandonment of distribution controls would result in inequities to consumers.

3. In the future, all requests for the abandonment of price controls (as differentiated from price changes) and distribution controls of essential commodities will be accompanied by the following detailed information for each specific item:

   a. Total amount of each of the raw materials used in production in the period of a year.

   b. Quantity available in stockpiles or at distribution points.

   c. Monthly production figures from January 1941 until month before request is made.

   d. Estimated current monthly demand.

   e. A clear and detailed statement of the distribution controls in existence at the time of the request.

   f. Figures showing in detail the actual distribution by

338

109 修身、日本史および地理の授業停止に関する指令

昭和20年12月31日　連合国最高司令官総司令部より日本政府宛

SCAPIN 519
AG 000.8 (31 Dec 45) CIE
MEMORANDUM FOR: IMPERIAL JAPANESE GOVERNMENT
THROUGH: Central Liaison Office, Tokyo
SUBJECT: Suspension of courses in Morals (Shushin), Japanese History, and Geography.

1. In accordance with the basic directive AG 000.3 (15 Dec 45) CIE proclaiming the abolition of government sponsorship and support of State Shinto and Doctrine, and

Inasmuch as the Japanese government has used education to inculcate militaristic and ultra-nationalistic ideologies which have been inextricably interwoven in certain textbooks imposed upon students,

It is hereby directed that:

　a. All courses in Morals (Shushin), Japanese History, and Geography in all educational institutions, including government, public, and private schools, for which textbooks and teachers' manuals have been published or sanctioned by the Ministry of Education shall be suspended immediately and will not be resumed until permission has been given by this Headquarters.

　b. The Ministry of Education shall suspend immediately all ordinances (Horei), regulations, or instructions directing the

FOR THE SUPREME COMMANDER:

H. W. ALLEN.
Colonel, A.G.D.,
Asst. Adjutant General.

31 December 1945
GENERAL HEADQUARTERS
SUPREME COMMANDER FOR THE ALLIED POWERS

months since January 1945.
　g. Monthly price changes since January 1937.
　h. Cost of production figures based on expenditures for goods and services at control rates.

manner in which the specific subjects of Morals (Shushin), Japanese History, and Geography shall be taught.

c. The Ministry of Education shall collect all textbooks and teachers' manuals used in every course and educational institution affected by 1, a. for disposal in accordance with the procedure outlined in Annex A to this memorandum.

d. The Ministry of Education shall prepare and submit to this Headquarters a plan for the introduction of substitute programs to take the place of courses affected by this memorandum in accordance with the procedure outlined in Annex B to this memorandum. These substitute programs will continue in force until such time as this Headquarters authorizes the resumption of the courses suspended herein.

e. The Ministry of Education shall prepare and submit to this Headquarters a plan for revising textbooks to be used in Morals (Shushin), Japanese History, and Geography in accordance with the procedure outlined in Annex C to this memorandum.

2. All officials, subordinates, and employees of the Japanese Government affected by the terms of this directive, and all school officials and teachers, both public and private, will be held personally accountable for compliance with the spirit as well as the letter of the terms of this directive.

FOR THE SUPREME COMMANDER:

H. W. ALLEN.

Colonel, A.G.D.,

Asst. Adjutant General.

3 Incls:

1 - Annex A - Procedure for Collection of Textbooks and Manuals

2 - Annex B - Plan for Submission of Substitute Programs

3 - Annex C - Procedure for Submission of Revised Program

ANNEX A

PROCEDURE FOR COLLECTION OF TEXTBOOKS AND MANUALS

The Ministry of Education shall collect all textbooks and teachers' manuals used in every course and educational institution for which teaching materials in the subjects of Morals (Shushin),

2　民主化・非軍事化政策への対応（昭和20年10月～21年5月）

Japanese History, and Geography have been prescribed, published, or sanctioned by the Ministry.

For the Tokyo, Kyoto, Osaka, and Kobe areas, the collection of these teaching materials shall be accomplished as soon as possible and, in any event, not later than the beginning of the Spring Term of School, 1946, at which time a report shall be submitted to this Headquarters, stating the total number of volumes collected, the gross weight of these volumes, and the specific location where these teaching materials have been collected.

In addition, a detailed report shall be submitted to this Headquarters, on 1 April 1946, for the collection of similar textbooks and manuals in all other areas of Japan. This plan shall include: the orders to competent prefectural authorities, reference to this Memorandum, and detailed instructions on the collections, number, weight, and availability for shipping of these teaching materials to designated pulping centers for the manufacture of paper.

ANNEX B

PLAN FOR SUBMISSION OF SUBSTITUTE PROGRAMS

The Ministry of Education shall prepare and submit as soon as possible to this Headquarters a plan for the introduction of substitute programs to take the place of courses affected by this Memorandum. These substitute programs will continue in force until such time as this Headquarters authorizes the resumption of the courses suspended herein.

This plan shall aim at presenting fundamental social, economic and political truths, relating them to the world and life of the students.

These truths shall be taught through classroom discussion based in part on materials sponsored by this Headquarters. Whenever possible, the discussion will be correlated with current events.

The Ministry of Education will issue teachers' manuals explaining the purpose of the program, prescribing discussion methods which will encourage independent thinking, outlining the major topics to be discussed and listing press, radio, pamphlet and other materials to be used.

ANNEX C

PROCEDURE FOR SUBMISSION OF REVISED PROGRAM

The Ministry of Education shall prepare and submit as soon as possible for approval to this Headquarters, a plan for revising textbooks and teachers' manuals used in Morals (Shushin), Japanese History, and Geography courses.

This plan shall have for its objective the preparation of temporary teaching materials which will be available for the Spring Term of the 1946 school year.

The details to be covered in this plan will include: personnel for the preparation of teaching materials, selection of suitable subject matter, translation into English, consultation with and approval from this Headquarters, printing, and distribution of materials.

General of the Army Douglas MacArthur's New Year Message

January 1, 1946

TO THE PEOPLE OF JAPAN:

A new year has come. With it, a new day dawns for Japan. No longer is the future to be settled by a few.

The shackles of militarism, of feudalism, of regimentation of body and soul, have been removed.

Thought control and the abuse of education are no more.

All now enjoy religious freedom and the right of speech without undue restraint. Free assembly is guaranteed.

The removal of this national enslavement means freedom for the people, but at the same time it imposes upon them the individual duty to think and to act each on his own initiative. It is necessary for the masses of Japan to awaken to the fact that they now have the power to govern and what is done must be done by themselves.

It is my hope that the New Year may be the beginning for them of "the way, and the truth, and the light."

110　昭和21年1月1日　連合国最高司令官総司令部発表
　　マッカーサー司令官の年頭メッセージ

2 民主化・非軍事化政策への対応(昭和20年10月～21年5月)

111 元日公布の詔書に関するマッカーサー司令官の声明

昭和21年1月1日　連合国最高司令官総司令部発表

付記　昭和二十一年一月一日公布

　　　右詔書

編注　本文書は、昭和二十四年三月、外務省特別資料部作成「日本占領及び管理重要文書集」第二巻より抜粋。

DOUGLAS MACARTHUR

General of the Army Douglas MacArthur's Statement concerning the Imperial Rescript of 1 January 1946

January 1, 1946

The Emperor's New Year's statement pleases me very much. By it he undertakes a leading part in the democratization of his people. He squarely takes his stand for the future along liberal lines. His action reflects the irresistible influence of a sound idea. A sound idea cannot be stopped.

（付記）

茲ニ新年ヲ迎フ。顧ミレバ明治天皇明治ノ初國是トシテ五箇條ノ御誓文ヲ下シ給ヘリ。曰ク、

一、廣ク會議ヲ興シ萬機公論ニ決スヘシ

一、上下心ヲ一ニシテ盛ニ經綸ヲ行フヘシ

一、官武一途庶民ニ至迄各其志ヲ遂ケ人心ヲシテ倦マサラシメンコトヲ要ス

一、舊來ノ陋習ヲ破リ天地ノ公道ニ基クヘシ

一、智識ヲ世界ニ求メ大ニ皇基ヲ振起スヘシ

叡旨公明正大、又何ヲカ加ヘン。朕ハ茲ニ誓ヲ新ニシテ國運ヲ開カント欲ス。須ラク此ノ御趣旨ニ則リ、舊來ノ陋習ヲ去リ、民意ヲ暢達シ、官民擧ゲテ平和主義ニ徹シ、教養豊カニ文化ヲ築キ、以テ民生ノ向上ヲ圖リ、新日本ヲ建設スベシ。

大小都市ノ蒙リタル戰禍、罹災者ノ艱苦、産業ノ停頓、食

糧ノ不足、失業者ノ増加ノ趨勢等ハ眞ニ心ヲ痛マシムルモノアリ。然リト雖モ、我國民ガ現在ノ試煉ニ直面シ、且徹頭徹尾文明ヲ平和ニ求ムルノ決意固ク、克ク其ノ結束ヲ全ウセバ、獨リ我國ノミナラズ全人類ノ爲ニ、輝カシキ前途ノ展開セラルルコトヲ疑ハズ。

夫レ家ヲ愛スル心ト國ヲ愛スル心トハ我國ニ於テ特ニ熱烈ナルヲ見ル。今ヤ實ニ此ノ心ヲ擴充シ、人類愛ノ完成ニ向ヒ、獻身的努力ヲ效スベキノ秋ナリ。

惟フニ長キニ亙レル戰爭ノ敗北ニ終リタル結果、我國民ハ動モスレバ焦躁ニ流レ、失意ノ淵ニ沈淪セントスルノ傾キアリ。詭激ノ風漸ク長ジテ道義ノ念頗ル衰ヘ、爲ニ思想混亂ノ兆アルハ洵ニ深憂ニ堪ヘズ。

然レドモ朕ハ爾等國民ト共ニ在リ、常ニ利害ヲ同ジウシ休戚ヲ分タント欲ス。朕ト爾等國民トノ間ノ紐帶ハ、終始相互ノ信賴ト敬愛トニ依リテ結バレ、單ナル神話ト傳説トニ依リテ生ゼルモノニ非ズ。天皇ヲ以テ現御神(アキツミカミ)トシ、且日本國民ヲ以テ他ノ民族ニ優越セル民族ニシテ、延テ世界ヲ支配スベキ運命ヲ有ストノ架空ナル觀念ニ基クモノニモ非ズ。朕ノ政府ハ國民ノ試煉ト苦難トヲ緩和センガ爲、アラユル施策ト經營トニ萬全ノ方途ヲ講ズベシ。同時ニ朕ハ我國民ガ時難ニ蹶起シ、當面ノ困苦克服ノ爲ニ、又産業及文運振興ノ爲ニ勇往センコトヲ希念ス。我國民ガ其ノ公民生活ニ於テ團結シ、相倚リ相扶ケ、寬容相許スノ氣風ヲ作興スルニ於テハ、能ク我至高ノ傳統ニ恥ヂザル眞價ヲ發揮スルニ至ラン。斯ノ如キハ實ニ我國民ガ人類ノ福祉ト向上トノ爲、絶大ナル貢獻ヲ爲ス所以ナルヲ疑ハザルナリ。

一年ノ計ハ年頭ニ在リ、朕ハ朕ノ信賴スル國民ガ朕ト其ノ心ヲ一ニシテ、自ラ奮ヒ自ラ勵マシ、以テ此ノ大業ヲ成就センコトヲ庶幾フ。

御名　御璽

昭和二十一年一月一日

内閣總理大臣兼
第一復員大臣第二復員大臣　男爵　幣原喜重郎
司法大臣　岩田宙造
農林大臣　松村謙三
文部大臣　前田多門
外務大臣　吉田茂
内務大臣　堀切善次郎
國務大臣　松本烝治

2　民主化・非軍事化政策への対応(昭和20年10月～21年5月)

112

ある種の政党、政治結社、協会およびその他の団体の廃止に関する指令

昭和21年1月4日　連合国最高司令官総司令部より 日本政府宛

編　注　本文書は、「官報號外　昭和二十一年一月一日」から抜粋。

厚生大臣　　　　　　芦田　均
國務大臣　　　　　　次田大三郎
大藏大臣　子爵　　　澁澤敬三
運輸大臣　　　　　　田中武雄
商工大臣　　　　　　小笠原三九郎
國務大臣　　　　　　小林一三

AG 091 (4 Jan 46) GS

GENERAL HEADQUARTERS
SUPREME COMMANDER FOR THE ALLIED POWERS
APO 500
4 January 1946

SCAPIN 548

MEMORANDUM FOR: IMPERIAL JAPANESE GOVERNMENT.

THROUGH: Central Liaison Office, Tokyo.

SUBJECT: Abolition of Certain Political Parties, Associations, Societies and Other Organizations.

1. You will prohibit the formation of any political party, association, society or other organization and any activity on the part of any of them or of any individual or group whose purpose, or the effect of whose activity, is the following:

　　a. Resistance or opposition to the Occupation Forces or to orders issued by the Japanese Government in response to directives of the Supreme Commander for the Allied Powers, or;

　　b. Support or justification of aggressive Japanese military action abroad, or;

　　c. Arrogation by Japan of leadership of other Asiatic, Indonesian or Malayan peoples, or;

　　d. Exclusion of foreign persons in Japan from trade, commerce or the exercise of their professions, or;

　　e. Opposition to a free cultural or intellectual exchange

between Japan and foreign countries, or;

f. Affording military or quasi-military training, or providing benefits, greater than similar civilian benefits, or special representation for persons formerly members of the Army or Navy, or perpetuation of militarism or a martial spirit in Japan, or;

g. Alteration of policy by assassination or other terroristic programs, or encouragement or justification of a tradition favoring such methods.

2. A list of organizations, some or all of whose purposes are prescribed under the provisions of paragraph 1 above, is given in Appendix A to this Memorandum. This list will not be regarded as inclusive. The organizations listed in that appendix and other organizations, whose purposes or activities are those above mentioned or similar to them, will be immediately dissolved, together with any organizations which they control or with which they are affiliated.

3. a. You will take such action immediately as may be required to prevent all transactions involving property owned or controlled, directly or indirectly, in whole or in part, by any organization dissolved or to be dissolved in accord with this Memorandum or of the type enumerated in paragraph 1 hereof. All such property, including all books, files and records of such organizations, will be seized and held in your custody. You will obtain complete records of all such property and will keep them available for inspection as public records. Officials receiving such records will be held personally responsible for their safe keeping and use in accord with this Memorandum. Any such property which is capable of use for the production of food, shelter or other necessities of life will be exploited as promptly as possible for those purposes.

b. You will promptly obtain and submit to this Headquarters the name and address and the position held by each person who has, at any time since 7 July 1937, served as an officer of any organization dissolved in accord with this Memorandum. Such information will also be kept available as a public record. Complete membership lists will also be furnished.

4. You will enact appropriate laws or ordinances to carry out the terms of this Memorandum and to prevent further activities contrary to its terms.

2　民主化・非軍事化政策への対応（昭和20年10月～21年5月）

5. Until further order of the Supreme Commander for the Allied Powers, any organization shall be deemed, regardless of its declared purposes, to further purposes or activities contrary to the terms of this memorandum if:

　a. Any of its principal officers were (i) members of organizations abolished in accord with this order, or (ii) former commissioned officers of the Imperial Japanese Regular Army or Navy or the Special Volunteer Reserve, who have been on active duty since 1 January 1930 or (iii) any person who has served in or with the military police (Kempei-Tai) or Naval Police, the TOKUMU KIKAN, KAIGUN TOKUMU BU, or other special or secret intelligence or military or naval police organizations.

　b. Its membership includes more than twenty-five percent of persons who were formerly members of an organization or organizations abolished or prohibited in pursuance of this Memorandum.

6. You will forbid the formation or activity of any party, society, organization, association or group whose purpose or activity consists of:

　a. Proposing or supporting candidates for public office.
　b. Influencing the policy of Government, or
　c. The discussion of the relations between Japan and foreign powers,

unless it shall first have filed a declaration of (a) its name, (b) its purposes, (c) the address of its principal offices, (d) the names and addresses of its officers together with a statement as to their military or police service and the names of any associations, societies or parties of which they are or have been members, (e) the names and addresses of substantial financial supporters and the amounts of their respective contributions, (f) a roster of the names and addresses of its membership in the office of the mayor of the town or city in which it has or intends to have its principal office. Such declarations will be kept up to date as changes in purposes and membership occur. Declarations with regard to changes of membership and substantial contributions will be made as required by the Supreme Commander; reports of changes in officers or purposes will be made immediately. You will direct that the mayor of any town or city receiving such a declaration or any change forward two copies to an appropriate office of the Imperial Japanese Government in Tokyo. Both the original and one of the copies of such declarations will be kept available for public inspection at all times during ordinary business hours. No fees will be charged in connection with any of the foregoing and the procedure fixed for filing such declarations shall be such as to make compliance with these directions as simple and easy as possible.

The provisions of this paragraph which require the filing of a roster of the names and addresses of members will not apply to groups or other organizations of workers or employees who meet for the purpose of the discussion of questions relating to wages, hours and working conditions or the choice of persons to represent them in negotiation with their employers in connection with such questions.

7. The purpose of the provisions of paragraph 6 of this Memorandum is to secure public knowledge of the character of political organizations in Japan and to prevent the formation of secret, militaristic, ultra-nationalistic and anti-democratic societies and organizations. It shall not be interpreted nor shall it be applied in a manner which interferes with freedom of assembly, speech or religion except with respect to the purposes and activities specifically mentioned herein.

8. You will present your programme for the execution of the directions of this Memorandum, together with any laws, ordinances or orders to be issued in accord with it, for the approval of the Supreme Commander for the Allied Powers. Any laws or ordinances which you will enact in compliance with this Memorandum will provide that upon such approval they will be effective from the date of this Memorandum, regardless of the date of their enactment.

FOR THE SUPREME COMMANDER:

H. W. ALLEN,
Colonel, A.G.D.,
Asst Adjutant General.

1 Incl:
　Appendix A

APPENDIX A

2 民主化・非軍事化政策への対応（昭和20年10月～21年5月）

List of Organizations to be Abolished referred to in Paragraph 2 of the Memorandum to the Imperial Japanese Government AG 091 (4 Jan 46) GS

Note: This list does not include all of the organizations which are to be dissolved in accord with the directions of the above Memorandum.

1. DAI NIPPON ISSHIN-KAI (Great Japan Renovation Society)
2. DAI NIPPON KOA RENMEI (Great Japan Rising Asia Alliance) and all its affiliated organizations
3. DAI NIPPON SEISANTO (Great Japan Production Party)
4. DAI NIPPON SEKISEI-KAI (Greater Japan True-hearted Society)
5. DAI TOA KYOKAI (Greater East Asia Association)
6. DAITO JUKU (Eastern Academy)
7. GENRON HOKOKU KAI (Literary Patriotic Society)
8. GENYOSHA (Dark Ocean Society)
9. JIKYOKU KAIGI KAI (Current Affairs Discussion Society)
10. KAKUMEI-SO (The House of the Cry of the Crane)
11. KENKOKU-KAI (National Foundation Society)
12. KINKEI GAKUIN (Golden Pheasant Institute)
13. KOKURYUKAI (Black Dragon Society)
14. KOKUSAI HANKYO RENMEI (Anti-Communist League)
15. KOKUSAI SEIKEI GAKKAI (International Political Economic Society)
16. KOKUSUI TAISHUTO (Ultranationalist Party)
17. KOKUTAI YOGO RENGO KAI (National State Protection League)
18. MEIRIN-KAI (Higher Ethics Society)
19. MIZUHO CLUB (Mizuho—archaic poetic term for Japan, literally "Fresh Rice Plant")
20. SONJO DOSHIKAI (Loyalist Comrades Society)
21. TAIKA KAI (Great Change Society)
22. TENKOKAI (Heavenly Action Society)
23. TOA RENMEI (East Asia League)
24. TOHO DOSHIKAI (Far Eastern Comrades Association)
25. TOHO KAI (Eastern Society)
26. YAMATO MUSUBI HONSHA (Yamato Solidarity Headquarters) or (Japanese Knot)

27. ZEN NIPPON SEINEN KURABU (All Japan Young Men's Club)

113 昭和21年1月4日 連合国最高司令官総司令部より 日本政府宛

望ましからざる人物の公職からの除去に関する指令

GENERAL HEADQUARTERS
SUPREME COMMANDER FOR THE ALLIED POWERS

APO 500

4 January 1946

AG 091.1 (4 Jan 46) GS
SCAPIN 550

MEMORANDUM FOR: IMPERIAL JAPANESE GOVERNMENT.
THROUGH: Central Liaison Office, Tokyo.
SUBJECT: Removal and Exclusion of Undesirable Personnel from Public Office.

1. The Potsdam Declaration states: "There must be eliminated for all time the authority and influence of those who have deceived and misled the people of Japan into embarking on world conquest, for we insist that a new order of peace, security, and justice will be impossible until irresponsible militarism is driven from the world".

2. In order to carry out this provision of the Potsdam Declaration, the Imperial Japanese Government is hereby ordered to remove from public office and exclude from government service all persons who have been:

a. Active exponents of militaristic nationalism and aggression.

b. Influential members of any Japanese ultranationalistic, terroristic, or secret patriotic society, its agencies or affiliates; or

c. Influential in the activities of the Imperial Rule Assistance Association, the Imperial Rule Assistance Political Society or the Political Association of Great Japan, as those terms are defined in Appendix A to this directive.

3. The term "public office" as used in this directive shall mean and include:

350

2 民主化・非軍事化政策への対応(昭和20年10月～21年5月)

a. Any position in the government service which is customarily filled by one with the civil service rank of Chokunin or above (or equivalent rank under any reorganization of the civil service system) ; or

b. Any other position in the government service not customarily filled by a member of the civil service which is equivalent or superior to the civil service rank of Chokunin (in the case of government corporations the term will include at least: Chairman of the Board of Directors, President, Vice-President, Director, Adviser and Auditor).

4. The term "government service", as used in this directive, shall mean and include all positions in the central Japanese and Prefectural Governments and all of their agencies and local branches, bureaus (including Regional Administrative Bureaus) and offices and all positions in corporations, associations and other organizations in which said Governments or any of their agencies have a financial interest representing actual or working control.

5. The term "remove from public office" as used in this directive shall mean to discharge the person from the public office which he holds and to terminate his influence and participation therein, directly and indirectly. Persons removed from public office will not be entitled to any public or private pensions or other emoluments or benefits without the consent of this Headquarters. An official removed under this procedure will be dismissed summarily and will not be entitled to the hearing or other procedures precedent to removal to which he may have been entitled under precedent in Japanese law.

6. The term "exclude from government service" as used in this directive shall mean to bar the person in question from any position in the government service. Thus, persons removed from public office will be disqualified from holding any other positions in the government service. Also persons who may not be holding public offices from which they must be removed, may nevertheless be disqualified from taking a position in the government service. This disqualification from holding public office shall be continued until the provisions of the Potsdam Declaration quoted in paragraph 1 have been fulfilled in Japan.

7. The mere removal of officials from public office and the

351

exclusion from government service of those persons described herein will not be sufficient to establish the new order of peace, security and justice envisaged by the Potsdam Declaration. If Japan is to achieve a peacefully inclined and responsible government, the greatest care must be taken to appoint new officials who will foster the revival and strengthening of democratic tendencies among the Japanese people and who will respect fundamental human rights and freedom of speech, religion and thought. If existing civil service qualification regulations provide obstacles to the appointment of such officials or unduly narrow the field from which appointments may be made, such regulations shall be amended or superseded.

8. The removals ordered by this directive shall be effected as expeditiously as possible, priority being given to the more important positions. Removal may be postponed in the case of individuals who are absolutely required to insure demobilization of the Japanese armed forces in the outlying theaters or to carry out the provisions of this directive. When their assistance is no longer absolutely required they will be dismissed. The names of such individuals, their positions, the reason for their disqualification, and the reasons for their temporary retention will promptly be reported to this Headquarters. The time of their final dismissal will also promptly be reported.

9. Appendix "A" contains a list of the categories of persons who must be removed from public office and excluded from government service by the Imperial Japanese Government in order to carry out the provisions of paragraph 2 of this directive. Persons included in the categories listed in Appendix "A" shall be removed from public office as provided in paragraphs 8 and 10 and shall thereafter be excluded from government service. However, if the Imperial Japanese Government represents that in order to carry on indispensable peaceful executive activities of such government, the temporary reinstatement of an individual so removed is essential and that it is impossible to obtain a suitable replacement, an application so stating, signed by a responsible official of the Imperial Japanese Government, may be filed with this Headquarters. Such application shall contain a statement of the name, rank, position, duties, and responsibilities of the individual involved; shall

2　民主化・非軍事化政策への対応（昭和20年10月〜21年5月）

state fully the reasons why such temporary reinstatement is regarded as essential, the requested period of temporary reinstatement and the efforts made to obtain a suitable replacement. Such application shall be accompanied by a copy of the questionnaire described in paragraph 10, below. No such temporary reinstatement will be effected by the Imperial Japanese Government until this Headquarters has registered its approval in writing.

10. In order to insure that the government service is cleansed of undesirable personnel the following action will be taken:

　a. The Imperial Japanese Government will instruct each of its Ministries or other appropriate agencies to remove from the positions described in paragraph 3 which are within its competence, any persons whom the records show or who are known to have been within the categories listed in Appendix "A". A Questionnaire (see below) will be obtained from each such individual before he is notified of his dismissal.

　b. In addition, the Imperial Japanese Government will instruct each of its Ministries or other appropriate agencies to prepare and distribute to all incumbents of positions described in paragraph 3 and to future applicants for government positions which are within its competence, the Questionnaire contained in Appendix "B". Such Questionnaires will be reviewed and on the basis of them and any other knowledge in possession of the Government, individuals will be removed from office or denied employment in accordance with the provisions of this directive.

11. Each Ministry or other appropriate agency will prepare a Plan for handling the Questionnaires which will provide for:

　a. Distribution.

　b. Collection.

　c. Review.

　d. Action on basis of information in Questionnaire.

　e. Classification and filing — this system should permit reference to the Questionnaire in terms of agency, rank of officials, and action taken (e.g. removal or retention.)

12. Each Plan will provide for screening of positions occupied by higher rank officials first. A duplicate set of completed Questionnaires will be provided at the Headquarters of each

Ministry or other agency where it will be available for inspection or removal by this Headquarters.

13. In addition to the Questionnaires each Ministry or other agency will maintain at its headquarters an alphabetical file of Questionnaire Record Cards substantially in the form indicated in Appendix "C" available for inspection or removal by this Headquarters. The cards will be filled out in English (also in Japanese if desired). Identical numbers, with an identifying symbol for each Ministry or other agency, will be assigned to each Questionnaire and the Record Card relating thereto.

14. In order that the forthcoming elections may provide a full opportunity for democratic elements in Japan to obtain memberships in the Imperial Diet denied them during the years of Japan's militaristic nationalism and aggression and in order to eliminate from the new Diet the influence of those who have deceived and misled the people of Japan into embarking on world conquest, any person who comes within the categories described in Appendix "A" shall be disqualified as a candidate for any elective position in the Imperial Diet. Any such person shall be disqualified from standing at any time as a candidate for Prefectural Governor or Mayor of a city (Shi). Also, all such persons shall be removed from and henceforth excluded from appointment to the House of Peers. The Imperial Japanese Government shall adopt measures to enforce this disqualification of candidates for elective office, including the issuance of necessary regulations, the publication of disqualification categories prepared in conformity herewith and the certification by each candidate that he is not thereby disqualified from standing for election. A comprehensive report of the measures proposed to be adopted will be furnished to this Headquarters.

15. The Imperial Japanese Government will make the following reports to this Headquarters (in English; in triplicate):

  a. Reports required by paragraphs 8 and 14 hereof.

  b. An initial report of the Plan of each Ministry or other agency called for by paragraph 11. This Headquarters may direct revision of any of these Plans if they are not considered adequate.

  c. A weekly report, divided into sections for the fields of competence of each Ministry or other agency, showing:

(1) Total number of positions whose incumbents are to be investigated.

(2) Number and type of positions investigated previously and during the current week.

(3) Number of persons removed or denied employment during the current week.

(4) Names, ranks, positions, and Questionnaire numbers of persons removed or denied employment during the current week.

16. This Headquarters will provide for inspections and investigations necessary to check compliance with this directive, and the Imperial Japanese Government will render any assistance required for the making of such inspections and investigations. Action taken by the Japanese Government with respect to removal or denial of employment and with respect to disqualification of candidates for elective office will be reviewed and may be reversed by this Headquarters.

17. Wilful falsification of or failure to make full and complete disclosures in any Questionnaire, report, or Application provided for in this directive will be punishable by the Supreme Commander for the Allied Powers as a violation of the Surrender Terms. In addition, the Imperial Japanese Government will make any provisions necessary to provide adequate punishment in Japanese courts and under Japanese law for such wilful falsification or non-disclosure and will undertake such prosecutions as may be required.

18. In addition to the general provisions of this directive covering all public offices, this Headquarters has made and may make more restrictive requirements respecting employment of certain classes of individuals at all levels in special fields.

19. All officials and subordinates of the Imperial Japanese Government affected by the terms of this order will be held personally responsible and strictly accountable for compliance with and adherence to the spirit and letter of this directive.

FOR THE SUPREME COMMANDER:

H. W. ALLEN,
Colonel, A.G.D.,
Asst Adjutant General.

Inclosures:

Appendix A - Removal and Exclusion Categories.

Appendix B - Questionnaire.

Appendix C - Questionnaire Record Card.

APPENDIX "A"

REMOVAL AND EXCLUSION CATEGORIES

A. War Criminals.

Persons arrested as suspected war criminals unless released or acquitted.

B. Career military and naval personnel; special police and officials of the war ministries.

Any person who has at any time held any of the following positions.

1. Member of:

   Board of Fleet Admirals and Field Marshals

   Supreme Military Council

   Imperial General Headquarters

   Army & Navy General Staffs

   Supreme Council for Direction of the War

2. Commissioned officer in the Imperial Japanese Regular Army or Navy or in the Special Volunteer Reserve.

3. Commissioned or non-commissioned officer, enlisted man or civilian employee who served in or with the Military Police (Kempei-Tai) or Naval police, the TOKUMU KIKAN, KAIGUN TOKUMU BU, or other special or secret intelligence or military or naval police organizations.

4. Ministry of War (unless appointed since 2 September 1945)

   Minister

   Permanent Vice-Minister

   Parliamentary Vice-Minister

   Parliamentary Councillor

   Chief Secretary

   All civilian officials of the civil service rank of Chokunin, or above, or who occupy positions normally held by persons of such rank.

5. Ministry of the Navy (unless appointed since 2

September 1945)

    Minister

    Permanent Vice-Minister

    Parliamentary Vice-Minister

    Parliamentary Councillor

    Chief Secretary

    All civilian officials of the civil service rank of Chokunin, or above, or who occupy positions normally held by persons of such rank.

C. Influential Members of Ultra-nationalistic, Terroristic or Secret Patriotic Societies.

    Any person who has at any time:

    1. Been a founder, officer, or director of; or

    2. Occupied any post of authority in; or

    3. Been an editor of any publication or organ of; or

    4. Made substantial voluntary contributions (a sum or property the value of which is large in itself or large in proportion to the means of the individual in question) to any of the organizations or their branches, subsidiaries, agencies, or affiliates (other than the organizations referred to in paragraph D below) described in the Memorandum to the Japanese Government on "Abolition of Certain Political Parties, Associations and Societies" AG 091 (4 Jan 46) GS.

D. Persons Influential in the Activities of IRRA, IRAPS, and the Political Association of Great Japan.

    1. Been a founder or national officer, a national director, national committee chairman, or a leading official of a prefectural or metropolitan subdivision of; or

    2. Been an editor of any publication or organ of:

        a. The Imperial Rule Assistance Association (Taisei Yokusankai) and any of its affiliates.

        b. The Imperial Rule Assistance Political Society (Taisei Seijikai) and any of its affiliates or agencies.

        c. The Political Association of Great Japan and any of its affiliates or agencies.

E. Officers of Financial and Development Organizations Involved in Japanese Expansions:

Any person who has at any time between 7 July 1937 and 2 September 1945, occupied any of the positions listed below:

Chairman of the Board of Directors, President, Vice-President, Director, Adviser or Auditor of any of the following or, in territory occupied by the Japanese armed forces since 7 July 1937, manager of a branch of:

South Manchurian Railway Company
Manchuria Development Company
North China Development Company
Central China Development Company
Southern Development Company
Taiwan Development Company
Manchuria Heavy Industry Development Company
Nanyo Development Company
Oriental Development Company
Wartime Finance Bank
United Funds Bank
Southern Development Bank
Overseas Funds Bank
Chosen Colonization Bank
Deutsche Bank Fuer Ostasien
Bank of Chosen
Bank of Taiwan
Bank of Manchukuo
Manchurian Development Bank
Korean Trust Company

Any other bank, development company or institution whose foremost purpose has been the financing of colonization and development activities in colonial and Japanese-occupied territory, or the financing of war production by the mobilization or control of the financial resources of colonial or Japanese-occupied territories.

F. Governors of Occupied Territories.

  1. Korea:

     Governor General
     Chief Civilian Administrator
     Members of Privy Council

358

2 民主化・非軍事化政策への対応（昭和20年10月～21年5月）

2. Formosa:
   Governor General
   Chief Civilian Administrator
   Inspector General of Police
   Director of Bureau of General Affairs
   Financial Charge d'Affaires

3. Kwantung:
   Governor General
   Chief Administrator
   Director of the Bureau of Pacification

4. South Seas:
   Governor General
   Director of South Seas Administration Office

5. Netherlands East Indies:
   Chief Military Administrator
   Chief Civil Administrator

6. Malaya:
   Chief Military Administrator
   Chief Civil Administrator
   Mayor of Singapore

7. French Indo-China:
   Governor General

8. Burma:
   Advisers to the Burmese Administration
   Chief to the Political Affairs Department of the Japanese Military Administration
   Chief of the Internal Affairs Department of the Central Administration

9. China:
   Advisers to the Nanking Puppet Government
   Ambassador

10. Manchukuo:
    Director of General Affairs Board
    Vice-Director of General Affairs Board
    Officers of the Central organization of the Concordia Society

11. Others:
    Responsible Japanese Officials controlling collabor-

ationist native governments in the Mongolian Federated Autonomous Government, the Philippine Puppet Republic, the Provisional Government of Free India, and Thailand.

G. Additional Militarists and Ultra-Nationalists

1. Any person who has denounced or contributed to the seizure of opponents of the militaristic regime.

2. Any person who has instigated or perpetrated an act of violence against opponents of the militaristic regime.

3. Any person who has played an active and predominant governmental part in the Japanese program of aggression or who by speech, writing or action has shown himself to be an active exponent of militant nationalism and aggression.

編注　本文書の「Appendix B」および「C」は省略。

114　エドワーズ財閥調査団の来日に関する総司令部発表

昭和21年1月7日　連合国最高司令官総司令部発表

付記一　昭和二十一年四月十五日、終戦連絡中央事務局経済部作成

〔四月十五日「ヘンダーソン」會談要領〕

二　昭和二十一年四月十六日、終戦連絡中央事務局経済部作成

〔ヘンダーソン氏懇談會要領（四月十六日）〕

Announcement by Public Relations Office, General Headquarters, United States Army Forces, Pacific concerning the Arrival of Edwards "Zaibatsu" Mission in Japan

January 7, 1946

An eight-man mission headed by Corwin Edwards of Chicago, appointed to make recommendations for the carrying out of the dissolution of the Zaibatsu and other Japanese business combines under directives issued by General MacArthur, has arrived in Tokyo from Washington.

The mission represents the War and State Departments jointly and will report to the two department secretaries when its work has been completed.

Its functions will include examination of the various combines, suggestions for expedients in their dissolution, analysis of facts and figures connected with the combines, and recommendations for meeting problems that might arise in dissolution plans.

Edwards, who is with the Economic Department of Northwestern University, although now a part-time employee of the State Department, emphasized that the mission's coming work will supplement the work that has already been done, and added:

"The mission expresses the interest and support which the American government feels for the policies toward the Zaibatsu already announced by SCAP, and the desire of those concerned with the matter in Washington to carry these policies through effectively."

Other members of the mission are:

James M. Henderson of San Mateo, Calif., special assistant in charge of the West Coast Offices, anti-trust division, Department of Justice.

Robert M. Hunter of Columbus, Ohio, recently transferred to the War Department from the Federal Power Commission.

William C. Dixon of Cleveland and Washington, special assistant to the Attorney General, Department of Justice.

Raymond Vernon of Philadelphia, assistant director of the Securities and Exchange Commission.

Samuel Neel of Washington, special assistant to the Attorney General, Department of Justice.

Benjamin Wallace of Washington, United States Tariff Commission.

Robert Dawkins of Washington, Federal Trade Commission.

編　注　本文書は、昭和二十四年八月、外務省特別資料課作成「日本占領及び管理重要文書集」第三巻より抜粋。

〔付記一〕

四月十五日「ヘンダーソン」會談要領（石原記）

一、澁澤同族ノ如ク財閥會社中ニ於テ比較的小ナルモノニ付テハ他ノ大ナル企業法令ノ處理トハ切離シ處理スルコト

考慮シ得、付テハ貴方ノ各財閥處理案ニ對スル極般（ママ）ノ意見ヲ承知シタシ

（當方ニテ目下概略聽取中ニシテ結論ヲ得ザル分ハ疑問ノママトシ參考迄ニ近ク提出スルコトニスベシト答ヘ置ケリ）

一、東芝、日本電氣ノ如ク部品ノ子會社ヲ擁シ相互間ニ密接ナル關聯ヲ有シ技術的ニモ子會社ノ技術向上ニ資スル形ナルモノニ付テモ子會社トノ關聯ヲ切離ス方却テ將來ノ發展ニ資スルモノト考フ、部品工場ノ如キ中小工場ノ技術ノ進步ニ付テハ「アメリカ」ノ「コンサルテイング、エンヂニア」ノ如キ制度ヲ考慮スルノ餘地アルベク又親會社トノ關係ニ付テモ契約關係及技術援助ノ方法ニテ十分目的ヲ達シ得ベシ

親會社ガ子會社ノ技術ノ進步ニ貢獻ストイフモソレハ當事者間ノ話ナルベク日本産業全体トシテハ必ズシモ然ラザルニ非ザルヤ卽チカカル財閥的ノ仕組ガ眞空管トイヘバ東芝ノミガ作レルトイフ如キ日本經濟ノ現狀ヲ來シタルモノナルベク日本ト「アメリカ」ハ近代産業ニ發足セル時期ニ大差ナシ素ヨリ資源ノ量ハ異ル故生產量ノ點ハ已

ムナシトシテ技術的發展ニ於テ今日ノ大差ヲ來シタルニハ日本ノ財閥的仕組ガ其ノ有力ナル原因ニ非ズヤ「アメリカ」ニ於テモ獨占ヲ發達セル事業ハ自由競爭ノ行ハレタル事業ノ間ニ技術的ノ進步ニ大ナル差アリ

一、財閥解体後個々ノ獨立會社ガ資產小トナルニ依リ輸入品ニ依ル競爭ニ對スル保護關稅ヲ以テ業ノ破滅ヲ救ハシムルコトハ理論トシテハ認メ難キモ「トレードアグリーメント」ノ問題トシテ考慮スルコト可能ナルヤモ知レズ、何レニセヨ自分ノ所管外ノコト故ハツキリシタコトハ申シ難シ

一、第二會社ノ設立案ニ關聯シ舊債務ヲソノママ舊會社ニ殘ツト完全ナル解決方法アルベキモ目下ノ處未定ナル事多キ爲カカル整理事項ハ不取敢ソノママトシ新會社ニ依ル民需增産ノ急ニ赴カザルヲ得ザル次第ナリト答ヘタルニ對シ國內賠償ニ對シ如何ナル補償ヲ爲スヤハ日本政府ノ問題ナルモ戰時中大イニ儲ケタル航空機工場ノ如キガ喪失資產ニ對シ完全ナル補償ヲ得ル如キコトアラバ聊カ

2　民主化・非軍事化政策への対応（昭和20年10月～21年5月）

可笑シカラズヤ又在外資産ノ損ト考ヘラルベク全部ニ付テハ或ハ疑問アルベキモ補償スベキ筋合ニ非ザル性質ノモノナルニ非ズヤ、素ヨリ之個人ノ意見ナルモカカル補償ガ齎ス「インフレ」的効果モ考ヘサル可ラズ、尚舊會社ニ於テ舊債務ノ整理ヲ爲ス場合モ半年カセイゼイ一年位ノ間ニ整理ノ片ヲツケルコト肝要ナリト思フ

（付記二）
ヘンダーソン氏懇談會要領（四月十六日）

日本側出席者
終連　小野、秋元、朝海、石原
大藏　木内
商工　山本、田中

一、日本經濟ノ將來ノ姿ニ付自分ハ正確ニ申シ上グベキ位置ニナク又國際經濟中ニ日本ノ占ムル地位ニ付テモ然リ、只方向ハ國民ノ所得ヲモツト廣汎ニ分布シ生活程度ヲ高メ國内ノ市場ヲ擴大スルノ要アルベシ素ヨリ輸入ノ必要ハ當然ニシテ此爲輸出ヲ行フノ要アルベク只戰前ノ如ク巨大ナル輸出ヲ行ヒテ屑鐵其ノ他ノ軍需品ヲ輸入スルトイフガ如キ國内軍備充足ノ爲ノ貿易依存ハ不可ナリ

社會主義的國家統制ノ形態ヲ將來ノ日本經濟ノ型トシテ考フルコトガ財閥ノ解體方針ニ如何ナル關係ヲ有スルヤ素ヨリ國家ガ統制ヲ行フ場合モ數個ノ巨大經營ニ集中サレアルコトガ數百ノ小單位ガ存スル場合ヨリモ統制上ノ便ポテンシヤリティーノ點ヨリシテ巨大支配ノ存在ハ否定本ノ戰爭可能性排除ノ點ヨリシテ巨大支配ノ存在ハ否定サルコトトナル

日本ノ將來ノ社會主義的國家統制ノ必要ヲ資源ノ不足ヨリ結論セントスルコトハ諒解ニ難キトコロナリカカル方向ガ日本ノ爲ニ必要ナリヤ否ヤハ判ラザルモ自分トシテハ贊成シ難シ

イギリスノ勞働黨下ノ國營方向ヨリシテ日本經濟將來ノ方向モ同樣ナラザル可ラズトノ所論ニ對シテハイギリスノ經濟（數十億ノ借金ヲアメリカヨリセザレバ成立タザル）ハ日本ノ範トスルベキモノニ非ズト思フ

安定ヲ恢復スル時期迄國家ノ統制ガ必要ナルコトハ勿論

之ヲ認メザルヲ得ズ

安定後ニ於テ自由競爭下ノ日本ノ不足經濟ニ於テ先ヅ充足サルベキ必要民需品ノ生產ノ確保ニ付テハ大ナル個人的消費購賣力ヲ殘サザル工夫ヲナサバ別ニ統制ハナクトモ之ヲ確保シ得ベシ一定ノ收入ナラバ當然贅澤品ヲ買フコトハナラズ最低限度生活ニ必要ナル商品ニ購賣力ガ向フベク贅澤品ハ買手ヲ發見スルニ困難ナルベシ之ニハ租稅制度ヲ高額所得ニ對シ重課スルコトニ依リ右ノ所得ノ調整ハ可能ナラズヤ

二、產業及銀行ニ許サルベキ一定ノ大イサノ標準ハ之ヲ與フルコト困難ナルニ非サルカ蓋シ一會社カソレ程大ナル割合ヲ占メサル場合ニモ他ノ競爭業者群小ナル場合ハ尙支配力ヲ振フコトヲ得ベク個人ノ產業全體ノ事情ヨリ判斷セラルルコトヲ要スレバナリ然ラバ如何ナル方法ニ依リ之ヲ定ムルカハ先ヅ「インスペクション」ニ依リ實情ヲ審査スルノ要アルベク「コート」ニ於テ右ノ機能ヲ果スベキヤゲーション、ユミション」ニ思フ

日本ハ政府勸獎ノ下ニ銀行ノ合併ヲ爲シ過ギタルニ非ズ

ヤ銀行ノ巨大ナルコトハ必スシモ銀行ノ能率或ハ預金者ノ保護ノ見地ヨリ說明スルコトヲ得ズ却テ逆トナル可能性アリ、巨大ナル銀行ハ槪ネスモールローンニ對シ不熱心ナル場合多シ

三、ヴァーティカルスノギリートシテ如何ナルモノヲ適法トスルヤ一義的ニ決定スルコトハ困難ナリ其ノ各分野ニ於ケル具體的行動ニ依リ之ヲ律スベクアメリカアルミニウム會社ノ場合ニ於テモ然ルトコロニ之ノ特許權ヨリ出發シテ一應適法ニ形成サルルコトトナリ集中モ其ノ後ノ實情ニ於テ適法トセラルルコトニナリ

今ヤ政府ノ戰時中建設セルアルミ工場ヲ獨立企業者ニ處分スルコトニ依リ此ノ獨占ヲ打破スルコトヲ考ヘ居ルニ次第ナリ

アメリカニ於テカイザーガウィローラン以下ノ自動車ノ部品工場ガフォード、G、Mト特別ノ關係ナク發達シアリタルガ爲ニシテ卽チカイザーハ直チニ自由競爭ノベーシスニ於テ部品工場ヨリ供給ヲ受ケ得タルニ依ルモノナリ

カカル形態ガ望マシキモノナリト云フ

2 民主化・非軍事化政策への対応（昭和20年10月～21年5月）

四、自然獨占ヲ生ズルコトガ直ニ止ムナキ場合ハ日本ニ具體的ニ如何ナル例ガ存スルヤ知レザルモカカル場合ハ寧ロ國營トナスコトガ可ナラズヤ

危險分散ノ爲ノ多角經營トイフコトハ諒解シ難シ單一經營ノ爲ニ破產ヲナスコトアリトスルモ其ガ直チニ國民經濟ノ爲ニ救ヒ難キ損失ナリトハ考ヘラレヌ會社ハ破產ヲナスモ設備ハ依然存在シ此ノ設備ヲ適當ニ下ゲラレタル價格ニテ讓受ケ新タニ其ノ事業ヲ再開スルコトニ依リ國民經濟ハ果シテ若干不利益ヲ蒙ルモノナリヤ、個人ノ投資家ハ會社ノ株式保有トイフクッションヲ通ジ危險ヲ間接化シアル譯ナリ日本ニ於テハ一部門ニ於ケル投資對象ノ小ナルコトノ爲ニ一部ニ對シ適當ナル範圍ノ投資ヲナシタル後其ノ以上ノ蓄積ガ當然他ノ部門ニ向ケラルルコトトナル點ニ付テハ其ハ金融機關其ノ他投資ノ專門家ノアルコト故銀行ニ金ヲ預ケルトカインヴェストナル(ママ)トラストノ如キモノニ投資スレバ足ルニ非ズヤ

「アメリカ」ニ於テ各都市ノ衛生其他ノ文化施設ノ狀態ヲ調查シタルコトアリ其時大都市ニ比シ中小都市ノ方カ優レタ狀態ニ在リタルコトヲ發見セリ巨大ナルモノカヨ

キモノニ非ズト考フ

五、制限會社ノ指令ノ意圖ハ「財閥及其ノ子會社ガ其ノ解體又ハ再編成前ニ「財產ノ不當ナル處分ヲ防止ス
ル」(during)」コトニ在リトイフ原則ハ「解體ニハ再編成ノ期間中ニ(before)資產ノ不當ナル處分ハ當時ノ新聞發表文等ヲ見タルモ右ノ如シ

六、財閥子會社ノ再編成ハ持株ノ解放ノ外企業ノ一部ヲ他ニ賣却又ハ數個ノ獨立會社ニ再編成セラルルコトヲ要スル場合アリ

七、制限會社ガ其ノ拘束ヲ解カルルニハ持株ヲ整理委員會ニ賣却スル外尙必要ナル要件トシテ
(一)「マネージメント」ガ變更セラルルコト
(二)軍國的、侵略的傾向ノアル人物ガ役員ニ殘存セヌコト等ガ數ヘラルベシ

昭和21年1月11日　連合国最高司令官総司令部より日本政府宛

ポツダム宣言受諾から降伏文書署名までの間の軍需物資処分に関し情報提供方指令

GENERAL HEADQUARTERS
SUPREME COMMANDER FOR THE ALLIED POWERS

11 January 1946

AG 386.3 (11 Jan 46) GD
SCAPIN 582

MEMORANDUM FOR: IMPERIAL JAPANESE GOVERNMENT.

THROUGH: Central Liaison Office, Tokyo.

SUBJECT: Disposition of Equipment and Supplies of the Japanese Armed Forces Between the Dates of 14 August 1945 and 2 September 1945.

1. Evidence has come to the attention of this Headquarters indicating that a large scale attempt to dispose of the supplies and equipment of the Japanese Armed Forces was made between the dates of 14 August 1945 and 2 September 1945. Actions such as the above are not considered to fall within the spirit of the Potsdam Declaration.

2. You will therefore furnish this Headquarters the following information:

a. A complete list of all equipment, supplies and materials of the Japanese Armed Forces which in any way were transferred from possession of the Japanese Armed Forces between the dates of 14 August 1945 and 2 September 1945. Information will also be included to show the location of the supplies and equipment at the time of transfer, their present location if known and the persons or agencies receiving them.

b. A complete file of English translations of all orders concerning disposition of property of the Japanese Armed Forces which were issued between the dates of 14 August 1945 and 2 September 1945 inclusive.

c. A list of the names of the officials of the Imperial Japanese Government or any agencies thereof who were responsible for the promulgation of the orders mentioned in paragraph 2b above.

3. A preliminary report will be forwarded to this Headquarters within 10 days from the date of receipt of this directive. A final complete report will be submitted on or before 10 February 1946.

FOR THE SUPREME COMMANDER:

2 民主化・非軍事化政策への対応(昭和20年10月〜21年5月)

116 三月十五日以降総選挙の実施を許可する旨の指令

昭和21年1月12日　連合国最高司令官総司令部より日本政府宛

GENERAL HEADQUARTERS
SUPREME COMMANDER FOR THE ALLIED POWERS

12 January 1946

AG 014.35 (12 Jan 46) GS
SCAPIN 584

MEMORANDUM FOR: IMPERIAL JAPANESE GOVERNMENT.
THROUGH: Central Liaison Office, Tokyo.
SUBJECT: Election.

1. You are hereby authorized to hold a general election of members of the House of Representatives, fixing the date of election not earlier than 15 March 1946.

2. It is of greatest importance that every step possible be taken looking toward a free and untrammeled expression of the people's will in this election. To such end you will give fullest publicity to the penal provisions of the law, and will take such steps as may be necessary to ensure their vigorous enforcement, to preserve inviolate the secrecy of the ballot, and to further such other safeguards as may from time to time be communicated to you by the Supreme Commander.

FOR THE SUPREME COMMANDER:

H. W. ALLEN.
Colonel, A.G.D.,
Asst. Adjutant General.

117 日本警察の武装に関する指令

昭和21年1月16日　連合国最高司令官総司令部より日本政府宛

GENERAL HEADQUARTERS
SUPREME COMMANDER FOR THE ALLIED POWERS

16 January 1946

AG 014.12 (16 Jan 46) GC
SCAPIN 605

MEMORANDUM FOR: IMPERIAL JAPANESE GOVERNMENT.

THROUGH: Central Liaison Office, Tokyo.

SUBJECT: Armament of Police Forces in Japan.

1. Information received at this Headquarters indicates that the Japanese Government has refrained from arming the Civil Police due to a misunderstanding of the disarmament directives. Directives issued by this Headquarters have not prohibited the arming of Japanese Civil Police with pistols where necessary nor has such prohibition been the intention of this Headquarters at any time.

2. The Imperial Japanese Government is hereby advised that the Japanese Civil Police are authorized to carry pistols in the performance of their duties, as deemed necessary by the Imperial Japanese Government, subject to the provision that the total number of pistols available to the Japanese Civil Police shall not exceed the strength of the Japanese Civil Police Force authorized by this Headquarters.

3. It is directed that all firearms, other than pistols authorized in accordance with the foregoing, currently in the hands of the Japanese Civil Police Force be delivered to United States Army Occupation Forces on or before 1 March 1946 in accordance with established disarmament procedures.

4. The Imperial Japanese Government is authorized to maintain a supply of 100 rounds of ammunition for each pistol authorized the Japanese Civil Police. Ammunition in excess of this amount will be turned over to United States Army Occupation Forces. Requests for resupply of ammunition may be submitted by police chiefs through local Occupation Force Commanders, as necessary.

FOR THE SUPREME COMMANDER:

H. W. ALLEN.

Colonel, A.G.D.,

Asst. Adjutant General.

昭和21年1月16日　連合国最高司令官総司令部より日本政府宛

警備隊の廃止に関する指令

GENERAL HEADQUARTERS
SUPREME COMMANDER FOR THE ALLIED POWERS

16 January 1946

AG 091.1 (16 Jan 46) GC
SCAPIN 606
MEMORANDUM FOR: IMPERIAL JAPANESE GOVERNMENT.
THROUGH: Central Liaison Office, Tokyo.
SUBJECT: Abolition of Keibei Tai.(編注)

The Imperial Japanese Government will take the necessary action to abolish and disband the Keibei Tai and all other organizations or mobile forces organized to augment the Japanese Civil Police Force. All weapons and ammunition currently in the hands of the Keibei Tai or similar organizations disbanded, will, with the exception of pistols and ammunition required for the Japanese Civil Police Force, be delivered to the United States Army Occupation Forces on or before 1 March 1946 in accordance with established disarmament procedures. This action is not intended to affect the over-all authorized strength of the Japanese Civil Police Force, which was established at a total of 93,935 as a result of the action directed by memorandum, this Headquarters, 11 October 1945, to the Imperial Japanese Government, subject: "Japanese Government Proposal to Increase Domestic Police Force."

FOR THE SUPREME COMMANDER:

H. W. ALLEN.
Colonel, A.G.D.,
Asst. Adjutant General.

編 注 本文書の「Keibei」は原文のままとした。

昭和21年1月16日 連合国最高司令官総司令部より
日本政府宛

119

地方行政予算に関する指令

GENERAL HEADQUARTERS
SUPREME COMMANDER FOR THE ALLIED POWERS
APO 500

16 January 1946

AG 123 (16 Jan 46) ESS/FI

SCAPIN 607
MEMORANDUM FOR: IMPERIAL JAPANESE GOVERNMENT.
THROUGH: Central Liaison Office, Tokyo.
SUBJECT: Local Finances.

1. Reference is made to the memorandum from the Ministry of Finance dated 8 December 1945 (L.O. 57) and attached memorandum from the Ministry of Home Affairs, with reference to the finances of Prefectures, Cities, Towns and Villages.

2. In the memorandum for the Imperial Japanese Government on the subject of Elimination of War Profits and Reorganization of National Finances, AG 121.7 (24 Nov 45) ESS/FI, the words, "Imperial Japanese Government, its subdivisions," include local governments, that is, the governments of prefectures, cities, towns, and villages. This definition applies to the use of the quoted words in paragraph 8 and wherever else they occur in the above mentioned memorandum.

3. This Headquarters disapproves the issuance of bonds in the total amount of ¥1,500,000,000 as requested. The issuance of bonds by local governments in the amounts and for the purposes shown below is approved:

Education	¥4,200,000
Sanitation	14,600,000
Encouragement of Industry	33,500,000
Public works (calamities)	63,600,000
Public works (ordinary)	77,000,000
Electricity and Gas	6,500,000
Measures to Prevent Property Damage	350,000,000
Rehabilitation Expenses	127,500,000
Revenue Deficits	111,400,000
All others	27,360,000
	¥815,660,000

The approval herewith applies to the borrowings necessary on the part of local governments to cover payments which have already been made by them or with respect to which they are legally committed. Such borrowing as may be necessary to cover local government requirements to the end of the fiscal year will be considered for approval upon submission of revised estimates and satisfactory evidence that all possible retrenchment has been made and

2 民主化・非軍事化政策への対応(昭和20年10月～21年5月)

all practicable economies have been effected.

4. Approval is granted for the flotation of loans to be paid from taxation or other revenues to be received in the same fiscal year or which are to be paid from the proceeds of bonds or other securities, the issuance of which has been permitted by this Headquarters.

5. The normal lending operations of public pawnshops may be continued.

6. Municipal or prefectural lending under the Officials' Mutual Relief System may be continued.

7. Approval is granted to direct lending by local governments, where the purpose is to promote or improve the security or standard of living or economic development within the community concerned.

8. Investments of local government funds or other assets in income bearing securities or profit making enterprises are approved, provided they are made in accordance with existing law.

9. Subsidies, tax exemptions, tax allotments, rebates or any similar benefits may be granted by local governments under existing or future laws provided they are consistent in all respects with the national government program.

10. Local government properties may be sold provided only that if the sale or transfer is to anyone except another governmental entity, the fair market value at the time of sale must be received.

11. This memorandum constitutes the authorization of this Headquarters required by paragraph 8 of the memorandum of 24 November 1945 referred to above. It should be clearly understood, however, that any payments, borrowing, lending, investment, or other measures taken pursuant to this authorization must be in conformity with paragraphs 4, 5, and 7 of the memorandum of 24 November 1945, as well as the applicable provisions of any other memorandums now or hereafter issued by this Headquarters. No financial measures shall be taken by local governments which are denied to the National Government.

12. Direct communication between the Ministry of Finance and interested Staff Sections of this Headquarters is hereby authorized to implement this memorandum.

120

政府借入金および歳出削減に関する指令

昭和21年1月21日 連合国最高司令官総司令部より日本政府宛

FOR THE SUPREME COMMANDER:

H. W. ALLEN.
Colonel, A.G.D.,
Asst. Adjutant General.

GENERAL HEADQUARTERS
SUPREME COMMANDER FOR THE ALLIED POWERS
APO 500

21 January 1946

AG 121 (21 Jan 46) ESS/FI
SCAPIN 635

MEMORANDUM FOR: IMPERIAL JAPANESE GOVERNMENT.

THROUGH: Central Liaison Office, Tokyo.

SUBJECT: Reduction of Government Borrowing and Expenditures.

1. Reference is made to memorandum this Headquarters, file AG 121.7 (24 Nov 45) ESS/FI, dated 24 November 1945, subject: "Elimination of War Profits and Reorganization of National Finances", and particularly to the provisions of paragraph 8 thereof which prohibited the Imperial Japanese Government, its sub-divisions, agencies or instrumentalities from issuing bonds or obtaining credit in any form except as authorized by this Headquarters.

2. It is noted that requests for approval of government borrowing, submitted in accordance with reference memorandum, propose a continuance of government expenditures at a high rate and the financing of the resulting deficit principally by sale of government bonds to the Bank of Japan, with resultant expansion of bank credit. To avoid the inflationary effect of such a policy, the Imperial Japanese Government will henceforth adhere to the following fiscal principles:

a. Government expenditures will be reduced to the absolute minimum essential to carry on necessary functions of government.

b. Government deficits will be financed to the fullest

372

extent possible by borrowing from the current savings of the people through the agencies already existing for the collection of such savings.

　c. Recourse to the resources of the ordinary banks and the Bank of Japan for financing deficits of the Imperial Japanese Government and its agencies or instrumentalities will be made only as a last resort. This restriction will not apply to the discount or rediscount of short-term government instruments, such as food certificates, issued directly in payment for goods or services.

　3. The provisions of paragraph 2 above will apply to all government borrowing authorized by this Headquarters since 24 November 1945, including, but not limited to, those authorized by the following memoranda:

　　a. AG 110.01 (12 Dec 45) ESS/FI, dated 12 December 1945, subject: "Supplementary Budgets 1 and 2 for Fiscal Year 1945–46".

　　b. AG 130 (13 Dec 45) ESS/FI, dated 13 December 1945, subject: "Government Borrowing".

　4. Effective immediately, the practice of financing the current deficit of the Imperial Japanese Government by overdraft on the government account with the Bank of Japan will cease. Upon receipt of this memorandum, a report of the approximate amount of such overdraft will be furnished this Headquarters. Thereafter that amount will not be increased except for payments already in process by branches and agencies of the Bank of Japan at the time of receipt of this memorandum. As soon as practicable thereafter, a final report will be submitted, showing the amount of the overdraft after all payments now in process have been completed. Application for funding of such amount by the issue of government bonds may then be submitted to this Headquarters.

　5. a. No further borrowing for, nor payments from, the Special Account for War Expenses will be made, except those already in process as indicated in paragraph 4 above. Future payments of the types which have heretofore been made from the Special Account for War Expenses and which have not been prohibited by this Headquarters and are not required to be made into blocked accounts, may be made from the General Account. Before any such payments are made, however, a detailed estimate of the

amount needed for the remainder of the fiscal year 1945–46 will be submitted to this Headquarters. Revenues which have heretofore accrued to the Special Account for War Expenses will hereafter be credited to the General Account.

b. Final settlement of the Special Account for War Expenses, including adjustment of records to conform with the provisions of paragraph 8 below, will be effected as rapidly as possible. A detailed report will be submitted to this Headquarters showing the final status of the account.

6. For the period from 1 January 1946 through 31 March 1946, the total of all payments from the General Account, including transfers to Special Accounts but not including payments authorized by paragraph 5a above, will not exceed an average of ¥2,000,000,000 per month without prior authorization by this Headquarters. Any request for such authorization will include a detailed estimate of total General Account payments for the remainder of the fiscal year, showing the amount needed for each major purpose. Immediate steps will be taken to effect the necessary economies.

7. a. Permission is hereby granted the Imperial Japanese Government and its agencies and instrumentalities to borrow for the following purposes without specific authorization from this Headquarters in each case:

(1) Working capital for government enterprises and activities which are completely self-sustaining from their own sources of income, exclusive of government grants or subsidies in any form.

(2) Short-term refinancing of debts presently outstanding.

(3) Sales of savings debentures and similar securities directly to the public, where the total of any one issue does not exceed ¥50,000,000.

b. The provisions of paragraph 2 will apply to loans made under the authority of this paragraph.

c. A report of loans made under authority of this paragraph will be included in the weekly report of the Minister of Finance.

8. a. A new Special Account will be created for all pay-

ments made by the Imperial Japanese Government under authority of paragraph 4 of Memorandum this Headquarters, file AG 121.7 (24 Nov 45) ESS/FI, dated 24 November 1945, subject: "Elimination of War Profits and Reorganization of National Finances". The unreleased balance of all government payments heretofore made into blocked accounts will be transferred to the new Special Account from the budget accounts from which they were originally paid.

　　b. Creation of government debt equal in amount to the total payments hereafter made from the new account is hereby authorized. Government debt for payments previously made into blocked accounts will be transferred to the new Special Account from the budget accounts where it has previously been carried. The debt authorized by this sub-paragraph will bear no interest.

　　c. Sums needed for actual payments or withdrawals from blocked accounts will be transferred from the General Account.

　9. The Imperial Japanese Government will submit to this Headquarters, as soon as practicable, a new government borrowing program for the remainder of the fiscal year 1945–46, based on the provisions of this memorandum. Borrowing authorized by paragraphs 7 and 8 above need not be included, except that an estimate of the total proceeds of sales under paragraph 7c is desired.

　10. The principles set forth in the preceding paragraphs will be followed in formulating the original and supplementary budgets for the fiscal year 1946–47, except that the provisions of paragraph 6 will not apply to the new fiscal year.

　11. Direct communication between the Ministry of Finance and interested Staff Sections of this Headquarters is hereby authorized to implement this memorandum.

FOR THE SUPREME COMMANDER:

H. W. ALLEN,
Colonel, A.G.D.,
Asst. Adjutant General.

121　昭和21年1月21日　連合国最高司令官総司令部より　日本政府宛

政府借入金に関する日本側承認要請への回答

GENERAL HEADQUARTERS
SUPREME COMMANDER FOR THE ALLIED POWERS
APO 500
21 January 1946

AG 130 (21 Jan 46) ESS/FI

SCAPIN 637

MEMORANDUM FOR: IMPERIAL JAPANESE GOVERNMENT.

THROUGH: Central Liaison Office, Tokyo.

SUBJECT: Government Borrowing

1. Reference is made to the following documents:

　a. Memorandum of the Minister of Finance, (LOF 21), dated 28 November 1945, subject: "Government Loans", requesting approval of borrowing by the Imperial Japanese Government to the extent of ￥9,235,000,000, for the month of November, 1945.

　b. Memorandum of the Minister of Finance, (LOF 117), dated 26 December 1945, subject: "Request for Approval of Government Loans", requesting similar approval in the amount of ￥9,358,000,000 for the month of December, 1945.

　c. Memorandum this Headquarters, file AG 121 (21 Jan 46) ESS/FI, dated 21 January, 1946, subject: "Reduction of Government Borrowing and Expenditures", which sets forth a new policy to be followed hereafter with respect to government expenditures and the financing of government deficits.

2. a. The loans proposed in paragraphs 1 (a) and 1 (e) of LOF 21 and paragraph 1a of LOF 117 are not approved. These loans will be reconsidered and included, to the extent still deemed necessary, in the program required by paragraph 9 of reference 1c above.

　b. No action will be taken on the request made in paragraph 1 (b) of LOF 21 until a full explanation is submitted.

　c. The loans proposed by paragraphs 1 (c) and 1 (d) of LOF 21 and paragraph 1b (1) of LOF 117 were authorized by memorandum from this Headquarters, file AG 130 (13 Dec 45) ESS/FI, dated 13 December 1945, subject: "Government Borrowing".

　d. The loan proposed by paragraph 1b (2) of LOF 117 is hereby authorized in accordance with paragraph 7a (2) of refer-

376

ence 1c above.

e. The loans proposed by paragraphs 1 (f) of LOF 21 and 1c of LOF 117 are hereby authorized in accordance with paragraph 8b of reference 1c above.

f. The loans proposed by paragraph 1d of LOF 117 will be reconsidered and included, to the extent still deemed necessary, in the program required by paragraph 9 of reference 1c above.

FOR THE SUPREME COMMANDER:

H. W. ALLEN,
Colonel, A.G.D.,
Asst. Adjutant General.

---

122 公娼制度の廃止に関する指令

昭和21年1月21日　連合国最高司令官総司令部より　日本政府宛

AG 726.7 (21 Jan 46) PH

SUPREME COMMANDER FOR THE ALLIED POWERS

GENERAL HEADQUARTERS

21 January 1946

SCAPIN 642

MEMORANDUM FOR: IMPERIAL JAPANESE GOVERNMENT.

THROUGH: CENTRAL LIAISON OFFICE, TOKYO.

SUBJECT: Abolition of Licensed Prostitution in Japan.

1. The maintenance of licensed prostitution in Japan is in contravention of the ideals of democracy and inconsistent with the development of individual freedom throughout the nation.

2. The Imperial Japanese Government is directed to forthwith abrogate and annul all laws, ordinances and other enactments which directly or indirectly authorize or permit the existence of licensed prostitution in Japan, and to nullify all contracts and agreements which have for their object the binding or committing, directly or indirectly, of any woman to the practice of prostitution.

3. English translations of the enactments issued in compliance with this Memorandum will be submitted in duplicate to this Headquarters immediately upon their final preparation and prior to publication.

FOR THE SUPREME COMMANDER:

H. W. ALLEN,

Colonel, A.G.D.,
Asst. Adjutant General.

123

昭和21年1月25日　終戦連絡中央事務局作成

「食糧輸入問題ノ現段階、見透シ及對策」

食糧輸入問題ノ現段階、見透シ及對策

一九四六、一、二五　CLO

目次

第一、食糧輸入問題ノ現段階、見透及對策

第二、GHQ、CLO間ノ手續キ關係ノ經緯

第三、華府方面ノ情勢

第四、GHQノ雰圍氣

第五、各期待國別ノ情況

　(一) 朝鮮
　(二) 臺灣
　(三) 佛印
　(四) 「シャム」
　(五) 滿洲
　(六) 合衆國其ノ他

第五、概括的結論及見透シ

第六、對策
　(一) 總論
　(二) 國內食糧資源ノ效率的活用
　(三) 食糧輸入ノ徹底的追進

食糧輸入問題ノ現段階、見透シ及對策

(二一、一、二五　CLO)

第一、GHQ、CLO間ノ手續キ關係ノ經緯

(一) 終戰直後GHQヨリノ慫慂モアリ昨年九月二十一日附差當リ一〇―一二月ニ輪入ヲ希望スル食糧物資ニ付他ノ棉花、石油、石炭、鐵鑛石等ト併セ左ノ輸入要請數字ヲ提出

　　穀　類　　　　二五〇千噸
　　砂　糖　　　　一〇〇千噸
　　油料子實　　　　三〇千噸
　　(鹽　　　　　二七〇千噸)

之ガ見返リトシテハ差當リノ輸出可能物資トシテ左ノ

2　民主化・非軍事化政策への対応（昭和20年10月～21年5月）

數字ヲ提示

生　糸　　四六千俵　　羽二重　　五、〇〇〇千米

其ノ他茶、賣藥等若干量

(二) 右ニ基キ「クレーマー」ヨリ對日船腹支援困難ノ指摘ト共ニ先ヅ支拂手段ノ最少限ノ確立ヲ要スベキ旨ヲ指示セラレ輸入物資ハ之ガ支拂手段ノ確立ヲ要スルコト明瞭トナリタルヲ以テ更ニ一〇月一日附特ニ緊急ヲ要スル必需物資ノ輸入要請ヲ左ノ通リ提出

米　　　　一〇〇千噸（佛印ヨリ）
小　麥　　一〇〇千噸（合衆國ヨリ）
（鹽）　　一〇〇千噸）（石油　約一二〇竏）

之ガ見返リ物資ニ付テハ前回提示ノ數量ニ依リ生糸、羽二重ニ止ムルト共ニ支拂決濟方法ニ關シ爲替消算勘定ノ設定、一時的借越ノ容認等ノ我方要望ヲ併セ申入ル

(三) 右數次ノ折衝ノ結論トシテGHQヨリ正式覺書ヲ以テ一〇月九日附國民生活必需物資（imports being vital to the maintenance of a minimum standard of living for the civilian population）輸入許可ニ關スル基本方針ノ指示ト共

ニ右生活必需物資輸入ニ先行スベキ見返リ物資ノ輸出確保ニ關スル諸種ノ國內的手段及輸入物資ノ一元的受入配給ニ關スル責任機關ノ確立並ニGHQノ輿ヘタル制約ノ下ニ其ノ可能性ヲ綜合的ニ說明スル一九四六年度ノ輸出入計畫ノ提出等ヲ指示

一〇月一〇日附各輸入物資ノ正式輸入許可申請ノ際ハ夫々其ノ消費、輸入及在庫實績、國內生產見込、用途、國內配給方法等詳細ヲ極メタル說明ヲ具備スベキ旨ヲ指示

(四) 右一〇月九日附覺書ニ基キ先ツ一一月九日附一九四六食糧年度我國食糧計畫（第二回ノ政府發表）一九四五年度米收穫推定數字四二、九七〇千石ヲ基礎數字トシテ採用シ一九四六食糧年度中三、〇〇〇千屯ノ食糧輸入ヲ見込ミタル場合辛ウジテ現行一般市民配給量二、九七瓦基準ヲ維持スルコトヲ得而モ此ノ場合國內米ノ政府買入ハ概ネ此ノ三月頃迄ニ計畫ノフルパーセント達成ヲ操作上ノ前提條件トセルモノ、今本食糧計畫中ニ提示セル數字ニ基キ輸入量ノ多寡ト國民ノ一人一日當リ平均的ニ攝取スルコトトナル綜合的ノ全食糧熱量ト

ノ相關係ヲ圖表示スレバ別紙圖表ノ如シ)ヲ提出、尚

一九四六曆年度ニ依ル食糧關係輸入要請數字ハ左ノ如シ

穀類　三、三九〇千屯(內三九〇千屯ハ一九四六年

　　　　一一―一二月期間ニ付期待

　　　　セラルモノ)

油脂　　四〇千屯

砂糖　　二〇〇千屯

コプラ　四三、四千屯　(飼料　四〇千屯

（燐鑛石　三三〇千屯）　（鹽一、〇五〇千屯）

次イデ一一月一五日附食糧關係以外ノ輸入要請物資棉花、石油、石炭、鐵鑛石、非鐵金屬ニ付書類ヲ提出而シテ右全輸入要請物資見込價額合計ハ併セテ提出セル左ノ如キ要請傭船見込料ヲ含メテ一應二、四〇六、三七〇千圓ト概定セラレタリ

一九四六年一―三月　　三三〇千重量屯

　〃　　　　四―六月　　六七〇〃

　〃　　　　七―九月　　六七〇〃

ノ基礎トスルトキハ

在庫品　　　　　　　　　　四七七、九六七千圓

一九四六年上期仕上リ品　　九五九、〇三〇千圓

　〃　　下期　〃　　　　一、五〇五、五二二〃

　　　總　計　　　　　　　二、九四二、五二一〃

ト算定セラレタル處輸入品見積リ價額ハ低キニ失スル虞レアルヲ以テ總價額ノ二〇%ヲ加算シ輸出品ニ付テハ生産ノ不振、先方需要ニ關スル見込違ヒ等ノ虞レアルヲ以テ總價額ノ三〇%ヲ差引キ安全率ヲ見タルバランスヲ推定シ

輸入　　二、八八七、六四四千圓

輸出　　二、〇五九、七六五〃

差引　　　　八二七、八七九〃

ノ支拂超過ヲ見込ム結論ヲ妥當トシ之ヲ提示セルヲ以テ之ガ補塡トシテハ金銀ダイアモンドヲ支拂手段ニ充當スルコト並ニ決濟方法上一時的借越ノ容認方要請セリ

而シテ右貿易計畫ハ計畫中ニ織込ミタル輸出産業用原材料トシテ國內資源又ハ國內在庫ノミナラズ輸入要請各物資ノ價額見込ハ一應當時ノ國內適正價格ヲ見積リ

2　民主化・非軍事化政策への対応（昭和20年10月～21年5月）

物資ノ使用ヲモ豫定セル相互依存因果關係ヲ包藏スルモノナリ

尚右十月九日附覺書ニ基クGHQノ指令内容ハ未ダ必ズシモ全部的ニ充足セラレ居ラズ貿易廳ハ形式的ニ開廳セラレタルモ實務ノ活潑ナル開始ヲ見ルニ至ラザルノミナラズ我方ニ於テ所謂貿易ノ「エーヂエンシイ」ノ解釋ニ付GHQ當局ノ眞意捕捉ヲ誤リタル嫌ヒアリテ其ノ眞意ニ付GHQ當局ノ眞意ニ副フ爲ニハ更ニ今一度貿易廳改組ノ要アリト認メラルルト共ニ（從テ輸出入決濟手段ニ關スル機構モ未解決）指令中ニ要求セラレタル輸出資源ノ國内保全方ニ關スル計畫ニ付テモ未ダ成案ヲ得ルニ至ラサルモノナリ

(五) 右一〇月一〇日附覺書指令ノ説明様式ニ則ル各輸入要請物資毎ノ正式輸入許可申請書ハ一二月八日附穀類、油脂、「コプラ」、燐鑛石、砂糖、棉花、鹽ニ付之ヲ提出シ一二月二六日附飼料、石油ニ付之ヲ提出セリ（其ノ他ノ物資ニ付テハ未提出）

(六) 其ノ後GHQ係官ヨリ右我方ノ提出セル貿易計畫ハ輸入品價額ヲFOBヲ以テ算出シアルモ之ヲCIFニ訂正スヘキ旨並ニ輸出品價額算定基礎ノ説明殊ニ一九三七年價格トノ比較表提示ヲ求メ來リタルヲ以テ夫々解答作成ノ上前者ハ一二月一八日附後者ハ一二月二四日附GHQ當局係官ニ之ヲ手交

(七) 既提出貿易計畫ノ輸出實施計畫トシテ一九四六年一―三月ニ於ケル輸出先別輸出可能物資表ヲ作成一二月二四日附GHQ當局係官ニ手交（本表ニ付テハ更ニ分推敲檢討ノ要アリテ目下再檢討中）

(八) 以上ハGHQニ對シ一九四六食糧年度中三、〇〇〇千屯ノ食糧輸入ヲ要請セル大筋ノ手續進行ノ經緯ナルモ我方トシテハ右以外ニ凡有契機ヲ逃サス之ヲ捕ヘ若干ニテモ食糧輸入ヲ實現セシムル手懸リトスノ要アリト思料シ別途正式ニ左ノ如キ食糧輸入要請書類ヲGHQニ對シ提出シアリ

(イ) 一一月二九日附及一二月一四日附北海道引揚朝鮮人復航船腹ノ利用ヲ提唱スル等ノ手懸リニ依リ石炭生產確保ノ爲ノ食糧増配用タルコトヲ名目トシ夫々一〇千屯、一〇〇千石ノ朝鮮米輸入許可方ヲ申請

(ロ) 一二月一四日附戰時中ヨリ懸案ノ「シヤム」向ケ見

返リ輸出品ノ仕上リ「リスト」提出ニ引懸ケ一、九四六年一──三月中ニ少クトモ四〇千屯以上ノ「シャム」米ノ輸入許可方申請
（中略）

第五、概括的結論及見透シ

要之「ポツダム」宣言ニ基ク「ハードピースポリシイ」ノ線ニ沿ツテ進止スヘキコトヲ宿命ツケラレタル敗戰國トシテノ我國當面ノ食糧輸入問題ハ此ノ冷嚴ナル制約ニ加フルニ聯合國側ニ於ケル次ノ三點ノ大イナル「ミスジヤツヂ」ヲ附加セラレアリ其ノ進展ノ見透シニ付重大ナル暗影ヲ投シ居ルモノト謂フヘキナリ

(イ)南半球ニ於ケル一九四五年農作物ノ早魃ニ因ル大不況
(ロ)東洋各輸入期待國ニ於ケル終戰ヲ契機トセル事情ノ急激ナル變更
(ハ)右事情ノ變更ヲ背景トシ聯合國側ノ之等ノ各國ニ於ケル「ソフトポリシー」、「ミリタリサーヴイス」、無經驗等ニ基ク統治方式ニ因ル食糧輸出促進工作ノ不手際乃至不成功

而シテ我方ニ於テモ右ノ第二點及第三點ニ付同樣ナル「ミスジヤツヂ」ヲ冒シ居リタルモノト云フヘク現在ノ事態ヨリ之ヲ觀ルトキハ漫然ト從來ノ統計數字ニ賴リ之等ノ東洋各期待國ニ於ケル既往ノ「ハンガーエキスポート」ノ實態ヲ無視シ事情ノ變更ト政策ノ更改ト二伴ヒ之等ノ各國ノ食糧輸出事情カ全ク相貌ヲ一變スルニ至ルヘキコトヲ見越シ得サリシ點アルハ否ムヘカラサルモノアリ而モ此ノ如キ政治上、經濟上ノ深キ縁由ニ基ク深刻ナル事態カ一朝一タニシテ好轉スルカ如キコトヲ期待シ得サルハ言ヲ俟タサル處

是ヲ以テ上述GHQ當局モ旣ニ自認シ居ルカ如ク大觀的ニハ東洋各期待國ニ付テハ始ト其ノ見込ナキモノトシテ食糧輸入見込數字推算ノ基礎ト爲スコト最モ安全妥當ナルヘシ唯我國ノ食糧需給操作上緊急避難ノ措置ノ手懸ハ之ヲ何トシテモ時間的、場所的ニ之等ノ各國ニ索ムルコトトセサルヲ得サルヲ以テ後述ノ如ク各種懸命ノ引出工作ヲ敢テ之ヲ試ミサルヘカラサルモノト思料スルモ其ノ成功ノ公算ハ極メテ少ク而モ其ノ成功スル場合ニ於テモ多クノ期待ハ勿論全ク不可能ニ屬シ東洋全地域ヲ合シテ多クトモ
（五字分アキ）
屯程度ノモノニ過ギズト判斷シテ誤

2　民主化・非軍事化政策への対応（昭和20年10月〜21年5月）

リナカルベキカ

其ノ反面合衆國ニ對スル食糧期待ハ其ノ一九四五年農作物ノ豊況ニ相俟チ合衆國自體ノ日本占領責任當事國トシテノ複雑ナル國際的利害關係ヲ反映スルト共ニ既述ノ如ク合衆國ガ獨占スル對日食糧供給事業ト之ニ伴フ見返リ物資輸出事業ノ採算的動機ニ刺戟セラレ相當好望ナルモノト判斷シテ支障ナカルベシ此ノ意味ニ於テハ舊秩序ヲ喪失セル東洋各國ニ於テニ非ズシテ合衆國ニ於テ一九四五年農作物ノ豊況ヲ呈セルハ敗戰國日本ニトリ洵ニ不幸中ノ幸ト謂フベキカ卽チ合衆國方面ニ對シ小麥ヲ中心トシ大豆、米、要スレバ玉蜀黍ヲモ敢テ之ヲ厭ハザルコトトシ之等ノ食糧物資ノ輸入工作ヲ強力執拗ニ追進スルニ於テハ略々期待量一、一五〇千屯程度ノ食糧輸入ヲ達成シ得ル公算極メテ大ナリト思料スルカ如何（前述ノ如ク本月二十一日附日本「タイムス」所載合衆國農務省發表ハ合衆國小麥輸出可能量ハ五、〇〇〇千屯程度ニ達スベキ旨ヲ述べ尚同日附星條旗紙所載ＵＰ華府電報ハ本年度合衆國小麥ノ極東向輸出ハ八〇〇千屯程度ニ達スベキ旨玆ニ支那ハ國內交通機關ノ破壞

ニ伴ヒ小麥輸入ヲ受入ルル可能性ニ乏シキ旨ヲ述べ居レリ）

結局目下ノ兩地域ノ綜合的結論トシテハ一九四六食糧年度ニ於テ多クシテ　　　　　（五字分アキ）　　屯少キ場合ハ　　　　　（五字分アキ）　　屯程度ノ食糧輸入ヲ見得ルニ過キザルモノト想定シ今ヨリシテ此ノ冷嚴ナル想定數字ヲ基礎トシ內外諸般ノ食糧對策ニ最善ノ手ヲ盡シ萬遺漏ナキヲ期スベキ段階ニ在ルヲ信ズルモノナリ（「マルカット」ハ最近西山次長ニ對シ日本ニ於テハ約六、〇〇〇千石程度ノ米カ政府公式數字以外ノモノトシテ銷流シツツアリト思料スル旨申述ベタリ以テ對日供給食糧ノ枠査定ノ一材料トシテ考慮セル點ヲ示唆セルモノト解シ得ルニ非ザルカ）〈以下略〉

124

昭和21年1月29日
連合国最高司令官総司令部より
日本政府宛

若干の外郭地域の日本からの政治上および行政上の分離に関する指令

付記一　右和訳文

二　昭和二十一年二月十三日、終戦連絡中央事務

383

局第一部第一課作成
「行政ノ分離ニ關スル第一回會談錄」

GENERAL HEADQUARTERS
SUPREME COMMANDER FOR THE ALLIED POWERS

29 January 1946

AG 091 (29 Jan 46) GS
(SCAPIN-677)

MEMORANDUM FOR: IMPERIAL JAPANESE GOVERNMENT.

THROUGH: Central Liaison Office, Tokyo.

SUBJECT: Governmental and Administrative Separation of Certain Outlying Areas from Japan.

1. The Imperial Japanese Government is directed to cease exercising, or attempting to exercise, governmental or administrative authority over any area outside of Japan, or over any government officials and employees or any other persons within such areas.

2. Except as authorized by this Headquarters, the Imperial Japanese Government will not communicate with government officials and employees or with any other persons outside of Japan for any purpose other than the routine operation of authorized shipping, communications and weather services.

3. For the purpose of this directive, Japan is defined to include the four main islands of Japan (Hokkaido, Honshu, Kyushu and Shikoku) and the approximately 1,000 smaller adjacent islands, including the Tsushima Islands and the Ryukyu (Nansei) Islands north of 30° North Latitude (excluding Kuchinoshima Island) ; and excluding (a) Utsuryo (Ullung) Island, Liancourt Rocks (Take Island) and Quelpart (Saishu or Cheju) Island, (b) the Ryukyu (Nansei) Islands south of 30° North Latitude (including Kuchinoshima Island) , the Izu, Nanpo, Bonin (Ogasawara) and Volcano (Kazan or Iwo) Island Groups, and all other outlying Pacific Islands [including the Daito (Ohigashi or Oagari) Island Group, and Parece Vela (Okino-tori) , Marcus (Minami-tori) and Ganges (Nakano-tori) Islands], and (c) the Kurile (Chishima) Islands, the Habomai (Hapomaze) Island Group (including Suisho, Yuri, Akiyuri, Shibotsu and Taraku Islands) and Shikotan Island.

4. Further areas specifically excluded from the gov-

384

ernmental and administrative jurisdiction of the Imperial Japanese Government are the following: (a) all Pacific Islands seized or occupied under mandate or otherwise by Japan since the beginning of the World War in 1914, (b) Manchuria, Formosa and the Pescadores, (c) Korea, and (d) Karafuto.

5. The definition of Japan contained in this directive shall also apply to all future directives, memoranda and orders from this Headquarters unless otherwise specified therein.

6. Nothing in this directive shall be construed as an indication of Allied policy relating to the ultimate determination of the minor islands referred to in Article 8 of the Potsdam Declaration.

7. The Imperial Japanese Government will prepare and submit to this Headquarters a report of all governmental agencies in Japan the functions of which pertain to areas outside of Japan as defined in this directive. Such report will include a statement of the functions, organization and personnel of each of the agencies concerned.

8. All records of the agencies referred to in paragraph 7 above will be preserved and kept available for inspection by this Headquarters.

FOR THE SUPREME COMMANDER:

H. W. ALLEN,
Colonel, AGD,
Asst. Adjutant General.

（付記 1）

若干の外郭地域を政治上行政上日本から分離することに關する覺書

二一、一、二九

一、日本國外の總ての地域に對し又その地域内にある政府役人雇傭員その他總ての者に對して政治上又は行政上の權力を行使すること及行使しようと企てることは總て停止する樣日本政府に指令する

二、日本帝國政府は已に認可されてゐる船舶の運航通信氣象關係の常軌の作業を除き當司令部から認可のない限り日本國外の政府の役人雇傭人其の他總ての者との間に目的の如何を問はず通信を行ふことは出来ない

三、この指令の目的から日本と言ふ場合は次の定義による日

本の範圍に含まれる地域として日本の四主要島嶼(北海道、本州、四國、九州)と對馬諸島、北緯三〇度以北の琉球(南西)諸島(口之島を除く)を含む約一千の隣接小島嶼

日本の範圍から除かれる地域として

(a)鬱陵島、竹島、濟州島(b)北緯三〇度以南の琉球(南西)列島(口之島を含む)、伊豆、南方、小笠原、硫黄群島及び大東群島、沖ノ鳥島、南鳥島、中ノ鳥島を含むその他の外郭太平洋全諸島(c)千島列島、齒舞群島(水晶、勇留、秋勇留、志發、多樂島を含む)、色丹島

四、更に日本帝國政府の政治上行政上の管轄權から特に除外せられる地域は次の通りである

(a)一九一四年の世界大戰以來日本か委任統治その他の方法で奪取又は占領した全太平洋諸島(b)滿洲、臺灣、澎湖列島(c)朝鮮及び(d)樺太

五、この指令にある日本の定義は特に指定する場合以外今後當司令部から發せられる總ての指令覺書又は命令に適用せられる

六、この指令中の條項は何れもポツダム宣言の第八條にある

小島嶼の最終的決定に關する聯合國側の政策を示すものと解釋してはならない

七、日本帝國政府は日本國内の政府機關にしてこの指令の定義による日本國外の地域に關する機能を有する總てのものの報告を調製して當司令部に提出することを要するこの報告は關係各機關の機能組織及職員の状態を含まなくてはならない

八、右第七項に述べられた機關に關する報告は總てこれを保存し何時でも當司令部の檢閲を受けられるやうにしておくことを要する

(付記二)

行政ノ分離ニ關スル第一回會談錄

(終戰第一部第一課)

昭和二十一年二月十三日黄田連絡官GS「ロッヂ」大尉及「プール」中尉ト標記ノ件ニ關シ第一回會談ヲ行ヒタリ要旨左ノ如シ

黄 「本日ハ領土ノ歸屬問題乃至ハ本指令ノ安當性等ニ付テハ觸レサルコトトシ單ニ疑義ニ付質問ヲ爲サンカ爲參

2　民主化・非軍事化政策への対応（昭和20年10月〜21年5月）

米「本指令ハ單ナル聯合國側ノ行政的便宜ヨリ出テタルニ過キス從來行ハレ來リタルコトヲ本指令ニ依リ確認シ示スモノナリ卽チSCAPノ行政及フ範圍ハ本指令ニ示セル日本國內ニ限ラレ其ノ他ハSCAPノ所管スルトコロニアラス例ヘハ大島ハCINPACノ所管、鬱陵島ハ第二十四軍團ノ指揮下ニ在リ從ッテ本指令ニ依ル日本ノ範圍ニ決定シ何等領土問題トハ關聯ヲ有セス之ハ他日媾和會議ニテ決定サルヘキ問題ナリ」

黃「本指令ニ關シ問題トナル點ハ未タ聯合軍側ノ機關ナク現地行政カ專ラ日本側ニ依リ行ハレアル地域例ヘハ伊豆大島等ニ關シテハ特ニ起ルヘシ先ッカカル地域ニ於テハ日本側機關ノ機能ヲ存續セシムル要アリト思料セラルルモ如何」

米「引續キ機能ヲ營ム要アリ何等カノ機關カ行政ヲ執行スル要アルヲ以テ從來ノモノカ引續キ之ヲ爲スヲ便トスヘシ」

黃「日本側官吏、傭人ノ身分ハ如何ナルヘキヤ」

米「日本政府ノ官吏トシテノ身分ハ之ヲ失フモノトス之等官吏ヲ定員外 (on leave) トシテ帳簿ノ上ニノミ存續セシメ敍位敍勳昇給等ハ他ノ官吏ト同樣ニ之ヲ爲シ置キ他日內地歸還ノ際其儘ノ身分ヲ保持セシムル如キコト可能ナラサルヤ」

黃「然ラハ其ノ間ノ俸給ハ何方ニテ支拂フヘキカ尙現在市町村吏員等ニ付十二月分ヨリ溯及シテ六割ノ物價手當增給ヲ決定シアルモ之ヲ實行シテ差支ナキヤ」

米「俸給ノ支拂ハCINPACト協議ノ上決定スヘシ增俸ニ關シテハCINPAC主義上「否」ト答ヘサルヲ得ス、日本側ニ於テ俸給及增俸分ヲ內地ニ credit シ置クコト可能ナラス」

黃「彼等ハ現ニ俸給ヲ以テ生活シアルヲ以テ左樣ナ悠暢ナルコトハ不能ナリ何等カノ便法ヲ講スル余地ナキヤ」

米「此等ノ點ニ付テハCINPACト協議ノ要アルヲ以テ卽答シ得ス」

黃「次ニ警察官、學校職員等ノ異動、特ニ內地ヘノ轉勤等ハ認メラレザルヤ」

米「主義上ハ出來ザル次第ナリ尙右ニ該當スベキ人員ノ數及東京都ガ之等警察官ヲ必要

黄「大島、新島、石垣島等七測候所ニ付テハ觀測繼續ヲトスルヤ否ヤヲ伺ヒタシ、警察官等ヲ引揚グルトセバ其ノ後ノ治安問題等ヲ考慮セザルヲ得ズ、當分之等ノ人員ハ之ヲ現地ニ殘スコト妥當ナルベシ」

米「右地域ニ居住スルモノニ對シ恩赦等ヲ行ヒ得ルヤ」

黄「具體例アリヤ主義上ノ質問ナリトセバ決定的ニ「否」ナリ」

米「從來通ニテ可ナリ」

黄「煙草、味噌、醬油、鹽等ノ配給ハ如何ニスベキヤ」

米「CINPACト連絡スル要アリ、具體的ニ不足品名ヲ承知シタシ」

黄「大島ニ漁港建設ノ計畫アルモ如何ニスベキヤ」

米「中止セラルヘシ既ニ着工セルモノナラバ其ノ程度ヲ承知シタシ」

黄「大島ニ於テハ生活必需品タル食料、調味料ハ節約スレバ三月末マデノ貯藏ハアルモ他ノモノニ關シテハ不足スルモノモアルベク右ニ付テハ日本政府ニ於テ之ヲ補給スルノ要アルベシ」

米「指令ナキ測候所ノ具體的ナ「リスト」竝ニ右ヨリノ「リポート」ガ直接東京ニ達スルヤ否ヤヲ承知シタシ此點ノ所管ハGSニ非ザル故所管課ト打合セノ上回答スベシ」

黄「第七項ノ日本ニ於ケル政府機關等ノ報告ノ範圍ニ付承知シタシ」

米「ハッシー」中佐ノ所管ナル故同中佐ト協議ノ上決定

尙最後ニ米側ヨリ左ノ點ニ付質疑アリタリ

一、伊豆七島ニCINPACガ未駐屯ナリト言フハ確ナリヤ奄美大島ニハ駐屯濟ナリ

二、日本內地ヨリ派遣セラレ居ル官吏ノ人數及職務ヲ承知シタシ

三、定員外 on leave ノ制度トシテ如何ナルモノガ考ヘラルルヤ

四、伊豆七島ノ自給自足ノ程度如何

黄「訴訟書類ノ送達、喚問、照會等ハ之ヲ爲シ得ルヤ」

米「否」

2 民主化・非軍事化政策への対応(昭和20年10月〜21年5月)

昭和21年2月1日　朝海(浩一郎)終戦連絡中央事務局総務部第一課長作成

「楊雲竹氏との會談覺」

楊雲竹氏との會談覺

（昭和二一年二月一日）

楊雲竹氏（現在外交部亞東司長）は昭和十年前後本官南京に在勤當時の外交部日本課長にて舊知なりしに付二月一日帝國ホテルに於て面會午前意見を交換せり、會談要旨左記の通り報告す。

一、今般朱世明中將と共に極東委員會中國代表として來邦せる楊雲竹氏（現在外交部亞東司長）は昭和十年前後本官が東京に於て代理大使として奮鬪せられその歸國官を閲したるが、斯る悲慘なる狀態にて再會見するとは思ひ掛けざりき、日本側は主として米側と接觸し居り其の日本管理に對する方針は略々承知し居るも、貴國代表者と接觸の機會乏しき爲め自然貴國の意向に付ては聞くこと少し、極東委員會管理理事會の活動等に付御意見を承り度し」

楊「極東委員會及日本管理理事會の設置は一種の妥協外交の所産なり、ソ聯側はマックアーサーは日本より降伏條件を受くる權限はあるも其の後の日本の管理は關係各國に於て之を行ふべしとの趣旨を強硬に主張せるも、右に對しては米側贊成せず、結局政策決定機關として極東委員會を設け右に理事會を置き總司令部に附しむる形にて落着きたる次第なり、日本は各國に分割占領せられ居らず、又其の政府も存在し居るを以て伯林に設置せられたるアライド・コントロール・カウンシルと日本管理理事會とは自ら相違し居ること勿論なり、管理理事會が其の活動を如何に規正せらるべきやは結局今後の運用如何に歸すべきも實際問題としてマックアーサーの相談機關たることを主たる職務とすべし、極東委員會は華府に於て政策を決定し右決定が國務省に移され、同省に於て陸海軍等とも連絡の上總司令部に訓令發出せらるる手順なり、本機構の運營付種々討論は行はれたるも何分前例のなき事に付動かして見ざれば判明せずと謂ふが現狀なり」

三、朝「新聞情報に依れば極東委員會内部に於て日本占領期間に付十年說二十年說等種々論議行はれ居る趣なる處

楊「各國委員に於て新聞記者に感想を述べたるものなるべく、委員會として本件を論じ得べきやは未だ明かならず、蓋し委員會討議事項より領土歸屬の問題と作戰事項とは除外せられ居れり、果して日本占領期間に關する問題が作戰問題なりや否やは疑問なき能はざるも委員會としては未だ正式には本件に付議論し非ず」

朝「英國軍の吳方面進駐は最近實現する模樣なるが、中國政府は日本占領の爲め軍隊を派遣する意向ありや如何」

楊「英國も自分が倫敦及華府に居りたる當時は未だ派兵に付自分等に明示し居らず内部に於ても派兵模樣なるが中國最高軍事方面にて如何に考慮し居られるや承知せず、朱世明將軍も對日派兵に付ては中國國内に於ても贊否の兩論あり、昨年八月頃は重慶に於て派兵論も相當出でたることあり、占領に參加するとしても米國以外の聯合國は大部隊を派遣することは困難にて象徴的兵力に止ると思考す」

朝「新聞情報に依れば中國側は共產軍問題、滿洲問題等國内問題に忙殺せられ日本に派兵方考慮し居らざる樣

如何」

楊「承知せり」

楊「國内問題に依るに非ずして派兵するとなれば相當の兵力に對する給養の問題あり、運輸の問題あり其の點にて忽ち困難に逢着する譯なり、日本側は中國兵の進駐を希望せざる次第なりや」

朝「中國兵の進駐を希望せざるが故に尋ねるものには非ず、聯合軍の進駐を出來る丈け早目に承知し、事前に手當し置くことは連絡事務局の職務なり、尚日本が如何に管理せらるべきやに付中國は隣接の大國として深甚なる關心を有すべき處派兵せざる結果其の發言權大ならざること豫想せられ焦慮の空氣無之や」

楊「武力を以て日本を壓伏することが日本に於ける中國の地位を高むる所以なりとは思ひ居らず」

四、朝「賠償問題に付ては米側より或程度方針を承り居るも聯合國内部の分前等は未だ決定せられ居らざる趣なるが如何、外國通信に依れば中國側は日本より勞務、鑛產物等特異なる賠償を要求し居る趣なるが如何」

楊「ポーレー大使其の他より相談を受け居るも中國としては今次戰爭に依り最も甚しき損害を受け居れり自分

2 民主化・非軍事化政策への対応（昭和20年10月〜21年5月）

等の賠償根本方針は日本產業に致命的打擊を與へ日本國民を不當に苦しむるものには非ざるも、同時に中國側の損害大なりしこと中國は日本を完全にディスアームすることに深甚の關心を有することを指摘せざるべからず、分前等は未だ決定し居らず賠償問題は全く初步的段階にあり中國側が勞務等の形にて賠償を要求すとの話は政府の話には非ず」

朝「ソ聯の態度に關し何等御話を聞き得べきや」

楊「ソ聯は賠償問題に付ても獨逸に對すると同樣日本に對し相當强硬なる態度を示し居るなり」

朝「ソ聯は獨逸に依り其の領土を侵略せられ多大の損害を受けたるものなるも日本よりは何等損害を受け居らざるに拘らず大なる要求を爲す根據は了解に苦しむ」

楊「ソ聯は獨逸に對して直接相當なる要求を爲し得るも、東亞に於ては日本に對し要求を爲し得る地位に在る他の國を極力支持支援すると言ふ形も執り得ることを指摘し得べし」

朝「日本產業は賠償問題の見透付かざる爲不安定なる狀態に在るに付至急決定方希望に堪えず」

楊「本件を急遽決定の要あることは極東委員會に於ても一致せる意見なるが何分に之が實施には複雜困難なる關係あり相當手間取るべしと思はる」

五、朝「日本は中國に近接し最も中國を識り得べき立場に在り乍ら所謂中國通の不合理極まる議論に迷され、結局最も中國を識らざりしものと謂ふを得べし、自分の經驗を申上ぐるに北支事變勃發の際自分は上司の命に依り陸軍省某中佐に對し保定軍結中の中國軍を爆擊せば事變は擴大して遂に收拾すべからざるに至るべき旨指摘せる處同中佐は右は中國の實際を知らざる一遍の常識論にして中國は單なる常識を以て判斷すべく餘りに複雜なり、此れ中國研究に十年二十年を要する所以にして、毆れば毆り返すと云ふは日本人の常識的判斷に過ぎず、毆れば引込むが中國人の心理なりと言へることあり、非合理なる中國論が橫行せる結果中國の本體を見誤りし今日の悲運を見たるは殘念なり」

楊「日本人は中國人に關する認識に乏しく、此の點は今日に於ても餘り變り居らざる樣なり、日本人は米國に對しては米國が實力を伴ひ存在し居る關係上極めて柔

朝「中國に對する日本人の認識を深むべしとの議論には同感なるも、終戰後の中國政府殊に蔣主席の態度は日本の朝野に深刻なる印象を與へ、日本人は今更の如く中國人を見直さざるを得ざりし次第にて、當時の新聞も社說等に依り斯る日本人の氣持を端的に表示せり、貴官の如く有力なる地位に在る方より斯る事情は十分蔣主席邊りに報告し置かるべきを切望す」

楊「相互の了解と云ふことは大事にて、自分等と一緒に來邦せる極東委員會の委員中には日本を理解せざる者

順なる一方英國に對しても殊に上層階級は歷史的に尊敬の念を抱き居れり然るに中國に對しては依然として多少の輕侮觀念を有し居る傾きあるは遺憾なり、中國人識者は大東亞戰爭に於て斯くも慘虐行爲の犧牲となり乍ら終戰に當り日本側に復讐すべからずと主張し殊に蔣主席の如きは內部に可成りの反對論ありたるにも拘らず暴に報ゆるに暴を以てして恨みを將來にのこすこと勿れと大乘的見解を聲明せられたり、斯る中國側態度に對し日本側より何等顯著なる反響なきは了解に苦しむ次第なり」

六、朝「尙華僑の取締問題にも言及致度し、嘗て所謂冀東貿易旺んなりし頃日本人進出の最尖端にありたる者はモヒ屋と密淫賣者にて、中國官憲を手古摺らせ又昭和十年銀國有令施行の際惡質日本人は上海より稅關吏を脅迫して銀の對日密輸出を行ひ、此等問題に付累次日本側は取締方貴官等より要望せられたり、然るに今や本官は逆に在日華僑の取締を中國に要望せざるを得ざる立場に在り因果は廻り來れりと言へば其れ迄なるも在留華人の不法行爲は日本政府として治安維持上放任し得ざる點御理解願ひ度」

楊「御趣旨は了承するも本件は中國政府に取りても相當

稍からず、マッコイ將軍が日本側と個人的に接觸し情報を蒐集し差支なしとの許可を出したる關係上、委員の或者は日本人を呼び通譯を通じ種々質問を行ひ居たるも、自分の觀る所に依れば斯る方法にて日本人が本當のことを言ふべしとは思はれず、仙臺に於て佛國の代表者が地方長官に對し占領期間の問題にて意見を求めたるが之も的外れにて、地方長官は斯る點を批評し得ず又批評する譯もなき次第なり」

392

2　民主化・非軍事化政策への対応（昭和20年10月～21年5月）

機微なる問題なり、華僑の取扱振り如何は直ちに中國一般に知れ渡り、之れが日本に於て取締の對象となり居れりと云ふこととなれば輿論は却々に收まらざるべし、此の點に留意され日本側は總て穩便に措置さるべきを希望す」

朝「穩便處か現在日本官憲は殆んど取締を行ひ居らざる實状なるも、華人勞務者中には集團を組み善良なる百姓を襲撃して其の貯藏食糧を強奪し、或は丸太を横へて列車の運行を妨害し、甚しきに至つては傷害殺人を敢てする者あり、勿論此等勞働者が日本に連れ來られたる當時の事情及び日本に於て勞働に服せしめられ居たる状況等に付ては日本側に相當の責任あることを認めざるを得ざるも去りとて右理由に依り治安の攪亂を放任することは許されず」

楊「華人は臺灣人朝鮮人と共に行動し居る處朝鮮人は其の遣る事遣り口極端且巧妙にして中國人も動ともすれば之に捲込まれ行く傾向あり、仍も中國政府としては臺灣人は同列なるも朝鮮人とは必ずしも行動を共にせざる樣華僑指導者に對し指示を與へ居る次第なり、御

説の如き行爲は勿論中國政府としても支持する所には非るに付此等取締のため最近外交部より適當の係官を日本に派遣することとなるべし、右係官には平常状態に於ける領事の如き職務を果さしめ度き方針なり、尚此の點に關聯し自分より貴官に對し個人的に希望あり、最近京都に於て看板引降し問題より日華人間に衝突起り警察部長は臺灣人「林」なる者を逮捕せり、斯ること先程お話せる通り輿論を刺戟し面白からざるに付至急釋放方内務省にお傳へあり度し」

朝「事情は判明せざるも貴意は關係方面に傳達し置くべし、尙華人に對する裁判管轄の問題は總司令部に於て研究中の模樣なる處如何、又臺灣人は華人と認むるや」

楊「華人に對する日本側の裁判管轄は認めず、日本側は犯罪容疑の華人をM・Pに引渡し得るに過ぎず引渡後の措置に付ては未だ決定し居らず、臺灣人は華人と看做し居れり」

七、朝「戰爭犯罪人名簿は各國別に出し居るものと思考せらるる處如何、中國のリストは出盡したりや、又總司令

楊「各國にて表を出し得る権限を有するの次第なりや」

部も選定の権限を有するの次第なりや」

慶を出たる時迄は中國側よりリストを出したる事實は知らず、最近重慶と本問題にて十分に連絡し居らずに付リストが出盡したりやの點もお答へし得ず、又總司令部は極東委員會に於て述べられたる政策の範圍内にて個々に選定し得る譯なり、戰爭犯罪人處分の問題に付ては倫敦のユナイテッド・ネーションズ・ウォア・クライム・コミッションに於て處分の原則、裁判所の構成等に付審議せられたり、此のコミッションはファー・イースタン・アンド・パシフイツク・サブコミッションを重慶に設け居り中國政府としても審議に參畫し居る次第なり、又日本に於て行はるべき裁判とは別に、特に其の國に關係ある犯罪に關しては當該國に於て犯罪人の引渡を受け、更に別個に裁判を爲し得る譯なり、中國側は戰爭犯罪人に對し苛烈なる取扱はせざる心算なるも、例へば傀儡政權に對し指導的役割を果し居たるが如き人物に對しては中國の輿論は相當強硬なるに付此の點考慮に入れざるを得ざる次第なり」

編注 本文書は、昭和二十一年八月、朝海終戦連絡中央事務局総務部長作成「報告書集録（その一）」より抜粋。

126

昭和21年2月19日
連合国最高司令官総司令部より日本政府宛

刑事裁判管轄権に関する指令

GENERAL HEADQUARTERS
SUPREME COMMANDER FOR THE ALLIED POWERS
APO 500

19 February 1946

AG 015 (19 Feb 46) LS
SCAPIN-756

MEMORANDUM FOR: Imperial Japanese Government.
THROUGH: Central Liaison Office, Tokyo.
SUBJECT: Exercise of Criminal Jurisdiction.

1. Japanese courts will henceforth exercise no criminal jurisdiction over United Nations Nationals or organizations, in-

2　民主化・非軍事化政策への対応（昭和20年10月〜21年5月）

cluding corporations. All pending criminal proceedings in which Nationals of the United Nations are defendants will be reported to this headquarters; further action by Japanese Courts with respect to such defendants will be stayed; and the defendants will be held subject to directions from authorized representatives of the Supreme Commander for the Allied Powers.

2. Japanese courts will henceforth exercise no criminal jurisdiction over the following offenses:

　a. Acts prejudicial to the security of the Occupation Forces, or any member thereof, or any person attached to or accompanying such forces.

　b. Killing or assaulting any member of the Occupation Forces, or any person attached to or accompanying such forces.

　c. Unauthorized possession, taking, receipt or disposal of property of the Occupation Forces or any member thereof, or of any person attached to or accompanying such forces.

　d. Interfering with or hindering the arrest of any person sought, or assisting in or furthering the escape of any person detained, by the Occupation Forces or by others pursuant to the direction of the Supreme Commander for the Allied Powers or his authorized subordinates.

　e. Interfering with, refusing information required by, making any false or misleading statement orally or in writing to, or defrauding in any manner, any member of the Occupation Forces or any person attached to or accompanying such forces in a matter of official concern.

　f. Acts on behalf or in support of any organization dissolved or declared illegal by the Supreme Commander for the Allied Powers or dissolved or declared illegal at the order of the Supreme Commander for the Allied Powers.

　g. Conspiracies to commit, or acts which aid or abet the commission of, any of the foregoing offenses.

3. Japanese courts will continue to exercise jurisdiction over acts prejudicial to the objectives of the occupation insofar as such acts constitute violations of Japanese law. However, military occupation courts may also assume jurisdiction over such acts or any other acts which are prejudicial to the objectives of the occupation.

4. The Commanding General of the Eighth Army and the Commander, Fifth Fleet, have been directed to appoint military occupation courts including commissions and provost courts with jurisdiction over the foregoing persons and offenses.

5. a. Military commissions are authorized to impose sentences which may include:- fines; imprisonment at hard labor, or both, or specified alternative imprisonment in lieu of payment of fines; expulsion; confiscation, padlocking and forfeiture of estates; and death.

b. Provost courts are authorized to impose sentences including:- fines not to exceed Seventy-five thousand (¥75,000) Yen; imprisonment at hard labor not to exceed five (5) years, or both, or specified alternative confinement in lieu of payment of fine; expulsion; confiscation and padlocking respecting properties not exceeding Seventy-five thousand (¥75,000) Yen in value.

6. The Imperial Japanese Government shall have no authority to arrest United Nations Nationals, except (a) in areas where Allied troops are not actually present on duty and there is a reasonable suspicion that a serious crime has been committed by a United Nations National, or (b) when otherwise directed by the Supreme Commander for the Allied Powers or his authorized subordinates; provided that, when such persons are taken into custody, the apprehending authority will immediately report the incident to the nearest Allied Military Authority and deliver such persons upon instructions from such Authority.

7. The Japanese people and all other persons in Japan will be informed of this directive.

For the Supreme Commander:

B. M. FITCH,

Brigadier General, AGD,

Adjutant General.

昭和21年2月26日　連合国最高司令官総司令部より　日本政府宛

民事裁判管轄権に関する指令

GENERAL HEADQUARTERS
SUPREME COMMANDER FOR THE ALLIED POWERS
APO 500

2 民主化・非軍事化政策への対応(昭和20年10月～21年5月)

AG 015 (26 Feb 46) LS
SCAPIN-777

26 February 1946

MEMORANDUM FOR: Imperial Japanese Government
THROUGH: Central Liaison Office, Tokyo
SUBJECT: Exercise of Civil Jurisdiction

1. a. Japanese tribunals will henceforth exercise no civil jurisdiction with respect to United Nations nationals or organizations (including corporations) attached to or accompanying the Allied Armed Forces.

b. Civil Claims against such persons or organizations will be presented to the Imperial Japanese Government, which, if it believes the claims to be meritorious and supported by good and sufficient evidence, will forward them to the Supreme Commander for the Allied Powers.

2. a. Decisions in all civil cases affecting other United Nations nationals or organizations, or in which such nationals or organizations are or may become parties, shall be subject to review, including revision or such other action as may be considered necessary, by the Supreme Commander for the Allied Powers or his authorized representatives.

b. The Supreme Commander for the Allied Powers or his authorized representatives will take such steps as are deemed necessary, including suspension of proceedings, to ensure that in the conduct of such civil cases the rights of the United Nations nationals or organizations parties thereto are adequately protected.

3. The Imperial Japanese Government will immediately report to the Supreme Commander for the Allied Powers, all civil cases hereafter instituted or now pending in Japanese tribunals affecting United Nations nationals or organizations (including corporations). Such reports will include names and nationalities of the parties, nature of the case, the relief sought and the status of the proceedings.

4. The Japanese people and all other persons in Japan will be informed of this directive.

FOR THE SUPREME COMMANDER:

B. M. FITCH,
Brigadier General, AGD,

128

昭和21年2月26日　連合国最高司令官総司令部より　日本政府宛

書籍およびその他刊行物の頒布制限撤廃に関する指令

GENERAL HEADQUARTERS
SUPREME COMMANDER FOR THE ALLIED POWERS

AG 000.73 (26 Feb 46) CIE
(SCAPIN - 776)

26 February 1946

MEMORANDUM FOR: IMPERIAL JAPANESE GOVERNMENT.
THROUGH: Central Liaison Office, Tokyo.
SUBJECT: Banned Books and Other Publications.

1. Upon receipt of this memorandum, the Imperial Japanese Government will abrogate all laws, ordinances, edicts, directives, or other governmental regulations expressed or implied which restrict the free circulation of books, pamphlets, periodicals, or other publications in public libraries or educational libraries.

2. The Imperial Japanese Government will submit to this Headquarters, on or before 1 April 1946, a statement of all actions taken by it or any of its subordinate agencies which have resulted in the removal of restrictions referred to in paragraph 1 above.

FOR THE SUPREME COMMANDER:

B. M. FITCH,
Brigadier General, AGD,
Adjutant General.

129

昭和21年2月27日　連合国最高司令官総司令部より　日本政府宛

社会救恤施策に関する指令

GENERAL HEADQUARTERS
SUPREME COMMANDER FOR THE ALLIED POWERS

AG 091.4 (27 Feb 46) PH/GS/GA/GD
(SCAPIN - 775)

APO 500
27 February 1946

MEMORANDUM FOR: IMPERIAL JAPANESE GOVERNMENT.

2　民主化・非軍事化政策への対応（昭和20年10月～21年5月）

THROUGH: Central Liaison Office, Tokyo.
SUBJECT: Public Assistance.

1. With reference to C.L.O. Memorandum 1484 (1.1), dated 31 December 1945, subject: "Relief and Welfare Plans", there is no objection to the Imperial Japanese Government proceeding with the proposed plan altered to conform to the following conditions:

　　a. The Imperial Japanese Government to establish a single National Governmental agency which through Prefectural and local governmental channels will provide adequate food, clothing, shelter, and medical care equally to all indigent persons without discrimination or preferential treatment.

　　b. Not later than 30 April 1946 financial support and operational responsibility for this program to be assumed by the Imperial Japanese Government and thereafter not to be rendered or delegated to any private or quasi-official agency.

　　c. Within the amount necessary to prevent hardship, no limitation to be placed on the amount of relief furnished.

2. The Imperial Japanese Government will submit the following reports to this Headquarters:

　　a. Copies of all legislation and instructions issued by the Imperial Japanese Government to accomplish the terms of this directive.

　　b. Commencing with the period March 1946, a monthly report delivered by the 25th day of the following month stating the number of families and individuals granted assistance and the amount of funds expended by Prefecture.

FOR THE SUPREME COMMANDER:

　　　　　　　　　　B. M. FITCH,
　　　　　　Brigadier General, AGD,
　　　　　　　　　　Adjutant General.

～～～～～～～～～

130　英連邦軍司令官との会談につき報告

昭和21年3月5日　服部（恒雄）終戦連絡呉事務局長より吉田終戦連絡中央事務局総裁宛

呉連第三八号

昭和二十一年三月五日

終戦連絡呉事務局長〔印〕

終戦連絡中央事務局總裁殿

英聯邦軍司令官トノ會談ニ關シ報告ノ件

英聯邦軍司令官「ノースコット」中將ハ二月二六日呉ニ着任セルニ付本官、廣島縣知事、中國復員監、呉地方復員局長官、廣島及呉兩市長等ニ於テ訪問敬意ヲ表シ度旨申入置タル處同中將ハ英聯邦軍駐屯宿舎及山口、島根兩縣ノ視察ヲ行ヒ三月二日歸呉シ四日午後四時楠瀬廣島縣知事鈴木警察部長及本官ノ三名ヲ指名シ官舎ニ於テ會見スベキ旨通知アリ仍ツテ本官ノ三名ハ同刻官舎ニ訪問シタルガ同中將ハ「アンダーソン」代將ト共ニ應接シ楠瀬知事ノ挨拶ニ應ヘテ占領任務遂行上日本側諸官ノ緊密ナル協力ヲ希望スル旨並ニ占領軍トシテ風光明眉ナル瀬戸内海ノ一角ヲ擔當スルコトハ仕合セナリ（本官ヲ顧ミテ官舎ヨリノ眺望ハ恰モ「シドニー」灣ヲ想起セシムルニアラズヤト語レリ）ト述ベ日本ノ習慣ハ知ラザルモ濠洲ノ習慣ナレバハトテ茶菓ヲ饗シ極メテ慇懃且打解ケタル態度ヲ以テ懇談セリ

右會談中「ノースコット」中將ノ語リタル要點左ノ如シ

一、英聯邦軍占領擔當地域

英聯邦軍ハ廣島縣ノ外山口縣及島根縣ヲ擔當スベシ山口縣等ニハ後續部隊ノ來着ヲ俟ツテ三週間以内ニ進駐スルコトトナルベシ四國ヲ管轄スルヤ否ヤニ付テハ未ダ確タル話ナシ

二、米第八軍第七十六軍政中隊トノ連繫同中隊ニ對シ連絡將校ヲ派遣シ司令部ト軍政中隊間及同中隊ヲ通ジ日本官廳トノ緊密ナル連絡ヲ保持スベシ

三、交通取締問題

警察部長ヨリ交通取締狀況ヲ聽取シタル後之ガ改善ノ爲ニハ占領軍車輛ノ取締ヲ行フ要アリ兵力來着後次第交通要點ニ憲兵ヲ配置シテ日本側ノ取締ト併行シ改善ニ協力スベシト述ブ

四、交歡問題

英聯邦軍將兵ニ對シテハ日本人民家ニ立入ルコトヲ「デイスカレッヂ」シアリ右ハ風習ニ通ゼザル間ニ思ハザル誤解ヲ惹起スルコト勿ラシメントスル趣旨ニ出ヅル次第ナレバ日本官民ニモ右方針ヲ周知セシメラレ度シ

尚ホ辭去ニ當リ本官ノ求ニ應シ市長等トノ會見ハ近日中ニ時間ヲ定ムベシト答ヘ又本官ニ對シ何事ニ據ラズ困惑ヲ感ズル樣ノ事案アリタル際ハ自分ニ申出テラレ度シ濠洲ニ在

2 民主化・非軍事化政策への対応(昭和20年10月〜21年5月)

131 離島所在気象台の業務開始方指令

昭和21年3月7日 連合国最高司令官総司令部より 日本政府宛

右何等御参考迄報告ス

勤セラレタル貴官ノ此地二在リタルハ悦バシト語リタリ

AG 000.93 (7 Mar 46) GC
SCAPIN - 801

MEMORANDUM FOR: IMPERIAL JAPANESE GOVERNMENT.
THROUGH: Central Liaison Office, Tokyo.
SUBJECT: Operation of Government Meteorological Stations Located on Detached Islands.

1. Memorandum for the Imperial Japanese Government, file no. AG 000.93 (13 Jan 46) GC, subject as above, dated 13 January 1946, is hereby rescinded.

2. The Imperial Japanese Government is directed to establish or rehabilitate and operate the following Island Meteorological Stations for a period of approximately six months:

Name	International Index No.	Lat - N	Long - E
Ishigaki Shima	645	24° 20'	124° 10'
Amami O Shima	650	28° 23'	129° 30'
Yaku Shima	651	30° 51'	130° 25'
Minami Daito Shima	649	25° 51'	131° 14'
Hachijo Shima	659	33° 06'	139° 50'
Tori Shima	099	30° 28'	140° 25'
Miyako Shima	640	24° 46'	125° 20'

3. The above stations will prepare and transmit hourly weather reports to the Central Meteorological Observatory, Tokyo in accordance with paragraph 1 of inclosure to Memorandum for the Imperial Japanese Government, file no. AG 000.93 (19 Nov 45) GC-P, subj: "Operation of Japanese Weather Service," dated 19 November 1945.

4. Arrangements have been made with The Shipping Control Authority For The Japanese Merchant Marine (SCAJAP) to

GENERAL HEADQUARTERS
SUPREME COMMANDER FOR THE ALLIED POWERS
APO 500
7 March 1946

furnish over-water transportation for establishment and maintenance of the above listed stations.

5. The Imperial Japanese Government will coordinate directly with Commanding Officer, 43rd Weather Wing, regarding transportation requirements and technical details.

FOR THE SUPREME COMMANDER:

Harold Fair
for B. M. FITCH,
Brigadier General, AGD,
Adjutant General.

輸出手続きに関する指令

昭和21年3月14日 連合国最高司令官総司令部より 日本政府宛

AG 091.31 (14 Mar 46) ESS/IE

GENERAL HEADQUARTERS
SUPREME COMMANDER FOR THE ALLIED POWERS
APO 500
14 March 1946

(SCAPIN 814)

MEMORANDUM TO: IMPERIAL JAPANESE GOVERNMENT

THROUGH: Central Liaison Office, Tokyo

SUBJECT: Export Procedure

1. It is directed that the Imperial Japanese Government follow the procedure outlined in the attachments hereto in preparing and delivering material for export.

2. General Headquarters, Supreme Commander for the Allied Powers, makes no commitment and assumes no liability in processing or validating Applications to Prepare for Export and Applications to Deliver for Export.

3. General Headquarters, Supreme Commander for the Allied Powers, will make every reasonable effort to cause Japanese export items to be disposed of suitably abroad. However, it is distinctly understood that if the commodities covered by any of these applications become unsuitable or ineligible for export or cannot be imported into or sold in another country, approval may be cancelled or modified as to part or all of such commodities.

4. The Imperial Japanese Government will be responsible

2 民主化・非軍事化政策への対応（昭和20年10月〜21年5月）

for the accuracy of all information presented in applications and for the availability of material as described therein. This includes:

　a. Responsibility for safeguarding any existing stocks of materials described as available for export, and preventing any disposal until and unless General Headquarters, Supreme Commander for the Allied Powers, determines that the material should not be exported.

　b. Responsibility for insuring that Applications to Prepare for Export describe material which can reasonably be expected to be available at the times indicated with due regard for the available supplies of raw materials, coal, labor and any other essential operating supplies and production facilities.

　c. Responsibility that the material actually shipped conforms to the specifications set forth in applications or shown in samples. Any deviations or substitutions will be made only with specific approval of General Headquarters, Supreme Commander for the Allied Powers.

　5. The Imperial Japanese Government will obtain clear title to any material to be exported, except that which is, or has been the property of governments or natural or legal persons outside Japan and of which General Headquarters, Supreme Commander for the Allied Powers, orders the restitution.

　6. Delivery of each shipment destined for the United States of America will take place on issuance of the on-board ocean bill of lading at the port of loading and title will pass to the U.S. Commercial Company on delivery. In the case of shipment destined for China or Korea in vessel of Japanese registry, delivery of each shipment will take place ex-vessel, port of discharge, and in the case of shipment in vessel of any other registry delivery will take place on issuance of the on-board ocean bill of lading. Title will pass upon delivery. Time of delivery and transfer of title of shipments to any other nation will be specified hereafter, either in general instructions or as each shipment is authorized.

　7. When samples of proposed exports are required, selection will be made by representatives of General Headquarters, Supreme Commander for the Allied Powers, from samples made available by the Imperial Japanese Government. One will be delivered directly to General Headquarters, Supreme Commander for

the Allied Powers. One will be catalogued by the Imperial Japanese Government, maintained in an accessible store room in the Tokyo area, and will be available at all times to General Headquarters, Supreme Commander for the Allied Powers, on request. The third sample will be packed for export and an Application to Deliver for Export, clearly marked SAMPLE in blocks 1 and 8, will be submitted. Simultaneously, the Application to Prepare for Export covering the material sampled will be submitted. If this Application to Prepare for Export has already been submitted, the Application to Deliver for Export covering the samples will be submitted as soon as the samples are packed and ready for export.

8. Specimen forms attached will be reproduced by the Imperial Japanese Government in English or bilingually in English and Japanese. Samples of the forms for reproduction will be furnished to General Headquarters, Supreme Commander for the Allied Powers, for approval prior to printing. All such applications submitted to General Headquarters, Supreme Commander for the Allied Powers, will be executed in English and insofar as feasible will contain all information required by the form.

9. All such applications will be signed by the authorized representative of the Imperial Japanese Government or his delegate as approved by General Headquarters, Supreme Commander for the Allied Powers.

FOR THE SUPREME COMMANDER:

B. M. FITCH,
Brigadier General, AGD
Adjutant General.

8 Incls:

Atchmt 1 - Export Procedure
Atchmt 2 - Specimen Form IE 100, Application to Prepare for Export
Atchmt 3 - Instructions for Submitting Specimen Form IE 100
Atchmt 4 - Specimen Form IE 200, Application to Deliver for Export
Atchmt 5 - Instructions for Submitting Specimen Form IE 200
Atchmt 6 - Specimen Form: Cargo Shipping Order
Atchmt 7 - Specimen Form: Invoice
Atchmt 8 - Bill of Sale to U. S. Com'l Co.

2 民主化・非軍事化政策への対応(昭和20年10月～21年5月)

Attachment 1

EXPORT PROCEDURE

1. Application to Prepare for Export

    a. When the Imperial Japanese Government or its official agency has reasonable assurance that a supply of a specific material is available for export in a given period, the Imperial Japanese Government or its officially authorized foreign trade agency will submit an Application to Prepare for Export (Specimen Form IE 100) to General Headquarters, Supreme Commander for the Allied Powers. Each application will be submitted in English and sextuplicate. One application will cover not only stocks of the material currently on hand and ready for shipment, but also quantities which can be available for shipment in the next few months. (See attachments 2 and 3: Specimen Form of Application to Prepare for Export and Instructions for Submitting Application.

    b. After processing by General Headquarters, Supreme Commander for the Allied Powers, two (2) copies of the validated application will be returned to the Imperial Japanese Government or its official agency. If the application is denied, the Imperial Japanese Government or its official agency will be notified.

    c. When General Headquarters, Supreme Commander for the Allied Powers wishes the export of material for which the Japanese Government has not submitted an Application to Prepare for Export the necessary directive will be issued by General Headquarters, Supreme Commander for the Allied Powers.

2. Application to Deliver for Export

    a. When the Imperial Japanese Government or its official agency has material actually ready for export, covered either by an approved Application to Prepare for Export or a directive, it will submit eight (8) copies of an Application to Deliver for Export (Specimen Form IE 200) (See attachments 4 and 5: Application to Deliver for Export and Instructions for Submitting Application). Several such applications may be submitted within the limits of one approved Application to Prepare for Export as quantities within the approved total are ready for shipment.

    In most cases, the time for submitting the Application to

Deliver for Export will be left to the Imperial Japanese Government or its officially authorized agency. However, in cases which require close coordination with shipping authorities, or in cases involving undue delay in delivery of material, covered by an approved Application to Prepare for Export, a Directive will be issued by General Headquarters, Supreme Commander for the Allied Powers, requiring submission of an Application to Deliver for Export.

    b. Each application will be processed by General Headquarters, Supreme Commander for the Allied Powers. Four (4) copies of the validated application will be returned to the Imperial Japanese Government or its official agency. Validation will include information as to country of destination, delivery of material, transfer of title, and time and place of shipment. If the application is denied the Imperial Japanese Government or its official agency will be notified.

    3. On receipt of the validated copies of the Application to Deliver for Export, the Imperial Japanese Government or its officially authorized agency will:

    a. Deliver the shipment to the agent of the carrier specified in the validation of the Application to Deliver for Export together with three (3) copies of a cargo shipping order (Specimen form attached, attachment 6) in accordance with instructions in the validation, and obtain from the agent, after the cargo is loaded, three (3) signed copies of an on-board ocean bill of lading and three (3) non-negotiable copies.

    b. Deliver four (4) copies of the validated Application to Deliver for Export to the United States War Shipping Administration at the port of shipment and receive back from the United States War Shipping Administration three (3) copies certified by them.

    c. Prepare the following documents:

    Five (5) copies of Bill of Sale and Transfer of Title. (see specimen form attached, for use in sales to U. S. Commercial Company, Attachment 8).

    Six (6) copies of Invoice. (See specimen form attached, attachment 7).

2 民主化・非軍事化政策への対応(昭和20年10月～21年5月)

Six (6) copies of Packing List and Weight and Measurement Lists.

Two (2) signed copies of on-board bill of lading and three (3) unsigned copies (received from the shipping company in 3a above).

The statement from the ship's master received in 3d above.

d. Deliver one (1) signed on-board bill of lading plus a complete set of the documents listed in 3c above (with the exception of the bill of sale) to the ship's master in an envelope addressed, in case of shipments to the U. S. A., to U. S. Commercial Company or its designee at U. S. port of entry as indicated in the validation of the Application to Deliver for Export. In the case of shipments to another country, the envelope will be addressed to the appropriate government agency. Obtain from the ship's master a statement that this envelope has been received.

e. Return immediately to the Eighth Army for transmittal to General Headquarters, Supreme Commander for the Allied Powers, the following documents:

One (1) copy of the certified Application to Deliver for Export as received from the port authority.

Five (5) copies of each of the documents prepared in 3c above.

f. In the case of shipments to China and Korea in vessels of Japanese registry, one less copy of all shipping documents will be submitted, and no bill of sale is necessary, and no validation of the Application to Deliver for Export by United States War Shipping Administration is required. If possible certification of actual shipment should be obtained from the Japanese port authorities or customs. In the case of shipments to China the set of documents given to the ship's master shall be addressed to COMGEN CHINA or his designee as indicated in the validation of the Application to Deliver for Export. In the case of shipments to Korea they shall be addressed to COMGEN USAFIK or his indicated designee. Documents may be returned directly to General Headquarters Supreme Commander for the Allied Powers, rather than to the Eighth Army

407

交易営団および日本雑貨貿易振興会社の解散方指令

昭和21年3月14日 連合国最高司令官総司令部より日本政府宛

編注　本文書の別添2〜8は省略。

GENERAL HEADQUARTERS
SUPREME COMMANDER FOR THE ALLIED POWERS
APO 500

14 March 1946

AG 323.31 (14 Mar 46) ESS/AC.
(SCAPIN - 815)

MEMORANDUM FOR: IMPERIAL JAPANESE GOVERNMENT.

THROUGH: Central Liaison Office, Tokyo.

SUBJECT: Dissolution of Koeki Eidan and Nippon Zakka Boeki Shinko Kaisha.

1. The Imperial Japanese Government is directed to liquidate the Koeki Eidan (National Trade Corporation) and its subsidiary organization, The Nippon Zakka Boeki Shinko Kaisha (Japan Miscellaneous Goods Trade Encouragement Company). In liquidation, however, no property in the following category will be sold, disposed of or transferred, without approval of this Headquarters:

a. All property in the custody of Koeki Eidan or Nippon Zakka Boeki Shinko Kaisha, formerly belonging to governments

---

for transmittal to General Headquarters, Supreme Commander for the Allied Powers. Otherwise, the procedure in 3a — 3e above shall be followed. In the case of all shipments to China or Korea in vessels of Japanese registry, the Imperial Japanese Government or its agent will obtain from consignee at the port of destination two (2) copies of the cargo receipt, which shall be returned to General Headquarters, Supreme Commander for the Allied Powers.

4. General Headquarters, Supreme Commander for the Allied Powers, will provide a receipt for the bill of sale and other shipping documents and will transmit it to the Imperial Japanese Government or its official agency as soon as feasible after receipt of documents.

2 民主化・非軍事化政策への対応(昭和20年10月〜21年5月)

or nationals of the United Nations, which was acquired after 7 July 1937 by any Japanese agency through duress, forced sale, confiscation, as booty of war, or transferred through the enemy property custodian.

b. All property held for or received from nationals or governments at war with the United Nations after 2 September 1939, which is now in custody of Koeki Eidan or Nippon Zakka Boeki Shinko Kaisha.

2. A complete inventory of the properties in the above-named categories showing the source from which each item was obtained, as well as the name of the prior owner, shall be submitted to this Headquarters on or before 15 May 1946 in quintuplicate, typed in English.

3. Such materials and goods as do not fall within the above-named excepted categories shall be distributed through the normal distribution channels in accordance with the present method of effecting such distribution.

4. The staffs of the named organizations shall be used for the purpose of liquidation under the direction of competent government authority. The name of such competent government authority shall be furnished this Headquarters on or before 20 May 1946. All records of the named organizations shall be preserved by the competent government authority directing the liquidation.

FOR THE SUPREME COMMANDER:

B. M. FITCH,
Brigadier General, AGD,
Adjutant General.

134
[聯合軍總司令部トノ連絡ニ關スル件]

昭和21年3月15日　閣議了解案

閣議諒解案

昭和二十一年三月十五日

聯合軍總司令部トノ連絡ニ關スル件

本件ニ關シ昭和二十年十一月十五日次官會議ノ決定ハアルモ聯合軍總司令部トノ折衝事項益々多岐ニ亘ルニ伴ヒ時ニ同司令部側トノ間ニ意思ノ疎通ヲ缺キ誤解ヲ生スルカ如キ事例モ生シ勝チナルニ付テハ今後ハ政府ノ重要政策、機構

409

135

「戦争と建設」など宣伝出版物の没収に関する指令

昭和21年3月17日 連合国最高司令官総司令部より 日本政府宛

改革若ハ重要ナル人事等ニ關シテハ事前ニ終戦連絡中央事務局總裁ニ通報シ同總裁ヲ通シテ豫メ總司令部側トノ連絡ヲ行フコトト致度シ

尚終戦連絡中央事務局總裁ニ對スル通報ハ誤リヲ避クル爲書物ニテ之ヲナスコトトス

SUPREME COMMANDER FOR THE ALLIED POWERS
GENERAL HEADQUARTERS
APO 500

17 March 1946

AG 311.7 (17 Mar 46) CI
(SCAPIN-824)

MEMORANDUM FOR: IMPERIAL JAPANESE GOVERNMENT.

THROUGH: Central Liaison Office, Tokyo.

SUBJECT: Confiscation of Propaganda Publications.

1. The Japanese Government is directed to collect from all public channels, including warehouses, book shops, book dealers, publishing companies, distributing agents and all commercial establishments, or agencies of the Japanese government where these publications are held in bulk, the following listed propaganda publications:

a. War & Construction (Asahi Newspaper Company) December 1943.

b. Senji Shimbun Tokuhon (Manual of Newspaper Reading in Wartime - Tokijiro Hirata) December 1940.

c. Kindai Kaisen (Modern Sea Battle - Mainichi Newspaper) October 1941.

d. Bei Ei Chosen No Shinso (The True State of the American-British Challenge to Japan - Hachiro Arita) October 1943.

e. Shomen Hikohei Tokuhom (Reader for Junior Air Corps - Army Information Department) November 1943.

f. Bei Ei No Toa Kokuran (American-British Disturbance of East Asia - Hachiro Arita) December 1943.

g. Bei Ei No Sekai Shinryoku (American World Agression - Kensuku Horiuchi) August 1944.

h. Dai Toa No Kensetsu (The Building of Greater East Asia - Eigi Amo) November 1944.

i. Fujin Asia (Asiatic Women - Mainichi Newspaper) Monthly January 1942 to September 1943.

j. Sakura (Cherry - Mainichi Newspaper Co.) Monthly.

2. These publications will be collected and stored in a central warehouse. Instructions for the disposal of these publications for pulping will be issued by this headquarters at a later date.

3. A periodic report will be submitted on the 15th and last day of each month to General Headquarters, Supreme Commander for the Allied Powers, beginning 31 March 1946. This report shall include:

a. The name and number of publications collected in the interim period

b. Source from which obtained, including the name and number of publications collected from each source

c. Total number of publications

d. Gross weight

e. Specific location of storage

4. Individual copies in private homes or libraries will be exempted from action directed above.

FOR THE SUPREME COMMANDER:

B. M. FITCH,
Brigadier General, AGD,
Adjutant General.

編注　本文書中のローマ字表記はすべて原文のままとした。

昭和21年3月22日　連合国最高司令官総司令部より日本政府宛

伊豆諸島および孀婦岩以北の南方諸島を日本の行政権下の地域に含める旨の指令

GENERAL HEADQUARTERS
SUPREME COMMANDER FOR THE ALLIED POWERS
APO 500

AG 091 (22 Mar 46) GS
SCAPIN 841

22 March 1946

MEMORANDUM FOR: IMPERIAL JAPANESE GOVERNMENT.
THROUGH: Central Liaison Office, Tokyo.
SUBJECT: Governmental and Administrative Separation of Certain Outlying Areas from Japan.

1. Reference is made to the following:

a. Memorandum to the Japanese Government AG 091 (29 Jan 46) GS - (SCAPIN 677), subject, "Governmental and Administrative Separation of Certain Outlying Areas from Japan."

b. Memorandum from the Japanese Government C.L.O. No. 918 (1.1) of 26 February 1946, subject, "Request for Information Regarding Status of Izu Islands."

2. Paragraph 3 of reference "a" is hereby amended so that the Izu Islands and the Nanpo Islands north of and including Lot's Wife (Sofu Gan) are included within the area defined as Japan for the purpose of that directive.

3. The Japanese government is hereby directed to resume governmental and administrative jurisdiction over these islands, subject to the authority of the Supreme Commander for the Allied Powers.

4. Nothing in this directive shall be construed as an indication of Allied policy relating to the ultimate determination of the minor islands referred to in Article 8 of the Potsdam Declaration.

FOR THE SUPREME COMMANDER:

B. M. FITCH,
Brigadier General, AGD,
Adjutant General.

〰〰〰〰〰〰

137

昭和21年3月22日 終戦連絡中央事務局より
連合国最高司令官総司令部宛

食糧輸入要請量の修正について

TO: GENERAL HEADQUARTERS OF THE SUPREME COMMANDER FOR THE ALLIED POWERS.
FROM: Central Liaison Office, Tokyo.
SUBJECT: Revised Demand and Supply Program of Staple Foodstuffs.

22 March 1946

C.L.O. No. 1330 (ET-A)

1. As the result of thorough investigation of the present food situation, the Japanese Government has been compelled to revise its 1945 rice year food program. The revised demand and supply program with the explanatory statement is submitted herewith to the General Headquarters.

2. The Japanese Government wishes to request that the General Headquarters would be good enough to give special consideration so that the importation of 2,000,000 tons of foodstuffs, which is the minimum requirement of Japan as shown in the revised food program referred to above, may be realized at the earliest date.

FOR THE PRESIDENT:

(S. Iguchi)
Director of General Affairs,
Central Liaison Office.

Enclosure: As stated in Para. 1 above.

編注　本文書の別添は見当たらない。

138

日本経済の全般的研究に関する総司令部係官との第一回会談要旨

昭和21年3月23日　調査局第三課作成

付記一　昭和二十一年三月二十五日、調査局第三課作成

　右第二回会談要旨

二　昭和二十一年四月一日、調査局第三課作成

　右第三回会談要旨

三　昭和二十一年五月六日、調査局第三課作成

　右第四回会談要旨

「ボグダン」トノ會見記録（第一回）

（調三、大來）

昭和二十一年三月二十三日午后三時半、GHQ、「フィナンシャル・デヴィジョン」「ボグダン」及「タマニヤ」、外務省大來、大藏省木内、商工省菅波

〔米〕日本經濟ノ全般的性格ニ就テ至急私的ニ研究致シ度

シ、カカル資料ナキヤ、特ニ工業生産及日本人ノ榮養ニ關シテ說明ヲ聽取致シ度シ

［日］榮養ニ關シテハ農林省審議室調査部長大野氏ヲ紹介致スベシ

尚ホ外務省ニ於テ經濟問題ニ關シ委員會ニテ審議中ナル「日本ノ賠償能力ニ關スル一研究」及「日本ノ食糧事情」（昭和二〇年一一月、農林省）ヲ提出ス

［米］外務省ニテカカル問題ヲ研究スル理由如何、尚ホ其ノ研究結果ヲ至急承知致シ度シ

［日］賠償及經濟民主化ニ關スル問題處理上右ノ如キ研究必要ナリ、且ツ他省ニテハ農林、商工、大藏等ニ分割セラレ綜合的研究ヲ擔當スル箇所ナキタメ外務省ニテ綜合的ニ研究シ居ル次第ナリ

［米］委員會報告書ノ英譯アリヤ、無ケレバ內容ノ梗槪ヲ提出セラレ度シ、次囘大野氏ヲ紹介セラレ度シ

［日］承知ス、尚ホ本日夕刊紙上ニ「ラチモア」氏ノ日本ノ政治經濟ニ關スル論說揭載セラル、內容日本ニ對シ非好意的且ツ不公正トノ印象ヲ受ケタリ

［米］其ノ感想ハ尤モナリ、「賠償委員團」ニ就テハ兎角ノ評判アリ他ニ貴方ニ於テ不愉快ナル經驗アラバ申述ベラレタシ

［日］別ニナシ

編注 大來佐武郎調査局第三課調査官。

（付記一）

「ボクダン」トノ會見記錄（二）

（調三、大來）

昭和二十一年三月二十五日午前十時GHQ「フィナンシヤル、デヴィジョン」「ボクダン」外務省大來、農林省大野、大藏省木內

［米］「日本ノ賠償能力」及「日本ノ食糧事情」讀了セリ、兩者トモ極メテ有用ナリ前者ニツイテハ意見必シモ全面的ニ同意ニハ非サルモ日本經濟ノ基本的問題ノ理解ニ極メテ有益ナリ

［米］「食糧事情」ニツイテハ左記ノ點說明アリタシ

1、年齢別、性別、勞作別人口構成及ソノ必要「カロ

2　民主化・非軍事化政策への対応（昭和20年10月～21年5月）

「リー」

2、日本人ハ植物性食物ヲ主トスルタメ欧米人ニ比シ栄養効率ノ見地カラ多量ノ食物ヲ必要トスルトアルモ其ノ意義如何

「日」（1）ニ就テハ次回ニ提出ス
（2）ハ植物性食物ハ動物性食物ニ比シ吸収率低キコト及植物性蛋白ハ動物性蛋白ニ比シ栄養上ノ効率低キコトヲ意味スルモノナリ

「米」日本國内ニ於テ食糧ヲ増産シ得ル限度如何又其ノ為ニ必要トセラレル措置如何

「日」増産ニハ新規耕地ノ開墾ト既耕地ノ収獲増加ノ二方法アリ前者トシテハ一五五萬町歩開墾ノ計畫アリソレニヨリ収獲増加ハ十年後ニ約一千萬石程度トナルヘシ開墾豫定地ハ現在如何ナル用途ニ使用セラレアリヤ

「日」原野、丘陵等力主ナリ

「米」既耕地ノ収量増加ハ肥料ニヨル増加ハ過去ニ於テ殆ント限界ニ近シ（過去ニ於ケル最大ノ米産額ハ約七千萬石ナリ）從ツテ残サレル途ハ品種ノ改良ト作付轉換ニヨル單位面積當リノ「カロリー」收穫増大ト土地改良等ノ手段ナリ

例ヘハ新鮮ナル土壤ヲ耕地ニ持込ムコト（客土）ヲ大規模ニ實行スレハ相當ノ増産可能ナルモ技術的經濟的ニ限度アリ

「米」開墾計畫ニヨル三年後五年後十年後ニ於ケル實際的増收可能量承知致シタシ

「日」次回ニ提出スヘシ

「米」今回ノ農地制度改革ハ現實ニ日本ノ農業生産力ヲ向上セシムルヤ又大地主ノ土地ヲ細分化スルコトノ生産力ニ及ホス影響如何

「日」小作農ノ自作化ニヨル生産増加ハ或ル程度期待シ得ヘシ土地細分化ハ適正規模以下ニ細分サレル場合ニハ總體的ノ生産力ヲモ低下セシムヘシ概括的ニ見テ日本ノ農業ノ形態ニトッテハ一農家當リ五「ホーカー」（ママ）程度ノ耕地カ適當ト認メラレソレ以下ニテハ人力ヲ如何ニ増加スルモ生産額ノ増加ハ期待シ難シ

「米」ソレハ收穫遞減ノ法則カ支配スルコトノ意味ナリヤ

「日」然リ

（付記二）

「ボクダン」トノ會見記録（第三回）

（調査局三課　大來）

［米］　經營規模別ノ農家戶數ト耕地面積ニ關スル統計アリヤ

［日］　次回ニ提出スヘシ

［米］　資料ハ一週間以內ニ提出セラレタシ

昭和二十一年四月一日午後二時GHQ「フィナンシャル、デヴィジョン」「ボクダン」及「タマニヤ」外務省都留、大來、產業大學中山伊知郎、朝日新聞土屋清、農林省大野數雄

「米」　特別調查委員會報告書ヲ受取リシトコロマデ讀ミセリ、極メテ有益ナリ、

（第三章日本經濟ノ特殊性）讀了セリ、極メテ有益ナリ、內容ノ一部ハ樂觀ニ過キ一部ハ悲觀ニ過クト認メラルルトコロアルモ全體トシテ極メテ「ソートフル」ナリトノ印象ヲ受ケタリ我々ハ入口ヲ示サレタルヲ以テ後篇「リコメンデーション」ノ內容ヲ一日モ早ク承知シ度ク待望シ居ル次第ナリ

尚ホ現在迄ニ讀了セルトコロニシテ最モ興味アリシ點ハ

日本カ後進國トシテ短縮サレタ期間ニ社會進化ノ過程ヲ經過セルタメ中間ノ段階卽チ眞實ノ資本主義ノ段階ヲ充分經驗セザリシ點ヲ指摘セル箇所ナリ

［日］　前回御要求アリシ日本人ニ必要カロリー、開墾計畫、肥料效果其ノ他ニ關スル資料持參セリ、內容御一覽迄

［米］　日本人ノ子供ト大人或ハ輕勞働者ト重勞働者トノ間ニ食料ノ構成上ノ相異ナキヤ

［日］　日本人ニ必要カロリーノ九六％迄ハ植物性食物ヨリ得ルヲ以テ年令或ハ勞作別ノ食糧構成內容ニ就テハ殆ト差異ナク量ガ相異スルノミナリ

［米］　意外ナルコトナリ、米國ニ於テハ小兒ト成人トノ食糧ノ質ノ內容ニハ著シク相異アリ

［米］　本日ハ委員會ノ「リコメンデーション」ノ概要ニ就テ說明セラレ度シ、我々特ニ關心ヲ有スル點ハ今後ノ日本ノ產業構成、及生活水準等ニ關スル事項ナリ

［日］　時間ノ關係モアリ重要ナル問題ヲ撰定シテ概要ヲ說明致スベシ

先ヅ農業ニ就テハ農業ノ外部ニ於ケル對策ト內部ニ於ケル對策トノ雙方アリ、外部的對策トハ數百萬ノ人口ヲ耕

2 民主化・非軍事化政策への対応(昭和20年10月～21年5月)

地ヨリ取リ除キ農業經營カ合理的規模ヲ持ツコトヲ可能トスルニアリ、內部的對策トハ土地制度ノ改革ヲ徹底セシムルニアリ

「米」外部的對策ト內部的對策ハ矛盾セザルヤ、土地制度ノ改革ニヨリ大地主ノ土地ヲ分割スレバ農業人口ノ增大ヲ齎スニ非スヤ

「日」日本ノ土地所有形態ハ歐米ト相異ス、大土地所有者ハ大經營者ヲ意味セス自己ノ所有地ヲ細分シテ小作ニ出スノガ普通ナリ、從ツテ今囘ノ土地制度改革ハ經營ノ分割ヲ意味セス寧ロ經營ノ擴大ヲ齎スモノナリ

「米」外部的對策ニヨリ農業ヨリ引出サルヘキ人口ハ何處ニ向クルヤ

「日」之ガ日本經濟ニトツテ最モ困難ナル點ナリ、工業及農業ニ於ケル各種ノ副業ヲ振興スルヨリ他ナシ其ノ點ニツイテハ和紙ノ製造等手數ヲ要スル農村工業モ奬勵サルヘキナラン

次ニ工業ニ關シテ承リ度シ、先ヅ日本ノ纖維工業ノ將來ヲ如何ニ考ヘルヤ、特ニ人絹工業ハ日本ニ有望ナリト認ムルヤ

「日」紡績工業ハ支那印度等ノ競爭ヲ受ケ戰前ノ如キ繁榮ヲ期待スルコトハ困難ナルヘシ、但シ織布、染色等ノ加工工業ハ日本ニ適當セル工業ナラン、人絹ニツイテハ相當高度ノ技術ヲ要スル化學工業ナルヲ以テ當分ノ間支那印度等ニ於ケル發展ハ豫想セラレサルヲ以テ日本ノ輸出工業トナリ得ルモノト思考ス

「米」人絹工業ハ戰爭中、南米ニ於テ顯著ナ發展ヲ遂ケタルヲ以テ日本ノ人絹製品ノ輸出ニハ相當ノ困難ヲ豫想セラルルトコロナリ、雜貨工業ニ就テハ如何、ドイツガ各種ノ重工業ヲ制限セラレル結果玩具其ノ他雜貨類ノ輸出ニ全力ヲ注グコトガ豫想セラレ此ノ點日本品ノ輸出ニ困難ヲ生スヘシ

「日」玩具、自轉車、ゴム製品、電球等ハ從來ノ重要輸出品目ニシテ日本ノ「低賃銀」ニ基礎ヲ置クモノナリ、今後低賃銀ハ改善ヲ要スルモ何トカ輸出ヲ維持シ度キトコロナリ

「米」日本ノ自轉車工業ハ今後モ有望ナリヤ、支那ニ於テモ盛ントナルコトハ豫想セラレサルヤ

「日」日本ノ自轉車工業ハ高度ニ發達セル組織的分業ニ基

クモノナルヲ以テ當分ノ間日本ガ優位ヲ保持シ得ヘシ

［米］機械工業ハ如何、工作機械ノ輸出等モ豫想スルヤ、

［日］若シ許容サレレバ工作機械モ輸出致シ度シ、機械工業ハ雇傭ノ點ヨリスルモ日本ニトッテ重要ナル工業ナリ、輸出先ハ支那印度等東亞諸國、種類ハ電氣機械、通信機器、鐵道車輛、鑛山機器、時計計器其他ノ精密機械等ナリ、概シテ云ヘバ成可ク材料ガ少ク勞働力ヲ多ク必要トスルモノガ適當ナラン

［米］今後米國ハ支那其他東亞ニ對シ大量ノ機械類ノ輸出ヲ計畫シアルヲ以テ日本ノ機械輸出ハ相當困難ヲ豫想サル、其點ハ如何ニ考フルヤ

［日］東亞ハ生活水準低ク社會的經濟的ニモ各種ノ特殊事情アリ、必シモ米國、ドイツ等ノ高級機械製品ノミニテハ不都合ニシテ品質ハ幾分劣ルモ安價ナル日本製ノ機械ヲ需要スルコトアルモノト豫想スル次第ナリ

［米］支那トシテハ必スシモ樂觀ヲ許ササルヘシ、化學工業ニツキテハ如何、主要ナル種類如何、又輸出ニハ何ヲ豫想スルヤ

［日］藥品類、調味料、染料等ノ輸出ヲ豫想ス、主要ナル化學工業トシテハ肥料、曹達、製紙、カーバイト、硫酸等ナラン

［米］肥料工業ハ國内向ケナリヤ或ハ輸出ヲモ豫想スルヤ

［日］出來得レハ輸出致シ度キトコロナリ

［米］肥料ノ輸出ハ日本ニトッテ有望ナラン

［米］次ニ日本ニ於テ牧畜業ノ發達セサル理由如何、羊ノ如キハ山地ヲ利用シテ大ニ飼養可能ナルニ非スヤ

［日］濕度高キコト、飼料不足ナルコト等カ日本ノ牧畜不振ノ原因ナラン、又政府ノ指導獎勵ノ方針カ一貫セサルコトニモ一半ノ責任アリ、日本ノ農業ハ畜力ノ使用カ必要ニシテ牛馬ハ其ノ爲ニ飼養セラルルモ羊ハ役畜ノ用ヲナササルル點モ其ノ飼養少キ一原因ナラン

［米］「アルゼンチン」ニテハ濕度高キトコロニテ盛ニ牧羊行ハル、英國ニ於テハ牛ト羊トヲ同時ニ飼養スル習慣アリ、日本ニ於テ羊ヲ飼養スルコトハ推獎セラルヘキモノト思考スルモ如何

［日］更ニ專門ノ方面ニ照會シ研究致シ置クヘシ

418

2 民主化・非軍事化政策への対応(昭和20年10月～21年5月)

〔米〕水產業ニ就テハ日本人ノ榮養上重要ナルヘキヲ以テ水產額ノ減退スル今後ニ於テ水產物ノ輸出ハ困難ナラスヤ

〔日〕物ニヨッテハ輸出可能ナラン、養殖等ニモ大ニ努カスル要アリ、鰯ノ如キモ從來飼料、肥料等ニ使用サレタモノヲ食用ニ向クルコトトナルヘシ

〔米〕觀光事業ニツィテハ「ホテル」、道路等ニ多額ノ資產ノ投資ヲ必要トスル點ヲ考慮スル要アルヘシ

〔リコメンデーション〕ハ翻譯原稿出來次第キ次ニ屆ケラレ度シ、早速讀了ノ上返却スルヲ以テ然ル後ニ

〔タイプ〕ヲ取リニ部御屆ケアリ度シ

(補遺)

〔米〕本日ハ之ニテ終了ト致シ度シ、委員會ノ報告書ノ一ケ月以上ヲ必要トスヘシ

〔米〕日本ノ現在人口ニ關スル統計ニハ二種アリ何レヲ採用スヘキヤ、一九四六年六月末七千四百萬人ト七千七百萬人トノ二種ナリ、當方トシテハ一應前者ヲ計算ノ基礎ニ考ヘオル次第ナリ、今次ノ人口再調査ノ結果ハ何時判明スルヤ

〔日〕人口統計ハ統計局發表ノ分ト厚生省推定ノ分トカア

リ統計局ハ昨年十一月一日ノ內地人口ヲ七千二百萬人ト發表セルモ此ノ調査ハ終戰時ノ動搖時ニ行ハレタルヲ以テ充分ノ信賴ヲ置キ難シ、當方ノ食糧計算ノ基礎トシテハ生省推定ノ數字ヲ使用シ居ル次第ナリ、人口再調査ハ四月二十日現在ニテ行ハレ總數ノ判明スルニハ少クトモ一ケ月以上ヲ必要トスヘシ

〔米〕ソレハ殘念ナリ、我方ノ作業ニ間ニ合ハス

〔米〕財閥問題ニ關シ委員會ハ如何ニ考フルヤ

〔日〕日本ニハ財閥發生ヲ必然的ナラシメタル經濟的、社會的ノ基礎アリ、從ッテ財閥カ演シタル日本經濟ニ對スル積極的役割ハ何等カノ形態テ存續セシムル要アリ、例ヘハ優秀ナル技術的ノ「スタフ」ノ養成等ハ今後ノ民間中小企業ニヨッテハ恐ラク困難ナラン

〔米〕日本ノ財閥ハ技術的ノ關聯ナキ各種ノ產業ヲ支配スルモノナルヲ以テ之ヲ各專門分野ニ解體スルモ技術的ノ能力ニ影響スルトコロハ少カルヘシ

〔日〕然ラス、例ヘハ我國造船業ノ例ヲトレハ造船噸數ハ一九一八年ニハ年間六十五萬噸、一九三二年ニハ六萬噸、一九四四年ニハ一七〇萬噸ナリ、斯クノ如キ變動甚シキ

419

工業ヲ單獨ノ專門化サレタル經營ニヨツテ維持スルコトハ困難ナリ、其ノ他ノ諸工業モ日本ニ於テハ市場ノ狹隘ト原料基礎ノ不安定等ノ結果單獨ニハ安定セル經營困難ナル場合多シ、經營ノ安定ナキトコロニ優秀ナル技術「スタフ」ノ養成ハ期待致シ難シ

尚詳細ハ報告書ニヨラレ度シ

（以上）

（付記三）

「ボクダン」トノ會談記錄（第四回）

（昭二一、五、六、調三、大來）

昭和二十一年五月六日GHQニ於テ「ボクダン」大來

「日」日本經濟再建ノ基本問題讀了セラレタリヤ

「米」讀了セリ、本「リポート」ニツキ詳細感想ヲ述ブル約束ナルモ、御承知ノ如ク當方ニ於テモ日本經濟ノ將來ニ關スル研究ヲ行ヒ既ニ取纏メヲ了シGHQニ提出シタル次第ニシテ余及「タマニヤ」ノ報告書ガGHQニ於テ正式ニ採用セラルルヤ否ヤハ未ダ確定セザル問題ナリ、從ツテ右事情ノ判明セル後ニ於テ余等ノ作業ノ内容及貴方「リポート」ニ對スル意見ヲ詳細申述ブルコトト致度

シ、余ハ次ノ日曜（十二日）中國ニ向ヒ二週間後二當地ニ歸來スル豫定ニシテ其ノ間ニ概ネGHQノ意向モ決定セラルベク又中國側ニ於テ日本經濟ヲ如何ニ考フルヤノ點ニ關シテモ聽取致スス所存ナルヲ以テ歸來後機會ヲ設ケ余ノ意見ヲ各章毎ニ詳細申述ベ貴方ノ參考ニ供シ度シ從ツテ本日ハ貴方「リポート」ノ一般的問題ニ關シ二、三ノ感想ヲ述ブルコトニテ止メタシ

一、本委員會ノ「メンバー」中數名ハ余モ面識ノ間柄ナリ、彼等ガ日本ニ於ケル眞摯ニシテ進步的且ツ「リベラル」ナ傾向ヲ有スル人々ナルコトハ余モ充分認識シ居レリ、本「リポート」ノ所說ハ眞劍且ツ「リアリスチツク」ニシテ日本側ノ見解ヲ極メテ率直ニ表明シ居ル點ハ余ノ頗ル「アプレシエイト」スルトコロナリ

内容ニ就テハ必シモ全面的同意ヲ致シ難ク余等ノ作業ノ結果ト相異スル點モ多々アリ特ニ日本ノ重工業ノ將來ニツイテ然リ

二、率直ニ申セバ本報告ハ「リアリスチツク」ナ態度ヲ取リナガラ「リアリズム」ニ一貫セザル點アルヲ指摘セザルヲ得ズ、其ノ意味ハ「敗戰」ノ現實ヲ充分考慮セ

ラレ居ラザル點ナリ斯ルコトヲ申述ブルハ余等ガ戰勝國民トシテ誇示センガ爲ノ意ニアラズ、又日本ハ過去ニ於テ敗戰ノ經驗ヲ持タズ今次戰爭モ本土ニ於ケル戰鬪ヲ經驗セズシテ終了セル結果「敗戰」意識稀薄ナルハ極メテ自然ト認メラルル次第ナリ、然シテラ敗戰ガ何ヲ意味スルヤハ冷靜ニ再考ヲ要スルトコロナリ、例ヘバ「ベルギー」ヤ「イタリー」ハ敗戰ノ意味スルトコロヲ數次ノ體驗ニヨリ現實的ニ自覺セルモ日本ノ場合ハ然ラズ、從ツテ余ガ貴下ニ勸メタキハ貴下ガ「ワシントン」ニ於ケル極東委員會ノ委員トシテ、特ニ中國側委員トシテ出席シ貴方「リポート」ノ提出ヲ受ケタル場合ヲ想定シテ右「リポート」ヲ再讀セラレンコトナリ

三、他ノ一點ハ本「リポート」ガ前半ノ敍述ガ極メテ卓越セルニ比シ後半ニ至ツテハ所論曖昧ト認メラルル點ナリ、更ニ數表其ノ他ヲ加ヘ「コンクリート」ナモノトセバ極メテ「ヴァリユアブル」ナ資料トナルベシ

「日」卒直ニシテ懇篤ナル御注意感謝ス我方ニ於テモ更ニ檢討致スベシ向ホ貴下歸來後ノ「デスカッション」ヲ大イニ期待致ス次第ナリ

139

外国人の日本入国および登録に関する指令

昭和21年4月2日　連合国最高司令官総司令部より　日本政府宛

SUPREME COMMANDER FOR THE ALLIED POWERS
GENERAL HEADQUARTERS

APO 500

2 April 1946

AG 053 (2 Apr 46) GA
SCAPIN-852

MEMORANDUM FOR: IMPERIAL JAPANESE GOVERNMENT.
THROUGH: Central Liaison Office, Tokyo.
SUBJECT: Entry and Registration of Non-Japanese Nationals in Japan.

1. From time to time non-Japanese nationals, not part of the Occupation Forces, will be granted permission to enter Japan. These persons will reside in Japan on a semi-permanent basis. Absence of Japanese consuls abroad and consequent impossibility

of obtaining visas, necessitates the establishment of a procedure for legal entry and residence.

2. It is desired that the Imperial Japanese Government take action to implement its part in the following procedure:

   a. This Headquarters will notify persons approved for entry of such approval, informing them that visa requirements are waived, but that they will report for registration to the Japanese Ministry of Home Affairs upon arrival in Japan.

   b. The Imperial Japanese Government will be furnished the names of persons approved as described in a above.

   c. When such persons report to the Ministry of Home Affairs the Imperial Japanese Government will register them and furnish them with identification and such documents as are necessary to legalize their residence in Japan.

FOR THE SUPREME COMMANDER:

          B. M. FITCH,
    Brigadier General, AGD,
      Adjutant General.

---

140 貿易庁設置に関する指令

昭和21年4月3日　連合国最高司令官総司令部より日本政府宛

GENERAL HEADQUARTERS
SUPREME COMMANDER FOR THE ALLIED POWERS
APO 500

3 April 1946

AG 334 (3 Apr 46) ESS-IE
(SCAPIN 854)

MEMORANDUM FOR: THE IMPERIAL JAPANESE GOVERNMENT.
THROUGH: Central Liaison Office, Tokyo.
SUBJECT: Board of Trade (Boeki Cho).

1. References are made to the following documents pertinent to the establishment of an agency by the Imperial Japanese Government which will represent that government in the performance of approved foreign trade functions:

   a. Paragraph 3d of Memorandum for the Imperial Japanese Government AG (091.31) ESS, dated 9 October 1945, which ordered the creation of an agency to be responsible for re-

2　民主化・非軍事化政策への対応(昭和20年10月〜21年5月)

ceiving, and for the distribution of, imports.

　b. Central Liaison Office No. 1176 (1.123) dated 18 December 1945.

　c. Imperial Ordinance No. 703 dated 14 December 1945.

　d. Imperial Ordinance No. 704 dated 14 December 1945.

　e. Foreign Trade Settlement Fund Law, Proceeding of the Diet No. XXVI (c) of 21 December 1945.

2. The Board of Trade, as indicated in C.L.O. 1176 (1.123) dated 18 December 1945, hereinafter referred to as Boeki Cho, is hereby recognized as the exclusive agency of the Imperial Japanese Government to handle all Japanese foreign trade transactions in accordance with the following:

　a. All of the transactions of Boeki Cho will be handled in accordance with, or in a manner consistent with, instructions of the Supreme Commander for the Allied Powers.

　b. All foreign trade will be handled by Boeki Cho on behalf of the Imperial Japanese Government, except as may be specifically authorized to the contrary by the Supreme Commander for the Allied Powers.

　c. No other agency of the Imperial Japanese Government, no quasi-governmental or other organization or association, and no natural or legal person under the jurisdiction of the Imperial Japanese Government will perform any foreign trade functions except through Boeki Cho or as specifically authorized by the Supreme Commander for the Allied Powers.

　d. Boeki Cho will deliver or cause to be delivered all export goods as instructed by the Supreme Commander for the Allied Powers. It will take delivery or cause delivery to be taken of import goods as instructed by the Supreme Commander for the Allied Powers. Boeki Cho will deliver or cause to be delivered for export only goods to which full and complete title has been vested in Boeki Cho on behalf of the Imperial Japanese Government, unless otherwise specifically authorized by the Supreme Commander for the Allied Powers, and Boeki Cho will transfer title thereto as the Supreme Commander for the Allied Powers may direct. Boeki Cho will take title on behalf of the Imperial Japanese Government to imported goods as directed by the Supreme Commander for the Allied Powers.

e. All commercial burdens, risks, claims and other responsibilities and liabilities as to foreign trade will be assumed by Boeki Cho.

f. All imports will be received "as is" and, except as approved by the Supreme Commander for the Allied Powers, Boeki Cho and the Imperial Japanese Government will assert no claims with respect to quality, quantity, condition or any other matter directly or indirectly affecting the receipt of such goods.

g. Boeki Cho and the Imperial Japanese Government will hold all other Governments and agencies and representatives thereof harmless from all loss, cost, damage or expense arising directly or indirectly out of any purchase, sale, disposition or other handling of export or import goods or arising in connection with any foreign trade transaction.

h. The appointment of all personnel of Boeki Cho of the rank of Chief of Bureau or higher, including Advisers and Counselors, will be subject to the approval of the Supreme Commander for the Allied Powers. Advice concerning personnel listed in the inclosure to your memorandum CLO No.1175 (1.123) dated 18 December 1945 will be furnished at an early date.

3. Imperial Ordinance No. 703, dated 14 December 1945, which established Boeki Cho, and other laws, ordinances and regulations pertinent thereto will be amended to give effect to the following:

a. Boeki Cho will purchase export goods only as authorized by the Supreme Commander for the Allied Powers by approval of an "Application to Prepare for Export" or an "Application to Deliver for Export" or by issuance of an export directive from the Supreme Commander for the Allied Powers.

b. Boeki Cho will receive all import goods made available by the Supreme Commander for the Allied Powers. It may allow others to perform acts connected with receipt of the goods, but title will first be vested in Boeki Cho on behalf of the Imperial Japanese Government, unless otherwise directed by the Supreme Commander for the Allied Powers.

c. Boeki Cho will handle, transfer, and receive all im-

2　民主化・非軍事化政策への対応（昭和20年10月～21年5月）

port and export goods in accordance with instructions of the Supreme Commander for the Allied Powers and authorizations and policies established by duly empowered agencies of the Imperial Japanese Government.

　d. Boeki Cho will be empowered to perform all of the acts and do all that is necessary to give full effect to paragraphs 2d, e and f above.

　e. Advisers will be appointed for one year terms.

　f. Advisers will in general act as a body (Board of Advisers). They will act upon a vote of a majority of the advisers, and minutes of all meetings shall be kept. The President of Boeki Cho will request their advice on all important matters. On occasion, they will upon the President's request, individually or as members of committees, assist him in the discharge of operations functions.

　4. Imperial Ordinance No. 704, dated 14 December 1945, which established the Committee for the Distribution of Imported Goods, and other laws, ordinances, and regulations pertinent thereto will be amended to give effect to the following:

　　a. The Committee for the Distribution of Imported Goods will advise and assist Boeki Cho and other duly empowered agencies of the Imperial Japanese Government in the distribution of imported goods, acting consistently with instructions of the Supreme Commander for the Allied Powers and policies of all duly empowered agencies of the Imperial Japanese Government.

　　b. Committee members may act individually or in groups to advise or assist the President of Boeki Cho.

　5. The Foreign Trade Settlement Fund, created by Proceeding of the Diet, No. XXVI (c) of 21 December 1945 will be sufficient in amount to meet the obligations of Boeki Cho, and laws, ordinances and regulations will be amended to give effect to the following:

　　a. Any loans or appropriations deposited in the fund are to be reported to the Supreme Commander for the Allied Powers.

　　b. The fund will be available solely to Boeki Cho and will be expended upon order of Boeki Cho only to discharge financial obligations reasonably assumed in the performance of the acts mentioned in paragraphs 3a, b, c and d, above, except as may otherwise be specifically authorized by the Supreme Commander for the Allied Powers.

c. All sums received by Boeki Cho arising directly or indirectly out of the sale or other disposition of imported goods will be deposited in the Foreign Trade Settlement Fund and will be available to Boeki Cho for the purposes defined above.

d. No loans for financing distribution of imports nor for processing or assembly of goods for export will be made out of the Foreign Trade Settlement Fund.

e. The Fund will not be used for any subsidy, direct or indirect, on any imported goods.

6. Direct communication between Boeki Cho, designated agencies of the Imperial Japanese Government and interested staff sections of the General Headquarters of the Supreme Commander for the Allied Powers is hereby authorized to implement the instructions contained in this memorandum.

7. Provisions of this memorandum do not apply to restitution, restoration or reparations directed by the Supreme Commander for the Allied Powers.

FOR THE SUPREME COMMANDER:

B. M. FITCH,
Brigadier General, AGD,
Adjutant General.

---

141 昭和21年4月19日　連合国最高司令官総司令部より　日本政府宛

略奪財産の没収および報告に関する指令

SUPREME COMMANDER FOR THE ALLIED POWERS
GENERAL HEADQUARTERS
APO 500
19 April 1946

AG 386.3 (19 Apr 46) CPC
(SCAPIN - 885)

MEMORANDUM FOR: IMPERIAL JAPANESE GOVERNMENT.
THROUGH: Central Liaison Office, Tokyo.
SUBJECT: Impounding and Reporting of Looted Property.

1. The Imperial Japanese Government is directed to seek out, inventory, and impound immediately, all identifiable looted

property which is now in Japan and which has been the subject of transfer under duress, wrongful acts of confiscation, dispossession or spoliation, whether pursuant to legislation or by procedure purporting to follow forms of law or otherwise, in areas occupied by the Japanese Armed Forces since 7 July 1937.

2. The completed inventory will be submitted to General Headquarters, Supreme Commander for the Allied Powers, by 1 June 1946, and will be compiled by territories or localities from which the property was taken, and will include:

   a. Complete description of property.
   b. Quantity.
   c. Name of owner at time of seizure.
   d. Disposition of property upon arrival in Japan.
   e. Present title holder and address.
   f. Present location of Property.

Five copies of this inventory will be furnished General Headquarters, Supreme Commander for the Allied Powers, and will be submitted in the English language.

3. The Imperial Japanese Government is directed to retain all such properties under custody and will not permit any transactions or movement of such properties.

4. The Imperial Japanese Government will issue an Official Ordinance covering the above instructions and providing adequate penalties for violators. Five copies of such Ordinance both in English and Japanese languages will be submitted to General Headquarters, Supreme Commander for the Allied Powers, by 7 May 1946.

FOR THE SUPREME COMMANDER:

B. M. FITCH,
Brigadier General, AGD,
Adjutant General.

昭和21年4月25日　極東委員会決定

対日食糧供給に関する極東委員会政策決定

Food Supply for Japan

〔FEC Policy Decision, April 25, 1946〕

In view of the world food shortage, which will be at its most critical stage over the next three months, and in view of the conditions prevailing in the territories of the Allied Powers, the Far Eastern Commission:

(1) decides as a matter of policy that, except to the extent that the Supreme Commander for the Allied Powers, with the advice of the Allied Council for Japan, determines that imports are essential immediately for the safety of the Occupation Forces, no imports shall be permitted which will have the effect of giving to the Japanese a priority or preferential treatment over the requirements of the peoples of any Allied Power or liberated area; and

(2) requests the United States Government, in the light of the policy set out above, immediately to review the food import program for Japan in consultation with the United Nations Relief and Rehabilitation Administration, the Combined Food Board, and other allocating authorities.

編　注　本文書は、昭和二十四年十二月、外務省特別資料課作成「日本占領及び管理重要文書集」第四巻より抜粋。

連合国軍人によって生じた損害の補償について

昭和21年4月26日　終戦連絡中央事務局より
　　　　　　　　　連合国最高司令官総司令部宛

付　記　昭和二十一年九月十一日付連合国最高司令官総司令部より日本政府宛公信SCAPIN第一一九五号

右損害補償はしない旨回答

TO: GENERAL HEADQUARTERS OF THE SUPREME COMMANDER FOR THE ALLIED POWERS.

FROM: Central Liaison Office, Tokyo.

SUBJECT: Compensation for Damage Caused by Allied Military Personnel.

26 April 1946

C.L.O. No. 1952 (PP-K)

1. With regard to the above subject the Central Liaison Office invited the attention of the General Headquarters in November 1945, by an informal letter addressed to Colonel F.P. Munson, G-2, from E. Sone, Director of the First Division, Central Liaison Office, to the following three cases, in which this Office

2 民主化・非軍事化政策への対応（昭和 20 年 10 月〜21 年 5 月）

deems compensation to be claimable:

　a. Cases in which actual violations of the law by the Allied Military Personnel have taken place and there is sufficient evidence therefor.

　b. Cases in which violations of the law by the Allied Military Personnel are established by witnesses but the offender cannot be traced.

　c. Cases where no violation of the law is involved but compensation for damage or injury is deemed equitable (e.g. damage caused by the disposal of explosives and gun powders).

　2. The Central Liaison Office inquired whether the General Headquarters, Supreme Commander for the Allied Powers, takes the view that compensation is claimable in the above cases, and, if so, whether it will be advisable for the Japanese side to set up some kind of commission to assist the Allied authorities in determining the extent of compensation.

　3. The Central Liaison Office was informed by Colonel Munson's informal letter dated 30 November 1945 that the matter of investigation, adjustment and payment of claims resulting from the occupation was presently being considered by the Chief, Claims Division, Office of the Judge Advocate General, Washington, D.C., who was then in Tokyo, and the Deputy Chief of Staff of the General Headquarters.

　And later on 13 December, 1945, Colonel Munson informed this office that a policy for the disposition of claims arising in Japan by reason of the occupation was under consideration by the U.S. War Department. Until such time as this policy was determined, no action by the General Headquarters could be taken.

　4. The Central Liaison Office has since been eagerly waiting for a determination of policy by the General Headquarters in this matter, but has not yet received any directive in this connection.

　5. On the other hand, misconducts and accidents involving Allied military personnel have reached considerable numbers, as set forth in the Enclosures 1 to 3, and not a few of the victims stand in need of speedy relief.

　6. In view of the above circumstances, the Central Liaison Office ventures to renew its request to the General Headquarters

for favourable consideration in this matter.

FOR THE PRESIDENT:

(S. Iguchi)
Director of General Affairs,
Central Liaison Office.

Enclosure: 3 tables.

編注　本文書の別添は見当たらない。

(付記)

GENERAL HEADQUARTERS
SUPREME COMMANDER FOR THE ALLIED POWERS
APO 500
11 September 1946

AG 150 (11 Sep 46) GS
SCAPIN-1195
MEMORANDUM FOR: IMPERIAL JAPANESE GOVERNMENT.
THROUGH: Central Liaison Office, Tokyo.
SUBJECT: Compensation for Damage Caused by Allied Military Personnel.

1. Reference is made to C.L.O. No. 1952 (PP-K) of 26 April 1946 requesting consideration of the establishment of procedure for the investigation, adjustment and payment of claims resulting from the occupation.

2. The Imperial Japanese Government is informed that the Supreme Commander for the Allied Powers recognizes no legal basis for liability with respect to such claims, and accepts no responsibility for the adjustment and payment thereof.

FOR THE SUPREME COMMANDER:

C. Z. Shugart
for JOHN B. COOLEY
Colonel, AGD
Adjutant General

144　昭和21年4月27日　連合国最高司令官総司令部より　日本政府宛
国際食糧事情に鑑み日本政府が提出した食糧輸入要請量に応じる確約はできない旨回答

2 民主化・非軍事化政策への対応（昭和20年10月〜21年5月）

GENERAL HEADQUARTERS
SUPREME COMMANDER FOR THE ALLIED POWERS
APO 500
27 April 1946

AG 091.31 (27 Apr 46) ESS/IE
(SCAPIN 1102-A)

MEMORANDUM FOR: THE IMPERIAL JAPANESE GOVERNMENT.
THROUGH: Central Liaison Office, Tokyo.
SUBJECT: Revised Food Import Requirements Program of Imperial Japanese Government.

1. Reference is made to letter from the Imperial Japanese Government, C.L.O. No. 1330 (ET-A), dated 22 March 1946, subject: "Revised Demand and Supply Program of Staple Foodstuffs".

2. The study of Japanese food requirements contained in above letter will be taken into consideration by the Supreme Commander for the Allied Powers. The extremely stringent world food situation makes impossible any assurance at this time of specific food importations.

FOR THE SUPREME COMMANDER:
J. W. Mann
for B. M. FITCH,
Brigadier General, AGD,
Adjutant General.

145

旧日本海軍艦艇の破壊に関する指令

昭和21年4月30日
連合国最高司令官総司令部より
日本政府宛

付記　昭和二十一年六月六日付連合国最高司令官総司令部より日本政府宛公信SCAPIN第一〇〇二号
右指令への補充指令

GENERAL HEADQUARTERS
SUPREME COMMANDER FOR THE ALLIED POWERS
APO 500
30 April 1946

AG 045.93 (30 Apr 46) GD
SCAPIN-910

MEMORANDUM FOR: IMPERIAL JAPANESE GOVERNMENT.

THROUGH: Central Liaison Office, Tokyo.

SUBJECT: Destruction of Former Japanese Naval Vessels.

1. All former Japanese surface combatant naval vessels which are:

   a. Within the Japanese Empire.

   b. Readily towable.

   c. Larger than destroyers.

   d. Not employed by the occupation forces or in the repatriation service,

are to be destroyed by scrapping or other approved manner within one (1) year of this date. All such vessels are hereby released to the Imperial Japanese Government for this purpose.

2. It is estimated that Naval Combatant vessels presently engaged in repatriation service will be available for destruction under a similar directive about November 1946.

3. The Imperial Japanese Government will:

   a. Coordinate action, in compliance with this directive, with the Commander Naval Activities, Japan and the Commanding General, Eighth Army.

   b. Submit to Commander Naval Activities, Japan:

   (1) An outline of the over-all plan for the accomplishment of this directive.

   (2) Quarterly reports indicating the status of the program and estimated date of completion.

   (3) Plans for specific scrapping operations.

   c. Submit to Commanding General, Eighth Army, applications of private contractors for newly established salvage and scrapping activities or applications as necessary to extend present industrial activity to include salvage and scrapping. Applications will be submitted as required by Occupational Directive No.3, dated 22 September 1945.

FOR THE SUPREME COMMANDER:

B. M. FITCH,
Brigadier General, AGD,
Adjutant General.

（付記）

2　民主化・非軍事化政策への対応(昭和20年10月～21年5月)

GENERAL HEADQUARTERS
SUPREME COMMANDER FOR THE ALLIED POWERS
APO 500

6 June 1946

AG 386.3 (6 Jun 46) GD
SCAPIN 1002
MEMORANDUM FOR: IMPERIAL JAPANESE GOVERNMENT.
THROUGH: Central Liaison Office, Tokyo.
SUBJECT: Destruction of Former Japanese Naval Vessels.

1. Supplementing Memorandum to the Imperial Japanese Government, AG 045.93 (30 Apr 46) GD (SCAPIN 910) the following ex-Japanese Naval Vessels are released to the Imperial Japanese Government for destruction by scrapping or other approved manner.

　　a. All remaining submarines, including partially constructed submarines.

　　b. All combatant vessels larger than Destroyers, not covered in SCAPIN 910 and not employed in repatriation or mine sweeping.

2. The provisions of paragraph 3 of the above-mentioned Memorandum to the Imperial Japanese Government are applicable to this directive.

FOR THE SUPREME COMMANDER:

B. M. FITCH,
Brigadier General, AGD,
Adjutant General.

146　昭和21年5月3日　連合国最高司令官総司令部より　日本政府宛

鳩山一郎の公職追放に関する指令

GENERAL HEADQUARTERS
SUPREME COMMANDER FOR THE ALLIED POWERS
APO 500

3 May 1946

AG 014.1 (3 May 46) GS
(SCAPIN 919)
MEMORANDUM FOR: IMPERIAL JAPANESE GOVERNMENT.
THROUGH: Central Liaison Office, Tokyo.

SUBJECT: Removal and Exclusion from Public Office of Diet Member.

1. Under the memorandum of 4 January 1946 "Removal and Exclusion of Undesirable Personnel from Public Office," (SCAPIN 550) the Japanese Government was directed to disqualify any candidate for the Diet who had deceived and misled the people of Japan within the spirit and letter of that directive.

2. After the election on 10 April 1946, the Central Liaison Office was informed that the eligibility of one Ichiro Hatoyama, (member-elect of the House of Representatives from the First Electoral District, Tokyo) to hold any public office being open to doubt in the light of evidence published subsequent to his screening by the Japanese Government, it was expected that his eligibility would be re-examined by the Government forthwith.

3. The Japanese Government having failed to act on its own responsibility, the Supreme Commander for the Allied Powers has determined the facts relative to Hatoyama's eligibility and finds that he is an undesirable person within the meaning of paragraphs 1 and 3 of Category "G", Appendix "A", SCAPIN 550 in that:

a. As Chief Secretary of the Tanaka Cabinet from 1927 to 1929, he necessarily shares responsibility for the formulation and promulgation without Diet approval of amendments to the so-called Peace Preservation Law which made that law the government's chief legal instrument for the suppression of freedom of speech and freedom of assembly, and made possible the denunciation, terrorization, seizure, and imprisonment of tens of thousands of adherents to minority doctrines advocating political, economic, and social reform, thereby preventing the development of effective opposition to the Japanese militaristic regime.

b. As Minister of Education from December 1931 to March 1934, he was responsible for stifling freedom of speech in the schools by means of mass dismissals and arrests of teachers suspected of "leftist" leanings or "dangerous thoughts." The dismissal in May 1933 of Professor Takigawa from the faculty of Kyoto University on Hatoyama's personal order is a flagrant illustration of his contempt for the liberal tradition of academic freedom and gave momentum to the spiritual mobilization of Japan

2 民主化・非軍事化政策への対応（昭和20年10月～21年5月）

which, under the aegis of the military and economic cliques, led the nation eventually into war.

c. Not only did Hatoyama participate in thus weaving the pattern of ruthless suppression of freedom of speech, freedom of assembly, and freedom of thought, but he also participated in the forced dissolution of farmer-labor bodies. In addition, his indorsement of totalitarianism, specifically in its application to the regimentation and control of labor, is a matter of record. His recommendation that "it would be well" to transplant Hitlerite anti-labor devices to Japan reveals his innate antipathy to the democratic principle of the right of labor freely to organize and to bargain collectively through representatives of its own choice. It is a familiar technique of the totalitarian dictatorship, wherever situated, whatever be its formal name, and however be it disguised, first to weaken and then to suppress the freedom of individuals to organize for mutual benefit. Whatever lip service Hatoyama may have rendered to the cause of parliamentarianism, his sponsorship of the doctrine of regimentation of labor identifies him as a tool of the ultra-nationalistic interests which engineered the reorganization of Japan on a totalitarian economic basis as a prerequisite to its wars of aggression.

d. By words and deeds he has consistently supported Japan's acts of aggression. In July 1937 he traveled to America and Western Europe as personal emissary of the then Prime Minister Konoye to justify Japan's expansionist program. While abroad he negotiated economic arrangements for supporting the war against China and the subsequent exploitation of that country after subjugation. With duplicity, Hatoyama told the British Prime Minister in 1937 that "China cannot survive unless controlled by Japan," and that the primary motive behind Japan's intervention in China involved the "happiness of the Chinese people."

e. Hatoyama has posed as an anti-militarist. But in a formal address mailed to his constituents during the 1942 election in which he set forth his political credo, Hatoyama upheld the doctrine of territorial expansion by means of war, referred to the attack on Pearl Harbor as "fortunately…a great victory," stated as a fact that the true cause of the Manchuria and China "incidents" was the anti-Japanese sentiment (in China) instigated by England and

America, ridiculed those who in 1928 and 1929 had criticized the Tanaka Cabinet, boasted that that cabinet had "liquidated the (previous) weak-kneed diplomacy toward England and America," and gloated that "today the world policy drafted by the Tanaka Cabinet is steadily being realized." This identification of himself with the notorious Tanaka policy of world conquest, whether genuine or merely opportunistic, in and of itself brands Hatoyama as one of those who deceived and misled the people of Japan into militaristic misadventure.

4. Accordingly, in view of these and other considerations not herein recited, the Imperial Japanese Government is directed to bar Ichiro Hatoyama from membership in the Diet and to exclude him from government service pursuant to SCAPIN 550.

FOR THE SUPREME COMMANDER:

B. M. FITCH,
Brigadier General, AGD,
Adjutant General.

~~~~~~~~~~

147 昭和21年5月6日　連合国最高司令官総司令部より　日本政府宛

在日連合国財産の返還手続きに関する指令

付記　昭和二十一年十一月二十二日付連合国最高司令官総司令部より日本政府宛公信ＳＣＡＰＩＮ第一三五四号　返還対象財産に関する改正指令

GENERAL HEADQUARTERS

SUPREME COMMANDER FOR THE ALLIED POWERS

APO 500

6 May 1946

AG 386.3 (6 May 46) CPC
(SCAPIN 926)

MEMORANDUM FOR: IMPERIAL JAPANESE GOVERNMENT.

THROUGH: Central Liaison Office, Tokyo.

SUBJECT: Procedure for Returning Property in Japan to Nationals of the United Nations.

1. The Imperial Japanese Government is directed to follow the procedure outlined below in the restitution of property in

2 民主化・非軍事化政策への対応(昭和20年10月〜21年5月)

Japan to nationals of the United Nations who are residing in Japan or who may hereafter return to Japan:

a. The present Japanese custodians or administrators of properties in Japan owned by United Nations nationals on 7 December 1941 will be instructed by the Imperial Japanese Government to inform any United Nations national who applies for return of his property that three copies of an application in the form attached marked Annex A should be submitted through the representative of his Government in Japan to General Headquarters, Supreme Commander for the Allied Powers.

b. One (1) copy of this application will be forwarded by General Headquarters, Supreme Commander for the Allied Powers to the Imperial Japanese Government for examination. The Imperial Japanese Government will, as promptly as possible, return the application to General Headquarters, Supreme Commander for the Allied Powers, furnishing complete information as to (1) complete documentary record of title to ownership on 7 December 1941; (2) the present physical condition and location of the property; (3) whether or not sold and if sold, all pertinent data relative to the sale including the name and address of the purchaser and present owner; (4) the financial status of the property, including proceeds of sales made, amounts credited to and withdrawn from the account and present balance of the account, and (5) any other pertinent data.

c. All the above (a and b) shall be in the English language except that data or evidence submitted by the nationals of United Nations may be in Japanese. In case of need and if available original documents may be exhibited but not filed with the Japanese Government authorities or custodians.

d. General Headquarters, Supreme Commander for the Allied Powers will subsequently instruct the Imperial Japanese Government as to what action will be taken in each case of restitution.

2. The term "property" as used in this Memorandum shall include money, checks, drafts, bullion, bank deposits, savings accounts, any debts, indebtedness, or obligations, financial securities commonly dealt in by bankers, brokers and investment houses, notes, debentures, stocks, bonds, coupons, bankers'

acceptances, mortgages, pledges, liens or other right in the nature of security, warehouse receipts, bills of lading, trust receipts, bills of sale, any other evidences of title, ownership, or indebtedness, goods, wares merchandise, chattels, vendors, stocks on hand, ships, goods on ships, real estate mortgages, vendors, sales agreements, land contracts, real estate and any interest therein, leaseholds, ground rents, options, negotiable instruments, trade acceptances, royalties, book accounts, accounts receivable, judgements, patents, trademarks, copyrights, contracts or licenses affecting or involving patents, trademarks or copyrights, insurance policies, safe deposit boxes and their contents, annuities, pooling agreements, contracts of any nature whatsoever, etc.

3. The filing of demands for restitution of property shall not prejudice the right of the claimant or applicant to claim for compensation at a subsequent time.

4. Direct communication between the appropriate agencies of the Imperial Japanese Government and the Civil Property Custodian, General Headquarters, Supreme Commander for the Allied Powers, is hereby authorized to implement this Memorandum.

5. Six (6) copies of all ordinances issued to comply with provisions of this Memorandum shall be furnished to General Headquarters, Supreme Commander for the Allied Powers by 27 May 1946. Such copies shall contain both the English and Japanese text.

FOR THE SUPREME COMMANDER:

B. M. FITCH,

Brigadier General, AGD,

Adjutant General.

1 Incl:

 Annex A in two parts

 Part-1-Demand for Return of Property

 Part-2-Receipt

編注　本文書の別添は見当たらない。

（付記）

GENERAL HEADQUARTERS

SUPREME COMMANDER FOR THE ALLIED POWERS
APO 500
22 November 1946

AG 386.3 (22 Nov 46) CPC/FP
(SCAPIN 1354)

MEMORANDUM FOR: IMPERIAL JAPANESE GOVERNMENT.

THROUGH: Central Liaison Office, Tokyo.

SUBJECT: Restitution of United Nations Nationals' Property Wrongfully Transferred.

1. Reference is made to Memorandum for Imperial Japanese Government, AG 386.3 (6 May 46) CPC, SCAPIN 926, 6 May 1946, subject "Procedure for Returning Property in Japan to Nationals of the United Nations," from General Headquarters, Supreme Commander for the Allied Powers.

2. The "Receipt Form" attached to the above referenced memorandum as Part 2, Annex A, is hereafter obsolete and the "Receipt Form" attached hereto as Annex A is substituted therefor.

3. The Imperial Japanese Government is directed to provide the necessary procedures for the restitution of properties owned by United Nations nationals in Japan on 7 December 1941, which have been the subject of transfer under duress, wrongful acts of confiscation, dispossession or spoilation, whether pursuant to legislation or by procedure purporting to follow forms of law or otherwise, and such restitution will be made under conditions as follows:

a. General Headquarters, Supreme Commander for the Allied Powers will issue a directive to the Imperial Japanese Government in each case of restitution, stating time and place for delivery of property to be restored and transfer of title thereto.

b. Receipt in the form of the "Receipt for Restitution to United Nation National of Wrongfully Transferred Property in Japan" attached hereto as Annex A, and containing all provisions therein, will be executed in original and seven copies and distributed in accordance with distribution as shown on the bottom of page 2 of the receipt form. All copies will be signed.

c. Separate pages will be used where space provided in "Receipt for Restitution to United Nation National of Wrongfully Transferred Property in Japan" is insufficient and notation to that effect inserted in space provided.

 d. Receipt will be the result of a joint inventory by the Restoree and Representative of the Imperial Japanese Government.

 4. In each case of restitution the Representative of the Imperial Japanese Government will present to the Military Government Officer in the locality in which the property to be restituted is located a copy of the Directive requiring the restitution. The Military Government Officer or his representative will witness the restitution.

FOR THE SUPREME COMMANDER:

JOHN B. COOLEY
Colonel, AGD,
Adjutant General.

Incl: "Receipt for Restitution to United Nation National of Wrongfully Transferred Property in Japan"

編　注　本文書の別添は見当たらない。

148

昭和21年5月7日　朝海終戦連絡中央事務局総務部総務課長作成

【食糧問題に關しフーヴァー氏來邦の件】

食糧問題に關しフーヴァー氏來邦の件

（昭和二一・五・七終連總務部朝海記）

一、五日フーヴァー特使は厚木に到着したが六日小野經濟部長、自分、松井連絡官は舊米國大使館□□（二字不明）にフェラース代將を訪問の際、圖らずもフーヴァー特使、ギブソン氏（前駐伯大使）、メーソン（前インターナショナル、ニュース總裁）等が「マ」元帥に送られて官邸より出て來るのを目撃する機會を得たが、フーヴァー特使は同日午後六時から放送會館に於て日米新聞記者に對し記者會見を行つた、自分等も右に列席してフーヴァー氏の謦咳に接することが出來たが、同氏は離米以來特別輸送機に依り歐亞□（一字不明）亘る二十四ヶ國を廻つてその元首等と會談を逐げ最も長く滯在せる場所でも四日を出でたることはなく、忙しい旅行を續けたので流石にフーヴァー氏も日本に於ては七十二歳の高齡でもあり流行に病氣も併發したさうで余り元氣はなかつたが出ると共に病氣も併發したさうで余り元氣はなかつた

2　民主化・非軍事化政策への対応（昭和20年10月～21年5月）

やうに見受けられたそれでも放送會館に現はれた同氏は約二十分に亘り記者團を前にして會見を遂げたのである、先づベーカー代將の紹介の辭に次ぎ世界食糧事情に付き次のやうな一般的説明を試みたその話振りは雄辯といふのではないが、極めて眞摯に諄々と話し出した態度には吾々も多大の感銘を受けたその要旨は次のやうであった即ち

世界の食糧危機は戰爭に依る荒廢のため極めて深刻であり世界歴史に前例のないやうな最惡の事態を現出して居る、現在の世界に於ける輸出可能の食糧は六億乃至七億屯であって各國が消費の節約を行へばこれを十億屯乃至十一億屯迄上昇せしめる希望なしとしない、各國が消費節約をする場合に最も影響を受けるのは米國であらう、而して若しロシアが滿洲に於て確保せる食糧を中國及朝鮮の爲にリリースすれば情勢は大分好轉するであらう、米國より輸出を期待し得るのは主として麥と脂肪であって、コーンは輸送中腐敗する惧れもあり長途の輸送には不適當であると思はれる、又後日これを確實に返濟する保障の下に現在一時的に食糧

に余裕のある國から借入れる方法も考慮して居る、來年度の北半球は豊作が豫想され從つて下半期には食糧の輸出も増大するであらうから問題は九月一日迄の危機を克服することに在る、此の點に於て食糧危機は戰爭の危機、政治的の危機とは性質が違ふのであつて九月一日を乘切り得れば問題は好轉し食糧の増配も可能であらうから各方面の協力が希望される、前世界大戰後にも食糧飢饉が存在したがこれと現在の食糧飢饉の相違を指摘すると、現在は一九一八年に比し農業生産が惡化し減少して居るのである、從つてこの二つの危機はその性質は同じであるが現在の危機に於ては余剰食糧が極めて少ないといふ點に相違がある。

といふ趣旨を述べた、即ち右に於て注目された點は(1)世界の食糧危機克服のためにロシアの滿洲に於ける協力を要請したこと(2)食糧危機を暫定的なりとして九月以降の見透しに付き樂觀的觀測を下したこと等の點であらう

二、次で總司令部の情報係官たるベーカー代將が總司令官よりフーヴァー特使に提出せる資料を讀上げた、要旨左の通り

「日本に於ける食糧飢饉は(1)一九四五年九月の颱風及洪水に依る損害(2)五年間肥料不使用に依り生ぜる土壌の貧困等に依り前例なき減収を示し一九四五年の収穫減は前年度に比し二七パーセントに達して居る

日本の食糧状況は更に(1)インフレーションに基く日本経済の混乱化(2)供出組織の崩壊(3)農民消費物資の欠乏(4)日本経済の不安定性(5)戦争に依る損害(6)人口の増加等の原因に基き愈々悪化された

若し食糧の輸入がなければ一九四六年の五月乃至九月の間に日本の非農業人口は七〇〇カロリー以下を摂取し得るに過ぎなくなり飢餓は免れ得ないであらう

最初総司令部は都市人口に対し一五五〇カロリーを供給するため三七〇萬屯の輸入を要請したのであるが右数字は七月一日迄に引渡さるべき数量六〇萬屯といふ数字に訂正せられ後半期に付ては更に新たなる要請が必要となつたのである、六〇萬屯にては今後五ケ月間に対し非農民に対し九〇〇カロリーを確保し得るに過ぎない

若し日本に適当たる輸入が行はれなければ大量飢餓が現はれ延いて占領の主目的を達成することは不可能となる

であらう」

三、次でフーヴァー氏は予ねて記者団から提出されて居つたらしい質問に対し丁寧に且つ一括答弁する所があつた、尚応答は概ね次の如きものであつた、その質疑応答は概ね次の如きものであつて政治には一切関与せず又行政的問題に付ても自分の答ふる限りでは自分は食糧問題に関する調査を任務とするものであつて政治には一切関与せず又行政的問題に付ても自分の答ふる限りではないことを明白に留保して居つた

(1) 肥料問題に関しこの問題も直接自分の検討の埓内には入つて来て居らない旨を答へた

(2) 九月一日以降は世界の食糧状況は心配要らぬ旨を答へた

(3) 有ゆる資源を利用して食糧を増産することが必要であり、従つて日本の北太平洋に於ける漁業は重大であつて之を拒否すべき理由はないと答へた

(4) 人口の或る一部分が餓死することは已むを得ないかも知れないとの質問に対してはフーヴァー氏は、自分はデモクラットであるから(後にメーソン氏はフーヴァー氏はレパブリカンなりと笑ひ居たり)一般が欠乏に置か

2 民主化・非軍事化政策への対応(昭和20年10月～21年5月)

るべきものであつて特定の人のみ良き状態に置かるることは反対であると答へた

(5) 如何にして日本の食糧不足を認定するかといふ質問に對しては、「マ」元帥の幕僚は極めて優秀な専門家である點を指摘してゐた

(6) 闇市場の質問に對して、闇市場で動く物資は極めて限定されてゐることはその價格の極めて高いことに依つても明かであり、これは余り問題にすることはないと思はれると答へた

四、尚、フーヴァー氏の書き物に依る聲明は次の通りである(日本新聞に報道せられて居るが、新聞は大事な點を落して聲明のニュアンスを失はしめて居るやうである)

「日本は食糧を輸入しなければならない、若し食糧の輸入がなければ日本國民の食糧割當數量はドイツ人がブッケンワルド、ベルゼンの集團收容所の拘禁者に與へた食糧の量と殆んど變らぬひどいものになる、斯る狀況の上にアメリカの國旗が飜るといふことは考へ得られざる觀念である、日本進駐の米軍が食糧不足に基く日本の秩序破壞或は惡疫流行のため結局危險に晒されないやうにするには單にキリスト教的人道上の問題としてのみでなく日本に食糧を輸入する要がある、現在の日本の食糧不足は日本の再建に障碍になるばかりでなく、日本の來るべき收穫期における收穫にも影響を與へるであらう、日本が必要とする輸入量はもし全世界における來るべき時期の食糧の需給が調整されれば決して中國、印度、フィリツピンあるひは朝鮮への食糧輸入割當を惡化せしめるほどのものでない、問題はソ聯が滿洲において獲得した食糧の一部を中國あるひは朝鮮へ廻送するか否かでソ聯のかかる措置は食糧事情改善に大いに役立つものであらう」

この聲明の中注意される點は「斯る狀況の上にアメリカの國旗が飜るといふことは考へ得られざる觀念である」と述べた點と「問題はソ聯が滿洲において獲得した食糧の一部を中國あるひは朝鮮に廻送するか否かで…」と述べた點である、殊に後者の字句の中には日本の名前がメンションされて居らない、この兩者のエキスプレッションを對比して見るとそこに興味のある政治的ニュアンスが示されて居ると思はれメーソン氏に指摘したところ、

同氏はフーヴァー氏は政治家でありその聲明文もよく練つてあると答へた

五、尚、小野經濟部長、自分及松井連絡官に於て右會見後フーヴァー特使に隨行して來邦したメーソン氏と會食し種々意見を交換し、又一行の旅中の印象を聽くことを得たが、一行は七日午前九時厚木飛行場を出發し、ミッドウェーに飛び更にハワイに飛んでハワイでは滿洲及北鮮狀況視察のため米國を出發したポーレー氏及びその隨員約十八名の一行と落ち合ふこととなつて居る由である、尚その際メーソン氏は、實はフーヴァー氏は滿洲に於ける食糧狀況に付き詳細なる資料蒐集方苦慮してゐたのであるが多少不快であつた關係もあり、又時間の都合もあり十分に資料を蒐集し得なかつた譯である、フーヴァー氏としては(1)過去十年間日本は滿洲より大豆たると家畜飼料たるとを問はず有ゆる形の食糧をどの程度に輸入してゐたやの資料(2)本年の滿洲に於ける收穫の見積、輸出力の見積に付き資料を蒐集いたし度い希望で右資料はハワイにおけるポーレー氏との會見上絶對必要であると逃べたので松井連絡官は米側自動車を借用し深夜の東京市街を十二時に至るまで急遽各方面に接觸を遂げたも時刻晩くして十分なる資料を蒐集するに至らず結局本件資料は七日午前中に取纒めフェラース代將を通じ在ハワイ米軍司令官宛打電することに打合せを遂げた

〔本項は取扱に注意を要す〕

〰〰〰〰〰〰〰〰〰〰

昭和21年5月11日 日本政府宛
連合国最高司令官総司令部より

149

公衆衛生および厚生関係政府機関の改組方指令

GENERAL HEADQUARTERS
SUPREME COMMANDER FOR THE ALLIED POWERS
APO 500
11 May 1946

AG 323.31 (11 May 46) PH
(SCAPIN 945)

MEMORANDUM FOR: IMPERIAL JAPANESE GOVERNMENT.

THROUGH: Central Liaison Office, Tokyo.

SUBJECT: Reorganization of Governmental Public Health and Welfare Activities.

2 民主化・非軍事化政策への対応(昭和20年10月～21年5月)

1. In order to cope adequately with the emergency health and welfare situation, as directed by Memoranda numbered (SCAPIN 48) 22 September 1945, and (SCAPIN 775) 27 February 1946, the Imperial Japanese Government will immediately reorganize the administration of health and welfare activities to provide for the following administration of functions:

　a. A Bureau of Health, the responsibility of which will be public health (maternity, child, and adult hygiene), health education, vital statistics activities and nutritional activities.

　b. A Bureau of Medical Treatment, the responsibility of which will be general affairs (medical relief programs), administration of hospitals, administration of sanatoria, medical affairs, pharmaceutical affairs (distribution) drug production (including biologicals) and pharmaceutical standardization.

　c. A Bureau of Preventive Medicine shall be established, the responsibility of which will be those concerned with sanitary engineering, communicable diseases and chronic infectious diseases.

　d. A Bureau of Social Affairs, the responsibility of which will be those in connection with public assistance, public welfare and the procurement and disposition of materials necessary to implement such functions.

2. The administration of other continuing activities and functions of the Ministry of Health and Welfare is not affected by this Memorandum and may be a matter for future consideration.

3. The Imperial Japanese Government will cause to be established in prefectural governments a Bureau of Health and a Bureau of Welfare whose functions will include those outlined for the Ministry of Health and Welfare, as shown in paragraph 1 of this Memorandum, which will act as the operating agency for public health and welfare activities.

4. Functions of operation in connection with this Memorandum will be performed as far as possible at prefectural and local levels. Matters of policy, technical matters and overall coordination of health and welfare activities are functions of the national government.

5. The reorganization as a result of this Memorandum will be subject to modification by action of the Japanese Diet.

445

150 対日理事会におけるアチソン議長の共産主義に関する演説抜粋

昭和21年5月15日　第四回対日理事会議事録（抜粋）

付記　昭和二十一年七月十一日、朝海終戦連絡中央事務局総務部総務課長作成

「對日理事會を通ずる米ソ關係の展望」

FOR THE SUPREME COMMANDER:

J. W. Mann
for B. M. FITCH,
Brigadier General, AGD,
Adjutant General.

Speech by Mr. George Atcheson, Jr., Chairman, at the Fourth Meeting of the Allied Council for Japan

May 15, 1946

THE CHAIRMAN: Yes, as I just mentioned, all complaints and statements and petitions of this sort which come into Headquarters are placed under investigation, and these statements are being investigated. And I would like to repeat again that if any Member of the Council has any concrete or definite information on matters of this sort, particularly allegations, the Supreme Commander would wish to have it at the earliest possible moment. This is a rather curious document to my mind. According to our translators who have been working over it, the original, which was received in Headquarters was not written in idiomatic Japanese, but gave the translators a rather clear impression that originally it had been drawn up in a foreign language and then translated into Japanese for presentation. It seems to me, further, that it is a document which is essentially concerned with internal politics in Japan. I may mention in that connection that it has been the firm policy of the Supreme Commander not to interfere with internal political activities except in cases of extreme necessity. The attitude of the Supreme Commander toward the activities of various political groups in Japan has –and rightly so, I believe –been one of great generosity in permitting every possible freedom of expression and action consistent with the occupation policies. By directive, political prisoners have been released from prisons in which some of

446

them were incarcerated for many years. These political prisoners have been released irrespective of their political beliefs. They have included avowed leaders and Members of the Communist Party. I do not need to tell you that the United States does not favor Communism either in the United States or in Japan but it has been our firm belief that in accordance with the Potsdam Declaration the Japanese people should be as free as possible to develop their political activities. The Communist Party has not been suppressed in the United States. It has not been suppressed in Japan. It has been allowed in Japan the same rights as other political parties, and members of the Communist Party have been elected to the Diet in Japan.

I offer as my personal opinion that this document which we have under discussion contains signmarks of Communist propaganda.

編注　本文書は、昭和二十四年三月、外務省特別資料部作成「日本占領及び管理重要文書集」第二巻より抜粋。

（付記）

對日理事會を通ずる米ソ關係の展望

（昭和二十一年七月十一日）

第一、緒言

日本管理のための機構として極東委員會及び對日理事會を設け前者を日本管理の最高政策決定機關としたが、之を華府に置き、後者は成程東京に存置されたが諮問機關であるに止まらせられた、此の複雜した徹底味を缺いたと思はれる日本管理機構の設置こそは米國のその他の聯合國殊にソ聯との妥協外交の所産であることは言を俟たない、而してこの極東委員會に現はれた列國の對日管理の見解なり、一般的雰圍氣なりと對日理事會に現はれて居る列國の見解や空氣とは必ずしも同一ではない様であらう、蓋しこれは兩者の權限の相違に基く當然の結果であらうと思はれるのであるが、我々が新聞報道等を通じて知り得るのみである極東委員會の樣子は姑らく措き、次に對日理事會四月五日第一囘開會以來今日に至るまでの討議經過を分析してその間に現はれた列國殊に米ソの意見の對立を吟味して見たいと思ふ、日本管理の問題に於

議が分れるのは單にその個々の問題に付米ソが見解を異にすると云ふ簡單なものではなくして米ソ兩國の全世界に互る關係が明治ビルの二階の一室にも如實に反映せられるのである、對日理事會に於ける列國代表の發言はこの一般外交關係の背景から行はれて居るものである點に於て注意に値ひすると思はれる。

第二、追放令及選舉問題

對日理事會の第一回會合はマッカーサー元帥の儀禮的開會の辭を中心としたものであり、特に論ずべきこともないので四月十七日開催せられた第二囘會議から檢討して見る、第二囘會議に於ては一體日本管理に發言權を有する各國は對日理事會に於て如何に論議し、如何なる態度を表明するであらうかといふことに付て全然不明であつたため日本側傍聽者に取つても多大の興味を持たれた次第である、然るにこの會議を傍聽した日本側が殊に奇異な感に打たれたことは、常に日本側を叱咤鞭撻する立場にある總司令部がソ英華、殊にソ聯の代表に對し極力日本の立場を辯護するの態度に出でたことであつて斯る態度は對日理事會開會劈頭に於て早くも會議の今後の波瀾

を豫想せしめたのであつた、卽ち日本に於ける追放令及び總選擧の狀況を說明してホイツトニー代將は「今次選擧は正にフリー・アンド・オネスト・エレクシヨンなりと謂ふべく、西歐に於ける民主主義國家に於てもこの程度の成績を誇り得るものは少いであらう、卽ち日本はフオームに於て又サブスタンスに於て民主主義を表示せるものと謂ひ得る」と述べてから「しかも自由にせられた國民は日本を今日の悲運に導いた極端なる右翼にも走ることなく、されどと云つて極端なる左翼にも雷同せず、兩者何れも排擊して居る、かかる明白なる事態を見ざる者はデモクラシーの眞義を理解せざる者か或は又プレジユデイスのため盲目にせられて居るかのいづれかである斷じ得る」と述べた、理事會に於ては四國が相當友好的雰圍氣の下に外交的辭令を用ひて事を審議すると豫想して居つた日本側傍聽人は此の米側のソ聯を目指したであらう露骨なインシニエーシヨンに驚いて思はずソ聯代表席を見て息を吞んだ次第である、又追放令に關し主として發せられたるソ聯の非難に對し「占領軍の目的達成は日本政府の現存フレームワークを基準として進めて居

2 民主化・非軍事化政策への対応（昭和20年10月〜21年5月）

る以上、追放を急いでこの機能を破碎するが如き措置を執ることは愚である」と喝破した邊りソ聯の批判的態度に對する米國の責任とこれに對するソ聯の批判的態度を表示して剩す處がなかったのである。

第三、メーデー文書問題

四月三十日第三回對日理事會に於て議題となった問題の中主要なるものは食糧問題であったが、食糧問題に付ては主として極東委員會に於けると同樣英國代表が積極的に發言して英帝國殊に印度に於ける食糧不安が看過せられ戰敗國日本に對し食糧供給の優先權が與へらるゝが如きことのない樣米國を牽制したのであるが、英ソ間には大なる議論もなく終つたのである。然るに第四回對日理事會に於てはソ聯代表から五月一日人民集會の際その代表なる者から總司令官及び對日理事會代表に宛てた書翰を議題にのせて來たゝめ此處に端なくも米ソ兩代表の間に一問一答的白熱した應酬が行はれたのである。本件が議題に上るや米國代表はかゝる投書は何等目新しいものでないこと、又この種の申立は何等事實に立脚して居らないことを述べ更に本件書類は原文を外國語で書いた

らしく飜譯臭が極めて強いことを無遠慮に言ひつつ滿場の空氣を緊張せしめた後「アメリカは合衆國に於ても又日本に於ても共産主義をフェーバーするものではない、今問題となつてゐる文書は共産黨の宣傳の臭ひを多分に含んで居るが理事會に於て斯る特定の政黨に對し支持を與へることは避けなければならない」と眞向にソ聯代表を見据ゑて言ひ切るに至つてその論旨は最高潮に達したのである。

そこでソ聯側もこれに屈せず第四回會議に於てのみならず五月二十九日第五回理事會に於て、又六月十二日第六回理事會に於て引續き本問題を採り上げ本件文書は少數團體に依り起草せられたといふが、五十萬民衆の意思表示ではないか、原文は外國語で起草せられ飜譯臭を有して居るといふ發言は適當でなからう、理事會は果して如何なる調査を行つたか、ソ聯は全く滿足しない、例へば總司令部代表者及び理事會構成各國から成る一定の集團を構成し、右をして本件の內容を調査せしめることが適當であらうといふやうに米側所說を論駁した、これに依てソ聯側が日本の一部分子に對する關心の度合を理事

會に於て表明せんとしたものであると思はれると同時に、反面出來得れば理事會が總司令官の行政的職能にも干與する手掛りを作らんとする狙ひを持つたものであらうことは想像し得る處であつた、之に對し米國代表は「元來少數の者が支配を行ふのがトータリテリアンの仕組であるが本件も少數者が支配を行はんとするものであるならば種類は違ふが矢張りレジメンテーションであることには變りがない、大衆が少數の分子に依つてオーガナイズされて行くことはデモクラシーの本義に反する」と述べたのである、かゝる比較的重要ならざる問題が而も三囘に互り理事會に於て討議せられたといふことは少しく了解に苦しむ所であつたが米國代表の言へる如く本件は大問題とは思はぬが、ソ聯代表が議題に上程したが故に採上げて論じて居るといふのが本音であつたらうと思はれる、六月十二日第六囘對日理事會に於て本件の締括りをつけた際米國代表は「自分に取つて最も不思議なことは吾々が此處で本問題を論議して居ることが日本の新聞に廣汎に報道せられて居るにも拘らず責任ある何人も自分の所に來つて斯る中立を支持するが如き具體

的事實を說明して居らない、これは實に奇妙な現象である」と皮肉り問題を打切らんとしこれに對しソ聯代表は「本申立を調査すべき機會を吾々に與へられなかつたのでこれ以上問題を研究すべき術がないから打切る」と述べて飽迄も對立した形に於てこのストーミーな問題の討議を終つたのである比較的小問題であるに拘らず米ソの意見が最も激しく交換せられた問題であつたと謂へやう。

第四、漁區擴張問題

六月十二日第六囘對日理事會に於ては日本の漁業區域擴張に關する議題が上程せられ、米國代表から日本に於て食糧問題が緊迫化して居る事情を述べ、他の聯合國の好意ある考慮を促したのに對し、ソ聯代表からはかかる漁區の擴張に依り何の程度の增獲あるべきや、又移出先は何處なりや、最近及び降伏當時の日本の漁船隊の構成狀況如何、戰前の漁船隊の大きさ如何等極めて微細なる點に亙り詳細なる說明を求めた後主義上暫定的措置としては本件に對し何等反對するものではないと述べたのである、然るに次囘の六月二十六日第八囘會議に於ては端なくもソ聯が漁區擴張問題にも反對的態度を持してゐることを

2　民主化・非軍事化政策への対応（昭和20年10月〜21年5月）

米國代表が明示したのである、即ち六月二十日附ソ聯代表から米國代表宛書翰に依れば「前回理事會に於て一定地域に於て日本の漁業及び捕鯨權を暫定的に行はしめることに付てはソ聯に於て異議がない旨述べて置いたが、本國政府から本件に付き訓令に接した、それに依れば一定の理由に基き日本側の現在漁區を擴張することに對してソ聯政府は反對である」と述べて漁區擴張に對するソ聯の態度を表示したのである、これに對し米國代表は「日本に於ける食糧状況は急速に措置する必要があり、漁場擴張の問題はこの解決に一歩を進めたものであるアメリカは日本に對し食糧供給の大負擔を負つてゐる事實に顧み、かかる食糧情勢を是正したいのである」といふ回答文を讀上げて米國の態度を明かにした。

第五、農地改革問題

此の問題に付總司令官からソ英華各國の意見の表示を求めたのに對し三國から共同勸告が行はれたのであるが、この共同勸告以外にソ聯側は單獨勸告を行つてゐる、この單獨勸告の内容中殊に注目すべきは支拂の點であつてソ聯案に依れば一種のスライディング・スキームに依り

地主保有農地三町歩迄は買上に際し公定價格で全額を地主に支拂ふが、三町歩以上六町歩迄は半額を支拂ふこれが以上は無償とすることになつて居る、これに對し共同勸告案が成立しなかつた理由でもあるのだが、此の點に對し米國から痛烈な反對が出たのである。即ち「土地及び他の財産を何等適當なる支拂なくして處分するといふ提案はポツダム宣言の趣旨に合致しない。眞の民主々義組織の主目的は基本的人權に付き規定し又これを保護することである。その權利の中には財産を獲得し且つこれを所有するといふ權利も含まれて居るのである、かかる財産を獲得し所有する權利を否認するが如き提案を容認することは適當でない」と述べたのである、之に對しソ代表は米國の言ふポツダム宣言の解釋には同意しないと述べ自己の最初の提案を固執し單獨勸告を行つたのである。

第六、日本人歸還問題

第八回對日理事會は六月二十六日開催せられた、その際米ソの間に議論の上下されたのは日本人歸還の問題であつた、即ちソ聯が日本人の歸還輸送に使用して居る船舶

を賠償に充てる問題を曾て理事會で論議したのに引掛けて逆に米國側から本件を理事會に上程して各國代表の意見を求めたものであつて、米國代表は「米國權力關係地域の歸還は九三パーセント終了し、滿洲を除く中國權力關係地區の歸還は六八パーセント終了し、英國權力關係地域の歸還は九四パーセント終了して居るに拘らず、ソ聯權力關係地區よりの歸還は零である」と數字を示してソ聯側の説明を求め更に「ポツダム宣言に依れば日本軍隊は完全に武裝を解除せる後は各自の家郷に歸還することを許され平和的にして生產的なる生活を送る機會を有せしめられるとあり、本件に關し英華は迅速にして十分なる協力を行ひ降伏條件の具體化に貢獻して居るが、ソ聯地區に於て抑留せられ捕虜となつた日本人の歸還問題に付ては何等決する所がない、降伏條件は自發的に各聯合國政府に依て出來得る限り速かに實施されるやうにといふ意見を開陳せざるを得ない、聯合國の一致を保つといふ上からも降伏宣言が一部なりとも一方的に廢棄せられたり若くは無視せられたりすることは面白くない」と述べソ聯の態度に付き強く反省を求めた。

第七、日本に於ける勞働立法問題

前記の如き米ソの論爭は七月十日第九囘對日理事會に於て日本の勞働立法を審議するに及び最高潮に達したのである、同日の理事會に於ては米ソは戰爭調査會問題と勞働立法問題の二問題に於て對立したのであつて、戰爭調査會設置に關しソ聯側は戰爭の原因を尋ねこれを處罰する仕事は國際軍事法廷の任務に屬するから日本政府の下に斯の如き機關を設置することの必要性は大いに疑問なしとしない、かかる委員會は今次戰爭を正當化する具になり得るかも知れない、依てこの委員會の解散を勸告するものであると述べたのに對し、米國代表は、若

之に對しソ聯代表は本日の議題としては復員者が如何に一般生活に融け込んでゐるかの問題を論議すべきであつて一般的に復員自體を論議するものではない、又本件の如き問題は對日理事會に於て論議解決し得ないといふ議論を述べ米國側はこれは一般還送の問題の一部であつて且對日理事會は降伏條件の具體化に付き論議し得る機關であるからこの席に於て問題を採上げ得ることは疑の餘地がなく明瞭であらうと述べて追及した。

2 民主化・非軍事化政策への対応(昭和20年10月～21年5月)

し日本人が戦争原因に付て探究せんと欲するならば、これを強ひて止めることは基本的自由を侵害するものであると思ふ、しかもかかる基本的自由を日本人に與へることが爲に今次戦争を戰ひ又かかる自由を日本人に與へることが我等政策の目的でもある、日本國民はその過去の侵略に對して言譯を求めんとしてゐるやうな態度を見せて居らないことは他の一部敗戦國の場合とは様子を異にする、この日本の態度は日本が戦争を破棄し又他國の平和的意圖と信義に信倚せんとする規定を憲法草案の中に織込むことを考へて居ることに依つても明かであると述べてソ聯の勸告に反對したのである。

乍然同日の理事會に於て最も米ソ間論争の中心となつたのはソ聯が議題に上程した日本に於ける勞働立法の問題で、ソ聯は總司令部係官の説明が終つてから二十三項目に亘つて詳細なる勸告を行つたのであるが、此の勸告が終るや否やアチソン氏から、諸般の状況に顧みるにソ聯の勸告には共産主義の宣傳のサインマークが看取される、日本に於ける勞働運動の最大の危險は勞働運動が極端にして利己的な分子の支配に落ち込みはせぬかとい

ふ點である、レジメンテーションは決して勞働者の友ではない。共産主義もファシズムも何れも勞働者の指導權を要求することは不當である、彼等は勞働者を指導するに非ずしてデストロイするものであると述べ更にソ聯はいろいろな事を日本側に勸告して居るが果して自國に於ては勞働組合の完全なる自由、一日八時間勞働等が嚴守されて居るであらうかと逆質問を行ひ、結論として理事會代表は共産黨の目標を支援して日本人に共産黨の意思を押し附けんとするものであるか、若は日本の民主化を達成するためにポツダム宣言を押し進めんとするものであるか、態度を明かにせよと述べて暑氣の溢れた滿場に一抹の凄氣を漂はせたのである。

これに對しソ聯代表は、ポツダム宣言の解釋を押し附けることこそ米國の宣傳であると述べアチソン代表の陳述に抗議をしてからこの問題に付ては後日再び論議するの權利を玆に留保するものであると述べたのである。

第三項所説のメーデー文書問題に於ても米ソは同じやうな意見の對立を見せたが、その場合と第九回理事會に於ける意見の對立の場合とはその性質を異にする點指摘

の要がある、蓋しメーデーの文書の場合にはその文書を提出した本人は日本側勞働者といふ第三者であつて、之れに對してアチソン氏が共產黨の宣傳文書であるといふ烙印を押したのであるが、今回の場合は理事會の代表たるソ聯代表の直接提出したる勸告自體を捉へて、共產黨のサインマークがあると述べたので此の點に於て兩者に性質上相違のあることは注意を要する。

米本國に於て米ソ關係の惡化することを憂へて居る一部論者は極東委員會に於て或は對日理事會に於て米國代表が公衆の面前で餘り容赦なくソ聯側をスラッシュすることは結局米ソ關係を不當に氣まづいものにする丈けであらうと云ふ批評を行つて居るが一方元駐英大使のジョセフ・ケネデイー氏の如き一米國雜誌上に於て「ソ聯と云ふ國は考へ方に於て物の言ひ方に於て又行動に於て齒に衣被せぬ直接的にして時にはブルータルでさへありアリズムを尊重するそして自分がそれを實行するのみならず他國もその通りであらうことを豫期して居る」と述べて居るのである、アチソン代表は正しく先輩の言を實行に移したものであると謂へやうか。

尙勞働立法を繞る米ソの論爭に關し外交的觀點から觀て興味のある點は (1) 四月三十日の論爭に於てアチソン代表が共產黨を批判したのに對し、直ちに國務省のデイーン・アチソン氏はこれを支持したのみならず、今般の言明に於ても同氏は「アチソン代表の見解は米國務省の十分な權限を得て居り同代表こそ米外交官中の卓越せる人物である」と述べてアチソン代表が一般的には國務省の方針を體して發言したものであらうことを示して居るのである (2) 但し今般の場合ソ聯は理事會の前日卽ち七月九日の夜勞働立法に關するその勸告內容を發表した由であるから、この發表を觀て直ちに反駁を起草した米側は之を事前に國務省に請訓する暇はなかつたであらうから (但しそれにも拘らず能く練られて居ることは米國外交の能率を示すものであらう) アチソン代表の反駁はその考慮の下に讀まるべきであらうと思はれる、ソ聯代表もそこを衝いて今の意思表示は個人的意見の表示かと突き込んだのに對しアチソン氏は自分のステートメントは自分の意見を表示したものであると述べて要領を得させなかつた邊り興味のある點である。

2 民主化・非軍事化政策への対応(昭和20年10月〜21年5月)

第八、英華の態度

以上が對日理事會に於て從來(七月十日までに)米ソが意見を異にした主なる點である、勿論前述せる如くこれ等はその一々の問題に對する單なる見解の相違に非ずして米ソの世界に於ける外交關係を大きく背景として兩者の意見の對立が對日管理の問題にも事毎に滲み出して居ると見るべきであらう、これに對して理事會の他の國、即ち英華の態度は如何といふに、例へば歐洲に於ける外相會議等に於てはソ聯に對し民主々義國家のグループ、即ち米英佛の諸國は一致してこれに對立し之が又ソ聯の不滿の對象となつて居る情勢であるが對日理事會に於ては不思議に現在のところその空氣がないのである、寧ろ總司令官即米國の對日管理政策に關し逆にソ英華が一致してこれを批判しその說明を求むるが如き態度を執つて居り、理事會の議事を傍聽して居る一英國婦人が「どうして皆で米國をあゝいふ風に攻擊するのであらう、又米國も讓らずどんどん頑張つて貰ひたい」と批評して居つた程英華の態度はソ聯に對しては「微溫的」であり殊に英國の態度は場合によりソ聯支持的でさへある。

例へば英國代表はメーデーの文書を繞つて米ソ代表が火花を散らして論爭してゐる際もその態度は明瞭でなかつたためアチソン氏から貴下は一體本文書を支持するのかしないのか態度如何と質問されこれに對しマクマホン・ボール氏は「理事會が斯るステートメントに耳を藉さないといふのは困る、但しソ聯代表も今少しく具體的なる證據を出すべきであらう」といふ風な應酬をして居るし、又アチソン氏からソ聯の六町步以上の農地無償取上の提案に關聯しこれはポツダム宣言の趣旨に反すると解せらるゝが英國側は如何に解するか、ソ聯の提案はデモクラシーに反すると思考するかと尋ねたのに對し英國代表は「自分は現在のところこれに關し確たる意見を述べることは出來ない、デモクラシーに於て果して所有權の尊重といふことが然く肝要であるかどうか議論があらうが、自分としてはソ聯の改革案に見るが如き財產に關する措置は尠くとも現在の日本に於ては望ましからずといひ得ると思ふ」といふやうな應酬をして居る。

又戰爭調查會問題に關聯し、調查會の存續を可とする米國と、否とするソ聯と意見が對立した際、英國代表は

自分は委員會を解散しろといふところまではリコメンドしないが委員會を設置する眞の意義は乏しく寧ろ危險であるとさへ思ふと、述べてソ聯に近い見解を示したし又日本に於ける勞働立法問題に關聯しアチソン氏が激しくソ聯代表を攻擊した際もソ聯代表に先立ち發言を求めた英國代表は、ソ聯の勸告に付いては非常な興味を以て承はつたがアチソン氏のこれに對する反駁に付いては更に一層大なる興味を以て承つた、自分の觀る所に依ればソ聯の提案にはアチソン氏の言ふ樣な共產黨の宣傳のサインマークは何處にもない、社會厚生の問題に關する提案を理事會の同僚が宣傳なりと云つて却けるのは殘念なやり方であると述べて完全にソ聯支援の態度を示して居たのである。

そこで前記英國の態度から類推せられることは（１）對日理事會に於て發言して居るのは「英國」と云ふのは不正確な表現で實は「豪洲」であるといふ點である、そもそも對日理事會の機構がモスクワ會議で決定せられその對蹠的機關である極東委員會は夙に華府に於て仕事を整備したに居つたに拘らず對日理事會の方はその機構

も拘らず却々當初に於ては開會の運びに立至らなかつた事は人の知るところであるが、即理事會の代表を英帝國側にあつたものではなからうか、その原因は主として英帝國內の何國より選出すべきかの問題が解決しなかつた經緯のあることは豫想せられるところで、英國代表としては當時東京にアトリー首相の個人代表たりガードナー中將も居つたのであるが、結局豪洲が英帝國を代表することゝなり、そこで結論せられることは、英國ならば對ソ關係に重大なる關心を有するからベヴイン外相の態度に於ても明かなる如き英米一體關係が出て來るのであるが、豪洲はその立場上ソ聯に對しては比較的無關心である、この邊に對日理事會に於ける豪洲代表の態度が歐洲に於ける英國外相の態度と必ずしも同一でない理由を見出し得るのであるが、（２）このことから更に又次の如きインフアレンスを抽き出し得ると思ふ、即ち極東問題に對する英本國の發言權は將來次第に減少し豪洲の發言權が增大して行くであらうと云ふこと之であつて、此の點は將來日本の外交關係に重大なる指針を暗示して居るものでは

2 民主化・非軍事化政策への対応（昭和20年10月〜21年5月）

あるまいか。

然らば中國代表は如何と言ふに之も亦日本人の歸還問題に關し「ソ聯代表の言へる如く本問題を理事會に於て論議し得ないといふことに反對であるが、但しソ聯の言ふ樣に日本側からインテグレーションに關する提案を出せといふ議論に付ては贊成である」といふやうな提案をして居り、積極的に米國代表を支持してソ聯の提案なりに發言なりに強く反對するといつたやうな空氣は見えて居らないが、その態度は英國代表とは相當異り英國代表の樣にはソ聯に近からず、より中立的である點が注意されるのである。

第九、結論

これを要するに對日理事會は世界の外交關係を如實に反映しつゝある英米ソ華が日本管理を論議する席上ではあるが、次第次第に米ソがその對日管理に關する意見の對立を鮮明にさしめて來て居り、囘を重ねるに從つて同理事會が兩國の論爭の舞臺となり、英華は寧ろ脇役として傍らに押しやられた觀がある、しかし脇役である英華はパリに於ける外相會議、國際聯合會議等とは多少異なり必ずしも全面的に米國と聯繋してソ聯と對立して居るものでもない、蓋しこれは主としては前述せる如く英ソ華がマッカーサー元帥の管理政策を批判しこれが質問に應ずるといふ立場を一にして居ることに基くものであらうと思ふが、果してこの空氣が何時迄持續せられるか、歐洲、中華民國、中東等に於ける英本國と豪洲の關係或は又英帝國に於ける各國の外交關係等も考慮するとき興味深き將來の問題たるを失はないのである。

尙本稿は事實の陳述を主としたもので、意見に付ては此種文書に於ても之を表示することは適當でなからうからその所々に於て簡單にヒントしてあるに過ぎない不徹底の點は御諒察あり度い。

編 注　本文書は、昭和二十一年八月、朝海終戰連絡中央事務局總務部長作成「報告書集錄（その一）」より拔粹。

3 経済諸施策への対応（昭和21年5月～24年4月）

151 経済安定本部の設置承認方回答

昭和21年5月17日　連合国最高司令官総司令部より日本政府宛

付記　昭和二十一年六月十二日、朝海終戦連絡中央事務局総務部総務課長作成
「經濟安定本部成立の經緯及び之が任務」

GENERAL HEADQUARTERS
SUPREME COMMANDER FOR THE ALLIED POWERS

APO 500

17 May 1946

AG 334 (17 May 46) ESS/PC
SCAPIN 960

MEMORANDUM FOR: THE IMPERIAL JAPANESE GOVERNMENT.
THROUGH: Central Liaison Office, Tokyo.
SUBJECT: Economic Stabilization Board.

1. Reference is made to letter and inclosures from the Central Liaison Office, subject: "Establishment of Economic Stabilization Board", (CLO No.1604) (GE) dated 6 April 1946.

2. There is no objection at this time to the establishment by the Imperial Japanese Government of the Economic Stabilization Board, to exist for a period of one year.

FOR THE SUPREME COMMANDER:

B. M. FITCH,
Brigadier General, AGD,
Adjutant General.

（付　記）

經濟安定本部成立の經緯及び之が任務

（昭和二一・六・一二）

一、經濟安定本部成立に關し米側と接觸中確め得たる點で將來本機構の圓滑なる運營上注意を要すと認められたる事項に付左の通り記錄する次第である。

3　経済諸施策への対応（昭和21年5月〜24年4月）

(1) 経済安定本部は政策事項に付ては各省に優越した存在でなければならないこと、

(2) 本機構は経済危機突破のための暫定的機構なること、そこで五月十七日の指令には一ケ年の期間を以て設立同意の旨回答があつたのであるが、これは決して日本の危機が一ケ年で克服されるであらうと見当を付したものでもなく、又一ケ年以上はこれが設立を許さぬとした趣旨でもないことは勿論である、一年の壽命しかない安定本部に人材の集まる理由がないふやうな議論を聞いたが、右は全く米側の意圖を了解せざるものに外なるもので總司令部が一年としたる趣旨は、日本の經濟は自由經濟が本則である、併し乍ら現在に於ては必要なる統制を加へざるを得ない。そこで米軍の自由經濟を本則とする原則はこれを留保して置きたいといふ趣旨が一ケ年を以て設立を許可するといふ形を採つて居るのに過ぎない。即ちこれは米側が原則を示したものに外ならない。

(3) 本機構は政變等に累されることなく繼續性を有するものであること、（繼續性は經濟安定會議の第二號議員たるため再修正が行はれたること、

(4) 總務長官の地位を極力強力ならしめ長官は名實共に國務大臣を指揮命令し得るが如き「カリバー」の人物たることを希望し居ること、

(5) 勅令第六條は必ずしも英文とコレスポンドせざるも日本側の意圖は總務長官を閣僚中より選定することに限らんとするものに非ずして適當なる人物を先づ國務大臣に任命し次で總務長官に任命せんとする趣旨なることを説明し總司令部側の了解を求めたること、

(6) 米側は總務長官の權限を強大ならしむることを希望し居り總裁たる總理大臣は形式的首長たるに止まらしめ勅令第六條に總務長官は總裁を佐け廳務を掌理すとありたるに關し「總裁を佐け」なる字句は總務長官の地位を輕からしむる印象を與ふべしとて斯る字句に拘泥するは意外と思はる、程にこれが削除を要求せること、

(7) 民意をも反映せる經濟安定會議の利用を圖りたること但し先方の意向を汲みたる當方案は餘りに經濟安定會議を強力ならしめ事務當局を牽制し過ぎる嫌ひありた

(8) 經濟安定本部第一部長は總務長官の兼任とすべき旨閣令中に明定方要求せるも日本側より右は閣令の體裁上適當ならざるを以て固執せざるやう致し度くその代り日本政府は總務長官に於て必ず第一部長を兼任するやうテークノートすべき旨約せること、

(9) 閣令第十四條議員の構成中米側は第二號の議員にアウトヴォートせられざるやう相互の人數を同數とすべき旨要求せるも當方より第十四條第二號は有能達識の士を以て第一號の議員に協力せしむることを主眼とし居り第一號第二號議員對抗して相爭ふが如き事態を豫見することは本條のスピリットに反すべき旨力說し米側右に同意せる經緯あること、

二、尚經濟安定本部が如何なる職務を行ふかに付て現下の重要問題である賃金問題に關し過般勞働委員會委員として滯邦中であつたアバソルド氏の如きは次の如く述べて居りその趣旨は勞働委員會から總司令官に對する勸告書の中に織り込まれて居ると思はれる。經濟安定本部に對する米側の氣持を知る上に參考とならう。

等の諸點である。

(一) 現在特に必要なのは一定の賃金統制であり、このやうな統制は經濟安定本部の機構を通じてこれを行ふことが必要である。而してこのやうな施策は前述したやうにインフレーションの防止及び日本の經濟再建に關する全般的政策と密接不可分的に檢討されることを要件とする。依て本委員會としては次のやうな勸告を總司令部に對して行はんとして居る。

(イ) 經濟安定本部を設立せる後は總括的價格統制計畫を實施すると共に次のやうな賃金に關する施策を講する必要がある。即ち法令に依り總ての賃金及俸給の上昇は經濟安定本部の承認を要することがこれである。茲に謂ふ賃金及俸給とは金錢に依ると現物に依るとを問はず一切の形のレミュネレーションを指す。依て或る企業家に於て賃金の增加を要求せられた場合右は經濟安定本部の容認がなければ賃金を引上げることが出來ぬことゝならう。而して經濟安定本部の任務は後に述べるやうに生產品の價格と賃金の上昇との關係を見極むることに在り、假に、三百圓の賃金增加の要求のあつた場合百圓に引上ぐ

3 経済諸施策への対応（昭和21年5月～24年4月）

るも價格に影響を及ぼさないといふ場合に於てはその限度に於て引上は許容せられるが三百圓の引上は許容せられないであらう。勿論百圓の引上を行ふ場合企業家の利潤のマージンは狹められることゝなるべきもコスト以下にて販賣せしめらるゝことはアンフェアなる故企業家には合理的な利潤は許されることは勿論である。

(ロ) 經濟安定本部は例外の場合を除いては價格の上騰を招來するやうな賃金の増加を否認する政策を一般的に堅持することを要する。

(ハ) 現在の價格水準に直接影響を及ぼさないやうな賃金の増加要求は經濟安定本部に於て容認せらるべきも而も各種の賃金増加は間接には一般價格水準殊に食糧價格に影響を及ぼす譯であるから直接物價を上昇させないやうな賃金の増加に對しても若干の制限を加へなければならない。而して如何なる制限を附するかは結局經濟安定本部に於て愼重檢討の要あり、而もこのやうな檢討は至急これを行ふを要することゝ過去及び現在に於ける一般賃金と價格水準との

レシオを考慮に入れること、の二點を特に銘記するの要がある。

(二) 現在日本の勞働者に對し特に關心があるのは金錢よりは寧ろ食糧である。而して食糧の配分は團體交渉に依て決定せしむべからざることを指摘する必要がある。蓋し團體交渉力のある勞働者が必要以上に大なる食糧を確保することゝなる惧れあるからである。他方重要産業に於ける勞働者はその能率を維持する爲にも十分なる食糧を與へられることが必要で、このやうな方法で勞働爭議を未然に防止することゝもなるであらう、依て本委員會としては次のやうな措置を總司令部に對し勸告して居る。即ち(イ) 經濟安定本部は出來る限り速かなる機會に職業又は産業に關するプライオリチー・リストを決定し日本の經濟復興に最も緊急なるものも重要なるものを選定する要あり(ロ) 經濟安定本部はプライオリチー・リストに掲げられたる種類の業務又は産業に從事する者に對し食糧の特配を行ふべく、このやうな食糧の特配を行ふべき源泉は米國よりの輸入食糧に俟つことゝなるであらう。而して生産の増強を確

保するがためには出來得る限りこのやうな食糧は現場に於て供給せしむる形を執ることが必要である。その結果不在者は恩典に浴することが出來なくなるからである。尚右配給を行ふに當つてはこの種食糧が他の闇市場に流れぬやう取締の要あることは勿論である。而して米國より十分な食糧を求め得ないやうな場合に於ては一般配給から取去る程の決意を要する。蓋しこのためには一般民の生存に多少の障碍を生ずることがあつても止むを得ぬところでこのやうな徹底した措置を執つて初めて日本の經濟的危機の期間を短くし且つ結局に於てはより少き人數が飢ゑるに過ぎない結果を收め得るのであつて經濟安定本部の責任の重大な所以も亦た實に茲に存すると謂はなければならない。

編 注 本文書は、昭和二十二年一月、朝海終戦連絡中央事務局総務部長作成「報告書集録（その二）」より抜粋。

昭和21年5月20日　連合国最高司令官総司令部発表

大衆による示威運動および無秩序な行動に対するマッカーサー司令官の声明

General of the Army Douglas MacArthur's Statement concerning Demonstrations and Disorders by Mass Mobs

May 20, 1946

I find it necessary to caution the Japanese people that the growing tendency towards mass violence and physical processes of intimidation, under organized leadership, present a grave menace to the future development of Japan. While every possible national freedom of democratic method has been permitted and will be permitted in the evolution now proceeding in the transformation from a feudalistic and military state to one of democratic process, the physical violence which indisciplined elements are now beginning to practice will not be permitted to continue. They constitute a menace not only to orderly government but to the basic purposes and security of the occupation itself. If minor elements of

3　経済諸施策への対応（昭和21年5月～24年4月）

Japanese society are unable to exercise such self restraint and self respect as the situation and conditions require, I shall be forced to take the necessary steps to control and remedy such a deplorable situation, I am sure the great mass of the people condemn such excesses by disorderly minorities, and it is my sincere hope that the sane views of this predominate public opinion will exert sufficient influence to make it unnecessary to intervene.

編注　本文書は、昭和二十四年三月、外務省特別資料部作成「日本占領及び管理重要文書集」第二巻より抜粋。

153　皇族の財産制限および特権廃止に関する指令

昭和21年5月21日　連合国最高司令官総司令部より　日本政府宛

GENERAL HEADQUARTERS
SUPREME COMMANDER FOR THE ALLIED POWERS
APO 500
21 May 1946

AG 386.7 (21 May 46) ESS/FI

SCAPIN-1298-A
MEMORANDUM FOR: IMPERIAL JAPANESE GOVERNMENT.
THROUGH: Central Liaison Office, Tokyo.
SUBJECT: Imperial Princes and Princesses.

1. Effective immediately the Imperial Japanese Government is directed to take the following action regarding the Imperial Princes and the Imperial Princesses.

    a. The securities listed in Annex "A" attached hereto, which are now being held in trust by the Imperial Household Ministry for the Imperial Princes and the Imperial Princesses, will be transferred to the several beneficiaries forthwith.

    b. No Imperial grants or loans of either money or property will be made to the Imperial Princes and the Imperial Princesses, or their households.

    c. No employee of the Imperial Household will be assigned duties involving service to the Imperial Princes or the Imperial Princesses, or their households.

    d. Upon the completion of the transfer directed under paragraph 1 a the Imperial Japanese Government will take all necessary action to divest the Imperial Princes and the Imperial Princesses of all right, title and interest in and to all property of every name and nature belonging to or held by the Imperial Household.

2. The Imperial Japanese Government is further directed to take all necessary action to divest the Imperial Princes and the Imperial Princesses of all special privileges and immunities, including all immunity from taxation.

3. As used in this directive the terms "Imperial Prince" and "Imperial Princess" do not include the Dowager Empress or the children of the Emperor.

FOR THE SUPREME COMMANDER:

J. W. Mann
for B. M. FITCH,
Brigadier General, AGD,
Adjutant General.

1 Incl: Annex "A"

ANNEX "A"

Securities Held in Trust by the Imperial Household for the Imperial Princes.

Type of Security	Amount
National Bonds	¥ 907,837
Prefectural Bonds	539,409
Debentures	4,222,882
Stocks	2,166,092
Total	¥ 7,836,220

154

昭和21年5月23日　連合国最高司令官総司令部より
日本政府宛

日本軍から引き渡される軍需品の用途変更方指令に関し返還品の再交付

GENERAL HEADQUARTERS
SUPREME COMMANDER FOR THE ALLIED POWERS

APO 500
23 May 1946

AG 386.3 (23 May 46) GD
SCAPIN 980

MEMORANDUM FOR: IMPERIAL JAPANESE GOVERNMENT

THROUGH: Central Liaison Office, Tokyo

SUBJECT: Materials, Supplies, and Equipment Received and to be Received from the Japanese Armed Forces.

    1. Reference is made to Memorandum for the Imperial Japanese Government, file AG 402.5 (24 Sep 45) GD (SCAPIN-53), dated 24 September 1945, subject: "Materials, Supplies, and Equipment Received and to be Received from the Japanese Armed Forces".

    2. Paragraph 5 of referenced Memorandum is rescinded and the following substituted therefor:

The supplies, materials, and equipment returned to the Imperial Japanese Government are for the purpose of civilian relief and for use towards restoration of Japanese civil economy to the extent that it can provide the essentials of food, clothing, and shelter for the Japanese civilian population; and to enable the Imperial Japanese Government to fulfill its responsibilities in connection with meeting the needs of Allied Occupation Force personnel and their dependents. The use of these supplies, materials, and equipment for any purposes other than the above is expressly forbidden.

FOR THE SUPREME COMMANDER:

J. W. Mann
for B. M. FITCH,
Brigadier General, AGD,
Adjutant General.

---

155 指令第三号における研究所報告の変更に関する指令

昭和21年5月25日　連合国最高司令官総司令部より　日本政府宛

GENERAL HEADQUARTERS
SUPREME COMMANDER FOR THE ALLIED POWERS
APO 500

25 May 1946

AG 091.3 (25 May 46) ESS/ST
(SCAPIN-984)

MEMORANDUM FOR: THE IMPERIAL JAPANESE GOVERNMENT.

THROUGH: Central Liaison Office, Tokyo.
SUBJECT: Amendment of SCAPIN 47, (Directive No. 3).

1. The Imperial Japanese Government is hereby advised that Directive No. 3, (SCAPIN 47) dated 22 Sep 1945, is amended as follows:

   a. Sub-paragraph 8a is deleted and the following is substituted:

   "8. a. You will require all research laboratories, research institutes and similar scientific and technological organizations, excluding those medical laboratories engaged solely in clinical diagnostic work, to submit a report through your office to the Supreme Commander for the Allied Powers, which will include the following information:

   (1) Name
   (2) Location
   (3) Ownership
   (4) Description of facilities
   (5) Number of employees
   (6) Detailed list of all projects studied from 1 Jan 1940 to 1 Sep 1945; and of all projects currently being studied."

   b. Sub-paragraph 8c is deleted and the following is substituted:

   "8. c. You will direct said agencies to render a report as of the first day of January and July of each year to the Supreme Commander for the Allied Powers, through your office, stating in detail the projects on which their facilities and personnel have been engaged during the preceding six months and the results of such work. You will also require them to list the projects upon which they desire to work for the following six months. These reports will reach the Supreme Commander for the Allied Powers on or before the first day of February and August respectively."

   c. The following sub-paragraphs are to be added:

   "8. e. Except where activities are directed towards developments in the fields of warlike activities, research and teaching for the extension of scientific and technical knowledge is permitted, in such agencies as have complied with the provisions of sub-paragraphs 8a or 8c.

466

3 経済諸施策への対応（昭和21年5月～24年4月）

156

昭和21年5月　終戦連絡中央事務局総務部総務課作成

［懸案事項］

昭和二十一年五月

懸案事項

總務部總務課

"8. f. Direct communication is hereby authorized between the interested staff sections of General Headquarters, Supreme Commander for the Allied Powers and the agencies of the Imperial Japanese Government to implement instructions contained in this paragraph."

FOR THE SUPREME COMMANDER:

B. M. FITCH,
Brigadier General, AGD,
Adjutant General.

一、政治部

　イ、新憲法草案ニ關スル件

來ル五月ノ特別議會ニ提出スベキ新憲法草案ハ去ル四月十八日公表セラレタガ、其ノ後ニ於テモ或ハ總司令部側ノ要求ニ依リ或ハ日本政府ノ發意ニ基キ司令部ト協議ノ上若干ノ修正ヲ加ヘツツアル。併シ議會ニ提出迄ニ今後重要ナ變更ハ加ヘラレナイ見込デアル

　ロ、復員省機構改正ニ關スル件

第一、第二復員省ヲ廢止シ内閣總理大臣ノ管理下ニ復員廳ヲ設置シ右兩省ノ殘務ヲ繼承サセル案ハ近ク總司令部ノ承認ヲ得タ上國内法上ノ手續ガ進メラレル豫定デアル

　ハ、救濟福祉計畫

昨年十二月八日附ノ總司令部覺書ニ從ヒ日本政府ハ本年一月ヨリ六月ニ至ル期間ノ救濟福祉計畫ヲ聯合國司令部ニ提出シタガ右政府計畫案ニ對シ總司令部ハ本年二月二十七日附ノ覺書ヲ以テ次ノ條件ニ於テ、本計畫案ノ遂行ニ反對シナイ旨回答シテ來タ

ソノ條件ハ(イ)單一ノ中央官廳（厚生省）ガ全責任ヲ以テ遂行スルコト(ロ)救濟ニ必要デアル以上ノ金額ヲ制限シナイコト

現在厚生省ハ右回答ニ基イテ綜合的救護法ノ立案ヲ急イデイル

　二、教職員適格審査ニ關スル件

昭和二十年十月二十二日竝ニ同月三十日附聯合國最高司令官覺書ニ基イテ、教職員ノ適格審査ヲ行フ爲、文部省ニ中心トシテ司令部ト折衝ノ重ネタ結果、之ニ必要ナ勅令、共同省令、訓令案ニツイテ承認ヲ得タノデ、近ク公布實施セラレルコトニナツタ

ホ、米國教育使節團報告書ニ關スル件

去ル三月來朝セル米國教育使節團ノ報告書ニ就テハ文部省ニ於テ目下ソノ內容ヲ檢討シ、日本教育制度ノ改革ニ就キ考究中

ヘ、教科書ニ關スル件

昭和二十年十月二十二日附竝ニ二十二月三十一日附覺書ニ基イテ、敎科書及ビ敎師用圖書ノ囘收、改訂及ビ新敎科書ノ編纂ハ文部省ニ於テ司令部ト連絡ノ下ニ進行中デアル

ト、掠奪品ノ押收及報告ニ關スル件

四月十九日附覺書ニヨリ日本軍ノ占領セル地域ヨリ掠奪シタル物件ノ目錄ヲ提出シ之ヲ押收スベキ旨ノ指令ニ接シタノデ官廳所有物件ニツイテハ各官廳ヨリ終戰連絡中央事務局ニ目錄ヲ提出シ之ヲ取纒メルコトトシ民間所有物件ニツイテハ新ニ勅令ヲ制定シ申告セシムルコトトシ內務省ニ於

テ之ガ省令制定手續ヲ進メツツアル

チ、神社問題

大筋ノ問題ハ解決シ目下神社財產ノ處理、神官ノ恩給、等ノ附隨的ノ小問題ノミガ殘ツテ居リ司令部ト折衝中デアリ、臨時法制調査會設置ニ關スル件

本件ニ關シテハ去ル三月二十六日司令部係官トノ會談ニ基キ四月上旬ヨリ同調査會ト司令部トノ間ニ常設的連絡措置ヲ講ズル豫定デアツタガ、同委員ガ未ダ正式ニ任命セラレテヰナイ爲、其ノ後司令部トノ間ニ連絡會議ハ開催セラレテヰナイ

ヌ、聯合軍將兵ニヨル邦人被害ノ賠償問題

右問題ハ民事裁判問題ト關聯シテ交涉中デアツタ處裁判管轄ニ關シテハ二月二十六日覺書デ一應決定シタガ、賠償ニ關シテハ目下聯合軍側ニ於テ別途考究中ニシテ、未決定デアル

ル、公務從事ニ適シナイ者ヲ公職カラ除去スル件

一月四日聯合國總司令部ヨリ來タ指令ニ基イテ二月二十七日勅令第百九號ト閣令、內務省令第一號ガ制定セラレソノ適用モ樞密顧問官等ヨリハジメテキル。然シ之ニヨツテ現

3　経済諸施策への対応（昭和21年5月～24年4月）

職ヨリ罷免サレル者ノ總數約千五百人ト豫定シテ居タ處、總司令部ニ於テ適用範圍ヲ擴大スルヤウニト申シ來タタメ、新タニ立案中デアル

二、經濟部

(一) 財務課

イ、財閥解體關係

一、證券整理委員會、設立委員任命閣令及定款　司令部ニ許可申請中

二、財閥自主的解體案檢討

大藏、商工ニ協議中（商工省ヨリ當方案ニ對スル修正案提出アリ大藏省ヨリハ未接受）

三、會社及個人ノ持株制限重役兼務禁止指令案ニ關スル日本側意見

商工省ニテ檢討中

四、財閥及事業獨占等ニ關スル審議會設置　內閣審議室ニテ立案中

五、制限會社各種申請　數十件司令部ニ申請中

ロ、其ノ他財政金融關係

一、復興金融會社案　閣議決定案說明金融會社具體案及政府ノ部分的保證案ニ付大藏省ニテ立案中

二、二十一年度豫算關係　先方查定案ニ對シ當方最後案檢討中（大臣カラ最高司令官宛書翰ヲ送ツテアル）

三、政府職員給與引上案　勞務部內示ニ基ク案許可申請中（正式許可ハ未着ナルモ實行ニ着手シテヰル）

四、財產稅、戰時利得稅及財產增價稅關係　チヤーン顧問ノ勸告案ニ付同顧問ト大藏當局トノ間デ檢討中

五、恩給及給與關係

(1) 海外引揚軍屬工員雇傭員ニ對スル退職金支給及旅費等ノ支給規則恩給停止指令抵觸トノ關係ニ付說明中

(2) 特高警察職員ニ對スル休職給、退職金ノ支給　近ク先方ニ說明ノ豫定（恩給停止指令ニ牴觸ノ問題）

(3) 恩給停止指令中「司令部ヨリ解散ヲ命ゼラレタ機關、法人ノ退職金支給禁止」ニ該當スベキ機關及法人ノ範圍確定方申請中

(4) 元軍人ノ在勤期間ニ關スル厚生年金ノ給付ヲ受クルコトニ對シ之ヲ拒否スル指令ニ接シタノデ目下善後處理手配中

六、正金銀行ノ第二會社案
　司令部ニ申請中

七、皇室財產關係
　皇室財產ノ一部解放ニ關シテハ大臣ト最高司令官及參謀長トノ話合デ暫ク留保皇室財產全般ノ處置ハ新憲法制定ト併行シテ進メル予定

(二) 貿易課
イ、輸出關係
一、石炭及坑木等積出ノ件
　(1) 石炭毎月八八千噸乃至九三千噸ヲ朝鮮及香港向積出サネバナラヌ
　(2) 坑木毎月二九七千本ノ支那向積出ニ付テハ農林課ノ項參照

二、生糸ノ積出ノ件
　農林課ノ項參照

三、「ゴム」、錫、「アンチモニー」輸出ノ件
　米國向輸出命令ヲ受ケ一定量ノ手配ハ了シダガ、指令ノ完成ニハ將來相當ノ困難ガアラウ

四、其ノ他各品目ノ積出方ノ件
　朝鮮支那向ニ通信機材鐵道車輛機關車「ピッチ」野菜種子其他數十品目積出方努力中ダガ相當困難ナルモノガアル

五、輸出準備申請書ニ關スル件
　五十有余件（金額五億二千百余萬圓）G・H・Qニ申請中

ロ、輸入關係
一、食料肥料輸入ノ件（農林課ノ項參照）

二、其他物資輸入ノ件
　二十一年間輸入希望表（客年十一月）四月—六月輸入希望表（三月末）提出中

三、余剰物資拂下ノ件
　(1) 旣ニ拂下ケラレタモノ、鑵詰小麥玉蜀黍等ノ項參照

3　経済諸施策への対応(昭和21年5月〜24年4月)

(2)近ク「トラック」拂下ゲラレル予定

八、其他

一、貿易廳ノ機構改正ニ關スル件(四月三日附覺書)
　細目ニ付司令部ノ意向照會中

二、稅關機構統合ノ件(四月八日附覺書)
　細目ヲ司令部ニ照會關係官廳間デ立案中

三、密輸入取締ノ件(二月二十八日附覺書)
　取締強化勅令案ヲ關係各省ニテ作成G・H・Qニ提出ノ予定

㈢　商工課

イ、賠償關係

一、航空機工場、軍工廠研究所關係賠償予定施設中我國經濟ノタメ最低限度ノ需要ヲ充足シ民生安定上絶對ニ必要トスル工場ニ付賠償對象カラノ除外乃至操業繼續ヲ認メラレル樣司令部ニ申入レ說明其他措置中

二、鐵鋼輕金屬工作機械等前項以外ノ產業部門ニ對スル賠償予定實施ノ指定近ク發セラルベキニ對シ其ノ際採ルヘキ措置ニ付關係各省デ準備中

ロ、戰后企業ノ再開促進ニ關スル件

商工省デ「ポツダム」勅令案及ビ商法ノ特例案ヲ作成司令部ニ對シ說明中、司令部側デ檢討中

㈣　農林課

イ、主要食糧輸入關係

一、四月—六月各月一五〇千屯輸入計畫實現ノ動キ「フォロー」

二、G4扱ヒ三月分輸入枠一〇〇千屯ノ實現確認

三、輸入濟ニ月分二五千屯(內旣解除ノ小樽入港米七、七六八屯ヲ除ク)

四、七月以降米國食糧輸入割當實現工作

五、ハワイ、マリアナ、沖繩等太平洋上ニ散在スル米軍集積餘剩食糧物資ノ引取確保

六、內地各地所在米軍餘剩放出食糧物資ノ引取確保

七、滿洲大豆、暹羅米輸入工作ノ繼續

八、隱退藏食糧摘發機構等輸入促進ニ關スル國內食糧機構ノ整備强化

ロ、其ノ他ノ輸入關係

一、比律賓「コプラ」「ハスクトココナット」ノ輸入工作

二、朝鮮、北支棉實ノ輸入工作

三、「アンガウル」、北大東島、海防、海州、埃及燐鑛石ノ輸入工作

四、米國硝安ノ輸入工作

五、北支、臺灣鹽等ノ輸入工作

六、南大東島、奄美大島砂糖ノ輸入工作

七、北、中支麩一三千屯ノ輸入確保

八、生糸輸出關係

生糸ハ三月十六日ヲ第一回トシテ米國向四月末迄ニ約二〇千俵ノ積出ガ爲サレタ、G・H・Qハ今後本年內ニ二三〇千俵月平均一三千俵ヲ目標トシ逐次輸出命令ヲ發出シ來ル模樣デアル、生糸ノ製造狀況ハ目下ノ處ハ殆ンド計畫通リニ進捗シテ居リ問題ハナイノデアルガ七月以降ハ新繭ノ增產ニ期待シナケレバナラナイノデアリ、從テ其ノ增產計畫ノ確保ト生產副資材ノ入手狀況如何ニ因リ難關ニ逢着スル危險ガ多分ニアリ其ノ對策ニ付テハ今カラ十分遺憾ナキヲ期スル必要ガアル

二、北支向坑木、枕木、朝鮮向木材ノ輸出

北支向枕木ノ輸出ハ確保セラルル見込デアルガ每月二

九七千本ノ坑木ノ輸出ハ難航ヲ續ケテキル、約六千屯ノ朝鮮向木材ノ輸出ハ北海道ニ現物ハアルト稱セラレテ居ルガ其ノ實現ニハ相當困難ヲ予想セラレル

ホ、農地制度改革

昨年末臨時議會開會中ニ發議セラレタG・H・Qノ指令ニ基イテ右議會ヲ通過シタ農地調整法中改正法律案等ノ內容等ヲ盛リ込ミ三月十五日附「コムプリヘンシーブ」且「ロングレンヂ」ノ農地制度改革計畫ヲ提出シテアルガG・H・Qデハ必ズシモ其ノ內容ニ滿足セズ例ヘバ五町步ノ面積制限ヲ更ニ三町步程度迄切下グルヲ適當ト認メテ居ルガ如クデアル

へ、木材統制關係

聯合軍宿舍建築用材ヲ始メ國內復舊用土木建築用材等ノ厖大ナ需要ヲ重點ノニ賄フ爲昨年十一月一部緩和シタ木材統制ヲ再ビ建テ直ス必要ガアリ目下新法案試案ヲG・H・Qニ提出其ノ下審議ヲ受ケテキル、右ハ現存ノ日本社、地木社ヲ中心トスル生產、配給統制機構ノ改善ト立木ノ強制賣渡命令ノ二點ヲ企圖シテ居ルノデアルガG・H・Qデハ右兩社ハ戰時機構ノ殘滓ダト

3 経済諸施策への対応（昭和21年5月〜24年4月）

三、交通部

イ、陸運關係

一、自動車輸送力ノ強化ニ關スルコト

米軍ヨリ中古自動車ノ拂下ヲ受ケルヤウ交渉中デアツタガ、貨物自動車四五〇輛、廢車三五〇輛ヲ第八軍ヨリ交付スル内連絡ガアツタ、更ニ四月二十六日貨物自動車及トレーラー合計九、八五〇輛（時價ヲ原價ノ三分ノ一トシテ約四、六〇〇、〇〇〇ドル）ノ拂下ニ就テモ總司令部關係者ヨリ内連絡アリ之ガ實現方努力中デアル

二、路面交通右側改變ニ關スルコト

二月中旬總司令部ヨリ運輸省ニ對シ路面電車、自動車及歩行者ノ右側通行ヲ六月十五日ヨリ實施スルヤウ獎漿（慫）ガアツタ

右ニ基キ調査シタ處、經費約一億圓、工事期間約二ケ年及多量ノ資材ヲ要スルコトガ明カトナツタ當事務局トシテハ種々ノ觀點ヨリ、右ガ實行困難デ

シテ其ノ存置ニ反對デ其ノ妥結ニハ相當困難ガ予想セラレ

アルコトヲ力説シ、實施ニ就テハ一應保留トナツテイルガ、今後更ニ接衝ノ必要ガアルモノト考ヘラレル

ロ、海運關係

一、税關機構移管ニ關スルコト

四月八日附覺書ニヨリ税關事務機構ヲ大藏省ニ移管スルヤウ指令ガアツタノデ目下運輸、大藏兩省間ニテ實施地方協議中デアルガ、港灣行政ノ一元化ガ破レルコトトナルノミナラズ、新設サレル沿岸警備ガ何レノ省デ擔當スルヤ等トモ關連シテ近日總司令部ニテ關係者ノ打合ヲナシ最後的決定ヲ見ル筈デアル

二、外地港ノ荷役増強ニ關スルコト

總司令部ノ指令ニヨル物資輸送ニ就テハ全力ヲ盡シテ完遂ヲ期シテヰルガ、外地港（例ヘバ朝鮮揚石炭デハ釜山）ニ於ケル揚不足等ノ問題ガアリ之ガ解決ニツキ努力中デアル

三、米國船舶借入ニ關スルコト

米國船舶二一五隻（LST一〇〇隻、リバテイ型一〇六隻、CI型九隻）ヲ我方ニ借入ヲ爲スコトトナ

リ、現在リバテイ型二隻ト、CI型一隻ヲ殘シ他ハ全部受取濟デアル

四、新造船ニ關スル件

新造船ニ關シテハ戰時中ヨリノ續行船一二三隻(三六六、九五〇總屯)ニ就テハ總司令部ヨリ建造許可ヲ得タガ、第二次計畫トシテ申請シタ六五隻(二二、九〇〇總屯)ノ新造ニ就テハ不許可トナッタ、其ノ理由ハ我國造船所ハ當分ノ間歸還輸送船ノ修理改裝ニ全力ヲ傾ケル必要ガアルト共ニ賠償等ノ根本問題ガ未決定デアリ、又世界的船腹過剩ノ問題モアリ今暫ク此ノ許否ヲ留保シタ模樣デアル

但シ右ノ中鐵道連絡船ノヤウナ特別ニ必要アルモノノ建造ニ就テハ司令部側ノ了解ヲ得テ再度要請スル方針デアル

尚漁船ニ付テハ鋼製漁船第一次建造計畫トシテ四一六隻(四八、五三三總屯)ノ許可ヲ申請中デアルガ、之ニ關シテハ目下好意的ニ考慮サレテヰル

八、遞信關係

一、通信料金ノ改正ニ關スル件

通信料金ヲ二倍値上ノ件ニ就テハ四月十九日ノ閣議決定ニ基キ四月二十二日總司令部ニ對シ申請シ、五月二日附デ許可ガアツタノデ目下實施準備ノ上小包料金等ハ五月六日ヨリ、郵便料金ハ七月一日ヨリ改正ノ豫定デアル

二、遞信院ノ省昇格ニ關スル件

遞信事業ノ戰後ニ於ケル重要性ニ鑑ミ遞信院ヲ省ニ昇格スル件ニ就テハ既ニ閣議ノ決定ヲ得タガ、三月四日總司令部ヨリ昇格ノ必要ヲ認メズトノ指示ガアリ昇格問題ハ停頓ノママ今日ニ至ツテヰル

三、對外通信連絡ニ關スル件

終戰後我國ノ對外通信連絡ハ全面的ニ停止ノ止ムナキニ至ツタガ、内外在住者ノ人心安定ヲ圖ルタメ必要最少限度ノ通信連絡ノ確保ヲ總司令部ニ對シ申請シタ結果ソノ許可ヲ得テ實施中デアル、尚今後ニ於テハ此ノ通信連絡ノ迅速ヲ期スルト共ニ進ンデハ新日本建設ノタメ必要ナ連絡圈ヲ確立スルヤウ總司令部ニ對シ接衝ノ方針デアル

二、歸還輸送及送還輸送關係

3　経済諸施策への対応(昭和21年5月～24年4月)

一、鐵道關係

(イ)在外邦人ノ歸還輸送ニ就テハ船舶ノ就航狀態ト揚陸地ノ收容狀態ト睨ミ合セ陸上輸送ヲ計畫シテヰルガ極メテ順調ニ進行シテヰル

(ロ)在日華、鮮、臺人等ノ本國送還輸送ニ就テハ總司令部二月十八日附覺書ヲ以テ登錄制ガ實施セラレタコトニヨリ更ニ強化セラレ陸海ニ亙リ計畫輸送ヲ實施シテ來テヰルガ、送還者ノ出足鈍キ爲其ノ實績ハ甚ダ低調デアル、從ツテ送還促進方ニ關シ新措置ヲ講ズル必要ガアル

二、海運關係

歸還輸送ニ就テハ在外邦人六八五萬人中四月末日迄ニ既ニ約四二％輸送シタ。臺灣、支那、南鮮、沖繩等ハ概ネ完了シ、目下南方地域竝ニ滿洲方面ヨリノ引揚(月間約九〇萬人)ニ重點ヲ移シテヰルガ、南方地域及北鮮ハ今秋迄ニ、滿洲モ今冬迄ニ終了スル見込デアル

歸還輸送ニ就テ船舶關係ノ最モ障碍トナルモノハ內地各受入港ニ於ケル船舶食糧ノ積込ガ容易デナイコ

トデ、之ニ就テハ目下關係省ト對策協議中デアル尚浦賀ニ於ケル「コレラ」解決ハ焦眉ノ急デアリ、吳ニ、佐世保ニ就テモ至急對策ヲ樹テル必要ガアリ準備中デアル

ホ、賠償關係

一、軍工廠、研究所及航空機工廠ノ轉換操業ニ關スル件
軍工廠、研究所及航空機工廠ノ轉換操業ニ就テハ一月二十日附指令ニヨリ再檢討ヲ要スルコトトナツタガ其ノ後檢討選定ノ結果ヲ聯合國軍ニ對シ申請シ實現ニ努力中デアル

二、其ノ他ノ賠償施設

(イ)以外ノ賠償施設及機械等ニ就テ近クソノ範圍ガ確定サレル筈デアルガ、「ポーレー」機關トノ交涉ニヨッテ判明シタ處ニヨリ、爾來特ニ民生安定上必須ノモノニ付テハ、總司令部及現地軍トノ認識ヲ深メテ來タ

鐵道車輛工場ノ撤去ニ就テハ、「ポーレー」聲明トシテハ此ノ點ニフレテ居ナカッタガ、其ノ後同機關ノ「マクスウエル」氏ニヨリ日本車輛工場ハ

ヲ説明シタ處(一)ニ付テハ先方ノ腹案トハ相當ノ隔リアルモノノ如ク(二)ノ點ニ付テハ大体了解シタモノノヤウデアル

約五割ノ過剰ニアル旨ガ指摘サレタ、ヨッテ當事務局トシテハ國民生活安定上必要トスル客貨輸送力ノ確保ヲ圖ルタメノ昭和二十五年度迄ノ車輛復興五ケ年計畫及修理方面ニ於ケル絶對的不足状態ヲ説明シ、此ノ間ノ認識ヲ深メ好意的考慮ヲ得タモノノヤウデアル

(ロ) 船舶關係ニ就テハ「ポーレー」大使ノ發表事項トシテ「日本占領上缺クベカラザル船舶修理ニ必要ナラザル範圍ニ於テ二十ケ所ノ造船所ノ全設備ト附屬品」ヲ賠償對象トスル旨ガ明カニサレタガ、我ガ方トシテハ

(一) 國民生活最低限度維持ニ必要ナ造船腹ハ四〇〇萬總屯デ之ガ損耗補充ニ當ツテハ大造船所ノミヲ撤去造船所ノ撤去ニ當ツテハ必要ナ造船ノ爲ニ二十ケ造船所ハ之ヲ殘置セラレタイコト

(二) 現有船腹ハ一一三萬屯デアルヲ以テ目標四〇〇萬屯ニ達スル迄ハ設備ノ撤去ヲ相當猶豫セラレタイコト

(八) 其ノ他工作機械ニ就テハ「ポーレー」聲明ニヨリ、工作機械製作能力ノ半分ヲ軍工廠其ノ他ノ設備ニツキ四〇萬近イ工作機械ヲ撤去スル旨ガ明カトナッタガ、特ニ「ボールベアリング」及「ローラーベアリング」ノ全工場ヲ撤去セラルル場合ハ自動車ノ新造修理ニ至大ナ影響ヲ生ズルノデ、此ノ點ニ就テハ鋭意説明ヲ爲シタガ、「ドイツ」ノ例ヨリ見レバ將來輸入ニ俟ツヨリ外ナイモノト思ハレル

四、設營部

イ、個人住宅接收ニ關スル件

聯合軍ニ依ル個人住宅ノ接收ハ家族呼寄ノ許可ニ伴ヒ佐官級ノ將校ノ爲ニモ行ハレ、且又「アライド、カウンシル、フオア、ジヤパン」代表、國際法廷首腦部及下級將官ノ爲ニモ行ハルルニ至ツタタメ其ノ影響範圍ハ著シク擴大シタ、目下接收通告ヲ受ケテ居ルモノハ佐官級住宅

3 経済諸施策への対応（昭和21年5月～24年4月）

五、管理部

(一) 概観

イ、在外邦人引揚ニ關スル交渉

聯合軍司令部（GⅢ主管）ノ在外邦人引揚ニ對スル態度ハ頗ル熱心且能率的ノデアツテ其ノ權限ニ屬スル限リ其ノ促進ノ為我方ノ希望ニ應ジテ大ナル便宜（引揚用船舶約百萬噸ノ貸與、之ガ南方英軍地域等ヘノ轉用、病院船ノ派遣、藥品類ノ供給、情報ノ供給、英、濠、華、等ノ諸國トノ連絡等）ヲ供與シテクレタルモ

(ロ) 援護局ニ於ケル檢疫防疫等醫療施設ノ不備及不履行ハ頗ル指令ノ不圓滑ニ基ク引揚船ノ出港延引ノ件

(イ) 食糧等供給ノ不圓滑ニ基ク引揚船ノ出港延引ノ件

(三) 先方カラ指令ノ不履行ヲ指摘セラレタ案件中重要ナルモノハ

今後トモ情勢ノ變化ニ伴ツテ適時申入ヲナス必要ガアル

(ロ) 漢口方面邦人（約三十萬人）ノ長江下航ノ問題等デアルガ右ハ何レモ米側ノ權限ノミデ解決シ得ナイ複雑ナ問題デアルカラ米側早急解決ヲ見ルニ至ラナイ

(イ)「ソ」聯地域殊ニ滿洲北鮮ニ在ル邦人ノ引揚促進及保護救援（三億五千萬圓送金ノ件、在京城及釜山日本人世話會資金ノ件等ノ）問題

(二) 我方カラ申入懸案中ノ主ナルモノハ

テキル

從ツテ司令部トノ交渉ハ目下ノ處我方カラ注文ヲ申入レル事項ヨリモ寧ロ我方ノ受入態勢ノ國内的非能率ノ為ニ先方カラ監視督促ヲ受クル案件ノ方ガ多數デアル

ロ、占領軍家族住宅及兵舎等ノ建設計畫ニ關スル件

總司令部ハ三月六日日本政府ニ對シ年間ニ約二萬家族ノ為ノ住宅ノ建築並ニ兵舎ノ新築（住宅ノ方ノ約半分ノ資材ガ見込マレテヰル）計畫ノ實施準備ヲ命令シ來リ先方ノ要求ニ從ヒ右ニ必要ナル諸機關ガ中央並ニ地方ニ設立セラレタガ本計畫ノ實施ニ付テハ特ニ資材ノ面ニ於テ多大ノ困難ガアルノデ、近ク聯合軍最高司令部及第八軍司令部ニ對シ好意的考慮ヲ懇請スルコトニナツテ居ル

トシテ八〇（七、八月接收ヲ豫想セラルルモノ二〇〇）其他三十八件アル

(ハ)引揚用船舶ノ不潔不衛生ノ問題、引揚港整備ノ遅延等

ロ、在日外國人(朝鮮人、臺灣人、中國人ヲ含ム)ノ故國送還問題

(イ)獨逸人ニ關シテハ本邦ニ於ケル登録ハ完了シタガ聯合國側ノ都合ニテ出發ハ延引シツツアル

(ロ)朝鮮人、臺灣人等ノ送還ハ日本側ノ計畫ニヨッテ歸還輸送ヲ行フベキコトトナッテヰルガ輸送ノ實績ハ諸般ノ事情ノ爲司令部カラ再三ノ注意ニモ不拘指令通リ行ハレズ著シク司令部係官ノ不滿ヲ結果シテヰル

八、其ノ他ノ司令部トノ交渉懸案

(イ)我カ國ノ在外利益代表國及在外邦人ニ關スル諸問題

(ロ)在日外國人ノ財産ニ關スル問題

之等邦人引揚ニ關聯スル諸問題及後述朝鮮人等送還ノ問題ニ關聯シテ政府トシテハ之ガ主管官廳ヲ此上トモ整備強化シ且關係各官廳カラノ援助ヲ一層積極的ナラシメテ萬全ヲ期スルコトガ喫緊ノ必要事デアルト考ヘラレル

(ニ)阿波丸ノ問題 等

(ホ)琉球人等ノ歸國問題

〰〰〰〰〰〰〰

昭和21年6月1日 連合国最高司令官総司令部より日本政府宛

復員局の設置承認方回答

GENERAL HEADQUARTERS
SUPREME COMMANDER FOR THE ALLIED POWERS
APO 500

1 June 1946

AG 388.3 (1 Jun 46) DCS
(SCAPIN -993)

MEMORANDUM FOR: IMPERIAL JAPANESE GOVERNMENT
THROUGH: Central Liaison Office, Tokyo
SUBJECT: Establishment of Demobilization Board.

1. Reference is made to Memorandum from Imperial Japanese Government, C.L.O. No.2473 (PP) subject: "Outline for Establishment of Demobilization Board", 22 May 1946.

2. The structural changes of the Demobilization Minis-

tries to Bureaus are approved by the Supreme Commander for the Allied Powers.

3. No exceptions to the provisions of Memorandum for the Imperial Japanese Government, AG 388.3 (10 Oct 45) DCSO subject: "Demobilization, Japanese Armed Forces", 14 October 1945, are to be made.

FOR THE SUPREME COMMANDER:

B. M. FITCH,
Brigadier General, AGD,
Adjutant General.

1 Incl:
Proposed Outline for Establishment of Demobilization Board

編 注 本文書の別添は見当たらない。

158 昭和21年6月3日 朝海終戦連絡中央事務局総務部総務課長作成
「石炭問題に關する總司令部との連絡會議(商工省)」

付記一 昭和二十一年六月十二日、朝海終戦連絡中央事務局総務部総務課長作成
「石炭問題等に關する商工大臣マーカット少將會談要點」

二 昭和二十一年七月五日、朝海終戦連絡中央事務局総務部総務課長作成
「石炭問題に關し商工大臣農林大臣總司令部側と會談の件」

石炭問題に關する總司令部との連絡會議(商工省)

(昭和二一・六・三 終連總務部朝海記)

三日、石炭問題に關する第一次會議は三菱商事ビルに於て開催せられたが、先方出席者シンウォルド、ベッカー、日本側出席者商工大臣、岡松、山本、山口、久武(以上商工)、朝海(終連)

一、シンウォルドより現下日本に於て食糧問題が最重要であるが産業の不振も重大關心事であり、これが根本原因は石炭の不足に求め得、自分は官廳會社等各方面と本件に付て話をしたが依然石炭増産はその緒に就いて居らない、依て問題の緊急性にも顧み御多忙なるべきも大臣に御足

勞を願ひたる次第であると述べ開會の挨拶を行ひ（大臣より答辭あり）次でベッカーより次の如く述べた、即ち

二、新內閣成立の機會に石炭生產に關し二、三の點に付て注意を喚起したい、自分の以下申述ぶることは既に石炭廳係官に對しては概ね指摘濟のことであるが、特にこの機會に大臣にもお話して置きたい

(1) 問題の一は勞働爭議であって、勞資の關係を安定化するやうに何等か適當なる措置を執る必要あり、例へば石炭の生產が月產一百萬屯といふが如く多少セーフ、レベルに到達するまでは勞資相互の休戰を提議するといふことも一案であらう、現に九州に於ては三月中二十二のストライキあり、これがため三萬屯の石炭を失ひ又スローダウンに依り八件乃至十件の所謂生產管理が行はれた又北海道に於ては八時間勞働の建前であるが實際上は四、五時間の仕事をしてゐるのに過ぎない、現場への往復に時間を取られて居るから實際上の勞働時間を八時間にすることが必要であらう、勿論これがために給料手當增加の問題が生ずべく又食糧問題もこれに關係を有して來るものと思はれる

(2) 炭坑勞務者に對する食料を確保せられたい、成程割當は現在の處良好であるけれども實際上の配給は特に北海道に於て甚しい、依て本問題に付き農林省、運輸省の關係が生じて來るのである

(3) 石炭の若干は闇市場に於て取引せられて居るから配供組織を分析研究の必要があらう

(4) 經營者側に於ける企業熱意の不足といふこともも石炭增產を阻害してゐる一因であるが、本件に關聯して補助金及び補助金を再檢討する必要があると思ふ、現在の石炭價格及制度を再檢討する必要があると思ふ、現在の石炭價格及が、現在の生產狀態は右數字より下廻はって計算であるから生產單價は從て高くならざるを得ない、業者の言に依れば平均原價は屯當り二百五十圓乃至三百圓であるさうであるが、大藏省は二百圓なりとして計算して居る、大藏省は補助金を押へたいといふ立場にあり、これに反して炭礦經營者は極力これを引上げようといふ意向にあるのであるから中立の第三者をして本問題を決定せしむる必要があらう、而して炭礦經營者は更に補助金の增額

3　経済諸施策への対応（昭和21年5月〜24年4月）

を請願して居るさうであるが、併し問題の解決は補助金の増額に依つては求められまい寧ろ逆の方法に依つてこれを發見し得るものと思ふ、補助金を増加するより補助金を全廢することゝ然るべしと思はれる、何となれば經營者が補助金を得る限り彼等は生産費を引下げる努力を行はぬと思はれるからである、成程石炭は各炭礦地域別にするためには寧ろ炭礦業者に補助金を與ふるよりと思ぼすことが考へられゐた然るにインフレーションを阻止するためには寧ろ炭礦業者に補助金を與ふるよりと思助金は石炭の消費者に廻はした方が適當であらうと思れる、而してこれに關聯し各炭礦地域別にクオーター・システムを勘案し、一定クオーター以上の超過出炭に付てはこれを自由市場に依てシーリング・プライスを設け賣捌くことを得しめては如何か、勿論斯るシーリング・プライスは炭坑勞務者の利益を確保し得る程度に十分高くなければならない

自分の今逑べた所は提案であり、而も問題は何れも簡單なものではないが、新政府の參考とならば幸ひである

尚最後に今一言したいのは勞資の關係が不安定な狀態に

あることは政府の方で責任を執る勇氣を缺いて居るからである、と云ふ點で商工省及び石炭廳は有能なる士を擁しては居るがその施策に付必ずしも政府の他の部面からの全面的な支持を受けてはゐなかつた、この結果勞資双方よりの政府に對する信頼の缺乏といふ結果が出て來たのである、依つて新内閣はこれ等の諸點を念頭に入れ、石炭生産の狀況か刻下の急務である點を十分に日本民衆に認識せしめられ度いと述べた

三、右に對し商工大臣から大要次の如く答へた

只今の適切なるお話に付き殊に重要なる三點に付き御返事したい、（一）勞働問題は單なる勞働問題から離れて民主主義を履き違へた政治問題となつてゐる傾きがあるが、限界を超えた運動は政府はこれを取締る方針である、尤も一方勞働者を或る程度經營協議會なるものに參加せしむることも適當であると考へ經營協議會なるものに付考慮を盡してゐる

（二）食糧問題は北海道は殊に悪い、これが思想問題と絡んで事態を悪化せしめて居るのであるが、關係方面と協議して食糧問題の改善方に付き格段の考慮を行つて居る、

尚本件に付ては米軍の援助を要請することゝならうから

481

宜しくお含み願ひたい

(三)價格問題は一昨日の自由進歩兩黨の政策協定の會議に於ても問題となり補助金制度よりは寧ろ消費する側に補助金を與へよといふ話も出た位であり、大藏大臣も又在野時代斯る意見を表示せることあり、商工省内部に於ても大體意見の一致を見てゐるが、御協力を得て措置を進めたい

尚勞資の協力は刻下殊に緊要である、又徵用といふやうなことではないが國民の愛國心に訴へて一定期間義務的に勞務に服せしむるといふことも考へてゐるのであるが、具體化した節は御協力を得たいといふ趣旨を述べた

(付記一)

石炭問題等に關する商工大臣マーカット少將會談要點

(昭和二一・六・一二　終連總務部朝海記)

六月十日の商工大臣とマーカット少將との會談先方の爲したる發言の中注目すべき點に若干の卑見を附して左の通り報告申上げる

一、食糧十萬屯輸入要請問題

(イ)食糧放出問題に關し自分の觀測する所では米側には日本側の配給機構の崩壞が現在の食糧危機に重大なる關係を有ってゐるとの見解から日本に主食の闇取引が存在する限りまだまだ食糧狀況緊迫なりとの日本政府の言ひ分には掛値があるとの主張が可なり強かったやうであるが現在に於て米側も事態の緊迫性は十分に認識して來て居ると思はれる(八日司令部食糧係官スミス氏及びエギキスト大尉の農林次官に對する發言)マーカット少將の六十余萬屯の商工大臣との會見に於ても同樣であった、但し六十万屯の輸入は未だ計畫であって必ずしも實現の目途が附いて居らないことと、アメリカに於ける經濟事情特殊に海運の罷業狀況等を睨み合せれば今直ちに手持ちの食糧を全部放出することに於てはその後の日本に於ける危機をタイド・オーバーすることが出來ないといふ憂慮からランプサムの食糧放出には躊躇して居るやうであった、卽ち一定の時期と一定の地域とを明示して放出を要請すれば考慮すると言って居るのである卽ち(a)問題の緊迫性を認めて來て居ることは例へば二週間前と格段に相違して居る但し(b)大量

3　経済諸施策への対応（昭和21年5月〜24年4月）

の放出に付ては先行に不安の要素が少なくないため躊躇して居る日本側の適當なる放出要望がタクトフルであるといふのが要點であらう

(ロ)米軍から放出された食糧を一般配給に廻はすべきか重要産業従事者に重點主義で配給すべきかの決定は先方は一切日本側に委して居る、自分の觀測する所では斯る事案こそ正に經濟安定本部の愼重なる研究に委せらるべき重大問題であらうと思ふ、而して「マ」少將の言外の趣旨は議事録で酌み取られたいが右「マ」少將の言外の含みとマッカーサー元帥に對して勸告を行つた勞働委員會の報告（未發表）を對比すれば其處に首尾の一貫した流れがある、蓋し同報告書は「プライオリティー・リスト」に掲げられて居るやうな種類の業務又は産業に従事する者に對し源泉の特配を行ふ必要があるが斯る食糧の特配を行ふべき源泉は米軍よりの輸入食糧に俟つべきこととならうが、米國より十分なる食糧を求め得ざるやうな場合に於ては一般配給より取り去てこの種勞働者に與ふることをも辭せざる程の決意を要する、蓋しこのために一般民の生存に多少の障碍を

來すことありと雖も止むを得ざるべく、斯の如き徹底した措置を執つて初めて日本の經濟的危機の期間を短くし且つ結局に於てはより少い人數が饑ゆるに過ぎざる結果を收め得る云々」と勸告して居るのである、勞働委員會は「マ」少將を長とするE・S・Sと緊密なる連絡を取り「マ」少將を經由して斯る最高司令官への報告を提出したであらうことは單なる想像ではない

二、石炭增産に必要な機械等資材の輸入に付てはロングレンジ・ポリシーであって急場の間に合はないといふことが指摘された

三、香港向輸出の取消し、朝鮮向輸出の量を減少せしめたことは總司令部が日本の現在の石炭危機を認識してくれた證左としこれ以上論ずることはサトルでない

四、生産管理問題に付ては總司令部の一部係官の意見なるものが新聞に傳へられたが（新聞に誤りがあったか係官が私見を發表したものであるかは知る由もないが）「マ」少將は明確に商工大臣に對し生產管理を總司令部に於て決して（デフィニットリーなる言葉を遣った）支持したこ

ともなければ現在に於ても支持しないと述べた、依て總司令部の生産管理に關する態度は極めて明確となったものと謂はなければならない、即ち米側は(イ)本問題は日本の裁判所に於て決定すべき問題ではあるが(ロ)尠くとも米側がこれを支持するといふことは絕對に有り得ないことを明示したのである、この問題に關する米側態度は從來極めて明確であったのであるが(バラード大佐所言、勞働委員會アバソルド博士所言等何れも報告の通り)再びアンミステーカブルにされたことは日本政府の今後の措置を容易ならしめるものであると思ふ

(付記二)
石炭問題に關し商工大臣農林大臣總司令部側と會談の件
　　　　　（昭和二一・七・五　終連總務部朝海記）

七月三日、商工大臣及び農林大臣求めに依り總司令部經濟科學部係官と會見要旨左の通り會談を遂げた、我方出席者兩大臣の外兩省係官、終聯係官、先方出席者ライダー（マーカット歸米不在中）ファイン、エギキスト、コーエン、ウォーカー等

一、先づライダー大佐から、本日は極めて非公式なる形式にてお話致したく御足勞を願つた、司令部としては或種の産業殊に石炭關係産業の生産增强に付き論議致し度い、日本の石炭は日本經濟の民需充実に必要なる半分量も生産されて居らざる實狀であってこれには各種の問題が關聯して居るが根本問題は食糧の問題である、占領軍に於て日本側に對し目下食糧を放出して居るが炭礦等の重要産業に食糧增配方に付き商工、農林兩大臣間に如何なる取極めを爲して居る次第であるか、米軍は今後輸入せらるべき食糧の數量をも睨み合せて着々放出を行つてゐるが日本に於ける全般的不足を輸入食糧に依り充足し得べしとは思はれざる次第で其處に重點配給の問題が生ずる、と述べたのに對し商工大臣から、一般的食糧不足の際司令部の食糧放出に付ては深謝に堪へざる所である、斯る放出に依られたる食糧の一部は先づこれを石炭增産に充てたき意向であつてその趣旨を閣議に於ても決定し居り一般の食糧不足にも拘らず坑夫六合、家族三合の配給を維持するに努めて居る、北海道はお蔭で狀況改善を見て居

3 経済諸施策への対応（昭和21年5月〜24年4月）

るが最近九州方面が少し旨く行かぬので心配であるが、これも改善させて石炭増産の目的を達したいと考へて居ると述べ、農林大臣からも食糧放出に付謝意を表示して居から石炭關係勞務者に對し必要ならば六合配給を維持して行きたい方針である、但し九州方面殊に福岡縣は少して事情を異にする、成程福岡縣は一般に窮屈ではあるが縣内に或る程度の持越食糧がある一方最近熊本縣、佐賀縣から各二萬石を福岡縣に移入方措置中であることを指摘致したい、尚この機會に了解を得て置きたいことは、成程食糧は石炭増産に必要であらうが、石炭生産不振の原因はこれのみに歸するを得ないといふ點であって、増産を阻む他の有力なる諸原因に付ても十分に研究の上對策を講ずる必要がある、尚福岡縣の状勢に關しては具體的な數字をも所有して居ると述べた、右に對しライダー大佐から、現下の經濟的非常事態に顧み日本政府が例へば一のグループに特惠的待遇を與へるとするも他よりの非難はなかるべく、余りに公正的に、且つ倫理的にのみ考へることは適當ではなからうと思ふ、何が重要産業であるかは定義を要するが、何れにするも重

要産業への特配は考慮に値ひすると思ふと述べ、エギキスト大尉より交通關係勞務者に對する特配問題にも觸れる所あり、右に對し商工大臣から炭坑勞務者をして食糧不安の状況から解放せしめ安全感を持たしめたいと思ってゐると述べ、農林大臣は石炭關係勞務者に對する特配の重要性は勿論熟知して居るが、食糧放出と一般状況を睨み合す農林大臣としての責任から言へば所謂基本産業に付てもそのウエイトに從ひ商工大臣とも連絡の上特配に付き再調整を行ふ必要があるのではないかと考へてゐると述べ、右に對しエギキスト大尉より、この問題は各省に關係ある重大問題である、食糧と基本産業の生産の關係は正しく經濟安定本部に於て各省の上に立って裁斷を下すべき問題であり、石炭増産の途を拓き、交通逼塞の危険を封殺せば日本經濟の困難を最小限度に止め終局に於ては困難克服を早め得る理であらうと述べ、ライダー大佐また經濟安定本部の急速なる活動に付き指摘する所があった

更にラ大佐から、本日お集りを願つた根本目的は食糧の特配問題に關聯し商工、農林兩省間に如何なる取極めを

作ることも結構であつて總司令部としては何等これに干渉するものではない、寧ろ反對に問題を解決せんと努力する日本側に總ゆる支援を惜しまないと云ふ趣旨を明かにする爲めである、總司令部から日本側に對し放出食糧を斯く斯くの如く配分せよと指令は出さぬが、兩省の斯る取極めに對しては總司令部として同意を與へこれに協力するの用意があると述べた

二、(イ)尚香港朝鮮向石炭輸出問題に關聯しライダー大佐から、本件に付ては日本側に對し文書も發出せられたが、香港は生鮮食糧五百屯を日本に送附して來て日本の食糧問題解決に關し總司令部を支援せんとして居る次第であるから七月は同地域に對し一萬五千屯を供給したいと思ふ又朝鮮に對しても同地域の實状に鑑み五萬屯を送附する必要があると思はれる、この邊の事情は日本政府にも解つて貰ひたい、結局七月は合計六萬五千屯を兩地域に輸出することとなるであらうと述べた（八月の輸出見込額に輸出することの日本側質問に對しては七月に比し如何にならうかとの日本側質問に對しては種々の條件もあり且つ本件は總司令官が決定する問題であるから現在に於ては何とも言へぬと答へた）

(ロ)製鹽關係産業への六月分の配炭減少に付き質問あり、我方から天候の關係で約一五〇萬屯と答へた

(ハ)日本全國の貯炭量に付き質問あり約一五〇萬屯と答へ、これが全量引取り不能の理由に付き交通の關係上アクセシブルでないこと、風化等に依て價値が下つてゐる物も尠くないことを答へた處アクセシブルでないといふのは如何なる狀態に在るのを意味するのか明かでないが、引取りに米軍トラックの協力が必要ならば申出でよ、無價値の物ならば貯炭として計上して置くこと自體が誤りで、却つて混亂を生ずる恐れがあると指摘した、本件に付ては(1)貯炭の數量(2)輸送し得るや否やの點(3)貯炭の品質等詳細石炭廳から報告することとなつた、尚この問題は六月十日商工大臣がマーカット少將と會見した際も先方から指摘された經緯があることを附言する

(二)商工農林兩大臣から食糧が相當量輸入せられたので議會に於て總司令部に對し感謝決議をやらうといふ考へがあるが國際關係も機微であり且つ米國内の輿論といふこともあるべく、日本政府としては總司令部側をエンバラスしたくないと思ふが此の點に關する貴見は如何かと尋

3　経済諸施策への対応（昭和21年5月〜24年4月）

ねた處ライダー大佐は、斯ることはやられぬ方が宜しからうと答へた（エゲクイスト氏と自分との會談參照せられ度くやらぬ方が好き事情は愈々明瞭である）

三、(イ)本日の會見の焦點が米側の食糧放出に伴ひこれを如何に配分するかは日本側に任せると云ふ原則を認めつつも總司令部としては政府がその一部を重要產業に優先的に配分することを間接的に慫慂したものであることは論を俟たない、前囘商工大臣がマーカット少將と會談の際もマ少將からこの話がそれとなく出た印象に付ては當時自分の報告を參照せられたい、ライダー大佐は右を今少しく明瞭に日本側に表示したものであり、アバソルド氏の勸告書にある通り「斯の如き徹底した措置を執り初めて日本の經濟的危機の期間を短くし且つ結局に於てはより少い人數が飢ゆるに過ぎざる結果を收め得る云々」と云ふ趣旨を述べたものである

(ロ)農林省としては一般配給の責任を有する次第でもあり農林大臣指摘の如く本問題を簡單に考へ得まいと思はれ結局經濟安定本部で決定する外あるまいが經濟安定本部は成立しても成立早々果して斯る重大問題に關し裁決を下し得るが如く動き出し得るか疑問である、然るに日本の經濟的危機は眼の前に迫つて居る、九州炭の鈍勢が北海道炭の增產をオフセットせんとして居るならば經濟安定本部の設立を待つことなく此の際至急惡循環を斷ち切るための思ひ切つた手段を講ずることが必要であらうと思はれる、卽ち福岡方面炭礦特配用なることを明示して

二、三千屯の食糧の放出を要望しては如何、三日の會議に於ても米側が重要產業に對する特配に協力しようといふ態勢にあることは明かであつた、本會談に列席した印象に基き敢て卑見を具申する次第である

〰〰〰〰〰〰〰〰〰〰

昭和21年7月6日
中國代表部王武大佐との會談覺
朝海終戰連絡中央事務局總務部總務課長作成

「中國代表部王武大佐との會談覺」

中國代表部王武大佐來訪會談したる覺左の通り

（昭和二一・七・六　終連總務部　朝海記）

一、中國軍人捕虜五名の入院治療費日本側負擔の問題（管理部で研究中）

五日、王武大佐と會談談した覺左の通り

三、中國軍進駐問題　自分から、最近中國軍が日本占領に參加するさうであるが現在如何なる段階にあるかと尋ねたところ同大佐は占領に參加することは確定的である、その兵力は凡そ一萬五千名程度とならう、時期は目下補給問題等に關しワシントンで米側と外交々渉中で未定である、占領地域に付ては祕密であると答へたので自分から、名古屋方面を中心とする地域であるといふ新聞報道を指摘したところ同大佐は敢て右を否定せず更に自分から中國軍の進駐は英濠軍の日本進駐と趣を異にし、日本には中國人居住者が多數存在して居る關係上これ等中國人が軍關係の身分を取得すると課稅の問題、警察取締りの問題等に於て困難なる問題を生ずると思ふから此の點は不合理のないやう豫めお含み置き願ひたいと申入れたところ同大佐は御趣旨は了承して置くと答へた

三、課稅問題　中國人が日本に於て營業稅等の稅金を支拂はぬ點を指摘し率直に言へばこの際中國人に全部歸つて貰ひたいが、殘る以上は日本の稅權に服して貰ひたい、これは日本の敗戰に關係がないこの點に付ては大藏省が總司令部と接觸中であらうと思はれるから總司令部より何等相談があつた場合は公正に處置ありたいと述べたところ同大佐は代表者として無法な要求は支持しない此の事案を研究する僑務處は最近歐米通の劉增華が去つて日本通の林定平が主宰者となつたから斯る問題に付て日本側としても非常に相談し易いことと思ふと答へた

〜〜〜〜〜〜〜〜〜〜〜〜

昭和21年7月12日　朝海終戰連絡中央事務局總務部總務課　長作成

160 「物價廳設立問題に關しマーカット少將、大藏大臣會談の件」

物價廳設立問題に關しマーカット少將、大藏大臣會談の件

（昭和二一・七・一二　終連總務部　朝海記）

本件に關し十二日會談が行はれたが出席者左の通り

米側、マーカット、ライダー、ノアーイン、エギキスト

日本側、石橋、工藤、片桐、柏木、朝海

マ少將より物價廳はいよいよ設立の運びとなつたが、本件が成功するか否かは重大問題であるからこれが任務に關し誤解のないやう次の點に關し確かめたいと述べた

3　経済諸施策への対応(昭和21年5月～24年4月)

(1) 物價廳は既に設立を許可されて居るに拘らず未だに運營されて居らぬ處の經濟安定本部の下にあるものと了解する、なお本件に關聯し本尊の經濟安定本部の構成と運營は如何になつて居るか、本機構の設立についての指令の出て居ることは御承知の通りである又經濟安定本部の長官は未だに決定しないのか(藏相から適當に應酬)

(2) 經濟安定本部と物價廳の關係は如何に規制するか、前者は政策を決定し後者はこれを實施する機關とりよう解する

(3) 遞信省等に於ては遞信關係費用を從來は同省に於て勝手に決め得た建前であるが今後は物價廳とその活動をコーデイネートすることゝなるべしと了解する、本件は重大な點であるが、日本側の方に誤解はないと思ふが念を押す次第である

(4) 物價廳は物價に關係あるすべての各省と協議して物價を決定すると了解する、併し物價決定の最終の責任者は物價廳であると了解する

(5) 地方に於ける價格に不均衝(衡方)があり、地方的に物資の不必要な移動が行はれることもあるが地方物價委員會に中央

とコーデイネートし地方に於ける不當な値段のために物資が不必要に移動することなきを期するものと了解する

(6) 物價廳の規模についてはこれを増大する考へはないが、自分等の見るところに依れば物價廳の機構は小に失する樣である(と逑べたのに對し大藏大臣から仕事を始めてからの規模についての研究等を逑べたのに對し)從來日本側の案を見ると紙の上では極めて有效の樣であるが、これが實施についても遺憾の點が少くない、その精神において部から發出される指令等についても、例へば司令部から發出される指令等についても有效でない場合が少くない、當初から適當な大きさの規模が必要であるが、よつてこの物價廳を適當な時期に擴充することについて大藏大臣のアッシユアランスを得たい(大藏大臣より本件の運營が有效に行はれることについては自分も同意であるからその意味において運營を有效ならしめるよう措置すると答へた)

以上を確認してマ少將から物價廳の設立を許可するという ことはもち論これによつて物價廳が營むあらゆる事務に自

161

昭和21年7月15日　条約局条約課作成

「日本（ドイツ）國の武装解除及び非軍事化に關する四國條約案について」

昭二一、七、一五、條條（小木曾事務官稿）

日本（ドイツ）國の武装解除及び非軍事化に關する四國條約案について

一、交渉の經緯

　去る六月二十一日發表された對日非武装四國條約案は、四月二十九日に發表された對獨條約案と殆ど全く同一の内容を有するものであるが、同條約案發表に關する放送は五月二十日のバーンズ國務長官のパリ外相會議に關する放送に據れば次の如くである。

　この條約の根本思想は既に一九四三年十月のモスコー宣言に現れてゐるのであってその全般的安全に關する四國宣言第二項において「右四國中共通の敵國と戰爭しつゝある國は該敵國の降伏及び武装解除に關する一切の事項に付協同して行動すべきこと」と記されてゐる。一九四五年七月のポツダム會談へ赴く途中トルーマンとバーンズはかゝる條約の必要につき討議した（因に對獨ポツダム協定、對日ポツダム宣言及び米國の初期の對日政策中の武装解除及び軍需生産禁止に關する諸原則はこの條約と同一の思想を現してゐる）。バーンズが初めてこの條約締結の必要を示唆したのは昨年九月のロンドン外相會議に於てであった。彼は更に昨年十二月モスコーに於てスターリンとこの問題について討議したが、これに對しスターリンは若し米國が提議するならば彼はこの提議を支持するであらうと述べた。尤もこれについては、ソ聯側は前記放送後に、當時バーンズは何ら草案を有してゐなかつたのであるから原則的支持

3　経済諸施策への対応（昭和21年5月～24年4月）

を約したことにはならぬと反駁してゐる。

本年二月バーンズは對獨條約案を英、ソ、佛に對日條約案を英、ソ、支各國政府に送つた。これに對しソ聯以外の各國は賛意を表したが、ソ聯は沈黙してゐた。

前回のパリ外相會議でこの條約案の審議が提議されたが、モロトフは先づポツダム宣言の武裝解除の實行されたかどうかを見ない中にかゝる條約を結ぶのは速やかな武裝解除を遅延せしめるものである、といつて審議に反對した。そこでバーンズは五月十三日のパリ會議にドイツの武裝解除調査のため四大國調査委員會の設置を提議し、全國一致承認された。しかし、この委員會は成立後米國側が調査範圍を狹く限定せず經濟的分野にまでも調査を行ふことを主張したのに對し、ソ聯が反對したため難關に逢着し（五月二十八日ロイター）その後進展せぬ模様である。

前記の如く對獨條約案は四月二十九日、對日條約案は六月二十一日それぞれ發表せられ、對獨案についてはバーンズは放送中で英佛兩國は同意なる旨述べ又對日案については發表と同時に英國及び支那は全面的に同意の旨が報道せられたが、ソ聯に關しては何等述べられなかつた。ただし間接的に政府の意向を反映してゐると思はれるもモスコー放送（五月三日）は對獨條約案に關して「四國條約案は何ら新味がない。それらは既にポツダム協定に含まれてゐたものである。米國案によればドイツがこれから武裝解除の條件を無條件に承認することは聯合國のドイツ占領を終結させる豫備行爲であるとし、二十五年間ドイツを處理する聯合國監督委員會を規定してゐる。しかしソ聯代表はこれに對し先づドイツ全占領域に亘る武裝解除の現状を調査することを提案した。これなくしては如何なる協定も一片の反古と化せざるを得ないにも拘らずドイツ全土に亘って武裝解除が四國協定の線に沿つて必ずしも遂行されてゐない幾多の事實を例證し得る」云々と述べ更に「四國條約の米國の企圖はドイツに於ける長期占領の義務履行からの逃避を隱蔽するものである」として非難した。

六月十五日以降繼續中の第二回パリ外相會議は七月九日初めてドイツ問題を取り上げたが、モロトフはこの條約案ではポツダム協定の目的を達することは出來ないとして、左の諸點を擧げてこの案に反對した。

一、ドイツの軍需産業抹殺についての規定を缺いてゐること。

二、ライン方面の非ナチ化を保障してゐないこと。
三、ソ聯に對する賠償支拂の繼續に關する規定を包含してゐないこと。
四、占領期間が短きに失すること。
そして有效期間を四十年に延長することを主張した。これに對しバーンズは期間の延長には同意したが他の點には反駁を加へたと傳へられる(七月九日ロイター七月十日SFAF放送)

三、條約案の內容と對日對獨兩案の差違
兩條約案の內容につきだつて、その差違を檢討すれば左の通りであるが、いづれも根本的のものではなく兩者は本質的には同一のものであると云つて差支ないであらう。

(一)締約國
對獨案の締約國は米、ソ、英、佛であるのに對し、對日案の締約國は英、支、ソ、米の四國である。
對獨處理の方針は、昨年二月クリミヤに於ける米、ソ、英會談において、更に同年七月のポツダム三國會談において決定されたが、佛はサン・フランシスコに

おいて開かれた聯合國會議に際し五大國の一に加へられ、ポツダム協定によつてドイツ國の占領に參加することとなつた。一方我國はポツダム宣言を受諾することによつて對獨案が米、ソ、支、英に降伏したのであり、從つて對獨案が米、ソ、英、佛を締約國としてゐることは當然である。

(二)準軍事組織
第一條甲において、對獨案ではエス・エス・アー及びゲシユタポの如き準軍事組織の武裝解除、復員及び解體を規定してゐるのに對し、對日案では憲兵隊、警備隊、特高課を準軍事組織として例示してゐる。

(三)占領期間中の武裝解除及び非軍事化の規定の實行
ポツダム協定政治的原則(一)は「ドイツ國に於ける最高權力はドイツ國に於ける管理機構に關する協定に從ひアメリカ合衆國、聯合王國、ソヴイエト社會主義共和國聯邦及フランス共和國軍司令官に依り其の政府よりの訓令に基き各自の占領地帶內においては各自に、又全體としてのドイツ國に關係ある事項に付ては其の管理理事會會員としての資格に於て共同して行使せら

3 経済諸施策への対応(昭和21年5月〜24年4月)

るものとす」と規定してゐる。即ちドイツ國の場合は、米、英、ソ、佛四國が各自の占領地帶內において各自占領地行政を行ふと同時に、ドイツ國全體に關係する事項については管理理事會を通じて共同權力を行使することとなつてゐたが日本の場合は、分割占領は行はれず聯合軍最高司令官の下に一體化されてゐる（註）。その結果第三條において占領期間中の第一條に揭げられた武裝解除及び非軍事化の規定の嚴格な施行について、對獨案では they (the high contracting parties) shall through, the Allied Control Council and in their respective Zones, enforce strictly……となつてゐるに反し、對日案では they shall support the strict enforcement of…となつてゐる。

註 モスコー公表文によれば極東委員會に關しては「委員會は合衆國政府より最高司令官への命令系統及び最高司令官の占領軍隊に對する指揮を含める日本國に於ける現存管理機構を尊重すべし。」とせられ、又委員會の表決は英、米、ソ、支を含む過半數によるのであつて、四箇國は否認權を有

してゐる。

又聯合國日本理事會については「一切の場合に於て行動は日本國に於ける唯一の聯合國の爲の執行權者たる最高司令官の下に行動すべし。最高司令官は事態の緊急性の許す限り重要事項に關する命令の發出に先ち理事會と協議し且之に諮問すべし。」とされてゐる。

次に條約案の內容を說明する。

前文

前文は次の三點より成る。

日本（ドイツ）國の全面的武裝解除及び復員の意圖が四國政府により宣言され、それは旣に相當程度實行されたこと。

日本（ドイツ）國の全面的武裝解除及び非軍事化の施行を確保することが依然として必要であること。

この目的遂行のため、四國が共同措置を執ること。

第一の點に關聯し、ソ聯はドイツ國の武裝解除が果して相當程度まで進捗してゐるか否かは不明である、かかる宣言を行ふことは武裝解除を遲らせる所以であると言

つて反對してゐる。第二の點はこの條約の目的を表したものであるが、これには「世界の平和及び安全が必要とする限り」といふ但書がついてゐる。これは必要なる場合には日獨軍備の保持を許すといふ意味ではないのであつて、日獨の非軍事化は四國の利益のためではなく世界平和及び安全のために必要であるといふことを明らかにしたにすきない。

前文中、對日案では「この保證のみがアジヤの諸國及び世界が心を一にして平和の習慣に復歸することを得しめるであらう」とするところを、對獨案では「――ヨーロッパの諸國及び世界が」となつてゐる。

第一條

日獨の武裝解除及び非軍事化を確保するための各種の措置を規定してゐる。

(甲) 一切の武裝兵力、準兵力及び補助組織の解體。

この項において、對日案では「憲兵隊、警備隊、特高課のやうな一切の準兵力」となつてゐるのに對し、對獨案では「ナチス親衞隊、突擊隊及び祕密警察のやうな一切の準兵力」となつてゐることは前に逃べた。

(乙) 參謀組織の解體。

この項において、對日案では The Japanese General Headquarters, the staffs of the army and the navy and the staffs of any para-military organizations となつてゐるが對獨案では The German general staff and staffs of any military organizations となつてゐる。

(丙) 軍事組織及び準軍事組織の存在の禁止。

(丁) 各種軍需品(兵器、爆藥、需品、艦艇、航空機等)の製作、生產、輸入の防止。

この中爆發物に關してはあらゆる種類の航空機、航空用裝備及び裝置が禁止されてゐる。又この項中では原子爆彈の重要性に鑑み、核分裂性物資(但し聯合軍により承認された條件の下では差支ない)も禁止されてゐる。

(戊) 軍事的構築物軍需工場等の建設利用の防止。

この中後者は丁項に列擧された種目の生產を行ふ一切の施設であり研究所、特許、設計等をも含んでゐる。

(己) 本條の除外例

治安維持に缺くことのできないやうな警察隊の編成

3　経済諸施策への対応（昭和21年5月～24年4月）

使用及び輸入小武器によるその武装並びに㈦一項中爆發物の如く建築、鑛業、農業その他平和的目的に必要なものの最少量の輸入は禁止より除外される。

以上の六原則中従前の宣言、指令等において既に述べられた事項を求めれば次の如くである。

㈲ポツダム協定第三部ドイツ甲政治的原則㈢の一の㈸、對日一般命令第一號の一、米國の初期の對日方針第三部政治の一。

㈼ポツダム協定ドイツ甲政治的原則㈢の一の㈸、初期の對日方針第三部政治一。

㈻右に同じ。

㈦ポツダム協定ドイツ甲政治的原則㈢の一、の㈹及び乙經濟の原則㈡一般命令第一號の一、指令第三號の四及び八の㈡、初期の對日方針第四部經濟の一。

㈼ポツダム協定ドイツ甲政治的原則㈢の一の㈹、初期の對日方針第四部經濟の一。

㈺ポツダム協定初期の對日方針にはなし。一般命令第一號の一（警察隊の維持につき）

第二條

第一條の規定を完全ならしむるため、占領終了と同時に實施される四國監察制度を設ける。そしてこれは監督委員會（commission of control）（註）を通じて運營せられる。この監督委員會は必要と思はれる檢査、審問及び調査を行ふことができる。

（註）ヴェルサイユ條約はザール河流域地方の施政を國際聯盟を代表する委員會に委任し、條約實施後十五年の期間滿了の時において人民投票によつて同地方の歸屬を決することとした。

ザールは一九三五年一月の人民投票によつて同年三月一日正式にドイツに復歸したが、それまでの十五年間ヴェルサイユ條約の規定する施政委員會（Government commission）による施政が行はれた。この委員會はザール地域に於て從來ドイツ帝國、プロイセン、バイエルンに屬した一切の施政權を保有し、公企業經營權、裁判權、租稅徴收權等の外、ザール施政の諸規定より生ずる一切の問題を解決する權限を有してゐた。この委員會は地域的な行政機關であり、國際聯盟を代表し、聯盟により委員が選定任命

締約國の行動を求める勸告を提出しなければならない。その報告及び勸告を受取つたときは、締約國は、その既遂又は未遂の違反の即時停止又は防止のため空海陸軍を含む行動を合意によつてすみやかに執る。締約國はその執つた行動又は執らうとしてゐる行動を安全保障理事會に直ちに報告しなければならない。

　締約國は特別の四國協定を結ぶため、この條約の効力發生の日から六箇月以内に協議する。その四國協定は(イ)監督委員會による檢査、審問及び調査(ロ)この條約の目的のため利用し得るやうにしなければならない兵力の數及び種類、出動準備程度及び一般的配置(ハ)各國が供與すべき便益及び援助の種類につき詳細に規定するものであつて、各自の憲法上の手續によつて批准される。

　この條約と安全保障理事會との關係について一言しやう。そもそも安全保障理事會は國際平和及び安全の維持について主要なる任務を負ふ機關であり、元來ならば國際聯合加盟國は安全保障理事會の許可なくしては強制措置を執ることは出來ぬのであるが、舊敵國に對してはその許可を必要としないこととなつてゐる（憲章五三條後

　第三條
　締約國は、占領期間中、武裝解除及び非軍事化の規定の嚴格な施行を支持しなければならない。日獨の管理形態の差異に因り、對獨案では「締約國は、、、聯合國管理事會を通じ及びその各自の占領地域内において嚴格に施行する」となつてゐることは前述した。又第一條及び第二條の規定の日獨による明白な受諾が占領終了の必須條件たることを規定してゐる。
　この條項は、この條約の成立が武裝解除及び非軍事化の進行を弱めるものでないことを確認せるものである（對獨案に對するソ聯の反對理由參照）

　第四條
　監督委員會は檢査、審問及び調査の結果を絶えず締約國及び國際聯合安全保障理事會に通報しなければならない。武裝解除及び非軍事化の規定違反が、既に生じ又は將に生じやうとしてゐるときは、締約國に報告しなければならない。
　その報告と共に委員會は過半數の委員が適當と認める

されるで今回の監督委員會と性質を異にしてゐる。

3 経済諸施策への対応（昭和21年5月〜24年4月）

段─現敵國に依る侵略政策の更新に對し向けられたる地域的取極に於て規定せられたるものを除くの外安全保障理事會の許可なくしては如何なる強制行動も地域的取極に基き又は地域的機關に依り執らるることなかるべし）。從つて、監督委員會及び締約國の安全保障理事會に對する報告は單に報告であつて意見や承認を求めるのではない。監督委員會が締約國の行動を求める勸告には報告すら必要としない。

監督委員會の勸告は過半數による。從つて、締約國は議決に關しては拒否權を有しない（安全保障理事會では五大國は手續問題以外については拒否權を認められてゐる）。尤も締約國は、違反の停止又は防止のため行動を執らうとする場合には、合意によつて執らねばならない。結局委員會の議決は一國の反對があつても成立するが、實際の行動は四國の一致を必要とする。一方、使用すべき兵力の種類その他の細い點については特別協定成立前にあつては、この條約は實際の效果を發生しない。

第五條　本條では批准手續及び有效期間を規定してゐる。この條約は二十五年間效力を有するが、締約國は有效期間滿了六箇月前に、この條約の定める監督を引續き施行することが必要であるか否かを決定するため、協議しなければならない。（この二十五年に對しソ聯は四十年を提議し米國が同意したと報道せられてゐることは前述の通りである）。

三、この條約案と平和條約との關係

この條約案は第一條に掲げられた武裝解除及び非軍事化が施行され、且つ第一條及び第二條の規定を日本が明白に受諾することを以て日本占領終了の必須條件とし（第三條）、聯合國の日本占領終了と同時に四國監察制度（System of quadripartite inspection）を設ける（第二條）ことを規定してゐる。換言すれば占領終了と同時に現在の管理制度が廢止され監察制度に移行するのである。

この條約は英支ソ米四國間の條約であつて、我國は當事國ではないが、この條約の内容は當然我國の受諾を前提としてゐるものではあり（第三條）、その我國の受諾がなされるのは平和條約においてでなければならないこと

はいふまでもない。從つて、この條約は實質的には對日（獨）平和條約の一部を成すものであつて、その上に四國が日本（ドイツ）による武裝解除及び非軍事化を監視し、違反の場合共同して制裁を加へることを約したものにほかならない。その意味からいつて、この條約第一條及び第二條は平和條約の内容を部分的に豫め示したものといへるのである。

第二條は占領終了と同時に監察制度が實施されるべきことを規定してゐるが、このことは進駐軍が全面的に撤退することを直ちには意味しない。占領が終了すれば聯合軍最高指揮官の制限の下に置かれてゐた天皇及び日本國政府の國家統治の權限（八月十一日附の四國政府囘答）は再び自由となるが、それは完全なる自由ではなく四國によつて一定期間監督を受けることになるのである。勿論占領が終了した上は、國家權力の總てが現在のやうに聯合國最高指揮官の指令に基いて運營せられることはなくなるが、監察制度（指令から内面指導に代る）をして實效あらしめんがためには、初期の間は相當の兵力を駐屯せしめるであらうことは想像に難くなく六月二十日の米

下院特別會計豫算分科會においてアイゼンハウアー參謀總長は「米國は五年乃至十年口獨に止る必要がある。但し順調にゆけば、日本における兵力は三年後には相當減少せられる可能性がある」と述べた趣である（六月二十一日ワシントンUP）。

監督委員會は、實質的には極東委員會及びその下にある對日理事會を繼承することとなるであらう。右委員會及び理事會には四國の他に佛、蘭、濠、加、ニュージーランド、印、比の七國が參加してゐるから、これらの諸國はこの條約の締約國ではないが何らかの形で監督委員會に代表せられることになるのではあるまいかと思はれる。第二條にも a commission of control to be established by the high contracting parties on a quadriparite basis とあつて必ずしも四國以外を排除する趣旨とは解されない。

四、この條約案の性格（ロカルノ條約との比較）

この條約案を前大戰後の安全保障條約たるロカルノ條約と比較すると、その根本的な差異を次の點に求めることが出來る。そしてそれは同時に本條約案の性格を表してゐる。

3 経済諸施策への対応（昭和21年5月～24年4月）

(一) 締約國の差異　ロカルノ條約の締約國は英、獨、佛、伊、白、波、チェッコで擔保國たる英伊を除いては總て獨と國境を接する國である。前大戰後、佛は自國の安全保障を初め英佛蘭及び米佛間援助條約により確保しやうとしたが失敗し、後ドイツの提議により國境保障の條約が商議され同條約が成立した。從つて、これは舊敵國たるドイツの主張が聯合國の意嚮に合致して成立したものであつて、同條約は佛白等に對し安全を保障するをのみならず獨に對しても安全を保障するものであつた。しかるに、今回の條約案は米國のイニシヤテイブにより、舊敵國たる日獨は全然除外され、その安全は全く顧みられてゐない。

(二) 對象の差異　ロカルノ條約は所謂ライン保障條約を中心に四つの仲裁裁判條約、二つの相互援助條約等より成つてゐるが、その内容をライン保障條約について見れば(1)國境の不可侵及び現狀維持、(2)正當防衞及び聯盟規約に基く以外戰爭に訴へざること、(3)紛爭の平和的處理（常設調停委員會、仲裁裁判又は國際司法裁判所等による處理）、(4)一方の國が他方より攻擊を受け

たる場合の他の締約國（英伊を含む）による援助であるが、この條約案はロカルノ條約の如く國境の不可侵、同國境に基く領土上の現狀維持を保障したものではなく、日獨の武裝解除及び非軍事化といふ敗戰國の內政監視を目的とし、その目的のために檢查、審問及び調查を行ふ權限を有する監督委員會を設置し、同委員會による監視及び違反の停止及び防止のための締約國共同の強制措置を規定してゐて全く對象を異にするのである。

編注　小木曽本雄条約局条約課事務官。

162

昭和21年7月18日

寺崎（太郎）外務次官より桃井（直美）岐阜県知事宛（電報）

付記一　昭和二十一年七月十五日発桃井岐阜県知事より寺崎外務次官宛電報

戦病死者・公務死亡者の弔慰法に関する総司令部との折衝を踏まえた対応方針について

右弔慰法につき政府方針照会

二 昭和二十一年十一月一日付山崎(匡輔)文部次
官より寺崎外務次官宛公信発宗五一号
公葬の實施方針について

本　省　7月18日後4時30分発

指示ありたし

マ司令部より貴電の趣旨の指令を受けた事はないが此の問題は目下折衝中で近く政府に於て一般的訓令を發出する筈それ迄とりあへず左記要領で實施ありたい。
一、國家機關、公共團体の葬儀主催は不可
二、戰死者に對する葬儀は私的に目立たないやう行ふこと
三、功勞者、公務死亡者の葬儀に官公吏が公の資格で出席し弔辭、弔慰金、花環を送るなどは差支へない。但し此の場合の功勞、公務等に軍功、軍務等を含まない事。

(付記一)

岐阜　7月15日後4時10分発
本　省　7月15日後7時44分着

(至急、警察無線經由)

戰病死者、公務死亡者に對する弔慰法マ司令部より日本政府に指令ありたる趣なる處是が内容及實施方法至急何分のに依つて實施するやう貴管下及關係諸團體等に對して徹底

(付記二)

發宗五一號

昭和二十一年十一月一日

外務次官殿

公葬等について

このことについて本日別紙の通り各地方長官及ひ各大學高等專門學校長宛通牒しましたから、御通知致します。

文部次官〔印〕

發宗五一號

昭和二十一年十一月一日

地方長官殿

公葬等について

このことに付ては政教分離の見地から今後左記の様な取扱

内務次官
文部次官

3　経済諸施策への対応（昭和21年5月～24年4月）

方配意せられ度
命に依つて通牒する

　　　　　記

一、地方官衙及び都道府縣市町村等の地方公共團體は、公葬其の他の宗教的儀式及び行事（慰靈祭、追弔會等）は其の對象の如何を問はず今後擧行しないこと。地方官衙及び地方公共團體の名において行ひ得るのは左の範圍に限る。

イ、文民としての功勞者の殉職者に對し宗教的儀式を伴はない慰靈式等を行ふこと（例へば學校、警察署等で僧侶、牧師等の參加なしに教員、警察官で殉職したものの慰靈を行ふ如きこと）

ロ、文民としての功勞者、殉職者に對し哀悼の意を表する爲の休業、喪旗の揭揚。但し國旗揭揚に際しては豫め現地聯合軍側の諒解を得ること。

ハ、文民としての功勞者、殉職者等に對して個人又は民間團體が行ふ葬儀、慰靈祭、追弔會等に弔慰金、花輪等を贈ること並びに官公長が公の資格で列席し又は弔辭を讀むこと。

二、文民としての功勞者、殉職者等に對して個人又は民間團

體が葬儀其の他の宗教的儀式及び行事を行ふことは差支へないが、此の場合と雖も地方公共團體又は公の機關がその施設を貸すことは原則として避けられたい。但し他に適當な施設がないときは例外として一般に貸す場合と同様の條件で學校又は公會堂等を使用せしめて差支へない。

三、戰歿者に對する葬儀其の他の儀式及び行事を個人又は民間團體で行ふことは差支へない。併し地方官衙又は地方公共團體が之を主催若は援助し又は其の名に於て許容される事項も戰歿者には之を適用しない。軍國主義者又は極端なる國家主義者に對する場合も同様である。

戰歿者の遺骨の輸送、保管、傳達に際しその取扱は禮を失せざるよう敬虔に行ふべきである。遺骨の傳達は政府の行ふものであるから公共建物又は公用地（學校及び其の構内を除く）を使用するのは差支へない。但し傳達式に一般公衆の參列は認められない。

又戰歿者の爲の葬儀其の他の儀式及び行事、遺骨の出迎

昭和21年7月23日　連合国最高司令官総司令部より
　　　　　　　　　日本政府宛

持株会社整理委員会関係法規の承認につき回答

等をなす場合教師が生徒児童を引卒して参加したり又は一般の者に対して参列を強制するが如きことのないやう又は軍國主義思想の鼓吹又は宣傳に渉らないやう注意せられたい。

四、忠靈塔、忠魂碑其の他戰歿者の爲の記念碑、銅像等の建設並びに軍國主義者又は極端なる國家主義者の爲にそれらを建設することは今後一切行はないこと。現在建設中のものについては直ちにその工事を中止すること。尚現存するものの取扱は左に依られたい。

イ、學校及び其の構内に存在するものは之を撤去すること。

ロ、公共の建造物及びその構内又は公共用地に存在するもので明白に軍國主義的又は極端なる國家主義思想の宣傳鼓吹を目的とするものは之を撤去すること。前項のことは戰歿者等の遺族が私の記念碑を建立することを禁止する趣旨ではない。

五、一般文民の功勞者、殉職者等の爲に記念碑、銅像等を建設することやその保存事業を行ふことは差支へない。

GENERAL HEADQUARTERS
SUPREME COMMANDER FOR THE ALLIED POWERS

APO 500
23 July 1946

AG 091.3 (23 Jul 46) ESS/AC
(SCAPIN - 1079)

MEMORANDUM FOR: IMPERIAL JAPANESE GOVERNMENT.
THROUGH: Central Liaison Office, Tokyo.
SUBJECT: Ordinances and Regulations Affecting the Holding Company Liquidation Commission.

1. Reference is made to the following:

　a. Central Liaison Office Memorandum No. 1171 (2.1), dated 12 March 1946, forwarding Memorandum from Ministry of Finance, LO 341 dated 9 March 1946, subject: "Organization Ordinance Concerning the Supervising Committee of the Liquidation of the Holding Companies," and attached final draft of the re-

3　経済諸施策への対応(昭和21年5月～24年4月)

ference Organization Ordinance;

b. Central Liaison Office Memorandum No. 2296 (EF), dated 13 May 1946, inclosing two (2) Memoranda from the Ministry of Finance, LO 522, dated 11 May 1946, subject: "The Regulations Concerning the Enforcement of the Holding Company Liquidation Commission Ordinance (The Ordinance of Cabinet, Ministry of Finance and Ministry of Justice)," with attached final draft of the reference Cabinet Ordinance, and LO 528, dated 13 May 1946, subject: "Articles of Incorporation of the Holding Company Liquidation Commission," with attached Articles of Incorporation.

2. No objection is offered to the proposed two (2) Ordinances nor to the Articles of Incorporation, provided that, with respect to compensation to the zaibatsu, adequate safeguards be established to provide against windfall or gain resulting from an increase in the market price or value of bonds received in compensation beyond the value assigned to such bonds when exchanged for receipts.

3. To further implement the program of deconcentration of economic power, and independently of proposals for the enactment of permanent legislation to effectuate such programs the Imperial Japanese Government is directed to take such immediate action as may be necessary, as a minimum, to insure the following:

a. The elimination of the influence of listed families or family members through security ownership or the holding of a position of business responsibility by either such family member or his appointee in any company; provided, however, that the Imperial Japanese Government may, with the approval of the Supreme Commander for the Allied Powers, permit certain families and individuals to be exempt or removed from this restriction upon a showing of necessity or good cause.

b. Limitation on intercorporate security holdings by Restricted Companies.

c. Prohibition of multiple directorates in all Restricted Companies except those of a financial nature, where adequate controls will be established.

d. Prohibition among Restricted Companies of contractual, service or patent arrangements which restrict competition or restrain trade and commerce.

4. The Imperial Japanese Government is, accordingly, directed to submit promptly, in quintuplicate, typed in English on 8" x 11" paper, to the Supreme Commander for the Allied Powers, its proposal for carrying out the requirements of paragraphs 2 and 3, above.

5. As used in this Memorandum, the term "Restricted Company or Companies" shall be construed to mean those companies which are listed in Memorandum for the Imperial Japanese Government from General Headquarters, Supreme Commander for the Allied Powers, file AG 004 (8 Dec 45) ESS/AC (SCAPIN-403), subject: "Establishment of a Schedule of Restricted Concerns," or subsequent additions thereto. The term "listed families or family members" shall pertain to those families whose activities are restricted by Memoranda for the Imperial Japanese Government from General Headquarters, Supreme Commander for the Allied Powers, file AG 004 (6Nov 45) ESS/ADM (SCAPIN -244), subject: "Dissolution of Holding Companies," and file AG 091.4 (3 Jun 46) ESS/AC (SCAPIN -995), subject: "Reports to be Made by Certain Families."

6. For the purpose of carrying out the objectives of this Memorandum, direct communication is authorized between the companies concerned and the Economic and Scientific Section, General Headquarters, Supreme Commander for the Allied Powers.

FOR THE SUPREME COMMANDER:

JOHN B. COOLEY
Colonel, AGD
Adjutant General

【對日貿易問題に關するフレミングとの會談要領】

昭和21年7月24日　都村（新次郎）終戰連絡中央事務局經濟部貿易課長作成

付記　昭和二十一年七月二十九日、都村終戰連絡中央事務局經濟部貿易部長作成

「G、H、Q貿易部長との會談」

對日貿易問題に關するフレミングとの會談要領

都村貿易課長

3　経済諸施策への対応（昭和21年5月〜24年4月）

七月廿四日司令部經濟科學部輸出入課長フレミングを、往訪第七回對日理事會（六月廿六日）に於て同課長より發表せられた對日貿易問題に關するステートメント中疑義を有する點に付、說明を得度き旨述べたところ、「フ」は、本件の如き事項に對し日本側より、何等說明を求めらるゝ理由はなしと答へたので重ねて、政府としてではなく個人的に不明の點を明にし度いのであると說明し添の如き質問事項を示した處「フ」は、然らば簡單に個人的の立場より御答へす。とて左の通り語つた。

一、弗表示の基礎は單に評價に留るものであつて、實際の賣買價格を示したものではない。

輸出額五千壹百萬弗と貿易廳の支拂へる額三億五千萬圓との間に何等關聯はない。自分側の計算では一弗は十四圓となる筈である。

二、バーターシステムは目下の處、考慮してゐない。

三、關稅の問題は米國の貿易政策とは何等の關係はなく單に便宜上行つてゐるに過ぎない。

四、日本の對外輸出は戰前（一三一年乃至一三六年）の實績を基礎として計畫されてゐる。

現在及將來の輸出を如何なる規模にするかに關しては、未だ考へてゐない。

五、例外はない。例へば日本の對朝鮮輸出も例外に非ず、總じて指令に基く通常の輸出である。勿論それらの中には、朝鮮の米占領軍用物資として、現在輸出に入らぬものもある。

六、決濟の方法に付ては何とも云へぬ。

七、現狀に於ては、所謂政府對政府を基礎として總てSCAPを通じて行ふ以外は認めない。

（別　添）

Re: The report of Mr. L.R. Fleming at the 7th meeting of the Allied Council for Japan.

1. The estimated amount in dollars of the Japanese foreign trade since the Occupation stated in report.

What is the basis of this estimate? Is it based on the current sale prices in the countries of destination and the purchase prices in those of shipment? Do they include freight and other charges?

According to the above report, the estimated export is 51,475,000 dollars, (estimated import is 27,844,000 dollars) while the amount paid by the Boeki-cho for export goods as of May 30.46 is 355,503,000 yen. This will mean that the exchange rate is 6.9 yen per one dollar.

2. "The United States Government has to take the initiative in providing Japan with needed materials and has disposed of exports to pay for such materials. The U.S. Government is endeavouring to get materials Japan needs from countries rich in these materials and interested in the Japanese export goods."

Does it mean that a barter system by countries will be adopted in the Japanese foreign trade?

3. "No customs are being collected by the Japanese on either exports or imports."

Is it a matter of principle that no customs should be collected? If so, is it a temporary measure or is it based on a principle U.S.A. has in mind for the reorganization of the world trade?

4. "Exports are programmed in ratio to Japan's pre-war trading pattern."

What does "pre-war" mean? What period before the war does it cover? On what scale is U.S.A. going to keep the present and future export of Japan?

5. "There are two exceptions, namely export which are in world short supply have been allocated by the combined Committee in Washington and exports which are directly bartered for essential imports."

Are there no other exceptions beside the above two? Isn't the export to Korea in compliance with the directives also an exception?

6. "The methods and dates for the settlement of foreign trade accounts have been under consideration for many weeks and it is expected that exact procedures for these transactions would be established shortly."

When is it expected to be established?

7. Has any formula been worked out for direct contact between the Allied Nations concerned and the Japanese concerning trade?

506

3 経済諸施策への対応（昭和21年5月〜24年4月）

If so, would it be possible to give us some idea what such a formula will be like before it is made public.

（付 記）

G、H、Q貿易部長との會談

終絡經濟部　都村

七月二十九日G、H、Q「フレイミング」貿易部長を往訪、我方秋元部長、都村課長

（一）我方より六月中迄七月十五日迄の輸出入に關するG、H、Q來信を「レヴイユー」するとて輸出に關しては現在の進行狀況を説明し輸入に關しては食料輸入の順調なることひとへに米國の好意的援助の賜であることとを謝し燐鑛石輸入も極めて貴重なることを述べたが我方質問に對する先方の回答中注意すべき點左の通り。

（二）朝鮮及香港向石炭輸出の件

朝鮮向については現地軍の要請に關して接渉したが八月も五萬屯の積出を必要とすべし見返りについては研究せるも思はしからず（我方より馬山に銑鐵の貯鑛ある由説明せるに對し）右があるとしても朝鮮自體必要とすべ

く對日輸出は問題となるまいと日本の片貿易は決濟しなくてはならないが朝鮮貿易問題は結局華府の決定に待つこととならう

香港向石炭の八月分は未決定であるが但し興國である香港側の要望の緊要性次第により日本側の生產狀況如何に不拘積出することが必要となる先般豆類六百二十屯の見返り輸入にあつたが之は先方の好意に依るものである（豆は米の八割五分程度のカロリーがある）G、H、Qとしては「トレード」してゐるのではない需要國の要請の緊要性によつて積出し先方から輸入可能ならば見返りを求むる譯で當面は借又は貸とし決濟は後日に殘される譯である

（三）輸入に關し

（イ）目下印度より綿花三十萬俵（見返りとしては生糸、レーヨン）輸入方交渉中にて出來れば今年秋以降實現せしめ度い

（ロ）「アデン」より鹽輸入に付接渉中

（ハ）米國より靴の輸入方計畫中なり（未發表に付極祕）

（四）尚「フレミング」は八月十一日歸米する由で後任は「マ

「ツクダーモット」(U、S、C副總裁)の由である

165

昭和21年7月25日　連合国最高司令官総司令部より　日本政府宛

外国人への課税承認につき回答

GENERAL HEADQUARTERS
SUPREME COMMANDER FOR THE ALLIED POWERS
APO 500

25 July 1946

AG 012.2 (25 Jul 46) ESS/FI
(SCAPIN - 1826-A)

MEMORANDUM FOR: IMPERIAL JAPANESE GOVERNMENT.
THROUGH: Central Liaison Office, Tokyo.
SUBJECT: Applicability of Ordinary Taxes to Non-Japanese Nationals.

1. References are memoranda for General Headquarters, Supreme Commander for the Allied Powers, from the Imperial Japanese Government, CLO No.2966 (EF), 19 June 1946, subject: "Taxation on Foreigners in Japan" and LO 627, 6 June 1946, subject: "Taxation on Chinese Residents in Japan."

2. There is no objection to the applicability of local and national ordinary taxation to all non-Japanese nationals except as specified in paragraph 3 below, provided that such taxes are not discriminatory against non-Japanese nationals.

3. No tax will be imposed by the Imperial Japanese Government on the official salaries of military personnel, of civilians attached to the occupation forces, and of personnel accredited by the Supreme Commander for the Allied Powers as having a diplomatic status.

4. For purposes of this memorandum the term "ordinary taxes" includes all general taxes presently imposed by the Imperial Japanese Government and by the various local governments. This memorandum will not apply to the impending Capital Levy Law and other taxes of an extraordinary nature.

FOR THE SUPREME COMMANDER:

A. J Rehe
for JOHN B. COOLEY
Colonel, AGD

3　経済諸施策への対応（昭和21年5月～24年4月）

166　昭和21年7月29日　連合国最高司令官総司令部より日本政府宛

食糧輸入に関する一般指令

付記　昭和二十二年三月六日付連合国最高司令官総司令部より日本政府宛公信SCAPIN第三六六A号

右に関する追加指令

Adjutant General

GENERAL HEADQUARTERS
SUPREME COMMANDER FOR THE ALLIED POWERS
APO 500
29 July 1946

AG 430 (29 Jul 46) ESS/FT
(SCAPIN 1844-A)

MEMORANDUM FOR: THE IMPERIAL JAPANESE GOVERNMENT.
THROUGH: Central Liaison Office, Tokyo.
SUBJECT: Shipments of Subsistence Stocks to Japan.

1. Shipments of cereals and other subsistence stocks arriving from the United States of America and other sources, will be made available for future Japanese consumption.

2. A Notice of Arrival (Specimen Form Attached), showing description of the cargo (insofar as particulars are available) quantity, name of vessel, port of discharge and estimated time of arrival, will be sent to the Imperial Japanese Government as early as possible prior to vessels' arrival, to enable the Imperial Japanese Government to take action and assume responsibility as follows:

a. Accept delivery from on board vessel at the port of discharge and furnish the Commanding General, Eighth United States Army, with quantitative receipts for the cargo at the point of delivery.

b. Store the cargo so that it is protected against spoilage, pilferage, theft or other hazards and is under proper custody at all times.

c. Insure that no distribution is made of the cargo until official authorization for release is given by the Supreme Commander for the Allied Powers. This does not preclude processing or the transportation of the cargo to areas of greatest anticipated need.

3. Reference is made to Memorandum for the Imperial Japanese Government from General Headquarters, Supreme Commander for the Allied Powers, file AG 430 (11 Apr 46) ESS/PC, (SCAPIN 960-A), 11 April 1946, subject: "Maintenance of Records of Storage and Distribution of Imported Foodstuffs." The information concerning the storage of this imported food required in paragraph 1 a of the above memorandum will be supplied to the Supreme Commander for the Allied Powers.

4. Terms of payment and accounting will be decided later.

FOR THE SUPREME COMMANDER:

R. G. Hersey
for JOHN B. COOLEY
Colonel, AGD
Adjutant General

1 Attachment:
Memo for the IJG fr GHQ, SCAP, subj: "Shipments of Subsistence Stocks to Japan, Notice of Arrival."

編注　本文書の別添は省略。

(付記)

GENERAL HEADQUARTERS
SUPREME COMMANDER FOR THE ALLIED POWERS
APO 500

6 March 1947

AG 430 (6 Mar 47) ESS/FT
(SCAPIN 3366-A)

MEMORANDUM FOR: IMPERIAL JAPANESE GOVERNMENT
THROUGH: Central Liaison Office, Tokyo
SUBJECT: Addendum to Memorandum

1. Reference is made to Memorandum for the Imperial Japanese Government from General Headquarters, Supreme Commander for the Allied Powers, AG 430 (29 Jul 46) ESS/IT, (SCAPIN 1844-A), dated 29 July 1946, subject: Shipments of Subsistence Stocks to Japan.

3　経済諸施策への対応(昭和21年5月～24年4月)

167　統制会の解散および特定産業内における政府割当機関・所要統制機関の設置に関する指令

昭和21年8月6日　連合国最高司令官総司令部より　日本政府宛

GENERAL HEADQUARTERS
SUPREME COMMANDER FOR THE ALLIED POWERS
APO 500

6 August 1946

AG 080 (6 Aug 46) ESS/AC
(SCAPIN‑1108)

MEMORANDUM FOR: IMPERIAL JAPANESE GOVERNMENT.

THROUGH: Central Liaison Office, Tokyo.

SUBJECT: Dissolution of Control Associations (Tosei Kai) and Authorization to Establish Government Allocation Agency together with Necessary Control Organs within Specific Industries.

1. In order to release industry from certain wartime production controls and to establish more democratic methods of increasing the production of essential materials and commodities for the reconstruction of a peacetime economy, the Imperial Japanese Government is directed to take the necessary action to accomplish the following within ninety (90) days from date of this Memorandum:

　　a. Dissolve existing Control Associations (Tosei Kai) and repeal or rescind all laws, ordinances, regulations and ministerial ordinances relating thereto.

　　b. Preserve the complete records of such Associations

2. Paragraph 2a of the memorandum referenced above is amended to read as follows:

　"a. Accept delivery from on board vessel at the port of discharge and furnish the local military government unit with quantitative receipts for the cargo at the point of delivery."

FOR THE SUPREME COMMANDER:

A. J. Rehe
for JOHN B. COOLEY
Colonel, AGD
Adjutant General

within the respective bureaus of the Government now supervising such Associations.

  c. Concurrently with the actions taken in accordance with the provisions of subparagraph 1a, above, establish such public agencies, divisions and procedures within or under the Economic Stabilization Board as may be necessary to effectuate, under the coordinated direction and supervision of said Board, and in cooperation with the particular ministries concerned, allocations to and within such specific industries as may be selected by such Board for the assured production of essential materials and goods, and to assure that such allocations are adjusted to meet desired production schedules; supervise the establishment and operation of democratically organized and operated trade associations to be used as temporary stabilization devices within the specified industries selected by the Economic Stabilization Board for the purpose of allocating essential raw and semi-processed materials within those industries.

  2. The Imperial Japanese Government will furnish the following information to the Supreme Commander for the Allied Powers, in quintuplicate, typed in English on 8" x 11" paper, within ninety (90) days from the date of this Memorandum:

  a. Complete list of all laws, ordinances, regulations and ministerial ordinances repealed or rescinded in compliance with the provisions of subparagraph 1a, above.

  b. Names of the responsible bureaus preserving the records of dissolved Control Associations (Tosei Kai) in compliance with the provisions of subparagraph 1b, above.

  c. Name, structure, composition and method of operation of the specified agencies and description of procedures established in accordance with the provisions of subparagraph 1c, above.

  d. List of the specific industries selected by the Government pursuant to authority granted in subparagraph 1c, above, to receive allocations of essential raw materials and goods.

  e. Report of actions taken by the Government to establish the necessary trade associations to be used as temporary stabilization devices pursuant to the provisions of subparagraph 1c, above, together with full information as to the structure, methods of operation and specific functions of each such trade association, and the measures taken to assure full, non-discriminatory participation in the decisions of such trade associations on the part of all small, medium and large-sized enterprises involved.

3. The existence of all industry trade associations as temporary stabilization devices within selected industries, and the public agencies established by the Imperial Japanese Government in compliance with the provisions of this Memorandum shall be limited to a period of one (1) year from date of this Memorandum, except as authorized by the Supreme Commander for the Allied Powers.

4. This Memorandum will not be construed as affecting in any respect whatsoever, the continued functioning of the Civilian Merchant Marine Committee, as created pursuant to Memorandum for the Imperial Japanese Government from General Headquarters, Supreme Commander for the Allied Powers, file AG 334 (9 Nov 45) GD (SCAPIN - 256), subject: "Appointment of Civilian Merchant Marine Committee."

FOR THE SUPREME COMMANDER:

C. Z. Shugart
for JOHN B. COOLEY
Colonel, AGD
Adjutant General

168

「戰爭調查會問題、臺灣人法權問題、經濟安定本部問題、生鮮野菜統制問題等に關し總司令部と連絡事項覺」

昭和21年8月10日　朝海終戰連絡中央事務局總務部長作成

（昭和二一・八・一〇　終連總務部　朝海記）

一、戰爭調查會問題　本件に關し八日同調查會青木長官私を來訪の次第もあつたので（幣原總裁御承知の由）九日總司令部外交局次席ビショップ氏と會談し左の通り話した即ち私から本調查會の目的とするところは決して今次戰爭

戰爭調查會問題、臺灣人法權問題、經濟安定本部問題、生鮮野菜統制問題等に關し總司令部と連絡事項覺

首題の件に關し八月九日總司令部に於て左の通り會談を遂げた

をジヤスチファイせんとするものでもなく、その構成員も占領軍に對しオブジエクショナブルならずと思考して居る、これ等に付てはアチソン大使が對日理事會で述べられた以上に日本側としても附加する所なく、同大使の發言には深謝して居るところである但し日本側としては米側をエンバラスしたくないと思ふから何等米側に於て本調査會に付サジエスシヨンがあればお示し願ひ度く右に從ふこととに致したい、有力な軍人が含まれて居るが舊軍人が戰爭を識つて居る以上彼等に依つて情報を求めざるを得ないのであるが、何れも臨時委員たるに過ぎない點を指摘致したいと申出たところビ氏は戰爭調査會存續の豫定期間、臨時委員の性格等に付て若干の質問を試みてから、米國としても殊に理事會の席に於てソ聯英國あたりから相當有力な非難あり公開の席に於ては辯護するに困難なる場合もあるが（ビ氏は理事會には常にアチソン議長の介添として出席してゐる）如何なるサジエスシヨンを日本側になすべきやその適否はアチソン大使及び總司令部關係の向とも連絡の上研究することと致し度いと答へ數日後の再會見を約した

三、臺灣人に對する法權問題　本件に關し私から、此の問題に關して先般貴官と會見の際貴官は(1)國籍の變更がデ・ジユーレにも實行せられたりと述べられ又(2)中國側は國籍決定の問題は國内問題であつて中國人と決定して來た場合これを容認せざるを得ないと述べ臺灣人を中國人と決定して頂きたが、右に對する日本政府の見解は最終的には講和條約で決定せらるべきものであつて本年一月バーンズ國務長官もヤルタ會談で決定された樺太南端と千島の歸屬は講和條約で最終的法的效果を與へられると言つて居り、現に歐洲に於てもフインランド、ルーマニヤ、ハンガリア等の諸國が休戰條約で約した領土の變更を再び講和條約草案の中に規定して居るのである、即ち講和條約が最終的に事態を決定すべきものと云はなければならない(2)國籍の決定といふことは或る場合に於ては國内事項であり得ない、一九二三年二月チユニスとモロツコの國籍法事件に於て英佛間に紛爭を生じた際常設國際司法裁判所は或る場合國籍問題が國内問題に非ざる旨の見解を表示して居る（以上條約局の研究に基く）と述べ常設國際司法裁判所記

録の一部を拔粹タイプしたものを同氏に手交して置いた
右に對しビショップ氏は、この問題は先般お話したやう
に吾々の頭痛の種であり、先日會見の際は數日中に御返
事出來るかと思つたが問題は國際關係も含んで居り然く
簡單でない、日本側の御趣旨は了解した、尚愼重な研究
を續けることと致したいと答へた

三、經濟安定本部問題　膳長官の意向に基き九日ライダー大
佐に對し左の通り申入れて置いた
(1) 安定本部各部長の人選は次の如く一應決定された（人
名略）
(2) 安定本部には次長二名を置きたき長官の希望があるこ
と
(3) 安定本部長官は差當り物價廰長官を兼ねたきこと
(4) 安定本部長官に個人的アドバイザースを有したき希望
があること
(5) 安定本部は八月十二日より發足の運びに至ること
等を通報し右の中最重要な點は安定本部長官が物價廰長
官を兼ぬる點であるが、この點に付ては貴方の了解
を得て居ると了承するが、その他の人事問題は追放令に該

當せざる限り日本側で定め得る理であらうと述べたとこ
ろ大佐は取敢ずの意見として人選に付てはいづれ正式
にスクリーンされることになるであらうから自分の方か
らも關係方面に連絡して置く、個人的顧問を置くことは
屋上屋の嫌ひもあるが諸般の人的關係に顧み或は賢明な
策であるかも知れない、經濟安定本部に依る解決を待つ
てゐる重大事案卽ち補償問題、賠償問題、食糧問題等が
山積して居るから同本部の責任は極めて重大であること
を知られたい、等の諸點を述べた

四、生鮮野菜統制問題　同日價格統制課長エギキスト氏の求
めに依り往訪したところ同氏は左の通り語つた
實は本日自由黨の代議士三名自分の許に來られ生鮮食糧
品に對する統制問題に付て論議したが、兩代議士はこれ
が統制に反對の見解を有し居り、自分の議論には納得し
なかつたやうに見受けられたが誤解を避けるため念の爲
め日本政府に自分の意思を傳へて置きたいと思ひお出を
願つた(1) 統制の枠を外せば價格も下り品物も出廻ると
いふ議論があるが、生鮮食料品である以上退藏は利かな
いから品物自體が豐富ならばシーリング・プライスがあ

つてもそれより下廻つた價格で相當に出廻り得る理であらう、又(2)日本政府としては次の點も考慮せられたい卽ちE・S・Sから目下ジョンソンが華府に赴き來年度對日食糧供給問題に付き華府に要請して居るが、ジョンソンの強い議論の一つは日本側は主食は勿論有らゆる食糧に付き強力なる統制を實施し、而も配給が可成り圓滑に行はれて居るといふ議論である、(3)然るに日本側が統制を緩和し又一々統制の枠を外すが如き措置を執り、例へば有力なる政黨が強權發動に反對し又生鮮食糧品の統制を緩和する等の措置は決して吾人の華府に對する手を強むるに役立たない(4)若し日本側が斯る統制の枠を外さうとするならば總司令部としてはその不可なる所以を正式に意思表示する外あるまいと思ふ、と述べこの點に付ては本日午前の會見に關聯し誤解のないやうにお傳へして置く次第であると述べたので私から、御趣旨は了承したと答へた

昭和21年8月15日　極東委員会決定

連合国国民に対する裁判管轄権に関する極東委員会政策決定

Exercise of Criminal and Civil Jurisdiction over Nationals of Members of the United Nations

〔FEC Policy Decision, August 15, 1946〕

1. The Supreme Commander for the Allied Powers should provide that no criminal jurisdiction of any sort will be exercised by the Japanese courts with respect to nationals of Members of the United Nations, but that such criminal jurisdiction will be exercised by military courts of Members of the United Nations as follows:

　a. In the case of military, naval or air force personnel and persons attached to or accompanying the armed forces, by courts of the nation of the forces of which they are a part. A national of a Member of the United Nations who is present in Japan on official business and for the purpose of performing functions in the interest of the occupation is to be regarded as "attached to or accompanying the Armed Forces".

　b. In the case of a national of one of the occupying pow-

3 経済諸施策への対応（昭和21年5月～24年4月）

ers, by a military court of his nationality; and

　c. In the case of other nationals of Members of the United Nations, by the Allied military court having jurisdiction in the particular territory. Such courts should be composed of three members appointed by the Supreme Commander for the Allied Powers, one of whom should be a representative of that nation whose national is held for trial, provided that if, in the judgment of the Supreme Commander, selection of such a representative would obstruct or unnecessarily delay the proceedings because of the non-availability of qualified personnel, then a representative of some other nation may be designated.

　2. The authority of the Japanese to take into custody any national of a Member of the United Nations should be strictly limited:

　a. To those areas of Japan not actually in Allied military occupation, and

　b. In such areas, only to those cases in which there is reasonable evidence that a serious offense has been committed. The Japanese authorities should be placed under specific orders to hand over such a person forthwith to the nearest Allied military authorities.

　3. Provision should be made that no civil jurisdiction of any sort will be exercised by the Japanese courts with respect to nationals of Members of the United Nations attached to or accompanying the armed forces. Civil jurisdiction in these cases should be exercised in a manner determined by the Supreme Commander.

　4. Decisions in all civil cases affecting other nationals of Members of the United Nations or in which such nationals are or may become parties, should be reviewed by the Supreme Commander or his representative, who may revise the decision or take such other action as may be considered necessary for the protection of their rights.

　5. The Supreme Commander should take such steps as he deems necessary, including suspension of proceedings, to ensure that in the conduct of such civil cases the rights of nationals of Members of the United Nations parties thereto are adequately protected.

　6. It is recognized that the available United States legal

officers will be barely sufficient to deal with such cases as involve United States nationals. The Supreme Commander may therefore advise the responsible commanders of other Allied forces that assistance in such cases as involve their nationals must be supplied by them.

7. The term, "nationals of the United Nations," as used in this document includes, wherever applicable, organizations and corporations of Members of the United Nations as well as persons.

編　注　本文書は、昭和二十四年三月、外務省特別資料部作成〈〈〈〈〈〈〈〈「日本占領及び管理重要文書集」第二巻より抜粋。

170
「經濟安定本部長官とマークワット代將會談の件」

昭和21年8月27日　朝海終戦連絡中央事務局総務部長作成

經濟安定本部長官とマークワット代將會談の件

（昭和二一、八、二七、終連總務部　朝海記）

膳長官二十七日マークワット代將と要旨左の通り會談を遂げた、我方出席者膳、白洲、朝海、石黒、米側マークワット、ライダー、エギキスト、ルデー、ルカウント、コーヘン、エーキンその他

一、膳長官から未拂込株金徴收に關し當該會社にして業績の惡い場合には拂込を行はしめるが、軍事補償打切りより生ずる損害のためには未拂込株金を徴收しない趣旨の提案が目下事務當局間に行われている旨を指摘して考慮を求めた

二、税金徴収の場合の密告制の採用問題、右につき膳長官から、本件は日本の風習にも反するし、社會秩序混亂を招く恐れがあるから考慮せられたいと述べ先方係官から反對的説明あり、よつて白洲次長及び私から交々(イ)本條項は經濟的に使用せられずして政黨により政治上の目的に利用せられる恐れがあること(ロ)從つて殊に治安關係閣僚において痛心をもつて成行を注視していること(ハ)日本のデモクラシーは米國の域に達しおらずかかる個人の權利義務の觀念が十分に自覺されておらずかかる米式方法をそのまま採用することは適當でないこと(ニ)誰でもせん索す

3　経済諸施策への対応（昭和21年5月～24年4月）

ればなにがしかの埃は出ること等を指摘し、これによつて社會混亂を惹き起すから、日本政府としてはかかる制度の實施に自信のないことを述べたところ先方は(イ)軍事補償の打切りは前例のないことであるから必ずしも従來の經験による自信をうんぬんする必要はない、(ロ)この問題を落すと四個の點に全面的影響を及ぼし又やり直しをしなければならない(ハ)本提案は日本の財產收入を向上せしめんとする見地からなされたものであると述べ殊に補償關係官はかかる問題のために又々遲延させられるのかといつた不快の面持を示した

マ代將は大藏大臣からもいろいろ意見の開陳はあるが問題は最早意見を上下する段階から進んで如何にして速に一致點に到達して實行するかである。日本側案には余りにループホールスが多く結局日本政府は資本家の利益のみを擁護するという非難に答えることが困難であると思う膳長官はこの點につき政府部內に大分のインフレンスを使用せられたいと述べ更にこの問題については事務當局において研究方約した

三、石炭問題　膳長官から殊に補助金の問題につきその後の

總司令部における研究の結果を尋ねたところマ代將は、本件は恐らく政府部內に對してさえも極祕に願いたい位であるが、併しこの點は政府部內に對しても承認せられることとなるであろうが、併しこの點は政府部內に對しても承認せられることとなるであろうが、併し蓋し日本側はこの問題につき既に新聞に發表しているため總司令部としてはまことにエンバラシシングな立場に置かれた譯である、蓋しこれを拒否せんか日本政府を窮地に陷れることとなるからである、總じてかゝる重大案件について事前に新聞に發表を行い、總司令部側の手を拘束せんとすることは不愉快であり事案を成就せしむる所以でない、日本側としては重大案件決定の際は事前に新聞に洩らす前我等に忌憚なく打明けるようにしてもらいたい、又かゝる補助金は決定せられるにしてもこれはひつきよう特別且つ暫定的措置であつて石炭増產の恆久的措置についてはいずれ彼我の事務當局において協議研究せしむることと致したいと述べた。

更に同代將は石炭問題については(イ)坑夫に對し食糧及び衣料を確保すること(ロ)坑夫の熱意及び能力を向上するが如き勞資協定を作ること(ハ)炭坑資材の優先的供給を確保すること、かゝる必要資材が確實に炭坑に到達する樣

政府は計画、コーディネーション、監督を行うこと㈡石炭增産を刺戟するよう石炭價格及び補助金につき檢討すること、これ等の調整は經濟安定に關する政府の施策と一致し矛盾なかるべきこと㈥石炭増産の急務なることを一般大衆及び石炭業界に教育する手段を執ること等の措置を講ぜられたいと述べた。

四、公共事業問題　本問題に關しマーカット代將から、軍事補償打切り等に伴う失業を最少限度に止めるために公共事業に失業者を吸收しこれを利用すべきであると考えるには賠償施設の撤去もこれを利用しなければならない度い。即ち、六の點に付て經濟安定本部をしてコーエン氏から、コーエン氏に左の通り説明せしめた。即ち、(1)經濟安定本部は總ての公共事業の企画及び監督に對して責任を有すべきこと(2)各省の計画に關しては、㈲重要物資の生産増強に役立つこと㈩失業者を救濟するに役立つこと等を考慮して、經濟安定本部において優先順位を決定すべきこと、(3)經濟安定本部において公正なる勞働雇傭基準を工夫すべきこと(4)資金がボスやパージせられたものや個人的な利益や政治目的の方向に流れざるよう嚴に注意すべきこと(5)經濟安定本部の特定者、出來得れば第四部長が公共事業計画の事務を掌理すること(これはもち論膳長官が最終の責任者であることを覆すものでもなければ、又第四部長と言うのは一應の考であるに過ぎない)(6)現在失業している者の不安を除去するために公共事業計画の進捗に付き十分にパブリシチーを行うこと、等の諸點を述べた。

右に對し膳長官から、(1)經濟安定本部の設立は一ケ年に限られているためにその基礎が比較的安定しておらないこと、依て(2)總ての公共事業を經濟安定本部において實施することとなれば現在の權限及び人員を以てしては處理し得べくもないから經濟安定本部の權限擴張に付き總司令部の支持を得たきことを述べ本日お話の趣旨は十分了解した、何れも經濟安定本部において實行したいと思うがなお詳細の點に付き吟味することと致したいと述べた。

五、右に關連しマーカット代將から、既存の各省に伍して貴官が内政的に困難なる立場にあることは十分了承する、

3　経済諸施策への対応（昭和21年5月〜24年4月）

併しながら貴官の地位は恐らく現政府において最も重要な地位であると思われる。しかも各種の計画なり決定なりは各省のゆう長なる研究を待つてはいられない、自分達は出来得る限り貴官に對して支援をする用意がある、各省に關係のある各般の問題についてはＥＳＳにおいて研究を遂げ適當にコーディネートしたが、緊急事案については各省と一々別々に接觸する方程を執らない方が事務處理上適當と考える、經濟安定本部及び物價廳が發展しつつあるように見られるのは結構であるかかる機關が日本の現在の緊急な經濟企画及び統制を實施することは總司令部の現在の方針にも卽する、かかる機關をしてその權限を無差別に移讓せしめないことは日本政府の責任である、經濟安定本部と物價廳をして責任を果し得るやう強力ならしめたいことは自分達の考えであると述べて經濟安定本部に對する總司令部の支援と信賴の意を表してから日本側と經濟問題に關し意見をきくため此の種會合を定期に開催することと致したい。總司令部においてエコノミック・コントロール・ボードなるものを作り自分がそのボードの長となつて部内の統合を圖り日本側との接觸を

も簡單迅速にしたいと思つている（八月二十六日エギキスト氏談話參照）卽ちこの方法によつて自分等の考えていることを事前に日本側に内報し（この場合パブリシチーは嚴に注意せられたいと念を押して注意あり）不必要な混亂を避けると同時に日本側よりも率直なる見解を示してもらいたいためであると述べたので當方から、右は結構な考えであるから是非左樣願いたい、いずれこの集會の日時、動かし方について事務的な連絡を遂げることに致したいと述べて會合を終つた。

171

昭和21年8月30日　外務省作成

平和産業の復興に關する吉田首相の總司令部に對する申し入れ内容

付記　右英訳文

八月三十日吉田總理の司令部に對する申入れ内容我が國の現下の經濟的苦況については多言を要せざるところであるが、主として今日の金融的措置による全般的な産業の再編成及び縮小に起因する失業者の激増により狀況は

急激に惡化すべきことを懸念せられてゐる失業者の概敷は本年末の以前に五百萬の大臺に到着すべく豫測せられてゐるが右の中百萬は戰時補償の打切、賠償のための産業設備の撤去等により職域より必然的に到來せらる斯くの如き巨大な失業は政府をしてその處理に苦しむ最大の問題に直面せしめた。もし本問題にしてその處理せられざるにおいてはこれはわが國經濟行動を更に敏速に處理せられざるものにして一般的な囘復を遲延せしむることを懸念せられてゐる、併し乍ら本問題を效果的に處理することは政府の現在の能力を超ゆるものなることは明白である、從つて日本政府としては失業増加の脅威に對處するため差當り左の措置を採ることを提案する

イ、直接の救濟を擴張すること。即ち援護資金へ Aid and protection fund の引用により百五十萬餘の失業者を處し得べき豫想である

ロ、公共事業の創設により二百萬餘の失業者を吸收する見込なり。

これらの手段を以てするもなほ百萬余の失業者を殘存する見込である、固よりその一部は鐵道、電話、電信施設の復舊等の事業により吸收せられるのであらうが日本政府としては愼重審議の結果大量失業に對處し得る最善且恐らくは唯一つの政策は正に平和産業の復活以外になしとの結論に到達した。この種の産業は綿その他の繊維製品の産業、陶磁器、ゴム製品、電球、ガラス製品、自轉車、醫藥品等の生産を含むであらう。これら産業の復活は失業者吸收するに十分なる大量の職場を創設するのと計算せられてゐる

この平和産業の復活は消費材生産の増加傾向が必ずや然らざる場合には益々増進すべき現下のインフレーション傾向の阻止に役立つであらうからこの意味においても經濟政策の安定に大いなる貢献をなすであらう。事實わが國の經濟的生存を維持するや否やはこれら主幹的な産業の復活及び發展如何にかゝるものと推測せられる。併し乍ら生産の希望する如き生産は現状においては基礎資材の甚しき拂底のために不可能となつてをるので日本政府としてはこれら基礎資材の供給について總司令部の援助を要請せざるを得ない。輸入を必要とせらるゝ物資一例へば鹽、染料製造のためのベンゾールその他の化學製品、ゴム、銅、その他の非鐵金屬、棉花、羊毛、揮發油、無煙突鐵鋼、木材等及び

3　経済諸施策への対応（昭和21年5月～24年4月）

これが數量は附屬表(編注)に計上せられてゐる。これらの物資の輸入が日本政府の希望する如くに許可せられるにおいては上述の通りこれが基本産業の復興に貢献し、失業者を吸収する見込である。更に又日本の産業の早期の恢復によつて日本の餘剰物資を東亞諸地域に供給する可能性を生ずべくその結果現在焦眉の問題になつてゐる消費材不足による世界のこの部門における經濟的困難は大いに緩和せらるゝ結果となりその經濟地域の民衆の福祉に貢獻するであらう。

即ち本措置はこれら諸地域の戰後の再建を容易ならしめ、更に危險なるインフレーションを處理するであらう。即ちこれを要するにわが國の平和産業の急速なる恢復は現にわが國を含む極東を脅威しつつある經濟的諸困難の解決の鍵を提供する見込である

特に留意を要する點は現在少からざる重要度を有する住宅建設の問題である。戰災者及び引揚者は住むに家なく、住宅の不足は焦眉の問題となつてゐるが、材木不足のため言ふに足る數の住宅を建設することは不可能である。冬期を控へてこの慘憺たる住宅状況が關係民衆の疫病及び不滿の根源となることが豫想せられるが、これら民衆の状態は正

に同情に値するものがある。更に又小學校の校舎を始めとして教育諸施設の再建はこれ亦建築資材の不足により困難なる問題と化してゐる。住宅建設計畫、校舎再建その他のに事情に基づく不足木材總數量は約五千萬立方呎に上るものと概算せられる。

日本政府は總司令部の體意によりこれら木材を輸入し、更に失業者に對する相當量の仕事を提供し得べきことを希望する。

上記諸物資の輸入の決濟についてはこれらの平和産業の生産する物資の輸出によつて生ずる賣上代金が輸入の經費を適時にカバーして餘りあるものと確信する。固よりこれらの輸出入勘定のバランスは從來と同樣日本の對外貿易の唯一の關係者たる總司令部の手によつて完全に把握せらるべきものと諒解してゐる。

編　注　「附屬表」は見當たらない。

（付　記）

吉田總理GHQ提示原稿

While there is no need to dwell upon the prevailing economic plight of the country, it is feared that the situation will be sharply aggravated by an enormous increase in the ranks of the unemployed due largely to the overall reorganization and retrenchment of various industries which is necessitated by the proposed financial measure. It is said that the aggregate number of the jobless will reach the 5,000,000 mark by the end of this year, including 1,000,000 who are expected to be thrown out of the work owing to the cancellation of war indemnities and the removals of industrial equipments for reparations. Such huge unemployment, inevitably attended by multifarious evils, presents the Government with a question of the first magnitude most baffling to cope with. If this problem is not dealt with speedily, it will, we fear, further dislocate our economic structure retarding the general recovery. Yet, it is apparently beyond the means now in our possession to dispose of it in an effective fashion. At present, we propose to counter the growing menace of unemployment in the following manner:

A) By extending direct relief, through the aid-and-protection fund, we hope to dispose more than 1,500,000.

B) By inaugurating public works we hope to absorb more than 2,000,000.

This still leaves over 1,000,000 jobless. Part of them could be taken care of by such works as rehabilitation of railways, telephone and telegraph services. But, we have come, after mature considerations, to the conclusion that the rehabilitation of peaceful industries is, indeed, the best perhaps the sole, policy to cope with the mass unemployment. Such industries may include manufacture of cotton and other textile goods, pottery and porcelain, rubber goods, electric bulbs, glassware, bicycles and pharmaceutical articles. The revival of these industries will, it is calculated, create a sufficiently large number of jobs to absorb the unemployed. It will also contribute powerfully to the stabilization of the economic life of our nation as rising increase in the output of consumer goods will certainly go far towards checking the present inflationary trend which would otherwise be accelerated. In fact, the maintenance of our economic existence, it seems, is predicated upon the revival and development of these key industries. However, the de-

3 経済諸施策への対応（昭和21年5月～24年4月）

sired production is impossible severely lacking, as we do, in essential materials for the supply of which we have to solicit the assistance of the General Headquarters. The principal commodities, and the quantities thereof, which need to be imported are salt, benzol and other chemicals for processing dye stuffs; rubber; copper and other non-ferrous metals; cotton, wool; benzine; anthracite coal; iron and steel; wood, etc. as contained in the attached tables. When the importation of these commodities are permitted, as we earnestly hope it will be, it will, as pointed out above, help restore our basic industries absorbing the jobless. Moreover, with the early rehabilitation of our above, help restore our basic industries absorbing the jobless. We may even count upon the possibility of supplying our surplus goods to other regions of East Asia with the result that the economic difficulties caused by the scarcity of consumer goods, now very acute, in these parts of the world will be substantially alleviated to the benefit of all concerned. Incidentally, this will also serve to facilitate the postwar reconstruction, besides forestalling dangerous inflation, of these regions. In short, therefore, a quick revival of our peaceful industries would seem to offer a key to the solution of economic difficulties now besetting the Far East, including our own Country.

Special consideration must be paid to the question of housing which is now assuming grave proportions. While there exists an acute shortage of houses for the war sufferers and the repatriated people who are deprived of shelters, we cannot build them in an appreciable number on account of the scarcity of timbers. With the approach of the cold season, we are apprehensive lest the deplorable housing situation may prove a source of disease and discontents on the part of the afflicted people whose fate certainly deserves sympathy. Again, the reconstruction of educational establishments, beginning with the primary school buildings, presents a difficult problem due also to the shortage of building materials. It is estimated roughly that the deficiency caused by the housing programme and the restitution of school buildings and other requirements will add up to some 50,000,000 cubic feet. These we would like to import by the good offices of the General Headquarters which, if allowed, would provide a considerable amount of works for the unemployed.

As for the payment for the import of above commodities, it can, we trust, safely be assumed that the proceeds to be realized by exporting the goods manufactured therefrom will amply cover the cost of import in due time, it is understood, of course, that the balancing of these accounts is, as hitherto, left entirely in the hands of the General Headquarters who are the sole authority in directing the external trade of this country.

172 アジア救済機関（ＬＡＲＡ）よりの救援物資の受領および配給に関する指令

昭和21年8月30日　連合国最高司令官総司令部より　日本政府宛

付記　右和訳文

GENERAL HEADQUARTERS
SUPREME COMMANDER FOR THE ALLIED POWERS
APO 500

30 August 1946

AG 400 (30 Aug 46) PH
(SCAPIN 1169)

MEMORANDUM FOR: IMPERIAL JAPANESE GOVERNMENT
THROUGH: Central Liaison Office, Tokyo.
SUBJECT: Receipt and Distribution of Relief Supplies from Licensed Agencies for Relief in Asia.

1. The Imperial Japanese Government, having verbally accepted the offer of relief supplies from the Licensed Agencies for Relief in Asia, will immediately prepare to accept title at dockside, guard, transport, store and distribute these relief supplies being donated by private agencies in the United States, to be used for Japan's destitute. These supplies will total not more than two thousand (2000) tons per month.

2. The Imperial Japanese Government will assume sole responsibility for the security, movement, allocation and distribution of these relief supplies from dockside to the using agency. Full police protection will be given the unloading, transportation, warehousing and distribution of these supplies, and the Imperial Japanese Government will be responsible to the Supreme Commander for the Allied Powers for any pilferage, wastage, or other preventable loss that occurs. Prompt removal of supplies from

3　経済諸施策への対応（昭和21年5月～24年4月）

shipside will be accomplished.

3. On or before 1 September 1946 the Imperial Japanese Government will present a general operational plan covering the distribution of these relief supplies, which is to include the following information:

a. Method of accounting.
b. Plan for storage.
c. Plan for distribution.
d. Detail of security plan.

4. Paragraph 3a above will include a report form which is to be sent monthly to General Headquarters, Supreme Commander for the Allied Powers, giving the following detailed information:

a. Record of total supplies received.
b. Total supplies distributed.
c. Agencies to whom distributed.
d. Amounts on hand.
e. Location of all the undistributed supplies.

5. Prior to distribution of these relief supplies, General Headquarters, Supreme Commander for the Allied Powers, will be informed of the plan of allocation, by the Imperial Japanese Government, and the agencies to whom the supplies are to be made available.

FOR THE SUPREME COMMANDER:

JOHN B. COOLEY
Colonel, AGD
Adjutant General.

（付　記）

一九四六年八月三〇日
聯合國最高司令部發
帝國政府宛　終連經由

一、さきにアジア救濟機關からの救濟物資の受領及び配給の件

　アジア救濟機關よりの救濟物資の供給を口頭をもつて受諾せる帝國政府は日本の困窮者用に合衆國の私設機關により與へられたる該救濟物資の權利を岸壁において管理し右物品を管理、輸送、貯藏並びに配給するよう直ちに手配すべし、右物資は總量一ヶ月二、〇〇〇噸を超えざるべし。

二、帝國政府は該救濟物資の岸壁より使用機關に渡す間の保管、移動、割當及び配給に關する全責任を負うものとす、右物資の積荷を卸す際輸送、倉庫に納める際並びに配給に當り警察の完全なる保護を與うべし。帝國政府は盗難、破損或は途中に起る其の他の損耗に對し聯合國軍最高司令官に責任を採るものとす物資を船から速に引き取るようなすべし。

三、一九四六年九月一日或はそれ以前に帝國政府は次の報告を含む該救援物資の配給に關する一般の實施計畫を提出すべし。

1. 會　計　方　法
2. 貯　藏　計　畫
3. 配　給　計　畫
4. 保護計畫の詳細

四、前記三1項は次の詳細なる情報を含む報告形式をとり、聯合國軍最高司令部宛毎月送付するものとす。

1. 受領せる全物資の記録
2. 配給せる全物資
3. 配給せる機關

4. 現　金　額

5. 全未配給物資の場所

五、右救濟物資の配給に先立ち聯合國軍最高司令部は、帝國政府により、割當計畫及び物資を利用する機關につき報告せらるべし。

最高司令官代

大佐、副將

ジヨン、B、クーリー

~~~~~~~

昭和21年9月5日　日本政府宛
連合国最高司令官総司令部より

173

付　記　昭和二十二年一月二日付連合国最高司令官総司令部より日本政府宛公信SCAPIN第一四三二号

右指令の變更について

ドイツを除く諸外国との国際郵便業務再開に関する指令

GENERAL HEADQUARTERS
SUPREME COMMANDER FOR THE ALLIED POWERS

3　経済諸施策への対応(昭和21年5月～24年4月)

AG 311.1 (5 Sep 46) CCS
(SCAPIN - 1177)

APO 500
5 September 1946

MEMORANDUM FOR: THE IMPERIAL JAPANESE GOVERNMENT.
THROUGH: Central Liaison Office, Tokyo.
SUBJECT: Resumption of International Postal Service between Japan and all other Countries except Germany.

　1. Resumption of International Postal Service between Japan and all other countries, except Germany, is authorized effective 10 September 1946 subject to the following provisions:

　　a. The service will be restricted to postal cards to and from Japan; one-way gift parcel post to Japan; and the mailing from Japan of such scientific and professional publications as may be approved by the Supreme Commander for the Allied Powers.

　　b. Communications on postal cards must be of a personal or family nature written in Chinese, English, French, Japanese, Korean, Russian, or Spanish. Letters (other than official mail pertaining to repatriation) and commercial and financial communications are prohibited.

　　c. Gift parcels to Japan will be limited to eleven pounds in weight and contents will be restricted to relief items such as non-perishable foods, clothing, soap, and mailable medicines.

　2. The regular-mail service will be governed by the provisions of the Universal Postal Union Convention of Buenos Aires, of 23 May 1939. The maintenance of records essential to settlement of accounts under the conditions of the Universal Postal Union Convention and the preparation of accounts for settlement will be the responsibility of the Japanese Government.

　3. Parcel post service, as authorized, will be operated by the Japanese Government under the terms of the bilateral or other agreements in effect between Japan and the respective countries at the time the service was suspended. The maintenance of records and preparation of the accounts required under the terms of the various agreements will be the responsibility of the Japanese Government.

　4. Amounts due Japan from the United States on bills for parcel post terminal charges will be deposited in the United States

Treasury trust fund receipt account "Deposits, proceeds of remittances to and exports from occupied areas" symbol 218905.1 Japan. Payments due from Japan in connection with international postal services will be made from that trust fund account upon recommendation of the Supreme Commander for the Allied Powers. Statements of such accounts will be prepared under direction of the Ministry of Communications, Imperial Japanese Government and certified to the Supreme Commander for the Allied Powers.

5. International mails will be dispatched from Japan on Japanese, or vessels of any other registration, excepting those of German registry.

6. All incoming and outgoing International Mail will be subject to censorship to the extent deemed advisable by the Supreme Commander for the Allied Powers. Mail will be made available to the Civil Censorship Detachment, G-2, General Headquarters, United States Army Forces, Pacific, and submitted for censorship as directed from time to time through the liaison officer of the Ministry of Communications assigned to censorship.

7. Repatriation mail service authorized 28 October 1945, (SCAPIN 202) will be discontinued effective 10 September 1946. Thereafter all repatriation mail, including official correspondence pertaining only to repatriation of Japanese forces and Japanese Nationals, will be handled as International Mail.

8. Direct communication between the Civil Communications Section, General Headquarters, Supreme Commander for the Allied Powers and the Ministry of Communications is authorized concerning all matters within the scope of this memorandum.

FOR THE SUPREME COMMANDER:

R. G. Hersey
for JOHN B. COOLEY
Colonel, AGD
Adjutant General.

GENERAL HEADQUARTERS
SUPREME COMMANDER FOR THE ALLIED POWERS
APO 500
2 January 1947

3 経済諸施策への対応(昭和21年5月～24年4月)

AG 311.1 (2 Jan 47) CCS (SCAPIN-1432)

MEMORANDUM FOR: IMPERIAL JAPANESE GOVERNMENT

THROUGH: Central Liaison Office, Tokyo

SUBJECT: Resumption of International Postal Service between Japan and all other Countries

1. Reference is made to memorandum from the Supreme Commander for the Allied Powers, (SCAPIN 1177), file AG 311.1, (5 Sept 46) CCS, dated 5 September 46, subject: "Resumption of International Postal Service between Japan and all other Countries except Germany".

2. Paragraph 1 of the reference memorandum is rescinded and the following substituted therefor:

"1. International postal service between Japan and all other countries is authorized effective 2 January 1947 subject to the following provisions:

"a. The service will be restricted to postal cards (including reply cards) and letters to and from Japan; one-way gift parcel post to Japan, and the mailing from Japan of such scientific and professional publications as may be approved by the Supreme Commander for the Allied Powers.

"b. Communications on postal cards and in letters will be restricted to personal and family messages, and to business, financial, and commercial correspondence, limited to ascertainment of facts and exchange of information, and subject to the following prohibitions:

"(1) Letters authorizing or effecting specific financial and commercial transactions.

"(2) Letters containing instructions or authorizations which effect property and financial transactions.

"(3) Letters which contain currency, securities, checks, drafts, payment orders or other financial instruments.

"c. Communications on postal cards and in letters must be written in Chinese, English, French, Japanese, Korean, Portuguese, Russian, or Spanish.

"d. Gift parcels to Japan will be limited to eleven

531

pounds in weight and contents will be restricted to relief items such as non-perishable foods, clothing, soap, and mailable medicines."

FOR THE SUPREME COMMANDER:

R. G. Hersey
for JOHN B. COOLEY
Colonel, AGD,
Adjutant General.

174 【重要資材の輸入申請に關する會談要領】

昭和21年9月11日 秋元(順朝)終戦連絡中央事務局経済部長作成

重要資材の輸入申請に關する會談要領（秋元部長）

昭和二十一年九月十一日

日本側　塚田貿易廰長官（商工大臣代理）、關事務官

終連秋元

司令部側　マーカット代將、ピケル少佐

「塚」本日は商工大臣が伺ふ筈のところ已むを得ない事情の爲伺ふことが出来ないので私が代理に罷り出た次第である商工大臣は昨日賠償問題に關して貴官と親しく會談

する機會を與へられ種々好意ある御意見を拜承したことを深く感謝し日本日參上出來ないことについては甚だ遺憾であるが不悪御了承願ひ度いと申述べる樣私に依頼された

さて日本政府としては御蔭を以て日本の對外貿易も漸次活潑となりつつあることに感謝をする。殊に食糧の輸入は七千萬國民を飢餓から救ふものであつて國民一同貴國の同情ある取計らひ厚く感謝して居るところである又棉花の輸入は日本のキー、インダストリーたる紡績業の活動を況しこの點赤感謝に堪えない

「マ」食糧については引續き輸入に努力してゐるが最近日本政府が一般配給の増配を企圖しこれを發表したことは頗る困つたことであつて現在米國に於ては日本への食糧輸入を停止しやうといふ空氣の濃厚な際かかることを企圖し而も之をGHQと連絡なしに發表することは甚だ危険である勞務加配用としての食糧輸入については司令部は完全に日本政府と協力一致の行動をとる必要があり且それに努めてゐるのであるが日本側單獨にかかる行動をされることは頗る遺憾である

3　経済諸施策への対応（昭和21年5月～24年4月）

「塚」御趣旨は克く農林、商工両大臣に御傳へする
さて米國其の他からの輸入に關してはかねて當方の計畫をたて司令部にも要請して居るが、今囘一方では軍需補償打切に伴ふ産業整理に直面し他方賠償工場の指定があり産業界の大變革を必要とするところから失業問題及社會不安を激成する虞がある。このことは吉田總理も大いに心配して居るのであるがこれを乗切る爲にはどうしても相當量の重要資材輸入を促進する必要があるので、それを御願に參上したのである

「マ」賠償工場については速に指定外の工場に生産を轉換することが必要であり、金融措置に關しては銀行の再組織と併行して新會社、新事業を興し産業を再組織して再出發することを切望する。この際相當血の出る面もあらうが將來の日本經濟の健全な發展の爲永い眼で見て再編成、再出發を斷行することが得策である。原料の輸入及失業問題の解決は共に重要問題であるから司令部としても最善の努力をする考であるが、經理、金融面の再組織と平行して新事業を興して増産に邁進し通貨と物資の均衡を圖ることが肝要である

「塚」今囘御願ひする輸入は木材を除き他は本年五月又はそれ以後に既に輸入申請をしてあるものであるがさきに述べた理由で重ねて輸入の促進を懇請するものである。木材は從來は進駐軍建設用の南洋材のみの輸入を要請してゐるがこれを追加する理由は食糧及棉花の輸入によって衣食住の内前二者の問題が解決するが「住」の問題として特に戰災者及海外からの引揚者の住宅問題を解決する必要があり又賠償施設の搬出の爲包装用として多量の木材を必要とするに至ったので新に輸入を懇請する次第である

「マ」賠償施設搬出に相當多量の木材を要することはよくわかるが、ESBが中心となって先づ國内産木材の充足を圖れば、相當程度賄ふことが出來るのではなからうか。又輸入はどこからする見込であるか

「關」加奈陀、米國を豫想してゐる

「ピ」輸入は困難であらう

「ピ」ロシアは如何

「マ」考へ得ることであるが必しも容易ではあるまい

「マ」賠償施設に必要な數量如何

「關」二年間に實施するものとして一年間の所要量最大八百萬石（BF約九〇、〇〇〇、〇〇〇）程度

「マ」賠償施設に關する木材の問題は非常に重要な問題と思ふ

「ピ」米、加よりの輸入には強い理由がなければ脈がない

「塚」失業問題については厚生省等からもお聞及びでよく御承知のことと思ふから省略したい

「マ」ある程度承知して居る。木材の件についてはピケル少佐によく話しておいて貰ひ度い

「塚」失業問題については生活保護法による援護資金、公共事業による救濟も行はれるが何といつても產業を復興して失業者を吸收することが必要であり、それには資材の輸入が必要である

「關」現在は縮小再生產の傾向にあり、鐵と石炭の相關關係の如きその適例で資材を輸入してこれを擴大再生產に轉換しなければならぬ

「マ」產業復興は司令部も最も力を入れてゐるところであり銀行の再編成と共に產業の再編成が必要であるが制限會社─財閥の所有株式の移轉には法律を要すると思ふが用意されて居るか

「關」「秋」既に施行した勅令によつて四大財閥のみならずその他の制限會社の所有株も持株會社整理委員會に讓渡して處理出來ることになつてゐる

「塚」資材の充足に關しては石炭肥料運輸等の方面に重點配給をしてゐるが何分にも絕對量が不足してゐるので極めて不十分である

「マ」どの位の資材を輸入してどの位の工場を動かさうとするのか知らないが、何れにしても五年計畫とかさういふ長い計畫は別として今直ちに輸入が必要であり直に增產に役立つ資材の輸入について知り度い。石炭の增產の如き强行せねばならぬ。又粘結炭及鹽の輸入も折角骨を折つて居るところである

「ピ」中國へ綿布、自轉車その他雜貨を輸出し粘結炭を輸入することが來週あたり決るであらう

「マ」これは目下來朝中のアンドレ、ヤング氏と話し合つてゐることで暫らく極祕にして日本側は直接には觸れず輸入について困つたことは米國の海員の總罷業が始つ

3 経済諸施策への対応(昭和21年5月～24年4月)

たことで直ぐには解決しないであらうから此處二ケ月位は輸入豫定が遅れるかも知れない

増產の爲には原材料の輸入も必要であらうが國內的にも爲すべきことが澤山ある。闇取引橫流れを防止すれば更に有效な重點配給が出來るであらう

米國に於ても陸軍省の豫算が削減された結果日本の輸入は日本の輸出で賄はねばならないといふことが從來よりも強く要請されて居り、今GHQでも研究中である

「塚」中國へは色々の物資を輸出してゐるが輸入が少くて困つてゐるところ御話のやうなことが實現すれば非常に幸である。輸入要請物資の細目は資料を準備してゐるから別途擔當官に說明致度い。基礎資材としては鋼材、鑄鐵管、人造ゴム其の他である（表を呈示す）

「關」鑄鐵管の如きは國內生產も相當あるではないか

「マ」本問題は重要であるからよく檢討して急速に輸入の必要なものから取上げて行くことにし度い

「關」石炭不足の爲十分でない

「マ」本問題はＥＳＢでも檢討したものであるが、賠償問題も考慮に入れ國內生產の豫想を立てた上輸入の要否を

檢討すべきであると思ふ

「塚」ＥＳＢでよく檢討し取纏めたものである

「マ」棉花は印度からも輸入出來るであらう

「ピ」若干見込んでゐる

「マ」羊毛は濠洲から來る筈と思ふ

「ピ」然り

「マ」人造ゴムは日本に入れて直ちに使へるであらうか、蘭印からゴムの輸入は出來ぬか

「ピ」人造ゴムの豫定は既に見當がついて居り產業課とも打合濟である

「塚」金融措置による整理が完了した後に於ても原材料が充足されなければ經濟再建は覺束ない原材料の充足如何が再建の成否を決すると思ふ

「マ」本問題は非常に重要であると思ふからピケル少佐のところで充分研究し來週會議を開いて決めることにし度い輸入も重要であるが第一は日本側で金融再編成と共に產業再編成を斷行することに在る、司令部としては輸入の繼續に努力し國民生活の維持及輸出產業に支障ない樣努力してゐる積りである

175

民事および刑事裁判権行使に関する改定指令

昭和21年9月19日　連合国最高司令官総司令部より　日本政府宛

「秋」輸入の時期は最も重要なことの一つである本日要請する物資は總て本年末迄に輸入實現することを希望する「マ」海員のストライキで遅れると思ふが失業問題との關聯においても輸入の時期を失しないことは重要なことである

～～～～～～

GENERAL HEADQUARTERS
SUPREME COMMANDER FOR THE ALLIED POWERS

APO 500

19 September 1946

AG 015 (19 Sep 46) LS-L

SCAPIN-1218

MEMORANDUM FOR: THE IMPERIAL JAPANESE GOVERNMENT

THROUGH: The Central Liaison Office, Tokyo

SUBJECT: Amendment of Memorandums on Civil and Criminal Jurisdiction

1. Reference is made to:

a. Memorandum for the Imperial Japanese Government, AG 015 (19 Feb 46) LS, subject: "Exercise of Criminal Jurisdiction," (SCAPIN 756), and

b. Memorandum for the Imperial Japanese Government, AG 015 (26 Feb 46) LS, subject: "Exercise of Civil Jurisdiction." (SCAPIN 777).

2. The following amendments are directed:

a. In Memorandum, subject: "Exercise of Criminal Jurisdiction," referred to in paragraph 1-a, above, delete in paragraph 6 thereof, "a reasonable suspicion" and substitute therefor, "reasonable evidence."

b. In Memorandum, subject: "Exercise of Civil Jurisdiction," referred to in paragraph 1-b, above, delete paragraph 1-b.

3. Except as otherwise provided herein, the provisions of the Memorandums referred to in paragraph 1, above, shall continue in full force and effect.

FOR THE SUPREME COMMANDER:

JOHN B. COOLEY,

3 経済諸施策への対応(昭和21年5月～24年4月)

176 昭和21年9月28日 連合国最高司令官総司令部より 日本政府宛

制限会社に関する規則に関する補足指令

GENERAL HEADQUARTERS
SUPREME COMMANDER FOR THE ALLIED POWERS
APO 500
28 September 1946

AG 004 (28 Sep 46) ESS/AC
(SCAPIN - 1238)

MEMORANDUM FOR: IMPERIAL JAPANESE GOVERNMENT.

THROUGH: Central Liaison Office, Tokyo.

SUBJECT: Supplementary Regulations Affecting Restricted Concerns.

 1. References are the following Memoranda for the Imperial Japanese Government from General Headquarters, Supreme Commander for the Allied Powers:

  a. AG 004 (8 Dec 45) ESS/AC, 8 December 1945, (SCAPIN - 403), subject: "Establishment of a Schedule of Restricted Concerns."

  b. AG300.8 (8 Dec 45) ESS/AC, 8 December 1945, (SCAPIN - 408), subject: "Regulations Affecting Restricted Concerns."

 2. The Imperial Japanese Government will take the necessary action to assure that, unless prior approval is obtained from the Supreme Commander for the Allied Powers, none of the following will directly or indirectly acquire any interest in or directly or indirectly participate in the management of any non-restricted concern:

  a. Any concern listed on the Schedule of Restricted Concerns established by reference Memorandum 1a, above.

  b. Any non-restricted subsidiary of a Restricted Concern.

  c. Any other concern or individual controlled by a Restricted Concern or a non-restricted subsidiary of a Restricted Concern.

Colonel, AGD
Adjutant General.

3. a. "Directly or indirectly acquire any interest" is defined to include, but not be limited to, acquiring any interest in any non-restricted concern through the directors, officers or other employees of a Restricted Concern, or through a non-restricted subsidiary of such Restricted Concern or the directors, officers or employees of such non-restricted subsidiary or through any other concern or individual controlled by such Restricted Concern or non-restricted subsidiary or the directors, officers or employees of such other concern. "Any interest" shall mean any shareholdings, indebtedness, certificates of indebtedness or other device through which any control over such other non-restricted concern is exercised or ownership of ten (10) percent or more of the shares of such other non-restricted concern.

b. "Directly or indirectly participate in the management" is defined to include, but not be limited to, any agreement or understanding between:

(1) A Restricted Concern, or the directors, officers or employees of such Restricted Concern, or

(2) A non-restricted subsidiary of a Restricted Concern, or the directors, officers or employees of such subsidiary, or

(3) Any other concern or individual controlled by a Restricted Concern or a non-restricted subsidiary thereof, or the directors, officers or employees of such other concern,

and: any other non-restricted concern whereby such Restricted Concern or non-restricted subsidiary thereof or such other concern or individual controlled by such Restricted Concern or non-restricted subsidiary participates in the management of such other non-restricted concern or exercises any control over the sales or production of such other non-restricted concern.

4. The Imperial Japanese Government will take the necessary action to assure that any concern or individual referred to in subparagraphs 2a, b and c, above, will, within thirty (30) days from the date of this Memorandum, submit plans to the Supreme Commander for the Allied Powers for the termination of any interest or participation as defined in subparagraphs 3a and b, above, if such interest or participation was acquired on or after 8 Decem-

ber 1945.

5. Direct communication is authorized between the interested Staff Sections of General Headquarters, Supreme Commander for the Allied Powers, and agencies of the Imperial Japanese Government concerned to implement all provisions of this Memorandum.

FOR THE SUPREME COMMANDER:

JOHN B. COOLEY
Colonel, AGD,
Adjutant General.

177

昭和21年10月9日　連合国最高司令官総司令部発表

不敬罪に関するマッカーサー司令官の見解

General of the Army Douglas MacArthur's Observation on lese majeste

October 9, 1946.

Commenting upon the action of Japanese procurators in absolving persons, including the editors of the Communist organ "Red Flag", from the charge of lese majeste, General MacArthur today observed:

"The decision of the Japanese procurators to drop accusations against men charged with lese majeste is a noteworthy application of the fundamental concept, embodied in the new constitution just adopted by the National Diet, that all men are equal before the law, that no individual in Japan —not even the Emperor— shall be clothed in legal protection denied the common man. It marks the beginning of a true understanding of the lofty spirit of the new national charter, which affirms the dignity of all men, and secures to all the right freely to discuss all issues, political, social, and economic, of concern to the people of a democratic nation. For, the free interchange of ideas, the free expression of opinions, the free criticism of officials and institutions is essential to the continued life and growth of popular government. Democracy is vital and dynamic but cannot survive unless all citizens are free thus to speak their minds.

"Such action, moreover, emphasizes the fact that from this land broken and ravaged by war, there is emerging a free people and a free nation. As the Emperor becomes under this new constitution the symbol of the state with neither inherent political power nor authority, the Japanese men and women are raised to a new status of political dignity and, in fact, will become the rulers of Japan.

"In his new role the Emperor will symbolize the repository of state authority —the citizen. The dignity of the state will become the dignity of the individual citizen, and the protection accorded him as the symbol of the state ought to be no more and no less than the protection accorded the citizen. To hold the contrary would constitute a direct negation of one of the basic principles of democratic government. It would but serve to perpetuate the pattern of feudalism and autocracy and do violence to those basic freedoms acknowledged by Japan and to which the Emperor himself has given most hearty accord.

"It should be needless to point out that it is for an enlightened public opinion to exert its great moral influence to the end that this right freely to criticize be exercised with decorum and restraint —that all public officials be protected against unwarranted defamation or vilification in licentious disregard of the respect to which they as free individuals in a free society and as the public representatives of a free people are fully entitled."

編 注　本文書は、昭和二十四年三月、外務省特別資料部作成「日本占領及び管理重要文書集」第二巻より抜粋。

178　昭和21年10月10日　終戦連絡中央事務局政治部政治課作成
行政制度改革に関する斎藤国務大臣と総司令部マーカムとの会談要旨

齋藤國務大臣、マーカム氏會談に關する件

昭和二一、一〇、一〇終連、政、政　藤崎記（編注）

齋藤國務大臣（今般新設せられる行政調査部の部長に内定）及び入江法制局長官（同部主幹）は本十日總司令部政治部パブリック・アドミニストレイション・デビジョンのマーカム氏を往訪し、約一時間半にわたり行政調査部の任務等について會談したが、その要旨左の通り。

一　「日本政府が今般行政制度の根本的な改革を企圖し行政

3　経済諸施策への対応（昭和21年5月～24年4月）

マ「我々の方では改革案を日本側に押しつけるやうな心算はない。アメリカの行政機構にも、固より缺陷があることだし、アメリカのある官廳機構をその儘日本に採用することを命じたりするやうなことは毛頭考へてゐない。

ただ新憲法の下において明確化された三權分立の線に沿ひ、又行政部門の内部における各廳間の權能を合理的に分配する。（例へば警察機能が教育乃至福利行政にまで不當に擴張されることがないやうにする）と言ふ様な根本的な點に興味をもつて居る。又新憲法では地方自治制度の強化が一つの原則として擧げられてゐるが、かうゆふラインにおいていかなる改革をなすべきかといふことも其の一つである。又公務員制度については、科學的なメリット、システムを採用して能率のよい行政が出來るやうにすることが眼目である。」

大臣「行政組織を考へるについて、三權分立といふことを基礎におかなければならないことは當然で、又地方自治體の強化も當然やるべきことであるが例へば警察の機能をどの程度まで地方自治體に移し、どの程度を中央政府に保留しておくかといふ様な具體的な點になると、問題

大臣「自分はこの行政調査部の部長になることになつて居るが、及ばずながら全力を懸けて出來る限りの成績を擧げたいと思つてゐる。行政制度の改革については、現在別に具體的な案は持つてゐないが、今後衆知を集め研究を遂行するについて總司令部側の協力をお願ひしたく、資料等も貰ひたいと思ふ。それについてはこの大きな仕事を進めることとしたい。アメリカ政治組織については大體のことは書物等で承知してゐるが、その國家組織が日本の國家組織とは非常に相異してゐることは相當承知してゐる。アメリカの制度をどの程度まで取入れるべきかは問題である。何れにしても自分は從來國民の非難の多かつた日本の官僚組織といふものを根本的に改革し、民主主義のラインに沿ふ體制を確立し、又行政の運營についても、これを極力簡易化して繁文縟禮をなくし、從來の様に國民に迷惑を掛けることのないやうな仕組みにしたいと思つてゐる。」

調査部を設置せられたことは誠に結構な企てで、又行政調査部の組織もこの仕事をやるに適當な組織であると思ふ。これからはその人的陣容を整へることが最も重要な點である。」

とすべきものがある。現在の議會で出來た地方制度改正法は固より完全なものではないので、次の議會か或はその次の議會に、もっと根本的な改正案が出されるものと思ふ。」

マ「行政調査部においては先づ公務員制度の問題に重點をおかるべきであると思ふ。即ち公務員制度の改革の基本的原則を先づ確立して、その實施に當つては、無用の混亂を來す等のことのない様逐次これを實施して行くべきである。行政機構の改革の方は、その時の必要に應じて機構の改廢新設に當り、最も合理的な權能の分配といふ見地からこれを立案して行くべきであると思ふ。尚自分は科學的な能率的な公務員制度の確立といふことが取りも直さず、吏員制度の民主主義化といふことであると思つて居る。」

大臣「いかに立派な制度を設けても、これを動かす人にその人を得なければ結局制度としても役に立たない。そして人の問題は結局教育の問題であつて、教育から改めてかからなければならないが、この教育を改めるといふことは一年や二年で出來る仕事ではなく、相當の年月を要する。アメリカでは政黨組織が非常に發達してゐて、大多数の公務員が選舉に依つて任命せられることになつてゐるやうに思ふが、現在の日本の實情から見て果して何の程度迄かう言ふ制度を取入れ得るか疑問であると思ふ。」

マ「諮問委員會としては、單にこの政治部を通じてレコメンディションをするに過ぎないので、日本の實情にそぐはない改革案を押しつけるやうなことは絶對しないから、その點の御心配は要らない。なほ今教育の重要性を言はれたがその點は自分も全く同感で今日特に大臣に御話したいと思つて居た點である。自分はこの行政調査部で優秀な青年を採用して、これを行政運營の專門家として養成することが極めて重要であると思ふ。これらの人々が言はば中核體となつて、將來はその一人一人が指導者になつて新知識を擴めて行くといふ様にすべきであると思ふ。そしてこの要員として優秀な者を得る爲には、彼等の任務が決して一時的のものではなくて、恆久的に政府部内で重要な職責を與へられるものだといふことをはつきりさせて置くことが必要であると思ふ。なほこの要員

3　経済諸施策への対応（昭和21年5月〜24年4月）

大臣「さういふ人を集めることは現在のところ却々困難である特に日本人は語學が下手で、さういふ適格者といふ者は却々ゐない。又調査部の仕事は一年位で完成したいと思つてゐるのであるがさういふ短期間で十分な教育が出來るかどうか疑はしいと思ふ。」

マ「行政制度の改正自體は長年を要するかも知れないが右の様な教育については半年か一年で十分であると思ふ。自分の經驗からすれば、假にこゝに十人の英語をよくする優秀な者を入れたとしたら、半年の後には基礎的な知識は充分に習得せしめ得るだらうし、一年の後には一人立ちになつて實態調査的な仕事を委せ得るやうになると思ふ。なほ將來においては大學等にさういふ講座を設けるといふことも考へるべきであらうと思ふ。」

大臣「アメリカのシビル、サーヴィスでは大統領の更迭に際して、どうなつてゐるか、又アメリカでは大統領の更迭に際して、どの程度に各廰の人事の異動が行はれるものか、さういふ點についてお伺ひしたい。」

は多数の者が英語を能く解するものであることが望ましい。」

マ「米國の政府部內の地位は、いはゆる unclassified のものと いはゆる classified のものとに別けられて居る。前者はいはゆる政治的任命によるもので各廰の長が勝手に任命出來、從つて政權の更迭毎に變へられることになる。後者はいはゆるシヴィル・サーヴィスであつて各地位の職務の種類、卽ち法律關係とか、土木關係とか言ふ種別によつて class に別けられ、職務の內容の上下によつて grade に別けられる。卽ち或る官廰の何の地位は何クラスの何グレイドと言ふことが決つて居る。他方シヴィル・サーヴィスに屬する各個人は適性を判定する各種試驗及經驗年數によつて各々のクラスとグレイドを與へられてゐる。卽ち classified の地位には、必ずそれに相當するクラスとグレイドを有するシヴィル・サーヴィス所屬員をつけなければならず又或る地位があけば、その地位につき得る者には何う言ふ者が居るかと直ぐ判る様な仕組になつて居る譯である。

これは大體の原則であつて、聯邦政府及び各州政府の採用して居る制度は各々異つて居り小さい州で聯邦政府より進んだ制度をもつて居るものもある。若し御希望な

179

隣組等による神道援助の禁止に関する指令

GENERAL HEADQUARTERS
SUPREME COMMANDER FOR THE ALLIED POWERS

APO 500

6 November 1946

AG 000.3 (6 Nov 46) CIE
(SCAPIN 1318)
MEMORANDUM FOR: IMPERIAL JAPANESE GOVERNMENT.
THROUGH: Central Liaison Office, Tokyo.
SUBJECT: Sponsorship and Support of Shinto by Neighborhood Associations.

1. Numerous complaints have been received concerning the continued use of neighborhood associations (chonaikai, burakukai, tonarigumi) to collect funds for the support of Shinto shrines and Shinto festivals and activities and to distribute amulets and charms. These practices violate paragraph 1-a of the Memorandum for the Imperial Japanese Government, AG 000.3 (15 Dec 45) CIE, SCAPIN 448, 15 December 1945, subject: "Abolition of Governmental Sponsorship, Support, Perpetuation, Control, and Dissemination of State Shinto".

2. The Imperial Japanese Government is directed to take appropriate action to remedy this situation.

FOR THE SUPREME COMMANDER:

JOHN B. COOLEY
Colonel, AGD,
Adjutant General.

編注 藤崎万里終戦連絡中央事務局政治部政治課連絡官。

昭和21年11月6日 連合国最高司令官総司令部より日本政府宛

らば、これらの點について希望の方々に集つて貰つて概略御話してもよい。」
大臣「本日は色々有益な御話を伺つて深く感謝する。又その中御目にかかりたい。」

180

昭和21年12月11日 連合国最高司令官総司令部より日本政府宛

3 経済諸施策への対応(昭和21年5月～24年4月)

臨時物資需給調整法による統制方式に関する指令

GENERAL HEADQUARTERS
SUPREME COMMANDER FOR THE ALLIED POWERS
APO 500

11 December 1946

AG 400 (11 Dec 46) ESS/AC
(SCAPIN - 1394)

MEMORANDUM FOR: IMPERIAL JAPANESE GOVERNMENT

THROUGH: Central Liaison Office, Tokyo

SUBJECT: Methods of Control under the Temporary Demand and Supply Adjustment Act

1. Reference is the Temporary Demand and Supply Adjustment Act.

2. The Imperial Japanese Government will withdraw from industry the powers of distribution control. The control of distribution of materials and products by the method of exclusive purchase and sale by a designated private company or association will be eliminated.

3. The Imperial Japanese Government will submit to the Supreme Commander for the Allied Powers plans for carrying on distribution functions through a government distribution corporation. The purpose of such corporation will be to exercise necessary control functions where adequate distribution cannot be accomplished through normal distribution channels.

4. No agency will be designated by the Economic Stabilization Board under the Temporary Demand and Supply Adjustment Act without approval of the Supreme Commander for the Allied Powers.

5. The officers and employees of agencies or corporations established or designated under paragraphs 3 and 4, above, will not be permitted to be stockholders or employees or to have any beneficial interest in any company or enterprise engaged in the production or distribution of goods and materials under the control of the agency or corporation.

6. The Imperial Japanese Government will submit to the Supreme Commander for the Allied Powers for approval, in quintuplicate, typed in English on 8″ x 11″ paper, within ten (10) days

from date of this Memorandum, proposed ministerial ordinances for the control of essential products and materials which are consistent with the policies set forth in this Memorandum.

FOR THE SUPREME COMMANDER:

      C. Z. Shugart
     for JOHN B. COOLEY
      Colonel, AGD,
      Adjutant General.

181　昭和22年1月1日　連合国最高司令官総司令部発表

マッカーサー司令官の年頭メッセージ

General of the Army Douglas MacArthur's New Year Message

January 1, 1947

TO THE PEOPLE OF JAPAN:

As we again bring one year to a close and enter upon the complexities of another, it is well that we calmly and carefully assay the past that we may the more realistically pattern the future.

For it is only by the fruits of experience with its successes and its failures, its strong points and its weak, its good and its bad, that we may re-orient ourselves toward that objective for which we have heretofore embarked.

In the year just past, none will fail to concede major advances toward the development of a social system in Japan designed along most progressive and liberal lines and resting upon that basic concept which seeks equality of opportunity and the maximum of human freedom, while elevating the dignity and the well-being and the happiness of the individual.

It has been a year of legislated reform, hardly surpassed in a comparable period during the evolution of civilized society, which has established the framework to popular government and, crashing through the barriers of tradition, prejudice and oppressive controls, has provided the Japanese people with the right and the opportunity to live in the full dignity of self-respect as free men.

It is for the historian of the future to judge just how fully the Japanese people avail themselves of this right and this opportunity which has come to them in wake of the blood sacrifice of countless thousands of Japan's sons. For it is not enough that this right and opportunity be bestowed. It must be fully understood, deeply cherished and resolutely preserved if that which is now written is to be transformed into meaningful and vital actuality —if from the bitterness and tragedy of Japan's past and present are to spring those strong roots of individual liberty upon which a future free society must rest.

Much has been accomplished, much yet remains to be done. There have been many successes, some failures; many strong points, some weak; much good, some bad. The great majority of Japan's leaders have displayed an exemplary approach to the realism of Japan's problems —an even greater majority of Japan's people resolutely have sought to remove the causes of Japan's ill-fated past and faithfully to build for Japan's happier future.

During this time, I have not been unmindful of these cross-currents of decision and indecision, of progress and retrogression, of steps both faltering and resolute, as the forces of liberalism and reaction have fought to establish a common ground for Japan's salvation. And I have confined my major effort to charting the course envisaged at hostilities end by both of our warring peoples, that would destroy entrenched totalitarian controls and raise the individual Japanese citizen to exert a dominant influence over his own destiny. For once the citizen has acquired the power of self-determination, limited only by rational convention and individual conscience, he may be counted upon firmly to preserve that power and to apply it fearlessly and intelligently, both for his own benefit and the common benefit of all.

Results in the year to come will have a profound bearing upon the well-being of the people of Japan during the generations which are to follow. For therein only can be brought to fruition those great reforms which are now just charted. The new constitution will take effect, placing all sovereign power in the hands of the people upon whom simultaneously will be conferred heretofore unknown rights and privileges and upon whom will be imposed new and most serious individual responsibilities. The agrarian reforms will be brought under implementation to the end that those who till the soil may reap the fruits of their toil. And the people throughout Japan will have the opportunity to select a new leadership through the exercise of their own free will, with entrenched restrictive controls inexorably swept aside.

The success of these and other projected reforms, designed to uplift the dignity and well-being of the individual and to establish here a free society, are dependent, however, in final analysis upon the manner in which the people themselves discharge their new political responsibilities, the type of leadership which the people select, and the faithfulness with which that leadership preserves inviolate the people's rights and furthers the people's interests. For unless the people assume in full reality the mantle and dignity of the sovereign power and proceed resolutely in the exercise of that power to build upon the ashes of decadence a new and enlightened social system, deeply rooted in a firm determination to remain free, there can be but superficial and temporary change from that which brought only tragedy in Japan's past.

Thus, on the people alone rests the solution to many of the pressing problems which harass Japan's present and will shape Japan's future. On their action as the year progresses will depend in large measure the course of Japan's destiny, and all peoples of good will everywhere will watch with intense interest and abiding hope the manner in which they meet these vital tests. It is my prayer, and indeed my firm anticipation, that the Japanese people will understand and grasp this opportunity and rise resolutely to meet its challenge. Therein lies Japan's salvation — therein lies the opportunity for future peace and happiness for Japan's people — and therein lies the hope of all of the peoples of the East for a better civilization.

DOUGLAS MacARTHUR

編　注　本文書は、昭和二十四年三月、外務省特別資料部作成「日本占領及び管理重要文書集」第二巻より抜粋。

182　昭和22年1月30日　極東委員会決定
原子力の研究・利用の禁止および制限に関する極東委員会政策決定

Japanese Research and Activity in the Field of Atomic Energy

3　経済諸施策への対応(昭和21年5月〜24年4月)

〔FEC Policy Decision, January 30, 1947〕

1. Japanese research or other activity in the field of atomic energy should be governed by the following:

　　a. such decisions by the United Nations on international control of atomic energy as are applicable;

　　b. additional restrictive policies established for the disarmament and control of Japan.

2. In view of continuing discussion of the foregoing, the Far Eastern Commission considers that the Japanese should not be permitted at present to conduct research in the field of atomic energy, or to develop or use atomic energy. The Commission accordingly establishes the following policy:

　　a. All research in Japan, of either a fundamental or applied nature, in the field of atomic energy should be prohibited, including:

　　　(1) all research or development which has for its purpose the production of fissionable atomic species;

　　　(2) all research or development which has for its purpose the separation or concentration of fissionable species of atomic isotopes from the naturally occurring isotope mixture of a chemical element.

　　b. All development or construction in Japan which has for its purpose the utilization of atomic nuclear energy should be prohibited.

　　c. The mining, processing, and refining of radioactive materials in Japan for authorized purposes, such as radium for medical uses, should be permitted only in those instances specifically approved by the Supreme Commander for the Allied Powers and under his surveillance.

～～～～～

編注　本文書は、昭和二十四年三月、外務省特別資料部作成「日本占領及び管理重要文書集」第二巻より抜粋。

183　昭和22年1月31日　連合国最高司令官総司令部発表

総罷業の禁止に関するマッカーサー司令官の声明

General of the Army Douglas MacArthur's Statement

concerning a General Strike

January 31, 1947

Under the authority vested in me as Supreme Commander for the Allied Powers, I have informed the labor leaders, whose unions have federated for the purpose of conducting a general strike, that I will not permit the use of so deadly a social weapon in the present impoverished and emaciated condition of Japan, and have accordingly directed them to desist from the furtherance of such action.

It is with greatest reluctance that I have deemed it necessary to intervene to this extent in the issues now pending. I have done so only to forestall the fatal impact upon an already gravely threatened public welfare. Japanese society today operates under the limitations of war defeat and allied occupation. Its cities are laid waste, its industries are almost at a standstill, and the great masses of its people are on little more than a starvation diet.

A general strike, crippling transportation and communications, would prevent the movement of food to feed the people and of coal to sustain essential utilities, and would stop such industry as is still functioning. The paralysis which inevitably would result might reduce large masses of the Japanese people to the point of actual starvation, and would produce dreadful consequences upon every Japanese home regardless of social strata or direct interest in the basic issue. Even now, to prevent actual starvation in Japan, the people of the United States are releasing to them quantities of their own scarce food resources.

The persons involved in the threatened general strike are but a small minority of the Japanese people. Yet this minority might well plunge the great masses into a disaster not unlike that produced in the immediate past by the minority which led Japan into the destruction of war. This in turn would impose upon the Allied Powers the unhappy decision of whether to leave the Japanese people to the fate thus recklessly imposed by a minority, or to cover the consequences by pouring into Japan, at the expense of their own meager resources, infinitely greater quantities of food and other supplies to sustain life than otherwise would be required. In the circumstances, I could hardly request the Allied peoples to assume this additional burden.

3　経済諸施策への対応（昭和21年5月〜24年4月）

184　総選挙実施方要求について

昭和22年2月6日　マッカーサー連合国最高司令官より吉田内閣総理大臣宛

編注　本文書は、昭和二十四年三月、外務省特別資料部作成「日本占領及び管理重要文書集」第二巻より抜粋。

〰〰〰〰〰〰〰〰〰〰〰〰〰〰〰〰〰

GENERAL HEADQUARTERS
SUPREME COMMANDER FOR THE ALLIED POWERS
OFFICE OF THE SUPREME COMMANDER

6 February 1947

The Prime Minister of Japan,
Tokyo, Japan.

〰〰〰〰〰〰〰〰〰〰〰〰〰〰〰〰〰

Dear Mr. Prime Minister:

I believe the time has come for a general election. Momentous changes in internal structure, in economic outlook, and in the whole fabric and pattern of Japanese life have occurred since the last general election nearly a year ago. It is necessary, in the near future, to obtain another democratic expression of the people's will on the fundamental issues with which Japanese society is now confronted. In this way we will once more advance in the process of democracy which now governs this state. The exact time and details are matters which I leave to the discretion of the Japanese Government, but the election should take place as soon as practicable after the close of the present session of the diet so that a new legislative body may initiate and synchronize with the introduction and effectivation of the new Constitution. The past year has been one of accomplishment. I look with equal confidence to the future.

While I have taken this measure as one of dire emergency, I do not intend otherwise to restrict the freedom of action heretofore given labor in the achievement of legitimate objectives. Nor do I intend in any way to compromise or influence the basic social issues involved. These are matters of evolution which time and circumstance may well orient without disaster as Japan gradually emerges from its present distress.

Very sincerely,
DOUGLAS MacARTHUR

在日連合国財産返還の暫定方針に関する極東委員会政策決定

昭和22年3月6日 極東委員会決定

Interim Principles for Restitution of Identifiable Property Confiscated in Japan From Allied Nationals

(FEC Policy Decision, March 6, 1947)

1. The Supreme Commander for the Allied Powers should be authorized to restore to nationals of any of the United Nations identifiable property, tangible or intangible, which was located in Japan prior to the outbreak of hostilities between their government and the government of Japan and owned by them at that time or lawfully acquired thereafter, and which was seized, confiscated, or sequestered, formally or otherwise, during the recent hostilities by the Japanese Government, members of its armed forces, or by official or private Japanese or other enemy individuals or groups; provided that:

　　a. subject to the discretion of the Supreme Commander, restitution should be made at this time only to:

　　　(1) natural persons present in Japan;
　　　(2) juridical persons where the holders of a controlling interest are nationals of Members of the United Nations now resident in Japan;
　　　(3) charitable and religious institutions financed primarily by non-Japanese funds, where a duly authorized agent or properly qualified person is resident in Japan to receive title;

　　b. without in any way prejudging the definitive policy later to be adopted by the Far Eastern Commission with respect to the disposition of large-scale enterprises, only small-scale commercial and industrial enterprises should be restored at the present time;

　　c. though title to gold, other precious metals and foreign exchange may be restored to the United Nations owners, they should remain subject to the laws and regulations in force at any time governing the custody, control and transfer of such assets;

　　d. the Supreme Commander is satisfied as to the identification of such property.

3 経済諸施策への対応（昭和21年5月～24年4月）

2. The policy for restitution of similar property to nationals of Members of the United Nations who are not resident in Japan at present will be dealt with in a future paper.

3. For the purpose of determining whether property was in fact confiscated it should be assumed that all property taken by the Japanese or other enemy Government, Armed Forces, or nationals during the recent hostilities from nationals of any of the United Nations was confiscated whether or not payment was made at the time of acquisition unless it can be definitely shown that no duress or fraud was involved.

4. The restitution of property should be made without expense for the owners and without prejudicing the claim of the original owners against the Japanese or other enemy Government and/or their nationals for damages to property, rent, depreciation, and other ascertainable losses. To facilitate the preparation and adjudication of claims, agreed statements as to the extent and condition of the property restored should be drawn up at the time of its return. The Japanese Government should be required to furnish to the owner a complete inventory of the property together with a report by the Japanese official administrator on the management of it and, in the case of industrial and commercial concerns, a closing balance sheet.

5. If payment to restoree was made at the time of confiscation the Supreme Commander for the Allied Powers should require persons repossessing the property to agree to remit such amounts to the Japanese Government as a prerequisite to restitution. However, actual payment of such amounts should be made only after settlement of claims as specified in paragraph 4 above.

6. If funds received in payment for confiscated property were blocked by the Japanese Government, such funds should be unblocked and the owner permitted to draw upon them on the same basis as depositors in general draw upon their bank funds, except that in the event that the confiscated property is returned such funds should be unblocked only in an amount sufficient to make the payment required in paragraph 5 above.

7. The right to restitution provided in the foregoing paragraphs and even the completion of restitution should not be considered as permission to operate properties where the Supreme

Commander for the Allied Powers considers the operation of such property injurious to occupying forces or to the purposes of the occupation. Similarly, the operation of properties considered by the Supreme Commander for the Allied Powers, upon consultation with the Allied Council for Japan in accordance with the Terms of Reference of the Allied Council for Japan, to be beneficial to the occupying forces and/or the accomplishment of the purposes of the occupation should not await restitution of title or the transfer of possession of such properties; but in such cases compensation for the use of the property should be paid for the account of the owner.

8. Japanese nationals injured by the provisions of the foregoing paragraphs should look to the Japanese Government for relief.

編注 本文書は、昭和二十五年四月、外務省・賠償庁共編「日本占領及び管理重要文書集」第五巻より抜粋。

昭和22年4月2日 国際連合安全保障理事会承認

旧日本委任統治地域に関する米国信託統治協定

United States Trusteeship Agreement for the Former Japanese Mandated Island; in the Pacific

Approved by the Security Council of the United Nations, April 2, 1947

Preamble

WHEREAS Article 75 of the Charter of the United Nations provides for the establishment of an International Trusteeship System for the administration and supervision of such territories as may be placed thereunder by subsequent agreements; and

WHEREAS under Article 77 of the said Charter the trusteeship system may be applied to territories now held under mandate; and

WHEREAS on 17 December 1920 the Council of the League of Nations confirmed a mandate for the former German islands north of the equator to Japan, to be administered in accordance with Article 22 of the Covenant of the League of Nations; and

WHEREAS Japan, as a result of the Second World War, has ceased to exercise any authority in these islands;

3 経済諸施策への対応(昭和21年5月～24年4月)

NOW, THEREFORE, the Security Council of the United Nations, having satisfied itself that the relevant articles of the Charter have been complied with, hereby resolves to approve the following terms of trusteeship for the Pacific Islands formerly under mandate to Japan.

Article 1

The Territory of the Pacific Islands, consisting of the islands formerly held by Japan under mandate in accordance with Article 22 of the Covenant of the League of Nations, is hereby designated as a strategic area and placed under the Trusteeship System established in the Charter of the United Nations. The Territory of the Pacific Islands is hereinafter referred to as the Trust Territory.

Article 2

The United States of America is designated as the administering authority of the Trust Territory.

Article 3

The administering authority shall have full powers of administration, legislation, and jurisdiction over the territory subject to the provisions of this agreement, and may apply to the Trust Territory, subject to any modifications which the administering authority may consider desirable, such of the laws of the United States as it may deem appropriate to local conditions and requirements.

Article 4

The administering authority, in discharging the obligations of trusteeship in the Trust Territory, shall act in accordance with the Charter of the United Nations, and the provisions of this agreement, and shall, as specified in Article 83 (2) of the Charter, apply the objectives of the International Trusteeship System, as set forth in Article 76 of the Charter, to the people of the trust territory.

Article 5

In discharging its obligations under Article 76 (a) and Article 84, of the Charter, the administering authority shall ensure that the Trust Territory shall play its part, in accordance with the Charter of the United Nations, in the maintenance of international peace and security. To this end the administering authority shall be entitled:

1. to establish naval, military and air bases and to erect fortifications in the Trust Territory;

2. to station and employ armed forces in the territory; and

3. to make use of volunteer forces, facilities and assistance from the Trust Territory in carrying out the obligations towards the Security Council undertaken in this regard by the administering authority, as well as for the local defense and the maintenance of law and order within the Trust Territory.

Article 6

In discharging its obligations under Article 76 (b) of the Charter, the Administering Authority shall:

1. foster the development of such political institutions as are suited to the Trust Territory and shall promote the development of the inhabitants of the Trust Territory toward self-government or independence as may be appropriate to the particular circumstances of the Trust Territory and its peoples and the freely expressed wishes of the peoples concerned; and to this end shall give to the inhabitants of the Trust Territory a progressively increasing share in the administrative services in the Territory; shall develop their participation in government; shall give due recognition to the customs of the inhabitants in providing a system of law for the Territory; and shall take other appropriate measures toward these ends;

2. promote the economic advancement and self-sufficiency of the inhabitants, and to this end shall regulate the use of natural resources; encourage the development of fisheries, agriculture, and industries; protect the inhabitants against the loss of their lands and resources; and improve the means of transportation and communication;

3. promote the social advancement of the inhabitants, and to this end shall protect the rights and fundamental freedoms of all elements of the population without discrimination; protect the health of the inhabitants; control the traffic in arms and ammunition, opium and the other dangerous drugs, and alcohol and other spirituous be-

3　経済諸施策への対応(昭和 21 年 5 月～24 年 4 月)

verages; and institute such other regulations as may be necessary to protect the inhabitants against social abuses; and

4. promote the educational advancement of the inhabitants, and to this end shall take steps toward the establishment of a general system of elementary education; facilitate the vocational and cultural advancement of the population; and shall encourage qualified students to pursue higher education, including training on the professional level.

Article 7

In discharging its obligations under Article 76 (c), of the Charter, the Administering Authority shall guarantee to the inhabitants of the Trust Territory freedom of conscience, and, subject only to the requirements of public order and security, freedom of speech, of the press, and of assembly; freedom of worship, and of religious teaching; and freedom of migration and movement.

Article 8

1. In discharging its obligations under Article 76 (d) of the Charter, as defined by Article 83 (2) of the Charter, the Administering Authority, subject to the requirements of security, and the obligation to promote the advancement of the inhabitants, shall accord to nationals of each Member of the United Nations and to companies and associations organized in conformity with the law of such Member, treatment in the Trust Territory no less favorable than that accorded therein to nationals, companies and associations of any other United Nations except the administering authority.

2. The Administering Authority shall ensure equal treatment to the Member of the United Nations and their nationals in the administration of justice.

3. Nothing in this Article shall be so construed as to accord traffic rights to aircraft flying into and out of the Trust Territory. Such rights shall be subject to agreement between the administering authority and the state whose nationality such aircraft possesses.

4. The administering authority may negotiate and conclude commercial and other treaties and agreements with Mem-

bers of United Nations and other States, designed to attain for the inhabitants of the Trust Territory treatment of the Members of the United Nations and other States no less favorable than that granted by them to the nationals of other States. The Security Council may recommend, or invite other organs of the United Nations to consider and recommend, what rights the inhabitants of the trust territory should acquire in consideration of the right obtained by Members of the United Nations in the Trust Territory.

Article 9

The administering authority shall be entitled to constitute the Trust Territory into a customs, fiscal, or administrative union or federation with other territories under United States jurisdiction and to establish common services between such territories and the Trust Territory where such measures are not inconsistent with the basic objectives of the International Trusteeship System and with the terms of this agreement.

Article 10

The administering authority, acting under the provisions of Article 3 of this agreement, may accept membership in any regional advisory commission regional authority, or technical organization, or other voluntary association of states, may cooperate with specialized international bodies, public or private, and may engage in other form of international co-operation.

Article 11

1. The Administering Authority shall take the necessary steps to provide the status of citizenship of the Trust Territory for the inhabitants of the Trust Territory.

2. The administering authority shall afford diplomatic and consular protection to inhabitants of the Trust Territory when outside the territorial limits of the Trust Territory or of the territory of the administering authority.

Article 12

The Administering Authority shall enact such legislation as may be necessary to place the provisions of this agreement in effect in the Trust Territory.

Article 13

The provisions of Articles 87 and 88 of the Charter shall be applicable to the Trust Territory, provided that the Administering

Authority may determine the extent of their applicability to any areas which may from time to time be specified by it as closed for security reasons.

Article 14

The Administering Authority undertakes to apply in the Trust Territory the provisions of any international conventions and recommendations which may be appropriate to the particular circumstances of the Trust Territory and which would be conducive to the achievement of the basic objectives of Article 6 of this agreement.

Article 15

The terms of the present agreement shall not be altered, amended or terminated without the consent of the administering authority.

Article 16

The present agreement shall come into force when approved by the Security Council of the United Nations and by the Government of the United States after due constitutional process.

編注一　本文書は、昭和二四年三月、外務省特別資料部作成「日本占領及び管理重要文書集」第二巻より抜粋。

二　本協定は昭和二十二年七月十八日発効。

187

昭和22年5月2日　　マッカーサー連合国最高司令官より
　　　　　　　　　　吉田内閣総理大臣宛

国会、最高裁判所、首相官邸および皇居における国旗掲揚許可について

General of the Army Douglas MacArthur's Letter to the Prime Minister of Japan

Tokyo, Japan.
May 2, 1947.

Dear Mr. Prime Minister:

With the effectuation of the new Japanese Constitution, there will be established in Japan a government, erected on democratic principles by a free expression of the popular will composed of coordinate organs of state power fully responsible to the people in whom the sovereignty now rests, and dedicated to the realization and safeguard of the sanctity of human freedom and the furtherance among men of lasting peace.

To mark this historic ascendency of democratic freedom which events have made possible, I believe it peculiarly appropriate that from henceforth the Japanese national flag be restored to the people of Japan for unrestricted display within and over the premises which house the National Diet, the Supreme Court, and the Prime Minister, as representative of the three main branches of constitutional government, and within and over the residence of the Emperor, who assumes his constitutional role as symbol of the State and of the unity of the people.

Let this flag fly to signify the advent in Japanese life of a new and enduring era of peace based upon personal liberty, individual dignity, tolerance and justice.

Very sincerely,
(Sgd.) Douglas MacArthur
DOUGLAS MacARTHUR.

The Prime Minister of Japan,
Tokyo.

編 注　本文書は、昭和二十四年三月、外務省特別資料部作成「日本占領及び管理重要文書集」第二巻より抜粋。

188 昭和22年6月10日　連合国最高司令官総司令部より　日本政府宛

連合国人が所有する特許権や著作権などの保護に関する指令

GENERAL HEADQUARTERS
SUPREME COMMANDER FOR THE ALLIED POWERS
APO 500

10 June 1947

AG 072 (10 Jun 47) CPC/PP
(SCAPIN 1726)

MEMORANDUM FOR: THE JAPANESE GOVERNMENT
THROUGH: Central Liaison Office, Tokyo
SUBJECT: Application of Directives to Patents, Utility Models, Trademarks, Designs and Copyrights.

1. Reference is made to the following:

   a. Memorandum for the Japanese Government, file AG

091.112 (13 Sep 45) MG, SCAPIN 26, 13 September 1945, subject, "Protection of Allied and Axis Property," from General Headquarters, Supreme Commander for the Allied Powers.

　b. Memorandum for the Japanese Government, file AG 130 (22 Sep 45) ESS, SCAPIN 45, 22 September 1945, subject, "Control of Financial Transactions," from General Headquarters, Supreme Commander for the Allied Powers.

　2. The Japanese Government is hereby notified that patents, utility models, trademarks, designs, copyrights and contracts or licenses affecting or involving patents, utility models, trademarks, designs and copyrights, fall within the scope of the definition of "property" given in Appendix A of reference 1b above.

　3. The Japanese Government is directed to take whatever steps are necessary to ensure inclusion of the property described in paragraph 2 above within the scope of measures taken in compliance with reference memoranda.

　4. Attention is directed to the fact that proper protection has not been afforded by the Japanese Government to trademarks registered on 7 December 1941 in the names of nationals of the United Nations as required by reference 1a above; infringement of trademarks of the Singer Sewing Machine Company (American) and the Dunlop Rubber Company, Ltd. (British) have been reported to General Headquarters, Supreme Commander for the Allied Powers.

　5. The Japanese Government is therefore directed, as one phase of its program to comply with reference memoranda and paragraph 3 above, to take immediate action to remedy the abuses set forth in paragraph 4 above, and to prevent the occurrence of similar abuses with respect to other trademarks registered on 7 December 1941 in the names of nationals of the United Nations.

　6. Details of action taken and to be taken in compliance with paragraphs 3 and 5 above will be submitted for approval to General Headquarters, Supreme Commander for the Allied Powers, prior to 15 July 1947.

FOR THE SUPREME COMMANDER:

A. J. Rehe
for R. M. LEVY

昭和22年6月19日　極東委員会決定

189 降伏後の対日基本政策に関する極東委員会政策決定（和訳文）

（一九四七年六月一九日極東委員會政策決定）

（一九四七年七月一一日極東委員會發表）

降伏後の對日基本政策

前文

この文書は、降伏後の日本國に關する一般的政策の聲明である。この文書は、日本國の占領に關する政策の決定を必要とする一切の問題を取り扱つているものではない。この文書に含まれていないか、又はこの文書で完全におおつくされていない問題は、別に取り扱われる。

一九四五年九月二日に、日本國は連合國に對して無條件で降伏し、現在においては、連合國最高司令官ダグラス・マックアーサー元帥の指揮の下にある右連合國の軍隊の軍事占領下にあるので、

次の諸國、すなわち日本國に對する戰爭に從事したオーストラリア國、カナダ、中華民國、フランス國、インド、オランダ國、ニュー・ジーランド、連合王國及びアメリカ合衆國の代表者が、日本國が降伏條項に基くその義務の履行を完成することのできるために準據する政策、原則及び基準を定めるために、モスコー外務大臣會議の決定に基いて、ワシントンにおいて極東委員會として會合したので、

右委員會を構成する諸國は、ポツダム宣言の意圖を遂行し、降伏文書を履行し並びに國際的安全及び安定を確立する目的をもつて、

右の安全及び安定は、第一には、日本國が過去數十年の侵略の遂行に用いた主な手段であつた軍事機構の完全な破壊にかかつており、第二には、日本國における軍國主義のいかなる復活をも不可能とするような政治的及び經濟的條件の確立にかかつており、第三には、日本人をして自己の戰爭意欲、自己の征服計畫及び右計畫の達成のために用いられた方法が自己を滅亡にひんさせたことを悟らしめるこ

3 経済諸施策への対応(昭和21年5月〜24年4月)

とにかかつていることを意識したゆゑに、日本國が、軍國主義をその一切の面において放棄することを決意し、且つ、世界の他の部分と平和に生活することを希望するに至るまで、又民主主義的原則が日本國の政治的、經濟的及び文化的生活の一切の分野において確立されるに至るまでは、日本國は再び自己の運命を支配することを許されることはできないことを決議し、

よつて、

連合國に對する日本國の義務の履行を確實にすること、全面的な武裝解除、戰爭能力を日本國から奪ふことを目的とする經濟的改革、軍國主義的勢力の除去、戰爭犯罪人に對する嚴重な處罰を含み、且つ、嚴重な管理の期間を必要とする措置によつて日本國の物質的及び精神的非軍事化の任務を完了すること、並びに

日本國民が自己をして自己の妥當な個人的及び國家的必要をみたすことを得しめ、且つ一切の國との永久に平和な關孫に自國をもたらすやうな經濟的及び文化的の線に沿つて、各自の間及び他國との間における交際を民主的社會のわく内において發展させることのできるやうな手段を自己の利益及び一般世界の利益のために見出すことについて日本國民を援助することに意見一致し、

日本國の處理に關し、次の基本的目的及び政策を採擇した。

第1部 究極の目的

1 日本國に對する降伏後の期間に關する政策が準據しなければならない日本國に關する究極の目的は、次のとほりである。

い 日本國が再び世界の平和及び安全に對する脅威とならないことを確實にすること。

ろ 自己の國際的責任を果し、他國の權利を尊重し、且つ、國際連合の目的を支持する民主的且つ平和的な政府をできるだけ早く樹立させること。日本國における このやうな政府は、日本國民の自由に表明された意思に從つて樹立されなければならない。

2 これらの目的は、次の主要な手段によつて達成される。

い 日本國の主權は、本州、北海道、九州、四國の諸島及び今後決定されることのある周邊の諸小島に限定さ

れる。

ろ　日本國は、完全に武裝解除され、且つ、非軍事化される。軍國主義者の權力及び軍國主義の勢力は、全面的に除去される。軍國主義及び侵略の精神を表明する一切の制度は、強力に抑壓される。

は　日本國民は、個人の自由に對する欲求並びに基本的人權特に信教、集會及び結社、言論及び出版の自由の尊重を發達させるよう獎勵されるべきである。日本國民は、民主的且つ代議的團體を組織するよう獎勵さるべきである。

に　日本國は、自己の經濟をささえ、且つ、公正な現物賠償の取立を可能ならしめるような產業を維持することを許されるべきであるが、自己をして戰爭のために再軍備することを得しめるような產業を維持すること支配とは區別して、原料の入手を許されなければならない。世界貿易關係への將來における日本國の參加は、許される。

第2部　連合國の權限

1　軍事占領

降伏條項を實施し、且つ、前記の究極の目的の達成を促進するため、日本國の本土諸島の軍事占領がなされる。右占領は、日本國に對する戰爭に參加した諸國のための軍事行動の性格を有する。右諸國の軍隊が日本國占領に參加するという原則は、確認されている。占領軍は、合衆國の任命する最高司令官の指揮の下に置かれる。

2　日本國政府との關係

天皇及び日本國政府の權限は、最高司令官に從屬するものであり、最高司令官は、降伏條項を實施し並びに日本國の占領及び管理の遂行のために確立された政策を實行するために必要な一切の權限を有する。

最高司令官は、天皇をも含む日本國政府の機構及び機關を通じて、その權限を行使する。但し、右は、ここに述べられている目的及び政策を滿足に促進する範圍に限られる。最高司令官の判斷と裁量とによつて、日本國政府は、國內行政事項において通常の統治の權限を行使することを許されることもできるし、又、最高司令官は、日本國政府の機關を用いないで、執るべき措置をいかなる場合においても

3　経済諸施策への対応(昭和21年5月～24年4月)

命ずることもできる。

連合國對日理事會における連合國代表者との適當な豫備的協議の後、最高司令官は、必要な場合には、日本國政府の個々の大臣の罷免に關し、又は個々の閣員の辭任によつて生じた空席の補充に關して決定を下すことができる。統治機構の變更又は全體としての日本國政府の變更は、極東委員會の付託條項に規定されている原則に從つてなされる。

最高司令官は、天皇又は他のいかなる日本國の統治權力者をも支持することを約束してはいない。政策は、日本國における現存の政治形態を支持することではない。降伏前における天皇制の形態を變更し、又政治形態の封建的且つ權威主義的性格を修正し又は除去し、且つ民主的日本國を確立する方向に向つてこれを變更することは、獎勵されるべきである。

3　連合國の利益の保護

一切の連合國及びその國民の利益、資産及び權利を保護することは、最高司令官の任務である。右保護が占領の目的及び政策の遂行と抵觸する場合には、關係國の政府は、外交手續によつて通知を受け、且つ、適當な調整の問題に

ついて意見を徴されなければならない。

4　政策の周知

日本國に對する戰爭に參加した國の國民、日本國民及び一般世界は、占領の目的及び政策並びにこれらのものの遂行の進ちよくについて絶えず充分に知らされなければならない。

第3部　政治關係

1　武裝解除及び非軍事化

武裝解除及び非軍事化は、軍事占領の最初の任務であつて、迅速に、且つ斷ことして遂行されなければならない。日本國民を欺き、これをして誤つて世界の征服に從事する役割を日本國民に至らしめた者及びこれを行うことに協力した者が果した役割を日本國民に徹底的に知らせるために、あらゆる努力がなされなければならない。

日本國は、陸軍、海軍、空軍、祕密警察組織又は民間航空又は憲兵隊を保有してはならないが、適當な非軍事警察隊を保有することはできる。日本國の地上、空中及び海上の兵力は、武裝解除され、且つ、解體されなければならず、又、日本帝國大本營、參謀本部(軍令部)及び一切の祕密警

察組織は、解消されなければならない。陸海軍の資材、陸海軍の艦船、陸海軍の施設、並びに陸海軍及び非軍用の航空機は、いずれの場所にあるを問わず、日本國軍隊の各降伏地帶の適當な連合國指揮官に引き渡されなければならず、且つ、既に採擇されたか又は採擇されることのある連合國の決定に從つて處分されなければならない。これらの規定の完全な履行を確實にするため、財產目錄が作成され、且つ、監査の權限が與えられなければならない。

日本帝國大本營及び參謀本部（軍令部）の高官、日本國政府の他の陸海軍の高官、超國家主義的及び軍國主義的團體の指導者並びに軍國主義及び侵略の他の重要な推進者は拘禁され、且つ、將來の處分のため留置される。軍國主義と好戰的國家主義の積極的推進者であつたことのある者は、公職からも、且つ、重要な私的責任を有する他のいかなる地位からも罷免され、且つ、排除される。超國家主義的又は軍國主義的な社會的、政治的、職業的及び商業的團體及び機關は、解散され、且つ、禁止される。

いかなる反民主主義的及び軍國主義的活動の復活も、特に日本國の職業的舊陸海軍將校、憲兵並びに解消された軍國に引き渡され、且つ、拘禁されなければならない。

2　戰爭犯罪人

連合國の捕虜又は他の國民を虐待した者を含む一切の戰爭犯罪人に對しては、嚴重な處罰が加えられなければならない。最高司令官又は連合國の適當な機關によつて戰爭犯罪人として告發された者は、逮捕され、裁判され、且つ、有罪の判決があつた場合には處罰されなければならない。他の連合國によつてその國民に對する犯罪を理由として要求された者は、最高司令官が裁判のためか、證人としてか又は他の理由で要求することのない場合には、右他の連

主義的、超國家主義的及び他の反民主主義的團體の舊會員によつて行われるものは、たとえ擬裝された形態においてでも、阻止されなければならない。

軍國主義的、超國家主義的及び反民主主義的の理論及び實踐は、準軍事訓練をも含んで敎育制度から除去されなければならない。職業的舊陸海軍將校及び反民主主義的理論及び實踐の推進者は、監督的及び敎育的地位から排除されるべきである。

3 経済諸施策への対応(昭和21年5月〜24年4月)

3 個人の自由及び民主主義的過程に対する欲求の奬励將來に對して保障されるべきである。又、超國家主義的、軍國主義的及び反民主主義的な團體及び運動は、宗敎といふ上衣のかげに隱れることを許されないといふことが日本人に對して明白にされなければならない。

日本國民は、民主主義國の歷史、制度、文化及び成果を熟知する機會を與えられ、且つ、熟知することを奬励されなければならない。

日本國民の間における民主主義的傾向の復活及び強化に對する障害は、除去されなければならない。

集會及び公開討論の權利を有する民主主義的政黨と勞働組合の結成とは、獎励されなければならない。但し、占領軍の安全の維持の必要に服さなければならない。

人種、國籍、信條又は政治的意見を理由として差別を設ける法律、命令及び規則は、廢止されなければならない。

この文書に概示されている目的及び政策と矛盾する法律、命令及び規則は廢止されるか、停止されるか又は必要に應じて修正されなければならないし、又、これらのものの施行を特にその任務とする機關は、廢止されるか又は適當に改組されなければならない。政治的理由によつて日本國官憲によつて不當に監禁されてゐる者は、釋放されなければならない。司法、法律及び警察制度は、この文書に揭げられてゐる政策に適合するやうできる限り速やかに改革されなければならないし、又、個人の自由及び人權を保護することは、一切の司法、法律及び警察官吏の任務でなければならない。

第4部　經濟關係

1　經濟上の非軍事化

日本國の軍事力の現存の經濟的基礎は、破壞されなければならないし、且つ、再興又は使用を目的とする何らかの軍隊又は軍事的設備の裝備、維持又は再興を許されてはならない。從つて、特に次の事項、すなわち、何らかの貨物の生產の即時停止及び將來における禁止、海軍艦船及び一切の種類の航空機を含む軍用器材の生產又は修繕のための施設に對する禁止の賦課、隠された又は擬裝した軍備の防止のための監察及び管理の制度の設定、戰爭のために再軍備する能力を日本國に與える諸產業又は生產部門の日本國か

らの除去並びに戰爭遂行力の發展に直接寄與する專門的の研究及び教育の禁止を含む計畫が實施せられる。平和的目的のための研究は、許されるが、戰爭の目的のためにはそれを使用することを防止するため、最高司令官によつて嚴重に監督されなければならない。日本國は、極東委員會によつて決定され、且つ、ポツダム宣言に反しない諸原則に從つて定められた經濟水準及び生活基準を保持することに制限されなければならない。

この計畫に從つて除去される日本國内の現存生産施設を賠償の目的のための外國への移轉、くず鐵化及び他の用途への轉換のうちのいづれかによつて究極的に處理することは、極東委員會の付託條項に從つて、明細表に基き決定される。右の決定あるまでの間は、外國への移轉のできるいかなる右施設も、緊急事態の場合を除いては、破壞されてはならない。

2 民主主義的勢力の促進

民主的な基礎において組織される產業及び農業における他の諸團體もそれ勞働團體は、獎勵されなければならない。民主的な基礎に

おいて組織される產業及び農業における他の諸團體もそれが日本國の民主化又は他の占領目的の促進に寄與する場合には、獎勵されなければならない。

所得並びに生産及び貿易の手段の所有の廣はん且つ公正な分配を確實にする目的をもつて、政策が定められなければならない。

日本國における民主的勢力を強化し、且つ、經濟活動が軍事的目的のために使用されることを防止するであらうと思はれる種類の經濟上の活動、組織及び指導に對しては、獎勵を與えなければならない。

右目的のため、最高司令官の政策は、次のとおりでなければならない。

い 過去の關係又は他の理由のために、日本國の經濟的努力を專ら平和的且つ民主的な目的に向つて指導することは信じられない個人を、經濟的分野における重要な地位に留めておくことを禁止すること。

ろ 産業及び金融の巨大な結合を解體して、管理及び所有權の基礎を擴張する組織によつてそれを漸進的に置き換えるための計畫を要求すること。

3 経済諸施策への対応(昭和21年5月～24年4月)

3 平和的經濟活動の再開

日本國の政策は、國民に經濟上の大破滅をもたらし、國民をして經濟的の困難と苦惱とに直面させた。日本國の苦境は、自己の行爲の直接の結果であつて、連合國は、損害修復の負擔を引き受けない。その損害は、日本國民が一切の軍事的目的を放棄し、勤勉且つ專心に平和的生活樣式に向つて努力する場合においてのみ、修復されることができる。日本國民は、物質的再建に着手し、且つ、自己の經濟上の活動及び制度の性格及び方向を根本的に改革することが必要である。ポツダム宣言に掲げられている保證につき、連合國は、右の事業を適當な期間内に完成することを妨げるような條件を課そうとする意思は有していない。

日本國は、飢餓、廣範圍の疾病及び激烈な肉體的苦痛を起させないで行われることができると最高司令官が判斷した程度まで占領軍の必要をみたすため貨物及びサーヴィスを提供することを期待される。

日本國官憲は、最高司令官の承認を條件として、次の目的に資するための計畫を維持し、發展させ且つ實施することを期待され、又必要な場合にはそうすることを指令される。

い 激烈な經濟上の苦痛を防止すること。
ろ 入手しうる物資の正當且つ公平な分配を確實にすること。
は 賠償引渡のための要求を滿たすこと。
に 供給しうる物資と連合國の國民及び從前日本國によつて占領されていた地域の人民に對する義務との雙方に照らして、極東委員會によつて作られた原則に從つて妥當と認められる供給を、日本の住民の必要のために行うこと。

4 賠償及び返還

賠償

日本國の行つた侵略行爲に對し、又、日本國の連合國に對し生ぜしめた損害の公平な賠償を目的として、又、戰爭遂行のための日本國の再軍備に導くことのできる産業における日本國の潛在的戰爭能力の破壞となるように、賠償は、現存の日本國の資本設備及び施設若しくは將來生産されることのある日本國の貨物であつて、極東委員會の掲げた方針に基き又は右委員會の付託條項に從つてこ

目的のために利用されるべきものの引渡によつて、日本國から取り立てられなければならない。右賠償は、日本國の非軍事化の計畫の完遂を危うくせず、又占領費の支辨及び國民の最低生活水準の維持を妨げることのないような形態のものでなければならない。日本國からの賠償總額中における個々の國の配分は、日本國の侵略の準備及び遂行の結果として、各請求國の被つた物的及び人的破壞及び損害の範圍を充分に考慮し、又、日本國の侵略に對する各國の抵抗の程度及び期間を含んで、日本國の敗北への各國の寄與をも充分に考慮して廣い政治的基礎の上で決定されなければならない。

返還

奪い取られたか、强迫によつて引き渡されたか又は無償値の通貨で支拂われた一切の識別しうる財産の完全且つ速やかな返還が要求される。

5　財政、通貨及び金融に關する政策

日本國官憲は、國內の財政、通貨及び信用に關する政策の管理及び指導について引き續き責任を有するが、この責任は、最高司令官の承認及び審査竝びに必要な場合には、

右司令官の指示を受けなければならない。

6　國際的の貿易關係及び金融關係

世界の貿易への日本國の究極の參加は、許される。占領期間中、適當な管理の下に、且つ日本國に對する戰爭に參加した國の國民の優先的な要求を留保し、日本國は、國が平和的用途に供するために必要とすることのある原料その他の貨物を外國から買い入れることを許される。日本國は、又承認された輸入に對して支拂をするため、適當な管理の下において、貨物を輸出することを許される。賠償勘定において又は返還として積み出されるよう指示されたもの以外の輸出は、見返りとして必要な輸入品を提供することに同意するか、又は輸入品の買入に使用することのできる外國爲替で右輸出品に對し支拂をすることに同意する仕向國に對してのみ、これをすることができる。日本國の輸出品の賣得金は、國民の最低生活水準を確保した後、占領に必要な非軍事的輸入であつて、降伏以來すでに行われていたものの費用に對し支拂をするためにこれを使用することができる。

統制は、一切の貨物の輸入及び輸出竝びに外國爲替及び

3 経済諸施策への対応(昭和21年5月～24年4月)

金融取引に對し維持されなければならない。極東委員會は、日本國からの輸出及び日本國への輸入を規律する政策及び原則を定めなければならない。極東委員會は、右管理の實施に當つて執らなければならない政策を定める。

7 日本國の在外資産

この文書中の賠償に關する條項及び賠償の問題に關して述べられたところは、在外資産問題に關する諸政府の見解を害するものではない。

8 日本國內における外國企業のための機會均等

いづれの連合國の商社も、すべて、日本國の海外貿易及び商業において、日本國內においては、連合國の一切の國民に對し均等の待遇が與えられなければならない。

9 皇室財産

皇室財産は、占領目的の遂行のために必要ないかなる措置からも免除されてはならない。

編 注 本文書は、昭和二十四年一月、外務省特別資料部作成「日本占領及び管理重要文書集」第一卷より抜粹。

190 昭和22年7月11日

対日平和条約のための会議に関する米国政府提案

United States Government's Proposal concerning a Conference for Japanese Peace Treaty

July 11, 1947

John H. Hilldring, Assistant Secretary of State for occupied areas, and John Carter Vincent, Director of the Office of Far Eastern Affairs, met on July 11 with Embassy representatives of the United Kingdom, Union of Soviet Socialist Republics, China, the Philippines, India, Australia, New Zealand, France, the Netherlands, and Canada to lay before them proposals in regard to a conference on a Japanese peace treaty.

The representatives were informed that the United States Government desires to hold a conference to discuss a peace treaty for Japan as soon as practicable. The conference would be composed of representatives of the eleven states members of the Far Eastern Commission, but the conference would be outside the Far

Eastern Commission. Such an eleven-power conference is advocated because it would provide a broad representative basis of participation to include all of those nations with a primary interest in Japan. It is the view of the United States Government that other states at war with Japan should be given an opportunity to present their views while the treaty is being drafted and that after the draft has reached a sufficiently advanced stage it should be considered by a general conference of all the states at war with Japan.

A tentative date of August 19, 1947, was suggested to the Embassy representatives for convening a conference. In view of the various commitments of the Foreign Ministers of the Governments concerned, it does not appear practicable to the Government of the United States to propose that such a conference be on the Foreign Minister level; therefore it is envisaged that the conference would initially be composed of the deputies and experts. The Government of the United States should be pleased to be host for such a conference if desired by other interested powers.

The Embassy representatives were informed of the United States desire to obtain the views of the other concerned governments on the various questions relating to the drafting of a peace treaty for Japan and were invited to consult to discuss the matter further after they had had an opportunity to consult with their respective governments.

編注　本文書は、昭和二十四年三月、外務省特別資料部作成「日本占領及び管理重要文書集」第二巻より抜粋。

191　昭和22年7月24日　極東委員会決定

対日貿易十六原則に関する極東委員会政策決定

Interim Import-Export Policies for Japan

〔FEC Policy Decision, July 24, 1947〕

I. *Long-range Policy Objectives*

1. As soon as possible participation by private individuals and corporations in Japanese foreign trade will be authorized. The policies set forth in this statement, therefore, should be regarded as applying to a fairly short period.

II. *Interim Controls*

3　経済諸施策への対応（昭和21年5月～24年4月）

2. All imports to and exports from Japan will take place exclusively under the direct control of the Supreme Commander for the Allied Powers acting in accordance with the policies formulated by the Far Eastern Commission or policies established in accordance with its terms or reference. For the present no government or individual will have contact with the Japanese Government or Japanese individuals except as authorized by the Supreme Commander.

3. The Japanese Government subject to the supervision of the Supreme Commander will be responsible for:

   a. Internal operations necessary to inspection, purchase, collection, and storage of goods for export, and the delivery of these goods to designated ports;

   b. Custody, sale and distribution of imported goods within Japan;

   c. Provision of all funds and conduct of internal financing arrangements necessary to these operations.

4. External purchases and sales will be on a government-to-government basis. The Japanese Government or its agent will make all sales and purchases and will guarantee title. Transactions should be carried out on behalf of the other governments by their trade representatives in Japan with the Japanese Government or its agents and should conform to general conditions determined by the Supreme Commander for the Allied Powers or alternatively, in respect of particular transactions to special conditions agreed with him. The purchaser from or seller to Japan will be a government agency or, if a non government firm, the transaction must be arranged for by an official trade representative who will take responsibility for the transaction.

5. The provisions of this section should not be taken to prevent the resumption of private trade.

III. *Development of an Import-Export Program*

6. The Supreme Commander for the Allied Powers will be responsible for ascertaining the types and amounts of goods available for export, and for recommending the types and amounts of goods to be imported. The trade program developed and recommended by the Supreme Commander will be reviewed by the U.S. Government, and forwarded to the Far Eastern Commission and

the Inter-Allied Trade Board for consideration in accordance with their respective terms of reference. The trade program when put into effect will contain only such items the inclusion of which are not contrary to any decision of the Far Eastern Commission.

7. The Supreme Commander will be notified by the United States Government, after consultation with the Inter-Allied Trade Board, of those export items for the disposal of which he will be directly responsible. In dealing with these he will be guided by the policies formulated by the Far Eastern Commission, or policies established in accordance with its terms of reference, relating to the destinations of exports and the terms of their sale. In the remaining cases the United States Government, after consultation with the Inter-Allied Trade Board, will reserve to itself the determination of allocations which will be notified to the Supreme Commander in due course. The disposition of exports will be for currencies which are acceptable in accordance with policies established in accordance with the terms of reference of the Far Eastern Commission or in exchange for imports necessary for Japan.

8. The Supreme Commander should make available to the Far Eastern Commission monthly returns showing completed imports and exports, and quarterly returns showing planned imports and exports and the state of Japan's balance of payments classified according to currencies.

IV. *Imports*

9. For the purposes of this paper imports are divided into the following three categories:

   a. Imports required to prevent such widespread disease and unrest as would endanger the occupying forces;

   b. Imports required to accomplish the objectives of the occupation;

   c. Other imports requested by the Japanese Government.

10. For the time being import programs under categories 9 a and b are authorized subject to the availability of items and funds and such other limitations as may be operative. Category 9 c imports are not authorized until it is possible to appraise more accurately than can be done at present such factors as the comparative need of the Japanese economy for such imports, the foreign trade

3　経済諸施策への対応(昭和21年5月～24年4月)

position of Japan, the amount of proceeds of exports required to pay for imports under a and b above, and other costs of the occupation to be paid for by export surpluses.

11. The commodity requirements for prevention of disease and unrest and to accomplish the objectives of the occupation will be met to the maximum extent by indigenous resources and to the minimum extent by imports.

V. *Exports*

12. For the present no fixed capital goods or equipment, except that which results from current production, should be exported to pay for imports.

13. Export industries should not be developed when the character of such industries would contribute significantly to the maintenance or development of Japan's war-making potential or if they would promote dependence of other countries on Japan for strategic products. Exports of textiles and other goods which are in world short supply, especially in Asiatic countries, should be stimulated to the maximum practicable extent.

14. The proceeds of export resulting from current production inclusive of current production of gold or other precious metals will be used in the first instance to pay for both past and current imports under categories 9 a and b.

15. The proceeds of exports of stocks of materials not subject to restitution in accordance with the Far Eastern Commission policy shall also be used in the first instance to pay for imports.

16. Stocks of gold, silver, cultural objects and other precious metals, precious stones and jewels should be disposed of as follows:

a. Cultural objects, produced prior to September 1, 1945, should not be exported.

b. Stocks of gold, silver, precious metals looted from occupied areas should be treated in accordance with Far Eastern Commission policy and pending establishment of a new restitution policy, items known to have been looted or probably looted, should not be exported from Japan.

c. Stocks of gold, silver, other precious metals, precious stones and jewels of clearly established Japanese ownership ultimately should be disposed of as reparations. In the meantime,

575

192

旧日本海軍艦艇の破壊に関する再指令

昭和22年8月12日　連合国最高司令官総司令部より　日本政府宛

編注　本文書は、昭和二十四年十二月、外務省特別資料課作成「日本占領及び管理重要文書集」第四巻より抜粋。

AG 388.3 (12 Aug 47) GD

GENERAL HEADQUARTERS
SUPREME COMMANDER FOR THE ALLIED POWERS
APO 500
12 August 1947

SCAPIN 1761

MEMORANDUM FOR: JAPANESE GOVERNMENT

THROUGH: Central Liaison Office, Tokyo

SUBJECT: Destruction of Former Japanese Naval Vessels.

1. Reference is made to:

   a. Memorandum, Supreme Commander for the Allied Powers, file AG 045.93 (30 Apr 46) GD (SCAPIN 910) subject: "Destruction of Former Japanese Naval Vessels".

   b. Memorandum, Supreme Commander for the Allied Powers, File AG 386.3 (6 Jun 46) GD (SCAPIN 1002), subject: "Destruction of Former Japanese Naval Vessels".

2. Supplementing the above memoranda, certain additional ships will be released from time to time for destruction by scrapping or by other method approved by the Supreme Commander for the Allied Powers.

3. Vessels released for scrapping will be designated by Commander Naval Activities, Japan. Destruction in each case will be accomplished within six (6) months of release to the Japanese Government, unless otherwise specified by Commander Naval

values of such Japanese assets should be preserved, but such assets themselves may be used as a means of acquiring foreign exchange to aid in financing production programs designed to contribute to the revival of productivity in a Japanese peace economy. In case of export of the above-mentioned assets equal opportunity to acquire these assets in return for acceptable currency should be granted to all member countries of the Far Eastern Commission.

3　経済諸施策への対応(昭和21年5月～24年4月)

Activities, Japan.

4. The provisions of paragraph 3 of reference 1a above will be complied with by the Japanese Government in carrying out the directive.

5. When specified by Commander Naval Activities, Japan, detailed accounting shall be kept of the scrapping operation, as follows:

　a. Costs of scrapping.

　b. Tonnage of various grades of ferrous scrap recovered.

　c. Weights of nonferrous scrap recovered. (Brass, Bronze, Copper, Lead).

　d. Proceeds from the sale of scrap, and value of unsold portion.

　e. Proceeds from the sale of equipment and machinery, and value of any unsold equipment and machinery.

Within sixty days of completion of scrapping of each vessel specified, detailed records containing the above listed information will be furnished to Commander Naval Activities, Japan.

FOR THE SUPREME COMMANDER:

R. M. LEVY
Colonel, AGD
Adjutant General

国際航空郵便の許可につき指令

昭和22年8月26日　連合国最高司令官総司令部より　日本政府宛

SUPREME COMMANDER FOR THE ALLIED POWERS
GENERAL HEADQUARTERS
APO 500

26 August 1947

AG 311.1 (26 Aug 47) CCS
(SCAPIN-1768)

MEMORANDUM FOR: JAPANESE GOVERNMENT
THROUGH: Central Liaison Office, Tokyo
SUBJECT: International Mail Service

1. <u>Rescissions</u>. The following Memorandums for the Japanese Government are rescinded effective 28 August 1947:

a. SCAPIN 1177, file AG 311.1 (5 Sept. 46) CCS, dated 5 September 1946, subject: Resumption of International Postal Service between Japan and all other Countries except Germany.

b. SCAPIN 1432, file AG 311.1 (2 Jan 47) CCS, dated 2 January 1947, subject: Expansion of International Postal Service between Japan and All Other Countries.

2. <u>Effective Date</u>. Effective 28 August 1947 International Postal Service between Japan and all other countries will operate in accordance with instructions embodied herein.

3. <u>Letters and Postal Cards</u>. Letters and Postal Cards containing personal and family messages; and business, financial, commercial, and transactional correspondence are mailable to and from Japan, subject to the following prohibitions:

    a. Messages which transfer currency, checks, drafts, payment orders, or other credit or financial instruments.

    b. Messages which relate to the conversion, transfer, or disguising of any Japanese external assets by powers of attorney, proxies, instructions, or other means intended to defeat SCAP regulations regarding foreign exchange or the conversion of external assets.

    c. Messages which grant or transfer translation, reproduction, performance or other rights concerning books, articles, plays, music, motion pictures, or other media of information and expression, and messages relating in any way to patents or copyrights except for description and explanation of the authorized channels and procedures for handling such matters and except for acknowledgment of rights arranged through the authorized channels.

4. <u>Commercial Papers</u>. Commercial Papers as defined by the Universal Postal Union Standards and Limitations are mailable to and from Japan, with the following exceptions:

    a. Scores or sheets of music in manuscript.

    b. Manuscripts of works or newspapers sent separately.

    c. All papers of legal procedure.

    d. Documents of all kinds drawn up by Ministerial officers.

5. <u>Prints</u>. The mailing of Prints, as defined by the Univer-

3　経済諸施策への対応(昭和 21 年 5 月～24 年 4 月)

sal Postal Union Standards and Limitations, is restricted to the following specific categories:

a. Photographs - (To and from Japan)
b. Drawings - (To and from Japan)
c. Plans - (To and from Japan)
d. Maps - (To and from Japan)
e. Patterns - (To and from Japan)
f. Catalogues - (To and from Japan)
g. Scientific and professional publications as may be approved by the Supreme Commander for the Allied Powers - (From Japan only)

6. Samples and Small Packets. These classifications of mail matter, as defined by the Universal Postal Union Convention, are mailable to and from Japan.

7. Air Mail. a. Letters and postal cards within weight limits prescribed by Universal Postal Union Regulations and Limitations, but subject to all restrictions set out herein covering ordinary mail, are mailable to and from Japan.

b. Transportation of International air mail both to and from Japan will be by Commercial Carriers only. Air mail destined to Japan will be dispatched in pouches labeled to Tokyo only.

8. Parcel Post. a. Parcel Post Service will be to Japan only. Parcels will be limited to twenty-two pounds in weight, and contents will be restricted to relief items such as non-perishable foods, mailable medicines in non-commercial quantities, soap, clothing and other relief items, in quantities which reasonably can be used by the addressee and/or his immediate family. The following specific limitations apply to each parcel:

(1) Only one of the following tobacco items can be included in a single parcel: Cigarettes - not more than 200 pieces; cigars - not more than 50 pieces; pipe tobacco - not more than one-half pound.

(2) Not more than 200 saccharine tablets in a single parcel.

b. Gift articles, as distinguished from relief items, such as watches, fountain pens, etc., will not be permitted entry.

c. Only one relief parcel per week may be mailed by any single sender to any one addressee.

579

d. Relief parcels which are undeliverable will not be returned to senders but will be turned over to designated relief agencies for disposition.

e. Excessive quantities of permitted items; that is, quantities in excess of the reasonable needs of the addressee and/or his immediate family, will be extracted by the Japanese Customs Service and delivered to the appropriate agency of the Eighth Army for distribution to recognized relief agencies.

9. <u>Censorship or Customs Inspection.</u> Incoming and outgoing International mails will be made available for censorship or customs inspection in accordance with instructions issued by the Supreme Commander for the Allied Powers.

10. <u>Governing Regulations.</u> a. The regular-mail service, embracing letters, postal cards, commercial papers, prints, samples and small packets, as authorized, will be governed by the provisions of the Universal Postal Union Convention.

b. Parcel post service, as authorized, will be operated by the Japanese Government under the terms of the Universal Postal Union Parcel Post Agreement, or bilateral or other agreements in effect between Japan and the respective countries at the time service was suspended.

c. The maintenance of records under the conditions of the Universal Postal Union Convention and the terms of the various bilateral parcel post agreements, and the preparation of the necessary accounts for settlement, will be the responsibility of the Japanese Government.

d. Amounts due Japan from other countries in the operation of the International Postal Service will be deposited in the United States Treasury Trust Fund Account, "Deposits, Proceeds of Remittances to and Exports from Occupied Areas," Symbol 218905.1 Japan. Payments due from Japan on International postal service operation will be made from that trust fund account upon recommendation of the Supreme Commander for the Allied Powers.

e. Statements of accounts showing amounts due Japan will be prepared under the direction of the Ministry of Communications and certified to the Supreme Commander for the Allied Powers.

f. International surface mail will be dispatched from Japan on vessels of Japanese or any other registration except German.

g. Articles of International mail addressed in Japanese, Korean, or Chinese characters must have an interlined address written in Roman characters if such articles are addressed for delivery in countries other than Korea, China, and the Ryukyu Islands.

11. Operational Correspondence. a. Form notices, bulletins of verification, inquiries, quarterly statements of terminal credits, and all other correspondence necessary in the operation of the International postal service as required by the Universal Postal Union Convention and bilateral parcel post agreements will be prepared by the Japanese Ministry of Communications and delivered unsealed to the Civil Communications Section, General Headquarters, Supreme Commander for the Allied Powers for examination, proper indorsement, and transmission. Indorsements on such communications will read "Authorized by SCAP for transmission through International mail channels."

b. Direct communication between the Civil Communications Section and other staff sections of General Headquarters, Supreme Commander for the Allied Powers and the Ministry of Communications is authorized concerning all matters within the scope of this memorandum.

FOR THE SUPREME COMMANDER:

R. G. Hersey
for R. M. LEVY
Colonel, AGD
Adjutant General

194

昭和22年9月16日　マッカーサー連合国最高司令官より
片山(哲)内閣総理大臣宛

警察制度改革および法務庁設置について

General of the Army Douglas MacArthur's Letter to the Japanese Prime Minister concerning the Reorganization of the Japanese Police System

Tokyo, Japan.
September 16, 1947.

Dear Mr. Prime Minister:

I have given careful consideration to your letter of September 3rd and to the plan for the reorganization of the police system submitted therewith. I fully understand your difficulty in reaching an acceptable compromise between the two divergent schools of thought of which you speak—a compromise which will prove adequately effective to meet the requisites for the preservation of law and order within Japan, and yet at the same time not impinge upon the ideal of human liberty to which the people of Japan are now committed, nor upon that fundamental principle indispensable to a democratic society so aptly stated in the Preamble of the Constitution of Japan, "Government is a sacred trust of the people, the authority for which is derived from the people, and the benefits of which are enjoyed by the people."

I am in full accord with the proposition that the realities of the situation require the maintenance of a national rural police unit to maintain law and order in the rural areas and available to the National Government to meet emergency conditions with which police forces available to the several local governments may be unable adequately to cope, and your suggested increase in the overall authorized police strength to 125,000 men, to provide for such a national rural police meets with my full approval. I am not in accord, however, with the idea of, nor the necessity for, delaying the decentralization of the police power now existing, as I feel that the preservation of that power in its present centralized form is wholly incompatible with the spirit and intent of the new Constitution and inimical to democratic growth.

It has been a dominant characteristic of modern totalitarian dictatorships, as it was in Japan's feudalistic past, to establish and maintain a strongly centralized police bureaucracy headed by a chief executive officer beyond the reach of popular control. Indeed, the strongest weapon of the military clique in Japan in the decade prior to the war was the absolute authority exercised by the national government over the thought police and the Kempei Tai, extending down to prefectural levels of government. Through these media, the military were enabled to spread a network of political espionage, suppress freedom of speech, of assembly, and even of thought, and by means of tyrannical oppression to degrade

582

the dignity of the individual. Japan was thus in the fullest sense a police state.

It is in recognition of this condition that the police system must be so reorganized as to provide what you so clearly describe in your letter as a "fundamental remedy of the misuse of the police by the state power as in the past." In the achievement of this objective, the potentiality of a police state inherent in centralized control must scrupulously be avoided. It should never again be possible for anti-democratic elements, either of the extreme right or the extreme left, to enmesh the freedom of the people in a web of police terrorism.

This basic objective can best be accomplished by the thorough decentralization of the police system in accordance with the principle of local autonomy embodied in the Constitution. Each city and town should be responsible for the preservation of law and order within its boundaries through its own local police system independent of the central government and headed by a police chief to be appointed and removable by a commission composed of three civilian members appointed by the mayor of the city or town with the consent of the local assembly and holding office for a fixed term of years. At the prefectural level there should also be a corresponding commission similarly appointed which will exercise operational control over the national rural police operating within the boundaries of that prefecture, reserving to the national government administrative authority over such national rural police wherever stationed.

Such a reformation of the Japanese police system would be in consonance with the general pattern of the reorganization of the Japanese governmental structure, integrating police officials and services as agencies of the people at the appropriate levels of government. Action toward such end should proceed immediately upon enactment of the appropriate statute.

The national government should allocate the necessary funds until such time as local financing is possible. So long as it is necessary for the national government to make allocations of funds, the strength of the police in the various localities should remain fixed at the present number, but after provisions have been made for the localities to assume the financial burden, the responsibility for determining the necessary numbers within their respective borders should belong to the cities and towns, in accordance with local requirements.

The necessary legislation should, of course, be enacted at the present session of the Diet. If vigorously prosecuted, I believe that completion of the plan may be accomplished within a period of ninety days thereafter.

As to an appropriate organization on the national level, I believe that there should be created directly under the authority of the Cabinet a Public Safety Commission composed of five members who have not been career officials, either in the police or the civil service. Such commission should be appointed by the Prime Minister, with the consent of the Diet, and should hold office for a fixed term of years.

To prevent the resurgence in disguised form of a centrally controlled national police network no channel of command should exist between the national rural police unit and the local police forces, but technical channels of communication should, of course, be permitted in the interest of overall efficiency and to facilitate a relationship of mutual assistance, liaison and coordination. The intervention by the national government in control over prefectural or local police affairs should temporarily be provided for, however, in the event of a national emergency when, upon the recommendation of the National Public Safety Commission, the Prime Minister might assume operational control over prefectural units of the national rural police force, subject to ratification by the Diet within twenty days. In this way the authority of the prefectural governor may be protected against arbitrary police interference by the national government, at the same time affording adequate safeguard for the national interest.

In the past, one of the ill-conceived aspects of the Japanese police system was the exercise by police officials of numerous administrative functions not related to the task of investigation and apprehension of criminals or the preservation of public order. All such functions should be exercised by non-police representatives of the particular ministry having responsibility for such matters, and wherever proper should be decentralized to local public entities in accordance with the provisions of the Constitution confer-

3 経済諸施策への対応（昭和21年5月～24年4月）

ring upon such entities "the right to manage their property, affairs and administration."

Closely related to the law enforcement process is, as you have specifically pointed out in your letter, the subject of reform in the judicial administrative system. Under the Constitution of Japan, the Supreme Court is now vested with the administration of judicial affairs and the rule-making power. With the establishment of an independent judiciary the Ministry of Justice no longer is responsible for the determination of rules of procedure and of practice, the internal discipline of the courts, or other attributes of the judicial process. Moreover, with the diminution of the role of the procurators in the administration of justice and their subordination to the rule-making power of the Supreme Court, the basic attributes of the procuratorial system under the Ministry of Justice have been radically revised.

On the other hand, to the Cabinet, as the executive branch of the government, is expressly delegated the responsibility for executing the provisions of the Constitution and of the laws enacted by the National Diet, as well as for determining questions of amnesty, commutation of punishment, and restoration of rights. To reflect adequately this constitutional separation of powers, it would seem desirable that the Ministry of Justice, within which authority over adjudicative functions has been traditionally intermingled with executive power, be replaced by an Attorney General, sitting in the Cabinet as a Minister of State and serving as the chief legal adviser to the executive branch of the government.

To administer the laws effectively requires the closest coordination between police officials charged with the apprehension of offenders against the national laws, and public attorneys charged with the prosecution thereof. The establishment of an Attorney General's Office with the responsibility of conducting all litigation, criminal and civil, in which the government has a direct interest, and of furnishing all legal advice to the Prime Minister and other Ministers of State in the discharge of their duties, would I believe provide a mechanism for such close coordination, facilitate the faithful execution of the laws, and support the independence of the judiciary as the bulwark of the liberties of the people. Consistent with this concept of an Attorney General, the present Legislative Bureau of the Cabinet can be dispensed with in the interest of governmental efficiency and economy.

Within the framework of the plan outlined in your letter, modified in the manner I have indicated, I feel confident that a law enforcement system may be evolved in Japan which will satisfy all requirements of public safety, which will provide for the definitive separation of the administrative from the judicial process, and which at the same time will comply meticulously with the underlying principles of the Constitution. In this connection it should be borne in mind that, in the final analysis, police power in the preservation of law and order in a democratic society does not attain its maximum strength through oppressive controls imposed upon the people from above, but rather does it find infinitely greater strength in the relationship of a servant of, and answerable directly to, the people. Thereby, and thereby alone, may it encourage respect for the people's laws through confidence and paternalistic pride in the police as the law enforcement agency of the people themselves.

I am hopeful that the legislation necessary to give effect to these programs in the reorganization of government can be completed in time for consideration at the current session of the National Diet. To such end do not hesitate to call upon this headquarters for any assistance which you believe would be helpful.

Sincerely yours,

(Sgd.) Douglas MacArthur

DOUGLAS MacARTHUR.

The Prime Minister,
Tokyo, Japan.

編注　本文書は、昭和二十四年三月、外務省特別資料部作成「日本占領及び管理重要文書集」第二巻より抜粋。本文書の別添は省略されている。

195　外国人への課税承認に関する指令

昭和22年11月29日　連合国最高司令官総司令部より日本政府宛

GENERAL HEADQUARTERS
SUPREME COMMANDER FOR THE ALLIED POWERS

3 経済諸施策への対応（昭和21年5月～24年4月）

AG 012.2 (29 Nov 47) ESS/FI
SCAPIN 4938-A

MEMORANDUM FOR: JAPANESE GOVERNMENT
THROUGH: Central Liaison Office, Tokyo
SUBJECT: Applicability of Taxes to Non-Japanese Nationals

1. SCAPIN 1826-A, dated 25 July 1946, subject: "Applicability of Ordinary Taxes to Non-Japanese Nationals" is hereby rescinded.

2. There is no objection to the applicability of local and national taxation to non-Japanese nationals except as specified in paragraph 3 below, provided that such taxes are not discriminatory against non-Japanese nationals. No tax, primarily designed to meet reparations or other charges falling upon the Japanese Government as a result of the war shall be imposed by the Japanese Government upon United Nations nationals or their properties.

3. No tax will be imposed by the Japanese Government on the official salaries of military personnel, of civilians attached to the occupation forces, and of accredited personnel of foreign diplomatic missions, delegations, and other official representation attached to the Supreme Commander for the Allied Powers. No tax based upon or measured by income lawfully received in non-yen currencies will be imposed by the Japanese Government. This shall not however be construed to prohibit the taxation of SCAP employees or SCAP licensee employees paid in yen currencies.

4. Direct communication between the Ministry of Finance and interested staff sections of this Headquarters is authorized to implement the provisions of this memorandum.

FOR THE SUPREME COMMANDER:

C. Z. SHUGART,
Colonel, AGD,
Asst. Adj. General.

APO 500
29 November 1947

〰〰〰〰〰

196 昭和23年1月1日　連合国最高司令官総司令部発表

マッカーサー司令官の年頭メッセージ

General of the Army Douglas MacArthur's New Year Message

January 1, 1948

TO THE PEOPLE OF JAPAN:

The design of a remodeled and reconstructed Japan is nearing completion. The pattern has been etched, the path has been laid. The development now lies largely in your own hands. Success or failure will depend upon your ability to practise the simple yet transcendental principles which modern civilization demands.

No occupation, however benevolent and beneficial, can substitute for the spiritual uplift which alone can lead to an invincible determination to build a future based upon the immutable concepts of human freedom — a social status under which full consciousness of individual responsibility must ever remain the keystone to the arch of success and progress.

Individual hardship is inevitable. Your economy, due to the disastrous war decisions of your past leaders, is now impoverished. This can only be relieved by employment to the maximum of the energies of your people, by wisdom and determination on the part of your leaders, and by the restoration of peace with its removal of existing limitations upon international trade. So long as your needs continue to be greater than your productive capacity, controls upon your internal economy will be essential lest the weaker segments of your population perish. Such controls must, however, only be temporary and subject to ultimate removal in favor of free enterprise.

Economically, allied policy has required the breaking up of that system which in past has permitted the major part of the commerce and industry and natural resources of your country to be owned and controlled by a minority of feudal families and exploited for their exclusive benefit. The world has probably never seen a counterpart to so abnormal an economic system. It permitted exploitation of the many for the sole benefit of the few. The integration of these few with government was complete and their influence upon governmental policies inordinate, and set the course which ultimately led to war and destruction. It was indeed so complete a monopoly as to be in effect a form of socialism in private hands. Only through its dissolution could the way be cleared for the emergence of an economy conducive to the well-being of all the people — an economy embodying the principle of

588

3 経済諸施策への対応(昭和 21 年 5 月～24 年 4 月)

private capitalism, based upon free competitive enterprise — an economy which long experience has demonstrated alone provides the maximum incentive to the development of those fundamental requirements to human progress — individual initiative and individual energy.

Politically, progress toward reform has been equally encouraging. Your new constitution is now in full effect, and there is increasing evidence of a growing understanding of the great human ideals which it is designed to serve. Implementing laws have reoriented the entire fabric of your way of life to give emphasis to the increased responsibility, dignity and opportunity which the individual now holds and enjoys. Government has ceased to be totalitarian and has become representative, with its functions decentralized to permit and encourage a maximum of individual thought and initiative and judgement in the management of community affairs. Control of every political segment has been shifted to permit the selection of a new leadership of your free choice capable of advancing democratic growth.

Socially, many of the shackles which traditionally have restricted individual thought and action have been severed and action has been taken to render the exercise of police power a matter for individual and community, rather than national, responsibility. The judicial system has been freed from executive and legislative controls, and laws have been enacted to temper inordinate bureaucratic power by requiring all public officials to justify the trust of public responsibility and answer for their acts directly to the people.

Every Japanese citizen can now for the first time do what he wants, and go where he wants, and say what he wants, within the liberal laws of his land. This means that you can select your own work, and when you have completed it you can choose your own method of relaxation and enjoyment, and on your day of rest you can worship as you please, and always you can criticize and express your views on the actions of your Government. This is liberty. Yet inherent in it are its obligations to act with decorum and self-restraint, and become acutely conscious of the responsibilities which a free society imposes upon its every segment.

The future therefore lies in your hands. If you remain true

197 昭和23年1月6日 米国の対日政策に関するロイヤル米国陸軍長官の演説

編 注　本文書は、昭和二十四年三月、外務省特別資料部作成「日本占領及び管理重要文書集」第二巻より抜粋。

付 記　昭和二十三年一月十八日付米国の対日政策に関するマッカーサー司令官のロイヤル長官へのメッセージ

Speech by Mr. Kenneth C. Royall, Secretary of the Army, on the United States Policy for Japan

Made in San Francisco, January 6, 1948

DOUGLAS MacARTHUR

To many American citizens —including myself —the most surprising development —and one of the most disappointing aspects of our victory over Germany and Japan has been the responsibility and cost which have been placed upon us in the matter of occupation. There were few who originally recognized the extent of this burden. And today every citizen of our country is justified in asking the "what" and the "why" of our occupation policies.

On this occasion I will speak specifically of Japan. Immediately after the surrender, the objectives of our policy were stated to be, first, "To insure that Japan will not again become a menace to the peace and security of the world," and, second, "to bring about the earliest possible establishment of a democratic and peaceful government which will carry out its international responsibilities, respect the rights of other states, and support the objectives of the United Nations."

to the great spiritual revolution which you have undergone, your nation will emerge and go on —if you accept only its benefits without its obligations, it will wither and go under. The line of demarcation is a simple one, understandable to all men —the line between those things which are right and those things which are wrong. The way is long and hard and beset with difficulties and dangers, but it is my hope and belief and prayer [on] this New Year's Day that you will not falter.

3 経済諸施策への対応(昭和21年5月〜24年4月)

The underlying idea was the prevention of future Japanese aggression —direct prevention by disarmament and indirect prevention by creating a type of government unlikely to develop again the spirit of aggressive war. The real well-being of Japan —or her strength as a nation —was decidedly a secondary consideration —secondary to protection of ourselves against Japan, and secondary to payment of reparations to the victorious Allies for the damages inflicted upon them.

This attitude is clearly shown by the emphasis in the original directive, which stated in part: "Japan shall be permitted" (not encouraged but permitted) "to maintain such industries as will sustain her economy and permit the exaction of reparations…but not…enable her to rearm…Access to, as distinguished from control of, raw materials shall be permitted. Eventual Japanese participation in world trade…shall be permitted."

It is clearly understandable —and it was fully in accord with the then feelings and opinions of our people —that in 1945 the main purpose of occupation should be protection against an enemy which had viciously attacked us and which had committed brutal atrocities against our troops and our private citizens.

Since then new conditions have arisen —in world politics and economics, in problems of national defense, and in humanitarian considerations. These changes must now be fully taken into account in determining our future course, but it should be remembered that these developments arose in large part after the original policies were set.

These original policies were promptly carried out. Within a few months after the end of hostilities, all Japanese tactical units had been dissolved and all implements of war destroyed or insulated. The top Japanese military organizations, as well as the infamous secret and terroristic societies, were abolished. Those who formulated the Japanese policies of conquest and aggression were removed from important political and economic positions.

War-making industries were marked for removal and reparation. This included arsenals, private munitions plants, aircraft factories, military research laboratories, synthetic rubber and oil plants, shipbuilding installations, and certain chemical, machine tool, precision bearing, thermo-electric, and metal factories, non-ferrous and others. Commitments were made to other nations for payment of reparations with those plants.

Other steps followed, including those leading to the dissolution of concentrations of property ownership and economic power. At the end of the war — and for a long period before the war — land ownership had been in the hands of a comparatively small part of the population. The system was analogous to the feudal system of past centuries, and in Japan the "land barons" used their power to encourage war.

In the business field, the Zaibatsu, or "money cliques," dominated completely and ruthlessly the Japanese economy — through holding companies and monopolies. A dozen families controlled over 75% of the country's commerce, industry and finance.

The influence over the Japanese Government of these and other monopolies was almost unbounded, and they were linked inseparably with the militarists. This joint group over a course of years — and particularly in the year and a half before Pearl Harbor — encouraged Japan toward war and destruction.

Steps were taken to break both types of concentrations. Under a directive issued by the Supreme Allied Commander, the Japanese Diet enacted in the Fall of 1946 a Land Reform Law under which, through local land commissions, the $5\frac{1}{2}$ million Japanese farm families could acquire land from the present owners at a reasonable price and pay for it over a period of years. This program will be completed by the end of 1948. Just as in America the small land-owner is symbolically and factually democracy in practice, so we expect that in time the strength of Japanese democracy will find roots in similar soil.

Action against the Zaibatsu has proceeded vigorously, and its control has now been virtually abolished. Sixty-seven holding companies, with 4,000 subsidiaries and affiliates, have been marked for liquidation. The two largest holding companies —Mitsubishi and Mitsui —have been closed. Others of the larger ones have been almost wholly liquidated.

The Japanese Government has been directed to prepare legislation prohibiting international cartels. Stringent anti-trust and deconcentration legislation has been prepared and passed in

3　経済諸施策への対応（昭和21年5月〜24年4月）

part. A Holding Company Liquidation Commission has been established and is functioning in the supervision of the entire program.

While these various steps were being taken, new developments were arising, and old factors were changing in importance. Japan had never been able to provide all of its own food — nor to produce enough of many other necessities of life. Seventy-eight million Japanese occupy an area smaller than California, and of that area only 16% is capable of cultivation.

The population is still growing at an enormous rate. It is expected to reach 84 million by 1951. The current troubled condition in Asia leaves practically no food available for import into Japan, even if the currency and Japanese export situation would make food purchases possible — which they would not.

And yet without food and other necessities, Japan would be faced with widespread starvation and disease — would seethe with unrest and disorder and hopelessness. Even aside from the simple principles of humanity, we could not, under such conditions, accomplish our original objective of a peaceful Japanese government. Nor could we hope that Japan would be other than susceptible to totalitarian demagogues from within and without. Without help the country would become a prey to non-democratic ideologies of aggression.

To meet this situation America has supplied Japan with food and other necessities. This assistance has given the country a base upon which to build, and it has been possible to supplant totalitarianism and Shintoism with democracy, to begin to replace educational regimentation with academic freedom, and to build the foundations for a peace-loving government of the people.

For this and other achievements in Japan, great credit must be given to General MacArthur and his staff. America was indeed fortunate that for this vital task, it had an outstanding leader who could bring the Japanese to a complete realization of their defeat and at the same time obtain their full cooperation in forming a free and stable government.

But the Department of the Army and the Department of State — which shares the policy responsibility of occupation — both Departments realize that for political stability to continue and for free government to succeed in the future, there must be a sound and self-supporting economy, and General MacArthur in command of the occupation can be depended upon to implement these policies.

We also realize that the United States cannot forever continue to pour hundreds of millions of dollars annually into relief funds for occupied areas, and that such contributions can end without disaster only when the occupied countries can pay for their own necessities with their own production and exports.

These factors have resulted in efforts to improve in many fields the economic situation in Japan. And with this increasing economic approach there has arisen an inevitable area of conflict between the original concept of broad demilitarization and the new purpose of building a self-supporting nation.

In the case of agriculture the two purposes do happen to run practically parallel. The breaking down of feudal holdings has ended a war-making influence. At the same time the wider division of lands tends to produce incentive on the part of the larger number of landowners and thereby to increase overall production.

But it is a different situation with manufacturing. The destruction of synthetic rubber or shipbuilding or chemical or nonferrous metal plants will certainly destroy the war potential of Japan, but such destruction may also adversely affect the peace potential.

The dissolution of the Zaibatsu may present in itself no serious economic problem, but at some stage extreme deconcentration of industry, while further impairing the ability to make war, may at the same time impair manufacturing efficiency of Japanese industry —may, therefore, postpone the day when Japan can become self-supporting.

Such is our dilemma. It is clear that Japan cannot support itself as a nation of shopkeepers and craftsmen and small artisans any more than it can exist as a purely agricultural nation. We can expect a continuing economic deficit in Japan, unless there is at least some degree of mass industrial production.

Another borderline situation between demilitarization and economic recovery is presented in the case of personnel. The men who were the most active in building up and running Japan's war machine —militarily and industrially —were often the ablest and

594

3　経済諸施策への対応（昭和21年5月～24年4月）

most successful business leaders of that country, and their services would in many instances contribute to the economic recovery of Japan.

What should we do about them now? We cannot afford to leave the Japanese war system intact nor forget that there is danger in retaining in power leaders whose philosophy helped bring on World War II. On the other hand we cannot afford to sterilize the business ability of Japan.

Nor can we believe without qualification individual Japanese protestations of war innocence or of peacetime reformation. One Senator said to me in Germany shortly after V-E Day: "I have inquired everywhere, and I have not yet found a single Nazi in Germany," to which could perhaps now be added, "Nor a war lord in Japan."

All these matters present questions of degree, and the decisions are matters of judgment. These decisions are not difficult at a cocktail party or on an easy chair or on a rostrum, if made by those who have no responsibility for the decisions or their results. It is somewhat different when you must live and suffer with any errors that you might make.

The Departments of State and Army are trying to draw the lines in the right place. And in doing so they are giving — and will give — full weight to the changes in political and military and economic considerations which have occurred since the initial days of occupation.

We realize that deconcentration must stop short of the point where it unduly interferes with the efficiency of Japanese industry. Earlier programs are being reexamined — as for example the details of the program stated in the paper submitted some months ago to the Far Eastern Commission, and recently given wide publicity as FEC-230.

We are not averse to modifying programs in the interests of our broad objectives. A bill recently submitted to the Japanese Diet setting up procedures for deconcentration of excessive economic power was changed before its final enactment — changed with a view of giving added weight to the economic needs of Japan.

In the case of plant dismantling and reparations — in addition to the matter of disarmament — we are bound by certain agreements with other nations —agreements which must be carried out unless breached by those others or altered by consent. However, since last summer we have had a competent group of industrial engineers in the Pacific selecting the specific plants which, consistent with our obligations, can be dismantled with the minimum of detriment to Japanese economic recovery. The report and recommendations of this committee should reach the Department of the Army during this month.

I would not leave the impression that questions of demilitarization or reparation or deconcentration or disqualification of personnel are the most immediate obstacles to Japanese recovery.

The principal difficulties arise from the destruction which war brought to Japan and to the chaotic condition which has existed in the Far East since V-J Day.

The flimsy nature of Japanese construction and the concentrated population centers made these islands most vulnerable target for our incendiary and other missiles. Even aside from the effects on Hiroshima and Nagasaki of the atomic bombs, many Japanese cities were largely destroyed. I believe that on a percentage basis greater Tokyo —with about 7 million peoples as of 1940 —was as badly damaged as any enemy city in the entire world.

Japan has long been dependent on the rest of Asia not only for foodstuffs but for raw materials needed in their manufacturing and business life, and it has relied largely on general commerce with China and other neighbors. With the war and its aftermath these sources of import and export become largely non-existent.

Many affirmative steps have been and are being taken to meet these and other difficulties —and to promote recovery and thereby hasten the day when Japan will cease to be a financial burden to the United States. I wish that time permitted me to discuss in detail our activities in many fields, including those of finance and credit and foreign trade.

Some results of our efforts are apparent. Overall Japanese industrial production has risen from 18 per cent of the 1930-34 level in January 1946, to 40 per cent in August 1947. In the case of coal —basically needed for business recovery —the present production is 86 per cent of the 1930-34 level. Fertilizer has increased four-fold during occupation. One-fourth of the war-destroyed

3 経済諸施策への対応（昭和21年5月～24年4月）

houses in Tokyo and vicinity have been replaced. Six hundred thousand acres of land have been reclaimed for cultivation, and a million more should be added by 1950.

In this whole picture of Japan do not forget that we are supervising an entire Government —and one disorganized by an unsuccessful war. We have all the many normal policy and operating problems of a stable and successful Government plus the added ones produced by the unusual and distressing conditions peculiar to present-day Japan.

The differences from our own country are such that we cannot expect to impose on the Japanese people an exact reproduction of American democracy. It follows that often there is no precise precedent for our problems, and the Departments must do as our forefathers did in the early days of our own government, reach the best results we can by trial and error.

The lines to be drawn are, of course, not always easy to draw, and as in the case of all decisions of importance one cannot be too dogmatic. There can be —and are likely to be —differences of opinion among sincere and informed people. Nor do I have any illusion that everything we do will be perfect.

But I can assure you that our decisions will be made with realism and with a firm determination of doing all possible to prevent Japan from again waging unprovoked and aggressive and cruel war against any other nation. We hold to an equally definite purpose of building in Japan a self-sufficient democracy, strong enough and stable enough to support itself and at the same time to serve as a deterrent against any other totalitarian war threats which might hereafter arise in the Far East.

（付　記）

編　注　本文書は、昭和二十四年三月、外務省特別資料部作成「日本占領及び管理重要文書集」第二巻より抜粋。

General of the Army Douglas MacArthur's Message to the Secretary of the Army concerning the United States Policy for Japan

January 18, 1948

Pursuant to the suggestion contained in radio W-93804, I

have sent General Fox to Washington to assist the Department of the Army in its detailed presentation before Congress of the budgetary requirements covering Japan and the Ryukyus for the fiscal year 1949.

As you know, neither of these areas have adequate indigenous food resources to sustain life. Prior to the war, they had direct call upon the resources of Formosa, Korea and Manchuria, and through highly successful industrial effort Japan was able to acquire additional food to meet any then existing deficiency, by trading her manufactured products in the markets of the world. This of course is no longer the case. Formosa, Korea and Manchuria have been taken away, the bulk of Japan's shipping afloat has been destroyed, home industries have been gutted, areas of deep-sea fishing previously available have been sharply curtailed, and the opportunities for foreign trade, beyond those on a government to government basis, are limited to such as private traders visiting Japan under fixed quotas are able to provide. Japan is therefore still under an economic blockade whose rigidity, while somewhat moderated to permit this limited field of government and private trade, yet prevents development of a self-sufficient economy.

Japan came under our custodial control in the aftermath of war and victory. Approximately six million Japanese citizens have been repatriated from abroad since the occupation started, but thus far none are permitted to leave for abroad from Japanese shores. The people therefore are, in all practical aspects, our prisoners of war, and as such entitled to our protection under the international conventions which we ourselves historically have never failed to respect. As a consequence, the custodial relationship which the United States assumed at the surrender embodied obligations and responsibilities having the most implicit legal basis. Such obligations and responsibilities will continue to dominate our relationship to Japan so long as, by force of restriction, we confine the Japanese people to their home areas and delimit their freedom of commerce and trade with others.

During the course of the occupation, the Japanese people have made diligent effort themselves to solve the deficiency problems involved. Sizeable tracts of land are being brought newly under cultivation, but Japanese terrain offers little hope for major

598

3　経済諸施策への対応（昭和21年5月〜24年4月）

relief in this direction. Amazing strides have been made toward industrial rehabilitation and recovery, despite the critically low inventory of essential raw materials available for such purpose. Traditionally a people exploited into virtual slavery by an oligarchic system of economic feudalism under which a few Japanese families, directly or indirectly, have controlled all of the commerce and industry and raw materials of Japan, the Japanese are rapidly freeing themselves of these strictures to clear the road for the establishment here of a more healthy economy patterned after our own concepts of free private competitive enterprise — to release the long suppressed energies of the people toward the building of that higher productivity of a society which is free. Agricultural land, long held within a similar vise of feudalistic control, with the productive energies of those who tilled the soil limited to the low standards which result from human serfdom, is being released through sale to those same persons who in future, as land owners themselves and sole beneficiaries of their daily toil, will find in the degree of their contribution to the soil the measure of their benefit from the soil. These and other measures, designed to set the pattern of a free Japan, in time will assert themselves in maximized productivity, but even then reliance must still be had upon resources abroad which are not available at home, and markets to absorb such goods as are produced beyond domestic needs as a medium of obtaining the resources essential to meet even such needs.

The answer to this vexatious problem of course lies in the effectuation of a treaty of peace which is now past due. Conflicts in the diplomatic sphere, however, dim the hopes that were once held that such a treaty may realistically be expected, with the concurrence of all of the Allied Powers, within a predictable future. This situation imposes upon the United States the continuance of the obligations and responsibilities inherent in our existing relationship, as we cannot afford to yield our position here until fully assured against any consequent power threat by others which might operate to destroy that which we have built, and thereby place our own country at consequent serious strategic as well as economic disadvantage. Meanwhile, it is essential to minimize by all available means the resulting burden upon the American people. With this in mind, we should, while progress toward the res-

599

toration of formal peace is stalemated, unilaterally or with other Allied governments similarly inclined, release as far as possible existing restrictions upon trade and commerce, and restore to the normal limits of diplomatic privilege the right of the Japanese citizenry to journey abroad and mingle with that of other lands, to study and absorb cultural and scientific advances made since the advent of war, and generally to be re-endowed with freedom of action in the solution of their own internal problems in the safeguard of their own domestic welfare.

By our resolute and faithful discharge in Japan of the obligations inherent in the relationship of victor to vanquished, we will fulfill the highest form of moral responsibility, and in so doing make an indelible impression which, more than all else, will gain converts to our own immutable concepts of life. It is not merely what we have done, but even more that we have done it. It will afford comfort and sustenance to human life —but, of immeasurably greater value, it will provide an example in human relationship which will continue to dominate men's thoughts for ages to come.

MacArthur

198 対日政策に関するマッコイ極東委員会議長の演説

昭和23年1月21日

編注 本文書は、昭和二十四年三月、外務省特別資料部作成「日本占領及び管理重要文書集」第二巻より抜粋。

Major General Frank R. McCoy's Statement on the United States Policy for Japan, at the Meeting of the Far Eastern Commission

January 21, 1948

U. S. Government has reviewed the accomplishments of the first two years of the occupation of Japan in the light of the ultimate Allied objectives as set forth in the Potsdam Declaration and elaborated in subsequent policy statement. This review has revealed that in implementation of the basic policy, SCAP (Supreme Commander for the Allied Powers) has destroyed Japan's ability to make war on the land, on the sea, and in the air. Excep-

3 経済諸施策への対応(昭和21年5月〜24年4月)

tional progress has been made in establishing political and economic institutions which will permit the development of a democratic and peaceful Japan capable of assuming the responsibilities of a member of the community of nations.

The framework of a democratic Japanese Government has been established in accordance with the provisions of a new constitution adopted by the Japanese people and a popularly elected Government is now in office.

However, the establishment of a self-supporting economy in Japan, without which the achievements of the occupation cannot be consolidated, has not yet been accomplished.

Japanese industry and commerce are not yet sufficient to sustain the Japanese economy, there is not yet final Allied determination of the reparations which Japan will be required today and Japan is not yet in a position to participate fully in world trade and to contribute its part to the rehabilitation of world economy.

Economic chaos in Japan has been prevented only at the expense of the American people who have financed the importation of vital food and other materials required to prevent widespread disease and unrest.

It is the view of the U. S. Government that if the fundamental objectives of the occupation are to be achieved, and if there are to be established the conditions necessary to enable Japan to make its proper contribution to the economic rehabilitation of world economy and to take its place in the community of nations, a much greater effort must be made to bring about the attainment of self-supporting Japan with a reasonable standard of living.

To this end, my Government believes that the Japanese Government and people, the Far Eastern Commission and its member states, and the Supreme Commander, recognizing the conditions which now require that more emphasis be placed on such a program, should take all possible and necessary steps, consistent with the basic policies of the occupation, to bring about the early revival of the Japanese economy on a peaceful, self-supporting basis.

The Japanese Government, under the supervision of SCAP, must prepare and implement plans under which Japan can become self-supporting at the earliest possible time. Progress has already been made in this direction. Although the primary responsibility [for the] preparation and execution of such a plan rests on the Japanese Government and people, SCAP must take the requisite steps to ensure that the Japanese Government and people energetically and effectively discharge that responsibility.

Greater efforts by the Japanese people, coupled with such assistance as the U. S. Government may be able to provide for a temporary period, should eliminate the burden on the American taxpayer of supporting the Japanese economy. While the American people will not continue indefinitely to subsidize the economy of Japan, the U. S. Government will shortly begin discussions in the Congress of a proposal to provide funds for the fiscal year 1949 in addition to funds requested for subsistence items for the procurement of such imports as industrial raw materials and spare parts to assist Japan to expand the output of its peaceful industries towards status of self-support.

The Far Eastern Commission has already agreed on a number of policies directed towards this goal. For example, it has already declared that measures should be taken or continued to stimulate Japan's production of goods required for export and to ensure that goods produced are those in demand in countries requiring supplies from Japan; it recently opened Japan to limited private trade and authorized the establishment of a revolving fund to aid in financing peaceful foreign trade. The U. S. Government, recognizing that the cooperation of the Far Eastern Commission and its member states is essential to the successful accomplishment of a program for bringing about a self-supporting economy in Japan, requests favorable consideration of future policies to be presented to the Commission towards this end.

編注　本文書は、昭和二十四年三月、外務省特別資料部作成「日本占領及び管理重要文書集」第二巻より抜粋。

199 農地改革の促進に関する指令

昭和23年2月4日　連合国最高司令官総司令部より　日本政府宛

GENERAL HEADQUARTERS
SUPREME COMMANDER FOR THE ALLIED POWERS

3　経済諸施策への対応(昭和21年5月〜24年4月)

APO 500
4 February 1948

AG 602 (4 Feb 48) NR/A
(SCAPIN 1855)

MEMORANDUM FOR: JAPANESE GOVERNMENT

SUBJECT: Rural Land Reform

1. Reference is made to:

a. Memorandum for Japanese Government, file AG 602.6 (9 Dec 45) CIE, (SCAPIN 411), subject as above, dated 9 December 1945.

b. Owner-Farmer Establishment and Special Measures Law, Law No.43, 21 October 1946.

c. Agricultural Land Adjustment Law, Law No.67, 2 April 1938, as revised by Law No.64, 28 December 1945, and by Law No.42, 21 October 1946.

2. The Owner-Farmer Establishment and Special Measures Law and the Agricultural Land Adjustment Law were enacted in accordance with the reference memorandum, in order to eliminate the feudal system of land tenure and remove economic obstacles to the redistribution of the land on an equitable and democratic basis. Since the enactment of these land reform laws, however, efforts have been made by certain adversely affected interests to obstruct the accomplishment of the rural land reform program.

3. The firm implementation of the Land Reform Program is essential to the creation in Japan of a society which is truly free and democratic and, as a consequence, it has become one of the foremost objectives of the Japanese people as well as of the Allied occupation. Therefore, the strict, vigorous and fearless enforcement of the above-mentioned laws is both imperative and indispensable.

4. Accordingly, it is directed that:

a. The Ministry of Agriculture and Forestry will instruct prefectural and local agricultural land commissions to purchase without delay all land subject to Land Reform Law in accordance with existing procedures and without regard to unauthorized action by pressure organizations seeking to impede the objectives of the Land Reform Program.

603

SCAPIN 1863

MEMORANDUM FOR: JAPANESE GOVERNMENT

SUBJECT: Inventory of Critical Materials

1. References:

a. Memorandum for the Japanese Government, AG 091 (15 Sep 45) MG, SCAPIN 29, subject: Production in Non-War Plants.

b. Economic Stabilization Board Instruction No. 6, dated 10 Feb 48, subject: Regulations Concerning the Procedure of Utilization of Idle Materials.

2. Reference 1a above requires the Japanese Government to "initiate, maintain and enforce production and other economic programs that serve the following purposes:.... b. The assurance of a just and impartial distribution of available supplies..... d. The restoration of Japanese Economy in order that the reasonable peacetime requirements of the population can be satisfied."

3. In order to assist in the most efficient utilization of indigenous resources in promoting economic rehabilitation, the Japanese Government is directed to take the necessary steps to

b. The Japanese Government will take prompt and vigorous action against any and all persons who, by bribery, intimidation or other unlawful means, obstruct the implementation of land reform measures. Reports of such action will be submitted to this headquarters.

FOR THE SUPREME COMMANDER:

C. Z. Shugart
for R. M. LEVY
Colonel, AGD
Adjutant General

200

昭和23年2月21日
連合国最高司令官総司令部より
日本政府宛

重要物資明細書の作成方につき指令

GENERAL HEADQUARTERS
SUPREME COMMANDER FOR THE ALLIED POWERS
APO 500
21 February 1948

AG 401.1 (21 Feb 48) ESS

make a comprehensive inventory of all goods and materials designated as critical materials in lists 1 to 4 of reference 1b, above presently held in industrial, commercial and distributive installations, including but not limited to factories, mills, mines, warehouses, storage yards and wholesale dealers' establishments, except the following:

a. Goods and materials in transit.

b. Goods and materials under production.

4. Inventories prepared in accordance with paragraph 3 above will be submitted within 60 days after the date of this Memorandum by the Japanese Government to the Military Government Unit for the prefecture concerned. Inventories will be as of a single date for the entire country. A complete copy of the inventory of stocks at each installation will be retained at the installation concerned.

5. All materials and stocks whose inventory is required by paragraph 3 above and which are not registered will be subject to confiscation without compensation as illegally held goods.

6. Direct communication is authorized between the Economic and Scientific Section and competent Ministries of the Japanese Government for implementation of this Memorandum.

FOR THE SUPREME COMMANDER:

C. E. Sheen
for R. M. LEVY
Colonel, AGD
Adjutant General

201

昭和23年3月29日

重要物資在庫緊急調査令の要旨につき通報

調整合第五〇號

本　庁　3月29日後2時30分発

曽禰（益）連絡調整中央事務局長官より
各連絡調整地方事務局長、各出張所長
宛（電報）

401. 1. ESS. SCAPIN 1863)に關する總司令部覺書（Feb. 21. AG 隠退藏物資の調査方に關する總司令部覺書（Feb. 21. AG 401. 1. ESS. SCAPIN 1863)に關する措置の經過については先に調整合第三三一號を以て速報した所であるが、今般「ポツダム」政令「重要物資在庫緊急調査令」が二十七日公布されたから要旨を通報する。政令本文、竝英譯は別に送付

政令第六六號

重要物資在庫緊急調査令(要旨)

一、目的　國內資源を最も有効に活用して、日本經濟の再建を圖るため、國內に存在する重要物資の在庫量の緊急調査を行う

二、調査期日並對象　三月三十一日午前零時現在、別表(略)所載物資を同表規定以上所有する者(國が所有者である場合を含む)

三、報告提出先　當該物資所在地を管轄する市區町村長―都道府縣知事(四月十五日迄)―都道府縣軍政部並報告義務者の事業の所管官廳(四月二十一日迄)

但し特別の事情あるときは提出期日の延期を申請し得る

四、報告義務者に對する、三月三十一日迄の期間の物資讓渡等の制限

五、違反者に對する處罰規定

六、卽日施行

猶、本令に基く商工省告示は三月二十三日各新聞紙に揭載されてゐるから參照されたい

202　昭和23年4月22日　連合国最高司令官総司令部より 日本政府宛

在日連合国財産の新しい返還手続きに関する指令

GENERAL HEADQUARTERS
SUPREME COMMANDER FOR THE ALLIED POWERS
APO 500

AG 386.3 (22 Apr 48) CPC/FP
22 April 1948

SCAPIN: 1880

MEMORANDUM FOR: THE JAPANESE GOVERNMENT

SUBJECT: Procedures for Restoration of Property in Japan to Nationals of the United Nations

1. Reference is made to the following:

   a. Memorandum to the Japanese Government, AG 386.3 (6 May 46) CPC, SCAPIN 926, 6 May 1946, subject, "Procedure for Returning Property in Japan to Nationals of the United Nations," from General Headquarters, Supreme Commander for the Allied Powers.

606

3 経済諸施策への対応(昭和21年5月～24年4月)

b. Memorandum to the Japanese Government, AG 386.3 (22 Nov 46) CPC/FP, SCAPIN 1354, 22 November 1946, subject, "Restitution of United Nations Nationals' Property Wrongfully Transferred" from General Headquarters, Supreme Commander for the Allied Powers.

2. Memorandum 1 b above is hereby rescinded and this memorandum substituted therefor.

3. The Japanese Government is hereby directed to provide the necessary procedures for restoration to nationals of the United Nations identifiable property, tangible or intangible, which was located in Japan prior to the outbreak of hostilities between their governments and the government of Japan and owned by them at that time or lawfully acquired thereafter, and which has been the subject of transfer under duress, wrongful acts of confiscation, dispossession or spoliation, whether pursuant to legislation or by procedure purporting to follow the form of law, or otherwise, during the event of hostilities by the Japanese Government, members of its armed forces or by official or private Japanese or other individuals or groups, enemies of the United Nations.

4. In the absence of definite proof that no duress or fraud was involved, it will be presumed that all property taken from United Nations nationals was wrongfully seized or transferred, whether or not payment was made at the time of acquisition.

5. Property will be returned as it exists on the date of restoration and, unless other provision is made, title will be restored as it existed prior to wrongful transfer or seizure. Vacant possession of real property will be provided in all cases unless the restoree elects to permit the occupants to remain on the premises or unless the premises are occupied by the Occupation Forces.

6. Property will be restored free of all legal incumbrances to which it may have become subject subsequent to wrongful transfer or seizure.

7. The restoration of property will be made without expense to the United Nation or United Nation national owner and will not prejudice the claim of such owner against the Japanese or other enemy government and/or their nationals for damages to property, rent, depreciation, and other losses.

8. Anyone injured by the above provisions will look to the

Japanese Government for relief.

9. Restoration will be made in accordance with the following provisions:

   a. General Headquarters, Supreme Commander for the Allied Powers, will issue a directive to the Japanese Government in each case of restoration stating the time and place for the return of specific property.

   b. Transfer of title will be made at the Judicial Bureau or its branch offices having jurisdiction prior to the date set for restoration.

   c. In each case of restoration, the representative of the Japanese Government will present to the Eighth Army Military Government officer in the locality in which the property to be restored is located a copy of the directive requiring the restoration.

   d. Receipt in the form of the "Receipt for Restoration to United Nation National of Property in Japan" attached hereto as Annex A and containing all provisions therein, will be executed in original and seven copies and will be distributed in accordance with the distribution indicated on the receipt form. All copies will be signed by the restoree and an authorized representative of the Japanese Government and will be witnessed by the Eighth Army Military Government Officer or by his representative. Additional provisions may be included if circumstances require.

   e. The Japanese Government will furnish at the time of restoration documentary evidence of transfer of title, a complete inventory of the property being returned and an official final report on the administration of the property from the date of wrongful transfer or seizure, to the date of restoration, said report to include a statement of financial transactions and, in the case of industrial and commercial concerns, a closing balance sheet. Copies of documentary evidence of transfer of title, inventory and report on administration will be attached to each copy of the receipt.

   f. An agreed statement as to the extent and condition of the property being returned will be drawn up at the time of restoration, will be signed by both the restoree and the authorized representative of the Japanese Government, and will be witnessed by the Eighth Army Military Government Officer or by his representative. A copy of this statement will be attached to each copy of the receipt.

10. Four copies of the accomplished receipt together with all attachments thereto will be submitted to General Headquarters, Supreme Commander for the Allied Powers, within ten days of the completion of the delivery of the property. Documents will be in English and those which are translations will bear a certification as to correctness and authenticity.

FOR THE SUPREME COMMANDER:

A. J. Rehe
for R. M. LEVY
Colonel, AGD
Adjutant General

1 Incl
Receipt for Restoration to United Nation National of Property in Japan

編注　本文書の別添は見当たらない。

203

重要物資在庫緊急調査に関する閣議決定につき通報

昭和23年5月19日

宛　各連絡調整地方事務局長、各出張所長

曽祢連絡調整中央事務局長官より

一地合祕第二五〇號

昭和廿参年五月拾九日

連絡調整中央事務局長官

各地方連絡調整事務局長殿
出張所長殿　　同

重要物資在庫緊急調査に關する件

先般實施された重要物資在庫緊急調査はその成績思はしくなく、去る五月十三日栗栖經濟安定本部長官と總司令部經濟科學局側との定例會談に於ても先方より嚴重なる警告があつたので、政府に於ては本件につき至急對策を講ずることとなり五月十八日別紙甲號の通り（英譯文併せて添付する。）閣議決定を見た。

尚前記栗栖長官と總司令部係官との會談要旨は別紙乙號の通りである。

本件取扱は發表ある迄注意せられたい。

右通報する。

（別紙甲號）

重要物資在庫緊急調査について

昭和二十三年五月十八日閣議決定

（二三、五　經濟安定本部）

先般のポツダム政令による重要物資在庫量の調査は遊休物資の徹底的活用を目的として行はれたのであつて、此の種類の廣汎な調査としては最後のものたらしめなければならない。各廳においては右の趣旨で大いに努力して居られることと思はれるが今囘GHQ關係部局からの注意もあり、右調査の目的を達成する爲、更に一段の努力を以て左の措置を採ることとしたい。

一、商工、農林其の他の主務官廳及びその出先機關が主體となり、經濟安定本部及地方經濟安定局が推進機關となつて、共に具體的實施計劃をたてて活潑に實地調査を行ひ、報告洩れ物資の總ざらへを期すること。

二、商工、農林その他の主務官廳は、報告書に基いて又前項

の實地調査によつて見出された過剩物資及不正保有物資を過剩物資等在庫活用規則によつて速かに活用すること。

三、各省は、速かにその保有する物資についてそれぞれの報告擔當官署より報告書（鐵道等の國營事業については經濟安定本部に提出すべき保有限度及過剩數量の報告書を含む）が提出されたか否かを調査し、若し未だ報告書を提出して居ない官署があれば嚴重に督促して直ちにこれを提出せしめること。但し、これは報告期限の延長を意味するものではない。

（別紙乙號）

緊急物資の在庫調査報告に關する會談要旨

（昭和二三、五、一三）

●コーヘン氏

緊急物資の在庫調査に關し二月二十一日附司令部のデイレクテイヴ第一八六三號が日本政府に對し發せられた際マーカツト局長より完全且つ正確な在庫報告を求められたのに對し、當時の和田經本長官は經本が責任を持つて右任務を果す旨答へた。右報告期間はすでに過ぎたに拘らず、報告

3　経済諸施策への対応(昭和21年5月～24年4月)

件数は予想件数八十萬中わづかに四萬程度にすぎない。右の不成績に對しては政府に一部の責任がある。最惡な點は遞信省、厚生省等の外多數公團も未だ報告を提出しないことで報告したのはわづかに船舶及び石油公團だけである。司令部としては報告の到着を待つと共に報告を怠るものに對しては所定の處分をする考である。經本は隱退藏物資處分に關する規則を發布したが問題はこれらの物資を正規のルートに乘せることである。かつて栃木縣の舊飛行機工場にアスベストが相當量存在し政府は右事實を知りながら輸入を懇請したことがある。こんなことが米國議會に知れると對日物資供給が困難になるであらう。これら物資の摘發及び利用狀況に關し、今後人を任命し時々報告をする要求するつもりであるからその旨他の閣僚にも傳へて一兩日に結果を報告してもらひたい。

⦿ 栗栖長官

今後十分注意して御期待に副ふやう努力する。他の閣僚にもよく話して置く。

（以上）

昭和23年5月28日　連合国最高司令官総司令部より日本政府宛

貿易庁と外国商社等との間の直接交渉許可に関する指令

204

GENERAL HEADQUARTERS
SUPREME COMMANDER FOR THE ALLIED POWERS
APO500

28 May 1948

AG 091 (28 May 48) ESS/EX
SCAPIN 1901

MEMORANDUM FOR: JAPANESE GOVERNMENT
SUBJECT: Authorization for Direct Communication Between Japanese Government Board of Trade and Firms, Persons, and Foreign Missions on Commercial Matters

1. References:

　a. Memorandum for Japanese Government, file AG 091.1 (4 Nov 45) GS, SCAPIN 237, subject: Official Relations Between Japanese Government and Representatives of Neutral Nations, 4 November 1945.

b. Paragraph 2, Memorandum for Japanese Government, file AG 091 (29 Jan 46) GS, SCAPIN 677, subject: Governmental and Administrative Separation of Certain Outlying Areas from Japan, 29 January 1946.

2. The Japanese Government Board of Trade (Boeki Cho) is hereby authorized to communicate direct with firms and persons (but not governments) outside of Japan and with firms, persons, and foreign missions in Japan on commercial matters directly connected with international trading operations. However, all contractual agreements including those concluded with foreign governments are subject to review and validation by or on behalf of the Supreme Commander for the Allied Powers.

FOR THE SUPREME COMMANDER:

GEORGE R. CONNOR,
Colonel, A.G.D.,
Asst. Adjutant General.

205

総司令部が提示した経済安定計画の基本原則（経済安定十原則）につき通報

昭和23年7月29日　曽禰連絡調整中央事務局長官より各連絡調整地方事務局長、各出張所長他宛

連絡調整中央事務局長官

一地合第四八三號
昭和廿參年七月貳九日

各地方連絡調整事務局長殿
同　　出張所長殿
岡山・山口駐在官殿

経済安定計画の基本原則送付に関する件

今般本件に關し總司令部経済科學局長「マーカット」少將より、「ワシントン」の意向に基くものとして、別添英文が栗栖経済安定本部長官に手交されたから、貴官限りの御含みとして參考迄に寫一部送付する。

尚「マ」少將は本英文を栗栖長官に手交した事實が外部に漏洩することなき様注意を喚起してゐる點に鑑み取扱には特に注意ありたい。

3　経済諸施策への対応（昭和21年5月～24年4月）

（別添）

GENERAL HEADQUARTERS
SUPREME COMMANDER FOR THE ALLIED POWERS
Economic and Scientific Section

15 July 1948

ESSENTIALS OF ECONOMIC STABILIZATION PROGRAM

In order to fulfill the requirements incidental to insuring the continuation of American aid and to hasten the realization of a self-supporting Japanese economy, the following basic elements for an effective economic stabilization program in Japan are indicated as imperative of immediate adoption and full implementation.

1. Increased production of all essential indigenous raw materials and manufactured products.

2. Improvement of effectiveness of present allocation and rationing system through rigorous enforcement and programing.

Complete elimination of the blackmarket.

3. Further improvement in the efficiency of the food collection program with more realistic determination of collection quotas.

4. Rigorous adherence to official price schedule with prompt punishment of all violators.

5. Prompt introduction of firm but flexible wage stabilization program.

6. Acceleration and strengthening of program to achieve substantially increased tax collection and vigorous criminal prosecution of tax evaders.

7. Introduction of new tax measures for raising additional revenue as well as effecting a redistribution of the tax load in the direction of greater equity.

8. Systematic reduction of deficits in the Special Account of the Budget.

9. Improvement in operation of foreign trade controls and administration and establishment of a foreign exchange control under appropriate agency of the Japanese Government.

10. Strengthening and effective enforcement of existing selective credit control program.

206 略奪財産の返還に関する極東委員会政策決定

昭和23年7月29日 極東委員会決定

W. F. MARQUAT
Major General, U. S. Army
Chief, Economic and Scientific Section

Restitution of Looted Property

(FEC Policy Decision, July 29, 1948)

1. This policy supersedes the Far Eastern Commission policy decision on Restitution of Looted Property approved 18 July 1946, as amended by the policy decision on Restitution of Looted Property approved 10 October 1946, and also supersedes the U. S. directive on Disposition of Captured Japanese Merchant Vessels filed with the Far Eastern Commission on 24 May 1946.

2. Immediate steps should be taken to restore to Allied countries property which is found in Japan and which is identified in accordance with this paper as having been located in an Allied country at or during the time of occupation of that country, and which was removed by fraud, force or duress by the Japanese or their agents. The fact that payment was made should be disregarded unless there is conclusive evidence that fraud, force or duress did not take place. Restitution of industrial and transportation machinery and equipment should be deferred, however, so long as its retention is required for the safety of the occupation forces. In such cases the Supreme Commander for the Allied Powers should provide an explanation of reasons for retention and an estimated date of restoration. Special policies with respect to ships are stated below.

3. Steps should be taken to restore to Allied countries ships of all types and sizes found in Japanese waters which are identified as having been registered in an Allied country at the time of seizure or sinking by the Japanese or their agents, or at the time of acquisition by the Japanese or their agents by fraud, force or duress. The fact that payment was made should be disregarded unless there is conclusive evidence that fraud, force or duress did not take place. Within the limits of feasibility ships found in Japanese waters whether seaworthy, sunk or damaged, should, on the re-

3 経済諸施策への対応(昭和21年5月～24年4月)

quest of the claimant country, be refitted, or salvaged, repaired and refitted, as a matter of priority in Japanese yards, to permit their return in a condition substantially similar to that at the time they came into Japanese hands. The foregoing costs should be borne by the Japanese Government.

4. The processing of claims for industrial and transportation machinery and equipment found in Japan should not be permitted in general to delay removals of machinery and equipment on reparations account, but no item for which restitution claim has been received by the Supreme Commander for the Allied Powers should be allocated on reparations account until the claim has been acted upon. On the other hand, no restitution claim should be recognized for articles already delivered to particular countries on reparations account.

5. The claimant government should take delivery at a point in Japan designated by the Supreme Commander for the Allied Powers except that at the discretion of the Supreme Commander and by agreement with the recipient country, (A) in the case of Allied vessels subject to restitution the Supreme Commander may make delivery at Western Pacific points outside Japan whenever delivery will thereby be facilitated, in which case any costs of supporting and repatriating ships' crews used for such delivery should not be borne by the recipient country unless it specifically agrees to do so; and (B) in the case of delivery of other items of looted property, unutilized outgoing shipping space of Japanese vessels being employed in the importation of goods or repatriation of Japanese from a restitution recipient country to Japan may be made available at the expense of the Japanese Government but at the risk of the recipient country to deliver such items at points outside Japan. Expenses incurred after delivery to the claimant government should be borne by that government, except that in the case of delivery within Japan, relevant transportation expenses within Japan and any dismantling, packing and repair necessary for proper transportation, including the necessary manpower, materials and organization, should be borne by Japan and be included in restitution. The recipient governments should indemnify the Supreme Commander for the Allied Powers against all claims made in respect of the property received.

615

6. Restitution claims for property other than ships should be made by the government of the Allied country from whose territory the property claimed was removed; and restitution made to that government. In the case of ships, restitution claims should be filed by, and restitution made to, the government of the country whose flag the vessels were wearing or on whose register of shipping the vessels were borne at the time of sinking, seizure or acquisition as specified in paragraph 3.

7. No property, including cultural objects, should be included in Japanese exports which the Supreme Commander for the Allied Powers considers as probably subject to restitution. If items later found to be subject to restitution should be exported or liquidated equitable compensation should be made to that country to which the items exported or liquidated should have been restored.

8. After full opportunities have been given for inspection of objects known to have been looted the Supreme Commander for the Allied Powers should be authorized to liquidate property including stocks of gold, silver, other precious metals, precious stones and jewels but not cultural objects, known to have been looted but not identified pursuant to the terms of this paper. The proceeds of such liquidation shall form a secured fund to be entrusted to the care of the Supreme Commander for the Allied Powers, which may be used, in the discretion of the Supreme Commander for the Allied Powers, as a basis for credit for the purposes of the occupation. The initial value of the secured fund is to be preserved by the Supreme Commander for the Allied Powers or his successor authority. The Governments of Australia, China, France, India, the Netherlands, the Philippines, and the United Kingdom should have a priority right to purchase items offered for liquidation by foreign exchange acceptable to the Supreme Commander for the Allied Powers up to but not exceeding their recognized national reparations percentage shares (adjusted to total 100%, applicable to this pool) of industrial assets available from among the countries herein specified in accordance with the percentage mentioned above, payable in United States dollars, or, at the discretion of the Supreme Commander for the Allied Powers, in foreign exchange acceptable to the recipient countries con-

3　経済諸施策への対応（昭和21年5月～24年4月）

cerned. The secured fund shall be distributed to the recipient countries not later than 1 October 1949.

9. Without prejudice to other arrangements which may be made between the interested parties, the foregoing restitution policies, especially those in paragraph 6 are not intended to give the Allied government concerned the right to withhold from a person who is a national of another Allied Power any property as to which he may establish a legitimate title.

10. The Far Eastern Commission should recommend to the Government of those countries within whose territories may be found objects looted or acquired by fraud, force or duress by the Japanese such as:

   a. Industrial and transportation machinery and equipment;

   b. Gold, other precious metals, precious gems, foreign securities, foreign currencies, and other foreign exchange assets;

   c. Cultural objects;

   d. Agricultural products and industrial raw materials;

   e. Ships;

that bilateral arrangements be drawn up providing for restitution according to these principles.

11. The Far Eastern Commission should request the United States Government to forward this statement of policy through the usual channels to States which are not represented on the Far Eastern Commission and within whose territories looted object may be found.

12. The Supreme Commander for the Allied Powers shall create an agency comprising one representative from each of the countries of the Far Eastern Commission to advise on restitution matters. In addition, the Supreme Commander or his deputy should act as the non-voting chairman of the agency. It may meet at the call of the Supreme Commander or at the request of any member. The Supreme Commander should notify the United States Government of the views of the agency when his views conflict with those of the majority of the member countries.

13. In applying standards of identification with respect to claims for looted property, the Supreme Commander for the Allied

Powers should observe the following principles:

a. In cases of doubt, the presumption should be in favor of the claimant country whenever permitted by the broadest application of law, equity and common sense.

b. In cases of doubt as to the adequacy of the evidence of ownership submitted to support a claim for an object known to have been looted, the Supreme Commander shall inform the other members of the advisory agency of the existence of the claim. The advisory agency, after examining the evidence, shall give its advice to the Supreme Commander as to whether the claim should be approved or the provisions of paragraph 8 above applied.

14. No claims for the restitution of looted property should be lodged with the Supreme Commander for the Allied Powers after eight months from the issuance of a directive to the Supreme Commander for the Allied Powers giving effect to this policy decision; provided that after such terminal date, claims may, with the concurrence of the Supreme Commander for the Allied Powers, be lodged for property known to have been looted but not yet identified pursuant to the provisions of this paper; and provided also that adequate opportunity be given to representatives of looted countries both before and after such terminal date to inspect property known to have been looted but not yet identified.

編注 本文書は、昭和二十五年四月、外務省・賠償庁共編 「日本占領及び管理重要文書集」第五巻より抜粋。

207 極東委員会構成国の技術代表に対し工業的ないし商業的価値がある日本の科学技術工程の情報提供方指令

昭和23年8月6日 連合国最高司令官総司令部より 日本政府宛

GENERAL HEADQUARTERS
SUPREME COMMANDER FOR THE ALLIED POWERS
APO 500

6 August 1948

AG 000.91 (26 Jul 48) ESS/ST
SCAPIN 1925
MEMORANDUM FOR: JAPANESE GOVERNMENT

3　経済諸施策への対応(昭和21年5月〜24年4月)

SUBJECT: Access to Japanese Scientific and Technical Information in Japan

1. The Japanese Government is hereby directed to make available from the date of this memorandum through 31 March 1949 all scientific and technical processes having industrial or commercial value of Japanese origin and ownership and developed prior to 31 December 1945 to technical representatives of governments of members of the Far Eastern Commission.

2. The following augmentation policies are promulgated to define the official relations of the technical investigators and Japanese nationals:

　a. All technical investigators and their parties will carry passes admitting them to the area of the factory, shop, laboratory, pilot plant, etc., in which processes being investigated are located. These passes will indicate that such investigations are recorded in General Headquarters, Supreme Commander for the Allied Powers. (See Inclosure 1)

　b. Technical investigators shall upon their request be furnished with opportunity to make or take copies of specifications, drawings, blueprints, manufacturing data, etc., provided, if permanent withdrawals are made, they do not reduce the number of copies in possession of the Japanese below three full sets, and shall be allowed such time as they deem necessary within the period of the pass to inspect shops, machinery, equipment, laboratories, pilot plants, etc., which are utilized in the process or processes being investigated.

　c. Japanese organizations or individuals who are using, or are in possession of, processes that lie outside the limitations of this directive, i.e., processes which are not of Japanese ownership and origin or which were developed after 31 December 1945, are advised that proof that such processes are not within those limitations is upon them. In the event of dispute, documentary proof will be requested from the Japanese Government by General Headquarters, Supreme Commander for the Allied Powers. Japanese organizations or individuals are prohibited from divulging or in any manner making available to technical representatives any technical or scientific information or processes, which are established as of other than Japanese origin or ownership, or access to

輸出手続きの簡素化に関する指令

GENERAL HEADQUARTERS
SUPREME COMMANDER FOR THE ALLIED POWERS
APO 500

AG 091.31 (9 Aug 48) ESS/FTC
SCAPIN 1926

9 August 1948

MEMORANDUM FOR: JAPANESE GOVERNMENT
SUBJECT: Export Trade

1. <u>Rescissions</u>:

a. The following memoranda for the Japanese Government from General Headquarters, Supreme Commander for the Allied Powers, are hereby rescinded:

　(1) File AG 091.31 (14 Mar 46) ESS/IE, SCAPIN 814, 14 March 1946, subject: Export Procedure

　(2) File AG 091.31 (25 Apr 46) ESS/IE, SCAPIN 900, 25 April 1946, subject: Freezing Material for Export

　(3) File AG 091.31 (16 Jul 46) ESS/IE, SCAPIN

information or processes having primarily military value.

3. The Japanese Government will give this directive the widest possible dissemination consistent with the prospective audience it will ultimately affect.

4. Direct communication between agencies of the Japanese Government and interested staff sections of General Headquarters, Supreme Commander for the Allied Powers is authorized.

FOR THE SUPREME COMMANDER:

　　　　　　　R. M. LEVY
　　　　　　　Colonel, AGD
　　　　　　　Adjutant General

1 Incl
　Sample pass

編注　本文書の別添は見当たらない。

昭和23年8月9日　連合国最高司令官総司令部より　日本政府宛

3 経済諸施策への対応(昭和21年5月～24年4月)

(4) File AG 091.31 (26 Aug 46) ESS/FT, SCAPIN 1156, 26 August 1946, subject: Export Procedure

(5) File AG 091.31 (30 Aug 46) ESS/FT, SCAPIN 1170, 30 August 1946, subject: Freezing Material for Export

(6) File AG 091.31 (3 May 47) ESS/FT, SCAPIN 1654, 3 May 1947, subject: Export Procedure

(7) File AG 091.31 (20 May 47) ESS/FT, SCAPIN 1688, 20 May 1947, subject: Infringement Claims for Form IE 100, IE 200 and IE 300

b. The following memoranda for the Board of Trade (Boeki Cho), Ministry of Commerce and Industry, Tokyo, from General Headquarters, Supreme Commander for the Allied Powers, Economic and Scientific Section, are rescinded:

(1) File 312.1 (27 May 47) ESS/FT, (BT 47-378), 27 May 1947, subject: Survey Reports of Packing on Export Shipments

(2) File 091.31 (18 Sept 47) ESS/FT, (BT 47-800), 18 September 1947, subject: Application for License to Export Form

2. Amendments:

a. The following memoranda for the Japanese Government from General Headquarters, Supreme Commander for the Allied Powers, are amended insofar as they conflict with the provisions of this memorandum:

(1) File AG 334 (3 Apr 46) ESS/IE, SCAPIN 854, 3 April 1946, subject: Board of Trade (Boeki Cho)

(2) File AG 091.31 (19 Nov 46) OGA, SCAPIN 1346, 19 November 1946, subject: Import-Export Accounting Control for Japan

b. The following memoranda for the Board of Trade, Ministry of Commerce and Industry, Tokyo, from General Headquarters, Supreme Commander for the Allied Powers, Economic and Scientific Section, are amended insofar as they conflict with the provisions of this memorandum:

621

(1) File 091.31 (20 Dec 46) ESS/FT, (BT 188), 20 December 1946, subject: Method of Authentication of Application to Prepare and Deliver for Export Forms IE 100 and 200

(2) File 311.1 (16 Jan 47) ESS/FT, (BT 47-21), 16 January, 1947, subject: Commercial Correspondence Between Private Individuals in Japan and in Other Countries

(3) File 091.31 (1 May 47) ESS/FT, (BT 47-303), 1 May 1947, subject: Export Procedure

3. The Japanese Government is directed to take necessary action to establish procedures under which direct sales of approved items for export may be made by exporters in Japan to foreign buyers after approval of the contract, and validation of the export license by the Japanese Government and the Supreme Commander for the Allied Powers, and in such quantities only as are allocated by the Japanese Government and approved by the Supreme Commander.

4. The Japanese Government may act as Seller in those cases where the potential foreign buyer appears to be prevented by restrictions imposed by his own Government from entering into a contract with a Japanese Seller, in government-to-government transactions, and in other cases of export of goods by the Japanese Government which cannot feasibly be handled in private trade.

5. Contracts for export will not be approved and export licenses will not be validated by the Japanese Government until that Government is assured that, in exchange for the goods exported, there will be paid into a SCAP Commercial Account the fair value of the merchandise in acceptable foreign exchange, at established prices, or such other compensation as may be specified in Trade Agreements duly approved by the Supreme Commander for the Allied Powers.

6. The Japanese Government will cause the Seller to be paid in yen the fair value of the merchandise exported plus necessary expenses incidental thereto. The Japanese Government shall be responsible for determining that applicable price control laws and regulations are complied with.

7. Responsibility rests with the Seller to fulfill the terms of

the export contract. Buyer and Seller may negotiate for the settlement of claims arising out of the contract, provided, however, that any settlement shall be subject to approval by the Japanese Government and the Supreme Commander for the Allied Powers.

8. The Japanese Government will safeguard material designated by it as available for export until determination by Supreme Commander for the Allied Powers as to whether or not material shall be exported.

9. The Japanese Government will eliminate functions of Governmental Foreign Trade Kodans and reduce personnel of such Kodans to the extent that functions previously performed by them are restored to private Sellers and Buyers under this memorandum. On or before 31 August 1948, the Japanese Government will submit a plan to General Headquarters, Supreme Commander for the Allied Powers, for the abolition of the four existing Foreign Trade Kodans and the establishment in their place of two Foreign Trade Kodans, one for the purpose of handling imports by the Japanese Government and one for the purpose of handling exports by the Japanese Government.

FOR THE SUPREME COMMANDER:

R. M. LEVY

Colonel, AGD

Adjutant General

209

昭和23年8月13日　　本庁　8月13日後4時45分発

極東委員会技術調査団の来日につき通報

曽祢連絡調整中央事務局長官より　各連絡調整地方事務局長宛(電報)

調整合第一九七號

今回極東委員会の決定に基き日本における科學技術にして關係國の興味を有するものに付調査を行う目的で同委員會構成國政府の技術調査團が來朝(期日未定)することとなり八月六日付の日より明年三月三十一日に至る間日本人が發案し且所有するもので昭和二十年十二月三十一日以前に發達した工業上又は商業上の價値を有する、すべての科學的技術的プロセスについて極東委員會構成國の技術調査員に情報を提供しなければならない

(二)日本人の發案並びに所有にかからないもの又は昭和二十年十二月三十一日以後に發達したものは調査對象とならないがその據證責任は日本側にある

(三)第一義的に軍事的價値を有する情報又はプロセスは提供してはならない

(四)調査員は調査日時、調査場所、調査對象等を記載した司令部發行のパスを携行する、これらのものに對しては視察を許し情報資料の提供に應じなければならない
調査團來朝の時期は未定であるが本件に關する公信急送するに付、その到着を待ち貴管下府縣廳等を通じ關係工場、研究所等に本件周知方取計われたい
管下各出張所及駐在官に轉報ありたい

昭和23年9月14日　連合国最高司令官総司令部より　日本政府宛

210
新たに制定された国民の祝日に国旗掲揚を許可する旨の指令

GENERAL HEADQUARTERS
SUPREME COMMANDER FOR THE ALLIED POWERS

APO 500
14 September 1948

AG 322.1 (30 Aug 48) GA

SCAPIN 1934

MEMORANDUM FOR: JAPANESE GOVERNMENT

SUBJECT: Display of Japanese National Flag

1. Reference is made to:

    a. Memorandum from the Japanese Government, C.L.O. No. 3044 (2PA), subject, "New National Holidays," dated 30 August 1948.

    b. General Headquarters, Supreme Commander for the Allied Powers, memorandum, file AG 322.1 (1 Mar 48) GA, (SCAPIN 1867), subject, "Display of Japanese National Flag," dated 1 March 1948.

2. Reference 1b above is rescinded.

3. Effective immediately permission is granted for the Japanese national flag to be displayed on occasion of the nine (9) Japanese national holidays as listed in Inclosure 1 hereto.

4. The Supreme Commander for the Allied Powers will

3 経済諸施策への対応(昭和21年5月〜24年4月)

211

昭和23年11月1日　連絡調整中央事務局作成
「民主化の進行について」

take under consideration requests from the Japanese Government to display the national flag on other occasions of national interest.

5. Occupation forces have been informed in this matter.

FOR THE SUPREME COMMANDER:

R. M. LEVY
Colonel, AGD
Adjutant General

編　注　本文書の別添は見当たらない。

1 Incl
List of National Holidays

民主化の進行について

第一　概説

一、日本の民主化は米占領軍當局の指導により、政治、經濟、社會及び文化の各方面に亘る法制上の改革によって開始された。この様な法制上の諸改革が、米軍三カ年の占領期間中著しく進捗したことは明白である。これ等の諸改革がどの程度まで日本國民の思想及び生活に滲透しつつあるかは諸改革の持つ各々の特性によって、自ら差異があるが、一般的にいつて日本國民の思想及び生活の民主化に貢獻しつつあることは否定し得ない。

二、この様な法制上の諸改革が、日本民族の生活にとけ込み社會革命が達成せられ、永續的な民主革命が日本に確立されるのは今後の最も重要な問題である。

三、敗戰を契機とする日本の民主化は次の如き諸要素を基礎として培養せられつつあるものと考へられる。

(1) 占領軍の指導
(2) 民主主義政治形態の優秀性に對する認識
(3) 日本の經濟能力
(4) 日本民族の性格
(5) 日本國民自身の過去に對する反省及び自主權回復への希望

右の中(1)の占領軍の指導は、戰後の日本の民主化に最も

重要な役割を有つ外部的原因であり(2)以下の理由は日本國民の内部にある民主革命を培養する社会的基礎である、したがつて占領軍の指導がいかに日本國民の中に根を下すかは占領軍の指導が如何に日本國民の内部にある社会的基礎に働きかけ、これを育てるかに依つて達成される。占領當初においては、占領軍の指導は敗戦後の混亂せる事態を収拾し、日本を民主化の方向に導く上において正に適切に行はれた。然し占領三カ年に及び平和の理想の下に社會秩序が次第に安定するに至つた現在においては、その指導方法に調整を要するものが生じて來るのは當然であり、かくして始めて日本國民の内部にある民主化の種子を育成することが出來る。然も此の様な民主化でなければ、外部の力の變更によつて簡單に抹殺されるであろう。

三、從て占領軍の指導が將來はどの様に行はれるべきかについては上記日本國民の内部に存在する民主化培養の基礎について考察する必要がある。

(1)民主主義政治形態の優秀性に對する認識

日本國民の民主化を培養する一社會的基礎は民主主義政治形態の優位である。民主主義政治形態は一方に於て今次戰爭を通じ獨裁主義及び共産主義に勝るものであることを立證し、他方において現在の高度の文化と繁榮を誇る米國は民主主義政治形態をとることによつて始めて可能であつたという確信を齎した。したがつて日本の民主化を行へば日本人も亦 American Standard of living に類する一定の生活安定を獲得し、各個人の經濟生活が現實に改善されるという希望を有する様になり且その希望が少しづゝでも實現されて行く事が必要である。若しこの希望が諸種の理想的改革にかゝわらず現實に達成されないならば、これ等の改革は軍のなき指導力の存在する限り繼續し得ても、これ等の力のない場合には、新らしい過激思想の浸入を喰止めることは出來ない。從つて日本の民主化に永續性を與へることは出來ない。

敍上の觀點からいつて米國の援助に依る食糧及び輸出用生産資材の輸入、並びに國内における生産分配の諸方式を含む經濟諸統制は最も重要な日本民主化の施策であるが、その効果は常に日本國民の日々の生活を直

3　経済諸施策への対応(昭和21年5月～24年4月)

接に改善する點を主眼として考へられなければならない。

然し日本國民の生活を直接に改善する點を主眼とするに當つては二つの矛盾した問題に留意しなければならない。その一つは自由競争の意慾であり、他は分配の公平化である。現在は日本の舊制度を破壊するに急なるあまり、單に分配の公平化のみならず、資本主義生産機構そのもの丶分散解体が行はれている。然し日本の如き頻死の經濟狀態ではこの樣な改革は勞資を共に困窮せしめる。從て經濟の民主化による勞働者の地位の向上は差當り利潤分配の公平化を限度とすべきであつて、生産機構そのもの丶改革による資本蓄積の制限及生産の低下は避けねばならない。この樣にすれば一方に於て民主主義の魅力たる自由主義經濟の迫力を生かして行くと共に他方勞働者の地位を向上させる事が出來ると考へられる。右の考へ方によれば勞働者の權利の擁護及勞働運動にも自ら限界が生ずる。

(2) 日本の經濟能力

民主化を培養する第二の社會的基礎はその國の經濟である。米國の民主主義を支えているものが、米國の資本であると同樣に日本の民主化は日本民族資本の大いさに依つて決定される。日本の資本蓄積が賄い得ないさにあっても、將來に於ける最高の目標を示すにしても、現實の生活苦に直面する日本國民からは遊離せざるを得ない。

例へば地方自治制度、警察制度及教育制度の改革は此點から觀察する必要があると考へられる。現に日本國民の間には此等の諸改革が過去の制度に勝るものであるとの確信が未だ生れて來ていない樣である。日本の地方は從來封建諸勢力の溫床であつた。然も困窮せる經濟狀態の下に於て道德の低下は爭はれない事實である。如何によい制度であつてもこれを實際に擔當する者の素質が低下している場合は制度の圓滑なる運用を期待し得ず、制度そのものに對する不信を高めるであろう。從て地方自治の尊重については多くの研究すべき問題があると考へられる。

(3) 日本民族の性格

日本の民主化は日本の民主化でなければならない。日

本の民主化でないならば社會的基礎を缺く故永續性を有たない。日本の民族的性格は、日本の歴史と、その地理的地位から、東洋文化を受入れて成立つている。したがつて日本の社會に存在する制度を悉く封建主義的なものとして排斥する場合には、日本に存在する東洋的なものをも排せつするおそれがある。殊に中國が世界の強國として存在する以上日本において東洋文化と歐米文化との調整が考へられなければならない。例へば宗教改革、教育内容の改革、國語改訂等の問題はこの點から觀察されねばならない。

又日本民主化の諸改革は歐米の法制そのまゝであつてはならない。この點からいつて、憲法その他の諸法律は餘りに歐米的色彩にとみ、日本民族の精神に觸れないものがある樣に考へられる。

(4) 日本民族自身の過去に對する反省及び自主權囘復への希望

日本の民主化の基礎の第三は日本民族の過去に對する反省及び自主權囘復への希望である。日本國民が民主化を達成することに依つて求めるものは生活の向上と

それを外部及内部の破壊から守る安定機構を民主化によつて達成しようとするからである。即ち民主化を達成すれば二度と再び戰爭の慘渦〔禍ヵ〕に卷込まれないとの希望を抱くからである。然るに日本がいかに民主化を達成しても現在の國際機構は平和を保證していない。この樣に保證のない場合には日本民族の民主化への熱意は動搖し懷疑的となる。

又日本は民主化を達成することに依つてポツダム宣言の規定に依り自主權を速に囘復せんとする希望を抱いている。管理機構が前途の見透しなく續く場合には民主主義そのものに對する希望を缺くに至る。

四、日本の民主化は占領軍の指導が上述の如き日本の内部にある狀勢に適應する樣に實施されることに依つて日本國民に對し廣く淺くではなくて範圍は狹くても深くその思想及び生活に滲透して行くであろう。右は指導の内容の問題であるが、指導方法についても上記の諸點に立脚し、綜合的な觀點から重要順位に從つて母體の負擔に堪えられる樣な新しき子孫が漸進的に生み出されなければならない。例へば中央においては各局毎に個別的指導が行は

3 経済諸施策への対応（昭和21年5月～24年4月）

れ、その局の仕事が最も重要であるとして、おしつけられるために、全体として日本経済の負擔を超過する種々の改革案が提出されるし、更に地方では各軍政部毎にこの様な傾向が見られる事は否定し得ない所である。

（欄外記入）

八軍ティルトンに提出のもの

212 輸出促進に関する極東委員会政策決定

昭和23年11月18日　極東委員会決定

Conduct of Trade with Japan

〔FEC Policy Decision, November 18, 1948〕

1. In so far as is compatible with the Basic Post Surrender Policy for Japan (approved 19 June 1947, and forwarded to the Supreme Commander on 26 June 1947), and other policy decision, of the Far Eastern Commission, including this policy decision, Japan's foreign trade should be so conducted as to:

a. foster the development and balanced growth of Japanese foreign trade to a level consistent with Japan's peaceful needs as defined by the Far Eastern Commission;

b. encourage an increase in Japanese exports:

(1) in order that those exports may, as soon as possible, pay for the imports required for the prevention of disease and unrest within Japan, and for the reestablishment of a self-sustaining economy; and

(2) in order that Japan may participate in providing goods for international trade;

c. insure competitive conditions in trade free of contracts or arrangements which limit access to markets or foster monopolistic controls, and prevent excessive concentration of economic power in Japan and monopolies in Japan of foreign trade, whether with the participation of Japanese or foreign capital.

2. In addition to Allied trade representatives whose entry into Japan has been or may be approved consequent upon policy decisions of the Far Eastern Commission, persons in the following categories should be permitted to enter and reside in Japan in

accordance with regulations established by the Supreme Commander for the Allied Powers:

a. Merchants and other traders (including representatives of commercial organizations, governmental or otherwise) who are prepared to purchase or to make arrangements for future purchases of potential exports, or to provide raw materials or other commodities which Japan must import;

b. Representatives of banks, insurance companies, airlines, shipping and other companies who are prepared to render necessary services in connection with Japan's foreign trade either to private non-Japanese businessmen, to the Supreme Commander for the Allied Powers, or to Japanese persons or agencies approved by him;

c. Representatives of companies or individuals who had prewar property interests in Japan, the renewed operation of which would contribute to the accomplishment of the objectives in paragraph 1;

d. Representatives of companies or individuals who had substantial prewar property interests in Japan, for the purpose of inspection of those interests.

3. Nothing in this policy decision is to be understood as requiring the reopening or operation of factories in Japan.

4. There should be no discrimination against any foreign trade representatives or businessmen in Japan and all should be accorded equality of opportunity to transact business. Accommodations should be allocated to such persons entering Japan under the provisions of this policy decision on an impartial basis.

5. Yen acquired by foreign nationals through activities envisaged in this policy should be usable for local expenditures in accordance with laws and regulations enforced in Japan.

6. The Supreme Commander for the Allied Powers may impose port and service charges upon foreign vessels entering Japanese ports for commercial purposes with the exceptions enumerated below:

a. No port charges should be imposed on vessels entering Japanese ports in so far as they are carrying occupation force cargo or are engaged in the removal of reparations or restitution goods. Where vessels are also engaged at the same time in normal

630

commercial operations, port charges should be imposed in proportion to the bulk of commercial cargo carried.

b. All port charges on commercial vessels as well as the services rendered to commercial vessels in Japanese ports should be subject to appropriate and nondiscriminatory payment in any foreign exchange useful for the purchase of imports for Japan or in local currency, in accordance with laws and regulations enforced in Japan.

7. The persons referred to in paragraph 2 should be afforded opportunity for direct access to individual Japanese firms of their own choosing, and should have the opportunity to move freely in Japan subject only to the availability of transports and accommodations. Any regulations pertaining to the participation of firms or government agencies, whether Japanese or foreign, in foreign trade should be non discriminatory in character and confined to measures essential to achieving the principles and objectives set forth in this policy and should be based upon criteria established by and under the supervision of SCAP.

8. Foreign trade may be conducted by the Japanese Government or agency thereof to the extent deemed by the Supreme Commander for the Allied Powers to be necessary for the purpose of maximizing export proceeds or for other purposes, consistent with the principles and objectives stated in this policy.

9. An exchange rate for the yen should be established as soon as practicable.

編 注　本文書は、昭和二十四年十二月、外務省特別資料課作成「日本占領及び管理重要文書集」第四巻より抜粋。

213

昭和23年11月24日　連合国最高司令官総司令部発表

極東国際軍事裁判所判決の審査に関するマッカーサー司令官声明

General of the Army Douglas MacArthur's Review of the War Crimes Sentences

November 24, 1948

No duty I have ever been called upon to perform in a long public service replete with many bitter, lonely and forlorn assignments and responsibilities is so utterly repugnant to me as that of reviewing the sentences of the Japanese War Criminal defendants adjudged by the International Military Tribunal for the Far East. It is not my purpose, nor indeed would I have that transcendent wisdom which would be necessary, to assay the universal fundamentals involved in these epochal proceedings designed to formulate and codify standards of international morality by those charged with a nation's conduct. The problem indeed is basically one which man has struggled to solve since the beginning of time and which may well wait complete solution till the end of time. In so far as my own immediate obligation and limited authority extend in this case, suffice it that under the principles and procedures prescribed in full detail by the Allied Powers concerned, I can find nothing of technical commission or omission in the incidents of the trial itself of sufficient import to warrant my intervention in the judgments which have been rendered. No human decision is infallible but I can conceive of no judicial process where greater safeguard was made to evolve justice. It is inevitable that many will disagree with the verdict, even the learned justices who composed the Tribunal were not in complete unanimity, but no mortal agency in the present imperfect evolution of civilized society seems more entitled to confidence in the integrity of its solemn pronouncements. If we cannot trust such processes and such men we can trust nothing. I therefore direct the Commanding General of the Eighth Army to execute the sentences as pronounced by the Tribunal. In doing so I pray that an Omnipotent Providence may use this tragic expiration as a symbol to summon all persons of goodwill to a realization of the utter futility of war—that most malignant scourge and greatest sin of mankind—and eventually to its renunciation by all nations. To this end on the day of execution I request the members of all congregations throughout Japan of whatever creed or faith in the privacy of their homes or at their altars of public worship to seek Divine help and guidance that the world keep the peace lest the human race perish.

編注　本文書は、昭和二十四年三月、外務省特別資料部作成「日本占領及び管理重要文書集」第二巻より抜粋。

昭和23年12月19日 マッカーサー連合国最高司令官より吉田内閣総理大臣宛

経済安定計画に関する米国政府の指令（経済安定九原則）通報について

付記１　右和訳文

二　作成日、作成局課不明
「経済安定計画指令に関する件」

三　昭和二十四年一月四日、作成局課不明
「日本経済復興九原則の政治的意味に付ての観測」

General of the Army Douglas MacArthur's Letter to Japanese Prime Minister concerning the Economic Stabilization Program

December 19, 1948

Dear Mr. Prime Minister:

I am just in receipt of an interim directive from the government of the United States forwarded to me in accordance with the terms of reference of the Far Eastern Commission. This directive establishes a series of objectives designed to achieve fiscal, monetary, price and wage stability in Japan as rapidly as possible, as well as to maximize production for export. Such objectives, which are listed as an inclosure to this letter are clear and explicit, and as pointed out in the public release of the United States State and Army Departments follow an objective pattern, the general aspects of which have heretofore been communicated to the Japanese Government as a means towards the ultimate desired stability.

The directive proceeds from the premises that the prompt economic stabilization of Japan is a primary objective common both to the Allied Powers and the Japanese people; that the prompt economic stabilization of Japan is a primary objective common both to the Allied Powers and the Japanese people; that the American people so long as called upon to underwrite existing deficits in the indigenous resources required to sustain Japanese life are entitled to the maximized industry of the Japanese people and the minimized loss incident to a maldistribution of available resources or failure vigorously to produce native raw products or curb extravagance and waste in the operation of government and industry; and that by positive Allied intervention may obstructions incident to improvidential political conflicts, unobjective labor strife and destructive ideological pressures best be avoided.

The fundamental objective of this action, reduced to language which all may understand, is the prompt achievement of that degree of economic self-sufficiency which alone can justify and insure political freedom. For there can be no political freedom so long as a people's livelihood is dependent upon the largess of others. Nor may a people fully mobilize the collective will as an impregnable barrier against evil and destructive ideological pressures and as an irresistible force toward progressively improved living standards, if lacking in that resolute dignity which alone springs from mastery over its own deficiencies.

Necessarily, the action of the United States is tied in to the problem of relief and recovery appropriations, which may be expected in future only in ratio to progress made through the combined efforts of the Japanese people toward achievement of the states objectives. This will call for a reorientation of Japanese thought and action, with both subordinated to a primary purpose common to all of the people. It will call for increased austerity in every phase of Japanese life and for the temporary surrender of some of the privileges and immunities inherent in a free society.

There will be no place for interference by management or labor with the acceleration of production, for the burden will be shared by every segment of Japanese society. There will be no place for political conflict over the objectives to be sought as these objectives are stated with crystal clarity. Nor will there be any place for ideological opposition as the purpose to be served is common to all of the people, and any attempt to delay or frustrate its accomplishment must be curbed as menacing the general welfare.

In keeping with my long established policy, insofar as is possible, I shall look to the Japanese Government and people for the vigorous and faithful fulfillment of this stabilization program. I have faith in their ability, however stern the requirement and great the personal sacrifice, to achieve so worthy a national goal. The course ahead may well prove difficult but its impact upon individual life will be minimized if the burden is equalized among all of the people.

It is my earnest hope and indeed my confident expectation that all Japanese men and women will rally with vigor and determination to the challenge of this objective. If they do, Japan will

3　経済諸施策への対応（昭和21年5月〜24年4月）

evolve a pattern of progressive stability for all of strife-torn Asia to emulate. If they do not, Japan may perish.

　　　　　　　　Very sincerely,
　　　　　　(Sgd.) Douglas MacArthur
　　　　　　　DOUGLAS MacARTHUR.

Mr. Shigeru Yoshida, Prime Minister of Japan, Tokyo.

OBJECTIVES SET FORTH IN INTERIM DIRECTIIVE OF THE UNITED STATES

1. To achieve a true balance in the consolidated budget at the earliest possible date by stringent curtailing of expenditures and maximum expansion in total governmental revenues, including such now revenue as may be necessary and appropriate.

2. To accelerate and strengthen the program of tax collection and insure prompt, widespread and vigorous criminal prosecution of tax evaders.

3. To assure that credit extension is vigorously limited to those projects contributing to economic recovery of Japan.

4. To establish an effective program to achieve wage stability.

5. To strengthen and, if necessary, expand the coverage of existing price control programs.

6. To improve the operation of foreign trade controls and tighten existing foreign exchange controls, to the extent that such measures can appropriately be delegated to Japanese agencies.

7. To improve the effectiveness of the present allocation and rationing system, particularly to the end of maximizing exports.

8. To increase production of all essential indigenous raw material and manufactured products.

9. To improve efficiency of the food collection program.

10. To develop the above plans to pave the way for the early establishment of a single general exchange rate.

編注　本文書は、昭和二十四年八月、外務省特別資料課作成「日本占領及び管理重要文書集」第三巻より抜粋。

（付記１）

經濟安定に關する吉田首相あてマ元帥書簡

昭和二十三年十二月十九日

親愛なる吉田首相へ

予は、極東委員會の付託條項（注）にしたがい、米國政府の送付した中間指令をまさに受領したところである。この指令は、日本の輸出生産を最大にするとともに、日本國内における財政、金融、物價及び賃金の安定をできる限り速やかに達成しようとする一連の諸目標を確立したものである。これらの諸目標は、この書簡に同封した別紙に明確に列擧されているが、これらは米國國務、陸軍兩省の發表に指摘されたように、一つの客觀的な雛形にしたがったものである。しかもこの雛形の一般的内容は、經濟安定という窮局目的の達成手段として、すでに日本政府に傳達ずみである。

この指令の發せられたのは次のようないろいろな事項を前提とするものである。すなわち、日本經濟の速やかな安定が連合國および日本國民に共通した第一義的目標であること、日本國民を養うために必要な國内資源の現在の不足を補給することが米國民に要請されている限り、米國民は

日本國民の最大限の勤勉を要求し、不正配給に伴う利用可能な物資の損失または生産増強の失敗による國產原料の損失を最少にし、行政費及び産業運營上の浪費または冗費を省くよう要求する權利を有すること、不見識な政爭、常軌を逸した勞働爭議、並びに破壞的な思想的壓迫に伴う諸障碍が斷乎たる連合國の干渉によって防止しうるよう最善をつくすこと、がこれである。

この措置の基本的な目標を簡單にいえば、それは、ただそれだけで、政治的自由を正當化し且つ保障しうる程度の日本の經濟的自給體制を速やかに確立することである。なぜならば、一國民の生計が他國の慈悲にたよっている限り、政治的自由はあり得ないからである。またもし、自國の欠乏をみずから克服することによってはじめて生まれる確固たる威嚴を欠いているならば、國民は邪惡且つ破壞的な思想の壓迫に對する強固な防壁として、さらに國民の生計を漸次改善してゆくための抗し難いほどの強い力として、集團の意志を充分に動員することもできない。この米國政府の措置は、必然的に救濟および復興援助費の問題と關連するもので、將來援助費は、上述の目標達成に向う日本人の

3　経済諸施策への対応（昭和21年5月〜24年4月）

結束した努力によって得られる進歩の實績に比例してのみ期待できることになろう。これはやがて全國民に共通な重要目的をまず第一に考え且つ行動するように、日本人の思想と行動の切りかえを要請することになろう。これはまた日本人の生活のあらゆる面において、より以上の耐乏を求め、自由な社會にそなわっている特權と解放を一時的ではあるがある程度放棄することを要求するものである。

今後、負擔は、日本社會の各層に分擔されることになるから、經營者にしても勞働者にしても生産の促進を妨害する余地は絶對にあり得ない。また今回の措置の諸目標は、非常に明確に述べられているから、この諸目標に關して政治的紛爭の起り得る余地もない。さらにここに實施される目的は、日本國民全體に共通なものである以上、これに對して思想的立場から反對を唱える余地も全然なく、その達成を遅らせたり挫折させようとする企圖は、公共の福祉をおびやかすものとして抑壓されなければならない。

予は、既定の政策に從って、この安定計画を日本政府と國民ができる限り強力且つ誠實に完遂することを見まもり、期待したい。予は、この要求がいかに苛酷なものであり、

これにともなう個人的犠牲がいかに大きいものであろうと
も、日本政府と國民がこの價値ある國家的目標を達成する能力があることを信じている。前途は、確かに困難であろう。しかし、その負擔が全國民に平等に課せられるならば、個人生活に對する衝撃は最少限度に喰い止めることができよう。

男たると女たるとを問わず、日本人のすべてがこの目標に向って勇氣と決意とをもって相協力することを、予は切望し、且つ確信をもって期待するものである。もし日本國民が、これを實行するならば、いま紛爭の眞っただ中に投げ込まれている全アジアがもって範とするに足るような進步的安定の型をつくりあげることができるであろう。しかし、萬一日本國民がこれを實行しないならば、日本は破滅するであろう。

　　　　　　　　　ダグラス・マックアーサー

中間指令に述べられた諸目標

1、支出を容赦なく削減し、必要且つ適切な新しい歳入をも含めて、政府の全歳入を最大限に増大し、一日も速や

637

三　合衆國政府は委員會によつてすでに作成された政策に網羅されなかつた緊急事項が發生するときは、常に委員會が行動をとるに至るまでの間、最高司令官に對し中間指令を發することができる。但し、日本國の憲政機構もしくは管理制度の根本的變革を規定する指令は、極東委員會の協議及び意見の一致を得た後においてのみ發せられるべきものである。

　かに總合豫算の眞の均衡を圖ること。
2、徵税計畫を促進强化し、脱税者に對しては卽時全面的且つ徹底的な刑事訴追の措置をとること。
3、融資は極力日本の經濟復興に貢獻する諸事業に限定すること。
4、賃金の安定を圖るため、有效な計畫を確立すること。
5、現行の價格統制計畫を强化し、必要あればその範圍を擴張すること。
6、外國貿易管理の運營を改善し、且つ現行の外國爲替管理を强化し、これらの措置を適宜日本側機關に委せうる限度まで徹底すること。
7、とくに輸出を最大限に振興することを目途として現行の割當配給制度の效果を改善すること。
8、すべての主要國產原材料及び製品を增產すること。
9、食糧供出計畫の能率を向上すること。
10、以上の諸計畫は一般的單一爲替相場の早期設定の準備として推進すること。

（注）極東委員會付託條項中米國政府の任務

編注　本文書は、昭和二十五年六月、外務省政務局特別資料課作成「日本管理資料（一）」より拔粹。

（付記二）

經濟安定計畫指令に關する件

一、米國の對日經濟援助の主たる目的は日本經濟をして速に自立せしめ、政治的及び經濟的なデモクラタイゼーションの急速なる實現によつて健全なる國民經濟を營ましめんとするにある。今度の指令もそのための大方策をはつきりと明示したものと思われ今後の日本の經濟政策に一大

3　経済諸施策への対応（昭和21年5月～24年4月）

指針を與えたものである。即ち來年一月に開かれる米國議會における予算審議において對日經濟援助費の増額方が考えられていると傳えられるが、今度の指令はその裏付け乃至保障として日本政府が今後相當に長期に亘つて強力に實行すべき項目をはつきりと決定したものである。

三、この指令の諸項目を檢討するに大部分はこの七月マックアーサー元帥から日本政府に與えられた經濟十原則の各項目の中に含まれているがそれに含まれていなかつた問題はその後急速に重要度を増した問題即ち一本爲替の決定を速かに行うべしというのが一點でありその二は貿易振興に最大の重點を置くべしとなす點である。一本爲替の決定は貿易の振興のため採らるべき措置として極めて重要な意味があり、且つこの際輸出産業を非常に重視する立場から思い切つて國際競争に耐えるように日本産業の再整備を實施することが要請されている次第であり日本として一度是非經過しなくてはならぬ過程である又輸出の最大限の振興のための原材料の割當等に最も合理的な措置を採るべきことが要請されている點も注意の要がある。

三、政治的に見れば、最近の國際政治情勢の急激な變化に應じ東亞における日本産業の重要性が増加する傾向に鑑みて速に日本經濟の世界經濟えの結び着きを實施させる為の措置と見られるのであつて、本月六日ワシントンの極東委員會において採擇された日本産業振興の為の趣旨も本件指令の精神と揆を一にするものと考えられる。過般ラプストンで開かれたアジア極東經濟委員會に於て日本産業の地位が論議された趣旨とも合致すると思う。

四、この指令の諸原則は米國が締結した對ヨーロッパ援助の實施の為の雙務協定の内容と趣旨を同じくしてをり、又本月十日京城において米國と朝鮮との間に結ばれた對朝鮮經濟援助協定の原則も大體このラインに從つて居る。これらの點に鑑みて、いわゆる「アジヤ・マーシヤル・プラン」とでもいうべきものと、今度の指令内容との間の關連性が一應考えられるのであるが、ヨーロッパに對するマーシヤル・プランのように、あの地域全般を對象とした包括的な經濟援助計畫というものは今の段階では東亞には適用され難く、寧ろ各國別にその特殊事情を十分に考慮に入れて、機動的な援助をするという米國の行

き方が端的に現われて居るものと思われる。

五、民間外資の導入は元より望ましいのであるが諸般の事情でなかなか容易でないとすれば、米國としては政府的な資金による援助が今の段階では重要なる要素になつて來るが、そのためには民間資本の導入を促進するための受入態勢として資本の安全性收益性を確保するということだけでは充分とは言えないのであってこれと並行して寧ろ政治的な受入態勢を速に整備することが目下の最も緊要な問題である。即ち日本政府の全能力を發揮して最も緊パキとこの指令に掲げられてある諸原則を強力に實施に移すということが差し當つては最大の經濟援助を期待する所以である。

六、予算の均衡とか、徴稅の強化とか、重點的金融等は十大原則の項目として政府としては着々と實施しつつあるが、(1)賃銀の安定と(2)一本爲替の早期設定と(3)輸出の最大限の振興という三點は今度いよいよ緊要性を増した新しい問題といえる。この三點は相互に關連性を持ち、これが有効なる實施は今後日本政府が最大の重要性を置いて極力實施に努力すべきである。

（付記三）

日本經濟復興九原則の政治的意味に付ての觀測

（昭和二四、一、四）

一、米國の對內政治的見地から米國政府としては對日援助の増額の必要性の増していている今日、租稅負擔者に對する申譯としても對日援助が單にその時々を賑はす救貧政策的のものでなく日本經濟の自立に資するものたらしめる爲に耐乏政策を日本國民に課しているということを印象付けなければならぬ立場にある。現在すでに相當の増額が對日援助予算に見込まれており追加的に一億六千五百萬弗、來會計年度においては對日援助費のみにて一億六千五百萬弗と傳えられる。今後もこの耐乏政策の實施熱度の如何によっては増額が期待できると思う。なお米國當局としては昨年一月ないし六月の原料輸入高が總輸入高の九％を占めるに至つたため、十一月には昭和五年ないし九年の平均生產高の六〇％以上になつたということを重視し、生產上昇に役立つ物資を適正に輸入させさえすればそれに相當した生產増強を期

3　経済諸施策への対応（昭和21年5月〜24年4月）

待し得るという見込を得たのではないかと思われる。
一説によればドクター・ファインがワシントンにおいて日本にこれ以上援助を増すも中國の情勢變化等の影響を被むり所詮日本の赤化を防ぎ得ないとするならば再考を要するとの消極論に遭遇し、困惑したこともあるとのことであるが、同博士としては援助のやり方と日本政府の受け方如何によっては斯る議論が杞憂であるということを示す必要に迫られ今度のような耐乏政策の決定となつたのではないかと推察される。

二、米國の對日政策の見地から

東亞の情勢が中共勢力の飛躍的増大の結果、東亞における米國の對ソ牽制壁の一角が大きく崩壊しつつあるわけであつて、この事態に對處するためトルーマン新政府が發足後適當の機會において極東情勢に關してソヴェトと政治的な話合を試みる公算がある。それまでの期間に外交交渉上ソ連を牽制し得る據點に對してはできるだけ力を注いで經濟援助を行い、自立への途を拓いておく態勢を作りソ連の出方に相當の壓力を加え米國の立場を改善せんとする考に出ているものと思われる。もし對ソ政

治的話合が付かぬということが明白になった場合は、米國は意を決して愈々準戰段階に入り込むものと思われるが、その場合には日本の軍需工業力と人的資源を活用する意味においてもまず日本人に獨立を與え、日本人の自主的な判斷に基いて對ソ戰列に立たしめんとの考慮があると考える。この意味において案外早い機會に單獨講和を結ぶという事態の到來も考えられない譯ではない。即ち米國としては進退何れの場合に處しても困らぬ様な手を打つておく必要がある譯で今度の耐乏政策は兩様の場合を予想して兎も角經濟自立の枠を與えて置かなくてはならぬという根本的な考え方に根ざしているともいえる。

從つて占領軍は作戰に専念し、産業行政の面では今度の耐乏政策の枠で米國から援助を與えつつ、なるべく日本人のイニシアテイヴを生かしながら極東における米國の立場を固めて行こうとする肚であると見られる。單獨講和が案外早く成立すればその直後において日本管理の機構を切替え對日經濟援助の實施面を例えばECAの支部を日本に作つてこれに委譲するということもあり得ることであるのみならず状況によつては對外經濟協力法の規定を

改正して占領中の地域と雖も經濟援助關係事項はこれをECAに委ねるという措置に出づる可能性も絶無とはいえない。

三、日本の國內的事情の見地から

耐乏政策はある意味では昨年三月ドレーパー陸軍次官來朝以來の宿題であつたといえるが從來の内閣は眞劍に實施する力も熱意もなく經過した嫌いがある。司令部は日本の戰爭の苛烈さにあきれ果て、この邊で政權を安定させ、いかなる政權でも安定したものに、他の政策を選ぶ余地なくこの耐乏政策の枠内で經濟自立への方策を眞面目に實施させようという考にははつきり態度を決めたものと推定される。占領開始直後の時期において勞働者に急激な權利主張を可能ならしめそれが行き過ぎになつたことは爭い難い所であるが今次指令の實施上必要と認められる場合は公共企業重要產業における勞資休戰を實現せしめる氣構えであると考える。

四、アジア經濟復興政策の見地から

世界の自由愛好國の經濟を健全化し、それによって共產化を防ぐという計畫をマーシャルプランと規定するな

らば、それには西歐型と東亞型とがあるといえる。西歐型は全域に亘つて綜合的一本の計畫を與えることに重點をおいているが、東亞型は國別に特殊事情を考慮に入れて機動的に（援助の增減を隨時情況に應じ調節し得る意味）行う方式に主眼を置いているということができよう。（尤もそれ以外にECAFE計畫というものが全般的計畫化の作用を持って徐々に表面へ出て來ることは考慮に入れなくてはならぬ。）今度の對日經濟援助に伴う耐乏政策の設定は、前記の東亞型の援助の現われといえるのであって、朝鮮に對しても援助に對する被援助國の義務としては大體日本に對する場合と似た一種の保障か雙務協定の形で規定されているところである。

たゞ米國の一部には東亞における防共態勢の重要な一環として日本經濟を早急に自立せしめ、その產業能力を東南アジア復興計畫の一つの鍵として活用するという考もあると思われる。卽ち昨年夏のオータカムンド及び秋のラプストンにおけるアジア極東經濟委員會の會議においてアジア產業復興五ヵ年計畫が論議された際、その計畫の中において日本經濟の占むる地位について突つ込ん

642

3 経済諸施策への対応（昭和21年5月～24年4月）

215

昭和23年12月20日　三宅（喜二郎）特別資料部第一課長作成

「日本管理の現段階とド・ファクト・ピース」

日本管理の現段階とド・ファクト・ピース

昭和二三、一二、二〇

特別資料部第一課長

〰〰〰〰〰〰〰〰〰〰

だ討議が行われ、その結果日本産業の復興と日本との貿易の促進方について重要な決定が行われたのは、その意味において重視すべきであると思う。

一、ポツダム宣言の條項受諾によって、日本は先ず國家及び個人の活動の内容について、大きな枠卽ち基本的制限を附せられることになつた。非軍事化及び民主化に關する制限が卽ちこれである。

しかして非軍事化及び民主化の實行は日本の自主的措置に一任せられることなく、連合國占領軍の管理を受けることになつた。卽ち日本の統治権は、ポツダム宣言の條項實施のため適當と認められる措置をとる連合國最高司令官の権限の下に從屬することになつた。その結果日本の國家及び個人の活動は各分野において最高司令官を始め占領軍各機關の命令、禁止、勸告、指導、監督に服している。非軍事化及び民主化實施のためのこれらの形式的及び内容的制限を便宜上實施的制限と呼ぶこととする。

前記の基本的制限は平和囘復後も講和條約に基ずいて殘るであろうが、實施的制限の大なる部分は平和が囘復すれば、取除かれる筈のものである。制限の或るものは實質上は猶殘るであろうが、少くともその形式は變るのである。卽ちサブヂェクト・トゥという形式の占領軍による管理は無くなり、非軍事化及び民主化は第一次的には日本の自主的措置によつて履行又は確保せられ、連合國は大使會議又は監視委員會によつて監督するという軽い意味の管理が一定期間續くことになるであろう。

然るに講和條約の早期成立の見込は少い。そこで一方においては日本の自主的政治體制の確立及び經濟的自立及び復興、他方においては連合國の負擔の軽減という見地から、講和條約前において各種の實施的制限を漸次緩和ないし撤廢し、本來ならば平和囘復後に實現するよう

な事態を事實上部分的に實現しようという考えが出て來た。これがド・ファクト・ピース・セットルメントのアイディアである。しかしながらサブヂェクト・トゥの根本方式は講和條約が成立する迄は續くのではなかろうか。

二、それは兎も角、現在事實上日本の國家及び國民が服している制限、換言すれば連合國による日本管理の目的としては、大體左の五つのことが考えられる。

(1) ポツダム宣言の根本目的の達成卽ち非軍事化及び民主化の確保
(2) 占領軍の安全確保及び維持給養
(3) 連合國財産の保全乃至返還、所謂りやく奪財産の返還及び賠償の取立
(4) 日本に對する經濟的救濟の有效なる實施及び日本の經濟的自立達成
(5) 防共基地としての確保及び東亞の工場としての復興

三、一般に、軍事占領の行われる場合、占領軍は作戰上の必要、自己の安全確保及び維持給養のため占領地住民に對して命令し、強制し得るのであるが、右のような軍事的必要の無い限り、現行の法令を尊重する義務を負い又住民の宗教に干渉せず、これを自由放任する義務がある。

四、しかるに連合國による日本占領は日本が受諾したポツダム宣言の條項履行を確保するためになされたものであり、日本はその統治權が、同宣言の條項を含む降伏條項を實施するため必要なる限度において連合國最高司令官の權限の下に從屬することを承諾した。從つて占領下の日本の國家及び國民は占領軍の軍事的必要のためのみならず、ポツダム宣言にかかげられた占領の根本目的達成のため必要なる限り、各分野においてその活動に制限を受けている次第である。右の根本目的は要するに非軍事化及び民主化の二つであるが、これらを再分すれば左の諸點となる。

(1) 軍隊の無條件降伏、武裝解除及び復員
(2) 軍事産業の破壞
(3) 領土の縮少
(4) 日本國民をして侵略の擧に出でしめた者の權力及び勢力の永久的除去
(5) 戰爭犯罪人の處罰
(6) 民主的傾向の復活及び強化に對する障碍の除去、言論

3 経済諸施策への対応(昭和21年5月～24年4月)

(7)日本國民の自由意思による平和的傾向の責任政府樹立

右の内、(1)及び(2)は占領直後完了しているのであるから、現在のところ占領の目的は(3)ないし(7)の達成を確保するにある次第であるしかしてこれらの事項についても着々目的達成への歩が進められていることは周知の通りであり、このことはマックアーサー元帥の屡次(一九四七年三月十七日等)の聲明、アイケルバーガー中將歸國後の談話、張群氏の訪日報告等にも逑べられている。昨年七月米國が對日講和豫備會議を提唱したことも、ソ連、中國、英連邦諸國が對日講和の早期締結を提唱していることも、本年十一月國連總會が對日講和の促進を決議したことも、みな日本の非軍事化が達成され、民主化が進ちよくし、その基礎が大體でき上つたことを列國が認めている證左であるといえよう。

終戰以來非軍事化及び民主化のため實施せられた主な措置は別紙(甲)に記載の通りである。

五、日本管理の第三の目的のうち、連合國財産及びいわゆりやく奪財産の返還についてはポツダム宣言は何ら言及していない。賠償の取立についても同宣言は直接これを條件としていない、ただ、同宣言を支持し且公正なる實物賠償の取立を可能ならしむる如き産業を維持することを許さるべし、、、、、、」とあり、賠償の取立を予定しているに過ぎないのである。

連合國財産及びいわゆるりやく奪財産の返還が非軍事化及び民主化と關係なきことは明かである。賠償については、軍事施設及び軍需産業施設の撤去という面においては非軍事化と關係があるが、損害賠償という賠償の固有の意義においては非軍事化とも民主化とも關係がない。從來の國際慣例においては、これらの措置は講和條約により正式に決定せられ、平和囘復後に實施せられるのが普通である。しかるに日本の場合は、これらの事項について既に種々の指令が發せられ、かつ現に實施せられつつあるものが少くない。すなわち、この分野においても管理が行われるとともにその結果日本にとつて消極的な意味におけるド・ファクト・ピースの一現象が起つているとも見られる。

六、次に、日本管理の目的の第四、すなわち日本に對する經濟的救濟の有效なる實施及び日本の經濟的自立達成という點について述べる。日本がその經濟を支持するに足る平和的產業を維持し得ることはポツダム宣言の認めた所であるが、占領の初期においては連合國は日本の經濟から復は日本國民自身の努力によつてなすべしとの方針をとっていた。米國の「初期對日方針」も極東委員會の「對日基本政策」も、現在の日本の苦境は自己の行爲の直接の結果であつて、連合國は損害修復の重荷を負擔しない旨を指摘した。しかるに一九四六年春食糧不足が日本の自力によつては到底克服し得ないものであることが明かとなつたので、疾病と社會不安を防止するため米國は取りあえず日本經濟の救濟に乘り出し、じ來年々約四億弗を國庫から支出して、食糧、肥料、醫藥、石油等を供給するに至つた。そこで占領軍當局としてはこの救濟が日本において有效適切に行われることに關心をもつのは自然であり、この見地からも日本經濟に對する管理が行われることとなつた。

しかしながら右の經濟的援助は應急的救濟という性質のものであり、未だ經濟自立のための恆久的措置ではない。のみならずポーレーの賠償案(一九四五年十二月及び四六年十一月)及びこれを基礎とした極東委員會の中間賠償計畫(一九四六年五月—十一月)はでき得る限り多くの賠償を取るという見地から最低限度の平和的國內需要を充すに必要な以外の一切の產業施設を撤去することを骨子としたものであり、日本の經濟的自立という見地から、輸入を賄うために必要な輸出產業施設を殘置せしめることに充分な考慮を拂ったものではなかった。しかるに日本が經濟的に自立しない限り、米國としては前記のような救濟の續行を餘儀なくされ、米國納稅者の負擔が嵩むのみならず、日本が平和的民主國家となる上に障碍となり、又共產主義の溫床となるおそれもあるとの考慮から、その後日本の經濟的自立の重要性が先ず米國陸軍省を中心として痛感せられるに至り、一九四七年には日本の經濟能力再調査が行われることとなり、その結果が、賠償は日本の經濟的自立を妨げない程度にとどめようというストライク調査團報告書(一九四八年二月)ともなつた次第である。從って日本の管理の面に

3　経済諸施策への対応（昭和21年5月～24年4月）

おいても経済的自立を速に達成せしめることを目的とする命令、勧告、指導、監督等が行われることになつた。かくて日本の経済は非軍事化及び民主化のための外、救済の有効なる実施及び経済的自立の達成という目的からも連合國の管理に服することとなつたのである。この點はポツダム宣言には直接述べてないことであるが、救済を受けている限りは或る程度やむを得ないことであるし、又ポツダム宣言の條項の實施と全然關係がないとはいえない。何となれば社會不安の防止は平穏なる占領實施のため必要であり、又經濟を支持するに足る平和的産業の維持は既述のごとくポツダム宣言も認めた所であるからである。ただ同宣言は經濟的自立達成のための管理、援助までも豫期していたとは思えないし、この問題については日本の立場から獨自の希望や意見もあるはずである。

七、次に日本管理の第五の目的、即ち防共基地としての確保及び東亞の工場としての復興と言う點について述べる。

米ソ關係の惡化及び東南アジア諸國の政治的、經濟的不安等に鑑み、その後米國においては單に日本の經濟的

自立を達成せしめるのみならず、更に日本を防共基地として確保し、且つ東亞の工場として復興せしめるため、積極的に援助するという方針をとるに至つたものと觀察せられる。このことを示す現象は一九四八年に入つてから特に多い。その主なるものを例示すれば左の通りである。

一、極東における全体主義の防壁としての日本の強化を主張したロイヤル陸軍長官の演説（一月六日）
一、日本の經濟復興のための措置を主張した極東委員會米國代表マッコイ少將の演説（一月二十一日）
一、經濟力集中排除に關するFEC文書第二三〇號原案の抛棄
一、ストライク報告書よりも更に輕い賠償を提案すると共に、日本經濟復興のため必要な各種の措置、特に米國からの經濟的援助の必要を主張したドレイパー使節團報告書（ジョンストン報告）の發表（五月十九日）
一、米國政府による對日救濟費の外、經濟復興援助費の支出、輸出入囘轉基金の設定及び米國民間銀行による棉花借款の成立

一、防共基地としての重要性を強調したアイケルバーカー中將の談話
一、賠償はジョンストン報告のラインによることに米國陸軍省及び國務省の意見が一致したとの報道（六月九日）
一、國家公務員法の改正（公務員の罷業禁止）を要求したマ元帥の書翰（七月二十二日）
一、日本は南鮮及びフィリピンと共に東洋における民主主義防壁の支柱である旨を述べたマックァーサー元帥の聲明（九月二日）

非軍事化の完了、民主化の進行及び右のような米國の對日方針轉換の結果、占領軍駐屯及びこれに伴う各種施設の意義も、ポツダム宣言の條項履行を保障するということに漸次權移し（從って占領費負擔の意義も變って來た）、又經濟管理の面においても非軍事化、民主化という目的よりも、經濟的自立達成、更に進んでは復興援助という目的が比重を増加して來たものと思われる。

共産主義勢力に對して占領軍の安全をはかり、日本の國內治安を維持して平穏なる占領を實施するということ

はポツダム宣言と關係があるが、それ以外の觀點は、ポツダム宣言や降伏文書には直接豫見されなかった所である。尤も復興援助という點は明らかに日本の利益であり、援助を受ける以上その有效適切な實施をはかるため勸告、指導、監督等を受けることはある程度やむを得ない。又防共という點も日本の治安及び國防の見地から言えば利益であるに相違ないが、その手段、方法等については日本としても希望や意見がある筈である。況んや米國の對ソ政策の手段ない至對ソ作戰の基地としての利用ということになると將來の日本の運命及び安全に關する重大問題である。日本の統治權は、ポツダム宣言の條項を含む降伏條項の實施に必要なる限りにおいては、連合國最高司令官の權限の下に從屬するが、それ以外の問題については、サブヂェクト・トゥではなく、獨自、對等の立場において話合をなし、自己の希望や主張を述べ得べき筈である。就中、その將來の運命及び安全に關する問題については、殊に然りと言わねばならぬ。（本來ならば、前記五、及び六、の問題の外、この點について正常な話合の出來るようなド・ファクト・ピースが特に望ましい）

3　経済諸施策への対応（昭和21年5月～24年4月）

八、なお、中立國との間の外交關係の全面的禁止は以上何れの目的から見ても理由薄弱である。よって中立國との外交關係は原則としてこれを復活せしめられることが望ましく、ただ占領軍の安全をはかり又占領目的の達成阻碍を防止するだけのために監督を行えば足りるものと思われる。

九、連合國の日本管理は以上のごとき目的をもって行われ、日本國家の統治權及び國民の活動は、對外關係、内政一般、軍事、經濟、文化、社會等各分野において各種の制限に服している。

管理には直接管理と間接管理とが考えられるが、日本の場合には、米國の「初期對日方針」及び極東委員會の「對日基本政策」に記されている通り、原則として日本政府を利用する間接管理が行われ、直接管理は例外である。直接管理の行われている主なる分野は國防、對外關係の大部分、裁判權の一部、貿易及び國際收支の相當大なる部分、言論、報道、通信の檢閲その他警察權の一部等である。

さて、日本管理の目的及びそれらの比重に既述のごとき變遷があり、又非軍事化は完了し、民主化の基盤もほぼ完成し、しかも他方、講和の成立が延引している結果、管理の態樣、方法、程度等に多少變化が見られつつある。一九四八年三月三十一日發表されたマ元帥の陸軍長官あて一月十八日付書翰は(1)通商貿易上の諸制限の緩和(2)日本國民の海外渡航權の囘復(3)國内問題の自主的解決を勸告したが、現在いかなる分野においていかなる管理が行われているか、又管理は實際上果して緩和されつつあるか、はたまた強化されつつあるか、その程度はどうか。各分野におけるこれらの點についての主なる事實は別紙(乙)號記載の通りであるが、大局的な傾向を要約すれば、大体次のようにいえると思う。

(1) 對外關係

講和の遅延及び經濟的自立ないし復興の必要に鑑み、外國との間の人的及び物的交通、通信及び公的關係は部分的に漸次囘復しつつある。例えば貿易、特に民間貿易の制限付再開、外國人及び日本人の來往に對する禁止の緩和、官吏の國際會議出席許可（但し總司令部員の顧問たる資格で）、郵便及び電氣通信の制限付再

開、萬國郵便條約及び國際電氣通信條約のごとき自働的加入條項を有する技術的、行政的事項に關する條約に對する加入等がこれである。しかしながら外交官及び領事官の派遣接受、外交交渉、一般の政治的及び經濟的條約の締結、國際機關及び國際會議への參加等正規の外交權は猶ほとんど全面的に停止されていることは周知の通りである。

(2) 國內事項

(イ) 政治、文化、社會等の分野

非軍事化及び民主化の基盤はほとんど完成したので、管理は漸次大綱から末梢部分に移行し、可なり微に入り細にわたっている。

命令という形よりも勸告、監督という內面指導の形が多く選ばれるようになったように見受けられる。實質的にほとんど制限緩和の事實はなく、むしろ強化されつつあるとさえ言える。

(ロ) 經濟の分野

非軍事化及び民主化に關する點においては、經濟の分野についてもほぼ前記と同樣のことが言えよう。

經濟的自立及び復興に關する點においては、米國の政策の積極化に伴い、管理は大綱についても強化されつつあると言うべきであろう。(但し日本の經濟全體に對する枠や經濟力集中排除等の實施的制限が緩和されつつあることは旣述の通り)

編注　本文書の別紙(甲)は省略、別紙(乙)は見当たらない。

216

マッカーサー司令官の年頭メッセージ

昭和24年1月1日　連合国最高司令官総司令部発表

General of the Army Douglas MacArthur's

New Year Message

TO THE PEOPLE OF JAPAN:

January 1, 1949

The period just concluded has been of great historical significance to Japan and to the other nations of the world. For in this period mankind has been groping for the solution to many ills which have beset the human race since the dawn of time. Steps have been halting and uncertain due to the confusion still engendered in the aftermath of war by the clash of opposed ideologies and the ambitions of selfish men who seek advantage from the universal will for peace. Encouragement is seen, however, from the fact that thinking men of all nations and all races, in increasing numbers, are firmly facing the historical realism that war, long tried, has never been and never will be a panacea for human ills, and are diligently searching for other means to orient mankind toward that human progress which alone can come from the abolition of war and the peaceful solution of issues between nations and men. Thus, on balance definite progress is being made in mobilizing the full power of world opinion in support of the general welfare of all mankind.

In Japan, despite freedom's convulsions on the Asiatic mainland, the situation has continued calm and well ordered as you have worked to lay imperishable foundation stones in the political mold of freedom and dignity and peace. You have established here a truly representative government in accordance with and responsive to the will of the majority. In no land anywhere are men more free or more safe and secure, and men here live in greater peace and greater tranquillity than do many of your neighbors. A serenity of calm has indeed enveloped your Islands for which every law-abiding citizen fully shares in the credit.

The period we now enter will test the invincibility of your will and the wisdom and capacity of your endowment to erect upon that political base an edifice of economic security, cast in the enlightened experience of time, which will fully support and preserve it. For political freedom and economic self-sufficiency are inseparable and of mutual support, as each is dependent for survival upon the spiritual strength of the other. Much that you have done in the fashioning of a strong and durable political base has earned the approval of other peoples, but now that the emphasis has shifted from political to economic reconstruction a world awaits with critical but not unfriendly eye your mastery of the problem. For as I pointed out in my letter of December 19th last to your Prime Minister, in which I set forth the intermediate objectives prerequisite to the attainment of your economic self-sufficiency, political freedom is impossible of achievement so long as your daily livelihood is dependent in any degree upon the beneficent energies of others. Furthermore, in past I repeatedly have affirmed to my own government that your will and your industry were such that given a reasonable opportunity for trade you could fully establish a self-supporting economy, producing for others no less than you received from others, and that this alone was the opportunity you asked and which you sought. You now have that opportunity. It is for you in gearing the forces of internal production to demonstrate the justification for my faith.

Your immediate response to the challenge of these new objectives has been most encouraging. On the labor front where the heavy burden of individual toil necessarily must fall there has emerged a high type of labor statesmanship, which has seen and fully accepted the need temporarily to lay aside some of labor's legitimate weapons in order to throw the full force of labor's energies in support of the national objective. In the ranks of management, too, the response has been similarly encouraging. Those who till Japan's soil, by their skill and industry already in past have won my sincere admiration, but even they are gearing themselves for renewed and greater effort to maximize Japan's indigenous food resources. And with the rapid and determined mobilization of Japan's public opinion now underway under the leadership of a sound and patriotic press, there is no room for doubt that these economic objectives progressively will be achieved.

This does not mean that the difficulties ahead will be light as the emphasis shifts from political to economic concern, but the measure of the individual burden to be borne will lie in the number of citizens who rally to assume their full share of the responsibility. And any who fail resolutely to do so must feel the full weight of an aroused public opprobrium. For none of right may shrink his equitable share of this, a whole people's burden.

The general election just ahead will test your wisdom in the selection of a leadership to whom you will in this crucial period entrust the sovereign power. The times require great dignity and capacity for wise statesmanship and such should be the measure of your choice — men capable of elevating your national legislative forum to the standard set by the finest of your traditions. Thereafter the issue will rest squarely upon the type of leadership they bring to the country and the resolute will by which each among your citizenry acquits his individual responsibility in the great task of ensuring that Japan may live. I have left this largely to your implementation without the slightest reservation of doubt concerning your ability to master its attending responsibility.

To enhance the spiritual strength necessary to carry on in the pattern which your general welfare now demands and in recognition of those advances you have heretofore made in establishing the sturdy base for a free political destiny, I now restore to you the unrestricted use and display of your national flag within your country's territorial limits. And I do so with the fervent hope that this flag shall ever stand in future before the world as a symbol of peace based upon those immutable concepts of justice and freedom universally sought by the human race; that it shall stand firm advocate for a concept of nationalism ever subordinate to the higher duty of obedience to the universal laws, written and unwritten, which establish the mutual obligations and responsibilities among peoples within the family of nations; and that it shall serve as a shining beacon to summon every Japanese citizen resolutely to the duty of building Japan's economic stature to ensure and preserve Japan's political freedom.

DOUGLAS MacARTHUR

編　注　本文書は、昭和二十四年三月、外務省特別資料部作成「日本占領及び管理重要文書集」第二巻より抜粋。

217　国旗の無制限掲揚に関する指令

昭和24年1月6日　連合国最高司令官総司令部より　日本政府宛

GENERAL HEADQUARTERS
SUPREME COMMANDER FOR THE ALLIED POWERS
APO 500

6 January 1949

AG 332.1 (29 Jan 46) GA
SCAPIN 1956
MEMORANDUM FOR: JAPANESE GOVERNMENT
SUBJECT: Display of Japanese National Flag

1. Reference is made to:

a. General Headquarters, Supreme Commander for the Allied Powers, memorandum, file AG 332.1 (30 Aug 48) GA, SCAPIN 1934, subject, "Display of Japanese National Flag," dated 14 September 1948.

b. General Headquarters, Supreme Commander for the Allied Powers, memorandum, file AG 332.1 (30 Aug 48) GA, SCAPIN 1934/1, subject, "Display of Japanese National Flag," dated 15 November 1948.

c. General Headquarters, Supreme Commander for the Allied Powers, memorandum, file AG 091 (29 Jan 46) GS, SCAPIN 677, subject, "Governmental and Administrative Separation of Certain Outlying Areas from Japan," dated 29 January 1946.

d. General Headquarters, Supreme Commander for the Allied Powers, memorandum, file AG 091 (22 Mar 46) GS, SCAPIN 841, subject, "Governmental and Administrative Separation of Certain Outlying Areas from Japan," dated 22 March 1946.

2. References 1a and b above are rescinded.

3. Effective 1 January 1949 permission is granted for the Japanese national flag to be displayed and used without restriction within the territorial limits of Japan, as defined by references 1c and d above.

4. Occupation forces have been informed in this matter.

FOR THE SUPREME COMMANDER:

R. M. LEVY
Colonel, AGD
Adjutant General

218

昭和24年1月21日　倭島（英二）管理局長作成

【ロイヤル陸軍長官と總理との會談に關する參考資料】

ロイヤル陸軍長官と總理との會談に關する參考資料

二四、一、二一

倭島

目　次

一、訪日に關する情勢判斷

二、マツクアーサー元帥との打合

三、ロイヤル長官との會談に注意すべき二點

3　経済諸施策への対応(昭和21年5月～24年4月)

ロイヤル陸軍長官と總理との會談に關する參考資料

二四、一、二一

一、今般のロイヤル陸軍長官の訪日は政策決定と密接に關係があるものと判斷せられる。差當りは一九五〇年度予算編成との關係であろうが、更にその根底においては尠くともさきに朝鮮の獨立を促進した方向の政策と一脈の繋りを持ち、更にその發展的の含みを持つものと思われる。

總理の話の内容は斯る先方の心構にピッタリとくる調子の高いものであるべきである。

二、High Policy に關することであるだけに、總理としてはロイヤル長官との會談の前に先づマックアーサー元帥と一應話して見て置かれる必要があろう。何れ總選擧直後結果報告等のため元帥を訪問せられることとなろうから、

その際然るべく耳打ちして置かれるのも一案である。

三、ロイヤル長官との會談では總理としては尠くとも次の二つの點に留意せられては如何かと思われる。

第一點は、この Personal Contact の好機をとらえて、總理の日頃の平和に關する信念とか政治的立場を充分説明せられ、米國政府の上層部に更に一人の知己を得られる様努力せられるのが肝要である。人間的信用が總ての基であるからである。

特に保守と言うことは、動もすれば反動とか國粋とか關連して考えられ、更にその裏面において米國との協力を涵るが如き誤解を受ける危ぐ必ずしもなしとしない。從って總理としては、この際米國と積極的に協力して遣ってゆく心組なることを率直に披瀝せられ、初對面にあり勝ちな警戒的な氣分をなるたけ和らげて、先方から何に彼に打明け話をする氣になるような風にせられることが最も大切であると思われる。

第二の點は、最近の我國情を率直に傳えて、これをあるべき方向へ引っぱって行くために是非米國側でも再考して貰いたい點、更に協力援助して貰いたい點を述べら

四、我國の安全保障問題
五、一般大衆の組織の問題
六、不消化人口の問題
七、我經濟再建の國際的條件
八、結語

れる必要があると思われる。

特に講和條約締結前においても、事實上速かに我國を自立せしむるために種々米國側において好意的考慮を進めてくれる點については深く感謝する處であるが、政治經濟社會各方面において未だ諸態勢に相當空白と凸凹とがあり、自立までには再調整を要するもの多々ある實情であると述べられ、從つてこれを未調整のままに過早に手離される様なことになると情勢の如何によつては收拾すべからざる様なことになるとも限らず、そうすれば結局共産主義者等の思う壺にはまることになることを恐れる旨を強調せられ、今後もどつしり腰を落ちつけて援助して格好をつける様にして貰いたいとの筋にて話して置かれることが必要であると思われる。(米國の現在における意圖と立場より見て、この際總理からひたすら講和條約締結促進の希望を表明せられると無用の誤解を招く恐れがないとも限らぬからである。)

總理から長官の注意を喚起せられる問題の中、特に政治に關連しては我國の安全保障と一般大衆の組織の問題、

經濟に關連しては不消化人口と我經濟再建の國際的條件について所見を披瀝せられロイヤル長官の意嚮と言うか、米國政府の底意を質して見られることが必要であると思われる。

四、我國の安全保障の問題は結局條約の締結までハッキリせぬ問題であるとも思われるが最近の國民感情は、國際政局の動きをも反映し、この問題について條約前においても何等か今少し安心の出來る様な風になることを欲していることは明らかで、更に換言すれば、本件について多少なりとも不安があるがために却つて共産主義者等に乗せられ、國民の氣持を日和見的にする傾向にあることは爭われぬ事實である。ソ連に對する考え方、憲法の永續性、再武裝の必然性等々に關する巷の私的論議の傾向は輕視すべきものでないと思われる。

Security Formula としては國際連合の枠内で集團保障的なものが考えられることになるのであろうが、要は米國がどの程度までそれに腰を入れてくれるかにかかるべく、而も現在の様子では米國の東亞に對する力の入れ方は西歐特に英國との關係に比し第二義的であつて、事あ

3 経済諸施策への対応（昭和21年5月～24年4月）

る際は一應棄てて又取返えせばよいではないかと言う様な態勢の據點にしか見えない。本當に我國を東亞における平和維持の據點として保持する氣なら作戰的見地からだけでも今少し施策や注文がありそうなものであると思われる。朝鮮の問題にしても、それが作戰的に見て結局保持出來ぬから何時でも棄て得る様にするために早く獨立態勢に入らしめたのだとの穿った觀察もあった。我國に對してもその様な傾向はないかどうか。もし我國を一つの據點として東亞の自立態勢を考える氣があるなら朝鮮の獨立に關しても我國の自立態勢との間に現在より更に考慮を加えねばならぬ點がある。なお我國の警察制度も、我國を骨抜きにすると言うのでなく新しい筋金を入れて新しい役割をさせると言う考えであるならば、警官の數丈けでなく制度そのものについても再考をしなくてはならぬ點を實狀に照して縷々說明せられることが必要と思われる。

五、一般大衆組織の問題は現在殘された政治上の空白の一番根本的なものと思われる。古い傳統と組織が急激に破壞されて新憲法の下に新しい秩序と組織が生れることには

なっているが、現實の狀況では未だ大きな空白として殘されている。

一般大衆の中で實質的に全國に强固な組織を張つているものは、現在第一は十六萬の黨員とシンパ百萬を擁する共產黨、第二は六百萬に達する勞働各組合位のようであって、その他の一般大衆は事實上 Unorganized の狀況に殘されている。

從來の方針によれば、新憲法の下に教育制度を刷新し教育と Trial and Error の實地訓練でこの大衆を民主的にたたき直すことになつている。もちろんそれは百年の大計として正しいものであろうが、しかし差當りの玆十年十五年の間の過渡期を如何にするかの問題がある。現在の空白は急激に左の傾向に蠶食せられて行きつつあるのであるが、これをこの儘座視するより外に方法はないかと言うことである。

事の極めて差迫つた際、大衆を急速に組織すると、かつてのナチとかファッショ型となるか或はソヴイエット張りの協和會又は新民會は我國で試みられた翼贊會とか隣組の様なことにならざるを得ない。しかもこれは今

の建前では總てRegimentationとして禁絶せられている方向である。

或る政治學者の研究では、我が現狀の儘に推移すれば、茲數年にして日本は共産主義に走るか又はファッショに再轉回するかの何れかを選ばねばならぬ傾向にあると見ている。つまり一般大衆の勢いが、現在の空白な狀況に居たたまれなくなって何等かのFormulaを欲求しそれにはまつて行くと言うことである。かかる見解の當否は別としても、總理としてはこの際一般大衆の組織が左のものを除き殆んど空白の狀態にあることを説明せられ、何んとかこれに對して民主主義の新しい建前の下にて據り所を與える様に出來ぬものかと考えている次第をなるべく話をせられ、右對策に關する先方の意見を求められては如何かと思われる。

六、不消化人口の問題は、一面には政治的の懸案であり、一面には經濟的の未決案件で一番解決困難なものであろう。我國の人口問題は今に始まったことではないが、戰後は特にその重壓が甚しい。まるで三疊か四疊半の室の中に五十人も六十人もインターンされたかの様である。

特に此の人口の中で正常なる生業につき得ないで其の場しのぎのことをして食いつないでいる人達、つまり現在の我經濟機構としては消化しきれないで不消化のままになっている人達の對策が更に問題である。

かかる不消化人口の大きな源を爲すと思われるものには、第一に海外からの引揚者があり、第二に戰災者がある。前者は一應六百萬と見積られるが關係家族を含めると尠くとも八百七十萬となり、後者は八百七十萬と見積られている。右二つでも合計千六百七十萬となり我現人口の約二割に達する譯である。

人口學者の調査によれば右引揚者、戰災者の外に正業からあぶれた失業者を加算して人口重壓は四割に達すると言う計算を述べているものもある。それが二割と言うか四割と見るかは別としても現在における我國の人口重壓と言うか不消化人口が甚だ高度のものであって、果してこれが貿易の再開等により何の程度に緩和せられるかが問題であると思う。

政治的觀點よりすればかかる不消化人口は共産主義の好餌であり經濟的の見地からは闇と不正の溫牀である。

3 経済諸施策への対応(昭和21年5月～24年4月)

總理としてはこの際かかる人口的の困難を説明せられ海外への大量渡航の問題について長官の考慮を願って置かれては如何かと思われる。

七、ロイヤル長官としては總選擧後の政治態勢と九原則の實現の見透しについて色々質問がして見たいであろうし、總理としてもこの點具體的に説明せられる必要があろうが、總理よりロイヤル長官の意見を質し又頼んで置いて貰いたいことは、寧ろその國外との關係で、つまり我經濟再建の國際的條件とも言うべきことに關してである。

第一に我國の經濟再建は從來一九三〇―三四年の生活水準の囘復が目標となっており五カ年計畫などもそれに調子を合せて立案せられている。外資導入の問題も一應我國内における需要とか購買力が直接の對象となっている如くである。

しかし此處で問題は昨年ドレーパー陸軍次官訪日の頃以來非公式ながら度々言われていることは、我國を東亞の工場たらしめると言うことである。つまり、我國の經濟再建と言うことが尠くとも東亞の經濟復興と言うこととの關連で考えられて居る點である。

事實これは單に非公式な發言に現われてくると言うばかりでなく、アジア及び極東經濟委員會の昨年における會合或はその決議の中にもその方向の具體的の表現が行われている。

從って對ソ關係やら條約締結前の機微なる關係はあるも、我國としては我國の經濟再建の基本的方向について米國政府の腹を打割った話を聞いておく必要がある。その考え方の如何によっては、基礎産業の復興の仕方にも根本的な相違を生ずるし、技術方面の人の養成訓練にも自ら心構が違ってくるからである。

第二に、尠くとも東亞の資源と市場とを對象として我經濟再建を目指す建前となるならば、更に米國の我國に對する投資の規模と性質が從來の考え方より一層擴大されてくると思われるが、その際における我國内の統制經濟と米國の自由奔放なる資本の繋りを如何につけるかと言う問題、自由港的な施設の問題、船舶の問題等を生じてくる。

總理としては米國の考え方一つによっては、我國の經濟を大きく開放して如何様にもこれに調子を合せる覺悟

を表明せられて先方の意見をたたいて見られては如何かと思われる。

第三に、國際的の視野と規模において我國の經濟を再建するならば、どうせ米國の中位の一州程度の面積と資源の賦存狀況であるから、この中の農業とか工業を從來の基礎の下に別々に復興する思想を棄てて、農業と工業とを密接に關連せしめて再建する全く新しい方向を選ぶことも一つの案であると思われる。つまり交通網を整備することにより工場を分業的に分散配置し、所謂「工場の農村化、農村の工場化」を徹底して遣ることである。

かかる徹底した再建方策は結局米國の了解と援助なしには到底實現できないのであるから、この際總理としては、ロイヤル長官とかかる案に對する米國側の意見についても質して置かれることが必要ではないかと思われる次第である。

八、以上を要するに、今般の總理とロイヤル長官との會談においては、Personal Contact の點に一つの重要なる意義あるに鑑みこの觀點よりこの機會をフルに活用する次第なるに鑑みこの観点よりこの機会をフルに活用する次第なるに

るに努むるとともに先方の直面する根本問題につき相互の首腦者間に腹藏のない意見の交換を行い特に我方としては眼前の諸指令、諸施策の據って來たる米國の根本政策につき先方の本當の腹を確かめる絕好の機會なるにつきその意味にても今回の會談をフルに活用する樣充分用意する要ありと認められる。

〜〜〜〜〜〜〜〜〜〜〜〜〜〜〜〜〜〜〜

219 【九原則の實施に關連する要望事項】

昭和24年1月28日　外務省作成

九原則の實施に關連する要望事項

外　務　省

二四、一、二八

一、貿易業者の海外渡航と通商領事關係政府機關の海外駐在

(イ)日本の貿易業者の海外渡航

最近における世界市場の動向を知得し、これにマッチする商品の生產及び輸出を促進するため、次の諸事項が出來得る限り廣範圍の地域にわたって、實現されることが望ましい。

3　経済諸施策への対応（昭和21年5月～24年4月）

(一) 貿易専門家よりなる海外市場調査團の派遣

(二) 貿易業者の海外渡航

(三) 貿易業者の海外における代理店、支店、出張所の設置

(ロ) 日本政府機關の海外駐在

一方において、諸外國との協定貿易の實施を圓滑にし及び保護を與えるため、政府の事務處理機關として、商務的機關又は領事的機關を主要市場に駐在させることを漸進的に許されることが望ましい。

三、通商上の最惠國待遇の保障と國際機關への加入

(イ) 通商上の最惠國待遇の保障

日本の輸出振興のため、日本の輸出品に對する關稅上の差別待遇が世界諸國によつて、行われることのないように、日本に對する通商上の最惠國待遇の確保につき、助力斡旋を得たきこと。

(ロ) 國際貿易機關（ITO）への加盟

右の問題に關連し、目下設立の途上にある國際貿易機關が發足した曉には、できる限り早い機會に、日本が

その一員として自由な多角的世界貿易の實現に貢獻することのできるように、これへの加盟を許されることが望ましい。日本政府は國際貿易機關憲章（Charter for an International Trade Organization）實現を企圖する理想に深い共鳴を感じ、今日からこれに合致する政策をとることに努めている。

(ハ) アジア極東經濟委員會への協力

日本とアジア地域との經濟的連帶關係にかんがみ、アジア極東地域の經濟の復興及び發展を促進する目的をもつて、國際聯合の社會經濟理事會の管下において目下進行中のアジア極東經濟委員會（Economic Commission for Asia and the Far East）の活動に何らかの形で日本人を協力せしめられるように取計はれんことを切望する。

(ニ) その他の政府間機關への加盟

國際貿易機關（ITO）とともに國際經濟協力の理想を追求する次のような政府間諸機關においおい加盟を許されるよう希望する。これらの機關、とくに國際勞働機關に協力することによつて、日本の「不公正な競

争」に對する世界の誤解ないし危惧を去ることが望ましい。

（一）國際通貨基金（International Monetary Fund）

（二）國際復興開發銀行（International Bank for Reconstruction and Development）

（三）國際勞働機關（International Labour Organization）

220　昭和24年2月2日　連合国最高司令官総司令部より　日本政府宛

為替管理委員会の設置等に関する指令

GENERAL HEADQUARTERS
SUPREME COMMANDER FOR THE ALLIED POWERS
APO 500

AG 386.7 (11 Dec 48) ESS/FIN　　　　　　2 February 1949
SCAPIN 1968
MEMORANDUM FOR: JAPANESE GOVERNMENT
SUBJECT: Foreign Exchange Controls

1. References are:

   a. Foreign Exchange Control Law (Law No.83, 11 April 1941) as amended.

   b. The following memoranda for the Japanese Government from General Headquarters, Supreme Commander for the Allied Powers:

   (1) AG 130 (22 Sep 45) ESS, SCAPIN 45, 22 September 1945, subject: Control of Financial Transactions.

   (2) AG 091.3 (22 Sep 45) ESS, SCAPIN 44, 22 September 1945, subject: Controls over Exports and Imports of Gold, Silver, Securities and Financial Instruments, and Appendix A thereto.

   (3) AG 160 (30 Oct 45) ESS/FI, SCAPIN 211, 30 October 1945, subject: Contracts by Persons in Japan with Foreign Concerns.

   (4) AG 334 (2 Apr 46) ESS/IE, SCAPIN 854, 3 April 1946, subject: Board of Trade (Boeki Cho).

2. The Japanese Government is directed to take the neces-

3 経済諸施策への対応（昭和 21 年 5 月～24 年 4 月）

sary steps promptly to establish coordinated control over the movement of foreign exchange and trade into and out of Japan, subject to the general supervision of the Supreme Commander for the Allied Powers. Such controls shall be flexible, so designed as to foster the furtherance of trade and investment programs essential to the economic rehabilitation of Japan and shall conform with the general characteristics of foreign exchange controls practiced by member nations of the International Monetary Fund. The measures taken shall include:

　a. Reorganization and regularization of control procedures, and clear allocation of functional responsibilities among the agencies of the Japanese Government concerned.

　b. Establishment of a Foreign Exchange Control Board to maintain administrative control of all Japanese Government funds, both foreign and domestic, resulting from international trade and exchange transactions; to establish administrative procedures for and coordinate clearance of all international exchange and trade transactions; make recommendations on foreign exchange policy; and maintain complete and current records of foreign exchange holdings, movements and commitments.

　c. Integration of Japanese and foreign banks into established control procedures.

　d. Appropriate utilization of the Japanese customs service in the application of foreign exchange controls.

3. The Foreign Exchange Control Board will be established independent of existing Japanese ministries and will consist of three to five persons of recognized merit, standing and general experience, appointed for such term of office and granted such compensation as will insure effective non-partisan service of the high order required. The Board will maintain a staff adequate to discharge its responsibilities effectively.

4. The Board will maintain its offices in the head office and branches of the Bank of Japan as required and will designate the Bank of Japan as its agent to conduct operations and maintain records and accounts and to make reports thereof as prescribed by the Board in the discharge of its functions and responsibilities. The Board shall also be authorized access to such records and facilities of the Bank of Japan, the Customs Service and other agencies of

663

the Japanese Government as are pertinent to the performance of its functions.

5. The Japanese Government will forward to General Headquarters, Supreme Commander for the Allied Powers, periodic reports prepared by the Board, showing the volume and nature of foreign exchange transactions, and the relation of the results thereof to economic rehabilitation of Japan.

6. All assignments of Foreign Exchange or Trade Control functions and responsibilities to Japanese agencies which have been directed by earlier memoranda for the Japanese Government are superseded by this memorandum insofar as they are in conflict with the terms specified herein.

7. Direct communication between interested staff sections of the Supreme Commander for the Allied Powers and appropriate agencies of the Japanese Government is authorized to facilitate implementation of this memorandum.

FOR THE SUPREME COMMANDER:

R. M. LEVY
Colonel, AGD

221　昭和24年2月2日　特別資料部作成

［民政移管問題］

昭和二四、一一、二

特　別　資　料　部

民政移管問題

一、従来の経緯

従来米国の責任ある当局者が自ら日本管理について民政移管の意見を発表したことはなかった。唯昨年三月国務省政策企画部長ケナン氏訪日の際、民政移管の問題が取上げられるのではないかと新聞紙上取沙汰せられ、又昨年九月、十月頃米国務省及び陸軍省が対日新政策を計画乃至準備中であり、右はケナン氏報告の線に沿うものであるとUP電やニュースウィークで伝えられた。当時伝えられた新政策の項目のうち、特に注目すべき点は左の通りであった。

(イ)占領軍の任務を軍事的役割だけに限定すること。

3　経済諸施策への対応（昭和21年5月～24年4月）

(ロ) 占領軍兵力を縮減すること。

(ハ) 日本に約十五萬の武装警察隊の保有を許すこと。

(ニ) 對日管理は占領目的の達成確保に必要な最少限度に縮少、緩和すること。

(ホ) 一流の米國實業家を日本政府へ政治顧問として派遣し、ある程度の經濟監督を續けること。

しかるに當時は總司令部筋は右樣のことはないと否定している旨新聞報道せられた。

今囘ローヤル長官の訪日に先ち、獨逸とともに日本の管理についても民政移管が問題となつている旨を海外通信は傳え、又總司令部がロ長官と協議するであろう四大事項の一に民政移管の問題がある旨を在京外國通信員は報道していた。

二月二日ロ長官の新聞記者會見で同長官はなるべく早く民政に移す方がよいという一般的意見をもっていることが明らかとなつた。

右の經緯から見て、予て米國の政府はなるべく早い適當の時期に民政に移すことを考慮していたものと思われ、これに對して總司令部は軍政の繼續を主張し、兩者の間に意見が一致しなかったのではないかと推測せられる。而してこの問題もロ長官訪日の機會に研究討議せられるのではないかと思われる。

三、民政移管論と反對論の理由

米國中央が民政移管を考慮する理由としては大体二つのことが考えられる。

(イ) 講和の遅延等に鑑み占領軍の任務を固有の軍務に限定し、その兵力及び經費を節約すること。

(ロ) 從來の管理政策は必ずしも一〇〇パーセント成功とは認められず、管理はやはり專門のシヴィリアンに任かせる方が適正、圓滑に遂行せられるであろうと考えるに至ったこと。

これに對し、現地軍が軍政繼續を希望する理由は、軍政の方が對ソ戦略態勢確立上における軍の要請をよりよく充足し得るというにあるものと思われる。

三、民政の態樣及び機構

民政の態樣及び機構としては一應次の三種類が考えられる。

(イ) 命令系統や首腦部は從來通りで、ただ下部の管理行政

擔當者をすべて軍人からシヴィリアンに取替えるだけの方法。

これは眞の民政ではなく、この方法は採られないであろう。

(ロ)軍事事項についてはもちろん從來通りであるが、管理行政については、從來と異り、國務省を通じてマ元帥の下に民政長官を設けて補佐せしめ、總司令部の參謀長以下軍人は一切これにタッチせしめない方法。

この場合マ元帥は依然連合國管理行政の最高責任者たる地位の外に、日本における連合國管理行政の最高司令官たる地位を兼ねる次第である。この點において、完全な純粹の民政とはいい難いが、この方法ならば、「管理制度の根本的變革」でないともいえるから、米國政府の指令だけで實行できるし、對日理事會の地位にも變更を加える必要がないし、又マ元帥によつて軍の要請と管理行政上の要請をある程度調整することができるから、實現の可能性が最も大なる方法である。

(ハ)前記第二の方法よりも更に徹底した方法で、連合國最高司令官も管理行政には一切タッチせず、軍事事項だけを擔當し合同參謀本部だけから指揮命令を受けることにする。

日本における管理行政の最高責任者としては(1)連合國民政長官を設ける方法と(2)連合國對日管理(又は民政)理事會を設け、その下に執行機關として事務總長又は民政長官を置く方法とが考えられる。

(1)の場合は民政長官は米國國務省の指揮命令を受けるものとすることが出來るが

(2)の場合は、直接極東委員會の指揮命令を受けることにしなければならぬであろうから、米國としては採らぬ所であろう。

```
                    ┌─(軍事事項)─合同參謀本部──參謀長─軍
極東──米國─────連合國
委員會 政府    最高司令官
   (管理行政)  └─────────────民政長官─民政官
        國務省
        對日理事會
```

3　経済諸施策への対応（昭和21年5月～24年4月）

この第三の方法は(1)(2)の何れにせよ、最高司令官及び對日理事會の地位の重大なる變更であり、一九四五年十二月二十六日のモスコー協定にいう「管理機構の根本的變革」であるから、極東委員會の決定を經ねばならない重要問題であり、且つ米國政府の中間指令では實施出來ない事項に屬するし、而も極東委員會の議に付したならば各國殊にソ連との意見一致を見ることは殆んど不可能であろう。又日本に對する關係においても、ポツダム宣言及び降伏文書は日本の統治權は連合國最高司令官に從屬することを規定して居るから、これを民政長官や對日管理（又は民政）理事會の權限の下に從屬せしめるためには、更めて日本の了解と關係連合國の同意とを取付けることを必要とする。

尚この方法はマ元帥の面子と立場に微妙な影響があるが、何れにしても、第三の方法は實現の可能性が乏しい。

四、民政移管の利害得失

前記三つの方法のうちでは、實現の可能性が最も多いと見られる第二の方法について、それが實現せられた場合の利害得失として一應考えられる諸點は次の通りである。

(イ) 米側

(1) 兵力は節減出來るが、その代り民政委員を必要とし、經費は余り節約されないであろう。

(2) 軍の要請が圓滑に又は充分に充されず、若くは軍の要請と管理上の要請とが對立する虞がある。

(ロ) 日本側

(1) 末梢的な部面では管理の緩和乃至撤廢を期待し得るであろうが、大綱においては、殊に經濟部面では管理は緩和されないであろう。

(2) 我が方の希望や意見について先方の理解を得ることは從來よりも容易となる。

(3) 軍は管理の責任者でなくなるから設營その他の要請について、日本の立場を考えず無理な要求をなすかも知れないが、その代り、民政擔當者が日本の立場をディフェンドしてくれる。

五、民政移管の時期

目下對ソ戰略態勢確立の必要上、日本の政治、經濟把

667

「民政移管の問題」

昭和24年2月5日　条約局条約課作成

民政移管の問題

一、はしがき

　今般來訪したロイヤル陸軍長官は、二月二日内外記者團との會見において、占領地行政の民政移管について發言を行つた。長官は、從來から持論として、民政移管を唱えているのであつて、今回の發言も個人としての意見の表明とは思われる。しかし、正式平和の遲延とともに昨年いらいの米國の對日新政策の推進となり、占領管理の緩和が米本國で考究されておるというような報道も傳わり、一方わが朝野におけるドファクト・ピース待望の聲の高まつている折柄、長官の發言は、一般の注目を惹いた。

　後記　二月三日ワシントン發ＡＰ電は、移管問題は約一年前には積極的に考慮されたが、現在では然らず、近い將來には實現しないであろうとの米國權威筋の觀測を傳えた。

　とであろう。見込薄で、若し實現するとしても、早くて一年位先のことであろうとの觀測記事もあり、マ元帥は來年の誕生日は本國で迎えるであろうが、旁々眞僞の程はわからないが、民政移管の早急實現は軍は管理面から手をひくことを好まないし、握に對する現地軍の要請は相當強いであろうから、當分

二、五　條約局條約課　二四、

左に民政移管の意味するところについて考察することにする。

三、民政移管の諸形態とその可能性

　現狀における政治的可能性並びに法律的可能性を一應考慮外として、カテゴリカリーに民政移管の形態を大別すれば次の二形態となる。

（一）民政の日本國政府への移管。

　占領軍は、依然そのまま、又は駐屯軍という形で殘り、その任務は、日本政府の行動監視及び必要な場合には、指導と勸告に限定され、一般民政は、日本政府の權限に囘復される。

3 経済諸施策への対応（昭和21年5月〜24年4月）

(二) 占領機關内部における占領行政部門の民政機關移讓。軍事以外の占領行政部門を占領國の一定の民政機關に移讓する。

第一の形態は、今次大戰後のイタリアが、平和條約の締結に至るまでの期間において、歩んだコースである。マ元帥もまた、昨年一月のロイヤル長官あての書簡において、國内問題に關する日本の自主性の囘復を要望するという形で進言している。しかしながら、このような意味での民政移管が早急に採用されると希望することは、時期尚早であろう。現在問題になっているドイツ占領行政の民政移管その他諸般の情勢から察するに、ロイヤル長官のいうところの民政移管は、占領地の軍による行政を占領國の民政機關に移讓するという第二の形態に屬するものを意味することは、疑いないところである。

さて第二の形態であるが、それには左の三の方式が考えられる。

(1) 最高司令官の權限を縮少して、純軍事に限定し、別個に民政機關を設置する方式。

(2) 最高司令官の權限は、そのままとし、軍事に關しては合同參謀本部の指揮を、軍事以外の占領地行政に關しては、國務省の指揮を受けることとし、更に行政に關しては、文官をもって構成する民政機關を設置して最高司令官に從屬させる方式。

(3) 最高司令官に對する指揮系統、最高司令官の地位には何らの變更を加えず、現在の占領行政擔當官をできる限り文官に切替える方式。

(1) の方式は、占領行政が最高司令官の下に一元的に行われていたのを廢し、最高司令官は、純軍事的權限のみを有するものとし、軍事以外の占領地行政は、純然たる民政機關に委ねるものであり、對日占領管理について軍事機關と民政機關が併存するいわば二本建の制度である。この場合、最高司令官は、在日占領軍の統帥權者としてもつぱら合同參謀本部の指揮下に立ち、他方民政機關は、もつぱら國務省の指揮下に立つ譯である。これは、最も徹底した形の民政移管といいうる。

この方式の法的な難點は、管理制度の根本的變革を行うことは、いわゆる米國の中間指令をもつてしても不可能であるとするモスコー公表文の規定である。最高司令

官の權限を縮少し、あらたな管理機關を別個に設立するということは、降伏文書、對日理事會、モスコー公表文によって示されている最高司令官、對日管理制度の地位權限を變更することであって、最高司令官、對日管理制度の根本的變革といわざるをえない。從って米國としては、このような變革を行うためには極東委員會の承認を是非とも必要とすることになる。現在の極東委員會の情況からみて、このような米國の動議が採用される見込はない。

(2)の方式であるが、これは、最高司令官に對する米國政府の指揮系統及び最高司令官の下部機構に對して變更を加えるだけで、最高司令官の地位には何らの變更を加えないのであって、對日理事會もその地位に何らの變更を受けないで濟む。

最高司令官に對する指揮系統の變化は、米國の國内上の問題であって、又下部機構の變化もまた、「管理制度の根本的變革」とはいいえないから、極東委員會との關係において問題となることはないであろう。從って(1)の方式に較べて法的にははるかに實現の可能性が多い。もっとも、これは、米國國内法上の問題であるが、最高司

令官が軍事に關して合同參謀本部の指揮下に立つことは、問題がないにしても、對日占領行政に關して、現役軍人たる最高司令官が、軍事以外の占領行政に關して、國務省の指揮を直接にうけるであろうかという疑問がある。何らかの形で、最高司令官という地位以外に、民政長官たる資格を附與しなければなるまいが、それは、可能であろうか。次に、最高司令官に對する指揮系統の二元化及び下部機構の民政、軍事の二分化の問題であるが、二本の指揮系統が最高司令官において集中するという結果、ある程度兩者の調節がうまく行われるということも可能であるが、反面において調節不可能な相反する指令に接する場合も考えられ、又、下部機構の二元化は、占領軍としての目的達成のための要求充足を不圓滑にする恐れなしとせず、兩者相待(俟力)つて最高司令官の立場を困難なものとする可能性がある。特に世界情勢の惡化に伴い、對日占領の純軍事的、戰略的意義が加重されている今日、現地軍當局の行動が阻害されるというような結果が豫見されれば、この方式の採用にも實際的な見地から種々の檢討が加えられるであろうと思われる。

3　経済諸施策への対応(昭和21年5月～24年4月)

最後に(3)の方式であるが、これは、もはや民政移管という語の本来の意味に含まれるものではない。しかしながら(2)の方式も早急に實現ができないことになれば、次善の方策としてとりあえずは行われるかもしれない。事實總司令部内における文人の數は、次第に増えてきているのであつて、ロイヤル長官の今囘の來訪に同道しているドッジ氏のごときも最高司令官の經濟顧問として日本に留ることになつている。

この點に關して、イタリアの管理機關であつた連合國管理委員會(後に連合國委員會と改稱)の人的構成が、當初はほとんど軍人であつたのが、次第に文官に切替えられて行つた事情は、顧みてはなはだ興味が深い。イタリアの場合においても占領の長期化に從い一般占領行政事務が複雑化し、その圓滑なる處理のためには、專門的知識を有する文人の登場が必要とされたのであり、又かかる軍人と文人の交替は、その後に來るべき民政移管への準備として行われた旨が記録されている。

三、結語

吾人が當面の目標として希望している民政の日本政府への移管ということは、既に述べたマ元帥の書翰にも明らかに要望されてをるところであり、米國始め連合國の究極の目標であろうと思われる。しかし現在問題となつている民政移管の問題は、右とはカテゴリーを異にするところのものであつて、吾人の希望達成までの前途は甚だ遼遠の感が深い。しかも現在の意味における民政移管にしても種々の困難が豫想せられ、又たまたま外電の傳うるところによれば、これが早急實現は困難であろうといわれている。しかし、もつとも微温的な單なる占領行政下部機構の人員の軍人から文人への切替えという方式でも採用されることになれば占領行政の一段の圓滑化が期待され、それは又更に徹底した民政移管、そして究極には、民政の日本政府への返還という過程における一歩前進を準備するものとしてわが國としては歡迎すべきこととではある。だが、わが國としては民政の日本政府への移管(換言すれば内政における政府の自主性の囘復)という究極の目標を頭において、この問題のうごきを見守る必要がある。

223 昭和24年3月7日 日本経済の安定に関するドッジ経済顧問の声明

Statement by Joseph M. Dodge, Finance Adviser to General MacArthur concerning the Japanese Economic Stabilization

7 March 1949

On a New Currency

There is no reason for any assumptions to arise from the fact that at one time I worked on the original plans for a German financial rehabilitation which included a drastic currency devaluation, since put into effect.

My presence in Japan does not indicate that any plans have been made for a similar monetary devaluation for Japan.

Whatever the problems may be here they will be approached and considered by everyone concerned solely on the basis of a local conditions and the fundamental requirements for achieving an effective financial and economic stabilization under the conditions relating to Japan alone.

I will state my personal conviction that, as a matter of principle, a currency devaluation should be avoided if any way can be found to do so. This will largely depend on the course of events. Principally, it will depend upon the sincerity and effectiveness with which the Japanese Government and the Japanese people meet the difficult problems connected with halting inflationary trends and achieving an actual financial and economic stabilization.

On the Foreign Exchange Rate

There exists a general desire for the early establishment of a single rate of exchange on foreign trade transactions. The urge to accomplish this is easily understood and there is an official objective to do so as soon as practicable.

While it is not too difficult a matter to compute a rate based on present circumstances, that is not all there is to the problem. There are other factors which should be considered.

It is one thing to establish a single official rate and another to defend it after it has been established. No one should want a rate which jiggles violently up and down.

Today the dollar rate is almost the sole consideration and concern because the present pattern of imports is overwhelmingly in dollars. However, that is not the historical pattern of Japanese foreign trade and may not and probably should not be the pattern of the longer term future. Thus the ultimate pattern of Japanese trade is a factor also deserving consideration.

Finally it should be remembered that the primary objective must be the accomplishment of a rate which will stimulate exports without unduly penalizing imports, and that an effective economic stabilization is closely related to achieving a sound and satisfactory result.

On Inflation and Stabilization

Real stability and progress has to be based on a sound fiscal and monetary approach to the nation's problems. An effective stabilization requires relating all policy decisions to the Government budget as a primary instrument of financial policy.

It is government which turns on the spigots of inflation and government which must turn them off. Inflation must first be sterilized at the source. This means that all economic and political decisions must be directly related to cost and the production needs of the economy.

It is not easy for a government to reduce its own spending in terms of subsidies, investments, and other general expenses. Nevertheless, it has to be done and awkward decisions cannot be set aside. Government expenditures have to be limited to the resources from available taxes. Reduction of taxes is the end result of reduction in Government expenditures.

Also it must not be overlooked that government investments and expenditures are rarely as productive as private investments and expenditures of the same amount. In a shortage economy every resource, whether money, labor or material, drawn off for unnecessary or non-productive purposes tends to add to inflationary pressures. Therefore the questions of absolute need, priority of need and the effective use of the funds absorbed by taxation and spent by the government have equal importance with the principle of their being covered by the revenues actually received.

To meet the problem it will be necessary for the Japanese Government to assume and exercise the power and find the means to discharge its responsibilities to the nation, to the United States, and to the Allied Powers. Restrictions on private consumption and expenditure cannot be advocated by the State and then most widely ignored by the State. The average man cannot be induced to practise thrift unless his government sets the example. No government can expect from its people virtues which it does not itself practise.

Some salutary anti-inflation readjustments and developments are not only necessary but desirable for the longer run good of the Japanese economy. It cannot afford to waste any existing elements of strength supporting the unrealistic distortions and dislocations of an inflationary trend. A postponed readjustment inevitably will be extremely serious and of much longer duration.

Everyone complains about the high price effects of inflation but wants to keep on getting his own slice of government funds. Inflation is always considered bad for other people but individuals want to keep for themselves whatever personal benefits they mistakenly believe arise from it. Increased subsidies, increased wages and increased government expenditures go hand in hand with higher prices to consumers and higher taxes. That is why wage stabilization is a fundamental factor in general stabilization. But it must be remembered that while wages increased by arithmetical progression, prices increased by geometrical progression. The consumer is always the loser.

Inflation burns the economic candle at both ends. The off end belongs to those who are being stripped of the value of their earnings and savings by rising prices. The near end belongs to those who are spending the values extracted from the public. They are spending other people's money.

Political and economic liberation has not increased the supply of goods and services as much as it has the demand for them. The facts are that the spending power in existence is too large for the supply of goods and services left over after satisfying the requirements of the government, exports, capital programs and war termination cost.

Under present conditions if the people are to have or to consume more it can only come from reducing these requirements or as a gift from the United States. Therefore, any relaxation in favor of the domestic economy must be offset by a tightening up some-

674

3 経済諸施策への対応（昭和21年5月～24年4月）

where else and every consideration in favor of the domestic economy must be accompanied by offsetting proposals of retrenchment.

There should be a general recognition that an increasing part of the national output will be needed for years ahead to replace the free goods now coming from the United States, which cannot come forever.

If this is to be accomplished, there must be less of thinking solely in terms of how much U. S. aid will be forthcoming and more thinking of increased production, decreased costs and greater exports. To substantially increase exports will require continued limitations on domestic consumption and an emphasis on the needs of the export consumer rather than that of the domestic consumer. While the domestic need for consumer and capital goods is real and apparent, internal rehabilitation and expansion necessarily falls into second place behind the need for a priority of exports. The objective must be to achieve self-support so as to warrant continuation of U. S. aid and ultimately create the conditions favorable for foreign credits.

It should be understood clearly that the U. S. Government is rightly concerned that lasting benefits to the Japanese economy and itself must result from grants of aid or credits.

These are the simple propositions governing economic policy. They are hard truths and not pleasant to hear but they are no more inexorable than the facts themselves.

The problems cannot be met by any form of monetary miracle or fiscal policy alone. They can be met only by increased production at less cost, sound fiscal and monetary policies, increased exports and a continued domestic self-denial.

Finally I urge every Japanese citizen to understand and remember these simple facts:

IN CONCLUSION:

First: The hundred of millions of dollars of aid received each year by Japan from the United States comes from the taxes imposed on the individual citizens and business enterprises of the United States. In turn these taxes have been paid from the wages of American workers and the production and profit of American business and industry. And the American citizen does not like to pay taxes any more than does the Japanese citizen.

Second: These dollars, or their equivalent in goods being received by Japan (which are so necessary right now to its economic life and rehabilitation) actually are only a temporary substitute for and supplement to the production and exports which Japan must provide for itself. Japan has met the requirements of its own livelihood and progress in the past and must prepare to do so again, as quickly as possible.

There can be no permanent substitute from the resources of another nation for the efforts required from the Japanese Government and the Japanese people to meet their own problems. To live as a self-supporting and not a dependent nation Japan must produce more at less cost, it must accumulate capital by savings and economy, it must supplement its limited internal resources with materials and products only available from other sources and it must be able to pay for them from expanding exports.

To put it briefly, the national deficit cannot be allowed to increase as production expands.

We have seen a rising production index, accompanied by a large and progressive increase in the amount of U. S. aid. The excess of imports has increased and the gap between import and export has substantially widened. The time must come when this national trend is completely reversed.

If individual enterprise continuously has to be subsidized to provide saleable exports, then increasing volume suggests only correspondingly increased subsidies and proportionally increased deficits.

To meet this problem the way has to be found to convert the dollar of imported materials into more, and not less, than a dollar of exports.

It is the height of folly to point with pride at an increasing production index or increasing exports which may actually represent only increased U. S. aid, increased subsidies and increased deficits. Too much attention is being given merely to raising the totals of production and exports without regard to cost or net results. Too little attention is being given to the need for creating the greatest possible net production and using imported raw materials so as to create the greatest possible amount of net exports.

676

3　経済諸施策への対応（昭和21年5月～24年4月）

It is for these fundamental reasons that every individual citizen has to make it a personal as well as national goal to produce more and to save more.

There is no other way for the individual or the nation to have more.

Trial of Japanese War Criminals

〔FEC Policy Decision, March 31, 1949〕

The Far Eastern Commission makes the following recommendations to member governments of the Commission:

If possible, investigations in connection with offenses falling under paragraph 1 b and 1 c of the policy decision of the Far Eastern Commission entitled "Apprehension, Trial and Punishment of War Criminals in the Far East," passed by the Commission on 3 April 1946, including such offenses alleged to have been committed by persons suspected of offenses falling under paragraph 1 a of the said policy decision, should be completed before 30 June 1949, and all trials thereof should be concluded if possible before 30 September 1949.

編　注　本文書は、昭和二十六年二月、外務省特別資料課作成「日本占領及び管理重要文書集」第二巻増補より抜粋。

224　昭和24年3月31日　極東委員会決定

日本人に対する戦争裁判の終結促進に関する極東委員会政策決定

付　記　昭和二十四年三月二十八日、吉村（又三郎）連絡調整中央事務局第三部戦争裁判課長作成「戦争犯罪と日本政府の立場」

編　注　本文書は、昭和二十四年八月、外務省特別資料課作成「日本占領及び管理重要文書集」第三巻より抜粋。

〰〰〰〰〰〰

（付　記）

戦争犯罪と日本政府の立場

（昭二四、三、二八）（追記昭二四、四、六）

第三部戦争裁判課長（印）

周知の如く戦争犯罪者を処罰することはポツダム宣言受諾

の結果日本政府がこれに協力すべき立場にあることは明白なるが、他面連合國各國も終戰處理の一として又その最高政策の一たる所謂民主化の一手段としてこれを徹底的に遂行するため、過去三年有餘に亘り最大の努力を傾け來りたる處なり。

然しながら今日に至るも未だ戰爭裁判終結せず、今後なお約一箇年に亘り俘虜虐待に關する戰時重罪を處罰せんとする段階にあり、この際日本政府と連合國との見解の一致點及び不一致點を明確にすると共に更に國內輿論の動向及び將來に對する見透しに關し一應の規準を「フォーミュレート」する要あるを感じ茲に卑見を具申し上司の御指導を俟つ次第なり。

本件に關する政府の立場は連合國に對する關係と國民輿論の判斷に對する關係とを規定することによりこれを說明するを得べし。

一、連合國の戰爭裁判は勝者が敗者を裁く結果となりたるためその裁判の公正を期する上において極めて困難なる諸條件を伴いおれり、即ち日本側としては徒らに犯罪人を庇護するが如き誤解を與えざるよう極めて細心にして論理的なるを要するに對し連合國としては自國輿論の壓力の前に裁判の公正を期すること困難なる場合も考えられ、更に連合國人の犯したる戰爭犯罪に關しては充分なる處置が採られておらずに拘らず戰爭裁判遂行者の個人的良心が團體意識と妥協せしめられる虞れあり、他方戰爭裁判が將來において歷史の評決に照されることを恐れおる氣配も觀取せられざるも未だ過去において下したる判決の輕重を再檢討し一般的減刑乃至釋放を斷行する氣運熟しおらざるものと認められる、然しながら一面において極東國際軍事裁判の判決のある部分に關しては米國輿論の中に早くも疑惑と懷疑を示しおるもの認められる（昭和二十四年一月十一日ワシントン・ポストの記事、同月十四日ワシントン・ポスト揭載のグルーの意見及び同紙社說に現われたる廣田處刑に對する懷疑的態度並に重光前外相減刑釋放論等參照）と共にキーナン檢事の重光有罪宣言に對する反對意志表示、旣報の如きブレークニー辯護人の極東國際軍事裁判多數判決に對する批評等に徵するに斯る反省に基く政治的な大轉換は相當長期間を要すべきも、いつかは實現するものと思料せ

678

3 經濟諸施策への對應（昭和21年5月～24年4月）

られる次第なり。

政府と總司令部法務局との今日までの連絡及び交涉の經緯との間に一致したる結論は(1)裁判は人間として可能なる限り公正なるべきこと、若しこの點において誤るにおいては裁判の敎育的價値及び建設的意義は沒却せられ却って將來において國交調整上有害となる虞あること(2)有罪と決定せられたる者はその刑に服するは當然なるも服役中の取扱は文明國の標準を維持し公正妥當なるべきこと、米國以外の外地戰犯者の服役に關してもこれが公正に運營せられるよう外交權を有せざる日本の現狀に鑑み總司令部が能う限り周旋（good offices）をなすこと(3)戰犯者の家族に對しては、その近親者が有罪となりたるため不當に取扱われること（unfair discrimination）なきよう日本人は勿論連合國人においても留意し、例えば家族の窮狀を奇貨とし金品を詐取するが如き行動は斷乎禁壓すること(4)服役者が釋放後社會的無能力者とならざるよう服役中はその敎育、修養、娛樂、運動等に關しては特別の配慮をなすこと、

政府と法務局との間に未だ一致せざる觀點は日本の軍隊においては上官の命令は絕對にして無條件にこれに服從せざるを得ざりしことは明瞭なるにつき、裁判の遂行に際しては責任者嚴罰主義を採り、命令服從者はこれを寬大に取扱い、能うれば無罪とせられたしとの我方の要請に對しては總司令部は戰犯裁判のチャーターに基き命令服從者はその刑の量定において情狀を酌量せられるも違法行爲は斷乎處罰すべしとの方針を維持しおれり。

二、戰犯旣決者及びその家族は俘虜虐待等の明白なる不法行爲を立證せられたる後においても未だその大部分は有罪意識を有しおらず、專ら斯の不遇は敗戰の事實に歸すべきものとし、或は連合國の復讐的手段と見做しおる結果、政府の無力を歎じ乃至は政府が冷淡無能力なりとして痛罵し强硬なる交涉を望む者相當多數あるものと判斷せられ、これら不平不滿の徒は早晚超國家主義又は共產主義の好個の鴨となる虞あり、戰犯旣決者及びその家族に對しては細心にして溫き配慮なかるべからず、右の如き不平と不滿は戰犯に問われざる一部舊陸海軍軍人の間にも存在するものと判斷せられ、斯る一部輿論の動向に對する處置は單なる事務當局の能力

を超えるものあるを恐れる次第なり、これを過去の實例に見るに復員局關係官が戰犯者の近親者に極端なる同情を示し、そのため言辭稍不穩當に走り、これが總司令部に傳はり徒らに法務局を刺戟し無用のイザコザを惹起せしめること多々あり、從つて復員局に對する良き助言者となることは連調第三部が重點を置き來りたる處なり。

他方前記既決者の修養、厚生、娛樂等に關しては政府としてはこれに優先的取扱を行い財政的支出をなすことは困難なる狀況に鑑みYMCA、佛敎連盟等の慈善團體、社會奉仕機關の健全なる活動を要請し、これが促進を圖らざるを得ざる次第にして、從來この方面との連絡は復員局が非公式に行いたる處なるが今後は連調第三部又は外務省が連絡を緊密にし善處すべきものと考えおる次第なり。

追記　なお本年四月二日極東委員會はBC級戰犯裁判はその調査を本年六月末までに完了すべしとの勸告案を決定せる趣なり、右月末までに終了すべく、一切の裁判は本年九月末までに終了すべしとの勸告案を決定せる趣なり、右勸告は連合各國に對して拘束力を有せざるも、米國に關

する限り右方針に關し、率先垂範するものと認められ、前記政治的大轉換えの一歩前進とも解釋せられる次第なり。

要するに戰犯問題を繞る連合國の對日方針の進展は連合國對日政策全般に關するバロメーターの一として注目すべきものと信ず。

〜〜〜〜〜〜〜〜〜〜

225

昭和24年3月31日　特別資料部第一課作成

「**連合國による日本管理の政治及び文化部門における變遷**」

連合國による日本管理の政治及び文化部門における變遷

昭和二四、三、三一
特別資料部第一課

一、占領開始以來現在までの管理政策を概觀するに、非軍事化及び民主化の大きな線は變らないが、右制限內において、內容的に變化のあつたのは主として次の諸點である。

(一) 經濟面では、當初日本の經濟的恢復は自力によつて行

3　経済諸施策への対応（昭和21年5月〜24年4月）

うべしという政策であったのが、一九四六年五月頃から先ず經濟的救濟に乘り出し、次いで一九四七年には經濟の自立を可能ならしめようとの考慮が加えられ、更に一九四八年には經濟的自立乃至振興のための援助を開始するに至つた。このような變化は、(イ)社會秩序の維持(ロ)赤化防止(ハ)米國の財政的負擔の早期解消(ニ)「東洋の工場」として、東亞諸國の經濟的安定及び復興に寄與せしめること(ホ)防共基地としての強化等の必要にもとずくものと思われる。

右のような内容の變化に伴つて、管理の形式面即ち制限についても、變化があり、ある部面においては管理が緩和されたが、ある部面においては管理が強化された。制限付民間輸出貿易の再開、貿易手續の簡素化、ドル地域以外との貿易增進、内外實業家の往來增加、單一爲替設定及び外資導入のための準備措置等は前者の例であり、經濟十原則、賃銀三原則、經濟九原則等は後者の例である。

(二) 一般政治面においては、その共産主義に對する態度及び政策の變化が見られる。これは國際關係及び日本の

三、(三) 戰略面についてはここに述べることを差控える。
(三) 一般政治面においては、前記赤化防止、治安維持等の目的に出た政策變化（敎育及び警察等の部門）の外は、主として便宜上の必要にもとづくものに過ぎない。例えば萬國郵便條約及び國際電氣通信條約への加入、國際會議に總司令部關係官の顧問又は正式講和の遲延に伴う實情的の必要から來ている。連合國人以外の者による占領軍關係物資不法所持等の行爲に對する裁判管轄權が日本側へ委讓されたのは、このような犯罪が多數に上つた實情に鑑み、便宜上の必要からとられた措置であると思われる。新聞その他の出版物に對する檢閱が事前から事後に變つたのは、有害なものが少くなつたのと便宜上の理由によるものと思われ、プレス、コードは依然存在するのである。

文書による指令よりも口頭の指示や勸告等による指導が漸次多くなって來たことは事實であるが、これは、主として、重要な指令は既に大體出盡したことに因る形式上の變化に過ぎないのであって、實質的には殆んど管理

國内狀態に因るものと思われる。

の緩和を意味しない。

政治面における管理の主な變化を部門別に示すと次の通りである。（經濟面については特別資料部第二課の調書が出る筈である）

對外關係

原則として、日本の對外關係は連合國の管理機關として總司令部の直接管理の下に立ち從つて連合國の管理機關として總司令部が自ら日本の對外關係を處理している。元々、日本の對外關係は次の覺書によつて連合國の管理を受けることとなつた。

一、一九四五年十月二十五日　日本の在外公館の文書財産の連合國側への移管及び在外公館員の召還

二、一九四五年十一月　四日　日本政府と中立國代表との公的關係の停止

この覺書は日本における中立國代表の存在が、連合國の占領管理の目的及び性質、並に連合國最高司令官の地位と兩立しないとの理由によつて、日本政府は中立國代表との公的關係を停止すべきことを指令した。

日本側は、日本の管理に關する基本的文書であるポツダム宣言、降伏文書、米國の初期對日方針には日本の對外關係について規定していないこと、及び日本側は中立國との友好關係の維持、利益保護關係事務の必要から中立國との友好關係の繼續を要請したが、總司令部はこれを峻拒した

（一九四五年十一月十八日總司令部覺書）

右によつて對外關係は全面的に總司令部の自ら處理するところとなつた（但し在日外交團の國際標準に合致する生活上の待遇供與は日本側の責任とされている）が、この管理の態樣は現在に至つても根本的變更を受けていない。ただ占領が長期化し、連合國の管理政策に關する日本側協力が、認められている現在、占領開始當時よりは次の二、三の點において變化が現われている。

一、政府間の國際會議に總司令部の代表がオブザーバーとして出席する場合に、日本人をそのテクニカル、アドバイザーとして會議に出席させることができる（四八年六月極東委員會の政策決定）

二、國際電氣通信條約及び萬國郵便條約への加入（四八年九月一日總司令部覺書）（四八年六月十二日總司令部覺書）

右兩條約はいずれも技術的行政事項に關するもので且

3　経済諸施策への対応（昭和21年5月〜24年4月）

つ日本、ドイツ、朝鮮の簡易加入手續を規定している特殊のものである。總司令部は日本側が、加入を希望する場合は、その加入を外交經路を通じて傳達すべきことを申越した。

三、國際電信電話主管廳會議に對する代表派遣

わが國は國際電氣通信條約加盟國として、一九四九年五月十八日からジュネーヴで開かれる第三地域無線主管廳會議及び同日からパリに開かれる電信電話主管廳會議への參加を招請せられ右會議に代表（總司令部係官の顧問としてでなく）を派遣することを三月二十一日總司令部から許可された。

なお、邦人の海外渡航は、最初總司令部は否定的であつたが、占領の長期化に伴い、漸次増加している。特に一九四八年一月十八日のマックァーサー元帥のロイヤル陸軍長官あてメッセーヂは、講和が長びいている現在においてできる限り通商に對する制限を緩和し、邦人の海外渡航を認むべきことを強調している、又極東委員會は一九四八年十一月日本の實業家の渡航を許可する政策決定を行つた。

裁判管轄及び非日本人の取扱

一、外國人に對する民事、刑事の裁判權

(1) 一九四六年二月十九日の「刑事裁判管轄に關する覺書」によつて、連合國人又は團体に對する日本側の刑事裁判管轄を排除し、逮捕權も原則として否認した。

なお特定の「占領目的に有害な行爲」については連合國以外の外國人及び日本人に對しても日本側裁判權を排除した。

(2) 一九四六年二月二六日の「民事裁判管轄に關する覺書」によつて、連合國人又は團体に對する日本側民事裁判管轄を排除する連合國人又は團体に對する日本側民事裁判管轄を排除すると共に、その他の連合國占領軍に對しては一應日本側の裁判權を認めるが、その判決に對してはすべて審査を行い、必要とあれば、事件進行中手續の停止等をも行い得ることとした。

(3) 一九四六年二月二八日の總司令部涉外局發表は、連合國占領軍に附屬し又は隨伴する者に對して日本側が民事裁判權を行使しないということは占領開始以來の事實であると逑べ、更に占領軍將兵及び占領軍に公的に附屬し又は隨伴する者が被占領國の民事及び刑事裁判

軍關係物資の闇取引行爲が増加し、漸く日本經濟秩序かく亂の一因ともならんとし、強力にこれが取締りを行う必要があつたことと、犯罪關係者や犯罪の性質上これが調査等も日本側においてこれを行うことが便宜であつたこと等によるもののようである。

三、朝鮮人に對する連合國側の取扱い方針の推移

(1) 連合國當局は終戰と共に、朝鮮人を「解放された民族」として、その政治犯人の釋放、勞働者の解放、集團歸國輸送の特典等種々の便宜を供與する外、一九四六年二月一九日の「朝鮮人及びその他のある國人に對する判決に關する覺書」によつて、特定の條件のもとに、朝鮮人に對する日本裁判所の刑事裁判判決を、連合國側が審査をすることとした。

(2) 右の如き連合國側の態度に影響されてか、終戰後各地において朝鮮人による集團暴行事件の發生をみた。これに對し日本側はあるいは列車内における集團暴行事件に關し、あるいはその他の不法事件に關して連合國總司令部に對し朝鮮人の取締りについての方針の明示を求めた。これに對し、總司令部はその都度單に「日

權から免除されることは國際法上當然認められるところである旨を述べている。

右によつてみれば、外國人に關する前記の裁判管轄方針は占領開始以來不變であり、これを前記覺書によつて明確にしたものと認むべきものであろう。

三、占領軍關係物資の不法所持等に關する犯罪に對する裁判權の日本側への移讓

(1) 一九四六年二月一九日の「刑事裁判管轄に關する覺書」第二項は「占領目的に有害なる行爲」として特定の行爲を列擧した中に、そのCにおいて「占領軍又はその將兵若くはこれに附屬し又は隨伴する者の財産を權限なくして所持、取得、受領若くは處分する行爲」を擧げ、これらの行爲に對しては、一切日本側に裁判權がないことを規定していた。ところが翌一九四七年六月二七日の覺書は、前記覺書第二項Cを削除して連合國以外の外國人及び日本人による右の行爲に對しては、裁判權を日本側へ移讓するに至つた。

(2) この改正の主な理由は、當時總司令部係官の日本司法當局に語つたところから判斷すれば、當時この種占領

3 経済諸施策への対応（昭和21年5月～24年4月）

本國内の秩序を維持することは日本側の責任」である旨を囘答してきたに止まつた。

その後朝鮮人の集團歸國が一段落し、殘留朝鮮人の地位や國籍問題が世上に喧論されるに至つた際、一九四六年十一月二〇日總司令部渉外局は一發表を行い、その中で「朝鮮人で歸國を拒み、引續き日本に滯留する者は日本の法律や諸規則に全面的に服する」旨を特に述べて朝鮮人の法的地位を明確にするところがあつた。

次いで一九四八年四月朝鮮人學校閉鎖問題に關して神戸、大阪等に朝鮮人による騷擾事件が發生した際、總司令部當局は重ねて朝鮮人が全面的に日本の法權に服すべき旨を確認し日本側に對しても、斷乎取締りを行うよう勸慫するところがあつた。

(3) 斯くて終戰以來稍もすればこれが取扱い方針を欠いた憾みのあつた朝鮮人問題もここに至つてその取締り方針の確立をみるに至つた譯である。

警察

旨、又日本側は「朝鮮人を取締る完全な權限」を有する

日本の警察力に關しては一般命令第一號（一九四五・九・二）において、「警察機關の人員及び武裝は規定せらるものとす」と定められていたが、終戰後の社會不安と軍隊解消後の秩序維持のため當時の警察力（九萬三千九百三十五人）では萬全を期しがたいので、日本政府（内務省）では昭和二十年十月五日警察力の増強に關して現在員を十八萬六千六百四十八人に増加することゝし、常設機動隊としての警備隊の設置、水上警察の強化に關する案を總司令部に提出したが十月十一日の覺書（AG○九一・一DCSO）によつて日本政府の提案に對しては好意ある考慮を拂うことはできない、その増強は目下のところ實施してはならないことを通達してきた。しかるにその後日本警察機構の民主的改革に關しては總司令部側及び日本政府において種々案を練つていたが日本政府の改革案は昭和二十二年九月三日、片山首相からマッカァーサー元帥に提出されその中で、日本の警察力を十二萬五千に引上げることを申請したところ、九月十六日付マ元帥の總理あて書簡によつて全面的に承認されたので、同年十二月十七日制定された警察法（法律第百九十六號）によつて、國家地方警察三萬人、地方（自治

685

警察九萬五千人の定員を決定した。

なお、一九四八年九月歸米後アイケルバーガー中將はしばしば日本警察力増強の必要を強調し約十五萬人の武裝警察隊の設置方を提唱したが、本年三月一日ワシントン發A・P電は、米國外交當局筋の言明によれば、日本警察の地方分權化に關する從來の政策を再檢討することを命じた指令がマ元帥に送られたが、右は共產黨その他による大規模な秩序の破壊に備へるためである旨報道した。

又他方、密入國及び密貿易の増加に鑑み、日本の沿岸水域における海上の安全を確保し、治安を維持するため、海上保安廳の設置方について二十二年春ごろから日本側において案を練つていたところ、同年秋總司令部からもこれを示唆され、その設置に關する法案は二十三年三月二十九日承認され、同年五月一日運輸省の外局として發足した。（海上保安廳法二三、四、二七法律第二八號）、海上保安廳法によれば、海上保安廳の職員の總數は一萬名を超えてはならず、保有船舶は港内艇を除いて、その隻數は百二十五隻を超えてはならず〈全トン數五萬總トン以下、一隻千五百排水トン以下、速力十五ノット以下〉、この法律のいかなる規定も、海上保安廳又はその職員が軍隊として組織され、訓練され、又は軍隊の機能を營むことを認めるものと解釋してはならないとされている。

　　　教　育

教育についての管理政策として根本的に變つて來た點は認められないが、反共的方策の面が最近特に明らかとなつて來ていることは爭われない。この傾向が漸次明確にされつつあつたのは昨年十月五日に行われた敎育委員の選擧に際で、CIEのオーア敎育部長は九月九日の記者會見においていかなる政黨の利益をも代表しない不偏不黨の人物立候補が望ましい旨を述べ、また地方軍政部のうちには左翼的日本敎職員組合の進出を阻止すべく種々方策を講じたところが少くなかつた。例えば東京軍政部はしばしば日本敎職員組合の暗躍を警告するとともに九月十六日には東京都敎員組合連合會役員執行委員會の立候補の取下げを勸告した。ホリングスヘッド大佐より敎員組合連合會役員執行委員會の立候補の取下げを勸告した。その後本年二月三日には東京軍政部敎育將校ボール・デュッツペル大尉は日大工科において學園における共產主義の脅威を警告、續いて同月十三日には東京軍政部は共產主義

3 経済諸施策への対応（昭和21年5月〜24年4月）

宣傳の教師は解雇せらるべき旨の見解を發表、三月二十二日の東京女子經濟專門學校の卒業式における祝辭中でも共産主義者は教員として不適當である旨を強調するところがあった。

一方文部省と協議の上、教育の政治活動は一切教育基本法第八條違反としてこれを禁止すべく、その具體的な行爲について明確なる方針を近く發表する運びとなっている。

言論報道

連合國は對日政策の一環として言論の取締りを行い、その手段として嚴重な事前檢閱制度を布いた。言論取締りの方針は一般的な言論及び放送、出版等をも對象に含めたものとしては、一九四五年九月十日付總司令部覺書（横濱終戰連絡事務局經由のもので件名は付せられていない）があり、また特に新聞を對象としたものに九月十九日付「プレス・コード」に關する覺書、ラジオ放送に對しては九月二十二日付「ラジオ・コード」に關する覺書がある。占領初期においては、檢閱は極めて嚴格に行われ、ことにラジオ放送等にあっては、檢閱資料、人選、放送時間等も總司令部側が自ら決定し、放送協會側の自主性はほとんど失われ

しかるに、一九四七年八月一日よりラジオ放送が事後檢閱制度に移されて以來、次第に他部門における檢閱も漸次事後檢閱への方向をたどり、同年末までには一部の極右、極左系のものを除いて地方の出版物は概ね事後檢閱の取扱いを受けることとなった。更に、一九四八年七月十五日以降、東京、大阪の主要十六新聞と三通信社が事後檢閱となり、同七月二十五日には、「アカハタ」をはじめ殘餘の全新聞がすべて事後檢閱となり、事前檢閱はここに全面的に廢止せられた。しかしながら、事前檢閱の廢止は言論取締り方針の緩和を意味するものではなく、占領軍にとつては、手續上の改正措置に過ぎないのであつて、「プレス・コード」等の效力は依然として存在し且つ總司令部民間檢閱係の結果は、何時でも干渉しうる體制にある。從つて、事前檢閱廢止の結果は、「アカハタ」及びその他の左翼系の新聞、雑誌を除くほかは、記事の取扱いぶりが一時むしろ愼重となり、また、「プレス・コード」違反の場合の停刊處分の脅威のため、疑いあるときは、その都度、新聞社側からあらかじめ掲載承認方を總司令部檢閱部に申請して萬全を期してい

總司令部民間諜報局長ブラット大佐は昨年四月、事前檢閱廢止を豫告した際、占領軍に對する破壞的批判と、共產黨宣傳の機會を最少限度に止めるために事後檢閱制度は今後も繼續されるとのべ、また民間情報教育局の新聞課長インボデン少佐は昨年九月二十五日、新聞週間の開催に先立つて「責任ある新聞は、新聞週間を通じて、よい新聞とゴロツキ新聞及びアカハタの類との區別をはつきり世に示すべきである」とのべるなど、米ソの對立關係日本の國內事情及びそれに基づく米國の對日政策の變化に伴つて、言論取締の對象はこゝ一年間に主として左翼關係のものに集中されてきた感がある。昨年三月三日、總司令部經濟科學局勞働課が、新聞における編集方針は經營者が決定すべきで、從業員は干與しえない旨聲明を發したことも、終戰後勞働運動の活發化につれて、從業員の發言權が增大した結果、新聞の編集方針が、しばしば左傾する傾向に終止符を打たんとする意圖に出たものとみることができよう。

付記　右和訳文

昭和24年4月1日　連合国最高司令官総司令部より　日本政府宛

ガリオア・エロア輸入物資に伴う見返資金の特別会計を日本銀行内に設定方指令

226

GENERAL HEADQUARTERS
SUPREME COMMANDER FOR THE ALLIED POWERS
APO 500

1 April 1949

AG 091.31 (1 Apr 49) ESS/EX
SCAPIN 1988
MEMORANDUM FOR: JAPANESE GOVERNMENT
SUBJECT: Yen Counterpart of GARIOA And EROA Imports

1. The Japanese Government will establish as of 1 April 1949 a special account in the Bank of Japan in the name of the Japanese Government to be designated the U.S. Aid Counterpart Fund for Japanese Stabilization (hereinafter called the Fund) and will make deposits in Japanese yen in this account in amounts commensurate with the dollar cost to the Government of the United

3 経済諸施策への対応（昭和 21 年 5 月〜24 年 4 月）

States of America aid (including any cost of processing, storing, transporting or other services incident thereto) furnished Japan by the United States.

2. The Supreme Commander for the Allied Powers will from time to time notify the Japanese Government of the dollar cost of the United States aid and the Japanese Government will thereupon deposit in the Fund a commensurate amount of yen computed at a rate of exchange which will be indicated to the Japanese Government by the Supreme Commander.

3. The Japanese Government will be permitted to draw from the Fund only such amounts and only for such purposes as may be approved by the Supreme Commander.

4. The Japanese Government will be required to submit to the Supreme Commander separate and specific proposals for any desired use of the Fund. In preparing these proposals the Japanese Government will take into account the imperative need for promoting and maintaining internal monetary and financial stability, for stimulating exports and for carrying out the other objectives set forth in the letter of 19 December 1948 from the Supreme Commander to the Prime Minister. To these ends the above mentioned proposals will take due cognizance of the need for effective retirement of the national debt, especially debt held by the Bank of Japan and other banking institutions and will coordinate such action with the legitimate needs of private and public enterprise for capital and credit. Such expenditures as the Japanese Government may be permitted to make from the Fund will not, in general, replace funds otherwise available from the normal revenues of the Government, savings of the Japanese people or from existing sources of credit. Whenever practicable, releases from the Fund will be repayable to the Fund in accordance with clearly defined interests and amortization schedules. However, this principle will not preclude approval of other categories of releases which will better contribute to the stabilization and export capacity of Japan.

5. In authorizing, limiting or disallowing applications for releases from the Fund, cognizance will be taken of the attainment by the Japanese Government, the Bank of Japan, and other financial institutions of prior established goals in the fields of budget, monetary and credit control. Furthermore, proposals by the

Japanese Government to advance counterpart funds for private and public investment programs will be considered in the light of achievement by the proposed recipients of specific programs of rationalization and economic stabilization.

6. Direct communication between the Economic and Scientific Section, General Headquarters, Supreme Commander for the Allied Powers and appropriate agencies of the Japanese Government within the scope of this memorandum is authorized.

FOR THE SUPREME COMMANDER:

R. M. LEVY,
Colonel, AGD,
Adjutant General.

(付 記)

對日援助見返資金特別勘定設定方に關する總司令部覺書

連合軍最高司令官總司令部
AG〇九一、三二(二十四年四月一日)ESS／EX
SCAPIN一九八八

APO五〇〇
昭和二十四年四月一日

件 名　對日援助見返資金特別勘定設定

覺書あて先　日本政府

一　日本政府は昭和二十四年四月一日付をもって、日本銀行内に日本政府名義で米國援助見返資金(以下資金と呼ぶ)特別勘定を設置し、米國より日本に與えられた米國援助の米國政府にとってのドル價格(加工、保管、輸送その他の附隨サーヴィスの價格を含む)と等額をこの勘定に日本圓をもって預金するものとする。

二　連合國總司令部は隨時米國援助ドル價格を日本政府に通報し、また日本政府はこれに基いて總司令部より日本政府に指示された交換率または爲替レートによって計算された等額の圓を資金に預け入れるものとする。

三　日本政府は總司令部によって承認された額と目的においてのみ資金から引出をなすことができる。

四　日本政府は最高司令部に對し、資金のいかなる使用の希望についても、各別の具體的な案を提出しなければならない。これらの案を準備するに際して、日本政府は、國

3　経済諸施策への対応（昭和21年5月〜24年4月）

内の通貨財政の安定、輸出の促進、その他昭和二十三年十二月十九日付最高司令部より總理大臣宛の書簡に規定されたところの諸目的の緊要性を考慮に入れなければならない。これらの目的達成のために、右の案は國の負債、とくに日本銀行その他の金融機關引受の債務の效果的な償還の必要性というものを充分考慮し、且つかかる措置と公私企業の資金並びに信用に對する正當な需要とを調整しなければならない。

日本國政府がこの資金から許されるところの支出は、一般的には、政府の通常の歳入や日本國民の貯蓄、或いはまた現存の信用資金によって賄い得る支出に代替するものであってはならない。この資金からの引出は能う限り明確に規定された利子並びに償還計画にしたがって、この資金に返還し得るようにせねばならない。

しかしながらこの原則は、より一層日本の安定及び輸出量に貢獻する他の範疇の引出があればこれを妨げるものではない。

五　資金よりの引出準備申請の許可、制限、不許可に當っては、日本政府、日本銀行その他金融機關による予算、

通貨及び金融統制の分野において予め立てられた目標の達成度の如何を考慮するものとする。

さらに見返り資金を民間並びに公共投資計画に用いるという日本政府の申請は、投資先が合理化と經濟安定の具體的計画に寄與する程度によって考慮される。

六　連合國最高司令部と日本の適當なる機關との本覺書の限度内における折衝が許可される。

最高司令官に代って

高級副官

副官部附大佐アール・エム・レヴィー

編注　本文書は、昭和二十五年六月、外務省政務局特別資料課作成「日本管理資料㈠」より抜粋。

〰〰〰〰〰〰〰〰〰〰

昭和24年4月4日　連合国最高司令官総司令部より日本政府宛

日本における外国人所有著作権の登録および保護に関する指令

GENERAL HEADQUARTERS

SUPREME COMMANDER FOR THE ALLIED POWERS
APO 500
4 April 1949

AG 072 (4 Apr 49) CPC/FP
SCAPIN 6499-A

MEMORANDUM FOR: JAPANESE GOVERNMENT

SUBJECT: Matters Affecting Registration and Protection of Foreign-Owned Copyrights in Japan

1. Reference is made to memorandum for the Japanese Government, file AG 130 (22 Sep 45) ESS, SCAPIN 45, 22 September 1945, subject, "Control of Financial Transactions," from General Headquarters, Supreme Commander for the Allied Powers.

2. Under present regulations commercial magazines, books (including translation and reproduction rights), motion pictures, news and photographic services and other media of mass communication, provided they are not detrimental to the purposes of the Occupation, may be introduced into Japan under license from foreign countries for sale to Japanese nationals.

3. Attention is directed to the following:
 a. Licenses have been issued to:
  (1) Individual copyright proprietors to contract with Japanese nationals, firms, and agencies in the normal business manner for the sale of translation and publication rights of their literary works
  (2) The Governments of the United States, United Kingdom, and France, and All Allied Union International Book, c/o Office of the Soviet Member, Allied Council for Japan to contract in Japan respecting the sale of translation and publication rights in copyrighted literary works originating in said nations and to conduct through General Headquarters, Supreme Commander for the Allied Powers all business necessary and incidental thereto
  (3) Individual publishers for importation of books printed abroad for sale to the Japanese public.
 b. All contracts entered into in Japan by the aforesaid

692

licensees are subject to approval of General Headquarters, Supreme Commander for the Allied Powers.

c. In addition, General Headquarters, Supreme Commander for the Allied Powers makes arrangements with foreign authors to authorize Japanese nationals to translate and/or publicly present their copyrighted dramatic and dramatico-musical works and to perform their copyrighted musical works.

d. Copies of the contracts referred to in paragraph 3b and of the arrangements referred to in paragraph 3c will be forwarded to the Japanese Government upon execution. Attached hereto, and marked "Exhibit 'A'," are copies of contracts and letters of authorization which have been approved heretofore by General Headquarters, Supreme Commander for the Allied Powers.

4. In the implementation of the program referred to in above paragraphs and notwithstanding the terms of reference, paragraph 1 above, the Japanese Government is directed to:

a. Authorize the Japanese publishers to take all necessary steps under the "Law of Copyright of Japan" and "The Enforcement Regulations of the Law of Copyright of Japan" to perform their obligations imposed by the contracts with reference to causing, at their own cost and expense, the copyrights in Japan of the translations to be duly assigned to the respective proprietors and registered in accordance with the copyright laws of Japan and to furnish to the contractor a certified copy (in English) of such registration

b. Extend to foreign copyright owners all the rights and privileges to which any national of any country is entitled under the Japanese copyright laws.

5. Direct communication is authorized between interested sections of General Headquarters, Supreme Commander for the Allied Powers and the Ministry of Finance and Ministry of Education, Japanese Government, regarding routine of administration in connection with the foreign-owned copyrighted material referred to in this memorandum.

FOR THE SUPREME COMMANDER:

A. J. Rehe
for R. M. LEVY

228

昭和24年4月23日 連合国最高司令官総司令部より 日本政府宛

正式為替レートの設定に関する指令

付記　右和訳文

編　注　本文書の別添は見当たらない。

SUPREME COMMANDER FOR THE ALLIED POWERS
GENERAL HEADQUARTERS
APO 500

23 April 1949

AG 123.7 (23 Apr 49) ESS/EX
SCAPIN 1997
MEMORANDUM FOR: JAPANESE GOVERNMENT

SUBJECT: Establishment of Official Exchange Rate for the Japanese Yen

1. The Japanese Government is directed to take the steps necessary to put into effect at 0001 hours, 25 April 1949, an official foreign exchange rate of 360 Japanese yen to one U.S. dollar. Rates for other currencies will be based on this rate translated into the U.S. dollar values of such currencies as registered with the International Monetary Fund. This rate will be the basis for all permitted foreign trade and exchange transactions, including transactions for which military conversion rate is now applicable, as well as deposits to the United States Aid Counterpart Fund for Japanese Stabilization.

2. Effective 0001 hours, 25 April 1949, foreign trade and exchange transactions will for the present continue to be executed through the Board of Trade at the above rate and in accordance with existing approved procedures. It is desired that the Japanese Government submit for approval of General Headquarters, Supreme Commander for the Allied Powers, at the earliest practicable date, recommended arrangements whereby transactions may be

1 Incl
Exhibit "A"

Colonel, AGD
Adjutant General

executed on the basis of this exchange rate through the Foreign Exchange Control Board.

3. Except as otherwise provided herein, export contracts which were approved by the Japanese Government prior to 25 April 1949 will be honored in accordance with yen payment terms which were agreed upon between the Japanese Government and exporters of Japanese goods under then existent export procedures. Any such contract now in force which requires use of imported raw materials for the execution thereof shall be discharged.

　　a. At yen prices specified under then existent export procedures to the extent that imported raw materials procured from the Japanese Government were paid for at yen prices effective at the time of approval of the contract.

　　b. At adjusted yen prices only to the extent that imported raw materials actually used for production of goods to be exported under the contract are procured from the Japanese Government and are paid for at yen prices in excess of those effective at the time of approval of the contract. Applications for such adjustments will be subject to review and approval by the Price Board.

4. The Japanese Government is hereby directed to take actions necessary to insure that exporters of Japanese goods fulfill all contracts approved prior to 25 April 1949 in good faith and in accordance with the provisions of this memorandum.

5. Direct communication between interested staff sections of the Supreme Commander for the Allied Powers and appropriate agencies of the Japanese Government is authorized to facilitate implementation of this memorandum.

　　　　　　FOR THE SUPREME COMMANDER:

　　　　　　　　　R. M. LEVY,
　　　　　　　　　Colonel, AGD,
　　　　　　　　　Adjutant General.

（付　記）

日本圓の公式爲替レート設定方に關する總司令部覺書
連合國最高司令官總司令部
AG 一二三、七（二十四年四月二十三日）ESS／EX
SCAPIN 一九九七

APO 五〇〇

昭和二十四年四月二十三日

覺書あて先　日本政府

件　名　日本圓の正式爲替レート設定

一　日本政府は昭和二十四年四月二十五日午前零時より一米弗に對し日本圓三六〇圓の公式外國爲替レートを實施するに必要な措置をとるようここに指令する。

米國以外の國の通貨に對するレートは、本レートを基準として國際通貨基金に登録されてある當該國通貨の對米弗比率をもって換算してこれを定めるものとする。本レートは許可されている外國貿易及び爲替取引の一切の基準となるものとし、現在軍用レート適用になっている取引もこれによるものとし、また日本安定の爲の米國援助見返り資金に對する預入れに際しても本レートを適用するものとする。

二　昭和二十四年四月二十五日午前零時より外國貿易及び爲替取引は當分の間は依然貿易廳を通じて上記のレートをもって現在通りの承認された手續に依って行われるものとする。日本政府は、本爲替レートに基き外國爲替管理委員會を通じて取引を行えるような案を作成し、可及的速やかに連合軍最高司令部に提出してその承認を受けなければならない。

三　昭和二十四年四月二十五日以前に日本國政府の認可があった輸出契約については、本指令において別段の定めある場合のほか日本國政府と日本商品の輸出業者との間において、契約の當時における輸出手續に基いて協定された圓價格をもって、支拂を行うものとする。

右の契約で、輸入原材料の使用を必要とするものについては、その價格は

(イ)日本政府より購入された輸入原材料の代金が、契約の認可のあった當時における圓價格をもってその支拂が完了している場合においては、契約の當時における輸出手續に基いて定められた圓價格。

(ロ)契約の下に輸出さるべき物資の生產のために、使用された輸入原材料が、日本國政府より購入され、その代金が、契約の認可の當時における價格をこえる圓價格をもって支拂われる場合においては、調整されたる圓價格。

によるものとする。

なお(ロ)にいう調整の申請は物價廳の審査並びに認可によるものとする。

3　経済諸施策への対応（昭和21年5月〜24年4月）

を受けるものとする。

四　日本國政府に對し、日本の物資の輸出者が昭和二十四年四月二十五日以前に認可されたあらゆる契約を本覺書の各條項に從つて忠實に履行することを保障するため必要なる措置をとるよう、ここに指令する。

五　總司令部關係各局と日本國政府該當官廳との間の直接交涉は、本指令の實施を容易ならしめるため認可するものとする。

最高司令官に代つて

　　高級副官

　　副官部附大佐アール・エム・レヴィー

編　注　本文書は、昭和二十五年六月、外務省政務局特別資料課作成「日本管理資料㈠」より抜粋。

229
「經濟關係事項」
昭和24年5月12日　総務局経済課作成

昭二四、五、一二

總務局經濟課

經濟關係事項

狹小且つ資源貧困な國土に八千萬の人口を抱えているわが國が自立するためには輸出の飛躍的振興を圖らねばならないことはまたぬところである。わが國は、いわゆる九原則の實行によつて、國民の耐乏生活を強行して右の目的を達成しようとしている。しかるに、輸出の增進のためにはわが國の國内の努力だけでは如何ともし難い問題がある。

その第一は海外市場の問題である。世界的ドル不足の問題もあり、又最近では世界各國の產業及び貿易の復興につれて、海外市場における競爭は漸次激化し、世界的に市場の問題が深刻な問題となりつつある。この點において、海外から完全に遮斷されているわが國の貿易は極めて不利な狀態に置かれている。海外市場の開拓こそ、わが輸出促進の成否を決定する決定的な問題である。第二は、市場問題と關連するが、輸出の促進に重要な貢獻をなすのみならず、それ自身見えざる輸出として、わが國際收支上重要な海運、保險、銀行等のいわゆるサーヴイス業（サーヴイスの輸出）の問題である。この點においては、現在全くわがサーヴイ

ス業の活動は認められておらず海外のサーヴィスに依存しているが、このことは日本の輸出を不利ならしめ且つ日本の國際收支に重大な負擔となつており、これを無視し得ない。これが解決の根本は講和條約の締結にあることはもちろんであるが、諸般の情勢上これが早期に行われること困難であるとしても、これらの問題丈は少くとも個別的な協定とか諒解とかの形でも解決しなければならない。今この見地に立つて見るとおうむね次のごとき諸點が早急に實施されることが必要であり、且つ極めて望ましい。

一、日本人の海外渡航

わが國の輸出が所期のごとく伸張しない原因としては、世界的ドル不足のようにわが國としてどうにもできない問題もあるが、長期の戰爭中外國と隔絶していたこと及び現在でもわが輸出業者が海外に眼と手足とを有たず、また海外に日本の貿易の利益を保護する政府機關もないために、次の如き結果を來たしていることも重要な原因である。

(イ)海外市場の流行、嗜好等に關する知識がかけており、従つて市場にマツチする適切な輸出商品の生産が行われない。

(ロ)進步した海外の技術に接せず技術が立ちおくれているために、商品の質においても價格においても世界的に劣つている。

(ハ)外國の輸入業者の信用狀態を確認する術がなく、従つて貿易取引は非常な危險が伴つている。

(ニ)適正な價格で輸出することができず、一方において外商により買い叩かれるとともに、他方においてダンピングの再現との非難を受けることも困難である。また、適切な輸入原料を安價に仕入れることも困難である。

(ホ)クレームをつけられても、それが正當なものであるか否かを認定し、これを公正に處理することが困難である。

(ヘ)外國政府の諸種の貿易規則(關稅引上、輸入制限、爲替制限等)の詳細が充分判明せず、また日本業者のために外國政府官憲に交渉あつせんする機關がないために不測の損害を被ることがある。

これらの點は、わが國業者(海運、保險、銀行業者を

3　経済諸施策への対応（昭和21年5月～24年4月）

含む）の海外渡航、海外支店又は代理店等の設置、商務官の派遣等によって、解決しなければならない。

二、日本船舶又は傭船の利用

現在の輸入品の運賃はきわめて高率であって、諸物資平均して約二割となって、殊に價格の内運賃の割合が大きいバルキーカーゴーたる鐵鑛石、ボーキサイト、鹽、石炭、棉花、羊毛など日本の輸入する原料は極めて割高となり、わが輸出産業の採算を世界の競争産業より不利にしていることは見逃し得ない。しかも輸送は大部分外國船であるために、それだけわが國の國際收支は不利となり、輸入し得る物資の數量が減少することとなる。これが解決には日本船舶をもって輸送することが必要であるが、わが國の大洋航行船舶の保有量は現在稼動し得るもの僅々十數萬トンにすぎないから日本船舶を最大限に利用する外に、たとえば米國のリバーティ、ヴィクトリー型船を裸傭船することができれば、わが保險業の參加と相まって、わが國の國際收支に及ぼす好影響は少くないであろう。

三、關税、通商、金融等に關する協定の締結

わが國は現在諸國との間に有效な通商航海條約をもっていないため、わが輸出品に對する最惠國待遇は原則として保證されておらず、また日本人の渡航も原則として認められていない。この中わが輸出品の最惠國待遇については、米國が「關税及び貿易に關する一般協定」及びECAに基く援助協定に關連して、その實現のため種々努力を拂っているが、戰前の如き日本品の競爭等の不安から、米國の提案を承認しない國が多いのが現狀である。しかし、わが國は、戰後勞働基準法等を制定し公正な競爭を行うことのみを念願とし、不當競爭を行う意志は毛頭ないのであるから、この點は杞憂にすぎない。從って單なる貿易協定の外に、關税協定を諸外國と個別的に締結する必要がある。次に、人、船舶、銀行等の待遇についても次のような問題がある。

(イ) 日本人（日本法人を含む）が渡航した後敵國人としての制限を受けず、商業活動を營み、財産を獲得し、訴訟當事者となりうることが必要である。

(ロ) 日本船舶を利用するには、日本船が外國港に寄港し、貨物の積取、積卸等を行い、これに關連する諸施設を

699

利用し、外國の業者と輸送契約を結び、これがため船舶會社が外國に支店又は代理店を設けることを許されるようにならねばならない。

(ハ)日本の銀行も敵國銀行としての制限を受けず、外國に支店を設け又はコルレス契約を結び、適法に外貨勘定を所有することを許されることが必要である。

(ニ)日本の保險會社が右と同樣外國保險會社と契約し、外貨建契約をなし、保險料を受拂する等營業活動を認められることが必要である。

右の諸點は、結局日本に對する敵國扱を部分的に修正することになるので、關係國との協定又はりよう解によつてこれを實現する必要がある。これらの點を實現することは、事實上一種の通商航海條約を締結することになるであろう。

四、國際機關への參加

國際連合等政治的な國際機關への加盟は講和條約を俟たねばならないであろうが、次の如き經濟關係機關又は條約への加盟は、なるべく早く認められることが、わが國の國際社會への復歸の點からも望まれる。

(イ)國際貿易機關ハヴァナ憲章
(ロ)國際通貨基金
(ハ)國際復興開發銀行
(ニ)關稅及び貿易に關する一般協定
(ホ)國際勞働機關
(ヘ)國際連合食糧農業機關

なおECAFE會議には、オブザーヴァーとして參加することを希望する。

五、移民問題

わが國民經濟の自立困難の根本原因の一つは過剰人口であるから、諸外國がわが移民を受け入れることが望ましいのはいうまでもない。しかしながら、この問題は、目下の國際情勢から見て、現在提起すべき問題ではないであろう。

4　制限緩和に向けた対応（昭和24年5月〜27年4月）

230

昭和24年5月25日　総務局作成
「對日管理緩和に關する米國の提案について」

對日管理緩和に關する米國の提案について

昭二四、五、二五、總務局

一、本月初めの外電は米國政府が極東委員會に對し對日管理を緩和し、外交と通商政策の面で自由を與えようとの勸告を出したと報じ、次いでその旨を國務省から發表したと報じたので當省員が司令部外交部のヒューストン參事官に會談の際この點に言及し

㈠本件に關するロンドン電と今次國務省聲明との間には實質的な相違がある次第なりや

㈡國務省の聲明によれば日本をして貿易促進の外、市民權及び財產權の諸問題についても處理するよう取計うべきだとあるが、之は貿易協定のみならず人、船舶、貨物等の待遇問題をも含む通商航海に關する全般的な取極の締結を考慮している趣旨か。

㈢又協定締結の上は領事官的な代表の派遣が予想されるか。

㈣文化關係、技術と科學に關する取極及び交換とあるが二國間の協定かユネスコ機關への加入と解すべきか。

㈤英、佛、フィリッピンは右勸告に反對したと報ぜられているが、その間の事情如何等の諸點を訊ねたところ、ヒューストン參事官は、本件については國務省へ連絡し、調べた上で答へたいと述べるところがあつた。

二、その後外交部ウェザビー二等書記官から他の當省員に對し、

㈠日本から領事官的な代表と貿易官を派遣する問題について國務省と連絡中であつたが、外務省として派遣場所と人數及び費用概算について具體案あらば承知した

い。特定の國（例えばブラジル、メキシコ）に派遣したいということになれば、日本とこれらの國との間に非公式の協定を最高司令官の仲介によって結ぶ必要があること。

（二）派遣が實現する場合實質的には領事であつても名稱は何か他に適當なものを選ぶべきであり、又非公式協定であるからなるべく紛議を醸さぬような形式をとるべきであること。

（三）極東委員會に對する勸告の原案では consular agreements とあつた筈であるが國務省が新聞發表の際關係國を刺戟することを避けるため「市民權及び財産權の分野における國際的責任」と修文したものと推測すること。

等の非公式な内話があつた。これらの諸點は先記我方の質問に對するヒユーストン氏からの責任ある正式の回答ではないから我方も愼重な態度で臨まなくてはならぬが米國政府の考え方の一端をうかがうことが出來ると思う。

三、領事官的な代表の派遣問題は暫定講和の一環として貿易官の派遣、交換學生の問題とも併行して昨年來外交部に

対し種々働き掛けて来た次第であつて場所によつては貿易官と領事官的代表とを併合的に考えて單一の事務所として開設することも策とする所もあるから、目下外務省において場所、人數、經費等從來計畫し來つた案に最後的檢討を加えつつあるので、最も早い機會に外交部え提示して話を更に具体的に進めたいと考えている。

（以 上）

～～～～～～～～～～

231

昭和24年6月9日　連合国最高司令官総司令部より日本政府宛

在外邦人の身分関係事項に関する日本政府と在外個人間の国際通信を許可する旨の指令

付記　右和訳文

GENERAL HEADQUARTERS
SUPREME COMMANDER FOR THE ALLIED POWERS
APO 500

AG 311.1 (9 Jun 49) DS
SCAPIN 2015

9 June 1949

702

4　制限緩和に向けた対応（昭和24年5月～27年4月）

MEMORANDUM FOR: JAPANESE GOVERNMENT

SUBJECT: Communications between Japanese Government and Persons Abroad in regard to Personal Status

1. Reference: AG 091 (28 Jan 46), GS, 29 January 1946, SCAPIN 677, subject: Governmental and Administrative Separation of Certain Outlying Areas from Japan.

2. Definition: Personal status is defined as those matters, listed in the inclosure hereto, which relate to the application of the Japanese Nationality Law, Family Law, Family Registration Law, and Succession Law.

3. The Japanese Government or any agency thereof is hereby authorized to communicate by international postal or telecommunications service with persons outside of Japan in regard to matters involving the personal status of Japanese nationals or former Japanese nationals, and to record changes of personal status in accordance with Japanese law. Such communications by the Japanese Government will be subject to all applicable restrictions. All documents pertaining to personal status are mailable to and from Japan, including papers of legal procedure and documents drawn up by Ministerial officials.

4. The Japanese Government is also authorized to transmit to appropriate agencies and individuals outside Japan information suitable for publication concerning Japanese personal status laws and regulations.

FOR THE SUPREME COMMANDER:

R. M. LEVY,
Colonel, AGD,
Adjutant General.

1 Incl (in trip)
List of Formal Acts Relating to Personal Status

（付 記）

編　注　本文書の別添は省略。

身分關係事項に關する日本政府と海外個人との間の通信に關する總司令部覺書

連合國最高司令官總司令部

ＡＰＯ五〇〇

AG三一一・一(二十四年六月九日)DS

昭和二十四年六月九日

SCAPIN二〇一五

覺書あて先　日本政府

件　名　身分關係事項に關する日本政府と海外個人との間の通信

一　參照　昭和二十一年一月二十九日付AG〇九一、SCAPIN六七七、件名、若干の外かく地域の日本からの政治上、行政上の分離。

二　定義　身分とは、ここに同封した別紙に記載の通り、日本國籍法、親族法、戸籍法及び相續法上の適用に關する事項をいう。

三　日本政府又はその機關が日本人又は元日本人の身分事項及び日本法律に基く身分上の記録の變動に關し、日本國外にある者と國際郵便又は電氣通信により通信することを許可する。日本政府からの右の通信は現行制限規定で該當するものはすべてこれを適用するものとする。身分事項に關するすべての書類は日本向け又は日本から郵送することができるが、この書類は訴訟用書類及び官吏の作成した文書を包含する。

四　日本政府は日本國外にある適當な機關及び個人に對し、日本人の身分に關する法律規則につき公告することに適する通知を送達することも許可する。

最高司令官に代つて

高級副官

副官部附大佐アール・エム・レヴィー

編　注　本文書は、昭和二十五年六月、外務省政務局特別資料課作成「日本管理資料(一)」より抜粋。

232　**「在外機關設置方に關する提案の件」**

昭和24年6月16日　大野(勝巳)政務局長作成

在外機關設置方に關する提案の件

昭二四、六、一六

大野記

本十六日午前外交部にウェザビー二等書記官を往訪し、別添案二部を提示し從來の經緯を述べ、本案は試案であるが

704

4 制限緩和に向けた対応（昭和24年5月～27年4月）

長い間の研究の成果であって、米國政府において特別の考慮を拂われたい、特にカバリング・ノートについても貴官のアドバイスを得てから決したいと思っている所、ウェ氏は一讀の上、案そのものはワーカブルな案であると思うし、實は國務省からは日本の對外活動に關して成るべく緩和する旨の一般的方針は既に二、三度到達しているが、問題はそれに對應して優れた具體案を華府に送ることにあるのであって、多くの場合一般の方針に適合した案をこちらから送れば採擇されて訓令の形でリピートされることが多い。その意味では丁度時宜を得ているものと考えられるので早速詳細に研究した上兩三日中に再度會見したい、この案並びにカバリングの取扱についてはその際に更に協議したい、と述べた。尚その案の内容を説明に取敢えずの意見としてウェ氏の指摘した點左の通り。

一、附屬第四號の公文交換方式は極めて適切と思う、その中で、日本側の機關にオフイシヤル・レコグニシヨン卽ち可能ならば領事官のタイトルの使用を許されたいとの件については領事官の現狀から見て容易でないと思う、（この點については領事官の享有すべき特權等について本官から應

答したが、結局現狀において日本政府の任命した正式の機關であることが判らなくては在留民關係の事務を公的に取扱うのに支障を來すので、この難點を除かんとする考慮であると述べた所、ウェ氏は、この點にこだわるために在外機關そのものの設置が後れるようならば寧ろスティックせざるを可とするに非ずやとの意見を述べた。）

三、經費の點については、ある程度の具體案が欲しいこと（この點については本官から外國爲替管理委員會が目下考えている輸出インセンティヴ・システムと全般的な輸出促進の爲の經費について輪廓を話し、後者の一部を使用させて貰うということも考えられるが、その外貨使用の仕組については同委員會の考えを訊いて次囘に何等かのインフオメーシヨンを述べることが出來ると思う、と述べておいた。）

尚本件書類は今の段階では非公式の會談における試案ということに取扱うことを申合わせた。

（以上）

（別添）

MEMORANDUM

TO: OFFICE OF THE UNITED STATES POLITICAL ADVISER FOR JAPAN.
FROM: Bureau of Political Affairs, Ministry of Foreign Affairs.
SUBJECT: Request for Establishment of Overseas Organs for Trade Promotion and for Disposal of Citizenship and Property Problems of Nationals Abroad.

June 16, 1949.

PG No. 3

1. By virtue of memorandum from the General Headquarters of the Supreme Commander for the Allied Powers to the Japanese Government on June 9, 1949 and by the press release of the Public Information Office, General Headquarters, Supreme Commander for the Allied Powers, on June 13, 1949, the Japanese Government or any agency thereof is now authorized to communicate with persons outside of Japan in regard to matters involving the personal status of Japanese nationals, and to record changes of personal status in accordance with Japanese law. The adoption of above measure is highly appreciated as it will enable the Japanese Government to dispose several hundreds of thousands of long-pending cases. However, in a desire to inform the Japanese nationals in the various remote places of overseas areas on the domestic situation and on the recent laws and regulations of Japan, it is urgently requested that appropriate organs would be established to realize the far-reaching and complete settlement of the long-pending cases at the earliest possible moment.

2. Although agreements relating to trade and its payment have been concluded between Japan and various countries under the supervision of the Allied Headquarters, a strong demand is lately increasing for the establishment of Japanese organs in the various places in the overseas areas not only for the promotion of trade by carrying out the negotiation and mediation in the overseas markets.

3. To fulfil the object cited in paragraph 1, Los Angeles and Lima could be listed and in case of paragraph 2, Calcutta, Karachi and Batavia are the probable places. It must be noted, however, that such centres as Buenos Aires, Rio de Janeiro and San Francisco embody the necessities cited in paragraphs 1 and 2. Even in the case when an organ is established in accordance with the

purport of paragraph 2, the increase of travel by Japanese nationals will eventually necessitate the organ to be charged with responsibilities as outlined in paragraph 1. By taking such a consideration in mind, a plan has been drafted for the establishment of one over-all organ in the various places in the overseas area which would unify the objectives of the preceding paragraphs. As a result of the study, four documents are attached hereunder.

Appendix 1 is entitled "Draft for the Organization and Personnel of Overseas Organs for Trade Promotion and for Disposal of Citizenship and Property Problems of Nationals Abroad."

Appendix 2 "Re Affairs to be Handled by Overseas Organ for Trade Promotion and for Disposal of Citizenship and Property Problems of Nationals Abroad."

Appendix 3 "Expenses Necessary for the Establishment and Maintenance of Overseas Organs for Trade Promotion and for Disposal of Citizenship and Property Problems of Nationals Abroad."

Appendix 4 "Re Form of Agreement between the Japanese Government and Each of the Governments Concerned in the Establishment of Overseas Organs for Trade Promotion and for Disposal of Citizenship and Property Problems of Nationals Abroad."

4. In spite of the present position which Japan is placed in, it is hoped that due understanding would be given to the true intention of fulfilling the responsibilities incurred in disposing the affairs which are long-pending and which are vitally important for the rehabilitation of Japan and for the welfare of Japanese nationals abroad. It shall be greatly appreciated if favorable consideration would be given to the realization of the plan as submitted.

5. A request for dispatching students abroad has been added as Appendix 5.

6. Name for overseas organs which is tentatively under consideration is "Agency for Trade Promotion and Overseas Japanese Affairs."

～～～～～～～

233　昭和24年6月21日　連合国最高司令官総司令部発表

軍政部の名称変更に関する総司令部発表

付記　昭和二十四年六月二十二日付鈴木連絡調整横浜事務局長より吉田外務大臣宛公信浜連機密本第二七号

右名称変更に関する第八軍幹部の内話報告

軍政部の名称變更に關する米國極東軍總司令部渉外局發表

昭和二十四年六月二十一日十三時三十分米第八軍の軍政局(ミリタリー・ガヴァメント・セクションズ)及び軍政部(ミリタリー・ガヴァメント・ティームズ)は、それぞれ民事局(シヴィル・アフェアーズ・セクションズ)及び民事部(シヴィル・アフェアーズ・ティームズ)と改稱され、昭和二十四年七月一日から實施されることが、本日連合國最高司令官總司令部から發表された。

この發表は次のようにのべてある。

軍政という語は、日本においても他の占領諸地域における同様な直接軍政が施かれていることを意味するというような誤解を常に與えていた。

占領の最初から、日本政府は、占領軍指令を実行する責を負い、正當な意味における軍政は、日本においてかつて一度も行われなかった。いわゆる軍政局及び軍政部の任務は、單に監視及び實情報告にとどまっていた。

占領の様相も變化してきたので、これと歩調を合せて、占領軍機關の眞の機能をより適切に表現するよう、民事という語が採用されたのであると指摘している。

編　注　本文書は、昭和二十五年六月、外務省政務局特別資料課作成「日本管理資料(一)」より抜粋。

(付記)

濱連機密本第二七號

昭和二十四年六月二十二日

横濱連絡調整事務局長(印)

外務大臣殿

「軍政部」の名稱を「民事部」に變更の件

六月二十一日總司令部より發表された進駐以来の「軍政部」なる呼稱を七月一日から「民事部」に變更するとの決定に付き同日第八軍軍政部副司令官ワッツ大佐の本官に對する内話要旨左の通

進駐の當時日本の所謂「軍政」をどういう形にするかに付問題があつたが實際は結局最初から眞の軍政ではなく日本政府が占領軍の指令にもとづいて直接行政面を擔當し所謂軍政部の任務は之が監視と實情報告だけであつて右は獨逸に於ける現在迄の軍政、伊太利に於て一時行はれた軍政又南朝鮮に於て政府が出來る迄の軍政とは全く異つていた。從て一九四六年の六月に既に事實に即し軍政部を民事部と變える案が出來たが當時としては右變更が與ふる事あるべき「サイコロジカル・エフェクト」を考慮して總司令部では六ケ月其の實行を延ばす事と成り爾來其のまゝに成っていたのを今囘實現する事にしたまでゝ實質には變りが無い。

尚陸軍省内部の書類には從來から「軍政部又は民事部」と書いてあり又陸軍省内の占領地の軍政又は民政を取扱う部は民事部（シヴイル・アフエアーズ・セクション）と云っている。

本信寫送付先　各地方連絡調整事務局長

〰〰〰〰〰〰〰

外国人出入国管理業務の実施に関する指令

昭和24年6月22日　連合国最高司令官総司令部より日本政府宛

付記　右和訳文

GENERAL HEADQUARTERS
SUPREME COMMANDER FOR THE ALLIED POWERS
APO 500

234

22 June 1949

AG 091.1 (28 May 49) GA
SCAPIN 2019
MEMORANDUM FOR: JAPANESE GOVERNMENT
SUBJECT: Establishment of Immigration Service

1. References:

 a. Circular 19, General Headquarters, Supreme Commander for the Allied Powers, 23 June 1948, subject, "Control of Entry and Exit of Individuals, Aircraft and Surface Vessels into and from Japan."

 b. Circular 1, General Headquarters, Supreme Commander for the Allied Powers, 1 January 1949, subject, "Private

Commercial Entrants."

c. Memorandum for the Japanese Government, AG 321 (8 Apr 46) ESS/IE, SCAPIN 941-A, 8 April 1946, subject, "Japanese Customs Organization."

d. Memorandum for the Japanese Government, AG 095 (22 May 48) GA, SCAPIN 1971, 11 February 1949, subject, "Entry of Personnel into Japan to Visit Relatives."

2. a. Effective 1 November 1949 and subject to the supervision of the Commanding General, Eighth Army, the Japanese Government will be responsible for the immigration surveillance of all individuals authorized by the Supreme Commander for the Allied Powers to enter into or depart from Japan (except occupation force personnel travelling under official orders).

b. Currently the Supreme Commander for the Allied Powers authorizes entry into Japan for individuals in the following categories:

(1) Compassionate entries
(2) Correspondents
(3) Commercial entrants
(4) Cultural entrants
(5) Dependents of mission members
(6) Dependents of commercial entrants
(7) Foreign diplomatic officials not assigned to Japan
(8) Government officials or employees
(9) In transit personnel
(10) Members of staff, Allied Council for Japan
(11) Members of foreign missions accredited to the Supreme Commander for the Allied Powers
(12) Military attaches of foreign missions in Japan
(13) Missionaries
(14) House-guests
(15) Tourists
(16) Miscellaneous

3. The Japanese Government will immediately take the necessary action to:

a. Assign the necessary immigration officials to the Customs Detachment currently operating under the supervision of

710

the Commanding General, Eighth Army, at each port of entry designated by Circular 19, General Headquarters, Supreme Commander for the Allied Powers, 1948, and amendments and supersedures thereto. The immigration officials will be under the direct supervision of the Commanding General, Eighth Army.

b. The Japanese Government will establish a central office of record for all clearances granted by the Supreme Commander for the Allied Powers to individuals entering or departing Japan, except occupation force personnel traveling under official orders. This office of record will be known as the "Central Locator Files" and will serve to inform the immigration officials of the Japanese Government working under the supervision of the Commanding General, Eighth Army, of all clearances granted by the Supreme Commander for the Allied Powers. The Central Locator Files will be maintained with sufficient English-speaking personnel on a twenty-four hour basis to receive information from the Supreme Commander for the Allied Powers concerning individuals authorized by him to enter or depart Japan. Upon receipt of such information, the Central Locator Files will notify the immigration officials of the Japanese Government of the clearances granted by the Supreme Commander for the Allied Powers.

4. In order that the Central Locator Files may receive information of clearances granted by the Supreme Commander for the Allied Powers, it is desired that a messenger visit the General Headquarters, Supreme Commander for the Allied Powers, promptly at 1200 each Tuesday, Thursday and Saturday to receive a list of clearances.

5. Effective 1 November 1949, the Japanese Government will be responsible for the prevention of the illegal entry of any individual into Japan. It is desired that particular emphasis be placed on entry of individuals through those ports not recognized by the Supreme Commander for the Allied Powers as official ports of entry. Necessary action will be taken by the Japanese Government to deport individuals apprehended as illegal entrants, or individuals who are otherwise in Japan without authority.

FOR THE SUPREME COMMANDER:

R. M. LEVY,
Colonel, AGD,

（付　記）

入國管理部設置に關する總司令部覺書

連合國最高司令官總司部

APO五〇〇

AG〇九一・一（二十四年五月二十八日）GA

昭和二十四年六月二十二日

SCAPIN二〇一九

覺書あて先　日本政府

件　　名　入國管理部の設置

一　參照

い、昭和二十三年六月二十三日付連合國最高司令官總司令部囘章第十九號、件名、「個人、航空機、水上船舶の日本への入國及び日本からの出國の統制」

ろ、昭和二十四年一月一日付連合國最高司令官總司令部囘章第一號、件名、「個人商用入國者」

は、昭和二十一年四月八日付日本政府あて覺書、綴込AG三三一（二十一年四月八日）ESS／IE、（SCAPIN九四一—A）件名、「日本の税關組織」

Adjutant General.

に、昭和二十四年二月十一日付日本政府あて覺書、綴込AG〇九五（二十三年五月二十二日）GA、（SCAPIN一九七一）件名、「親族訪問者の日本入國」

二

い、昭和二十四年十一月一日から、米軍第八軍司令官監督の下に、日本政府は、連合國最高司令官の許可を受けて日本へ入國し又は日本から出國するすべての個人（官命により旅行する進駐軍要員を除く）に對する出入國監督の責任を負う。

ろ、現在連合國最高司令官により日本入國を許可されている個人は、次のとおりである。

(1) 呼寄家族
(2) 通信員
(3) 商用入國者
(4) 文化的入國者
(5) 使節團員家族
(6) 商用入國者家族
(7) 日本に駐在しない外國外交官

4　制限緩和に向けた対応（昭和24年5月～27年4月）

(8) 政府官吏及び使用人
(9) 通過旅客
(10) 對日理事會職員
(11) 連合國最高司令官に派遣された外交使節團員
(12) 駐在外交團附武官
(13) 宣教師
(14) 近親訪問者
(15) 遊覽旅行者
(16) その他

三　日本政府は、即時次のため必要な措置をとらなければならない。

い、昭和二十三年連合國最高司令官總司令部囘章第十九號により指定された各入國港において米第八軍司令官の監督下に運營されている税關に必要な入國管理官を配置する。

ろ、日本政府は、官命により旅行する進駐軍要員を除き日本へ出入國する個人に連合國最高司令官の與えたすべての許可を記録する中央官署を設立しなければならない。當該官署は「セントラル・ロケーター・ファイルズ」と

稱し、米第八軍司令官の監督下に勤務する入國管理官に對し、連合國最高司令官の與えたすべての許可に關する情報を提供する。「セントラル・ロケーター・ファイルズ」には連合國最高司令官が日本へ出入國を許可した個人に關する情報を受けるため充分な英語會話に堪能な人員を二十四時間勤務で配置すること。このような情報を受けたときは遲滯なく連合國最高司令官により與えられた許可を日本政府入國管理官に通告すること。

四　連合國最高司令官により與えられた許可の情報をうるために傳書使を每週火、木、土曜の正午に連合軍最高司令官總司令部へ出頭させ許可の「リスト」を受領すること。

五　昭和二十四年十一月一日より日本政府は個人の日本への不法入國の予防の責任を負う。このような措置に際して、特に連合國最高司令官により正式に入國港として認められない港からの入國に重點をおくことが望ましい。日本政府は、不法入國者として逮捕された者及び權限がなくて日本に在留する者の追放に必要な措置をとることを要する。

最高司令官に代って
高級副官

編 注 本文書は、昭和二十五年六月、外務省政務局特別資料課作成「日本管理資料㈠」より抜粋。

235 【在外事務所設置等に關する件】

昭和24年6月24日　大野政務局長作成

在外事務所設置等に關する件

昭和二四、六、二四　大野

本二十四日午後外交部にウェザービー氏を往訪し、標記の件についての話合を續行した結果、曩に（十六日）提示した我方案の取扱方については前囘（二十日）の話合の通りだが、（内容については修文を要せず）外交部宛のカヴァリング・ノートを附する案に關しては、字句を整理した上で會談の、覺書の形式にすることが本件處理上最も得策であるということになった。よってカヴァリング・ノート案を持歸って修文を加え（修文を加えた箇所は〔　〕内。日附は六月二十七日にした。）別添書き物の通りのものとして先方へ手交することに諒解を遂げた。その際ウェ氏は、この非公式會談の覺書には參加者として通産省の人の名を擧げておき得れば取扱上便宜と思うが如何。これは通産省側から案が出る場合も結局外交部或は國務省の意嚮が徵取される次第であるから、斯うした案の形で國務省系統において基礎的に研究を進めておくことは通産省にとっても有利であり、適當で もあると考える。實は北原事務官とは前に本件の樣なことに付て意見を交換したことあり、同氏の名を掲げることは通産省としても別段支障あるまじと思うが貴見如何、との話であったので、本官から、外務省としても通産省との連絡をとる必要を感じていた次第であるから、至急通商局長に從來の經緯を連絡して大體の諒解を得るようにし、その上で通産省側關係官の名をも覺書に記載し得るように努めようと逑べて辭去した。

236 輸出代金の外貨購入を一定割合で許可する旨の指令

昭和24年6月24日　連合国最高司令官総司令部より日本政府宛

副官部附大佐アール・エム・レヴィー

4 制限緩和に向けた対応(昭和 24 年 5 月〜27 年 4 月)

GENERAL HEADQUARTERS
SUPREME COMMANDER FOR THE ALLIED POWERS
APO 500

AG 091.31 (17 Jul 48) ESS/FTC 24 June 1949
SCAPIN 2020

MEMORANDUM FOR: JAPANESE GOVERNMENT

SUBJECT: Purchase of Foreign Exchange Credits for the Purpose of Stimulating Exports

1. Reference is Memorandum for the Japanese Government from General Headquarters, Supreme Commander for the Allied Powers, AG 386.7 (2 Feb 49) ESS/FIN, SCAPIN 1968, 2 February 1949, subject: Foreign Exchange Controls.

2. It is desired that the Japanese Government submit plans and procedures not later than 27 June 1949, to permit purchase of foreign exchange credits by exporters of Japanese goods in accordance with the principles outlined herein.

3. Exporters of Japanese goods (other than government agencies) will be permitted to purchase with yen foreign exchange credits resulting from any private export transaction in accordance with the following allowable percentages and commodity categories:

　　a. Category I (see Incl 1) – 3%
　　b. Category II (see Incl 2) – 6%
　　c. Category III (see Incl 3) – 10%

In cases where a commodity is not listed under categories indicated above, separate prior approval of the Supreme Commander for the Allied Powers will be obtained for the right to purchase an appropriate percentage of foreign exchange credit resulting from the export thereof.

4. Foreign exchange retention credits may be available only as a result of transactions financed by Letters of Credit or remittances received from outside of Japan. Transactions financed through open accounts may be a source of such credits only if relative foreign government's concurrence is obtained and to the extent of such concurrence. Such retention credits as do result from open account transactions will be available only for and/or in the country with which the contract has been made.

715

5. Foreign exchange credits purchased by private exporters of Japanese goods may be used for the following purposes:

a. Travel and living expenses abroad of Japanese or foreign personnel sent abroad for the purpose of increasing Japanese trade and/or production.

b. Compensation for foreign agents merchandising Japanese goods.

c. Payment for sales promotion expenses.

d. The importation of such industrial raw materials, machinery, tools, or other items designed to maximize export production.

e. Purchase of credit information, samples, catalogs, and other trade publications.

f. Purchase of patent rights and services furnished by foreign technical and engineering consultants.

g. Other purposes as may be specifically approved by the Supreme Commander for the Allied Powers.

6. The establishment and operation of a system under which foreign exchange credits in the currency of the export contract are allowed under this memorandum will be implemented by the Foreign Exchange Control Board in accordance with reference 1 above. Such credits may be purchased subject to the following controls:

a. Rights of purchase will not be effective beyond a six (6) months' period.

b. Rights of purchase may be transferred only once and to not more than three persons within the chain of supply.

c. No foreign currencies or instruments negotiable within Japan will be made available to any person.

d. Such other safeguards as may be prescribed by the Supreme Commander for the Allied Powers.

7. Appropriate Japanese Government agencies will be designated to submit to the Supreme Commander for the Allied Powers for approval names of Japanese nationals requesting travel abroad under provisions of this memorandum subject to the following limitations:

a. The travel requested must be demonstrated to be confined to trade activities.

716

4 制限緩和に向けた対応（昭和24年5月～27年4月）

b. The individual concerned will not be acting as sole sales or purchasing agents for the Ministry of International Trade and Industry or for Japanese trade associations.

8. Direct communication among the Ministry of International Trade and Industry, designated agencies of the Japanese Government and interested staff sections of the General Headquarters of the Supreme Commander for the Allied Powers is hereby authorized to implement the instructions contained in the memorandum.

FOR THE SUPREME COMMANDER:

R. M. LEVY,
Colonel, AGD,
Adjutant General.

3 Incls
as indicated

CATEGORY I

1. METAL, MACHINERY & INSTRUMENTS
   a. Non-ferrous metals
      Mercury, Cadmium, Zinc, etc.
   b. Ferro-alloys, alloy steel scrap
   c. Coal
   d. Vessels
   e. Railway rolling stock
2. TEXTILES:
   a. Cotton
      (1) Yarn
      (2) Grey goods
   b. Silk
      (1) Raw Silk
      (2) Yarn
      (3) Fabrics, greige and bleached
   c. Rayon
      (1) Staple fiber
      (2) Yarn (Filament & spun rayon)
   d. Woolens & Worsteds
      (1) Yarn
      (2) Tops

3. CHEMICALS & DRUGS:
   a. Fertilizer
4. FARM AND MARINE PRODUCTS:
   a. Mining timbers, railway-sleepers, telephone poles
5. IRON & STEEL PRODUCTS:
   a. Alloy steel
   b. Bars, ingots & billets
   c. Bars, all shapes & types
   d. Cast iron pipes
   e. Rails
   f. Sash bars
   g. Seamless tube
   h. Sheets (plain & galvanized)
   i. Wire rope
   j. Structural shapes

CATEGORY II

1. METALS, MACHINERY & INSTRUMENTS:
   a. Textile machinery
       (1) Spinning, weaving, knitting, preparing & finishing machinery
   b. Industrial machines
       (1) Chemical machines
       (2) Mining machines
       (3) Printing & bookbinding machines
       (4) Boilers
   c. Agricultural machines
   d. Electrical machines
       (1) Generator and motor
       (2) Transformer
       (3) Turbine
   e. Construction & conveying machines
   f. Well & pumping machines
   g. Food processing machines
   h. Machine Tools
   i. Metal products
       (1) Semi-fabricated
       (2) Cable

4　制限緩和に向けた対応(昭和24年5月～27年4月)

   (3) Copper & copper alloy products

2. TEXTILES:

  a. Cotton

    (1) Fabrics: bleached, piece dyed, yarn dyed and printed

    (2) Nets and netting

    (3) Towels, toweling, blankets, blanketing, thread, sheets, pillow cases, handkerchiefs

    (4) Knit fabrics

    (5) Velveteens, corduroys

    (6) Rag rugs

  b. Silk

    (1) Fabrics: dyed and printed

  c. Rayon

    (1) All fabrics

    (2) Scarfs

  d. Woolens and worsteds

    (1) All fabrics

    (2) Blankets and rugs

  e. Miscellaneous

    (1) Linen yarn, twine and fabrics

    (2) Ramie yarn, twine and fabrics

    (3) Cordage

    (4) Jute yarn, twine, fabrics & bags

3. SUNDRY GOODS:

  a. Porcelain insulators, porcelain tile, porcelain sanitary ware

  b. Paper

  c. Automobile tires & tubes

4. CHEMICALS & DRUGS:

  a. Caustic Soda, soda ash

  b. Portland cement

5. FARM & MARINE PRODUCTS:

  a. Tea

6. IRON & STEEL PRODUCTS:

  a. Barbed wire

  b. Conduit pipe

  c. Nails

  d. Rivets

  e. Galvanized wire

f. Galvanized iron wire netting
g. Enamelled iron wire netting
h. Iron wood screws

CATEGORY III

1. METALS, MACHINERY & INSTRUMENTS:
   a. Light machinery
   (1) Bicycles & parts
   (2) Optical instruments:
      (a) Binoculars
      (b) Cameras
      (c) Microscopes
   (3) Communication equipment:
      (a) Amplifying systems
      (b) Radio receivers
      (c) Radio transmitters
      (d) Switch Boards
      (e) Telephone sets
      (f) Vacuum tubes
   (4) Electric apparatus:
      (a) Batteries
      (b) Desk & reading lamps
      (c) Fans
      (d) Light bulbs
      (e) Lighting fixtures
      (f) Wire & wiring apparatus
   (5) Gauges & Indicators:
      (a) Ammeters, barometers, magnetic volt meters
      (b) Scales
   (6) Photographic equipment: (roll-film, sensitized paper)
   (7) Medical instruments:
      (a) Surgical instruments
      (b) Injection needles
      (c) Clinical and household thermometers
      (d) X-ray equipment (film-hangers, portable X-ray apparatus, X-ray film and others)
   (8) Wire netting (brass, copper)
   (9) Agricultural goods and machines:

720

4 制限緩和に向けた対応(昭和24年5月～27年4月)

2. TEXTILES:

a. Cotton

(1) Apparel and household goods (except towels, blankets, sheets, pillow cases, handkerchiefs, and rag rugs)

b. Silk

(1) Apparel and household goods (except scarfs)

c. Rayon

(1) Apparel and household goods (except scarfs)

d. Woolens and worsteds

(1) Apparel and household goods (except blankets and rugs)

e. Miscellaneous

(1) All other textiles and textile products

3. SUNDRY GOODS:

a. Porcelain ware (except porcelain insulators, porcelain tile and porcelain sanitary ware)

b. Glass & glass ware

c. Enamel ware

d. Agricultural implements

e. Musical instruments

f. Metallic goods:

(1) Cast iron goods

(2) Aluminum ware

(3) Antimony ware

(4) Sewing needles

(5) Galvanized bucket

(6) Metal leaf

(7) Metal powder

(8) Cutlery

(9) Hand tools

(10) Smoking articles

g. Fountain pens & pencils

(a) Hand type cultivators

(b) Hoes

(c) Hand type plows

(d) Sickles

(e) Spades

(10) Carpenter Tools:

h. Motion pictures
i. Bamboo & bamboo ware
j. Paper goods
k. Leaf-tobacco
l. Brushes
m. Matches
n. Fishing guts and fishing hooks
o. Imitation pearls
p. Buttons
q. Foot wear
r. Umbrellas
s. Papier-mache tray
t. Fans & lanterns
u. Incense
v. Art & curios (including lacquer ware, etc.)
w. X'mas lamps & miniature electric lamps
x. Toys
y. Artificial flowers

4. CHEMICALS & DRUGS:

a. Chemicals (except fertilizer, caustic soda, soda ash and Portland cement)
b. Medicines
c. Celluloid goods (including celluloid sheets)
d. Rubber goods (except auto tires & tubes)
e. Leather goods

5. FARM & MARINE PRODUCTS:

a. Dried Aquatic products:

Sharksfin, Cuttlefish, Scallops Abalone, Sea weed, Kazunoko, Dried-slugs, Agar-agar

b. Aquatic products:

Seed oysters, Frozen goods, Fish liver oil (Vitamin A & D, Natural Coral tree, Living fish)

c. Miscellaneous Foods:

Japanese pickle, miscellaneous food & drink, Ajinomo-

d. Agricultural products:

Fruits, bulbs, vegetable-wax, chillies, persimmon juice, seed, menthol crystals, peppermint oil, refined camphor,

4 制限緩和に向けた対応（昭和24年5月〜27年4月）

e. Hard-wood lumber, flooring, plywood chest
f. Furs (including angora-wool)
g. Canned goods
iles-iles flour, onion

237 地方軍政部廃止に関する神奈川県知事と第八軍幹部との意見交換につき報告

昭和24年6月28日　鈴木連絡調整横浜事務局長より吉田外務大臣宛

濱連機密本第三三一號

昭和二十四年六月二十八日

横濱連絡調整事務局長（印）

外務大臣殿

地方軍政部廃止に關する件

六月二十七日内山神奈川縣知事地方財政の問題に付き第八軍司令官ウォーカー中將を往訪河崎次長立會の下に會談したがその際司令官から地方軍政部廢止の問題を持出され大要左の如き意見の交換が行われた。

先づウォーカー中將から最近マクアーサー元帥より日本側に行政を可及的に移讓する方針の内示があり目下第八軍に於て之が具體案を研究中であるが地方の比較的重要でない縣例えば福井、秋田縣等に於て縣單位の軍政部を引揚げた場合知事として困る事態を生ずるや否やの質問あり、知事よりかゝる場合心配されるのは治安の點丈けであると答えた處司令官は軍政チームは數挺のピストル以外には別に武器を有せず從って之が廢止は治安上影響なしと思はるゝがと述べたるが知事はそれは米軍の威信乃至はモーラル・サポートの問題で殊に終戰後の警察の弱體化、民衆の官憲に對する反抗氣分等に鑑み米軍のモーラル・サポートを必要とする次第を説明した。右に對し司令官はかゝる問題は日本警察隊の強化により解決可能なりと思考すと述べ次で例えば東北地方にて秋田、山形、青森等の縣單位の軍政部を廢して仙臺丈けに軍政部を存置した場合日本側に不便を感ぜらるゝやと重ねて質問あり、之に對し知事より米軍は機動性に富むを以て地區單位の軍政部丈けでも充分なりと思考する旨を答え會談を終つた。

右會談中ウォーカー中將は少くとも邊すう縣の軍政部廢止

238

「海外事務所設置方の件」

昭和24年6月30日　大野政務局長作成

付記　昭和二十四年六月二十七日付

　　　右に関する非公式会談覚書の和文原案

海外事務所設置方の件

昭和二四、六、三〇　大野

一、本件に関する非公式會談の覺書に通産省係官を參加者として記載することにつき、六月二十九日通産省武内通商局長より同意を取付けたので別添の通り覺書を作成し、本三十日午後ウェザービー氏を往訪の際に提示したところ、同氏はこれを多として受取り、先般の案は米國政府に於て第八軍と緊密なる連絡を保ち情勢を注視すべきも中央に於てもかゝる動きに對し豫め對策を御考究置相成度。

本信寫送付先　地方各連絡調整事務局長

に付ては極めて熱心なる樣見受けられ偶々同中將は前日東北地方巡視から歸任せる許りにて同旅行中本件に付て研究したものと推察される。本件に付ては今後とも本官

の最近の方針に鑑み、丁度時機を得たものであって、自分達もこれを極力推進するつもりであると述べた。

その際本官から、外電によればベヴィン英外相が、目下極東委員會に於て對日方針の改訂方を研究中であるとの趣旨を述べた由であるが、これは五月初めに國務省から極東委員會に提出されたと傳えられる對日緩和案を指すか、と尋ねたところウェ氏はこれを肯定した。

二、ウェ氏は、米國政府が日本の對外的行動に對する制限をなるべく緩和せんとする方針に出ている次第は、今回のパリーの電氣通信條約關係の會議においても看取される通りであって、殘念ながら日本の地位に關する票決は二十四對二十三で米案が否決されたが、今夏開催のI・T・Uの管理理事會において取扱う際は是非とも勝つようにあらゆる努力を拂う方針である旨華府からの通報に接している、と述べたので、本官から、同管理理事會の票決については樂觀し得るやと問うたところ、ウェ氏は、先般一票の差で破れたのは票決が急であったために當然支持する筈の國（例えば南米の諸國）の中で欠席國が相當あったからであり、今度は事前に手ぬかりなく手配する

4 制限緩和に向けた対応(昭和24年5月~27年4月)

つもりであるから結果は良いと思っている。何しろソ連とその衛星國の外に極東委員會構成國の多くが必ずしも米案に同調せぬことが頭痛の種である、と語った。

編 注　本文書の別添覚書は省略。同覚書の和文原案を本文書付記として採録。

（付　記）

（件名）　會談覚書

（出席者）　連合國最高司令部外交局二等書記官

　　　　　　　　　　メレディス・ウェザビー

　　　　　外務省政務局長　　大野　勝巳

　　　　　通商産業省事務官　北原　秀雄

　　　　　　昭和二十四年六月二十七日

通商振興及び制限付領事事務のための在外機關設置に關する要請提出の件

一、一九四九年六月九日付日本政府あて連合國最高司令部の覺書及び一九四九年六月十三日の連合國最高司令部渉外局の新聞發表により、日本政府又はそのいかなる代行機關も海外にある日本人の身分上の問題について通信を行い、日本法に從つて身分上の變動を記録することを許せられた。右措置の採用は數十萬件に上る懸案を日本政府をして處理せしめることを得るものとして高く評價せられるものである。しかしながらこの措置は領事機關の欠如に起因する多數の問題を極く一部分解し得るにとどまる。完全な領事機關の設置はなお決定的な解決に俟たなければならないが、過渡的な措置として領事事務を處理し又海外僻遠の各地にある日本人に國内情勢及び最近の日本法律を周知せしめるための適當な在外機關を設置することが強く要望せられるのである。

二、連合國管理下に各國との間に貿易及び支拂上の取極が成立しているが、最近その圓滑な實施のため海外各地に日本側の機關を設置し、海外市場における折衝及びあつ旋により貿易の振興を圖ることを要望する向がますます増加している。

三、以上の如き目的を達成するためには、先づもつて緊急の

必要ある地點にこの種機關を設置することが要望せられる。例えば、制限付領事事務についてはロスアンゼルス及びリマ、通商振興についてはカルカッタ、カラチ及びバタヴィア、又兩者についてはブエノスアイレス、リオデジャネイロ及びサンフランシスコが擧げられる。一般に第二項のための機關においても海外に渡航する日本人の數が增加するにしたがつて必然的に第一項のための任務を帶びる必要がある。この意味において日本政府は海外各地に兩者を統合した總合的機關の設置を要望する。

ここに研究の結果として別添一、通商振興及び制限付領事事務のための在外機關機構人員表案二、同機關設置及び維持のための經費四、同機關事務の內容三、同機關設置及び維持のための經費四、同機關設置に關する日本國政府と關係各國政府との間の合意の形式について、を提出する。

四、日本の置かれている現在の地位に拘らず、旣に長年に亘る懸案となつており且つ日本の復興及び在外日本人の福祉にとつて極めて重大な意義を持つ事項を處理すべき責任を充分に果さんとする眞意を了解せられるならば幸甚

五、なお附屬五、として留學生派遣に關する計畫を附加した。

六、右提案に基く在外機關の名稱は「通商振興及び在外日本人關係事務のための機關」としたい。

編　注　本文書の別添はすべて省略。

239

昭和24年7月9日　外務省作成

「パリ外相會議以後の國際情勢についての一考察」

パリ外相會議以後の國際情勢についての一考察
（昭和二十四年七月九日）

パリ外相會議は今春以來活潑となつたソ連の「平和」攻勢の一環であり、ソ連はこれにより、最近とみに强化した西歐におけるアメリカ側の體制の軟化を計り、東歐及び東亞に延びた共產圈の政治的および經濟的體制强化のための時をかせぎ、また東西兩獨間の通商をさそい水として東西兩歐間貿易を促進し、ソ連圈强化のため資本主義諸國の經濟力の利用を意圖する。而して外交面における情勢緩和の

4　制限緩和に向けた対応（昭和24年5月～27年4月）

ふん囲氣を醸成するとともに、ソ連としてはその對外政策の重點をますます共産黨を通ずる活動に移し、資本主義諸國の内部攪亂とソ連防衛を計る。したがって戦争は極力間避するが、本質的讓歩はこれを行わない。

右ソ連側の政策は今後當分の間定數と看做してもよく、これに對する「西方」の出方と態度が今後における情勢の推移を決定する。アメリカ側としては、かかるソ連の平和攻勢の眞意につき警戒を怠らず、ソ連の本質的讓歩なき限り西歐強化の既定方針をゆるめない。

したがって「冷い戦争」はなお解消せず、重點は外交面からしだいに經濟面、思想面に移行する。またアメリカ經濟の足どりは必ずしも樂觀を許さず、東西貿易の成果は對ソ連圏貿易の特質上さして大きくなく、マーシャル・プランは各國の生産の増大とともに貿易面の困難から袋小路に入った傾向が強くなる。

アジアにおいては中共制覇の確立にともない、アメリカ側の受身の狀態が當分繼續し、全面的對日講和は當分實現しない。

一、ソ連側の觀點と政策

外交面における強硬政策の效果はすでに限界に達したと見られるので、西方陣營側の對抗措置を牽制し遲延させる目的をもって「平和」攻勢を一段と強化する。從って今次外相會議に見られた如き誘引的態度を絶えず繰返すが、それと同時に國力の急速な復興發展ならびに共産圏（中共をふくむ）内の體制確立のため資本主義諸國の經濟力を利用する必要上、東西通商の擴張に努める。

かくて外交面におけるソ連の態度は一見いよいよ協調的となるが、要するに時をかせがんとする戰術的要請にもとづくものであるから、本質的讓歩はこれを行うことなく、かえってドイツ問題、日本問題などにおける發言權の増大をねらうとともに、ソ連の「平和性」の宣傳、米外交ないし占領政策の「侵略性」に對する批判などにより西方陣營の指導者層と一般大衆との離間を策し、合せて各國共產黨の扇動工作により對ソ戰爭の防止を計り、萬一の場合に備え「戰爭を内亂へ」轉化するための準備を行う。

（イ）ドイツに對しては、西獨政府の建設を阻止しえないことが明らかとなったので、やむをえざる對抗手段

の形を装い、東獨に「統一」ドイツ政府を樹立するための實效的措置を講じつつも、表面ドイツの分裂を促進するような言動は嚴にこれを愼しみ、むしろドイツ人の民族感情に直接訴えるような宣傳を盛んに行い、かつ講和に關し相當寬大な條件をもつて臨むが如き態度を以してドイツ民心の收攬を試みるとともに、西方陣營との間にドイツ統一問題に關する交渉を繼續して、できる限り全ドイツに對する發言權の增大を計る。それと同時に東西兩獨間の通商再開を東西兩歐間の通商擴大のさそい水とするべく努力する。

オーストリアに對する講和條約締結問題は「平和」攻勢の大きな持駒として、かつ對東歐政策と關連して愼重かつ效果的に利用する。

(ロ)東歐諸國に對しては、東西通商をも考慮し、政治的內面工作を一層强化する。ユーゴに對しては、マケドニア問題などを利用して攪亂工作を强化する。

(ハ)西歐諸國に對しては、ソ連の「平和性」、なかんず

く危機緩和のためのソ連側の「協調的態度」と東西兩歐通商擴大の熱意に關する宣傳を行うことによつて、對ソ不信を解消し、逆に一般民衆のソ連に對する親しみの感情を育成するに努め、それと竝行して共產黨を中心とする「平和」擁護運動を大規模に展開する。

(ニ)アジアにおいては、民族意識を動力とする赤色勢力の進出を反米鬪爭に直結すべく努める。
中共の連合政權が樹立された場合には直ちにこれを承認し、その國際政治的利用を計るが、大規模な物質的援助は行わない。また南鮮の完全把握を目標として攪亂工作を强化する。

(ホ)日本に對しては、講和攻勢をもつて臨み、アメリカ勢力の後退と自己の發言權の增大を策する。また九原則の結果生ずる經濟の逼迫および社會不安、中共との貿易問題、引揚問題などを巧みに組合せることによつて、日共の黨勢擴大を計るばかりでなく、しばしば治安を脅威し、占領軍に對する威力偵察を行い、暴力革命準備のための模擬演習的行動をとらせ

二、アメリカの觀點と政策

アメリカはパリ外相會議の成果は從來の對ソ強硬政策の妥當性を示す證左に外ならず、又ソ連が右會議において未だ何等實質的讓步を行つていない點に鑑み、アメリカとして今後とも西獨の建設、マーシャル・プランの完遂、武器援助の實施等の政策を推進するよう努め、ヨーロッパにおいて東方陣營に對し壓倒的優位を確立することを計る。

又ソ連の「平和」攻勢及び今間の外相會議の結果米ソ間の緊迫緩和の一般的印象に鑑み、アメリカは西歐諸國の紐帶弛緩を戒める一方、ソ連の眞意、ソ連國民生活の實態等につき民主諸國の大衆の啓蒙に努め、ソ連側の「平和」宣傳に對抗する。

しかし右の政策を推進するに當り、その基盤となるアメリカの經濟は昨秋以來下降狀況を示し、またこれに伴つて議會の一部に經費削減の動きが見られ、これ等はアメリカ政府の對外政策實施上或程度の制約となる恐があるので、アメリカはその景氣の維持を圖り、議會一部の反對を排して既定の政策を進めるよう努力する。

かくの如くアメリカは米ソ關係の一時的安定感に拘わらず從來の對ソ政策を引續き推進し、國內經濟の維持に努めて、自己に有利な客觀情勢の形成を圖るが、同時に對ソ交涉を排除するものではない。但しパリ外相會議に見られた如く、アメリカとしては對ソ讓步を行つて迄も交涉妥結を計る意圖はない。

(イ)西獨をヨーロッパ復興の重要な一環たらしめる從來の政策を續行するとともに、ドイツ民心の獲得を計り、西獨政府を將來の統一ドイツ政府の母體または典型たらしめるよう努力する。

オーストリアの講和條約をなるべく早期に成立せしめ、これに引續き經濟援助を與える。

(ロ)東歐については基本的人權蹂躙に對する抗議、オーストリア條約成立の際のソ連軍の撤退要求、反ソ宣傳等を行うであろうが、これ等は何れも將來の對東歐政策の伏線たる程度に過ぎない。ユーゴに對しては通商上の利益をもつてソ連圏からの事實上の離脫を計る。

(八)西歐に對してはマーシャル・プラン完遂、北大西洋條約批准、武器援助實施、西歐諸國間の軍事協力の方針をもつて臨み、ソ連の工作や宣傳に對しては反共啓蒙宣傳をもつて對抗し、西歐の結束弛緩を防ぐ。殊にマーシャル・プラン完遂の見地から西歐諸國間の交易增大、非ドル地域との交易增進等を強く要望し、また一定の制限はあるが、東西兩歐の貿易交流を促進する。

(二)中共に對しては西歐諸國と協議を行いその行動を一致せしめるよう努め、また徒らに中共を刺戟することを避けて將來の行動の自由を確保するよう圖る。中共が聯合政府を樹立した場合にも、當分これを承認せず、臺灣及び對外貿易に關するその出方を注視する。

南鮮からの撤兵はその抛棄を意味せず、南鮮の育成はアメリカのアジア全體に對するプレスティージの問題でもあるから、これに繼續的經濟援助を與え、かつ軍事使節團を置く。

南方諸國における赤色勢力に對してはヨーロッパ

植民諸國をして極力現地民主政權の育成に努めしめる。

(ホ)對日講和はここしばらくは遲延させることを得策とし、單にソ連の講和攻勢に對應するため、及び日本の自立と民心維持、經費節約等の目的に必要な限度において管理政策を形式的に緩和し、事實上の講和に近づけて行く、ただし經濟面、治安對策における實際のグリップは一層強化する。

三、ヨーロッパの情勢

統一ドイツに關する米、ソの對立は解消せず、オーストリア講和條約成立の氣運はヨーロッパにおける緊迫感を表面的には幾分解消することにはなつても、ヨーロッパにおける「冷い戰爭」は依然繼續する。

マーシャル・プランは第二年度に入り、生產の增大という面における一應の成功にも拘わらず、貿易は停滯し、復興は頭打ち狀態となつているが、アメリカのマーシャル援助の增額は望めない狀況であるから、ポンド貨を初めとする歐州各國通貨の對ドル價値の再調整、多角的決濟制度の擴張、東西兩歐の交易量の增大等の手段による

4 制限緩和に向けた対応(昭和24年5月～27年4月)

貿易の振興を計る。しかしこれが實施に當つては各國の利害關係が對立し、根本的な解決はできないにしても何等かの妥協的解決策が成立する。

(イ)東西兩獨間の經濟交流は改善されるが、西獨政府に對應する東獨の「統一」ドイツ政府の具體化により、ドイツの分裂は一層明確となり、對獨講和は成立しない。

(ロ)オーストリア講和條約は一般の予想よりは多少遅延する。

(ハ)共産黨はマーシャル・プランの難行に乗じて攪亂工作を繼續するが大した影響はなく、西歐の政情は安定をつづける。

(ニ)ギリシャの内亂は混迷状態をつづけるが、幾分改善する。

(ホ)イランは當分現状のままであり、パレスタインの平静化と相まつて、中近東にはさして變化はない。

四、アジアの情勢

アジアにおいては秋頃中共の中央連合政府が成立し、國民黨政府はしだいに衰滅の一途を辿る。同時に中共制

覇の東亞に及ぼす影響がいよいよ顯著となる。南方の政情はいぜん不安を繼續し、南鮮は治安惡化が深刻となる。

(イ)廣東は今夏陷落すべく、これと前後して新政治協商會議が召集され、秋頃には中華人民民主主義共和國政府が出現する。ソ連はこれを承認するが、アメリカやイギリスは當分これを承認しない。現政府は一應西南奥地に敗退し、右派の大部分は臺灣を最後の據點とする。

中共は國内經濟建設の必要上商工政策に重點を置き、この間貿易等の對外關係においては比較的妥協的態度を示す。しかしその輸入するものはもつぱら經濟建設に役立つものであり、自由貿易の範圍はほとんどない。

(ロ)南方の政情は、インドシナ、インドネシア等にかんするヨーロッパ本國の努力およびアメリカの意圖にもかかわらず容易に平静化しない。

(ハ)南鮮においては、米軍の撤退後北鮮系からする統一のための政治攻勢は秋頃を目標として一層強化され、現政府はアメリカの援助にもかかわらずいよいよ弱

体化する。

五、對日關係

(イ)「冷い戰爭」は本質的にはなお解消するに至らないから、對日講和は對獨講和とともにここ當分實現しない。

ソ連は對日問題における自己の發言權の增大ならびに日本國民の反米感情育成のために對日講和を促進することをもつて有利と判斷している。從つて今後も對日講和攻勢を繰返し、日共を通じて日本國民に働きかけ講和促進氣運を醸成する一方、講和豫備會議早期開催の必要上手續問題その他で若干形式的讓步を行うことをも辭さない(ただし機會をとらえて中共承認を誘致する)。しかしこれに對し米ソ關係の現段階においてはむしろ日本における現狀維持を有利とするアメリカ側としてはたとえ講和豫備會議開催に同意しても、撤兵その他にかんするソ連側の條件を容認することはないと思われる。またソ連としてもなんら實質的讓步を行う意圖はないから結局ソ連をもふくむ全面的對日講和條約成立の可能性はほとんど存しない。

(ロ)アメリカの對日援助は、對外經費節約の必要もあり、現在までの傾向とは逆に今後はだんだん切りつめられこのため日本國內經濟の合理化はつよく要請されるが、日本の保持に必要な最小限度の援助は常に與えられる。

(ハ)アメリカの景氣後退、西歐經濟の行きづまり、東亞の政情等により、輸出の振興は行き惱み、經濟不安は容易に解消せず、失業者は增大する。かかる內地の情勢と、南鮮の不安及び中共制覇の傾向と相まつて相する日共の活動はその暴力破壞的傾向と相まつて相當深刻な不安を醸成する。アメリカ側はこれに對しますます抑壓的態度をもつて臨むほかないが、その結果日共は加速度的に地下運動、非合法的暴力行動に走ることとなる。

(二)かかる狀況において、アメリカは對日講和を考え得る段階にはないが、日本國民一般の獨立欲求や經濟界の行詰りに對する現狀打破の要望がソ連の講和攻勢に動かされ易い下地を形成して來る。アメリカは

4　制限緩和に向けた対応（昭和24年5月～27年4月）

240

昭和24年7月28日　連合国最高司令官総司令部発表

民事部の漸減命令に関する総司令部発表

渉外局發表

民事部の漸減命令に關する米國極東軍總司令部

昭和二十四年七月二十八日

これに對し、管理政策の形式的緩和等により日本人の自立心の作興と、對米感情の維持に努め、なかんずく賠償の打切り、日本人の海外渡航、日本側のイニシアティヴの尊重等の面においては僅かながら事實上の講和に近い狀態に移行するが、治安對策や經濟の運用の實際面においては反って把握が強化されている。

種々な指示が發せられている。

地方民事部及び地區民事部は、現在とほぼ同程度の定員が存置される予定であるが、そのスタッフは、できるだけ米國陸軍省軍屬をもってし、行政部門擔當の軍人の数は最少限にとどめることになろう。

この計画は、更に第八軍民事部を廢止し、連合國最高司令官總司令部に小規模な民事局を設置することを規定している。

この計画は、昭和二十四年十二月三十一日までに實施され、第八軍司令官は、同日以後民事遂行の責を解かれ、各地方民事部の指揮權は連合國最高司令官に引き繼がれる。

地方民事部は、宿營管理、部內行政、規律に關しては依然第八軍に從屬する。

編 注　本文書は、昭和二十五年六月、外務省政務局特別資料課作成「日本管理資料㈠」より抜粋。

241

昭和24年7月29日　大野政務局長作成

各府縣民事部の仕事を漸次減らして、究極においては、七地方民事部及び北海道地區民事部に、その任務と責任とを統合するという計画が、本日連合國最高司令官總司令部から發表された。

既に、この變更に直ちに着手するよう、第八軍司令官に

「日本政府の海外機關設置方に關し會談の件」

日本政府の海外機關設置方に關し會談の件

昭和二四、七、二九　大野

本二九日午後外交部にウェザービー氏を往訪し、本日の華府發ＵＰヘンスレイ特電を提示し、この内日本政府の在外通商領事機關設置の問題は、六月末我方から外交部に提案された具體案と關連あるものと思ふが、その後の本件進展振り如何と尋ねたところ、ウェ氏は丁度今自分が起案中のものを絕對極祕の含みで内示すべしとて、日本政府の在外機關設置（通商促進及制限的領事事務）に關する司令部の日本政府宛覺書案の草案を原稿のまま本官に示し、右に關しアドヴァイスを承知したいと述べた。右草案の要點は大体左の趣旨であった。

(一) 日本政府は覺書受領後は、通商促進と制限的領事事務の處理のために、相手國の同意を條件として在外機關を設置することを得ること。

(二) 本件在外機關設置のために日本と相手國との間に合意が成立するを要すが、右は一切總司令部外交部が斡旋仲介に當るべきこと。

(三) 在外機關の設置許可は、日本の外交的自主權の囘復と解せらるべきではないこと。

(四) 在外機關の設置を具體化するに當っては、所要外貨の入手方については總司令部經濟科學局の同意を要すべきこと。

(五) 本件實施以後は、司令部の指定する關係日本政府機關は當該外國の政府機關と直接連絡し得べきこと。

(六) 在外機關の運營に當っては通商促進事務については經濟科學局、制限的領事事務については外交部と密接な連繫をとるべきこと。

本官は右草案を一讀後、これは外務省の提案が基礎になっているとの印象を得て、甚だ嬉しく思ふが、具體化の手順如何と尋ねたところ、ウェ氏は、自分の目下の計畫では外交部としての確定案を得た上は司令部內の關係各部局と協議して、司令部の成案とし、華府に請訓したく、然る場合は最後的承認を得ることは困難ではないと思ふ。しかし華府の承認を得ることちにこの覺書を日本政府に送付することは暫く控えておき、先づ第一番の實例を示す意味で、米國政府と日本政府との

4　制限緩和に向けた対応（昭和24年5月～27年4月）

間に、在外機關設置方に關する合意を成立せしめたく、その形式は予て貴方提案の通り交換公文によりたく、準備成つて愈々公文交換の實行の一週間位前に初めて本件覺書を日本政府へ送付し、これを公表すると共に、總司令官から在京諸外國代表部に對し、この覺書の本旨と米國政府の方針とを闡明し、諸外國政府に於ても速かに日本政府の在外機關設置方に關して合意が成立する様勸奨する旨の書信を送り、米國に引續き他の二、三の國に渡りをつけるようにすることにしては如何と思うと述べたので、本官から大体その段取りで結構と思うが、本件と極東委員會との關係如何と尋ねたところ、

ウェ氏は、本年四月二十一日に國務省から日本の對外活動制限の除去乃至緩和方に關し、極東委員會に提案したままになつているので米國政府としては、改めて新提案をすると云うことでなく、具体的に國別に扱つて行く趣旨と思うと答えた。

仍つて本官から外務省としては、更に通産省と協議を重ね貴方の好意的處理に應へたいと思うが本會計年度内に具体化するとすれば予算の問題もあり、およそ何時頃か見當

をつけたい次第であるが、これは所謂八月十五日又は九月二日の朗報説と時期的に關連ありやと問えるに、

ウェ氏は、所謂朗報説の時期には關連がないと思うが、八月十五日乃至九月二日に千のステートメントが出るよりも、少し遅れてもこの案一つが成立する方が有意義であると思うが如何と述べ、且つこの件は所要の方面との連絡調整の必要があり、年内一杯位かかると見る方が安全と思うと答えた、尚米國政府としては貴方提案の通り差當り三ヶ所（ニューヨーク、サンフランシスコ、ロスアンゼルス）に事務所を設置することで進みたい考えであるが爾余の諸國についても先方次第であるから貴方の案で一應進み、必要に應じ適當調整を加へることとすればよいと思う。ただ自分の心配する點は、此の件は司令部の内部では、外交部と經濟科學局、日本政府の方では外務省と通産省と云うように四者に關連する問題であるから日本側においては通産省の間に圓滑に進むよう調整を遂げておいて貰いたいことであると述べた。

仍つて本官から從來の本問題に關する外務省と通産省との連絡状況を更に詳細に述べた。實は一兩日前の外務通産

両省の幹部（外務次官、政務局長、連絡局長、通産次官、通商監、通商局長等）間の定例懇談會に於て、近く何等かの形で政府の在外機關の設置が許されるとすれば補正予算で所要の經費の予算化を圖る必要があるとの議が出たが、外務省側からこの問題は外交部において四月二十一日の極東委員會に對する國務省の方針提案以來種々の經緯があり、外交部はこの線に沿い折角推進中であるから通商監からマーカット少將に提案したままになっている案（總司令部のニューヨーク貿易事務所への日本人派遣案及び他の若干の箇所への總司令部貿易事務所の設置案）は客觀的情勢に合致しない嫌があるから暫く靜觀を希望する旨の提言をしておいた經緯ありと述べ、殊に予算化の場合の兩省の措置については事態の進展した際に初めて表面化し得る問題であつて、過早に閣議に具體的數字を出す譯に行かぬがいよよ實施の場合に如何なるスタッフを兩省から出すか、又出先に對する指揮命令權の問題等につき兩省間に協定を成立させて、圓滑なる運營を期し得る積り故懸念に及ばないが、ただ本官の氣にかかることは、外交部で斯くの如く努力中である際に通産省から經濟科學局の方へ別の案が出て、採用されるようなことになっては國務省案が停滯する結果を招く甚だ不本意なことになる惧れがあることである。勿論通産省方面に對しては、なお念を押して連繫をとられ萬全を期していただきたいと希望して辭去した。

〰〰〰〰〰〰〰〰〰

昭和24年7月30日

鈴木連絡調整橫濱事務局長より
吉田外務大臣宛

242

民事部の廢止に關する第八軍幹部の内話報告

橫濱連絡機密本第九二號

昭和二十四年七月三十日

橫濱連絡調整事務局長（印）

外務大臣殿

民事局部機構改組の件

七月二十八日附拙信濱連機密本第八二號に關し自分が七月三十日第八軍民事局次長ワッツ大佐（二週間程の公用旅行より歸濱せる）に面會種々懇談した際本件に付ての内話御參考迄に左の通

局長のシェパード少將及自分は都府縣の民事部を漸次廢止

4　制限緩和に向けた対応(昭和24年5月〜27年4月)

する考であつたが總司令部は一時に廢止する事に決した。府縣單位の民事部は十一月三十日迄に軍團民事部に十二月三十一日迄に夫々廢止する。第八軍民事局が總司令部に移るのが十二月三十一日で明年一月一日から同部の管轄に入る。第八軍民事局の人員は總司令部としては縮減を希望して「スモール、セクション」と云つているが何の位に成るかは未だ決定していない。

移管の當時は相當の人員で行くが次第に減らしてゆく事になるかと思う。

二十八日の本件新聞發表にあつた最後の一項 The Regional Teams will remain attached to Eighth Army for logistic support, administration and discipline 中ロジステイツク、サポートとは必要な住宅、事務所、衣類、食事の供給等の事で總司令部が地方に之に必要な組織をもつていないから當然で第五空軍の如きも第八軍に對して同樣の地位にある。デイシプリンとは民事部員が不法行爲を犯した時地方の第八軍部隊に屬する軍法會議を利用して之を裁判し又上級司令官が其判決をルヴイユーする事をを指しアドミユニストレーションは民事部要員につき總司令部と第八軍側との權限の限界

の問題でそれはこれから決るものである。(ワツツ大佐以外の一局員は之は要員の人事健康等の問題で尤もプロモーションの點は總司令部の權限と成るうと云う)

尚CICは各府縣に依然として維持されるので今後は地方民事部の無い縣のCICには當該地方民事部から下士官二名位が派遣され自働車をもつていて地方民事部又は總司令部民事局から巡視する要員を世話する事になろう。

將又總司令部各局特に經濟科學局と當民事局との間には從來密接な連絡があり凡て方針決定に先立つて非公式に當民事局に相談があり兩者の間に意見の相違等があれば總司令部副參謀長が之を調整していた。此の方針は過去二年間圓滑に動いていて其の意味で第八軍の民事局は事實上總司令部の一局の形であつたとも云える。云々

本信寫送付先　各連絡調整事務局長

〜〜〜〜〜〜〜〜〜

243

昭和24年8月1日
連合国最高司令官総司令部より
日本政府宛

日本人技術者の海外渡航許可に関する指令

GENERAL HEADQUARTERS

SUPREME COMMANDER FOR THE ALLIED POWERS
APO 500

1 August 1949

AG 680.2 (25 Aug 48) GA
SCAPIN 2035
MEMORANDUM FOR: JAPANESE GOVERNMENT
SUBJECT: Travel of Japanese Technicians Outside Japan

1. As a measure designed to assist the Japanese economy through deposits in the Supreme Commander for the Allied Powers Commercial Accounts, broadening Japanese participation in world-wide industry, advertising Japanese technical skills and products abroad and accruing good will, the restrictive policy of the Supreme Commander for the Allied Powers concerning travel abroad of Japanese technicians is now liberalized as hereinafter provided.

2. For the purpose of this program the term "Technician" is defined as any individual possessing a skill or capable of rendering a service which is saleable outside of Japan as an invisible export. The term "Technician" does not include "Common Labor" in the generally accepted sense of the latter term.

3. The Supreme Commander for the Allied Powers will in general give favorable consideration to the travel of any technician:

a. When the presence of the technician in the country to be visited will contribute to the economic or cultural advancement of the country concerned, providing the absence of the technician from Japan will not be harmful to Japanese cultural and/or economic advancement because of the loss of his skill, and/or will not contribute to an unreasonable degree to the development of an industry abroad which may impair the position of peculiarly Japanese industries which are essential to the achievement of a self-supporting economy.

b. When the personal attributes of the individuals are such that his actions and associations while abroad will be likely to further the objectives of the occupation.

4. Requests for travel abroad of technicians must be submitted by or with the indorsement of the government of the country of destination. The employment of these individuals will be on a

4 制限緩和に向けた対応（昭和24年5月〜27年4月）

contract basis between the business concern or individual of the country of destination which desires their services and a business concern in Japan which will provide the technicians or the technician himself. A sample model contract is attached for information. Contracts will be modified to suit individual cases, but will conform as closely as possible to the inclosed model; they will be subject to ratification by the Supreme Commander for the Allied Powers, with the advice of suitable agencies of the Japanese Government.

5. The business concern hiring the technicians will be required to pay the total costs of transportation and allied expenses from and to Japan. The salaries of these technicians will be paid partially in the indigenous currency of the country of destination to meet day-to-day expenses with the remainder of the salary being deposited in acceptable currencies into the Supreme Commander for the Allied Powers' Commercial Accounts. By arrangement with the Foreign Exchange Control Board this deposit will be converted into yen which will be deposited into the account of the business concern in Japan which furnishes the technicians or the technician himself. This business concern will support the dependents of such technicians while they are abroad or deposit the yen salary of the technician to his credit in Japanese banks. For the present dependents will not be authorized to accompany such technicians abroad. The salaries of these technicians will be arrived at on a case by case basis and will be based on prevailing worldwide standards for technicians of comparable experience and training.

6. The Supreme Commander for the Allied Powers contemplates placing no limitations on the number of these technicians who may be authorized to travel abroad for employment subject to the conditions outlined above.

7. The appropriate agency of the Japanese Government will be responsible for securing the services of technicians when they are not requested for by name, and will otherwise maintain closest liaison with Economic and Scientific Section, General Headquarters, Supreme Commander for the Allied Powers in advising whether or not the travel of certain technicians will be inimical to Japanese industry for any of the reasons provided in paragraph 3 above.

FOR THE SUPREME COMMANDER:

R. M. LEVY,
Colonel, AGD,
Adjutant General.

1 Incl
Sample Model Contract

~~~~~~~~~~

244
昭和24年8月3日　連合国最高司令官総司令部発表
過度経済力集中排除審査委員会の任務完了に関する総司令部発表

経済力集中排除審査委員會の任務完了に關する
總司令部渉外局發表

（昭和二十四年八月三日）

本日マックアーサー元帥は集中排除審査委員會が集中排除法に基く一切の審査事項について勸告を行う任務を完了したと聲明したが、これは占領使命のさらにまた一つの主要局面が達成され、また日本經濟を平時の基礎の上に再興し民主化するために多くの論議をかもしつつなされた總司令部の努力が結實したことを示すものである。集中排除審査委員會は最終報告を提出したので即時解散されるであろう。

同委員會を構成する專門家のグループは、昨年五月四日、日本に到着したが、その委託された權限は、日本の法律の規定によリ過度經濟力集中として指定された會社につき持株整理委員會の提出した一切の改組計畫を審査することにあり、ま一元帥の要請に基いて結成された權限は、マックアーサた右改組が一般經濟に及ぼすかも知れない衝撃に關して連合國最高司令官に勸告を提出する責任を有している。さらに同委員會は、ポツダム宣言及び昭和二十二年六月十九日極東委員會によって政策協定として發せられた對日占領及び管理のための降伏後の指令に従って、陸軍省が發した諸指示の實行上適切と思われる集中排除の他の局面について勸告を行う權限を認められた。操業中の諸會社の集中排除の基本計畫は一年余で終了し、戰前日本人の生活を支配した獨占的經濟力の排除は、金融または産業に有害な影響を與えずに、またその「細分化」をもたらすことなく、效果的に完了したことを占領軍總司令部は強調している。權威

740

4　制限緩和に向けた対応(昭和24年5月～27年4月)

ある觀測者は、むしろ日本經濟の健全さが增大した證據として、過去一年に安定化に向って著しい進步を示したこととともに生產の五〇％增大したことを指摘している。このような重要な任務を果した委員會のメンバーは次のとおりである。

ジョセフ・ロビンソン
（委員長、ロビンソン連結器會社會長）

ロイ・S・キャンベル
（初代委員長、ニュー・ヨーク造船會社前社長）

エドワード・J・バーガー
（オハイオ公共事業會社取締役兼副社長）

バイロン・D・ウッドサイド
（かつて連邦通商委員會及び證券爲替委員會に參與していた企業經營の專門的研究家）

ウォルター・R・ハッチンソン
（米國檢事總長の元特別顧問）

ジョージ・F・ブルーエット
（法律顧問官かつて極東國際軍事法廷に配屬していたフィラデルフィア州弁護士）

基本的諸指令に從って多面的な集中排除計畫を實施するに當り、最初にとられた措置は、少數の家族が日本の商工業及び金融に對して全面的に行き渡った統制を行う手段とともになっていた舊財閥持株會社の所有權を解消し、それを廣く分散させることであった。財閥の支配した機關以外の持株會社も同樣に解體された。右目的のために制定された法律のもとに改組された。戰前及び戰時中各產業に對して廣汎な統制力を行使し、生產及び自由經濟活動を人爲的に制限していた多くの統制組合は廢止された。

財閥の支配的連鎖に關係していた約一二〇〇の會社は「制限會社」として指定され、財閥との關係が斷たれるまで、日本の法令に從って細かい點まで監督を受けることとなった。

昭和二十二年初期獨占禁止法が日本の立法機關によって制定されまた財閥同族支配力排除法も昭和二十三年一月國會を通過した。集中排除審査委員會の設置に先だってとられたこれらの措置によって、戰爭を計畫しこれを遂行した政治的・軍事的・經濟的結合體の强大な力は有效に破壞され、また同じような極めて强力な組織の再生を防止する法

昭和二十二年十二月國會を通過した法律第二〇七號は自由企業と自由競爭を制限していた日本における操業中の會社の過度經濟力集中を除去することを目的とした。この法律に從って特定の過度經濟力集中を指定する標準とした集中排除審査委員會が積極的な活動を開始した後最初に行った仕事は、持株會社整理委員會が會社を指定した基準と手續を檢討し、法律上の解釋が正確であったか否か、手續が連合國指令に合致していたか否かを決定することであった。

最初三二五の操業中の會社が、事實上、過度の經濟力集中と認められる根據があるか否かを一般的基準に照らして詳しく檢討するために「指定」されたが、豫備審査の結果、五十社は過度集中でないとして持株會社整理委員會による指定から解除され、さらに他の一〇七社は機構に影響のない比較的重要でない調整を受けることを條件として指定を解除された。その後、集中排除審査委員會が勸告した四基本原則に從い、數囘に亙り、さらに一一一社が種々の理由

によって指定を解除された。

金融・商業・工業など二二二の業種を代表する五七社については、審査委員會が詳細に檢討を加えた後、勸告をそえて連合國最高司令官に提出したのであるが、これらは、金融機關・鐵鋼會社・製紙工場・重電氣機械・電氣器具・ビール・ガラス・通信・石油・綿紡織・絹・化學製品・造船・鐵道用設備・器具・金物・農業用機械・製粉・セメント・食糧容器・倉庫・漁業・製氷・冷凍・ガス・酪農・石炭・金屬鑛業及び精錬・映画・演劇・通運・發電及び配電會社などであった。

上記五七社について調査の結果、そのうち十一社は機構の改組を勸告され、三社は特定の工場または持株の處分を必要とされ、二社はその取引慣習に關する特別の勸告を添えて公正取引委員會に付託され、二社は斯業全體にわたる措置による完全な改組、一社は政府機關としての特權の放棄を勸告され、殘りの三十七社は指定會社の表から解除するよう勸告された。

會社が全般的または部分的に改組される場合には、すべてその改組要求に適合する自己の案を提出することを認め

4 制限緩和に向けた対応(昭和24年5月～27年4月)

245

昭和24年8月25日 鈴木連絡調整横浜事務局長より吉田外務大臣宛

米軍民事機構の縮小に関する第八軍司令官の内話につき報告

濱連機密本第一三三號

昭和二十四年八月二十五日

横濱連絡調整事務局
局長　鈴木　九萬〔印〕

外務大臣　吉田　茂殿

米軍民事局部機構縮少の件

編　注　本文書は、昭和二十五年六月、外務省政務局特別資料課作成「日本管理資料㈠」より抜粋。

られ、また會社組織をいかに變える場合でも、すべて生産低下を齎さないように行わねばならぬことが強調された。集中排除審査委員會及び他の總司令部の特別顧問による調査中、日本の産業はその技術及び技術的手續の改善のために價値ある技術的情報を提供された。

八月二十四日朝自分が第八軍司令官ウォーカー中將に面會の際本問題に付き左の趣旨を陳べて置いた。

七月二十八日本件につき總司令部特別發表があつて以來一ケ月近くに成る處政府としては公式には本件につき聲明を出して居ないけれども吉田總理を始め政府側に於ては今囘の府縣單位民事部撤收の措置をとられた本當の意味を充分に理解して居る次第であるが從來地方民事部より多大の同情的援助と助言とを得て來た知事の大多數は現在の地方行政が治安と云い勞働と云い經濟と云い其他各方面に多大の困難があるので突然撤收した後の事につき不安を感じて撤收後も幾人かの民事要員を殘して欲しいと云う陳情等が多くあつた譯で去る八月十一、十二日の知事會議に於ても種々話が出た。然して知事側の最も關心を有つのが治安問題で地方の自治體警察については從來から其の改革案となっていた様だが民事部廢止の此の機會に一つの改革案(府縣に自治體警察をおく、町村の治安は其の府縣自治體警察の管下に置く)を決議し之が實現を政府に要請する事になつたとて其の内容を説明し而も右實現を府縣單位民事部廢止前に實現

を要望している。勿論之は國家警察との關係もあり政府の之に對する意向も未だ明かではないが知事會議側としては之を總司令部及第八軍にも通じ同情と援助とを要請して居るとて昨日知事會議代表がシェパード少將に會つた事に言及した。次で民事部廢止其のことについては知事側一般に民事部要員を幾人かでも殘して欲しいと云ふ希望があり特に治安問題の困難な縣に此の要望が強く山口縣の如きが夫れであるる旨を口頭で知事側代表者から説明する所があつた

と述べて置いた。
右に對し司令官は左の趣旨を述べていた。

實はマック、アーサー元帥から最初に本問題に關連して話のあつたのは約八ケ月前で同元帥は占領軍としては現在の樣な形で日本側を指導援助するのでは何年やつても切りがなく最早や日本側を特に地方行政につき一人立ちをさせる時機が來たと確信すると云われて自分に對し問題の研究を命ぜられた。知事の中には何か地方行政等に失敗のあつた場合これは民事部側の命令だと云つて言譯する樣な場合や面倒な場合のあつた事も事實である。然し同元帥の氣持は決して日本人側を一人立ちにさせたからと云つて適

當な指導と援助とを打切るわけでは決して無い。自分は貴下も御承知の如く七月二十八日總司令部から本件について發表があつた前後を通じ全國知事の半數以上と本問題について意見を交換して居り警察の問題については同情もし現に出來る丈け多くのピストルを持たせる樣に努力して現も御承知の通りで山口縣の如き其の實情はよく判つているので何とか警察力が增强される事を希望する。

尙之れは極祕に願いたいが自分としては府縣民事部の現在の如きサーヴェーランスは漸次問題の容易なもの容易な場所より之を外してゆき今後一ケ年位で結局府縣民事部が完全に撤收される事を總司令部に禀申したのだが同司令部は本年一杯でそこ迄行く事に決めたわけである。就いては貴下は知事や市長とも色々連絡があるのだから此の自分達の氣持を機會ある每に徹底さして貰い度い。

右に對し自分より右は努力いたすべくタイミングの問題については意見も岐れ得たであろうが事態がプレシピテートしつつあり獨逸では九月十五日より軍政を民政に切り替えると傳えられて居る此の際でもあり且つ民事局方面できいた所によるも本年一杯で府縣單位等の民事部完全撤收に

4 制限緩和に向けた対応(昭和24年5月～27年4月)

246 「政府の在外機關設置に關する件」

昭和24年9月15日

大野政務局長、北原(秀雄)通商産業省事務官作成

本信寫送付先　各地方連絡調整事務局長(幸便による)

政府の在外機關設置に關する件

　　　　　　　　昭和二四、九、一五
　　　　　　　　外務省　大野政務局長
　　　　　　　　通産省　北原事務官

標記の件に關し總司令部外交局の求めに依り本官等兩名は十五日午前經濟科學局に參集し通商貿易課ケンプ氏外一名及び外交同オヴァトン氏と會合した處先方から豫て計畫中の日本政府の通商領事事務代表事務所の米國に於ける設置の案件は愈々ファイナル・ステージに到達したので貴官等と共に主として經費の問題を中心として具體的に相談致したいと前置きし總司令部側事務當局の腹案を逐次説明し日本側の意見を承知し討議を進めたいと述べたので我方から首相に於かれては豫て本件實施を見る場合は

(1) 人件費は出來得る限り節約するが事務費は成るべく潤澤にして機動的に働き得るように取計ひたきこと

(2) 日本からの派遣員は少數にても有能なる者を充て成るべく駐在國の人を雇入れ能率をあげるようすることを心掛くべしとの御意見を述べた處先方は極めて適切なる御考へである自分達の腹案も大體それに則つているものと思うからその趣旨で協議致したしとて細目を具體的に討議した結果腹案に若干の修正を加へ左の様な案で先方上司に報告し決定案を得るよう取計うべしとのことであつた。
(從つて細部に亘つてはまだ今後多少の變更があり得る)

尚同司令官の話ではヴォーリーズ陸軍次官は八月二十九日來日九月六日、七日が横濱の行事に豫定されているとの事である。

將の民事局とも出來る丈け協力したいと思っていると陳べて置いた。

事が望ましく此の點については自分としてもシェパード少將の民事局とも出來る丈け協力したいと思っていると陳べて置いた。

事務が占領軍側と日本側との間にうまく行く樣工夫する事が望ましく此の點については

が至急實現されん事を希望すると共に民事部機構縮少後民事事務が占領軍側と日本側との間にうまく行く樣工夫する

央政府に於て警察問題につき案を作り能率的な適當な改革が至急實現されん事を希望すると共に民事部機構縮少後民

ついては變更を加へ得られないと了解される以上一方に中央政府に於て警察問題につき案を作り能率的な適當な改革

一、設置の場所

紐育、桑港、ロスアンゼルス

（第一回としてはこの三箇所とするがホノルルに付てはシカゴ、ニユーオルリーンズに付ては第一回分實施後將來適當の時期に考慮すること）

二、人員數（一館當り）

〇日本人（三名）

　領事　　　　一名

　貿易官　　　一名

　副領事　　　一名

〇現地採用（五名）

　顧問（テクニカル・アツシスタント）＝大學卒業級の相當高級な補助者　　　　一名

　書記生代りの館務補助員（オフイスマネージヤー）　　　　　　　　　　一名

　速記兼タイピスト　　二名

　雑役書記　　一名

（右は基準數であつて紐育に付て考へたのであるが桑港、ロスアンゼルスに付ても大體同規模としたく又貿易官一名は少な過ぎるとの意見に對しては實は紐育には總司令部の貿易事務所あり職員九名を擁し相當の經費を配賦してあるので貿易促進の業務に付ては全面的に援助すべきに付き之と連繋を密にせらるれば充分目的を達し得べき見込にして貿易官は差當つては市況報告等の事務に主眼を置くことゝせられたしとのことであつた。）

三、通信及び連絡系統の問題

通商領事代表事務所と日本政府との通信連絡等の爲には相當額の通信費を計上するから外務省を通じ通信を行ひ現地に於ては館長たる領事が之を統轄するは勿論であつて領事は外部に對しては事務所を代表すべきこと。通信事項に付ては總司令部に留保すべきもの若干ある由。

（戰前日本の出先機關に於ては館長たる本廳と連絡して不始末を生じたことは米國に於ても著聞しているが今後は日本政府の對外事項は一切外務省に於て統轄することに制度を確立すべきであると云ふのがシーボルト氏の堅持する方針である旨を先方は強調した。尙右に關連し

247 昭和24年10月17日 大野政務局長作成「日本政府の在外機關設置に關する件」

日本政府の在外機關設置に關する件

昭和二四、一〇、一七

大野

十月十七日求めにより外交局にオヴァトン氏を往訪したる處同氏は日本政府の在米機關設置案は參謀長の所で最後的に檢討中であつたが原案の主要點はその儘で、人員等に付て輕微な修正が加へられたから、米國政府は之を採決次第日本政府に對し紐育、桑港、羅府の三個所に領事貿易代表事務所設置方のインヴィテーションを寄せる筈であり、それは本月一杯には接到する段取と予想されると告げた。仍つて本官から外交局今日までの盡力に對し深甚なる謝意を表明した上各般の質問をしたのに對しオ氏は絕對極祕の含みで左の諸點を內話した。

一、本件の重要なる意義に鑑み米國政府よりのインヴィテーションが接到後最も早い機會に司令部から公表する筈であつて、その際は相當大きくパブリシテイを與える方針である。シーボルト公使は談話を發表するものと思はれるが、事前に內示するから日本政府からも直ちに之に應

(次頁へ続く)

―――

て國務省に於ける「レザーヴド・オフィサー」の制度の說明を行ひ貿易官等について參考としては如何と示唆するところがあつた。）

（中略）

四、經費

五、日本人職員の身分及び特權

日本人職員については關稅その他通常領事職員に認められる日常の特權は認められるものと諒解してよいかとの質問に對してはオヴァトン氏は全般的な原則論としては今卽答出來ないが事實問題としては關稅免除は勿論であらう然し戰前日本では米國の領事職員に對し必ずしも滿足すべき待遇を與へていなかつたことを自分は良く知つているとの發言があつたので我方より我々の知つている限り決つしてそんな扱ひをした覺えはない筈であるがと應酬して置いた。

（以上）

諾する旨の返翰を用意して米側と共に公表し、併せて米國政府の態度にレシプロケートするような聲明乃至談話を發表すること望ましく、右に付き具体的な打合せを行いたきこと。

（先方は本件の持つ政治的重要意義に鑑み公表の時期—十月末か十一月初頃—に付て總理の御考えを承りたいとのことであった。）

二、日本側としては極祕裡に人選に着手されたく、又公館長及び館員の名稱は對外的には事務所長、貿易事務代表等と呼稱するのが適當であるが、日本側の官制上外務省において有する官名即ち總領事、乃至領事、商務書記官、副領事等を日本側限りで使用することは差支えなきものと思うこと。

三、本案は紐育及び桑港に付ては、各々日本人職員三名、現地採用職員四名、羅府に付ては、日本人職員二名（貿易代表は落ちた）、現地採用職員三名を予定しているが、所に依り副領事又は書記生とするか、或は現地採用のオフィス・マネージャースは書記生とすること、及び一名は現地採用予定の速記兼タイピストの代りに婦人職員を

以て充て得るようせられたし、との日本政府の希望に鑑み經費予算の範圍内で日本政府の裁量により實施出來るような余地を殘してある。但し現地採用を日本からの派遣に替える場合には赴任旅費が問題になるが、大した額でもないから予算全体の範圍内で他の費目から融通されたく、例えば所により現地採用者の俸給等を多少鹽梅して捻出すれば可能となるべきこと。

四、本件公館の性格上未だ外交的な性格乃至機能を附與し得ないことは勿論であるが、細目に亘つては次の樣な諸點に付ては權限がない。

(a) 日本人の海外における旅行の許可（之は司令部の手にある。）

(b) 占領軍人員の渡日

(c) 總司令部から特に許可される場合を除く貿易協定その他政府間交渉（事務所そのものの行政的運營に關連するものは例外）

(d) 米國連邦政府に對し直接日本を代表して行動すること及び特に總司令部から許可を與えられている場合を除き、日本政府を公に代表して行動すること（在外邦人は現地採用予定の

4　制限緩和に向けた対応（昭和24年5月〜27年4月）

248　民間輸入に関する指令

昭和24年10月21日　連合国最高司令官総司令部経済科学局より通商産業省宛

の利益保護の爲に地方官憲と交渉することは出來る。（以下省略）

GENERAL HEADQUARTERS
SUPREME COMMANDER FOR THE ALLIED POWERS
Economic and Scientific Section
APO 500

091.31 (21 Oct 49) ESS/FTC
(BT 49-5927) A　　　　　　　　　21 October 1949

MEMORANDUM FOR: Ministry of International Trade and Industry Attention: Mr. A. Kodaki, International Trade Administrator

SUBJECT: Private Imports

1. Reference are:

　a. Memorandum for Japanese Government from General Headquarters, Supreme Commander for the Allied Powers, AG 091.31 (9 Mar 49) ESS/FTC, SCAPIN 1982, 9 March 1949, subject: Import Procedure;

　b. Memorandum from Ministry of International Trade and Industry to General Headquarters, Supreme Commander for the Allied Powers, Economic and Scientific Section, 20 September 1949, subject: Programming & Import Quota for Limited Private Import;

　c. Memorandum from the Ministry of International Trade and Industry to General Headquarters, Supreme Commander for the Allied Powers, Economic and Scientific Section, 22 September 1949, subject: Procedure for Limited Private Import.

2. References 1 b and 1 c are not favorably considered.

3. It is directed that the Ministry of International Trade and Industry submit within ten (10) days a plan for establishing private imports on or before 1 January 1950.

4. There is attached hereto an outline of a private import procedure which may be used by interested agencies in the formalization of an effective plan.

右制限解除に関する通報

二　日本政府とアジア救済機関との契約案

GENERAL HEADQUARTERS
SUPREME COMMANDER FOR THE ALLIED POWERS
APO 500

AG 400 (26 Jul 49) PH　　　　　25 October 1949
SCAPIN 2054

MEMORANDUM FOR: JAPANESE GOVERNMENT

SUBJECT: Receipt and Distribution of Relief Supplies from Licensed Agencies for Relief in Asia

1. Reference:

   a. Memorandum for the Japanese Government from General Headquarters, Supreme Commander for the Allied Powers, file AG 400 (30 Aug 46) PH, SCAPIN 1169, dated 30 August 1946, subject same as above.

   2. Reference Memorandum is rescinded effective 1 April 1950 with the exception of that portion of paragraph 4 therein concerning monthly reports which will continue in effect until all

---

FOR THE CHIEF, ECONOMIC AND SCIENTIFIC SECTION:

(Sgd.) F. E. Pickelle

F. E. PICKELLE
Chief
Foreign Trade & Commerce Division

1 Incl:
as indicated

編注 一　本文書の別添は省略。
　　 二　本文書は、昭和二十四年十二月、外務省特別資料課作成「日本占領及び管理重要文書集」第四巻より抜粋。

249

昭和24年10月25日　連合国最高司令官総司令部より日本政府宛

アジア救済機関（LARA）よりの救援物資の受領および配給の制限解除に関する指令

付記 一　昭和二十四年十月二十五日付連合国最高司令官総司令部よりアジア救済機関宛公信和訳文

4 制限緩和に向けた対応（昭和24年5月～27年4月）

FOR THE SUPREME COMMANDER:

K. B. BUSH,
Brigadier General, AGD,
Adjutant General.

LARA relief goods in possession of the Japanese Government have been allocated and distributed.

（付記一）

連合國軍總司令部

　軍郵　五〇〇

總司令部公衆衛生福祉部氣付

　　　LARA御中

一九四九、一〇、二五

日本に於けるララの計畫活動は連合國軍最高司令官の同國における任務遂行上言外の效果と援助を提供したものである。

海外における民間の有志團体がそれぞれの救援物資を送るに當り一つの認可された團体卽ちLARAを通じて實現し而して救護が最も必要であり廣範圍にこれを要した當時に一括的に日本政府の救援分配分野に合流し無差別平等に行われたことは特筆に價する處である。

今や日本の社會、經濟事情は順次恢復し多くの統制、制限はこれを解除撤廢し得る時に立ち到つている。海外より民間の救援物資を割當又は分配のため日本に於ける特定の代表者或は代理者に直送する場合の從來の制限もその一つである。

此の制限の解除によつてLARAの計畫もその遂行上從來の方針によらなければならないという必要はなくなるのである。しかしLARAが新しい方針に卽應する態勢を整えるため十分な時日を採り得るために日本政府との現在のとりきめ、卽ち日本政府がLARA救援物資を受取り、その安全な受渡し、運搬、割當及び分配に關して責任を有することは昭和二十五年（一九五〇）三月卅一日まで繼續するものとする。

昭和二十五年四月一日以降LARAは希望によつて在日認可民間社會福祉團体（　数文字分アキ　）として日本において割當、無償分配のため海外より救援物資の送付を受けることを繼續し得るのである。LARAは昭和二十五年四月一日

以降從來實施の計畫通り活動を遂行し得るのであるが割當及び（或は）救援のため分配するためLARA救援物資を受入れるための日本政府の協定は總てLARAと日本政府との間のものであつて尚右の協定は總司令部の審査承認を要するものとする。

LARA及び日本政府或はその一方が上述の如き協定を好まない場合においてもLARAは救援物資を繼續して輸入することが出來る。但しこの場合は輸入に許可證（数文字分アキ）を要する。

右の救援物資の受領後はその割當、配分についてはLARAにおいてその責任を負うのである。昭和二十五年三月卅一日以降LARA及び（或は）その代表者は他の認可民間社會福祉團体の分野に屬することとなり、占領軍としての援助を受けないこととなるのである。

LARAの計畫に對し又その代表の方々が我々當局者及び地方關係官に對して示された御友情と御協力とに對し厚く感謝致す次第であります。

我々は四月以降のLARAの卽活動計畫に關してなるべく速に伺いたく存じます。

准將 K、B、ブッシ

副官部

（付記二）

The Contract between the Japanese Government and the Representatives of LARA (the Licensed Agencies for Relief in Asia)

The Japanese Government and the Representatives of LARA have this day entered into a contract as follows on the receiving and distribution of LARA relief supplies in Japan in accordance with the letter from GHQ, SCAP to LARA dated 25 October 1949, a copy of which is annexed, and the Memorandum from SCAP to the Japanese Government file AG 400 (26 Jul 49) PH, SCAPIN 2054, dated 25 October 1949, subject "Receipt and Distribution of Relief Supplies from Licensed Agencies for Relief in Asia", a copy of which is annexed.

Article 1. Purpose

All the LARA relief supplies shall be distributed gratis, with a view to assisting in the reconstruction of Japan, without discrimination by nationality, religion, race or political faith, equitably, effectively and appropriately as occasion needs, to persons who are really in need of relief.

Article 2. Method of Transfer and Distribution of the Supplies

(a) The Representatives of LARA shall deliver LARA relief supplies to the Japanese Government at the port of Yokohama, the Japanese Government shall receive them on behalf of beneficiary organizations or individuals.

(b) The Japanese Government shall distribute them adequately for realization of the purpose mentioned in Article 1 upon consultation with Representatives of LARA.

Article 3. The Responsibility of the Japanese Government

(a) The Japanese Government shall take all responsibility of security, movement, allotment and distribution of LARA relief supplies from receipt by the Government to the delivery to the beneficiary organizations or individuals, and shall bear necessary expenses therefor.

(b) The Japanese Government shall take every precaution in unloading, transportation and storage so that robbery, damage or any other preventable damages shall be avoided.

(c) The Japanese Government shall give first priority to unloading, storing and transportation of LARA relief supplies.

Article 4. Exemption from Taxation

(a) The Japanese Government shall take measures to exempt LARA relief supplies from import duty and any taxes to be imposed by any public authorities.

(b) The Japanese Government shall take measures to exempt income taxes upon salaries and remunerations which are paid in foreign countries to LARA Representatives who are not Japanese nationals.

Article 5. Term of the Contract

The present agreement shall be effective from April 1st, 1950 to the date when the activities of LARA in Japan are finished.

Article 6. Alteration

Alteration of the present contract and addition of any other necessary matters not mentioned in the preceding articles of the present contract shall be decided upon agreement between the two parties.

SIGNED THIS ___ DAY OF ___, 1950

Shigeru Yoshida, Premier,
Japanese Government.

G. E. Bott, Representative, LARA
E. Rhoads, Representative, LARA
Fr. Felsecker, Representative, LARA.

250

「日本政府の在外公館設置に關する件」

昭和24年11月17日　大野政務局長作成

日本政府の在外公館設置に關する件

昭和二四、一一、一七　大野

本十七日午後求めにより外交局にオヴァトン氏を往訪したところ、在米三館設置の問題に關し、國務省が極東委員會構成國に送ったエイドメモアールの概要を國務省から電報越した趣を以て、右電報を極祕の含みを以て一讀を求めた後、本件は極東委員會諸國に將來のことを考慮し最後的に念を押しているため、予定より手間取った次第であるが、この際外交局としては外務省と協力してこの種公館の設置が現下の狀況に鑑み如何に價値ありやの點を、できるだけ具體的にワシントンに申送り、問題の推進に資するよう致したいので一つの書物を作成したく、非公式に書き物を提出されればこれを基本として一つのステートメントを作りたしと考えているから協力を得たいと逃べた。よって右の趣旨に基き如何なるポイントを上げて論據を强むべきやにつき話合った結果、次の諸點につき具體的な事項を書き物にし明後十九日(土曜)朝、暫定草稿として外交局に持參し、右を基礎として更に修文を加ふることに話合った。

(一)日本の經濟再建のための重要な一環として貿易を振興する必要上、日本の實業家達が海外の消費者の嗜好とかデザインを知る必要が絕對にあるのみならず、米國における最近の關稅手續法規、貿易關係の國內課稅法規その他最近の立法を知ることが必要であるが、そのためにも政

4　制限緩和に向けた対応（昭和24年5月〜27年4月）

府機關を米國に置いて的確かつ迅速に日本に報告する必要があることは勿論のこと、最近數年間在留邦人の一身上及び財產上の變更を適法に處理することの不可能な事態及び戰後における日本の新立法中在外邦人に直接間接適用あるものを知らしめるためにも領事館的機能を持った政府機關が駐派されることが必要であることを強調すること。

(二) 在外邦人の身分上及び財產上の諸問題の法律上の未解決狀況から來る實際上の困難が如何に大であるかの實例をできるだけ具體的に掲記し、かつその件數等をも併記すること。（又本年六月日本政府と在外邦人との間に直接の通信が許されて以來、屆出等の件數があまり多くないのは、要するに從來のように在外領事官が手を取るように手續的事項につき助言して來たのが全然今は存在しないためであると思われるが、斯る事實はできるだけ詳細かつ的確に書上げること。）

(三) 政治的な部面からして今まで日本がおかれて來た封鎖的な地位から漸次脫却して、制限された形とはいえ國際諸關係に入って行くことは日本國民の最も熱望していると

ころであり、國際社會への復歸が如何に日本國民の等しく希望しているところであるかは、日本人の間に國際連合とかユネスコなどに對する關心が諸外國に比して著しく高いのに徵して明かであるが、斯る在外公館の設置により日本人がどれくらいエンカレッジされるか計り知れざるものあり、これにより日本人の自立心と責任感をますます深める結果となり、日本再建のために良好なる效果があること。

(四) 在外邦人の利益保護にはスエーデン等が當っているが、經費の點で何等か措置をとらなくては困る段階に到達しており、かつ利益保護國の從來の努力に對しては大いに感謝する所であるが、それにも拘らず經費の問題もあり又その在外公館の活動範圍も限られているため、立入った問題までは到底その解決を期待し得ない次第であって、すでにそのリミットに達しており、その面からも在留民の多い所では日本政府獨自の機關が駐派されて、從來の莫大な數に上る懸案を解決するために努力を集中する必要があること。

なおオ氏が本件會談の冒頭に內示した國務省からの來電の

極東委員會構成國のエイドメモアールの内容は、「ニューヨーク、サンフランシスコ、ロスアンゼルスの三地に貿易及び領事事務代表の事務所を置くことをSCAPから米國政府へリコメンドして來ている」とてその趣旨を述べ、本件当初からの設置趣旨を再び繰返した上、「極東委員會構成國政府においても右に同調せられんことを希望する」との趣旨のものであったので、本官から、最近の外電の一つから得た印象では極東委員會では狭義の領事的事務代表よりも貿易官的代表に重點を置いているやに思えたが、斯る傾向ありや、又本日話合った本件共同作業の一つの目的は狭義の領事官的事務代表の必要性をも強調する點にありやと尋ねたところ、才氏は、その後のワシントンにおける推移については詳しい情報に接しないので分らぬが、通商代表的事務に比較的重點を置く方が政策的に通りがいいという考慮も多少動いているやに感じている。しかし外務省が、そうなれば通産省の方が主體になりはしないかとの危惧の念を懐かれるならば、それは当らない。何となれば、建前の問題については外交局は決して通産省に事務所の主導權は渡さぬつもりであるし、すでに得點を上げているつもりである。自分達の差当りの最大の關心事は、東京からも有力な論拠を送って、当初の計画通りに一日も速かに實現せしむることにあるとの趣旨を述べた。（以下省略）

〜〜〜〜〜〜〜〜〜

251

昭和24年12月1日　連合国最高司令官総司令部より日本政府宛

自由輸出貿易の許可に関する指令

GENERAL HEADQUARTERS
SUPREME COMMANDER FOR THE ALLIED POWERS
APO 500

AG 091.31 (1 DEC 49) ESS/FTC
SCAPIN 2059

1 DEC 49

MEMORANDUM FOR: JAPANESE GOVERNMENT
SUBJECT: License Free Exports

1. Rescissions:

　a. The following Memoranda for the Japanese Government from General Headquarters, Supreme Commander for the Allied Powers are rescinded:

4 制限緩和に向けた対応(昭和24年5月～27年4月)

(1) AG 091.31 (9 Aug 48) ESS/FTC, SCAPIN 1926, 9 August 1948, subject: Export Trade;

(2) AG 091.31 (9 Aug 48) ESS/FTC, SCAPIN 1926/3, 27 January 1949, subject: Procedures for Handling Private Export Contracts and License to Export.

b. The following Memoranda for the Board of Trade (Boeki Cho) Ministry of Commerce and Industry, Tokyo, from General Headquarters, Supreme Commander for the Allied Powers, Economic and Scientific Section, are rescinded:

(1) 091.31 (20 Dec 46) ESS/FT (BT 188), 20 December 1946, subject: Method of Authentication of Application to Prepare and Deliver for Export Forms IE 100 and 200;

(2) 311.1 (16 Jan 47) ESS/FT (BT 47-21), 16 January 1947, subject: Commercial Correspondence Between Private Individuals in Japan and in Other Countries;

(3) 091.31 (1 May 47) ESS/FT (BT 47-303), 1 May 1947, subject: Export Procedures;

(4) 091.31 (21 Sep 48) ESS/FTC (BT 48-3033), 21 September 1948, subject: Recommendation of Contract Forms for Export Transaction;

(5) 091.31 (16 Oct 48) ESS/FTC (BT 48-3160), 16 October 1948, subject: Use of Application Forms Relative to Yen Pricing Under Private Export Procedures;

(6) 300.6 (31 Jan 49) ESS/FTC (BT 49-3818), 31 January 1949, subject: Implementation of SCAPIN 1926/3;

(7) 160 (4 Mar 49) ESS/FTC (BT 49-4241), 4 March 1949, subject: Program for Investigation of Applications for Cargo Shipment;

(8) 091.31 (31 Mar 49) ESS/FTC (BT 49-4519), 31 March 1949, subject: Invisible Exports;

(9) 120.1 (21 Apr 49) ESS/FTC (BT 49-4753), 21 April 1949, subject: Terms of Payment;

(10) 091.31 (21 Apr49) ESS/FTC (BT 49-4738), 21 April 1949, subject: Extension of Time Under Export Contracts.

c. The following Memoranda for the Ministry of International Trade and Industry from General Headquarters, Supreme Commander for the Allied Powers, Economic and Scientific Section, are rescinded:

(1) 140.2 (13 June 49) ESS/FTC (BT 49-5117)

A, 13 June 1949, subject: Processing of Cargo Shipment Forms;

(2) 091.31 (29 Aug 49) ESS/FTC (BT 49-5641)

A, 29 August 1949, subject: Export Procedure.

2. Amendments:

   a. Memorandum for the Japanese Government from General Headquarters, Supreme Commander for the Allied Powers, AG 334 (3 Apr 46) ESS/IE, SCAPIN 854, 3 April 1946, subject: Board of Trade (Boeki Cho), is amended insofar as it conflicts with the provisions of this memorandum.

   b. Memorandum for the Japanese Government from General Headquarters, Supreme Commander for the Allied Powers, AG 091.31 (6 Nov 47) ESS/FT, SCAPIN 1813, 6 November 1947, subject: Procedure for the Export of Samples, is amended by deleting paragraphs 3, 4, and 5.

   c. Memorandum for the Imperial Japanese Government from General Headquarters, Supreme Commander for the Allied Powers, AG 091.31 (19 Nov 46) OGA, SCAPIN 1346, 19 November 1946, subject: Import-Export Accounting Control for Japan, is amended by deleting paragraphs 3 and 4.

3. Effective this date:

   a. The Japanese Government will supervise and authorize export of goods from Japan in accordance with provisions of "Foreign Exchange and Foreign Trade Control Law".

   b. Prior validation of the Supreme Commander for the Allied Powers will be required only for those items contained in the Japanese Government list of designated goods as may be specified by this Headquarters.

4. Changes and modifications of the initial list of designated goods will be subject to prior approval of this Headquarters.

5. Payments collected from export proceeds will be credited to such foreign exchange accounts as may be specified by this Headquarters.

6. Direct communication between appropriate agencies of the Japanese Government and General Headquarters, Supreme Commander for the Allied Powers, is authorized to implement this memorandum.

4　制限緩和に向けた対応（昭和24年5月～27年4月）

252 「外国為替及び外国貿易管理法」の制定経緯・特色につき通報

昭和24年12月12日　吉田外務大臣より　各連絡調整地方事務局長宛

〜〜〜〜〜

FOR THE SUPREME COMMANDER:
K. B. BUSH,
Brigadier General, AGD
Adjutant General.

連地合第一〇六八號

昭和廿四年十二月拾貳日

外務大臣　吉田　茂

各連絡調整事務局長殿

外國爲替及び外國貿易管理法送付の件

第六臨時國會を通過した本件法律を御參考迄に英譯文と共に別添（省略）の通り送付する。

なお此の法律の制定經緯及び其の特色は左記の通りで、本法に基く政令は逐次送附する。

記

我國貿易問題に關しては、本年九月中旬米國商務省「オーモンド、フリール」氏を團長とする貿易使節團一行が來朝し、當時不振狀態に立至つてゐた我國貿易を種々な角度より檢討してこれが振興策に付總司令部を援助した。又右一行と前后して現西獨合同輸出入機關理事長として同國貿易伸張に多大の貢獻をした「ウィリアム、ローガン」氏が特派されて來朝し、これ又同一問題を檢討して總司令部を援助して來た。「フリール」氏一行が貿易手續上より我國貿易問題を取り上げる一方、「ローガン」氏は所謂「ドッヂ、ライン」による日本經濟再建に繋がるより高い觀點から之を研究したもので、其の執れもが貿易振興に依り我國經濟の戰後に於ける病弊を除去して其の自立を計る爲の米國の對日經濟政策に關連してゐる事は疑いない。

其の後「フリール」國際貿易團長は總司令部に對して行つた貿易振興策に關する勸告の內容を發表したが、其の勸告の結果、現在迄に屢次公信を以て通報した通りの措置が採られて來た次第で、（一）從來行はれて居つたフロア、プライス（輸出最低價格制）を十月二十六日以降撤廢し（二）現在迄總司令部が扱つて居た銀行事務を日本側銀行に移す目的を以て、

外國爲替の集中を計り、日本側外國爲替銀行の地位を確立する「外國爲替銀行の臨時措置等に關する政令」を十月二十五日公布して卽日實施した。更に㈢外國貿易を米國の援助資金で賄はれてゐるもの以外は民間の手に移し、實務上の手續を最大限度簡易化するため、總司令部は十月二十一日、二十二日附覺書を以て、從來の管理貿易方式を改變すべき旨示して來た。

卽ち、右覺書に依れば、輸出に付ては從來通商產業省の許可を必要としたが、特定物資を除き事前許可はこれを全廢し、輸出手續を著しく簡素化し、輸入に於ては、これ迄は政府輸入に限られて居たが㈠「ガリオア」「イロア」兩資金に依る物資は從前通り政府が輸入するが㈡統制を全面的に撤廢出來ぬ特定物資は、通產省が需要者に爲替の事前割當をして輸入せしめ㈢前記以外の物資は、經濟安定本部內に新設される輸入諸問委員會が四半期每に輸入計畫及び爲替割當計畫を樹立し、通產省を通じ指定商品の明細と商品別爲替豫算總額を公示する。輸入業者は其の範圍內で外國爲替銀行に輸入を申請する。但し一件に付、割當てられた爲替總額の二十「パーセント」を超える事を得ない。申請

を受けた銀行は外國爲替委員會に資金利用を申し込む。同委員會は所要事項を調查して、利用可能の場合は支出割當を記錄して銀行宛許可を通知することとなる。結局早い者勝式輸入方式で、業者は外國爲替銀行に輸入を申請するだけで自由に輸入し得る事になる。

政府は、以上の輸出入に關する兩覺書を受領して以來、其の背景をなす「ローガン」氏の所謂「ローガン、ライン」に付總司令部と逐次連絡して成案を得、第六回臨時國會に「輸出貿易臨時措置法案」又遲くとも第七回通常國會には「輸入貿易臨時措置法案」を提出出來る樣準備を整えた。

其の後、米國より國際通貨基金「ムラディック」委員が來朝して、總司令部に於て獨自の立場から更に前記二法案を檢討するに及び、將來日本が國際社會への參加を認められ、國際通貨基金に加盟する場合を考慮して、斯かる國際的見地からの修正を加えた改革案を政府宛通告して來た。卽ち十一月十日總司令部經濟科學局「ライダー」中佐より手交された所謂「ライダー」試案がこれである。

右試案の要點は㈠外國に對し權威を持たせるため、從來の局長級の輸入委員會に代り、新たに閣僚級のメンバーで構

4 制限緩和に向けた対応（昭和24年5月〜27年4月）

成する委員會を設置し、此の委員會に於て輸出入を含む外貨の收支豫算を決定する。（二）爲替レートの承認は凡ゆる種類を通じて單一とし、レートの變更は閣議の承認を必要とし、賣物取引に於ける賣買相場は公定標準相場より一「パーセント」以上開いてはいけない。（三）大藏大臣は外國爲替銀行を指定する等である。十一月十五日更に總司令部より法案の形式に關する申入れがあつた。即ち政府は、貿易に關する法案は前述の通り二本建てとし、とは別個に外國爲替に關する法案を用意して、既に外國爲替委員會に於て「涉外取引法案」として總司令部と接衝の上、第四次案の完成を見て居たが、此の度は之等三法案を綜合し簡單な一本建恆久的法律とすべき旨示唆された譯である。その理由は、國際通貨基金に參加する場合及び外國人の對日投資或は外人觀光客の訪日等に備えて複雜難解な法律を避ける爲である。よつて政府は、諸外國の管理法に倣つて骨組だけを成文化することに止め、詳細の運用規定は後日政令に委ねることとし、早速關係機關に於て具體的檢討に入り、漸く脫稿の上、十一月二十一日の閣議に於て之を決議し、「外國爲替及外國貿易管理法案」として第六回臨時國會に提出した。

斯くして、同月三十日を以て兩院を通過の上、法律となつた次第である。

此の法律は、七十三條及附則よりなり、其の內容の特色に付ては、前述の經緯より容易に了解し得る所であつて、第一の特色は閣僚審議會の組織及び運營を政令に委任する規定（第三條）を初めとして、大部分の詳細な運用規定を政令に委任した一大委任立法である事で、之等委任を受けるべき政令中には所謂「ローガン」構想が織り込まれて、それが漸次實現されて行くことが期待される次第である。又國際的感覺を採り入れた事も第二の特色として擧ぐべきで、國際通貨基金協定の規定する原則を採用して、外國爲替相場に付ては基準相場すべての取引を通じて正しい裁定外國爲替相場を決定、維持し（同條第二項）直物取引の相場の開きを一「パーセント」以內に限定した（同條第五項）。

第三の特徵は、第三章に於て外國爲替に付予算制度を採用した點で、予算を對外收入と睨み合はせて、對外支拂いを最も有效にする樣之を作成する事が必要とされ、從つて其の操作如何により對外支拂いが如何なる輸入に向けられる

かは、貿易外收支に對する配分額の如何と相俟つて、國内經濟に大きな影響を及ぼすものである。此の點は、各國との貿易協定方式により輸入を增進し相手國に購買力を賦與する事により延いては輸出の振興を狙ふ。これがため從來の貿易協定を益々擴大せんとする政策と共に、從來の物の面からの「ブレーキ」を、爲替を通じて之を行はんとする「ローガン」構想の二大眼目の一であると考えられてゐる。

第四の特色は、この法律は一應爲替及び貿易の全般を網羅し、其の運營には彈力性を持たせ、能率的管理を狙つた事である。卽ち、この法律は屬地主義を採用し、居住者の持つ對外支拂手段、貴金屬、外貨債權、外貨證券のみでなく、本邦内に在る非居住者が本邦内に持つ對外支拂手段、貴金屬等に付ても保管、登録又は賣却の義務を課し、更に非居住者が有する内國支拂手段、本邦通貨表示の證券、債權等に付ても同樣の義務を課し、(第二十一條、第二十二條、第二十三條)爲替集中措置に遺漏ない樣、萬全を期した。

又第二條に於て、この法律に於ける制限を、其の必要の減少に伴い逐次緩和する目的を以て、再檢討する餘地を與え、或は國際經濟事情の急變があつた場合、緊急の必要がある

と認めたときは政令に依り、本法の適用を受ける取引を停止する權限を主務大臣に賦與する規定(第九條)を設ける等有效適切な運營を認めた事である。

なおこの法律の施行期日は、附則により、各條に付政令で定め、其の期日は昭和二十五年三月三十一日以前となつて居る。

〰〰〰〰〰〰〰〰〰〰

253

不要な統制の撤廢に關する指令(和譯文)

昭和24年12月19日

1949年12月19日附

連合軍最高司令部經濟科學局覺書

青木經濟安定本部總務長官

稻垣通商産業大臣

森農林大臣

―――宛

連合国最高司令官総司令部経済科学局より

経済安定本部、通商産業省、農林省宛

不要な統制の撤廢に關する件

一、日本政府のインフレ抑制經濟安定計畫實施が滿足すべき成果をあげた結果今やこれまで經濟的窮乏のため必要で

4　制限緩和に向けた対応（昭和24年5月～27年4月）

あった統制の廃止に向って大きな歩みを進め得ることになった。

二、不要な規制を撤廃する原則に従い順次價格及び補給金の分野において統制撤廃の處置が取られて来たが今や外國貿易の分野においてもそれが實施せられつつある。

三、この時にあたり、特に來るべき民間輸入手續の實施に鑑み一九五〇年一月一日までに一切の不要な割當統制を廃止することは特に重要である。一般にその供給が國内的に又は輸入を通じて適切な又は近く適切ならしめられる商品の割當を行う必要はないのであり次のような結果を生ずる場合を除き割當統制は廃止さるべきである。

a、生計費に著るしい影響を與ふべき品目の價格を大幅に吊上げる場合

b、日本國家予算から補給金を交付されている商品が不要不急の使用者に流れる場合

c、不足外國爲替特に弗爲替をもって購入された物資が不要不急の使用者に流れる場合

四、現在割當指定の「重要品目リスト」中にある品目を仔細に檢討すると割當統制中の三十品目中七は完全に更に十

一は部分的に一九五〇年一月一日より統制を廃止しても日本経済に悪影響のないことが分る。

右品目の詳細は附表Ａに示されている。

五、新な民間輸入手續及び正常な自由競争的壓力による生産の合理化を支持するため出來るだけ統制を簡易化し少くするという観點から不要な割當統制を解除するため關係閣令、省令、訓令等の適當なる改正措置を講じ右措置を本歴年末迄に廣く公表することが緊要である。

経済科學局長米國陸軍少將　Ｗ・Ｆ・マーカット

〰〰〰〰〰〰〰〰〰〰〰〰

昭和24年12月23日
鈴木連絡調整横浜事務局長より
吉田外務大臣宛

対日講和問題に関する第八軍司令官の内話につき報告

昭和二十四年十二月二十三日

濱連機密本第三四六號

横濱連絡調整事務局
局長　鈴木　九萬（印）

外務大臣　吉田　茂殿

第八軍司令官と會談の件

十二月二十日ウオーカー中將と猪狩の爲神奈川縣下青野村方面に赴き獵場にて種々話合つたが其の中左の點何等御參考迄に內報する。

同中將より明年以內に對日平和條約は成立すると思うや等種々質問あり自分より之れは當方からこそ聞き度い質問であるが對日講和問題が本當に持上るのは一月のコロンボに於ける英國側の極東外交官會議又二月に延期された由のジエサツプ大使主宰のバンコツクに於ける米國外交官會議の後かとも察せられる。尤も對日講和の內容は對獨講和のそれに比べたら或る意味では比較的簡單であるから對日講和の成立は米國側の腹一つでは明年中に出來得ると思う。問題はソ連と中國政府(其の頃中共政權が中國政權として實際上認められる場合)を除外してもやるかやらぬかの點であり此の點に關しては國內に於ても大體現政府黨側は已むを得ねば所謂單獨講和でも結構ということに對し反對黨側は全面講和を強く主張しているようである。又國內輿論は講和成立後如何なる方法で國の安全を保つかという方法に付ても分れていると說明しておいた。

右に對し同中將は最近マック、アーサー元帥に會つた際元帥が日本は一切の武備を捨てた關係上國費を全然軍備に使わなくて濟むから日本の復興は非常に早いだらう。又現在の國際情勢でいざ第三次戰爭という時本當に自國を防禦し本當の戰爭の出來るのは米、ソの二國だけであり、從て僅か許りの兵備を持つ持たぬはどちらでも大した違いはない。又日本の輿論中には瑞西の永世中立式の形で國の安全を計らうとするものがあるが、瑞西は第一に其地理的又歷史的條件が永世中立を全うさせた事と、あのような小國にしては非常な立派な軍備をもつているという事を忘れてはならない。(之れから見ればマック、アーサー元帥の「日本は極東の瑞西たるべきである」との聲明は國際連合乃至地域的安全保障條約等に依る安全保障を排除する意味でないというのが同中將の意見と解された)云々と述べた。

又自分より朝鮮問題と同樣對獨問題でも米、ソの妥協は出來ず、過般の巴里米英佛三國外相會議では獨逸に對し「戰爭狀態終止聲明」を研究することと成つた由であるが、日本に付ても成るべく早く少くとも希望國の間丈けでも「戰爭狀態」を終止してはどうかと思うと私見を陳べておいた。

尚ウォーカー中將は右に關聯して今後少くとも一年位は在任する豫定の様な口吻であった。(客年九月來任の際は少くとも三年間は在任すべき旨を内話した)

將又同中將は今後は毎月二日程度宛司令部をフィールドに移す筈であるとて丁度二十一、二十二日の兩日厚木飛行場に赴き演習する旨を内話した。現に同中將は兩日間幕僚と共に同飛行場に過した。第八軍は愈々明年一月一日以後民事事務を離れ、大体純軍務に專念することとなり横濱方面もヘルメット、野戰靴の姿が多きを加える情勢である。

本信寫送付先　各地方連絡調整事務局長(幸便に依る)

255

昭和24年12月27日　連合国最高司令官総司令部発表

民間輸入貿易の正常化に関するマッカーサー司令官の声明

付記　右和訳文

General of the Army Douglas MacArther's Statement concerning Return of Private Import to Normal

December 27, 1949

The Supreme Commander has authorized the transfer of control of the equivalent of $67,000,000 in pounds sterling and U. S. dollars to the Japanese government. The Bank of Japan, acting as agent for the Foreign Exchange Control Board, will take control of these funds for the account of the Supreme Commander with full authority to delegate and redelegate its powers of operation to the Foreign Exchange Bank in order to facilitate the implementation of private imports in accordance with the Foreign Exchange Control Law and under SCAP surveillance.

Appropriate government agencies will publish lists of goods and payments for which import licenses will be considered. Importers may apply directly to designated foreign exchange banks for licenses with which to effect private procurements in accordance with such lists.

Licenses will be considered by banks in accordance with fund availabilities as determined by the Bank of Japan as agent for the Foreign Exchange Control Board, and in general be issued on a first-come-first-served basis. The license will assure the importer that he may purchase with yen the foreign exchange needed to consummate his approved import.

Prior approval of appropriate government agencies are required for specified import transactions of a special nature. These requirements will be relaxed as rapidly as possible.

Goods and payments to be authorized have been programmed in a quarterly foreign exchange budget which has been carefully prepared by the Japanese government and reviewed by General MacArthur's Headquarters.

The budget itemizes expected proceeds from Japanese visible and invisible exports and programs imports and payments in accordance with the foreign exchange or trade arrangement credit determined to be available.

Using agencies or individuals are permitted to apply for funds within budget allocations. Working reserves are provided in the budget to permit consumption of "spot" transactions not listed in the import program but of immediate benefit to the economy. A monetary reserve is provided which may be expended for special purposes approved by the Japanese government and validated by SCAP.

The Bank of Japan as agent for the Foreign Exchange Control Board will take title to the transferred funds on behalf of the Japanese government and will be responsible for maintaining central records and determining funds and credit availabilities upon which banks can issue import licenses.

Open accounts under Trade Arrangements will be operated as at present until agreements can be finalized to permit such accounts to be maintained by the Japanese government. In the interim Japanese banks will be permitted to draw on such accounts in accordance with approved procedures and principles.

Adequate funds and specified portions of export proceeds will be retained in SCAP Accounts to safeguard outstanding liabilities against these accounts. As liabilities are liquidated, additional funds will be released from the SCAP Account.

Negotiations are being initiated immediately to open correspondent relations between Japanese and outside banks to normalize commercial practices and to pave the way for future credit lines to Japanese banks.

SCAP officials indicated that this action reflects the final

766

4 制限緩和に向けた対応(昭和24年5月〜27年4月)

編　注　本文書は、昭和二十四年十二月、外務省特別資料課作成「日本占領及び管理重要文書集」第四巻より抜粋。

major step in returning Japan's trade to normal channels. The details of licensing procedures will be announced by agencies of the Japanese government.

(付　記)

貿易正常化に關するマ元帥聲明

(昭和二十四年十二月二十七日、總司令部渉外局特別發表)

本日マックアーサー元帥は、日本の民間輸入貿易が昭和二十五年一月一日から開始される旨發表した。

連合國最高司令官は同時に六千七百萬ドルに相當するポンド及びドル貨資金の管理權を日本政府に移管することを許可した。日本銀行は外國爲替管理委員會の代行機關として、この資金を總司令部勘定として管理し、外國爲替管理法に從い、且つ總司令部の監督下に、民間輸入の實施を圓滑にする目的をもって、この資金の操作を外國爲替銀行に委任及び再委任する全權を與えられる。

關係政府機關は輸入許可書を發行しうる物資の種類及び支拂方法に關するリストを發表することになっている。輸入業者は直接に指定外國爲替銀行に輸入許可書の發注を申請し、これによって前記リストに基き民間輸入が實施されることになる。

指定外國爲替管理委員會の代行機關としての日本銀行が、どれだけの外貨資金を割當てるかによって輸入許可書の發行を考慮し、原則として先着順に處理することになる。業者は輸入許可書の發行を受けたならば、これによって承認された輸入を完了するのに必要な外國爲替を圓貨で買入れることができる。

特殊の輸入取引については、關係政府機關の事前許可が必要であるが、これらの取扱いはできるだけ早く解除される筈である。

許可される輸入物資及びその支拂は四半期ごとの外國爲替予算に組みこまれているが、この予算は日本政府が愼重に策定し、總司令部の審査を經たものである。

この予算は、商品輸出及び商品外輸出から期待される賣上代金と、入手できることが確定している外國爲替、貿易

または貿易協定に基くクレヂットに見合う計画輸入及びその支拂とに分類仕譯されている。

右予算の割當の範圍内でならば、代理機關でも個人でも資金割當の申請を行うことができる。この予算の中には特別の運轉予備金が組まれており、これによって輸入計画のリストの中に含まれてはいないが、それによって直ちに日本の經濟に役立つようになっている。また日本政府の許可と總司令部の認可を受けた特別の目的のために支出すべき予備金の制度もつくられている。

外國爲替管理委員會の代行機關としての日本銀行は、日本政府に代って移管された資金を管理し、且つ記録の保持や爲替銀行が輸入許可書を發行する基礎となる資金およびクレジット額の決定について責任を負う。

各國との通商協定に定められたオープン・アカウントは、これらの勘定を日本政府が直接運營することができるような協定が結ばれるまで、現在のまま操作される。その間日本の諸銀行は、規定の手續と原則に從い、これらの勘定を利用されることを許される。

總司令部勘定の中にはその勘定に對する未拂債務を保證

するのに十分な資金を殘し、さらに輸出代金から一定の比率で、この資金に繰入れることになっている。これらの債務が支拂われたならば、さらに多くの資金が總司令部勘定から日本政府に引き渡されるはずである。

日本の銀行と海外諸銀行の間にコルレス契約を結び、これによって通商慣行を正常化し、日本の銀行に對するクレジット設定への途を開くための交渉が直ちに開始される予定である。

今回のこの措置は日本の通商活動を正常なルートにもどすためにとられる重要措置の最後のものである。なお輸入許可書發行の手續に關する詳細は日本政府關係機關が發表することになっている。

編注 本文書は、昭和二十五年六月、外務省政務局特別資料課作成「日本管理資料(一)」より抜粹。

256

昭和25年1月1日　連合国最高司令官総司令部発表

マッカーサー司令官の年頭メッセージ

4 制限緩和に向けた対応（昭和 24 年 5 月〜27 年 4 月）

General of the Army Douglas MacArthur's
New Year Message

January 1, 1950

TO THE PEOPLE OF JAPAN:

On this fifth New Year's Day following hostilities' end, one fact inescapably stands out — although Japan is still technically at war, there are few places on earth more completely at peace.

In keeping with my announced purpose to transfer the authority of government to your chosen representatives just as rapidly as they demonstrated the will and the capacity firmly to discharge the attending responsibility, the past year has witnessed progressive and far-reaching relaxation of Occupation controls. We have, indeed, gone a long way and internally have virtually arrived at a de facto peace. Your new leadership, strengthening under the stimulus of responsibility, is rapidly becoming safe guarantee against either the re-emergence of those institutions which brought your race to the brink of destruction or the substitution of alien concepts no less provocative of disaster. The ideal of human freedom, vigorously taking root in Japanese hearts, is progressively asserting itself through expression of the public mind whenever suppressive forces arise to challenge it. The myth of an unbridgeable gulf between the ways of the East and the ways of the West has been thoroughly exploded by the lesson of experience and no longer dominates man's thinking. For men now know that humanity, whatever the origin, race or cultural environment, is fundamentally the same in the impelling universal desire for higher personal dignity, broader individual liberty and a betterment of life. Given the opportunity, any segment of the human race thus will draw upon the best of the East and the best of the West, and from the resulting blend of tried and proved ideas will fashion a way of life best adapted to advance its own well being. If, therefore, out of the bankruptcy, chaos and despair left in war's wake there emerges an ethical base for New Japan, embodying many sound ideas which in practice have raised the standard of Western life and provided the moral basis of Western thought, it will be but another triumph of common sense in its age-old struggle to apply enlightened knowledge as the guide to human decision.

During the past year Japan has scored impressive gains

along almost every front and the confidence reflected in my message to you of a year ago has found complete support in ensuing events. Despite the convulsions in many lands where the concept of human freedom is suppressed or under assault, Japan's free institutions progressively have strengthened. The individual citizen is grasping with increasing understanding and firmness the political responsibility which attaches to the sovereign power. The public opinion is giving striking evidence of its insistence upon responsibility in government and public officials are showing a growing consciousness of their responsibility for the stewardship of public affairs. The police of Japan have made rapid strides in organization and training and proved that they can adequately cope with the problems of enforcing the law and preserving the public order as servants, rather than masters, of the citizenry.

With the continuation of the noble support of the American people tendered a prostrate Japan in her hour of most desperate need, a further broad advance has been made toward the self-supporting economy which is the goal of every Japanese citizen. The adoption of a truly balanced consolidated budget in the last fiscal year and the projection of one similarly balanced for the next has largely corrected the inflationary fiscal practice which persisted in the immediate post-war years, strengthened the Government's financial position and established the foundation for a sound system of public finance based on the capability of the people's support. The volume of currency outstanding has been stabilized, and for the second consecutive year provision has been made for debt retirement. Marked improvement in tax collections evidences an increasing consciousness of the individual's responsibility to support the operation of his public institutions. The implementation of the Government's plans to establish a more equitable tax structure and a fair and more efficient system of tax administration, will equalize the burden and, it is my hope, will permit substantial future tax reductions over a broad base.

Production has continued the forward march initiated in 1946. Coal, utilities and other basic components of industrial activity are gradually approaching their pre-war levels, thus furnishing the sinews for overall industrial recovery. Consumer goods have become available in increasing quantities, and the production and collection of foods, benefited by good crops and a large catch of marine products, have reached new post-war highs. The farmers and fishermen thus are not only acquitting well their responsibilities toward securing the people's livelihood but are providing a striking demonstration of the fruits of free enterprise.

Labor, too, by its energy and patriotism is making a splendid contribution to the national recovery. Turning from an irresponsible leadership of the past, it is now becoming well oriented toward an objective and healthy future. And its demand for moderation evidences that labor is coming to understand that in a society which is truly free the individual standard of life must bear a direct relationship to the constructive energies the individual contributes to life —that every segment of society must earn its own way, as the arbitrary advancement of one segment at the expense of another inevitably weakens political and economic freedom.

Correction of the fiscal maladjustment and elimination of many shortages have made it possible to approach a condition where stability of the price structure derives from the equilibrium of normal economic forces rather than from artificial devices.

Thus, the economic control exercised through rationing, price ceilings and subsidies during the period of acute shortages and inflationary pressure has been lifted as rapidly as conditions in the various fields have warranted. With the latest relaxation of control, export trade was returned to a private basis on December 1st, as is import trade being returned today, retaining in the hands of the Government only such control as is necessary to safeguard Japan's foreign exchange position, the stability of her currency, and the equitable distribution of essential commodities still in short supply. Japan thus rapidly is approaching that economic ideal —free private competitive enterprise —which alone can provide hope for progressive advancement of the living standard.

In foreign trade the gains initiated with the post-war resumption of exports have continued. Reflecting the accelerated industrial production and reopening of foreign trade outlets, exports this year approximately doubled those of the last. Coincident with the expansion of international trade, definite gains are being made toward attaining a balance between imports and exports. All this, indeed, shows healthy progress in the building of New Japan and foretells the day not long hence when political maturity, social justice, and economic self-sufficiency will make of Japan a sturdy and highly respected member of the society of free nations.

This synopsis of the present etches the pattern of the future. It reflects the steady, unswerving progress of a people who, with backs to a discredited past, see a lofty goal ahead and are determined to achieve it. It gives unmistakable answer to those voices of men — the uninformed or misinformed, the informed but pathological cynic; the indoctrinee of Japan's old and discredited order, so blind that he "will not see"; and the subversive who would sabotage the people's faith — raised during the four years and more of occupation in self-ordained omniscience to forecast from time to time with insatiable persistence the imminence of economic disaster, the re-emergence of political reaction, the widespread absorption of the Communist hypocrisy, and the social convulsions inevitable from any effort to integrate Western ideals with Eastern culture. It is to the credit of both the American and Japanese peoples that these prophets of gloom have had their say without marring in the least the pattern of steady progress.

As we enter the new year, two basic and yet unresolved problems cause concern in every Japanese mind — the global ideological struggle brought close to Japan by the Communist roll over China, and the international procedural conflict delaying call of a Japanese peace conference. Such concern is indeed most natural. But the solution of these problems does not lie within Japan's present capability, and should not directly be drawn within the orbit of Japan's internal politics. Pending such solution, however, Japan's road ahead is clearly delineated. She must continue steadfastly and invincibly forward along the course so well charted by the constitutional precepts. To do so is not only to strengthen Japan's own free institutions, but by example to strengthen the free institutions of others as well.

Some contemporary cynics deride as visionary Japan's constitutional renunciation of the concept of belligerency and armed security. Be not overly concerned by such detractors. A product of Japanese thought, this provision is based upon the highest of moral ideals; and yet no constitutional provision was ever more fundamentally sound and practical. While by no sophistry of reasoning can it be interpreted as complete negation of the inalienable right of self-defence against unprovoked attack, it is a ringing affirmation by a people laid prostrate by the sword, of faith in the ultimate triumph of international morality and justice without resort to the sword. It must be understood, however, that so long as predatory international banditry is permitted to roam the earth to crush human freedom under its avarice and violence, the high concept to which you are pledged will be slow in finding universal acceptance. But it is axiomatic that there must always be a first in all things. In this historic decision, you are the first. The opportunity, therefore, is yours to exemplify before mankind the soundness of this concept and the inestimable benefit resulting from the dedication of all energy and all resource to peaceful progress. In due course other nations will join you in this dedication, but meanwhile you must not falter. Have faith in my countrymen and other peoples who share the same high ideals. Above all, have faith in yourselves.

DOUGLAS MacARTHUR

編注　本文書は、昭和二十六年二月、外務省特別資料課作成「日本占領及び管理重要文書集」第二巻増補より抜粋。

257

昭和25年1月1日　連合国最高司令官総司令部より　日本政府宛

外国為替および貿易統制に関する修正指令

GENERAL HEADQUARTERS
SUPREME COMMANDER FOR THE ALLIED POWERS
APO 500

AG 010 (1 JAN 50) ESS/FTC　　　1 JAN 50
SCAPIN 2070

MEMORANDUM FOR: JAPANESE GOVERNMENT
SUBJECT: Foreign Exchange and Foreign Trade Control

1. The following memoranda for the Japanese Government from General Headquarters, Supreme Commander for the Allied Powers are rescinded:

　　a. AG 091.3 (22 Sep 45) ESS, SCAPIN 44, 22 September 1945, subject: Controls over Exports and Imports of

Gold, Silver, Securities and Financial Instruments;

b. AG 130 (22 Sep 45) ESS, SCAPIN 45, 22 September 1945, subject: Control of Financial Transactions;

c. AG 091.31 (9 Oct 45) ESS, SCAPIN 110, 9 October 1945, subject: Import of Essential Commodities;

d. AG 160 (30 Oct 45) ESS/FI, SCAPIN 211, 30 October 1945, subject: Contracts by Persons in Japan with Foreign Concerns.

e. AG 091.31 (10 May 46) ESS/IE, SCAPIN 943, 10 May 1946, subject: Reports Relative to Import-Export Commodities;

f. AG 091.31 (9 Aug 48) ESS/FTC, SCAPIN 1926/1, 19 November 1948, subject: Return from Abroad of Commercial Quantities of Manufactured Articles for Repair and Return to Owner.

g. AG 091.31 (9 Mar 49) ESS/FTC, SCAPIN 1982, 9 March 1949, subject: Import Procedure.

2. Effective this date the Japanese Government will supervise and authorize the import of goods into Japan in accordance with the "Foreign Exchange and Foreign Trade Control Law", and provisions of this memorandum.

3. The Japanese Government will obtain approval of General Headquarters, Supreme Commander for the Allied Powers:

a. For trade plans and foreign exchange budgets approved by the Ministerial Council prior to their implementation by the Japanese Government.

b. For initiation of negotiations for procurement by the Japanese Government of imports for the Japanese Government account.

c. For all changes in the basic rate of exchange.

d. For the designation of currencies to be authorized for foreign exchange purposes.

e. For measures pertaining to the manner or degree of concentration of foreign exchange.

f. For the export or import of gold, silver or other precious metals.

g. For transactions relative to property which is within

774

4　制限緩和に向けた対応(昭和24年5月～27年4月)

the jurisdiction of the Civil Property Custodian by reason of the existence therein of the interest of a non-Japanese national on or since 7 December 1941 with the exception of those transactions which have already been authorized by memorandum to the Japanese Government or agencies thereof.

　　h. For such other matters as may be designated later by General Headquarters, Supreme Commander for the Allied Powers.

　4. Property or cargo owned by the occupation forces or agencies thereof, cargo derived from American aid programs, and cargo reimbursed in part or wholly from American aid programs or for which transportation has been paid from such programs will not be subject to the provisions of the "Foreign Exchange and Foreign Trade Control Law" unless specifically stipulated by the Supreme Commander for the Allied Powers.

　5. Direct communication between appropriate agencies of the Japanese Government and General Headquarters, Supreme Commander for the Allied Powers is authorized to implement this memorandum.

FOR THE SUPREME COMMANDER:

　　　　　　　K. B. BUSH,
　　　　　Brigadier General, AGD,
　　　　　　Adjutant General.

258　昭和25年1月5日　連合国最高司令官総司令部より日本政府宛
日本人の海外渡航申請の受理事務を日本政府へ移管する旨の指令

SUPREME COMMANDER FOR THE ALLIED POWERS
GENERAL HEADQUARTERS
APO 500

AG 014.331 (5 Jan 50) AG　　　　　　　　5 January 1950
SCAPIN 2072
MEMORANDUM FOR: JAPANESE GOVERNMENT
SUBJECT: Applications for Travel of Japanese Nationals Abroad

　1. References:

　　a. Memorandum for the Japanese Government, AG

014.331 (14 Apr 47) GA, SCAPIN 1609, subject: Travel Documents for Japanese Nationals Traveling Abroad, dated 14 April 1947.

b. Memorandum for the Japanese Government, AG 014.331 (14 Apr 47) GA, SCAPIN 1609/1, subject: Issuance of Passports or Certificates of Identity or Nationality to Japanese Nationals, dated 25 August 1948.

c. Memorandum for the Japanese Government, AG 014.331 (26 Oct 48) GA, SCAPIN 6163–A, subject: Orientation of Japanese Nationals Who May be Authorized to Travel Outside Japan, dated 8 November 1948.

d. Memorandum for the Japanese Government, AG 680.2 (25 Aug 48) GA, SCAPIN 2035, subject: Travel of Japanese Technicians Outside Japan, dated 1 August 1949.

e. Memorandum for the Japanese Government, AG 091.31 (17 Jul 48) ESS/FTC, SCAPIN 2020, subject: Purchase of Foreign Exchange Credits for the Purpose of Stimulating Exports, dated 24 June 1949.

f. Memorandum for the Japanese Government, AG 680.2 (25 Aug 48) GA, SCAPIN 7008–A, subject: Travel of Japanese Technicians Outside of Japan, dated 15 December 1949.

2. The Supreme Commander for the Allied Powers hereby authorizes the Japanese Government to accept applications from Japanese nationals for travel abroad for the purposes authorized by the Supreme Commander for the Allied Powers.

3. It is desired that effective 21 January 1950 the Japanese Government designate a single agency to administratively process applications for travel abroad for submission to the Supreme Commander for the Allied Powers for approval.

4. The designated agency will be responsible for:

a. Ascertaining from the applicant all information necessary to his travel as required by the Supreme Commander for the Allied Powers and the Japanese Government.

b. The individual's completion of the Application for Passport form in triplicate and supporting documents as specified.

c. Obtaining necessary approvals from other Japanese Government agencies.

d. Forwarding the completed application and support-

776

4　制限緩和に向けた対応（昭和24年5月～27年4月）

ing documents to Supreme Commander for the Allied Powers, for approval.

e. Issuing passport to individual whose application for travel has been approved by the Supreme Commander for the Allied Powers.

f. Marking all passports as follows: "This passport is invalid for use in any country into which the Supreme Commander for the Allied Powers has authorized travel unless on succeeding pages a visa or entry permit into the country to be visited has been affixed by the appropriate authorities."

g. Complying with the requirements of memorandum for the Japanese Government, AG 014.331 (26 Oct 48) GA, SCAPIN 6163-A, subject: Orientation of Japanese Nationals Who May be Authorized to Travel Outside Japan, dated 8 November 1948.

h. Directing the individual to the appropriate diplomatic representative in Japan of the country of destination to obtain necessary visa in the passport.

FOR THE SUPREME COMMANDER:

K. B. BUSH,
Brigadier General, AGD,
Adjutant General.

5 Incls
1. Application for Passport
2. Personal History Form
3. Application for Approval of Foreign Employment Agreement
4. Instructions for Cultural Tvl Applicants
5. Instructions for Coml Tvl Applicants in 3 parts

編注　本文書の別添は省略。

259

昭和25年2月9日　連合国最高司令官総司令部より　日本政府宛

米国に在外事務所の設置を許可する旨の指令

付記　右和訳文

GENERAL HEADQUARTERS
SUPREME COMMANDER FOR THE ALLIED POWERS

APO 500
Diplomatic Section
Tokyo, February 9, 1950.

MEMORANDUM FOR: JAPANESE GOVERNMENT
SUBJECT: Establishment of Japanese Overseas Agencies in the United States of America.

The Government of the United States of America has requested General Headquarters, Supreme Commander for the Allied Powers, to transmit to the Japanese Government an invitation to establish in the United States certain Overseas Agencies for the purpose of promoting trade relations between Japan and the United States and handling citizenship and property problems relating to Japanese nationals residing in the United States.

It is proposed that the functions of the Overseas Agencies consist of the following:

1. Promotion of Trade
   a. Promotion of trade between the United States and Japan.
   b. Research on market conditions and trade opportunities in the United States.
   c. Extending good offices and answering trade and travel inquiries.
   d. Transmission of information to Japan concerning local commercial procedures and regulations.
   e. Making available to local businessmen information concerning Japanese laws and regulations governing import-export, customs, exchange control, investments, and other similar matters.
   f. Displaying samples and exhibits of Japanese manufactures and providing information on trade opportunities in Japan.
   g. Supplying tourist information.

2. Affairs Pertaining to Japanese Nationals and Property
   a. Disposal of matters pertaining to the retention and renunciation of Japanese nationality.
   b. Handling of notifications of birth, death, marriage, and other changes of status or name requiring recording in Japanese family registers.

778

4 　制限緩和に向けた対応(昭和24年5月〜27年4月)

c. Drawing up documents in accordance with Japanese legal requirements and administering oaths relating to Japanese civil status or property matters.

d. Protection and administration of property of deceased Japanese nationals in so far as such action is in conformity with state laws.

e. Bringing to the attention of local Japanese nationals all Japanese laws and regulations, as well as SCAP regulations, with which Japanese nationals residing in the United States might be directly concerned.

The Government of the United States further proposes that the agencies be officially entitled "Japanese Overseas Agencies" and that the officials assigned to these agencies be designated as "Japanese Overseas Representatives"; that initially the agencies be established at New York, San Francisco, Los Angeles, and Honolulu; and that pending firsthand determination of actual personnel needs, each agency be staffed with not more than three officers and four clerks.

With reference to the foregoing invitation, the Japanese Government is informed that the Supreme Commander for the Allied Powers has no objection to Japan's establishing overseas agencies in the United States, such agencies to be operated under the supervision of and to report directly to the Japanese Foreign Office subject to the following limitations:

1. The Japanese Overseas Representatives shall not act in a diplomatic or quasi-diplomatic capacity. They are to refrain from engaging in propaganda activities and from direct representation functions such as acting on behalf of the Japanese Government in making representations to the United States authorities, except in so far as the administrative conduct of the agencies themselves may require.

2. The Representatives shall have no consular titles or immunities; they shall receive no exequatur; they shall not use codes other than standard commercial codes; they are not to interpose with the local authorities for the protection of any Japanese nationals beyond making courteous inquiry to local officials; and they shall have no jurisdiction in controversies involving seamen.

3. The Representatives shall not issue, renew, or amend

Japanese passports, visas, or other travel documents.

4. The activities of the Japanese Overseas Agency in New York are not to conflict with those of the SCAP Foreign Trade New York Office.

5. The total cost of establishing and operating the four agencies shall not exceed $276,600. Attached hereto is a suggested budget for the offices computed on the basis of a manning level of three Japanese officials and four assistants for the New York, San Francisco, and Honolulu agencies, and two Japanese officials and three assistants for the Los Angeles Agency. The cost estimated for the Los Angeles Agency does not contemplate the inclusion of a trade representative at that location.

6. The agencies are to be financed as follows:

a. In the event that salaries are to be used for making payments in Japan, such as for the support of family in Japan, payments shall be made by the Japanese Government in yen and an appropriate amount of dollars shall be deducted from salary payments.

b. All fees and other income received by the Agencies shall be deposited in a special account in a United States bank to be used only for operating costs of the Agencies. After a reserve has been accumulated sufficient to cover anticipated expenses for a twelve (12) month period, the balance over and above such reserve shall be deposited in a SCAP Commercial Account.

c. Expenses in excess of receipts will be defrayed by payments out of a SCAP Commercial Account. Funds will be deposited in United States banks to the account of each Agency. Members of the Agency staff, who shall be bonded, will be authorized to draw on those accounts. Bank accounts and records of the offices shall be subject to a quarterly audit by a Certified Public Accountant in the United States and review by the Foreign Exchange Control Board and the Controller, ESS, GHQ, SCAP.

It is requested that the Japanese Government inform General Headquarters as to its views in the foregoing matter at the

4 制限緩和に向けた対応(昭和24年5月～27年4月)

earliest possible date in order that an appropriate reply may be made to the United States Government.

　　　　　　　　　　　Cloyce K. Huston
　　　　　　　　　　　Acting Chief
　　　　　　　　　　　Diplomatic Section

Enclosure:
Suggested budget for Japanese Overseas Agencies

編　注　本文書の別添は省略。

(付記)
連合國最高司令官司令部外交局發日本政府あて覺書
一九五〇年二月九日

件名　アメリカ合衆國に日本政府在外事務所を設置する件

アメリカ合衆國政府は、連合國最高司令官總司令部に對して、日本と米國との間の貿易關係の促進並びに米國内に居住する日本人の身分及び財産に關する問題の處理のため在外事務所を米國に設置するよう日本國政府に招請狀傳達方要請した。

在外事務所の職務は、左の通りと致したい。

(一) 貿易の促進
(a) 米國と日本との間の貿易の促進
(b) 米國における市況及び商機の調査
(c) あつせんを行うこと及び貿易及び旅行に關する照會に答えること
(d) 出先の取引手續及び諸規則に關する情報を日本へ傳達すること
(e) 出先の業者に對して、輸出入、關稅、爲替管理投資及びその他のこれに類する諸事項に關する日本の諸法令について情報を提供すること
(f) 日本製品の見本を展示すること及び日本における商機に關する情報を提供すること
(g) 旅行に關する情報を提供すること

(二) 日本國民及びその財産に關する事務
(a) 日本國籍の留保及び離脱に關する事務の處理
(b) 出生、死亡、婚姻、その他日本の戸籍に記載すること を要する身分又は名稱の變更の通知を取扱うこと

(c) 日本人の民法上の身分又は財産上の事項に關して日本の法令上の要件にしたがつて文書を作成すること及び宣誓を行わしめること

(d) 米國の州法に抵しよくしない場合に限り日本人の遺産を保護し管理すること

(e) 出先の日本人に對して彼等に直接關係するようなすべての日本の法令及び連合國最高司令官の指令を周知せしめること

アメリカ合衆國政府は更に、在外事務所の正式名稱を「日本政府在外事務所」にすること、在外事務所に置かれる職員の名稱を「日本政府在外代表」にすること、在外事務所は、先づ、ニューヨーク、サンフランシスコ、ロスアンゼルス、及びホノルルに設置せられること及び現地における實際的な人的要求の決定があるまでは、各事務所の構成は、三人の職員と四人の事務職員を越えないことを提案する。

叙上の招請狀に關連して、連合國最高司令官は、日本が米國に在外事務所を設置し、右事務所が左記制限のもとに日本國外務省の指揮監督に服し、直接これに報告を行うこ

とに異議がない旨を日本國政府に通報する。

一、日本政府在外代表は、外交官、又は外交官に準ずる資格で行動してはならない。宣傳的活動に從事すること及び日本政府のために米國官憲に申し入れを行う等直接日本國政府を代表する職務を行うことは差し控えるべきである。但し、在外事務所の行政上の運營に必要な範圍においてはこの限りでない。

二、日本政府在外代表は、領事の稱號又は免除を有しない。標準商業電信暗號以外の電信暗號を使用してはならない。日本人の保護のため地方官憲に丁寧に照會する以外に地方官憲と交渉すべきではない。又海員に關連する紛爭については、管轄權を有しない。

三、日本政府在外代表は、旅券、査證又はその他の旅行に關する書類を發給し、書き換え、又はそれらの記載事項を變更することはできない。

四、ニューヨークの在外事務所の活動は在ニューヨーク連合國最高司令官外國貿易事務所のそれと抵觸してはならない。

4 制限緩和に向けた対応(昭和24年5月～27年4月)

五、四カ所の在外事務所の設置及び運營に要する經費の總額は、二十七萬六千六百ドルを超過してはならない。

司令部が提案する在外事務所の予算は附表の通りであるが、これはニューヨーク、サンフランシスコ及びホノルルの在外事務所にはそれぞれ三人の日本人職員及び四人の事務職員を置きロスアンゼルスの在外事務所には二人の日本人職員及び三人の事務職員を置くという基礎に立つて計算されたものである。ロスアンゼルス在外事務所の見積り經費は、貿易代表者を當該事務所に置くことを考慮していない。

六、在外事務所の經理は左の各號に從つて行われなければならない。

(a)日本に居住する家族の扶養等のために俸給が日本國内での支拂に充てられる場合には、支拂は日本國政府によつて圓でなされ、それに相當する額のドルが俸給から差引かれねばならない。

(b)在外事務所が受領するすべての手數料その他の收入は、米國の銀行の特別勘定に預金されて在外事務所の運營費としてのみ使用されねばならない。將來十二カ月の期間に予期される經費を賄うのに充分な額の予備金が蓄積された後、その額を超過する殘額は聯合國最高司令官商業勘定に拂いこまれねばならない。

(c)收入額を超過する經費は聯合國最高司令官商業勘定から支拂われるであろう。

資金は、米國の銀行に、當該在外事務所の勘定として預金されるであろう。

保證の手續を了した在外事務所の職員はこれらの勘定から預金を引出す權限を與えられるであろう。在外事務所の銀行勘定及び記錄は、米國の特許會計士の年四囘の會計檢查並びに外國爲替管理委員會及び聯合國最高司令官總部經濟科學局資金統制官の審查を受けねばならない。

適當な囘答がアメリカ合衆國政府になされるように、日本國政府は前記の事項に關するその見解を出來るだけ早い時期において聯合國最高司令官總部に通知されたい。

外交局首席代理

クロイス・K・ヒューストン

添付書類 總司令部の提案する日本政府在外事務所の予算

編注　本文書の別添は省略。

260　昭和25年2月14日　外務省より連合国最高司令官総司令部宛

在外事務所の設置に関する日本政府回答

TO: GENERAL HEADQUARTERS, SUPREME COMMANDER FOR THE ALLIED POWERS. (Attn: Diplomatic Section).

FROM: Ministry of Foreign Affairs.

SUBJECT: Establishment of Japanese Overseas Agencies in the United States of America.

14 February 1950

FOM No. 274 (PG)

1. The Japanese Government has received the memorandum dated 9 February 1950 from General Headquarters, Supreme Commander for the Allied Powers, with reference to the establishment of Japanese Overseas Agencies in the United States of America.

2. The memorandum transmitted an invitation of the United States Government to the Japanese Government to set up Overseas Agencies at four places, namely, New York, San Francisco, Los Angeles, and Honolulu, for the purpose of promoting trade between the United States and Japan and for dealing with citizenship and property problems relating to Japanese nationals residing in the United States.

The memorandum also contained the stipulations laid down relative to the functions, organization, appropriations and finances of the proposed Overseas Agencies.

The Japanese Government is happy to accept the foregoing invitation under the general conditions laid down. Legal and financial measures will be taken with a view to assuring the smooth and prompt execution of plans relative to the Overseas Agencies, and the appropriate authorities of General Headquarters will be contacted, as the occasion arises, on details concerning personnel, appropriations, finances, and other pertinent matters.

3. On this occasion, the Japanese Government wishes to express anew its profound gratitude for the unfailing good will of the United States Government and the Supreme Commander for the Allied Powers, as is demonstrated by their present action.

4　制限緩和に向けた対応（昭和24年5月〜27年4月）

261

昭和25年2月20日　連合国最高司令官総司令部より　日本政府宛

出入国管理業務の日本政府への移管に関する指令

GENERAL HEADQUARTERS
SUPREME COMMANDER FOR THE ALLIED POWERS
APO 500

20 February 1950

AG 014.331 (3 Feb 50) GA
SCAPIN 2082

MEMORANDUM FOR: JAPANESE GOVERNMENT

SUBJECT: Immigration Service

1. a. Rescission. Memorandum for the Japanese Government, AG 091.1 (28 May 49) GA, SCAPIN 2019, subject: Establishment of Immigration Service, 22 June 1949.

b. References:

(1) Circular 3, General Headquarters, Supreme Commander for the Allied Powers, subject: Control of Entry and Exit of Individuals, Cargo, Aircraft and Surface Vessels into and from Japan, 3 February 1950.

(2) Memorandum for the Japanese Government, AG 000.5 (21 May 49) GB, SCAPIN 2055, subject: Suppression of Illegal Entry into Japan, 3 November 1949.

(3) Memorandum for the Japanese Government, AG 720.4 (3 Feb 50) GA, SCAPIN 2083, subject: Customs, Immigration and Quarantine Operations, 20 February 1950.

2. The Japanese Government will immediately assign the necessary immigration officials to ports of entry designated by Circular 3, General Headquarters, Supreme Commander for the Allied Powers, 3 February 1950, to insure adequate immigration surveillance of all individuals authorized by the Supreme Commander for the Allied Powers to enter or depart from Japan (ex-

---

(Shigeru Yoshida)
Minister for Foreign Affairs.

cept occupation force personnel traveling on official orders).

3. The Japanese Government will establish a central office of record for all clearances granted by the Supreme Commander for the Allied Powers to individuals entering or departing Japan, except occupation force personnel traveling under official orders. This office of record will be known as the "Central Locator Files," and will serve to inform the immigration officials of the Japanese Government of all clearances granted by the Supreme Commander for the Allied Powers. The Central Locator Files will be maintained with sufficient English-speaking personnel on a twenty-four hour basis to receive information from the Supreme Commander for the Allied Powers concerning individuals authorized by him to enter into or depart from Japan. Upon receipt of such information, the Central Locator Files will notify the immigration officials of the Japanese Government of the clearances granted by the Supreme Commander for the Allied Powers.

4. Effective 25 February 1950, the Immigration Service of the Japanese Government at Tokyo, Yokohama and Kobe is directed to receive applications for exit from Japan and/or exit from and reentry into Japan for any individual in Japan, except occupation force personnel, submitted in accordance with the provisions of reference 1b (1) above.

5. The Immigration Service of the Japanese Government at Tokyo, Yokohama and Kobe is authorized to indorse the passports or other valid travel documents of persons from whom applications have been received in accordance with paragraph 4 above, indicating thereon that permission has been granted by the Supreme Commander for the Allied Powers to depart from Japan and/or depart from and reenter into Japan. Such individual passports may be so indorsed only after completion of the following procedures:

a. Nonoccupation personnel, as defined in paragraph 3b, reference 1b (1) above:

(1) The Japanese Government will indicate its approval or disapproval on one copy of each application received and forward that copy to the Supreme Commander for the Allied Powers daily except Sundays and holidays.

4　制限緩和に向けた対応（昭和24年5月～27年4月）

(2) Passports of nonoccupation personnel may be indorsed forty-eight hours after one copy of the individual application has been forwarded to and received by the Supreme Commander for the Allied Powers, PROVIDED that the Immigration Service of the Japanese Government has not been informed that the subject application has been denied or that action on the application has been delayed.

(3) After action has been completed by the Immigration Service of the Japanese Government, a second copy showing action taken will be forwarded to the Supreme Commander for the Allied Powers within twenty-four hours.

b. Residents of Japan as defined in paragraph 3c, reference 1b (1) above:

(1) The Japanese Government will forward three copies of such applications with its approval indicated thereon to the Supreme Commander for the Allied Powers for consideration and decision. Approved applications will be returned to the Immigration Service of the Japanese Government for necessary action.

(2) Passports of residents of Japan may be indorsed only after receipt of approved applications from the Supreme Commander for the Allied Powers by the Immigration Service of the Japanese Government.

(3) After action has been completed by the Immigration Service of the Japanese Government, a copy of the application showing action taken will be forwarded to the Supreme Commander for the Allied Powers within twenty-four hours.

6. Necessary stamps in the form and size indicated in Inclosure 1 will be procured by the Japanese Government for use in indorsing passports of individuals for exit from and/or exit from and reentry into Japan.

7. The Japanese Government is authorized to collect the

税関、出入国管理および検疫業務の運営に関する指令

GENERAL HEADQUARTERS
SUPREME COMMANDER FOR THE ALLIED POWERS
APO 500

AG 720.4 (3 Feb 50) GA　　20 February 1950
SCAPIN 2083

MEMORANDUM FOR: JAPANESE GOVERNMENT
SUBJECT: Customs, Immigration and Quarantine Operations

1. References:

　a. Circular 3, General Headquarters, Supreme Commander for the Allied Powers, subject: Control of Entry and Exit of Individuals, Cargo, Aircraft and Surface Vessels into and from Japan, 3 February 1950.

　b. Memorandum for the Japanese Government, AG 130 (18 Jan 49) ESS/FIN, SCAPIN 1966, subject: Property Individuals are Authorized to Carry on Entering and Leaving Japan, 18 January 1949.

　c. Memorandum for the Japanese Government, AG

sum of ¥1000 for each indorsement placed on the passport of an individual in accordance with the provisions of this directive.

　8. Direct communication between the Japanese Government agencies concerned and appropriate sections of General Headquarters, Supreme Commander for the Allied Powers, is hereby authorized to implement this directive.

FOR THE SUPREME COMMANDER:

K. B. BUSH,
Brigadier General, USA,
Adjutant General.

2 Incls: (in trip)
1. Form indicating type of stamps
2. SCAP Circular 3, 3 Feb 50

編注　本文書の別添は見当たらない。

昭和25年2月20日　連合国最高司令官総司令部より　日本政府宛

4 制限緩和に向けた対応(昭和24年5月～27年4月)

386.7 (11 Dec 48) ESS/FIN, SCAPIN 1968, subject: Foreign Exchange Controls, 2 February 1949.

d. Memorandum for the Japanese Government, AG 311.1 (28 May 48) CCS, SCAPIN 1900/9, subject: International Postal Service, 26 May 1949.

e. Memorandum for the Japanese Government, AG 095 (22 May 48) GA, SCAPIN 1971, subject: Entry of Personnel into Japan to Visit Relatives, 11 February 1949.

f. Memorandum for the Japanese Government, AG 321 (8 Apr 46) ESS/IE, SCAPIN 941-A, subject: Japanese Customs Organization, 8 April 1946.

g. Memorandum for the Japanese Government, AG 014.331 (3 Feb 50) GA, SCAPIN 2082, subject: Immigration Service, 20 February 1950.

h. Memorandum for the Japanese Government, AG 000.5 (21 May 49) G-2 CIS PSD, SCAPIN 2055, subject: Suppression of Illegal Entry into Japan, 3 November 1949.

i. Memorandum for the Japanese Government, AG 680.2 (25 Aug 48) GA, SCAPIN 2035, subject: Travel of Japanese Technicians Outside of Japan, 1 August 1949.

j. Memorandum for the Japanese Government, AG 710 (22 Sep 45) MG, SCAPIN 48, subject: Public Health Measures, 22 September 1945.

k. Memorandum for the Japanese Government, AG 567 (1 Oct 47) PH, SCAPIN 1787, subject: Quarantine Installations and Procedures, 1 October 1947.

4 (14 Oct 47) CTS-W, SCAPIN 1801, subject: Quarantine Installations and Procedures, 14 October 1947.

1. Memorandum for the Japanese Government, AG 720.

2. Effective this date and in accordance with directives promulgated by the Supreme Commander for the Allied Powers, the Japanese Government is responsible for customs, immigration and quarantine operations attendant to the entry into and exit from Japan of individuals, cargo, surface vessels and aircraft, except for occupation force personnel, cargo, surface vessels and aircraft entering or leaving Japan.

3. Designated agencies of the Supreme Commander for the Allied Powers will regulate, by surveillance over the operating

agencies of the Japanese Government, the implementation of the provisions of paragraph 2 above.

4. The Japanese Government is directed to review existing procedures pertaining to customs, immigration and quarantine to take such actions as may be necessary to establish effective customs, immigration and quarantine controls in agreement with generally accepted international practice. These actions will be coordinated with the appropriate agencies of the Supreme Commander for the Allied Powers.

5. Direct communication between the Japanese Government agencies concerned and appropriate agencies of the Supreme Commander for the Allied Powers is hereby authorized to further the implementation of this memorandum.

6. The provisions of all earlier memoranda for the Japanese Government pertaining to customs, immigration and quarantine operations in conflict with the instructions contained herein are superseded by this memorandum.

FOR THE SUPREME COMMANDER:

K. B. BUSH,

Brigadier General, USA,
Adjutant General.

1 Incl (in trip)

SCAP Circular 3, 3 Feb 50

編注　本文書の別添は見当たらない。

263

昭和25年2月26日　連合国最高司令官総司令部発表

日本の国際会議参加に関する総司令部発表

付記　右和訳文

Statement by Public Information Office, General Headquarters, Far East Command on the Interim Directive from the United States Government for SCAP concerning Permission Granted Japan of Participation in International Agreements, Conventions and Conferences

February 26, 1950

General Headquarters, Supreme Commander for the Allied Powers, announces receipt of the following interim direc-

4　制限緩和に向けた対応(昭和24年5月～27年4月)

tive from the United States Government:

　"The Supreme Commander for the Allied Powers, subject to his discretion and continued control, should permit Japan to participate with other nations or groups of nations in such international agreements, conventions, and conferences of a technical character as Japan may be invited to enter into, accede to, or attend, and as the Supreme Commander shall consider to be in the interests of the occupation.

　"Before leaving Japan, Japanese Representatives appointed in accordance with the provisions of this policy decision, should be instructed to refrain from engaging in propaganda or subversive activities of any kind.

　"The Supreme Commander should direct the Japanese Government to fulfill any obligations which it assumes in accordance with the provisions of this policy.

　"The Supreme Commander should inform the Far Eastern Commission of any action taken in accordance with the provisions of this policy."

編注　本文書は、昭和二十六年二月、外務省特別資料課作成「日本占領及び管理重要文書集」第二卷增補より拔粹。

(付　記)

日本の國際會議參加に關する米國政府の總司令部あて中間指令に關する總司令部涉外局發表

　　　　　昭和二十五年二月二十六日

　總司令部は米國政府から次の中間指令を受け取ったと發表した。

　連合國最高司令官は、自己の判斷およびその引き續き保持する管理權限にもとづき、日本が參加、加入または出席の招請を受け、かつ總司令官が占領に役立つと考える專門的性格の國際協定、協約および會議などに各國別にまたは數力國とともに参加することを許可すべきである。

　この政策決定の規定により任命される日本代表に對しては、いかなる種類のものといえども宣傳あるいは破壞的祕密活動を一切しないようにとの訓令が日本出發に先立って與えられなければならない。

　最高司令官は日本政府に對し、この政策の規定に從い、

264

日本船舶の船主への返還および自主的運航に関する指令

昭和25年3月3日　連合国最高司令官総司令部より日本政府宛

編　注　本文書は、昭和二十五年十一月、外務省政務局特別資料課作成「日本管理資料(二)」より抜粋。

日本政府が負うべき責務は、いかなるものといえども完全に果すよう指令すべきである。またこの政策の規定に従い執られるべき処置は、いかなるものといえども最高司令官から極東委員會に通告されなければならない。

GENERAL HEADQUARTERS
SUPREME COMMANDER FOR THE ALLIED POWERS
APO 500

3 March 1950

AG 544 (3 Mar 50) CTS
SCAPIN 2086

MEMORANDUM FOR: JAPANESE GOVERNMENT
SUBJECT: Japanese Merchant Shipping

1. References:

　a. SCAPIN 1931, AG 544 (27 Jul 48) CTS, 2 Sep 48, subj: Japanese Merchant Shipping.

　b. SCAPIN 1931/1, AG 544 (27 Jul 48) CTS, 5 Aug 49, subj: Japanese Merchant Shipping.

2. Memorandums, references 1a and 1b, are hereby rescinded, effective 31 March 1950.

3. Effective 1 April 1950, present time charter arrangements for vessels under Civilian Merchant Marine Committee shall be cancelled. All cargo vessels over 800 gross tons shall be divided into two categories: Category A covering vessels employed in overseas trade and Category E covering all other vessels over 800 gross tons. Relaxation of controls of these two categories shall be effected as indicated below:

CATEGORY A

4. Steel cargo vessels engaging in trade outside Japan

4 制限緩和に向けた対応(昭和24年5月〜27年4月)

shall be released commencing 1 April 1950, to their respective owners, for owners' account under private operation (without government subsidy). Shipowners operating vessels in accordance with the above will be required through the Civilian Merchant Marine Committee to:

   a. File application with Supreme Commander for the Allied Powers for clearance of vessels in foreign trade.

   b. Submit proposed rates to Supreme Commander for the Allied Powers for review.

   c. Process through Supreme Commander for the Allied Powers settlement of all freight monies and accounts in connection with shipping, husbandry or brokerage with agents outside Japan.

   5. All vessels meeting International requirements, (Load line Certificate, Safety of Life at Sea and Communications Certificates) shall be eligible for release of controls. Additional vessels may be added to this category upon approval of Supreme Commander for the Allied Powers. Vessels placed in this group shall not be returned to Category B once approval has been given for inclusion in Category A (vessels engaged in overseas trade).

   6. The Japanese Government will take the following action in the administration of the subsidy funds appropriated for the Civilian Merchant Marine Committee.

   a. Effective at the beginning of JFY 1950-51, end all payment of charter hire of any kind for any vessel, except charter hire paid for the actual carriage of wholly Government-owned cargo.

   b. Commence the payment of standby subsidy to the owners of steel cargo vessels of over 800 gross tons according to the following regulations:

   (1) Basic standby subsidy shall be fixed by the Civilian Merchant Marine Committee to provide for each vessel only the minimum standby crew, fuel and supplies required to keep it in operating order, and covering cost of minimum insurance but not interest or any profit or other payment to owners. In general, for craft over 800 but less

CATEGORY B

All vessels over 800 gross tons not included in Category A

than 2,000 tons, the standby crew will be limited to four, of whom one may be the master of the vessel. For larger vessels, the crew will be kept to a similar minimum.

(2) For the purpose of standby subsidy, the Japanese Merchant fleet over 800 gross tons will be divided into the following groups:

(a) Group I. Vessels complying with International Classification Society rules.

(b) Group II. Vessels complying with Japanese Classification Society rules but not meeting the standards of (a) above.

(c) Group III. Vessels not meeting the standards of Group II but capable of operating at the same average cost as those listed in Group II. The minimum test for placing a vessel in Group III shall be the completion of one or more voyages under pay load totalling at least 500 miles since 30 September 1949.

(d) Group IV. Vessels not in condition to operate or not meeting the standards of Group III.

(3) For a period of six months from the beginning of JFY 1950–51, the standby subsidies shall be paid to all vessels in Groups I, II, III and IV.

(4) Effective not later than 1 October 1950, the following standby subsidies shall be paid.

(a) Group I. – the basic subsidy.
(b) Group II. – the basic subsidy.
(c) Group III. – the basic subsidy less 20 percent.

No subsidy shall be paid to vessels in Group IV or to any vessel for time within thirty days after its most recent employment.

(5) Effective not later than 1 January 1951, the following standby subsidies shall be paid.

(a) Group I. – the basic subsidy.
(b) Group II. – the basic subsidy.
(c) Group III. – the basic subsidy less 50 percent.

7. Through the Civilian Merchant Marine Committee, all

794

Japanese merchant vessels will continue to be subject to administrative control of Administrator, United States Shipping Control Authority for Japanese Merchant Marine. The Ministry of Transportation will collect, compile and submit such reports as may be required.

8. To permit orderly and gradual return of operating responsibilities for the Japanese merchant fleet to normal channels as outlined above, direct communication in implementation of this directive is authorized between Civil Transportation Section, General Headquarters Supreme Commander for the Allied Powers; Commander, United States Naval Forces, Far East (Administrator, United States Shipping Control Authority, Japanese Merchant Marine) and the Japanese Government.

FOR THE SUPREME COMMANDER:

　　　　K. B. BUSH,
　　Brigadier General, USA,
　　　Adjutant General.

～～～～～～～～～～

昭和25年3月9日　政務局総務課長作成

[在外事務所設置に關するポツダム政令に關する件]

在外事務所設置に關するポツダム政令に關する件

昭二五、三、九　政務局総務課長八日本官總司令部外交局オーヴァートン書記官を他用をもって往訪し、本件に關し國内各官廳との折衝の模様等を説明し、その助言を求めた。會談内容左の通り

一、在外事務所設置に關し外務省としては急速に實現するため、國會開會中ではあるが、總司令部覺書に基くポツダム政令を制定することを準備中であるが、この點に關し、法務府、人事院方面に若干の疑義があり、法律によらず、ポツダム政令によることの根據の問合を受けている。これに對して外務省としては本件の早急實現を強く要望されている關係もあり、ポツダム政令をもって行いたい旨を説明している。

これに對してオ書記官は司令部最近の政策としてディレクティヴもしくはSCAPINの發出を極力手控え日

本政府に自主權を與える形をとる趣旨からSCAPINのないメモランダムの形式をもって申入れをなすことが多いが、殊に本件の如きは總司令部政策の一環として、その早期實現を強く要望するものである。また經濟科學局が通商促進の見地から一日も早く事務所を開設すべきを要望していることは御承知と思うが、元來本件はアメリカ政府において極東委員會において決定を見なかったにも拘らず、獨自の立場から敢えて強行した次第である。またマッカーサー元帥としても本件を日本の對外關係における自主性恢復の一歩として重要視せられているが、日本國内部の事情、これを法律で設置する場合の手續、國會における諸論議等國内の法制的、政治的理由からその實現が遲延するが如きことは司令部としては到底忍び得ないところであり、面子の問題でもある。從ってポツダム政令をもって本件を早急に實現しようとする外務省の主張には全面的に賛成であり、これらの事情を日本側關係當局にも強く申入れられることを希望すると述べた。

二、通產省との關係において通產大臣の通商に關する權限と外務大臣の權限との關係の問題が法務府、通產省及び外務省の間で問題となっているが、これには二つの考え方があると思う。一つは、外務大臣が通商に關係ある事項について通產大臣と協議した上在外事務所長を指揮監督するとの規定を設けるのと、もう一つは通產大臣が外務大臣と協議し且つ外務大臣を經て在外事務所所長を指揮監督することができるとする二案であるが、通產省としては是非通產大臣の指揮監督權を確保したいという線を主張している。

これに對してオ書記官は、自分の考としては司令部の覺書の趣旨もあり、外務大臣が指揮監督權を有するわけであるから、第一案を支持するものであり、第一案の方が遙かによいと思う。もし實際上通產大臣の指揮が必要となった場合には、それは外務大臣との間に事務上の了解を取付ければよいのであり、法令の文面にこれを入れることには賛成できないと述べ、今後も一二、その他の問題で日本側内部に本件の早期實現に對する困難が起る場合には、外交局としてできる限りの御援助をいたしたいと結んだ。

266 昭和25年5月23日 連合国最高司令官総司令部より 日本政府宛

日本政府・在外事務所間の通信許可に関する指令

GENERAL HEADQUARTERS
SUPREME COMMANDER FOR THE ALLIED POWERS
APO 500

AG 311.23 (23 MAY 50) CCS　　　　　　　　　　23 MAY 50
SCAPIN 2098

MEMORANDUM FOR: JAPANESE GOVERNMENT

SUBJECT: Communications with Japanese Overseas Agencies

1. Reference is made to:

　　a. Memorandum for the Japanese Government, AG 091 (29 Jan 46) GS, SCAPIN 677, 29 January 1946, subject: Governmental and Administrative Separation of Certain Outlying Areas from Japan.

　　b. Memorandum for the Japanese Government, AG 311 (24 Feb 50) CCS, SCAPIN 2085, 24 February 1950, subject: Rationalization of Japan's International Telecommunications Services.

　　c. Memorandum for the Japanese Government from Diplomatic Section, General Headquarters, Supreme Commander for the Allied Powers, 9 February 1950, subject: Establishment of Japanese Overseas Agencies in the United States of America.

　　d. Memorandum for the Japanese Government, AG 311.1 (28 May 48) CCS, SCAPIN 1900, subject: International Postal Service, 28 May 1948, as amended.

2. Communications between the Japanese Government and Japanese Overseas Agencies established pursuant to and in accordance with reference memorandum 1c above are authorized.

3. Receiver-to-pay messages from Japanese Overseas Agencies and Japanese Overseas Representatives, to the Japanese Government or its agencies in Japan, are authorized.

4. Direct communication between Civil Communications Section, General Headquarters, Supreme Commander for the Allied Powers, and the Ministry of Telecommunications and the Ministry of Postal Services, concerning matters within the scope of

267 日本共産党中央委員の公職追放に関するマッカーサー司令官の吉田首相への書簡

昭和25年6月6日 マッカーサー連合国最高司令官より吉田内閣総理大臣宛

付記 右和訳文

General of the Army Douglas MacArthur's Letter to Japanese Prime Minister concerning Purge of Full Membership of the Central Committee of the Japan Communist Party

Tokyo, Japan
6 June 1950

Dear Mr. Prime Minister:

It has been a fundamental purpose of the Occupation to assist the Japanese people to meet their commitments under the Potsdam Declaration, foremost of which requires the establishment in Japan of a new order of peace, security and justice upon which may firmly stand a peacefully inclined and responsible government. To such end the Japanese Government is specifically enjoined in the Potsdam Declaration to 'remove all obstacles to the strengthening of democratic tendencies among the Japanese people.'

In the implementation of this requirement, carried forward as one of the basic objectives of Allied policy as determined and prescribed by the Far Eastern Commission, the structure of the Japanese Government has been redesigned, its laws and institutions where undemocratic have been revised, and those persons whose public record gives warning that their continued influence would be inimical to democratic growth have been removed and excluded from Japan's public affairs.

The guiding philosophy of this phase of the Occupation has been protective, not punitive. Its purpose and effect has been to provide assurance that the aims of Allied policy in the democra-

this memorandum is authorized.

FOR THE SUPREME COMMANDER:

K. B. BUSH,
Brigadier General, USA
Adjutant General.

798

4 制限緩和に向けた対応(昭和 24 年 5 月～27 年 4 月)

tization of Japan would not be thwarted by the influence and pressure of anti-democratic elements. The area of its application for the most part has embraced those persons who because of position and influence bear responsibility for Japan's totalitarian policies which led to adventure in conquest and exploitation. Recently, however, a new and no less sinister groupment has injected itself into the Japanese political scene which has sought through perversion of truth and incitation to mass violence to transform this peaceful and tranquil land into an arena of disorder and strife as the means of stemming Japan's notable progress along the road of representative democracy and to subvert the rapidly growing democratic tendencies among the Japanese people.

Acting in common accord, they have hurled defiance at constituted authority, shown contempt for the processes of law and order, and contrived by false and inflammatory statements and other subversive means to arouse through resulting public confusion that degree of social unrest which would set the stage for the eventual overthrow of constitutional government in Japan by force. Their coercive methods bear striking parallel to those by which the militaristic leaders of the past deceived and misled the Japanese people, and their aims, if achieved, would surely lead Japan to an even worse disaster. To permit this incitation to lawlessness to continue unchecked, however embryonic it may at present appear, would be to risk ultimate suppression of Japan's democratic institutions in direct negation of the purpose and intent of Allied policy pronouncements, forfeiture of her chance for political independence, and destruction of the Japanese race.

Accordingly, I direct that your government take the necessary administrative measures to remove and exclude the following named persons, constituting the full membership of the Central Committee of the Japan Communist Party, from public service, and render them subject to the prohibitions, restrictions and liabilities of my directives of January 4, 1946, (SCAPINS 548 and 550) and their implementing ordinances:

HAKAMADA Satomi
HASEGAWA Hiroshi
ITO Kenichi
ITO Ritsu

KAMEYAMA Kozo
KAMIYAMA Shigeo
KASUGA Shoichi
KASUGA Shojiro
KONNO Yojiro
KISHIMOTO Shigeo
KURAHARA Koreto
MATSUMOTO Kazumi
MATSUMOTO Saneki
MIYAMOTO Kenji
NOSAKA Ryu
NOSAKA Sanzo
SATO Satoji
SHIDA Shigeo
SHIGA Yoshio
SHIRAKAWA Seiichi
TAKAKURA Teru
TAKENAKA Tsunesaburo
TOKUDA Kyuichi
TOSAKA Hiroshi.

Sincerely yours,

(Sgd.) Douglas MacArthur
DOUGLAS MacARTHUR.

Mr. Shigeru Yoshida,
Prime Minister of Japan, Tokyo.

編 注 本文書は、昭和二十六年二月、外務省特別資料課作成「日本占領及び管理重要文書集」第二巻増補より抜粋。

(付記)

共産黨中央委員の公職追放に關するマ元帥の吉田首相あて書簡に關する總司令部渉外局發表

昭和二十五年六月六日

内閣總理大臣殿

日本國民がポツダム宣言に基いて負っている公約を果すよう援助するのが占領軍の根本的目的であった。その日本國民の公約のうち最も重大なものは平和と安全と正義の新秩序が樹立されることであり、右の基礎の上にはじめて

800

4 制限緩和に向けた対応（昭和24年5月～27年4月）

平和的傾向を有しかつ責任ある政府は確立されるのである。この目的のために日本政府は「日本國民の間における民主主義的傾向の強化に對する一切の障碍を除去する」ことをポツダム宣言中において特に命ぜられている。

この條件は極東委員會によって決定され指令された連合國政策の基本的目的として推進されてきたものであって、これを履行するため日本政府の機構は改編され、法律及び制度の非民主的なものは改正され、また過去の閲歴から見てそのままにしておけば民主主義の成長に有害な影響を及ぼすおそれのある人物は日本の公職から追放された。

この局面での占領指導原理は保護にあって、懲罰ではなかった。その意圖と效果は連合國の日本民主化政策の目的が反民主主義的分子の影響と壓力によって阻まれることがあってはならないとの保障を與えることであった。その適用の範圍は、日本を征服と搾取の冒險に導いた全體主義的政策に對しその地位及び影響力よりして責任を有する人々を主に包含していた。ところが最近にいたり日本の政界には新しくこれに劣らず邪惡な一派が入り込んできた。かれらは代議政治による民主主義の線に沿って日本が著しい進

歩を遂げているのを阻止し、日本國民の間に急速に成長しつつある民主主義的傾向をくつがえすための手段として、眞理をゆがめることと大衆の暴力行爲をあおることによって、この平和で靜穩な國土を無秩序と鬪爭の場に轉化しようとしている。

かれらは一致協力して憲法上の權威に挑戰し、法と秩序による手續を蔑視し、虛僞や煽動その他の攪亂手段によって社會的混亂を引き起し、ついには日本の立憲政治を力によって轉覆する段階をもちきたらすような社會不安を生ぜしめようと企んでいる。かれらの高壓的な方法は、過去の軍國主義的指導者が日本國民を欺き、道を誤らせたのと驚くべき類似點を持っており、その目的がもしも達成されたならば、なお一層惡性の災厄に日本を陷れるにちがいない。

この不法行爲への煽動をこのまま放置するということは、たとえそれが現在は萌芽にすぎなくても、ついには日本の民主主義的諸制度の抑壓を招き、連合國が宣言してきた政策の目的と意圖を直接否定し、日本の獨立の機會を失わせ、日本民族を破滅させる危險を冒すことになろう。

それ故に私は日本政府が左記氏名の日本共産黨中央委員

268

昭和25年6月7日　外務省作成

［在外事務所設置に關する件］

編　注　本文書は、昭和二十五年十一月、外務省政務局特別資料課作成「日本管理資料㈡」より抜粋。

全員を公職から追放し、昭和二十一年一月四日付の私の指令（SCAPIN五四八及び五五〇）の禁止、制限、責任事項及びその施行令をかれらに適用するため、必要な行政措置をとることを命ずるものである。

ダグラス・マックアーサー

袴田里見、長谷川浩、伊藤憲一、伊藤律、亀山幸三、神山茂夫、春日正一、春日庄次郎、紺野與次郎、岸本茂雄、藏原惟人、松本一三、松本三益、宮本顯治、野坂龍、野坂參三、佐藤佐藤次、志田重男、志賀義雄、白川晴一、高倉テル、竹中恆三郎、德田球一、遠坂寛

在外事務所設置に關する件

昭和二十五年六月七日

一、米國以外の諸國に在外事務所を設置する件に關してかねて總司令部外交局よりインド、パキスタン、アルゼンチン、ブラジル、シャム、スウェーデン、フランス、韓國及びインドネシヤの諸國の內意を問い合せ中であったが、ブラジル（リオ及サンパウロの二個所）フランス、スウェーデン及びパキスタンより應諾の旨司令部に内報があったので五月十八日付覺書をもって右四國政府に正式申入れの手續きをとった。

なおブラジル政府に對しては、二在外事務所職員の人選を內報し、司令部外交局を通じ申入れの手續きをとった。

一方これら在外事務所に要する經費についても檢討のうえ、予算案を外交局に提示した。

しかるに、その後外交局係官の談によれば、連合國總司令官參謀長において、ブラジル政府に對する日本政府申入れは伯國政府の申出に基きリオ・デ・ジャネイロ及びサン・パウロの二ケ所に在外事務所を設置するよう要請してあるがブラジルには一ヶ所にて足りるとの意響を有している旨連絡があったので外交局係官の希望により、

802

4 制限緩和に向けた対応(昭和24年5月～27年4月)

五月二十七日、メモをもつて貿易の振興及び在外邦人保護の関係上、是非とも二ヶ所に設置する必要がある旨説明して置いた。

また予算の面についても司令部E・S・Sにおいて若干異見もある趣で、事務的レベルで目下折衝中である。

本七日司令部外交局係官の談によればブラジル、サン・パウロの問題につき参謀長の諮問に対しE・S・Sマーカット少将も設置の必要性に関し消極的回答をなしたためブラジルに二ヶ所の在外事務所を設置する件は、まつたくデッド・ロックに陥つた趣である。同係官の私見によれば他方ウルグァイ、ベルギー等より在外事務所設置方の要請もあり、且つ、日本政府の要請があつてから既に二週間も経過しているのでブラジルについては、とりあえずリオ・デ・ジャネイロの一ヶ所につき参謀長の決裁をとり直ちにブラジル、フランス、スウェーデン、パキスタン各政府に覚書を送ることとし、サン・パウロは後日再び問題を提起することとしては如何かと思うと語つた趣である。

なお、同係官談によればマッカーサー元帥よりロンドンに在外事務所を設置する件に関し諮問があつたが過去の経緯に徴し非常に困難であると思はれる、尤も米英両国政府首脳部の話合に移せば打開の道があるかも知れないと答えた由である。

とりあえず御報告まで。

〰〰〰〰〰〰〰〰〰

269

昭和25年6月26日　連合国最高司令官総司令部より
　　　　　　　　　日本政府宛

外国人の入国要件および日本における商業活動に関する指令

付記　昭和二十六年二月七日付連合国最高司令官総司令部より日本政府宛公信SCAPIN第二
一〇五／一号
右指令の一部取り消しに関する指令

GENERAL HEADQUARTERS
SUPREME COMMANDER FOR THE ALLIED POWERS
APO 500

AG 004 (26 Jun 50) FIB　　26 June 1950

SCAPIN 2105

MEMORANDUM FOR: JAPANESE GOVERNMENT

SUBJECT: Entry Requirements and Business Activities in Japan

1. References and supersessions.

   a. Reference is Circular 11, General Headquarters, Supreme Commander for the Allied Powers, subject: Entry Requirements and Business Activities in Japan, 16 June 1950.

   b. The following memoranda for the Japanese Government are superseded:

   (1) AG 004 (27 Apr 48) ESS/EX, SCAPIN 1961, 14 January 1949, subject: Business Activities of Non-Japanese in Japan.

   (2) AG 004 (27 Apr 48) FIB, SCAPIN 1961/1, 21 October 1949, subject: Business Activities of Non-Japanese in Japan.

2. Referenced circular details the conditions:

   a. Under which non-occupation personnel may enter Japan, and

   b. Under which non-Japanese nationals, foreign-controlled firms and non-resident Japanese nationals other than occupation personnel may conduct themselves and their commercial, professional, and investment activities within Japan.

3. In order to facilitate the restoration of normal economic relationships for the purpose of establishing the Japanese economy on a self-supporting basis, it is desired that the Japanese Government implement the principles set forth in the referenced circular in the following manner:

   a. Take the necessary legal steps to assure non-Japanese nationals and firms permitted to engage in business activities in Japan equal and non-discriminatory treatment with Japanese nationals and firms.

   b. Receive and approve or disapprove, applications by non-Japanese nationals and foreign controlled firms to engage in business of banking, insurance, communications, transportation, public utilities, professional services, or other businesses as hereafter may be designated. Prior to issuance of any license or disapproval of an application to engage in any of the above-mentioned business activities, the Japanese Government shall sub-

4 制限緩和に向けた対応(昭和24年5月～27年4月)

mit its proposed action, including application, to the Supreme Commander for the Allied Powers for concurrence. Each license shall contain a provision that licensee is not authorized to conduct a business activity with occupation force agencies and personnel involving the transfer of foreign exchange or transfers between convertible accounts without specific written authority of General Headquarters, Supreme Commander for the Allied Powers.

c. Applications by non-Japanese nationals and foreign-controlled firms engaging in business activities involving the admission or dissemination of magazines, books, motion pictures, news and photograph services, and other media of mass communication, and all applications by military personnel and personnel attached to or accompanying the occupation forces and their dependents to engage in business activity will be filed directly with the Supreme Commander for the Allied Powers.

d. Maintain an appropriate system providing for the registration upon entry of all persons entering Japan, except (a) occupation personnel, and (b) persons whose stay in Japan is less than 72 hours. Such registration offices as may be required will be easily accessible to ports of entry into and exit from Japan.

e. Obtain from all persons entering Japan, except (a) occupation personnel and (b) persons entering Japan for less than 72 hours, the following information: Name (both in English and native letters or characters); nationality; race; passport number, date and country of issue; permanent residence; sex; height; weight; color of hair; color of eyes; complexion; build; identifying scars or marks; date and place of birth, name, address and business of employer; country from which approved for entry into Japan; port of entry; date of entry; name of carrier; residence and/or commercial address while in Japan; and such additional information as may be required under this and other applicable regulations. The Japanese Government will forward, within forty-eight (48) hours after entry, to the Supreme Commander for the Allied Powers, a copy of the registration form required from persons entering Japan.

f. Obtain records of all persons exiting from Japan except (a) occupation personnel and (b) persons whose stay in Japan has not exceeded 72 hours, as follows: Name (both in English and native letters or characters), nationality, race, date of departure, destination, name of carrier, passport number and country of issue. A copy of the form executed by persons exiting from Japan will be forwarded to the Supreme Commander for the Allied Powers within forty-eight (48) hours after such departure.

g. Provide commercial entrants and missionaries entering Japan with a copy of referenced circular and obtain and retain receipt therefor. Provide tourists entering Japan with a brochure containing essential tourist information and pertinent rules of conduct.

h. Conduct reasonable inspections of records, or other necessary examinations of businesses for the purpose of discovering whether the business is conducted according to applicable Japanese law and the regulations of the Supreme Commander for the Allied Powers. Supervise compliance, investigate, and upon discovery, report to the chief of the nearest Civil Affairs Region of GHQ, SCAP, violations of the provisions of all laws, regulations, licenses or written authorizations issued by the Supreme Commander for the Allied Powers or the Japanese Government to non-Japanese nationals and foreign-controlled firms; EXCEPT THAT, in the investigation and enforcement measures heretofore mentioned, the Japanese Government will be limited by the provisions of Memorandum to the Japanese Government, AG 015 (19 Feb 46) LS, subject: Exercise of Criminal Jurisdiction, SCAPIN 756, 19 February 1946, as amended. Whenever the Japanese Government is prevented or restricted from carrying into execution the foregoing directives by the limitations imposed upon the Japanese Government by the provisions of Memorandum to the Japanese Government, AG 015 (19 Feb 46) LS, subject: Exercise of Criminal Jurisdiction, SCAPIN 756, 19 February 1946, as amended, the Japanese Government is directed to request the assistance of the chief of the nearest Civil Affairs Region of General Headquarters, Supreme Commander for the Allied Powers.

i. Take necessary action to make it a punishable offense for any person to become a party or accessory to illegal transactions as defined in para 34, reference circular.

j. Receive and either approve, with concurrence by the Supreme Commander for the Allied Powers, or disapprove applications by non-Japanese nationals and foreign-controlled firms

4　制限緩和に向けた対応（昭和24年5月〜27年4月）

for validating acquisition from Japanese nationals, from firms in which Japanese nationals or firms have a proprietary interest, or from Japanese Government agencies of property interests or rights in the following categories:

(1) Acquisition of title to stocks and shares other than acquisition of new stock issues based upon prior valid stock acquisitions.

(2) Acquisition of title to land and/or residence for business purposes, and to commercial and industrial buildings and installations, and plant and facilities attached thereto. (Land and residences reasonably required by an individual for his full or part time residence are not considered business properties.)

(3) Leases for periods in excess of five years, mortgages or other hypothecations, and arrangements or options for future acquisition of properties in the categories indicated in subparagraphs (1) and (2) above.

(4) Acquisition of patents of Japanese origin and rights thereunder.

(5) (a) Acquisition of rights to a proportion of the profits, sales, sales price or output of an enterprise for a period in excess of one year by transfer of patent rights or technology; continuing technical or factory managements assistance agreements; patent license agreements or otherwise.

(b) Acquisition of rights to a specified periodical payment covering a period in excess of one year, as consideration for transfer of patent rights or technology; continuing technical or management assistance agreements; patent license agreements or similar contracts.

k. The Japanese Government, when validating transactions indicated in subparagraph 3) above, will state

(1) That it has investigated the acquisition of such

property interest or right thereby validated and finds the same is not taking place under conditions of fraud, duress or undue influence assignable in any way to the occupation, and

(2) That adequate budgetary provision has been or will be made in the foreign exchange budget for any foreign exchange remittance abroad licensed or authorized in the acquisition of such property.

1. It is desired that the Japanese Government declare legally void all acquisitions, leases, hypothecations, mortgages, options, and arrangements for future acquisition of properties and rights for which validation is required by referenced Circular 11, which have been or are made after 14 January 1949 and which have not been specifically validated by the Japanese Government with the concurrence of the Supreme Commander for the Allied Powers.

4. Direct communication between the appropriate agencies of the Japanese Government and appropriate agencies of the Supreme Commander for the Allied Powers is authorized for the implementation of this memorandum.

5. Nothing herein contained shall be deemed to affect any right acquired or action taken pursuant to superseded memoranda to the Japanese Government, SCAPIN 1961, 14 January 1949, and SCAPIN 1961/1, 21 October 1949.

FOR THE SUPREME COMMANDER:

K. B. BUSH,
Brigadier General, USA,
Adjutant General.

(付記)

GENERAL HEADQUARTERS
SUPREME COMMANDER FOR THE ALLIED POWERS
APO 500

7 February 1951

AG 004 (26 Jun 50) FIB
SCAPIN 2105/1
MEMORANDUM FOR: JAPANESE GOVERNMENT

4 制限緩和に向けた対応（昭和24年5月～27年4月）

270 国際郵便業務に関する指令

昭和25年6月29日　連合国最高司令官総司令部より　日本政府宛

GENERAL HEADQUARTERS
SUPREME COMMANDER FOR THE ALLIED POWERS
APO 500

AG 311.1 (29 JUN 50) CCS　　　　29 JUN 50

SCAPIN 2110

MEMORANDUM FOR: JAPANESE GOVERNMENT

SUBJECT: International Postal Service

1. a. Rescission: Memorandum for the Japanese Government, AG 311.1 (28 May 48) CCS, SCAPIN 1900, 28 May 1948, subject: International Postal Service, as amended.

   b. References:

   (1) Memorandum for the Japanese Government, AG 091 (29 Jan 46) GS, SCAPIN 677, 29 January 1946, subject: Governmental and Administrative Separation of Certain Outlying Areas from Japan.

   (2) Memorandum for the Japanese Government, AG 311.1 (9 Jun 49) DS, SCAPIN 2015, 9 June 1949, subject: Communications Between

SUBJECT: Entry Requirements and Business Activities in Japan

1. Reference is Memorandum for the Japanese Government from General Headquarters, Supreme Commander for the Allied Powers, AG 004 (26 Jun 50) FIB, SCAPIN 2105, subject: Entry Requirements and Business Activities in Japan, 26 June 1950.

2. Referenced SCAPIN is amended by deleting paragraph 3h.

3. Those parts of referenced SCAPIN not hereby specifically amended, are not affected by this memorandum.

FOR THE SUPREME COMMANDER:

K. B. BUSH
Brigadier General, USA
Adjutant General

Japanese Government and Persons Abroad in Regard to Personal Status.

(3) Memorandum for the Japanese Government, AG 720.4 (3 Feb 50) GA, SCAPIN 2083, 20 February 1950, subject: Customs, Immigration and Quarantine Operations.

(4) Memorandum for the Japanese Government, AG 311.23 (23 May 50) CCS, SCAPIN 2098, 23 May 1950, subject: Communications with Japanese Overseas Agencies.

(5) Memorandum for the Japanese Government, AG 311 (24 Feb 50) CCS, SCAPIN 2085, 24 February 1950, subject: Rationalization of Japan's Telecommunication Services.

2. International Postal Services between Japan and all other nations will be operated in accordance with the Universal Postal Union Convention and Agreements and all other international or bilateral postal agreements to which Japan is now, or with approval of the Supreme Commander for the Allied Powers shall in the future become, a signatory; subject to provisions of references 1b (1) to 1b (5), inclusive, above, any other directives promulgated by the Supreme Commander for the Allied Powers, applicable Japanese laws and regulations including, but not limited to those governing mail, customs, foreign exchange and foreign trade, and to instructions embodied herein.

3. The Japanese Government or any agency thereof is prohibited from corresponding with other governments, persons outside Japan or diplomatic missions and/or representatives in Japan, except as authorized in references 1b (1), (2), (4), and (5) above; and except that:

a. The Japanese Government and/or agencies thereof are authorized to communicate with all international organizations to which Japan is now, or with approval of the Supreme Commander for the Allied Powers shall in the future become, a signatory, on administrative and fiscal matters necessary in the operation of such organizations.

b. The Japanese Government, Ministry of Postal Services, is authorized to communicate with the International Bureau

810

4 制限緩和に向けた対応(昭和24年5月〜27年4月)

of the Universal Postal Union, foreign postal administrations, shipping companies and air lines on matters necessary in the operation of all postal services covered by international conventions or agreements to which Japan is signatory. Agreements or decisions to expand or contract services within these agreements will be subject to prior approval of the Supreme Commander for the Allied Powers.

c. The Philatelic Agency, Ministry of Postal Services, is authorized to communicate with persons abroad on philatelic matters and to export postage stamps, souvenir stamps and stamped paper on receipt of orders and payments therefor.

d. The Japanese Government and/or agencies thereof are authorized to send and receive manuscripts or publications covering results of scientific research and activity and to correspond with persons outside Japan on matters contained in such manuscripts or publications.

e. The Japanese Government and/or agencies thereof are authorized to communicate with foreign government patent offices on procedures, administrative matters, laws and regulations concerning copyrights and industrial property registrations, and to send and receive publications related to same.

4. The mailing of "relief" or "gift" parcels to Japan only is authorized, in addition to regular parcel post service under international agreements, subject to the following provisions:

a. Weight – limited to 22 pounds or 10 kilograms.

b. Contents – restricted to assorted non-perishable foods, clothing, clothes-making materials and mailable medicines, in non-commercial quantities, for the personal use of the recipient and his immediate family, or for the use of bona fide orphan asylums, asylums for the aged, and charity hospitals and/or institutions. (See Annex I attached for list of permissible quantities.)

c. Indorsements – wrappers of such parcels must be indorsed "Relief Parcel" or "Gift Parcel."

d. Customs – parcels complying with the provisions of paragraphs 4a, b and c above will be admitted duty free but will be subject to customs examination and a customs clearance fee.

e. Parcels containing assorted food items, not exceeding the weight limit, will not be considered as being in commercial quantities.

f. Parcels found to contain clothing or clothes-making materials in commercial quantities will not be permitted entry duty free but will be treated in the same manner as regular parcels, in accordance with applicable international agreements and Japanese laws and regulations.

g. Parcels found to contain mailable medicines in commercial quantities will be treated as undeliverable.

h. Parcels found to contain gift articles, as distinguished from relief items, such as watches, fountain pens, tobacco products, soap, etc., or any article other than those listed in paragraph 4b above, will be delivered only on payment of applicable customs duties, taxes and/or penalties that may be assessed. Failure of addressees to pay same will cause entire parcel to be treated as undeliverable.

i. All parcels must be accompanied by appropriate Customs Declarations, containing full and precise details as to contents.

5. All international mails will be made available for examination, in accordance with instructions issued by the Supreme Commander for the Allied Powers.

6. Except as otherwise authorized by the Supreme Commander for the Allied Powers, settlement of accounts between Japan and other countries, shipping lines and air lines will be in terms of dollars or pounds sterling, subject to provisions of the Foreign Exchange and Foreign Trade Control Law of 1949, Japan.

7. Direct communication between Civil Communications Section and other Staff Sections of General Headquarters, Supreme Commander for the Allied Powers and the Ministry of Postal Services is authorized concerning matters within the scope of this memorandum.

FOR THE SUPREME COMMANDER:

K. B. BUSH,
Brigadier General, USA
Adjutant General.

1 Incl

Annex I – Permissible Quantities in Relief Parcels

812

4 制限緩和に向けた対応(昭和24年5月～27年4月)

ANNEX I

to

Memorandum for the Japanese Government, SCAPIN 2110 dated 29 June 1950

Standard of Permissible Quantities of Items

For Any Single Relief Parcel Destined for Japan

1. Relief packages cannot exceed 22 pounds or 10 kilograms in weight.

2. Specific Limitations:

Assorted foodstuffs	up to weight of package
Medicines:	
Penicillin	up to 9 million units
Santonin	up to 1 gram
Phenacetin	up to 1/8 pound
Streptomycin	up to 100 grams
Vitamins	100 ampules or 1 pound of tablets
Aspirin	2 ounces
Sulfa drugs	150 tablets
Clothing, new:	
Suits or dresses, adults	1 of each size
Suits or dresses, children	2 of each size
Shirts	3 of each size
Underwear	6 pairs
Gloves	3 pairs
Socks or stockings	1 dozen pairs
Hats, caps and the like	2 items
Boots or shoes	2 pairs of each size
Handkerchiefs	1 dozen
Towels	1 dozen
Sheets and similar coverings	5 items
Textiles for clothing:	
Woolen	sufficient for 2 suits
Cotton	sufficient for 2 dresses
Others	reasonable amounts not in commercial quantities

Silk	sufficient for 2 dresses
Woolen yarn	5 pounds
Cotton thread (yarn)	2 dozen small rolls
Sewing needles	2 small packets

Used clothing, in moderate quantities using above new goods standard as a basis.

Dear Mr. Prime Minister:

In keeping with my established policy to re-invest autonomous authority in the Japanese Government as rapidly as the situation permits, I have visualized the progressive development of law enforcing agencies adequate to the maintenance of internal security and order and the safeguard of Japan's coastline against unlawful immigration and smuggling.

By letter of September 16, 1947 I approved the recommendation of the Japanese Government for an increase in the overall strength of Japan's police force to 125,000 men, making provision for a new national rural police force of 30,000 men. It was then the view of the government, in which I fully concurred, that the strength recommended and authorized was not an arbitrary determination of future police requirements but designed to provide an adequate force around which might be built a modern and democratic police system oriented to an effective decentralization of the police responsibility in harmony with the constitutional principle of local autonomy.

Subsequent action in the recruitment, equipping and train-

General of the Army Douglas MacArthur's Letter to the Japanese Prime Minister concerning Establishment of National Police Reserve and Expansion of Strength of Personnel serving under the Maritime Safety Board

Tokyo, Japan
8 July 1950

271　警察予備隊設置および海上保安庁増強に関するマッカーサー司令官の吉田首相への書簡

昭和25年7月8日　マッカーサー連合国最高司令官より
吉田内閣総理大臣宛

付記　右和訳文

4　制限緩和に向けた対応（昭和 24 年 5 月～27 年 4 月）

ing of the police force then authorized has proceeded with commendable efficiency. The concept of autonomous responsibility has been faithfully observed, essential coordination has been carefully developed and the proper relationship between the police and private citizenry has been progressively forged. As a consequence, the Japanese people today may take justifiable pride in this agency for the enforcement of law at all levels of government. Indeed, it may be credited to both organizational police efficiency and the law-abiding character of the Japanese people that, despite a much lower police strength in relation to population here than is to be found in most of the other democratic states and the general postwar impoverishment and other adverse conditions usually conducive to lawlessness, Japan stands out with a calmness and serenity which lends emphasis to the violence, confusion and disorder which exist in other nearby lands.

To insure that this favorable condition will continue unchallenged by lawless minorities, here as elsewhere committed to the subversion of the due processes of law and assaults of opportunity against the peace and public welfare, I believe that the police system has reached that degree of efficiency in organization and training which will permit its augmentation to a strength which will bring it within the limits experience has shown to be essential to the safeguard of the public welfare in a democratic society.

Insofar as maritime safety in the harbors and coastal waters of Japan is concerned the Maritime Safety Board has achieved highly satisfactory results but events disclose that safeguard of the long Japanese coastal line against unlawful immigration and smuggling activity requires employment of a larger force under this agency than is presently provided for by law.

Accordingly, I authorize your government to take the necessary measures to establish a national police reserve of 75,000 men and expand the existing authorized strength of the personnel serving under the Maritime Safety Board by an additional 8000.

The current year's operating cost of these increments to existing agencies may be made available from funds previously allocated in the General Account of the National Budget toward retirement of the public debt. The appropriate sections of this Headquarters will be available, as heretofore, to advise and assist in the technical

昭和二十二年九月十六日付の書簡で、私は新たに三萬五千名の國家地方警察隊を設けて日本警察總力を十二萬五千名に増員する日本政府の勸告を承認した。

當時、政府の所見としては、この勸告され承認された警察力は將來必要とする警察力を獨斷的に考慮して決定されたものでなく、憲法に基く地方自治確立の原則に合致させ、警察機能の責任を地方に分散するために近代的な民主的警察制度を作り上げるに十分な警察力を規定するのがその目的であったのであり、私も又これにまったく同意したのである。

警察官の募集、装備ならびに訓練に關するその後の措置は、きわめて有効に實施された。自治的責任の精神は忠實に守られ、必要な連絡調整は注意深く行われ、警察と一般市民の間の正しい關係は漸次強化されてきた。この結果、今日の日本國民は、政府のこれら各級の法令執行機關を持っていることを十分誇りとしてよいであろう。

當時の日本の警察力は、人口との比率では、他の多くの民主々義諸國よりはるかに低いものであり、さらに、普通ならば無秩序状態になりやすい一般的な戰後の窮迫その他

aspects of these measures.

　　　　　Very sincerely,

　　　　　(Sgd.) Douglas MacArthur
Mr. Shigeru Yoshida,
Prime Minister of Japan,
Tokyo.

　　　　　　　　　　DOUGLAS MacARTHUR.

編　注　本文書は、昭和二十六年二月、外務省特別資料課作成「日本占領及び管理重要文書集」第二卷増補より抜粹。

(付記)
　警察力増強に關するマ元帥の吉田首相あて書簡
　昭和二十五年七月八日總司令部渉外局特別發表

内閣總理大臣吉田茂殿

私は情勢の許す限り一刻も早く日本政府に自治權を許すという既定の方針に基き、國内の保安と秩序を維持し、かつ不法入國と密輸に對し、日本の沿岸を防衞するに十分な法令執行機關を徐々に發展させる構想を持っていた。

4 制限緩和に向けた対応(昭和24年5月～27年4月)

の悪條件があったにもかかわらず、日本が靜穩を維持し、しかもそうした狀態が隣接諸國の暴動、混亂、無秩序と對照的なものになってきたということは、實際組織的警察力の高能率と日本國民の違法精神に負うものといえよう。かかる好ましい狀態が、他國におけると同樣に法律の正當な運營を覆えし、かつ平和と公共福祉を侵害するを事とする不法な少數者の挑戰を受けることなく堅持されてゆくために、私は警察制度が組織と訓練において十分な能力あるに段階に達し、その結果民主主義社會の公共福祉を防衞するに必要欠くことのできないものと經驗上明らかな限度内において警察力を增大し得るものと信ずる。

日本の港灣及び沿岸水域における海上保安に關する限り海上保安廳はきわめて滿足な成果をあげてきたが、その後の諸情勢により、長い日本の沿岸線を不法入國及び密輸入活動から守るためには、現行法律が定めているよりも多くの海上保安廳職員を雇用することの必要性が明らかにされた。

以上の理由により、私は日本政府に對し七萬五千の國家警察予備隊を設けるとともに、現在認められている海上保安廳職員をさらに八千名增强するために必要な措置をとることを許可する。これら職員の增强にともなう本會計年度の運營費は、國家予算の一般會計中の債務償還費を流用してよい。總司令部の關係各局においては從來と同樣にこれら措置の技術面について勸告、並びに援助を行うつもりである。

ダグラス・マックアーサー

編注 本文書は、昭和二十六年二月、外務省政務局特別資料課作成「日本管理資料(三)」より拔粹。

〰〰〰〰〰

昭和25年7月18日　マッカーサー連合国最高司令官より吉田内閣総理大臣宛

272

日本共産党機関紙『アカハタ』の発行禁止に関するマッカーサー司令官の吉田首相への書簡

付記　右和訳文

General of the Army Douglas MacArthur's Letter to Japanese Prime Minister concerning Indefinite Suspension Imposed upon Publication of AKAHATA

Tokyo, Japan
18 July 1950

Dear Mr. Prime Minister:

Since my letter to you of June 26th designed to curb the dissemination of false, inflammatory and subversive Communist propaganda, the international forces with which the Japan Communist Party is publicly affiliated have assumed an even more sinister threat to the preservation of peace and supremacy of the rule of law in democratic society, giving clear warning to free peoples everywhere of their purpose by violence to suppress freedom. In these circumstances, it becomes obvious that the free and unrestricted use of the media of public information for the dissemination of propaganda to such end by a minority so dedicated in Japan would be a travesty upon the concept of press freedom, to be permitted only at hazard to the vast proportion of the free Japanese press faithful to its public responsibility, and jeopardy to the general welfare.

In the great struggle which is now engaging the forces of the free world all segments must accept and faithfully fulfill their share of the attendant responsibility. That share as to none is greater than such as falls upon the media of public information. For there rests the full responsibility of insuring dissemination of the truth, and based upon the truth the development of an informed and enlightened public opinion. History records no instance where a free press failed in the discharge of its responsibility without inviting its own doom.

I am not concerned over any destructive influence Communist propaganda may have upon the great mass of Japan's responsible citizenry, for it has already given ample evidence of its devotion to the cause of right and justice and its ability to penetrate the mask of Communist hypocrisy. But passing events warn of distinct danger in the use by Communism of the media of public information to propagate its tenets of subversion and violence as a means of inciting the irresponsible and lawless minority elements of society to oppose law, disturb order, and subvert the general welfare. Therefore, so long as Communism in Japan continues in the abuse of freedom of expression through incitation to such lawlessness, its free use of the media of public information must be

818

4 制限緩和に向けた対応(昭和24年5月～27年4月)

昭和二十五年七月十八日渉外局特別發表

(昭二五・七・一八、官報號外第九〇號所載)

拝啓

　虚偽、煽動的、破壊的な共産主義者の宣傳の播布を阻止する目的をもった私の六月二十六日付貴下宛書簡以來、日本共産黨が公然と連繋している國際勢力は民主主義社會における平和の維持と法の支配の尊嚴に對して更に陰險な脅威を與えるに至り、暴力によって自由を抑壓する彼等の目的について至る所の自由な人民に對し警告を與えている。

　かかる情勢下においては、日本においてこれを信奉する少數者がかかる目的のために宣傳を播布するため公的報道機關を自由且つ無制限に使用することは新聞の自由の概念の惡用であり、これを許すことは公的責任に忠實な自由な日本の報道機關の大部分のものを危險に陷れ、且つ一般國民の福祉を危くするものであることが明らかとなった。現在自由な世界の諸力を結集しつつある偉大な闘いにおいては、すべての分野のものはこれに伴う責任を分擔し、且つ誠實に遂行しなければならない。かかる責任のうち、公共的報道機關が擔う責任程大きなものはない。何故なら、

denied in the public interest.

Accordingly, I direct that your government vigorously continue the measures being taken in the implementation of my aforesaid letter, and maintain indefinitely the suspensions heretofore imposed upon publication of Akahata and its successors and affiliates employed in the dissemination in Japan of inflammatory Communist propaganda.

Very sincerely,

(Sgd.) Douglas MacArthur

DOUGLAS MacARTHUR.

Mr. Shigeru Yoshida
Prime Minister of Japan
Tokyo

編注　本文書は、昭和二十六年二月、外務省特別資料課作成「日本占領及び管理重要文書集」第二卷增補より拔粹。

(付記)

アカハタ發行禁止に關するマ元帥の吉田首相あて書簡

そこには眞實を報道し、この眞實に基いて事情に通じ、啓發された世論をつくりあげる全責任があるからである。歷史は自由な新聞がこの責任を遂行しなかった場合必ず自ら死滅を招いたことを記録している。

私は共產主義者の宣傳が責任を自覺した日本國民大衆に與えるかもしれない破壞的な影響については憂慮してはいない。蓋し日本國民大衆が正義と公正の目的に獻身し、共產主義の僞善の假面を見破る能力を有することをすでに充分に立證してきているからである。しかしながら現實の諸事件は共產主義が公共の報道機關を利用して破壞的暴力的綱領を宣傳し、無責任、不法の少數分子を煽動して法にそむき秩序を亂し公共の福祉をそこなわしめる危險が明白なことを警告している。それ故日本において、共產主義が言論の自由を濫用して公的報道の自由を使用させることは公共の利益のため拒否されねばならない。

よって私は日本政府に對し先の私の書簡の實施のために現在とられている措置を引續き強力に實施し、日本國内において煽動的な共產主義者の宣傳の播布に當ってきたアカハタ及びその後繼紙竝びに同類紙の發行に對し課せられた停刊措置を無期限に繼續することを指令する。

　　　　　　　　　　　　　敬具

一九五〇年七月十八日

　　　　　　　ダグラス・マックアーサー

内閣總理大臣吉田茂殿

編　注　本文書は、昭和二十六年二月、外務省政務局特別資料課作成「日本管理資料㈢」より抜粋。
　　　　〰〰〰〰〰〰〰〰〰〰〰〰〰〰〰〰

昭和25年8月1日
連合国最高司令官総司令部より日本政府宛

273 日本商船乗組員の海外航行許可申請手続きに関する指令

APO 500

SUPREME COMMANDER FOR THE ALLIED POWERS

GENERAL HEADQUARTERS

AG 544 (1 Aug 50) GA

1 August 1950

SCAPIN 2118

MEMORANDUM FOR: JAPANESE GOVERNMENT

SUBJECT: Travel of Japanese Mariners Outside of Japan

1. Effective 1 August 1950, all Japanese nationals to be employed as mariners on Japanese merchant vessels authorized to engage in private overseas trade shall be required to obtain the approval of the Supreme Commander for the Allied Powers for travel in the waters and areas outside of Japan.

2. Individuals shall make application in person to the Marine Authority of the Ministry of Transportation for the Supreme Commander for the Allied Powers' permission to travel as mariners. The attached application form will be used and will contain a certification by the Ministry of Transportation that the individual is a qualified mariner. Applications, accompanied by Personal History Statements, shall be forwarded to the Supreme Commander for the Allied Powers for consideration.

3. Upon receipt of the Supreme Commander for the Allied Powers' approval of the application, the Marine Authority of the Ministry of Transportation shall cause the following indorsement to be made in the Mariner's Pocket-Ledger which is issued under the provisions of Japanese Law No. 100, Mariners' Law and Regulation for the Enforcement of the Mariners' Law:

"I, the undersigned, Minister of Transportation, identify _____, whose photograph and description are affixed hereto, as a Japanese National who has been authorized to travel in waters and areas outside of Japan and return to Japan in the capacity of mariner under instructions AG 544 (1 Aug 50) GA, SCAPIN 2118, 1 August 1950, delivered at _____ date _____.

Signature of Bearer (Seal)   Ministry of Transportation (Seal)

This indorsement shall be printed in both English and Japanese on Page 2 of the Mariner's Pocket-Ledger.

4. Crew members of Japanese merchant vessels engaged in overseas trade shall be restricted to such vessels while in foreign ports unless specific authorization for shore privileges is included

in the vessel clearance (sailing orders) granted for each voyage by the Supreme Commander for the Allied Powers.

5. In the event of an emergency, resulting from illness or other contingency, at a foreign port of call, the master of the vessel through the local authorized agents shall make the necessary arrangements with the competent government authorities to place the crew members on shore and to arrange for their subsequent repatriation.

6. Only bona fide crew members authorized by the Supreme Commander for the Allied Powers shall be signed on any vessel engaging in Japanese overseas trade.

FOR THE SUPREME COMMANDER:

K. B. BUSH,
Brigadier General, USA,
Adjutant General.

1 Incl
Appl Form

編注　本文書の別添は省略。

昭和25年8月2日　鈴木連絡調整横浜事務局長より　吉田外務大臣宛

朝鮮情勢に関する第八軍関係者等の内話情報につき報告

付記　昭和二十五年八月十九日、情報部作成〔朝鮮の動亂とわれらの立場〕

濱連機密本第一八五號

昭和二十五年八月二日

　　　　　　　　横濱連絡調整事務局
　　　　　　　　　局長　鈴木　九萬〔印〕

外務大臣　吉田　茂殿

朝鮮問題に關する件

(一)第八軍關係の一大佐内話(七月三十一日)。自分の米國側乃至國連側としてどこ迄やったら一應はこを収めるか(尤もソ連が安保理事會で平和解決と稱して何を云い出すかは判らぬが)との間に對して三十八度線を超えて陸兵を動かすとソ連と衝突の可能性が出て來るので仁川邊へ敵前上陸をして南下した北鮮軍に大打撃を加えてから國連の保障の下に事件を収めるとい

4　制限緩和に向けた対応(昭和24年5月〜27年4月)

(二)佛國大使ドジヤン氏の内話(八月二日)。

今日の見通しでは米軍は尚幾分後退しようが釜山を中心に何とか橋頭堡を確保して攻勢に移り北鮮軍を押し返し得ようかと思う。如何なる形で朝鮮問題を解決するかは北鮮軍も南北統一を呼號して事を起したが結局三十八度線が余りに人工的で沒常識な境界だから國連の手で之を廢し民主政府を樹て國連が或る期間之を守り立ててゆくという風に持つてゆき度いのだろうがソ連が何う出るか。北鮮の後ろ又は仲に中共が居りソ連も同様な事は云う迄もないが、之れは彼我兩方とも今の處余り觸れぬ方が都合がよい然し此のようなカラクリは何時迄もは續き得ない米が目下人員、物資を動員している程度及英、佛のやつている所も朝鮮問題丈けの解決よりはずつと上廻つた所を目標にしている。之れは朝鮮問題を解決した後ソ連に対し戰争か平和かの對決的態勢に入る氣構えである。自分から他方面へ更にソ連が出る形勢は見えぬかとの問に対しては米の第七艦隊が臺灣海峽に頑張つた事は中共の行動を著しく妨害する事勿論で最近中共が上海邊の兵

を臺灣對岸に移したという情報は多分に神經戰かと思う。佛印は最う四年にも亘つて雙方對立して居り今急に大きな変化は無いかと思う。蔣政權側の内部からの崩壞あるか(之れも今は其の危險性がへつたとおもう)又は比島、印度等で共產黨の大きな騒ぎでも起らぬ限り今直ぐ日平和條約の見通し如何との質問に対して自分が日本人なればこの方面に手は出せぬかと思うと逃ぶ。此の際ハツキリ西歐デモクラシー側に與して之を早むべきだと思うとの事だつたので其の點は少數論は兎も角國民の大勢は既に西歐に興しているに対し総理や政府要人の屢次の聲明をきくと漸次其の方向に動いてはいるが、ヂツク・ザツクの組があるとの事故それに対し自分等は未だ連合國の占領下にあり連合國側の對日平和乃至將来の日本の安全問題等に対する氣持もよく解らぬのと他方新憲法の條項等の關係もあつて余り突進んだ事の云えぬ事情はよく理解される必要があると説明した。右に対し同大使は今度の朝鮮問題で國連のコレクチブ・セキユリテイも実際に迅速に動いたので將来にとりよい前例と

成った。憲法の條項で工合の悪いところがあれば之も改正して一日も早く西歐に與し國連の枠内に這入る事を希望すると逃べていた。

（付　記）

昭和二十五年八月十九日　　　　外務省情報部

朝鮮の動亂とわれらの立場

一、朝鮮動亂の背景

今から丁度五年前、敗戰の現實によって戰爭中の軍國主義的迷夢からさめたわれわれが、翻然として悟ったものは自由の貴さであり平和の有難さであった。ひとりわれわればかりではない。第二次世界大戰の終了とともに二十三億全人類はひとしく永久平和への希望を新たにしたのである。第一次大戰のあとでついに世界平和維持の使命を果すことができなかった國際連盟に代って、新たに發足した國際連合に寄せられた期待はまことに絶大なものがあった。どの國民もすべて平和をのぞみ、どの國も自由を基調とする民主主義を欲しているかぎりは、こうした期待は白日夢に終るはずがなく、全人類はようやくにして永久平和をわがものにしたかに思えたのである。

しかし不幸にして自由と平和への待望はつぎつぎと裏切られていった。東ヨーロッパでは自由が粉碎され、滿州や中國では平和が容易にもたらされなかった。北緯三十八度線で二分された朝鮮では、國際連合の努力にもかゝわらず統一が實現しないばかりでなく、事態はますます對立を深めてきた。西ヨーロッパでも、米國の經濟援助に對して意識的なかく亂が行われ、わが國でも一時、無秩序が世間を支配するかの觀を呈した時すらあった。このようにして戰後全人類の期待に反して自由と平和を基調とする民主主義は、自由と平和を破壞せんとする共産主義によってあらゆる妨害を受けているのである。

われわれの待望する講和條約もこうした情勢を背景にして急速な實現が見られなかった。マックアーサー元帥が昭和二十二年三月十七日、對日早期講和の締結を提唱したにもかゝわらず、全連合國間の話合いはとうてい望むべくもなく、徒らに自主獨立へのわれわれの焦慮をかきたてているばかりである。いな、日本の講和條約ができないばかり

824

4　制限緩和に向けた対応（昭和24年5月～27年4月）

ではなく、國際連合自体すら期待通りの活動をしえない實情であつた。戰後しばしば開催された連合國の外相會議も、平和の道を切り開かなかつたばかりか、かえつて「二つの世界」の對立を深刻化しているようにさえ思われる。一昨年から昨年へかけてのベルリン封鎖や、本年五月の東獨青年團のベルリン行進デモは、あたかも世界平和がまさに危殆に瀕するかの心配をわれわれに與えた。この危機を救つたものは米英佛三國の毅然たる態度であつた。すなわちベルリン封鎖に對し西歐側は總額一億七千萬ドルに達したといわれる大規模な空輸を行つて西ベルリン市民の苦境を救うとともに、封鎖を解除しないうちはドイツ問題について一切ソ連と話合いを行わずとの強硬な態度を持したため遂に約一ヵ年にわたつた封鎖問題も大事に至らずして收まつた。また東獨の自由ドイツ青年團も、西ベルリン乘取りの氣勢をあげた際にも、米英佛三占領軍は東獨青年の挑發行爲に對しては發砲も辞さないという強い決意を示したため、五月二十八日のデモは平穩裡に終了したのである。

今春以來、アジアが「二つの世界」の焦點になるのではないかといつた徴候がいろいろな方面でみうけられていた。

アジア各地域の共産勢力が歩調をそろえて武力闘争の準備をはじめてきたのである。わが國においてもいずこともなく叫ばれてきた「戰争近し」という聲とともに、「平和を守ろう」といつたポスターが街頭に汎濫しはじめた。われわれの待望する自主獨立を一日も速かに達成しようという早期多數講和の主張に對して、全面講和、局外中立等の議論がわが國一部に次第に強く叫ばれるようになつた。去る二月十四日に調印された中ソ友好同盟及び相互援助條約がわが國を「侵略日本」と呼び「日本と侵略行爲について連合する國家」を目標としていたことは、ひとえに平和を欲するわれわれに異様な感じを與えた。また同條約第二條が中ソ兩國は「日本との平和條約をできるだけ早く結ぶために相互の合意の下に努力することを約束する」と謳つているのも、共産國家間の條約であるだけに日本をめぐるアジア情勢のただならぬことを思わせたのである。

六月二十五日未明、突如として北鮮共産軍は北緯三十八度線を怒濤の如く突破して侵略を開始した。「自由と平和を守る」と自ら唱える共産勢力がいまや明かにアジアの平和をやぶり、ひいてはわが國の自由をも奪わんとしてきた

のである。これはまことに解しがたいことのように思えるが、不思議でも何でもない。「二つの世界」という言葉が端的に表現しているように、「自由」についても、考え方に「二つの世界」があるからである。「平和」についても、考え方に「二つの世界」があるからである。

基本的人權の尊重を基盤とする民主主義的な世界は、地上のすべての國で國民の意思が自由に表明される體制が整えられるならば、世界の平和は必ず達成されると確信している。それは各國内における不合理は民主的な議會を通じる平和的方法で調整されるべく、國家間の對立は外交交渉や國際連合を通じて平和的に解決されることを理想とするものである。

これに反して、共産主義的な世界は、そうした民主主義的な考え方を全面的に否定する。階級闘爭の見地にたつ共産主義は全世界の共産化が實現するまでは平和はもたらされないと主張する。國際連合についても、とうてい世界の平和を維持するに役立たないと考えるだけでなく、それは世界の共産化を妨害するものとさえ解するのである。共産主義にとつては世界の共産化を進めるための行動は、現實にはそれによっていかに社會の秩序が亂され、あるいは戰

火がもたらされても、すべて「正義の行爲」であり「解放の事業」なのである。いわゆる「平和闘爭」とはこの謂である。政治的なデモヤスト、昨夏起つた如きもろもろの事件、北鮮軍の侵略など、すべてこの「平和闘爭」に屬するものであり共産主義世界にあつてはそれに賛成する自由のみが認められるにすぎない。

このようにして、共産主義世界の唱える「平和」がもたらされ「解放」が實行されるためには、民主主義世界の欲する平和は破壞され、自由は壓殺されなければならないのである。朝鮮の國民が家を燒かれ、飢に泣き、血にそまつて倒れている現實が、すなわち共産主義のいう「平和」であり、「解放」なのである。自由と平和の貴さを否定し、自己の主張を無理やりに他人に押付けんとする共産主義の暴力が身近に迫つている場合に、われわれがまん然、手を拱いて唯々傍觀しているとすれば、それは民主主義の自殺にほかならない。それについて思い出されるのは第二次大戰勃發前のミユンヘン協定のことである。事態の擴大を防止せんとする自由世界のあらゆる努力にもかゝわらず、協定の成立後半年を出でないでドイツのチエツコ併合が行わ

4 制限緩和に向けた対応（昭和24年5月～27年4月）

れ、ドイツ軍のポーランド進撃となつて第二次世界大戰の火蓋は切つて落されたのである。かくして自由の世界はミユンヘン協定から一つの敎訓を學びとつた。それは全體主義、共產主義的國家の野望に對しては絕對に意味をなさず、野望はその銳鋒の現われた最初の機會に斷固これを粉碎しなければならないということであつた。

二、立ち上つた國際連合

北鮮共產軍が韓國を攻擊したという報道を聞いて、われわれの胸を搏つたものは、日本の將來に對する不安と焦慮であつた。われわれの心から嫌惡する戰爭が、わが國と僅かに海峽を隔てるだけの朝鮮で不幸にも勃發したのである。もしこの戰鬪がさらに大規模なものとなる場合、憲法によつて軍備を放棄した日本人がどのような運命に陷るか、という心配はもはや單なる假定の問題ではなくなつた。われわれの關心が米國政府と國際連合の動きに向けられたのは當然である。昨年六月末に韓國から軍隊を撤收して後は少數の軍事顧問を殘留せしめていたにすぎない米國がいかなる措置にでるかは、日本自身の安全保障問題との關係においても等閑視できないところであつた。

果して米國は世界の平和と民主主義を守るために、武力に對しては武力をもつて立ち上つた。北鮮軍の攻擊に先だつと五日、ダレス米國務長官顧問が京城で言明した「人類の自由という偉大な目的に向つて十分に努力をつくすかぎり、韓國は決して孤立無援に陷ることはないであろう」との言葉が、現實の措置によつて裏づけられたのである。

米國ばかりではない。いままでわれわれの期待を充すに足りないとさえ思われていた國際連合も、民主主義世界の强力な支持のもとに、俄然實效的な措置に乘り出してきた。米國は直ちに韓國に對する武器援助の方針を決定すると共に急遽國連安保理事會の召集を要請した。この六月二十五日の緊急安全保障理事會は、北鮮の行動をもつて平和の破壞と斷定し、㈠戰鬪行爲を直ちに停止すること、㈡北鮮軍は三十八度線まで撤退することを連絡してあらゆる援助を與えかつ北鮮援助を差控えることを內容とする米國提出の決議案をソ連代表缺席のまま九對〇、棄權一（ユーゴ）で採擇した。さらに二十七日の同理事會は、國連

加盟國が北鮮軍の武力攻撃を擊退し、朝鮮における平和と安全が回復されるため必要な援助を韓國に與えるよう勸告することを內容とする米國提出の決議案を同じくソ連代表缺席のまま七對一(ユーゴ)、棄權二(エジプト、インド)で採擇した。

國際連合のこうした一連の強硬措置と並行して、トルーマン大統領は二十六日夜、米海空軍に出動を命じ、さらに翌二十七日には、二十五日の安全保障理事會の決議に則つて米海空軍に韓國軍援助を命じ、それと同時に「共產勢力がいまや地下運動に賴る段階を超え、侵略と戰爭に訴えた事情にかんがみ」第七艦隊に臺灣に對するいかなる攻擊をも阻止するよう命ずるとともに、在フイリツピン米軍の增强とフイリツピン政府に對する軍事援助の促進及び在インドシナ・フランス軍、バオダイ軍に對する軍事援助の促進と軍事使節團の派遣を聲明した。ついでトルーマン大統領は三十日には、二十七日の安全保障理事會の決議に則つて(イ)米空軍に北鮮の軍事目標攻擊を許可したこと、(ロ)海軍に全朝鮮沿岸の封鎖を命じたこと、及び(ハ)マックアーサー元帥に對して地上部隊の使用を許可したことを發表した。

このようにして米國政府は國際連合の決議にしたがつて急速な實力的援助を韓國に與えることになつたが、この措置が廣く民主主義世界の贊意と支持の上に立つものであることは、前記三十日の安全保障理事會の決議が國連加盟國五十九カ國のうち實に五十二カ國の多數によつて支持されていること、またそのうち十カ國が國連派遣軍に參加を申出たことによつても明らかである。すでにイギリス、カナダ、オーストラリア、ニュージーランド、トルコ、タイ、フイリツピン、ニカラグワは地上部隊の提供を約し、イギリス、フランス、オーストラリア、ニュージーランド、カナダ及びオランダは海軍部隊を派遣しているし、イギリス、オーストラリア、カナダ、ギリシヤ、ベルギーは空軍の協力を提供している。その他中國も陸兵派遣を申出で、デンマーク、ノルウェー、フイリツピン、チリなど多數の國が醫藥品その他の援助を申出ている。

さらに七月七日の安全保障理事會は(イ)朝鮮作戰軍の合同司令部設置を勸告すること、(ロ)國連旗の使用を許可することと、(ハ)米國に司令官任命を委任する決議を同じくソ連代表缺席のまゝ七對〇、棄權三(インド、ユーゴ、エジプト)で

4 制限緩和に向けた対応(昭和24年5月～27年4月)

採擇し、トルーマン大統領はマックアーサー元帥を國連軍最高司令官に任命した。かくて「闘う民主主義」の象徴として往時の十字軍にも匹敵すべき國連軍が誕生し、國連旗は高くマックアーサー司令部の屋上に、あるいは朝鮮前線の第一線でひるがえつている。

だが國際連合側のこうした努力に對してソ連がいかなる措置に出るかは非常に注目されたところであるが、リー國連事務總長が前記安全保障理事會の勸告を傳え、また米國政府が六月二十六日に朝鮮における戰闘の終止についてソ連政府が北鮮政權に影響力を及ぼすよう要請する覺書を送つたのに對して、ソ連政府は全面的にこれを拒否したのである。ソ連政府の主張は「安全保障理事會の朝鮮問題に關する決議は國連憲章の手續を無視して採擇されたものであるから法律的效果を有しない」とし、また朝鮮動亂の責は南鮮側にあるから米國政府の韓國援助に反對するというにあつた。

これを見ても明かなように、世界革命を目標とする共産主義世界と個人の自由を基盤とする民主主義世界との間には尋常の手段では到底話合いが成立せず、假に話合いが出來たとしても決して永續きはしないのである。戰後平和を望むが故に自らの軍事體制強化を極力差控えてきた米國政府が、擧國一致とも稱すべき國民各層の支持のもとにいまや現實的立場から軍事體制の確立に乘り出さざるをえなくなつたゆえんもまたここにある。

米國議會が多額に上る追加軍事豫算や對外軍事援助費を承認しまた米國政府が徵兵法の發動による徵兵の開始をはじめとする國防の強化に乘り出したこと、あるいは北大西洋條約參加國が眞劍に西歐軍事體制の確立を討議しはじめたことなどは、民主主義世界が朝鮮動亂を全世界にわたる民主主義體制に對する直接の脅威と判斷したことを如實に物語るものである。

三、動亂の見透しと思想戰

「二つの世界」の對立は、かくて北鮮軍の侵略を契機として、全世界にわたる實力的對決にまで進展しつつあるかの觀を呈してきた。動亂の地朝鮮を一衣帶水の彼方に控えたわれわれ日本國民として朝鮮の危機が米ソ兩國間の直接的武力闘爭にまで發展するかどうかについて多大の心配を抱くことはけだしやむをえないところである。

もちろん、われわれとしてはかかる事態の發生は絶對に望むところではない。しかし民主主義の旗のもとに結集する國際連合軍とコミンフォルムの旗のもとに結集する國際革命軍との鬪爭は、今後ますます激化してゆくにちがいない。國際連合側は自ら欲しないままに實力をもって立ち上ることを餘儀なくされたのであるから、自ら進んで戰局の擴大を圖ることのないのはいうまでもない。一方、コミンフォルム側としても、一度立ち上れば絶對的な力量を示す米國の軍事力と民主主義世界の不退轉の決意を前にして無謀な戰局擴大は仲々決心がつかぬにちがいない。ここにわれわれが全世界を覆う暗雲のもとにあっても、なおかつ事態の不擴大に一縷の期待をかけうるゆえんがある。

ところで上述のように侵略阻止のため毅然として立ち上った國際連合は、もはや姑息な手段で共產主義世界との一時的、局地的妥協を圖ろうと欲するものではないようである。すなわち國際連合は決して朝鮮問題のみの解決に焦慮しているわけではなくて、世界の他の地域に對する共產主義のこれ以上の侵略を強力に阻止しつゝ世界の平和を確保する基盤を作り上げようとしているのである。そのために

は、共產主義世界の軍事體制に對抗するに足る強力な軍事體制と世論の決然たる支持を背景とすることが絶對に必要である。目下國際連合はこうした見地から萬全の準備をととのえつゝ、その一環としての朝鮮問題の解決を圖ろうとしているのである。

さてこのような「二つの世界」の實力的對決に際してわれわれの最も注意すべきは思想戰である。民主主義世界の武器たる原爆戰は事態が最惡の段階に立ち至るまでは行われないであろうが、共產主義世界の武器たる思想戰はすでに最も重要な武器として世界の津々浦々にまで展開されている。共產主義は民主主義世界の「寬大」さにつけこんで自らに不利な影響を及ぼすべき全面的な武力對決を巧みに囘避しつゝ、戰爭の切迫感をあおりたてることによって、民主主義世界の團結と決意を混亂させようと企圖している。そのための最も重要な武器がこの思想戰なのである。朝鮮動亂は一見したところ、朝鮮半島の局地的問題であるかのように思えるが、實はそうではない。思想戰との關連において、民主主義世界に住むわれわれすべてがすでに戰場にあり、その中でも共產主義は、日本に特別

4　制限緩和に向けた対応(昭和24年5月～27年4月)

の關心をもっているのであるから、われわれ日本人は完全に朝鮮動亂の渦中に立っているといっても過言ではない。こうした状況はまことに不幸なことであるが、否定しえない現實である。しかもわれわれは平和を欲するのであるから、もし許されるならば、あくまで紛爭の局外に立ちたいと願うのも無理からぬところである。しかしながら民主主義と共産主義というとうてい相容れない二つの勢力が全世界にわたって拮抗している情勢のもとでは、いかにわれわれが「不介入」や「中立」を唱えてもそれはとうてい出來ない相談である。共産主義は全世界にわたる民主主義の絕滅を終極の目標としているから、共産主義に全面的に屈伏しない限り、その國はすべて共産主義の「敵」であり、共産主義國の辭典には「中立」や「不介入」などという言葉はありえないのである。思想戰の見地からみて、すでに戰場にあるともいうべきわれわれがあいまいな態度をとることは、實戰における敵前逃亡と同じ結果をもたらし、われわれの希望にもかかわらずかえって自由と平和を破壞せんとする勢力に利益を提供することゝなり、眞の意味における自主獨立の回復にはなんら役立たないのである。

共産主義の行う思想戰は、民主主義の寬容とわれわれの素朴な平和愛に乘じて侵略の步を進めてくるのである。われわれは何人も平和を望み戰爭を欲するものではないから、「反戰平和」という合言葉は全く魅惑的である。しかし「二つの世界」の間には共通の「平和」もなければ、一致した人類愛も存在しないのであるから、單なる合言葉を唱えるだけでは、われわれの欲する眞の平和はもたらされないのである。それのみでない。共産主義の侵略を前にして、平和が現實にかく亂されている原因がどこにあるかを見定めないで、徒らに共産主義世界の「反戰平和運動」に同調することは、民主主義を崩壞させるに役立つだけである。われわれが眞に平和の回復をのぞむならば、まず平和かく亂の原因そのものを明確に認識する要がある。更にこうした思想戰と關連して各種の破壞工作が行われてくる。國際連合軍が平和を回復するために多大の犧牲を拂っているにもかかわらず、背後から國際連合軍の活動を麻痺させようとする工作が全世界にわたって行われている。とくに國際連合軍の重要な據點であるわが國において、一部の共産主義者によってこうした破壞工作が現に行われ

つゝあるばかりでなく、今後益々計画化されてゆく危険があるのである。これらの破壊工作を粉砕することは決して警察ばかりに任しておいてよいことではない。われわれ一人一人がこれを阻止してわが國で、そして全世界で守られることを欲するならば國際連合の意圖するところを正確に認識することそれに協力することが必要であるばかりか、それこそ朝鮮動亂を契機として展開されつゝある不幸な事態を速かに解消せしめる唯一の途であることを知らなければならぬ。

四、むすび

從來わが國民の一部の間に全面講和論が眞面目に取上げられた原因の一つは、多數講和成立後における日本の安全に關し、漠然たる不安があつたからである。この國民の不安を巧みに利用して殊更に戰爭の恐怖を宣傳したのが共産黨の謀略工作であり、局外中立、戰爭不介入、軍事基地化反對等の議論はその手段であつたのである。しかしながら今回の朝鮮動亂に際して逸早く取られた國際連合軍の活動と臺灣防衞に關するトルーマン大統領の命令とは、さきに發表された「アメリカはアリユーシヤンから日本、琉球、

フイリッピンにわたる防衞線について直接その防衞の任に當る」というアチソン長官の聲明の經緯にも鑑み、わが國の安全保障に對し重要な示唆を與えるものである。われわれが過去の過ちを清算し民主主義に徹底するならば、もし日本に對し朝鮮における如き不挑發の侵略が行われた場合、民主主義國は共同してわれわれに救援の手を差しのべてくれるであろう。

朝鮮の動亂は「二つの世界」が一致して希望するわが國の在り方もなければ、兩者が共同でわが國の安全を保障してくれる基盤もないことをはっきりと教えてくれたのである。日本が平和的な民主主義國家としてとどまるかぎりは、いかに媚態を呈しても、共産主義世界の滿足をかちとることはできない。したがつて、民主主義を放棄して、全體主義、共產主義に屈從するまでは、われわれはたえず「戰爭の脅威」にさらされる運命にある。しかしてわれわれを共產主義の暴力から防ぐものは民主主義國の團結の力以外にはないのである。憲法で交戰權を放棄したわが國が民主主義國の團結に協力しその強化を助けるのは、すなわち自らを衞るゆえんであると考うべきである。

4　制限緩和に向けた対応（昭和24年5月～27年4月）

かくてわれわれの進むべき道は二つに一つしかない。すなわちわが國における民主主義の達成をあきらめて、共産主義世界に屈服するか、あるいはできるかぎりの協力を國際連合に致すことによつて、その安全保障のもとに平和的な民主日本を建設するか、このいずれかである。朝鮮における民主主義のための戰いはとりもなおさず日本の民主主義を守る戰いである。朝鮮の自主と獨立を守るために闘つている國際連合軍に許されるかぎりの協力を行わずしてどうして日本の安全を守ることができようか。第三次世界大戰が起つたならば、日本ばかりではなく、世界の文明が破滅するのである。われわれの最も心すべきことは世界の大動亂が再び起らないようにすることである。それには暴力による世界革命を目的とする全体主義、共産主義國をして戰爭が商賣にならぬことを知らせる外に途はない。

七月二十一日のロンドン・タイムス紙も「努力と犠牲を回避して、自らの義務を忘れ、現實の基礎のない平和への夢に眠るものは、より大きな災害を自ら招かんとするものに外ならない。これはわれわれが幾度も經驗した道程であり、全面的な災害、無鐵砲な敵との死闘に再びわれわれを

導く道でしかない」と論じている。今日のように相對立する二つの世界の間に處して兩方より好かれようというが如きは余りにも虫のよい注文である。このようなあいまいな態度は、それがいかに眞面目なものであつても、結局において共産主義の乘ずるところとなり、民主主義の挽歌を奏する結果になるにすぎないことをわれわれは篤と銘記すべきである。

〜〜〜〜〜〜〜〜〜〜〜〜〜〜〜〜〜

275　昭和25年8月14日　連合国最高司令官総司令部発表

朝鮮での作戦の費用支払いに関する総司令部発表（和訳文）

朝鮮作戦の費用支拂いに關する總司令部渉外局特別發表　昭和二十五年八月十四日

朝鮮事變發生直後にマックアーサー元帥が確立した政策の下では、朝鮮における作戰のために必要となった費用は、それがたとい日本本土内で必要とされるものであつても、これをまかなうために占領軍維持費として予算に計上されている日本政府資金は、全然流用されていない。

その政策の一つの結果として、在鮮國連軍が必要とする補給物資と資材調達のために日本ですでに三千萬ドル以上の經費が支出された。朝鮮作戰遂行のために必要となった日本における不動産の賃借料と建設費用は、一切米國が負擔することになろう。

朝鮮作戰の結果、日本における軍用施設への出入道路は輸送の増大によって損傷がひどくなったので、その維持については、日本の道路建設五ヵ年計画から除外されて關係軍事施設がこれを維持することになろう。

要するに結論としていえることは、米國は北鮮共産軍の行動によって、間接的にもせよ、日本における占領軍の第一の使命である日本經済の復興が阻害されるようなことは許さない決意である。

編注　本文書は、昭和二十六年二月、外務省政務局特別資料課作成「日本管理資料（三）」より抜粋。

昭和25年8月15日　連合国最高司令官総司令部発表

日本船舶の米國港出入許可に關する總司令部発表（和訳文）

日本船舶の米港出入許可方に關する總司令部渉外局特別発表

昭和二十五年八月十五日

總司令部民間運輸局長ミラー大佐は本日、次のように聲明した。

米國政府はすべての日本船舶に對し、米國の港に出入する許可を與えた。

米國の港に向けて輸送され、また米國の港から積み出される貨物、及びこの輸送に従事する日本船舶は、このような貿易に對して通常課せられている規則及び規定に従うこととなろう。

初めのうちは、米國の港を訪れるのはバルキー・カーゴーの輸送に當る日本船舶と思われ、そして現在のところ定期的な運航は考えられていない。

なお、ミラー大佐は、日本船舶はすでに極東、中東及び南米諸國との貿易に従事していることを指摘した。

4 制限緩和に向けた対応（昭和24年5月〜27年4月）

277 日本貿易商社の支店または代表者の海外設置に関する指令

昭和25年8月25日 連合国最高司令官総司令部経済科学局 より 通商産業省宛

編注　本文書は、昭和二十六年二月、外務省政務局特別資料課作成「日本管理資料㈢」より抜粋。

GENERAL HEADQUARTERS
SUPREME COMMANDER FOR THE ALLIED POWERS
Economic and Scientific Section
APO 500

091/31 (23 Aug 50) ESS/FTC 25 August 1950
MEMORANDUM FOR: Ministry of International Trade and Industry
ATTENTION: Mr. R. Takeuchi, International Trade Administrator
SUBJECT: Establishment of Japanese Trading Firms' Branch Offices or Representatives Abroad

1. Reference is memorandum from the Ministry of International Trade and Industry, ITII No. 473-VII-B-227, 11 August, 1950, subject: Establishment of Japanese Commercial Firms' Branch Offices or Representatives in United States.

2. The Supreme Commander for the Allied Powers interposes no objection to the following announcements by the Ministry of International Trade and Industry:

　　a. The establishment abroad of branch offices or representatives of Japanese trading firms is authorized in those countries whose governments permit.

　　b. In accordance with existing procedures, representatives of Japanese trading firms may apply to the diplomatic missions in Japan which are accredited to the Supreme Commander for the Allied Powers to be advised whether or not the establishment of such branch offices or representatives is acceptable, and if so, to be informed of the legal requirements and procedures that must be complied with to obtain the appropriate visas.

　　c. All the necessary foreign exchange expenditures, including all business and personal expenses, must be financed by

835

authorized foreign exchange funds.

d. Those applicants who desire visas for the United States of America may apply to the Consular Offices of the Office of the United States Political Adviser for Japan located in Tokyo, Yokohama, Kobe, Nagoya, Fukuoka and Sapporo.

FOR THE CHIEF, ECONOMIC AND SCIENTIFIC SECTION:

R. W. HALE
Chief, Foreign Trade and Commerce Division

278

昭和25年9月15日
連合国最高司令官総司令部より
日本政府宛

出入国管理業務の強化に関する指令

付記　右和訳文

GENERAL HEADQUARTERS
SUPREME COMMANDER FOR THE ALLIED POWERS
APO 500

15 September 1950

AG 014.39 (15 Sep 50) GA

SCAPIN 2122
MEMORANDUM FOR: Japanese Government
SUBJECT: Immigration

1. References:

a. Memorandum for the Japanese Government, AG 000.5 (21 May 49) GB/CIS/PSD, SCAPIN 2055, subject: Suppression of Illegal Entry into Japan, 3 November 1949.

b. Memorandum for the Japanese Government, AG 014.331 (3 Feb 50) GA, SCAPIN 2032, subject: Immigration Service, 20 February 1950.

c. Memorandum for the Japanese Government, AG 720.4 (3 Feb 50) GA, SCAPIN 2083, subject: Customs, Immigration and Quarantine Operations, 20 February 1950.

d. Letter from the Supreme Commander for the Allied Powers, to Prime Minister Yoshida, 8 July 1950. (Inclosure 1)

2. The Supreme Commander for the Allied Powers in letter referenced in paragraph 1d called attention to certain weaknesses in governmental structure with respect to the control of unlawful immigration activities and enumerated certain measures to be

4 制限緩和に向けた対応（昭和24年5月〜27年4月）

taken to correct these weaknesses. In addition to the measures specifically enumerated in referenced letter, the Japanese Government is hereby directed to:

a. Apprehend and detain individuals entering or remaining in Japan in violation of the regulations of the Supreme Commander for the Allied Powers and Japanese laws pertaining to entry of individuals into Japan.

b. Establish for retention of individuals apprehended for unlawful immigration necessary processing centers which are in no way a part of or affiliated with penal corrective institutions or national or local police organizations.

c. Establish procedures in these processing centers to:

(1) Insure compliance with customs and quarantine regulations of the Supreme Commander for the Allied Powers and the Japanese Government.

(2) Take into protective custody and deliver receipt for property in the possession of persons detained for unlawful immigration except that property necessary for their personal use in processing centers. In this connection all arms, military material, military equipment, military supplies, aircraft and vessels will be immediately taken into custody and reported to the nearest military authority.

(3) Obtain complete information concerning the identity of the individual and the circumstances of his entry. This information will be forwarded immediately to the Supreme Commander for the Allied Powers.

d. Report to the Supreme Commander for the Allied Powers for appropriate negotiation with interested governments those illegal entrants who are to be deported. Upon receipt of information from the Supreme Commander for the Allied Powers that clearances to permit the travel of the deportee have been obtained, the Japanese Government will take the necessary measures including arrangements for transportation to effect immediately the deportation of such persons.

3. The Japanese Government is further directed to estab-

lish organizations to provide the policy and procedural direction to and effect positive coordination of immigration matters including those enumerated in references listed in paragraphs 1a, b, and c, as well as those enumerated herein.

4. Since expeditious implementation of this directive is mandatory, the Japanese Government will within 15 days after receipt of this SCAPIN submit to the Supreme Commander for the Allied Powers for concurrence drafts of plans and directives necessary to its implementation.

5. The draft plans and directives referred to in paragraph 4 above should, if necessary to the implementation of the plans, include recommendations for readjustment of personnel ceilings and reallocation of budgeted funds.

6. Direct communications between the Japanese Government agencies concerned and appropriate occupation force agencies are hereby authorized to implement this memorandum.

FOR THE SUPREME COMMANDER:

K. B. BUSH,
Brigadier General, USA,
Adjutant General.

1 Incl
Cy Ltr to PM Yoshida

編　注　本文書の別添は見当たらない。

（付　記）

連合國最高司令官總司令部
APO五〇〇

昭和二十五年九月十五日

SCAPIN二一二二
AG〇一四・三九（二十五年九月十五日）GA

覺書あて先　日本政府

件　名　出入國

1　參照

い、日本政府あて覺書、AG〇〇〇・五（二十四年五月二十一日）GB／CIS／PSD、SCAPIN一〇五五、昭和二十四年十一月三日付、件名、「日本への

4　制限緩和に向けた対応（昭和24年5月〜27年4月）

「不法入国の抑制」

ろ、日本政府あて覚書、AG〇一四・三三二一（二十五年二月三日）GA、SCAPIN二〇八一一、昭和二十五年二月二十日付、件名、「出入國管理事務」

は、日本政府あて覚書、AG七二〇・四（二十五年二月三日）GA、SCAPIN二〇八三、昭和二十五年二月二十日付、件名、「税關、出入國及び檢疫事務」

に、昭和二十五年七月八日付、連合國最高司令官の吉田首相あて書簡（同封書類一）

2　連合國最高司令官は前記第一項にの書簡において不法出入國行爲の取締に關し、政府機構の弱點について注意を喚起し、この弱點を矯正するためにとるべき手段を列擧した。右の書簡に特に列擧された手段に加え、ここに日本政府に左記事項を指令する。

い、個人の日本入國に關する連合國最高司令官の取締規定及び日本の法律に違反して日本に入國し又は居留した者を逮捕し拘留すること。

ろ、不法入國により逮捕された者を抑留するため矯正保護組織又は國家警察ないし自治警察組織にまったく屬さず又はなんら關係のない所要の入國收容所を設置すること。

は、この入國收容所においては、次の事項を處理すること。

(1) 連合國最高司令官及び日本政府の關税及び檢疫に關する取締規則に確實に從わせること。

(2) 不法入國により拘留された者の所有する所持品は入國收容所において私用に供する所有物品を除き保護的に保管し、保管證を交付すること。この點に關しあらゆる兵器、軍事物件、軍事資材、兵站施設、飛行機及び船舶は直ちに保管し、もよりの軍機關に報告すること。

(3) 入國者の身元と入國の状況に關し、完全な情報を取得すること。右情報は、直ちに連合國最高司令官に提供すること。

に、連合國最高司令官が關係國政府に適切に交渉するため、送還される不法入國者を同司令官に報告すること。送還者の旅行を許可する出國許可が出された旨連合國最高司令官から情報を受領した場合、日本政府は直ちにこれらの者の送還を行うため輸送手配を含む所要の

3 右のほか、日本政府に對し、この覺書に列擧された事項とともに前記第一項い、ろ、はに參照として列擧された事項を含む出入國事務にかかる政策をたて、手續上の管理を行い、又積極的調整を行う機構を設置することを指令する。

4 この指令を速やかに實施することは至上命令であるから、日本政府はこの指令受領後十五日以内に連合國最高司令官に對し、この指令實施上必要な計畫及び指令の草案を提出し、その同意を得なければならない。

5 前記第四項に言及した計畫及び指令の草案は、右計畫實施上必要ならば定員と予算の再調整に對する勸告を含むべきである。

6 この覺書を實施するため、日本政府關係機關は占領軍當該官憲と直接連絡することができる。

　　　　　最高司令官に代って
　　　　　米國陸軍代將
　　　　　高級副官
　　　　　ケー・ビー・ブッシュ

編注　本文書は、昭和二十六年二月、外務省政務局特別資料課作成「日本管理資料（三）」より抜粋。

〰〰〰〰〰〰〰〰〰〰

昭和25年10月18日　連合国最高司令官総司令部より日本政府宛

279 **連合国人に対する裁判管轄権に関する指令**

GENERAL HEADQUARTERS
SUPREME COMMANDER FOR THE ALLIED POWERS
APO 500

18 October 1950

AG 015 (6 Oct 50) LS-L
SCAPIN 2127

MEMORANDUM FOR: JAPANESE GOVERNMENT
SUBJECT: Exercise of Civil and Criminal Jurisdiction

1. Criminal Jurisdiction over Persons in Japan. Japanese courts will henceforth exercise criminal jurisdiction over all nationals of members of the United Nations, (hereinafter referred to as United Nations nationals), in Japan except for the following,

4 制限緩和に向けた対応(昭和24年5月～27年4月)

designated as occupation personnel:

a. Members of the armed forces of any member of the United Nations;

b. United Nations nationals officially attached to or accompanying and in the service of the occupation forces;

c. United Nations nationals on official business in Japan;

d. Members of the immediate families and dependents accompanying the above.

2. Arrest. a. All persons in Japan not within the category of occupation personnel as designated in paragraph 1 (hereinafter referred to as nonoccupation personnel) are subject to arrest by the Japanese law-enforcement authorities.

b. Occupation personnel shall be subject to arrest by the Japanese law-enforcement authorities only if both of the following circumstances exist at the same time:

(1) Where occupation police are not physically present to perform the arrest, and,

(2) Where the offense or threatened offense involves bodily harm or serious damage to property.

c. Occupation personnel arrested by the Japanese police under the circumstances set forth in paragraph 2 b. shall be turned over immediately to the nearest occupation authorities.

3. Pre-Trial Confinement. a. When any United Nations national is confined to prison, is awaiting trial, or is otherwise detained in custody by Japanese authorities, the Japanese Government will:

(1) Forward to the Supreme Commander for the Allied Powers immediately a brief statement of the circumstances involved for transmission to the Head of the Mission charged with the protection of the interests of said national;

(2) Give written advice to the United Nations national concerned, in a language he understands, of his right to inform the Mission charged with the protection of his interests of the circumstances of his detention. Said United Na-

841

tions national will be given reasonable facilities to communicate with the interested Mission. Any such communication will be forwarded without delay;

(3) Upon due presentation of credentials, permit a representative of the Mission charged with the protection of the said United Nations national's interest, to visit without delay, to confer privately with, and to arrange legal representation for, the United Nations national concerned.

b. Nothing contained in this paragraph shall be construed to delay the orderly progress of the proceedings against the person detained, nor shall noncompliance therewith be deemed to affect the jurisdiction of the court.

4. Post-Trial Confinement. a. Where a United Nations national has been convicted by a Japanese court and is serving a sentence of imprisonment, a representative of the Mission charged with the protection of his interests, upon due presentation of credentials, will be permitted to visit said United Nations national in prison, upon notice, that need not exceed twenty-four hours, to the official in charge of the institution having custody of such national. There will be no limit to the number of such visits within reasonable hours and said representative will be allowed to converse privately with the United Nations national concerned.

b. Subject to the appropriate prison or institutional regulations, said representative may transmit written communications between the prisoner and other persons

c. Any person heretofore or hereinafter sentenced to imprisonment by a military occupation court will be received for confinement by the Japanese authorities upon direction of the occupation court appointing authority exercising jurisdiction over the prisoner. Except on expiration of sentence, no prisoner will be released without approval of the said occupation authority.

5. Sentences. a. Any sentence imposed by a Japanese court on a United Nations national will be reported immediately to this headquarters for transmission to the Head of the Mission concerned. Said report will include a brief statement of the circumstances involved.

842

4　制限緩和に向けた対応（昭和24年5月〜27年4月）

b. A sentence to death or life imprisonment imposed on a United Nations national by a Japanese court shall not be carried into execution until the same shall have been confirmed by the Supreme Commander for the Allied Powers. A complete and final record of such case shall be submitted to this headquarters for review and appropriate action.

6. <u>Exclusive Occupation Court Offenses</u>.　a. It shall be unlawful for any person in Japan to:

(1) Commit an act prejudicial to the security of the occupation forces or occupation personnel;

(2) Kill or assault occupation personnel;

(3) Interfere with or hinder the arrest of any person sought, or assist in, or further the escape of any person detained by the occupation forces, or by others pursuant to the direction of the Supreme Commander for the Allied Powers, or his authorized subordinates;

(4) Interfere with, refuse information required by, make any false or misleading statement orally or in writing to, or defraud in any manner, any of the occupation personnel in a matter of official concern;

(5) Commit an act in behalf or in support of any organization dissolved or declared illegal by the Supreme Commander for the Allied Powers, or dissolved or declared illegal at the order of the Supreme Commander for the Allied Powers;

(6) Conspire to commit any of the foregoing offenses or commit any act which aids or abets the commission of such offenses.

b. Japanese courts will exercise no criminal jurisdiction over the offenses enumerated in paragraph 6 a.

c. It shall be unlawful for any person in Japan to commit any act prejudicial to the objectives of the occupation. Japanese courts will continue to exercise criminal jurisdiction over such acts in so far as they constitute violations of Japanese law.

7. <u>Jurisdiction over Vessels</u>.　Japanese courts and government agencies may exercise jurisdiction over vessels within its

territorial waters if, in the case in which the vessel is involved, said courts and agencies would be authorized to exercise jurisdiction over both the owner and the charterer or other authorized user or possessor of the vessel, and, also, would be authorized to exercise jurisdiction over the particular criminal or civil proceeding involving the vessel.

8. <u>Civil Jurisdiction</u>. Japanese courts will exercise no civil jurisdiction of any sort with respect to any case in which any of the parties is a person within the category designated as occupation personnel in paragraph 1.

9. <u>Review of Decisions</u>. All decisions of the Japanese courts with respect to United Nations nationals, may be reviewed by the Supreme Commander for the Allied Powers or his designated representatives, who may take such further action as is considered necessary in respect thereto.

10. <u>Protection of United Nationals' Rights</u>. The Supreme Commander for the Allied Powers, or his designated representatives, will take such steps as are deemed necessary to insure that the rights of the United Nations nationals subject to Japanese jurisdiction are protected.

11. <u>Military Occupation Courts</u>. a. Military occupation courts may assume criminal jurisdiction, as authorized by the Supreme Commander for the Allied Powers, over any or all nonoccupation personnel in Japan for any and all offenses committed by them.

b. Military occupation courts are authorized to impose sentences which may include death, imprisonment, or revocation of privileges or licenses.

c. Any case pending in a military occupation court, which has been referred for trial, will be concluded by said court in accordance with the rules and regulations in effect at the time such case was first referred.

12. <u>Expedite Trials</u>. The Japanese Government is directed to take immediate action to expedite the trial of criminal and civil cases.

13. <u>Definition</u>. The term "United Nations national" as used herein includes, wherever applicable, organizations and corporations of present or future members of the United Nations as

844

4 制限緩和に向けた対応(昭和24年5月～27年4月)

well as natural persons.

14. <u>Dissemination</u>. The Japanese people and all other persons concerned in Japan will be informed of this directive.

15. <u>Prior Actions</u>. Nothing contained herein shall be construed to invalidate or otherwise affect any action, pending or concluded, taken pursuant to any law, directive, order, or regulation hereby superseded.

16. <u>Liaison</u>. Direct communication between Legal Section, General Headquarters, Supreme Commander for the Allied Powers, and Japanese Government agencies concerned, is authorized on matters within the scope of this memorandum.

17. <u>Supersession</u>. a. This memorandum shall supersede the following:

 (1) SCAPIN 756, 19 Feb 46, subject: Exercise of Criminal Jurisdiction;

 (2) SCAPIN 777, 26 Feb 46, subject: Exercise of Civil Jurisdiction;

 (3) SCAPIN 853, 25 Mar 46, subject: Exercise of Criminal Jurisdiction;

 (4) SCAPIN 1218, 19 Sep 46, subject: Amendment of Memorandums on Civil and Criminal Jurisdiction;

 (5) SCAPIN 1740, 27 Jun 47, subject: Amendment to Exercise of Criminal Jurisdiction, paragraph 1;

 (6) SCAPIN 1758, 5 Aug 47, subject: Exercise of Jurisdiction over Vessels;

 (7) SCAPIN 1921, 17 Jul 48, subject: Exercise of Criminal Jurisdiction;

 (8) SCAPIN 1937, 9 Oct 48, subject: Amendment to Exercise of Criminal Jurisdiction;

 (9) SCAPIN 1941, 9 Nov 48, subject: Exercise of Criminal Jurisdiction.

b. Any provision of law or regulation in conflict with the contents of this memorandum is hereby superseded, or shall be deemed amended to conform hereto.

18. <u>Effective Date</u>. This memorandum is effective 1 November 1950.

280 輸出銀行の設立許可に関するドッジ顧問の覚書（和訳文）

昭和25年11月9日

FOR THE SUPREME COMMANDER:

K. B. BUSH
Brigadier General, USA
Adjutant General

〜〜〜〜〜〜〜〜〜〜

輸出銀行の設立許可方に關するドッヂ氏のメモ

昭和二十五年十一月九日

日本の將來、その進步及び生活水準における究極的改善は、繼續的な輸出の積極的發展に依存するところすこぶる大なるものがある。

このような輸出は消費財及び半消費財だけでなく、他國の生産上の必要を充たすに役立つ設備及び重量機械類によって構成されるであろう。設備及び重量機械類を吸收するような可能性が漸次展開することは、日本の基本的な利害と合致する。

この種輸出品の少からざる部分の生産及び引渡は、他の大部分の輸出品に對して必要とされるよりも長い時日を必要とする。それ故に、輸出向資本財の生産者に對して、必要な場合には長期の圓資金の貸付できるような機構をつくることが望ましい。このような貸付金が巨額になるのが適當でないものがある。

この問題の解決を助けるために、總司令部は輸出銀行の設立に同意した。昭和二十五年度補正予算中には右財源のため二十五億圓の政府出資が計上されているが、これと同額の出資が米國の對日援助見返資金の中から行われる。このようにして、同銀行のために五十億圓の當初資本金が設けられる。

昭和二十六年度予算には同銀行の追加資本金として五十億圓の政府出資が行われ、これと相應じて見返資金より同額の出資が行われる計画である。翌年度末には、同銀行の總資本金は百五十億圓となる。

同銀行は、その貸付業務を擴張するための資金を民間の市場に輸出の發展を遂げうる可能性は大いにある。そのよ

4 制限緩和に向けた対応（昭和24年5月～27年4月）

金融機關又は日本銀行に仰がない。その資金は、それが同銀行の目的のために利用しうるものである限り、政府出資及び見返資金より供給されるものである。

同銀行が實際に設立され業務を開始するに先き立ち、その經營と業務及び貸付を行いうる場合の制限及び條件に關する各種詳細事項を決定し、同意を得なければならぬ。

しかしながら、右最後的決定をなすに當っては左の諸原則の支配を受けるものであるとの取極めが行われた。

1 輸出銀行は能う限り簡單な構成、最少限度の營業組織をもって能う限り直接の政府統制よりは能う限り獨立して設立されること。すなわち、獨立の金融機關として業務を行うことである。

2 同銀行の業務は、同銀行が據ってもって設立される法律により特別な制限を受ける。

3 同銀行に關する國會の憲法上の責任は、大藏大臣を通じて遂行され、行政的經費の豫算は、大藏大臣及び國會に對し承認を得るため毎年同銀行より提出される。

4 同銀行は、數ヵ年の期間内、内閣の承認を經て總理大臣によって任命された卓越した個人首腦者を總裁と

して仰ぐ。

5 同銀行の取締役はその數を五名とし、同銀行の總裁と、總裁によって選定され任命された他の同銀行の責任及び經驗ある個人四名を包含する。總裁及び取締役は、職員を雇傭し、指揮及び監督する。

6 同銀行は、日本の輸出業者に對し短期貸付を行う上において日本の商業銀行と競爭することなく、適當な現行利率で割引又は協調融資の方法によって日本の輸出業者に對する必要な長期貸付を取扱う。

7 同銀行の主要な職能及び第一の責務は、日本における輸出向資本財の生産及びその輸出の資金調達のため必要な長期貸付を許可することにある。しかしながらもしも充分な資金が利用し得られ、かつ必要と思われる場合には、一定金額の同銀行資金を外國から輸出する取引が日本側及び輸入者側の外國爲替制限に抵觸しないことと、確實かつ信用し得べき契約であることが必要とされる。

8　同銀行は、その貸付業務擴張のための資金を得るため日本銀行及び、民間金融機關または民間資本市場と交渉を持つものではない。

編　注　本文書は、昭和二十六年二月、外務省政務局特別資料課作成「日本管理資料㈢」より抜粋。

~~~~~~~~~~

281

マッカーサー司令官の年頭メッセージ

昭和26年1月1日　連合国最高司令官総司令部発表

付　記　右和訳文

General of the Army Douglas MacArthur's

New Year Message

January 1, 1951

TO THE PEOPLE OF JAPAN:

As the dawn of another year breaks upon New Japan, every Japanese citizen may review the past with satisfaction at progress achieved, and look forward with added self-assurance to the difficult tests which lie ahead. For this land in the past year has witnessed advances in every field of human and social endeavor and the Japanese citizen has undoubtedly emerged with added individual liberty and higher personal dignity. From this period of trial has, indeed, come a measure of the moral stature of the Japanese nation and people who have met the challenge of a flaming Asia with calm deliberation, unruffled composure and quiet determination.

Politically, economically and socially Japan has continued to make uninterrupted and significant progress toward the goal of national stability. Representative democracy in its added maturity now stands as guardian over the rights and liberties of the people, and impressive strides have been made in the development of autonomous responsibility. Under the impetus which alone springs from the pursuit of free private competitive enterprise, production in agriculture and industry has achieved new post-war highs and Japan has again been able successfully to operate under a government fiscal policy centering on a truly balanced budget, curtailment of subsidies, and sound credit practices. For the first time since the war's end the index of industrial production exceeded the 1932-36 base level by an appreciable margin. In foreign trade, im-

4　制限緩和に向けた対応(昭和24年5月〜27年4月)

pressive and encouraging gains also were made, the volume of exports exceeding by about 50 percent the volume achieved during the previous year, with the gap between imports and exports being further narrowed to a very heartening degree. Socially, progress has been no less notable. Despite increased international tensions, this land has been an oasis of tranquility and progress. It has fully merited the respect and faith of men of goodwill everywhere and proved its right to equal partnership in the family of free nations of the earth.

Your constitution renounces war as an instrument of national policy. This concept represents one of the highest, if not the highest ideal the modern world has ever known and which all men must in due course embrace if civilization is to be preserved. This self-imposed limitation has meticulously guided your thought and action on the problem of national security, even despite the menace of gathering storms. If, however, international lawlessness continues to threaten the peace and to exercise dominion over the lives of men, it is inherent that this ideal must give way to the overweening law of self-preservation and it will become your duty within the principles of the United Nations in concert with others who cherish freedom to mount force to repel force. It is my fervent hope that such an eventuality will never come to pass, but should it, Japan's security would be the deep concern of all the other free nations of the Pacific area.

I sincerely trust that this year will bring to New Japan the blessings of complete political freedom through a treaty effectively erasing the remaining scars of war, and that thereafter, a Japanese nation firmly rooted in immutable concepts of political morality, economic freedom and social justice evolved from a blend of ideas and ideals of the west and your own hallowed traditions and time-honored and universally respected culture, may be counted upon to exercise a profound influence upon the course of destiny in Asia.

DOUGLAS MacARTHUR

編注　本文書は、昭和二十六年二月、外務省特別資料課作成「日本占領及び管理重要文書集」第二巻増補より抜粋。

（付　記）

マックアーサー元帥の年頭聲明に關する
總司令部渉外局發表

昭和二十六年一月一日

日本國民諸君

新しい日本に新年の夜明けを迎えるに當り、日本國民の一人一人は過去における進歩のあとを滿足感をもって振りかえり、前途に横たわる困難な試錬を新たな自信の念をもって待ち迎えるであろう。この國においては過去一年間に人道的、社會的努力のあらゆる分野において進歩がみられ、さらに日本國民は疑いもなく從來に増して個人的自由と高度の個人的尊嚴とをもつにいたった。この試錬期を經た結果、日本の國家および國民は、戰火に燃えるアジアのちょう戰にたいし冷靜なる熟慮、物に動じない落着きと沈着な決意とをもって對處することができるほど、確固たる精神をきずき上げたのである。

日本は政治的に、經濟的に、また社會的に、國家の安定という目標に向ってひたすら目ざましい進歩を續けてきた。代議制民主主義は次第に成熟の度を加え、現在では國民の權利と自由に對する守護者として嚴存し、自治の責任を高めてゆく點においても目ざましい進歩が續けられてきた。自由な民間企業が互いに競争を續けていくことによっての
み生ずる刺戟を受けて、日本の農業および工業の生産は戰後最高の水準に達し、また日本は眞の均衡予算、補助金の削減および健全な金融操作などに重點を置く政府の財政政策により、ふたたび以前のようにうまく運營されるようになっている。昨年は工業生産指數も戰後はじめてかなりの差をもって一九三二─三六年度の水準を上囘った。また外國貿易も目ざましく且つ人の心を明るくするような進展を示し、輸出量は一昨年を五〇パーセント方上囘り、輸入の開きは一段と縮まって將來に明るい見通しがもてるようになった。社會的な分野における進歩も同樣に著しかった。

國際關係の緊張が高まってきたにもかかわらず日本はずっと平穩と進歩のオアシスとして存在している。日本は全世界のすべての善意の人人の尊敬と信賴を受けるに値するようになり、全世界の自由な諸國家の家族に、平等な一員として參加する權利があることを實證したのである。

日本國憲法は國策の具としての戰爭を放棄している。こ

4 制限緩和に向けた対応(昭和24年5月〜27年4月)

の理念は近代世界がかつて經驗した最高の理想とはいえなくとも、最高の理想の一つを現わしており、かつ文明が維持されるべきであるならば、すべての人人は信奉しなければならないものである。この自ら課した制約は、次第に強まりつつある嵐の脅威にもかかわらず、國家の安全保障の問題に關する諸君の思慮と行動を細部にいたるまで導いてきたのである。しかしながら、もし國際的な無法律狀態が引續き平和を脅威し、人人の生命を支配しようとするならば、この理想がやむを得ざる自己保存の法則に道を讓らねばならなくなることは當然であり、自由を尊重する他の人人と相携えて、國際連合の諸原則のわく內で力を擊退するに力をもってすることが諸君の義務となるであろう。このような事態が決して起らないことを私は熱烈に希望するが、萬一起った場合、日本の安全保障は太平洋地域の他のすべての自由諸國家の深い關心事となるであろう。私は一九五一年には、新しい日本がまだ殘っている戰爭の打擊を十分ぬぐいさることができるような講和條約を通じて、完全な政治的自由の恩惠を受けることになるものと心から信じている。またさらにその後、西歐の思想や理想と日本國民自身の尊い傳統や、世界が尊重する古來の文化とが交流したものから生れ出た政治的道義、經濟的自由および社會正義の不變の理念にしっかり根をおろした日本國民が、今後のアジアの運命に大きな影響を與えるものと考えられることを心から信じている。

ダグラス・マックアーサー

編 注 本文書は、昭和二十六年四月、外務省政務局特別資料課作成「日本管理資料(四)」より拔粹。

昭和26年1月27日 鈴木連絡調整橫浜事務局長より 吉田外務大臣宛

282 朝鮮動亂に關する仏國大使の內話情報につき報告

濱連機密本第一九號

昭和二十六年一月二十七日

橫濱連絡調整事務局

局長 鈴木 九萬〔印〕

外務大臣

吉田　茂殿

佛國大使の朝鮮動亂に關する內話の件

佛國大使の朝鮮動亂に關する內話の件一月二十六日面會の際ドジヤン佛國大使は自分に對し朝鮮動亂に關し次の樣な趣旨の觀想を內話した。御參考迄。

客年十一月初に國聯軍が鮮滿國境近くで中共の大軍に突然直面した時は西歐側特に米國にとつて多大の衝動を與え中共軍の實相が誇張して傳えられたが折角包圍した國聯軍に大した損害も與えずに逃がした事（國聯側が少くとも二、三師團をせん滅させらるべき情勢であつたにも拘わらず）はソ連としては十月末迄の戰鬭で北鮮軍乃至中共軍に供給した飛行機、戰車等の武器が多數の損害を受けたのでその後は武器彈藥の供給を非常に澁つて居るにもよるが其の後の中共軍の作戰ともにらみ合わして見ると兵數こそ多いが中共軍も思つた程で無いという考が次第に出て來て居る。國聯軍としては巧みに出來る丈け速に南鮮に引揚げてしまつたが今や國聯軍側の地步は相當強く中共軍の神祕性を西歐側に強く印象附けて國聯軍を海へ追い落す可能性を信ぜさせ朝鮮問題、臺灣問題、中共の國聯參加問題等のバーゲンに使おうとした、又其

の脅かしの利いた時機は既に去つたかに見える。過日コリンズ陸軍參謀長等が來日した意味は今や逆に補給線ののびた中共軍に對して一寸でも攻擊に出れば出來る丈け出血させ今後は一尺の地を讓るにも尙數十萬位の犧牲を拂わせ理に國聯軍を追落そうとすれば尙數十萬位の犧牲を覺悟せねばならぬという事を悟らせるという態勢を固めた事にあるかと思う。又西歐側としても出來れば朝鮮で不法な侵略が決してそろばんに合わぬという事を示したいという點では變りはないと思う。兎に角茲數週間は一時に比べれば事實上の停戰狀態みたいなものであるが政治的に見て西歐と中共との間に今すぐ話合がまとまる程には氣運が熟して居ない。然し其の中何とかまとまる可能性が無いとは思えない云々。

昭和二十六年二月一日　連絡局調査課作成

「戰犯問題連絡協議會議事要錄」

戰犯問題連絡協議會議事要錄（昭二六、二、一）

連絡局調査課

4　制限緩和に向けた対応（昭和24年5月～27年4月）

出席者　外務省　小田部連絡局次長、吉村調査課長、石田事務官

引揚援護廳（一復）橋本法務調査部長、井上第三科長、野尻第一科長

（二復）豊田法務調査班長、市來崎事務官、宮崎事務官

一、比國關係戰犯死刑執行

(1) 一月十九日比國政府は十四名の死刑囚に對し銃殺刑を執行した旨在比加賀尾教誨師より報告があり右は昨日の朝刊各紙に報道された。

(2) 死刑囚七十八名に對し、當初三名の死刑を執行して以來長らくこれを中絶しており、昨秋は再審の結果一名を無罪とし、最近においては全員内地服役早期實現の可能性に關する樂觀的情報すら報道されていた際とて

今囘突然の處刑は家族は勿論一般に相當の衝撃を與えたものと思われる。

(3) 比國政府がかかる處刑を行ったことは、對日講和實現の可能性が急速に濃化して來た今日の情勢に鑑み、戰犯問題の總決算を行う必要に迫られて、懸案の死刑囚に對する措置を急ぎ始めたものと思われ、同時にまた對日賠償打切問題とも關連して、國民の對日感情を抑制する手段であるとも推測される。

(4) 殘餘の死刑囚六十名に對し執行が續けられるか否かは豫斷を許さないが、家族よりこれ以上の處刑停止を歎願しても、既に提出された幾多の助命歎願書の效果は最早限界點に達している。

(5) 今囘の處刑が齎した家族の衝動乃至輿論の失望を比國政府に表明することは、徒らに同國及び同國民を刺戟する以外の效果はないのみならず、却つて面白からざる逆效果を來たす怖れがある。日本政府としてもこの際何等の意思表示を行うことは差控えるべきである。

(6) 宗教團体殊にカトリック教徒より人道的宗教的見地より助命歎願を試みることは妨げない。

二、ダレス特使と戦犯問題

(1) ダレス特使今回の來朝は來るべき對日講和への準備工作として日本の經濟自立、安全保障等の根本問題に關する日本側の見解を調査するのが目的であり、從つて戦犯に對する日本側の希望を持ち出すことは適當でない。

(2) 戦犯は講和條約に附隨する問題であるから、結局は講和成立と共に何らかの措置が講ぜられるべきものであるが、これらに關しては講和の基本的構想が決定されて後に論議に上る問題で、今直ちに正面切つての交渉議題として持ち出すのは時期尚早である。

(3) 特使一行は比國を訪問することとなつているから、隨員中適當な人に何等かの機會を捉えて今囘比國の處刑による家族の衝撃の情を傳えて置くことは差支えない。

三、內地服役問題

內地服役に關しGHQは原則的にはこれを承認しているが、再審その他懸案未決のまゝ引き受けることには反對している。濠は目下尙裁判中、比國は再審中であり、英國關係のみが早期實現の可能性がある。但し英領中香港には濠州關係服役者がいる關係上、濠州の裁判が終了するのを俟つて英濠同時に內地服役を實施することに兩國間に了解があるやの情報もある。

四、講和後の戦犯管理

講和條約締結後或は時期において巣鴨服役者の釋放が行われるものと豫想されるが、その間の服役者の管理は、これを全面的に日本側の責任に歸することは服役者に與える心理的影響に鑑みて好ましくなく、最終の責任は米側が取る如き形態とすることが望ましい。

五、すがも新聞

最近「すがも新聞」に現われた論調には、やゝ穩當を欠く傾向があり、拘置所當局により削除されたものもあつた。右は服役者全部の傾向を代表するものではないとしても、拘置所乃至GHQ當局に無用の疑惑誤解を抱かしめ、却つてマイナスの効果を生ずることとなるから、編輯には特に愼重を期するよう注意を與える必要がある。

4　制限緩和に向けた対応（昭和24年5月〜27年4月）

昭和26年2月13日　連合国最高司令官総司令部より　日本政府宛

連合国最高司令官に対して派遣された在日外交代表との直接連絡を日本政府に許可する旨の指令

付記　右和訳文

GENERAL HEADQUARTERS
SUPREME COMMANDER FOR THE ALLIED POWERS
APO 500

13 February 1951

AG 091 (26 May 50) DS
SCAPIN 2142

MEMORANDUM FOR: JAPANESE GOVERNMENT

SUBJECT: Authorization for Direct Communication Between the Japanese Government and Foreign Diplomatic Representatives Accredited to the Supreme Commander for the Allied Powers

1. References:

a. Memorandum for Japanese Government, file AG 091.1 (4 Nov 45) GS, SCAPIN 237, subject: Official Relations Between Japanese Government and Representatives of Neutral Nations, 4 November 1945.

b. Memorandum for Japanese Government, file AG 091 (29 Jan 46) GS, SCAPIN 677, subject: Governmental and Administrative Separation of Certain Outlying Areas from Japan, 29 January 1946.

c. Memorandum for Japanese Government, file AG 091.112 (2 Dec 46) GB, SCAPIN 1372, subject: Contact with Japanese Officials, 2 December 1946.

d. Memorandum for Japanese Government, file AG 091 (28 May 48) ESS/EX, SCAPIN 1901, subject: Authorization for Direct Communication Between Japanese Government Board of Trade and Firms, Persons, and Foreign Missions on Commercial Matters, 28 May 1948.

2. The Japanese Government is hereby authorized direct communication with the diplomatic representatives of foreign governments accredited to the Supreme Commander for the Allied Powers, subject to the provisions listed below, the restrictions

embodied in referenced memoranda being relaxed only to the extent of permitting such limited contact.

3. The Japanese Government may receive from and dispatch to the diplomatic representatives referred to above, written communications on the following subjects. Oral consultation is permissible only on matters on which written communication has been made.

a. Exit and reentry matters involving foreign nationals, except occupation force personnel, in Japan, as provided in Circular 3, General Headquarters, Supreme Commander for the Allied Powers, 1950, and SCAPIN 2082, 20 February 1950.

b. Logistic facilities such as housing, office space, and supplies and services for foreign missions such as are not furnished by this headquarters.

c. Matters involved in protection of Japanese nationals and their interests abroad such as are handled by neutral foreign diplomatic missions on behalf of the Japanese Government.

d. Whereabouts and welfare cases; arrests and trials; financial and property matters (except war claims); rations; registration of nationality, births, marriages; deaths and estates; repatriation and deportation; and other routine individual status problems involving respective individual foreign nationals in Japan and individual Japanese nationals abroad.

e. Copyright, trade mark, and patent matters involving solely transmittal of correspondence and publications relating to procedural and administrative matters connected with copyright and industrial property registrations, laws and regulations, and excluding correspondence having to do with specific copyrights or copyrighted materials, trade marks, or patent matters or transactions relating thereto.

f. Routine correspondence of an administrative, including fiscal, nature regarding transportation and communication facilities already authorized between Japan and foreign countries, such as authorized for telecommunications in SCAPIN 2085, 24 February 1950.

g. Routine correspondence of an administrative, including fiscal, nature between the Japanese Government and international organizations in which Japan maintains membership or

4　制限緩和に向けた対応（昭和24年5月～27年4月）

has affiliations, or with which such correspondence is necessary.

h. Details concerning establishment of Japanese representation abroad, after agreement regarding such establishment has been approved by the Supreme Commander for the Allied Powers.

i. Details regarding Japanese representation at and participation in international conferences, after attendance has been approved by the Supreme Commander for the Allied Powers.

j. Routine correspondence concerning the execution of bilateral or international treaties or agreements, after their conclusion has been approved by the Supreme Commander for the Allied Powers.

k. Requests for official publications normally exchanged between governments; arrangements for exchange of scientific, educational, and cultural publications prepared by semi-official and educational institutions.

l. Trade matters such as authorized by SCAPIN 1901 of 28 May 1948.

4. It is understood that communications on all other subjects, including those mentioned above when they involve interpretation of or deviation from standing policies, will continue to be submitted to the Supreme Commander for the Allied Powers.

5. The present authorization for direct written communication is a specific delegation of responsibility to the Japanese Government which will, therefore, submit to Diplomatic Section, General Headquarters, Supreme Commander for the Allied Powers, copies of all communications it receives or dispatches under the provisions of this memorandum. The Japanese Government is instructed to use the English language, with such Japanese or Chinese characters as may be required to facilitate the reading of romanized names, in all communications authorized by this memorandum.

6. The accreditation of foreign diplomatic representatives in Japan remains unchanged, being solely to the Supreme Commander for the Allied Powers.

7. This direct channel of written communication does not in any way deprive the foreign diplomatic representatives of their right to continue transmitting communications authorized in para-

graph 3, through this headquarters if they so desire. Both the accredited foreign diplomatic representatives and the Japanese Government may, when either deems it advisable in any particular case and without direct reply on their part, refer any communication received which may be considered controversial, or as involving policy to the Supreme Commander for the Allied Powers for the latter's consideration, clarification, or reply.

8. The foreign diplomatic representatives accredited to the Supreme Commander for the Allied Powers with which the Japanese Government may communicate directly under the provisions of this memorandum, unless this list is modified by subsequent memoranda, are:

    a. The Australian Mission in Japan
    b. The Belgian Mission in Japan
    c. The Brazilian Diplomatic Mission in Japan
    d. The Canadian Liaison Mission in Japan
    e. The Chinese Mission in Japan
    f. The Danish Diplomatic Mission in Japan
    g. The French Mission in Japan
    h. The Indian Liaison Mission in Japan
    i. The Italian Diplomatic Mission in Japan
    j. The Korean Diplomatic Mission in Japan
    k. The Netherlands Mission in Japan
    l. The Norwegian Diplomatic Mission in Japan
    m. The Philippine Mission in Japan
    n. The Portuguese Diplomatic Agency in Japan
    o. The Spanish Diplomatic Mission in Japan
    p. The Swedish Diplomatic Mission in Japan
    q. The Swiss Diplomatic Mission in Japan
    r. The Thai Diplomatic Mission in Japan
    s. The United Kingdom Liaison Mission in Japan
    t. The Uruguayan Diplomatic Agency in Japan.

9. In the absence of contrary indications from the Japanese Government, it will be understood that the channel of all correspondence between the Japanese Government and the foreign missions on the subjects specified will be the Japanese Ministry of Foreign Affairs, except that correspondence on international trade operations may pass directly between the missions and the Minis-

4 制限緩和に向けた対応（昭和24年5月～27年4月）

try of International Trade and Industry.

10. The provisions of this memorandum will become effective thirty (30) days after its publication.

FOR THE SUPREME COMMANDER:

K. B. BUSH
Brigadier General, USA
Adjutant General

（付記）

連合國最高司令官總司令部發日本國政府あて千九百五十一年二月十三日付覺書譯文

一、参照
件名　日本國政府と連合國最高司令官に對して派遣された外國の外交代表との直接通信の許可

a、日本國政府あて千九百四十五年十一月四日付覺書、ファイルAG091・1(4Nov45)GS、SCAPIN237、件名　日本國政府と中立國代表との公的關係

b、日本國政府あて千九百四十六年一月二十九日付覺書、ファイルAG091(29Jan46)GS、SCAPIN677、件名　若干の外かく地域の日本からの政治上及び行政上の分離

c、日本國政府あて千九百四十六年十二月二日付覺書、ファイルAG091・112(2Dec46)GB、SCAPIN1372、件名　日本官憲との接觸

d、日本國政府あて千九百四十八年五月二十八日付覺書、ファイルAG091(28May48)ESS/EX、SCAPIN1901、件名　貿易上の事項に關する日本國政府貿易廳と商社、個人及び外國使節團との直接通信の許可

二、日本國政府は、以下に掲げる規定に從うことを條件として、連合國最高司令官に對し派遣された外國政府の外交代表との直接通信をここに許可され、参照覺書に含まれた諸制限は、このような制限された接觸を許す範圍においてのみ、緩和される。

三、日本國政府は、次の事項に關する書面による通信を、前記の外交代表から受領し、又はこれに發送することができる。口頭の協議は、書面による通信がなされた事項に

ついてのみ、許される。

a、外國人(千九百五十年連合國最高司令官總司令部間章第三號及び千九百五十年二月二十日付SCAPIN第二千八百二號に定めた在日占領軍軍人を除く。)の出國及び再入國に關する事項

b、住宅、事務所用地及び食糧のような居住便益並びに本司令部の供與しない外交使節團に對する奉仕

c、中立國外交使節團が日本國政府のために行つている在外日本人及びその利益の保護に關する事項

d、在日外國人及び在外日本人に關する居所及び福利狀況、逮捕及び裁判、財產上及び資產上の事項(但し、戰爭に基く賠償請求を除く。)、食糧、國籍と出生と婚姻の登錄、死亡及び遺產、送還及び移送、並びに他の常務的な個人の私的地位の問題

e、著作權、商標及び特許權に關する事項で、著作權及び工業所有權の登錄と法律及び規則とに關連する及び執行上の事項に關する通信及び出版物の傳達にもつぱら關係あるもの。但し、特別の著作權若しくは著作權取得物件、商標又は特許權の事項に關する通信並

びにこれに關する事務を除く。

f、千九百五十年二月二十四日付SCAPIN第二千八十五號において電氣通信について許可されたような日本國と外國との間に既に許可された運輸及び通信に關する執行的性質(財政的なものを含む。)の常務的通信

g、國際機關であつて、日本國がこれにおいて構成員としての地位を維持し、若しくはこれに加入し、又はこれと通信をすることが必要であるものと、日本國政府との間の執行的性質(財政的なものを含む。)の常務的通信

h、日本の在外代表の設置に關する協定が連合國最高司令官によって承認された後におけるこの設置に關する細目

i、日本の國際會議への出席が連合國最高司令官によつて承認された後における日本の同會議への代表派遣及び同會議への參加に關する細目

j、雙務的又は國際的な條約又は協定の締結が連合國最高司令官によつて承認された後におけるこれらの條約又は協定の實施に關する常務的通信

860

4 制限緩和に向けた対応（昭和24年5月～27年4月）

k、政府間に通例交換される公の刊行物の要請、半官の且つ教育的な機關の作成した科學的、教育的及び文化的刊行物の交換のための取極

1、千九百四十八年五月二十八日付のSCAPIN第千九百一號によつて許可されたような通商事項

四、すべての他の事項（現存の政策の解釋問題を含み又はこれを逸脱するときは、前記の事項を含む。）に關する通信は、引き續き連合國最高司令官に提出されるものとする。

五、書面による直接通信のこの許可は、日本國政府への責任の特定委任であり、從つて、日本國政府は、この覺書の規定に基いて受領し又は發送するすべての通信の寫を、連合國最高司令官總司令部外交局に提出するものとする。日本國政府は、この覺書によつて許可されたすべての通信においては、イギリス語を、ローマ字名の讀方を容易にするために必要な日本字又は漢字と共に、使用するよう指令される。

六、外國の在日外交代表の派遣先は、連合國最高司令官であつて、引き續き不變である。

七、書面による通信のこの直接の經路は、いかなる方法によつても、外國の外交代表から、第三項において許可された通信を、同代表が希望するときに、引き續き本司令部を通じて轉送する權利を奪うものではない。外國の派遣外交代表と日本國政府とは、共に、その受領した通信で紛議を豫想せられ又は政策問題を含んでいると考えられるものを、個々の場合において適當と思うときに、自らの直接の囘答をせずに、連合國最高司令官に對して、その考慮、明瞭化又は囘答のために、照會することができる。

八、連合國最高司令官に對して派遣された外國の外交代表で、日本國政府がこの覺書の規定に基いて直接通信することのできるものは、この表が今後の覺書によつて修正されない限り、次のとおりである。

a、在日オーストラリア使節團
b、在日ベルギー使節團
c、在日ブラジル使節團
d、在日カナダ連絡外交使節團
e、在日中華民國使節團
f、在日デンマーク外交使節團

g、在日フランス使節團
h、在日インド連絡使節團
i、在日イタリア外交使節團
j、在日大韓民國外交使節團
k、在日オランダ使節團
l、在日ノールウェー外交使節團
m、在日フィリピン使節團
n、在日ポルトガル外交事務所
o、在日スペイン外交使節團
p、在日スウェーデン外交使節團
q、在日スイス外交使節團
r、在日タイ外交使節團
s、在日連合王國連絡使節團
t、在日ウルグァイ外交事務所

九、日本國政府からの反對の指示のない限り、日本國政府と外國使節團との前記特定事項に關するすべての通信の經路は、日本國外務省とするものと了解される。但し、通商活動に關する通信は、諸使節團と通商産業省との間に直接送受することができる。

十、この覺書の規定は、その公表の日から三十日後に效力を生ずる。

最高司令官に代り
高級副官
ケー・ビー・ブッシュ
アメリカ合衆國陸軍准將

285

昭和26年4月10日 連合国最高司令官総司令部より 外務省宛

在外事務所の権限強化に関する指令

GENERAL HEADQUARTERS
SUPREME COMMANDER FOR THE ALLIED POWERS
APO 500

Diplomatic Section

AG 095 (10 Apr 51) DS   10 April 1951

MEMORANDUM FOR: Japanese Ministry of Foreign Affairs
SUBJECT: Additional Functions for Japanese Government Overseas Agencies.

4　制限緩和に向けた対応(昭和24年5月〜27年4月)

1. Japanese nationals permanently residing abroad are encountering difficulty in obtaining entry clearance into Japan under present procedures. In order that these requests for entry may be expeditiously processed, effective immediately the Japanese Government Overseas Agencies are authorized to act as agents for the Supreme Commander for the Allied Powers and process applications for entry into Japan from Japanese nationals residing abroad.

2. The aforementioned authority will be implemented by the Agency concerned in the following manner:

　a. Receive application and verify information therein.

　b. Verify that applicant possesses a valid reentry permit into the country concerned which will also be construed as a valid travel document insofar as entry into Japan is concerned.

　c. Forward application to Japanese Ministry of Foreign Affairs who submits application to this Headquarters with recommendations of the Japanese Government.

　d. Approved application will be returned to the Japanese Government who will forward it to the appropriate Overseas Agency.

　e. Provided no objection is interposed by the country concerned, the Agency will indicate in applicant's travel document that Supreme Commander for the Allied Powers clearance has been given and cite the authority for entry into Japan.

　f. In the event the country concerned objects to the Agency placing clearance authority in the travel document, the Agency will notify the applicant of his clearance by returning to him an approved copy of the application and advise him of the requirements to be fulfilled on arrival in Japan.

3. Enclosed are applications for entry as tourists from Japanese nationals resident in Brazil as forwarded to the Headquarters by the Ministry's memoranda nos. FOM 246 (CP) dated 7 February 1951, FOM 326 (CP) dated 17 February 1951, FOM 379 (CP) dated 27 February 1951, and FOM 641 (CP) dated 2 April 1951, and by travel agencies. These applications are approved with the understanding that they will be processed in accordance with the aforementioned procedures except that they will not have to be returned to this Headquarters.

For the Chief, Diplomatic Section:

MEMORANDUM FOR: JAPANESE GOVERNMENT
SUBJECT: Applications for Travel of Japanese Nationals Abroad

1. Reference is SCAPIN 2072.

2. The Supreme Commander for the Allied Powers desires that the Japanese Government assume a more normal function in the processing of applications for travel abroad by determining and certifying the acceptability of the individual applicant as a traveler from the standpoint of the interests of the occupation, of Japan, and of the country of destination prior to submitting the individual's application for the approval of the Supreme Commander for the Allied Powers.

3. In order to determine whether or not an applicant is a person whom the Japanese Government is willing to acknowledge as fully qualified to represent Japan as a traveler abroad, the Japanese Government will take appropriate action to verify the authenticity of the statements made by the applicant and to ascertain that the personal attributes of the applicant are such that the proposed travel would not be prejudicial to the interests of the occupation, of Japan, or of the country of destination.

4. Effective immediately the certificate on the applicant's Personal History Form, attachment 2 to application for passport, is amended to read as follows:

SCAPIN 2072/2
AG 014.331 (5 Jan 50) GA

SUPREME COMMANDER FOR THE ALLIED POWERS
GENERAL HEADQUARTERS
APO 500

12 April 1951

Niles W. Bond
Deputy Chief

Inclosures:
71 applications

編　注　本文書の別添は見当たらない。

286　昭和26年4月12日　連合国最高司令官総司令部より日本政府宛

海外渡航日本人の申請に関する指令

864

4 制限緩和に向けた対応(昭和24年5月〜27年4月)

Certificate

Adjutant General

I certify that the above is the true signature and seal of the individual concerned, that the applicant is acceptable to the Japanese Government from every standpoint and that there is nothing in the applicant's past or current activities which would indicate that the travel as planned would be prejudicial to the interests of the occupation, of the country to which applicant desires to travel, or of Japan.

For the Ministry of Foreign Affairs

5. The Japanese Government is reminded of its responsibility for the orientation of Japanese nationals who may be authorized to travel outside Japan as prescribed in SCAPIN 6163-A, 8 November 1948.

FOR THE SUPREME COMMANDER:

K. B. BUSH
Brigadier General, USA

---

287 昭和26年4月18日　吉田内閣総理大臣よりリッジウェイ連合国最高司令官宛

占領管理下において制定された法令の改廃に関する要望書

付記　右和文原案

I. Laws

Laws and Ordinances Promulgated under Occupation of which repeal or Revision is desired.

Enumerated below are the principal laws, ordinances and orders, which in the light of the opinions expressed from various circles as well as actual experience in their enforcement, are considered as requiring revision. The purpose of the proposed revisions is to adapt our national legislation to the current realities of the country without deviating from the spirit of the Constitution and at the same time to promote the economic self-support of Japanese economy.

A. The National Public Service System

The National Public Service Law.

This law in its operation has revealed several points not only unsuited to the existing conditions of the country but also detrimental to the enhancement of efficiency. It is desired:

(a) To put in the Special Positions category such part-time officials as commissioners and advisers and also to render the personnel administration regulations more elastic with respect to high rank officials such as vice ministers of various ministries.

(b) To simplify the structure of the National Personnel Authority and to make it an organ of the Cabinet with its functions limited to giving advices and recommendations and to supervision and readjustment.

(c) To curtail the scope of the matters delegated to the Authority under the present law.

(d) To extend the scope of appointment by reelection, to introduce the efficiency basis to a degree into the pay system, and to give more elasticity to the Position Classification System.

B. The Local Self-Government System

The Local Autonomy Law.

Because of the emphasis placed on the importance of local autonomy a considerable number of affairs which intrinsically belong to the State have been delegated to local public entities. Under the existing system the Cabinet's position is too weak without adequate authority for unified execution of these affairs. It is desired to render more effective the Cabinet's directive authority over local public entities with respect to these State affairs.

C. The Family System

The Civil Code.

The present Civil Code lays too great an emphasis on marriage — or the husband-and-wife relationship — as the central factor of family life. This has produced a mistaken notion that it is proper to disdain or reject the old virtues of filial piety, deference to elders and kindness to the young, which had characterized the social and spiritual life of Japanese people. They are fast losing the sense of family honor and dignity and veneration for ancestors. The need is felt with special urgency today to preserve and

866

4 制限緩和に向けた対応(昭和24年5月～27年4月)

foster the institution of family built on the traditions of ages, while seeking to harmonize it with the basic Constitutional principles of individual dignity and equality. It is desired:

(a) To recognize legally the head of a household as the center of family life with authority necessary for ensuring unity and harmony.

(b) To let the kinsmen's council solve family disputes, instead of leaving the settlement of such disputes solely to family courts as under the existing system.

(c) To make special provisions in the Property Succession Law for the person who succeeds to the family genealogical records and tombs and conducts memorial rites for ancestors, and must shoulder the financial burden thereof.

(d) To ensure the preservation of small farms and business enterprises by providing against the dispersion of their meagre assets through succession by equal division.

D. The Police System

The Police Law.

The existing police system is defective in more than one ways for the preservation of law and order. For rectification it is considered necessary:

(a) To effect readjustment in the system for mutual assistance between the National Rural Police and the Autonomous Police.

(b) To bring about closer relationships among the Public Safety Commission, the Cabinet and the heads of local public entities.

(c) To create a Capital Police system under State control; and to raise the population limit for cities, towns and villages required to maintain an autonomous police force.

E. The Educational System

1. The Board of Education Law.

(a) The present system under which a Board of Education is made an independent body while other similar organs are subject to the authority of governor or mayor, does not operate satisfactorily. It would seem advisable to make the Board of Education an advisory organ to the head of local public entity.

(b) In order to simplify the country's educational administration it is desired to repeal the existing provision requiring every city, town and village to set up a Board of Education and to limit such requirement to prefectures (To, Do, Fu and Ken).

2. The School Education Law and Related Laws and Orders.

It is desired to re-examine the 6-3-3-4 System and the respective curricula with a view to adapting them to the actual conditions of the country.

F. Economic Laws

1. The Law relating to Prohibition of Private Monopoly and Preservation of Fair Trade.

In view of the backwardness of Japanese economy and the scarcity of accumulated capital and of the country's need to achieve a self-supporting economy, it would be desirable to relax certain of the provisions of this anti-monopoly legislation.

2. The Enterprise Organization Law.

To be relaxed for the same reasons as above.

G. The Legal Procedure

The Code of Criminal Procedure.

Experience in the enforcement of this code has shown the need of substantial relaxation with respect to several points including the provisions such as those relating to the requirement to inform the suspect of the charges against him upon his detention for prosecution; the collection of evidence; the right to parole, and the right of the suspect or defendant not to testify against himself.

H. Labor Laws

1. The Labor Standards Law.

This law and especially its Rules of Procedure are unadapted to the realities of Japan's labor situation, so that violations are inevitable, inviting distrust of all laws, and sowing the seeds of unwarranted labor disputes. It is deemed imperative to relax the restrictions on female, young, and outdoor workers, to expand the scope of exemptions from the Safety and Sanitation Standards, and to relax their application to small enterprises.

2. The Mariners Law.

For the same reasons as stated above, this law requires

4 制限緩和に向けた対応（昭和24年5月～27年4月）

modifications. It is especially necessary to incorporate special provisions relating to fishing boats and other small craft.

II. Potsdam Ordinances.

It is desired to preserve permanently the Potsdam Ordinances listed below by enacting them into national laws with slight adjustments in certain cases. All the others are slated for repeal, excepting those of which retention may be required under the peace treaty.

1. Price Control Ordinance
2. Land and House Rent Control Ordinance
3. National Police Reserve Order
4. Poisonous Comestibles, etc. Control Ordinance
5. Organization Control Ordinance (including the Cabinet Order concerning Administration and Disposal of dissolved Organizations)
6. Cabinet Order concerning the Maintenance of Order among Repatriates
7. Order re Internal Air Transportation
8. Cabinet Order concerning the transfer of Land under the Owner-Farmer Establishment Special Measures Law and the Agricultural Land Readjustment Law.
9. Cabinet Order concerning Acquisition of Properties by Foreign Nationals.
10. Cabinet Order concerning Business Activities of Foreign Nationals.
11. Cabinet Order concerning Acquisition of Real Property and/or Rights thereto by Foreign Governments.
12. Cabinet Order concerning Immigration Surveillance.
13. Aliens Registration Ordinance
14. Immigration Agency Establishment Order
15. Repatriation Relief Agency Establishment Order
16. (Imperial) Ordinance Prohibiting the Possession of Fire Arms and Other Weapons.

III. Revision of the Administrative Structure

1. Concerning the National Administrative Organization Law and the Laws for the establishment of various Ministries and Agencies, it is considered in the light of experience that they will require rather extensive changes inasmuch as not only do they contain fea-

tures unadapted to the actual conditions of the country but also they tend to be too complex and unwieldy for efficient operation.

A. Simplification of the Central Government Machinery

The Postal Services Ministry and the Tele-Communications Ministry to be amalgamated into a single ministry.

The Attorney General's Office to be organized similar to other ministries.

The external organs of various ministries, such as the Tax Administration Agency, Smaller Enterprises Agency, Economic Research Agency, Agency of Industrial Science and Technology, Reparations Agency, and National Fire Defense Agency, should either liquidated or simplified as much as possible and made internal organs of the respective ministries.

With the reform of the Public Service System, the National Personnel Authority should be simplified and made an auxiliary organ of the Office of the Prime Minister, with its functions confined to giving recommendations and advices and to supervision and readjustment.

B. The System of Independent Commissions

The system of independent commissions conflicts in certain respects with the responsibilities of the Cabinet in a parliamentary government established under the Constitution. Accordingly, these commissions should be abolished as far as possible in order to make clear that these responsibilities rest with the Cabinet. For instance, the Foreign Exchange Control Commission, Statistics Commission, Radio Regulatory Commission, Public Utilities Commission, Land Adjustment Commission, National Offenders' Prevention Rehabilitation Commission, Securities and Exchange Commission, Foreign Investment Commission, Local Finance Commission, etc., should be transferred to the respective ministries concerned as their internal organs. The National Public Safety Commission and the Fair Trade Commission require reorganization with a view, the former, to establish close relationship with the Cabinet; and the latter, to confine its function to the role of

870

4　制限緩和に向けた対応（昭和24年5月～27年4月）

referee, all the other functions being transferred to the Ministry of International Commerce and Industry.

編注　本文書はマッカーサー司令官に手交する予定で準備されていたが、同司令官が四月十一日に解任されたため、同十八日にリッジウェイ新司令官に手交された。

（付記）

（欄外記入）

占領管理下において制定された法令の改廢について

一、連合軍最高司令官の終始變らざる熱烈なる支援により、近い将來において講和條約が締結されるという見透しを持つに至つた今日、日本國政府は占領管理下において制定された以下に述べるような法律の改正及び政令の改正又は廢止について總司令部の意向を伺ひ、助言を求め度いと思う。

二、この改正又は廢止は日米兩國の友好關係の爲め成る可く占領の終了前になされることが望ましい。

一、法律

従來における法律實施の經驗と、國內各方面の意向に徵し、改正の論議の對象となるべき法律のうち重なるものは次の通りである。これらの改正は、日本國憲法の精神を尊重しつゝ、法制を我が國現在の實情に卽せしめ併せて我が國經濟自立を促進せしめようとするにある。

例えば

A、國家公務員制度

国家公務員法

本法運用の經驗に鑑み我が国の実情に副わないのみならず能率の昂上を阻害している點がある。仍つて

(a) 委員顧問の如き非常勤公務員を特別職とし、各省次官の如き高級公務員について任用、給與、分限等において、一般職より融通性を持つ人事管理制度をとること。

(b) 人事院を簡素化し、專ら勸告、助言、統轄、調整的機能を擔任する總理府の一機關とすることにより、内閣との連繋を緊密にすること。

(c) 現行の人事院規則に委任する事項の範圍を縮少すること。

(d) 国家公務員の任用については詮衡任用の範圍を

擴大し、給與については能率給制度を加味し、職階についてはその融通性を持たせること。

B、地方自治制度

地方自治

本來國家事務に屬する事柄を地方自治尊重の建前から、地方公共團體の長に委任しているものが少くないが、現行制度では、その統一的運營を圖る手段として内閣に與えられた權能は弱きに失するので、この種の國の委任事務については内閣の地方公共團體の長に對する具體的指揮權を一層實效的にすること。

C、家族制度

現行民法の制度は婚姻、即ち夫婦關係を中心とし、あまりにこれを强調し過ぎている爲めに、その反動として、從來日本人の社會生活、精神生活の一つの良き據點となつていた親子間、長幼間の敬愛關係は、むしろ輕視、否認することが正しいというような誤解を一般に與え、又家の名譽とか、尊嚴とかあるいは祖先崇拜というような觀念が一般國民の念頭から離れつゝある。

仍つて憲法の基本原則とする個人の尊嚴及び平等の調和を求めつゝ、よき傳統に基く家及び家族生活の維持助長を考慮すべきことは、今日特に必要であると思われる。

例えば

(a) 家長制度を認め家族共同生活の中心として統合上必要な機能を擔任せしむること。

(b) 家族間の紛爭を專ら家庭裁判所が審判する現行制度に對し、その第一段階として親族會にその解決を計らしむること。

(c) 系譜、墳墓等を承繼して祖先の祭祀を主宰する者に對しその經濟的負擔を考慮して或る程度の遺産承繼上の特例を認めること。

(d) 實質上、家の存續を保障する意味で、中小商工業者の零細な營業用資產、農業用資產とか、が均分相續のために分散することを防ぐこと。

D、警察制度

警察法

4 制限緩和に向けた対応（昭和24年5月〜27年4月）

警察の現行制度は治安維持上遺憾の點があるので、これを是正するため
(a) 國家自治警察相互間の應援制度を更に整備すること。
(b) 公安委員會制度と内閣及び地方自治團體の長との關係を緊密にすること。
(c) 首都警察の制度を創設し、自治警を維持する市町村の範圍を縮少すること。

E、教育制度
1、教育委員會法
(a) 獨立的委員會たる教育委員會の制度は地方公共團體の長その他の機關との關係上、現狀においては地方事情に卽さない點が多い。仍つて教育委員會は地方公共團體の長の諮問機關とすべきであると思う。
(b) 教育行政の簡素化を圖るため、すべての市町村に教育委員會を置かなければならない點を改正し、都道府縣程度に止め度い。

2、學校教育法及びその關係法令
六、三、三、四制及びその教科内容を本邦の實情に副うよう再檢討すること。

F、經濟關係
1、私的獨占の禁止及び公正取引の確保に關する法律
日本經濟の後進性と資本の蓄積の不充分なこと及び日本經濟が速かに自立する必要から見て、現在の獨占禁止法の規定を緩和する必要がある。

2、事業者團體法
獨占禁止法と同樣の理由により緩和すること。

G、訴訟關係
刑事訴訟法
本法實施の經驗に鑑み、起訴前の勾留理由開示制度、採證制度（證據法の問題）、權利保釋の制度、被疑者及び被告人の默祕權等の諸點につき相當緩和して、本法の適正なる運用を可能にすること。

H、勞働關係
1、勞働基準法
本法特に施行規則は、我國勞働事情の現實に卽しない點があり從つて法律違反を不可避ならしめ、かえつて法秩序全般に對する不信を招くお

それあり、且つ過度の勞働爭議の因ともなっている。よって現實に卽應するように女子、年少者、屋外作業者等に對する制限の緩和、安全衞生基準の適用除外の範圍の擴大、小規模事業に關する適用の緩和等を行う必要に關する適用の緩和等を行う必要がある。

2、船員法

勞働基準法について逑べたと同様の理由で、調整し、特に漁船その他小船舶について特例を設ける必要がある。

I、行政機構

行政機構の改正については別途に申請する予定。

二、ポツダム命令

ポツダム命令の中次にあげたものは、將來法律として存續する措置をとりたいと考える。尤もこの措置をとるに當つて内容に若干の調整を加える必要はある。

その他については、講和條約實施上必要なものを除き原則として廢止すべきものと考える。

1、物價統制令

2、地代家賃統制令

3、警察予備隊令

4、有毒飲食物取締令

5、團体等規正令（解散團体の財産の管理及び處分等に關する政令も含めて。）

6、引揚者の秩序保持に關する政令

7、國內航空運送事業令

8、自作農創設特別措置法及び農地調整法の適用を受けるべき土地の讓渡に關する政令

9、外國人の財産取得に關する政令

10、外國人の事業活動に關する政令

11、外國政府の不動産に關する權利の取得に關する政令

12、出入國の管理に關する政令

13、外國人登錄令

14、出入國管理廳設置令

15、引揚援護廳設置令

16、銃砲刀劍類等所持取締令

三、行政組織の改正

一、國家行政組織法及び各省府設置法については、これらの法律實施の經驗に鑑み、わが國の實情に副わない點が

4　制限緩和に向けた対応（昭和24年5月～27年4月）

あるばかりでなくその機構の複雑と、非能率等のきらいがあり、相當改正を要すると認められる。

A、中央行政機構の簡素化をはかること

例えば郵政省、電通省を統合して一省とすること。法務府を各省と同様のものとすること。國税廳、中小企業廳、經濟調査廳、工業技術廳、賠償廳、國家消防廳、等各省の外局を整理して、出來る限り簡素なる内局とすること。公務員制度の改正と相俟って人事院を簡素化し、專ら勸告、助言、統轄、調整的機能を擔任する總理府の附屬機關とし、内閣との連携を緊密にすること。

B、獨立委員會制度について

獨立委員會制度は憲法上の制度である議院内閣制度における内閣の責任と合致しない點がある。よって獨立委員會はなるべくこれを廢止し、責任の歸屬を明らかにすること。例えば外國爲替管理委員會、統計委員會、電波監理委員會、公益事業委員會、土地調整委員會、中央更生保護委員會、證券取引委員會、外資委員會、地方財政委員會等は廢止して、それぞれ關係府、省の内局の權限に移し、國家公安委員會（内閣との関係をより密接なものとする。）公正取引委員會（審判的機能を残し、他は通産省へ移管する。）等は改組を要する。

（欄外記入）

三月二十日午后目黒官邸で管野官房副長官から受領、副長官と佐藤法制意見長官との間で加筆訂正されたるもの、本官の意見を求められたるに對し、全然贊成なる旨答えおきたり。三月二十二日西村記

米国政府の占領費一部負担に関する総司令部発表（和訳文）

昭和26年5月14日　連合国最高司令官総司令部発表

米國政府の占領費一部負擔に關する總司令部渉外局發表

昭和二十六年五月十四日

連合國最高司令官は、本日次のとおり發表した。米國防

日米経済協力に関するマーカット経済科学局長の声明(和訳文)

昭和二十六年五月十六日

日米経済協力に関するマーカット経済科学局長声明に關する總司令部渉外局發表

リッジウェイ大將は、本日、最近米國から歸還した日米經濟協力に關する總司令部使節團の業績に關する報告の發表を許可した。マーカット經濟科學局長を團長とする占領軍總司令部使節團は、ワシントンで三週間を費し、國務、國防、財務の各省、國防動員總本部、國防生產局、軍需委員會、緊急調整局、輸出入銀行、經濟協力局、連邦準備委員會、需給調整委員會その他を含む米國政府の高官と協議した。

使節團は、將來の日米經濟關係について、大統領特別補佐官アヴェリル・ハリマン氏、對日平和條約交渉に關する大統領使節ジョン・フォスター・ダレス大使、對日經濟金融顧問ジョセフ・ドッジ公使その他の權威筋と協議した。

最高司令官は、マーカット少將から報告書を受取り、その內容を吉田首相に傳達し、その上で新聞に發表するよう指令した。報告の主要點は、次のとおりである。

省は、トルーマン大統領が最近行った決定に從って、近く議會に對し、米政府は現在日本が負擔している日本駐在の米占領軍維持費のうち、七月一日からその一部を支拂うこと、及び、それと同時に、對日經濟援助費を減額することを提案することとなろう。

日本が經濟自立と安定經濟という目標に向って現在に成しとげた進步から見て、本日發表された新政策のもとに取得を豫想される外貨は、他の方面から取得する外貨と相まって、米國の對日ガリオア經濟援助が米國の現會計年度末で打切られても差支えないほど充分なものとなるであろう。

右の新措置が議會の承認を得た場合には、對日平和條約の效力發生の日まで實施されるであろう。

編注 本文書は、昭和二十七年二月、外務省國際協力局特別資料室作成「日本管理資料(五)」より抜粋。

289 昭和26年5月16日 連合国最高司令官総司令部発表

4 制限緩和に向けた対応（昭和24年5月〜27年4月）

連合軍占領下における日本の復興は、米國官民から尊敬と稱贊とを受けている。

米國は、日本が他國と平等な條件で、且つそうした取扱いを受けるだけの正當な理由をいぜんとして示しうる限り、世界市場と原料入手の途とを與えられることに深い關心をもっている。

米國は、製品の質と價格競争との基礎に立って日本を歐州諸國及び他の西半球諸國とともに米國の緊急調達計画に參加させることに伴う利益を充分認識している。米國産業は、生產力増強のため犠牲を拂い、且つそのための投資を行った。その結果、米國産業は、米國の緊急調達計画上、優先權を要求することとなるであろう。しかし、現在過剰な工業力を持ち、また地理的に有利な立場にある日本は、計画の當初から充分な需要に恵まれ、しかもこの需要は將來急角度に増大するであろう。米國の調達計画は、資金が入手可能となり、發注がつぎつぎと行われるにつれ加速度的に膨脹する。調達命令が長期的に發しうる單一な總合計画は、存在していない。國際的工業發展にはつきものの、漠然として捕捉し難いものが多々あるので、發注は自由競

争に基いた契約をつぎつぎに結ぶという基礎の上に行われることが大切である。

最も支配的な要素は、外國爲替の入手と、世界的に不足を告げている基礎的及び戰略的原料の入手とである。現下においては、原料事情のほうが一層と重大であって、嚴格な割當手續が設けられつつある。これら稀少物資の新資源の開發は、割當及び融資という點からみて、優先的な考慮を必要とするであろう。日本にとって、このような新資源を探求し開發する機會は、これを利用した結果相當な利益となりうるものである。

米國においては、生產及び貯藏の活動は、最大能力を發揮しているが、現在はまだ概して計画の段階にある。種種の機關が設けられ、割當、統制その他の承認された手段によって主要な經路を通じて全國民の努力を指導している。もし世界の他の國國が、製品の國內價格を國際水準に合致させるような政策を採ることを考えるべきであって、さもなければ、日本もまた同様な行動を採ることを考えるべきであって、さもなければ、諸國と太刀打ちできなくなるであろうことはきわめて明らかである。もしなんらかの理由で、日本がこの國際的計画

に寄与し得ないならば、適當な國内の消費水準維持のための原料及び食糧の確保にも響くことになるであろう。日本は、現存の諸機關を通じて、適當な監督の効果を最大限度まであげる必要がある。

日本に對しては、クレジット供與に伴うリスクを引受けるという方式で、國際的な、米國政府による、および民間の融資を與えることができる。日本が國際金融機關に加盟を申請するに當っては、まずその資格を整えることが必要である。リッジウェイ最高司令官は、すでにこの點に關し、占領當局が充分に援助する旨を日本人に約した。國際金融機關加盟の前提條件を若干あげれば、次のとおりである。

1　今後採るべき對外的支拂政策を決定し、かつ公表すること、この問題についてはすでに考慮が拂われつつある。

2　國内インフレの抑制に關し恆久的な施策を公表すること。國際金融機關の一基本目的は各國通貨の安定を援助することであるから、無統制なインフレに因る減價から自國通貨を守る計畫をもたない國に加盟を認めることは到底考えられない。非常時的需要を満たすための生産は、本來インフレ的であり、こうして國内で消費できないよ

うな物資を生産することから生れる個人的購買力の膨脹を相殺するような措置を講ずる必要は、今日すべての國が認めている。それと同時に、國内の生活水準を最大限度に向上させることが必要かくことのできないことである。

3　擔保的預託の問題も、重要である。國際機關への加盟が考慮される前に、まず加盟に必要な基本預託金の財源をはっきり確保する必要がある。

4　國家予算政策も、重要である。國内の安定が維持されなければ、無統制なインフレから通貨の減價と、これにつれて、物價の高騰が起る危險がある。國内物價高のため、世界市場から脱落しないような状態では、國際的クレジット供與もあり得ない。

米國の國内金融機關としては、既定方針のわく内で日本に對し融資を考慮する用意がある。これらの機關は、多くの場合、米國の國庫から出資をうけているため、その行いうる融資の型を法律によって限定されている。その型の融資は、米國とその企圖される取引の相手方の双方とを盆する場合に限り、考慮されるのが通常である。

4　制限緩和に向けた対応(昭和24年5月～27年4月)

米國の民間投資機關は、商業的貸付の方式で日本に貸付を行う氣構えがある。この型の融資にとって最大の關心事は、今日行われるすべての對日投資に對し、將來平和條約締結後日本に接收されるような場合に備えて、承認と適當な保護とを與える旨日本側が保證することである。占領終結後に及ぶ外資處遇方針を公表することは、外資導入奬勵上肝要である。米國では、目下産業擴張期を迎えて、企業家に對し、短期償却その他の助成措置を講ずるなど、米國内にいくらでも有利な投資の機會がある現狀であるから、對外投資はそのリスクが釣り合に大きいときは、米國資本として大して氣乘りがしない。

日本の將來の通商政策は、米國の政府及び民間にとって相當な關心事である。米國政府の對日貿易に關する立場は、ずっと前から占領政策の中に具體的に示されている。それは、實際に米國との通商にあたって、不公正な通商上の慣行に對して自國の利益を保護する米國政府としての責任をとる一方、他の第三國となんら差別のない待遇を日本に與えることである。いかなる方面からの競爭をも退けようとする特殊な利害關係がすべての國に常に存在する。しかし

ながら、これらの國や商社は日本から買うばかりでなく賣ることも希望しているわけだから、國内の商業又は工業に對してなんらかの保護を與えることは、日本の場合と他の國の場合とを問わず、必ず國家間の互惠的な協定で決めるべき問題である。

連合國最高司令官總司令部・極東軍使節團は米國における發注の機關ではなかったが、協議の結果、關係兩國の間に直ちに取引關係ができないかもしれない數個の分野が展開された。これを詳しくいえば、適正な品質と價格を有する日本製消費財の販賣を増加する機會がある程度與えられるかもしれない。しかし、これは米國の會社がこれらの製品の生産を再開するまでの一時的の現象とみるべきである。それだけでなく、日本の産業が特需物資に對する一部の國際市場を引受けることもありうるわけで、これによって米國の産業は軍需品生産のかたわら、ある程度まで消費財の生産能力を保持するように援助されるであろう。

米國では、日本の現下の海運事情の重大性が一般に了解されている。米國と國際海運の運營との關係については、日本を差別的に待遇するような傾向はない。反對があるの

は、日本の海運自體に對してではなく、戰前日本が行ったような運賃の切崩しが海運界において復活することをおそれるがためである。この活動分野においても、もし日本が明確な海運政策を示すならば、それは限りなく價値のあることがあるであろう。米國の繋船中の遊休船を賃貸ないし用船することについては、いかなる外國にも使用させることに對し嚴重な法律上の制限があり、これはあえて日本に對する差別的な政策ではない。これについては、米國當局者において、日本にとって有利な特別の考慮をなすべく強力且つ積極的な努力をしたのであるが、法制上の改正の成否は非常に疑問とみられるばかりでなく、もしこれができたとしても、目下の緊急の問題に間に合いそうにもない。日本としては、このような「棚からぼた餅」的なことを期待するよりもむしろなんらか他の解決法を求めることが一層實際的であるように思われる。

今後の日本の産業上の進歩については、米國民間會社は、すでに商業的基礎において技術上の援助を與えることに對し、全幅の贊意を表明した。恆久的な一般政策の發表と、投下資本の保護とをもってする適正な誘因があれば、株式

所有に對する非常な關心が起るであろう。日本は特許權を保護する保證のもとに、直接購入することを前提として技術上の大きな進歩を企てることができる。現在米國製の特殊用途工作機械に對する需要がきわめて活潑であるが、日本は日米經濟協力計畫に適用すべき工業能力を増進するためのこれら工作機械に對する需要につき考慮を與えられるであろう。

日米經濟協力計畫による調達の實務は、現在の調達機關と民間買付機關とを通じて行われる。これらの諸機關は、各自獨立別個の豫算會計資金を擁しているので、中央機關による統一的調達はできない。米國が日本で行う調達のすべてを總括調整する機關も考慮中ではあるが、これは米國側の需要を一つにまとめて日本側政府と工業生産の計畫及び施設動員の問題に關し折衝するのが主目的である。

米國は、日本の可能な工業力を東南アジアの原料生産の増加と可能な工業力の増強とに最大限に利用できると考えている。日本は現在軍需生産に從事している平時の仕出國が供給できない資本財及び消費財を東南アジアその他の地域に輸出する好機會に惠まれている。このためには、日本

880

4 制限緩和に向けた対応（昭和24年5月～27年4月）

は、全面的な日米經濟協力計画に結び付いて諸計画を發展させるため、多方面にわたる米國の經濟援助と東南アジアに派遣されている技術顧問團からの援助とを得るよう努力すべきである。

總括的にいえば、米國は日本に發展性のある存立可能な經濟を維持しうるように完全な自主を認める平和條約の早期締結を明らかに望んでおり、日本を自由國家族の一員として迎え、日本が健全な國內的發展と自由世界の平和及び發展とのために使用する限り、日本に市場と資源とを獲得させることを切望している。平和條約締結後も、日本の幸福と不斷の進步とに對して引續き關心がもたれることは至極明白である。米國は歷史上まれにみる寬大さで占領下の日本の再建に盡したが、米國は日本が平和條約締結後、これまでになし遂げた健全な經濟的發展を後退させるようなことが萬一あるとしても、日本を窮境から救出する責任があるとは考えていない。過度のインフレは、日本製品の價格を高騰させ、日本製品が世界の市場から閉め出される結果となるとともに日本が適量な原料輸入の途を阻まれることになるであろう。

總司令部使節團による調査の結果、日本はきわめて滿足すべき速度で經濟的進展を續けうる大きな機會があることが明らかに示された。しかし、日本は直ちに長期的經濟政策を樹立し、これを世界に發表する絕對的な必要がある。この政策は、原則において健全なものであるならば、必しも米國で實行されているものとか、占領當局によって提唱されたものである必要はない。このことは、すでにずっと以前から總司令部の主張であった。日本の將來は、將來の健全な經濟政策を採用し、自由世界との產業上の協力を行う上において、日本自身が妥當な行動を採ることによって確立される。その成功の可能性は、大いにあるように思われる。

リッジウェイ最高司令官は、占領の殘りの期間において、總司令部の諸經濟機關は長期にわたる互惠的關係の問題としての日米經濟協力體制の進展に全力をあげて努力することを明らかにした。

編　注　本文書は、昭和二十七年二月、外務省國際協力局特別資料室作成「日本管理資料㈤」より拔粹。

昭和26年5月31日　政務局経済第一課作成

「對外經濟政策の大綱(案)」

對外經濟政策の大綱(案)

昭和二六、五、三一

政・經・一

一、わが國の對外經濟政策は外交政策の一環として、わが國の基本的外交政策の推進に寄與するものでなければならない。この意味において、對外經濟政策の基調は

(1) 國際連合との協力
(2) 西歐民主主義諸國との協同動作に置かれなければならない。

(1) 國際連合との協力については、わが國が憲章第五十五條に掲げられた原則「諸國間の平和的且つ友好的關係に必要な安定と福利との條件」を創造するために國際連合と協力することである。

このことは、對日講和條約米國草案前文でもわが國がこのような意圖を宣明することになつているので講和條約上の義務としてもわが國が對外經濟政策上第一に遂行しなければならないところである。

このことは又わが國ができる限り國際連合の專門機關及びその他の國際機關(例えば國際通貨基金、食糧及び農業機關、貿易及び關稅に關する一般協定等)への早期加入を實現し、これら專門機關の目的を推進することに協力しなければならないことを意味するのである。

(2) 西歐民主主義諸國は今や共產主義圈に對抗する防衞體制の整備强化をはかるとともに共產主義圈諸國の戰力の增强を防止するための努力を續けつつある。この西歐諸國の現在執りつつある兩面に積極的に協力することはわが國の執るべき第一次的施策であるといわねばならない。この意味においてわが國としては一面西歐民主主義國が共產主義圈に對抗する防衞體制(諸國の政治及び經濟的安定を保持することが防衞體制確立のための前提條件とされている)確立のためにわが國に要望するところに欣然として應じ(いわゆる日米協力の問題)他面わが國の經濟にとつて不利であつても共產主義圈の戰力を增强

4 制限緩和に向けた対応(昭和24年5月～27年4月)

する結果となる措置を回避する努力を續けなければならない。後者の見地からわが國としては中共地區に對する禁輸を當分の間繼續していかねばならない。

二、わが國の對外經濟政策上、重點を置かなければならない第二の點は後進地域（特にアジアにおける）の開發に對して寄與することである。

第一次世界大戰後の國際經濟協力が成功しなかった一つの原因として夙に國際連盟は後進國の開發計畫が樹立遂行されなかつたことを指摘したが、こういう考え方を反映して後進國開發の問題は第二次戰爭終了直後から檢討されて來た。特に最近においては、これら地域の開發がその經濟的政治的安定に必要であり又歐米の再軍備上不可缺の稀少戰略物資の供給を増大するという見地からも必要であるとして非常な努力がなされつつある。「アメリカ」の「ポイント・フォア」、國際連合及びその地域的經濟委員會たる極東アジア經濟會議の後進國開發計畫はこういう努力のあらわれであり、又、最近國際連合の經濟社會理事會でも本件についての大規模な計畫を檢討中であるといわれている。後進地域特に東南アジア地域では第二次戰爭およびこれに引き續く内亂のため未だその經濟的復興すら完全に行われていない。その經濟的復興及び開發に寄與することは、歴史的、地理的及び人種的に緊密な關係に立つているわが國の神聖な使命であると考えなければならない。

東南アジア地域は現在先進諸國への原料の供給源である。特に外國貿易に對する依存度の高いわが國としては、これらの地域からの原料の輸入をえて經濟を維持發展せしめることができているのである。これらの地域は進んでその生産する原料及び半製品を供給してくれている。然るに先進諸國は、再軍備の衝撃のために、これらの地域がその經濟開發のために切望しつつある生産財及び消費財を充分に供給しえない立場に置かれている。これらのことを考えれば、わが國として、たとい國内的の不自由をしのんでもこれらの地域の必要とする資材の供給を確保するための措置を執らなければならない。この意味においてわが國としては特需もさることながら差當りこれら地域への輸出を確保し、これら地域の經濟開發

の速度を遅緩せしめないような適當な措置を執ることが必要である。

以上に述べた必需資材の供給から更に一歩を進めて、わが國としてはこれら地域の經濟開發に更に積極的に參加しなければならない。これらの地域は現在必要な技術と資本を欠除している。わが國としてはこれらの地域への技術的援助と民間投資の進出及び必要に應じて直接又は間接の長期借款の供與の形式による援助によつてこれら地域の經濟開發に積極的に寄興しなければならない。わが國將來の產業構造は終局において、これら地域との經濟的紐帶の強化の方向に執らざるを得ない立場にあることを考えれば、これらのことは更に重要である。

三、對外經濟政策の第三の基調は通商の自由、通商障碍の低減及び差別待遇の撤廢に置かれなければならない。この意味においてわが國は進んで國際貿易憲章の早期成立を支持すると共に、國內施策上、この目標と背馳する如き措置（高率な保護關稅、輸出及び輸入割當又は爲替制限の強化等）はできるだけこれを避けなければならない。

四、對外經濟政策の第四の基調は、公正な通商上の慣習を遵守することである。わが國は過去においてしばしば不公正な方法で通商の伸張をはかつたとの非難を受けて來たのである。わが國は將來においては斯くの如き非難を拂底するように努力しなければならない。この意味で輸出補助金ダンピング（海運を含む）等は絕對にこれを避け又工業所有權、商標權等を尊重しなければならない。このことは講和條約草案においても前文において日本は遵守する意圖を表明し又第五章で公正取引を規定する多邊的取極に參加すべきことを約束することになつているので講和條約上の義務としても絕對に違守しなければならない。

〰〰〰〰〰〰〰

291

旅券発給権限に関する指令

昭和26年6月2日　連合国最高司令官総司令部より
　　　　　　　　日本政府宛

GENERAL HEADQUARTERS
SUPREME COMMANDER FOR THE ALLIED POWERS
APO 500

2 June 1951

AG 014.331 (2 Jun 51) GA
SCAPIN 2155

MEMORANDUM FOR: JAPANESE GOVERNMENT

SUBJECT: Authority for Issuance of Passports

1. Rescissions:

   a. Memorandum for the Japanese Government from General Headquarters, Supreme Commander for the Allied Powers, AG 000.74 (14 Apr 47) GA, SCAPIN 1609, 14 April 1947, subject: Travel Documents for Japanese Nationals Traveling Abroad.

   b. Memorandum for the Japanese Government from General Headquarters, Supreme Commander for the Allied Powers, AG 014.331 (14 Apr 47) GA, SCAPIN 1609/1, 25 August 1948, subject: Issuance of Passports or Certificates of Identity or Nationality to Japanese Nationals.

2. References:

   a. Memorandum for the Japanese Government from General Headquarters, Supreme Commander for the Allied Powers, AG 014.331 (5 Jan 50) AG, SCAPIN 2072, 5 January 1950, subject: Applications for Travel of Japanese Nationals Abroad.

   b. Memorandum for the Japanese Ministry of Foreign Affairs from Diplomatic Section, General Headquarters, Supreme Commander for the Allied Powers, AG 095 (10 Apr 51) DS, 10 April 1951, subject: Additional Functions for Japanese Government Overseas Agencies.

3. The Japanese Government is hereby granted authority to issue passports and to establish regulations for issuance of such passports, which comply with the following:

   a. Japanese nationals residing in Japan and desiring to travel abroad will continue to receive approval from the Supreme Commander for the Allied Powers in accordance with established regulations. The following indorsement will be placed in the passport:

   The bearer has been authorized by the Supreme Commander for the Allied Powers under instructions AG 014.331 (5 Jan 50) AG, SCAPIN 2072, 5 January 1950, to depart from Japan in order to proceed to _____ for the purpose of _____.

This authorization is valid until _____ and may be extended only upon the express authorization of the Supreme Commander for the Allied Powers.

b. Japanese nationals residing abroad and desiring to travel to Japan may be issued a passport. To facilitate travel of these individuals, the Japanese Government or agencies thereof are authorized to indicate in the passport that the Supreme Commander for the Allied Powers has granted entry clearance into Japan for such nationals. The Supreme Commander for the Allied Powers assumes no responsibility in the matter of reentry into the country of origin or travel in countries en route to or from Japan.

c. Japanese nationals residing abroad may be issued Japanese passports as established by Japanese passport regulations. However, recognition of the validity of such passports as a travel document is a matter of concern of the country of residence or the country to or through which individuals desire to travel.

4. Overseas Agencies may be designated by the Japanese Government to accept applications for passports from Japanese nationals residing abroad and to issue passports to Japanese nationals abroad in accordance with such regulations as the Japanese Government may prescribe.

5. The proposed passport and regulations will be submitted to this headquarters for approval.

FOR THE SUPREME COMMANDER:

K. B. BUSH
Brigadier General, USA
Adjutant General

292 昭和26年6月4日 連合国最高司令官総司令部より 外務省宛

国際会議への日本の参加許可に関する指令

付記 右和訳文

GENERAL HEADQUARTERS
SUPREME COMMANDER FOR THE ALLIED POWERS
APO 500

Diplomatic Section

AG 092 (4 Jun 51) DS

4 June 1951

MEMORANDUM FOR: Japanese Ministry of Foreign Affairs
SUBJECT: Authorization for Japanese Attendance at International Meetings

1. The Ministry is advised that it will no longer be necessary for the Japanese Government to secure the approval of this Headquarters in each individual instance prior to the consideration of invitations to regular meetings of recognized international organizations of which Japan is, or in the future shall become, a member.

2. The normal travel documentation procedure applicable to individuals who may attend such meetings as the official representatives of the Japanese Government will remain unaltered. The processing of travel documentation in such instances will be authorized if the pertinent papers bear an indication that the traveller is designated to attend, as an official Japanese Government representative, a meeting of an international organization of which Japan is an authorized member.

3. This Headquarters should be notified immediately of any invitations of the foregoing nature which the Japanese Government may accept, but communication with the secretariat of the relevant international organization should be conducted as authorized in paragraph 3 (a) of SCAPIN 2110, dated 29 June 1950 and paragraph 3 (g) of SCAPIN 2142 of 13 February 1951.

4. This in no way alters the requirement that the Japanese Government shall secure the approval of this Headquarters in each individual instance prior to the consideration of invitations to attend meetings of international organizations of which Japan is not an authorized member.

For the Chief, Diplomatic Section:

Niles W. Bond
Deputy Chief

（付 記）

國際會議の日本參加許可に關する總司令部外交局覺書
連合國最高司令官總司令部外交局
APO 五〇〇

昭和二十六年六月四日

AG○九二(二十六年六月四日) DS

覺書あて先　日本外務省

件　名　國際會議への日本參加許可

1　日本外務省に對し、日本政府は、日本が現在加盟國であるか、又は將來加盟國となる公認國際機關の定期會議への招請につき考慮するに先立ち、その都度當總司令部の承認を得ることは最早必要でないことを通告する。

2　右のような諸會議に日本政府の公式代表として出席する個人に適用する通常の渡航書類作成手續は、いぜんとして變更されない。右のような場合における渡航書類の作成は、もしも關係書類に渡航者は日本が加盟國として認められている國際機關の會議に日本政府の公式代表として出席するよう命ぜられた者である旨の表示がある場合には、許可される。

3　日本政府の受諾しうるような前記性質の招請については、遅滞なく當司令部に通告しなければならない。しかしながら、關係國際團体の事務局との通信は昭和二十五年六月二十九日付SCAPIN二一一〇號第三項（い）及び昭和二十六年二月十三日付SCAPIN二一四二號第三項（と）に許可されているところに從って行わなければ

ならない。

4　右は、日本が公認加盟國でない國際機關の會議に出席するための招請を考慮するに先立ち、その都度當司令部の承認を得なければならないという要件をなんら變更するものではない。

外交局長に代って

局長代理

ナイルス・ダブリュー・ボンド

〜〜〜〜〜〜〜〜〜〜〜〜〜

編　注　本文書は、昭和二十七年二月、外務省国際協力局特別資料室作成「日本管理資料（五）」より抜粋。

293

昭和26年8月27日　連合国最高司令官総司令部より
　　　　　　　　　日本政府宛

在外日本政府官吏または代表者との通信に関する指令

GENERAL HEADQUARTERS
SUPREME COMMANDER FOR THE ALLIED POWERS
APO 500

27 August 1951

AG 311 (27 Aug 51) CCS
SCAPIN 2164

MEMORANDUM FOR: JAPANESE GOVERNMENT

SUBJECT: Communications with Japanese Government Officials or Representatives Abroad

1. Reference is made to:

   a. Memorandum for the Japanese Government, AG 091 (29 Jan 46) GS, SCAPIN 677, 29 January 1946, Subj: Governmental and Administrative Separation of Certain Outlying Areas from Japan.

   b. Memorandum for the Japanese Government, AG 311 (24 Feb 50) CCS, SCAPIN 2085, 24 February 1950, Subj: Rationalization of Japan's International Telecommunications Services.

   c. Memorandum for the Japanese Government, AG 311.23 (23 May 50) CCS, SCAPIN 2098, Subj: Communications with Japanese Overseas Agencies.

2. In addition to the specific authorization to communicate with Japanese Overseas Agencies pursuant to paragraph 2 of reference 1c above, the Japanese Government is authorized to communicate with Japanese Government officials or official representatives abroad not connected with Japanese Overseas Agencies.

3. Direct communication between the Civil Communications Section, General Headquarters, Supreme Commander for the Allied Powers, and the Ministry of Telecommunications, concerning matters within the scope of this memorandum is authorized.

FOR THE SUPREME COMMANDER:

C. C. B. WARDEN
Colonel, AGC
Adjutant General

294　昭和26年8月30日　連合国最高司令官総司令部より　日本政府宛

金融および貿易協定の交渉ならびに締結を許可する旨の指令

付記　右和訳文

GENERAL HEADQUARTERS
SUPREME COMMANDER FOR THE ALLIED POWERS
APO 500

30 August 1951

AG 091.31 (30 Aug 51) ESS/FTC

SCAPIN 2166

MEMORANDUM FOR: JAPANESE GOVERNMENT

SUBJECT: Authority to Negotiate and Sign Financial and Trade Agreements

1. The Japanese Government is hereby authorized to enter into negotiations, on its own behalf, with other countries, with a view toward concluding financial and trade agreements or arrangements, trade plans and memoranda, side letters and other documents in implementation thereof.

2. The Japanese Government is hereby authorized to sign and to exchange with the representatives of the governments concerned, documents resulting from negotiations as authorized, to be effective upon the coming into force of the treaty of peace between the Allied Powers, or any of them, and Japan.

FOR THE SUPREME COMMANDER:

C. C. B. WARDEN
Colonel, AGC
Adjutant General

（付記）

金融及び貿易取極を交渉し署名する權限に關する

總司令部覺書

連合國最高司令官總司令部

APO 五〇〇

AG〇九一・三一(二十六年九月三十日)ESS/FTC

SCAPIN二一六六

覺書あて先　日本政府

件　名　金融及び貿易取極を交渉し署名する權限

昭和二十六年八月三十日

1　日本政府に對し金融及び貿易協定又は取極、その實施のための貿易計畫及び覺書、副文書並びに他の文書を締結する目的をもって、自らのために他國と交渉を開始することをここに許可する。

2　日本政府に對し、平和條約が連合諸國またはそのいずれかの一國と日本との間に効力を發生すると同時に有效となるべき、許可されたような交渉の結果生ずる文書に署名し及び關係國政府の代表者との間にそれを交換することをここに許可する。

最高司令官に代って

高級副官

副官部附大佐　シー・シー・ビー・ウォーデン

編注　本文書は、昭和二十七年二月、外務省国際協力局特別資料室作成「日本管理資料(五)」より抜粋。

〰〰〰〰〰〰〰〰〰〰

昭和26年9月13日　連合国最高司令官総司令部より　日本政府宛

295　連合国最高司令官に対して派遣された在日外交代表との直接連絡の許可に関する指令

付記一　右和訳文

二　昭和二十六年九月十三日

「對外交渉權擴大措置についての外務大臣談話」

GENERAL HEADQUARTERS
SUPREME COMMANDER FOR THE ALLIED POWERS
APO 500

13 September 1951

AG 091 (6 Sep 51) DS
SCAPIN 2170

MEMORANDUM FOR: JAPANESE GOVERNMENT

SUBJECT: Authorization for Direct Communication Between the Japanese Government and Foreign Diplomatic Representatives Accredited to the Supreme Commander for the Allied Powers

　1. Rescission. Memorandum for Japanese Government AG 091 (26 May 50) DS, SCAPIN 2142, subject: Authorization for Direct Communication Between the Japanese Government and Foreign Diplomatic Representatives Accredited to the Supreme Commander for the Allied Powers, 13 February 1951.

　2. References. a. Memorandum for Japanese Government, AG 091.1 (4 Nov 45) GS, SCAPIN 237, subject: Official

Relations Between Japanese Government and Representatives of Neutral Nations, 4 November 1945.

b. Memorandum for Japanese Government, AG 091 (29 Jan 46) GS, SCAPIN 677, subject: Governmental and Administrative Separation of Certain Outlying Areas from Japan, 29 January 1946.

c. Memorandum for Japanese Government, AG 091. (2 Dec 46) GS, SCAPIN 1372, subject: Contact with Japanese Officials, 2 December 1946.

d. Memorandum for Japanese Government, AG 091 (28 May 48) ESS/EX, SCAPIN 1901, subject: Authorization for Direct Communication between Japanese Government Board of Trade and Firms, Persons, and Foreign Missions on Commercial Matters, 28 May 1948.

3. The Japanese Government is hereby authorized direct communication with the diplomatic representatives of foreign governments accredited to the Supreme Commander for the Allied Powers, subject to the provisions of this memorandum, the restrictions embodied in referenced memoranda being relaxed only to the extent of permitting such limited contact.

4. The Japanese Government may receive from and dispatch to the diplomatic representatives referred to in paragraph 9 written communications on subjects of mutual concern except that all agreements between Japan and other countries are subject to prior approval of the Supreme Commander for the Allied Powers. Oral consultation is permissible only on matters on which written communication has been made.

5. Communications on subjects which involve interpretation of or deviation from standing policies will continue to be submitted through Diplomatic Section, General Headquarters, Supreme Commander for the Allied Powers.

6. The present authorization for direct written communication is a specific delegation of responsibility to the Japanese Government which will, therefore, submit to Diplomatic Section, General Headquarters, Supreme Commander for the Allied Powers, copies of all communications it receives or dispatches under the provisions of this memorandum. The Japanese Government is instructed to use the English language, with such

4 制限緩和に向けた対応(昭和24年5月～27年4月)

7. This direct channel of written communication does not in any way deprive the foreign diplomatic representatives of their right to continue transmitting any communications through this headquarters if they so desire. Both the accredited foreign diplomatic representatives and the Japanese Government may, when either deems it advisable in any particular case, refer any communication received which may be considered controversial, or as involving policy to the Supreme Commander for the Allied Powers for the latter's consideration, clarification or reply.

8. The accreditation of foreign diplomatic representatives in Japan remains unchanged, being solely to the Supreme Commander for the Allied Powers.

9. The Japanese Government may communicate directly with the foreign diplomatic representatives accredited to the Supreme Commander for the Allied Powers, who are listed below, under the provisions of this memorandum. This list will be modified by subsequent memoranda as may become necessary.

a. The Australian Mission in Japan
b. The Belgian Mission in Japan
c. The Brazilian Diplomatic Mission in Japan
d. The Canadian Liaison Mission in Japan
e. The Chinese Mission in Japan
f. The Danish Diplomatic Mission in Japan
g. The French Mission in Japan
h. The Indian Liaison Mission in Japan
i. The Indonesian Mission in Japan
j. The Italian Diplomatic Mission in Japan
k. The Korean Diplomatic Mission in Japan
l. The Netherlands Mission in Japan
m. The Norwegian Diplomatic Mission in Japan
n. The Peruvian Diplomatic Mission in Japan
o. The Philippine Diplomatic Mission in Japan
p. The Portuguese Diplomatic Agency in Japan
q. The Spanish Diplomatic Mission in Japan
r. The Swedish Diplomatic Mission in Japan

Japanese or Chinese characters as may be required to facilitate the reading of romanized names, in all communications authorized by this memorandum.

s. The Swiss Diplomatic Mission in Japan
t. The Thai Diplomatic Mission in Japan
u. The Turkish Diplomatic Agency
v. The United Kingdom Liaison Mission in Japan
w. The Uruguayan Diplomatic Agency in Japan.

10. In the absence of contrary indications from the Japanese Government, it will be understood that the channel of all correspondence between the Japanese Government and the foreign diplomatic mission on the subjects specified will be through the Japanese Ministry of Foreign Affairs, except that correspondence on international trade operations may pass directly between the missions and the Ministry of International Trade and Industry.

FOR THE SUPREME COMMANDER:

C. C. B. WARDEN
Colonel, AGC
Adjutant General

連合國最高司令官總司令部覺書
連合國最高司令官總司令部
APO　五〇〇
　　　　　昭和二十六年九月十三日
AG〇九一(二十六年九月十三日)DS
SCAPIN 二二七〇
件　名　日本政府と連合國最高司令官に對して派遣された外國の外交代表との直接通信の許可
覺書あて先　日本政府

1　廢止、日本政府あて覺書、AG〇九一(二十五年五月二十六日)DS、SCAPIN二一四二、昭和二十六年二月十三日付、件名、「日本政府と連合國最高司令官に對して派遣された外國の外交代表との直接通信の許可」

2　参照
い　日本政府あて覺書、AG〇九一・一(二十年十一月四日)GS、SCAPIN二三七、昭和二十年十一月四日付、件名、「日本政府と中立國代表との公的關係」
ろ　日本政府あて覺書、AG〇九一(二十一年一月二十九日)GS、SCAPIN六七七、昭和二十一年一月

(付記一)
日本政府と連合國最高司令官に對して派遣された外國

4　制限緩和に向けた対応（昭和24年5月～27年4月）

二十九日付、件名、「若干の外かく地域の日本からの政治上及び行政上の分離」

は日本政府あて覺書、AG〇九一・一一二（二十一年十二月二日）GS、SCAPIN一三七二、昭和二十一年十二月二日付、件名、「日本官憲との接觸」に日本政府あて覺書、AG〇九一（二十三年五月二十八日）ESS／EX、SCAPIN一九〇一、昭和二十三年五月二十八日付、件名、「貿易上の事項に關する日本政府貿易廳と商社、個人及び外國使節團との直接通信の許可」

3　日本政府は、この覺書の規定に從うことを條件として、連合國最高司令官に對し派遣された外國政府の外交代表との直接通信をここに許可され、參照覺書に含まれた諸制限は、このような制限された接觸を許す範圍までにおいてのみ、緩和される。

4　日本政府は、相互に關係あるすべての問題について書面による通信を、第九項に記された外交代表から受領し、又はこれに送付することができる。但し、日本國と他の諸國家との間のすべての取極は連合國最高司令官の事前の承認を要する。口頭の協議は、書面による通信がなされた事項についてのみ、許される。

5　既定の政策の解釋問題にかかわるか又はそのような政策より逸脱する事項に關する通信は、引き續き連合國最高司令官總司令部外交局を經由して提出されるものとする。

6　書面による直接通信の許可は、日本政府への責任の特定委任であり、從って、日本政府は、この覺書の規定に基いて受領し又は發送するすべての通信の寫を、連合國最高司令官總司令部外交局に提出するものとする。日本國政府は、この覺書によって許可されたすべての通信においては、英語を、ローマ字名の讀方を容易にするために必要な日本字又は漢字とともに、使用するよう指令される。

7　書面による通信のこの直接の經路は、外國の外交代表が希望する場合には、いかなる通信をも、引き續き本司令部を通じて轉送する權利を少しも外國の外交代表より奪うものではない。外國の派遣外交代表も日本國政府も、共に、その受領した通信で紛議をかもし易いか又は政策

問題にかかわると考えられるものを、いずれかが個個の場合において適當と思うときは、連合國最高司令官の審議、解明又は同答を求めるために、連合國最高司令官に照會することができる。

8 外國の在日外交代表の派遣先は、もっぱら連合國最高司令官であって、いぜんとして變らない。

9 連合國最高司令官に對して派遣された外國の外交代表で、日本國政府がこの覺書の規定に基いて直接通信することのできるものは、次の表のとおりである。この表は、必要が起り次第今後の覺書によって修正される。

a 在日オーストラリア使節團
b 在日ベルギー使節團
c 在日ブラジル外交使節團
d 在日カナダ連絡使節團
e 在日中華民國使節團
f 在日デンマーク外交使節團
g 在日フランス使節團
h 在日インド連絡使節團
i 在日インドネシア使節團
j 在日イタリア外交使節團
k 在日大韓民國外交使節團
l 在日オランダ使節團
m 在日ノールウェー外交使節團
n 在日ペルー外交使節團
o 在日フィリピン使節團
p 在日ポルトガル外交事務所
q 在日スペイン外交使節團
r 在日スウェーデン外交使節團
s 在日スイス外交使節團
t 在日タイ外交使節團
u トルコ外交事務所
v 在日連合王國連絡使節團
w 在日ウルグァイ外交事務所

10 日本國政府と外國使節團からの特定事項の指示のない場合には、日本國政府と外國使節團との特定事項に關するすべての通信は、日本外務省を經由するものと了解される。但し、通商活動に關する通信は、諸使節團と通商産業省との間に直接送受することができる。

896

4 制限緩和に向けた対応（昭和24年5月～27年4月）

最高司令官に代って
高級副官
副官部附大佐　シー・シー・ビー・ウォーデン

編　注　本文書は、昭和二十七年二月、外務省国際協力局特別資料室作成「日本管理資料㈤」より抜粋。

（付記二）

昭和二十六年九月十三日

外務省情報部

對外交渉權擴大措置についての外務大臣談話

平和條約の調印に續いて、今般、日本にある外國ミッションとの間の交渉權が大幅に擴大され、かくていよいよわが國が諸外國ミッションとの交渉の面において自らの責任で行動することができるようになつたことは、誠に意義深いものがある。

從來より、特定の事項のみについては交渉權が認められていたが、この措置によって、條約發效までに果すべき懸案の解決は大いに促進されるものと確信する。

296　昭和26年9月22日　連合国最高司令官総司令部より日本政府宛

外国人に対する裁判管轄権に関する指令

GENERAL HEADQUARTERS
SUPREME COMMANDER FOR THE ALLIED POWERS
APO 500

22 September 1951

AG 015 (6 Oct 50) LS-L
SCAPIN 2127/1
MEMORANDUM FOR: JAPANESE GOVERNMENT
SUBJECT: Exercise of Criminal Jurisdiction

1. Reference is made to memorandum for the Japanese Government from General Headquarters, Supreme Commander for the Allied Powers, AG 015 (6 Oct 50) LS-L, SCAPIN 2127, subject: Exercise of Civil and Criminal Jurisdiction, 18 October 1950.

2. Subparagraphs 6a and b of reference memorandum are rescinded and the following substituted:

"6. Offenses.　a.　It shall be unlawful for any person in

Japan to:

(1) Commit an act prejudicial to the security of the occupation forces or occupation personnel;

(2) Kill or assault occupation personnel;

(3) Interfere with or hinder the arrest of any person sought, or assist in, or further the escape of any person detained by the occupation forces, or by others pursuant to the direction of the Supreme Commander for the Allied Powers, or his authorized subordinates;

(4) Interfere with, refuse information required by, make any false or misleading statement orally or in writing to, or defraud in any manner, any of the occupation personnel in a matter of official concern;

(5) Commit an act in behalf or in support of any organization dissolved or declared illegal by the Supreme Commander for the Allied Powers, or dissolved or declared illegal at the order of the Supreme Commander for the Allied Powers;

(6) Conspire to commit any of the foregoing offenses or commit any act which aids or abets the commission of such offenses.

b. Japanese courts will exercise criminal jurisdiction over offenses enumerated in subparagraph 6a unless jurisdiction is assumed by a military occupation court."

3. Except as otherwise provided in this memorandum, the provisions of the reference memorandum shall continue in full force and effect.

4. Any provision of law, regulation, or directive in conflict with the provisions of this memorandum is hereby superseded, or shall be deemed amended to conform therewith. Reference is made to memorandum for the Japanese Government from General Headquarters, Supreme Commander for the Allied Powers, AG 386.5 (5 Sep 51) LS-L, SCAPIN 2167, subject: Exercise of Jurisdiction over Property, 5 September 1951. No provision of SCAPIN 2167 shall be construed to divest the Japanese criminal courts of jurisdiction over persons in cases involving the categories of

4 制限緩和に向けた対応(昭和24年5月～27年4月)

297

昭和26年9月24日

連合国最高司令官総司令部経済科学局 より

外務省、通商産業省宛

貿易および金融協定に関する指令

GENERAL HEADQUARTERS
SUPREME COMMANDER FOR THE ALLIED POWERS

Economic and Scientific Section
APO 500

24 September 1951

091.31 (24 Sept 51) ESS/FTC

MEMORANDUM FOR: Ministry of International Trade and Industry
　　　　　　　　　　　Ministry of Foreign Affairs

SUBJECT: Trade and Financial Agreements

1. Reference is memorandum for the Japanese Government from General Headquarters, Supreme Commander for the Allied Powers, AG 091.31 (30 Aug 51) ESS/FTC, SCAPIN 2166, 30 August 1951, subject: Authority to Negotiate and Sign Financial and Trade Agreements.

2. When the Government of Japan negotiates new trade and/or financial agreements with other countries to become effective with the coming into force of the peace treaty, but desires the provisions of the new agreements become effective prior to the coming into force of the peace treaty, the Government of Japan should transmit the final drafts of the agreements to this office for consideration.

property enumerated in paragraph 2 thereof.

5. Nothing contained herein shall be construed to invalidate or otherwise affect any action, pending or concluded, taken pursuant to the deleted portions of the reference memorandum.

6. Direct communication between Legal Section, General Headquarters, Supreme Commander for the Allied Powers, and Japanese Government agencies concerned, is authorized on matters within the scope of this memorandum.

FOR THE SUPREME COMMANDER:

　　　　　　　　　　　　C. C. B. WARDEN
　　　　　　　　　　　　Colonel, AGC
　　　　　　　　　　　　Adjutant General

3. In order to conform the provisions of any agreements that are desired to come into force prior to the effective date of the peace treaty with those which the Government of Japan negotiates for the post treaty period, certain technical changes will be necessary so as to assure that the agreements which the Supreme Commander for the Allied Powers signs in respect of Occupied Japan adequately conform with the Supreme Commander for the Allied Power's area of responsibility. After these technical changes have been made, the Supreme Commander for the Allied Powers will sign such agreements in respect of Occupied Japan unless the provisions of such agreements are contrary to the policy of the Supreme Commander for the Allied Powers; in which case, a conference would be convened with the interested parties for the purpose of negotiating the necessary changes in order that the agreements could become effective prior to the coming into force of the peace treaty.

4. The foregoing procedure has been adopted in order to permit negotiations free from any possible prejudice by Headquarters representation on either the Japanese Government's or the other countries' position during the negotiation of agreements which are to become effective with the coming into force of the peace treaty. However, when negotiating agreements which are to become effective prior to the coming into force of the peace treaty, it is requisite that Headquarters personnel be present at the negotiations.

FOR THE CHIEF, ECONOMIC AND SCIENTIFIC SECTION:

C. C. CAMPBELL
Chief
Foreign Trade and Commerce Division

298

在外事務所の権限および機能強化に関する指令

昭和26年9月28日　連合国最高司令官総司令部より
日本政府宛

付記　右和訳文

GENERAL HEADQUARTERS
SUPREME COMMANDER FOR THE ALLIED POWERS
APO 500

28 September 1951

AG 092 (20 Sep 51) DS
SCAPIN 2173

MEMORANDUM FOR: JAPANESE GOVERNMENT

SUBJECT: Abilities and Functions of Japanese Government Overseas Agencies

1. References. a. Memorandum for the Japanese Government, subject: Establishment of Japanese Overseas Agencies in the United States of America, 9 February 1950.

b. Memorandum for the Japanese Government, AG 311.23 (23 May 50) CCS, SCAPIN 2098, subject: Communications with Japanese Overseas Agencies, 23 May 1950.

c. Memorandum for the Japanese Government, AG 091.31 (30 Aug 51) ESS/FTC, SCAPIN 2166, subject: Authority to Negotiate and Sign Financial and Trade Agreements, 30 August 1951.

d. Memorandum for the Japanese Government, AG 091 (6 Sep 51) DS, SCAPIN 2170, subject: Authorization for Direct Communication Between the Japanese Government and Foreign Diplomatic Representatives Accredited to the Supreme Commander for the Allied Powers, 13 September 1951.

2. All restrictions imposed upon the abilities and functions of Japanese Government, with respect to the abilities and functions of Japanese Government Overseas Agencies, by the Memorandums referred to in references 1a and b are rescinded.

3. The Japanese Government is authorized to conclude agreements, with the various Governments concerned, which will define the abilities and functions of the individual Japanese Government Overseas Agencies in terms mutually satisfactory to the Japanese Government and to the several host Governments.

4. The functions to be exercised by the Japanese Government Overseas Agencies under the terms of such agreements will constitute a specific delegation of responsibility to the Japanese Government. The Japanese Government will therefore, submit to Diplomatic Section, General Headquarters, Supreme Commander for the Allied Powers, copies of all communications of a diplomatic or quasi-diplomatic nature which the several Japanese Government Overseas Agencies may dispatch to, or receive from, the several host Governments. All agreements between Japan and

other countries to be concluded by the Japanese Government Overseas Agencies are subject to prior approval of the Supreme Commander for the Allied Powers, with the exception of financial and trade agreements authorized by SCAPIN 2166, dated 30 August 1951.

FOR THE SUPREME COMMANDER:

C. C. B. WARDEN
Colonel, AGC
Adjutant General

(付記)

日本政府在外事務所の能力と機能に關する
總司令部覺書
連合國最高司令官總司令部
APO 五〇〇
AG〇九二(昭和二十六年九月二十日)DS
SCAPIN二一七三
覺書あて先　日本政府
昭和二十六年九月二十八日

件　名　日本政府在外事務所の能力と機能

1　參照

い　日本政府あて覺書、昭和二十五年二月九日付、件名、「アメリカ合衆國における日本政府在外事務所の設置」

ろ　日本政府あて覺書、AG三一一・二二三(二十五年五月二十三日)CCS、SCAPIN二〇九八、昭和二十五年五月二十三日付、件名、「日本政府在外事務所との通信」

は　日本政府あて覺書、AG〇九一・三一(二十六年八月三十日)ESS／FTC、SCAPIN二一六六、昭和二十六年八月三十日付、件名、「金融及び貿易取極を交渉し署名する權限」

に　日本政府あて覺書、AG〇九一(二十六年九月六日)DS、SCAPIN二一七〇、昭和二十六年九月十三日付、件名、「日本政府と連合國最高司令官に對して派遣された外國の外交代表との直接通信の許可」

2　日本政府在外事務所の能力と機能について參照覺書1(い)及び(ろ)に述べられた覺書によって日本政府に課せられたすべての制限は、撤廢される。

4 制限緩和に向けた対応（昭和24年5月～27年4月）

3 日本政府は、關係諸國の政府との間に、日本政府とそれぞれの相手國政府とが相互に満足する條件で、個個の日本政府在外事務所の能力と機能とを規定する取極を締結することを許される。

4 このような取極の條項に基き日本政府在外事務所によって行使される機能は、日本政府への責任の特定委任である。従って、日本政府は、それぞれの日本政府在外事務所がそれぞれの相手國政府へ發送し又は準外交的性質のすべての通信の寫を連合國最高司令部外交局に提出するものとする。日本政府在外事務所によって日本國と他の諸國との間に締結されるすべての取極は、昭和二十六年八月三十日付SCAPIN二一六六によって許可された金融及び貿易取極を除き、連合國最高司令官の事前の承認を要する。

最高司令官に代って

高級副官
　　副官部附大佐　シー・シー・ビー・ウォーデン

編　注　本文書は、昭和二十七年二月、外務省国際協力局特別資料室作成「日本管理資料㈤」より抜粋。

〜〜〜〜〜〜〜〜〜〜〜〜〜〜〜〜〜〜〜

連合国最高司令官総司令部より日本政府宛

299

昭和26年10月22日

出入国管理業務に関する指令

GENERAL HEADQUARTERS
SUPREME COMMANDER FOR THE ALLIED POWERS
APO 500

22 October 1951

AG 014.331 (3 Feb 50) GA
SCAPIN 2082/1

MEMORANDUM FOR: JAPANESE GOVERNMENT

SUBJECT: Immigration Service

1. References. a. Circular 14, General Headquarters, Supreme Commander for the Allied Powers, subject: Control of Entry and Exit of Individuals, Cargo, Aircraft, and Surface Vessels Into and From Japan, 22 October 1951.

b. Memorandum for the Japanese Government, General Headquarters, Supreme Commander for the Allied Powers, AG

300

昭和26年10月22日

連合国最高司令官総司令部より日本政府宛

税関、出入国管理および検疫業務に関する指令

GENERAL HEADQUARTERS
SUPREME COMMANDER FOR THE ALLIED POWERS
APO 500

AG 720.4 (3 Feb 50) GA   22 October 1951
SCAPIN 2083/1

MEMORANDUM FOR: JAPANESE GOVERNMENT

SUBJECT: Customs, Immigration and Quarantine Operations

1. References. a. Circular 14, General Headquarters, Supreme Commander for the Allied Powers, subject: Control of Entry and Exit of Individuals, Cargo, Aircraft and Surface Vessels Into and From Japan, 22 October 1951.

b. Memorandum for the Japanese Government, General Headquarters, Supreme Commander for the Allied Powers, AG 720.4 (3 Feb 50) GA, SCAPIN 2083, subject: Customs, Immigration and Quarantine Operations, 20 February 1950.

2. Effective 1 November 1951, the Japanese Government will assume full responsibility for the following customs, immigration and quarantine operations pertaining to other than Allied Forces activities:

a. Inspections of all individuals, cargo, aircraft and merchant vessels for compliance with Japanese quarantine and customs laws except for exit of cargo requiring a license validated by the Supreme Commander for the Allied Powers.

b. The issuance of landing permits to crew members 014.331 (3 Feb 50) GA, SCAPIN 2082, subject: Immigration Service, 20 February 1950.

2. Effective 1 November 1951, individuals departing Japan permanently will not be required to obtain exit clearance. Reference 1 b is amended accordingly.

FOR THE SUPREME COMMANDER:

C. C. B. WARDEN
Colonel, AGC
Adjutant General

4 制限緩和に向けた対応（昭和24年5月～27年4月）

and passengers of commercial carriers subject to the following conditions and such other regulations the Japanese Government may impose:

(1) The Captain of the carrier or the representative of the carrier in Japan must make application to the Japanese immigration authorities at the port of entry.

(2) On arrival in Japan, the individual must possess a ticket or a guarantee in writing by the commercial carrier of onward transportation and a valid travel document permitting individual's entry into some country other than Japan.

(3) The individual will be required to depart Japan within 72 hours and will be informed that the landing permit will not be the basis for entry into Japan in some other category. For cogent reasons, a landing permit may be extended for an additional maximum period of 72 hours.

(4) Prior to departure of the carrier from Japan, the Captain will certify to the immigration authorities that all passengers and crew members granted landing permits are aboard, except for individuals authorized to depart on a different carrier in which case the immigration authorities will determine that the individual boards the new carrier.

(5) Individuals granted landing permits are subject to all rules and regulations promulgated by the Supreme Commander for the Allied Powers and Japanese law not in conflict therewith.

(6) Individuals failing to depart Japan within 72 hours, or within the additional period of 72 hours, may be subject to prosecution as illegal entrants.

(7) In addition to the certificate required by subparagraph 2b (4), the immigration authorities will take positive action to insure that only bona fide crew members and passengers are authorized

301

昭和26年11月26日 連合国最高司令官総司令部より日本政府宛

海外渡航許可権の日本側への移譲に関する指令

SUPREME COMMANDER FOR THE ALLIED POWERS
GENERAL HEADQUARTERS
APO 500

AG 680.2 (31 Oct 51) GA
SCAPIN 2185

26 November 1951

MEMORANDUM FOR: JAPANESE GOVERNMENT

SUBJECT: Japanese Travel Abroad

1. Rescissions:

　a. Memorandum for the Japanese Government, AG 014.331 (5 Jan 50) AG, SCAPIN 2072, 5 January 1950, subject: Applications for Travel of Japanese Nationals Abroad.

　b. Memorandum for the Japanese Government, AG 014.331 (5 Jan 50) GA, SCAPIN 2072/1, 5 May 1950, subject: Applications for Travel of Japanese Nationals Abroad.

　c. Memorandum for the Japanese Government, AG 014.331 (5 Jan 50) GA, SCAPIN 2072/2, 12 April 1951, subject: Applications for Travel of Japanese Nationals Abroad.

　d. Memorandum for the Japanese Government, AG 680.2 (25 Aug 48) GA, SCAPIN 2035, 1 August 1949, subject: Travel of Japanese Technicians Outside of Japan.

　e. Memorandum for the Japanese Government, AG

---

landing permits and to physically determine that individuals granted landing permits depart Japan. Landing permits will be written in both Japanese and English and will provide for positive identification of the individual.

　c. The entry into Japan of Japanese nationals residing abroad.

　d. The entry into Japan of plants, animals and birds.

FOR THE SUPREME COMMANDER:

C. C. B. WARDEN
Colonel, AGC
Adjutant General

4　制限緩和に向けた対応(昭和24年5月～27年4月)

680.2 (25 Aug 48) GA, SCAPIN 7008-A, 15 December 1949, subject: Travel of Japanese Technicians Outside of Japan.

　　f. Memorandum for the Japanese Government, AG 544 (1 Aug 50) GA, SCAPIN 2118, 1 August 1950, subject: Travel of Japanese Mariners Outside of Japan.

　　g. Memorandum for the Japanese Government, AG 014.331 (26 Oct 48) GA, SCAPIN 6163-A, 8 November 1948, subject: Orientation of Japanese Nationals Who May be Authorized to Travel Outside Japan.

　2. Effective 1 December 1951 applications for the travel of Japanese nationals abroad will not be forwarded to this headquarters. The issuance of Japanese passports will be the sole responsibility of the Japanese Government in accordance with such regulations as the Japanese Government shall prescribe.

　3. It will be the responsibility of the individual applicant to secure the necessary visas for entry into foreign countries.

　4. General Headquarters, Supreme Commander for the Allied Powers, upon receipt of an applicant's personal history data form will process application for entry into areas under military control where military authorization for entry is required in lieu of visa.

　5. In implementing the foregoing authorization, direct communication between agencies of the Japanese Government and the appropriate section of General Headquarters, Supreme Commander for the Allied Powers, is authorized.

FOR THE SUPREME COMMANDER:

C. C. B. WARDEN
Colonel, AGC
Adjutant General

302　若干の外郭地域の日本からの政治上および行政上の分離に関する指令の一部改正について

昭和26年12月5日　連合国最高司令官総司令部より　日本政府宛

付記　右和訳文

GENERAL HEADQUARTERS
SUPREME COMMANDER FOR THE ALLIED POWERS
APO 500

AG 091 (29 Jan 46) GS
SCAPIN 677/1

MEMORANDUM FOR: JAPANESE GOVERNMENT

SUBJECT: Governmental and Administrative Separation on Certain Outlying Areas from Japan

1. Reference:

    a. Memorandum for the Japanese Government, AG 091 (29 Jan 46) GS (SCAPIN 677), 29 January 1946, subject, "Governmental and Administrative Separation of Certain Outlying Areas from Japan".

    b. Memorandum for the Japanese Government, AG 091 (22 Mar 46) GS (SCAPIN 841), 22 March 1946, subject, "Governmental and Administrative Separation of Certain Outlying Areas from Japan".

2. Paragraph 3 of reference a, as amended by reference b, is further amended so that the Ryukyu (Nansei) Islands north of 29° north latitude are included within the area defined as Japan for the purpose of that directive.

5 December 1951

3. The Japanese Government is directed to resume governmental and administrative jurisdiction over these islands, subject to the authority of the Supreme Commander for the Allied Powers.

FOR THE SUPREME COMMANDER:

C. C. B. WARDEN
Colonel, AGC
Adjutant General

（付　記）

若干の外かく地域の日本からの政治上及び行政上の分離に關する總司令部覺書
連合國最高司令官總司令部
APO 五〇〇

昭和二十六年十二月五日

AG〇九一（二十一年一月二十九日）GS
SCAPIN 六七七／一
覺書あて先　日本政府
件　　名　若干の外かく地域の日本からの政治上及び行

4 制限緩和に向けた対応(昭和24年5月～27年4月)

政上の分離

副官部附大佐　シー・シー・ビー・ウォーデン

1　參照

い　昭和二十一年一月二十九日付連合國最高司令官總司令部覺書、AG〇九一(二十一年一月二十九日)GS(SCAPIN六七七)、件名、「若干の外かく地域の日本からの政治上及び行政上の分離」

ろ　昭和二十一年三月二十二日付連合國最高司令官總司令部覺書、AG〇九一(二十一年三月二十二日)GS(SCAPIN八四一)、件名、「若干の外かく地域の日本からの政治上及び行政上の分離」

2　參照(ろ)によって修正された參照(い)の第三項は、北緯二十九度より北にある琉球(南西)諸島が右指令の適用上日本として限定された地域内に含まれるようさらに修正される。

3　日本政府は、連合國最高司令官の權限に服することを條件として、これら諸島に對する政治上及び行政上の管轄權をふたたび行使するよう命ぜられる。

最高司令官に代って

高級副官

編　注　本文書は、昭和二十七年二月、外務省国際協力局特別資料室作成「日本管理資料(五)」より抜粋。

303

昭和27年1月8日　国際協力局第四課作成

「第十三囘國會答弁資料(戰犯關係)」

第十三囘國會答弁資料(戰犯關係)

昭和二七、一、八

國際協力局第四課

一、戰犯裁判概觀

終戰以來極東國際軍事裁判所(東京)を始め米、英、佛、中、濠、比、蘭の連合各國軍事法廷(米は東京、横濱、グアム、マニラ、上海、英はシンガポール、クアラルンプール、ペナン、北ボルネオ、ラングーン、香港等、佛はサイゴン、中は北京、南京、上海等、濠はラボウル、モロタイ、香港、マヌス島、比はマニラ、蘭はバタヴィア、メダン等)において行われた日本人戰犯裁判は、昭

909

和二十六年四月九日マヌス島における豪軍裁判の終結をもって全部終了した。總司令部公報その他の情報を綜合すれば、全連合國(ソ連を除く)の戰犯裁判の判決狀況は左の通りである。

判決	件數
死刑	一、〇八三(二〇・七三%) 執行濟 九八
終身刑	四七三(九・〇三%)
有期刑	二、九六四(五七・五四%)
無罪	五六六(一一・〇四%)
起訴却下	一六(〇・三〇%)
判決却下	一三(〇・二三%)
計	五、二二

(註) 1. 確定判決に據った。從って再審の結果別種の刑に減刑されたものは、その原判決は計上されていない。
 2. 同一人が二箇以上の同種又は別種の判決を受けた場合は、その各の判決を計上した。
 3. 情報洩れのものも予想されるので本表の數字はもとより正確を保し難い。

なお死刑の原判決と再審の結果による減刑及び執行、未執行等の狀況を各國別に示せば左の通りである。

死刑原判決措置狀況一覽表 (二六、一二一現在)

地區別	國別	原判決	減刑	執行	欠席裁判	逃亡	死亡	未執行
東京	國際	七		七				
横濱	米	一二四	七二	五一				
グアム	米	三一	八	一四				
マニラ	比	七九	二	一七			六〇	
中國	米	六		六				
中國	中	一四九	一三	一四二		一	一〇	六
香港	英	二四	一	一三				
馬來	英	一〇六	二	一〇二	五	一		
ビルマ	英	三〇	六	二三				
蘭印	蘭	二四一	二三	二二六	二一	一五	五	一
サイゴン	佛	六七	三	六三			一	
ラボウル	濠	一三〇	五	一二三			二	

4　制限緩和に向けた対応（昭和24年5月～27年4月）

（註）
1. マニラ（比）六〇名は審査中
2. 中國（中）六名は執行の有無不明
3. 蘭印一名は現在マヌス島にて服役中

二、内外地戰犯關係收容者數

昭和二十七年一月一日現在における内外地戰犯關係收容者數は左表の通りである。

内外地戰犯關係收容者數一覽表

地區別	收容場所	裁判國別	人員 有期	終身	計	摘要
外地	マニラ	比	三	三〇	三三	
	マヌス	濠	一二四	一〇	一三四	
	小計		一二七	四〇	一六七	
内地	巢鴨	國際	〇	三	三	○内松澤病院入院中の者一名（米、終身）
		米	四〇九	一九六	六〇五	○假出所され自宅服役中の者三七三名
		英	四一	一四	一五七(※)	○假出所者總計 五二一名
		中	二五	四一	一二九	
		蘭	一五	一二	二七	
		佛	一八	五	二三	
		濠	九六	三三	一二九	
	小計				一、二二一	

註
1. 朝鮮人、臺灣人及び沖繩人を含む。
2. 巢鴨收容者中最終公報の未接到が若干あり、從つて刑期別人員數に多少の差異あるものと認められる。

（中略）

内外地全收容者數	有期	終身	死刑	計
	一、二〇九	三二九	六〇	一、六〇八

三、内地服役

外地において有罪の判決を受けた戰犯者は、當該裁判國の拘置所において服役するのが原則であるが、戰犯者及び家族の切實なる要望及び當該國の國内事情等により、既に外地戰犯者大部分の内地服役は實現され現在外地には前表の通りフイリピン（マニラ）に一二三名、濠州（マヌス島）に一二三四名を殘すのみとなつた。從來迄に實現

を見た内地服役の状況は左の通りである。

國名	服役地名	巣鴨移送年月日	移送服役者數
中國	中國各地	昭和二四、三、四	二五一
蘭國	蘭印各地	昭和二五、一二、三	六二三
佛國	サイゴン	昭和二六、六、三	八二
英國	ホンコン	昭和二六、五、一七	四二
濠州	ホンコン	昭和二六、五、一七	二五
英國	ラングーン、シンガポール、マレイ、英領北ボルネオ	昭和二六、八、一七	二三
計			一、〇三七

政府としてもその間屢々總司令部に對し內地服役實現方を要請したが、總司令部においては當該裁判國において再審を完了し判決が最後的に確定し且つ當該國からの希望があるならば、內地移送を受容れることには何等異存がないとの立場を取つている。

フイリピンにおいては、判決殊に六〇名の死刑判決が、目下キリノ大統領の下において各ケース每に審査中であるから、内地服役の急速な實現は困難と思われるが、政府としては今後とも機會ある每に本件實現方努力する所存である。

濠州においては、その裁判が他の諸國よりも後れ、漸

く昭和二六年四月九日に終了したが、再審も既に終つた模様であり且つ前述の通り既に一部香港の抑留者の內地服役の實現を見たのであるから、マヌス島服役者の內地移送についても、機會あるごとに關係方面の好意ある取計を要請する所存である。

四、戰犯服役者に對する恩典

戰犯服役者に適用される各國の恩典制度には種々のものがあるがこれを大別すれば左の四つに分けることが出來る。米國及びその他の國についてその概要を述べれば左の通りである。

(一)未決通算 (二)善行特典 (三)宣誓假出所 (四)恩赦その他の四つに分けることが出來る。

(1) 米 國

一九五〇年三月七日總司令部囘章をもつて統一的恩典制度が制定され、巣鴨服役者全部に適用されている。その要點は左の通りである。

A、拘留期間の特典

いわゆる未決通算で容疑者又は戰犯者として拘留された全期間が刑期に通算される。

B、善行特典

912

4　制限緩和に向けた対応（昭和24年5月～27年4月）

服役者が拘置所の諸規則を遵守し、懲罰を受けなかった場合に與えられる特典でそれぞれの刑期に應じ次のように減刑される（終身刑を除く）。

六月以上一年未滿の刑　　一月に付五日
一年以上三年　〃　　　　　　六日
三年以上五年　〃　　　　　　七日
五年以上十年　〃　　　　　　八日
十年以上　　　〃　　　　　　十日

C、宣誓假出所（パロール）

宣誓假出所は服役狀態良好な戰犯者が、刑期の三分の一（終身刑の場合は十五年）を服役した場合、本人の申請により、パロール委員會（總司令部法務局内に設置）の勸告に基き最高司令官の許可を得て實施される。假出所の資格を決定するに當つては未通算が行われるが、善行特典による減刑は適用されない。即ち刑期の三分の一とは、判決刑期より未決期間を控除したものゝ三分の一である。假出所は刑そのものゝ輕減でなく、殘餘の刑を拘置所外で服役するもので、出所者は中央更生保護委員會（法務府の外局）の選定しパロール委員會の承認した保護觀察者の監督の下に生業を營み、保護觀察者を通じ毎月パロール委員會に對しその動靜を報告することになっている。

昭和二十五年五月九日第一回宣誓假出所實施以來、昭和二十六年十二月二十七日第六十九囘までに累計五二一名が假出所の恩典に浴している。右假出所者數の刑期別及び裁判國別の内譯は左の通り。

刑期別内譯
十五年　　七　　十四年　　二　十二年　二六
十一年　　五　　十年　　二二四　　九年　一四
八年　　九二　　七年　　八〇　　六年　二六
五年　　四〇　　四年　　九　　三年　六

裁判國別内譯
國際　　一　　米國　一七一　　中國　九九
蘭國　一八〇　　佛國　二一　　英國　四八
濠州　　一

なお實施以來每月平均出所者數は約二〇名であつたが、昭和二十六年十一月より急增して六二名に達

し、更に十二月には八十五名の出所者を出しており右は講和條約發效までになるべく多くの有資格者（現在推定六百餘名）を出所せしめようとの總司令部側の意圖の現われとも見ることが出來よう。

(2) 中　國

未決通算のみが附與された。

(3) 蘭　國

昭和二十三年八月ウエルヘルミナ女王の卽位五十週年に當つて一律に一ケ月乃至八ケ月の恩赦減刑が行われ、また翌年四月女王誕生日に當り數名の者が更に三ケ月の減刑を受けた。

(4) 佛　國

未決通算が行われ、また昭和二十四年七月フランス革命記念日に當り、五年未滿の刑に對しては六ケ月、五年以上十年未滿に對しては一ケ年、十年以上二十年の刑に對しては二ケ年の恩赦減刑が一律に行われた。右はいづれも終身刑には適用がなかったのであるが、昭和二十六年七月十六日のフランス大統領令により終身刑の戰犯十六名を五年乃至十五年の有期刑に減刑し

た（同年十一月二十日附書翰をもつて在日フランス使節團より通告）。なお佛國關係戰犯で巢鴨服役者中この恩典に浴さなかった終身刑のもの二名があるが、右はいづれもその刑の言渡が佛印裁判の最終段階たる昭和二十五年三月末に行われ、今回の減刑措置には含まれなかったものである。

(5) 英　國

未決通算は認められなかつたが、服役狀態良好のものには、八ケ月の服役をもつて一年とされた。卽ち刑期の三分の二を服役すればよい。また終身刑は二十一年とみなされ、從つて右原則により十四年を服役すれば滿期となる。

以上中、蘭、佛、英の四國關係戰犯者は、ホンコンより移送された濠軍關係戰犯者とともに、米軍關係戰犯者と同一の恩典を適用されている。

(6) 濠　州

未決通算を始め恩典制度は認められていない。

(7) フイリピン

昭和二十五年末より比國改正刑法の未決通算（二日

4 制限緩和に向けた対応（昭和24年5月〜27年4月）

五、比島死刑囚減刑問題

比島裁判における死刑言渡数は前表の通り七九件で、うち二名は減刑され、三名が死刑を執行された後、しばらく處刑を行わなかつたが、昭和二十六年一月突如十四名が處刑され、爾餘六〇名の死刑囚の運命が氣遣われていたがその後執行は續行されず今日に至つており、その間家族よりの助命歎願書に對し、大統領より適當な考慮が拂われる旨の囘答が寄せられ、またしばしば、大統領の下において個々のケースにつき再審査が行われている旨が傳えられている。これら死刑囚の減刑に關しては同國政府よりまだ正式の意思表示には接していないが、政府としては、同國政府及び國民の寛容の精神に信頼し、その好意ある措置を希求している。

六、戰爭犯罪人に對する恩赦減刑等の問題

平和條約第十一條により、日本は連合國戰爭犯罪法廷の裁判を受諾し、日本國で拘禁されている日本國民にこれらの法廷が課した刑を執行することになつている。更に恩赦減刑等の措置を實施するに當つては、日本國の勸告と關係連合國の決定とを必要とすることになつている（第十一條實施上の國内法的措置については法務府において立案中）。

もし關係連合國において、條約發效前又は發效と同時に、自發的にこれらの恩典を廣汎に賦與する措置をとつてくれたならば、日本國民はその寛容を深く感謝し、民主主義諸國との全面的協力の決意を一層固めるものと思われるのであるが、各國ともそれぞれの國民感情、政治情勢、國際關係その他諸般の要素を愼重に考慮する必要のあることは充分推察し得る所である（部分的の恩典はあるが、前述の通り實施され良好な結果を生じている）。從つて政府としては、性急の措置によつて不測の不利を招くことのないよう、細心の注意を以て事態の推移を檢討している次第である。

七、巣鴨拘置所及び戰爭犯罪人の管理移轉の問題（主管、法務府）

客年十二月三十一日附覺書第二一九二號により、平和條約發效の日か本年三月三十一日か、何れか早い日から、

304

昭和27年1月24日　連合国最高司令官総司令部発表

都市地区にある接収財産の返還に関する総司令部発表（和訳文）

総司令部渉外局発表

都市地区にある接収財産の返還に関する総司令部渉外局は都市地區にある接収財産の返還に關し、本日次のような政策聲明を發表した。

目下の計画では帝國ホテルは、昭和二十七年三月三十一日頃日本側に返還される予定である。

平和條約の批准と日本安全保障條約の實施に伴って、在日米軍の再編成及び再配置についての計画はこの幾月かの間進捗しつつあった。

本問題は困難かつ多岐にわたっている。それは今正確に對比考量することの出來ない種種の要因により複雑であったし、現在もなお複雑である。これらの要因のおもなるものは、朝鮮における戰鬪作戰の支援である。

現在保持されている施設を引き續き使用することは、新らしく建設する資金がないこと及び代りとして必要な施設を建設するに要する時間的要素がないためにより複雑なものとなっている。

これらの多くの困難にもかかわらず、總司令部は米極東軍司令部の使命と矛盾しない限りできるだけ速やかに、縮少、再編成、整理及び再配置による解除できるあらゆる種類の施設を返還する政策をとって來ている。現在もそのような政策をとっている。

この政策の一部として、この數カ月間行われてきた休養ホテル及び娯樂施設の漸進的解除を引き續き行う予定である。この範圍に入る施設は結局主として朝鮮から歸還する人員の休養及び囘復途上にある病人の必要に應ずるために保持されるに過ぎない。

總司令官の政策に基いて、一般に〝USハウス〟といわ

916

巣鴨拘置所及び同所に收容中の戰爭犯罪人の管理を日本側に移す旨指示され、これが爲に必要な立法的、行政的並に予算上の措置については、法務府において準備中である。

4 制限緩和に向けた対応（昭和24年5月～27年4月）

れている日本全國の私有日本人住宅は平和條約發効後所有者の要求により、占領者が立退き次第、できるだけ速かに返還される。

また、この政策に基いて、貸事務所、ホテル、住宅、娯樂施設及び割愛し得る他の一切の施設返還の措置を、特に帝都中心地域において、強化するために引き續き研究が行われまた實際行動がとられている。

にある日本郵船ビルは近い將來に返還されるであろうが、その正確な日時は目下建築中の代るべき建物が何時完成するかにかかっている。

この範圍に屬する他の都市施設の返還は代るべき施策が建設され、軍の全面的な責任の支障なき遂行のために利用されるようになり次第行われるであろう。

總司令官の政策遂行を時間の上で必然的に制約している主要原因は都市地域以外において、新しく建設するか又は現存施設を取得又は復舊してこそ初めて現在占有している設備にとってかわることが出來るという事實である。しかし新建設又は取得及び復舊の資金は合衆國議會においての
み計上され、そして大統領の裁可を受けることのできる特別の予算支出から生れるものでなければならない。

編　注　本文書は、昭和二十七年五月、外務省國際協力局特別資料室作成「日本管理資料㈥」より抜粋。

〰〰〰〰〰〰〰〰〰〰〰〰〰〰〰〰〰〰〰〰〰

305 出入國管理業務の日本側への移管について

昭和27年2月5日　連合国最高司令官総司令部より日本政府宛

GENERAL HEADQUARTERS
SUPREME COMMANDER FOR THE ALLIED POWERS
APO 500

AG 720.4 (3 Feb 50) GA　　5 February 1952

SCAPIN 2083/2

MEMORANDUM FOR: JAPANESE GOVERNMENT

SUBJECT: Customs, Immigration and Quarantine Operations

1. References. a. Circular 14, General Headquarters, Supreme Commander for the Allied Powers, subject: Control of Entry and Exit of Individuals, Cargo, Aircraft and Surface Vessels Into

and From Japan, 22 October 1951.

b. Memorandum for the Japanese Government, from General Headquarters, Supreme Commander for the Allied Powers, file AG 720.4 (3 Feb 50) GA, SCAPIN 2083, 20 February 1950, subject: Customs, Immigration, and Quarantine Operations, as amended by SCAPIN 2083/1, 22 October 1951.

2. Effective 15 February 1952, the Japanese Government will assume full responsibility for the following immigration operations pertaining to other than Allied Forces personnel:

a. Extensions of stay in Japan
b. Changes of status
c. Exit-reentry clearances.

3. General Headquarters, Supreme Commander for the Allied Powers, will continue to process applications of individuals desiring to change their status to that of Allied Forces personnel.

FOR THE SUPREME COMMANDER:

C. C. B. WARDEN
Colonel, AGC
Adjutant General

306 昭和27年4月28日 吉田内閣総理大臣談話

平和条約発効に際しての吉田総理談話

講和發效當日內閣總理大臣談

桑港平和條約は規定せられた數を超える連合國がその批准書の寄託を完了しまして本日めでたく發効致します。わが國は遂にこゝに自由と獨立とを囘復し得たのであります。日本は平等の主權國として國際社會に復歸致したのであります。これに對して私は慶賀と感謝の念禁ずる能わざるものがあります。卽ち終戰以來わが國をよく助けよく導き更に史上かつて見ざる寛大なる平和を與えてくれた米英其の他の連合國に對して厚く感謝致すものであります。そしてこの講和の完成するためにわが國民の永い間の辛苦がこの見事な實を結びましたことを大いに慶賀するものであります。われわれは、今や喜び勇んで撓ゆむことなく平和と民主主義の大道を進めばよいのであります。

然しながらわれわれの前途には一團の暗雲が横たわっています。それは巧妙なる宣傳戰と浸透謀略を用い、はたまた暴力そのもの―武力侵略によって世界征服を企圖する共

918

4 制限緩和に向けた対応（昭和24年5月〜27年4月）

産主義の脅威であります。その故に武装なき日本を護るためにも且つ太平洋地域の共同防衛の目的をもってわれわれは米國と安全保障條約を結びわれわれの要請に應じて米國の陸海空軍がわが領土内とその周邊に駐在致すことに致したのであります。勿論かゝる取り極めは無期限に存續されるべきものでないことは言を俟たないことで、その故にわれわれは國情と國力の増進に順應してわが國自らの自衛力を作り上げ、進んで他の自由諸國と共に世界の平和と自由を擁護する決意をなすべきであります。今や自由諸國は今後のわが國の存在、行動に新たなる期待をかけつゝあるのであります。わが國民が此の期待に背かず徐ろに國力を蓄え、更に德性を涵養し文化を發揚し、以て新日本建業の名譽ある偉績を後世子孫に遺すの抱負と覺悟を獨立恢復のこの日に當つて更に新しくすべきであると存ずるのであります。

〰〰〰〰〰〰〰〰〰〰

307

昭和27年4月28日　外務省発表

平和条約発効に関する外務省発表

付記　昭和二十七年五月八日付岡崎外務大臣より各在外公館長他宛公信総合第三三一九号

平和条約非署名国・批准書未寄託国との国交回復状況につき通報

外務省發表（昭和二十七年四月二十八日）

本日、すなわち、昭和二十七年四月二十八日午後十時三十分（日本時間）、アメリカ合衆國政府は對日平和條約の批准手續を完了した。さきに日本國政府は、昨年十一月二十八日平和條約の批准書をアメリカ合衆國政府へ寄託したが、その後連合王國、オーストラリア、ニュー・ジーランド、カナダ、パキスタン、フランス各國政府も相ついで批准書を寄託しているので、ここにアメリカ合衆國政府の批准書寄託をもって、昨年九月八日サンフランシスコにおいて調印された平和條約は、同條約第二十三條所定の手續を了し、效力を發した。

平和條約の發效と同時に日本國は、前記七箇國とのほか、すでに批准書の寄託を終えているメキシコ、アルゼンチン兩國との間に正常な國交關係を回復したのはもとより、平和條約調印國で手續の關係上まだ平和條約の發效を見ていた

昭和二十七年五月八日

外務大臣　岡崎　勝男

國交回復に關する件

一、本件に關し、平和條約非署名國及び同條約署名國中批准書未寄託國との國交回復の經緯は左のとおり。

(一) 平和條約非署名國關係

1 タイ、本年一月二十五日バンコック在外事務所を通じ平和條約の最初の效力發生の日よりの國交回復、大使交換につき申し入れ、四月十一日タイの同意あり、四月二十八日吉田外務大臣と在日タイ公使との間に右を確認する書簡を交換した。

2 インド、戰爭狀態終了宣言と同時の國交回復、大使交換を申し入れ、大使交換については四月十五日それぞれ在京ミッションより同意の回答あり、四月二十八日吉田外務大臣とチェートウール在日インド連絡使節團長との間に右を確認する書簡を交換した。

3 ドイツ、平和條約の最初の效力發生の日より國交間

ないベルギー、ブラジル、セイロン、オランダ、ノルウェーとの間にも國交を再開する取極めが成立した。中華民國とは本日平和條約の調印を終り、外交使節を交換する交渉が行われている。インドネシア、フイリピンとの間にも使節を交換する運びとなつた。また平和會議に參加しなかつたインド、ユーゴスラヴイアとの間にも、本日をもつて戰爭狀態は終了し、互に友好關係に入つた。さらにデンマーク、ドイツ、イタリア、スペイン、スウェーデン、スイス、タイ、ヴアチカンなどとの間にも、本日をもつて、正常な國交關係が樹立された。

なお日本國がアメリカ合衆國との間に締結した安全保障條約の批准書は、アメリカ合衆國政府の平和條約批准書の寄託と同時刻、すなわち本四月二十八日午後十時三十分（日本時間）、ワシントンにおいて日米兩國政府間に交換を了した。ここに安全保障條約も、平和條約と同時に效力を發した次第である。

(付　記)

總合第三三九號

4 制限緩和に向けた対応（昭和24年5月～27年4月）

復、大使交換する旨の書簡を四月十一日アデナウア首相兼外相と吉田首相兼外相との間に交換した。

4 イタリア、昨年九月二十七日右と同趣旨の書簡を交換した。

5 スペイン、本年二月十二日右と同趣旨の書簡を交換した。

6 デンマーク、本年二月二十七日右と同趣旨の書簡を交換した。

7 ヴァチカン、本年一月二十三日右と同趣旨の書簡を交換した。

8 スウェーデン、平和條約の最初の効力發生の日より國交回復、公使交換を申し入れ、四月十五日同國外務次官より同意の旨回答があつた。

9 ユーゴースラヴィア、平和條約の最初の効力發生の日に戰爭狀態を終了し國交を回復する旨のエドヴアルド・カルデリ外務大臣より吉田外務大臣あて一月二十三日付書簡に對しこれを確認する吉田外務大臣の二月二十七日付書簡を交換した。

10 スイス、平和條約の最初の効力發生の日よりの國交回復、公使交換につき本年一月十六日在京ミッションの口頭了解があつたが四月二十四日スイス政府より同意の旨の正式回答があつた。

(二) 批准書未寄託國關係

1 ベルギー、本年三月六日在京ミッションより同國による批准は遲延の見込なるも特に平和條約の最初の効力發生の日より國交回復、大使交換を希望する旨の口頭申入れがあり、四月一日同趣旨のエード・メモワールを交換した。

2 オランダ、四月二十四日右と同趣旨のエード・メモワールを交換した。

3 ノールウェー、右同

4 ブラジル、四月二十一日在京ミッションより平和條約の最初の効力發生の日より大使館として認められたき旨口頭申入れあり、リオデジャネイロ在外事務所長へ訓電の結果四月二十四日ブラジル政府より同意の旨回答があつた。

5 ペルー、平和條約の最初の効力發生の日よりの國交回復、公使交換を希望する旨の四月二十八日グラ

ウ 在京ペルー外交代表よりの書簡に對し四月三十日これを確認する岡崎外務大臣の書簡を交換した。
（なお、ドミニカについては、未だ國交囘復の手續は完了していない。）

二、ビルマ政府は四月三十日對日戰爭狀態終了宣言を發し、若干の遲延はあるが二國間平和條約の締結前に國交を囘復し大使交換のことに合意が成立する見込である。

三、從來の大韓民國駐日代表部は平和條約の發效に伴いその地位を喪失したので日韓間に正規の外交關係の樹立されるまで、相互主義に基き暫定的に領事機關なみの特權を與える旨の合意が四月二十八日成立した。

中華民國については四月二十八日日華平和條約が調印され、兩國間に外交使節を交換する交涉が行われているが、とりあえず相互主義に基き暫定的に從來通りの地位及び特權を四月二十八日付をもって認めることとした。

インドネシヤ駐日外交使節團についても、正式の國交囘復、使節交換ができるまでの間、相互主義に基き暫定的にこれに事實上從來通りの地位及び特權を四月二十八日付をもって認めることとし、フィリピン外交使節團に

ついても同樣の措置がとられた。

本信送付先　各在外公館長及び在外事務所長（三十三ヵ所）

| 日本外交文書 | 占領期　第一巻
（占領政策への対応） |

2017年5月10日　初版発行

編　　者　外　務　省
発 行 者　八　木　唯　史
発 行 所　株式会社 六 一 書 房
　　　　　〒101-0051　東京都千代田区神田神保町 2-2-22
　　　　　電話 03-5213-6161　FAX 03-5213-6160　振替 00160-7-35346
　　　　　http://www.book61.co.jp　E-mail info@book61.co.jp
印刷・製本　株式会社　三陽社

ISBN 978-4-86445-085-0 C3021　　Ⓒ the Ministry of Foreign Affairs, Japan 2017
Printed in Japan